Structuring Venture Capital, Private Equity, and Entrepreneurial Transactions

2003 Edition

Jack S. Levin
Kirkland & Ellis

Special Editors

Martin D. Ginsburg
Georgetown University Law Center

Donald E. Rocap
Kirkland & Ellis

This volume is current through March 1, 2003

PUBLISHERS

1185 Avenue of the Americas, New York, NY 10036
www.aspenpublishers.com

Permissions
Aspen Publishers
1185 Avenue of the Americas
New York, NY 10036

1 2 3 4 5 6 7 8 9 0

Printed in the United States of America

ISBN 0-7355-3845-X

Library of Congress Catolog No. 95-75867

About Aspen Publishers

Aspen Publishers, headquartered in New York City, is a leading information provider for attorneys, business professionals, and law students. Written by pre-eminent authorities, our products consist of analytical and practical information covering both U.S. and international topics. We publish in the full range of formats, including updated manuals, books, periodicals, CDs, and online products.

Our proprietary content is complemented by 2,500 legal databases, containing over 11 million documents available through our Loislaw division. Aspen Publishers also offers a wide range of topical legal and business databases linked to Loislaw's primary material. Our mission is to provide accurate, timely, and authoritative content in easily accessible formats, supported by unmatched customer care.

Other Aspen Publishers products treating tax issues include:

Mergers, Acquisitions, and Buyouts

Multistate Corporate Tax Guide

**Corporate Tax Planning: Takeovers,
    Leveraged Buyouts, and Restructuring**

Venture Capital and Public Offering Negotiation

Corporate Finance and Securities Laws

Tax Planning for Troubled Corporations

Financial Products: Taxation, Regulation, and Design

To order any Aspen Publishers title, go to *www.aspenpublishers.com* or call 1-800-638-8437.

For more information on Loislaw products, go to *www.loislaw.com* or call 1-800-364-2512.

For Customer Care issues, e-mail *CustomerCare@aspenpublishers.com*; call 1-800-234-1660; or fax 1-800-901-9075.

**Aspen Publishers
A Wolters Kluwer Company**

SUBSCRIPTION NOTICE

This Aspen Publishers product is updated on a periodic basis with supplements to reflect important changes in the subject matter. If you purchased this product directly from Aspen Publishers, we have already recorded your subscription for the update service.

If, however, you purchased this product from a bookstore and wish to receive future updates and revised or related volumes billed separately with a 30-day examination review, please contact our Customer Service Department at 1-800-234-1660 or send your name, company name (if applicable), address, and the title of the product to:

ASPEN PUBLISHERS
7201 McKinney Circle
Frederick, MD 21704

About the Author

Jack S. Levin, through his professional corporation, is a senior partner in the law firm of Kirkland & Ellis, where it is widely rumored that the professional corporation does more of the work than does Mr. Levin. In person he has also long been a lecturer at the University of Chicago Law School and the Harvard Law School, teaching a course on *Structuring Venture Capital, Private Equity, and Entrepreneurial Transactions.*

Mr. Levin graduated summa cum laude from the Northwestern University School of Business in 1958, where unlike Professor Ginsburg—whose meager lifetime accomplishments are painstakingly chronicled under Special Editors below—Mr. Levin was regrettably not on the golf team. In May 1958 Mr. Levin won the Illinois Gold Medal on the CPA examination, an accomplishment secretly admired by Professor Ginsburg.

In 1961 Mr. Levin graduated summa cum laude from the Harvard Law School, ranking first in a class of 500, and served as Recent Case Editor of the Harvard Law Review, accomplishments that required no athletic prowess at all.

After graduation Mr. Levin served as law clerk to Chief Judge J. Edward Lumbard of the United States Court of Appeals for the Second Circuit and later as Assistant to the Solicitor General of the United States for tax matters under Archibald Cox and Thurgood Marshall, where he argued numerous cases to the U.S. Supreme Court and the Federal Courts of Appeals and slowly began to develop the modest tennis game in which he still takes immodest pride.

Mr. Levin is co-author (along with Professor Ginsburg) of an exciting 3000 page multi-volume treatise *Mergers, Acquisitions, and Buyouts* (Aspen Publishers), which they have updated and republished semi-annually since 1989, allowing Professor Ginsburg to claim credit for the many creative and few well written portions.

Mr. Levin is a frequent speaker at major tax institutes, Practising Law Institute programs, and ALI-ABA seminars, mainly in warm climates, and private equity/venture capital conferences, mainly at ski resorts, and has authored numerous articles and chapters of books on a variety of interesting tax and venture capital topics, although, to the best of anyone's knowledge, no one has ever read any of them.

Mr. Levin is a member of the American College of Tax Counsel and the Tax Advisory Group to the American Law Institute's Federal Income Tax Project on the Revision of the Corporate Tax Laws.

Over past times Mr. Levin has also served as a member of the Harvard Board of Overseers Committee for visiting the Harvard Law School, Chairman of the ABA Subcommittee on Corporate Distributions, Chairman of the Chicago Federal Tax Forum, Chairman of the Harvard Law School Fund Raising Drives in 1986, 1991, 1996, and 2001, a member of the Little, Brown and Company and the

CCH Tax Advisory Boards, an Executive Committee member of the Chicago Bar Association's Taxation Committee, Chairman of the Lawyers Division of the Chicago Jewish United Fund, president of the Birchwood Club, board member of the Mid-America Club, and, more important, for 13 years as Parliamentarian of the Winnetka Town Meeting (Winnetka, Illinois, being for the very few who do not know, the nation's model for honest and efficient government as described further below).

Through many patient years of practice and the selection of an extraordinary partner, Mr. Levin won the Kirkland & Ellis doubles tennis tournament four successive times during the summers of 1987 through 1991, and it has been downhill ever since.

Overcoming a lifetime of fear, Mr. Levin some years ago at age 45 (through his professional corporation, in case of debilitating injury) took up downhill skiing, a sport he enthusiastically pursues shoulder-to-shoulder with a number of his private equity clients, who (unlike Mr. Levin) are professional risk takers.

In May 2000 the American Jewish Committee presented Mr. Levin the Learned Hand Award for contributions to his profession and the community. Although disagreeing with AJC's selection, Professor Ginsburg nevertheless delivered a warm keynote address entitled A Salute To Imperfection, while Justice Ruth Bader Ginsburg, the family's better part, presented the award.

In December 2002 the Illinois Venture Capital Association presented Mr. Levin with a lifetime achievement award for service to the venture capital industry, an honor Professor Ginsburg questioned, only in small part because not asked to speak at the awards dinner.

While neither Mr. Levin nor Professor Ginsburg has ever achieved election to any public office, Mr. Levin's wife Sandy (the family's socially useful member) has at various times been elected President of the Winnetka Public School Board and a Trustee of the Winnetka Village Council. As Winnetka elected officials serve without monetary compensation, Mr. Levin devotes most of his time to the remunerative practice of law, less to teaching, none to the professional tennis or skiing circuits. Jack and Sandy have four daughters, two with law degrees and three with MBAs, four sons-in-law, one with a law degree and three with MBAs, and ten grandchildren, none of whom have yet graduated from anything.

About the Special Editors

Martin D. Ginsburg is Professor of Law at Georgetown University Law Center in Washington, D.C. His professional corporation is of counsel to the firm of Fried, Frank, Harris, Shriver & Jacobson.

Professor Ginsburg attended Cornell University, stood very low in his class, and played on the golf team. He graduated magna cum laude from Harvard Law School which, in those years, did not field a golf team.

Professor Ginsburg entered private practice in New York City in 1958. Although beloved by partners, clients, and opposing counsel, including Mr. Levin, he withdrew from full-time practice when appointed the Beekman Professor of Law at

About the Authors

Columbia Law School. He moved to Georgetown University in 1980 when his wife obtained a good job in Washington.

In addition to Columbia and Georgetown, Professor Ginsburg has taught at New York University School of Law, Stanford Law School, the University of Leiden in Holland, the Salzburg Seminar in Austria, Harvard Law School, and the University of Chicago Law School.

In 1986, someone who probably prefers never to be identified endowed a Chair in Taxation in his name at Georgetown; no one appears willing to occupy the Ginsburg Chair, and it remains vacant. In 1993 the National Women's Political Caucus gave Professor Ginsburg its "Good Guy" award; history reveals no prior instance of a tax lawyer held to be a "Good Guy," or even a "Decent Sort."

Professor Ginsburg is co-author (along with Mr. Levin) of a multi-volume treatise *Mergers, Acquisitions, and Buyouts* (first published in January 1989 and currently updated and republished semiannually by Aspen Publishers), in which he claims to have written all the entertaining and intellectually challenging portions. He is a frequent speaker at tax seminars mainly in warm climates, and the author of a ghastly number of articles on corporate and partnership taxation, business acquisitions, and other stimulating things. Professor Ginsburg has served on many bar association and government advisory committees, managing in each case to perform no useful service at all.

Professor Ginsburg's spouse was a lawyer before she found better work. Their older child was a lawyer before she became a schoolteacher. The younger child, when he feels grumpy, threatens to become a lawyer.

Donald E. Rocap is a partner in the Chicago office of Kirkland & Ellis, where he specializes in the tax aspects of complex transactions. He is a lecturer at the University of Chicago Law School.

Mr. Rocap received his undergraduate degree from Duke University and his J.D. from the University of Virginia Law School, where he was a member of the Order of the Coif and, more noteworthy, a member of the Law School's championship soccer team. Prior to joining Kirkland & Ellis, Mr. Rocap was Deputy Tax Legislative Counsel (Regulatory Affairs) at the U.S. Treasury Department's Office of Tax Policy. Since joining Kirkland & Ellis, he has studiously avoided playing competitive tennis with Mr. Levin.

Acknowledgments

In addition to special editors Martin D. Ginsburg and Donald E. Rocap, the author wishes to thank Emile Karafiol, William R. Welke, H. Kurt von Moltke, Bruce I. Ettelson, Scott A. Moehrke, Vicki V. Hood, Alexandra Mihalas, Olga A. Loy, Walter H. Lohmann, Jr., Edward T. Swan, James D. Sonda, Patrick C. Gallagher, Theodore L. Freedman, Keith E. Villmow, Andrew M. Kaufman, Margaret A. Gibson, Brian Land, Mark E. Grummer, Daneen Jachino, Robert R. Zitko, Toni B. Merrick, Carter W. Emerson, and Karl E. Lutz of Kirkland & Ellis; Paul F. Jock II, Mark B. Tresnowski, Richard A. Lang, Richard E. Peterson, Thomas M. Zollo, Robert H. Kinderman, and Richard E. Aderman, formerly of Kirkland & Ellis; Mark V. Sever and James F. Somers of Ernst & Young LLP; and Sean S. Sullivan, formerly of Ernst & Young LLP, for their assistance in the preparation of this volume.

The author is grateful to Gary R. Wendorf, senior legal assistant at Kirkland & Ellis, without whose tireless efforts in organizing this book and moving it from scribbled notes to polished product it would not have seen the light of day and without whose Herculean efforts the hundreds of updates to this book would be so much waste paper.

Summary of Contents

Contents

Chapter 1

Introduction

Chapter 2

Structuring Start-Up Transaction

Contents

Chapter 3

Structuring Newco as Flow-Through Entity

Contents

Chapter 4

Structuring Growth-Equity Investment in Existing Company

Contents

Chapter 5

Structuring Buyout

Contents

Contents

Chapter 6

Terms and Tax Ramifications of Debt and Equity Securities

Contents

Chapter 7

Structuring Consolidation of Fragmented Industry

Contents

Chapter 8

Structuring Turn-Around Investment in Overleveraged or Troubled Company

Contents

Chapter 9

Exit Strategies: Structuring IPO or Sale of VC-Financed Portfolio Company

Contents

Chapter 10

Structuring Formation of Private Equity Fund

Appendix

Statutes, Regulations, and Other Precedents

Contents

Contents

Contents

Contents

CHAPTER 1

Introduction

¶101 NATURE AND USE OF THIS BOOK

This book addresses (1) the general nature of venture capital, private equity, and entrepreneurial transactions and (2) the legal, tax, economic, and practical concerns in structuring these transactions.

This book is suitable for use by a lawyer, accountant, investment banker, venture capitalist, private equity investor, mezzanine lender, or anyone dealing with these professionals who desires to learn more about the nature of these transactions and the principal considerations in structuring them. It is also designed to be used in a law school or business school course focusing in whole or in part on venture capital, private equity, and entrepreneurial transactions.

This book covers many of the entrepreneurial transactions in which venture capital and private equity professionals typically engage, including:

- Structuring a start-up transaction.
- Using a tax flow-through entity, such as an S corporation, a partnership, or an LLC, rather than a C corporation which attracts tax at both the corporate and the shareholder level.
- Structuring a growth-equity investment in an existing company.
- Structuring a leveraged or management buyout of:

  - a wholly-owned subsidiary or division of a big company,
  - a privately-held company which is not a subsidiary of a big company,
  - a publicly-held company, or
  - any company so as to qualify for recapitalization accounting.

- Structuring an industry consolidation.
- Structuring a bankruptcy or non-bankruptcy workout of an over-leveraged or troubled VC portfolio company, including a turn-around investment into such a company.
- Designing subordinated debentures, preferred stock, various types of common stock, warrants, and convertible securities suitable for purchase by venture capitalists and private equity investors.
- Designing an equity-based executive compensation arrangement for a venture-capital financed portfolio company.
- Effectuating the venture capitalist's or private equity investor's exit from a successful investment.
- Structuring the formation of a venture capital, private equity, or buyout fund.

The abbreviations most frequently used in this book are set forth at ¶107 below.

Most of the precedents necessary for an understanding of the principles discussed in this book are reproduced in the Appendix, including tax, SEC, bankruptcy, fraudulent conveyance, and Delaware corporate, partnership and LLC statutes, as well as tax and SEC regulations and rulings, a few court decisions, and other precedents.

¶102   GENERAL DESCRIPTION OF VENTURE CAPITAL AND PRIVATE EQUITY INVESTING

This book generally uses the terms venture capital and private equity transactions interchangeably. Professional venture capitalists ("VCs") generally plan and execute private equity investments, including start-ups, growth-equity investments, leveraged and management buyouts, leveraged recapitalizations, industry consolidations, and troubled-company turn-arounds.

The VC community includes venture capital or merchant banking subsidiaries (or divisions) of large institutions, such as bank holding companies, insurance companies, investment banks, or even large industrial companies. The VC community also includes many free-standing specialized investment entities formed solely or principally to make venture capital or private equity investments, such as publicly-held or privately-held SBICs, publicly-held BDCs, or privately-held funds formed (generally as partnerships or LLCs) to make such investments.

A private fund generally raises its capital from a limited number of sophisticated investors in a private placement (including public and private employee benefit plans, university endowment funds, wealthy families, bank holding companies, and insurance companies) and splits the profits achieved by the fund between the VC professionals and the capital providers on a pre-negotiated basis (typically with 20% of the net profits going to the VC professionals as a carried interest and the remaining 80% of the profits to the VC professionals and the capital providers in proportion to the capital supplied).

¶103 DISTINGUISHING VENTURE CAPITAL/ PRIVATE EQUITY INVESTING FROM OTHER TYPES OF INVESTING

The *first* feature distinguishing venture capital/private equity investing is the VC professional's active involvement in identifying the investment, negotiating and structuring the transaction, and monitoring the portfolio company after the investment has been made. Often the VC professional will serve as a board member and/or financial adviser to the portfolio company. Hence, venture capital/private equity investing is significantly different from passive selection and retention of stock and debt investments by a money manager.

A *second* distinguishing feature is that venture capital/private equity investments generally are not intended to be held indefinitely. Rather, they are intended to be held for a limited number of years with the expectation that there will be substantial growth in value followed by sale. For example, a venture capital or private equity fund ordinarily has a limited term, often 10 to 13 years, and hence goes through cycles, with venture capital/private equity investments being made during the first 5 years, value-added monitoring and growth continuing during the several years following each investment, most investments sold within 3 to 7 years after the original investment in the portfolio company, and all investments sold (or distributed in kind to the investors) within 10 to 13 years after the fund's formation.

The VC professional normally does not make an investment seeking to maintain long-term control over the portfolio company or to build a career running the portfolio company. Rather, VC generally evaluates alternative exit strategies at the time the initial investment in the portfolio company is made. Often the original investment documents contain the terms or at least the outline of VC's anticipated exit strategy. Hence, venture capital/private equity investing is significantly different from acquiring a company with the intent of managing it for the indefinite future and profiting from the operating cash flow produced by the business.

A *third* distinguishing feature of venture capital/private equity investing is that the securities purchased are generally privately held as opposed to publicly traded.

- When a VC professional organizes a new business start-up, the newly-formed company ("Newco") is almost always privately held at the outset.
- Even where the target company in a buyout is publicly held (before the buyout), the new company formed to effectuate the buyout ("Newco") is almost always privately held after the buyout.
- Where a VC professional makes a growth-equity investment in an existing company ("Oldco"), Oldco is usually privately held. In those few circumstances where a VC professional makes a growth-equity investment in a publicly-held Oldco, VC generally buys a type of Oldco securities that is not publicly traded. For example, where Oldco's common stock is publicly traded, VC may buy Oldco (1) convertible preferred stock or convertible subordinated debentures or (2) straight preferred stock or straight subordinated debentures with warrants. And even when VC infrequently buys garden-variety Oldco common stock (of the type publicly traded), VC typically acquires such stock from Oldco in a private placement subject to SEC restrictions and with special negotiated rights (e.g., registration rights, preemptive rights, options or warrants to buy additional stock at a fixed price, one or more board seats, etc.) which make VC's stock different from Oldco's publicly-traded common stock.

In sum, a venture capital/private equity investment is normally made in a privately-held company, and in the relatively infrequent cases where the investment is into a publicly-held company, VC generally holds non-public securities.

While VC's exit strategy often involves taking the portfolio company public and ultimately selling VC's stock into the public market, public trading for the portfolio company is generally part of the end game, not the opening gambit. Thus, venture capital/private equity investing is considerably different from buying, holding, and selling publicly-traded equity securities.

A *fourth* distinguishing feature is that venture capital/private equity investors generally seek a very high return on their capital. VCs do not purchase debt instruments simply to obtain an interest yield. Rather, the principal goal of a venture capital/private equity transaction is to obtain geometric returns when the portfolio company is successful and its common stock or common equivalents soar in value. Hence, a venture capital/private equity transaction will generally involve the purchase of one or more of the following:

- Common stock.
- Convertible preferred stock or convertible subordinated debentures with a relatively low yield (all or a portion of which may be deferred) but with attractive conversion features.
- Straight preferred stock or straight subordinated debentures with a relatively low yield but with warrants.

VC generally purchases a relatively risky slice of the portfolio company's capital structure (and is frequently subordinated to a substantial amount of leverage), risks losing most or all of its investment if the portfolio company does not prosper, and expects to be handsomely rewarded if the portfolio company does prosper. VC requires a high return on successful investments to cover its losses suffered on portfolio companies which fail—i.e., to provide a high compound internal rate of return ("IRR") on its *aggregate* invested capital to compensate VC for the high risk of such investments.

This feature—purchasing risky equity-oriented securities and seeking a high compound yield on successful transactions—distinguishes venture capital/ private equity transactions from the purchase of debt securities.

One type of transaction which falls just short of the venture capital/private equity transactions featured in this book is mezzanine lending, i.e., a layer of financing which is more risky than senior bank debt but less risky than VC's investment, thus occupying a mezzanine halfway between the ground floor and the balcony. The mezzanine lender (like the VC professional) generally employs active investment professionals who negotiate the purchase of privately-placed securities in venture capital/private equity transactions, such as buyouts, but the securities purchased are normally from the portfolio company and are predominantly debt securities—generally high-yield subordinated debt with an explicit equity kicker, i.e., a slice of common stock, warrants, or conversion rights.

The senior bank lender generally locks in its entire yield in the form of contractual interest payments (albeit often at rates which fluctuate with market interest indexes) and specified fees, although the senior lender may occasionally take a small equity kicker when financing a buyout. The mezzanine lender, by contrast, normally takes a portion of its yield in the form of an equity kicker, and thus shares an interest (with VC) in the portfolio company's future equity value. However, mezzanine debt is at least one level more senior in the capital structure than VC's investment and hence is significantly less risky than VC's. Moreover, the mezzanine lender's focus, more like the senior lender's and less like VC's, is on its high interest yield and relative safety of principal. The mezzanine lender's equity kicker is designed to augment its interest yield but does not play the central role that it does with the VC.

The venture capital/private equity investor, on the other hand, focuses on common stock or common equivalent securities, with any purchase of subordinated debentures and/or preferred stock generally designed merely to fill a hole in the financing or to provide VC with some priority over management in liquidation or return of capital.

A *fifth* distinguishing feature of venture capital/private equity investing is that VC generally invests in a portfolio company only when convinced that the company has (or that the VC has recruited) a superior management team. VC generally can not be induced to put its money behind a management team in which it does not have confidence, no matter how attractive the portfolio company's product, concept, or business plan. A frequently heard VC maxim is that an attractive portfolio company has 3 key attributes: superior management, superior management, and superior management.

Where VC disregards this maxim and backs weak management, the VC too often is faced with an unpalatable choice before long: *either* continue with suboptimal management and risk the portfolio company's falling behind its business plan *or* fire management and seek better replacements, risking significant business disruption during which well-managed competitors will often overcome the portfolio company's early lead. A second, but less obvious, reason to avoid weak management is that, when management must be replaced mid-stream, VC will spend an inordinate amount of time recruiting and training new management, diverting VC from its other portfolio companies.

A *sixth* (although not inevitable) distinguishing feature of venture capital/ private equity investing is that VC often seeks in the early years control of the portfolio company or, if control is not obtainable, at least board representation. This is because VC does not view itself as supplying capital alone, but also as providing important advice on financial and strategic planning and oversight for the portfolio company's management in order to add value to VC's investment.

Where a portfolio company needs more money than the lead VC is willing to commit, the lead VC may bring one or more additional VCs into the deal. The lead VC will normally play the principal role in structuring and negotiating the investment, but each VC (at least each VC with a substantial investment) will monitor its own investment, and the VCs will not inevitably act in concert (except insofar as their interests coincide) on issues involving the portfolio company.

¶104 HIGH COST OF VENTURE CAPITAL/PRIVATE EQUITY MONEY

Venture capital/private equity money may not on its face cost the portfolio company as much as a bank loan, a private placement of senior debt securities, or a public issuance of senior debt securities. That is, there may be little or no fixed interest or debt service payments on the VC money. However, if the portfolio company is successful, VC money will inevitably be more expensive to the portfolio company's other common shareholders. This is because VC, as a condition to investing in the portfolio company, will demand a substantial portion of the portfolio company's common equivalents—common stock, warrants, and/or conversion privileges—which will have substantial value if the portfolio company is successful.

Hence, as a general rule, where a portfolio company can obtain traditional debt financing, it will find this route less expensive to its existing common shareholders than venture capital/private equity financing. However, the very factors which make a portfolio company attractive to a professional VC—a speculative situation with substantial opportunity for value enhancement if the business succeeds—will often make the portfolio company too risky to qualify for unsupported bank or other traditional debt financing. Once the portfolio company obtains venture capital/private equity financing, it usually can leverage its new-found VC equity by obtaining bank (or mezzanine) loans senior to the new VC money.

Moreover, obtaining a venture capital/private equity investor generally brings the portfolio company more than capital. As discussed above, the portfolio company generally ends up with one or more top-flight VC professionals on its board, who are capable of providing the portfolio company with high quality financial and strategic advice and management oversight. Thus, a venture capital relationship gives the portfolio company substantial benefit not normally obtainable

ng or a private or public debt floatation (although
management not desiring any such oversight
uch advice can, of course, be a two-edged sword,
s control of the portfolio company can mean, in
y which fails to meet its business plan, that the
nt will be seeking new jobs.

JRE CAPITAL/PRIVATE
ACTIONS

rt-Up Transaction

ital" is sometimes used narrowly to refer only to
w business, a transaction which generally involves a
negotiation between ... nore professional VCs and one or more entrepreneurs
seeking to start the business. Such a Newco start-up transaction is discussed in
Chapter 2, and the pros and cons of organizing Newco as a S corporation, a
partnership, or an LLC, rather than as a traditional C corporation, are discussed
in Chapter 3.

In this book, however, the term "venture capital" refers to a broader spectrum
of investing, encompassing not only start-ups, but also growth equity, leveraged
and management buyouts, leveraged recapitalizations, industry consolidations,
and turn-around investments into over-leveraged and troubled companies.

Venture capital start-up transactions can be categorized into (1) seed money
and (2) early stage. Seed money refers to financing a potential business which
requires substantial research, development, and/or other threshold activities before the entrepreneur can begin revenue-generating activities. Early-stage venture
capital, on the other hand, refers to financing an entrepreneur who has passed
the seed-money stage and is ready actually to begin (or has recently begun)
revenue-generating activities.

Start-up transactions can further be broken down into high tech, low tech, and
no tech, depending on the degree of cutting edge technology necessary for the
business to succeed. Businesses financed by venture capital/private equity investors can range from a high-tech bio-genetic engineering company to a low-tech
manufacturing enterprise to a no-tech retail or fast food chain.

Naturally, a VC professional will be more likely to supply start-up money
where the entrepreneur is a successful inventor and/or executive with a proven
track record.

¶105.2 Growth-Equity Transaction

Frequently, an existing business enterprise needs money for expansion—to
build a new plant, to develop a new product, to begin national distribution of a
local or regional product, to acquire an add-on business, etc. The enterprise's

capital requirements may exceed the amount it is able to raise from traditional sources, such as a secured loan from a bank lender, a private placement of debt with an insurance company, a private equity offering to Oldco's shareholders, their friends and family, or a public offering of debt or equity securities (or, with respect to the last alternative, it may be premature for the company to go public).

In these circumstances, a business seeking money for expansion might turn to venture capital/private equity investors to supply its capital needs, or perhaps to supply enough equity capital to serve as a base for borrowing the remainder of its capital needs from traditional lenders. Such a venture capital/private equity investment in an existing company ("Oldco") is called a growth-equity investment.

While a VC growth-equity investment is generally into a privately-held Oldco, VC may under certain circumstances invest in a publicly-traded Oldco. In this case, VC is likely to buy securities of a type not publicly traded (e.g., preferred stock convertible into publicly-traded common stock). Less commonly, VC may buy securities of the publicly-traded class (typically common stock), but at a substantial discount from the public-market price and/or with other valuable rights (e.g., preemptive rights, options or warrants to buy additional stock at a fixed price, one or more board seats, etc.). Although Oldco is publicly traded, VC's stock acquired in a private transaction (rather than in the public market) is subject to SEC restrictions on resale; VC therefore normally obtains registration rights from Oldco as a condition of making the investment.

Where VC is making a relatively large investment in Oldco, VC may organize a consortium or syndicate of venture capital/private equity investors, who will usually co-invest in the same strip of securities.

While a growth-equity investment is generally designed to provide Oldco with expansion capital, there are cases where Oldco is seeking the new VC investment so that it will have cash to redeem Oldco stock from existing large shareholders. One or more Oldco shareholders may be seeking such a stock redemption to pay estate tax (where a large stockholder has died) or for liquidity (where the shareholder has recently retired or is engaged in estate planning). Such a growth-equity investment to finance a redemption is called a recapitalization and, when financed primarily with borrowed money, a leveraged recapitalization.

Because Oldco in a growth-equity investment is generally more mature than is Newco in a start-up, a growth-equity transaction is often called a later-stage investment (as compared to a seed-money or early-stage investment in a start-up). Where VC invests in a more mature Oldco seeking growth-equity money, VC's investment risks and potential gains are generally lower than in a start-up.

A traditional growth-equity investment into Oldco is examined in Chapter 4.

In many proposed growth-equity investments, VC concludes that the key management executives do not own sufficient Oldco stock to incent their future performance, i.e., that too large a percentage of Oldco's stock is in the hands of passive shareholders and too small a percentage is in the hands of key managers. In this case, a front-end restructuring of Oldco's equity ownership is often an essential step to induce VC to invest in Oldco. Chapter 4 discusses several ways of achieving this equity restructuring objective.

¶105.3 Troubled-Company Turn-Around Investment

Occasionally, VC may make a growth-equity investment in a company ("Badco") which is suffering losses, is over-leveraged, and/or is experiencing other financial or business reverses.

VC may make such a "turn-around" investment into an unrelated Badco in which VC has not previously invested. Or VC may have been Badco's original sponsor, i.e., today's Badco may, a few years ago, have been the Newco which, with much optimism and with VC's money, acquired Target in a highly-leveraged buyout.

Whether or not VC made a prior investment in Badco, VC's new turn-around investment generally presents the same issues, except that, where VC was Badco's original sponsor, there is greater pressure on VC to make the new turn-around investment, to protect both its original Badco investment and its business reputation. Such turn-around financing into a troubled Badco is almost always riskier than traditional growth-equity financing of a sound, well-managed company.

A turn-around investment in an over-leveraged, financially-troubled Badco is analyzed in Chapter 8.

¶105.4 Leveraged or Management Buyout

When an established business ("Target") is for sale, there are at least 3 classes of potential buyers:

- A *strategic buyer* is a company which already owns a business similar or complementary to Target's and believes that combining the buyer's existing business with Target's business will produce a synergistic increase in value.
- A *long-term personal buyer* is a person or group desiring to enter Target's industry (e.g., a company in other businesses seeking diversification or the former managers of another company in Target's industry) which has (or can borrow) the capital necessary to buy Target.
- A *financial buyer* is a venture capital/private equity investor (or group of such investors) able to raise the funds necessary to buy Target, generally with the goal of holding Target for 3 to 7 years, improving Target's business performance, and then reselling Target at a substantial profit.

Where a venture capital/private equity investor or group is planning a leveraged buyout (an "LBO"), VC generally forms a new company ("Newco") to buy Target, arranges for Newco to borrow a majority of the necessary funds (hence the use of the term "leveraged" buyout), and contributes a minority of the necessary money as equity capital. In one variation where VC desires to structure the LBO for "recap" (rather than "purchase") accounting, VC generally does not form Newco but instead invests directly in Target, which borrows additional funds and redeems most of its old shareholders.

Newco frequently arranges its borrowings in several tranches—from senior lenders, senior subordinated lenders, and junior subordinated lenders. In order to obtain each successively more junior layer of debt financing, Newco must offer a progressively higher interest rate and/or a progressively larger equity kicker (Newco common stock, warrants, a conversion privilege, or contingent interest based on Newco's results) to each more subordinated layer.

However, the essence of an LBO is that only Newco and/or Target is liable to the lender for the borrowed money. That is, no venture capital/private equity investor guarantees Newco's debt (other than possibly a guarantee with recourse only to Newco's stock owned by the guarantor, which does not expose the venture capital/private equity investor's assets other than its investment in Newco).

Typically, as part of the LBO arrangements, VC obtains top management talent (either newly-recruited executives or Target's most talented existing executives) to run Newco-Target after the LBO and incents them with cheap common stock or with common equivalents, such as stock options, often subject to complex time and/or performance vesting.

Sometimes, Target's management (rather than VC professionals) originate the deal, and Target's management executives then seek to recruit a venture capitalist/private equity investor (or group) to provide equity financing for the acquisition. This most often happens where Target's old owners have offered to sell Target to Target's existing management team if they can raise the necessary financing. In such case, the transaction is generally called a management buyout (an "MBO"). Throughout this book the term "buyout" is used to include both traditional VC-led LBOs and management-led MBOs.

Buyouts come in at least 4 varieties, with the applicable tax, SEC, accounting, and other legal and practical implications of each varying significantly from the other 3.

- The simplest version of a buyout is the purchase of a Target division or wholly-owned subsidiary from a large corporation ("Bigco"), generally where Bigco has concluded that the division or subsidiary no longer fits Bigco's long-term business strategy.
- A somewhat more complicated buyout variation is presented where Target is privately held by a family or reasonably small group of persons, i.e., Target is not a Bigco division or consolidated subsidiary.
- The most complicated buyout variation is presented where Target is itself a publicly-traded corporation, in which case Newco's purchase of public Target is a going-private transaction.
- A fourth complex buyout variation is presented where VC structures its buyout of Target (described in any of the 3 preceding bullets) as a recapitalization of Target seeking to obtain the benefits of "recap" accounting and thereby maximize Target's post-buyout GAAP book earnings.

These 4 forms of buyout are discussed in Chapter 5. Chapter 6 discusses the terms and tax ramifications of debt and equity securities frequently used in buyouts, as well as in other VC transactions.

¶105.5   *Industry Consolidation*

Often a VC professional identifies a fragmented industry, i.e., an industry where there are many small or relatively small competitors and no or few market leaders have appeared. VC then recruits a top-flight management team with experience in the industry. VC and the management team form Newco as a "platform" to assemble a significant, or perhaps even leadership, presence in the fragmented industry by (1) acquiring selected strategically located industry players in a series of buyouts or roll-ups, (2) starting up new businesses in those markets where there is no desirable target business or the existing businesses in such market are overpriced, and (3) amalgamating the buyouts and start-ups into a regionally or nationally important player in the otherwise fragmented industry.

Often the term platform is used where the consolidation begins with a reasonably large buyout of an established business, followed by numerous add-on acquisitions, and the term roll-up is generally used where there is no large initial acquisition but only a series of reasonably small acquisitions.

Chapter 7 discusses industry consolidations, including the advisability of using a holding corporation, partnership, or LLC as an umbrella entity over the various business enterprises being assembled.

¶105.6   *Exit Strategies*

When a VC professional invests in a transaction of the types identified above, VC's goal is to liquefy its investment at a substantial profit when portfolio company's value has been maximized through astute management and VC supervision, add-on acquisitions, and the like (i.e., when portfolio company has matured to the point where its value is no longer growing geometrically), generally 3 to 7 years after VC's initial investment in portfolio company.

When structuring its original investment—in a start-up, growth-equity, buyout, industry consolidation or troubled company—VC will already be planning its ultimate exit strategies. Indeed, contracts signed at the time of VC's initial investment will generally give VC certain future rights to control its exit strategy. This is especially important where VC will not (or may not) control portfolio company at the back end when the exit strategy is executed. Even where VC will control portfolio company at the time of the end game, the actual exit strategy employed (e.g., a sale of portfolio company's stock) may require cooperation from some shareholders who will not (or may not) be in agreement with the timing, price or other terms as proposed by VC. For these reasons, it is important that VC obtain, at the front end when making its investment, contractual rights to control the back-end exit strategy.

VC's exit scenarios may include (1) sales of portfolio company stock to the public in an IPO or a post-IPO registered offering or pursuant to SEC Rule 144 *or* (2) sale of portfolio company to a large company ("Bigco") in exchange for Bigco stock (in a tax-free reorganization), for cash, or partly for cash and partly for Bigco debt instruments on the installment method *or* (3) sale of VC's securities back to portfolio company, possibly at a fixed time and price (e.g., a scheduled redemption of VC's preferred stock) or possibly at VC's option and for FV determined by appraisal or by formula (e.g., a common stock variable-price put).

Chapter 9 discusses exit strategies.

¶105.7 Formation of Venture Capital, Private Equity, or Buyout Fund

Where the VC professionals are employed by a large institution, such as a bank holding company or an insurance company, they will generally be investing the institution's money and hence will not form a fund. Frequently, however, a group of individuals experienced in venture capital investing (often former executives of a large institution's venture capital operation) will form a venture capital, private equity, or buyout fund (a "PE fund").

In this case the VC professionals will often raise capital from a limited number of sophisticated investors, including public and private employee benefit plans, university endowment funds, wealthy families, insurance companies, and bank holding companies. Such a PE fund will generally be formed as a partnership or LLC (to avoid entity level taxation) and will generally split the fund's profits between the VC professionals and the capital providers on a pre-negotiated basis, typically with 20% of the net profits going to the VC professionals as a carried interest and the remaining 80% to the VC professionals and the capital providers in proportion to the capital supplied.

A PE fund may or may not seek to qualify as an SBIC. Occasionally a PE fund may offer equity interests to the public (rather than only to a limited number of sophisticated investors), in which case the fund will generally seek to qualify as a publicly-held BDC.

Once these VC professionals have formed a PE fund, the fund will generally make new investments for a limited period of time, e.g., 5 years after formation, engage in value-adding monitoring during the several years following each investment, sell each investment as soon as it matures, distribute the proceeds to the fund's partners as sales occur, and complete the sale of virtually all its investments (or distribute in kind to the investors) within 10 to 13 years after the fund's formation. Hence, approximately 5 years after a PE fund's formation, the VC professionals, if they have developed (or are able to convince investors that they are developing) a successful track record, will generally seek to form a second fund, so that they have money for future investments, with future funds to follow every 5 years or so.

Chapter 10 discusses the formation of a new PE fund.

¶106 HISTORY OF VENTURE CAPITAL/PRIVATE EQUITY INVESTING

¶106.1 Ancient History

While professional venture capital investing as described above is a fairly recent phenomenon, "venture capital" in the broader sense of "private risk capital" has existed in one form or another in every society that had significant commercial activity. A few examples:

- Marcus Licinius Crassus, reputedly the richest man in Julius Caesar's Rome, financed many enterprises, including a private fire department. Though most of Rome's buildings were made of wood in the first century B.C., republican Rome had no public fire department. Crassus capitalized on this deficiency: When a building caught fire, his business agents and firefighters would repair swiftly to the scene of the conflagration. If they believed the building (or the adjoining structures) worth saving, the agents would offer to buy it (or them) for cash (at an appropriate discount). If the owner(s) refused, the firefighters would leave without taking remedial action. If the owner agreed to sell the building(s), Crassus' agents would close the purchase and his firefighters would then attempt to save the building(s). While not every such Crassus investment was a success, Crassus apparently did very well on a fully-distributed portfolio basis.
- In 1492, Christopher Columbus obtained from Ferdinand and Isabella of Spain the venture capital necessary to finance his exploration of the New World.
- In 16th and 17th century England, the aristocrats and other wealthy families financing risky commercial and industrial enterprises—mostly foreign trade, exploration and privateering, the high-tech of that era—were known as "adventurers." For example, the Merchant Adventurers, licensed by Henry VII, played an important part in opening trade with "Muscovy" and was a model for companies formed later to exploit the New World.

¶106.2 Industrial Revolution and Merchant Bankers

With the industrial revolution in the 19th century, banks became the main source of business financing. Business enterprise had become so common that it was no longer viewed as inherently high-risk.

Hence, venture capital began to focus on financing a business that lacked access to bank financing, frequently by providing equity capital as the underpinning for a bank loan. As before, venture financing was largely provided by amateur venture capitalists—wealthy families, the entrepreneur's friends and local business acquaintances, etc.

However, as the scale of business endeavors, and hence their capital needs, escalated (building railways, shipping wheat from the Ukraine or the American West to the growing cities of Europe, etc.), venture capital became more institutionalized. In England, merchant banks emerged as the principal providers of high-risk capital to business enterprises around the world. They invested both capital obtained from their partners and capital obtained from other rich individuals and families. While the aristocracy and other wealthy families of England had long invested in risky business enterprises, the merchant banks were more professional and could raise more capital than the amateur venture investors.

English merchant banks helped to finance the industrial revolution in the U.S. and provided a model for U.S. merchant banks (such as J.P. Morgan) that financed new industries, like steel and oil. However, merchant banks tended to focus more on new enterprises requiring substantial capital from the start than on small business. Hence, the latter continued to rely on family, friends, and wealthy amateurs willing to take a flyer on a new enterprise.

¶106.3   U.S. in the 1940s and Thereafter

Venture capital/private equity investing in the U.S. today largely reflects the marriage of the 2 traditions discussed above: "professional" merchant banking and "amateur" venture investing by wealthy individuals and families.

Beginning in the 1940s, several very wealthy American families began the move from amateur to professional venture capital status by developing the continuity of focus and the staffing which enabled them regularly to find, evaluate, consummate, and monitor risk-oriented investments.

Passage of the Small Business Investment Act in 1958 was a critical event, because it gave public recognition—and government financial backing—to professional venture capital investing as an independent, profitable activity. The Act also permitted banks (and bank holding companies[1]) to invest in SBICs. The entry of banks into venture capital investing in the late 1950s, and the growth of these endeavors through the 1960s and 1970s, were key steps in the formation of a professional, institutionalized, venture capital/private equity industry in the U.S. Today, approximately two-thirds of SBIC capital is supplied by banks, and many professionals throughout the venture capital industry obtained their training at bank SBICs.

Beginning in the late 1970s, private and public employee benefit plans and university endowment funds began investing a small portion of their enormous available funds in venture capital/private equity. As this huge pool of previously risk-averse capital began to seek skilled VC professionals to handle a slice of their investment capital, the formation of private venture capital/private equity funds—frequently staffed by experienced executives from the venture capital subsidiaries of banks and insurance companies—received a tremendous boost.

¶106   [1] For purposes of this ¶106, a reference to banks includes bank holding companies.

Today the venture capital/private equity industry is an extraordinary mixture of institutional venture subsidiaries (investing money supplied by a parent bank or insurance company) and private funds (investing money supplied by a small group of sophisticated investors, including public and private employee benefit plans and university endowment funds, wealthy families, insurance companies, and banks). These institutional venture capital/private equity entities and private funds focus on a wide range of risk-oriented investment opportunities from seed money and early-stage start-ups to later-stage growth-equity investments, recapitalizations, buyouts, turn-arounds, and industry consolidations.

¶107 FREQUENTLY USED DEFINITIONS

"AFR" means applicable federal rate (published monthly by IRS in short, medium, and long-term versions), as defined in Code §§1274 and 7872.

"AIP" when used to describe a debt instrument means adjusted issue price as defined in Code §1272(a)(4) and as used in Code §108(e)(3).

"AMT" means alternative minimum tax under Code §55.

"AR" means attribute reduction, as determined under Code §108(b).

"Asset COB" means asset carry-over tax basis in a transaction structured for carry-over rather than asset SUB under the Code.

"Asset SUB" means asset stepped-up tax basis in a transaction structured to achieve a new tax basis for acquired assets reflecting the purchase price for the assets rather than asset COB under the Code.

"Badco" means a company which has fallen upon hard financial times.

"BDC" means a Business Development Company as defined in the Investment Company Act of 1940 or the Investment Advisers Act of 1940, as the case may be.

"BHC" means a bank holding company.

"BHCA" means the Bank Holding Company Act.

"BIG" means built-in gain (i.e., the excess of FV over tax basis) under the Code.

"Bigco" means a large corporation, generally engaged in many businesses.

"BIL" means built-in loss (i.e., the excess of tax basis over FV) under the Code.

"Buyout" means an LBO or an MBO.

"C corporation" means a corporation which is taxed under Code §11 and subchapter C (and thus generally subjected to double tax under the Code), rather than a corporation which has elected to be taxed as a flow-through entity under subchapter S of the Code.

"CG" means capital gain.

"CL" means capital loss.

"COB" means carry-over tax basis in a transaction structured for carry-over rather than asset SUB under the Code.

"Code" means the Internal Revenue Code of 1986, as amended.

"CODI" means cancellation of debt income, as determined under Code §108.

"CYTM" means constant yield to maturity.

"DC" means debt cancellation, as determined under Code §108.

"DER" means debt-equity ratio.

"DRD" means dividends received deduction under Code §243.

"E" is an entrepreneur who wishes to start or has started a business.

"E&P" means earnings and profits, as described in Code §312.

"ERISA" means the Employee Retirement Income Security Act of 1974, as amended.

"FASB" means Financial Accounting Standards Board.

"Fed" means the Board of Governors of the Federal Reserve System

"FP" means a foreign person.

"FTC" means the Federal Trade Commission.

"FV" means fair value.

"GAAP" means generally accepted accounting principles.

"Ginsburg and Levin M&A book" means Mergers, Acquisitions, and Buyouts, published by Aspen Publishers, updated and republished semiannually.

"GP" means general partner.

"IA" means investment adviser.

"IAA" means the Investment Advisers Act of 1940, as amended.

"IB" means investment banker.

"ICA" means the Investment Company Act of 1940, as amended.

"IPO" means initial public offering.

"IRR" means compound internal rate of return.

"IRS" means the Internal Revenue Service.

"ISO" means an incentive stock option, as defined in Code §422.

"LBO" means leveraged buyout.

"LLC" means a limited liability company which, unless otherwise stated, is treated as a partnership for federal income tax purposes under the Code §7701 check-the-box regulations.

"LP" means limited partner.

"LTCG" means long-term capital gain, i.e., gain from the sale or taxable exchange of a capital asset held more than one year.

"LTCL" means long-term capital loss, i.e., loss from the sale or taxable exchange of a capital asset held more than one year.

"Market traded" when used to describe a debt instrument for purposes of Code §108 means publicly traded on an established securities market as defined at ¶803.4.

"MBO" means management buyout.

"Newco" means a newly-formed company, which is a regular C corporate entity, unless the phrase "Newco S" or "Newco partnership" or "Newco LLC" is used.

"NOL" means net operating loss.

"NOLCF" means net operating loss carryforward.

"NQO" means non-qualified stock option, that is, a stock option which does not meet the Code §422 requirements for ISO status.

"NQ Pfd" means non-qualified preferred stock as defined in Code §351(g) and §354(a)(2)(C) and discussed in ¶403.1(9) through (15) of this book.

"OI" means ordinary income (i.e., taxable income which is not CG).

"OID" means original issue discount, as defined in Code §1273.

"Oldco" means an existing company, which is a regular C corporate entity, unless the phrase "Oldco S" or "Oldco partnership" or "Oldco LLC" is used.

"PBGC" means the Pension Benefit Guaranty Corporation.

"PE fund" or "PE Fund" means a fund (generally formed as a partnership) which is engaged in making venture capital/private equity investments.

"PIK" means payment in kind for a debenture or preferred stock which pays interest or preferred yield in additional debentures or preferred stock ("bunny debentures" or "bunny preferred").

"Preferred OID" means the excess of preferred stock's liquidation/redemption amount over its issue price, as defined in Code §305(b)(4) and (c).

"Prop. Reg." means Proposed Treasury Regulation.

"PV" means present value.

"RULPA" means the Revised Uniform Limited Partnership Act of 1976 or 1985, as the case may be.

"S corporation"or "SCo" means a corporation which has elected to be taxed as a flow-through entity under subchapter S of the Code.

"SAR" means stock appreciation right.

"SBIC" means a small business investment company, licensed by the Small Business Administration (the "SBA").

"SEC" means the Securities and Exchange Commission.

"SUB" means stepped-up tax basis (1) under Code §1012 for an asset purchase or a stock purchase structured to achieve a tax basis reflecting the purchase price for the assets rather than COB under the Code, or (2) under Code §1014(a) for assets owned by an individual who has died or, in certain circumstances, owned by a partnership when an individual partner has died.

"Target" means the acquired company in a buyout.

"TEO" means tax-exempt organization, as defined in Code §501.

"Treas. Reg." means Treasury Regulation.

"UBTI" means unrelated business taxable income, as defined in Code §511 through §514.

"ULPA" means the Uniform Limited Partnership Act of 1916 or 2001, as the case may be.

"VC" means a professional venture capital investor.

"1933 Act" means the Securities Act of 1933, as amended.

"1934 Act" means the Securities Exchange Act of 1934, as amended.

"80-80 test" means the 80%-or-more-by-value and 80%-or-more-by-vote test for Code §1504 affiliation between two or more corporations, satisfaction of which allows them to file a consolidated federal income tax return if they so elect, and (whether or not a consolidation return is filed) to liquidate tax-free (and with COB) the subsidiary into its corporate parent under Code §332.

CHAPTER 2

Structuring Start-Up Transaction

Chapter 2. Structuring Start-Up Transaction

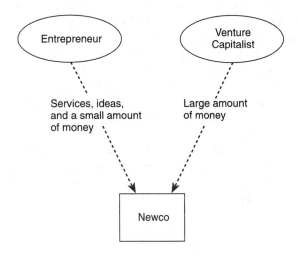

E, an entrepreneur, wishes to start a business. E may have a new high-tech invention or a low-tech improvement on an existing product, or E may merely have a new no-tech approach to the manufacture or marketing of an established product or service.

E's concept may require substantial research, development, and/or other activities before the proposed business will be ready to begin actual sales of goods or services, so that E is seeking seed money. Or E may have passed the seed money stage and may now need early-stage venture capital to begin producing goods or providing services.

In either event, E has approached VC seeking $1 million to start the proposed new business (or to enhance a business which E recently commenced). E and VC have decided to form Newco as a C corporation.

Where Newco is formed as a C corporation, Newco is generally subjected to federal income tax on its income at the corporate entity level, at rates ranging up to 35%. When Newco-C corporation distributes its after-tax accumulated income to its shareholders as dividends, individual shareholders are subjected to a second federal income tax—at OI rates ranging up to 38.6% for 2002 and 2003.

Thus, C corporation earnings are subjected to double tax under the U.S. federal income tax system for C corporations.[1] Indeed, even where the C corporation accumulates its after-tax income rather than distributing dividends (so that there is no shareholder-level tax on the C corporation's accumulated earnings), there is a second shareholder-level federal income tax (albeit at a 20% LTCG rate) when the shareholder sells his or her stock for a price which reflects the corporation's accumulated income, i.e., for a price which is larger than it would have been if the corporation had distributed its accumulated income, unless the shareholder retains the stock until his or her death produces SUB for the stock.[2]

(The possibility of forming Newco as a tax flow-through entity, i.e., a S corporation, a partnership, or an LLC none of which are subject to double tax, is explored in Chapter 3.)

E's proposal to VC on how their ownership interests in Newco should be structured (all common stock) and VC's 7 objections to E's all common stock proposed structure are set forth in ¶201 below. VC's more complex counterproposal to E (under which VC would purchase non-convertible debentures and preferred stock in addition to common stock) is set forth in ¶202 below. Just in case E does not accept VC's counter proposal, VC is considering 2 alternative ownership structures (under which VC would purchase either (1) convertible debentures or convertible preferred stock or (2) participating double dip preferred stock), as set forth at ¶203 below.

Although VC has not accepted E's initial proposal, VC believes that E's business concepts are very promising, that E is an extraordinarily able manager and/or inventor, and that Newco will prosper. Hence VC is interested in investing in Newco if mutually acceptable terms can be negotiated with E.

---

[1] One of the traditional methods for blunting the double tax imposed with respect to C corporations is the C corporation's payment of substantial deductible compensation to its shareholder-executives. However, compensation paid by a corporation is deductible only to the extent it constitutes "reasonable . . . compensation for personal services actually rendered." Excessive compensation (i.e., compensation in excess of this "reasonable" standard) to a shareholder is treated as a non-deductible dividend. Thus, where the economic arrangement between VC and E is that (1) Newco will pay E $100,000 per year as recompense for E's services and (2) VC and E will share Newco's profits in excess of $100,000 proportionately to their stockholdings, it is difficult to transmute Newco's taxable income in excess of $100,000 to deductible compensation when VC is not performing substantial services for Newco.

[2] A Bush administration 1/03 legislative proposal would, if enacted, (1) abolish the shareholder-level tax on dividends paid in 2003 and later by a C corporation to the extent of the corporation's after-tax profits earned in 2002 or later on which the corporation paid tax (either federal income tax or tax paid to a foreign country which qualifies for the U.S. foreign tax credit) ("taxed profits") and (2) increase shareholder-level tax basis in the corporation's stock to the extent of each shareholder's proportionate share of the corporation's taxed profits not paid out as dividends. Because future prospects for this controversial legislative proposal are highly uncertain, the text of this book is based on current law and does not further discuss this legislative proposal.

¶201   E's PROPOSED STRUCTURE—ALL COMMON STOCK

E, being very aggressive and desiring simplicity, makes the following proposal to VC regarding their contributions to, ownership of, and control positions in, Newco corporation:

	VC	*E*
Amount invested in Newco	$1 million	E's ideas, experience, and future services
Newco common stock received	40 shares	60 shares

E sees no need for any additional contractual arrangements among E, VC, and Newco regarding (e.g.) control of Newco corporation's board of directors.

There are at least 7 reasons VC rejects E's all-common-stock structure for Newco, as discussed below.

¶201.1   Code §83(a) Adverse Tax Effect on E

¶201.1.1   E's Code §83(a) OI on Bargain Purchase of Newco Stock

Under E's proposal, E may immediately owe tax on $600,000 or more of OI.

Under Code §83(a), a service provider receiving "property" "in connection with the performance of services" recognizes OI (when he or she receives the property) equal to the property's FV less the amount paid for the property (the "spread"). Here Newco is worth at least $1 million immediately after the transaction (i.e., the amount of cash Newco receives from VC) and E receives 60% of Newco's stock. Thus E arguably receives at least $600,000 FV of Newco stock (60% × $1 million = $600,000) "in connection with the performance of services" but makes no payment in exchange for such stock.

OI tax would be imposed on this $600,000 at the front end when E receives his or her Newco stock, even though E receives no cash with which to pay the OI tax.

Indeed, an especially unpleasant IRS agent might argue that, since sophisticated VC was willing to invest $1 million for 40% of Newco, Newco must therefore be worth $2.5 million ($1 million ÷ 40%), so that E's 60% of Newco's stock must be worth $1.5 million, rather than $600,000, in which event E would owe OI tax on $1.5 million.

The top federal tax rate on an individual's OI is 18.6 points higher than the top federal rate on an individual's LTCG. Thus, E is disadvantaged by paying tax at the higher OI rate rather than the lower LTCG rate and also by paying that tax at the front end when the Newco stock is issued to E rather than many years later at the back end when E sells the Newco stock.

- An individual's 2002 and 2003 OI is taxed at a top federal rate of 38.6%.
- Where the service provider is an employee (rather than an independent contractor), current compensation is subject to immediate income tax withholding.
- In addition to normal income tax as detailed above, an individual's compensation income is subjected to an uncapped medicare tax (i.e., with no ceiling on the amount subject to the tax) equal to 1.45% (non-deductible) on the employee and 1.45% (deductible) on the employer (with the full 2.9% [one-half deductible] imposed on a self-employed person's earnings).
- By contrast, the top federal tax rate on an individual's LTCG (i.e., CG from the sale or taxable exchange of a capital asset held more than one year)[1] is 20% and CG is not subject to the 1.45%/2.9% uncapped medicare tax.
- Indeed, under certain circumstances, LTCG realized by an individual qualifies for a special lower rate (18% for property acquired after 12/31/00 and held more than 5 years, 14% for "small business stock" held more than 5 years, and a tax-free rollover opportunity for "small business stock" held more than 6 months). See ¶906 below for details.
- In addition, an individual's itemized deductions are generally disallowed in an amount equal to 3% of his or her adjusted gross income in excess of approximately $139,500 for 2003 (adjusted each year for inflation). This adds at least 1.2 additional points of tax (38.6% × 3%) on an individual's OI and LTCG (.6 additional points of tax on an individual's LTCG which qualifies for the Code §1202 reduced rate).

¶201.1.2 Several Approaches for Avoiding or Minimizing Code §83(a) OI

(1) Code §351. E can escape tax on this bargain purchase of Newco stock to the extent E contributes to Newco "property" rather than services. E's receipt of Newco stock in exchange for "property" is tax-free under Code §351, dealing with tax-free corporate formations. While "property" within the meaning of Code §351 includes patents, copyrights, secret formulas, confidential knowhow, and other legally protectable intangible assets, "property" does not for this purpose include E's past services to, or E's agreement to perform future services for, Newco. Hence in many VC-financed start-ups E's contribution to Newco does not rise to the level of Code §351 "property" but rather consists of only a promise to bring his or her experience to bear on behalf of and to perform services for Newco.

Even where E's contribution to Newco does consist in part of "property," to the extent the FV of E's Newco stock exceeds the FV of E's contributed "property" E nevertheless recognizes Code §83(a) OI equal to such excess. Indeed, where E does contribute valuable property to Newco, the FV of such property (in addition

---

¶201 [1] An individual's gain from the sale or taxable exchange of a capital asset held one year or less (short-term CG) is taxed at OI rates up to 38.6% for 2002 and 2003.

to VC's cash contribution to Newco) must be taken into account in valuing Newco's stock and hence in valuing E's Newco stock.

(2)   **Temporal differentiation.** A second approach by which E might escape Code §83(a) OI is where there is a sufficiently wide temporal gap between (a) E's formation of Newco and receipt of 60 Newco shares and (b) VC's subsequent investment in Newco. In the case discussed in this chapter 2, there is no temporal gap, that is, E and VC are forming Newco together, with VC paying a substantially greater price for each Newco common share than E is paying, thus creating a patent Code §83(a) issue for E.

However, if E had formed Newco and began to develop Newco's business on (e.g.) 1/1 year 1 and E first began negotiations with VC 6 months later on 6/30 year 1, E could then take the position that (a) when E formed Newco on 1/1 year 1, contributing very little to Newco in exchange for 60 Newco common shares, E's 60 Newco common shares were worth very little, i.e., there was on 1/1 year 1 no Code §83(a) excess of stock FV over the price E paid for his or her 60 Newco shares, (b) over the 6 months subsequent to Newco's 1/1 year 1 formation, Newco's stock appreciated substantially in value, and (c) when VC paid $1 million cash for 40 Newco common shares on 6/30 year 1, VC paid a higher price for each Newco common share than had E on 1/1 year 1 because Newco's FV on 6/30 year 1 was far greater than it had been 6 months earlier. Under this approach, E recognizes no 1/1 year 1 Code §83(a) OI upon receipt of 60 Newco common shares (because E paid an amount equal to the 1/1 year 1 FV of such shares), and E recognizes no 6/30 year 1 Code §83(a) OI when VC buys 40 Newco common shares for a much larger per share price (because E received no additional Newco shares at that time).

Could E obtain this desirable tax result in the case discussed in this chapter 2—even though E and VC had already reached agreement on the terms of both Newco's formation and VC's Newco investment—by quickly forming Newco and buying 60 Newco shares for a low price on 1/1 year 1 and then waiting a few days (e.g., until 1/15 year 1) before VC consummates its $1 million Newco investment? Where VC and E had already reached agreement before E formed Newco, and indeed even where negotiations were in progress and on track, IRS would likely argue (with success) that, under the step transaction doctrine, E's receipt of 60 Newco shares upon Newco's 1/1 year 1 formation should be viewed as a single integrated transaction along with VC's $1 million 1/15 year 1 investment in Newco. Indeed, even if for some reason the step transaction doctrine did not apply, IRS would likely argue (with success) that, where VC's investment occurs within a relatively short time after E's receipt of 60 Newco shares (and without the temporal gap necessary for E's shares thereafter to appreciate substantially in value), VC's 1/15 year 1 purchase price for 40 Newco shares (shortly after E's 1/1 year 1 purchase of 60 Newco shares at a lower price) constitutes probative evidence of the shares' FV when E received his or her 60 shares.

Obviously, the likelihood that E can avoid or minimize Code §83(a) OI by such a temporal gap is enhanced to the extent the temporal gap between E's purchase of Newco stock and VC's subsequent purchase grows longer, the negotiations between E and VC at the time of E's purchase are more nascent (or better yet non-existent), and significant positive events occur after E's purchase and before VC's purchase providing reasons for Newco's stock to appreciate between E's and VC's purchase.

(3) Substantive differentiation. The third approach for avoiding or minimizing E's Code §83(a) OI is to issue VC different and more valuable securities (e.g., Newco preferred stock) than the Newco common shares purchased by E, so that E can claim that VC's higher purchase price per share for Newco's more senior and more valuable securities is not probative (or at least only minimally probative) as to the value of E's more junior and less valuable common shares. This approach is reviewed in ¶202 and ¶203.

¶201.2   Split of Proceeds If Newco Not Successful

If Newco is *not* successful and liquidates before Newco has spent all of VC's $1 million investment, VC wants a preference for most of its $1 million investment (i.e., VC does not want to receive only 40% of the remaining money).

EXAMPLE

If Newco's project becomes unfeasible and Newco prematurely liquidates after spending only $100,000 (i.e., while Newco still has $900,000), the entire $900,000, rather than only $360,000 (40% of $900,000), should go to VC.

¶201.3   Split of Proceeds If Newco Successful

If Newco *is* successful and is profitably sold several years later, VC wants a preference for most of its $1 million investment and wants only the *profits* to be shared (i.e., under E's proposal 40% to VC and 60% to E).

EXAMPLE

If Newco is sold after 3 years for $2 million (i.e., double the $1 million invested), VC should *not* receive $800,000 (40% of $2 million), but rather should receive its $1 million investment (perhaps plus an interest yield) plus a percentage of the remaining profit ($1 million profit less a possible interest yield on VC's investment).

¶201.4   *Interest Deduction*

VC wants at least a portion of its $1 million investment in Newco to be debt, so that VC's yield on the amount so invested will be tax deductible to Newco as interest expense and hence will reduce Newco's corporate-level income tax.

¶201.5   *VC's Internal Rate of Return*

VC wants more than 40% of Newco's common stock because (1) VC is supplying 100% of Newco's funding, (2) VC's money is worth a full $1 million, (3) E's services and ideas are not so novel (in VC's humble view), and (4) VC wants a higher IRR than it expects to realize from simply owning 40% of Newco's common stock.

¶201.6   *E's Good-Faith Investment*

VC wants E to invest (i.e., put at risk) in Newco enough money to show E's faith in the project.

¶201.7   *E's Conditional Right to Retain Newco Stock*

VC wants E to realize the benefits from E's Newco common stock only if E stays with Newco for a substantial period *and* the project is successful, i.e., VC wants E's stock to be subject to vesting.

¶202   VC's PROPOSED STRUCTURE— NON-CONVERTIBLE DEBENTURES AND PREFERRED IN ADDITION TO COMMON

In order to cure VC's 7 objections to E's all-common-stock structure for Newco, VC proposes the following capital structure:

	VC	E
Non-convertible subordinated debenture	$ 500,000	$ —
Non-convertible preferred stock	440,000	—
Common stock		
60% VC: 60 shares at $1,000 per share	60,000	—
40% E: 40 shares at $1,000 per share	—	40,000
Total	$1,000,000	$40,000

VC advances numerous reasons for and explanations of this more complex capital structure, as set forth below.

¶202.1   *VC Senior Claim*

Under VC's proposed structure, VC has a senior claim to Newco's first $940,000 (plus accrued interest on VC's subordinated debenture and accrued preferred dividends on VC's preferred stock) of distributions and any excess available for distribution by Newco will be distributed 60% to VC and 40% to E.

A portion of VC's $940,000 senior claim is structured as debt, which will allow (1) Newco a deduction for the yield (i.e., interest) accruing to VC on the debenture and (2) VC return of capital treatment (i.e., to avoid Code §302 OI treatment) on redemption of the debenture.

The remainder of VC's senior claim is structured as preferred stock, so that Newco's DER will not be excessive, in order to maximize the likelihood that the debenture will be treated as debt for tax purposes.

See ¶602.8 below regarding Newco's interest deduction on borrowed money and ¶603.8 below regarding OI tax aspects of a preferred stock redemption.

There is some risk that, in case of Newco's bankruptcy, VC's debentures might be equitably subordinated to Newco's obligations to its other creditors because of VC's control position.

Under this (or any of the other complex capital structures discussed below), VC and E (and any other equity owners) would generally enter into a shareholders' agreement specifying that if Newco's ultimate disposition is effectuated by a stock sale (rather than by an asset sale plus Newco liquidation), the aggregate sale proceeds will be allocated among Newco's security holders in the same fashion as if Newco had sold its assets and distributed the proceeds pursuant to Newco's capital structure (so that the debenture plus accrued interest would first be paid in full, then the preferred stock plus accrued dividends would be paid in full, and then the common shareholders would share any remaining sales proceeds proportionally to their common stock).

¶202.2   *E's Purchase of Common Stock*

Where E has a substantial personal investment in Newco's common stock, E will be less likely to walk away from Newco in frustration should the development of Newco's business progress more slowly than expected (as often happens).

Hence under VC's proposed structure, E will either pay $40,000 cash to Newco or give Newco a combination of cash and E's personal note totalling $40,000, to purchase E's 40 common shares.[1] Thus, E will pay (in cash or by note) the same price per common share as VC ($1,000 per share), but E will not be required to buy the more expensive and less desirable (because of limited upside potential) non-convertible debenture and non-convertible preferred stock.

¶202.2.1 No Significant Code §83(a) OI

Under this approach E should not have any significant Code §83(a) OI, because E is paying (or agreeing to pay) $1,000 per share for 40 Newco common shares which appear for 2 reasons to be worth $40,000:

- *First*, E is paying the same price ($1,000 per share) for E's Newco common stock as is VC.
- *Second*, Newco has assets of $1,040,000 immediately after the transaction ($1 million received from VC and $40,000 from E). After subtracting Newco's $940,000 in senior obligations (the debenture and the preferred), Newco's aggregate common stock appears to be worth $100,000. This is $1,000 for each of Newco's 100 outstanding common shares. Hence, the common shares purchased by E appear to have an FV equal to the price paid by E.

¶202.2.2 Modest Code §83(a) OI Risk

There is, however, some slight risk IRS may take the position that E's common shares have a somewhat higher FV than E's $1,000 per share cost. This risk is exacerbated to the extent:

- the dividend rate on the VC preferred stock, or the interest rate on the VC debenture, or both, is below a market rate, so that the preferred stock and/or debenture purchased by VC are worth less than face and hence the common stock purchased by E is worth more than its purchase price, and/or
- the aggregate purchase price for the common stock is disproportionately low compared to the aggregate purchase price for the preferred stock and debenture, so that the common derives an "option" value from the substantial leverage provided by the debenture and preferred.

¶202 [1] Under the corporation laws of many states, E must pay in cash or property (but not by a note) an amount at least equal to the par value of the Newco shares purchased.

Under Sarbanes-Oxley Act of 2002 ("SO") §402 E is apparently prohibited from paying any part of the Newco stock's purchase price by a note where Newco is an "issuer" as defined in SO §402 (generally a company with publicly-issued or publicly-traded securities, as described in more detail in ¶501.5.4.2).

¶202.2.3   Recourse Note

For tax reasons (as well as to achieve the business goal of placing E at risk), where E pays part or all of the purchase price for Newco stock by issuing a note to Newco, E's note should be full (or at least partial) recourse, and not merely a non-recourse note secured only by E's 40 Newco common shares. If E were to deliver only a non-recourse note or a small amount of cash plus a non-recourse note for the balance, IRS would undoubtedly take the position that E has not really purchased the stock but merely has an option to purchase the stock, with less-advantageous tax results. See Code §83 regulations treating a purchase of stock for a non-recourse note as an option and ¶407 below describing taxation of options.

However, where E has a substantial amount at risk with respect to Newco stock purchased for a non-recourse note, the arrangement is not the economic equivalent of an option and hence, we believe, should not be treated as an option for income tax purposes. This is generally the case where:

- E's note is partially recourse to E, or
- E pays a portion of the purchase price in cash and all the purchased Newco stock (both the stock purchased for cash and the stock purchased for a non-recourse note) secures the non-recourse note, or
- the non-recourse note is secured by property in additional to the Newco stock purchased by E with the non-recourse note (including other Newco stock owned by E), so long as the partial recourse features, the cash down payment, and/or the other property securing the note are "substantial" in relation to the price of the stock.[2]

¶202.2.4   Interest-Bearing Note

To avoid imputed interest and imputed Code §83(a) consequences for tax purposes, E's note should bear interest at least equal to the AFR—see Code §1274, §483, and §7872. Newco can agree to pay E annual bonuses to defray E's interest payments to Newco on the note.

¶202.2.5   E's Interest Deduction

Because of Code §163(d)'s limitation on the deductibility of "investment interest," E may not be able to deduct interest expense against compensation (including

---

[2] See ¶407.3.5 for a discussion of the accounting aspects of Newco's stock sale to E, including the possibility that Newco may be forced to apply variable accounting under APB 25 where E purchases Newco stock with a note, resulting in increased compensation charges to Newco's income for financial accounting purposes.

See ¶501.5.4.2 for a discussion of SO §402 prohibiting E from paying for Newco stock with a note generally where Newco has public-issued or publicly-traded securities.

bonus) income received from Newco. Hence, from a tax standpoint, it may be desirable for the note to be secured by a second mortgage on E's residence in order to avoid the Code §163(d) limitation on deductions for investment interest. See Code §163(h) allowing a deduction for interest on up to $100,000 of debt secured by a personal residence even where the loan proceeds are not used to acquire or rehabilitate the personal residence.[3]

If this is not feasible, it may be desirable, from E's viewpoint, for Newco to "gross up" the bonus (i.e., pay E an amount equal to the income tax imposed on the bonus *plus* the income tax imposed on the gross-up payment).

¶202.3   *Vesting*

To insure that E will realize the benefits from E's Newco common shares only if E stays with Newco for a substantial period, 50% of E's 40 common shares (i.e., 20 shares) will *"time vest"* based solely on E's continued employment.

To insure that E will realize the benefits from at least a part of E's Newco common shares only if the Newco project is successful, 50% of E's 40 common shares (i.e., 20 shares) will *"performance vest"* based upon Newco's performance during E's continued employment.

¶202.3.1   Option to Repurchase from E at Cost

Time and/or performance vesting is implemented by granting Newco and/or VC the option to repurchase at cost (or perhaps at the lower of cost or FV):

- E's *time vesting shares* which have not yet time vested when E leaves Newco's employ, and
- E's *performance vesting shares* which have not yet vested when E leaves Newco's employ because the performance goal has not yet been satisfied (and, even while E remains in Newco's employ, E's performance vesting shares as to which the performance goal has been failed).

¶202.3.2   Time Vesting

Twenty of E's shares time vest over 5 years, so long as E's employment continues. There are a number of approaches to structuring a time vesting schedule:

- Daily prorated vesting (a pro-rata portion of the shares vests each day E's employment continues) *vs.* annual cliff vesting (no shares vest in a year

---

[3] However, for purposes of calculating E's AMT (rather than E's regular income tax), E's interest expense would continue to be subject to the Code §163(d) deduction limitation, because the AMT rules do not allow a home mortgage interest deduction when the money was borrowed for a purpose other than acquiring or rehabilitating the home.

unless E is employed on the last day of the year) *vs.* cliff vesting at the end of 5 years (no shares vest unless E is employed on the last day of the 5-year period).

- Straight-line vesting (4 shares vest each year for 5 years) *vs.* back-end-loaded vesting (2 shares vest the first year, 3 shares vest the second year, 4 shares vest the third, 5 shares the fourth, 6 shares the fifth) *vs.* front-end-loaded vesting (6 shares vest the first year, 5 shares vest the second year, 4 shares vest the third year, 3 shares the fourth, 2 shares the fifth).

- Possible special accelerated vesting for unvested Newco stock upon E's death or disability, E's termination by Newco without cause, or E's resignation for good reason (e.g., substantial reduction by Newco in E's status, authority, or compensation, or E's forced relocation to a different geographic region, perhaps northern Alaska).

- Possible special accelerated vesting upon sale of Newco or Newco's IPO at a price which produces more than a stated IRR on VC's investment.

In the case of special accelerated vesting upon sale of Newco, the golden parachute tax rules may impose on E an extra 20 percentage points of federal tax on the spread in the Newco shares at vesting (whether E makes a Code §83 election or not) and deny Newco a deduction for amounts otherwise deductible (i.e., the spread in the Newco shares at vesting where E did not make a Code §83(b) election), because the compensation (here the vesting) occurs on account of a change in control of Newco or a change in ownership of its business. Code §280G and §4999.

Hence, it is desirable for as many Newco shares as possible to be regularly vested before Newco is sold, i.e., for as few shares as possible to specially vest because of Newco's sale. This goal is advanced by daily prorated straight-line or front-end-loaded vesting as opposed to back-end-loaded cliff vesting.

In addition, a special 75% vote of Newco's voting shareholders may nullify the golden parachute tax, but harsh IRS rules make it difficult to utilize this escape: Newco must be privately held at the time of Newco's sale, failure to obtain the requisite 75% shareholder vote must defeat E's accelerated vesting on Newco's sale, failure to disclose all material facts to Newco's shareholders would negate the vote, and changes in ownership of Newco's voting stock between the 75% shareholder vote and Newco's sale may negate the vote.

Thus, it is often feasible to hold a vote of privately-held Newco's shareholders at the front-end when Newco first enters into the vesting agreement with E. However, this front-end vote will be negated from a golden parachute tax standpoint if (1) Newco goes public before the accelerated vesting at sale occurs, *or* (2) there is a more than 25% change in ownership of Newco's voting stock between the shareholder vote and the sale of Newco so that the persons who voted in favor of the special vesting at the front-end do not own at least 75% of Newco's voting stock at back-end when Newco is sold, *or* (3) the facts at sale have changed so that the disclosures to shareholders at the time of the front-end shareholder vote were not a sufficiently accurate and complete description of the situation at the back-end when Newco is sold.

If Newco is still privately held at the time Newco is being sold, its shareholders could hold a new back-end vote, but such a back-end vote is effective for golden parachute tax purposes only where E agrees in advance of the vote to give up his or her right to accelerated vesting at Newco's sale unless the new 75% shareholder approval is obtained.

¶202.3.3   Performance Vesting

Twenty of E's shares performance vest based on several goals which must be satisfied within specified time periods while E's employment with Newco continues. For example:

- 5 shares vest if a working prototype is developed within 9 months.
- 7 shares vest if sales reach $5 million within 2 years.
- 8 shares vest if net income reaches $1 million within 3 years.
- Possible accelerated vesting for death, disability, termination without cause, resignation for good reason, sale of Newco, or Newco IPO. See ¶202.3.2 above for a discussion of the golden parachute tax that may apply if vesting is accelerated by a sale of Newco.
- Perhaps special cumulative vesting if Newco misses one performance goal but meets a subsequent goal.

¶202.3.4   No Code §83(b) Election

As discussed in ¶201.1.1 above, a service provider receiving "property" "in connection with the performance of services" normally recognizes OI under Code §83(a) (equal to the spread between the purchase price and the FV of the property) when he or she receives the property. However, §83(a) postpones both recognition and measurement of the service provider's OI where the property is subject to vesting at the time the service provider receives the property and the service provider does not make a timely Code §83(b) election.

Where E receives 40 Newco shares subject to vesting and makes no §83(b) election, E will recognize §83(a) OI (and Newco will generally be entitled to a §83(h) deduction) when each Newco common share vests (i.e., when there is no longer a set of events which allows Newco or VC to buy a share from E at a forfeiture price, that is, a price substantially below FV), equal to the share's FV at the time of vesting *less* E's purchase price for the share.

The tax cost could be substantial if Newco is successful, because E will owe OI tax (not lower LTCG tax) on the spread at the time of vesting (which should be substantially greater than the spread at the time E purchased the shares).[4] However, Newco may still be privately held at vesting, so that E may not then

---

[4] E's compensation OI is subject to immediate income and uncapped medicare tax withholding at the time of vesting where E is an employee (rather than an independent contractor).

be able to sell the stock in order to obtain cash with which to pay the OI tax due at vesting.

Where E contributes "property" to Newco in exchange for part or all of the Newco common shares received by E, so that E's receipt of such Newco shares in exchange for property is covered by Code §351 (see ¶201.1.2(1) above), but such shares are subject to time or performance vesting and E fails to make a timely §83(b) election, E will subsequently recognize §83(a) OI (and Newco will subsequently be allowed a §83(h) deduction) equal to the FV of such shares at time of vesting in excess of the FV of the property contributed to Newco by E (measured at the time of E's original contribution of the property to Newco). This result likely follows because E received the shares "in connection with the performance of services" for Newco (as demonstrated by the vesting attached to the shares), even though the original issuance of the shares was covered by §351.

Where there are multiple vesting events with respect to the same Newco share and E has not made a timely §83(b) election, E's OI (and Newco's §83(h) deduction) will be recognized and measured only when the last vesting event with respect to the share occurs. For example, assume that Newco has 3 options to repurchase E's Newco shares, each of which 3 options has a different exercise price and is exercisable by Newco only upon the occurrence of a different specified event:

- Newco's first option to repurchase E's Newco shares is exercisable only if E leaves Newco's employ before the first anniversary of the stock sale to E and this option has an exercise price equal to E's *cost* for the shares ($1,000 per share).
- Newco's second option to repurchase E's Newco shares is exercisable only if E leaves Newco's employ on or after the first anniversary of the stock sale to E but before the fifth anniversary of the stock sale to E and this option has an exercise price equal to the *book value* of the shares (which is, and the parties reasonably believe will continue to be, substantially below the shares' FV).
- Newco's third option to repurchase E's Newco shares is exercisable only if E leaves Newco's employ on or after the fifth anniversary of the stock sale to E and this option has an exercise price equal to the *appraised FV* of the shares.
- E does *not* make a timely Code §83(b) election.

In this case, the §83 measurement date occurs (and hence E's OI is calculated and taxed) only on the fifth anniversary of the stock sale to E, so long as E is then still employed by Newco (because on the fifth anniversary the cost and book-value buy-back options both expire and the only remaining buy-back option is at full appraised FV).

¶202.3.5   Code §83(b) Election

If E *does* make a timely Code §83(b) election, E will recognize Code §83(a) OI[5] (and Newco will be entitled to a §83(h) deduction) when E purchases the 40 Newco common shares but only to the extent the shares' FV at the time of purchase (ignoring the vesting provisions) exceeds their cost—presumably here the excess is zero for the reasons discussed at ¶202.2.1 above—and there will be no further tax ramifications when the shares vest.

See ¶202.2.2 above for a discussion of the slight risk IRS may argue for a higher FV at purchase.

To be effective, E's Code §83(b) election must be filed with IRS within 30 days after E purchases the Newco common shares and a copy must be filed with E's federal income tax return.[6] No extension for filing a Code §83(b) election is permitted.

Where Newco and E have entered into a contractual vesting arrangement with respect to E's Newco stock (e.g., Newco has the option to repurchase E's stock at a forfeiture price under specified circumstances), the arrangement would (under state corporate law—see, e.g., Del. Gen. Corp. Law §202) generally not bind a transferee of E's stock who is ignorant of the arrangement, unless E's stock certificate contains a legend referring to the contractual vesting arrangement. Hence it is typical to place such a legend on the certificate representing unvested shares. Where, however, there is no such legend, IRS regulations treat E's ability to transfer the shares as the equivalent of a Code §83(b) election, although two murky court decisions, dealing with confused facts, might be read (erroneously in our view) as inconsistent with this result.

¶202.3.6   Newco Deduction

Newco's §83(h) deduction is equal in amount to E's OI.

The exact timing of Newco's §83(h) deduction can be a bit tricky where Newco uses a fiscal year (but E uses a calendar year, as do almost all humans). Where the stock is vested at the time transferred to E, Newco's deduction is recognized at the time the stock is transferred to E. However, where the stock is not vested at the time transferred to E, E makes no §83(b) election, and the stock vests later, Newco's deduction is recognized on the last day of E's tax year during which the stock vests. Hence if Newco and E are on different tax years and the stock vests after the end of E's tax year but before the end of Newco's tax year, Newco's deduction is postponed until Newco's tax year following vesting. When the stock is not vested at the time of transfer to E and E does make a §83(b) election, it

---

[5]Such OI is subject to immediate income and uncapped medicare tax withholding where E is an employee (rather than an independent contractor).

[6]Where E enters into an executory contract to purchase Newco shares on a future date (which shares are subject to vesting), it is possible (in light of a questionable 1996 court decision—Theophilos v. Commissioner, 85 F.3d 440 (9th Cir. 1996)) that E's 30-day period to file a §83(b) election begins to run on the contract date, rather than on the date the contract is closed and E buys the Newco stock.

appears that Newco's deduction is recognized on the last day of E's tax year during which E recognized §83(b) OI.

Under IRS regulations, the service recipient (here Newco) is permitted a Code §83(h) deduction only if the Code §83(a) income is "included" in the service provider's gross income, explained in the regulatory preamble to mean that the Code §83(a) income is either (1) reported on the service provider's original income tax return *or* (2) reported on the service provider's amended income tax return *or* (3) included in the service provider's gross income by IRS on audit.

Recognizing that it is generally difficult for the service recipient to ascertain whether a service provider has included an amount in gross income, the regulations contain a safe harbor, under which the service provider is "deemed to have included the amount as compensation in gross income" if the service recipient timely files form W-2 (with respect to a service provider who is an employee) or form 1099 (with respect to a service provider who is an independent contractor) with the service provider and IRS. To meet this rule the service recipient must generally file form W-2 or form 1099, as applicable, with the service provider by 1/31, and with IRS by 2/28, of the year following the year in which the income was taxable to the service provider.[7] These safe harbor rules apply equally whether the service provider is an employee or an independent contractor.

If the service recipient has not timely complied with the form W-2 or form 1099 requirements, it is still entitled to a deduction if it can "demonstrate that the [service provider] actually included the amount in income," according to the regulatory preamble.[8]

---

[7] When the service recipient's gross payments to a service provider fall within the form 1099 reporting exception for payments aggregating less than $600 in a taxable year, the service recipient is, according to the regulatory preamble, entitled to rely on the safe harbor without reporting.

However, when the service provider is a corporation so that the payments fall within the form 1099 reporting exemption for payments to a corporation, the service recipient can invoke the safe harbor, according to the regulatory preamble, only by filing a voluntary form 1099.

A special timing rule applies to the safe harbor with respect to a disqualifying disposition of ISO stock, under which the W-2 form must be furnished to the service provider and IRS by the time the service recipient files its tax return claiming the deduction.

[8] The §83(h) regulations described in text above (the "post-1994 regulations") condition Newco's Code §83(h) deduction on *either* Newco issuing a timely W-2 or 1099 covering E's Code §83(a) OI *or* E including the §83(a) OI in E's income (original return, amended return, or IRS audit adjustment). The post-1994 regulations superseded earlier §83(h) regulations (the "pre-1995 regulations") which had conditioned Newco's §83(h) deduction (with respect to a Newco employee) on whether Newco "deducts and withholds upon" E's corresponding §83(a) OI.

In a 1998 case, the Tax Court (in a decision reviewed by the full court) wrote 5 separate and conflicting opinions on the validity of the pre-1995 regulations. A bare majority of the Tax Court (9 judges) interpreted (1) Code §83(h) as conditioning the employer's deduction on the employee actually including the §83(a) OI in his or her taxable income and (2) the pre-1995 regulations as granting the employer a safe harbor under which the employer's deduction would be allowed without regard to whether the employee included the §83(a) OI if the employer satisfied its withholding requirement. A bare minority of the Tax Court (8 judges) reached a contrary conclusion, (a) 2 judges on the ground that the §83(h) statute automatically granted Newco a deduction whenever the Code *required* E to recognize §83(a) OI, so that the pre-1995 regulatory condition to a §83(h) deduction (employer withholding) was invalid, *and* (b) 6 judges on the alternative grounds that the statute automatically granted Newco a deduction whenever E was required to recognize §83(a) OI or that the pre-1995 regulations (which these 6 judges read in a strained fashion) did not impose employer withholding

Where E, the service provider, is an employee of Newco, the service recipient, Newco is required to withhold income and uncapped medicare taxes on the amount of E's OI.

Where the services for which E is being compensated are treated for tax purposes as producing future-year benefits for Newco, Newco's §83(h) deduction may be subject to capitalization.

¶202.3.7   E's LTCG on Sale

When E sells the Newco stock, E will recognize CG equal to the sales proceeds *less* the sum of the original purchase price ($40,000) and any §83 OI recognized at purchase (if the stock was fully vested or there was vesting on the stock but a §83(b) election was filed) or at vesting (if there was vesting on the stock and no §83(b) election was filed), i.e., any §83 OI recognized by E is added to E's tax basis in the stock and hence reduces E's CG on sale of the stock.

For example, if E receives fully vested stock (or stock with vesting but files a §83(b) election) and E recognizes no OI at purchase (because the stock's FV did not exceed its purchase price), all of E's profit on sale of the stock (i.e., the excess of E's sales proceeds over the price E paid for the stock) will be LTCG.

However, if E receives stock subject to vesting, files no §83(b) election, and recognizes substantial OI at vesting (because the stock's FV at vesting substantially exceeds E's purchase price), only the portion of E's profit on sale of the stock (i.e., the excess of E's sales proceeds over the stock's vesting date FV) will be LTCG (the remainder, equal to vesting date FV over the price E paid for the stock, having previously been taxed as §83 OI).

¶202.3.8   Vesting Subsequently Imposed On Outstanding Stock

E may form Newco and receive 40 Newco common shares, and VC may subsequently invest in Newco. See ¶201.1.2 for discussion of at least one tax reason for a temporal separation between (1) E's formation of and investment in Newco and (2) VC's subsequent investment in Newco.

What if E's original 40 Newco shares are fully vested (i.e., unrestricted) when received by E at the time of Newco's formation but, when VC subsequently invests in Newco, VC requires E to enter into a vesting agreement, i.e., VC requires E to

---

as an absolute condition to Newco's §83(h) deduction in the case of property that was vested when transferred to the employee. Venture Funding, Ltd. v. Commissioner, 110 T.C. 236 (1998), aff'd, 198 F.3d 248, 99-2 U.S.T.C. ¶50,972 (6th Cir. 1999).

The 9 judges in the Tax Court majority gave every indication that they would read the post-1994 §83(h) regulations (described in text above)—requiring *either* Newco to issue a timely W-2 or 1099 *or* E to include in income the §83(a) OI—a valid condition to Newco's §83(h) deduction, while the 8 Tax Court minority judges seemed likely to apply their dissenting views to the current (post-1994) regulations.

grant Newco and/or VC an option to repurchase E's 40 Newco shares at cost (or at the lower of cost or FV) if E does not meet specified time or performance goals?

Where E's unrestricted Newco shares are later subjected to vesting, can E successfully assert that, because E's 40 Newco shares were fully vested at the time of Newco's formation, (1) §83(a) applies to E's 40 shares only at the time they were issued (even without a timely §83(b) election), so that E recognizes OI only if (and only to the extent) the unrestricted shares were worth more than E's cost at the time of Newco's formation and (2) E recognizes no OI when the shares later vest?

There is risk IRS may reject this approach and argue that E (absent a timely §83(b) election) recognizes OI at vesting on one (or more) of 3 grounds:

(1) **Newco a shell company when E initially purchases stock.** IRS may take the position that E purchased cheap stock in a shell company (Newco) prior to making arrangements essential to Newco's future operations (such as obtaining commitments for necessary VC financing), so that Newco's initial transfer of the fully vested stock to E is disregarded as essentially meaningless and the transfer of Newco shares to E is viewed as occurring at the later date, when the essential business arrangements are settled (e.g., when the VC financing is arranged and vesting imposed), at which time the Newco stock is subject to vesting. If IRS were to succeed in this argument, E would recognize (absent a timely Code §83(b) election) OI equal to the spread in the Newco shares when they vest (i.e., the excess of the stock's FV at vesting over the price paid by E).

(2) **Vesting imposed shortly after E's initial stock purchase.** IRS may take the position, where Newco's subsequent financing is arranged and vesting imposed shortly after E's initial purchase of unrestricted Newco stock, that the step transaction doctrine applies to treat E's initial stock purchase and the subsequent imposition of vesting as a single transaction, especially where Newco is in the process of (or perhaps well along in) negotiating the subsequent financing when E initially buys the Newco stock. If IRS were to succeed in this argument, E's Newco stock would (absent a timely Code §83(b) election) be treated as subject to vesting from the outset and E would recognize OI equal to the spread when vesting expires (i.e., the excess of the stock's FV at vesting over the price paid by E).

(3) **Constructive exchange even where Newco not shell company and vesting not imposed shortly after E's initial stock purchase.** IRS may take the position that, although E first held fully vested stock (i.e., from Newco's formation until consummation of the VC financing), E subsequently engaged in a constructive exchange of fully vested Newco shares for new unvested shares, so that §83 applies to E's receipt of the unvested Newco shares. If IRS were to succeed in this argument, E would recognize (absent a timely Code §83(b) election) OI when the Newco shares vest equal to the excess of (a) the FV of the unvested Newco shares when they vest over (b) the price E paid for the unvested Newco shares (i.e., the FV of the initial fully vested stock at the time E engaged in the constructive exchange).

To avoid these tax risks, E should make a "protective election" under §83(b) within 30 days after imposition of vesting. The protective election should state that (1) a §83(b) election is not necessary because E owned fully vested stock from the outset, but that a protective election is being made in case IRS seeks to invoke §83 and (2) the price E paid for the unvested shares (i.e., the price E paid for the fully vested shares at the outset in (1) and (2) above and the FV of the fully vested shares deemed to have surrendered in the constructive exchange in (3) above) is equal to the FV of the unvested shares received or deemed received (ignoring, as required by §83(a), the effects of vesting restrictions on the shares' FV), so that E recognizes no OI as a result of the election.

In several private letter rulings and an information letter, beginning 6/00 IRS has adopted the pro-taxpayer position that where an executive holds fully vested stock (or partnership/LLC interest) and subsequently at the behest of a new financing party agrees to impose vesting on the stock (or partnership/LLC interest), "the subsequent imposition of the forfeiture provisions on the founder's [Newco] shares [or partnership/LLC interest] must necessarily have been accomplished in the *absence* of a section 83 transfer (i.e., the shares were *already owned* for section 83 purposes), and that, therefore, these provisions had no effect for section 83 purposes."[9]

While we welcome IRS's conclusion, we are cautious about recommending that E not file a §83(b) election, because, first, private letter rulings and an IRS information letter are not authority on which a taxpayer may legally rely, and second, the private letter rulings and information letter merely indicate IRS would not assert ground 3 (the constructive exchange argument) and do not address the possibility IRS could, depending on the facts, argue that E recognizes OI on vesting expiration on ground 1 or 2.

¶202.3.9   Other Issues

¶202.3.9.1   *Post-Vesting Buy-Back from E*

Newco and/or VC would like to have an option to purchase E's *vested* Newco shares at *appraised FV* when E leaves Newco's employ. This option will not have Code §83 tax significance, because it is at full FV.

¶202.3.9.2   *Accounting Charge*

For a discussion of the possible adverse accounting aspects of (1) sales of stock to E at less than FV *or* (2) sales of stock to E subject to performance vesting, see ¶407.3 below.

---

[9] IRS Letter Ruling 200212005 (11/8/01) (corporate stock), IRS Letter Ruling 200204005 (10/12/01) (LLC interest), IRS Information Letter (6/12/00) from Robert Misner, Assistant Branch Chief.

¶202.3.9.3   Granting Stock Option to E

For a discussion of the tax and accounting aspects of granting an NQO or an ISO to E (or another Newco employee), see ¶407 below.

¶202.3.9.4   Newco Sale of Stock to VC

Neither Code §83 nor the possible adverse accounting aspects referred to immediately above should apply where Newco sells stock to VC, because these rules apply to stock sales to a service provider (like E) rather than to an investor (like VC).

¶203   SEVERAL ALTERNATIVE CAPITAL STRUCTURES

Under the simple Newco capital structure initially proposed by E (¶201), VC and E receive only common stock, so that they share any proceeds on disposition of Newco pro rata to their ownership of common stock. Hence VC does not obtain any preferential position by virtue of its $1 million investment.

Under the more complex Newco capital structure proposed by VC (¶202), VC receives $940,000 of non-convertible non-participating senior securities, so that VC is entitled to $940,000 of proceeds (plus accrued interest and preferred dividends) before any remaining Newco proceeds are shared proportionally to ownership of VC's and E's common stock. Hence VC obtains *both* $940,000 (plus accrued yield) on its senior securities *and* a percentage (here 60%) of remaining proceeds.

Numerous other Newco capital structures could be utilized, some of which are discussed below.

¶203.1   *VC Convertible Debenture or Convertible Preferred*

Under a third structure, VC receives (in exchange for its $1 million) a Newco convertible subordinated debenture and/or convertible preferred shares:

	VC	E
Convertible subordinated debenture and/or convertible preferred stock— convertible into 60 common shares	$1,000,000	
Common stock—40 shares at $1,000 per share		$40,000
Total	$1,000,000	$40,000

If VC does not convert its convertible securities, VC has a senior claim for $1,000,000 plus any accrued yield, in which case E is entitled to 100% of Newco's remaining sale proceeds. On the other hand, if VC chooses to convert its convertible senior securities, VC receives 60 common shares and forfeits its senior position. Hence, with convertible securities VC is entitled to *either* its $1 million senior position *or* its 60 common share position (as contrasted with ¶202 where VC was entitled to *both* its $940,000 senior position *and* its 60 common share position).

Under this convertible approach, VC may structure a portion of its senior position as convertible debt, which will allow (1) Newco a deduction for the yield (i.e., interest) accruing to VC on the debenture and (2) VC return of capital treatment (i.e., to avoid Code §302 OI treatment) on redemption of the debenture. VC may structure the remainder of its senior claim as convertible preferred stock, so that Newco's DER will not be excessive, in order to maximize the likelihood that the debenture will be treated as debt for tax purposes.

Upon conversion, there are several methods for handling accrued interest (on the convertible debenture) and accrued preferred dividends (on the convertible preferred stock): such accrued yield could be paid in cash on conversion, could be paid in additional Newco common stock, or could evaporate.

If VC converts, VC is in effect paying $16,667 per common share (i.e., $1 million debenture purchase price ÷ 60 common shares received on conversion) while E (at the time of Newco's formation) paid only $1,000 per common share. This dichotomy is certainly to E's advantage from an economic standpoint. However, this approach presents some Code §83(a) OI risk for E (assuming E purchased fully vested Newco shares or filed a Code §83(b) election with respect to unvested Newco shares). E would argue that Newco's common stock is worth no more than the $1,000 per share E paid at Newco's formation, since (1) VC had the right not to convert and hence to receive back VC's $1 million plus yield and (2) only in the event VC chose to convert would E obtain some economic enhancement from VC's high $16,667 conversion price. The extent of E's Code §83(a) OI risk turns on such factors as whether VC is entitled to a fair yield on its convertible securities, whether the yield is payable in all events or evaporates on conversion, and the relative ratio of VC's conversion price to E's common stock purchase price.

¶203.2   VC Participating Double Dip Preferred Stock

Under a fourth structure, VC receives (in exchange for its $1 million) Newco participating preferred stock:

	VC	E
Participating preferred stock, with a 60 common share participation	$1,000,000	
Common stock—40 shares at $1,000 per share		$40,000
Total	$1,000,000	$40,000

Under the terms of VC's participating preferred stock:

- If Newco's exit scenario is a sale of Newco, VC's participating preferred would be entitled to a double dip: *both* an amount equal to its $1 million preference—perhaps plus a specified yield, e.g., 10% per year, or a specified return multiple, e.g., 2 times original cost—*plus* a common-stock-like participation in residual proceeds consisting of the share of residual proceeds the preferred shareholder would have received if it owned 60 Newco common shares.

- If Newco's exit scenario is an IPO of Newco's stock to the public, VC's preferred stock would generally automatically convert into 60 common shares (i.e., the preferred stock's double dip would evaporate) and the accrued preferred dividends would either be paid in cash, paid in common stock, or evaporate as specified in the preferred stock terms.

¶204   TERMS AND TAX ASPECTS OF VC's DEBENTURE AND PREFERRED STOCK

See Chapter 6 below for a discussion of the terms and the tax aspects of VC's $500,000 Newco subordinated debenture and its $440,000 Newco preferred stock.

¶205   STRUCTURING CONTROL OF NEWCO's BOARD

¶205.1   *No Relationship Between Equity Split and Board Seats*

E and VC can agree upon an allocation of directors completely different from the equity split through the use of:

- A voting agreement.
- A voting trust.
- Voting and nonvoting common.
- Voting and nonvoting preferred.
- Election of different classes of directors by different classes of stock.

¶205.2   *E's Proposal*

E believes that Newco is E's baby and that E should therefore be entitled to elect 2 directors while VC should be satisfied with only 1 director.

¶205.3   VC's Proposal

VC, on the other hand, believes that the $1 million of cash it is investing in Newco entitles VC to elect 2 directors while E should be content with only 1 director.

¶205.4   Neutral-Director Compromise

One possible compromise between E's and VC's conflicting views as to control of Newco's board is an agreement under which:

- E has the right to elect 1 director,
- VC has the right to elect 1 director,
- a third neutral director will be selected by both E and VC or, if they can not agree, by a designated third party.

¶205.5   Veto-Power-Plus-Shifting-Director Compromise

A second possible compromise is an agreement under which E begins with 2 directors and VC begins with 1 director, except that:

- Unanimous director vote (or consent of the preferred shareholder[1]) is required for specified decisions outside the ordinary course of business (so that VC has veto power over such decisions), e.g., merger, acquisition, large capital expenditure, large borrowing, stock issuance, entering new business, plant expansion, new product, E's bonus, or E's salary increase greater than cost of living adjustment, and
- Third director shifts from E to VC (i.e., VC will have 2 directors and E will be reduced to only 1 director) if Newco fails to meet any one of several stated goals (e.g., working prototype within 9 months, sales of $5 million within 2 years, net income of $1 million within 3 years), so that control shifts from E to VC upon Newco's nonperformance.

¶205.6   Protecting Newco's Directors from Personal Liability

Regardless of the composition of Newco's board, the directors (and VC, who has surely agreed to indemnify VC's nominees on Newco's board for any liability

---

¶205   [1] Because a director owes a fiduciary duty to all shareholders, VC has less risk of a suit by E (or another shareholder) if VC obtains its veto rights not as a director but rather as a preferred shareholder. However, if VC holds Newco stock with a majority of Newco's voting power, VC may still have some fiduciary duty to Newco minority shareholders.

suffered by them as Newco board members) undoubtedly want Newco's certificate of incorporation to (1) require Newco to indemnify its directors to the full extent allowed by applicable state law and (2) absolve its directors from liability for damages for good faith breach of their fiduciary duty to the full extent allowed by applicable state law (and Delaware corporate law specifically allows such absolution except for breach of the duty of loyalty).

To protect Newco's directors against such indemnified liability in case Newco should go bankrupt, it is desirable for Newco to obtain directors and officers insurance, if obtainable at reasonable cost.

¶206 CONTROL OVER SUBSEQUENT PRIVATE OFFERING, IPO, OR SALE OF NEWCO

Subsequent to VC's start-up investment in Newco, Newco will often require additional rounds of private equity financing before it has matured sufficiently so that it either can be sold at the desired profit or is ready for an IPO. Typically, new investors (often introduced to Newco by VC) will provide a majority of the capital in later rounds of financing, and VC's influence over Newco will thereby be diluted. Therefore, it is desirable that VC's contractual arrangements with Newco at the front end, when VC makes its start-up investment in Newco, grant VC some of the protections VC may need later, when VC has become a Newco minority shareholder. See ¶408 and the introduction to Chapter 9 below.

In order to give VC some control over a future Newco IPO or a sale of Newco, a shareholders' agreement (entered into at the front end when VC makes its start-up investment in Newco) may state that (1) during the first 3 years after Newco's formation either E or VC can veto a proposed Newco IPO or sale and (2) after 3 years VC has the right to require an IPO or a sale of Newco but E has the right to preempt VC by purchasing all of VC's Newco stock at its appraised FV or at a formula price. See also ¶207.7.3 below regarding VC's contractual SEC registration rights.

To implement VC's right to require a sale of Newco beginning 3 years after Newco's formation, the shareholders' agreement will generally state that if VC finds a buyer for Newco, VC has the right (1) to require E to vote in favor of the transaction if it is to be consummated by a merger or sale of assets requiring a shareholder vote *and* (2) to require E to sell E's stock if the transaction is to be consummated by a stock sale (called a "drag-along" right).

The shareholders' agreement may also state that if E finds a buyer for part or all of E's Newco stock at any time, VC has the right to participate in the stock sale, i.e., VC has a right (but not an obligation) to sell part or all of VC's Newco stock along with E, with the number of Newco shares to be sold by VC and E, respectively, being pro rata to the number of Newco shares owned by each (called a "tag-along" right).

Similarly, to cover the situation where VC finds a buyer for Newco, the shareholders' agreement may give E a tag-along right.

¶207   SEC COMPLIANCE

¶207.1   *Obligation to Register Securities with SEC*

When Newco issues securities (debentures, preferred stock, or common stock)—to E, VC, other financing parties, other Newco employees, and the like—Newco must first register the issuance of the securities with SEC under the 1933 Act, unless the issuance fits within an exemption. Because a 1933 Act SEC registration is time consuming and expensive, it is desirable to fit each issuance of Newco securities into an exemption.

¶207.2   *Exemptions from SEC Registration*

Newco may be able to comply with the private placement exemption from SEC registration *either* by meeting the "safe harbor" contained in SEC Regulation D, as described at ¶207.3 immediately below, *or* by fitting into the more amorphous statutory exemption contained in 1933 Act §4(2).

If the offering is to persons who provide services to Newco (e.g., directors, employees, consultants), Newco may be able to comply with SEC Rule 701, as described at ¶207.4 below.

In very limited circumstances, Newco may be able to comply with the intra-state exemption of 1933 Act §3(a)(11) and SEC Rule 147.

Also where Newco has substantial California contacts, it may be able to comply with SEC Rule 1001, as described at ¶207.5 below.

If the offering is an "offshore transaction" with no "directed selling efforts" into the U.S. market, Newco may be able to comply with SEC Reg. S.

If no other exemption is available, Newco may be able to use the exemption contained in SEC Regulation A, which permits Newco to comply with abbreviated SEC filing procedures, as described at ¶207.6 below.

¶207.3   *SEC Reg. D*

Reg. D's safe harbor exemption from 1933 Act registration contains 3 operative rules—Rule 504, Rule 505, and Rule 506—with the stringency of the prerequisites for Reg. D qualification escalating as the size of the offering increases. As discussed further below, generally all securities issued at approximately the same time and for the same purpose (e.g., here to finance Newco's start-up) are "integrated" and treated as one offering.

¶207.3.1   Rule 504

(1) Sales can not exceed $1 million, *less* sales during the 12 months before the start of the Rule 504 offering (and during the Rule 504 offering) which are:

- pursuant to any exemption under 1933 Act §3(b) (other than Rule 701), including Rule 504, Rule 505, and Reg. A, or
- in violation of the 1933 Act.

(2) There is no limitation on the number of purchasers and no requirement that they be sophisticated investors.

(3) There is no express disclosure requirement (i.e., no formal private offering memorandum is required). However, the offering (like all sales of securities) is nevertheless subject to the general anti-fraud provisions of the federal securities laws requiring that all "material" information be made available to purchasers and that any offering materials neither misstate a material fact nor omit a material fact necessary to prevent the offering materials or any other statements from being misleading (see, e.g., SEC Rule 10b-5).

(4) Newco can not be a 1934 Act reporting company, an investment company required to register under the Investment Company Act of 1940, *or* a so-called blank check company.

- A **1934 Act reporting company** is generally one which meets any one of the following three tests:

  (a) Has a security (debt or equity) listed on a national securities exchange.

  (b) Has consolidated gross assets of $10 million or more (based on its balance sheet prepared in accordance with generally accepted accounting principles) *and* 500 or more holders of a class of equity securities (although a reporting company can de-register if it is subsequently held by less than 300 persons *or* less than 500 persons where the company's assets have not exceeded $10 million on the last day of each of its three most recently ended fiscal years).

  (c) Has made a 1933 Act registered public offering (although such a reporting company can, after the first fiscal year as a reporting company, de-register if it is held by less than 300 persons *or* less than 500 persons where the company's assets have not exceeded $10 million on the last day of each of its three most recently ended fiscal years).

- An **investment company** required to register under the Investment Company Act of 1940 is a company the primary activity of which is investing in securities which meets at least one of the following tests: the company (a) has more than 100 beneficial owners of its securities *and* has at least one security holder which is neither a "Qualified Purchaser" nor a "Knowledgable Employee" *or* (b) has made (or plans to make) a public offering of its securities. See ¶1008 below.

- A **blank check company** is a start-up company with no specific business plan or purpose except to merge with or acquire an unidentified company.

(5) No general solicitation of and no general advertising for potential purchasers are permitted unless the offering is (a) solely to "accredited investors" (as defined below) pursuant to state securities law exemptions permitting general solicitation and advertising so long as sales are made only to "accredited investors" (and at least 30 states have such exemptions) *or* (b) registered pursuant to each applicable

state securities law requiring public filing and delivery to investors of a pre-sale public disclosure document, the offering is so registered in at least one state, and such registration document is delivered to purchasers in all states (including those states that do not require such registration). Hence, for an offering meeting the requirements of (a) or (b) above, there is no prohibition on seminars or meetings with potential purchasers invited by general solicitation or advertising.

(6) Securities issued pursuant to Rule 504 are restricted securities (see ¶207.7 and ¶¶901 through 903 below regarding resales of restricted securities), unless the offering is (a) solely to "accredited investors" (as defined below) pursuant to state securities law exemptions permitting general solicitation and advertising so long as sales are made only to "accredited investors" (and at least 30 states have such exemptions) *or* (b) registered pursuant to each applicable state securities law requiring public filing and delivery to investors of a pre-sale public disclosure document, the offering is so registered in at least one state, and such registration document is delivered to purchasers in all states (including those states that do not require such registration). For an offering meeting the requirements of (a) or (b) above, the securities are not restricted and generally can be freely resold by the holder—see ¶904 below regarding resales of unrestricted securities by Newco affiliates (i.e., members of Newco's control group).

(7) A Rule 504 offering is not exempt from state blue sky laws, and not all states have conformed their blue sky laws to SEC's Rule 504.

¶207.3.2   Rule 505

(1) Sales can not exceed $5 million, *less* sales during the 12 months before the start of the Rule 505 offering (and during the Rule 505 offering) which are:

- pursuant to any exemption under 1933 Act §3(b) (other than Rule 701), including Rule 504, Rule 505 and Reg. A, or
- in violation of the 1933 Act.

(2) Sales can be made to an unlimited number of "accredited investors" *plus* up to 35 additional investors.

- In determining whether there are more than 35 non-accredited investors, (a) all relatives of a purchaser with the same principal residence as the purchaser are ignored, (b) a trust or estate in which a purchaser and his or her relatives with the same principal residence own in the aggregate more than 50% of the beneficial interest is ignored, and (c) any entity in which a purchaser and his or her relatives with the same principal residence own in the aggregate more than 50% of the equity securities is ignored.

(3) There is no requirement that investors be sophisticated.

(4) If any purchaser is not an accredited investor, a substantial disclosure document (i.e., a private offering memorandum) must be delivered to such non-accredited investor.

(5) No general solicitation of and no general advertising for potential purchasers are permitted. Hence no seminars or meetings may be held with potential purchas-

ers invited by general solicitation or advertising. While nothing on this issue has been heard from SEC since 6/95, SEC had then announced that it was considering revising or eliminating the prohibition on general solicitation.

(6) Securities issued pursuant to Rule 505 are restricted securities—see ¶¶207.7 and 901 through 903 below regarding resales of restricted securities.

(7) *"Accredited investor"* means:

- *Certain institutional investors*, e.g., a bank, an S&L, or a similar financial institution, whether acting in its individual or fiduciary capacity, an insurance company, an SBIC, a registered investment company, a public or private BDC, *or* a registered broker-dealer.
- *An ERISA plan* (a) with a fiduciary which is a bank, an S&L, an insurance company, or a registered investment adviser, *or* (b) with total assets in excess of $5 million, *or* (c) which is a self-directed plan with investment decisions made solely by accredited investors.
- *A corporation, partnership, business trust, or Code §501(c)(3) charitable organization*, in each case with total assets in excess of $5 million and not formed for the specific purpose of acquiring the securities offered. SEC takes the perfectly logical interpretative position that while not specifically enumerated in Reg. D's list of entities, an LLC may be treated as an "accredited investor" as long as it meets the other requirements, i.e., total assets in excess of $5 million and not formed for the specific purpose of acquiring the securities. For purposes of the $5 million test, a general partnership is treated as owning assets owned by its GPs.
- *A trust* with total assets in excess of $5 million and not formed for the specific purpose of acquiring the securities offered, whose purchase is directed by a sophisticated person (i.e., a person who has such knowledge and experience in financial and business matters that he or she is capable of evaluating the merits and risks of the prospective investment or who uses a sophisticated purchaser representative not affiliated with the issuer of the securities being sold).
- *A director or an executive officer of the issuer* (or, if the issuer is a partnership, a GP of the issuer or a director, executive officer, or GP of the issuer's GP).
- *An individual* with more than $1 million net worth or joint net worth with the individual's spouse.
- *An individual* with more than $200,000 of income in each of the two most recent years, or joint income with such individual's spouse in excess of $300,000 during such periods, who reasonably expects income in excess of such amount in the current year. In general, income means adjusted gross income for tax purposes *before* any deduction for LTCG or depletion or partnership losses allocated to an LP *plus* tax-exempt interest income.
- *An entity* in which all of the equity owners are accredited investors.

¶207.3.3   Rule 506

(1) There is no limitation on the dollar size of the offering.

(2) Sales can be made to an unlimited number of accredited investors *plus* up to 35 additional investors (defined and counted as described in ¶207.3.2).

(3) A non-accredited investor must be sophisticated or use a sophisticated purchaser representative not affiliated with the issuer of the securities being sold.

(4) If any purchaser is not an accredited investor, a substantial disclosure document (i.e., a private offering memorandum) must be delivered to such non-accredited investor.

(5) No general solicitation of and no general advertising for potential purchasers are permitted. Hence no seminars or meetings may be held with potential purchasers invited by general solicitation or advertising. While nothing on this issue has been heard from SEC since 6/95, SEC had then announced that it was considering revising or eliminating the prohibition on general solicitation.

(6) Securities issued pursuant to Rule 506 are restricted securities—see ¶¶207.7 and 901 through 903 below regarding resales of restricted securities.

¶207.3.4   Integration

Except as described below, SEC's normal factually-based integration doctrine (which applies to all securities offerings) is applicable in determining whether Newco's offering qualifies under Reg. D. Under the integration doctrine, the following factors are considered in determining whether one sale of securities by Newco will be integrated with (i.e., treated as part of the same offering as) a prior or subsequent offer or sale of Newco securities:

- Whether the sales are part of a single plan of financing.
- Whether the sales involve issuance of the same class of securities.
- Whether the sales occur at or about the same time.
- Whether the same type of consideration is received.
- Whether the sales are for the same general purpose.

Where the integration doctrine applies to treat two ostensibly separate sales as one, the Reg. D standards (e.g., limitation to 35 non-accredited investors for a Rule 505 or 506 offering, prohibition on general solicitation or advertising) are applied to both sales viewed together.

Reg. D sets forth a safe harbor exception to SEC's normal integration doctrine: Sales of Newco securities more than 6 months before the beginning of the Reg. D offering *or* more than 6 months after the completion of the Reg. D offering are *not* integrated with the Reg. D offering where, during those 6-month periods, Newco makes no offers or sales of the same or a similar class of securities as those sold in the Reg. D offering.

In some cases, Newco may begin a private offering and subsequently determine that a registered public offering would be a better alternative. Conversely, Newco may begin a registered public offering and subsequently determine that a private offering would be better (e.g., because of insufficient public interest). SEC Rule 155 sets forth conditions that must be met in order to allow Newco to convert a private offering into a public offering, or a public offering into a private offering, without risk the offerings will be integrated and violate the 1933 Act. In the case of a private offering converted into a public offering: no securities may be sold in the private offering, the private offering must be terminated and all selling activities terminated, there must be a 30-day waiting period prior to filing the registration statement (unless the securities in the private offering were offered only to accredited and sophisticated persons), and the public offering prospectus must disclose certain information about the abandoned private offering. In the case of a public offering converted into a private offering: no securities may be sold in the public offering, the registration statement must be withdrawn, there must be a 30-day waiting period prior to commencement of the private offering, certain information about the abandoned public offering must be provided to each offeree in the private offering, and the private offering memorandum must contain current information about Newco.

Three additional types of sales are never integrated with a Reg. D offering:

- Sales pursuant to SEC Rule 701 (as discussed at ¶207.4 below).
- Sales pursuant to SEC Reg. A which are consummated *subsequent* to the Reg. D offering *or* which are consummated more than 6 months *prior* to the Reg. D offering (as discussed at ¶207.6 below).
- Sales to foreign persons made outside the U.S. in compliance with SEC Reg. S, i.e., in an "offshore transaction" where there have not been any "directed selling efforts" into the U.S. market with respect to such securities and the securities are restricted from resale to a U.S. person for a specified period, one year in the case of equity securities and 40 days for debt securities.

¶207.3.5 Look Through

Where an entity (e.g., a corporation, partnership, LLC, or trust) purchases Newco securities and such entity purchaser "is organized for the specific purpose of acquiring the [Newco] securities," Reg. D looks through such entity and treats each of the entity's equity owners as a purchaser for purposes of Reg. D. Those of the entity's equity owners who are not accredited investors therefore count toward the 35 non-accredited investor limitation in Rule 505 and Rule 506 (and each such non-accredited investor must be sophisticated or must use a sophisticated purchaser representative not affiliated with the issuer of the securities being sold where the offering is pursuant to Rule 506 and each such non-accredited investor must also receive a substantial disclosure document if the offering is pursuant to either Rule 505 or 506). Those of the entity's equity owners who are accredited investors cause no harm to the Reg. D offering, since Rules 505 and 506 permit an unlimited number of accredited investors.

Reg. D offers no guidance on when an entity purchaser is treated as organized for the specific purpose of acquiring Newco securities. However, important factors include:

- The percentage of the entity's assets devoted to purchasing Newco securities. In an analogous context (see ¶1008(5) below, dealing with the ICA), SEC generally regards an investment of 40% or less of an entity's assets as not giving rise to an inference that the entity was formed for the purpose of making the investment. However, there is no clear guidance (under either the ICA or Reg. D) on how much more than 40% of its assets an entity could invest in Newco without creating an inference that the entity was formed for the purpose of investing in Newco.
- Whether the entity, in raising its capital, announced in advance to the persons from whom it was raising money its intent to invest in Newco.
- Whether the entity is operated in a manner designed to facilitate individual decision-making by its equity owners as to whether (or how much of the equity owner's contribution to the entity) each equity owner desires to invest in Newco. Where the entity permits each of its equity owners to make such an individual investment decision, the entity will likely be treated *either* (1) as "organized" for the purpose of investing in Newco *or* (2) as "reorganized" for such purpose.

Thus, for example, look through is likely where *either*:

- An entity is formed for the announced purpose of investing 90% of its newly-raised capital in Newco and 10% in other securities and does so promptly after its formation, *or*
- An "old and cold" entity with diversified investments grants each of its equity owners the right to decide whether any of such owner's share of the entity's assets (and, if so, how much) are to be invested in Newco and thereafter maintains separate accounts reflecting each equity owner's profit or loss from such investment in Newco.[1]

On the other hand, look through is not likely where an entity is formed for the announced purpose of investing 40% of its newly-raised capital in Newco and 60% in other securities, does so promptly after formation, but does not offer its equity owners any opportunity to vary the percentage interest each holds in the entity's various investments.

¶207 [1] However, several SEC no action letters take the position that there is no Reg. D look through where a group of individuals with pre-existing affinity (e.g., all such individuals are key employees of a single business enterprise or are members of a single professional partnership) form a general partnership to make investments, even though each participant then has the right to specify the amount of his or her contribution to each investment by the partnership (or to opt out of an investment entirely), so long as all the participants are liable under state law (as general partners in the investment partnership) for all of the investment partnership's unpaid debts.

¶207.3.6   Reg. D Notification

Newco is required to file a Reg. D notification with SEC within 15 days after the first sale of securities, but failure to file does not destroy the Reg. D exemption.

¶207.4   *SEC Rule 701*

SEC Rule 701 exempts from 1933 Act registration an offering of Newco securities to Newco employees, directors, officers, consultants and advisers (or those of its majority-owned subsidiaries) where the following requirements are met:

(1) Newco can not be *either* a 1934 Act reporting company (see ¶207.3.1(4)) *or* an investment company required to be registered under the Investment Company Act of 1940 (see ¶1008 below).

(2) The securities must be issued in compensatory circumstances, not to raise capital, and must be issued pursuant to a written compensatory benefit plan or a written compensatory contract. Each purchaser must receive a copy of the written plan or contract. Securities can be issued, for example, pursuant to:

- An outright stock purchase program.
- A stock option plan.
- A stock award program.
- An employment agreement with a single employee.

However, it is not necessary to issue the securities at a price below FV.

(3) The amount of securities sold under Rule 701 (*including* sales during the prior 12 months in reliance on Rule 701) may not exceed the *greater of*:

- $1 million, *or*
- 15% of Newco's total assets measured at its most recent balance sheet date, *or*
- 15% of Newco's outstanding securities of the class being issued (including securities issuable under currently exercisable or convertible warrants, options, rights or other securities not originally issued pursuant to Rule 701) at its most recent balance sheet date.

For purposes of calculating whether Newco's Rule 701 sales are within this maximum amount, options are treated as securities sold by Newco on the date of grant and at the exercise price, without regard to whether the option is then vested or exercisable.

(4) Rule 701 contains no limitation on the type of distribution in which Newco may engage, the number of offerees or purchasers, or the sophistication of the offerees or purchasers. However, each purchaser must be a Newco employee, director, officer, consultant, or adviser or, in certain cases such as an option exercise, a person who formerly held such a position when the option was granted or a family member of such a person.

(5) There are no specific disclosure requirements (i.e., no formal private offering memorandum is required). However, the offering (like all sales of securities) is nevertheless subject to the general anti-fraud provisions of the federal securities

laws requiring that all "material" information be made available to purchasers and that any offering materials neither misstate a material fact nor omit a material fact necessary to prevent the offering materials or any other statements from being misleading. In addition, if Newco sells more than $5 million of securities in reliance on this exemption in any 12-month period, or believes that its sales will exceed $5 million in a 12-month period, Newco must deliver to purchasers a written disclosure of risks associated with an investment in the Newco securities, a summary of material terms of the compensatory plan, and certain Newco financial statements. For an option, such disclosure is required a reasonable period before option exercise.

(6) Offerings under Rule 701 are not integrated with any other offering or sale of securities, whether or not registered under the 1933 Act. In addition, a Rule 701 offering is not subtracted in determining the permissible amount of sales under other SEC rules adopted pursuant to 1933 Act §3(b), such as Rules 504 and 505.

(7) Securities received in a Rule 701 offering are restricted securities which can not be resold without 1933 Act registration or an exemption. See ¶¶207.7 and 901 through 903 below regarding resales of restricted securities. However, 90 days after Newco becomes a 1934 Act reporting company, securities issued by Newco under Rule 701 (unlike other restricted securities) will be free of most of the requirements of SEC Rule 144, as discussed at ¶903 below.

(8) A Rule 701 offering is not exempt from state blue sky laws, and not all states have conformed their blue sky laws to SEC's Rule 701.

¶207.5   SEC Rule 1001

Rule 1001 exempts from 1933 Act registration offers and sales of up to $5 million of Newco securities made in accordance with California Corporations Code §25102(n).

This California exemption applies where *either* (1) Newco is organized or incorporated in California *or* (2) Newco has more than 50% of its property, payroll, and sales attributed to California *and* more than 50% of Newco's outstanding voting securities are held of record by persons with California addresses. Where this California exemption applies, Newco can sell its securities to a somewhat broader group than is allowed by Reg. D., i.e., SEC Rule 1001 allows California to define a "qualified purchaser" (which is treated like a Reg. D accredited investor) and California has defined qualified purchaser to include (e.g.) a natural person buying more than $150,000 of an offering who is either sophisticated or investing less than 10% of his or her net worth in the offering. In addition, this California exemption is broader than Reg. D in that it allows Newco to make certain general solicitations similar to the "test the waters" communications allowed under Reg. A. However, California allows offers and sales only to qualified purchasers, i.e., there is no Reg. D-like exemption for up to 35 non-qualifying persons.

Securities issued by Newco pursuant to Rule 1001 are "restricted securities" for purposes of Rule 144.

SEC Rule 1001's exemption for such offerings permitted by California law may well be the beginning of a trend under which additional SEC rules will exempt offerings pursuant to other state securities exemptions.

¶207.6   SEC Reg. A

If an offering of Newco securities does not qualify for Reg. D, Rule 701, or any other 1933 Act exemption, Newco can nevertheless avoid a full-blown SEC registration by complying with Reg. A, in which case Newco is exempt from 1933 Act registration but is required to file an offering statement with SEC:

(1) The maximum amount Newco can sell under Reg. A is $5 million, *less* sales pursuant to Reg. A during the 12 months before the start of (and during) the Reg. A offering. Up to $1.5 million of the $5 million can be secondary sales by Newco security holders.

(2) Newco can not use Reg. A if it is *either* a 1934 Act reporting company *or* an investment company required to register under the Investment Company Act of 1940 *or* a blank check company (see ¶207.3.1(4) above).

(3) While a Reg. A offering requires Newco to file an offering statement with SEC and to respond to SEC's comments on the offering statement, a Reg. A offering statement is generally shorter and less complex than a full-blown 1933 Act registration statement, and the Reg. A process is generally less expensive and less time consuming.

(4) A Reg. A offering is a public offering. Hence, (a) there is no limitation on the type of distribution which may be engaged in, the number of offerees or purchasers, or the sophistication of the offerees or purchasers and (b) securities purchased in a Reg. A offering are *not* "restricted securities," so that they can generally be freely resold. See ¶904 below regarding sales of unrestricted securities by Newco affiliates (i.e., members of Newco's control group).

(5) SEC's normal factually-based integration doctrine applies in determining whether an offering qualifies for Reg. A, except that:

(a) offers or sales of Newco securities *prior* to the Reg. A offering are never integrated with the Reg. A offering, and

(b) offers or sales of Newco securities *subsequent* to the Reg. A offering are never integrated with the Reg. A offering where such subsequent sales are:

- made more than 6 months after completion of the Reg. A offering, *or*
- registered under the 1933 Act, *or*
- pursuant to Rule 701, *or*
- made to foreign persons outside the U.S. in compliance with SEC Reg. S, i.e., in an "offshore transaction" where there have not been any "directed selling efforts" into the U.S. market with respect to such securities and the securities are restricted from resale to a U.S. person for a specified period, one year in the case of equity securities and 40 days for debt securities.

(6) If Newco were selling securities in a full-blown 1933 Act registered public offering, Newco could not (because of the SEC "gun-jumping" rules) communicate with potential purchasers regarding the offering until filing its full-blown registration statement with SEC. However, where Newco is planning a Reg. A offering, Newco can "test the waters" before preparing the Reg. A offering circular. By filing a very simple statement with SEC, Newco can communicate with potential purchasers—orally, in writing, or by advertising (in newspapers, on radio or TV, or by mail)—to determine whether they have any interest in purchasing Newco securities. If there is not sufficient interest, Newco can drop the idea of a Reg. A offering without incurring the expense of preparing and filing a Reg. A offering statement.

¶207.7   Restrictions on Resale of Newco Securities

At the time E, VC, and others are purchasing Newco's securities, they will be interested in knowing any restrictions on their ability ultimately to resell the securities. In addition, at the time of purchase, they may wish to negotiate with Newco to obtain contractual registration rights.

¶207.7.1   Restricted Securities

Newco securities purchased—by E, VC, other financing parties, other employees, and the like—without SEC registration in a §4(2) private placement, a Reg. D offering (other than in limited circumstances pursuant to Rule 504 as described in ¶207.3.1) or a Rule 701 sale are restricted securities. The holder of a restricted security can resell it only:

- in a subsequent private sale exempt from 1933 Act registration, *or*
- in a public offering registered with SEC under the 1933 Act, *or*
- in a public sale pursuant to SEC Rule 144, *or*
- in a public sale pursuant to a Reg. A offering statement filed with SEC, *or*
- in an "offshore transaction" pursuant to SEC Reg. S when there have not been any "directed selling efforts" into the U.S. market.

¶207.7.2   Unrestricted Securities

Securities issued by Newco in certain limited circumstances pursuant to SEC Rule 504 (as described in ¶207.3.1) or pursuant to a Reg. A offering statement filed with SEC are not restricted securities.

Normally the federal securities laws do not prevent the holder of an unrestricted security from reselling it freely, subject to the anti-fraud provisions of the federal securities laws requiring that all "material" information be made available to purchasers and that any offering materials neither misstate a material fact nor omit a material fact necessary to prevent the offering materials or any other statement from being misleading. However, where the holder of an unrestricted Newco security is a Newco affiliate (i.e., a member of Newco's control group), see ¶904 below regarding an SEC restriction on resale.

¶207.7.3 Contractual Registration Rights

A purchaser of Newco restricted securities would be wise to obtain from Newco (at the time of purchase) contractual SEC registration rights, obligating Newco to register with SEC the holder's resale of the restricted securities *either* at the holder's demand (a "demand registration right") *or* as an add-on to another SEC registration statement being filed by Newco (a "piggy-back registration right").

¶207.7.3.1 *Newco Resistance*

An SEC registration statement for a secondary offering of restricted securities must be effective when the holder actually sells the Newco securities to the public. Because SEC registration is generally time consuming and expensive, Newco may resist granting contractual SEC registration rights to a purchaser of Newco restricted securities, at least until Newco is able to utilize the less expensive short-form registration formats described at ¶207.7.3.4 below.

If Newco does grant contractual registration rights, it may seek some or all of the following limitations:

- No demand registration until after Newco has first had an IPO, so that a Newco shareholder can not force Newco to go public.
- Limitation on the number of demand registrations.
- Limitation on the timing of a demand registration.
- Requirement that a large percentage of the holders who have registration rights join in the demand registration.
- Demand registrations limited to the less expensive short-form registration formats described below.
- No demand registration, only piggy-back registration rights.

¶207.7.3.2 *Piggy-Back Offering*

A piggy-back SEC registration is, of course, not as expensive as a demand registration, because Newco is registering with SEC the holder's resale of Newco restricted securities only as an add-on to an SEC registration being filed by Newco to sell new securities in a primary offering or to allow other existing holders to sell their securities in a secondary offering. However, a piggy-back registration

right does not give the holder flexibility to choose the time of the registration or
to choose the underwriter (if any is used).

¶207.7.3.3 *Underwritten Offering*

If the offering of Newco securities is being underwritten (i.e., an investment
banker has contracted to buy the Newco securities and resell them to the public),
there may well be an underwriting limitation on the number of Newco shares
which can be included in the offering (because the underwriter limits the number
of Newco securities it is willing to buy). Such an underwriting limitation can be
especially troublesome for those piggy-backing on a large primary offering.

Hence, contractual SEC registration rights should generally specify proration
priorities among the holder exercising the demand registration right, other holders
seeking to exercise piggy-back registration rights, and Newco seeking to sell
shares in a primary offering. Similarly, in a primary offering initiated by Newco,
the contractual registration rights should specify priorities among Newco and
various holders of secondary registration rights. Where the contractual registration
rights allow Newco to preempt VC's demand registration in favor of a Newco
primary offering, they may also require that a portion of such offering be reserved
for VC's securities.

The order of proration priorities will often differ depending on whether the
registration is (1) a VC demand, (2) a demand by other holders with VC exercising
piggy-back rights, or (3) a primary offering initiated by Newco with VC and other
holders exercising piggy-back rights.

Moreover, the underwriter will undoubtedly require that Newco and each
major shareholder (and possibly each holder who was offered the opportunity
to participate in the registration, whether or not such holder actually does sell in
the offering) agree not to sell additional Newco shares (including under SEC Rule
144) for a specified (and often lengthy, e.g., 90 to 180 days or occasionally longer)
period after the underwritten offering (a "hold-back period"). Hence, contractual
SEC registration rights should generally require that Newco, each major shareholder, and any other holder who has the right to participate in the offering agree
to any such hold-back requested by the underwriter.

¶207.7.3.4 *Short-Form S-2 or S-3*

If Newco has been a 1934 Act reporting company for a specified period and
meets certain other requirements, Newco can use a short-form registration statement to register with SEC the holder's resale of Newco securities:

- *Form S-3* incorporates most information by merely referring to Newco's
  periodic 1934 Act filings.
- *Form S-2* requires that certain of Newco's periodic 1934 Act filings actually
  be delivered to buyers.
- See ¶902 below for a discussion of the prerequisites to use of S-2 and S-3.

¶207.7.3.5   Reg. A

An offering statement under Reg. A—which is generally shorter, less complex, less expensive, and less time consuming than a full-blown SEC registration statement—can be used for up to $1.5 million of secondary securities in any 12-month period where Newco is not a 1934 Act reporting company and meets other Reg. A requirements. See ¶207.6 above.

¶207.7.4   Rule 144

Where Newco has not registered the holder's resale of its restricted securities, the holder can nevertheless resell such restricted securities publicly under Rule 144, so long as:

(1) the holder has at least a 1-year SEC holding period for limited quantity resales and Newco is a 1934 Act reporting company *or*

(2) the holder has at least a 2-year SEC holding period for unlimited resales by a non-affiliate of Newco, whether or not Newco is a 1934 Act reporting company.

While nothing on this issue has been heard from SEC since 2/97, SEC had then announced that it was considering shortening the holding periods to six months and one year, respectively. SEC was also considering how to address hedging transactions involving restricted securities and may reinstate the concept of tolling the holding period where the holder engages in puts or short sales or acquires other options to sell securities.

For a more detailed description of SEC Rule 144 and certain other requirements which must be satisfied, see ¶903 below.

¶208   COMPLIANCE WITH STATE SECURITIES LAWS

An offering of Newco securities must also comply with each applicable state securities (blue sky) law. This includes a primary sale by Newco to existing or new stockholders (such as E or VC), as well as a secondary resale by any stockholders to third parties.

While many state securities laws contain exemptions from registration similar to the federal exemptions described at ¶207 above, many states impose additional conditions. Also, many states do not have the equivalent of Rule 504 or Rule 701.

In addition, while federal securities laws focus on disclosure of information about Newco and the manner of sale, some state securities laws go further and seek to regulate the substantive fairness of the offering.

However, (1) where Newco issues securities pursuant to SEC Rule 506, no state may impose merit review or require any filing other than a filing substantially similar to that required by SEC Rule 503 and (2) where Newco or a Newco shareholder sells securities to be traded on the NYSE, AMEX, or Nasdaq National Market, no state may impose merit review or require any filing. This does not affect any required state broker-dealer filings.

¶209 NATURE OF VC

¶209.1 VC as SBIC

Small business. Generally, where VC is an SBIC, VC can invest only in a "small business," i.e., one which meets at least one of the following two "size standards":

- has tangible book net worth not in excess of $18 million and prior 2 fiscal years' average net income not in excess of $6 million *or*
- meets certain employee or revenue standards published by SBA for the industry in which the SBIC portfolio company is principally engaged.

If the SBIC portfolio company's business is principally located in a labor surplus area (as determined by the Department of Labor), each of the size standard tests is increased by 25%.

The SBIC portfolio company's tangible net worth for purposes of the $18 million size standard test is apparently calculated in accordance with GAAP by reducing the portfolio company's book net worth by the carrying value of its intangible assets (including goodwill, patents, trademarks, know-how).

In determining whether the SBIC portfolio company meets the size standards, the portfolio company is measured together with its "affiliates." In determining who are the portfolio company's affiliates:

- The portfolio company's affiliates include a company which the portfolio company controls, a company which is controlled by the portfolio company, or a company which is under common control with the portfolio company.
- "Control" means not only ownership of 50% or more of a portfolio company's voting stock, but also includes ownership of a block of voting stock which is large compared to others (e.g., two 40% shareholders, or perhaps even three 30% shareholders, of a portfolio company would each be treated as affiliates of the portfolio company).
- Affiliation is generally measured on a pro forma basis after giving effect to the SBIC's investment and related transactions.
- Rights to acquire portfolio company voting stock (e.g., by exercise of a warrant, option, or conversion privilege) outstanding immediately after consummation of the transaction in which the SBIC and its co-investors make their investment are taken into account only where a deemed exercise causes a person with such rights to become a portfolio company affiliate.
- Rights to acquire a portfolio company's business (e.g., by exercise of an option or consummation of an asset purchase or merger agreement) outstanding immediately after consummation of the transaction in which the SBIC and its co-investors make their investment are also taken into account

only where a deemed exercise causes the person with such rights to become a portfolio company affiliate.

- Interlocking directors or officers, contractual relationships, family relationships, etc., may also create affiliation.
- Certain types of portfolio company investors are not treated as portfolio company affiliates, broadly described by the statute as "a venture capital firm, investment company" (including an SBIC), and certain tax-exempt entities, although SBA's regulations are longer and somewhat more detailed than the statutory language.

Once the portfolio company's affiliates have been identified (in the manner described immediately above), the size standards are generally applied by looking at the portfolio company together with its post-investment affiliates based on the size of each immediately *before* the SBIC makes or commits to make its investment (i.e., without giving effect to the SBIC's and its co-investors' investment in the portfolio company and related transactions).

- The first set of size standards (related to net worth and net income) is normally applied to the portfolio company and its affiliates viewed as a single group, and the group must meet both the net worth and the net income tests.
- The second set of size standards (relating to either number of employees or size of revenue, depending on the industry) is normally applied twice (and both tests must be met), once to the employees or revenue of the portfolio company (apparently although not explicitly including its affiliates) based on the industry in which the portfolio company is primarily engaged and once to the portfolio company (apparently although not explicitly including its affiliates) based on the industry in which the group is primarily engaged. A proposed regulatory amendment would, if adopted, substitute a single test applied to the employees or revenue of the portfolio company (explicitly including its affiliates) based on the industry in which the portfolio company viewed alone is primarily engaged.

Change of ownership. When an SBIC finances a portfolio company "change of ownership," two additional tests must be satisfied:

- The size standards are applied to the portfolio company both *before* and *after* giving effect to such change, including all related financings, mergers, and acquisitions (whereas in a transaction which is not a change of ownership, the size standards [except for the identification of affiliates] are generally applied only *before* giving effect to the SBIC's investment and related transactions).
- In addition, when the resulting portfolio company (apparently but not explicitly including its affiliates) will have over 500 full-time equivalent employees, the portfolio company is required to meet one of two DER tests:
  - DER not exceeding 5 to 1 if the SBIC has SBA financing.
  - DER not exceeding 8 to 1 if the SBIC has no SBA financing.

For this purpose, "equity" means common and preferred stock (contributed capital in the case of a partnership and membership interests in the case of an LLC), not including retained earnings, and "debt" means long-term debt and short-term working capital loans not containing a 30-day-per-year clean-up clause, but not subordinated debt issued to the seller in payment of all or a portion of the purchase price in the change of ownership transaction.

- While these two additional tests clearly apply where an SBIC finances a *newly-formed* portfolio company (Newco) acquiring target company, they apparently do not apply where an SBIC finances an *existing* company (Oldco) acquiring target company as part of Oldco's normal growth.

Repealed restrictions on portfolio company control. Under SBA regulations which were effective until 11/20/02, the SBIC venture capitalist, alone or together with other SBICs (and their "associates"), could not control the portfolio company except in certain limited situations, including:

(1)   there has been "a substantial change in [the portfolio company's] operations or products during the past 2 years, or such a change is the intended result of" the SBIC's investment in the portfolio company and the SBIC (together with other SBIC investors) is the portfolio company's "major source of [debt and equity] capital,"

(2)   a start-up (not an LBO) financing and the SBIC (together with other SBIC investors) is the portfolio company's "major source of [debt and equity] capital,"

(3)   subsequent to the SBIC's financing of the portfolio company, the portfolio company commits a material breach of its financing agreements with the SBIC or other circumstances make it reasonably necessary for the SBIC to take control of the portfolio company to protect its existing investment, or

(4)   the portfolio company's business is principally located in a low and moderate income (LMI) zone as determined by various government agencies.

Under these pre-11/21/02 SBA regulations, an SBIC that took control of a portfolio company was required to file with SBA a "control certification" agreeing to relinquish control within 5 years.

Current 7-year control regulations. SBA interpreted a somewhat opaque 12/00 statutory amendment as overruling the above SBA regulations limiting circumstances when one or more SBICs can control a portfolio company. The SBIC statute as amended in 12/00 states "an investment [in a small business] by a venture capital firm, investment company . . . , [or certain tax-exempt entities] . . . shall not cause [the small] business . . . to be deemed not independently owned and operated *regardless of the allocation of control during the investment period under any investment agreement between the [small] business . . . and the entity making the investment*" (12/00 amendment in italics).[1]

Almost 2 years after enactment of this 12/00 statutory amendment SBA published final regulations, effective 11/21/02, allowing an SBIC (and its associates) to

---

¶209   [1]15 USC §662(5)(a)(i) as amended 12/00.

exercise control over a portfolio company (through ownership of voting securities, management agreements, voting trusts, majority board representation, or otherwise) for 7 years, subject to extension with SBA's prior written approval where reasonably necessary to complete divestiture of control or to ensure the portfolio company's financial stability.

Under both the current SBA regulations and under the now-repealed pre-11/21/02 SBA regulations, an SBIC is generally treated as taking control of a portfolio company if the SBIC, together with other SBICs, has 50% or more of the portfolio company's voting securities or otherwise has a majority of the portfolio company's board. Where the portfolio company has 50 or more shareholders, the 50%-or-more test is reduced (1) to a more-than-25% test and (2) to a 20%-or-more test if no other party holds a larger block. However, even if the SBIC(s) fail this 50% or 25%/20% test, the SBIC is not treated as controlling the portfolio company where the portfolio company's management owned at least 25% of the portfolio company's voting securities, management can elect at least 40% of the portfolio company's board, and the SBIC(s) can elect no more than 40%, in which case the balance of the board can be elected by mutual agreement of the SBIC(s) and management or by management alone or by third parties.

Further investment after portfolio company ceases to be small. Once an SBIC has invested in the portfolio company (while the portfolio company met the size standards), the SBIC can continue investing in the portfolio company (even after the portfolio company has ceased to meet the size standards) until the portfolio company's first public offering of equity or debt securities. Thereafter, the SBIC may continue investing in the portfolio company (which no longer meets the size standards) only if pursuant to (1) a written commitment made before such first public offering or (2) exercise of stock options, warrants, or similar rights.

Smaller enterprise requirement. At least 10% of the total dollar value of an SBIC's financings (including pre-licensing financings approved by SBA for inclusion in Regulatory Capital) as of the first anniversary of licensing, and at least 20% of the dollar value of an SBIC's financings on a cumulative basis measured each subsequent anniversary of licensing, must be in "**Smaller Enterprises,**" i.e., businesses which meet the old SBA size standard: $6 million net worth and $2 million average net income for proceeding 2 fiscal years *or* the applicable employee/revenue test.

- Exceptions: (1) 20% is 50% for an SBIC with less than $10 million of capital. (2) 100% of all financings made in whole or in part with leverage in excess of $90 million must be in Smaller Enterprises.

A change of ownership which creates a Smaller Enterprise qualifies as a Smaller Enterprise financing.

Other restrictions. Investments by an SBIC in a portfolio company are subject to numerous SBA regulations, dealing with, among other things:

- the business in which a portfolio company is permitted to engage (e.g., not principally the real estate or banking business, with limited exceptions),
- the extent to which the portfolio company's business must be domestic (i.e., in the U.S.),

- fees the SBIC may charge the portfolio company,
- the maximum interest rate on and schedule for amortizing the SBIC's loans to the portfolio company (1 year minimum life under 12/00 legislation, rather than former 5 years),
- the maximum dividend rate on and schedule for redeeming the SBIC's redeemable preferred stock in the portfolio company (1 year minimum life under 12/00 legislation, rather than former 5 years),
- the timing and pricing of the SBIC's equity puts, i.e., the circumstances under which the SBIC may require the portfolio company to repurchase portfolio company stock held by the SBIC, generally not during the first year after the investment under 12/00 legislation, and the permissible methods for determining the price for such a redemption,
- restrictions on the SBIC's sale of portfolio company securities to an "associate" of the SBIC, and
- restrictions on the SBIC investing in a portfolio company with which the SBIC's "associates" have prescribed relationships.

Former restrictions on an SBIC selling portfolio securities to a competitor of the portfolio company were repealed in 11/02.

See ¶1011 below for a discussion of the pros and cons of forming VC as an SBIC.

¶209.2   VC as BHC Subsidiary

¶209.2.1   BHCA

Where VC is a BHC or a BHC subsidiary, the BHCA does not permit VC to invest in a portfolio company unless the investment falls into at least one of the four permissive baskets discussed below.

¶209.2.1.1   Reg. Y and the 5/25 rules

Reg. Y under the BHCA permits a BHC or its U.S. subsidiary (other than a bank or its subsidiary)—which group is referred to as a "BHC" throughout this ¶209.2.1.1—to hold portfolio company securities so long as such securities meet the 5 and 25 rules, i.e., such securities do not constitute more than:

- 5% of any class of the portfolio company's voting stock (including rights to acquire portfolio company stock by conversion, warrant exercise, and the like) *or*
- generally 25% of the portfolio company's equity measured by value, but it is not wholly clear (1) whether this means book value, FV, or dollars invested and (2) whether or under what circumstances subordinated debt should be included as equity,

and so long as VC does not otherwise control the portfolio company.

The Fed has sometimes taken the position that a BHC with the legal right to elect a director (either by contract or pursuant to the terms of the portfolio company stock it holds) has impermissible control of the portfolio company. The Fed has occasionally taken the position that a BHC whose designee is elected a director (where the BHC has no legal right to a board seat) presumptively controls the portfolio company if the BHC owns a substantial equity position (15% or more), even if the BHC holds no voting stock.

The Fed generally treats non-voting stock as voting if *either*:

- the BHC has the right to convert it into voting stock, *or*
- the non-voting stock is freely transferable and the transferee has the right to convert it into voting stock,

unless such conversion is permitted only after a widespread distribution of the stock or in certain other special circumstances. Similarly, the Fed generally applies the rules set forth immediately above to determine whether a warrant exercisable directly or indirectly for voting stock constitutes voting stock.

The Fed may treat non-voting stock as voting if it carries substantial covenants relating to management of the business.

¶209.2.1.2   VC as SBIC

Where VC is both an SBIC and a BHC subsidiary (including a subsidiary of a bank), VC can make any investment permitted by the SBIC rules described in ¶209.1 above.

¶209.2.1.3   Reg. K

Reg. K under the BHCA permits a BHC or its U.S. or foreign subsidiary (other than a bank and most of the bank's subsidiaries) to invest in a foreign portfolio company so long as such investment meets each of three tests, i.e., the investment does not exceed:

- $25 million (including portfolio company subordinated debt if the BHC holds more than 5% of the portfolio company's equity) *nor*
- 40% of portfolio company's equity (including convertible debt, warrants, other rights to acquire portfolio company stock, and loans which participate in portfolio company profits) *nor*
- 19.99% of portfolio company's voting power.

These limits can be exceeded with prior Fed consent.

To qualify as foreign, the portfolio company (and certain portfolio company affiliates) must not be "engaged in business" or "engaged in activities" or have an office (other than a "representative office") in the U.S., although the portfolio company need not be formed outside the U.S. (e.g., the portfolio company can be a Delaware corporation or LLC).

¶209.2.1.4   Merchant Banking Activity

The 11/99 Gramm-Leach-Bliley Act (the "GLB Act") repealed the depression-era Glass-Steagall Act and amended the BHCA to insert a significant fourth basket for BHC venture capital investments, by allowing VC to invest in a portfolio company (including a PE fund) where *all* of the following tests are met:

- The BHC qualifies as a "financial holding company," meaning that all of the BHC's subsidiary depository institutions are "well capitalized" and "well managed" and meet certain standards for investing in their local communities (the so-called CRA or Community Reinvestment Act requirement).
- The BHC elects "financial holding company" status.
- The investment in the portfolio company is made and held by the BHC's "securities affiliate or an affiliate thereof" and not by "a depository institution or subsidiary" thereof.
- The investment in the portfolio company is "part of a bona fide . . . merchant or investment banking activity, including investment activities engaged in for the purpose of appreciation and ultimate resale or disposition of the investment."
- The portfolio company securities "are held for a period of time to enable the sale or disposition thereof on a reasonable basis consistent with the financial viability of" such merchant or investment banking activity.
- The BHC and its securities affiliates as defined in (a) below—which group is referred to as a "BHC" throughout this ¶209.2.1.4—do "not routinely manage or operate such [portfolio] company . . . except as may be necessary or required to obtain a reasonable return on investment upon resale or disposition."
- Each company in which the BHC invests pursuant to the GLB Act's merchant banking authority is engaged primarily in non-financial activities (but a BHC can often invest in a company engaged in financial activities under other statutory and regulatory provisions).

Subject to satisfying the above, the BHC may own portfolio company securities "directly or indirectly . . . whether as principal, on behalf of 1 or more entities . . . , or otherwise . . . (including debt or equity securities, partnership interests . . . , or other instruments representing ownership) . . . , whether or not constituting control."

While the GLB Act is very broad, many of its statutory phrases are vague and inevitably attract Fed interpretation:

(a) **Securities affiliate.** The Act authorizes a portfolio company investment only if made by the BHC's "securities affiliate or an affiliate thereof." The Fed has interpreted this to mean that a BHC merchant banking investment can be made by the financial holding company or any of its subsidiaries other than a bank and its subsidiaries, so long as (1) the financial holding company or one of its subsidiaries is a registered broker or dealer or a registered municipal securities dealer (including a division or department of a bank registered as a municipal securities dealer) under the 1934 Act *or* (2) the financial holding company controls both an insurance under-writer and a registered investment adviser providing investment advice to an insurance company.

(b) **10-year maximum holding.** The Act authorizes the purchase of portfolio company securities as "part of a bona fide . . . merchant . . . banking activity . . . for appreciation" where the securities "are held for a period of time to enable the sale . . . on a reasonable basis. . . ." The Fed has interpreted this to mean that a financial holding company normally can not retain a merchant banking investment more than 10 years including tacking (i.e., the 10-year period begins when the financial holding company or any subsidiary or affiliate (including an affiliated PE fund) acquires an invest-ment in the portfolio company). In order to hold an investment longer than 10 years, the financial holding company must obtain Fed permission.

(c) **Prohibition on routine management or operation.** The Act authorizes the BHC to "control" a portfolio company, so long as it "does not routinely manage or operate such [portfolio] company except as . . . necessary . . . to obtain a reasonable return upon . . . resale." The Fed has interpreted this to mean, among other things, that, in general, no director, officer, or employee of a financial holding company or its subsidiaries can serve as, or have the responsibilities of, a portfolio company executive officer, and there is a rebuttable presumption that no such person can serve as a portfolio company employee below the level of executive officer (although, as described below, such persons can be portfolio company directors).

In addition, the financial holding company can not have covenants or other contractual arrangements restricting the portfolio company's "ability to make routine business decisions" (including "entering into transactions in the ordinary course of business or hiring" persons below the level of executive officers). The financial holding company may, however, have covenants restricting portfolio company action "outside . . . the ordinary course of . . . business," including:

- Acquisition of significant assets or control of another company.
- Selection of an independent accountant or investment banker.
- Significant business plan changes.
- Replacement of executive officers (i.e., "person[s] who participate . . . in major policy making functions" other than as a director).
- Redemption or issuance of equity or debt securities.
- Borrowing outside the ordinary course of business.
- Amending the articles of incorporation or by-laws.
- Sale, merger, spin off, recapitalization, or liquidation of the portfolio company or a significant subsidiary.

Moreover, the financial holding company may appoint any or all of a portfolio company's directors (or persons exercising similar functions) and these directors may "participate fully in those matters . . . typically presented to directors" at formal or informal meetings.

In addition, the Fed does permit the financial holding company to manage or operate the portfolio company so long as "intervention by the financial holding company is necessary . . . to obtain a reasonable return on the financial holding company's investment . . . upon resale or other disposition of the investment, such as to avoid or address a significant operating loss or in connection with a loss of senior management," although where such control lasts beyond 9 months, the financial holding company must notify to the Fed and justify its actions.

(d) **Investment in PE fund.** The Fed explicitly permits the financial holding company to invest in a PE fund.

Where the financial holding company does not "control" PE Fund (i.e., is passive), PE Fund's "actions [and portfolio company shares owned by PE Fund] should not be attributed to the financial holding company," so that PE Fund can routinely manage or operate its portfolio companies without violating the BHCA and the GLB Act.

However, where the financial holding company does "control" PE Fund, the "financial holding company is considered to be acting through [such] fund that it controls," so that PE Fund can not manage or operate its portfolio companies except under circumstances which would allow the financial holding company to exercise such rights with respect to one of its portfolio companies (i.e., "intervention . . . necessary . . . to obtain a reasonable return") as described in (c) above.

For this purpose, the financial holding company "controls" PE Fund if the financial holding company or any employee, director, or principal shareholder:

- serves as PE Fund's general partner (or person exercising similar function), *or*
- owns or controls at least 25% of any class of PE Fund voting shares, *or*
- selects or constitutes a majority of PE Fund's directors (or persons exercising similar functions), *or*
- owns or controls more than 5% of any class of PE Fund's voting shares *and* serves as PE Fund's investment adviser.

If PE Fund constitutes a "qualifying" fund, a 15 year rather than a 10 year maximum investment duration applies, i.e., without Fed approval (1) the financial holding company can hold its investment in PE Fund for as long as 15 years and (2) PE Fund (even if controlled by the financial holding company) can hold its portfolio company investments for as long as 15 years. For this purpose, PE Fund constitutes a "qualifying" fund where, among other requirements, (1) the financial holding company and its employees, directors, and principal shareholders do not own or control more than 25% of PE Fund's "total equity" *and* (2) PE Fund's maximum term (including all potential extensions, except as approved by the Fed) does not exceed 15 years.

If PE Fund is not a qualifying fund, (e.g., because the financial holding company and its related persons own more than 25% of PE Fund's "total equity" *or* PE Fund has more than a 15 year maximum term including potential extensions), a 10-year (rather than a 15-year) maximum investment duration applies to the financial holding company's investment in PE Fund and, where the financial holding company controls PE Fund, also applies to PE Fund's investment in each of its portfolio companies.

The Fed interpretations do "not impose any limits on advisory fees or . . . incentive compensation" that the financial holding company may receive for services rendered to PE Fund.

¶209.2.2   Federal Reserve Act §23A

Where a BHC seeks to be both a substantial equity investor in the portfolio company (through one of the BHC's venture capital subsidiaries or a PE fund controlled by the BHC) and also a lender to the portfolio company (through the BHC's banking subsidiary), Federal Reserve Act §23A may prohibit the BHC from holding both debt and equity positions. In brief, the §23A prohibition is most likely to apply (and hence to prohibit the BHC's banking subsidiary from lending to the portfolio company) where (1) the BHC or its subsidiaries (other than bank subsidiaries) acquires 25% or more of a class of portfolio company voting stock (or in some cases 15% or more of portfolio company's total equity) and (2) the BHC's bank subsidiary makes a loan to the portfolio company.

In more detail, the §23A prohibition generally applies where *all* 5 of the following conditions are met:

(1)   VC (an equity investor in a portfolio company) is under common control with a bank (the "VC-related bank") which is either a member of the Federal Reserve System or a federally-insured non-member bank.

(2)   VC-related bank is a lender to the portfolio company.

(3)   VC is not an SBIC which is a bank subsidiary, i.e., a direct or indirect subsidiary of VC-related bank (or of a sister bank controlled by the BHC), but rather VC is either (a) the BHC which controls VC-related bank, or (b) a non-bank subsidiary of the BHC, or (c) a "financial subsidiary" of the bank. A financial subsidiary of a bank is generally a bank subsidiary engaged in financial activities in which the bank itself can not engage, but not activities permitted by a specific statute (e.g., SBIC activities in which a bank subsidiary is permitted to engage by a specific statute).

(4)   VC "controls" the portfolio company, defined by §23A as meaning that:

(a)   VC owns or controls, directly or indirectly, 25% or more of any class of the portfolio company's voting securities, *or*

(b)   VC controls the election of a majority of the portfolio company's directors, *or*

(c)   the Fed has determined that VC has a controlling influence over the portfolio company's management or policies, *or*

(d)   where VC's investment relies upon the financial holding company rules (as described in ¶209.2.1.4 above) and VC owns 15% or more of the portfolio company total equity (but does not fall within (4)(a) through (c) above), VC is presumed to control the portfolio company, unless the presumption is rebutted based on all the facts and circumstances, and the presumption is deemed rebutted:

- where no financial holding company officer, director, or employee serves as a portfolio company director (or person exercising similar functions), *or*
- where one financial holding company officer, director, or employee serves as a portfolio company director (or similar position) *and* a person not affiliated or associated with the financial holding company owns or controls more of the portfolio company's total equity than the financial holding company, *or*
- where more than one financial holding company officer, director, or employee serves as a portfolio company director (or similar position) but less than a majority of the portfolio company's directors (or similar positions) *and* a person not affiliated or associated with the financial holding company owns or controls 50% or more of the portfolio company's voting power.

Where VC "controls" a portfolio company, §23A refers to the portfolio company as an "affiliate" of VC and VC-related bank.

(5)   VC-related bank's loan to the portfolio company fails to meet any one or more of the following 3 tests (generally at any time while the loan is outstanding):

(a)   The loan is secured by collateral with a market value of at least 130% of the loan (somewhat less than 130% under certain circumstances, e.g., 120% if the collateral consists of satisfactory quality debt instruments, including receivables).

(b)   VC-related bank's loans to (and certain other transactions with) the portfolio company are 10% or less of VC-related bank's capital stock and surplus.

(c)   All of VC-related bank's loans to (and certain other transactions with) all "affiliates," including the portfolio company, are 20% or less of VC-related bank's capital stock and surplus.

In sum, where a VC-related bank is a lender to a portfolio company and VC "controls" the portfolio company, VC must be a direct or indirect subsidiary of VC-related bank (or of a sister bank controlled by the BHC), assuming (as is invariably the case) that the bank loan fails to meet at least one of the three tests described in (5) above.

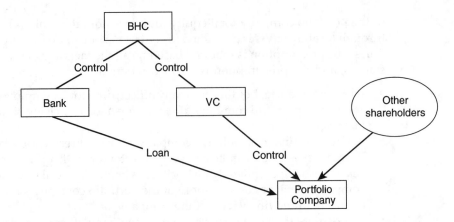

Some BHCs offer one-stop shopping, supplying a portfolio company with both equity and debt capital. Where a BHC offers one-stop shopping and its banking subsidiary supplies debt capital to a portfolio company while its VC subsidiary acquires 25% or more of a class of the portfolio company's voting stock (or otherwise controls the portfolio company), the BHC must generally acquire the portfolio company stock through an SBIC subsidiary of its banking subsidiary.[2] This is because none of the other types of entities through which the BHC could acquire the portfolio company stock (i.e., a ¶209.2.1.4 merchant banking entity, a ¶209.2.1.1 Reg. Y entity, or generally a ¶209.2.1.3 Reg. K entity) are permitted to be direct or indirect subsidiaries of a bank.

Where BHC's equity investment in a portfolio company is made through a Reg. Y subsidiary which is *not* an SBIC, the BHCA generally prohibits VC from owning more than 5% of any class of the portfolio company's voting stock, as described in ¶209.2.1.1. Hence in this circumstance §23A would seldom apply, because BHC and its Reg. Y subsidiary would not be viewed as controlling the portfolio company as defined by §23A. However, §23A can apply where BHC's equity investment in the portfolio company is made through an SBIC (which is not a subsidiary of the lending bank or of a sister bank to the lending bank) or through a financial holding company engaged in merchant banking, since neither an SBIC's nor a financial holding company's ownership of portfolio company voting stock is limited by the BHCA 5% rule.

¶209.3 VC as Insurance Company

State law generally imposes restrictions on the amount of voting power an insurance company (or an affiliate thereof) can hold in a non-insurance company.

---

[2] Assuming the bank loan fails to meet at least one of the three tests described in (5) above.

¶210   SPECIAL LTCG ADVANTAGES FOR INDIVIDUALS

The top normal federal tax rate for an individual's LTCG (i.e., gain on sale of a capital asset, including stock, held more than one year) is 20%, which is 18.6 percentage points below the top individual OI rate (38.6% for 2002 and 2003). However, three Code provisions grant further tax relief to an individual who owns stock either directly or through a partnership, LLC, or S corporation and who recognizes LTCG in special circumstances:

(1) A 14% top rate for LTCG on sale of "qualified small business stock" held more than 5 years.

(2) A tax-free rollover on sale of stock that would have qualified for the 14% special rate (except that the necessary holding period is more than 6 months rather than more than 5 years) where the proceeds are then reinvested in new qualified stock within 60 days.

(3) An 18% top rate for LTCG on sale of property (not merely "qualified small business stock") acquired after 12/31/00 and held more than 5 years (with a taxpayer election to treat pre-12/31/00 property as sold and reacquired in 1/01).

See ¶906 for a more detailed discussion of these CG tax breaks for individuals.

¶211   KEY ISSUES AND REFERENCES

Overview of a Start-Up Transaction

What are E's principal legal, tax, and economic goals in negotiating and structuring a start-up transaction? What are VC's principal legal, tax, and economic goals? How do VC's goals differ from E's?

How will the use of different types of securities (e.g., common stock, preferred stock, debentures, convertibles, warrants, options) help to achieve E's and VC's goals?

Key Tax Issues

Will E recognize OI when Newco is formed?

Will E recognize OI as his or her stock vests? If so, where will E obtain cash with which to pay the tax? Can E defer the tax until E sells the stock?

Is E disadvantaged by recognizing OI?

What is "vesting"? What is a "substantial risk of forfeiture" (an "SRF")? Are the two concepts different?

What is "time vesting"? What is "performance vesting"? How are the two different? Will E prefer one type of vesting rather than the other? Will VC's preference be different than E's?

Where E's stock is subject to vesting, should it make a difference why E's employment with Newco ends?

E quits—with or without "good reason."
E is fired—with or without "cause."
E dies.
E becomes disabled.
Newco is sold.
E becomes Secretary of State.

References:

- Code §§1(a), (h)(1), (h)(2), and 1202
- Code §83
- Code §351
- Treas. Reg. §1.83-1 through §1.83-8
- Treas. Reg. §1.351-1 and §1.351-2
- Ginsburg and Levin M&A book ¶901 (re Code §351), ¶¶1502.1.1, 1502.1.3, 1502.1.4, and 1502.1.6 (re Code §83)
- Sheffield and Kimball, Organizing the Corporate Venture §§301 through 304 (Practising Law Institute, "Tax Strategies for Corporate Acquisitions, Dispositions, Spin-Offs, Joint Ventures, Reorganizations and Restructurings," vol. 8, 2000)
- Del. Gen. Corp. Law §202
- Ginsburg and Levin M&A book ¶604.1.6 (discussing in a Code §368 context the tax rules which likely apply where E receives Newco stock subject to vesting in a Code §351 contribution of property for Newco stock)

Key Delaware Corporate Law Issues

What steps should Newco take to protect its directors from liability?

References:

- Del. Gen. Corp. Law §102(b)(7) and §145

Key SEC and Blue Sky Issues

Is there a securities law impediment to selling Newco stock to E or VC?

How about sales to Newco executives, sales persons, secretaries, factory workers?

How about sales to E's idiot golfing buddies, bright tennis partners, retired next-door neighbor, widowed mother, or truck-driver brother living in Nebraska?

What if VC is really a group of individuals who have formed (or are forming) an informal investment club?

Is there a securities law impediment to E, VC, and the other buyers of Newco's stock reselling the stock in the future?

References:

- 1933 Act §§4(2) and 5
- SEC Reg. D
- 1933 Act §3(a)(11)
- SEC Rule 147
- SEC Rule 701
- SEC Rule 144
- 1934 Act §10(b)
- SEC Rule 10b-5
- Ginsburg and Levin M&A book ¶1702.2.8

Attorney Ethical Considerations

Is there any impediment to one attorney representing all the parties—E, VC, Newco, various Newco employees, E's golfing buddies, E's widowed mother, etc.?

References:

- ABA Model Rule 1.7 and Comments thereunder

Shareholder Interest Deductions

If E (or any other individual buyer of Newco stock) pays for the Newco stock with a note (or borrows money from a third-party lender to buy the Newco stock), is there any impediment to the individual deducting the interest expense?

References:

- Code §163(a), (d), and (h)
- Ginsburg and Levin M&A book ¶1308

Newco Interest Deductions

Where VC makes part of its investment in Newco by purchasing a Newco debenture, is there any impediment to Newco deducting the interest expense on the debenture issued to VC?

References:

- ¶602.8 of this book
- Ginsburg and Levin M&A book ¶1403

Deductibility of Newco's Pre-Opening Start-Up Expenses

A special harsh IRS rule applies to Newco's pre-opening start-up expenses.

References:

- ¶304 of this book

CHAPTER 3

Structuring Newco as Flow-Through Entity

E and VC have reached agreement on the economic and certain of the structuring terms of the Newco start-up, as discussed in Chapter 2. However, they are now exploring whether Newco should be formed as a regular C corporation subject to double tax under the U.S. federal income tax system (as Newco was structured throughout Chapter 2) or whether it might be more advantageous to form Newco as a tax flow-through entity, i.e., a S corporation, a partnership, or an LLC none of which are subject to double tax.[1]

---

[1] As discussed in a footnote in chapter 2's introduction, a controversial Bush administration pending legislative proposal would, if enacted, largely repeal the double tax on C corporations. Because future prospects for this legislation are highly uncertain, the text of this book is based on current law and does not further discuss this legislative proposal.

¶301 NEWCO AS S CORPORATION

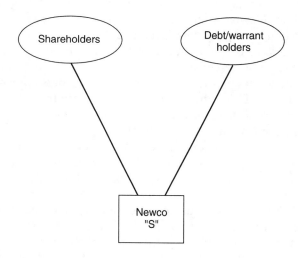

¶301.1 No Entity-Level Tax

Where Newco is formed as an S corporation, Newco is generally *not* subject to federal income tax on its income at the entity level. Rather each of Newco's shareholders reports a pro rata share of Newco's profits—whether or not distributed—and (subject to numerous qualifications) a pro rata share of Newco's losses on his or her personal tax return. Thus, Newco is not subject to federal corporate tax rates (up to 35%); instead each of Newco's shareholders is taxed at the appropriate federal rate—e.g., up to 38.6% for an individual's 2002 and 2003 OI.[1]

¶301.2 S Compared to C and Other Entities

¶301.2.1 S Compared to C

An S corporation (as opposed to a regular C corporation) has one significant tax disadvantage and several significant tax advantages:

(1) The initial tax on the S corporation's taxable income (payable by its shareholders, not by the corporation) is generally at individual tax rates (ranging up

---

¶301 [1] The top individual 2002 and 2003 federal OI rate is really higher than the 38.6% nominal rate because of the 3% itemized deduction disallowance, as described in ¶201.1.1 above.

In addition, the individual top rate is increased on any income subject to the uncapped medicare tax, which is imposed at a 1.45% (non-deductible) rate on an individual receiving compensation from an employer (e.g., an employee of an S corporation) and at 1.45% (deductible) rate on the employer, but does not apply to the income of an S corporation not paid out as compensation (i.e., income accumulated at the S corporation level or paid out as dividends).

to a federal rate of 38.6% for 2002 and 2003), as opposed to the lower 35% top federal corporate rate.

Hence, Newco S generally distributes to its shareholders approximately 38.6% of its taxable income (plus an additional amount to cover state income tax). This exceeds the amount Newco would pay if it were a C corporation (approximately 35% of its taxable income plus state income tax).

Indeed, a minority S corporation shareholder would be well advised to seek a mandatory distribution agreement with the S corporation, requiring the S corporation periodically to make distributions to all shareholders approximately equal to their income tax liabilities attributable to S corporation stock ownership.

(2) There is no second level of tax on distributions by the S corporation to its shareholders of earnings while an S corporation.

(3) There is no second level of tax when a shareholder realizes on previously taxed S corporation income by selling his or her stock, because the undistributed S corporation income is added to the shareholder's tax basis in his or her stock as earned.

(4) When the S corporation's business is ultimately sold, the sellers can deliver asset SUB to the buyer while recognizing only one tax (i.e., S status avoids double federal income tax on a properly structured sale of the business).

This result can be achieved *either* by (a) sale of the S corporation's assets, (b) forward taxable merger of S corporation into buyer, *or* (c) sale of the S corporation's stock to a corporate buyer where both the buying corporation and all of the S corporation's selling shareholders jointly elect under Code §338(h)(10) to treat the stock sale as an asset sale for federal income tax purposes.

This SUB-with-one-tax result is achieved for two reasons:

- *First*, as discussed above, an S corporation's taxable income (including its asset-sale gain) normally is not subject to federal income tax at the S entity level, but only at the shareholder level.
- *Second*, the mechanics of subchapter S protect the shareholders from liquidation gain. Under Code §331, a shareholder (including an S corporation shareholder) has CG equal to the *excess* of his or her liquidating distributions from the corporation *over* his or her tax basis in the corporation's stock. With a C corporation, a shareholder's tax basis in the stock is generally his or her original cost for the stock (plus any subsequent contributions to the corporation), i.e., C corporation frozen stock basis. However, with an S corporation, a shareholder's tax basis in the stock is flexible, generally consisting of:

  - original cost,
  - *plus* the shareholder's subsequent contributions to the corporation,
  - *plus* S taxable income taxed (and any S tax-exempt income attributed) to the shareholder,
  - *less* distributions by the corporation to the shareholder,
  - *less* S taxable losses deducted by the shareholder.[2]

---

[2] With either a C or an S corporation, when a shareholder dies, his or her estate or beneficiaries take a new tax basis for the stock equal to FV at death, although in the case of an S corporation there is a basis reduction equal to the decedent's share of any Code §691 income-in-respect-of-a-decedent

Thus each shareholder's tax basis in his or her S corporation stock increases by his or her share of the S corporation's asset-sale gain. Accordingly, when the S corporation liquidates and distributes the sales proceeds to its shareholders, they do not recognize liquidation gain under Code §331.

However, in the case of an S corporation which was formerly a C corporation, Code §1374 imposes a corporate-level tax on any sale of the corporation's assets occurring during its first 10 years as an S corporation (based on the *lesser* of (a) the built-in gain in an asset at the time the corporation became an S corporation *or* (b) the actual gain recognized on the sale of such asset).

This rule also applies to assets acquired from a C corporation by an S corporation (even though the latter was never itself a C corporation) in an asset COB transaction (e.g., a tax-free merger of a C into an S corporation), based on the lesser of (1) the built-in gain in a COB asset at the time acquired by the S corporation or (2) the actual gain recognized on the sale of such asset.

As discussed in ¶301.6.4 below, an S corporation is permitted to treat a 100%-owned corporate subsidiary as a division of the parent S corporation, so that the taxable income of the 100%-owned subsidiary escapes C corporation tax and flows through to the parent S corporation's shareholders. Where, for example, an S corporation acquires 100% of a pre-existing C corporation's stock and elects to treat such subsidiary as a division of the parent S corporation, the S corporation is treated as acquiring the subsidiary's assets in a COB transaction, so that the Code §1374 corporate-level tax applies to any sale of the subsidiary's assets during the next 10 years (to the extent of the built-in asset gain at the time the subsidiary ceased to be a C corporation and became a deemed division of the parent S corporation).

Where Code §1374 applies, there is thus double federal income tax on the portion of the S corporation's gain covered by §1374.

(5) As described above, each shareholder of an S corporation is taxed on his or her pro rata share of the S corporation's income. However, where a person holds only a right to acquire stock in the future (e.g., a warrant or conversion privilege), such potential shareholder is generally not treated as a shareholder for tax purposes. Hence, such potential shareholder is not taxed on a share of the S corporation's income; rather the S corporation's actual shareholders are taxed on the share of the entity's income which would have been allocated to the potential shareholder if he or she had actually acquired the stock. Similarly, where an individual actually holds stock in an S corporation, but the stock is subject to vesting (see ¶202.3) and a timely Code §83(b) election (see ¶202.3.4 and ¶202.3.5) was not made, the individual is not treated as a shareholder for federal income tax purposes until the shares vest.

Thus, a potential shareholder (including a holder of unvested shares as to which no Code §83(b) election was timely made) is not taxed on the S corporation's income and consequently such person's tax basis in the S corporation's stock does not increase as the S corporation recognizes income.

---

items held by the S corporation. A similar rule applies when the pass-through entity is a partnership or an LLC classified as a partnership. Code §1014(a), (c).

¶301.2.2   S Compared to Partnership or LLC

Although an S corporation is similar to a partnership or an LLC in that all 3 forms of organization are flow-through entities for tax purposes and hence are generally not subject to an entity-level federal income tax, there are nevertheless significant differences among them, including the following:

(1) An S corporation must comply with arbitrary rules limiting the number and identity of its shareholders. See ¶301.6 below. These rules do not apply to a partnership or LLC, which can have an unlimited number of partners/members of any type (e.g., individual, entity, foreign, TEO), so long as the partnership or LLC is not publicly traded. See ¶302.3 and ¶302.8.5 below.

(2) An S corporation is permitted to issue only a single class of plain vanilla common stock (although differences in voting rights between shares are permitted) and hence its shareholders must share all S corporation income, gains, losses, and distributions in proportion to their stock ownership. See ¶301.6.1 below. In contrast, a partnership or LLC may issue an unlimited number of different classes of equity and hence may allocate income, gains, losses, and distributions flexibly among their partners/members, so long as those allocations have "substantial economic effect." See ¶302.4 below.

(3) When an S corporation distributes appreciated property to its shareholders in kind, the S corporation recognizes (for tax purposes) the appreciation inherent in the property and such recognized gain flows through and is taxed to its shareholders.[3] In contrast, no gain or loss is generally recognized to a partnership or LLC and its partners/members when a partnership or LLC distributes appreciated property in kind to its partners/members.[4] See ¶302.4 below.

(4) An S corporation is a corporation and hence can acquire another corporation or be acquired by another corporation in a tax-free Code §368 reorganization. In contrast, a partnership or LLC can not be a party to a tax-free reorganization. See ¶302.10 below.

(5) All shareholders of an S corporation and all members of an LLC are generally entitled to "limited liability" under state statute. See ¶301.5 and ¶303.3 below. In contrast, at least one partner of a partnership must be a general partner with unlimited liability for the obligations of the partnership (although that partner may itself be a corporation—including an S corporation—or an LLC). See ¶302.6 below.

(6) An S corporation's service provider who receives stock must apply the Code §83 rules by reference to the stock's FV (as must a C corporation's service provider). In contrast, a partnership's or LLC's service provider receiving a partnership or LLC interest generally applies the Code §83

---

[3] See Code §§311 and 336.
[4] See Code §731.

rules by reference to the equity interest's liquidation value (not its FV). See ¶302.14 below.

(7) Two additional differences: (1) the Code §1374 corporate-level tax applies only to an S corporation, not to a partnership or LLC, and (2) entity-level liabilities affect each equity owner's basis in his or her partnership or LLC interest, but not in an S corporation's stock. In addition, an S corporation shareholder is entitled to treat the shareholder's basis in S corporation debt held by the shareholder as stock basis in determining whether the shareholder has sufficient stock basis to deduct S corporation losses allocable to the shareholder. See ¶302.2 below.

¶301.3   State Taxation

The tax law of each state and local jurisdiction where the S corporation does business must be checked to see whether an S corporation is a flow-through entity for *state* or *local* tax purposes or whether the S corporation must pay full or partial entity-level income tax.

Although most states (and cities, when there is a city income tax) automatically follow the federal treatment of an S corporation, this is not always the case. Some states do not recognize an S election and tax S corporations in the same manner as C corporations. Other states impose entity-level tax at a reduced rate on S corporations. Other states require a special *state* S election filing and/or impose eligibility requirements that differ from the federal requirements. Hence, local tax law in each jurisdiction must be reviewed when a federal S election is made.

¶301.4   Loss Pass-Through

While an S corporation's losses generally pass through to its shareholders for federal income tax purposes, there are significant restrictions on a shareholder's ability to deduct the flow-through losses, including the basis limitation rule of Code §1366(d), the "at risk" rules of Code §465, and the passive activity loss rules of Code §469.

¶301.5   Limited Liability

An insolvent S corporation's shareholders have the same protection from corporate debts as the shareholders of a regular C corporation.[5] Thus, neither S nor C shareholders are personally liable for the corporation's debts absent invocation

---

[5] See, e.g., Del. Gen. Corp. Law §102(b)(6) making no distinction between a "C" and an "S" corporation.

of the "piercing-the-corporate-veil" doctrine or a statutory-liability doctrine or shareholder participation in a negligent or wrongful act.

¶301.5.1 Piercing the Corporate Veil

Under the traditional common law doctrine of piercing the corporate veil, there is a slight risk that one or more Newco shareholders may be held responsible for Newco's liabilities. Some of the significant factors leading to such a finding of responsibility are:

- Undercapitalization of Newco.
- Newco's failure to observe corporate formalities (such as regular board and shareholder meetings, maintenance of corporate records, etc.).
- Commingling of the shareholder's and Newco's funds or other assets.
- Failure to maintain an arms-length relationship between Newco and the shareholder (or the shareholder's other businesses).
- Common business enterprise between Newco and the shareholder, i.e., both engaged in portions or segments of an integrated business activity.
- The shareholder's fraudulent intent to avoid liability.

In a well-structured VC transaction, there should be little risk of piercing-the-corporate-veil liability.

¶301.5.2 Environmental Cleanup

Under CERCLA (the principal federal environmental cleanup statute), each person who is an "owner or operator"of a contaminated facility is liable for cleaning up the facility. There has been a long-standing dispute whether Newco's CERCLA liability may reach a Newco control shareholder otherwise protected by Newco's corporate shield. In an important 1998 case the Supreme Court held it could, but only in limited circumstances where a Newco shareholder is involved in pollution-related operations (i.e., the shareholder exercises control over operations involving leakage or disposal of hazardous waste or over decisions about compliance with environmental regulations) and takes actions outside the norms of corporate behavior or beyond those actions consistent with mere investor status. See the discussion of this topic at ¶501.5.3.2 below.

¶301.5.3 Pension Plan and Other ERISA Liabilities

Where an entity shareholder owns 80% or more of Newco's stock (by vote *or* by value, excluding from the denominator certain third-party stock, such as stock owned by a Newco employee if that stock is subject to vesting or other transfer restrictions), such entity shareholder (as well as any other entity in such entity shareholder's 80% ERISA control group) is generally liable for (1) Newco's delinquent pension contributions, (2) Newco's liability for a terminated underfunded pension plan, (3) Newco's multiemployer union pension plan withdrawal liability, (4) Newco's delinquent PBGC premiums, and (5) Newco's continuation medical coverage ("COBRA") obligations, all as described in more detail in ¶501.3.5.2, ¶501.3.5.3, and ¶501.5.3.1 below.

¶301.5.4 Shareholder Participation in Negligent or Wrongful Act

The doctrine of corporate limited liability protects a Newco shareholder from Newco's liabilities (absent invocation of a superseding doctrine such as those discussed above), but does not absolve a Newco shareholder from liability along with Newco where the shareholder (in his or her capacity as a Newco officer, director, employee, or agent) actually participates in a negligent or wrongful act toward a third party, in which case such shareholder would generally be directly liable to the third party.[6] The same is true where a non-shareholder (e.g., a Newco officer, director, employee, or agent who owns no Newco stock) actually participates in a negligent or wrongful act toward a third party.

¶301.6 Arbitrary Tax Limitations on Use of S

The Code imposes a number of arbitrary limitations on S qualification (which generally prevent a VC from investing in an S corporation). These include:

¶301.6.1 One Class of Stock

An S corporation can issue only plain vanilla common stock (although differences between the shares as to voting power, e.g., non-voting shares, low-vote shares, high-vote shares, etc., are permissible if the shares are identical except for voting power). Hence, the shareholders must share all items of the S corporation's income, gains, losses, dividends, and liquidating distributions in proportion to their ownership of the S corporation's plain vanilla stock, and preferred stock is not permissible.

¶301.6.2 75-Shareholder Limitation

An S corporation can have no more than 75 shareholders (treating husband and wife as a single shareholder). In counting shareholders, each beneficiary of a permitted trust is generally taken into account as a separate shareholder.

---

[6] For example, Del. Gen. Corp. Law §102(b)(6)'s absolution of a corporation's shareholders from the corporation's debts expressly states "except as [the shareholders] may be liable by reason of their own conduct or acts."

Some states impose even more extensive liability on shareholders of a corporation engaged in one or more specified professional activities, e.g., all shareholders liable for malpractice or shareholder liable for malpractice committed by shareholder or person under shareholder's supervision.

¶301.6.3   Prohibition on Entity and Foreign Shareholders

Except as described below each shareholder of an S corporation must be either an individual (who is either a citizen or resident of the United States[7]), a deceased U.S. individual's estate, or the estate of a bankrupt U.S. individual, i.e., no shareholder of an S corporation can be either a corporation, partnership, or LLC (including a partnership or LLC composed solely of individuals).

A trust can be an S corporation shareholder if it fits into one of 5 permissive rules:

- Any trust (whether it accumulates or distributes income, including a trust with more than one beneficiary) so long as all beneficiaries (with one minor exception) are either U.S. individuals or estates, and the trust files an election with IRS to be taxed at the trust level on its flow-through income from the S corporation and its gain or loss on disposition of the S corporation's stock (as if such portion of the trust were a separate entity) at the maximum rate (i.e., 20% for LTCG and 38.6% for 2002 and 2003 OI).
- A trust with only one income beneficiary at a time, who is a U.S. individual and to whom all the trust's income is distributed or required to be distributed currently.
- A trust which is a "grantor" trust under the Code so that all of the trust's taxable income is taxable to either the trust's grantor or beneficiary who, in either case, is a U.S. individual, but only so long as the U.S. individual is alive or for a limited period after his or her death.
- A mere voting trust all the beneficiaries of which are qualified S corporation shareholders.
- A trust which receives S corporation stock pursuant to a will, but only for a limited period.

A TEO (e.g., a §501(c)(3) charitable organization or a §401 qualified retirement plan, but not a Code §408 IRA) can be an S corporation shareholder (beginning 1/1/98), in which case the TEO's flow-through income from the S corporation and the TEO's gain or loss on disposition of the S corporation's stock are automatically treated as UBTI (with certain exceptions for a shareholder which is an ESOP). See ¶302.1 for a description of UBTI.

Hence, if VC is a corporation, partnership, or LLC (other than a single member disregarded LLC), it can not be an S shareholder, but can be a creditor (e.g., a holder of a Newco subordinated straight or convertible debenture), and/or a holder of rights to acquire Newco stock in the future (e.g., warrants) so long as such debt instruments and stock rights held by the entity VC do not (under applicable tax principles) constitute stock for tax purposes.

---

[7] In discussing persons who are qualified to (1) hold stock of an S corporation or (2) be the beneficiary of a trust qualified to hold S corporation stock, the term "U.S. individual" means a human being who is either a U.S. citizen or a U.S. resident.

Treasury regulations make it feasible in some circumstances for an entity VC to own an interest in an S corporation through debt with warrants or conversion privileges. For example, under these regulations, warrants will not be treated as stock (and hence the entity VC will not be a disqualifying shareholder as a result of holding the warrants) if any *one* of the following tests is met:

(1) VC is actively and regularly engaged in the business of lending and the terms of the debt-with-warrants transaction are commercially reasonable.

(2) The warrant exercise price is at least 90% of the stock's FV at the time the warrants are issued.

(3) The warrants are not substantially certain to be exercised, judged at the time the warrants are issued. Reg. §1.1361-1(*l*).

However, if the entity VC supplies most of Newco's money as "debt" (with warrants or a conversion feature), Newco's DER may be so high as to risk the "debt" being treated as equity under applicable tax principles, in which case Newco would be disqualified as an S corporation.[8] This risk may be exacerbated where VC's conversion privileges or warrants are substantially in the money or the debt has other equity-like terms. See ¶602.8.1 below discussing the subjective debt/equity test.[9]

Where this approach is used, there can be no flow-through of Newco's taxable income or loss to the entity VC, because it is not, for tax purposes, a Newco shareholder. Moreover, when the entity VC's warrant or conversion privilege is actually exercised, so that the entity VC becomes a shareholder for tax purposes, Newco's S status terminates immediately.

A second route for an entity VC to circumvent the prohibition on an entity shareholder of an S corporation is for the operating business to be owned by a partnership or LLC, which is in turn owned in part by the S corporation and in part by the VC entity, so that the VC entity does not own any interest in the S corporation.

---

[8] Pursuant to a statutory exception, the S corporation would not be disqualified under such circumstances where (1) the debt holder is an individual U.S. citizen or resident, an estate, a trust qualified to be an S corporation shareholder, or a person actively and regularly engaged in the business of lending money *and* (2) the debt is nonconvertible, bears interest at a fixed rate, and meets certain other statutory requirements ("straight debt").

[9] Under the actual but somewhat complex wording of the applicable S corporation regulations, straight debt (whether or not issued with warrants) is treated as a second class of stock if (1) the debt instrument "constitutes equity or otherwise results in the holder being treated as the owner of stock under general principles of federal tax law" (see, e.g., ¶602.8.1 below) and (2) "a principal purpose of issuing . . . the instrument . . . is . . . to circumvent the limitation on eligible shareholders" (i.e., the prohibition on entity shareholders). When, however, the debt is convertible into stock (rather than straight debt issued with warrants), the regulations treat it as a second class of stock if *either* (1) it would fail the test for straight debt described immediately above *or* (2) "it embodies rights equivalent to those of a call option that would be treated as a second class of stock under [the rules applicable to warrants as summarized in text above]." Reg. §1.1361-1(1)(4)(ii)(A) and (iv).

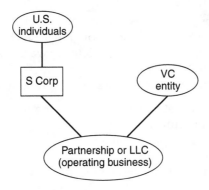

¶301.6.4   Corporate Subsidiaries

An S corporation is permitted to own one or more C subsidiaries.

In addition, where an S corporation owns 100% of the stock of one or more U.S. corporate subsidiaries, the S corporation is permitted (with minor exceptions) to elect to treat any such subsidiary as a division of the parent S corporation, (commonly referred to as a "QSub"), so that the taxable income of each such 100%-owned electing subsidiary escapes C corporation tax and flows through to the parent S corporation's shareholders.

¶301.7 *Key Issues and References*

How does a corporate statute work?

References:

• Delaware General Corporate Law

How is an S corporation taxed differently than a C corporation and when do the C rules also apply to an S corporation?

References:

• Code §11(a) and (b)
• Code §1363 through §1378
• Code §311
• Code §336
• Code §1014(a)

How are an S corporation and its shareholders taxed on profits, losses, and the sale of the corporation?

References:

• Code §338(h)(10)

With respect to shareholder deductions for an S corporation's losses, see also:

References:

- Code §465
- Code §469

Are there some corporations which can not qualify as an S?

References:

- Code §1361 and §1362
- Treas. Reg. §1.1361-1

Are shareholders of an S corporation more likely to be held liable for the S corporation's debts than shareholders of a C corporation?

Is it best to elect S status at the outset when Newco is formed, or to wait a year or even a few years?

References:

- Code §1374
- Code §1375
- Ginsburg and Levin M&A book Chapter 11

¶302   NEWCO AS PARTNERSHIP

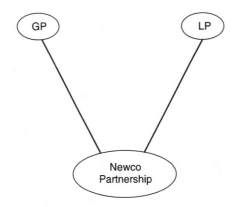

¶302.1   *No Entity-Level Tax*

Newco (as a partnership) will not be subject to federal income tax on its income at the entity level. Rather each of Newco's GPs and LPs will report his, her or its share of Newco's profits and losses on its own tax return. Thus, Newco will not be subject to federal corporate rates (up to 35%); instead, each of Newco's partners is taxed at the appropriate federal rate—up to 38.6% for an individual's 2002 and

2003 OI,[1] up to 35% for a corporation, and 0% for a TEO unless the partnership's income constitutes unrelated business taxable income ("UBTI").

The partnership's income will generally be UBTI to a TEO (1) where it derives from an active business (i.e., does not constitute passive income from interest, dividends, CGs, real property rents, royalties, and certain other asset-sale gains) (active business UBTI), or (2) even if it constitutes such passive income, to the extent the partnership borrows money to finance the investment giving rise to the passive income (debt-financed passive UBTI).[2]

A few state and local jurisdictions impose a partial entity-level tax on a partnership's income.

See ¶301.2.1(1), (2), (3), and (5) for certain S corporation characteristics which apply to a partnership as well, and see ¶301.2.2 for a description of additional partnership characteristics.

¶302.2   *Delivering SUB to Buyer*

When the partnership business is ultimately sold, the seller can deliver a stepped-up tax basis in the partnership's assets ("asset SUB") to the buyer (either through a sale of the partnership's assets or through a sale of the partners' interests in the partnership) while recognizing only one tax (i.e., partnership status avoids double federal income taxation on a sale of the business structured for asset SUB).

¶302 [1] The top individual federal OI rate is really higher than the 38.6% nominal rate because of the 3% itemized deduction disallowance, as described in ¶201.1.1 above.

In addition, the individual top rate is increased on any income subject to the uncapped medicare tax, which is imposed at a 2.9% rate (one-half deductible and one-half non-deductible) on a partner's share of partnership income (other than passive income such as rents from real estate, interest, dividends, and CGs, which are excluded from the definition of earnings from self-employment). While this rule applies in full force to a GP, there is a taxpayer-favorable rule for LPs, who are subject to medicare tax only on guaranteed payments for services rendered by the LP to the partnership. Code §1402(a)(13).

In 1997, IRS issued proposed regulations (effective for taxable years beginning after the regulations are finalized) that would generally treat an LP in the same manner as a GP for purposes of applying the medicare tax if the LP (1) participates in the partnership's business for more than 500 hours during the taxable year *or* (2) provides services to the partnership and substantially all of the activities of the partnership involve the performance of services in the fields of health, law, engineering, architecture, accounting, actuarial science, or consulting *or* (3) has personal liability under state law for the partnership debts by reason of being a partner (an unlikely situation) *or* (4) has authority to contract on behalf of the partnership (also an unlikely situation).

Although a Congressionally imposed moratorium on finalization of the proposed regulations expired 7/1/98, the regulations remain in proposed form.

[2] These debt-financed UBTI rules do not apply to certain TEOs (generally pension plans and educational institutions) where the partnership's borrowing finances a specified type of investment in real property (e.g., a fixed purchase price for real property where the amount payable on indebtedness which financed the purchase of the real property is not dependent upon rents or other cash flow from the real property and the partnership agreement satisfies certain tax requirements).

This asset SUB-with-one-tax result is achieved for two reasons:

First, as discussed above, a partnership's taxable income (including its asset-sale gain) is not subject to federal income tax at the partnership entity level, but only at the partner level.

Second, the mechanics of partnership taxation protect the partners from liquidation gain. Under Code §731, a partner has CG equal to the excess of his or her distributions of cash or certain marketable securities from the partnership over his or her tax basis in the partnership interest. A partner's tax basis in his or her partnership interest is generally:

- original cost,
- *plus* the partner's subsequent contributions to the partnership,
- *plus* the partner's share of partnership liabilities (as described below),
- *plus* partnership taxable (or tax-exempt) income allocated to the partner,
- *less* distributions by the partnership (measured by the basis of any property distributed, the amount of any cash distributed, or the issue price of any partnership debt distributed),[3] treating as a cash distribution any net reduction in the partner's share of partnership liabilities (as described below),
- *less* partnership taxable loss (and non-deductible non-capitalizable expense) allocated to the partner.[4]

Thus, each partner's tax basis in his or her partnership interest increases by his or her share of the partnership's asset sale gain. Accordingly, when the partnership liquidates and distributes to its partners proceeds of an asset sale, they do not recognize liquidation gain under Code §731.

The above rules are quite similar to the S corporation rules discussed in ¶301.2.1 above except for two dramatic differences.

First, as noted in the foregoing summary of the partnership basis rules, each partner's basis in his or her partnership interest includes his or her share of the partnership's liabilities. Thus, as the partnership's liabilities increase, each partner's basis in the partnership increases by the partner's share, just as if the partner had borrowed money from the third party creditor and contributed the money to the partnership. This rule enables a partnership, which has borrowed in order to effectuate a leveraged recapitalization, to make cash distributions in excess of the partners' pre-recapitalization tax bases in their partnership interests without triggering immediate partner-level tax.

However, as the partnership's liabilities decrease, each partner's basis in the partnership decreases by the partner's share, just as if the partner had received a cash distribution from the partnership and used the money to repay the amount borrowed by the partner from the third party creditor. Concomitantly, when a partner's percentage interest in the partnership is reduced and his or her share of the partnership's liabilities correlatively declines, the reduction in such partner's

---

[3] See ¶1001.1(3) below for a further discussion of the tax ramifications to a partner of a distribution of cash, marketable securities, or other property by a partnership.

[4] When a partner dies, his or her estate generally takes a new tax basis for the partnership interest equal to FV at death (Code §1014), *less* the deceased partner's share of the partnership's unrealized receivables and similar so-called Code §691 items.

(or when the partner's percentage interest in the partnership is reduced to zero, such ex-partner's) share of liabilities causes a decrease in his or her basis in the partnership. Indeed, since a reduction in a partner's share of partnership liabilities is treated as a distribution of cash, he or she recognizes taxable gain to the extent such constructive cash distribution would otherwise cause the partner's basis in the partnership to fall below zero, generally CG.

By contrast, an SCo shareholder's basis in his or her SCo stock is not affected by the SCo's liabilities.

Second, unlike the Code §1374 rules applicable to an S corporation that has a C corporation history, no Code provision imposes entity-level tax on a partnership.

On the other hand, if a corporation (either S or C) holding appreciated assets is converted mid-stream to a partnership (or LLC), the conversion is treated as a liquidation of the corporation. Such a deemed liquidation of a C corporation triggers double tax, i.e., a corporate-level tax on the net BIG in the C corporation's assets and a shareholder-level tax on the FV of the assets distributed (in excess of the shareholders' stock basis). Code §§336 and 331. See discussion at ¶1001.4 below. Such a deemed liquidation of an S corporation (not subject to Code §1374) holding appreciated assets triggers single tax, i.e., a shareholder-level tax on (1) the corporate-level BIG and (2) the shareholder's stock gain if the FV of the corporate assets deemed distributed exceeds the shareholder's stock basis (after such basis has first been increased to reflect the shareholder's recognition of the corporate-level BIG).

¶302.3 No Arbitrary Tax Limitations on Partnership Qualification

A partnership (unlike an S corporation) can have owners which are entities and foreigners, can have multiple classes of ownership, and can have more than 75 owners (so long as it is not a "publicly-traded partnership" under Code §7704).

¶302.4 Flexible Sharing and No Recognition of Gain on Property Distributions

The partnership format allows flexible sharing of Newco's profits and losses between VC and E (i.e., different types of profits and losses can be allocated, and distributions can be allocated, in any fashion specified in the partnership agreement), so long as the partnership allocations have "substantial economic effect," as defined in the Code §704(b) regulations.

In general, neither a partnership nor its partners recognize gain or loss when the partnership distributes property in kind to its partners. Code §731.[5] A partner

---

[5] See ¶1001.1(3) below for a discussion of rules which may, in some cases, require the recognition of gain by a partner who receives a distribution of marketable securities from a partnership. See Code §704(c)(1)(B) and Code §737 for rules which may trigger gain where a partner contributes appreciated property to a partnership and, within 7 years, (1) the partnership distributes the contributed property

generally takes asset COB for property received from the partnership, i.e., the partner generally takes the lesser of the partnership's basis in the property or the partner's basis in his or her partnership interest, thus deferring, but not eliminating, recognition of the gain or loss inherent in the property.

¶302.5   Loss Pass-Through

While partnership losses generally pass through to its partners for federal income tax purposes, there are significant restrictions on a partner's ability to deduct the flow-through losses, including the basis limitation rule of Code §704(d), the "at risk" rules of Code §465, and the passive activity loss rules of Code §469.

¶302.6   Difficulties in Achieving GP Limited Liability

If Newco partnership is ultimately unable to pay all of its recourse liabilities (even after taking into account its applicable insurance coverage), each Newco GP (e.g., E) has unlimited liability for such unpaid Newco debts.

Use of entity intermediary. Risk of unlimited GP liability can generally be eliminated where the person or entity which would otherwise be Newco's GP forms an LLC to hold the GP interest (or where a U.S. individual who would otherwise be Newco's GP forms an S corporation to hold the GP interest). However, see ¶301.5 and ¶501.5.3 for a discussion of piercing-the-veil and other doctrines that might make a corporate GP's shareholder(s) liable for the corporation's liabilities, which doctrines should apply equally to make an LLC GP's member(s) liable for the LLC's liabilities.

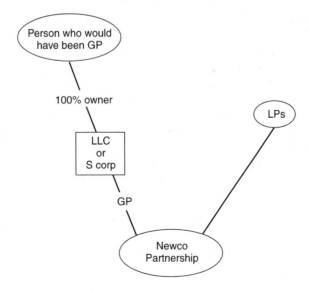

_____

to a partner other than the contributing partner or (2) the contributing partner receives a distribution of property (other than the contributed property) from the partnership.

Qualification as LLP. Between 1991 and 1999 all 50 states and the District of Columbia adopted the concept of a "limited liability partnership," generally allowing either a limited partnership or a general partnership to elect also to be a limited liability partnership (an "LLP"). In most states (approximately 32 plus the District of Columbia) the GP(s) of a partnership electing add-on LLP status are absolved from any liability for the partnership's obligations, whether arising in contract, tort, or otherwise—so-called "full shield" protection. In approximately 14 states the GP(s) of a partnership electing add-on LLP status are absolved from liability only for the partnership's negligence, malpractice, misconduct, or wrongful acts liabilities—so-called "half shield" protection.[6] In addition, 4 states allow a partnership to elect add-on LLP status only if the partnership renders professional services (e.g., law practice).[7]

Most of the approximately 14 half shield states (all except 3) allow a limited liability partnership organized in a full shield state to apply the law of the state in which the partnership is organized (the "organization state") in determining a GP's liability to third parties.[8] Thus if a partnership organized in a full shield state incurs an obligation in one of the 11 half shield states (the "liability state") that apply organization state law to determine GP liability, the GP is entitled to full shield protection.

While many LLP statutes (e.g., Delaware's) explicitly allow either a general partnership or a limited partnership to elect also to become a limited liability partnership, other state statutes have added the LLP concept only to their general partnership law, thus creating some ambiguity whether a limited partnership can elect LLP status for its GP(s) in such a state. Because RULPA explicitly states that a limited partnership's GP(s) have the same liabilities as a general partnership's GP(s),[9] it appears that a limited partnership should be able to qualify as an LLP (so as to reduce or eliminate the liabilities of its GP(s)) in a state which allows a general partnership to do so but is silent on a limited partnership's ability to do so, although the issue is not wholly free from doubt.

Finally, the 2001 Uniform Limited Partnership Act (if and when adopted by a state) clearly grants full shield protection to GPs of any partnership (general or limited) electing LLP status and clearly states that the organization state's law applies in determining a GP's liability to third parties.

Thus, in summary, an LLP limited partnership organized in a full shield state that explicitly allows a limited partnership to qualify as an LLP (e.g., Delaware), when conducting business in other states, can obtain full shield protection for its GP(s) (assuming positive resolution of the issue, discussed immediately above, whether a limited partnership can qualify as an LLP in states which are silent on

---

[6] The half shield states are Illinois, Kentucky, Louisiana, Maine, Michigan, New Hampshire, Ohio, Pennsylvania, South Carolina, Tennessee, Texas, Utah, and West Virginia, with North Carolina ambiguous as to whether it is half or full shield.

[7] These states are California, Nevada, New York, and Oregon.

[8] The 3 half shield states which do not clearly apply organization state law in determining GP liability are Pennsylvania (clearly allows GPs of foreign LLP no greater protection from liability than the half shield protection available to GP(s) of a Pennsylvania LLP) plus Illinois and Louisiana (LLP statute silent or ambiguous).

[9] See, e.g., Del. RULPA §17-403(b).

qualification of a limited partnership as an LLP) in approximately 43 states and the District of Columbia, i.e., all except (1) the 4 states which recognize the limited liability partnership concept only for professional services (California, Nevada, New York, and Oregon) and (2) the 3 half shield states which do not apply organization state law in determining GP liability (Pennsylvania clearly, plus Illinois and Louisiana silent or ambiguous).[10]

¶302.7   *Difficulties in Achieving LP Limited Liability*

If Newco partnership is unable to pay all of its recourse liabilities (even after taking into account its applicable insurance coverage), the question arises whether (and under what circumstances) a Newco LP (e.g., VC) risks unlimited liability for Newco's unpaid debts. Under the 1916 version of the Uniform Limited Partnership Act ("ULPA"), an LP which "takes part in the control of the [partnership] business" was liable as if such LP were a GP.

This risk of LP liability (and the ambiguity of the takes-part-in-control test) long made the limited partnership format less attractive to an active LP (such as VC), because of fear that VC's exercise of customary VC approval and veto powers (such as the power to veto or approve cash distributions, mergers, acquisitions, asset sales, borrowings, capital expenditures, entering a new business, hiring and firing key executives, and other significant transactions) could be viewed as taking part in the control of Newco partnership's business.

However, by 1998 all 50 states and the District of Columbia had adopted the 1985 version of the Revised Uniform Limited Partnership Act ("1985 RULPA") under which the risk of unlimited LP liability has been substantially eliminated for three reasons.

First, under 1985 RULPA, an LP participating in control of the partnership business only in the manner specified in statutory safe harbors is absolved from unlimited liability. While the 1985 RULPA statutory safe harbors as enacted by the 50 states and the District of Columbia vary, Delaware's expansive version[11] includes:

- An LP serving as an agent or employee of the partnership or its GP.
- An LP serving as a consultant or adviser to the GP.
- An LP serving as an owner of or service provider to an entity GP.
- An LP's action which causes any person to take any action with respect to the partnership's business or any other matter.
- An LP serving on a committee of LPs.
- An LP acting (including approving or disapproving, by voting or otherwise) on any "other matters as are stated in the partnership agreement or in any other agreement or in writing."

---

[10] See ¶301.5 and ¶501.1.5.3 for discussion of piercing-the-veil and other doctrines that might cause partners (who are otherwise absolved from liability for the partnership's liabilities) to be liable for partnership liabilities.

[11] Del. RULPA §17-303.

Second, under 1985 RULPA, an LP who participates in control of the partnership business beyond the RULPA statutory safe harbors is generally liable only to a person who:

- transacts business with the partnership *and*
- is reasonably misled by the LP's conduct into believing that the LP is a GP (but it is not clear whether LP conduct falling within the statutory 1985 RULPA safe harbors discussed above is disregarded for this purpose).

Third, where a limited partnership incurs liabilities in a state (the "liability state") which has enacted RULPA §901 (as all 50 states and the District of Columbia have now done), the law of the state where the partnership is organized (the "organization state") governs the liability of the partnership's LPs to the partnership's creditors. Hence, if the LP's organization state has enacted 1985 RULPA with expansive safe harbors (as Delaware has done[12]), the LPs are protected from liability to the partnership's creditors in all 50 states and the District of Columbia (by RULPA §901), so long as the LPs satisfy the organization state's safe harbors (even when the liability state's safe harbors are less expansive).[13]

Indeed, any small residual risk of unlimited LP liability can generally be eliminated where one or more LPs form an LLC or a corporation to hold their LP investment in Newco partnership and such holding entity has sufficient status to avoid the piercing-the-veil doctrine. See ¶301.5 and ¶501.5.3 for discussion of piercing-the-veil and other doctrines that might make an entity LP's owner(s) liable for the entity's liabilities.

An LP (or a GP) that holds its partnership interest through a holding *corporation* which is a C (rather than an S) corporation would generally lose the flow-through tax benefits, while those GPs and LPs who hold their partnership interests through an LLC or S corporation would continue to receive flow-through tax benefits. An LP which is itself a C corporation can hold its LP interest through a subsidiary C corporation (which meets the 80-80 test of Code §1504) and still preserve its flow-through tax benefits by filing a consolidated federal income tax return with its subsidiary.

Finally, the 2001 Uniform Limited Partnership Act (if and when adopted by a state) entirety abandons the concept of LP liability for participation in control of the partnership's business and simply states that an LP "is not personally liable . . . for an obligation of the limited partnership solely by reason of being [an LP], even if the [LP] participates in the management and control of the limited partnership."

---

[12] Del. RULPA §17-303.

[13] The language of RULPA §901 generally makes the provision's protection subject to any limitations in the foreign state's constitution and, in Montana, to the state's public policy. It is not readily apparent that these exceptions increase LP exposure in any meaningful way.

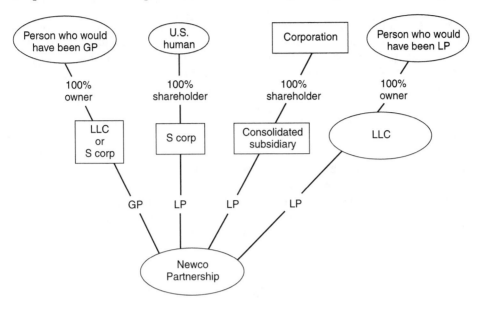

¶302.8 Achieving Flow-Through Tax Status

¶302.8.1 Check-The-Box Classification Rules

While the Code explicitly recognizes a partnership as a flow-through entity, the Code does not automatically accept state-law characterization as establishing the federal income tax status of an entity formed under a state partnership statute. Prior to 1/1/97, a partnership was entitled to flow-through tax status (i.e., was treated as a partnership rather than as an "association" taxable as a corporation) for federal income tax purposes only if it met several strange tests set forth in IRS regulations (the "old *Kintner* regulations").

In 12/96 IRS repealed the old *Kintner* regulations effective 1/1/97 and dramatically simplified the procedure by which an unincorporated organization, such as a partnership (or an LLC), achieves flow-through (i.e., partnership) status for tax purposes. Under the 12/96 regulations, a domestic noncorporate entity (as well as many types of foreign entities) can simply choose (i.e., "check the box") whether to be taxed as a partnership (so long as the entity is not a PTP as discussed in ¶302.8.5 below) or as a corporation. In general, a domestic partnership is taxed as a partnership absent an affirmative election to be taxed as a corporation.

A foreign partnership is generally (1) taxed as a partnership for U.S. federal income tax purposes (absent an affirmative election to be taxed as a corporation) where at least one of its partners has personal liability for some or all of the debts of the partnership by reason of being a partner and (2) taxed as a corporation (absent an affirmative election to be taxed as a partnership) where none of its partners has such personal liability.

An election by a domestic partnership to be taxed as a corporation (or by a foreign partnership to be taxed in a manner other than its default classification) is made on IRS Form 8832. The election is effective on the date specified by the partnership on Form 8832 (but a specified retroactive or prospective effective date can not be more than 75 days before, or more than 12 months after, the form is filed). The election must be signed *either* by (1) each partner who is an owner at the time the election is filed *or* (2) any officer or partner (e.g., the general partner of a limited partnership) authorized under local law to make the election who so represents under penalties of perjury. In the case of a retroactive election, the election also must be signed by each person who was not a partner at the time the election is filed but was a partner on or after the retroactive effective date. Once having made an election, the partnership can not change its tax classification by making a new election for 60 months following the effective date of the election, although IRS may permit an earlier change in election if the partnership has an intervening more-than-50% ownership change.

¶302.8.2 Determining Who Is a Partner

The check-the-box regulations do not address the issue of when an owner of an interest in a partnership "will be respected as a bona fide [partner] for federal tax purposes" (rather than treated as a mere service provider to the partnership). Rather, the preamble to the regulations indicates that resolution of this issue "is based on all the facts and circumstances" of each case.

Only if a service provider to the partnership is treated as a partner would its share of the partnership's LTCG qualify for flow-through LTCG treatment on its tax return; conversely if a partner/service provider were treated merely as a service provider to (and not a partner in) the partnership, its share of the partnership's LTCG would constitute OI (i.e., a fee for services rendered) on its tax return, and would give rise to an equivalent deduction for the partnership.

Under the old *Kintner* regulations, IRS took the position for ruling purposes that the GP of a limited partnership would not be treated as a general partner of the partnership where the GP's interest (or, if there is more than one GP, the GPs' aggregate interest) in the partnership was too small. In order to meet IRS guidelines (the "minimum-GP-interest test"), the GP's interest (or the GPs' aggregate interest) in the partnership was required to meet both of two tests:

- The GP must have had at least a 1% interest (counting both its GP and any LP interests) in each item of the limited partnership's income, gains, deductions and losses (with a scale down from 1% if the partnership's capital exceeded $50 million, reaching 0.2% at $250 million of capital, but never declining below 0.2%), ignoring special allocations required by Code §704(b) and §704(c).
- The GP must have contributed capital to the limited partnership (apparently including any contribution as an LP), and maintained a capital account balance, equal to 1% of the partnership's capital (with a $500,000 ceiling when the partnership's capital exceeded $50 million) *or* (for a GP providing

substantial services) the GP must have been obligated, upon dissolution of the limited partnership, to contribute the lesser of the GP's deficit capital account balance *or* the excess of 1.01% of the limited partners' total capital contributions over the aggregate capital previously contributed by the GP.

Even under the check-the-box regime, there is some possibility IRS may seek to retain some version of these old *Kintner* rules, i.e., IRS may take the position (at least for ruling purposes) that for a service provider to be treated as a partner entitled to flow-through treatment, such service provider must *either* (1) make a substantial investment in the limited partnership *or* (2) share in allocation of net losses and have an obligation to make up a substantial portion of any deficit in the service provider's capital account upon termination of the partnership.

¶302.8.3   Publicly Traded Partnership Taxed as Corporation

Under Code §7704, a publicly traded partnership (a "PTP") is generally taxed as a corporation. Hence, a PTP can not qualify for flow-through taxation, even where it checks the partnership box as described in ¶302.8.1 above.

A PTP is not, however, taxed as a corporation where at least 90% of the partnership's gross income consists of certain types of income, including interest, dividends, real property rents, income derived from mineral and natural resources, and gains from the disposition of property producing such types of income, for each year after 1987.

A partnership is "publicly traded" if interests in the partnership are either (1) traded on an established securities market or (2) readily tradable on a secondary market (or the substantial equivalent thereof), a factual issue on which neither the Code §7704 legislative history nor IRS regulations offer clear guidance. The regulations do, however, set forth two safe harbors that allow most partnerships to avoid PTP status.

First, interests in a partnership will not be treated as tradable on a secondary market or the substantial equivalent if (1) all interests in the partnership were issued in one or more transactions that were not required to be registered as public offerings under the 1933 Act (e.g., issuances which qualify for the private placement exemption)[14]—see ¶207 above—and (2) the partnership does not at any time have more than 100 partners. A person who holds an indirect interest in a partnership through a flow-through entity (i.e., a partnership, LLC, grantor trust, or S corporation) is for this purpose counted as a partner in the underlying partnership if (a) substantially all the FV of the person's interest in the flow-through entity is attributable to the underlying partnership and (b) a principal purpose for using the flow-through entity is to satisfy the 100-partner limitation of the safe harbor.

---

[14] The safe harbor does not apply, however, to a foreign-targeted offering exempt from SEC registration under Regulation S that would have been subject to SEC registration under the 1933 Act if offered in the U.S.

Second, interests in a partnership will not be treated as tradable on a secondary market or the substantial equivalent if the aggregate transfers of interests in partnership capital or profits during any partnership taxable year (disregarding "private" transfers described below and certain other exempted transfers) do not exceed 2% of total capital or profits. For this purpose, certain "private" transfers are disregarded, including:

- any "block transfer" (i.e., a transfer by a partner or group of related partners during a 30-day period aggregating more than 2% of partnership capital or profits interests),
- a transfer at death or between family members,
- any issuance by the partnership of additional interests, and
- any transfer not recognized by the partnership (i.e., where the partnership does not admit the transferee as a partner or recognize the transferee's right to receive partnership distributions).

¶302.9   IPO

If Newco partnership desires to go public, it generally should incorporate before an IPO. Incorporating would trigger gain for any partner who has deducted flow-through losses in excess of its investment in Newco, so that the partner has a "negative" tax basis in its partnership interest.

For a surprisingly hostile SEC Rule 144 interpretation where Newco is originally formed as a partnership and subsequently incorporates either in anticipation of an IPO or otherwise, and for a method of solving the problem, see ¶903.4.6 below.

As discussed in ¶302.8.5 above, even if Newco partnership did not incorporate, the Code would generally treat a publicly-traded partnership as if it had incorporated (with several specific, limited exceptions), in which event the IPO would trigger gain for a negative-tax-basis partner as described above.

¶302.10   Incorporation

Newco partnership must incorporate substantially in advance of a Code §368 tax-free merger with another corporation, because only a corporation (not a partnership) is permitted to use the tax-free reorganization rules and the step-transaction doctrines preclude a tax-free incorporation of Newco immediately before the merger. As discussed above, incorporation would trigger gain for a partner whose deduction of flow-through losses has created a negative basis in its partnership interest.

¶302.11   UBTI

Any TEO which is a partner in Newco partnership (or any TEO which is a partner in a partnership fund which is a partner in Newco partnership) will have UBTI to the extent that Newco partnership has active business income or debt-financed passive income as described in ¶302.1 above.

¶302.12   Foreign Person

Any FP which is a partner in Newco partnership (or any FP which is a partner in a partnership fund which is a partner in Newco partnership) will be taxed in the U.S. to the extent that Newco partnership has:

(1)   U.S. active business income,
(2)   gain from the disposition of a U.S. real estate interest, or
(3)   gain from the disposition of a portfolio company predominantly owning U.S. real estate (generally as determined under a 50%-by-FV-at-any-time-in-the-past-5-years test, but treating as a reduction in the FV of such property, for purposes of the 50% test, any mortgage liability or other debt secured by any property and either (a) "incurred to acquire" or (b) "incurred in direct connection with" such property).

Active U.S. business income (described in (1) above) may cause the FP to be taxed on other U.S. income which is "effectively connected" with such active U.S. business income.

¶302.13   Use of Holding Corporation

A TEO or FP may form a holding corporation to hold its investment in Newco and thereby avoid direct exposure to U.S. income tax (on a TEO's UBTI and an FP's active business income). However, there are many tax complexities to forming such a holding corporation and, indeed, this approach is normally undertaken only to avoid tax reporting requirements, rather than to reduce the amount of income tax borne by the TEO or FP, because the holding corporation would be taxable in full on its entire share of Newco partnership's taxable income plus its gain on disposition of its interest in Newco partnership.

¶302.14   Taxation of Service Provider on Receipt of Partnership Interest

Where a service provider to Newco partnership purchases (or is granted) a Newco partnership interest (either a GP or an LP interest), the rules of Code §83 generally apply (as discussed in the corporate context at ¶201.1, ¶202.2, and

¶202.3), except that the §83 OI of a service provider to a partnership (and the partnership's §83(h) deduction) are (subject to the qualifications discussed below) measured not by the partnership interest's FV but rather by its liquidation value ("LV"), i.e., by (1) the amount the service provider would receive if the partnership were to sell its assets at FV (determined at the time the service provider receives the partnership interest) and distribute the proceeds in complete liquidation of the partnership over (2) the purchase price paid by the service provider for the partnership interest.

Thus, the service provider is (subject to the qualifications discussed below) taxed only to the extent his or her "capital interest" exceeds his or her purchase price for the partnership interest and is not taxed to the extent he or she received a mere profits interest.

EXAMPLE 1

E and VC form Newco as a partnership, with VC contributing $1 million and E contributing E's ideas, experience, and future services. VC receives 60 class A partnership units entitling VC to the first $1 million of Newco's distributions (without interest) plus 60% of any distributions in excess of $1 million. E receives 40 class B partnership units entitling E to 40% of any distributions in excess of $1 million.

E's 40 class B units are fully vested at issuance (or alternatively the 40 units are subject to vesting—contingent upon E's continued performance of services for Newco—but E either makes a timely §83(b) election or (as discussed below) is treated as making a §83(b) election).

E's 40 units have substantial FV because they entitle E to 40% of the future profits and appreciation from Newco's new business, which has $1 million of funded capital (i.e., E will receive 40% of Newco's distributions, including sales proceeds, in excess of $1 million, with no interest-like compensation to VC for the use, possibly for many years, of VC's $1 million contributions to the Newco business).

However, under the LV approach to valuing the partnership interest, E has no OI upon receipt of the 40 units (nor does E have any OI upon vesting). This result follows because if (at the time E received the 40 class B units) Newco sold its assets ($1 million cash) for FV and liquidated, VC would (by virtue of its $1 million class A liquidation priority) receive the entire $1 million liquidating distribution and E would receive nothing.

EXAMPLE 2

VC1 and VC2 each owns a 50% interest in Newco partnership, which operates a business with a $10 million FV. To induce E to leave E's old job and become CEO of Newco partnership, the parties rearrange Newco's ownership as follows: VC1 and VC2 each receives 30 class A partnership units (total 60 class A units) entitling them in the aggregate to the first $10 million of Newco's distributions (without interest) plus 60% of any distributions in excess of $10 million. E receives 40 class B partnership units entitling E to 40% of any distributions in excess of $10 million.

E's 40 units are fully vested (or alternatively the 40 units are subject to vesting—contingent upon E's continued performance of services for Newco—but E either makes a timely §83(b) election or (as discussed below) is treated as making a §83(b) election).

E's 40 units have substantial FV because they entitle E to 40% of the future profits and appreciation from Newco's business, which has an existing value of $10 million (i.e., E will receive 40% of Newco's distributions, including sales proceeds, in excess of $10 million, with no interest-like compensation to VC1 and VC2 for the time value, possibly for many years, of the $10 million FV of the Newco business which they owned before the equity rearrangement.

However, under the LV approach to valuing the partnership interest, the tax result is the same as in Example 1.

Where the service provider's share of future partnership profits is disproportionately large in relation to his or her capital contribution (generally referred to as a "carried interest"), this pro-taxpayer LV (rather than FV) approach minimizes the service provider's OI, so long as the OI is measured at the front end when the service provider receives the partnership interest (i.e., before the partnership's business appreciates in value). However, the service provider's right to use this pro-taxpayer LV approach is subject to several qualifications:

(1) IRS's taxpayer-favorable LV approach to valuing a service provider's partnership interest was announced in Rev. Proc. 93-27, which states that where "a person receives a profits interest in exchange for providing services to (or for the benefit of) a partnership in a partner capacity (or in anticipation of being a partner), [IRS] will not treat the receipt of such an interest as a taxable event." IRS added, however, that this taxpayer-favorable rule would not apply in any of the following circumstances:

- Where the service provider receives "a capital interest," defined as "an interest [in the partnership] that would give the [service provider] a share of the proceeds if the partnership's assets were sold at fair market value and then the proceeds were distributed in complete liquidation of the partnership." It is possible (but illogical) to read Rev. Proc. 93-27's words and conclude that IRS intends the taxpayer-favorable LV rule not be available where either (a) the service provider's partnership interest is in the money (even by a small amount) at the time he or she receives the partnership interest (e.g., the service provider pays $100 for a partnership interest that would yield the service provider $101 if the partnership immediately sells its assets and liquidates) or (b) the service provider pays an amount for the partnership interest and, immediately after such purchase, the service provider's partnership interest is worth (on an LV basis) exactly the amount paid for the interest (e.g., the service provider pays $100 for a partnership interest that would yield $100 if the partnership immediately sells its assets and liquidates). However, a far more rational reading is that IRS intends the taxpayer-favorable LV rule not be available only to the extent the service provider's partnership interest is in the money at receipt (i.e., $1 in example (a) and zero in example (b) above), so that the taxpayer-favorable rule is available for a "profits interest" even if combined with a "capital interest."

- Where "the profits interest relates to a substantially certain and predictable stream of income from partnership assets, such as income from high-quality debt securities or a high-quality net lease."
- Where the service provider "disposes of the profits interest" within 2 years after receipt.
- Where the profits interest is a limited partnership interest in a publicly-traded partnership.

Hence, in the typical case where (a) a service provider purchases a partnership interest for a nominal amount (or even for a substantial amount) and, at the time of such purchase, the interest is in the money by an amount equal to the price paid by the service provider, (b) the service provider does not dispose of the partnership interest within 2 years, and (c) the service provider makes a timely §83(b) election, the service provider should recognize no front-end OI and no back-end OI.

(2) Rev. Proc. 93-27 is not entirely clear on the treatment of a service provider receiving a partnership interest subject to vesting who makes no §83(b) election. If §83 does apply to a partnerships profits interest and no §83(b) election is made (or deemed made, as described below) the service provider would recognize OI *at vesting,* when the partnership's business may have appreciated substantially, in which case the service provider's OI will be very substantial even if a Rev. Proc. 93-27 LV approach is used at the time of vesting.

(3) However Rev. Proc. 2001-43 gives a surprisingly pro-taxpayer answer to the question whether Rev. Proc. 93-27's taxpayer-favorable LV rule applies where the service provider's partnership interest is subject to vesting but the service provider makes no §83(b) election: a service provider "need not file [a §83(b)] election" (i.e., IRS will treat the service provider as if he or she had filed such an election—a deemed election), so that the Rev. Proc. 93-27 "determination . . . whether an interest granted to a service provider is a profits interest is . . . tested at the time the interest is granted, even if, at that time, the interest is substantially nonvested" (i.e., is subject to vesting). However, Rev. Proc. 2001-43 conditions this *deemed* §83(b) election on surmounting several hurdles:

- The *partnership* and *all partners* must consistently report their taxes for all tax periods as if the service provider partner had made a §83(b) election. Thus, a service provider who relies on a *deemed* §83(b) election (i.e., who does not make an *actual* election) is at risk if the partnership or any partner (perhaps a former active partner who left the enterprise on poor terms but retains an economic interest causing him or her to continue to be treated as a partner for tax purposes) disregards the deemed §83(b) election and claims a deduction upon the vesting of the service provider's partnership interest, as is clearly permitted by Code §83 and the regulations.

• The service provider's partnership interest must meet all the requirements of Rev. Proc. 93-27 (discussed in (1) above), some of which (as discussed in (1)) are a bit problematic or the satisfaction of which cannot be predicted with certainty when the service provider receives the partnership interest (e.g., no disposition within 2 years).

• Because it is often impossible for a service provider to foresee perfectly (when he or she receives a partnership interest) whether a deemed §83(b) election may later turn out to be unavailable and because the cost of filing an actual §83(b) election is low, a service provider receiving a partnership interest subject to vesting should generally file an actual §83(b) election. If such an actual election is made, it will be clear that the service provider receives the partnership interest (for tax purposes) at the front end, when it is more likely to constitute a pure interest in future profits, rather than later at vesting when it may have grown into a capital interest. In addition, even if the service provider's equity interest does not qualify for Rev. Proc. 93-27's taxpayer-favorable LV rule (e.g., if the service provider disposes of the interest within 2 years or if the interest is in the money to some extent and Rev. Proc. 93-27 is interpreted as not applying to such an interest), it will be clear that the FV of the partnership interest is determined at the front end, rather than later at vesting when the partnership's assets may have appreciated substantially in value.

(4) The precedents are reasonably clear that where a service provider receives an equity interest for services to be performed as a partner (which equity interest is fully vested or with respect to which a §83(b) election is made or deemed made) and the partnership subsequently recognizes OI or CG (e.g., earns profits from its business or sells a partnership asset at a gain), the character of the income in the partnership's hands (OI or CG) passes through to the service provider, i.e., the equity interest holder.

¶302.15   Key Issues and References

How does a limited partnership statute work?

References:

• Delaware Revised Uniform Limited Partnership Act excerpts set forth in appendix.

How is a partnership taxed differently than a C or an S corporation?

References:

• Code §701 through §761
• Ginsburg and Levin M&A book Chapter 16

How are a partnership and its partners taxed on profits, losses, and the sale of the partnership?

With respect to partners' deductions for partnership losses, see also:

References:

- Code §465
- Code §469

Can any partnership qualify as a partnership for tax purposes?

References:

- Treas. Reg. §301.7701-2, -3 ("Check-The-Box" regulations)
- Code §7704

Are the arbitrary S corporation qualification rules (no more than 75 shareholders, very limited types of entity shareholders, no foreign shareholders, only one class of stock) applicable to a partnership? If not, why not?

Can a partnership have different classes of partnership interests, for example, analogous to straight preferred stock or convertible preferred stock in a corporation?

What non-tax disadvantages does a partnership present? When is a GP (e.g., E) liable for the partnership's liabilities to the extent the partnership is unable to pay them? Can a GP protect itself from liability by forming a corporation? If so, should it be a C or an S corporation?

When (and to what extent) are LPs (e.g., VC) liable for the partnership's liabilities? To what extent can an LP protect itself by forming an intermediary corporation to hold the LP interest?

References:

- Del. Revised Uniform Limited Partnership Act §17-303, §17-607, and §17-901(a)
- 1916 Uniform Limited Partnership Act §7
- 1985 Revised Uniform Limited Partnership Act §303, §607, §608, and §901
- 2001 Uniform Limited Partnership Act §201(a)(4), §303, §404, §508, §509, §901(a)

How is an FP taxed if it is a partner? How is an FP taxed if it is a shareholder in a corporation?

References:

- Code §871(a) and (b)
- Code §875
- Code §881(a)
- Code §882(a), (b), and (c)

How is a TEO taxed if it is a partner? How is a TEO taxed if it is a shareholder in a corporation?

References:

- Code §511(a)(1)
- Code §512(a)(1)
- Code §512(b)(1), (4), and (5)
- Code §512(c)(1)
- Code §513(a)
- Code §514(a), (b)(1), and (c)(1)

How is a service provider to a partnership taxed on receipt (or vesting) of a partnership GP or LP interest?

References:

- Rev. Proc. 93-27
- Rev. Proc. 2001-43

¶303 NEWCO AS LLC

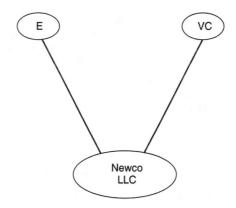

¶303.1 *LLC General Characteristics*

An LLC is a relatively recent creation of state statutory law, generally treated like a partnership for federal tax purposes and like a corporation with limited liability for state law and other non-tax purposes.

While a few state LLC statutes were enacted before 1988, a 1988 favorable IRS tax ruling—that a properly structured LLC satisfying IRS's complex *Kintner* regulations would be treated as a partnership for federal income tax purposes—encouraged an increasing number of states to enact similar statutes, and by 1997 all 50 states and the District of Columbia had adopted LLC statutes. Finally, as of 1/1/97 IRS repealed the excessively complex *Kintner* regulations and adopted a check-the-box approach, allowing an LLC simply to choose to be treated as a partnership for federal tax purposes and making the LLC format highly desirable.

¶303.2 No Entity-Level Tax and Other Tax Attributes

So long as an LLC does not affirmatively elect to be taxed as a corporation and interests in the LLC are not publicly traded under the Code §7704 rules discussed at ¶302.8.5 above, the LLC will not be subject to federal income tax on its income at the entity level, because it will be treated as a partnership (i.e., a flow-through entity). Rather, each of Newco LLC's equity owners (called "members" under a typical LLC statute) will report his, her, or its share of Newco's profits and losses on its tax return and pay tax at the appropriate federal rate—up to 38.6% for an individual's 2002 and 2003 OI, up to 35% for a corporation, and 0% for a TEO unless the LLC income constitutes UBTI.[1]

¶303 [1] The top individual federal OI rate is really higher than the 38.6% nominal rate because of the 3% itemized deduction disallowance, as described in ¶201.1.1 above.

In addition, the individual top rate is increased on any income subject to the uncapped medicare tax, which is imposed at a 2.9% rate (one-half deductible and one-half non-deductible) on an LLC member's share of LLC income (other than passive income such as rents from real estate, interest, dividends, and CGs, which are excluded from the definition of earnings from self employment).

When this 2.9% medicare tax is applied to a partnership, Code §1402(a)(13) contains a taxpayer-favorable rule for LPs, who are taxed only on guaranteed payments for services rendered by the LP to the partnership. Because an LLC is treated as a partnership for federal income tax purposes, it is arguable that the taxpayer-favorable LP rule (which covers an LP in a partnership) should also cover an LLC member. Clearly an LLC is treated as a partnership for federal income tax purposes generally, but it is not as clear that an LLC member should be treated as an LP for purposes of Code §1402(a)(13). There are at least 3 possible approaches for determining whether an LLC member should be treated as an LP for purposes of this taxpayer-favorable partnership rule:

- First, an LLC member could be treated as an LP if he or she is not personally liable for the LLC's debts — under this rule virtually all LLC members would constitute LPs since under all 50 state LLC statutes LLC members are not liable for LLC debts, absent a member's agreement to be liable for the LLC's debts.
- Second, an LLC member could be treated as an LP only if he or she was a non-managing member of the LLC.
- Third, an LLC member could never be treated as an LP because an LLC member does not *under state law* constitute a "limited partner" of a partnership.

IRS apparently rejects the first approach and, while we regard the second approach as sensible in the context of an LLC, it is not clear whether IRS would agree, and instead may assert the third approach, i.e., an LLC member is never treated as an LP for purposes of Code §1402(a)(13).

In 1997, IRS issued proposed regulations (effective for taxable years beginning after the regulations are finalized) that would generally treat an LLC member like a partnership GP—thus subjecting the LLC member to the uncapped medicare tax on the member's share of LLC income (other than passive income such as rents from real estate, dividends, and CGs, which are excluded from the definition of earnings from self-employment) if (1) the member has authority to contract on behalf of the LLC (i.e., is a manager of the LLC) *or* (2) the member participates in the LLC's business for more than 500 hours during the taxable year *or* (3) the member provides services to the LLC and substantially all of the activities of the LLC involve the performance of services in the fields of health, law, engineering, architecture, accounting, actuarial science, or consulting *or* (4) the member has personal liability under state law for the LLC's debts by reason of being a member (an unlikely situation). Under the proposed regulations an LLC member who was not covered by any of these 4 tests would be treated like a partnership LP—thus subjecting the LLC member to the uncapped medicare tax only on guaranteed payments for services rendered by the member to the LLC.

Although a Congressionally imposed moratorium on finalizing of the proposed regulations expired 7/1/98, the regulations remain in proposed form.

Generally, all the federal income tax issues discussed in ¶302 in the context of Newco partnership (including ¶302.2 through ¶302.5 and ¶302.9 through ¶302.14) apply equally to Newco LLC.

The tax law of each state, local, and foreign jurisdiction where the LLC does business must be checked to see whether an LLC is a flow-through entity for *state,local,* and *foreign* tax purposes or whether the LLC must pay full or partial entity-level state, local, and foreign income tax. For example, Texas treats an LLC (but not a partnership) as a corporation for state tax purposes, as does Canada for Canadian tax purposes. Similarly, Pennsylvania subjects an LLC (but not a partnership) to the Pennsylvania Capital Stock and Foreign Franchise Tax if the LLC does business within Pennsylvania.

¶303.3   Limited Liability

Between 1977 and 1997 all 50 states and the District of Columbia adopted LLC statutes under which an insolvent LLC's equity owners (like shareholders of an S or C corporation) are not personally liable for the LLC's liabilities even if they participate in the management of the LLC,[2] absent invocation of the piercing-the-veil or a statutory liability doctrine (see ¶301.5 and ¶501.5.3), any of which doctrines should apply equally to a corporation or an LLC. Thus, LLC statutes do not contemplate personal liability equivalent to exposure under the GP-unlimited-liability or the LP-treated-as-a-GP rules (see ¶302.6 and ¶302.7).

While every state has adopted an LLC statute (the last of which became effective in 1997), the LLC statutes adopted in the various states are not wholly uniform. Hence, there is slight risk that the members of an LLC, properly formed under the LLC statute in the state where the LLC is organized (its "organization state"), but with characteristics not permissible for an LLC organized in a different state in which the LLC conducts business activities (the "liability state"), may not be accorded limited liability in the liability state.

However, 46 of the 50 LLC state statutes (plus the District of Columbia's) contain provisions (1) similar to RULPA §901 (discussed at ¶302.7)[3] utilizing organization state law to determine the liability of an LLC's members to the LLC's creditors and (2) explicitly allowing an LLC to register in the liability state notwithstanding differences between organization state and liability state law. The four exceptions are Florida (which, although ambiguous, is somewhat favorable to organization state law) plus Montana, Pennsylvania, and Wyoming (which are totally ambiguous). Thus, this slight risk arises only with respect to LLC liabilities incurred in the four LLC states with no §901-like provision.

---

[2] See, e.g., Del. LLC Act §18-303(a).

[3] Indeed the Delaware LLC law provision is §901, although other states use different numbering systems.

¶303.4   Achieving Flow-Through Tax Status

¶303.4.1   Check-The-Box Classification Rules

As discussed in ¶302.8.1 above in the context of a partnership, IRS regulations effective 1/1/97 permit a domestic noncorporate entity (as well as many types of foreign entities) to simply choose (i.e., "check the box") whether to be taxed as a partnership (so long as the entity is not a PTP as discussed in ¶302.8.3 above) or as a corporation for federal income tax purposes. In general, a domestic LLC is taxed as a partnership absent an affirmative election to be taxed as a corporation, so that, absent such corporate-tax election, all of the tax characteristics of a partnership (as described in ¶302 above) apply equally to an LLC.

A foreign unincorporated entity is generally (1) taxed as a partnership for U.S. federal income tax purposes (absent an affirmative election to be taxed as a corporation) where at least one of its members has personal liability for some or all of the debts of the entity by reason of being a member and (2) taxed as a corporation (absent an affirmative election to be taxed as a partnership) where none of its members has such personal liability.

IRS had long taken the position that an LLC could qualify as a partnership for federal income tax purposes only if it had two or more members, so that it was unclear whether a single-member LLC would be treated for federal income tax purposes as a corporation (subject to entity-level tax) or as a sole proprietorship or division (disregarded for tax purposes). The check-the-box regulations generally treat a single-member domestic unincorporated entity as a sole proprietorship (disregarded for tax purposes) unless it affirmatively elects to be taxed as a corporation. A single-member foreign unincorporated entity is generally (1) taxed as a sole proprietorship or division for U.S. federal income tax purposes (absent an affirmative election to be taxed as a corporation) where the member has personal liability for some or all of the debts of the entity by reason of being a member and (2) taxed as a corporation (absent an affirmative election to be taxed as a sole proprietorship or division) where the member does not have such personal liability.

¶303.4.2   Determining Who Is a Member

As discussed in ¶302.8.2 above in the context of a partnership, the check-the-box regulations do not address the circumstances when an owner of an interest in an LLC will be respected as a member for federal income tax purposes (rather than as a mere service provider to the LLC). Only if a service provider to the LLC is treated as a member would its share of the LLC's LTCG qualify for flow-through LTCG (rather than OI) treatment on its tax return. Hence there is some possibility IRS may seek to retain some version of its old *Kintner* rules to treat a member/ service provider as merely a service provider to (and not a member of) the LLC if he or she does not *either* (1) make a substantial investment in the LLC *or* (2) share in allocation of net losses and have an obligation to make up a substantial portion of any deficit in his or her capital account upon termination of the LLC.

¶303.5   Non-Tax Disadvantages

Because most LLC statutes are recent, there is little or no judicial guidance as to their interpretation. This may create uncertainty regarding the rights and obligations of and among LLC members, managers, and officers. Also, the small lingering doubt as to state law liability of LLC members in a state with no RULPA §901-like provision, combined with the absence of case law on the point, may discourage some from using an LLC.

The discussion in ¶302.9 through ¶302.13 in the context of a partnership applies equally to an LLC.

For a surprisingly hostile SEC Rule 144 interpretation where Newco is originally formed as an LLC and subsequently incorporates, and for a method of solving the problem, see ¶903.4.6 below.

¶303.6   Key Issues and References

Should Newco be structured as an LLC?
How does an LLC statute work?

References:

- Delaware Limited Liability Company Act excerpts set forth in appendix

Will Newco LLC be taxed as a partnership?

References:

- Precedents cited at ¶302.15 above as to when a state law partnership qualifies as a partnership for tax purposes
- See the discussion at ¶302.8 above

Under what circumstances will the members of an LLC (VC and E) be liable for the LLC's recourse liabilities to the extent the LLC is unable to pay them?

¶304   TAX LIMITATIONS ON NEWCO's DEDUCTIBLE EXPENSES

¶304.1   Capitalization of Pre-Opening Start-Up Expenses

Newco's pre-opening start-up expenses (i.e., Newco's expenses incurred "before the day on which the active trade or business begins, in anticipation of such activity becoming an active trade or business") cannot be deducted as incurred but rather must be capitalized. Code §195. However, if Newco makes a timely Code §195 election, Newco can deduct these expenses over 60 months after start-up.

This rule applies regardless of Newco's form of organization, e.g., it applies whether Newco is an S corporation, a partnership, an LLC, or a C corporation.

¶304.2 Exceptions

The capitalization rule described at ¶304.1 above does not apply to expenses deductible under Code §174 as R&D, Code §163 as interest, or Code §164 as taxes.

Nor does the rule described at ¶304.1 above—which allows 60-month amortization—apply to Newco's "syndication" costs, i.e., Newco's expenses of raising money from equity owners (i.e., promoting the sale of equity interests), which costs are never deductible or amortizable. Code §709(a).

¶304.3 Key Issues and References

What does "start-up" mean for federal income tax purposes? When does "start-up" end? Why is this special rule in the Code?

Does this rule apply regardless of whether the start-up entity is an S corporation, a partnership, an LLC or a C corporation? If so, why?

References:

- Code §195
- Ginsburg and Levin M&A book ¶1407

CHAPTER 4

Structuring Growth-Equity Investment in Existing Company

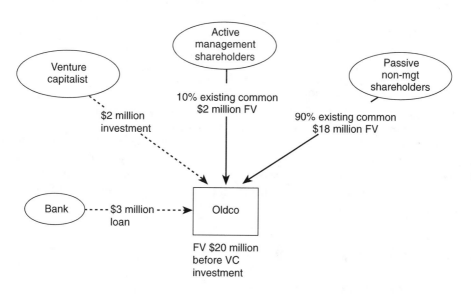

Oldco is an existing, reasonably successful C corporation. Oldco needs more money to expand its business than it is able to raise from traditional sources, such as a bank loan, an insurance company private debt placement, a private offering of debt or equity securities to Oldco's shareholders, their friends and family, or a public offering of debt or equity securities.

Hence, Oldco has approached VC (or a group of VCs) to make a later-stage growth-equity investment in Oldco, i.e., to supply enough equity capital (or equity capital plus subordinated debt) to enhance Oldco's existing borrowing base so that Oldco can obtain the balance of its needed cash from traditional lenders (e.g., banks).

VC believes that Oldco's value will rise quickly and geometrically once Oldco has the necessary money for expansion and Oldco's stock ownership is rearranged to incent able younger managers (who may include new managers located by VC).

While a growth-equity investment is generally designed to provide Oldco with expansion capital as described above, there are cases where Oldco is seeking the new VC investment in order to obtain cash with which to redeem Oldco stock from existing large shareholders. One or more Oldco shareholders may be seeking such a stock redemption to pay estate tax (where a large shareholder has died) or for liquidity (where the shareholder has recently retired or is engaged in advance estate planning). Such a growth-equity investment to finance a redemption is called a recapitalization and, when financed in large part with borrowed money, a leveraged recapitalization.

A VC growth-equity investment is generally more complex than the start-up discussed in Chapter 2 where VC had only E with whom to negotiate. In a growth-equity transaction, VC is investing in an existing company, which generally has a number of shareholders (some active and some passive) with differing interests and goals.

Moreover, Oldco in this Chapter has far more in the way of assets, contingent liabilities, and operating history than did Newco in Chapter 2. Hence it is more important that VC and its advisers (1) undertake a substantial business, legal, and accounting due diligence review to uncover unanticipated Oldco problems and (2) draft a more extensive agreement allocating the risks of unknown liabilities and other contingencies between VC and Oldco's old shareholders.

In this chapter, Oldco is a C corporation. If Oldco were an S corporation, a partnership, or an LLC, many of the applicable tax rules would be different, as discussed in Chapter 3.

¶401 PROPOSED GROWTH-EQUITY TRANSACTION

¶401.1 *Oldco's Characteristics*

(1) Sales $20 million.
(2) Net income $2 million.
(3) 100 shares of common stock outstanding.
(4) 10 stockholders, consisting of 4 active management stockholders owning only 10% of Oldco's 100 common shares and 6 passive non-management stockholders—Oldco's founders, retired executives, and their heirs—owning 90%.

(5) Oldco seeks $5 million of new money to:

- acquire an existing company ("Target") engaged in a complementary business,
- expand Oldco's business nationwide,
- develop a new product, and/or
- build a new plant.

¶401.2 VC Proposed Investment

VC is considering an investment in Oldco of $2 million to support a new $3 million bank loan.

In preparation for this growth-equity investment, VC conducts legal due diligence on both Oldco and Target, including the following:

(1) Contingent liabilities:

- Environmental/pollution violations and other cleanup obligations.
- Employment discrimination claims.
- Pension underfunding and unfunded retiree medical benefits.
- Uninsured or under-insured product liabilities.
- Product warranties.
- Patent/copyright/trademark infringements.
- Antitrust violations.
- Tax deficiencies.
- Breach of contract claims.
- OSHA violations.
- Guarantees.
- Other lawsuits, claims, and contingent liabilities.

(2) Material contracts and debt agreements.
(3) Product liability insurance and other insurance.
(4) Prior acquisition agreements and joint ventures.
(5) Capital structure, outstanding securities (including convertibles, warrants, and options), and prior securities law compliance.

After its due diligence examination, VC believes that Oldco has an FV (prior to the new VC investment) of approximately $20 million.

Hence, the 90% of Oldco's common stock owned by the passive non-management shareholders has an FV of approximately $18 million and the 10% owned by the active management stockholders has an FV of approximately $2 million.

If VC were to make a $2 million common stock investment into Oldco, Oldco's common equity would be worth $22 million ($20 million FV before VC investment + $2 million new VC common stock investment). Hence, VC's $2 million investment would purchase only 9.1% of Oldco's common stock (i.e., $2 million VC investment divided by $22 Oldco common stock FV after VC investment = 9.1%), so that VC would own only 10 common shares out of 110 outstanding Oldco common shares. However, VC seeks a larger share of Oldco's common stock (i.e., a larger share of Oldco's future appreciation) and VC also wants some Oldco fixed securities (i.e., subordinated debentures and/or preferred stock) in exchange for a portion of its $2 million investment.

In addition, VC wants Oldco's active management shareholders to own a larger percentage of Oldco's common stock than the 10% they currently own (or the 9.1% they would own if VC simply made a $2 million common stock investment), so that the active management shareholders will have a greater incentive to perform.

In order to achieve these goals, VC would like Oldco to engage in a front-end rearrangement of its shareholdings so that (1) the passive non-management shareholders own a smaller share of Oldco's common stock (plus some fixed preferred stock or debentures), (2) the active management shareholders own a larger share of Oldco's common stock (50% in the examples below), thus giving them greater incentive to stay with Oldco and perform, and (3) VC is able to acquire for its $2 million of new money a larger share of Oldco's common stock (25% in the examples below) plus some subordinated debentures and/or preferred stock.

There are several methods of achieving this front-end rearrangement of Oldco's equity:

- A common stock redemption from the passive shareholders for subordinated notes.
- A preferred stock recapitalization (i.e., an exchange of new preferred stock for old common stock) with the passive shareholders.
- A pro rata dividend of preferred stock to all of Oldco's shareholders combined with formation of a new holding company ("Newco") to hold all of Oldco's common stock (and the active management shareholders' Oldco preferred stock), with Newco's common stock owned in the desired 25-50-25 ratio.
- Any of these 3 techniques can also be combined with an issuance to active management of additional common shares or options to acquire new common shares (with each dollar of stock purchase price, or option exercise price, purchasing a far higher percentage of post-transaction common stock interest than it would have purchased pre-transaction because each of the above 3 techniques has transformed much of Oldco's common equity value into preferred stock or subordinated notes).

¶402   REARRANGING OLDCO's EQUITY THROUGH REDEMPTION

Under a redemption approach, Oldco's passive shareholders swap some or all of their old common stock for new subordinated notes in order to increase active management's and VC's percentage of Oldco's common stock. The passive shareholders' taxable gain on the exchange is reported on the installment method.

¶402.1 *Principal Tax Characteristics*

(1) The passive shareholders' redemption exchange of old common stock for new subordinated notes is a taxable exchange to the passive shareholders, generally producing CG reportable on the installment method. Under the installment method, the exchanging shareholder recognizes no CG at the time of the redemption and thereafter recognizes a proportionate part of the deferred CG from the redemption as he or she receives principal payments on the notes. Thus, a holder's receipt of (e.g.) 40% of the principal payments on the notes triggers recognition of 40% of the holder's LTCG from the redemption.

(2) A passive shareholder's redemption exchange of old common stock for new subordinated notes qualifies for installment method tax reporting, only if (a) neither the common stock surrendered nor the new notes received in exchange are publicly traded and (b) the new notes satisfy other installment method requirements (such as not payable on demand and not secured by cash). Code §453. If the redemption does not qualify for installment reporting, the passive shareholder's entire CG on the exchange is taxable at the time of the redemption.

(3) A taxpayer who receives more than $5 million of §453-qualifying installment notes in a year owes IRS an annual interest charge calculated on the deferred income tax on the gain attributable to the portion of the notes in excess of $5 million. Code §453A.

- For purposes of the $5 million per person exemption from the annual interest charge on deferred installment method tax, each individual owner of Oldco stock is treated as a different person, even in the case of spouses filing a joint tax return. Indeed, it appears a shareholder can expand his or her exemption by gifting Oldco stock to a relative (including the shareholder's spouse—to whom a gift can be made without gift tax) immediately before signing the installment sale contract.
- If an Oldco shareholder is a pass-through entity (e.g., a partnership, LLC, or S corporation) and such pass-through entity sells its Oldco stock, the $5 million per person exemption is calculated at the owner (not the pass-through entity) level.

(4) If the sales price for the Oldco stock exceeds $150,000, the redeemed shareholder's §453 installment gain is triggered by a subsequent pledge of the installment note. For purposes of determining whether the $150,000 threshold is met, it appears that all sales by Oldco's shareholders pursuant to a single plan are aggregated. Code §453A.

(5) If a redeemed shareholder gifts his or her §453 installment note, the previously deferred installment gain is triggered, but a transfer by death does not trigger immediate installment gain. Code §453B.

(6) Where a noteholder dies owning a §453 installment note, his or her estate or heirs are *not* entitled to a stepped-up tax basis for the note. Thus when his or her estate or heirs collect on the §453 installment note, the deferred CG is recognized. However, the portion of the deceased noteholder's federal estate tax attributable to the amount of installment gain included in his or her estate is deductible for

income tax purposes by his or her estate or heirs when the installment gain is recognized. Code §§691(c) and 1014(c).[1]

(7) A redeemed shareholder is entitled to CG treatment on the redemption and to utilize the §453 installment method only if the shareholder surrenders sufficient old common stock to prevent recharacterization of the redemption as an immediately taxable dividend. Dividend characterization for the redemption is highly unlikely so long as the transaction causes the passive shareholder's percentage ownership of Oldco's common stock (and voting power) to drop significantly, so that the exchange qualifies as a substantially disproportionate redemption. Code §302(b).

- The Code §302(b) determination whether a redemption is treated as a dividend is made on a shareholder-by-shareholder, rather than an aggregate, basis.
- However, if any active management shareholder is related to a passive shareholder, the §302-§318 attribution rules must be reviewed to ascertain whether (a) common stock owned by the active management shareholder is attributed to the passive shareholder and (b) if so, whether this attribution means that such passive shareholder's receipt of the subordinated notes is "essentially equivalent to a dividend," in which case the notes received by such passive shareholder are taxed as a dividend (with no right to use the installment method).
- Certain additional attribution rules are also applied in making this determination, e.g., attribution from an entity shareholder to its owners, attribution from a person to an entity owned by such person, and attribution from an optionor to an optionee. Code §318(a).

(8) Oldco *is* entitled to a deduction for interest on the notes so long as the notes qualify as "debt" for tax purposes and surmount several other tax hurdles. See ¶602.8 below.

(9) If the notes grant Oldco an interest holiday (i.e., a period during which interest accrues but is not paid), the interest is nevertheless taxable to the holder and deductible to Oldco as it accrues, although not paid. See ¶602.5 below. If the notes do not bear interest of at least 100% of the AFR, there will be imputed interest. Code §1274.

(10) Even where the notes' FV is less than face, there will be no imputed OID (as there would be with preferred stock in comparable circumstances—see ¶403.1 below), so long as the notes bear interest of at least the AFR and are not part of a class of publicly-traded notes. Code §1274.

¶402   [1] The top federal estate tax bracket for 2003 is 49% (gradually decreasing to 45% in 2007, then dropping to 0% in 2010, and then returning to 55% in 2011). However, Code §2011 allows a credit against federal estate tax for a sliding percentage of state death tax, approximately 5 to 8 points in 2003, decreasing to approximately 2 to 4 points in 2004. After 2004 the credit is replaced by an estate tax deduction for the amount of state death taxes actually paid. (Virtually all states impose a death tax at least as large as the Code §2011 federal credit.) The amount of state death tax credited against the federal estate tax is not deductible for federal income tax purposes under Code §691(c). Hence, for a larger estate, the §691(c) income tax deduction is approximately 41% to 44% in 2003 and approximately 44% to 46% in 2004 of the installment gain included in the deceased noteholder's estate.

(11) Redemption of the notes should give rise to no risk of Code §302 dividend treatment (as would a preferred stock redemption) so long as the notes qualify as "debt" for tax purposes. See ¶603.8(1) below.

¶402.2   *Principal Non-Tax Issues*

(1) Will the passive shareholders' notes bear interest at a fixed rate payable periodically (e.g., quarterly, semi-annually, or annually)? At what rate? Will there be sanctions if the interest is not paid timely, e.g., an increased interest rate, a right for the holders to accelerate the notes, and/or a right for the holders to take control of Oldco?

(2) On what date or dates will the principal on the notes be payable? Will Oldco be obligated to pay all or a portion of the principal on the notes earlier upon the occurrence of specified events, e.g., IPO of Oldco common stock, change in control of Oldco, sale of more than a prescribed portion of Oldco's assets, realization of cash flow in excess of specified levels?

(3) Will the passive shareholders'notes be secured by any or all of Oldco's assets, making them superior in liquidation to Oldco's unsecured creditors with respect to such assets *or* will the noteholders agree to be subordinated to Oldco's general creditors or to specified Oldco creditors *or* will they neither take a security interest nor agree to be subordinated, in which case they will be pari passu with Oldco's general creditors?

(4) What will be the relative priority on liquidation between the passive shareholders' notes and any fixed security (preferred stock or debt instrument) purchased by VC? If the passive shareholders receive subordinated notes and VC buys preferred stock, the passive shareholders would be senior to VC in bankruptcy. Hence VC may want to buy *senior* subordinated debt and insist that the passive shareholders take *junior* subordinated notes.

If it is important to Oldco that any amount invested by VC for a fixed Oldco security constitute equity (i.e., preferred stock) in order to enhance Oldco's accounting net worth (e.g., so that Oldco can comply with senior bank loan covenants or so that Oldco's unsecured creditors are willing to extend credit to Oldco), VC and the passive shareholders could enter into a side agreement making VC's preferred stock effectively senior to the passive shareholders' subordinated notes in case of bankruptcy (e.g., by obligating the noteholders in case of bankruptcy to use a portion of their proceeds from the notes to purchase preferred stock from VC). Such a strategy would, however, pose some risk of IRS seeking to recharacterize the transaction, e.g., attempting to treat VC and the passive shareholders as each owning a portion of the preferred stock and a portion of the notes from the outset *or* attempting to treat the notes as equity rather than debt.

(5) If Oldco goes into bankruptcy soon after the redemption, is there any risk the passive shareholders have received a fraudulent conveyance? See ¶501.4.3.8 below. Is there any risk that the equitable subordination doctrine may apply to the passive shareholders' notes in case of bankruptcy?

(6) Will the transaction qualify for "recap" accounting so that Oldco's GAAP accounting basis for its assets remains unchanged as a result of the transaction? If the transaction qualifies for recap accounting, no accounting write-up and Oldco's post-transaction GAAP book earnings are not reduced by amortization of the write-up in tangible and intangible assets other than goodwill. In contrast, if the transaction does not qualify for recap accounting and if there has been a change in control of Oldco, purchase accounting or partial purchase accounting may apply, causing a write up (for accounting purposes) in all or a portion of Target's assets, including goodwill. Such a write up will generally increase Oldco's post-transaction accounting charges for depreciation and amortization of tangible and intangible assets other than goodwill, reducing Oldco's post-transaction GAAP book earnings.

See ¶501.8 regarding "purchase" accounting and FASB's 7/01 decision to eliminate amortization of purchased goodwill and to substitute a "non-amortization approach" under which goodwill is reviewed for impairment, that is, written down and expensed against earnings when the recorded value of goodwill exceeds its FV, although Oldco's tangible assets and intangible assets other than goodwill (as written up by the purchase transaction) continue to be amortized/depreciated for accounting purposes. See ¶504 regarding "recap" accounting.

¶402.3   Redemption Example

Before the redemption, Oldco's FV is $20 million, the 6 passive shareholders own 90% of Oldco's common stock (FV $18 million), and the 4 active management shareholders own 10% (FV $2 million).

In the redemption, the 6 passive shareholders swap $17 million of their $18 million of Oldco common stock for new straight subordinated notes with a $17 million face amount, fixed interest at least equal to the AFR, and 10-year maturity, leaving the passive shareholders with only $1 million FV of common stock.

Before the redemption, the passive shareholders own 90 of Oldco's 100 common shares. In the redemption, they swap 85 of their 90 common shares for the new subordinated notes leaving them with 5 common shares out of 15 common shares outstanding (before the new VC investment) or 33% of Oldco's common shares (plus $17 million of Oldco subordinated notes).

Before the redemption, the 4 active management shareholders own 10 common shares out of 100 common shares outstanding. After the redemption (and before the new VC investment), they own 10 common shares out of 15 now outstanding or 67% of Oldco's common shares.

Hence, after the redemption and before the new VC investment, Oldco still has an enterprise FV of approximately $20 million, of which $17 million is now represented by the new subordinated notes (held by the passive shareholders) and $3 million is now represented by the 15 common shares—held 33% or $1 million FV by the passive shareholders and 67% or $2 million by the active shareholders.

VC then purchases (1) 5 new shares of Oldco common stock (which will then constitute 25% of Oldco's 20 common shares outstanding) for $1 million and (2) $1 million of fixed securities (either straight preferred stock or subordinated debentures).

These transactions can be summarized as follows:

Passive shareholders	*FV (millions)*
Common FV before redemption	$ 18
Surrender common for subordinated notes in redemption	(17)
Common FV after redemption	$ 1

VC purchases	*FV (millions)*
Common	$ 1
Preferred or subordinated debt	1
Total	$ 2

Summary of ownership after redemption and VC investment			
	Common		*Preferred or debentures FV (millions)*
	No. of shares	*FV (millions)*	*%*	
Passive shareholders	5	$1	25	$17
Active mgmt shareholders	10	2	50	—
VC	5	1	25	1
Total	20	$4	100	$18

¶402.4   Key Redemption Issues and References

How is a redemption—an exchange of old common stock for new notes—taxed? Under what circumstances is a passive shareholder entitled to CG treatment rather than OI-dividend treatment? When can a passive shareholder elect Code §453 installment treatment?

If the holder of a Code §453 installment method note transfers the note as a gift or by bequest, is the deferred §453 gain triggered?

If the holder of a §453 installment method note dies while still holding the note, does his or her estate or beneficiary take an SUB for the note?

Compare all of these tax ramifications to those resulting from a recapitalization swap of old common stock for new preferred stock discussed at ¶403 below.

References:

- Code §302
- Code §318(a)
- Code §317
- Code §301
- Code §316(a)
- Code §453(a) through (d), (f), (k)(2)
- Code §453A
- Code §453B (except §453B(e))
- Code §691(a) through (c)
- Code §1014(c)
- Ginsburg and Levin M&A book ¶203.4

Are there securities law impediments to such a redemption?

References:

- 1933 Act §3(a)(9), §3(a)(11), §4(2)
- SEC Reg. D
- SEC Rule 147
- 1934 Act §10(b)
- SEC Rule 10b-5

Are there any state corporate law impediments to such a redemption? What is "surplus" under Delaware corporate law, and why is it necessary?

References:

- Del. Gen. Corp. Law §154, §160, §170(a), §172, §173, §244
- In re International Radiator Co., Del. Ch., 1914

What are the tax ramifications to the note holder when the notes are later redeemed by Oldco? Compare to redemption of preferred stock in the recapitalization discussed at ¶403 below.

Can Oldco deduct interest on the debentures? Could it deduct dividends on the preferred stock in the recapitalization discussed at ¶403 below?

Might there be imputed interest if the debentures do not bear adequate stated interest?

References:

- Code §1272 through §1275
- Code §483
- Ginsburg and Levin M&A book ¶203.6

Will the transaction qualify for recap accounting?

References:

- ¶501.8 and ¶504 of this book regarding purchase and recap accounting

¶402.5   Issuing Additional Oldco Common Shares (or Options) to Executives

Simultaneous with Oldco's redemption of common stock from the passive shareholders or shortly thereafter, Oldco may (in order to provide additional incentive to Oldco key executives) (1) issue additional Oldco common shares to particular Oldco executives who are expected to play a key future role in Oldco's management (perhaps those executives who did not previously own Oldco common stock or who owned only a small amount of Oldco common stock) for cash and notes or (2) issue options (NQOs or ISOs) to purchase Oldco common shares to such executives. Each common share, or option, so issued represents a much larger percentage interest in future Oldco appreciation than would have been the case without the $17 million common stock redemption from the passive shareholders because the redemption has metamorphosed $17 million of Oldco's common equity into subordinated notes.

See ¶202.2 above regarding the need for recourse and adequate interest on any note given by an executive to pay for Oldco common stock, ¶202.3 above regarding vesting, desirability of a Code §83(b) election where the Oldco common stock is subject to vesting, and an executive's OI if the purchase price for Oldco common stock is below FV, and ¶407.3 below regarding possible adverse accounting aspects of Oldco stock sales to executives.

See ¶407.1 below regarding tax aspects of NQOs, ¶407.2 below regarding tax aspects of ISOs, and ¶407.3 below regarding possible adverse accounting aspects of executive options.

¶403   REARRANGING OLDCO's EQUITY THROUGH TAX-FREE RECAPITALIZATION

Under a tax-free recapitalization approach, Oldco's passive shareholders swap some or all of their old common stock for new preferred stock in order to increase active management's and VC's percentage of Oldco's common stock.

¶403.1   Principal Tax Characteristics

(1) A passive shareholder who exchanges old common stock for new preferred stock qualifies for tax-free "recapitalization" treatment, except to the extent the new preferred stock constitutes NQ Pfd, as discussed in (9) through (14) below. Code §§368(a)(1)(E) and 354(a). Unless otherwise stated, discussion of preferred stock in this ¶403 assumes such stock is not NQ Pfd.

(2) A passive shareholder who exchanges old common stock for new preferred stock with recapitalization treatment takes a tax basis in the new preferred stock equal to his or her tax basis in the old common stock, thus postponing the LTCG inherent in the old common stock until the new preferred stock is sold. Code §354(a).

(3) Where a passive shareholder dies while owning the new preferred stock, his or her estate or beneficiaries are entitled to a stepped-up tax basis equal to the stock's FV at death, thus wiping out the holder's deferred LTCG. Code §1014(a).

(4) After the recapitalization, Oldco is entitled to *no* deduction for dividends paid on the preferred stock.

(5) There is some risk that the preferred stock (issued in a tax-free recapitalization to the passive shareholders in exchange for a large portion of their common stock) may be §306-tainted. A §306 taint would generally cause the holder's proceeds from a later sale or redemption of the preferred stock to constitute OI (without reduction for the shareholder's basis in the redeemed shares) rather than LTCG.

Preferred stock received in a recapitalization is §306-tainted (unless it participates significantly in corporate growth) where, had the shareholder received cash in lieu of the preferred stock, such cash would have been "substantially the same as the receipt of a . . . dividend" under Code §302. Such a result is highly unlikely so long as the recapitalization causes the passive shareholder's percentage ownership of Oldco's common stock (and Oldco's voting power) to drop significantly. In this case the transaction (if Oldco had issued cash in lieu of preferred stock) would have qualified for non-dividend treatment as a substantially disproportionate redemption. Code §§306(c)(1)(B)(ii) and 302(b).

- The Code §302(b) determination whether a cash redemption of common stock would have qualified for non-dividend treatment is made on a shareholder-by-shareholder, rather than an aggregate, basis.
- If any active management shareholder is related to a passive shareholder, the Code §302-§318 attribution rules must be reviewed to ascertain whether (a) common stock owned by the active management shareholder is attributed to the passive shareholder and (b) if so, whether this attribution means that cash in lieu of the preferred stock received by such passive shareholder would have been "substantially the same as the receipt of a . . . dividend," in which case the preferred stock received by such passive shareholder would be §306-tainted.
- Certain additional attribution rules are also applied in making this determination, e.g., attribution from an entity shareholder to its owners, attribution from a person to an entity owned by such person, and attribution from an optionor to an optionee. Code §318(a).

Even where the passive shareholder's Oldco preferred stock is §306-tainted, §306's OI result can generally be avoided where:

- The passive shareholder dies while holding the §306-tainted preferred, thus cleansing the §306 taint and also delivering to the shareholder's estate or beneficiaries death SUB equal to the preferred stock's FV at death,

- the passive shareholder disposes of all his or her non-§306-tainted Oldco stock at the same time as, or prior to, disposing of the §306-tainted preferred stock, so that the passive shareholder completely terminates his or her stock interest (both actual and §318-constructively owned), *or*
- the passive shareholder establishes to IRS's satisfaction that the transaction was not part of a tax avoidance plan.

(6) Even if a passive shareholder's later sale or redemption of his or her Oldco preferred stock previously received in a recapitalization is not covered by Code §306, there is some risk that a future redemption of the Oldco preferred stock while the redeemed shareholder retains his or her Oldco common stock may result in Code §302 OI dividend treatment for the shareholder's full redemption proceeds (without reduction for the shareholder's basis in the redeemed shares). However, LTCG tax on the redeemed shareholder's gain (i.e., proceeds less tax basis) is likely, because only the passive shareholders hold preferred stock being redeemed, so that the future distribution of cash in redemption of preferred would be disproportionate to common shareholdings. See ¶603.8 below. Nevertheless, this LTCG result is not certain because (a) the redeemed shareholder's common percentage would not be reduced where only preferred is redeemed and (b) the Code §302-§318 attribution rules must be applied in making this determination.

(7) A preferred shareholder who receives more than $5 million of preferred stock does not owe IRS any interest charge on the deferred tax. Nor does a preferred shareholder who borrows money and pledges the preferred stock thereby trigger the gain inherent in the preferred stock. Cf. Code §453A discussed at ¶402.1 above, which is applicable to installment method notes, not to preferred stock.

(8) To the extent the preferred stock's issue price (generally the FV of the common stock surrendered in exchange for the new preferred stock) is below the preferred stock's redemption/liquidation price, there is preferred OID. In general, the preferred holder will recognize phantom dividend income (calculated each year on a CYTM basis), over the life of the preferred, in an aggregate amount equal to the preferred OID. Code §305(b)(4) and (c).

- In any year, the preferred OID amortization for such year constitutes dividend income to the preferred holders only to the extent of Oldco's E&P.
- No annual preferred OID amortization is required where the preferred stock is evergreen, i.e., never subject to call or mandatory redemption by Oldco or to put by the holder. Although not entirely clear, IRS regulations can arguably be read as taking the position that stock which must be redeemed only upon a specified event (e.g., an IPO or change of control), rather than at a specified time, qualifies as evergreen—see Treas. Reg. §1.305-5(b)(2) mandating preferred OID amortization where "the issuer is required to redeem the stock at a *specified time* or the holder has the option (whether or not currently exercisable) to require the issuer to redeem the stock [unless there is] a contingency . . . beyond the . . . control of either the holder or the holders as a group . . . and that . . . renders remote the likelihood of redemption . . ." (emphasis added).

- Where the preferred qualifies as evergreen (as described immediately above) except that the issuer has the right to call the preferred (whether immediately exercisable at issuance or exercisable only at a future time)—i.e., there is no mandatory redemption at "a specified time" and no holder put—the §305 regulations require preferred OID amortization only if it is "more likely than not" that the issuer will exercise the call right. Even in such circumstances, preferred OID amortization is not required when the redemption premium—in the event the preferred is called—is "solely in the nature of a penalty for premature redemption," i.e., "a premium paid as a result of changes in economic or market conditions over which neither the issuer nor the holder has control" (such as "changes in prevailing dividend rates or in the value of the common stock into which the [preferred] stock is convertible").

- No OID amortization is required where the excess of the preferred stock's redemption/liquidation price over the preferred stock's FV at issuance is below a specified (but small) de minimis amount.

- No annual preferred OID amortization is required when the preferred stock has a significant participation in corporate growth (through a variable dividend rate or a redemption price based on Newco's success). Although illogical, according to the §305 regulations a conversion privilege does not constitute such a participation in growth (unless the preferred holder participates in common dividends and redemption proceeds on an as-if converted basis even where the preferred stock is not converted into common stock).

(9) The 1997 Tax Act imposed a new barrier to achieving the tax results described above in this ¶403.1. Specifically, the 1997 Tax Act created a new category of non-qualified preferred stock or "NQ Pfd." A shareholder who exchanges Oldco common stock for Oldco NQ Pfd in what would otherwise be a tax-free recapitalization ordinarily must recognize gain up to the FV of the NQ Pfd. Code §§351(g), 354(a)(2)(C)(i), and 356(e). Subject to the exceptions discussed immediately below, NQ Pfd is preferred stock that meets any one of the following 4 tests:

- *Puttable preferred.* The holder has the right to require the issuer (or a related person)[1] to redeem or purchase the stock within 20 years after the issuance date.

- *Mandatorily redeemable preferred.* The issuer (or a related person) is required to redeem or purchase the stock within 20 years after the issuance date.

- *Callable preferred.* The issuer (or a related person) has the right to redeem or purchase the stock and, as of the issuance date, it is more likely than not that the right will be exercised within 20 years after the issuance date.

- *Indexed preferred.* The dividend rate on the stock varies in whole or in part (directly or indirectly) with reference to interest rates, commodity prices, or other similar indices, regardless of whether such varying rate is provided

---

¶403 [1] Persons are "related" for this purpose if a 50% overlapping ownership test is met. Code §§267(b) or 707(b). See discussion in ¶602.8.4(4) below.

as an express term of the stock (e.g., adjustable rate stock) or as a result of other aspects of the stock (e.g., auction rate stock).

For purposes of the first 3 tests, a right or obligation to redeem or purchase the preferred stock, even though it may be exercised or mature within the 20-year period, will be disregarded if it is subject to a contingency which, as of the issue date, renders remote the likelihood of redemption or purchase.

(10) Stock otherwise meeting one of the 4 tests in ¶403.1(9) above is treated as NQ Pfd only if it is "limited and preferred as to dividends and does not participate in corporate growth to any significant extent." Code §351(g)(3)(A). Although early versions of the legislation were clear that preferred stock could participate significantly in corporate growth through a conversion privilege, the final statutory language is silent on this point and the Conference Committee Report states:

> The conference agreement also clarifies the treatment of certain conversion or exchange rights, by deleting any statutory reference to the existence of a "conversion privilege." The conferees wished to clarify that in no event will a conversion privilege into stock of the issuer automatically be considered to constitute participation in corporate growth to any significant extent.

The most sensible reading of this legislative history is that a conversion privilege does not *automatically* constitute significant participation, rather the conversion privilege must be (a) analyzed, so that if vastly out of the money, it is likely not significant participation, and (b) viewed in conjunction with the preferred stock's other terms, so that if at or near the money, it can constitute significant participation for an otherwise non-participating preferred stock.

Alternatively, the passive shareholder's preferred stock could be amalgamated with their retained common stock in a single instrument which (because of the common stock portion) participates in corporate growth.

(11) If an Oldco passive shareholder receives (and is taxed on) NQ Pfd in an Oldco recapitalization:

- such shareholder's gain on receipt of the NQ Pfd is generally LTCG, because (even when the passive shareholders receiving the NQ Pfd is related to the active shareholders retaining substantial common stock) the Code §302(b) "essentially equivalent to a dividend" test for OI (described in ¶402.1(1) above) apparently does not (absent an amendment of Code §317 or, possibly, regulations to the contrary) apply to the passive shareholder's receipt of NQ Pfd which is instead governed by Code §1001, and
- such NQ Pfd is not (absent regulations to the contrary) §306-tainted (as described in (5) above) in the passive shareholder's hands, because such NQ Pfd was not received by the passive shareholder tax free, and thus a subsequent sale or redemption of the NQ Pfd would not produce Code §306 OI to the passive shareholder disposing of such NQ Pfd (although a redemption might produce Code §302 OI—see ¶402.1(1)).

(12) For purposes of applying the first 3 tests of ¶403.1(9), "a right or obligation to redeem or purchase [preferred] stock transferred in connection with the per-

formance of services for the issuer or a related person . . . which represents reasonable compensation" is disregarded if "it may be exercised only upon the holder's separation from service from the issuer or a related person." Code §351(g)(2)(C)(i)(II). The statutory requirement that the preferred stock "represents reasonable compensation" creates confusion regarding the scope of this exception since, if the preferred stock were received as payment for services and not as payment in exchange for common stock, the tax-free exchange provisions of the Code would not apply in the first place. The exception should simply be read as applying where a service provider receives the stock in connection with his or her performance of services (as an employee or an independent contractor), broadly interpreted in a manner consistent with Code §83 and the words "which represents reasonable compensation" should be read as meaning Congress did not want the exception to apply if the stock represented unreasonable compensation, a situation that should not exist where the stock is received in exchange for property under Code §354 and hence does not represent compensation at all.

However, 2000 IRS regulations apparently attempt to limit this exception (wrongly in our view) to the situation where (a) a service provider first receives Oldco stock which is taxed as OI, (b) the service provider subsequently exchanges such "reasonable compensation" Oldco stock for Bigco stock in a tax-free reorganization (or for Oldco stock in a recapitalization), and (c) both the old stock and the new stock have similar redemption, put, or call features. One of the many unfortunate aspects of this approach is that where the service provider purchased Oldco stock at a bargain price, the exception could apparently apply only to the bargain portion of the Oldco stock taxed as OI and not to the portion for which the service provider paid.

(13) A redemption or purchase right or obligation is also disregarded where "it may be exercised only upon the death, disability, or mental incompetency of the holder," but only if, at the time the preferred stock is issued, neither the issuer (Oldco) nor a related party has outstanding a class of stock which is "readily tradable on an established securities market or otherwise," and the issuance of the preferred stock is not "part of a transaction or series of transactions in which [any such] corporation is to become a corporation" with a class of readily tradable stock. Code §351(g)(2)(C)(ii).

(14) The requirement that a taxpayer recognize gain upon an exchange of common stock for NQ Pfd does not apply to NQ Pfd received in a recapitalization under Code §368(a)(1)(E) of a "family-owned corporation." A corporation is family-owned for this purpose only if 50% or more of its stock by vote and 50% or more of each class of its non-voting stock is owned by members of one family throughout the 8-year period beginning 5 years before the recapitalization. Code §§354(a)(2)(C)(ii), 447(d)(2)(C)(i).

(15) As discussed in ¶402.1 above, a passive shareholder's exchange of Oldco common stock for Oldco subordinated notes is taxable, but the taxable gain may be reported under Code §453 on the installment method, subject to the general limitations on use of the installment method. Because NQ Pfd is not debt, the installment method rules do not, by their terms, apply to gain recognized upon a passive shareholder's receipt of NQ Pfd. The 1997 Tax Act's legislative history

authorizes IRS to issue regulations applying installment sale-type rules to NQ Pfd. It seems clear that installment method reporting is appropriate in all cases where the receipt of NQ Pfd triggers gain and the receipt of a debt instrument from the issuer of the NQ Pfd stock in lieu of the NQ Pfd would have been reportable on the installment method.

If IRS does permit installment reporting upon the receipt of NQ Pfd, the collateral taxpayer-unfavorable installment sale provisions discussed at ¶402.1(3) through (6) presumably will also apply: (a) Code §453A interest charge for NQ Pfd in excess of $5 million, (b) immediate gain triggered on a pledge or gift of NQ Pfd, and (c) no death SUB.

Although one can hope that IRS will allow installment reporting for NQ Pfd retroactive to the 6/97 effective date of the NQ Pfd provisions, in the absence of regulations well-advised taxpayers may prefer to receive an Oldco debt instrument, which in most cases will clearly be reportable on the installment method, rather than NQ Pfd. Of course, the substitution of debt for NQ Pfd would alter a number of other tax and non-tax consequences (e.g., with debt Oldco is entitled to an interest deduction for the instrument's yield, but with preferred stock, including NQ Pfd, Oldco has no interest deduction).

¶403.2   *Principal Non-Tax Issues*

(1) Will the passive shareholders' preferred stock bear a fixed dividend payable periodically (e.g., quarterly, semi-annually, or annually)? At what rate? Will the dividend be cumulative if not paid? Will there be sanctions if the dividend is not paid timely, e.g., an increased dividend rate, a right in the holders to demand that Oldco redeem the preferred, and/or a right in the holders to elect one or more Oldco directors (or even take control of Oldco)?

(2) Will the passive shareholders' preferred stock have a fixed liquidation value, e.g., $100 per share plus accrued unpaid dividends? Will Oldco be obligated to redeem the preferred stock (for a price equal to the fixed liquidation value plus accrued unpaid dividends) at a specified date (e.g., 7 years after issuance or half on the seventh and the balance on the eighth anniversaries of issuance), either mandatorily or upon the demand of the holders, or will the preferred stock be evergreen (i.e., no Oldco obligation to redeem the preferred stock until Oldco liquidates)? Will Oldco be obligated to redeem all or a portion of the preferred, either mandatorily or upon the demand of the preferred holders, earlier upon the occurrence of specified events, e.g., IPO of Oldco common stock, change in control of Oldco, sale of more than a prescribed portion of Oldco's assets, failure to pay preferred dividends timely, realization of cash flow in excess of specified levels?

(3) Will Oldco have the right to call the preferred stock at any time (for a price equal to the fixed liquidation value plus accrued unpaid dividends)? Will Oldco be obligated to pay a stated premium if it exercises this call option before a specified date (or a sliding call premium which declines periodically according to a specified schedule)? Will there be a front-end no call period?

(4) Will the passive shareholders' preferred stock have any rights to participate in Oldco's success, e.g., a participating dividend (which increases as Oldco's earnings or common dividends increase), a participating liquidation value (which increases as the value of Oldco's common stock increases), or a right to convert the preferred stock into common stock at a fixed price?

(5) What will be the relative priorities on liquidation between the passive shareholders' preferred stock and VC's fixed security (preferred stock or debt instrument)? If VC receives a debt instrument, VC would be senior to the passive shareholders in bankruptcy. If VC receives preferred stock, VC will desire its preferred stock to be senior to the passive shareholders' junior preferred stock, and the passive shareholders will desire the opposite. Similarly, VC will desire that its fixed security have a payment date prior to the redemption date for the passive shareholders' preferred stock, and the passive shareholders will desire the opposite.

(6) Will the transaction qualify for "recap" accounting? See discussion at ¶402.2(6) above.

¶403.3   *Recapitalization Example*

Same as in ¶402.3 above, except that passive shareholders swap old common stock for new preferred stock (instead of swapping old common stock for new subordinated notes).

¶403.4   *Key Recapitalization Issues and References*

Does a swap of old common stock for new preferred stock qualify as a tax-free recapitalization? Would a swap of old common stock for new debentures qualify?

References:

- Code §368(a)(1)(E)
- Code §354(a)
- Code §356 (other than §356(b) and (f))
- Code §351(g)
- Code §358(a)
- Code §447
- Code §1001

Is the preferred stock §306-tainted? What does §306 taint mean?

References:

- Code §306
- Code §302
- Code §318(a)
- Code §317

Are there securities law impediments to such a recapitalization?

References:

- 1933 Act §3(a)(9), §3(a)(11), and §4(2)
- SEC Reg. D
- SEC Rule 147
- 1934 Act §10(b)
- SEC Rule 10b-5

If a shareholder (who swapped old common for new preferred stock in a recapitalization) dies while still holding the preferred, does his or her estate or beneficiaries obtain SUB for the preferred stock equal to the new preferred stock's FV at death?

References:

- Code §1014(a)

What are the tax ramifications if the preferred is later redeemed by Oldco?

References:

- Code §302
- Code §318
- Code §§301, 316(a), 317(a)
- Ginsburg and Levin M&A book ¶1310
- ¶603.8 of this book

What is preferred OID? How is it taxed?

References:

- Code §305
- Treas. Reg. §§1.305-1, -5, and -7
- Ginsburg and Levin M&A book ¶1309.3

For the additional issues raised where Oldco (in order to provide additional incentive to key executives) issues additional Oldco common shares to particular Oldco executives for cash and notes, or grants such executives options to purchase additional Oldco common shares, see ¶402.5.

¶404   REARRANGING OLDCO's EQUITY THROUGH PREFERRED STOCK DIVIDEND PLUS FORMATION OF NEWCO TO HOLD ALL OF OLDCO'S COMMON (AND PART OF OLDCO'S PREFERRED) STOCK

Under this approach, Oldco first issues new preferred shares pro rata to all of Oldco's common shareholders in order to make Oldco's old common stock less valuable, and then newly-formed Newco—organized by VC and to be owned by VC, the active management executives, and the passive shareholders in the desired 25-50-25 ratio—acquires all of Oldco's common stock (and the portion of Oldco's preferred stock held by the active management executives) in exchange for Newco common stock.

¶404.1   *Principal Tax Characteristics of Oldco's Pro Rata Preferred Stock Dividend*

(1) The pro rata distribution of Oldco preferred stock to all Oldco common stockholders is tax free. Code §305. This result is not changed even if the distributed preferred is NQ Pfd (as described in ¶403.1(9) through (15) above). The NQ Pfd statutory provisions as enacted by the 1997 Tax Act do not apply to stock dividends under Code §305. While IRS has authority to issue regulations to prescribe the treatment of NQ Pfd under other statutory provisions (presumably including Code §305), IRS has not yet issued any such regulations and any such regulations, if ultimately issued, should have only prospective effect.

(2) To the extent the new preferred stock has an FV at the time of distribution below the preferred stock's redemption/liquidation price, there is preferred OID. In general, the preferred holder will recognize imputed dividend income, to the extent of Oldco's current or accumulated E&P, over the life of the preferred stock equal to the preferred OID, unless the preferred stock either (a) is evergreen or (b) enjoys a significant participation in corporate growth (other than through a conversion privilege). See ¶403.1(8) above.

(3) Preferred stock received as a pro rata stock dividend is generally Code §306-tainted (unless it participates significantly in corporate growth). Thus, a holder who sells or redeems his or her preferred stock would recognize OI equal to the full sales proceeds (or, if less, his or her share of Oldco's E&P measured (1) in a sale, at the earlier time when the preferred stock was distributed as a dividend and (2) in a redemption, on the redemption date). See ¶403.1(5) above.

Even where the passive shareholder's Oldco preferred stock is §306-tainted, Code §306's OI result can generally be avoided where:

- The passive shareholder dies while holding the §306-tainted preferred, thus cleansing the §306 taint and delivering to the shareholder's estate or beneficiaries a death SUB equal to the preferred stock's FV at death,
- the passive shareholder disposes of all his or her non-§306-tainted Oldco stock at the same time as, or prior to, disposing of the §306-tainted preferred stock, so that the passive shareholder completely terminates his or her Oldco stock interest, *or*
- the passive shareholder establishes to IRS's satisfaction that the transaction was not part of a tax avoidance plan.

As discussed in ¶404.3(2) if Newco (a C corporation) is interposed between Oldco's old shareholders and Oldco (as described in ¶404.2), the likelihood that a passive shareholder will qualify for the second of these exceptions to §306 OI treatment is greatly enhanced. Where a passive shareholder transfers all his or her Oldco §306 common stock to Newco and such passive shareholder does not own 50% or more of Newco's total stock by value (actually and by §318-attribution), Oldco shares held by Newco are (somewhat surprisingly) not attributed to the passive shareholder. Thus, a passive shareholder who transfers all his or her Oldco common shares to Newco and later disposes of all his or her Oldco §306 preferred shares is likely to qualify for the second of these §306 exemptions (although such passive shareholder's Code §318 relationships with other Newco and Oldco shareholders must be taken into account in making this determination).

(4) Where a preferred holder dies while holding §306-tainted preferred stock, his or her estate or beneficiaries are entitled to stepped-up basis for the preferred stock equal to the stock's FV at death and (as discussed above) the §306 taint is eliminated. Code §1014 and §306.

(5) Even if a passive sharholder's later disposition of Oldco preferred stock received as a pro rata stock dividend is not covered by Code §306 (e.g., because the original preferred shareholder has died), there is some risk that a future redemption of Oldco preferred stock while the redeemed shareholder retains (actual or §318-constructive) ownership of Oldco common stock may result in Code §302 OI dividend treatment for the shareholder's full redemption proceeds (without reduction for the shareholder's basis in the redeemed shares). However, LTCG tax on the redeemed shareholder's gain (i.e., proceeds less tax basis) is likely, for the reasons set forth in ¶403.1(6) and ¶404.1(3).

¶404.2 Example of Preferred Stock Dividend Plus Interposition of Newco to Own All of Oldco's Common (and Part of Oldco's Preferred) Stock

Before the equity rearrangement, Oldco's FV is $20 million, the 6 passive shareholders own 90% of Oldco's common stock (FV $18 million), and the 4 active management shareholders own 10% (FV $2 million), as described above.

Oldco pays a pro rata stock dividend consisting of $18,888,889 face (i.e., redemption/ liquidation amount) of new preferred stock to all of its old common shareholders—$17 million (90%) to the passive shareholders and $1,888,889 (10%) to the active management shareholders—reducing the FV of Oldco's aggregate common stock to $1,111,111 (i.e., $20 million FV before VC investment less $18,888,889 of newly-issued preferred stock), assuming that Oldco's new preferred stock is worth face. At this point Oldco's passive shareholders own 90 common shares worth $1 million and Oldco's active management shareholders own 10 common shares worth $111,111. In addition, the passive shareholders own $17 million face amount of Oldco preferred stock (90% of $18,888,889) and the active management shareholders own $1,888,889 face amount of Oldco preferred stock (10% of $18,888,889).

VC organizes Newco as a C corporation. VC invests $1 million cash in Newco and receives in exchange 100 Newco common shares. Simultaneously (1) Oldco's passive shareholders transfer all of their Oldco common shares (FV $1 million) to Newco in exchange for 100 Newco common shares (with Oldco's passive shareholders retaining their $17 million of Oldco preferred stock) and (2) Oldco's active management shareholders transfer all of their Oldco common shares (FV $111,111) plus all of their Oldco preferred shares (FV $1,888,889) to Newco in exchange for 200 Newco common shares. Finally, VC purchases from Oldco for $1 million cash Oldco preferred stock or debentures (or some of each) having a total face amount and FV of $1 million.

These transactions can be summarized as follows:

	FV of Oldco common before preferred dividend (millions)	Face amount of Oldco preferred distributed	FV of Oldco common after preferred dividend
Passive shareholders	$18	$17,000,000	$1,000,000
Active mgmt shareholders	2	1,888,889	111,111
Total	$20	$18,888,889	$1,111,111

Summary of ownership after equity rearrangement and VC investment	Newco common			Oldco preferred or debentures FV (millions)
	No. of shares	FV (millions)	%	
Passive shareholders	100	1	25	17
Active mgmt shareholders	200	2	50	-
VC	100	1	25	1
Total	400	4	100	18

¶404.3   Tax Effects of Newco's Interposition

(1) In an integrated transaction all of the participants are transferring property to Newco—VC is transferring cash, passive shareholders are transferring Oldco common stock, and active management shareholders are transferring both Oldco common and Oldco preferred stock—solely in exchange for Newco common stock, and immediately after the transfer the transferors as a group (i.e., VC, the passive shareholders, and the active management shareholders) are in control of Newco—defined in Code §368(c) to mean at least 80% of Newco's stock by vote and at least 80% of each non-voting class of Newco's stock. Under these circumstances Code §351(a) directs that none of the transferors recognize gain or loss on the exchange, and Code §1032 directs that Newco recognizes no gain or loss on its issuance of Newco shares for property (here cash and Oldco stock). Thus neither

Oldco's passive shareholders nor its active management shareholders recognize gain on the transfer of their appreciated Oldco stock to Newco in exchange for Newco stock.

(2) Each former Oldco shareholder takes a substituted basis for his or her Newco stock equal to the basis he or she had in the Oldco stock surrendered to Newco in exchange for the Newco stock, deferring recognition of gain on the exchange of his or her Oldco stock until disposition of his or her Newco stock (unless the shareholder dies before disposing of the Newco stock and hence obtains an FV basis at death).

(3) Each Oldco passive shareholder continues to own Oldco preferred shares, but at the close of the transaction no passive shareholder owns directly any Oldco common shares. Are Oldco common shares now owned by Newco attributed to an Oldco passive shareholder under Code §318? The somewhat surprising answer is no: Under Code §318(a)(2)(C) Oldco shares held by Newco are attributed to a Newco shareholder only if such shareholder owns (directly and by, e.g., family attribution from spouse, parent, child, or grandchild) at least 50% in value of Newco's total outstanding stock. So long as none of the 6 passive shareholders own or are deemed to own 50% or more of Newco's stock by FV, all of the passive shareholders are, in the integrated transaction, deemed to have disposed of all interest in Oldco's common stock.

As a result, neither Code §306 nor Code §302 should impose OI treatment on the passive shareholder's later sale or redemption of his or her Oldco preferred stock.

(4) In order to allow Newco's expenses to be offset against Oldco's earnings for tax purposes, it will often be desirable for Newco and its partially owned subsidiary Oldco to file a consolidated federal income tax return. Although Newco does not own all of Oldco's stock, Newco and Oldco can nevertheless elect to file such a consolidated return so long as the Oldco preferred stock owned by the passive shareholders and any Oldco preferred stock owned by VC is sufficiently debt-like so that it meets a set of statutory tests (e.g., non-voting, limited and preferred as to dividends, no significant participation in corporate growth, non-convertible, face amount not significantly greater than FV).

¶404.4   Issuing Additional Newco Common Shares (or Options) to Executives

Simultaneously with Oldco's preferred stock dividend and Newco's interposition or shortly thereafter, Newco may (in order to provide additional incentive to key executives) (1) issue additional Newco common shares to particular executives (perhaps those executives who did not previously own Oldco—now Newco—common stock or who owned only a small amount of Oldco common stock) for cash and notes or (2) issue options (NQOs or ISOs) to purchase Newco common shares to such executives. Each share, or option, so issued represents a much larger percentage interest in future Oldco appreciation than would have been the case without the $18,888,889 preferred stock dividend, because so much common equity has been metamorphosed into Oldco preferred stock owned by the passive shareholders.

See ¶202.2 above regarding the need for recourse and adequate interest on any note given by an executive to pay for Newco common stock, ¶202.3 above regarding vesting, desirability of a Code §83(b) election where the Newco common stock is subject to vesting, and an executive's OI if the purchase price for Newco common stock is below FV, and ¶407.3 below regarding possible adverse accounting aspects of stock sales to executives.

See ¶407.1 below regarding tax aspects of NQOs, ¶407.2 below regarding tax aspects of ISOs, and ¶407.3 below regarding possible adverse accounting aspects of executive options.

¶404.5   Key Issues and References on Preferred Stock Dividend Plus Interposition of Newco and Selective Issuance of New Common Stock or Options

Preferred stock dividend. What are the tax ramifications of a preferred stock dividend paid pro rata to all Oldco common shareholders?

References:

• Code §305(a) through (c)
• Code §306(a) through (c)

Is the preferred stock Code §306-tainted? What does §306 taint mean?

References:

• Code §306
• Code §302
• Code §318(a)

Are there securities law or Delaware law impediments to such a preferred stock dividend?

What is the reason for paying a dividend of preferred stock to all Oldco shareholders before selectively issuing management new common stock or options on common stock?

How will the Oldco shareholders be taxed on a later redemption of their preferred stock?

Will Oldco shareholders be entitled to an SUB for preferred stock still held at death?

Interposition of Newco to hold all of Oldco's common (and part of Oldco's preferred) stock. Do Oldco's passive shareholders recognize gain on transfer of Oldco common shares to Newco in exchange for Newco common shares? Do Oldco's active management shareholders recognize gain on transfer of Oldco common shares and Oldco preferred shares to Newco in exchange for Newco common shares?

Reference:

- Code §351

Do the former Oldco shareholders take a substituted basis for their Newco stock (i.e., the same basis as they had in the Oldco stock surrendered to Newco in exchange for the Newco stock)?

Reference:

- Code §358(a)

Does Newco recognize any gain on the receipt of Oldco shares (from the passive shareholders and active management shareholders) and cash (from VC) in exchange for Newco stock?

Reference:

- Code §1032

Can Newco and Oldco elect to file a consolidated federal income tax return?

References:

- Code §1501
- Code §1504(a)(1), (2), (4)

Selective sale of common stock to executives. How is a sale of common stock to an active management executive taxed? Does it matter if the stock is subject to vesting? Does it matter if the executive pays FV for the stock? How is Oldco taxed?

References:

- Code §83
- Treas. Reg. §1.83-1 through §1.83-8
- Ginsburg and Levin M&A book ¶1502.1 (except ¶1502.1.2)
- ¶202 of this book

Is there an accounting charge to Oldco's net income when stock is sold to an executive?

References:

- ¶407.3 of this book
- Ginsburg and Levin M&A book ¶1502.1.7

If an executive pays for the stock with a note, can the note be non-recourse? Must it bear interest?

Are there securities law impediments to such an issuance of stock?

Reference:

- SEC Rule 701

Accounting treatment. Will the transaction qualify for "recap" accounting?

Reference:

- See discussion at ¶402.2(6) above.

¶405 PASSIVE SHAREHOLDER INCENTIVE TO REDUCE COMMON OWNERSHIP

Why would a passive shareholder exchange part of his or her old common stock for a new fixed security (i.e., debt or preferred stock) as described in ¶402, ¶403, and ¶404 above?

- Higher current yield on the new fixed security.
- Less downside risk on the new fixed security than on the old common stock.
- Better to have a smaller common percentage in Oldco with happy management and capital from new VC rather than a larger common percentage in Oldco with dissatisfied management and inadequate capital.

¶406 IRS ANTI-ESTATE-FREEZE RULES

¶406.1 Code §2701 Imputed Gift

If the active management shareholders (i.e., the persons whose common equity percentage in Oldco increases in the examples discussed above) and the passive shareholders (i.e., the persons whose common equity percentage in Oldco decreases) are related to each other and certain other tests are flunked, the extraordinarily complicated chapter 14 "anti-estate-freeze" rules of Code §2701 might apply. If so, a passive shareholder might be treated as making a taxable gift to an active shareholder to whom the passive shareholder is related in one of several statutorily-specified ways. A taxable gift may result under §2701's mechanical rules even where there is no gift economically and where, under traditional gift tax principles, no gift would result.

As described in more detail in ¶406.3.1 below, where Code §2701 can not be avoided, its impact generally can be reduced or eliminated by issuing to the passive shareholders (1) preferred stock (as in ¶403 above) which bears cumulative dividends, payable at least annually, at an adequate fixed rate, or (2) a debt instrument (as in ¶402 above).

The Code §2701 rules discussed below apply where any person who receives an increased common equity interest is related to any person who suffers a reduced common equity interest, irrespective of whether either or both are active or passive with respect to the entity and whether the entity is a corporation, partnership, LLC, or other type of business organization.

¶406.2   *Avoiding Code §2701*

A passive shareholder generally can avoid the Code §2701 rules if at least one of the following 5 exceptions applies:

¶406.2.1   No-Family-Relationship Exception

Code §2701 does not apply where no active shareholder is a member of the passive shareholder's "descendant family," defined for this purpose as:

(1)   the passive shareholder's spouse,
(2)   a lineal descendant of the passive shareholder or his or her spouse, and
(3)   the spouse of any such descendant.

¶406.2.2   No-Applicable-Retained-Interest Exception

Code §2701 does not apply where immediately after the transaction neither the passive shareholder nor any member of his or her "ancestral family" holds an "applicable retained interest."

The passive shareholder's **"ancestral family"** is defined as:

(1)   the passive shareholder's spouse,
(2)   any ancestor of the passive shareholder or his or her spouse, and
(3)   the spouse of any such ancestor.

An" applicable retained interest" is defined as an equity interest in Oldco with respect to which there is *either* of the following:

- **An "extraordinary payment right."** An extraordinary payment right is a right to cause Oldco to be liquidated, a right to put Oldco stock to Oldco, or a right to acquire Oldco stock (through a conversion privilege, an option, or otherwise), if the exercise or nonexercise of any such right affects the value of the Oldco stock transferred to (or in some cases held by) an active shareholder who is a member of the passive shareholder's "descendant family." The regulations, however, treat a non-lapsing right to convert into a fixed number or a fixed percentage of Oldco's common stock as not creating an extraordinary payment right.
- **A "distribution right" where Oldco is a "controlled" entity.** A distribution right is a right to receive distributions with respect to an equity interest in Oldco, other than a right with respect to a class of stock the same as or subordinate to the stock owned by the active shareholders. Oldco is consid-

ered a controlled entity where *immediately before* the transaction 50% or more of Oldco's stock is owned (by vote or value) in the aggregate by the passive shareholder, his or her "ancestral family," and lineal descendants of any parent of the passive shareholder or his or her spouse.

The 1996 Tax Act amended Code §2701 in an ambiguous fashion. A *pro-taxpayer interpretation* of the 1996 amendment would broaden the no-applicable-retained-interest exception so that the passive shareholder (and his or her ancestral family) could (without invoking Code §2701) retain Oldco preferred stock with a cumulative dividend payable at least annually at a fixed rate (i.e., a "qualified payment right"), with no extraordinary payment right (e.g., with no put right and no right to require Oldco's liquidation). Unfortunately the 1996 amendment's language (which states that in the case of such a cumulative preferred stock, "the value of the distribution right shall be determined without regard to [§2701]") does not quite say that the no-applicable-retained-interest exception remains available (and thus Code §2701 is not invoked) where the passive shareholder (or his or her ancestral family) retains such a preferred stock (which appears to be a prohibited distribution right where Oldco is a controlled corporation).[1]

On the other hand, *an anti-taxpayer interpretation* of the 1996 amendment would construe it as simply reconfirming the rule discussed in ¶406.3.1 below to the effect that, once Code §2701 is applicable (i.e., where neither the no-applicable-retained-interest exception nor any of the other 4 exceptions applies), such an Oldco retained cumulative preferred stock's FV will be calculated under normal valuation principles, i.e., such preferred stock will not be arbitrarily assigned a zero value as Code §2701 often does with other retained rights (as explained in ¶406.3.1 below). However, pre-1996 Code §2701 already appeared to reach this result, thus suggesting that the 1996 drafters may have intended the pro-taxpayer interpretation, although the statutory language seems to fall a bit short.

EXAMPLE 1

Oldco has a $1 million FV. Passive shareholder A owns all of Oldco's 100 common shares.

¶406 [1] Unfortunately, the legislative history of the amendment does not help to resolve this ambiguity. However, should this pro-taxpayer interpretation prevail and should Oldco thereafter fail timely to pay a cumulative dividend on such stock (generally within 4 years after the dividend date), another 1996 amendment clarifies that the holder's taxable gifts or taxable estate would be increased by the amount of such unpaid dividends plus interest.

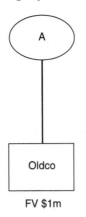

A swaps all 100 of the Oldco common shares to Oldco in exchange for $1 million face amount of newly-issued Oldco preferred stock. At the same time A's descendant, B, pays $1,000 to Oldco to purchase 1 newly-issued Oldco common share.

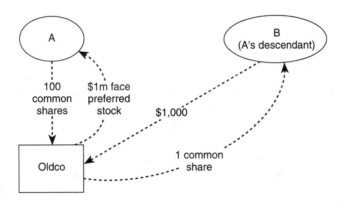

A's preferred stock has one or more of the following "extraordinary payment rights":

- A's preferred stock has the right to require Oldco to be liquidated, *or*
- A's preferred stock can be put to Oldco at A's option, *or*
- A's preferred stock has a lapsing conversion right into Oldco common stock, *and*

A's exercise or non-exercise of such described extraordinary payment right(s) affects the value of B's 1 common share.

Code §2701 treats the foregoing change in Oldco's capital structure as a transfer from A to B of B's 1 common share. A's extraordinary payment right(s) renders the no-applicable-retained-interest exception unavailable, whether or not A's retained preferred stock bears a fixed cumulative dividend. Hence Code §2701 applies and A is treated as making a gift to B equal to Oldco's $1 million FV *less* the value of A's retained preferred stock. Moreover, in many cases §2701 would cause A's retained preferred stock to be valued substantially below FV calculated under traditional gift tax principles. See ¶406.3.1 below.

EXAMPLE 2

Same as Example 1, except that (1) A has none of the extraordinary payment rights described in Example 1 and (2) A's retained preferred stock bears a fixed cumulative dividend payable at least annually.

A controlled Oldco before the transaction and holds an equity right to receive distributions from Oldco which are preferred to B's. Thus it appears that A fails the no-applicable-retained-interest exception because A holds a distribution right in a controlled entity.

However, under the pro-taxpayer interpretation of the 1996 amendment, the no-applicable-retained-interest exception would nevertheless apply and Code §2701 would not be applicable (except for missed dividends as illustrated in Example 6 below). In this case, A is treated as making a taxable gift to B under traditional gift tax principles only to the extent that A's cumulative preferred stock (taking into account the dividend rate and all other factors) has an FV less than face. See Examples 5 and 7 below regarding valuation of A's preferred stock under traditional gift tax principles.

On the other hand, under the anti-taxpayer interpretation of the 1996 amendment, the no-applicable-retained-interest exception would be unavailable and Code §2701 would apply. Because A's retained "distribution right" (i.e., the right to the preferred dividends) meets the test for a qualified payment right described in ¶406.3.1, it is valued under traditional gift tax principles, but a number of other Code §2701 rules nonetheless apply, including (a) the subtraction method valuation procedure described in ¶406.3.1, (b) the common-stock 10%-minimum-value rule described in ¶406.3.2 below, and (c) as in the pro-taxpayer interpretation, the inclusion of the unpaid preferred dividends plus interest in the passive shareholder's transfer tax base.

EXAMPLE 3

Same as Example 1, except that (1) before the transaction Oldco's 100 common shares are owned $\frac{1}{3}$ each by A1, A2, and A3, three unrelated individuals, (2) each of A1, A2, and A3 swaps his or her 33 $\frac{1}{3}$ common shares for $333,333 face amount of preferred stock, and (3) A1's descendant B1, A2's descendant B2, and A3's descendant B3 each buys $\frac{1}{3}$ of an Oldco common share from Oldco for $333.

If the Oldco preferred stock has an extraordinary payment right, the result is the same as in Example 1.

However, if the Oldco preferred stock does not have any extraordinary payment right, the no-applicable-retained-interest exception applies (i.e., A1's, A2's, and A3's distribution rights do not render the exception unavailable), regardless of whether the pro-taxpayer or the anti-taxpayer interpretation of the 1996 amendment is adopted. This is because neither A1 nor A2 nor A3 had 50% or more control of Oldco (by vote or value) immediately before the transaction and hence their distribution rights are not with respect to a controlled entity.

¶406.2.3   Same-Class Exception

Code §2701 does not apply where immediately after the transaction the "applicable retained interest" held by the passive shareholder and his or her "ancestral family" is of the same class as (or is proportional to the class of) Oldco equity transferred (or treated as transferred) to the active shareholder who is a member of the passive shareholder's "descendant family."

¶406.2.4   Proportionality Exception

Code §2701 does not apply where the transaction results in a proportionate reduction of each class of Oldco equity held by the passive shareholder and his or her "ancestral family" in the aggregate immediately before the transaction.

¶406.2.5   Market-Quoted Securities

Code §2701 does not apply where there are readily available market quotations on an established securities market for either the transferred interest (or the interest treated as transferred) *or* the "applicable retained interest."

¶406.3   *Calculating Code §2701 Gift*

If none of the 5 exceptions discussed in ¶406.2 above applies, a passive shareholder is treated as making a Code §2701 taxable gift in an amount calculated under a complex four-step method set forth in the regulations (and generally summarized immediately below), the effect of which generally is to increase the value of the taxable gift above the amount calculated under traditional gift tax principles.

¶406.3.1 Four-Step "Subtraction Method"

(1) Calculate the after-transaction FV (using traditional gift tax principles) of all "family-held" equity interests in Oldco[2] without regard to the §2701 rules and treating all such interests as held by one person.

(2) Subtract from the amount determined in (1) the after-transaction value of family-held Oldco "senior equity interests" (using traditional gift tax principles), i.e., Oldco equity interests carrying a right to distributions of income or capital that is preferred over the rights of the equity interests held by the active shareholders in the family.

In making this calculation, "extraordinary payment rights" held by the passive shareholder and his or her "ancestral family" are treated as having a zero value, i.e., they are ignored.

In addition, "distribution rights" in a controlled entity held by the passive shareholder and his or her "ancestral family" are treated as having a zero value, with one important exception. Under this important exception for a "qualified payment right," Oldco preferred stock is valued under traditional gift tax concepts where (a) such preferred stock bears a cumulative dividend, payable at least annually, at a fixed rate (or a rate which bears a fixed relationship to a specified market rate), *or* (b) the holder of the preferred stock elects to treat the distribution right as if it were a cumulative preferred stock of the type described in (a), in which case such election must specify the amounts and times for such hypothetical "cumulative dividend payments," which can not be "inconsistent with the underlying legal instrument."[3]

Where an "extraordinary payment right" and a "qualified payment right" both exist, the value of the retained preferred stock is calculated by assuming that all extraordinary payment rights are exercised in a manner that produces the lowest total value for all such rights.

Where the family's aggregate percentage ownership in the applicable retained interests (i.e., generally the senior equity interests) exceeds the family's aggregate percentage ownership in subordinate equity interests, the excess applicable retained interests are valued under traditional gift tax principles (rather than assigned a zero value).

(3) The amount remaining after subtracting (2) from (1) is allocated (generally on the basis of FV determined without regard to Code §2701) among the transferred interests and the other family-held equity interests in Oldco held by, among others, the passive shareholder, the active shareholders who are members of the passive shareholder's "descendant family," and certain other family members.

---

[2] "Family-held" means held directly or indirectly by the passive shareholder, his or her "ancestral family" members, and lineal descendants of any parent of the passive shareholder or his or her spouse.

[3] Whenever the fixed cumulative preferred stock is held by the passive shareholder, zero value treatment for such distribution right is automatically avoided, unless the holder makes a contrary election. Conversely, whenever the fixed cumulative preferred stock is held not by the passive shareholder, but rather is held by an ancestral family member, zero value treatment for such distribution right applies, unless the holder elects otherwise.

(4) Minority and similar discounts as described in the regulations and consideration received by the passive shareholder (and presumably by Oldco) are deducted from the amount allocated to the transferred interests under (3) to arrive at the taxable gift from the passive shareholder to the active shareholders who are members of the passive shareholder's "descendant family."

Hence, the §2701 valuation rules often ascribe a zero value to elements of Oldco equity rights retained by the passive shareholder and his or her "ancestral family," thus increasing the taxable gift from the passive shareholder to the related active shareholder who owns the Oldco subordinate equity interest.

However, where Code §2701 can not be avoided, the parties can generally reduce or eliminate its gift tax effects by issuing to the passive shareholders (1) preferred stock in a recapitalization (as described in ¶403 above) which bears cumulative dividends, payable at least annually, at an adequate fixed rate, or (2) a debt instrument in a redemption (as described in ¶402 above).

EXAMPLE 4

Same as Example 2 (i.e., A has no extraordinary payment right), except that where A's post-transaction preferred stock does not bear cumulative fixed preferred dividends, payable at least annually (and A does not elect to treat the preferred stock as if it had such rights). A's preferred stock will be valued at zero for Code §2701 purposes, in which case A will be treated as making a taxable gift to B equal to $1 million.

EXAMPLE 5

Same as Example 2 (i.e., the Oldco preferred stock bears cumulative dividends payable at least annually). In addition, (1) the cumulative dividend rate is 5% and (2) the FV of the Oldco preferred stock (taking into account the 5% cumulative dividend rate and all other factors) is $700,000.

A has made a $300,000 taxable gift to B (i.e., Oldco's pre-transaction $1 million FV *less* $700,000 FV of A's retained preferred stock). A's preferred stock is not valued at zero, because it meets the annual-cumulative-fixed-dividend test.

Note that if A's preferred stock bore a cumulative dividend at a full market rate (instead of a 5% rate), the preferred stock's FV would have been its face amount and there would have been no taxable gift to B (subject to the 10% minimum valuation rule discussed in ¶406.3.2 below).

Where preferred stock meets the annual-cumulative-fixed-dividend test (so that such preferred stock is not valued at zero) and Oldco subsequently fails timely to pay a dividend on such stock (generally within 4 years after the dividend date), the holder's taxable gifts or taxable estate are increased by the amount of the unpaid dividend plus interest.

EXAMPLE 6

Same as Example 5, except that Oldco fails to pay the first year's $50,000 preferred dividend (i.e., 5% x $1 million preferred face amount) within the prescribed 4-year period.

A's taxable gifts or taxable estate are increased by $50,000 plus interest when A dies, gifts the preferred stock, or elects to recognize the deemed gift, whichever occurs first.

¶406.3.2 Common-Stock-10%-Minimum-Value Rule

In addition, if §2701 applies, there is a special minimum valuation rule which requires that Oldco's common stock be deemed to have a value no less than 10% of the sum of (a) the total value of all Oldco's equity interests *plus* (b) the total Oldco debt held by the passive shareholder and his or her "ancestral family." This minimum common valuation will be relevant where steps (1) through (4) in ¶406.3.1 above result in a lower valuation for Oldco's common stock. This rule would create a taxable gift, for example, where the 10% minimum value rule results in a higher value for any Oldco common stock transferred (or treated as transferred) to the active shareholders than the amount (if any) paid by the active shareholders for such common stock.

EXAMPLE 7

Same as Examples 2 and 5 (i.e., the Oldco preferred stock bears cumulative dividends payable at least annually), except that (1) the cumulative dividend rate is 10% and (2) A's $1 million face amount of preferred stock has an FV (by reason of its adequate fixed dividend rate and other terms) equal to $1 million.

If Code §2701 does not apply to the transaction, A has made no taxable gift to B. This is because B paid $1,000 for 1 Oldco common share with an FV of $1,000 (i.e., Oldco's $1 million pre-transaction FV *plus* $1,000 B paid to Oldco for 1 common share *less* $1 million post-transaction preferred stock FV held by A).

If Code §2701 applies to the transaction, the 10% minimum value rule causes B's common stock to be valued arbitrarily (for §2701 purposes) at $100,100 (10% x $1,001,000). Since B paid only $1,000 for the 1 Oldco common share, A has made a Code §2701 taxable gift to B of $99,100 (i.e., $100,100 deemed FV of B's Oldco common stock under the 10% minimum value rule *less* $1,000 paid by B for the Oldco common stock).

Where (as described in ¶406.2.2 above) A holds only a distribution right in a controlled entity, consisting of cumulative preferred stock (with a fixed dividend payable at least annually), and A holds no extraordinary payment right, there are two possible interpretations of the change made to Code §2701 by the 1996 Tax Act. Under the pro-taxpayer interpretation, A nevertheless qualifies for the no-applicable-retained-interest exception, and hence A's transaction would be outside Code §2701, so that the 10% minimum value rule would not apply. Under the anti-taxpayer interpretation, on the other hand, A flunks the exception but A's fixed cumulative preferred stock (being a qualified payment right) is valued under traditional gift tax principles (i.e., such preferred stock is not automatically valued at zero); however, the transaction is then subject to the 10% minimum value rule. Under either interpretation, however, failure to pay a dividend within the 4-year grace period triggers an increase in A's taxable gifts or taxable estate as illustrated in Example 6.

¶407 TAXATION OF AND ACCOUNTING FOR OPTIONS

In order to provide incentive to an executive, Oldco (in this Chapter 4) or Newco (in Chapters 2 and 5) may sell common shares to such executive for cash and notes as described in ¶202.2 and ¶202.3. Alternatively, where the executive is not willing to put his or her money (or credit) at risk, Oldco (or in Chapters 2 or 5 Newco) may issue to such executive options to purchase a specified number of Oldco shares at a specified price for a specified period (generally cut short by termination of executive's employment with Oldco). This ¶407 discusses the tax ramifications of an Oldco stock option issued to such an Oldco service provider (with ¶407.1 discussing an NQO and ¶407.2 discussing an ISO), which differ significantly from the tax ramifications of an outright sale of Oldco stock to an Oldco service provider as described in ¶202.2 and ¶202.3. (For the very different tax ramifications of an investor warrant, see ¶501.5.2.)

¶407.3 discusses the accounting aspects of *both* (1) an option grant to a service provider and (2) a sale of stock to a service provider, which often have an adverse effect on Oldco's GAAP earnings.

¶407.1 NQO Tax Ramifications

¶407.1.1 Income Tax Ramifications

Any option issued to a service provider is an NQO unless it meets the ISO rules described in ¶407.2 below.

(1) No OI to executive or deduction to Oldco at the time of the option grant.

(2) At exercise of the option, executive recognizes OI equal to the *spread at exercise* and Oldco is entitled to an equal deduction,[1] unless (3) immediately below applies.

(3) If the stock received by executive upon exercise is subject to further vesting after exercise (and the stock is non transferable or transferable only subject to the vesting restriction), executive recognizes no OI at exercise but instead recognizes OI at the time of vesting equal to the *spread at vesting* and Oldco is entitled to an equal deduction.

(4) However, if executive makes a Code §83(b) election within 30 days after exercise, the rule set forth in (3) immediately above does not apply and instead the rule set forth in (2) above applies, so that executive recognizes OI *at exercise* (and Oldco is entitled to a deduction) equal to the *spread at exercise*.

(5) The exact timing of Oldco's Code §83(h) deduction can be a bit tricky where Oldco uses a fiscal year (but the executive uses a calendar year, as do nearly all humans). Where the stock is vested at the time the option is exercised, Oldco's deduction is at the time of exercise. However, where the stock is not vested at exercise, E makes no Code §83(b) election, and the stock vests later, Oldco's deduction is recognized on the last day of E's tax year during which the stock vests. Hence, if Oldco and E are on different tax years and the stock vests after the end of E's tax year but before the end of Oldco's tax year, Oldco's deduction is postponed until Oldco's tax year following vesting. Where the stock is not vested at exercise and E does make a Code §83(b) election, it appears that Oldco's deduction is recognized on the last date of E's tax year during which E recognized Code §83(b) OI.

(6) Under IRS regulations, the service recipient (here Oldco) is permitted a deduction only if (a) the service recipient timely files form W-2 (with respect to a service provider who is an employee) or form 1099 (with respect to a service provider who is an independent contractor) with the service provider and IRS (by 1/31 for the former and 2/28 for the latter of the year following the year in which the income was taxable to the service provider) or (b) the service provider actually reports the income on his or her original or amended tax return (or IRS includes such amount on audit). See ¶202.3.6 above.

(7) Executive recognizes CG (or CL) on sale of the stock equal to the excess (or deficiency) of the sales proceeds over the sum of the option price paid and the OI previously recognized (except that if the stock never vests, executive is entitled to no loss or deduction on account of any OI previously recognized because of a §83(b) election).

(8) Oldco could lend part or all of its tax saving (from the NQO deduction) to executive to pay executive's tax at exercise (with the loan due when executive sells the stock, or possibly earlier if executive's employment ceases), charge interest on such loan at the AFR (in order to avoid the Code §7872 imputed interest rules), and agree to pay an annual bonus to executive to reimburse executive for interest expense on the loan at the AFR. Because the top individual federal income tax

---

¶407 [1]Where the services for which E is being compensated are treated for tax purposes as producing future-year benefits for Oldco, Oldco's Code §83(h) deduction may be subject to capitalization.

rate exceeds the top corporate rate, Oldco would have to go out of pocket (i.e., loan executive more than Oldco's tax saving) if executive is in the top federal tax bracket and Oldco's loan is meant to cover executive's entire tax bill.

Moreover, if Oldco is in an NOL position before taking account of its NQO deduction, Oldco's tax saving will be postponed until Oldco utilizes the NOL generated by the NQO deduction. In this case, Oldco would have to go further out of pocket to fund a current loan to executive.

(9) If executive's OI tax rate at exercise exceeds executive's expected LTCG tax rate at sale, Oldco could pay executive part of Oldco's tax saving as a tax offset bonus (to compensate executive for the actual OI tax on the spread at exercise in excess of the amount executive's LTCG would have been on such amount). Oldco would still end up with cash in its pocket (because its tax saving—which might be delayed if Oldco has NOLs—will very likely exceed the bonus to executive). However, GAAP would cause a reduction in Oldco's accounting net income, as described in ¶407.3 below.

(10) These NQO rules generally apply whether Oldco is a C corporation, S corporation, partnership, or LLC, except that:

- If Oldco is a flow-through entity, Oldco's Code §83(h) deduction does not reduce any Oldco entity-level income tax; rather the deduction flows out to Oldco's equity owners and reduces their taxable income.
- If Oldco is a partnership or LLC, executive's Code §83 OI (and Oldco's Code §83(h) deduction) are generally calculated based on the liquidation value (rather than the FV) of executive's Oldco equity interest at exercise (or, if the equity interest is subject to post-exercise vesting and no timely Code §83(b) election is filed (or deemed to be filed), then such liquidation value measurement is likely made at vesting). See ¶302.14 and ¶1006.

¶407.1.2   Transfer Tax on Gift

(1)   Vested NQO. Where an NQO is vested and exercisable at the time an executive gifts the NQO to a family member, the tax consequences of such NQO transfer and of the subsequent NQO exercise (as confirmed by a number of IRS private letter rulings) are as follows:

(a) For gift tax purposes, the NQO transfer constitutes a completed gift on the transfer date, at the NQO's FV on the transfer date, so long as the transfer is irrevocable and executive retains no rights or powers associated with the transferred NQO (e.g., the right to determine whether or when to exercise).

(b) For estate tax purposes, the transferred NQO is not included in executive's estate upon his death, so long as the conditions in (a) above are met.

(c) For income tax purposes, the NQO transfer does not cause executive to recognize taxable income. However, when the transferee exercises the NQO, executive recognizes OI under Code §83 equal to the excess of the NQO shares' FV on the exercise date over the NQO exercise price, and executive's employer (Oldco) is entitled to a corresponding deduction under Code §83(h).

(d) For income tax purposes, the transferee's basis in the NQO shares acquired upon exercise is the FV of such NQO shares at the time of exercise.[2]

In consequence, where the underlying stock is expected to appreciate substantially, the gift of a vested NQO to family members immediately or shortly after grant (plus cash to exercise) can result in substantially lower overall gift and estate taxes—with no increase or shift in income tax liability—as compared to a gift of the underlying shares after the NQO exercise.

EXAMPLE 1

Oldco grants executive A a vested and exercisable 7-year NQO to purchase 100 Oldco common shares at $10 per share (or a total option price of $1,000), at a time when the FV of an Oldco common share is $10. A promptly gifts the NQO to family member B, along with $1,000 cash. Assuming A's effective gift tax rate is 50% and the NQO's FV is $300 (i.e., 30% of the underlying stock's FV—see discussion of option valuation techniques below), A owes $650 of gift tax ($1,300 x 50%), $150 of which is attributable to the option ($300 option value x 50%). B later exercises the NQO when Oldco stock FV is $50 per share.

When B exercises the NQO, A owes income tax (generally at a 38.6% rate for 2002 and 2003) on the $4,000 spread at exercise ($5,000 FV at exercise less $1,000 exercise price).

B's tax basis in the Oldco stock should be $5,150 ($1,000 exercise price paid by B, plus $4,000 OI recognized by A, plus $150 gift tax on option transfer paid by A).

EXAMPLE 2

Same as Example 1, except that A retains the NQO, exercises the NQO when Oldco stock FV is $50 per share, and immediately gifts the option shares to B.

A's cash outlays in this Example 2 are the same as in Example 1 ($1,000 NQO exercise price plus OI tax on the $4,000 NQO spread at exercise),

---

[2] Although not addressed in the letter rulings referenced above, the transferee's basis in the NQO shares should also include the amount of gift tax paid, if any, with respect to the transferred NQO. *See* the last sentence of Reg. §1.83-4(b)(1) (basis of nonvested property acquired reflects amount paid for the property, amount of OI recognized, and any Code §§1015 and 1016 adjustments) and Code §1015(d) (adding gift tax to the basis of property transferred). Code §1015(d) states that the basis of gifted property is increased by the gift tax "but not above the fair value of such property at the time of the gift." This limitation should not apply to the gift of an NQO, since the executive generally has a zero basis for the NQO at the time of the gift and the gift tax is a percentage (not greater than 50% for 2002) of the NQO's FV at the time of the gift. Thus, the basis of the NQO in the transferee's hands immediately after the gift is generally the gift tax paid, which by definition is a percentage (not greater than 50% for 2002) of the NQO's FV. The Code §1015(d) limitation does not by its terms apply at the later time the NQO is exercised (but only at the time the NQO is gifted).

except that A's gift tax, calculated when A gifts the option shares to B, is $2,500 ($5,000 stock FV x 50%), i.e., $1,850 more than in Example 1 ($2,500 less $650).

B's tax basis in the Oldco stock should be $5,000 ($5,000 tax basis of stock in A's hands, not increased by $2,500 gift tax paid by A because of Code §1015(d) limitation).

For gift tax purposes, the FV of a gifted NQO is not simply the spread between the NQO exercise price and FV of the underlying stock at the time of the gift. An IRS Revenue Procedure sets forth a safe harbor methodology for valuing a compensatory stock option (either NQO or ISO) for gift and estate tax purposes, applicable only to a nonpublicly traded option to acquire stock that is traded on an established securities market on the valuation date permitting a taxpayer to determine the FV of a compensatory stock option "using a generally recognized option pricing model (for example, the Black-Scholes model or an accepted version of the binomial model)" that takes into account (1) the exercise price of the option, (2) the expected life of the option, (3) the current trading price of the underlying stock, (4) the expected volatility of the underlying stock, (5) the expected dividends on the underlying stock, and (6) the risk-free interest rate over the remaining option term.[3] While the Revenue Procedure does not cover an option to acquire non-publicly-traded stock, executive should be allowed to apply the factors set forth in the Revenue Procedure in good faith to value such an option.

Use of the Black-Scholes or similar option pricing model typically produces an option FV (for an option that is at-the-money on the valuation date) equal to 20% to 40% of the underlying stock's FV, depending on such factors as the option's expected life and the price volatility of the underlying stock. Thus, in Example 1 above (where executive A received a 7-year option to purchase 100 Oldco common shares at $10 per share, at a time when the FV of an Oldco common share was $10), executive A's NQO might be valued at $300 ($1,000 x 30%) at the time of grant. The higher the stock's price volatility and the longer the expected life, the higher the value of the option, because of the higher probability of a large option gain. For options that are substantially in-the-money on the valuation date, the option's FV as a percentage of the underlying stock's FV may be significantly greater than 20% to 40%.

Thus, executive may not find it advantageous to utilize the Revenue Procedure safe harbor.

(2)   Unvested NQO. What if the NQO is not vested and exercisable at the time of the gift, e.g., where the NQO does not become vested and exercisable until executive subsequently satisfies an employment-related condition, such as executive's continued employment for a specified period following grant? Such vesting/exercisability restrictions are a common feature of NQOs. Until early in 1998, there had been hope IRS would treat a gift of an unvested/unexercisable

---

[3] Rev. Proc. 98-34, 1998-1 C.B. 983.

NQO in the same manner as a gift of a vested and exercisable NQO. However, a 1998 Revenue Ruling takes the position that the transfer of an unvested/unexercisable NQO is *not* a completed gift, and therefore is not valued for gift tax purposes, until expiration of the vesting/exercise restrictions.[4]

EXAMPLE 3

Same as Example 1, except that A's NQO is exercisable only if A remains continuously employed by Oldco for two years following grant. A immediately gifts this non-vested, non-exercisable NQO to family member B. Two years later the vesting condition is satisfied and the NQO first becomes exercisable, when the FV of the stock underlying the NQO is then $50 per share, or a total of $5,000.

Under the 1998 Revenue Ruling, A's NQO gift is treated as complete for gift tax purposes (and the gift is valued) on the second anniversary of grant when the NQO first becomes vested and exercisable.

IRS's position in the 1998 Revenue Ruling appears to be inconsistent with the estate tax regulations which state that a gift is complete when "the donor has so parted with dominion and control over the property transferred as to leave him no power to change its disposition, whether for the donor's own benefit or the benefit of another."[5] Nevertheless, the 1998 Revenue Ruling asserts that an unvested NQO does not constitute an "enforceable property right" for gift tax purposes until the right to exercise the NQO becomes "binding and enforceable," although such an unvested NQO (1) clearly has value and (2) clearly gives the transferee (not the executive) the legal right to exercise the NQO and receive the stock, so long as the condition of the executive's continued employment during the vesting period has been satisfied.[6]

The 1998 Revenue Ruling addresses a vesting/exercise restriction that lapses with the performance of additional services. What about a vesting/exercise restriction that lapses based on the attainment of a pre-determined performance goal regardless of whether the executive renders any additional services? A 3/99 IRS Letter Ruling holds that transfer of an NQO that would become exercisable upon achievement of a pre-determined appreciation target with respect to the underlying stock (without regard to whether additional services are performed by the gifting executive) constitutes a completed gift, because "the ability to exercise the

---

[4] Rev. Rul. 98-21, 1998-1 C.B. 975.

[5] Reg. §25.2511-2(b).

[6] The term "property" has generally been given a broad definition by courts in applying the gift tax. See, e.g., Smith v. Shaughnessy, 318 U.S. 176, 180 (1943) ("the language of the gift tax statute, 'property . . . real or personal, tangible or intangible,' is broad enough to include property, however conceptual or contingent."); Galt v. Commissioner, 216 F.2d 41, 50 (7th Cir. 1954) (transfer of interest in a percentage of future profits from leased property is a completed gift as of the transfer date even though such future profits were "speculative, uncertain and contingent upon future developments").

options is not conditioned on [executive's] continued future employment . . . by the Company."

¶407.2   ISO Tax Ramifications

(1) No OI to executive or deduction to Oldco at the time of the option grant or at the time of the option exercise.

(2) Surprisingly, the spread at exercise is subjected to AMT, at a rate potentially as high as 28% (if the spread is large enough and/or the executive has sufficient other AMT preference items).

(3) On resale of the stock, executive recognizes LTCG or LTCL based on sales proceeds compared to option price paid. Thus, the executive may pay a 28% AMT at exercise and a 20% LTCG tax at sale on the same income, subject to the possibility that a complex AMT credit carryforward may be available to offset all or part of the 20% LTCG tax.

(4) To constitute an ISO, a number of requirements must be met, including

- Option price is at least 100% of stock FV at grant.
- Executive does not have more than $100,000 of ISOs vesting (i.e., first becoming exercisable) in any calendar year (measured by the FV of the option stock at the time of grant).
- Executive holds the stock for more than one year after option exercise (or, if longer, more than 2 years after option grant).
- Option does not state that it is not an ISO.
- Option is non-transferable (other than by executive's death) and does not last more than 10 years.
- Optionee is an employee of Oldco or a 50%-or-more parent or subsidiary corporation (measured by voting power).
- Option is granted pursuant to a plan which has Oldco shareholder approval and meets certain other requirements.

(5) While an ISO allows executive to save taxes (LTCG rate 18.6% lower than 2002 OI rate and no 1.45%/2.9% uncapped medicare tax), the desirability of ISOs is questionable because:

- Oldco obtains no tax deduction.
- Executive may be subject to AMT at option exercise.
- Executive must hold Oldco stock more than one year after exercise to obtain ISO tax benefits.

(6) The ISO rules apply only where Oldco is a corporation, not where Oldco is a partnership or LLC.

¶407.3   Accounting for Options, Stock Sales, and Stock Grants

Under GAAP rules, Oldco's accounting net income may be substantially reduced by the sale or award of Oldco stock or by the grant of options on Oldco stock to an executive. These GAAP rules generally apply (1) whether Oldco is a C corporation, S corporation, partnership, or LLC and (2) whether Oldco is a long-standing entity or a newly formed entity (e.g., Newco in Chapters 2 or 5).

APB 25. For many years prior to 10/95, the governing set of GAAP rules for such stock-based compensation emanated from APB Opinion 25 (published in 1972). APB 25 sharply distinguishes between non-variable (i.e., fixed) and variable compensation (as described in ¶407.3.1 and ¶407.3.2 below). Under APB 25 (which utilizes the so-called "intrinsic value approach"), the accounting charge for non-variable compensation turns on stock FV at the time of the stock sale or award or the option grant (generally charging accounting income for the excess (if any) of the stock's FV at sale or grant over the purchase or option price for the stock), while the accounting charge for variable compensation turns on stock FV at the time of vesting, exercise, or other specified event (generally charging accounting income for the stock's FV at time of vesting or other specified event over the purchase or option price for the stock). Thus, with variable compensation, where the FV of the stock increases from the time of the stock sale or award or the option grant to the time of vesting, the accounting charge increases, whereas with non-variable compensation the charge does not increase.

FASB 123. In 10/95, after several years of vigorous and heated debate, FASB Statement 123 was published, creating an elective set of alternative GAAP rules in lieu of APB 25. If Oldco elects FASB 123 (which utilizes the so-called "fair value approach"), the accounting charge in all cases (both variable and non-variable) is based on the stock's FV at the time of the stock sale or award or the option grant (as discussed in ¶407.3.3 below) *plus,* in the case of an option grant, the estimated FV of the option privilege at the time of the grant. Thus, electing FASB 123 rather than APB 25 increases the accounting charge for a non-variable option (by the estimated FV of the option privilege at grant date) but generally decreases the accounting charge for a variable stock-based arrangement.

Choosing between APB 25 and FASB 123. If Oldco elects to utilize FASB 123, it must account for all of its stock-based compensation under FASB 123 (as described in ¶407.3.3 below) and hence can not utilize APB 25 for any such compensation at any time thereafter.

If instead Oldco chooses to continue utilizing APB 25, Oldco must account for all of its stock-based compensation for employees under APB 25 (as described in ¶407.3.1 and ¶407.3.2 below), in which case (1) Oldco is required to disclose prominently in its financial statements as to the accounting effect if Oldco had instead adopted FASB 123, including pro forma net income under FASB 123 and pro forma earnings per share, and (2) Oldco has the choice at any time in the future to switch from APB 25 to FASB 123, in which case Oldco must thereafter account for all of its stock-based compensation under FASB 123.

In the past, most companies continued to account for their stock-based compensation arrangements using APB 25. However, as reaction to the corporate accounting scandals of the early 2000s reached crescendo in mid-2002, there was substantial pressure from Congress and the press to "expense" stock options, and during 2002 a number of large public companies announced plans to adopt FASB 123.

Possible future change. As of this writing, FASB appears ready to take up again the controversial issue of appropriate accounting for stock-based compensation, including whether to mandate the fair value approach of FASB 123. It is not clear when or whether such deliberations will result in changes to U.S. accounting rules for stock-based compensation. Past discussions of potential changes to stock-based compensation accounting were lengthy and controversial. However, there currently is additional political pressure for change arising out of the corporate accounting scandals of the early 2000s.

Two legislative proposals in 2002 would, if enacted, affect a company's choice between APB 25 and FASB 123. Senator McCain's proposed amendment to the Sarbanes-Oxley Act of 2002 would have required companies to expense stock options as granted. The amendment did not pass. A second proposal by Senators Levin and McCain would, if enacted, limit a company's income tax deduction upon exercise of a stock option to the amount of the company's GAAP compensation charge for such option.

An additional source of potential change is the Public Company Accounting Oversight Board, created by the Sarbanes-Oxley Act of 2002, which is empowered to create accounting standards that SEC may adopt for entities reporting under the federal securities laws.

The remainder of this ¶407.3 is organized as follows:

- ¶407.3.1 and ¶407.3.2 explain in more detail the GAAP rules applicable under APB 25 to a non-variable and a variable stock-based compensation.
- ¶407.3.3 explains in more detail the GAAP rules applicable under FASB 123 to any stock-based compensation (whether non-variable or variable).
- ¶407.3.4 through ¶407.3.9 explain a number of sub rules and nuances applicable to APB 25 and FASB 123.

¶407.3.1   APB 25 Rules for Non-variable Stock-Based Compensation

If Oldco chooses to utilize APB 25 (rather than FASB 123), it must account for non-variable (i.e., fixed) stock-based compensation (i.e., each stock-based compensatory arrangement in which both the number of shares to be received by the executive and the executive's purchase price are known at the date of the stock sale or award or the option grant) as follows:

(1) **Stock sale:** where Oldco sells stock to an executive, Oldco is treated as having compensation expense equal to the excess of the stock's FV (at the time of the sale) over the price paid by the executive for Oldco's stock (under the so-called "intrinsic value approach"), so that Oldco's accounting net income is reduced by this charge, *less* Oldco's expected tax savings, if any, from any tax deduction (up to the amount of accounting compensation expense) created by the stock sale.

(2) **Stock award:** where Oldco issues stock to an executive without consideration, Oldco is treated as having compensation expense equal to the stock's FV at the time of such award (under the intrinsic value approach), so that Oldco's accounting net income is reduced by this charge, *less* Oldco's expected tax savings from any tax deduction (up to the amount of accounting compensation expense) created by the stock award.

(3) **Stock option:** where Oldco grants an option to an executive, Oldco is treated as having compensation expense equal to the excess of the stock's FV (at the time the option is granted) over the option exercise price, whether the option is an ISO or an NQO (under the intrinsic value approach), whether the option is an ISO or an NQO for tax purposes, so that Oldco's accounting net income is reduced by this charge, *less* Oldco's expected tax savings from any tax deduction (up to the amount of accounting compensation expense) which will be created by the option exercise.

Where the stock purchase price (in (1) above) or the option exercise price (in (3) above) equals or exceeds the stock's FV on the stock purchase date or option grant date, there is no spread (i.e., no excess of stock FV at grant over purchase price or option exercise price) and hence under APB 25 Oldco has no compensation expense to reduce its accounting net income.

Under APB 25, the charge to Oldco's accounting net income (calculated on the intrinsic value approach as set forth in (1) through (3) above) is accrued (i.e., recognized for accounting purposes) "over the period(s) in which the related employee services are rendered . . . if the award is for future services . . . [which is generally] presumed to be the period from the grant date to the date the award is vested and its exercisability does not depend on continued employment service." Where there is a difference between the length of the executive's employment agreement and the length of the executive's vesting period for the stock-based compensation, APB 25 generally uses the vesting, rather than the employment, period.

If Oldco chooses to continue using APB 25 rather than switching to FASB 123, it must prominently disclose in its financial statements the accounting effect had Oldco instead adopted FASB 123 (calculated as described in ¶407.3.3 below).

Where Oldco grants an option, sells stock, or awards stock to an executive (a stock-based compensatory transaction) shortly before an IPO of Oldco's stock and the IPO offering price substantially exceeds the earlier price utilized in the stock-based compensatory transaction, SEC may (as a part of its review of Oldco's IPO filing) seek to increase Oldco's accounting charge for the earlier stock-based compensatory transaction. In 1998 and 1999 SEC became more aggressive in challenging such "cheap stock" transactions—seeking an explanation of the difference between the higher IPO price and the lower value utilized by Oldco in calculating the accounting charge for the earlier stock-based compensatory transaction. While SEC frequently challenges anything more than a trivial discount off the IPO price where the earlier stock-based compensatory transaction occurred within a year before the IPO, SEC has also sought justification for such pricing differences for stock-based compensatory transactions occurring as much as 9 years before the IPO.

APB 25 generally applies only to stock-based compensation to Oldco's employees and to Oldco's non-employee directors, not to independent contractors (other than directors). Hence stock-based compensation for Oldco's non-employee service providers (other than directors) is generally covered by FASB 123, regardless of whether Oldco uses APB 25 for employee stock-based compensation.

¶407.3.2   APB 25 Rules for Variable Stock-Based Compensation

If Oldco chooses to utilize APB 25 (rather than FASB 123) and the stock sold or awarded or the option granted to an executive is pursuant to a variable arrangement (i.e., an arrangement where the number of shares to be received by the executive or the executive's purchase price is not known at the outset), the accounting charge to Oldco's net income may be substantially increased (over the accounting charge described in ¶407.3.1 above for a non-variable arrangement).

A stock-based arrangement is variable if the stock or the option is subject to performance vesting (generally based on the achievement of one or more specified goals), because the accounting measurement date for determining Oldco's compensation expense is deferred until the performance goals are satisfied, so that the spread at the time of vesting is treated as compensation expense (under the so-called "intrinsic value approach") as further described in ¶407.3.4 below. Hence, where the FV of Oldco's stock rises between a stock sale or award or an option grant, on the one hand, and vesting on the other, Oldco's compensation expense increases.

By contrast, where the stock sold or awarded or the option granted to an executive is subject only to time vesting (based on continued employment for a specified period), the accounting measurement date generally is not postponed, so that the non-variable rules described in ¶407.3.1 above apply and only the spread at sale or grant is treated as compensation expense (again as further described in ¶407.3.4 below).[7]

However, other factors (including Oldco's payment of a tax-offset bonus to the executive or repricing of a previously granted option as described in ¶407.3.6 and ¶407.3.7 below), when added to a stock sale or award or an option grant, can cause the arrangement to be treated as variable, so that Oldco's compensation

---

[7] As also discussed in ¶407.3.4 below, many of the practical effects of performance vesting can be obtained while achieving the favorable accounting effects under APB 25 of time vesting by use of a TARSAP arrangement.

expense increases as the FV of Oldco's stock increases after the stock sale or award or the option grant.

Where a non-variable stock sale or award or option grant is subject to time vesting and Oldco subsequently grants the executive accelerated vesting, there is generally a new accounting measurement date with additional compensation expense, although the stock or option is not thereby rendered variable (as further described in ¶407.3.8 below).

If Oldco chooses to utilize APB 25 (rather than FASB 123), a stock appreciation right (an SAR)—under which an executive receives either in cash or in Oldco stock an amount equal to the spread between the FV of Oldco stock at the time the SAR is exercised and the base price established at grant—is also treated as variable compensation. Hence, Oldco recognizes compensation expense equal to the amount payable under the SAR, whether payable in cash or Oldco stock.

With any variable arrangement, the portion of Oldco's compensation expense attributable to the spread in the stock at the time of the sale, award, or grant must be accrued over the service/vesting period (as described in ¶407.3.1 above), and the amount of Oldco's compensation expense caused by post-sale, post-award, or post-grant changes in stock FV must be accrued quarterly as Oldco's stock fluctuates in value (as discussed in ¶407.3.9 below). Hence, (1) Oldco's accounting net income is reduced (over the service/vesting period) by the compensation charge, *less* Oldco's expected tax savings from any tax deduction (up to the amount of such accounting compensation expense), and (2) as Oldco's stock fluctuates in value, Oldco's accounting net income is reduced (where the stock increases in value) or increased (where the stock declines in value subsequent to an increase in value) each quarter by the compensation charge, as adjusted for changes in Oldco's expected tax savings from any tax deduction (up to the amount of accounting compensation expense) created by the variable arrangement.

If Oldco chooses to continue using APB 25 rather than switching to FASB 123, it must make footnote disclosure to its financial statements as to the accounting effect had Oldco instead adopted FASB 123 (calculated as described in ¶407.3.3 below).

¶407.3.3   Elective FASB 123 Rules for Non-variable and Variable Stock-Based Compensation

If Oldco elects to account for all of its stock-based compensation under FASB 123 rather than continuing under APB 25, Oldco has significantly greater accounting charges for some stock-based arrangements and significantly lower accounting charges for others (as compared to the results under APB 25).

For those electing out of APB 25 or otherwise unable to use APB 25 (e.g., nonemployee compensation), FASB 123 abolishes the sharp distinction (created by APB 25's intrinsic value approach) between non-variable and variable compensation (under which the accounting charge for non-variable compensation turns on stock FV at the time of the stock sale or award or the option grant, while the accounting charge for variable compensation turns on stock FV at the time of vesting). Rather, FASB 123 bases the accounting charge on the FV of the stock-based compensation at the date of a stock sale or award or option grant, including in the case of an option grant the FV of the option privilege (under the FV approach). Thereafter, compensation expense is *not* adjusted to reflect changes in the stock FV, whether or not the stock arrangement contains performance vesting, a tax-offset bonus, etc.

(1)   FV of stock sale or award. In the case of a stock sale or award, the amount of Oldco's compensation expense is equal to the FV of the stock on the sale or award date *less* the price paid by the executive and Oldco's expected tax saving from any tax deduction (up to the amount of accounting compensation expense) created by the stock sale or award,[8] so that Oldco's accounting net income is reduced by this amount.

Under FASB 123 neither a stock sale nor a stock award is an option, so that there is no option value to the executive because the executive is not deferring payment of the price. Hence, FASB 123 compensation expense for a stock sale or stock award is equal to the stock's spread at the sale or award date, regardless of whether there is performance vesting or a tax-offset bonus.

Where, however, stock is sold to an executive for a non-recourse note, the transaction is generally treated as the grant of an option, so that the FASB 123 accounting charge is increased by the value of the option privilege, although any nonrefundable interest the executive is required to pay on the non-recourse note reduces the value of the option privilege.

(2)   FV of stock option. In the case of an option, the amount of Oldco's compensation expense is equal to the FV of the option at the grant date, taking into account both (1) the spread (if any) at grant and (2) the value to an executive of being able to defer payment of the option price, i.e., the value of the option privilege, *less* Oldco's expected tax saving from any tax deduction (up to the amount of accounting compensation expense) created by the option grant and exercise,[9] so that Oldco's accounting net income is reduced by this amount.

FASB 123 states that Oldco must use an option-pricing model to estimate the FV of an option (for example, Black-Scholes or a binomial model) that takes into account the current price of the underlying stock, the exercise price, the expected option holding period (which FASB calls the "expected life") (i.e., not the stated term of the option but the shorter period Oldco expects the option actually to be outstanding before exercise or expiration, but which does not take account of any possibility of forfeiture), expected dividends on the stock, the stock's expected volatility, and the risk-free rate of return for the expected life of the option. The most commonly mentioned valuation technique, the Black-Scholes model, typically produces an option FV (for an option that is not significantly in the money at grant) equal to 20% to 40% of the option stock's grant date FV, depending

---

[8] The tax saving from any tax deduction in excess of the accounting expense is generally credited directly to net worth.

[9] The tax saving from any tax deduction in excess of the accounting expense is generally credited directly to net worth.

on such factors as the option's expected life and the price volatility of the underlying stock. The higher the stock's price volatility and the longer the expected life, the higher the value of the option, because of the higher probability for a large option gain.

Because a non-public company generally has no information on which to base an estimate of expected future volatility, a non-public company may estimate the value of its options using a method (the minimum-value method) that does not take into account expected volatility. For this purpose, a company is non-public if none of its equity securities (and none of its parent's equity securities) are traded on an exchange or over the counter (including local quotations).

See (3) below for a discussion of the possibility of using actual bid quotations to value an option under FASB 123.

With respect to an option that under APB 25 is *non-variable,* electing FASB 123 would result in a *higher* accounting charge than under APB 25 accounting rules. This is because the APB 25 accounting rules for a non-variable option create compensation expense only for the spread at grant, whereas FASB 123 creates compensation expense for the full option FV, taking into account not only the spread at grant but also the value to the option holder of being able to defer payment of the option price, i.e., the value of the option privilege. Moreover, because compensation expense is measured at the grant date under FASB 123, expense is recognized even if the stock price subsequently declines and the option expires unexercised.

With respect to an option that under APB 25 is *variable* (e.g., because of performance vesting), so that the APB 25 compensation charge is the spread at the time of vesting, FASB 123 results in a *lower* accounting charge, as compared to APB 25, where the FV of the stock increases significantly from grant date to vesting.

(3) Using bid quotations to value option under FASB 123. When Coca Cola Company in 7/02 announced adoption of FASB 123, it stated that:

> To determine the fair value of the stock options granted, the company intends to use quotations from independent financial institutions. The option value to be expensed will be based on the average of the firm quotations received from the financial institutions to buy or sell Coca Cola shares under the identical terms of the stock options granted.[10]

Coca Cola's plan thus attempts to determine the FASB 123 FV of stock options without resort to Black-Scholes or other option pricing formulas dependent on variables that can only be estimated, not directly observed, which are, in the view of some critics, open to inconsistent application from company to company.

Coca Cola's plan to expense stock options using independent price quotes raises a number of complex issues under FASB 123 and hence is likely to attract substantial attention.[11] It seems likely that such issues will be further addressed

---

[10] See Coca Cola Company press release 7/14/02.
[11] See Ginsburg and Levin M&A book, ¶1502.1.7.3(3) for a detailed discussion of these issues.

as FASB reconsiders U.S. accounting rules for stock-based compensation. See ¶407.3 Possible future change.

(4)   Vesting rules. Under FASB 123 (as under APB 25), the charge to Oldco's accounting net income (calculated under the FV approach as set forth above) is accrued (i.e., recognized for accounting purposes) over the executive's service/vesting period.

Moreover, under FASB 123 the charge is based on the number of options or shares that actually vest. Oldco can calculate this charge based on its best estimate as to the number of options or shares likely to vest, in which case Oldco would take additional compensation charges (or credits) in subsequent years as actual vesting experience results in fewer (or greater) forfeitures than originally expected (calculated based on the option value at time of grant or the stock value at time of sale or award). Alternatively, Oldco can calculate the front-end compensation charge on the assumption that all options or shares will vest, in which case Oldco would take into account compensation credits as options or shares are forfeited (again calculated based on the option value at time of grant or the stock value at time of sale or award).

If a vested option expires unexercised (e.g., because the option is out of the money), there is no downward adjustment in compensation expense.

(5)   SARs. Under FASB 123, an SAR which is payable in cash results in compensation expense equal to the cash payment (accrued as Oldco's stock rises in value), just as under APB 25. However, an SAR payable in Oldco stock is treated under FASB 123 similar to an option so that Oldco's only compensation expense is the FV of the SAR arrangement measured at the time of grant, i.e., the amount (if any) by which the SAR is in the money at grant plus the value of the option privilege determined under a Black-Scholes or similar formula (generally 20% to 40% of the stock's FV at grant where the option is at the money). By contrast, APB 25 treats an SAR payable in Oldco stock like an SAR payable in cash.

(6)   Choice between FASB 123 and APB 25. In the past, most companies (particularly those with non-variable arrangements) continued to account for their stock-based compensation arrangements using APB 25 (with footnote disclosure under FASB 123). However, as the corporate accounting scandals of the early 2000s reached crescendo in mid-2002, there was substantial pressure from Congress and the press to "expense" stock options, and during 2002, a significant number of companies announced plans to adopt FASB 123, including Coca Cola, General Motors, AT&T, General Electric, Bank One, P&G, AIG, Citigroup and Amazon.com.

If Oldco's stock-based compensation arrangements are predominantly variable (e.g., because of performance vesting), election of FASB 123 may well prove advantageous. This is because the compensation charge under APB 25 for a variable arrangement is the spread at the time of vesting, so that FASB 123 (which bases the accounting charge on the spread at grant plus, in the case of an option, the FV of the option privilege) would likely result in a lower accounting charge where the FV of Oldco's stock increases significantly from grant date to vesting. Unfortunately Oldco can not adopt FASB 123 piecemeal (i.e., Oldco can not adopt FASB 123 for its performance vesting arrangements but retain APB 25 for its non-variable arrangements), and once having adopted FASB 123 Oldco can not subsequently switch back to APB 25.

See ¶407.3 (Possible future change) for discussion of two legislative proposals that would, if enacted, affect Oldco's APB 25-FASB 123 choice.

¶407.3.4 APB 25 Rules for Vesting and TARSAP

Under APB 25 (described in ¶407.3.1 and ¶407.3.2 above), a number of factors affect whether stock-based compensation is variable or non-variable and how the compensation charge is accrued.

(1) When Oldco sells or awards stock to an executive or grants an option to an executive *and* on the sale/award/grant date the purchase price, option price and the number of shares are fixed (not variable), the arrangement can generally qualify as non-variable and hence receive the more favorable accounting treatment described in ¶407.3.1 above rather than the less favorable treatment described in ¶407.3.2 above.

(2) The rule set forth in (1) applies even where the arrangement vests over a series of years based on the executive's continued employment, i.e., the arrangement is treated as non-variable where it is subject to vesting based only on the executive's continued rendition of services for a specified period.

(3) However, if vesting of the arrangement is based on specified performance goals (e.g., Oldco achieving specified earnings levels, stock values, or other goals), the arrangement is treated as variable and hence there will be a charge to Oldco's accounting net income equal to the spread in the stock at the time the arrangement vests (i.e., the stock's FV at vesting less the purchase/exercise price) reduced by Oldco's tax savings from the stock transaction, i.e., the accounting "measurement date" is deferred until satisfaction of the performance goals (as described in ¶407.3.2 above).

(4) If the arrangement is variable so that the accounting measurement date is postponed, the charge to Oldco's accounting net income must generally be accrued by Oldco periodically (e.g., quarterly) as the FV of Oldco's stock fluctuates.

(5) Oldco may be able to obtain the favorable time vesting/non-variable accounting treatment (described in (1) and (2) above), while at the same time obtaining some of the practical effects of performance vesting (described in (3) above) by using a "time accelerated restricted stock award plan" or TARSAP approach. Under a TARSAP arrangement, the arrangement will vest if the executive is in Oldco's employ (i.e., is still rendering services to Oldco) on a specified future date, i.e., solely a time-vesting standard. However, if Oldco meets specified performance goals while the executive is still in Oldco's employ, the vesting date will be accelerated.

SEC staff has expressed concern over use of a TARSAP arrangement to disguise what is in substance a performance plan and has indicated that (1) the time vesting period for a TARSAP arrangement can not *significantly* exceed the time vesting period in Oldco's other stock based arrangements (and can in no event exceed 10 years), i.e., if Oldco's regular stock based arrangements have 5-year vesting, TARSAP time vesting can not significantly exceed 5 years (subject to acceleration if performance goals are achieved) and (2) to qualify for the TARSAP rule, time vesting must be "more likely than not" even if the performance goals are not achieved.

(6) The rules (set forth in (1) through (5) above) apply whether Oldco grants an option to an executive subject to vesting or Oldco sells stock to an executive subject to vesting or Oldco awards stock to an executive (i.e., the executive's purchase price for the stock is zero) subject to vesting. Hence, for example, if Oldco sells stock to an executive subject to performance vesting (so that Oldco has the right to repurchase the stock if performance targets are not met), Oldco's accounting charge is measured as described in (3) and (4) above (generally based on the stock's FV at vesting), unless the TARSAP rules described in (5) above are satisfied.

¶407.3.5 APB 25 Rules for Paying Stock Purchase Price or Option Exercise Price by Note

Where an executive uses a note, rather than exclusively cash, as part or all of the consideration to purchase Oldco stock or to exercise an Oldco stock option, a number of additional complex APB 25 rules (which frequently reach results inconsistent with economic reality) come into play as described in (1) through (4) below. These rules in application often arbitrarily fail to take into account important economic differences with respect to the executive's form of payment for the stock-based compensation (cash, non-recourse note, non-recourse note with recourse interest, or recourse note).

For example, as described in (1)(b) below, an executive who pays for Oldco stock with an interest-free non-recourse note is deemed to have paid the same amount for APB 25 purposes as a second executive who buys the same Oldco stock with a non-recourse note bearing recourse interest, even though the first executive receives a significantly more attractive economic deal. Similarly, APB 25 takes below-market-interest-rate features into account for *recourse* loans used to purchase stock or to exercise options (creating variable accounting or other compensation charges) but generally does not take below-market-interest-rate features into account on *non-recourse* notes used to purchase stock or exercise options, although the below-market-interest-rate feature generates for the purchaser an equivalent economic benefit in each case. Compare (1) and (2) below with (3) and (4) below.

These inconsistencies between APB 25 accounting and economics are largely attributable to three features of APB 25 accounting: (1) under APB 25 a non-recourse note used to purchase stock or to exercise an option is generally treated as an option, not a purchase and loan, (2) APB 25 non-variable accounting (in contrast to FASB 123) has never taken into account option value beyond the current spread (i.e., APB 25 ignores the value of owning a share of future appreciation without risking current capital) in measuring compensation expense, and (3) APB 25 accounting views non-recourse interest as part of the stock purchase price but recourse interest as not part of the stock purchase price.

As described more fully below, the accounting consequences of paying for a stock purchase or option exercise with a note turn, in part, on whether the note is recourse or non-recourse. EITF has stated that "the legal form of a recourse note arrangement should be respected . . . unless:"

(i)   the employer "does not intend to seek repayment beyond the shares issued,"

(ii)   the "employer has a history of not demanding repayment of loan amounts in excess of the fair value of shares,"

(iii) the "employee does not have sufficient assets or other means (beyond the shares) to justify the recourse nature of the loan," or

(iv)   the employer has in the past (even if on only one occasion) accepted a recourse note to purchase shares and subsequently converted the note into a non-recourse note.

If any of these four factors is present, the loan is to be treated as non-recourse.

As noted in (iv) above, if Oldco forgives all or part of a recourse note or converts a recourse note into a non-recourse note, on even one occasion, EITF applies a one-strike-and-you're-out approach, (a) treating as non-recourse all recourse notes subsequently given by executives to Oldco in payment for stock or the exercise price of an option and (b) treating each recourse note previously given by executives in payment for stock or the exercise price of an option as if it were converted into a non-recourse note. See ¶407.3.5(5) for a discussion of the consequences to Oldco of converting (or being deemed to convert) a recourse note originally given in connection with an executive's purchase of stock or exercise of an option into a non-recourse note. SEC advances a potentially different view, stating that all facts and circumstances must be considered and noting that if a note is ultimately forgiven, SEC will generally "challenge whether the conclusion that the note was recourse was appropriate."[12]

As discussed in more detail in ¶501.5.4.2, Sarbanes-Oxley Act of 2002 ("SO") §402 generally prohibits a company with publicly issued or publicly traded securities (an "issuer" as defined by SO) from extending or maintaining credit or arranging for the extension of credit in the form of a personal loan to or for any director or executive officer. Absent a favorable, and unlikely, SEC interpretation, an executive officer's (or director's) note to such a company as the consideration (or as part of the consideration) for such executive's purchase of the company's stock (either an outright purchase or upon a stock option exercise) likely constitutes such a prohibited extension of credit in the form of a personal loan.

---

[12] See EITF 00-23, ¶151. Although EITF and SEC statements in EITF 00-23 technically refer to whether a note issued in connection with a stock option exercise is considered recourse or non-recourse, the standard should be the same for a note issued in a stock purchase without an option.

Discussion in this ¶407.3.5 regarding accounting treatment where an Oldco executive pays for his or her stock purchase from Oldco with a note assumes that either Oldco is not an "issuer" covered by SO §402 or the executive is not an Oldco executive officer or director covered by SO §402, so that paying for the stock with a note is permissible.

(1) Stock purchase using non-recourse note. Where an executive purchases Oldco stock in exchange solely for a non-recourse note secured only by the purchased stock, accountants generally take the position that the purchase is, in substance, the issuance of a stock option.[13]

(a) Where interest on the note is non-recourse to the executive (as is typically the case with a non-recourse note), accountants treat the interest as part of the purchase price for the stock, in which case accountants further take the position that the award is subject to variable accounting (on the ground that the purchase price is not fixed) where the total amount of interest payable under the note may vary because (1) the note is prepayable at the executive's option, or (2) the note is mandatorily prepayable upon the occurrence of specified events (e.g., Oldco sale or IPO), or (3) the note bears a floating interest rate.[14]

(b) Fixed, rather than variable, accounting applies, however, notwithstanding the rule set forth in (a), if the award would otherwise qualify as a fixed award apart from the note terms and:

- the interest on the note (although not the principal) is a recourse obligation of the executive (because accountants generally do not treat interest which is a recourse obligation as part of the stock purchase price, so that in such case the stock purchase price for accounting purposes is a fixed amount, i.e., the note principal), or
- the interest rate on the note is fixed and the note is not prepayable under any circumstances (so that the total amount of interest payable under the note, and hence in such case the stock purchase price for accounting purposes, is a fixed amount),[15] or
- the note does not bear any stated interest (so that the stock purchase price for accounting purposes is a fixed amount, i.e., the note principal).[16]

---

[13] See ¶202.2.3 for a discussion of the risk IRS will treat the purchase of Oldco stock in exchange for a non-recourse loan secured only by the purchased stock as an option for income tax purposes.

[14] EITF 95-16, entitled Accounting for Stock Compensation Arrangements with Employer Loan Features under APB Opinion No. 25.

[15] In some states a clause prohibiting prepayment of the executive's note may be unenforceable. To the extent that the executive's note is governed by the law of such a state, this technique would probably not avoid variable accounting.

[16] If the note does not bear adequate interest but the note is respected for tax purpose (i.e., the transaction is not recharacterized as the mere issuance of a stock option), the tax rules set forth in ¶202.2.4 would apply, causing the executive to be treated for tax purposes as buying the stock for a lower price than the face amount of the note, with the difference treated for tax purposes as additional interest (technically OID), potentially deductible by the executive and includable in income by Oldco. The lower purchase price for tax purposes would also increase the income recognized by the executive under Code §83 and the correlative deduction allowed to Oldco. These tax rules should not affect the accounting conclusions set forth in text above.

With a non-recourse (principal and interest) note, even where the interest rate is below market, there is apparently no APB 25 charge for the below market element (as there is with a recourse note—see (3) and (4) below) because accountants view a stock purchase solely for a non-recourse note as an option.

(c) If the note is non-recourse but principal and interest are fully secured by property owned by the executive (other than Oldco stock and, in the view of at least some accountants, by property other than Oldco securities of any kind), the note should generally be treated the same as a recourse note and should not result in variable accounting if the stock purchase otherwise qualifies as a fixed award. See (3) below dealing with stock purchase with recourse note.

(d) If the note is partially recourse or there are other features (such as a cash down payment on the purchase price for the Oldco stock securing the non-recourse note or additional property owned by the executive pledged as security for the non-recourse note—including in the view of some accountants other Oldco securities owned by the executive) so that the executive has substantial amounts at risk with respect to the purchased stock, the proper accounting was not clear (unless the note had one or more of the features described in (b) or (c) above so that fixed accounting clearly applied):

- Some accountants took the position—unreasonably harsh in our view—that the entire stock purchase was subject to variable accounting if any portion (however small) of the purchase price was paid with a non-recourse note or a partially non-recourse note.
- Other accountants bifurcated the stock purchase into two pieces, based on the amount the executive had at risk with respect to the purchase, so that only a portion of the stock was treated as purchased with a non-recourse note and hence potentially subject to variable accounting.
- Other accountants took the position that no part of the stock purchase was subject to variable accounting on the ground that the substantial amounts the executive had at risk made the transaction similar in substance to a purchase with a recourse note, although some accountants may take this position only with respect to a privately held company.

In 7/01, EITF adopted the harshest view. EITF 00-23 takes the position that a part-recourse/part-non-recourse note is treated as *entirely* non-recourse, "regardless of the relative percentages of . . . recourse and non-recourse," where the non-recourse portion gives Oldco a claim on all of the Oldco shares purchased (as is typical in order to avoid unfavorable income tax results) rather than merely a pro rata portion.[17] We believe EITF's position is irrational and ignores the economic substance of part-recourse/part-non-recourse financing.

(2) Option exercise using non-recourse note. Where an executive exercises a stock option and pays the exercise price solely with a non-recourse note, accountants generally treat Oldco as issuing a new stock option to the executive—

---

[17] EITF 00-23, ¶154. Although this portion of EITF 00-23 explicitly addresses notes issued in connection with a stock option exercise, the standard should be the same for notes issued in a stock purchase without an option.

triggering a new measurement date for APB 25 purposes—unless the non-recourse note is viewed as part of the original option because (i) the terms of the original option permitted exercise with a non-recourse note or (ii) the non-recourse note is due not later than the expiration of the original option so that the non-recourse note is not viewed as extending the term of the original option.[18]

(a) Where the original option terms permit exercise of the option for *either* cash or a non-recourse note with non-recourse interest (i.e., so that the interest is considered part of the option price under the rules described in (1)(a) above), the option is considered variable (even if the note is not prepayable) because it is not known until exercise whether the executive will pay with cash or with a non-recourse note reflecting a higher price from an accounting point of view (because the non-recourse interest is treated as part of the exercise price).[19] On the other hand, if the note either does not bear interest or bears recourse interest, fixed accounting applies because the option price (determined under the rules described in (1)(b) above) is the same, whether the executive pays cash or exercises the option using the note.

(b) Where the original option terms permit exercise of the option only for a non-recourse note (i.e., the option cannot be exercised for cash), the option is subject to variable accounting for the reasons set forth in (1)(a) above, unless the non-recourse note has one or more of the features described in (1)(b) above.

(c) Where the original option terms do not permit exercise of the option for a non-recourse note, but Oldco allows executive to exercise the option for a non-recourse note, the option is subject to variable accounting for the reasons set forth in (1)(a) above, unless the non-recourse note has one or more of the features described in (1)(b) above (except as set forth in (d) below). Even if variable accounting does not result, a new measurement date is required where the note term extends beyond the option term.

(d) Where the original option terms do not permit exercise for a non-recourse note, but Oldco allows executive to exercise the option for a non-prepayable non-recourse note bearing fixed-rate non-recourse interest, exercise of the option for the note is viewed as an increase in the option exercise price. This is because exercise of the option for the non-recourse note is viewed as either continuing the original option (where the note term does not extend beyond the original option term) or issuing a new option (where the note term extends beyond the original option term) and, in either case, non-recourse interest is part of, and hence an increase to, the option exercise price as described in (1)(a) above. Thus, under EITF 00-23 a new measurement date results and, in addition, the option is forever variable unless facts and circumstances indicate that "future changes to the exercise price . . . will not occur."[20]

Moreover, the original option is apparently considered canceled for purposes of Interpretation 44 and hence can be matched with a new option issuance at a price below the original option price (generally within 6 months before or after

[18] EITF 95-16.
[19] EITF 95-16.
[20] EITF 95-16 and EITF 00-23.

the deemed cancellation) to create an indirect option price reduction, triggering variable accounting. See ¶407.3.7(1).

(e) Where use of a non-recourse note with a below-market interest rate does not cause variable accounting under the rules described in this (2)(a)-(d), there is apparently no APB 25 charge for any below-market element (as there is with a recourse note—see (3) and (4) below) because accountants view option exercise for a non-recourse note as either continuing the original option or as issuing a new option.

(f) Where the non-recourse note's principal and/or interest is secured as described in (1)(c), the principal and/or interest is regarded as recourse for purposes of applying the rules set forth in (2)(a)-(d) and (3). Where the note is partial recourse and partial non-recourse, the conflicting interpretations described in (1)(d) apply. EITF 00-23 takes the position that a part-recourse/part-non-recourse note is treated as *entirely* non-recourse, "regardless of the relative percentages of the recourse and non-recourse," where the non-recourse portion gives Oldco a claim on all of the Oldco shares purchased (as is typical for income tax reasons) rather than merely a pro rata portion. As noted in (1)(d) above, we believe this approach ignores the economic substance of part-recourse/part-non-recourse financings.

(3)   Stock purchase using recourse note. Purchase of stock with a full recourse note should not result in variable accounting if the award otherwise qualifies as a fixed award. However, where an executive purchases stock using a recourse note with a face amount equal to the Oldco stock's FV, but bearing interest at a below-market rate, it is likely that accountants will require a compensation charge based on the reasoning of EITF 00-23, with the charge calculated to reflect the present value of the below-market interest rate advantage.

(4)   Option exercise by recourse note. Under EITF 00-23, a stock option that permits exercise of the option with a recourse note bearing interest that may not represent a market rate on the *date of exercise* is subject to variable accounting. The EITF treats the exercise price as variable until option exercise because it is not known until exercise whether the executive will pay the exercise price in cash or with a note the FV of which may be less than the option's stated exercise price due to an interest rate which is below market at time of exercise.

Under EITF 00-23, a stock option that permits exercise with a recourse note bearing interest at a fixed rate specified at grant (even if such interest rate is a market rate at grant) is apparently subject to variable accounting because the interest rate may be below market rate at exercise. On the other hand, if the option allows exercise with a recourse note bearing interest at a market rate to be established *at exercise*, the option is accounted for as fixed (assuming the option otherwise meets the test for a fixed award).

Determining a market interest rate for this purpose apparently requires difficult judgements. EITF 00-23 states that "a statutory rate such as the IRS Applicable Federal Rate does not necessarily represent a market rate" and a market rate "at the date of exercise should consider the credit standing of the [executive] and be determined such that the [executive] would be indifferent as to whether a loan for the exercise price is obtained from [Oldco] or from another unrelated lender."

If a stock option is modified after grant to allow exercise with a recourse note bearing (or which may bear, at exercise) interest at less than a market rate, the modification is generally a repricing which triggers variable accounting.

(5) Stock purchase or option exercise with recourse note followed by conversion to non-recourse note. Where an executive purchases stock or exercises an option with a note qualifying as recourse for accounting purposes and Oldco later converts the recourse note into a non-recourse note (or, as discussed below, Oldco is deemed to convert the recourse note into a non-recourse note), EITF 00-23 views Oldco as repurchasing the original stock and simultaneously issuing a stock option to the executive in the form of new stock purchased by the executive with a non-recourse note.[21]

Oldco is viewed as repurchasing the original stock for an amount equal to the sum of (a) the principal balance of the recourse note, (b) any accrued interest on the recourse note, plus (c) the spread in the new stock option (i.e., the excess of the new stock's FV over the amount of the non-recourse note) at the time the note is converted (or deemed converted) from recourse to non-recourse.

Stock held at least 6 months at conversion. If the conversion from recourse to non-recourse occurs at least 6 months after the executive purchased the stock or exercised the option (so that the executive has held the shares for at least 6 months), Oldco's repurchase of stock is considered independent of the executive's original purchase or exercise. Oldco recognizes compensation expense if the repurchase price (as defined above) exceeds the original stock's FV at the time of conversion (i.e., where the stock has declined in FV or failed to rise in FV by the amount of the accrued interest, assuming the executive originally gave a recourse note for the stock's full purchase price and thereafter made no principal payment thereon). Thus, assuming that the amount of the new non-recourse note equals the amount of the old recourse note (including accrued interest), Oldco recognizes compensation expense equal to the excess, if any, of the recourse note (including accrued interest) over the original stock's FV at conversion.

Stock held less than 6 months at conversion. If the conversion from recourse to non-recourse occurs less than 6 months after the executive purchased the stock or exercised the option, the original shares deemed repurchased are considered "immature" and the repurchase transaction is generally integrated with the original purchase or exercise. Oldco generally recognizes compensation income equal to the excess, if any, of the purchase price (as defined above) over the sum of (a) the original cost of the stock and (b) the lesser of the spread in the arrangement measured at original grant or measured at conversion (using the original cost of the stock). However, if the purchase price (as defined above) exceeds the stock's

---

[21] Accountants generally treat an executive's acquisition of stock for a non-recourse note as equivalent to the grant of a stock option. See ¶¶407.3.5 and 407.3.5(1).

FV at conversion, Oldco's compensation expense cannot be less than the excess of the purchase price over such FV.

As a simple illustration, assume that the executive gave a recourse note for the stock's full purchase price and thereafter made no principal payments. If the stock's FV at conversion exceeds the amount of the recourse note (including accrued interest) and the new non-recourse note equals the amount of the old recourse note (including accrued interest), Oldco recognizes compensation expense equal to the excess of the stock's FV at conversion over the amount of the executive's original purchase price for such stock (reduced by any compensation recognized by Oldco on the original purchase or option grant). If the amount of the recourse loan (including accrued interest) exceeds the FV of the stock at conversion, Oldco recognizes compensation income equal to the excess of the old recourse note (including accrued interest) over the lesser of (a) the stock's original cost or (b) its FV at conversion.

New option. In either case, the new stock option deemed issued has an exercise price equal to the amount of the non-recourse note. Thus, unless the non-recourse note meets one of the tests outlined in ¶407.3.5(1) and (2) above, the new option is subject to variable accounting (because non-recourse interest on the note is treated as part of the option exercise price, making the option exercise price uncertain).

Effect on other notes. Once Oldco has converted a recourse note into a non-recourse note (on even one occasion), accountants treat as non-recourse all recourse notes subsequently given by executives to Oldco in payment for stock or the exercise price of an option. In addition, if Oldco holds other previously issued recourse notes which have not actually been forgiven or converted, EITF treats each such note as if it were deemed converted into a non-recourse note. See ¶407.3.5(1).

¶407.3.6   APB 25 Rules for Tax-Offset or Other Cash Bonus

(1) FASB Interpretation No. 44, issued 3/31/00, states that "[a] cash bonus and a stock option award shall be accounted for as a combined award if payment . . . of the cash bonus is contingent on the exercise of the option."[22] Where a cash bonus is contingent on exercise of the option and is not fixed in amount (e.g., a tax-offset cash bonus as discussed in (3) and (4) below), the bonus is viewed as causing the exercise price to be variable so that the option is subject to APB 25 variable accounting.

(2) Where a fixed-amount cash bonus (established at the time the option is granted) is contingent on option exercise, the cash bonus is treated as reducing the stated option exercise price (potentially producing additional compensation

---

[22] Thus, a cash bonus contingent on the vesting of a stock option, rather than its exercise, would not be linked to the stock option for accounting purposes.

at grant of the option), but such bonus does not, by itself, cause variable accounting. However where a cash bonus feature contingent on option exercise is added after the option was granted, such bonus would generally constitute a repricing of the option, triggering variable accounting.

Under EITF 00-23, a cash bonus not contingent on option exercise is not combined with the option award and is instead treated as a separate compensation item. Thus, for example, a cash bonus to be paid only if a stock option (a) vests *and* (b) is in-the-money at vesting is not integrated with the stock option. On the other hand, a cash bonus contingent on sale of stock received on option exercise is integrated with the option and tested as a combined award because the cash bonus is effectively subject to two conditions, one of which is option exercise and the other of which is subsequent sale of the stock.

(3) As discussed in ¶407.1 above, upon exercise of an NQO, an executive recognizes OI equal to the spread (i.e., equal to the stock's FV at exercise less the option exercise price). Thus, the option agreement, or a separate agreement between Oldco and the executive, may call for Oldco to pay the executive a cash bonus upon exercise equal to the OI tax on the spread (plus the OI tax on the cash bonus) *or* the option agreement may call for Oldco to pay the executive a smaller bonus equal to the withholding tax on the spread (plus the withholding tax on the bonus). Such a tax-offset cash bonus is combined with the option award and (because the amount is uncertain at grant) subjects the option to APB 25 variable accounting, so that there is a reduction in Oldco's accounting net income equal to (a) the spread in the stock at exercise *plus* (b) the bonus payment *less* (c) Oldco's tax savings from the stock sale and bonus. This can produce a very substantial reduction in Oldco's accounting net income.

(4) If there is never any tax-offset bonus agreement at all, but Oldco simply pays the executive a voluntary, discretionary bonus at or shortly after the executive exercises the option, and such bonus is not pursuant to any prior oral understanding that the executive would receive a tax-offset bonus (i.e., until the option exercise there was no understanding that the executive would receive a tax-offset bonus), it is not clear whether accountants would link the voluntary post-option-exercise bonus with the earlier option to create a variable price option, although the case for such linking is certainly stronger where the bonus amount correlates with the amount of the executive's income tax triggered by the option exercise.

(5) There is no APB 25 adverse accounting effect if Oldco agrees to make a normal recourse loan to the executive to cover withholding, income taxes, or option exercise price, although accountants may seek some assurance from Oldco that it actually plans to enforce the note.

¶407.3.7   APB 25 Rules for Option Repricing, Rescissions and Other Modifications

(1)   APB 25 repricing rule. Where Oldco grants an executive an option qualifying as non-variable for APB 25 purposes, but the trading price for Oldco's stock thereafter declines, Oldco may reprice the option, i.e., reduce the option exercise price to the new lower trading value. Or alternatively Oldco may cancel the original option and grant the executive a new option at the new lower trading value.

The pre-2000 APB 25 accounting rules did not contain a special rule dealing with such option repricing, so that an option qualifying as a non-variable option at grant could continue as a non-variable option for APB 25 purposes after repricing. Thus, if the original non-variable option had an exercise price equal to the Oldco stock's FV at grant and the repriced option has an exercise price equal to the Oldco stock's lower FV at time of repricing, Oldco would generally not record a compensation charge on either the original grant of the option or its repricing.

Under FASB Interpretation No. 44, issued 3/31/00, "[i]f the exercise price of a fixed stock option is reduced, the award shall be accounted for as variable from the date of the modification." The exercise price of an option is considered reduced if "the fair value of the consideration required to be remitted by the grantee upon exercise is less than or potentially less than the fair value of the consideration that was required to be remitted pursuant to the award's original terms." Variable accounting is required even if the reduction is contingent on the occurrence of a future event—whether or not the future event ever occurs.

Variable accounting is also required (even where the stated terms of the option remain unchanged) if Oldco "indirectly" reduces the option exercise price, e.g., where:

- Oldco grants the executive a cash bonus payable only if the option is exercised or the underlying stock is sold.
- Oldco allows the executive to pay the option exercise price with a recourse note bearing below-market interest.
- Oldco cancels (or settles for cash or other consideration) the original option and grants a new option to the same executive at a lower price, either before or after the cancellation (settlement). Cancellation or settlement of an original option is combined with issuance of new option at a lower price to create an indirect option price reduction where the new option is issued within 6 months before or 6 months after cancellation/settlement of the original option, which time period is extended where there is agreement between Oldco and executive to compensate the executive for increases in Oldco's market price after a cancellation/settlement.
- Oldco grants the executive a new option at a lower price than the original option and the new option expires 30 days after Oldco's stock price increases to the exercise price of the original option, in which case variable accounting applies to both the original option and the new option from the grant date of the new option until exercise, forfeiture, or expiration of the old option, on the ground that "the new award, through its cancellation provisions, provides an indication of direct linkage to a previously granted out-of-the-money award. . . . [so that] economically, the impact of the above-described sequence of actions is initially similar to a direct reduction to the exercise price of the previously granted [original] stock options." FASB's conclusion that a repricing has occurred seems far from compelling, since the executive is entitled to retain the original option with its terms unchanged. However,

according to FASB, if the new option remains exercisable for at least six months (rather than 30 days) after Oldco's stock price increases to the exercise price of the original option, the new option would be "uncoupled" from the old option and there would be no indirect repricing.

Where Oldco (and the executive) (1) cancel an outstanding option and (2) agree that Oldco will issue the executive a new option more than 6 months later at an exercise price equal to the FV of Oldco stock on the reissuance date, the cancellation and reissuance do not result in an indirect repricing, rather the replacement option is "decoupled" from the cancelled option, so long as Oldco has not otherwise agreed to compensate the executive for any increase in the FV of Oldco stock.

EITF 00-23 states that "grant of an in-the-money option award subsequent to a cancellation of a previous option award creates a presumption that an agreement or implied promise existed to compensate the grantee for increases in the market value of the stock after the cancellation date (even if the market price of the stock has not increased) and, therefore, results in variable accounting for the new award. This presumption may be overcome if the relevant facts and circumstances clearly indicate that the in-the-money option is not related to the prior cancellation."

FASB refused to enunciate a general rule identifying all transactions treated as indirect option repricings, because "it is not practical to address every potential set of facts or sequence of actions that could cause an effective reduction to the exercise price of a stock option award."

Under EITF 00-23, Oldco's mere offer to reduce the exercise price of an option or enter into an exchange of options having the effect of a repricing apparently causes variable accounting for all options eligible for the offer, even options held by executives who do not accept the offer.

A modification that increases the option price results in either a new measurement date or variable accounting under EITF 00-23. In addition, under the interpretation, the increase is treated as a cancellation of the original option that may be matched with another option issuance at a lower price than the original option (generally within 6 months before or after the deemed cancellation) to create an indirect option price reduction, triggering variable accounting. Any other modification of an option's terms making it less likely to be exercised is also treated as a cancellation for this purpose.

Under EITF 00-23, "a modification that increases the exercise price or reduces the number of shares under a fixed stock option award should always result in an accounting consequence." If facts and circumstances indicate that "future changes to the exercise price and or number of shares will not occur . . . the award continues to be fixed after the modification . . . [and] the accounting consequence of the modification would be only a new measurement date. In other situations, the nature of the modification and the reasons for it may indicate that there is no practical way to ascertain whether the price is fixed or whether further modifications will occur in the future. In those cases, variable accounting is required for the modified award."

Where Oldco settles or replaces a fixed stock option with a stock award (rather than an option), a new measurement date is required. However, variable accounting does not apply to the new replacement stock award, on the ground that the exercise price of the original option has been reduced to zero and no further reductions to the exercise price are possible.

FASB is silent on whether repricing a stock sale (as opposed to an option grant) originally accounted for as an APB 25 non-variable transaction might cause the repriced sale to be accounted for as an APB 25 variable transaction, e.g., when Oldco sold stock to an executive, the stock FV declined, and Oldco then reduced the original purchase price by refunding a portion of the cash paid by the executive for the stock or canceling a portion of a note given by the executive for the stock.

EITF 00-23 notes that a stock award (i.e., a grant of stock where the employee pays no purchase price) "could be considered to be an option with a zero exercise price." Thus, where Oldco exchanges new stock options for a previously issued, but unvested, stock award, EITF 00-23 states that the exchange is treated as an "upward repricing" of the stock award, resulting either in a new measurement date or variable accounting under the rules described above for modifications that increase the exercise price of a stock option. While not addressed by EITF 00-23, this position suggests that a similar approach would be taken for repricing an unvested stock purchase.

(2) APB 25 extension or renewal rule. APB 25 states that a measurement date (but not full variable treatment) is required if a fixed stock option or purchase right is renewed or extended.

FASB Interpretation No. 44 states that where the terms of an option, purchase, or award are modified to extend the time period beyond the original maximum time period, including a modification contingent on a future separation from service, the modification triggers a new measurement date at the time of the modification. However, if the modification extends the time period, contingent on a future separation from service, but not in excess of the original maximum time period, a new measurement date is triggered at the modification, but additional compensation expense attributable to the new measurement date is ultimately taken into account only if the separation event actually occurs and extends the time period.

A modification that decreases the life of an option does not, by itself, cause variable accounting. However, under the interpretation, the decrease in life is considered a cancellation of the original option that may be matched with another option issuance at a lower price than the original option (generally within 6 months before or after the deemed cancellation) to create an indirect option price reduction, triggering variable accounting.

For a modification that accelerates vesting for a stock option or award, see ¶407.3.8.

(3) APB 25 change in number of shares rule. FASB Interpretation No. 44 states that where Oldco "increases the number of shares to be issued under a fixed stock option award, the award shall be accounted for as variable from the date of the modification." Similarly, a fixed stock option is treated as variable from the date of modification if it is modified to grant the executive a new option conditioned on exercise of the old option (a "reload feature").

Oldco's mere offer to increase the number of shares issuable under an option will apparently cause variable accounting for all options eligible for the offer, even options held by executives who do not accept the offer.

The interpretation does not generally address the consequences of a decrease to the number of shares issuable under an option, unless the decrease is combined with a grant of a new option that is in substance a repricing of the original option. Under EITF 00-23, a modification that decreases the number of shares issuable under an option results in either a new measurement date or variable accounting. See the discussion in (1) above of modifications that increase the exercise price of an option.

(4) APB 25 equity restructuring rule. Adjustments to an option's exercise price, number of shares, or both may be made as a result of a stock dividend, spin-off, stock split, rights offering, recapitalization through a large non-recurring dividend, or similar transaction (an "equity restructuring transaction" in accounting parlance) without triggering variable accounting or a new measurement date if:

- the aggregate spread (i.e., the difference between the option exercise price and the FV of the underlying stock) in the option is not increased, and
- the ratio of the exercise price per share to the stock FV per share is not reduced.

(5) APB 25 rules for other modifications. FASB Interpretation No. 44 states that "[a] modification to a fixed stock option or award that does not affect the life of the award, the exercise price, or the number of shares to be issued has no accounting consequence."

For a modification which accelerates vesting for a stock option or award, see ¶407.3.8.

(6) APB 25 rules for stock option rescission. Where stock prices fall sharply after an executive exercises an Oldco stock option, the executive may end up holding Oldco stock worth less than the taxes triggered by option exercise. In such case, the executive may wish to "unexercise" the option.

For income tax purposes, if executive and Oldco "unexercise" the option not later than end of the taxable year in which the option is exercised, executive and Oldco should be treated as if the option had never been exercised, eliminating executive's OI recognized on exercise (and Oldco's corresponding compensation deduction).[23]

SEC announced in 1/01 that it would require variable accounting in situations where Oldco allows an executive to unexercise or rescind the prior exercise of a stock option.[24] SEC treats the rescission as involving two elements: (1) repurchase

---

[23] Where Newco and executive use different taxable years, it is not entirely clear whether the rescission must occur before the end of the taxable year for *both* executive and Newco in order to be given tax effect.

[24] SEC Staff Announcement, Accounting for the Rescission of the Exercise of Employee Stock Options (2001).

of the previously issued stock and (2) issuance of a new option subject to variable accounting. According to SEC, Oldco is required to recognize, on the rescission date, compensation expense equal to (a) the cash paid to the executive, *plus* (b) the positive spread in the new options deemed issued, *plus* (c) the tax benefits lost by Oldco,[25] *less* (d) the FV of the repurchased shares. In addition, the restored option is subject to variable accounting until it is no longer possible to rescind the exercise of the restored option for tax purposes, generally the earlier of expiration or forfeiture of the option or the end of the tax year in which the restored option is exercised.

(7)   FASB 123 repricing and other modification rule. Under FASB 123, "[a] modification of the terms of [stock-based compensation] that makes it more valuable shall be treated as an exchange of the original award for a new award. In substance, [Oldco] repurchases the original instrument by issuing a new instrument of greater value, incurring additional compensation cost for that incremental value." Thus, where Oldco reprices an option (or otherwise modifies an option to increase its value), Oldco recognizes additional compensation equal to the excess of (a) the FV of the newly modified option at grant over (b) the FV of the original option (determined immediately before the repricing or modification). In each case, the option FV is determined under the Black-Scholes model or another option-pricing model as discussed in ¶407.3.3. The additional compensation is recognized immediately if the new or modified option is vested and is recognized (together with any unrecognized cost from the original option grant) over the executive's remaining service/vesting period if the new or modified option is subject to further vesting.

A change to an option's terms "in accordance with antidilution provisions that are designed, for example, to equalize an option's value before and after a stock split or a stock dividend" is not considered a modification for this purpose.

¶407.3.8   APB 25 Rules for Accelerated Vesting

When Oldco grants an executive an option or sells or awards an executive stock subject to vesting, the terms of the option or the stock vesting agreement may explicitly provide for accelerated vesting upon occurrence of a specified event, e.g., a change in Oldco's control or the executive's death or retirement ("mandatory acceleration"). Even when the option or stock vesting agreement does not explicitly provide for such accelerated vesting, Oldco may nevertheless grant the executive accelerated vesting upon the occurrence of such an event ("discretionary acceleration").

---

[25] In effect, SEC's formula forces Oldco to recapture on rescission the tax benefits attributable to the previous option exercise. This seems harsh to us, since Oldco likely did not receive any benefit on its GAAP income statement for the tax benefits. That is, typically under APB 25 Oldco would not record any compensation expense on its GAAP income statement upon issuance or exercise of the option, and hence Oldco would have no GAAP compensation expense to be reduced to reflect tax benefits; rather the tax benefits would merely have been recorded for GAAP purposes as an increase in shareholder net worth.

The pre-2000 APB 25 accounting rules did not contain a special rule dealing with mandatory or accelerated vesting for options or stock. However, under FASB Interpretation 44, issued 3/31/00:

(1)   No new measurement date is required where vesting is accelerated for an option or stock in accordance with the original terms of the option or stock vesting agreement (i.e., mandatory acceleration pursuant to the original agreement).

(2)   A new measurement date occurs (when the option is modified) if acceleration is not pursuant to the original terms of the option or stock vesting agreement (i.e., discretionary acceleration), but only where it ultimately turns out that the acceleration permits the executive to retain stock or exercise an option in circumstances where a forfeiture or expiration would otherwise have occurred according to the original terms. Thus, if vesting is accelerated, but the executive continues in Oldco's service so that the stock would have vested or the option would have become exercisable under its original vesting provisions, no additional compensation charge is triggered by the acceleration.

(3)   Accelerated vesting that is permitted, but not required, by the original option or stock vesting agreement is treated in the manner as set forth in (2) above, i.e., a new measurement date occurs at the time of the discretionary decision to accelerate, but only where it ultimately turns out that the acceleration permits the executive to retain stock or exercise an option in circumstances where a forfeiture or expiration would otherwise have occurred according to the original terms.

Where a new measurement date is required, the additional charge to Oldco's net income is based upon the FV of Oldco's stock on the new measurement date (generally the date Oldco agrees to give the executive accelerated vesting), reduced by any prior charge which was measured by the FV of Oldco's stock when the option was granted or the stock was sold or awarded to the executive. However, these acceleration rules do not cause the option or stock to become a variable award, i.e., there are no additional charges to Oldco's net income for increases in Oldco's stock FV subsequent to the new measurement date.

¶407.3.9   Timing of Accounting Charges

Whenever there is an APB 25 or an FASB 123 charge to Oldco's accounting net income under the rules set forth above, Oldco must generally accrue it (e.g., quarterly), based on reasonable estimates.

¶407.4   Illustration—NQO Tax and Accounting Aspects

Oldco grants executive an NQO on 1,000 shares of common stock at $100 per share (such stock's FV at grant date), executive exercises the option 5 years later when the stock's FV is $500 per share, and executive sells the stock 2 years later for $600 per share.

¶407.4.1 Tax Aspects

Executive recognizes no OI at grant.

At exercise of the NQO, executive recognizes $400,000 of OI ($400 spread at exercise × 1,000 shares), assuming that the stock is then fully vested (or if the stock is then subject to further vesting, that executive makes a timely §83(b) election), so that executive owes $158,400 of federal income tax (38.6%[26] × $400,000). Oldco is entitled to a $400,000 ordinary deduction, so that it saves $140,000 of federal income tax (35% × $400,000) if it is then in a tax paying position.

When executive sells the stock for $600,000, executive recognizes a $100,000 LTCG and owes an additional $20,000 of federal income tax (20% × $100,000), but Oldco is entitled to no corresponding deduction.

On the other hand, if the stock is subject to post-exercise vesting and executive makes no §83(b) election within 30 days after exercise, there are no tax ramifications at exercise and instead, executive recognizes OI at the time of vesting equal to the spread at vesting, Oldco has an ordinary deduction at the same time in the same amount, executive's basis for computing CG on a later sale of the stock would be the stock's FV at vesting, and executive's IRS holding period begins at vesting.

¶407.4.2 APB 25 GAAP Aspects

Under APB 25, if the only vesting requirement for the NQO and/or the stock is executive's continued employment at Oldco for a specified period, there is no reduction in Oldco's accounting net income, because the option price was at least 100% of the stock's FV at grant. Oldco's tax saving because of its ordinary deduction for the spread in the stock at exercise (or if the stock is not vested at exercise and executive makes no §83(b) election, at later vesting) is credited directly to Oldco's net worth and does not increase its accounting net income (although it increases Oldco's net cash flow).

However, if vesting is also dependent on specified performance goals (rather than solely on executive's continued employment for a specified period), Oldco's accounting net income under APB 25 will be reduced by the spread at the time of vesting ($400,000 assuming the stock cliff vests at the end of 5 years, shortly before executive exercises the option) *less* Oldco's tax saving of $140,000 ($400,000 × 35%), for a $260,000 net reduction of Oldco's accounting net income. Oldco generally must accrue this accounting charge to net income quarterly as the FV of Oldco's stock fluctuates.

---

[26] The top individual 2002 and 2003 federal rate is really higher than the 38.6% nominal rate because of (a) the 3% itemized deduction disallowance and (b) the 1.45%/2.9% uncapped medicare tax, as described at ¶202.01 above.

Even where there is no performance vesting, if Oldco has agreed to pay executive a tax-offset bonus (i.e., to pay executive all or part of Oldco's tax saving to offset executive's tax on the NQO exercise), so that the option price is not fixed (in the FASB's view), Oldco's accounting net income under APB 25 is reduced by the spread at exercise ($400,000) *plus* the bonus payment to executive *less* Oldco's tax saving from deducting the $400,000 and the bonus. Oldco generally must accrue this accounting charge to net income quarterly as the FV of Oldco's stock fluctuates.

¶407.4.3   FASB 123 GAAP Aspects

If Oldco has chosen to account for stock-based compensation under FASB 123 (rather than APB 25), Oldco's accounting net income will be reduced (over the executive's service/vesting period) by the FV of the NQO at the grant date—taking into account both (1) the spread at grant (here zero) and (2) the value to the executive of being able to defer payment of the option price, i.e., the value of the option privilege—*less* Oldco's expected tax savings arising from its tax deduction (up to the amount treated as accounting compensation expense) at exercise.

The FV of the option, calculated by the Black-Scholes or other appropriate model, is generally between 20% and 40% of the option price where (as here) there is no spread in the option at grant, depending on the stock's expected future volatility (if Oldco is a public company), the expected option life, and other factors, here approximately $20,000 to $40,000 (i.e., $100,000 option exercise price × 20% to 40%).

Oldco's expected tax saving on exercise of the NQO arising from the tax deduction (up to the amount treated as accounting compensation expense) will be approximately $7,000 to $14,000 ($20,000 to $40,000 × 35%). Hence, Oldco's accounting net income will be reduced over the executive's service/vesting period by approximately $13,000 to $26,000. Where Oldco's ordinary deduction exceeds the Black-Scholes FV of the option, tax savings on account of the excess deduction are credited directly to Oldco's net worth and do not increase Oldco's accounting net income (although increasing Oldco's net cash flow).

This accounting result under FASB 123 is the same whether the option is fully vested from the outset, is subject only to time vesting for the executive's continued employment, or is also subject to performance vesting.

¶407.5   Stock Sale

The tax aspects of an executive's purchase of stock (without the grant of an option) are discussed at ¶¶202.2 and 202.3 above. The accounting treatment is discussed at ¶407.3 above.

¶407.6   Key Issues and References on Options, Stock Sales, and Stock Grants

NQO grant to executive. How are NQOs taxed—at grant, at exercise, at resale of the stock?

References:

- Code §83
- Treas. Reg. §1.83-1 through §1.83-8
- Ginsburg and Levin M&A book ¶¶1502.1.2, 1502.1.4, and 1502.1.5

Are there securities law impediments to such an option grant or exercise?

Is there an accounting charge to Oldco's net income at grant or exercise of an NQO?

Reference:

- Ginsburg and Levin M&A book ¶1502.1.7

Gift of NQO. How is an executive taxed when he or she gifts an NQO to a family member and when the transferee ultimately exercises the NQO?

Reference:

- Rev. Rul. 98-21

ISO grant to executive. How are ISOs taxed—at grant, at exercise, at resale of the stock? What distinguishes an ISO from an NQO?

References:

- Code §422
- Code §421
- Code §424
- Ginsburg and Levin M&A book ¶1502.2

Are there securities law impediments to such an option grant or exercise?

Do the accounting rules for an ISO differ from the accounting rules applicable to an NQO?

Stock sales to executive. How are stock sales to executives taxed—with or without vesting?

Reference:

- See ¶201 and ¶202 above

Do the accounting rules for a stock sale to an executive differ from the accounting rules applicable to NQOs and ISOs?

¶408   NEGOTIATING POSTURE AS COMPARED TO START-UP TRANSACTION

There are a number of important differences between VC's negotiating posture in the Oldco growth-equity transaction discussed in this chapter and in the Newco start-up discussed in Chapter 2.

(1) In the Oldco growth-equity transaction, VC is more likely to receive real debentures and/or preferred stock, i.e., (a) a better yield on the debentures or preferred stock and current payment of the yield, because Oldco's cash flow is better than Newco's and (b) near-term redemption dates, because Oldco is more mature and therefore closer to an IPO or a sale of the company.

- If VC is an SBIC, it must comply with specific SBA rules regarding amortization of loans and redemption of equity securities.

(2) In the Oldco growth-equity transaction, VC generally receives a smaller percentage of common stock because Oldco's existing shareholders are contributing more value than did E in the Newco start-up transaction.

(3) In the Oldco growth-equity transaction, VC is less likely to obtain board control and more likely to get minority board representation or mere observer rights.

VC may seek contractual rights to receive periodic financial statements and other information about Oldco.

VC may seek a contractual right to take board control if there is a payment default or a covenant breach on VC's securities. Thus, it is more important in the Oldco growth-equity transaction for VC to obtain contractual covenants and default provisions.

(4) In the Oldco growth-equity transaction, there is increased importance, when drafting the investment agreement, that VC do an extensive due diligence review of Oldco and obtain extensive representations and warranties (along with adequate disclosure schedules) so that VC has a snapshot of Oldco, because Oldco's business is far more complex than Newco's in Chapter 2.

(5) In the Oldco growth-equity transaction, there is increased need for default remedies, because VC has less control over, and less equity in, Oldco, including:

- Default warrants and/or reduced conversion or warrant price.
- Increased dividend and/or interest rate.
- Board control.
- Acceleration of preferred and/or debenture redemption.

(6) In a growth-equity transaction as contrasted with a start-up, (a) VC is likely to make a larger capital investment but to devote less time to Oldco's affairs after making the investment and (b) the investment is likely to be less risky and to mature more quickly.

(7) VC's exit strategies in the growth-equity transaction.

  (a) VC's contractual SEC registration rights are even more important than in a start-up, because Oldco is more likely to have an IPO and VC has less control over Oldco. See ¶207.7.3 above.

(b) VC's right to force a sale of Oldco.

(c) VC's right to put to Oldco VC's common stock at specified times and specified or formula prices or at appraised FV.

- If VC seeks a put, Oldco may seek a call on VC's stock. If VC grants Oldco a call on VC's stock, VC will prefer that Oldco's call becomes exercisable only after VC's put has become exercisable, that the call price be at a premium over the put price, and that if the call is exercised, VC receive an additional payment if Oldco is sold or has an IPO within a specified period (e.g., 12-24 months) after exercise or consummation of the call at a valuation higher than the call price.

- If VC is an SBIC, it must comply with specific SBA rules regarding puts of equity securities.

(d) VC will want a tag-along right if the active management shareholders sell Oldco stock. See ¶206 above.

(e) If Oldco has a right of first refusal (an "RFR") on VC's common stock, such RFR will generally have a chilling effect on VC's ability to find a third-party buyer willing to negotiate to buy VC's Oldco stock. There is less chilling effect where Oldco has merely a right of first offer (an "RFO").

- An RFR means that once VC has a concrete offer from a third-party buyer, Oldco has the right to preempt the third-party buyer and to purchase VC's common stock merely by matching the third-party's offer.

- An RFO means that once VC notifies Oldco that VC wishes to sell its Oldco stock at a price stated in VC's notice, Oldco has a limited period (e.g., 30 to 90 days) to buy VC's stock at the price stated in the notice, but if Oldco does not buy VC's stock, VC has the right to sell to a third-party buyer at the price stated in VC's notice or a higher price for a specified period (e.g., 6 to 9 months). An alternative method for drafting an RFO is that VC sets no price in its notice to Oldco of intent to sell but rather Oldco sets an offering price in its response to VC's notice and VC then has a limited period (e.g., 30 to 90 days) to accept Oldco's offer, but if VC does not accept Oldco's offer, VC has the right to sell to a third-party buyer at a price higher than Oldco's offer price for a specified period (e.g., 6 to 9 months).

(8) Because Oldco is more mature and larger at the time of VC's investment than was Newco in Chapter 2, (a) Oldco is less likely to qualify for Code §1202's special 14% tax rate because VC is less likely to hold its stock for more than 5 years and Oldco is less likely to meet the $50 million asset limitation at the time of VC's investment (see ¶906 below) and (b) Oldco is less likely to meet the SBIC "small business" requirements (described at ¶209.1 above), in which case a VC which is a BHC subsidiary would have to comply with the BHCA restrictions (described in ¶209.2.1 above).

(9) If other VCs previously purchased some Oldco stock (in a first-round investment) and a new VC is participating in this second-round investment in

Oldco, blending the rights of the first and the second-round VCs requires substantial negotiation.

¶409 TERMS OF VC's DEBENTURES AND PREFERRED STOCK

See Chapter 6 below for a discussion of the terms and tax ramifications of VC's debentures and preferred stock.

Key Issues and References:

If VC purchases Oldco debentures, is VC taxed on interest income even if Oldco does not pay the interest?

References:

- Code §7872
- Code §1272(a), (c), (d)
- Code §1273
- Code §1274 and §1275
- Code §483
- Ginsburg and Levin M&A book ¶1309

Might VC's Oldco debentures be treated for tax purposes as preferred stock? What are the tax ramifications if they are so treated?

References:

- Code §385
- Ginsburg and Levin M&A book ¶1302, ¶1310

If VC purchases Oldco preferred stock, is VC taxed on cash dividends received? Does it matter whether VC is a corporation, an individual, or a partnership? What is a DRD? Does it matter whether Oldco has E&P?

References:

- Code §301
- Code §316(a)
- Code §317
- Code §312
- Code §243(a) through (c)
- Code §246A
- Code §1059

Is VC taxed on accrued preferred dividends not yet received?

References:

- Code §305(b)(4) and (c)
- Treas. Reg. §1.305-5

How is VC taxed when its Oldco preferred stock is redeemed?

References:

- Code §302
- Code §318(a)
- Rev. Rul. 85-106
- Ginsburg and Levin M&A book ¶1310

¶410 COMPLYING WITH FEDERAL AND STATE SECURITIES LAWS

See ¶207 and ¶208 above.

After Oldco has gone public, are there securities law impediments to VC's sale of Oldco common stock into the public market?

References:

- SEC Rule 144
- SEC Rule 701
- ¶902 through ¶904 of this book

¶411 NATURE OF VC

See ¶209 above.

¶412 SPECIAL LTCG TAX ADVANTAGES FOR INDIVIDUALS

The top normal federal tax rate for an individual's LTCG (i.e., gain on sale of a capital asset, including stock, held more than one year) is 20%, which is 18.6 percentage points below the top individual 2002 and 2003 OI rate (38.6%). However, three Code provisions grant further tax relief to an individual who owns stock either directly or through a partnership, LLC, or S corporation and who recognizes LTCG in special circumstances:

(1) A 14% top rate for LTCG on sale of "qualified small business stock" held more than 5 years.

(2)   A tax-free rollover on sale of stock that would have qualified for the 14% special rate (except that the necessary holding period is more than 6 months rather than more than 5 years) where the proceeds are then reinvested in new qualified stock within 60 days.

(3)   An 18% top rate for LTCG on sale of property (not merely "qualified small business stock") acquired after 12/31/00 and held more than 5 years (with a taxpayer election to treat pre-12/31/00 property as sold and reacquired in 1/01).

See ¶906 for a more detailed discussion of these CG tax breaks for individuals.

CHAPTER 5

Structuring Buyout

Chapter 5. Structuring Buyout

The existing owners of a reasonably successful business ("Target") have decided to dispose of the business.

- In ¶501, Target is wholly owned by Bigco, a large corporation which operates many businesses as subsidiaries and divisions. Bigco acquired Target in the days of conglomerization but now wishes to sell Target and concentrate on Bigco's core businesses.
- In ¶502, Target is owned by an individual or group, and is not a Bigco subsidiary. Target's principal shareholders, unable to locate the fountain of youth, are focusing on estate planning and would like to liquify their estates.
- In ¶503, Target is a publicly traded company. Target's board of directors has concluded that (1) although Target's business is sound, the stock market does not properly value a company of Target's size in Target's industry and (2) Target's shareholder value can be maximized by selling Target. In addition, Target's CEO, who is also its largest shareholder (owning 15% of Target), has tired of the game and is ready to seek sunnier climes.
- In ¶504, VC structures the buyout of Target (which may be a Bigco subsidiary, a free-standing company owned by an individual or a group, or a publicly traded company) as a recapitalization in order to obtain the benefits of "recap" accounting, which will maximize Target's post-buyout GAAP book earnings. By contrast, in ¶501 through ¶503 VC forms Newco to acquire Target which generally results in "purchase" accounting and hence reduces Target's post-buyout GAAP book earnings.

In each of these circumstances, VC (or a group of VCs) believes that, with additional capital for expansion, some add-on acquisitions over several years, proper VC supervision, and more incentive for Target's younger executives (or new executives located by VC), Target's business will rise geometrically in value. Hence VC forms Newco to purchase Target's business.

In this Chapter 5, unless otherwise stated Target is, and long has been, a C corporation subject to double tax under the U.S. federal income tax system, and Newco also is formed as a C corporation. If either or both were a tax flow-through entity, i.e., an S corporation, a partnership, or an LLC none of which are subject to double tax, many of the applicable tax rules would be different, as discussed in ¶502.1 and in Chapters 3 and 7.[1]

¶501   BUYOUT OF BIGCO SUBSIDIARY OR DIVISION

In this ¶501 (as described above) Bigco, a large corporation operating many businesses as subsidiaries and divisions, now wishes to sell Target—originally acquired in the days of conglomerization—so that Bigco can concentrate on Bigco's core businesses, while VC (or a group of VCs) believe that Target's business will—with additional capital for expansion, some add-on acquisitions, proper VC supervision, and more incentive for Target's younger executives (or new executives located by VC)—rise geometrically in value. Thus, one or several VCs—along with Target's management (or new executives located by VC) and several lenders—begin the task of structuring Newco to acquire Target from Bigco.

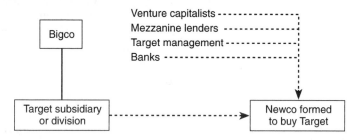

¶501.1 $50 Million Purchase Price and Financing Therefor

VCs, believing Bigco would be willing to sell Target for $50 million, have formed Newco and arranged $50 million of financing for Newco corporation in 4 tranches:

Securities to Be Issued	Millions
Senior bank notes	$30.0
Subordinated debentures	12.5
Preferred stock	6.5
Common stock	1.0
Total	$50.0[1]

---

[1] As discussed in a footnote in chapter 2's introduction, a controversial Bush administration pending legislative proposal would, if enacted, largely repeal the double tax on C corporations. Because future prospects for this legislation are highly uncertain, the text of this book is based on current law and does not further discuss this legislative proposal.

¶501   [1] This example ignores for simplicity the additional amounts Newco must raise for transaction expenses and working capital.

Sources of Funds	Millions			
	Total Financing	Straight Debt	Straight Preferred	Common
Bank lenders	$30.0	$30.0		
Mezzanine lenders and/or seller paper	12.6	12.5		$ .1
VCs	7.2		$6.5	.7
Management	.2			.2
Total	$50.0	$42.5	$6.5	$1.0

Split of Securities	Normal Transaction	Alternate Transaction
Bank lenders	$30.0 million of straight debt	Same
Mezzanine lenders and seller paper	$12.5 million for straight subordinated debentures *plus* $.1 million for 100 common shares (i.e., 10% of Newco's common)	$12.6 million for subordinated debentures *plus* warrants or conversion rights to acquire 100 common shares upon either (a) surrender of $.1 million of debentures or (b) $.1 million cash payment
VCs	$6.5 million for straight preferred and $.7 million for 700 common shares (i.e., 70% of Newco's common)	$7.0 million for preferred *plus* warrants or conversion rights to acquire 700 common shares upon either (a) surrender of $.7 million of preferred or (b) $.7 million cash payment
Management	$.2 million for 200 common shares (i.e., 20% of Newco's common)	Options to buy 200 common shares for $.2 million, in which case Newco would now have to raise an additional $.2 million elsewhere

¶501.2   *Three Separate Transactions*

A buyout is really 3 separate transactions, each complex and time consuming and all mutually interdependent in their consummation.

¶501.2.1   Acquisition

The first transaction—Newco's acquisition of Target from Bigco—presents all of the issues inherent in any corporate acquisition:

(1) Negotiating the purchase price for the Target business.
(2) Negotiating representations and warranties, indemnification, closing conditions, covenants not to compete, etc. between Newco and Bigco.
(3) Newco's due diligence on the Target business.
(4) Structuring federal income tax aspects of the acquisition transaction, including:

- The pros and cons of structuring the acquisition as a purchase of assets, a purchase of stock, or a forward or reverse merger.
- Whether the structure selected will result in single tax or double tax to the seller.
- Whether the structure selected will give Newco asset SUB or asset COB.

(5) Analyzing other legal aspects of the acquisition transaction, including:

- Liabilities to be inherited by Newco or its subsidiaries, including contingent liabilities.
- Transferability of Target's assets, including its contract rights.
- Sales and transfer taxes.
- State income tax issues.

¶501.2.2   Debt Financing

The second of the three transactions comprising a buyout—Newco's debt financing—includes negotiating the terms of Newco's senior and subordinated/mezzanine debt, as well as any seller financing, and is critically important (unlike a start-up or growth-equity investment discussed in Chapters 2 and 4 above).

¶501.2.3   Equity Financing

Newco's equity financing is the third of the three transactions comprising a buyout. Negotiating Newco's complex equity financing arrangements is similar to (but more complex than) negotiating the equity structure of a start-up or growth-equity investment, as discussed in Chapters 2 and 4 above, including:

- The common stock split among VCs, management, subordinated lenders, and possibly the seller.
- Whether management buys common stock (or receives ISOs) to obtain LTCG tax treatment, or receives NQOs.
- Vesting arrangements on management's stock or options, including Code §83(b) tax issues and APB 25/FASB 123 accounting issues presented by such vesting.
- Whether Newco's securities are structured so that VC is entitled first to receive back its investment plus a fixed yield (through straight debentures and/or preferred stock) before splitting the residual (common stock) profits with management and the subordinated lenders.
- Board control of Newco and veto powers for certain equity owners and creditors.
- Right of certain Newco equity owners to mandate or veto a Newco sale or IPO.
- Whether Newco is formed (1) as a regular C corporation subject to double tax *or* (2) as a flow-through entity (i.e., an LLC, partnership, or S corporation) subject only to single tax, in which case ultimate sale of Newco to BuyerCo can be structured to deliver asset SUB to BuyerCo with single (not double) tax to Newco and its equity owners.

¶501.2.4 Key Issues and References on Buyouts in General

How does a buyout differ from other mergers or acquisitions?

References:

- Ginsburg and Levin M&A book ¶101 (definition of a buyout) and ¶102

What does it mean when one layer of invested money (debt or preferred stock) is "subordinated" to another layer? Why would an investor be willing to take an instrument (debt or preferred stock) which is subordinated to other instruments?

What are the typical terms of the debt and equity securities issued in a buyout?

References:

- Chapter 6 of this book

Will all of the interest on Newco's debt be deductible for tax purposes? What tax hurdles must be overcome?

References:

- ¶602.8 of this book (regarding terms and tax ramifications of subordinated debentures) and the precedents cited therein

Was the highly-leveraged buyout craze of the late 1980s good for America?

Was the hi-tech and internet start-up craze of the late 1990s thru early 2001 good for America?

Do our current tax laws encourage highly-leveraged buyouts?
Should our tax laws be changed?

References:

- Testimony Before the House Ways & Means Committee of Jack S. Levin, 2/2/89
- American Law Institute, Federal Income Tax Project, Reporter's Study Draft 6/1/89 Subchapter C Supplement Study, by Professor William D. Andrews, pp. 13-37

¶501.3   Key Acquisition Issues

¶501.3.1   Purchase Price and Related Issues

¶501.3.1.1   Purchase Price

After the parties have agreed on the nominal purchase price, a number of pricing issues remain to be negotiated, including:

(1) Amount payable in cash.

(2) Amount payable in the form of Newco subordinated note or preferred stock (i.e., seller paper or seller financing).

(3) Purchase price adjustments to reflect such items as (a) Bigco's retention of Target's cash on hand at closing *or* (b) changes in Target's net book value or net working capital between date of Target's financial statements relied upon in negotiating the purchase agreement and closing.

- Requirement of an audit and right of appeal to an independent CPA firm, to arbitration, or to court.
- Reference to GAAP consistently applied or to Target's accounting principles consistently applied.

Where there is no purchase price adjustment for Target's closing date net book value or net working capital, it may be desirable (although not as effective) for Newco to seek covenants (a) forbidding distributions from Target to Bigco prior to closing and/or (b) obligating Bigco to conduct Target's business prior to closing in the ordinary course and in accordance with past custom and practice, especially with respect to activities the deferral of which would allow Bigco to generate and retain more cash from Target's business, including covenants:

- Requiring normal repairs, maintenance, clean-up.
- Requiring normal purchases of new capital assets.
- Requiring normal purchases of inventory.
- Prohibiting accelerated or discounted sales of inventory.
- Prohibiting accelerated or discounted collection of receivables.
- Requiring normal payments to trade creditors.

If the parties can not agree on a fixed purchase price, they may want to use a contingent purchase price or earn-out based on the future performance of Target's business, although such an approach will generally raise complex issues as to (a) whether buyer or seller controls management decisions during the earn-out period, (b) whether adjustments to actual earnings will be made for unanticipated events, (c) whether to include earnings (losses) from subsequent Target add-on acquisitions (and, if not, how to allocate certain expenses between Target's original businesses and any businesses subsequently acquired), and (d) the like.

¶501.3.1.2   *Reps & Warranties*

There are at least 3 reasons Newco would seek contractual representations and warranties from Bigco:

- Disclose information useful to Newco in deciding (a) whether to buy Target, (b) what price to pay for Target, and (c) whether to insert specific contract clauses dealing with specific items.
- Allow Newco to call off the deal after contract signing and prior to closing (where signing and closing are not simultaneous) if Target's business fails to conform to the contractual representations and warranties.
- Allow Newco to seek to recover money damages from Bigco, or in an extreme case to rescind the transaction, if the representations and warranties turn out to be incorrect.

Some of the key representations and warranties Newco may seek from Bigco:

(1) No Target liabilities not shown on Target's balance sheet or listed on the disclosure schedules (including known and unknown contingent liabilities), such as:

- Environmental/pollution violations and other clean-up obligations.
- Employment discrimination claims.
- Pension underfunding and unfunded retiree medical benefits.
- Uninsured or under-insured product liabilities.
- Product warranties.
- Patent/copyright/trademark infringements.
- Antitrust violations.
- Tax deficiencies.
- Breach of contract claims.
- OSHA violations.
- Guarantees.
- Other lawsuits, claims, and contingent liabilities.

(2) Target's inventory good and salable in the ordinary course of business.
(3) Target's receivables collectible in the ordinary course of business within a specified period.
(4) Target's plants, equipment, and other tangible assets in good condition and without defect.

(5) Target's financial statements either true and correct or fairly presented in all material respects.

(6) Target's good title to its assets and Bigco's good title to Target's stock.

(7) Target has committed no violations of law or governmental regulations (especially important where Target is engaged in a regulated industry).

(8) No governmental or third party consents necessary to complete the buyout, except as listed on a schedule.

Such Bigco representations and warranties can be unqualified *or* qualified by references either to Bigco's knowledge (or to the knowledge of specified Bigco executives) or to a materiality standard *or* both.

Only if Bigco's representations and warranties survive the closing can Newco make a contractual claim against Bigco for damages, in which case the 3 principal issues are (1) the time period permitted to make claims, (2) the stated basket (*either* a deductible amount *or* a threshold amount which must be reached before a claim can be made for the entire amount), and (3) the maximum claim amount.

Security for Newco claims against Bigco (e.g., escrow, holdback, setoff on seller note or preferred stock, lien on Bigco assets) is more or less important, depending on Bigco's financial health.

Persons who are interested in the extent of Bigco's representations and warranties, and Newco's rights to recover for breach, include not only Newco and its shareholders, but Newco's lenders as well.

The parties' negotiating positions on these issues will generally be as follows:

- In the typical negotiation, Newco will seek extensive representations and warranties from Bigco regarding Target. Bigco, however, will seek to give Newco far fewer representations and warranties (or possibly none at all—i.e., an "as is" sale) and to qualify them with concepts of materiality and knowledge.

- Newco will seek to have these representations and warranties survive the closing for a lengthy period (possibly forever) and will seek to have Bigco indemnify Newco against any breaches Newco discovers during the survival period. Bigco, however, will seek to have the representations and warranties expire at the closing (i.e., to give Newco no right whatsoever to sue Bigco after the closing for breaches of representations and warranties) or, at least, to have the representations and warranties survive only for breaches discovered by Newco within a short period (e.g., 6 to 12 months).

- Newco will seek indemnification which begins with the first dollar of damages from breach and is unlimited in amount. Bigco, however, will seek to have its indemnification obligation subject to (1) a deductible so that it pays claims only in excess of (e.g.) $1 million and (2) a ceiling so that it pays no more than (e.g.) $10 million.

- Newco will seek security for Bigco's indemnification obligation, e.g., a holdback of part of the purchase price, escrow part of the purchase price, set off rights against any seller paper, and/or liens against Bigco assets. Bigco, however, will not desire to provide any such security for its indemnification obligation.

- Newco will seek to assume responsibility for only specified Target liabilities and leave behind the remainder (including unknown and contingent liabilities) for Bigco to pay (or, in a stock purchase, to have Bigco agree to indemnify Newco and Target for the remainder). Bigco, however, will desire that Newco assume responsibility for all of Target's liabilities, known and unknown, liquidated and unliquidated.

One particularly difficult issue regarding representations, warranties, and indemnification relates to whether Newco or Bigco should bear the cost of a tax deficiency (imposed by IRS after the acquisition) arising out of the disallowance of Target's pre-acquisition tax deductions for such items as depreciation and repairs:

- Newco buys Target's stock from Bigco in an asset COB transaction.
- Bigco represents to Newco that Target has no tax liabilities for prior years.
- In fact, it turns out that Target incorrectly claimed a tax deduction (in a taxable year prior to the acquisition) for $100 of depreciation (and/or $100 of repair expense), which amount was not properly deductible by Target (and hence by Bigco on its pre-acquisition consolidated return), but rather is deductible by Target (and hence by Newco, as Target's consolidated parent or successor) in a taxable year subsequent to the acquisition.
- IRS's post-acquisition audit of Target and Bigco results in disallowance of the $100 pre-acquisition deduction.
- The $100 disallowed pre-acquisition deduction results in a $35 federal income tax deficiency plus interest. IRS asserts the $35 tax plus interest against either (1) Target (now a Newco subsidiary) or Newco (if Target has merged with or liquidated into Newco) *or* (2) Bigco as Target's consolidated parent for the year in which the deficiency arose (see Treas. Reg. §1.1502-6, discussed at ¶501.3.5.1 below).
- Either (1) Newco pays the $35 tax deficiency plus interest and seeks indemnification from Bigco *or* (2) Bigco pays the deficiency and seeks indemnification from Newco.
- In either case, Bigco asserts that in a year subsequent to the buyout Newco (which took asset COB in the acquisition) will be entitled to the $100 deduction (because Target's post-acquisition tax basis for the asset will be $100 greater than anticipated) and hence Newco will save $35 of federal income tax (assuming tax rates stay the same).
- A well-drafted indemnification agreement in this situation might (1) make Bigco liable for the interest due to IRS on the $35 deficiency *plus* the excess of the $35 tax over the discounted PV of Newco-Target's future tax deduction and (2) make Newco liable for the remainder.

¶501.3.1.3 *Closing Conditions*

Newco will seek expansive closing conditions that will allow Newco to bow out of the transaction (after the acquisition agreement has been signed) if things do not go as Newco anticipated (i.e., Newco will seek a contract which is in effect an option to acquire Target), for example:

- Successful completion of Newco's financing (i.e., a financing out).
- Satisfactory completion of Newco's due diligence examination of Target (i.e., a due diligence out).
- Compliance with all applicable laws and regulations, including Hart-Scott-Rodino antitrust clearance from FTC.
- Necessary third-party consents.
- No material adverse change to Target's business.

Bigco will generally resist both a financing out and a due diligence out or will at least attempt to limit the time during which Newco can exercise such outs.

¶501.3.1.4   Transition Services

Newco may seek a contract obligation for Bigco to supply transition services to Newco for a reasonable period at reasonable prices:

- Computers.
- Purchasing.
- Employee benefit administration.
- Insurance administration.
- Space rental.
- Accounting services.
- Receivables collection or payables management.

¶501.3.1.5   Seller Paper

If Newco can not raise all the financing necessary to purchase Target, Newco may need to fill its financing hole by issuing a Newco subordinated note or preferred stock to Bigco as part of the purchase price. See ¶501.4 for some of the issues such seller paper raises, including subordination to, and maturity after, Newco's other financing.

¶501.3.2   Transferring Target Assets and Contracts

¶501.3.2.1   Hard to Transfer Assets and Contracts

- Long-term low-rent leaseholds.
- Long-term low-interest borrowings.
- Long-term low-royalty patent and other technology licenses.
- Large number of vehicles.
- Large number of real estate parcels.
- Governmental licenses and permits.

Where Target is a Bigco subsidiary (rather than a division), structuring the acquisition as a purchase of Target's stock by Newco or a reverse subsidiary cash merger of a Newco subsidiary into Target will generally ease the burdens of transferring such Target assets, unless the contract (or governmental regulation) treats a change of Target's control like an asset transfer. A forward cash merger of Target into Newco or a Newco subsidiary may ease the burdens, depending on the contractual (or governmental regulatory) language. However, a purchase of assets seldom will ease the burdens. It is necessary to read each contract (or governmental regulation) to ascertain whether a third-party consent is necessary for a sale of stock, a reverse subsidiary merger, a forward merger, a sale of assets, and, where the contract (or governmental regulation) is silent, to review applicable legal precedents. However, buyer sometimes ignores the need for advance consent with respect to contracts which are not individually material to the business in the expectation that the other parties to those contracts will have no interest in cancelling them.

¶501.3.2.2   *Sales Tax and Real Estate Transfer Taxes*

Many states impose sales tax (perhaps 6% to 8%) on a sale of tangible assets which will not be held by the buyer for resale, i.e., fixed assets.

- Some states also tax transfers of computer software.
- Some states exempt the sale of a business in bulk or other casual sale.

Some governmental entities impose real estate transfer tax (state, county and/or municipal) at rates which vary greatly from jurisdiction to jurisdiction.

Where such a sales tax or real estate transfer tax is imposed, it generally applies to a sale of assets. Whether the tax applies to a forward cash merger depends on state law. Such tax generally does not apply to a sale of stock or a reverse subsidiary merger, except that some jurisdictions may impose real estate transfer tax even on a stock transfer where the corporation's assets are predominantly real estate located in the jurisdiction.

¶501.3.2.3   *Real Estate Title Insurance*

Normally relatively clean title insurance can be obtained on real estate in a purchase of assets.

It is often possible to obtain a special endorsement (at extra cost) giving relatively clean title insurance on real estate in a purchase of stock or merger.

If real estate is pledged as collateral to secure acquisition financing, the lender will generally require title insurance payable to the lender, in which case an additional owner's policy to protect Newco can be obtained for a nominal additional charge.

Premium costs vary significantly from state to state (e.g., between $1 and $5 per $1,000 of coverage).

¶501.3.2.4   Union Contracts

A union contract may contain a successor clause or otherwise seek to bind Newco even in a purchase of assets. In any event, Newco probably must deal with Target's unions.

¶501.3.3   Hart-Scott-Rodino Antitrust Reporting Act

¶501.3.3.1   Filing and Waiting Period

Unless the transaction qualifies for exemption as described in ¶501.3.3.4, an HSR filing is required if (1) the size of the transaction as described in ¶501.3.3.2 exceeds $200 million *or* (2) the size of the transaction exceeds $50 million and the size of person test described in ¶501.3.3.3 (one person at least $10 million and one at least $100 million generally measured by sales or assets) also is satisfied. There is generally a 30-day waiting period after making the required HSR filing which is extended if FTC or Department of Justice issues a request for additional information.

Newco must pay a filing fee to the FTC:

Fee	Transaction value
$ 45,000	less than $100 million
$125,000	at least $100 million but less than $500 million
$280,000	$500 million or more

If other HSR reportable events are occurring, additional fees may be due.

In addition, the parties must file a substantial amount of information with the antitrust agencies, including each study, analysis, and report prepared by or for an officer or director of Bigco, Target, or Newco (or by or for an officer or director of a controlling parent or controlled subsidiary) which was prepared for the purpose of evaluating the transaction with respect to market share, competition, or the potential for market expansion.[2]

---

[2] FTC takes the position that (1) an "analysis" includes any interoffice memorandum, handwritten note, correspondence, computer file, slide presentation, or board minutes, if such document contains even a brief evaluation or analysis of the acquisition's competitive advantages, even where such document contains substantial other information not required to be filed with FTC, (2) failure to include any such analysis renders the HSR filing deficient, so that the HSR waiting period restarts when the omitted analysis is subsequently submitted (unless FTC waives a restart), and (3) FTC can require a substantial civil penalty for such failure, as it did (approximately $3 million to $4 million) in 1996, 1999, and 2001 cases where FTC discovered Newco's failure only after the acquisition had been consummated, even though Newco's failure apparently was not deliberate in any of the cases.

¶501.3.3.2   Size of Transaction

The size of the transaction (for purposes of the $200 million test and the $50 million test described in ¶501.3.3.1) is the value of all Target voting securities that will be held by Newco and all assets acquired by Newco from Target or from Target's ultimate parent entity (as defined in ¶501.3.3.3), whether acquired in one or a series of transactions. Generally, transaction size is measured by the price paid for voting securities and by the greater of the price paid or market value for other acquired assets.

¶501.3.3.3   Size of Person

This test is met if either Target (along with its affiliates as described below) or Newco (along with its affiliates as described below) has annual net sales or total assets of at least $100 million *and* the other has annual net sales or total assets of at least $10 million.

(1) This test is modified where Target (along with its affiliates as described below) is not engaged in manufacturing, in which case no filing is required where Target (along with its affiliates as described below) has total assets less than $10 million and annual net sales less than $100 million.

(2) Total assets and net sales are measured by the most recent regularly prepared (a) balance sheet and (b) annual income statement whether audited or not.

(3) In measuring net sales and total assets, the measurement is made at the level of ultimate parent, including any controlled corporation, partnership, or LLC.

- A corporation is controlled by a person *either* holding voting securities with 50% or more of its voting power for directors *or* having the contractual right to designate 50% or more of its directors.
- A partnership or LLC is controlled by a person having the right to receive 50% or more of its profits (or its assets upon dissolution).
- Hence, where Target is controlled by Bigco, Target sales and assets are measured by looking at Bigco and all of Bigco's controlled corporations, partnerships, and LLCs (including Target).
- If VC controls Newco, Newco's sales and assets are measured by looking at VC and all of VC's other controlled portfolio companies.
- If Newco is not controlled by VC (or any other person) and (because newly formed) Newco has no regularly prepared balance sheet when it acquires Target, Newco must include in its HSR assets all assets held by Newco at the time of the Target acquisition, including all cash provided by lenders or equity investors, but can subtract *both* (a) cash used as consideration for Newco's acquisition of Target or for incidental expenses in connection with such acquisition *and* (b) any Target securities held by Newco before the acquisition.

¶501.3.3.4   Exemption

The more important exemptions from HSR filing include:

(1)   acquisition of goods and realty in the ordinary course of business,
(2)   acquisition of voting securities solely for the purpose of investment where the acquiring person will hold 10% or less of Target's voting securities and will not have a board seat or participate in Target's management, and
(3)   acquisition of certain non-U.S. assets from a foreign entity and acquisition of certain voting securities of a foreign issuer.

¶501.3.3.5   No Antitrust Exemption

Even if the rules described above do not require an HSR filing, the transaction is not exempt from the antitrust laws. Moreover, the government's failure to respond to an HSR filing is not an antitrust exemption.

¶501.3.3.6   References

•   Ginsburg and Levin M&A book ¶1707

¶501.3.4   Protecting Newco from Target Liabilities

¶501.3.4.1   Stock Acquisition

Where Newco (or a Newco subsidiary) purchases Target's stock, Target (which becomes a Newco subsidiary) remains liable for all of its fixed and contingent liabilities. If the parties intend Bigco to retain some of Target's liabilities in the context of a stock acquisition, Bigco can agree to indemnify and hold harmless Newco and its new subsidiary Target against such liabilities.

However, should Bigco fall upon financial hard times, its indemnification may be worthless and Newco's new subsidiary Target may hence bear such liabilities.

¶501.3.4.2   *Asset Acquisition*

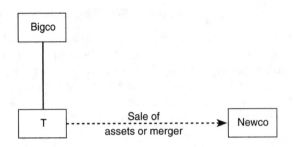

Where Target merges into Newco (or a Newco subsidiary), state merger law generally causes the corporation which survives the merger (Newco or NewSub) automatically to become liable for all of Target's liabilities. If the parties intend Bigco to retain some of Target's liabilities in the context of a merger, Bigco can agree to indemnify and hold harmless Newco (or NewSub) against such liabilities, in which case Newco is protected, subject to the risk that Bigco falls upon hard times and is unable to fulfill its indemnification obligation.

Where Newco (or a Newco subsidiary) purchases Target's assets, the parties can tailor the asset purchase agreement so that buyer expressly assumes only specified liabilities and leaves all other liabilities behind in Target, which remains a Bigco subsidiary. However, even in an asset purchase, there are several legal doctrines (discussed below) under which buyer may involuntarily inherit a Target liability if Target (which is still a Bigco subsidiary) falls on financial hard times and is unable to pay its liabilities. Hence, it is desirable for Bigco to agree in the asset purchase agreement to indemnify Newco (or NewSub) against the Target liabilities not assumed by Newco (or NewSub). Nevertheless, there is still risk to Newco if (1) both Target and Bigco fall upon financial hard times and are unable to pay such liabilities *and* (2) one of the following legal doctrines applies to make Newco (or NewSub) involuntarily liable for the Target liability not expressly assumed by Newco (or NewSub).

(1)   **Bulk sales act.** In an asset purchase (where Target transfers its inventory in bulk to Newco (or NewSub) in a state which has a bulk sales act in force), a buyer of Target's assets in bulk is generally liable for Target's liabilities (up to the FV of the inventory and equipment purchased) unless notice is given to all of Target's creditors at least a specified period before the sale (in some states by registered mail and in others by publication) and other specified procedures are followed.

Under older versions of the bulk sales act (still in effect in 5 states), the act's protection extends to each person with a claim against Target (including a contract or tort claim) based on a transaction or event occurring prior to the bulk sale. These older versions make the bulk sale of inventory and equipment "ineffective" against Target's creditors if the notice requirements are not satisfied, with the result that buyer may have to pay for the inventory and equipment a second time. However, these versions are ambiguous as to whether all creditors, or only those who were not given the required notice, are entitled to a remedy.

Newer versions of the act (now in effect in 4 states and the District of Columbia) generally exclude from the protection of the act (1) claims incurred outside Target's business, (2) unasserted tort and warranty claims, (3) unmatured claims for salary, benefits, and similar employment compensation, and (4) tax claims. In addition, the newer versions clarify that a creditor is entitled to a remedy only if buyer has not given the creditor the required notice (unless buyer has agreed to distribute all or a portion of the net contract price directly to Target's creditors, in which case a creditor is also covered if buyer fails to make such distribution). Furthermore, the newer versions clarify that buyer's liability to a creditor is limited to money damages for the loss actually resulting from buyer's non-compliance, and that buyer's cumulative liability to all creditors is limited to (1) twice the net value of the inventory and equipment purchased *less* (2) any amount buyer paid to or applied for the benefit of Target or a Target creditor which is allocable to the inventory and equipment.

To recover under either the older or newer version of the act, an eligible creditor must sue buyer within a specified period after the acquisition (usually 6 or 12 months, depending on applicable state law). Although almost all states at one time enacted a bulk sales act, in recent years more than 80% of the states have repealed their bulk sales provisions.

(2)   De facto merger and successor liability. Some courts have held a bulk asset buyer responsible for some Target liabilities (especially tort liabilities for defective products, underfunded pension liabilities, and environmental liabilities) under the vague common law doctrines of "de facto merger" and "successor liability" where Target's business is transferred to buyer as a going concern and Target goes out of existence, especially, but not exclusively, where Target's stockholder(s) receives a substantial equity interest in buyer.

Because of bulk sales act, de facto merger, and successor liability risks, it is often desirable, where Newco is making or intends to make several acquisitions (or where Newco already has other assets), for a Newco subsidiary (NewSub) to acquire Target's assets, so that if buyer is unexpectedly held liable for Target liabilities not expressly assumed by buyer, the exposure is limited to NewSub and Newco's other assets are insulated.

¶501.3.5   Some Special Target Liabilities

¶501.3.5.1   Bigco's Unpaid Consolidated Federal Income Taxes

Where Bigco files a consolidated federal income tax return, the federal tax law (Reg. §1.1502-6) creates a surprising liability: each entity (including Target) that was a member of Bigco's consolidated group for any part of a year is liable for all of the Bigco group's federal income tax for such year (even on income generated by other members of the group) if Bigco ultimately does not pay IRS.

Hence, where Newco buys Target's *stock*, Target remains liable for the entire Bigco group's federal tax deficiencies for each year in which Target was a Bigco subsidiary for any part of the year, if Bigco falls on hard financial times and does not ultimately pay IRS.

The situation would be even worse if (after Newco purchased Target's stock) Newco caused Target to merge upstream into Newco, because under state merger law Newco would become liable for all of Target's obligations (including the §1.1502-6 obligation for the Bigco group's federal income tax liabilities), thus infecting Newco's assets (if Newco has assets in addition to Target).

This rule does not apply where Newco buys Target's *assets* (rather than Target's stock). However, there is some risk in an asset acquisition that the bulk sales act, de facto merger doctrine, or successor liability doctrine may cause buyer involuntarily to inherit Target's §1.1502-6 liability to IRS.

Newco may seek to protect itself by:

- Obtaining representations and warranties from Bigco regarding the status of the Bigco consolidated group's tax liabilities.
- Obtaining the right to indemnification from Bigco (with no basket, cap, or contractual expiration date) if IRS pursues Newco and/or Target (Newco's subsidiary) for any of the Bigco group's tax liabilities.
- Obtaining security interests in Bigco group assets and/or a bank standby letter of credit to secure Bigco's indemnification obligation.

References:

- Treas. Reg. §1.1502-6
- Ginsburg and Levin M&A book ¶210

¶501.3.5.2   Target's and Bigco's Pension Plan Liabilities

Target is liable for its own (i) delinquent pension contributions, (ii) multiemployer union pension plan withdrawal liabilities (as described in ¶501.3.5.3 below), (iii) unfunded benefit liabilities for a terminated pension plan, and (iv) delinquent premium payments to the PBGC.

In addition, where Target is an 80% or greater Bigco subsidiary (by vote *or* by value, excluding from the denominator certain third-party-owned stock, such as stock owned by a Target employee if that stock is subject to vesting or other transfer restrictions), ERISA and the Code cause Target also to be liable for certain pre-acquisition pension plan liabilities of related entities, specifically: (1) where any member of Bigco's 80% control group is delinquent in its pension contributions, Target is jointly and severally liable for such pre-acquisition pension contribution delinquencies, (2) where any member of Bigco's 80% control group has previously incurred liability for a terminated pension plan, Target is jointly and severally liable for such pre-acquisition plan termination liability, (3) where any member of Bigco's 80% control group has previously incurred withdrawal liability from a multiemployer union pension plan, Target is jointly and severally liable for such pre-acquisition multiemployer plan withdrawal liability, and (4) where any member of Bigco's 80% control group has failed to pay PBGC premiums, Target is jointly and severally liable for such unpaid pre-acquisition PBGC premiums.

Hence, where Newco buys Target's *stock*, Target remains liable for such pre-acquisition liabilities of the entire Bigco 80% control group if Bigco and Bigco's continuing control group members fall on financial hard times and do not pay the pre-acquisition liabilities.

Where Newco buys Target's *assets*, there is some risk that Newco involuntarily inherits these Target liabilities under either the bulk sales act, de facto merger doctrine, or successor liability doctrine in states which maintain such approaches (unless such state law doctrines are preempted by ERISA) or in certain circumstances under the complex provisions of ERISA.

¶501.3.5.3 *Withdrawal Liability for Underfunded Multiemployer Union Pension Plan*

Where Target participates in an underfunded multiemployer union pension plan, a sale of Target's *assets* triggers immediate withdrawal liability for Target and Bigco (generally equal to Target's portion of the pension plan's unfunded vested benefits) unless certain ERISA requirements are met, including (1) Newco must assume the obligation to make ongoing pension plan contributions, (2) for a period of 5 years after the asset sale Newco must provide a bond or escrow securing its ongoing contribution obligation, and (3) the asset purchase agreement must state that should Newco withdraw from the plan during the 5 years following the asset sale, Target is secondarily liable for any withdrawal liability (and should Target liquidate, additional procedures must be followed and Bigco may be secondarily liable).

In addition, under several federal cases, where Newco buys Target's *assets*, Newco becomes liable for delinquent contributions and withdrawal liability with respect to Target, even if Newco does not intend to assume the obligation in the asset purchase agreement. The same result might be reached under the bulk sales act, de facto merger doctrine, or successor liability doctrine in states which maintain such approaches, unless such state law doctrines are preempted by ERISA.

In a *stock* sale, Target's withdrawal liability is not triggered by the sale, but Newco's new subsidiary, Target, remains liable to make pension plan contributions and retains withdrawal liability upon a future shutdown or sale.

¶501.3.6 Effect of Target's Retiree Medical Benefits on Newco's Financial Statements

Unless Target has clearly and unambiguously reserved the right to amend or terminate its retiree medical benefits, retirees may have a right to lifetime continuation of medical benefits.

For financial accounting purposes, an employer must accrue, over each employee's working life, the liability and expense for such employee's future post-retirement medical benefits.

¶501.3.7 Bigco Public Announcement

Where Bigco's securities are publicly traded, timing of a Bigco public announcement of the transaction turns on relative size and importance of Target to Bigco.

¶501.3.8 Regulated Industry

Additional issues may arise if Target is engaged in a regulated industry (e.g., telecommunications regulated by the Federal Communications Commission and by state and local cable commissions, railroad transportation regulated by the Federal Department of Transportation, health care, banking, insurance, utility, etc.).

¶501.4 Key Debt Financing Issues

¶501.4.1 Negotiating Bank Loan

Fixed *vs.* floating interest rate.

Fixed repayment schedule *or* requirement to use free cash flow to make principal payments *or* both.

Required repayment of the bank loan (in whole or in part) upon the occurrence of certain events (IPO, sale of a division or subsidiary, sale of the company, change of control, issuance of new equity, issuance of additional debt).

Financial covenants to measure and monitor Target's financial health (i.e., to give the bank an early warning signal).

- Setting financial covenant ratios based on (1) Target's pre-acquisition financial statements *or* (2) Target's post-acquisition financials as affected by APB 16 purchase accounting. See ¶501.8 below for a discussion of purchase accounting for an acquisition.

Security interests in Newco/Target assets.

Bank information and inspection rights and Target required reporting of covenant breach.

Restrictions on Newco dividends, stock redemptions and possibly payments on junior debt (restricted payments).

Restrictions on Newco mergers, acquisitions, capital expenditures, borrowing, new businesses, and other specified activities and uses of funds.

¶501.4.2   Negotiating Subordinated Debentures (or Seller Paper)

Same issues as in ¶501.4.1 above (except that senior bank lender will want junior debt to have fewer and weaker covenants), plus the following additional issues. Interest issues.

- Payable in cash *vs.* accreting *vs.* payable in bunny debentures (i.e., payment-in-kind or PIK debentures).
- If accreting or PIK, ultimately payable in all events *vs.* contingent on Newco's earnings.
- Compound *vs.* simple interest.
- Usury issues.

OID tax rules.

- If the face amount of the debenture exceeds the loan proceeds, the difference is OID.
- If the debenture is a zero coupon instrument, the accreting build-up in face is also OID.
- With a PIK debenture, PIK bunny debentures issued as interest payments are also OID.
- OID is amortized for tax purposes as ordinary income to the holder and as a deduction for Newco on a constant-yield-to-maturity or CYTM basis. Newco's tax deduction for amortized OID is subject to the qualifications discussed at ¶602.8 below.
- OID may be created by an IRS reallocation of tax basis away from the debentures to common stock or warrants issued in conjunction with the debentures (but there is no such IRS reallocation to a conversion privilege).

Scheduling principal payments on the junior debt around the senior debt.

Determining the Newco debt to which debentures will be subordinated. Generally the debentures are expressly subordinated only to specified Newco debt for borrowed money, although infrequently also to trade creditors.

Extent to which payments of principal and interest on junior debt can be cut off by a default on senior debt.

- Cut-off trigger may be different for a payment cut-off on the junior debt and a remedies cut-off (or "standstill") on the junior debt.
- Cut-off triggers on junior debt could include:

    (1)   Insolvency or bankruptcy event.
    (2)   Money default on senior debt.

    (3)   Financial covenant default on senior debt.

    (4)   Technical default on senior debt.

    (5)   Default on junior debt (through a cross-default clause in the senior debt).

- Subordinated lenders will seek to limit the total amount of senior debt, any extensions of the senior debt's maturity date, the type of cut-off events, and the length of the cut-off period.
- Subordinated lenders will seek a requirement that senior debt holder diligently prosecute its rights in order to continue cut-off on junior debt.
- Basket concept, e.g., payments of interest and/or principal to junior debt are permitted only from a percentage of earnings.
- Senior lenders will seek a give-back of payments on junior debt for any interest and principal payments made during the cut-off period.
- In case of bankruptcy: senior debt holder will desire that post-petition interest on its debt constitute senior debt.
- Newco and the senior lender will want new debt which refinances the old senior debt to inherit all the seniority rights vis-a-vis the junior debt.

Junior lender may receive equity rights in Newco as an inducement to supply the junior financing.

- Common stock *vs.* warrants *vs.* conversion rights issued as an inducement to purchase subordinated debentures. See ¶501.5.2 for a discussion of the tax and SEC differences between common stock, warrants, and convertibles.
- Preemptive rights on Target's future sales of new stock (statutory or by agreement) and first refusal or first offer rights on transfers of Target stock.
- Anti-dilution protection (generally only for convertibles and warrants).

    (1)   Simple anti-dilution only for stock splits, stock dividends, recapitalizations, and reorganizations.

    (2)   Institutional weighted average (proportional price and equity protection).

    (3)   Half rachet (full price protection only).

    (4)   Full rachet (full price and equity protection).

    (5)   Protection for spin-offs and large cash or property distributions.

- Registration and other liquidity rights.

    (1)   Demand and piggyback registration rights.

    (2)   Put to Newco or ability to force sale of Newco.

    (3)   Take-along or drag-along rights.

Newco's interest deduction may be disallowed or deferred if Newco and/or Newco's debt instruments fail one or more of the 6 tests described at ¶602.8 below.

¶501.4.3 Negotiating Relative Rights of Various Financing Parties

¶501.4.3.1 Priorities, Express Subordination, and Structural Subordination

Priorities. Priorities among Newco's lenders and preferred shareholders in case of bankruptcy or liquidation will be established through security interests in Newco/Target assets, contractual subordination clauses, and state law priorities for debt over equity, generally as follows:

- Bank lenders.
- Subordinated or mezzanine lenders and trade creditors.
- Junior subordinated seller note or preferred stock.
- VC preferred stock.

No Newco shareholder liability. The essence of an LBO is that no entity above Newco is liable on the acquisition debt, i.e., that neither VC nor any other Newco shareholder guarantees or is otherwise contractually liable for the acquisition debt (other than possibly a guarantee with recourse only to a pledge of Newco's stock, which does not expose any assets held by Newco's shareholders other than their Newco stock).

Express subordination and cut-offs. Under the contractual subordination agreements, a money default or a technical default on one layer will generally cut off payments to lower layers (see ¶501.4.2 above).

Structural subordination. Relative priorities among creditors can be affected by structuring some creditors into a Newco operating subsidiary (so they have first claim on such subsidiary's assets) and some creditors into Newco holding company (so they are structurally subordinated by operation of law to the subsidiary's creditors with respect to the subsidiary's assets), in which case lenders at the subsidiary level can foreclose on and sell subsidiary assets free of the Newco holding company debt.

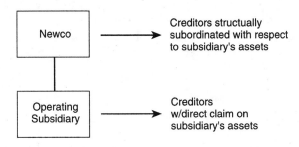

Bank lender usually insists on lending to the operating subsidiary in order to obtain a direct claim against its assets and a more defensible lien.

Mezzanine lender usually prefers to be at the same level as bank lender.

If Newco borrows money and simply purchases Target's *stock*, the acquisition debt (in Newco holding company) is structurally subordinated to all of Target's creditors (with respect to Target's assets). Several methods to avoid such structural subordination of the acquisition debt are illustrated below.

Alternative acquisition structures. Any acquisition can be normally structured in several radically different forms, but the structure selected will generally have a significant effect on a series of important issues, including the relative rights of the financing parties and the tax ramifications to buyer and seller. Several of the alternative structures are discussed below.

¶501.4.3.2   *Purchasing Target's Stock*

Newco can purchase all of Target's stock with money borrowed at the Newco holding company level.

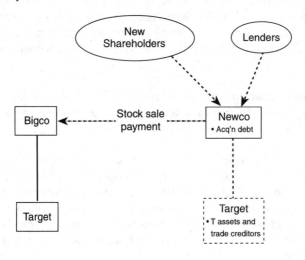

As long as Target does not liquidate or merge into Newco and Target does not guarantee Newco's acquisition debt, Newco is the only entity liable for the acquisition debt. Hence, Target's trade and other creditors are not affected by the acquisition and the acquisition debt is structurally subordinated to Target's trade and other debt.

¶501.4.3.3   *Purchasing Target's Assets*

Newco can purchase all of Target's assets (*or* Newco and a Newco subsidiary can each purchase part of Target's assets) with money borrowed by the entity buying the assets.

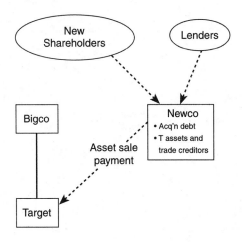

In the structures discussed in ¶501.4.3.3 through ¶501.4.3.7, much or all of the new acquisition financing ends up a liability of the same entity that is liable to Target's old trade and other creditors. Hence, there is no structural subordination as to such new acquisition debt and Target's trade and other creditors are disadvantaged by the acquisition to the extent that the post-acquisition entity which is liable to them has also become liable for the new acquisition debt incurred to finance Newco's purchase of Target, i.e., because such new acquisition debt becomes a pari passu claim against the purchased Target assets, or may even become a senior claim if the acquisition lender receives a lien on such assets, thereby diluting the assets available to service Target's pre-acquisition debt.

¶501.4.3.4   *Purchasing Target's Stock Plus Target Liquidation*

Newco can purchase Target's stock with money borrowed at the Newco level and immediately thereafter (1) liquidate Target by distributing its assets (subject to its liabilities) upstream into Newco *or* (2) merge Target upstream into Newco. Target's pre-acquisition creditors are disadvantaged by the acquisition because Newco ends up liable for both Target's pre-acquisition debts and the new acquisition debt, thereby diluting the assets available to service the Target's pre-acquisition debt.

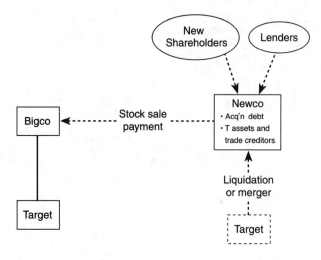

¶*501.4.3.5 Reverse Subsidiary Cash Merger*

Newco can merge a transitory subsidiary into Target, with money borrowed at either the Newco level or the transitory subsidiary-Target level, so that (1) Target survives the merger, (2) Target's old shareholder(s) (Bigco) receives the stated merger consideration in cancellation of its old Target stock, (3) Newco receives new Target shares in exchange for its Transitory Subsidiary shares, and (4) after the transaction Newco owns 100% of Target's stock. Target's pre-acquisition creditors are disadvantaged to the extent the acquisition debt is at transitory subsidiary-Target level, so that in the merger the acquisition debt is inherited by Target, thereby diluting the assets available to service Target's pre-acquisition debt.

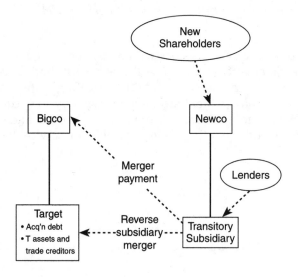

¶501.4.3.6   Reverse Two-Party Cash Merger

Newco can merge directly into Target, with (1) Target surviving the merger, (2) Target's old shareholder(s) (Bigco) receiving the stated merger consideration in cancellation of its old Target stock, and (3) Newco's shareholders receiving new Target shares in exchange for their Newco shares, so that after the transaction Newco's shareholders own directly 100% of Target's stock.

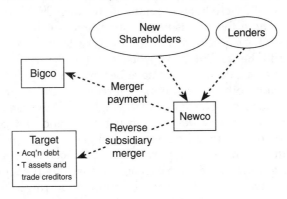

¶501.4.3.7   Part Purchase Plus Part Redemption of Target's Stock

Newco can purchase a portion of Target's stock from Bigco (with money borrowed at the Newco level) and Target can simultaneously redeem the remainder of its stock from Bigco (with money borrowed at the Target level), so that after the transaction Newco owns 100% of Target's stock. Target's pre-acquisition creditors are disadvantaged to the extent the money is borrowed at the Target level to finance the redemption, thereby diluting the assets available to service Target's pre-acquisition debt.

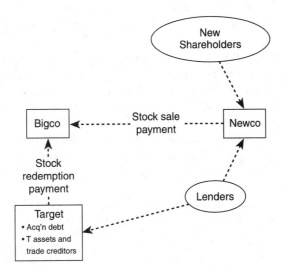

¶501.4.3.8   Fraudulent Conveyance Risk

(1) Where the acquisition is structured so that the new acquisition lenders are structurally subordinated to Target's trade and other creditors (such as where Newco purchases Target's stock, see ¶501.4.3.2 above), there should be no fraudulent conveyance problem (unless Target and Newco are thereafter combined by merger or liquidation or Target guarantees Newco's acquisition debt), because Target's trade and other creditors are not disadvantaged by the acquisition.

(2) However, where the acquisition is structured so that the same entity is liable both for the new acquisition debt and for Target's trade and other liabilities, Target's trade and other creditors are worse off after the transaction than before (because the new acquisition lenders have become pari passu with or senior to Target's trade and other creditors). Moreover, under the collapse (or step-transaction) doctrine, Newco's borrowings from the acquisition lenders, Newco's acquisition of Target's assets and liabilities, and Newco's payments to Target's old shareholders are all treated as a single transaction. Thus, Newco is viewed for fraudulent conveyance purposes as not receiving adequate consideration from the acquisition lenders in exchange for issuing them debt instruments (and possibly security interests), because the amount borrowed from the acquisition lenders is promptly paid out to Target's shareholders (rather than used to pay Target's creditors or to acquire additional assets for Target[3]).

In order to prevent the transaction from constituting a fraudulent conveyance where the same entity is (after the acquisition) liable for both the new acquisition debt and Target's trade and other liabilities, the entity which ends up liable to Target's trade and other creditors must meet all 3 of the following tests immediately after the acquisition:

- **Solvency:** Asset FV exceeds liabilities, including reasonably anticipated contingent liabilities.

    There are at least 2 highly subjective issues in this determination: (1) the FV of intangible assets (including goodwill, going concern value, customer lists, etc.) and (2) the reasonably anticipated amount of any contingent liabilities.

    Where Target slips into bankruptcy soon after the buyout, 20-20 hindsight may undermine optimistic valuations of Target's intangible (and possibly even tangible) assets made shortly before the buyout, especially with respect to goodwill and going concern value. Hence, where Target's business is liquidated soon after the buyout and the court finds that the parties should, at the time of the buyout, have anticipated the liquidation, the court will generally value intangible assets (as well as tangible assets) at their lower *liquidation* values rather than at *going concern* values. In particular, values

---

[3]On the other hand, where (as discussed in (1) above) the acquisition is structured as Newco purchasing Target's stock (without Target becoming liable for the new acquisition debt), Newco's acquisition of an additional asset—the Target stock—should be respected, so that the collapse doctrine should not apply and in any event Target's trade and other creditors are not prejudiced (because Newco's acquisition debt is structurally subordinated to Target's trade and other creditors).

given to goodwill and similar assets under GAAP purchase acquisition accounting rules are likely to be substantially discounted or reduced to zero if the court finds that such items would yield little or no value in a liquidation.

- **Adequate capital:** Asset FV exceeds liabilities (including reasonably anticipated contingent liabilities) by enough to give the entity a reasonable amount of capital.

  There are at least 3 highly subjective issues in this determination: the 2 mentioned in the solvency discussion above plus the amount which is reasonable for capital.

- **Ability to pay debts:** Cash flow projections indicate that the entity will have the ability to pay its obligations as they mature in the ordinary course of business.

  There are many highly subjective issues in this determination: future sales levels, future expense levels, the success or failure of existing or planned products, the outcome of lawsuits, claims, and other contingent liabilities, ability to borrow additional amounts or to refinance maturing debts, the anticipated contributions toward contingent liabilities by co-defendants, ability to sell surplus assets or unwanted businesses (and at what price), etc.

Where the acquisition structure prejudices Target's trade creditors, Newco generally supplies the acquisition lenders with carefully prepared asset appraisals, contingent liability estimates, cash flow projections, and other data designed to make the lenders comfortable that all 3 tests described above are satisfied. It is also common for Newco to supply the acquisition lenders with a solvency opinion from an IB or an experienced appraiser.

If the transaction is a fraudulent conveyance and the acquisition entity fails to pay its debts, there is risk that the new acquisition lenders are aiders and abettors (hence both losing their liens and becoming subordinated to other creditors) and that Target's selling shareholders (at least insider shareholders who knew that the transaction involved adding substantial leverage (i.e., debt) to the acquiring entity's balance sheet) must give back their sales proceeds. There is even some risk that a fraudulent conveyance may cause Newco's new shareholders to be liable as aiders and abettors.

The fraudulent conveyance rules, if found to apply, will often help not only trade and other creditors at the time of the acquisition, but also subsequent creditors.

References:

- Bankruptcy Code §101(32), §544(b)(1), §548, §550
- State fraudulent conveyance laws: Uniform Fraudulent Conveyance Act, Uniform Fraudulent Transfer Act, and South Carolina and Virginia laws utilizing Statute of Elizabeth approach (intent to delay, hinder, or defraud creditors in South Carolina and insolvency in Virginia)
- Ginsburg and Levin M&A book ¶1706

¶501.4.3.9   Other Issues

(1) Upstream guarantees. There are significant issues regarding the validity of an upstream guarantee of Newco-level debt by a Newco subsidiary (and liens to support such guarantees) under the fraudulent conveyance doctrine (and perhaps under the equitable subordination doctrine and some state corporate laws).

(a) If the subsidiary is insolvent or undercapitalized when it guarantees Newco debt (or becomes insolvent or undercapitalized because of the guarantee), the guarantee will be invalid (under federal bankruptcy, state fraudulent conveyance, and/or state corporate law) unless the subsidiary received reasonably equivalent value for giving the guarantee.

(b) To minimize these risks, the subsidiary's guarantee agreement may state that the subsidiary is guaranteeing Newco's debt to the lender but not more than a specified maximum guarantee dollar amount, which the parties would calculate based on the FV of the subsidiary's assets less the amount of its liabilities at the time the guarantee is given. Whether the FV of the subsidiary's assets is calculated based upon going concern or liquidation value is often hotly contested and generally turns on whether (with 20-20 hindsight) the subsidiary's business was reasonably expected, at the time of the guarantee, to remain a going concern or should have been expected to be liquidated.

(c) Under a more conservative approach, after the maximum guarantee dollar amount is calculated based on the subsidiary's asset FV net of its liabilities at the time the guarantee is given (as described in (b) above), a further reduction is made for a reasonable capital amount for the subsidiary's business.

(d) Under another more conservative approach, the maximum guarantee dollar amount is the amount calculated (either under (b) or (c) above) at the time the guaranty is given or, if less, such an amount recalculated when the guarantee is called.

(e) In an effort to avoid the drafting and calculation issues inherent in (b) through (d) above, the subsidiary's guarantee agreement could simply state that the subsidiary is guaranteeing the maximum amount of Newco's debt that the subsidiary is permitted by law to guarantee without causing the guaranty to be voided under the fraudulent conveyance doctrine, the equitable subordination doctrine, state corporate law, or any other similar doctrine.

(f) There have been very few court decisions interpreting the legal nuances discussed above, and hence the actual contours of the legal principles remain vague.

If a foreign subsidiary guarantees or pledges assets to secure Newco debt (or if a foreign subsidiary's stock is pledged to secure Newco debt), Newco may be treated for U.S. tax purposes as receiving a dividend from the foreign subsidiary. See Code §956 and Ginsburg and Levin M&A book ¶1404.

(2)   Effect of tax law on choice of acquisition structure. Substantial federal income tax issues turn on choice of acquisition structure, including:

- Asset SUB vs. asset COB on the buyer's side.
- Single tax vs. double tax on the seller's side.

These important issues are discussed at ¶501.7 below.

At least one important *state* income tax issue may turn on the acquisition structure: some states prohibit a parent corporation and its subsidiaries from filing a consolidated *state* income tax return (perhaps unless they are engaged in a "unitary business"). In such a case, there will be a state income tax problem if some or all of the acquisition debt (and the corresponding interest deduction) is at the parent level but the earnings are at the subsidiary level.

See ¶701.2.2 below regarding the use of management fees or parent-subsidiary interest-bearing loans as possible techniques to transfer income from an operating subsidiary to the parent level where it can be offset for state income tax purposes against the parent's interest deductions on the acquisition debt.

¶501.5   Key Equity Financing Issues

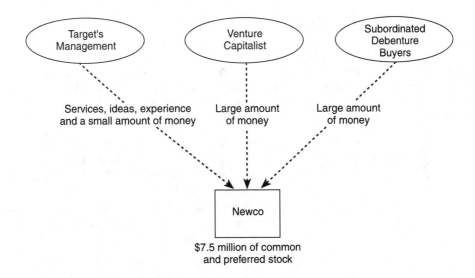

¶501.5.1   VC's and Subordinated Debenture Buyers' Equity

VC and subordinated debenture ("SD") buyers may purchase any one or a combination of the following:

- Straight subordinated debentures.
- Straight preferred stock.

- Common stock.
- Warrants.
- Convertible subordinated debentures.
- Convertible preferred stock.

VCs and SD buyers may seek additional equity rights:

- Right to one or more demand and/or piggyback public offerings.
- Priorities on a public offering in case of underwriting limitation.
- Right to force sale of Newco or put investment back to Newco.
- Preemptive rights.
- Right to take control of Newco's board.

¶501.5.2 Tax and SEC Issues in Evaluating Convertible vs. Warrants vs. Cheap Common

¶501.5.2.1 Purchasing Common Stock

Money spent is at risk and has no yield.

¶501.5.2.2 Warrants—Tax Aspects

No money spent and hence nothing at risk until exercise. However, IRS more-than-12-month tax holding period for LTCG generally starts only when warrant is exercised (which is generally relevant only to a non-corporate holder, to whom federal tax law grants a lower tax rate on LTCG—currently 20% rather than 38.6%[4]), subject to the following qualifications:

- The reason the tax holding period for stock received on a warrant exercise generally begins anew at the time of exercise is that long-standing Code §1223(6) states that where "stock [is] . . . acquired . . . by the exercise of rights to acquire such stock . . . , there shall be included [in the stock's holding period] only the period beginning with the date on which the right to acquire was exercised." There are, however, two arguments that at least a portion of the warrant stock takes a tacked holding period:

  - First, if the warrant exercise price is paid by surrender of another Newco security (long-term debt, preferred stock, or common stock) (i.e., a gross cashless exercise), it is probable (but not certain) that a portion of the new stock received on exercise (equal to the FV of the surrendered security used to pay the warrant exercise price) takes a tacked IRS holding period from the surrendered security (as a tax-free recapitaliza-

---

[4] The top individual 2002 and 2003 federal rate is really higher than the 38.6% nominal rate because of the 3% itemized deduction disallowance, as described in ¶201.1.1 above.

tion or, where the surrendered security is common stock, a Code §1036
common-for-common exchange), and the remaining new stock received
on exercise (equal to the amount by which the warrant was in the
money) starts a new IRS more-than-12-month tax holding period.

- Second, a 1/98 change in IRS regulations (treating a warrant as a "security" for tax purposes) now allows an exchange of old warrants for new
  stock to be treated as a tax free recapitalization; thus it is now strongly
  arguable (but not certain) that a net cashless exercise of a warrant
  without payment of any exercise price (where common stock is issued
  with an FV equal to the warrant spread) qualifies as a recapitalization
  with tacked holding period from the warrant to all of the stock received
  upon exercise. It is possible (but less likely) that this argument could
  also be applied to a gross cashless exercise to give all of the stock
  received upon exercise a tacked holding period.

- Independent of the two arguments above, if the warrant has a nominal
  exercise price (in relation to the FV of the underlying stock on the date the
  warrant is issued), it is strongly arguable (but not certain) that the warrant
  should be treated as stock for federal income tax purposes, and hence
  exercise of the warrant should not start a new holding period.
- Sale of unexercised warrant held more than one year to an underwriter or
  other person qualifies for LTCG.
- These tax rules apply only to an investor warrant. For the very different
  tax rules applicable to an option issued to a service provider in connection
  with the performance of services, see ¶407.

¶501.5.2.3   Convertible—Tax Aspects

No money at risk in no-yield common stock until convert. Conversion does
not start new IRS one-year holding period; rather, IRS holding period tacks from
convertible debenture or convertible preferred stock to common stock, which is
generally relevant only to a non-corporate holder.

¶501.5.2.4   Tax Allocation to Warrant or Common But Not
             Conversion Feature

With convertibles, there is no separate tax allocation of consideration to the
conversion privilege.

However, if the holder buys straight debenture or straight preferred stock plus
a valuable warrant or common stock (an investment unit), there is a tax allocation
to the warrant or common stock, which will generally create OID for the straight
debt or preferred stock.

- Under IRS regulations, if the holder purchases debt plus a valuable warrant
  or common stock, the issuer's allocation of the purchase price between the

debt and the warrant or common stock (whether or not specified in the contract) is binding on the holder (absent disclosure on the holder's tax return that it has taken a position inconsistent with the issuer) but is not binding on IRS.

- If the holder purchases preferred stock plus a warrant or common stock, no IRS regulations govern allocation for tax purposes. Contractual allocation to prevent the holder and issuer from taking inconsistent positions is helpful but not binding on IRS.

IRS rules under which the holder recognizes OID amortization income differ between debt OID and preferred OID as discussed at ¶602.5 and ¶603.7 below.

¶501.5.2.5   SEC Rule 144 Holding Period

Where VC or the SD buyer holds restricted securities (see ¶207 above), VC's or the SD buyer's SEC holding period for such securities is relevant for Rule 144's 1-year/2-year public sale provisions, as discussed at ¶903 below.

- **Purchase from Newco or affiliate.** If the holder purchases the securities from Newco or a Newco affiliate (i.e., a member of Newco's control group), the SEC holding period generally does not begin until the holder has paid the full purchase price, although a full recourse note from the purchaser, secured by assets (other than the Newco securities being purchased) with an FV at least equal to the note, will also generally start the SEC holding period, so long as the note is paid before resale of the securities.
- **Purchase from non-affiliate.** If the holder does not purchase the securities from Newco or a Newco affiliate, the holder tacks the transferor's SEC holding period.
- **Convertible.** When a convertible debenture or preferred stock is converted into common stock, the SEC holding period for the convertible security tacks to the SEC holding period for the new common stock.
- **Warrant.** A warrant holder starts a new SEC holding period for the new common stock received upon warrant exercise, *except* (1) where the warrant exercise price is paid by surrender of another security of the same company (debentures, preferred stock, common stock) (i.e., a gross cashless exercise), the holder tacks the shorter of the SEC holding period for the surrendered security or the SEC holding period for the warrant to the SEC holding period for the new common stock and (2) where the warrant is exchanged for common stock with an FV equal to the spread in the warrant (i.e., a net cashless exercise without payment of any warrant exercise price), the holder tacks the SEC holding period for the warrant to the holding period for the new common stock.
- **Incorporation of partnership or LLC.** If Newco was originally formed as a partnership or LLC (e.g., in order to obtain flow-through tax treatment) and was later transformed into a corporation (e.g., in anticipation of an IPO), SEC takes the illogical position that (1) the holders' SEC holding

period in the partnership or LLC interests does not tack to the corporate stock received in exchange, because the decision to incorporate is a new investment decision, but (2) the holders' SEC holding period does tack where (i) at the time of the holder's original investment in the partnership or LLC, a written agreement contemplated that the entity would be transformed into corporate form in connection with an IPO, (ii) no additional consideration is paid at the time of the transformation, (iii) the incorporation causes no shift in the holders' economic interests not contemplated by the original documents, and (iv) the holders do not retain any veto power or other voting power with respect to the transformation. However, SEC takes the position that there is no tacking for any equity owner of the partnership or LLC (e.g., the general partner) who did have a veto power or other voting power with respect to the incorporation.[5]

¶501.5.2.6   Recapitalization, Merger, or Other Tax-Free Reorganization

Under 1/98 IRS regulations, applying to exchanges on and after 3/9/98, an exchange of outstanding Newco warrants for stock or warrants of an acquiring corporation as part of a tax-free reorganization qualifies as a tax-free exchange. For an exchange prior to 3/9/98, an outstanding Newco warrant did not qualify for tax-free exchange for new securities under the tax-free reorganization rules, but if the warrant was exercised before the acquisition, the newly purchased common stock would qualify.

¶501.5.2.7   Anti-Dilution Provision

See ¶501.4.2 above.

¶501.5.3   Liabilities Which Migrate Upstream Where One Person Owns Large Amount of Newco Stock

¶501.5.3.1   Pension Plan and Other ERISA Liabilities

Where VC owns 80% or more (as defined below) of Newco's stock, VC is contingently liable under ERISA and the Code (except as set forth below) if (1) Newco fails to make a required pension plan contribution when due, (2) Newco terminates an underfunded pension plan, (3) Newco withdraws from an un-

---

[5] If Newco partnership or LLC has an IPO (see Code §7704) or checks the box for corporate tax treatment (see ¶302.8.1), Newco will (although still a partnership or LLC for state law purposes) be treated as a corporation for federal tax purposes, but no new SEC holding period will begin. However, this technique will not transform Newco into a state law corporation (which is generally desirable for IPO purposes).

derfunded multiemployer union pension plan, (4) Newco fails to pay a PBGC premium, or (5) Newco fails to discharge a continuation medical coverage ("COBRA") obligation to former employees (collectively, "ERISA group liabilities").

Where VC owns 80% or more of Newco and Newco in turn acquires 80% or more of Target, VC is (except as set forth below) similarly contingently liable for Target's ERISA group liabilities.

Likewise, where VC owns 80% or more of Newco's stock and 80% or more of other portfolio companies, VC and each of VC's 80%-or-more-owned portfolio companies are (except as set forth below) similarly contingently liable for the ERISA group liabilities of all other 80%-or-more-owned portfolio companies. See ¶501.3.5.2 and ¶501.3.5.3 above for a more detailed discussion of these liabilities.

These rules clearly apply where VC is a corporation, so that if Newco (or its new subsidiary Target) falls upon financial hard times, VC and its other 80%-or-more-owned portfolio companies are liable for Newco's (or Target's) ERISA group liabilities.

However, where VC is a partnership or an LLC (rather than a corporation) not engaged in a "trade or business," (1) there is a strong argument based on the regulatory language that VC itself is not liable and (2) there is also an argument (albeit weaker) that VC's 80%-or-more-owned portfolio companies are not liable for each other's ERISA group liabilities, although PBGC has informally indicated its likely disagreement with the second argument.

If income tax precedents are applied in determining whether non-corporate VC is engaged in a "trade or business," then a VC engaged only in long-term investment activities, even though actively conducted by a staff of professionals, would not be engaged in a trade or business. However, several cases dealing with the ERISA-group-liability issue have declined to apply income tax trade-or-business precedents, (1) holding instead that ERISA should be construed liberally to provide maximum protection to workers covered by pension plans and (2) seizing upon language in a Supreme Court income tax decision interpreting trade or business as an activity with continuity, regularity, and a primary purpose of income or profit. Hence it is not clear whether for ERISA purposes a VC engaged in long-term active investing with a professional staff might be treated as engaged in a trade or business.

The above-described 80%-or-more ownership test is satisfied (so that an upper-tier entity (and its 80%-or-more-owned subsidiaries) are (except as set forth above) liable for a lower-tier entity's ERISA group liabilities) (1) where the upper-tier entity owns 80% or more of the lower-tier entity's stock by vote or value if the lower-tier entity is a *corporation* and (2) where the upper-tier entity owns 80% or more of the lower-tier entity's capital or profits if the lower-tier entity is a *partnership or LLC*.

In computing whether VC owns 80% or more of Newco (or another portfolio company), (1) VC is treated as owning a pro rata portion of stock owned by an entity in which VC has an interest, (2) VC is treated as owning stock owned by a third party where VC has an option to purchase such stock, (3) VC apparently is not treated as owning unissued stock VC could acquire from the issuer upon exercise of warrants, conversion privileges, and the like, and (4) if VC owns 50% or more of Newco (or another portfolio company), certain stock owned by third parties (including, most importantly, stock owned by an employee of such company which is subject to vesting or other transfer restrictions) is treated as not outstanding.

For example, where VC owns 79% of Newco's stock and a Newco executive owns the other 21%, but one-half the executive's stock is subject to *either* vesting or a right of first refusal (or both) on the part of Newco, VC is treated as owning 88% of Newco (79 ÷ [100 − 10.5]).

¶501.5.3.2 *Environmental Cleanup*

(1) Owner/operator liability. Under CERCLA (the principal federal environmental cleanup statute), each person who is an "owner or operator" of a contaminated facility is liable for the cleanup of the facility. Under some circumstances a control shareholder (here VC) can be liable for cleanup of a facility owned or operated by the company it controlled (here Newco, VC's portfolio company).

A 1998 Supreme Court decision (*United States v. Bestfoods*)[6] replaced a variety of inconsistent tests that had grown up under previous lower court decisions and set forth two routes to liability for a control person.

(2) Veil-piercing. Like any other liability, CERCLA owner or operator liability can reach a shareholder if usual common law standards for "piercing the corporate veil" are met (see ¶301.5.1 above).

(3) Direct "operator" liability. Although the *Bestfoods* case cut back on the control shareholder liability established by some prior lower court decisions, it left open the possibility that, in certain circumstances, a shareholder can be liable under CERCLA as a facility "operator" even where veil piercing tests are not met. Those circumstances are quite limited:

- *Bestfoods* restricted such shareholder "operator" liability to situations where the shareholder is involved with the portfolio company's contaminated facility and the facility's "operations related to pollution," i.e., where the shareholder exercises control over "operations having to do with the leakage or disposal of hazardous waste, or decisions about compliance with environmental regulations." *Bestfoods* thus rejected prior cases suggesting shareholder liability results from a more generalized exercise of control.
- *Bestfoods* relied heavily on whether the shareholder's conduct fell within "norms of corporate behavior." If so, the conduct is probably safe, while behavior which is "eccentric" by such norms or unduly favors the shareholder's interest over the portfolio company's interest is more likely to result in liability.

---

[6] 524 U.S. 51, 118 S. Ct. 1876 (1998).

- A shareholder's involvement with a portfolio company is probably safe if limited to what is "consistent with investor status," e.g.:

  - monitoring the portfolio company's performance,
  - supervising the portfolio company's finance and capital budget decisions, and
  - articulating general policies and procedures.

- Contrary to suggestions in some prior cases, "dual" officials (those with formal roles in both the control shareholder and the portfolio company) are not inherently suspect, but rather are presumed to be acting on behalf of the portfolio company when their actions affect the portfolio company's facility.
- However, a red flag goes up where shareholder representatives who lack a formal role with the portfolio company nonetheless take actions affecting the portfolio company's facility, particularly its "operations related to pollution."
- *Bestfoods* implies that a shareholder should not be liable for an acquired portfolio company's pre-acquisition contamination (i.e., contamination resulting *exclusively* from actions of the company's prior owners).

(4) Meaning of control. In contrast to the underfunded pension rules discussed at ¶501.5.3.1 above, the CERCLA cases do *not* require a person to own *80%* of a company to potentially constitute a liable party for CERCLA purposes, and indeed there is risk that liability may be imposed even where VC owns *less than 50%* but enough of the other factors giving rise to such liability are present.

¶501.5.3.3   Other Liabilities

Under the traditional common law doctrine of piercing the corporate veil, there is a slight risk that a control person may be held responsible for a portfolio company's liabilities of all types. See ¶301.5.1 for a discussion of the principal factors leading to a finding that a control person should bear such derivative liability.

¶501.5.4 Management's Equity

¶501.5.4.1   General Considerations

Serial vesting on management's 20% of Newco common, so that Newco has an option to repurchase unvested common shares at cost (or perhaps at the lower of cost or FV) when executive leaves Newco's employ.

ISO *vs.* NQO *vs.* cash purchase of stock *vs.* purchase of stock for recourse note bearing interest at IRS imputation rate.

See ¶¶202.2, 202.3 and 407 above for a discussion of these techniques and their tax and accounting aspects.

¶501.5.4.2 *Sarbanes-Oxley Act §402 Executive Loan Prohibition*

Frequently Newco's executives pay for Newco common stock with a note or partly in cash and partly for a note, as described in ¶202.2.

However, Sarbanes-Oxley Act of 2002 ("SO") §402 prohibits any company covered by SO's "issuer" definition (generally a company with publicly-issued or publicly-traded securities, as described in more detail below) from:

> directly or indirectly, including through any subsidiary, . . . extend[ing] or main-tain[ing] credit, . . . arrang[ing] for the extension of credit, or renew[ing] an extension of credit, in the form of a personal loan to or for any director or executive officer (or equivalent thereof). . . .[7]

Where a company falling within SO's "issuer" definition sells stock to an executive officer (or director) for a note (or partially for cash and partially for a note), the note likely constitutes an extension of credit in the form of a personal loan and hence falls within SO §402's loan prohibition. This is because (absent a favorable, and unlikely, SEC interpretation) the note issued to the company by the executive in exchange for the company's stock (like a personal borrowing of cash) is an obligation of the executive to pay money at maturity, generally with interest.

SO defines "issuer" (i.e., a company subject to SO §402's loan prohibition) as:

(1) a company with a class of equity or debt securities traded on a national securities exchange (a 1934 Act §12(b) company), or

(2) a company with (a) a class of equity securities (or warrants or options) held by 500 or more holders of record and (b) consolidated gross assets of $10 million or more (based on its balance sheet prepared in accordance with GAAP) (a 1934 Act §12(g) company), or

(3) a company which has sold equity or debt securities pursuant to a 1933 Act registration statement and hence is "required to file [10-K, 10-Q, and other] reports [with SEC] under [1934 Act] section 15(d)" (a 1934 Act §15(d) company), except that such a company's status as a §15(d) company (and thus as an "issuer") is automatically suspended for each year (subsequent to the year in which the 1933 Act registration becomes effective) when the company has (on the first day of such subsequent year) fewer than 300 record holders of such 1933 Act registered security, or

(4) a company which has filed with SEC a 1933 Act registration statement covering equity or debt securities that has not yet become effective but has not yet been withdrawn.

If a company falls within any one of these 4 "issuer" definitions, the company is prohibited from making a loan to an executive officer (or director) or continuing

---

[7] SO §402 adds this loan prohibition as §13(k) of the 1934 Act.

a loan previously outstanding (except for a loan outstanding before SO's 7/30/02 enactment and not thereafter materially modified or renewed). As discussed above, this prohibition likely includes (absent a favorable, and unlikely, SEC interpretation) executive's note for the purchase of company stock.

There are several circumstances where a company might become a covered "issuer" (subject to SO §402's loan prohibition) even though the company has no publicly traded equity securities:

(a) Under (2) above, a company with 500 or more record holders of a class of equity securities and $10 million or more of assets is an "issuer" even if there is no public trading in the company's stock.

(b) Under (4) above, a company which files a 1933 Act registration statement with SEC to sell equity or debt securities (even though the registration statement has never become effective) immediately becomes an "issuer" at the time of filing with SEC, unless and until the 1933 Act registration becomes effective (in which case the company becomes an "issuer" under (3) above) or the company takes affirmative steps to withdraw the not-yet-effective 1933 Act registration statement (so that a company whose 1933 Act registration statement is on hold should generally withdraw the registration statement if the company desires to avoid SO §402's loan prohibition).

For example, a company filing a 1933 Act registration statement for (i) an equity IPO or (ii) an issuance of high-yield bonds—either for cash in the public market or in an A/B exchange for bonds previously issued in a private placement or offshore transaction—is immediately covered at the time of its 1933 Act filing with SEC.

(c) Under (3) above, where a company's 1933 Act registration statement for equity or debt securities (including high-yield bonds) actually becomes effective and the securities are sold, the company is thereafter required to file 1934 Act §15(d) periodic SEC reports and is an "issuer." However, such a §15(d) company—which has not become a §12(b) company (listed on a national securities exchange) or a §12(g) company (with 500 or more record holders of a class of equity securities and $10 million or more of assets)—ceases to be required to file §15(d) SEC reports, and hence ceases to be covered by SO §402, with respect to any year subsequent to the year its 1933 Act registration became effective if, on the first day of such subsequent year, such class of 1933 Act registered securities is held by fewer than 300 record holders.

Thus, where Newco sells stock to an executive officer for a note (or partly for a note) and then acquires Target in an LBO financed in part by 1933 Act registered high-yield bonds, Newco (i) becomes an "issuer" under (4) above (so that the executive must pay the note) immediately upon filing with SEC the 1933 Act registration for the high-yield bonds, (ii) continues to be an "issuer" under (3) above once the 1933 Act registered bonds are issued, but (iii) ceases to be an "issuer" once the bonds are (on the first day of a Newco fiscal year subsequent to the year of the bond sale) held by fewer than 300 record holders. The reason Newco ceases to be an issuer once it drops below 300 record holders of the 1933 Act registered bonds is that Newco is no longer "required to file reports under [1934 Act] section 15(d)." However, it is unclear whether Newco continues to be an "issuer" for approximately an additional 3 months, i.e., until Newco files its 10-K report for its last §15(d) year.

EXAMPLE

VC-financed (calendar year) Newco files with SEC a 1933 Act registration statement for high-yield bonds on 8/1 year 1 to finance Newco's acquisition of Target. The registration statement becomes effective and the bonds are sold to 20 institutional buyers on 12/1 year 1. Newco has no securities listed on a national securities exchange and no class of equity securities held of record by 500 or more persons. On 1/1 year 2 Newco has fewer than 300 record holders of the bonds.

On 8/1 year 1 when Newco files the 1933 Act registration statement, it becomes an "issuer" under (4) above and hence is covered by SO §402.

On 12/1 year 1 when Newco sells the bonds, it remains an "issuer" under (3) above and hence continues to be covered by SO §402.

However, on 1/1 year 2 Newco (with fewer than 300 record holders of the bonds on the first day of a year subsequent to the year the bonds' 1933 Act registration became effective) automatically ceases to be covered by 1934 Act §15(d) with respect to years subsequent to year 1, i.e., the year in which Newco sold the 1933 Act registered bonds (although SEC requests that Newco file a form 15 notifying SEC that Newco has ceased to be a §15(d) company). Notwithstanding this cessation: (1) Newco is still required to file its 10-K for year 1 with SEC (in approximately March of year 2) and (2) if Newco's 1933 Act registered bonds are ever held by 300 or more record holders in the future, Newco would again be covered by 1934 Act §15(d).

Arguably Newco ceases to be an "issuer" under (3) above—i.e., a company "required to file reports under [1934 Act] section 15(d)"—on 1/1 year 2, since it has only one report (year 1's 10-K) to file with SEC, and is no longer required to file "reports" generally. However, SEC has not yet indicated its view on this timing issue and hence there is risk SEC may take the position that Newco's obligation to file a last 10-K for year 1 (in March of year 2) means that Newco is still required to file "reports" until that final 10-K is actually filed.

Most high-yield indentures for 1933 Act registered bonds require Newco (even after dropping below 300 record holders and thus ceasing to be required by the 1934 Act to file periodic SEC reports) to continue filing with SEC the 1934 Act §15(d) reports which Newco would have been required to file with SEC if Newco still had 300 or more holders of such bonds. This raises the question whether such a "voluntary filer" (i.e., a company required to file 1934 Act reports with SEC by indenture but not by law) is, by virtue of filing SEC reports not required by law, covered by part (3) of the "issuer" definition (i.e., a company "required to file reports under [1934 Act] section 15(d)"). On 11/8/02 SEC announced that "required to file" means required by law, not by contract, so that a voluntary filer is not an "issuer."

Where Newco proposes to issue high-yield bonds to finance its LBO of Target, Newco may adopt 3 alternative courses of action to avoid SO §402's loan prohibition:

First, Newco can issue the bonds in the private Rule 144A market (rather than in a 1933 Act registered public offering) without any agreement to effect a subsequent 1933 Act registered A/B exchange of the private bonds for similar SEC registered bonds.

Second, Newco can adopt a two-tier holding company/operating company structure—with 1933 Act registered high-yield bonds issued by operating subsidiary—so that parent holding company, which sells holding company stock to executives, never becomes an SO §402 covered "issuer" at all. Under this approach, holding company must not guarantee operating subsidiary's bonds, because the guarantee is itself a security that must be registered, which would cause holding company to become an "issuer."

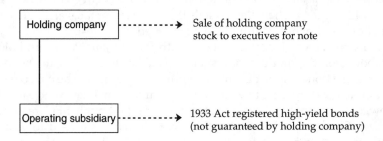

This approach should not violate the spirit of SO §402's loan prohibition, which is designed to prevent a covered "issuer" from risking assets belonging in part to the issuer's public holders by making risky loans to the issuer's executives. Where only the operating subsidiary has public holders (the high-yield bondholders), the parent holding company's loan to an executive does not put at risk any of the operating subsidiary's assets (just as a loan from a VC investor in holding company to holding company's executives—not guaranteed by operating company—would not put at risk any of operating company's assets).

Because SO §402 also prohibits an "issuer" from "arranging" a loan to an executive officer (or director) of the "issuer," operating subsidiary (which is an "issuer") should not "arrange" for executive's loan from holding company (or from holding company's VC investor). Because holding company and operating subsidiary likely have many overlapping employees, there may be uncertainty on this "arranging" issue where one or more employees of both companies are involved in holding company's sale of stock to a person who is an executive of both. However, it would clearly be helpful if (a) the borrowing executive—although also an operating company executive—has some duties to holding company which make it rational for holding company to extend credit (i.e., engage in a stock sale for a note) to such executive and (b) the holding company officials who approve and document the stock sale for a note are not operating company employees (e.g., the holding company directors who vote for the stock sale and receive the executive's note in exchange are not operating company employees, although they could be employees of the VC investor serving as part-time holding company officials).

Third, Newco's VC investor or some other third party can lend money to the executive (so that the executive can purchase the Newco stock for cash, rather than for a note), with Newco subsequently lending money to executive (so executive can pay off the VC or third party loan) once Newco ceases to be an "issuer" "required to file" 1934 Act §15(d) reports (because the bonds are held by fewer than 300 record holders).

An executive officer covered by SO §402's loan prohibition (under 1934 Act Rule 3b-7) is:

- issuer's president
- each of issuer's vice presidents in charge of a principal business unit, division, or function (such as sales, administration, or finance)
- each of issuer's officers performing policy-making functions for issuer
- each executive officer of a subsidiary of issuer performing policy-making functions for issuer

Where Newco is not an "issuer" at the time of Newco's post-7/29/02 stock sale to an executive officer for a note, but becomes an "issuer" subsequently (e.g., because Newco subsequently files a 1933 Act registration statement), the loan becomes a §402 violation as soon as Newco becomes an issuer. Similarly, where Newco is an "issuer" at the time of Newco's post-7/29/02 stock sale to a lower level employee (i.e., not an executive officer) for a note but the lower level employee is subsequently promoted to executive-officer level, the loan becomes a §402 violation as soon as the executive is promoted. Hence any loan documents should require payment of the note immediately before any event that would make the loan illegal under SO §402.

Reference:

- 1934 Act §13(k)(1) [Sarbanes-Oxley Act §402]

¶501.5.5   Board Control and Related Issues

Voting agreement on board seats: mezzanine lenders, VCs, management.
Veto powers through negative covenants: banks, mezzanine lender, VCs.
Public offering registration rights and rights to require eventual sale of Newco.
Rights of a specific stockholder or group of stockholders to veto particular Newco actions, such as mergers, acquisitions, sale of Newco, sales of additional

Newco stock, borrowing, expansion, entering new business, change in top executives.

Board seats and board control—initially and in case of default or failure to meet specified goals.

See ¶205 above for a discussion of structuring control of Newco's board.

See ¶206 above for a discussion of establishing control over an IPO or a sale of Newco.

¶501.5.6   SEC and State Securities Law Compliance

See ¶¶207 and 208 above.

¶501.6   Nature of VC

See ¶209 above.

¶501.7   Federal Income Tax Aspects of Buyout

¶501.7.1   Overview

Newco would prefer to structure the acquisition so that, for tax purposes, Newco obtains asset SUB for the Target business acquired from Bigco, equal to *the sum of*:

- the purchase price Newco pays to Bigco, *plus*
- the Target liabilities assumed by Newco or its subsidiaries, *plus*
- Newco's acquisition expenses.[8]

Bigco, on the other hand, may prefer to structure for asset COB, for tax purposes for the reasons discussed below.

Where the transaction is structured to achieve asset SUB for tax purposes Bigco pays tax as if it had sold Target *assets*. However, where the transaction is structured for asset COB, Bigco pays tax as if it had sold Target's *stock*.

Where Target is a Bigco subsidiary (filing or eligible to file a consolidated return with Bigco under the 80-80 test[9]), it is generally feasible to structure the transaction so that Newco takes asset SUB while Bigco pays only one tax, i.e., tax on a sale of Target's assets.[10] This can be achieved *either* (1) by an asset sale, (2) by a forward cash merger of Target into Newco or its subsidiary NewSub, *or* (3)

---

[8] This book focuses on the typical situation where the FV of Target's assets exceeds their pre-acquisition tax basis. The tax structuring would be different if Target's assets were worth less than their tax basis, because Newco would then seek to structure for asset COB.

[9] The 80-80 test is met where Bigco owns 80% of Target's stock *both* by vote and by value (ignoring non-voting debt-like preferred stock). See ¶701.2.1.

[10] Bigco as a C corporation pays federal income tax at rates ranging up to 35% on both OI and CG.

by a stock sale with Code §338(h)(10) election (under which all parties to the transaction are treated as if there were an asset sale rather than a stock sale).[11]

- In the SUB transaction discussed in this ¶501, Target is a Bigco subsidiary or division before the transaction. By contrast, where Target (before the transaction) is not a Bigco subsidiary or division (see ¶502 and ¶503 below), structuring Newco's purchase of Target for asset SUB results in double tax on the transaction (unless Target is a seasoned S corporation, a partnership, or an LLC).

- The SUB transaction described in this ¶501 results in only single tax—on Target's asset-sale gain—because Code §332 exempts Bigco from paying a second level of tax when Bigco receives a liquidating distribution (consisting of Target's asset-sale proceeds) from its 80-80 subsidiary, Target. On the other hand, where Target is a C corp owned by a group of shareholders (as discussed in ¶502 and ¶503 below) Code §332 does not apply to exempt the shareholders from paying a second tax on their liquidating distribution from Target.

- However, if Bigco (in this ¶501) were to redistribute the sale proceeds to its shareholders, there would be a second tax at the Bigco shareholder level, regardless of whether Bigco's sale of Target was structured for SUB or COB. Code §301, §302, §331.

One situation where Bigco would resist an asset SUB structure is where Bigco's outside basis in Target stock substantially exceeds Target's net inside basis in its assets, generally because Bigco (1) acquired Target some time in the past in a stock purchase structured for asset COB and (2) paid a substantial premium over Target's inside net asset tax basis at the time of the stock purchase. In this case, Bigco's taxable gain on sale of Target's stock to Newco (with no Code §338(h)(10) election) is calculated using Bigco's higher tax basis in Target's stock, whereas Bigco's taxable gain on a sale of Target's assets to Newco (or Bigco's sale of Target's stock to Newco with Code §338(h)(10) election) would be calculated using the lower tax basis in Target's assets.[12] See ¶501.7.3 below.

Whether it is worthwhile for Newco to raise its purchase price for Target in order to induce Bigco to structure for asset SUB (where Bigco's outside tax basis in Target's stock exceeds Target's net inside asset tax basis) depends on the discounted PV of Newco's expected tax savings from the additional tax deductions

---

[11] A Code §338(h)(10) election is permitted only where Newco is a corporation (not a partnership or LLC), Target is either a Bigco 80-80 subsidiary or an S corporation, both Newco and Target's old shareholders elect (where Target is a Bigco 80-80 subsidiary, Bigco must consent and where Target is an S corporation, all of Target's shareholders must consent), and certain other technical requirements are met. A Code §338(h)(10) election should not be confused with a regular Code §338 election, which has significantly different tax ramifications.

[12] However, where Bigco or Target has a substantial NOL which could shelter Bigco's asset-sale gain, Bigco may be willing to structure for asset SUB even where Bigco's tax basis in Target's stock substantially exceeds Target's inside net asset tax basis. Where Bigco and Target do not have a substantial NOL, Bigco may be willing to structure for asset SUB if (and only if) Newco increases the purchase price for Target to adequately compensate Bigco for Bigco's larger tax on an asset SUB transaction.

for cost of goods sold, depreciation, and amortization resulting from asset SUB, as discussed in ¶501.7.4 below.

¶501.7.2 Alternative Acquisition Structures

¶501.7.2.1 Summary

- Newco purchases Target's stock with no regular §338 election or §338(h)(10) election—asset COB.
- Newco purchases assets from Target or Bigco—asset SUB.
- Newco purchases Target's stock with regular §338 election or §338(h)(10) election—asset SUB.
- Forward cash merger of Target into Newco or NewSub—asset SUB, like purchase of assets.
- Reverse cash merger of a transitory Newco subsidiary into Target—asset SUB if regular §338 election or §338(h)(10) election and asset COB if no regular §338 election or §338(h)(10) election, like purchase of Target's stock.
- Reverse cash merger of Newco into Target—asset COB, like purchase of Target's stock, but regular §338 election or §338(h)(10) election not permitted because no one corporate entity purchases at least an 80-80 amount of Target's stock (unless Newco is itself an 80-80 subsidiary of another corporation).

*¶501.7.2.2 Purchasing Target's Stock With No Code §338 Election
        or §338(h)(10) Election*

If Newco purchases the stock of a Bigco subsidiary (Target) and no regular Code §338 election or §338(h)(10) election is filed, Newco takes asset COB and Bigco is taxed on the stock gain (i.e., the difference between the sales price for the stock and Bigco's basis in its Target stock).

¶501.7.2.3 Purchasing Target's Assets

If Newco purchases the assets of a Bigco 80-80 subsidiary (Target) included in Bigco's consolidated return, Newco obtains asset SUB for the purchased assets and Bigco is taxed on the asset gain (i.e., the difference between the asset sale price and Bigco's asset basis).

If Target is a division (rather than a subsidiary of Bigco), Newco has no choice about structuring the transaction and must purchase Target's assets, so that the transaction is taxed as set forth immediately above. Indeed, even if Bigco incorporates Target in anticipation of the sale to Newco and sells stock to Newco, the transaction may be treated as an SUB transaction (because Bigco's transfer of assets to Target may fail to qualify as tax-free under Code §351 or, possibly, because the transaction may be treated as an asset sale under the step-transaction doctrine).

¶501.7.2.4 Purchasing Target's Stock With Code §338(h)(10) Election

If Newco purchases the stock of a Bigco subsidiary (Target) included in Bigco's consolidated return and the parties file a Code §338(h)(10) election, the tax ramifications are the same as in ¶501.7.2.3 above, i.e., Newco obtains asset SUB and Bigco is treated as if it had sold assets, not stock.

- For state tax purposes, Target, rather than Bigco, may be liable for state income tax on the deemed asset sale resulting from a §338(h)(10) election.

A §338(h)(10) election is permitted only where (1) a single corporate entity (or a consolidated group of corporations), here Newco, purchases an amount of Target's stock which satisfies the 80-80 test *and* (2) before such purchase, Bigco's ownership of Target satisfied the 80-80 test.[13]

Where a single corporate entity (or consolidated group of corporations), here Newco, purchases at least an 80-80 amount of Target, Newco is permitted to make a regular §338 election for Target (whether or not Target was a Bigco 80-80 subsidiary). A regular §338 election yields a far different—and less desirable—tax result than does a §338(h)(10) election. With a regular §338 election Target, now a Newco subsidiary, is treated as purchasing Target's assets, and hence obtains asset SUB (just as with a §338(h)(10) election). However, Target's shareholders are treated as selling Target's stock and thus Target's shareholders are taxed on their stock gain. Because Target's shareholders are taxed on their stock sale gain and Target itself is also taxed on its asset-sale gain, there is double tax on the transaction (once at the Target corporate level and once at the Target shareholder level), making a regular §338 election undesirable in almost all circumstances.

With a §338(h)(10) election for Bigco's 80-80 subsidiary or for an S corporation, by contrast, all parties are treated as if there had been an asset sale from Target to a Newco subsidiary followed by a liquidating distribution by Target of its sales proceeds to its old shareholders, and hence only a single tax is imposed on the transaction (i.e., on the asset-sale gain). This is because (1) where Target is a Bigco 80-80 subsidiary, Code §332 protects Bigco from shareholder-level tax on the deemed liquidating distribution and (2) where Target is an S corporation, the increase in shareholder tax basis for Target's taxable income (the asset-sale gain) normally fully protects against shareholder-level tax on the deemed liquidating distribution.

¶501.7.2.5 Forward Cash Merger

A forward cash merger of Target into Newco or NewSub is taxed as Newco's purchase of Target's assets, as described in ¶501.7.2.3 above (with Target's asset-sale gain generally taxed on Bigco's consolidated tax return) followed by Target's liquidation into Bigco.

---

[13] As discussed below, a §338(h)(10) election is also available where Target is an S corporation.

The transaction is not a tax-free reorganization under Code §368, because the judicial continuity-of-interest doctrine precludes reorganization treatment unless a substantial portion (generally at least 40%) of the consideration issued in exchange for Target's stock is stock of the acquiring corporation or its parent (and certain other technical requirements are met).

¶501.7.2.6   *Reverse Subsidiary Cash Merger*

A reverse subsidiary cash merger of a newly-formed transitory Newco subsidiary into Target is taxed as if (1) Newco purchased Target stock where no §338 election or §338(h)(10) election is made, as described in ¶501.7.2.2 above or (2) Newco's subsidiary purchased Target's assets where a §338(h)(10) election is made, as described in ¶501.7.2.4 above.

This is because IRS (1) disregards Newco's transitory subsidiary and hence disregards the merger and (2) views the transaction as if Newco had purchased Target's stock from Bigco.

Where no §338(h)(10) election and no regular §338 election is made, so that the transaction is taxed as a sale of Target's stock:

- To the extent the cash paid to Target's old shareholder(s) (here Bigco) comes from Target (e.g., out of Target's accumulated working capital or borrowings for which Target ends up liable), the transaction is taxed as if Target redeemed that much of its stock from Bigco.
- On the other hand, to the extent the cash paid to Target's old shareholder(s) (here Bigco) comes from equity contributions to Newco or from borrowings for which Newco, rather than Target, ends up liable, the transaction is taxed as if Newco purchased Target stock from Target's old shareholders.
- The tax ramifications to Target's old shareholder(s) (here Bigco), i.e., LTCG on the disposition of the Target stock, are generally the same whether the transaction is treated (1) only as a purchase by Newco of Target's stock *or* (2) as if Newco purchased part of Target's stock from Bigco and as if Target redeemed part of its stock from Bigco (a part-purchase, part-redemption). In the unusual situation where Bigco owns (actually or constructively) substantial Newco (or Target) stock *after* the transaction, the proceeds received under (1) or (2) may be treated as an OI dividend, although the standard for dividend recharacterization is somewhat different for (a) the portion treated as a purchase (where the Code §304 OI rules apply with broad aggregation and attribution rules so that there is more risk of OI dividend treatment) and (b) the portion treated as a redemption (where the Code §302 OI rules apply with narrower attribution rules so that there is less risk of OI dividend treatment).

¶501.7.2.7   *Reverse Two-Party Cash Merger*

A reverse two-party cash merger of newly-formed Newco into Target is taxed as if Newco's shareholders had purchased Target's stock from Bigco.

This is because IRS (1) disregards Newco as transitory and hence disregards the merger and (2) views the transaction as if Newco's shareholders had purchased Target's stock from Bigco.

In this case no §338(h)(10) election is permitted because a single corporate entity did not purchase at least an 80-80 amount of Target's stock (unless Newco is itself an 80-80 subsidiary of another corporation).

The transaction may be taxed partly as a Newco purchase of Target stock from Target's old shareholder(s) (here Bigco) and partly as a redemption by Target of its stock from Target's old shareholder(s) (here Bigco), depending upon the source of the funds paid to Target's old shareholder(s) (here Bigco), as described in ¶501.7.2.6 immediately above.

¶501.7.3   Taxation of Bigco's Gain

Bigco's sale of Target's stock without a Code §338(h)(10) election or regular §338 election generally produces CG.

Bigco's or Target's sale of assets (or stock sale with §338(h)(10) election) produces part OI/part CG, depending on the nature of the assets sold. The OI/CG distinction is relevant for a corporation (like Bigco) only if (1) Bigco has a CL which can only be used to offset its CG or (2) there is in the future a higher tax rate on corporate OI than on corporate LTCG (currently the corporate OI and LTCG rates are the same).

Where Bigco sells Target's stock without a Code §338(h)(10) election, its CG is the excess of the sales proceeds over Bigco's basis in Target's *stock*. Where Bigco sells Target's assets *or* sells Target's stock with a §338(h)(10) election, Target (and thus Bigco as consolidated return parent) recognizes part OI/part CG equal to the excess of the sales proceeds over Target's basis in its *assets*. However, in some circumstances Bigco's outside basis in Target's stock exceeds Target's net inside basis in its assets (i.e., inside asset basis minus liabilities), so that Bigco prefers a stock sale with no §338(h)(10) election, while Newco prefers an asset SUB transaction (either an asset purchase or a stock purchase with §338(h)(10) election).

- Bigco has a higher outside basis in Target's stock than Target's net inside basis in its assets where Bigco (1) acquired Target at some time in the past in a stock purchase structured for asset COB and (2) paid a premium over Target's inside net asset basis at the time of the stock purchase.

There may thus be 2 reasons for Bigco to favor a stock sale with no §338(h)(10) election (i.e., an asset COB structure):

First, the amount of gain on such a stock sale would be lower than on a sale structured for asset SUB (an asset sale or stock sale with §338(h)(10) election) if Bigco had previously purchased Target's stock in an asset COB transaction at a price which constituted a premium over Target's inside net asset basis.

Second, stock gain is all CG while asset gain is part OI/part CG, which is relevant (as long as corporate CG and corporate OI continue to be taxed at the same rates) only where Bigco has otherwise unusable CL from other transactions.

However, if Bigco or Target has a substantial NOL which could shelter its asset-sale gain, Bigco may be willing to structure for asset SUB even in the circumstances described above.

If Bigco does not have a substantial NOL, it may be willing to structure for asset SUB in the circumstances described above if (and only if) Newco raises the purchase price for Target so as to compensate Bigco adequately for the larger tax on an asset SUB transaction. Whether (and how much) Newco is willing to raise the acquisition price in order to obtain asset SUB turns on the factors set forth in ¶501.7.4 below.

Of course, if Bigco's outside basis in Target's stock does not exceed Target's inside net asset basis, Bigco in most cases should have no objection to structuring for asset SUB.

Where Bigco sells stock of a consolidated subsidiary (here Target) at a loss with no Code §338(h)(10) election, unfortunate and complex IRS regulations severely limit Bigco's ability to claim the loss on the stock sale for tax purposes. Treas. Reg. §1.1502-20.

State tax consequences to Bigco and Target may also differ depending on whether a Code §338(h)(10) election or regular §338 election is made.

¶501.7.4   Newco's Tax Savings from Asset SUB

Whether it is worthwhile for Newco to raise its purchase price for Target in order to induce Bigco to structure for asset SUB (where Bigco's outside basis in Target's stock exceeds Target's inside net asset basis) depends on the discounted PV of Newco's expected tax savings from the additional deductions for cost of goods sold, depreciation, and amortization resulting from asset SUB, which in turn depend upon:

- The amount of step-up allocable respectively to inventory, depreciable assets, and amortizable intangibles.
- The useful life of the depreciable/amortizable assets.
- Whether Newco elects FIFO or LIFO for stepped-up inventory.
- The degree of risk that IRS successfully challenges (on audit) Newco's SUB allocation among the assets.
- The amount and timing of future taxable income Newco expects to generate which can be sheltered by the additional deductions.
- The applicable corporate tax rates in the future years when the additional deductions are allowable.
- The appropriate discount rate for computing the PV of the future tax savings.
- Whether Newco can obtain sufficient financing to pay the front-end tax cost, if any, of structuring for asset SUB (by paying Bigco the enhanced purchase price necessary to cover Bigco's extra tax burden from so structur-

ing, including a gross-up for additional tax on the additional purchase price).

The result achieved by applying these tax considerations to specific transactions changed radically with the 1993 enactment of Code §197, under which virtually all purchased intangibles (acquired in an SUB transaction) are now amortizable for tax purposes over a 15-year period.[14] Section 197's pro-taxpayer aspect is tax amortization (over 15 years) for goodwill, going concern value, and other similar intangibles which previously were not amortizable at all for tax purposes. Code §197's anti-taxpayer aspect is the automatic 15-year life on virtually all purchased intangibles, including those which generally had much shorter tax lives before §197's enactment.

- In an asset SUB acquisition, §197's 15 year amortization applies to virtually all purchased intangibles. Even in a COB acquisition, §197 applies to covenants not to compete purchased from Target's employees and shareholders.
- Where Newco and Target are more than 20% related by vote or by value, calculated by comparing Target's pre-acquisition ownership to Newco's pre- or post-acquisition ownership, Code §197's illogical and arbitrary anti-churning rules may prevent 15-year amortization of those intangibles held by old Target before 9/93 that would have been non-amortizable before §197's enactment (goodwill and going concern value or any other intangible with no reasonably ascertainable useful life).

  - Where Target and/or Newco is a partnership or LLC, the anti-churning rules are slightly different.
  - In addition, although there are strong arguments under the statute and certain prior precedents that the corporate anti-churning rules should not apply unless Target and Newco are *50% or more* related by vote or value, IRS regulations (effective for transactions after 1/00) take the position that the anti-churning rules generally apply where Target and Newco are more than *20% related*.
  - In a buyout of a Bigco subsidiary, there may be such more-than-20% overlapping ownership between Target and Newco where Bigco buys a portion of Newco's stock.

- Prior to §197's 1993 enactment, many taxpayers enjoyed a degree of success allocating a portion of the purchase price (in an asset SUB transaction) to intangibles such as covenants not to compete, patents, computer software, customer lists, order backlog, advantageous customer and supplier contracts, know-how, and the like (as opposed to goodwill and going concern value which were then clearly non-amortizable) and amortizing such amount over a reasonably short estimated useful life, although the result in litigation (where IRS challenged the deduction) was often quite fact-specific.

---

[14] Code §197 contains limited exceptions for certain assets, including (1) customized computer software not acquired as part of the acquisition of a business and (2) off-the-shelf computer software, whether or not acquired as a part of a business, both of which are amortizable over a 36-month period.

In the unusual situation where Target's assets have an FV below their tax basis (i.e., Target's assets have declined in value more than the depreciation/amortization deductions allowed for tax purposes), Newco may wish to structure for asset COB, i.e., to purchase Target's stock with no Code §338(h)(10) election or regular §338 election, so that Target retains its high asset basis. However, where there is built-in loss ("BIL") in Target's assets at the time Target suffers a change in control, Code §382 may limit future use of Target's pre-acquisition BIL as well as Target's pre-acquisition NOL. See ¶809 below.

¶501.7.5 Allocating Asset SUB

¶501.7.5.1   Newco's Aggregate Basis

Where Newco has acquired Target in an asset SUB transaction, Newco is entitled to an aggregate basis for Target's assets equal to:

- the purchase price Newco pays to Bigco, *plus*
- the Target liabilities assumed by Newco or its subsidiaries, *plus*
- Newco's acquisition expenses.

¶501.7.5.2   Residual Allocation

Newco values the purchased assets (other than §197 intangibles) and allocates its aggregate basis among them proportionally, with no asset taking a basis greater than its FV:

- Finished goods inventory is valued at FV (e.g., selling price *less* selling expenses and a reasonable portion of the profit).
- Raw materials inventory is valued at FV (e.g., replacement cost).
- Receivables are valued at FV.
- Other tangible assets are valued at FV.
- Bargain leaseholds are valued at discounted PV of the bargain element, while off-the-shelf software, favorable financing arrangements, and a few other intangibles excluded from Code §197 are valued at FV.

§197 intangible assets are allocated the residual amount not allocated to the other purchased assets as discussed above.

Where Newco's aggregate basis exceeds the FV of the purchased assets (other than §197 intangibles), the residual method allocates as basis to each such asset an amount equal to such asset's FV and the excess is allocated to §197 intangibles, which are amortizable over 15 years.[15]

---

[15] In a few cases it makes a difference how basis is allocated between different elements of Newco's purchased Code §197 intangibles—e.g., where overlapping stock ownership between Newco and Target cause the anti-churning rules (discussed at ¶501.7.4 above) to deny Code §197 amortization for goodwill, going concern value, or any other asset not amortizable before Code §197's enactment

Where the FV of Target's assets (other than §197 intangibles) exceeds Newco's aggregate basis, the residual method allocates basis first to cash, marketable securities, receivables, and inventory before allocating the residual to fixed assets, so that each of Target's fixed assets takes a basis less than such asset's FV, i.e., aggregate basis available is spread over fixed assets proportionately to their FV, and no amount is allocated to §197 intangibles.

Example of Residual Method Allocation

	Millions
Aggregate basis:	
Amount paid for Target	$50
Liabilities assumed	9
Expenses of acquisition	1
Aggregate basis	$60

Where Aggregate Non-§197 Asset FV Exceeds Aggregate Basis			Where Aggregate Basis Exceeds Aggregate Non-§197 Asset FV		
		Residual Method of Allocation (Millions)			*Residual Method of Allocation (Millions)*
Asset	*FV*	*Basis*	*Asset*	*FV*	*Basis*
Receivables	$18	$18	Receivables	$12	$12
Inventory	18	15	Inventory	12	12
Fixed assets	36	24	Fixed assets	24	24
§197 intangibles	—	0	§197 intangibles	—	12
Total	$72	$60	Total	$48	$60

¶501.7.6   Key Issues and References on Tax Aspects of Bigco Subsidiary or Division Buyout

If Target is a Bigco *division*, how will the buyout be taxed?

If Target is a Bigco *subsidiary*, are there tax choices to be made?

(i.e., any intangible that does not have a reasonably ascertainable useful life absent Code §197). In these cases, available basis (after allocation of basis to assets other than Code §197 intangibles) is allocated first to Code §197 intangibles other than goodwill and going concern value up to their FV, and the residue is allocated to goodwill and going concern value.

References:

- Code §197
- Code §332
- Code §334
- Code §337
- Code §338
- Code §1504(a) and (b)
- Treas. Reg. §1.338(h)(10)-1
- Rev. Rul. 69-6
- Rev. Rul. 73-427
- Rev. Rul. 78-250
- Rev. Rul. 79-273
- Rev. Rul. 90-95
- Ginsburg and Levin M&A book ¶107, ¶201, ¶202, ¶211.1, ¶301
- Ginsburg and Levin M&A book Chapters 2 through 4

Which costs of the acquisition or the financing for the acquisition incurred by Newco, Target, or Target's shareholder(s) are (1) immediately deductible, (2) amortizable over a period (e.g., the term of the acquisition financing), or (3) never deductible?

References:

- Ginsburg and Levin M&A book ¶403

When is it desirable from a tax standpoint to structure a bifurcated acquisition where Newco purchases a portion of Target's assets and then purchases Target's stock?

References:

- Ginsburg and Levin M&A book ¶203

¶501.8 GAAP Purchase Accounting Rules

¶501.8.1 Currently Effective GAAP Rules

GAAP purchase accounting generally applies to the acquired company in a buyout regardless of whether the acquisition transaction is structured as an asset purchase, stock purchase, or merger. Where the GAAP purchase accounting rules apply, Target's assets take a new aggregate book value equal to the amount Newco paid for Target, *plus* Target liabilities assumed by Newco or its subsidiaries, *plus* Newco acquisition costs. This aggregate book value amount is allocated first to current assets at FV, second to fixed assets at FV, next to specific intangibles at FV, and the residual to goodwill.

FASB eliminated goodwill amortization for accounting purposes in 7/01. Thus, amounts allocated to purchased goodwill are not amortized but rather are periodically written off (or down) only if and only to the extent "impaired" (i.e., to the extent carrying cost exceeds FV). Prior to FASB's 7/01 decision, purchased goodwill was amortized over a period not to exceed 40 years.

However, even after FASB's 7/01 decision, Target's tangible assets and Target's intangibles other than goodwill (as stepped up by the purchase transaction) must be amortized/depreciated for accounting purposes, thus reducing Newco-Target's post-buyout accounting net income. In addition, Newco-Target's post-buyout accounting net income is reduced (from time to time) if and to the extent purchase accounting goodwill subsequently becomes impaired and hence is written down.

Because goodwill is no longer amortizable, Newco generally has an incentive to maximize the allocation to Target's goodwill, since depreciation and amortization charges for all of Target's other assets (i.e., tangible assets and identifiable intangible assets other than goodwill), including the effect of any purchase accounting step-up, continue to be subtracted from income on a current basis. However, Newco is required to identify, and allocate purchase price to, any Target intangible that either (1) arises from contractual or legal rights or (2) is capable of being separated from Target and sold, transferred, licensed, rented, or exchanged (whether in isolation or together with related contracts, assets, or liabilities).

Where the acquisition has been structured for tax purposes to achieve asset COB (e.g., a stock purchase with no §338 election or §338(h)(10) election), Newco's post-acquisition GAAP earnings are doubly impacted—asset COB for tax and hence no tax saving for increased depreciation/amortization coupled with GAAP write up of assets and hence increased accounting depreciation/amortization.

If Newco-Target were subsequently to go public, such GAAP purchase accounting would decrease Newco-Target's valuation.

The purchase accounting rules described above are subject to a number of qualifications and exceptions, including:

First, Newco is not required to apply complete purchase accounting where there is substantial overlap between the shareholders of Target before the transaction and the shareholders of Newco after the transaction. In this case GAAP accounting rules call for "part purchase" accounting, so that the assets take a part FV/part carryover book value and net worth is reduced (from the amount it would be under 100% purchase accounting) by the same amount as the reduction in asset carrying value from full purchase accounting.

A second exception to purchase accounting (referred to as "recapitalization" or "recap" accounting) applies where Target remains alive (i.e., the acquisition is structured as a purchase of Target's stock or as a reverse subsidiary merger) and Target's old shareholders continue to own a "significant" stake in recapitalized Target's common equity. See ¶504 below. As a practical matter, accounting firms generally take the position that where Target's old shareholders as a group own somewhere between 5.5% and 10% of recapitalized Target's common equity, depending on the circumstances, such as the number and type of old Target shareholders with a continuing interest in Target's common equity, the significant continuing stake test is satisfied.

Where Target qualifies for recap accounting, the book value of Target's assets on its post-acquisition financial statements does not change at all (i.e., there is no purchase accounting or part purchase accounting on Target's financial statements).

However, where one of Target's new shareholders (e.g., Newco) is an entity owning sufficient Target stock so that Newco must account for its Target investment on the equity method of accounting (generally where Newco owns 20% or more of Target's voting power) or on the consolidated method of accounting (generally where Newco owns more than 50% of Target's voting power), Newco must use purchase accounting principles in preparing its financial statements, even though Target can use recap accounting in preparing its separate financial statements.

Recap accounting may also apply in two circumstances where Target's old shareholders do not retain a significant (or indeed any) continuing interest in recapitalized Target's common equity: *First*, where Target has publicly held debt or publicly held preferred stock outstanding prior to and independent of the recapitalization and such public debt or preferred stock remains outstanding after the recapitalization. *Second*, where at least one of the new investors purchasing a significant stake in Target's recapitalized equity as part of the LBO is "independent" of the investors sponsoring the recapitalization transaction.

FASB's 7/01 elimination of goodwill amortization reduces (but does not eliminate) the desirability of recapitalization accounting. First, under a non-amortization/impairment approach, goodwill created by purchase accounting does not reduce earnings unless and until goodwill's FV is subsequently impaired. Thus, using recapitalization accounting to avoid goodwill creation eliminates the possibility of a future earnings reduction, should goodwill become impaired. Second, recapitalization accounting also avoids an accounting basis step-up for both tangible assets and intangible assets other than goodwill and hence avoids an earnings reduction due to increased depreciation and amortization charges for these non-goodwill assets.

Third, where Newco's acquisition of Target is subject to purchase accounting but a portion of Target's assets consist of an R&D project(s) in process (e.g., a new product in the development stage), Newco can (and indeed must) write off the amount allocated to such in-process R&D assets immediately after Newco consummates its purchase accounting acquisition of Target (just as accounting rules require Newco to write off its internal R&D costs as incurred). Indeed, in numerous purchase accounting acquisitions of software companies during the 1990's the acquirors immediately wrote off significant portions of the purchase price as in-process R&D, thereby reducing their post-acquisition goodwill amortization. However, starting in 1998 SEC began to challenge numerous acquisitions on the ground that R&D write offs exceeded the portion of the purchase price properly allocable to Target's in-process R&D. In response many companies challenged by SEC drastically scaled back their proposed in-process R&D write-off.

Fourth, Newco's pre-7/01 acquisition of Target is not subject to the purchase accounting rules at all if the acquisition qualifies for pooling accounting, i.e., (1) 90% or more of the consideration for the acquisition of Target common stock and common stock equivalents consisted of Newco voting common stock and (2) numerous other arbitrary pooling requirements were satisfied. In this case, Newco picks up Target's assets at their historic book values as reflected on Target's GAAP financial statements. FASB abolished pooling accounting in 7/01. Thus, Newco's acquisition of Target initiated after 6/30/01 is generally accounted for as a purchase unless part purchase or recapitalization accounting applies.

¶501.8.2   FASB Proposed Changes

FASB's project to study accounting for business combinations (begun in 8/96) resulted, after a number of conflicting tentative decisions and a contentious debate, in the final 7/01 decisions described in ¶501.8.1 above abolishing pooling accounting and eliminating goodwill amortization (substituting an impairment approach). FASB's business combinations project continues in two separate areas.

First, FASB is studying purchase accounting procedures in light of its 7/01 decisions. As part of this process, FASB tentatively decided in 10/01 and 10/02 to abolish part purchase accounting, although the exact scope of this tentative decision is currently unclear (e.g., whether it applies to leveraged buyouts).

Second, FASB previously stated that it will review recapitalization accounting (see ¶504) as part of a second phase of its business combinations project. In 9/00, as part of this second phase, FASB started deliberations on "new basis issues," including push-down accounting.

Thus, the long-term viability of recapitalization accounting may be in some doubt. By analogy to FASB's 7/01 decision to abolish poolings prospectively, we believe that any change to current recap accounting rules should apply only to transactions occurring after FASB final rules are published.

References:

- ¶504 of this book, discussing recap accounting in far more detail
- Ginsburg and Levin M&A book ¶1703 and in particular:
  - ¶1703.2 on purchase accounting
  - ¶1703.3.1 through ¶1703.3.5 on part purchase accounting
  - ¶1703.3.6 on recapitalization accounting (containing recap accounting examples not contained in ¶504 of this book)
  - ¶1703.4 on pooling accounting

¶502   BUYOUT OF PRIVATE COMPANY

In this ¶502, Target is a private company owned by a person or group of persons (but is not a Bigco subsidiary). Target's principal shareholders, unable to locate the fountain of youth, are focusing on estate planning and would like to liquefy their estates. In other respects, the facts are the same as at ¶501, including the $50 million buyout price.

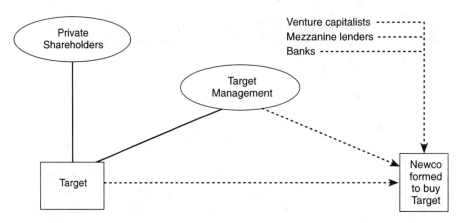

¶502.1   *Federal Income Tax Aspects*

Just as in ¶501, Newco would prefer to structure the acquisition to obtain, for tax purposes, asset SUB for Target's business. However, depending upon whether Target is a C corporation, an S corporation, a partnership, or an LLC, Target and its owners may prefer to structure for asset COB, for tax purposes, as discussed below.

¶502.1.1   Target Is C Corporation

If Target is a C corporation and the transaction is structured for asset SUB—e.g., Target's sale of assets to Newco followed by Target's liquidation—the sellers shoulder double tax, i.e., (1) Target owes corporate-level tax on its asset-sale gain, (2) Target shareholders owe shareholder-level tax on their liquidation proceeds less their stock tax basis, and (3) Target's old shareholders generally bear the economic burden of both taxes.

Double tax also obtains where the transaction is structured for asset SUB as a taxable forward merger of Target into Newco or a taxable forward subsidiary merger of Target into NewSub. However, in these cases the incidence of Target's corporate-level tax falls on Newco because in the merger Newco (or NewSub) inherits Target's corporate-level tax liability.

- Similarly, where the asset SUB structure is Newco's purchase of Target's stock (or Newco's acquisition of Target's stock in a taxable reverse subsidiary merger) with a regular §338 election, there is double tax on the transaction. In such case Target's shareholders are treated as selling Target's stock, while "new" Target is treated as purchasing "old" Target's assets, so that Target's shareholders are taxed on their stock-sale gain and, in addition, Target itself is taxed on its asset-sale gain, resulting in double tax, but with the economic burden of Target's corporate-level asset-sale tax falling on the buyer (Newco). No §338(h)(10) election is available in these circumstances, because §338(h)(10) applies only where Target is either a Bigco 80-80 subsidiary or an S corporation.

• By contrast, in ¶501 above (where Target was a Bigco 80-80 subsidiary and Bigco retained the sale proceeds), structuring the acquisition for asset SUB (either as an asset sale or a stock sale treated as an asset sale by virtue of a §338(h)(10) election) did not result in double tax because the liquidation (or the §338(h)(10) deemed liquidation) of Target into Bigco was a tax-free Code §332 liquidation. Where, however, Target is a C corporation but not a Bigco 80-80 subsidiary, structuring for asset SUB results in double tax, i.e., Target-level tax on the asset-sale gain and shareholder-level tax on Target's liquidation.

Where Target is a C corporation and does not have a substantial NOL to shelter its asset-sale gain, it is generally not advantageous to structure for asset SUB because the PV of the seller's corporate-level tax (payable immediately) exceeds the PV of Newco's tax savings on account of asset SUB (which occur over a number of years—15 years in the case of Code §197 amortizable intangibles—as described in ¶501.7.4 above).[1]

Where Target is a C corporation and the acquisition is structured for asset SUB, there may be a threat to Newco's asset SUB where any one of the following four "SUB-threat" rules applies:

(1)   Target shareholders (and their attributees) own 50% or more of Newco's stock by vote *or* by value, because the transaction may be treated as covered by either Code §304 (if structured as a stock purchase) or Code §368(a)(1)(D) (if structured as an asset purchase), *or*

(2)   Target sells assets to Newco and receives part cash and part Newco stock as consideration, because the transaction is covered by Code §351 which may afford only partial asset SUB, *or*

(3)   Target sells assets to Newco solely for cash but Target shareholders use a portion of the cash received on Target's liquidation to buy Newco stock, in which case IRS may seek to invoke the step transaction doctrine to treat the transaction as described in (2) above, *or*

(4)   Newco acquires Target's stock (in a stock purchase or a reverse subsidiary cash merger) with the intent of making a regular §338 election or a §338(h)(10) election *and* one or more of Target's shareholders receive part of their consideration for Target in the form of Newco stock (or use part of their cash proceeds to buy Newco stock and IRS seeks to invoke the step transaction doctrine to treat the transaction as if such Target shareholders received part cash and part Newco stock in exchange for Target), in which case (a) such old Target shareholders who end up with some Newco stock

---

¶502   [1] One exception: Target might be willing to structure for asset SUB by an asset sale where Target's shareholders are elderly and contemplate near-term death SUB for their stock. In this case double tax on the sellers can be avoided where Target sells assets to Newco and Target remains in existence as an investment company until its shareholders obtain SUB for their Target stock by reason of death.

A second exception arises where Target is a foreign corporation.

may be treated as contributing their Target stock to Newco in a Code §351 transaction (which does not constitute a "purchase" under §338) and (b) Newco may thus fail to "purchase" an 80-80 amount of Target stock (as required for a §338 election or a §338(h)(10) election)—especially where Newco's lenders lend all or a part of the acquisition financing to Target, which is treated as redeeming a part of its stock.

Moreover, where Newco's acquisition of Target violates rule (1) above, there may be a threat to Target's shareholders' LTCG treatment on sale of Target, i.e., they may be subjected to OI tax by either Code §§304 and 302(d) (if the acquisition is structured as a stock purchase) or Code §§368(a)(1)(D) and 356(a)(2) (if the acquisition is structured as an asset purchase).

Where the parties structure for asset COB, it is generally tax efficient from Newco's standpoint to pay as much of the purchase price as possible directly to Target's shareholders as (1) compensation for future executive or consulting services and/or (2) covenant-not-to-compete payments. Such payments are:

(a)   taxable to the recipients as OI,
(b)   not taxable at the Target level, and
(c)   as long as reasonable in amount, deductible by Newco over (i) the life of the employment or consulting arrangement (in the case of employment or consulting payments) or (ii) 15 years under Code §197 (in the case of noncompete payments).[2]

However, because Target's individual shareholders are taxed at substantially higher rates on OI (including a consulting or noncompete payment) than on LTCG—a 38.6% top federal income tax rate for 2002 and 2003 OI compared to a 20% top federal income tax rate for LTCG—Target's shareholders seek to minimize allocation to consulting or noncompete payments and/or seek a gross-up payment from Newco to compensate them for the higher tax rate.

¶502.1.2   Target Is S Corporation

Where Target is a seasoned S corporation (rather than a C corporation), Newco can structure for asset SUB—either a sale of Target's assets followed by Target's liquidation or a sale of Target's stock with §338(h)(10) election—without imposing the burden of double tax on the sellers.[3] See ¶301 above.

IRS now takes the position that all T-SCo shareholders must consent to the §338(h)(10) election (although formerly IRS appeared to require consent only from T-SCo shareholders who sold their stock to Newco). Under IRS's current position, Newco needs consent from a T-SCo shareholder who (1) retains his or her T-SCo

---

[2] Prior to the 1993 enactment of §197, a covenant not to compete was amortizable over the life of the covenant, generally far shorter than 15 years.

[3] A §338(h)(10) election is permitted in only two circumstances: where Target is an 80-80 Bigco subsidiary as discussed in ¶501 or where Target is an S corporation as discussed in this ¶502.1.2.

If Newco were to purchase Target's stock with a regular §338 election, the unfortunate result would be double tax because Newco's purchase of Target's stock would terminate Target's S election.

stock or (2) is squeezed out in a reverse subsidiary cash merger after (or simultaneously with) Newco's purchase of T-SCo's remaining stock, but apparently not from a T-SCo shareholder squeezed out in a cash merger *before* Newco purchases the remainder of T-SCo's stock.

However, in the case of an S corporation which was formerly a C corporation, Code §1374 causes at least partial double tax on the sellers by imposing corporate-level tax on any sale of the S corporation's assets occurring during its first 10 years as an S corporation, based on the *lesser* of (1) the built-in gain in an asset at the time the corporation became an S corporation or (2) the actual gain recognized on the sale of such asset.

- This Code §1374 tax also applies to assets previously acquired from a C corporation by the S corporation (even though never itself a C corporation) in an asset COB transaction (e.g., a tax-free merger of a C into an S corporation), based on the *lesser* of (1) the built-in gain in a COB asset at the time acquired by the S corporation or (2) the actual gain recognized on the sale of such asset.
- Where Code §1374 applies, there is double federal income taxation on the portion of S corporation's gain covered by Code §1374 (the built-in gain).

Where Target is an S corporation (whether or not subject to the Code §1374 corporate-level tax) and the acquisition is structured for asset SUB, there may be a threat to Newco's asset SUB where any of one or more of the four SUB-threat rules (discussed in ¶502.1.1) applies.

¶502.1.3   Target Is Partnership or LLC

Where Target is a partnership or LLC, Newco can structure for asset SUB without double tax to the sellers, either by a sale of Target's assets or a sale of all Target's ownership interests. In this case, there is no need for a §338(h)(10) election to achieve asset SUB and there is no Code §1374-like penalty tax.

Where Target is a partnership or LLC and the acquisition is structured for asset SUB, there may be a threat to Newco's asset SUB where SUB-threat rule #2 or #3 (as discussed in ¶502.1.1) applies.

¶502.1.4   §197 Amortization

In an asset SUB transaction, Code §197's anti-churning rules (as discussed in ¶501.7.4) may prevent 15-year amortization of certain intangibles where persons who owned more than 20% of Target's stock before the buyout own more than 20% of Newco's stock after the buyout.

There may be such more-than-20% overlap where, for example, Newco sells stock to Target's executives who were Target shareholders before the buyout. See ¶501.7.4.

¶502.1.5 Summary

It is generally not advantageous to structure for asset SUB unless Target is an S corporation not subject to a substantial Code §1374 penalty tax, a partnership, an LLC, a Bigco 80-80 subsidiary, a C corporation with a large NOL to shelter its corporate-level gain, or a C corporation with elderly shareholders contemplating near-term death SUB for their stock and willing to operate Target as an investment company until then.

Where the parties are considering structuring for asset SUB, the analytical approach described at ¶501.7.4 above should be utilized to evaluate the tax benefits of asset SUB and to compare them to the front-end costs of structuring for SUB.

¶502.2 Target Management Tax-Free Rollover

A Target executive who owns appreciated Target stock and plans to invest in Newco corporation could escape LTCG recognition on a disposition of his or her Target stock by engaging in a tax-free rollover of appreciated Target stock in exchange for Newco stock pursuant to Code §351 (which deals with the tax-free formation of a new corporation), i.e., the executive could contribute appreciated Target stock to Newco in exchange for Newco stock with an FV equal to the FV of the Target stock contributed, at approximately the same time as Newco's other shareholders (including VC) form Newco.

- This approach is feasible only where the acquisition is structured for asset COB, i.e., Newco corporation purchases Target's stock *or* Newco corporation acquires Target's stock by a reverse subsidiary merger *or* Newco's shareholders acquire Target's stock by a reverse two-party merger.
- An executive swapping low basis Target stock tax free (in a Code §351 transaction) for high FV Newco stock takes COB for the Newco stock (equal to his or her low basis in the Target stock) and hence defers LTCG until disposition of the Newco stock, but permanently avoids LTCG recognition if he or she dies while owning the low basis Newco stock.
- An executive receiving any Newco "Nonqualified Preferred Stock" ("NQ Pfd") (i.e., most redeemable debt-like preferred stock, discussed in more detail in ¶403.1(9) through (15) above) in such an otherwise tax-free rollover would recognize gain up to the NQ Pfd's FV unless one of the statutory exceptions applies. In general, this rule applies to preferred stock which (1) does not participate significantly in corporate growth and (2) (within 20 years of issuance) is either (a) puttable by the holder, (b) mandatorily redeemable, or (c) callable (if it is more likely than not at issuance that the call will be exercised), unless contingencies render the chance of a put, call, or redemption "remote." In addition, any preferred stock with a dividend rate that varies with market indices is treated as taxable NQ Pfd. Where old Target shareholders roll their Target stock into a "strip" of Target debt-like preferred stock which constitutes NQ Pfd and common stock, the

Target NQ Pfd would be taxable boot, triggering gain on the exchange. This adverse tax result can be avoided in three ways:

- The Target preferred stock may be designed so that it has a significant stake in corporate growth (e.g., by amalgamating Target preferred stock and Target common stock together in a single instrument) and hence is not NQ Pfd.
- The Target preferred stock is designed to be evergreen (i.e., not mandatorily redeemable, puttable, or callable) and hence is not NQ Pfd.
- The redemption, put, or call features with respect to the Target preferred stock are limited to those that qualify for Code §351(g)(2)(i)(I)'s death-or-disability exception or Code §351(g)(2)(i)(II)'s issued-in-connection-with-services exception, so that in either case the Target preferred stock is not NQ Pfd.

Where Newco is a partnership or LLC, a Target executive who owns appreciated Target stock can escape LTCG recognition by engaging in a tax-free rollover of appreciated Target stock in exchange for Newco partnership or membership interests pursuant to Code §721 (which deals with tax-free contributions to a partnership) without regard to the NQ Pfd rules.

¶502.3   *Shareholder Vote and Dissenters' Rights*

In a *merger or asset sale* of corporate Target, a vote of Target's shareholders by a requisite majority[4] binds all of Target's shareholders (subject to a dissenting shareholder's right to claim appraisal rights, i.e., a cash payment equal to the court-determined FV of the dissenter's Target stock). However, where the transaction is structured as a *sale of Target's stock*, any recalcitrant old Target shareholder has the right to retain his or her Target stock, so that Newco may end up owning less than 100% of Target.

This recalcitrant-minority-shareholder problem is generally solved—where the parties intend the acquisition to be taxed as a stock purchase but one or more old Target stockholders refuse to sell—by structuring the transaction as a reverse subsidiary merger (an "RSM") of Newco's newly-formed transitory subsidiary (NewSub) into Target, with Target's old shareholders receiving cash in exchange for their Target stock and Newco receiving Target stock in exchange for its New-Sub stock.

---

[4]Most states require only a majority shareholder vote, although a few require a higher vote (e.g., two-thirds), and Target's charter may require a higher vote than normally required by state law.

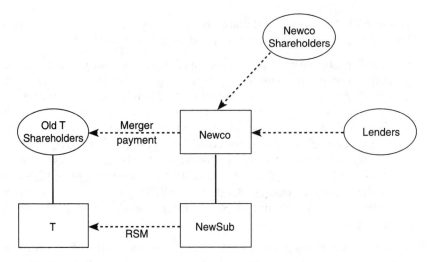

Such an RSM requires the affirmative vote of a requisite majority of Target's old shareholders and generally allows dissenting Target shareholders to claim appraisal rights. However, after the RSM Newco owns 100% of Target's stock and, for tax purposes, such an RSM is generally taxed as if Newco had purchased Target's stock, because IRS (1) disregards Newco's transitory subsidiary and hence disregards the RSM and (2) views the transaction as if Newco had purchased Target's stock from Target's old shareholders.

- To the extent the cash paid to Target's old shareholders comes from Target (e.g., out of Target's accumulated working capital or borrowings for which Target ends up liable), the transaction is taxed as if Target redeemed that much of its stock from the old Target shareholders.
- On the other hand, to the extent the cash paid to Target's old shareholders comes from equity contributions to Newco or from borrowings for which Newco, rather than Target, ends up liable, the transaction is taxed as if Newco purchased Target stock from Target's old shareholders.
- The tax ramifications to Target's old shareholders, i.e., LTCG on the disposition of the Target stock, are generally the same whether the transaction is treated (1) only as a purchase by Newco of Target's stock *or* (2) as if Newco purchased part of Target's stock from the old Target shareholders and as if Target redeemed part of its stock from the old Target shareholders (a part-purchase, part-redemption). In the unusual situation where the old Target shareholders own (actually or constructively) substantial Newco (or Target) stock *after* the transaction, the proceeds received under (1) or (2) may be treated as an OI dividend, although the standard for dividend recharacterization is somewhat different for (a) the portion treated as a purchase (where the Code §304(b) OI rules apply with broad aggregation and attribution rules so that there is more risk of OI dividend treatment) and (b) the portion treated as a redemption (where the Code §302 OI rules apply with narrower attribution rules so that there is less risk of OI dividend treatment).

An alternative method for squeezing out 100% of Target's old shareholders is a reverse two-party cash merger of newly-formed Newco into Target in which Target's old shareholders receive cash while Newco's shareholders receive Target stock in exchange for their Newco stock and Newco disappears.

This transaction (like an RSM) requires the affirmative vote of a requisite majority of Target's shareholders and generally allows dissenting Target shareholders to claim appraisal rights. However, after the transaction Newco's shareholders own 100% of Target's (rather than Newco's) stock and, for tax purposes, IRS (1) disregards Newco as transitory and hence disregards the merger, (2) treats Target as redeeming a portion of its stock, and (3) treats Newco's shareholders as purchasing the remainder of Target's stock from Target's old shareholders, generally as described above in an RSM.[5]

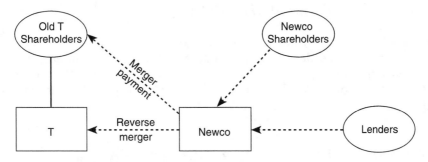

If Target's stock were publicly traded, a vote of Target's shareholders would be covered by the SEC proxy rules, requiring extensive factual disclosure about Target, Newco, and the transaction and entailing delay often as long as four months (while proxy materials are drafted and go through SEC review, followed by a 20-day waiting period under Delaware law after mailing the proxy statement to Target's shareholders and before the shareholders' meeting). See ¶503.3.2.7 and ¶207.3.1(4).

Where (as in this ¶502) Target is not publicly traded, SEC's proxy rules do not apply. Nevertheless, where Target is a Delaware corporation and Target's shareholders have the opportunity to take some action—e.g., (1) to vote on a Target merger or sale of assets or (2) to claim or forego statutory appraisal rights—Delaware courts have concluded that Target's directors have a duty to disclose all material facts to Target's shareholders before Target's shareholders take such action, causing at least some delay while any necessary disclosure materials are prepared and delivered, although the far greater delay inherent in SEC review is obviated.

Where Target is not incorporated in Delaware, the state law duty to provide disclosure to Target's shareholders is generally far less clear, because few state courts have articulated this duty as clearly as have the Delaware courts. Indeed, even in Delaware it is unclear whether there is a duty of disclosure to shareholders

---

[5] In this case no §338(h)(10) election is permitted (even where Target is an S corporation) because a single corporate entity did not purchase at least an 80-80 amount of Target's stock (unless Newco is itself an 80-80 subsidiary of another corporation).

whose action is not required—e.g., where one or a few fully informed shareholders have acted to approve the merger by written consent and statutory appraisal rights do not apply.

¶502.4   Purchase Accounting

For a discussion of purchase accounting, part purchase accounting, recap accounting, and (for pre-7/01 transactions) pooling accounting, see ¶501.8 above and ¶504 below.

¶502.5   Golden Parachute Tax Rules

IRS golden parachute rules may impose an extra 20 percentage points of federal tax on executives and deny Target a deduction for payments to executives (or special vesting of non-vested stock or options) in connection with a change in control of Target or a sale of its assets. Code §280G and §4999. See the discussion of the golden parachute tax rules at ¶202.3.2 above.

¶502.6   Special LTCG Tax Advantages for Individuals

The top normal federal tax rate for an individual's LTCG (i.e., gain on sale of a capital asset, including stock, held more than one year) is 20%, which is 18.6 percentage points below the top OI 2002 and 2003 individual rate (38.6%). However, three Code provisions grant further tax relief to an individual who owns stock either directly or through a partnership, LLC, or S corporation and who recognizes LTCG in special circumstances:

(1) A 14% top rate for LTCG on sale of "qualified small business stock" held more than 5 years.
(2) A tax-free rollover on sale of stock that would have qualified for the 14% special rate (except that the necessary holding period is more than 6 months rather than more than 5 years) where the proceeds are then reinvested in new qualified stock within 60 days.
(3) An 18% top rate for LTCG on sale of property (not merely "qualified small business stock") acquired after 12/31/00 and held more than 5 years (with a taxpayer election to treat pre-12/31/00 property as sold and reacquired in 1/01).

See ¶906 for a more detailed discussion of these CG tax breaks for individuals.

¶502.7   Other Issues

Generally the same as ¶501 above.

¶502.8 Key Issues and References on Private Company Buyout

Tax aspects of acquisition. Does Newco always desire to structure for asset SUB? Do Target and its shareholders always desire to structure for asset COB? Why?

References:

- Ginsburg and Levin M&A book ¶101's definition of a buyout, ¶¶104, 105, 107, 403.1
- Code §331
- Code §336
- Ginsburg and Levin M&A book Chapters 2, 3, 4 and 14

What structure minimizes taxes for all parties as a whole?
What structure preserves most flexibility?

References:

- Rev. Rul. 69-6
- Rev. Rul. 73-427
- Rev. Rul. 78-250
- Rev. Rul. 79-273
- Rev. Rul. 90-95

Deductible payments to Target's shareholders. When is it desirable from a tax standpoint for Newco to make payments directly to Target's shareholders for post-acquisition consulting and/or covenants not to compete?

References:

- Ginsburg and Levin M&A book ¶404

Management rollover. If Target management owns appreciated Target stock and plans to use the proceeds to buy Newco stock, is it possible for them to save the income tax on their gain in the Target stock by a stock-for-stock swap?

References:

- Code §351
- Ginsburg and Levin M&A book ¶1403
- Ginsburg & Levin M&A book ¶902 and ¶903

Corporate, SEC, and other considerations. What non-tax considerations may play a role in deciding whether to structure the acquisition as a purchase of stock, purchase of assets, or merger?

References:

- Del. Gen. Corp. Law §251, §252, §259(a), §261, §262
- Ginsburg and Levin M&A book ¶1702

Where Target is a private corporation being acquired by Newco in a merger or asset purchase, what type of disclosure (if any) to Target's shareholders is prerequisite to Target's shareholders' (1) vote on Newco's acquisition of Target or (2) exercise of their statutory appraisal rights?

References:

- *Malone v. Brincat*, 722 A.2d 5 (Del. S. Ct 1998).
- *Turner v. Bernstein*, 1999 WL 66532 (Del. Ch. 1999).

Limitations on deductibility of executive compensation. What are the golden parachute tax rules and when do they apply? Who is harmed when these special tax rules apply?

References:

- Code §280G
- Code §4999
- Ginsburg and Levin M&A book ¶1505

¶503 BUYOUT OF PUBLIC COMPANY

In this ¶503, Target is a publicly traded C corporation.[1] Target's board of directors has concluded that (1) although Target's business is sound, its stock is trading (and is expected to continue trading) at a disappointing price, because the stock market does not properly value a company of Target's size in Target's industry and (2) Target's shareholder value can be maximized by selling Target. In addition, Target's CEO, who is also its largest shareholder (owning 15% of Target), has tired of the game and is ready to seek sunnier climes. In other respects, the facts are the same as in ¶501, including the $50 million buyout price.

¶503 [1] Under Code §7704, every publicly traded company—even if formed as a partnership or LLC—is taxed as a C corporation, with only very minor exceptions.

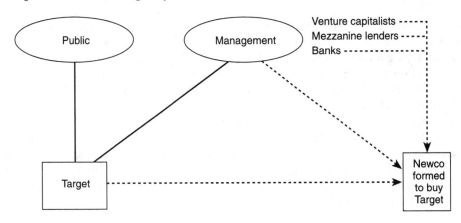

¶503.1   One-Step vs. Two-Step Buyout

There are two principal methods for structuring Newco's buyout of public Target: In a *one-step merger structure*, Newco (or Newco's subsidiary NewSub) merges into Target with Target's shareholders receiving cash for their Target stock in a two-party reverse cash merger (or a reverse subsidiary merger). With such a one-step approach, Newco does not gain control of Target until the merger is completed, often as long as four months, principally because SEC's proxy rules apply since Target's shareholders must vote on the merger. See ¶503.2.2.7 below.

In a *two-step approach*, Newco first makes a cash tender offer for Target's stock followed by a squeeze out reverse cash merger of Newco or NewSub into Target, with Target's remaining shareholders (who did not sell in the cash tender offer) receiving cash for their Target stock in the squeeze-out merger. Under a two-step approach, SEC's tender offer rules allow Newco to complete the first step tender offer quickly (approximately one month) and hence gain control over Target. See ¶503.2.2.4 below.

¶503.2   Federal Income Tax Issues

The federal income tax issues in acquiring publicly traded Target are generally the same as those discussed at ¶502 above regarding the buyout of a private C corporation (i.e., a company which is neither a Bigco subsidiary nor an S corporation, partnership, or LLC). Whether Newco acquires Target in one step or in two steps, the transaction is generally structured for asset COB so that only one tax is imposed on the sellers, i.e., a CG tax on Target's shareholders.

By contrast, if the transaction were structured for asset SUB—with Newco purchasing Target's assets, or Newco acquiring Target in a forward cash merger, or Newco acquiring Target's stock in a reverse cash merger with a §338 election— double tax would be imposed (i.e., corporate-level tax on Target's inherent asset appreciation and shareholder-level tax on the Target shareholders' stock gain).

The double tax is wholly borne by the sellers in an actual asset sale, while the corporate-level tax is borne by Newco in a forward cash merger or a reverse subsidiary cash merger (with or without a first step tender offer) with a regular §338 election. As discussed in ¶502, it is generally not tax advantageous to structure the acquisition of a C corporation for asset SUB (because the PV of Target's corporate-level tax exceeds the PV of Newco's tax saving), unless Target has a substantial NOL to shelter its corporate-level asset-sale gain.

As discussed in ¶202.3.2 and ¶502.5 above, IRS golden parachute penalties may apply if there are substantial payments to Target executives (or special vesting of non-vested stock or options) in connection with Newco's acquisition of Target. These penalties cannot be avoided by the special 75% shareholder vote procedure, because Target's stock is publicly traded.

¶503.3 Securities and Corporate Law Issues and Negotiating Strategies

In addition to the buyout issues discussed in ¶501 above (buyout of a Bigco subsidiary or division) and ¶502 above (buyout of a private company), a going private buyout of a publicly traded target implicates a large number of federal securities law issues, state corporate law issues, and practical negotiating issues.

¶503.3.1 Practical Scenario

VC may prefer to approach Target's CEO with a firm offer at a stated premium price, fully backed by financing commitments, in order to induce Target to accept the VC-Newco offer as quickly as possible. However, to delay Target's public disclosure obligation (see ¶503.3.2.1 below), VC may decide to approach Target's CEO with merely an expression of interest.

If an approach to Target management is not productive, VC may decide to approach Target board members either directly through general contacts or by delivering a "bear hug" letter proposing a friendly combination on terms to be negotiated.

During this process, VC may begin accumulating Target stock in the open market. VC must file a schedule 13D (pursuant to 1934 Act §13) once VC acquires more than 5% of a class of Target's voting stock registered under 1934 Act §12 (see ¶207.3.1(4) above and ¶503.3.2.2 below) and must generally make a Hart-Scott-Rodino Antitrust Reporting Act filing with the FTC once VC acquires $50 million of Target voting securities (see ¶501.3.3 above). In addition, VC must file a schedule 13D even before acquiring more than 5% of a class of Target's voting stock when (1) VC is acting in concert with other Target shareholders who, in the aggregate together with VC, own sufficient Target shares to exceed the 5% reporting threshold or (2) VC obtains an option to acquire Target stock, whether from Target or from Target shareholders, which causes VC to be treated as owning sufficient Target shares to exceed the 5% reporting threshold.

When Target's management is investing in Newco there is a conflict between management's duty to obtain the highest price for Target's public shareholders and management's apparent desire for Newco (which will be partly owned by Target's management) to purchase Target at the lowest possible price. Thus, Target's board may utilize some or all of the following protective devices to protect themselves against liability to Target's public shareholders for breach of fiduciary duty: (1) appoint an independent board committee (which in turn selects independent legal counsel and an independent investment banker for the committee), (2) obtain an IB fairness opinion, (3) seek a majority vote of disinterested directors, and (4) seek a majority vote of disinterested shareholders. See ¶503.3.3.1 below.

Newco may desire some or all of the following *protective devices* to discourage competing bidders and/or to compensate Newco should another bidder ultimately triumph:

- a no-shop clause,
- an exclusivity clause,
- a break-up fee, covering Newco's expenses plus a profit element,
- a topping fee payment to Newco if Target is sold to another buyer at a higher price (often based on the amount by which the third party buyer's price exceeds Newco's original bid),
- an option to buy unissued Target shares at a fixed price,
- an option to buy outstanding Target shares at a fixed price from one or more large Target shareholders, and
- a crown-jewel option to buy a Target division or other key Target asset at a fixed price.

Questions may arise as to the validity of these protective devices under state corporate law, especially where Target management is investing in Newco. Ideally, these protective devices should be negotiated and signed *before public announcement of Newco's offer.*

If public announcement of Newco's bid can not be postponed until Newco and Target have negotiated and signed a definitive agreement which includes some form of protection for Newco, Newco may attempt to negotiate an agreement which contains limited protection immediately before Target's public announcement of Newco's bid, after which the parties can negotiate the final deal containing more extensive protective devices.

¶503.3.2   Federal Securities Laws

¶503.3.2.1   *Disclosing Negotiations with Target*

For some years the generally accepted time for making a public announcement regarding the Target-Newco transaction was when firm agreement had been reached, including agreement on price and structure. However, the Supreme

Court's 1988 *Basic Incorporated v. Levinson* decision[2] established a case-by-case, facts-and-circumstances test, essentially weighing the public's need for disclosure against Target's need for confidentiality. The Court sanctioned silence or a no-comment response from Target during preliminary negotiations, stating that silence in such circumstances is not misleading when Target does not otherwise have a duty to disclose. However, the Court stated that when Target otherwise has a duty to disclose material information, disclosure of preliminary merger negotiations is required if there is substantial likelihood a reasonable investor would consider the existence of such negotiations significant in reaching an investment decision, considering the total mix of available information.

Such a duty to disclose preliminary negotiations may arise from Target's prior statements (e.g., a denial that any unusual transaction is pending) or in response to unusual fluctuations in Target's stock price which might indicate that information about the Newco-Target transaction has leaked.

The NYSE, AMEX, and Nasdaq National Market all have rules requiring prompt disclosure of any material information that may affect the value of an issuer's securities or influence an investor's decision, including preliminary merger negotiations, and failure to comply with such rules could subject the issuer to delisting.

¶503.3.2.2 *Ownership Disclosure*

Any person (a "5% shareholder") who acquires beneficial ownership of more than 5% of a class of voting equity securities registered under the 1934 Act (see ¶207.3.1(4) above) generally must file a schedule 13D or, in certain cases, a less burdensome schedule 13G. The 5% shareholder's intent characteristics and percentage ownership determine the type of filing required (e.g., schedule 13D or 13G) and the timing of the filing, as discussed below. Multiple persons acting in concert are treated as a "group" and the holdings of each member of the group are aggregated in calculating such person's percentage ownership. Beneficial ownership is defined broadly to include the right to acquire stock, and thus the holder of a currently exercisable option would generally be treated as beneficially owning the shares which can be acquired upon exercise.

The filing must disclose the 5% shareholder's intent with respect to Target and, for a schedule 13D, substantial additional information, including the source and the amount of the 5% shareholder's financing, the 5% shareholder's contacts with the issuer, and a detailed explanation of any proposed acquisition.

Each 5% shareholder is required to file schedule 13D, except (1) certain institutional investors (e.g., insurance companies, registered investment companies, registered broker dealers, employee benefit plans) (an "Institutional Investor") acquiring securities in the ordinary course of business and with no purpose or intent of changing or influencing control of the issuer are permitted to file schedule 13G and (2) another investor beneficially owning less than 20% of a class of voting

---

[2] 485 U.S. 224 (1988).

securities is permitted to file schedule 13G if such investor does not intend to change or influence control of the issuer (a "Passive Investor").

Under SEC Rule 13d-1, a schedule 13D or a Passive Investor's schedule 13G must be filed within 10 days after the person or group beneficially owns more than 5% of the outstanding class of voting securities. Any changes in ownership or purpose following an initial schedule 13D filing must be promptly reported on a supplemental 13D. An Institutional Investor is required to file a schedule 13G within 45 days following the end of the year in which the investment occurred, unless such investor has acquired more than 10% of the outstanding class of voting securities, in which case the filing is due within 10 days following the end of the month in which that threshold was crossed. A Passive Investor that changes its investment intent or crosses the 20% threshold is required to file a schedule 13D within 10 days after the event, and is subject to a 10-day cooling off period during which such investor is prohibited from voting its securities and acquiring additional securities.

¶503.3.2.3   Limits on Insider Trading

The "antifraud" provisions of SEC Rule 10b-5 under the 1934 Act prohibit a person (an "insider" or a "temporary insider") from (1) trading on material non-public information unless the information is publicly disclosed or (2) "tipping" others who do so. Information is "material" if a reasonable investor would consider it relevant to his or her investment decision. Thus, if VC has held substantial discussions with Target management, VC must be cautious about purchasing Target stock from a Target shareholder who is not privy to material non-public information obtained by VC.

VC and Newco should consider the effects of 1934 Act §16, covering disgorgement of short-swing profits on a purchase and sale (or sale and purchase) of Target stock (or certain derivatives) within a six-month period by a person who is an executive officer, director, or 10% beneficial owner of Target. §16 could apply to VC's or Newco's purchase of Target stock made in the 6 months prior to Newco's acquisition of Target, because Newco's acquisition of Target generally constitutes a sale of Target stock by Target's shareholders.

Under SEC Rule 14e-3, when Newco has taken a substantial step to commence, or has commenced, a tender offer, any person (other than Newco) who possesses material non-public information relating to such tender offer is prohibited from purchasing or selling Target stock or securities convertible into or exchangeable for Target stock or any option or right to obtain or to dispose of the foregoing securities.

¶503.3.2.4   Tender Offer Rules

Where Target's stock is publicly held and Newco is purchasing Target stock from a number of people, Newco must comply with the 1934 Act's tender offer provisions (also known as the Williams Act) and SEC's tender offer rules, governing timing and disclosure of tender offers. All tender offers, whether the consideration offered by Newco consists of cash or stock, are made on SEC schedule TO, with substantive disclosure as required by SEC Reg. M-A.

(1) The old rule that within 5 business days after Newco publicly announces its intention to make a tender offer for Target stock (a) Newco must formally "commence" or renounce the offer to Target's shareholders and (b) Newco must file a schedule 14D-1 with SEC describing the tender offer and deliver a copy to Target was repealed 1/00. Thus, there is now no limit on the period Newco can wait after announcing its intention to tender for Target stock before "commencing" its tender offer, but Newco must send Target's shareholders the information required by SEC schedule TO and SEC Reg. M-A no later than the time Newco sends to Target's shareholders a letter of transmittal to be used by them in tendering their Target stock to Newco.

(2) Target must file a schedule 14D-9 with SEC within 10 business days after Newco commences its tender offer for Target stock containing Target's recommendation to its shareholders regarding acceptance of, rejection of, or no position on Newco's tender offer.

(3) Newco's tender offer must remain open for at least 20 business days.

(4) Newco's tender offer must be open to all Target shareholders and must offer each Target shareholder the highest consideration Newco paid to any other Target shareholder during such tender offer.

(5) Newco can first begin purchasing Target shares 20 business days after commencing its tender offer and can not purchase (or agree to purchase) Target shares outside the tender offer once it has commenced.

(6) If Newco's tender offer is not for "any and all" Target shares, Newco must purchase Target shares on a pro rata basis from all Target tendering shareholders.

   • If Newco seeks (e.g.) 51% of Target's stock, Newco cannot accept the first 51% tendered and reject the excess. Rather, where more than 51% of Target's stock is tendered during the tender offer and Newco chooses to buy only 51%, Newco must buy a pro-rated portion from each tendering Target shareholder.

(7) A Target tendering shareholder may withdraw any tendered Target shares prior to expiration of the tender offer.

(8) If Newco makes a material change in the terms of its tender offer (e.g., a change in the percentage of Target shares sought or the amount of consideration to be paid), the tender offer must remain open for at least 10 business days thereafter.

(9) Newco must announce any extension of the tender offer's expiration date by 9:00 a.m. EST on the day following scheduled expiration.

(10) Newco must pay the consideration offered or return the Target shares tendered promptly after consummation, termination, or withdrawal of Newco's tender offer.

(11)   Newco (after consummating its initial tender offer which was for any and all Target shares) may elect to make a second tender offer at the same price as the initial tender offer without a 20-business-day waiting period and without allowing tendering Target shareholders any withdrawal rights. This second tender offer must be open for at least 3 business days and no more than 20 business days. Newco must immediately accept and promptly pay for Target shares as tendered during the second tender offer.

(12)   The rules are somewhat different for a tender offer by Target for its own stock (a "self tender").

¶503.3.2.5   *Federal Margin Regulations*

Where Newco makes a tender offer for Target stock or purchases Target stock in the open market (rather than simply acquiring Target in a one-step merger with no tender offer or open market stock purchases), Newco's borrowings to purchase such publicly traded stock may be subject to the Fed's margin regulations (promulgated pursuant to the 1934 Act) limiting the amount of debt which may be incurred to purchase publicly traded equity securities. The margin regulations would be violated where (1) Target's stock is "publicly traded" (i.e., constitutes "margin stock"), (2) the margin stock constitutes *either* "direct" *or* "indirect" *or* "presumed indirect" security for an extension of credit to Newco (the borrower), and (3) Newco borrows more than 50% of the current market value of Newco's Target shares.

For purposes of (1) above, stock is "publicly traded" and hence constitutes "margin stock" only if registered (or afforded unlisted trading privileges) on a national securities exchange or qualified for trading in the Nasdaq National Market.

For purposes of (2) above, the Target stock constitutes (a) "direct" security for a borrowing where Newco pledges the stock to the lender, (b) "indirect" security for a borrowing where the loan becomes due and payable upon a sale of the Target stock (a due-on-sale clause) or Newco agrees not to pledge the Target stock to any other lender (a negative-pledge clause), and (c) "presumed indirect" security for a borrowing where the borrower is a shell corporation with no substantial assets or business operations (other than the Target stock being acquired), as Newco generally is in a buyout.

However, there are two potential exceptions to this "presumed indirect" security rule (i.e., so long as there is no actual pledge and no due-on-sale or negative-pledge clause, the borrower's Target stock is not presumed to be security for the borrowing merely because the borrower is a shell corporation):

The first potential exception applies where, at the time Newco borrows money to purchase Target shares (in a tender offer or open market purchases), Newco has a signed merger agreement with Target.

The second potential exception applies where Newco's loan agreement permits Newco to borrow money to purchase Target shares only if Newco acquires sufficient Target shares so that Newco can effectuate a Newco-Target merger without a vote of Target's shareholders. Where Target is a Delaware corporation, such a short-form merger without a vote of Target's shareholders is permissible (under Del. Gen. Corp. Law §253) if Newco (through a tender offer or open market purchases or a combination thereof) has acquired at least 90% or more of Target's stock.

In summary:

(1) Where Newco acquires publicly traded Target in a one-step reverse subsidiary cash merger with no tender offer and no open market purchases of Target stock, the margin regulations are not a problem because Target's publicly traded stock is extinguished in the merger and the borrowing is therefore not secured in any respect by "margin stock."[3]

(2) Where Newco acquires Target in a two-step cash tender offer plus a reverse subsidiary squeeze-out cash merger, the margin regulations are applicable—because when the tender offer closes (and thereafter) Newco holds publicly traded Target (margin) shares—and hence if Newco wishes to borrow more than 50% of the current market value of the Target shares purchased, Newco must structure the transaction so that (a) Newco borrowing which is directly or indirectly secured by Target stock does not exceed this 50% limit and (b) with respect to any borrowing in excess of the 50% limit, the Target stock is not presumed indirect security for such borrowing because the transaction fits within either the signed-merger-agreement exception or the sufficient-stock-ownership-for-a-short-form-merger exception.[4]

(3) Where Newco makes open market purchases of publicly traded Target stock as a prelude to either a one-step or a two-step acquisition of Target, the margin regulations apply in the same way as set forth in (2) above regarding a tender offer.[5]

¶503.3.2.6   Going Private Rules

If the buyout constitutes a "going private" transaction, as defined in SEC Rule 13e-3, Target must file schedule 13E-3 with SEC containing extensive disclosure

---

[3] The same conclusion—margin regulations not a problem—obtains where Newco acquires Target in a one-step *forward* cash merger of Target into Newco or a Newco subsidiary; however, a forward merger format is generally not desirable because such an acquisition structure implicates corporate-level tax on the inherent gain in Target's assets. See ¶503.2 and ¶502.1.1 above.

[4] The same conclusion—margin regulations not a problem — obtains in these circumstances where Newco acquires Target in a two-step cash tender offer plus a *forward* cash merger of Target into Newco or a Newco subsidiary, which can generally be effectuated without corporate-level tax on the inherent gain in Target's assets so long as Newco has first acquired at least 80% of Target's stock.

[5] The discussion in this ¶503.3.2.5 above relates to the margin regulation (Reg. U) governing loans by banks and other lenders which are not brokers or dealers. A broker or dealer (subject to Reg. T, which is more restrictive than Reg. U) generally can not make a loan to Newco for the purpose of purchasing any stock (whether publicly traded or not) unless (a) Newco actually pledges the stock to the broker or dealer as security for the loan to Newco and (b) the loan to Newco does not exceed 50% of the current market value of the publicly-traded stock serving as collateral for the loan (i.e., there is no margin credit for any stock which is not publicly traded). In the case of a broker or dealer lender, the "indirect" security concept as well as the two exceptions to the "presumed indirect" security rule discussed in text above are thus not available.

about the history and fairness of the transaction. Newco's acquisition of Target is a going private transaction when:

(1) one or more specified acts (including a tender offer, a purchase of stock, or a solicitation of proxies in connection with a merger) is

(2) undertaken by either Target or a Target affiliate (i.e., a person controlling, controlled by, or under common control with Target, and hence Newco may be a Target affiliate if any member of Target's top management will be a Newco key employee and/or a significant Newco stockholder) which

(3) either has a reasonable likelihood or the purpose of causing (a) a class of Target's equity securities subject to 1934 Act reporting (see ¶207.3.1(4)) to be held of record by fewer than 300 persons or (b) a class of securities traded on a securities exchange or interdealer quotation system to be neither listed nor authorized for quotation.

¶503.3.2.7 *Proxy Rules*

Any required Target shareholder vote on a merger, sale of assets, or similar transaction will be subject to the SEC proxy rules if Target's common stock is registered under 1934 Act §12 (see ¶207.3.1(4)). In addition, if Newco is listed on the NYSE, AMEX, or Nasdaq National Market or certain regional exchanges and Newco is issuing 20% or more of its common stock in connection with its acquisition of Target, the NYSE, AMEX, Nasdaq National Market, or certain regional exchange rules require Newco's shareholders to approve the stock issuance.

Prelude to Target's shareholder vote, Target must first draft an extensive proxy statement containing disclosures about Target, Newco, and the transaction. Target must then file the preliminary proxy statement with SEC at least 10 calendar days prior to mailing the proxy statement to shareholders, but SEC review of the proxy statement often results in a far longer waiting period. Target must file the definitive proxy statement with SEC when it is sent to shareholders.

Under Delaware and most state corporation laws, Target's shareholders' meeting to approve the merger can not be held for at least 20 days after mailing the proxy statement. A cumulative delay of as much as four months between execution of the merger agreement and the actual vote of Target's shareholders is not unusual.

If Newco has completed its tender offer and owns 90% or more of Target (which is incorporated in Delaware or another state permitting a short-form merger), Target's shareholders need not vote on the squeeze-out merger and hence no proxy statement is necessary for Target's shareholders. However, a Delaware (not an SEC) information statement must be sent to Target shareholders after the merger.

¶503.3.3   State Corporate Laws

¶503.3.3.1   Target Board's Fiduciary Duty

Under state corporate law, the business and affairs of a corporation are managed by or under the direction of its board of directors. In general, a board's business judgment is respected and accorded deference if the board acted on an informed basis, in good faith, and in the honest belief that the action was taken in the best interests of the company and its shareholders.

In order for the board to claim the benefit of this judicial "business judgment rule," the board must be able to demonstrate that it acted with due care after thorough study and conscientious deliberation.

However, when Target's sale is being considered, its directors have an enhanced duty to ensure that the interests of Target's shareholders are being maximized, and courts typically subject the directors' conduct to enhanced scrutiny to ensure that it is reasonable. Where this standard is not met and a court concludes that the directors did not undertake a thorough review of the proposed sale, directors have been held personally liable for breaching their fiduciary duty and agreeing to sell the company for too low a price.

A corporation incorporated in Delaware or certain other jurisdictions may eliminate director monetary liability for breach of fiduciary duty, including the duty of care (through a provision in the certificate of incorporation), except for (1) a breach of the director's duty of loyalty, (2) acts or omissions not in good faith or which involve intentional misconduct or a knowing violation of law, or (3) a transaction from which the director derives an improper personal benefit.

When some board members have an interest in the transaction different from the interest of Target's shareholders generally (e.g., some Target board members will become significant Newco shareholders or executives), a committee of Target independent directors is usually advisable to foster an arm's length negotiation between Newco and Target. The independent committee typically selects its own investment bankers and legal counsel. The independent committee must be composed of directors who have no interest in Newco, must be fully informed, and must have freedom to negotiate with Newco at arm's length. If such procedural and substantive measures are not taken or followed, the interested parties are required (in case of a lawsuit) to demonstrate that the transaction was entirely fair to Target's public shareholders.

An IB fairness opinion and some form of (pre- or post-agreement) auction or market check helps to demonstrate that the board acted in an informed and reasonable manner. However, courts look carefully at such investment banking opinions, particularly when two competing bids are being considered.

A board may not discriminate among rival bidders in the absence of a reasonable relationship to shareholder interests. In contrast, a board may use defensive measures to allow the company to complete a transaction considered to be strategically important and under consideration for a substantial period.

When Target is attempting to choose between rival bidders after a decision has been made to sell control of Target or to enter into a transaction that results in a change of Target's control, the directors' overriding duty is to obtain for Target's shareholders the best value reasonably available.

¶503.3.3.2 Negotiations with Target

Some of the clauses which might be included in an acquisition agreement between Target and Newco are:

No-shop/fiduciary-out clause. A no-shop clause prevents Target from seeking third-party offers for Target, while a fiduciary-out clause allows Target to pursue a more favorable unsolicited offer if one is received. Courts look carefully at the enforceability of any provision that purports to limit the ability of Target's board to explore unsolicited bids. For example, a court may well hold invalid a contract provision prohibiting the board from negotiating with a rival making a bid which is not fully financed.

Lockup. Newco may obtain options to buy outstanding stock at a fixed price from key Target shareholders, an option to buy newly issued Target stock at a fixed price from Target, or an option to buy a Target division or subsidiary or other "crown jewel" from Target at a fixed price. NYSE rules require shareholder approval for the grant of an option to buy stock from Target where *either* (1) exercise of the option would result in a change of Target's control *or* (2) the option covers more than 20% of Target's common shares (not including the option shares). AMEX rules contain only rule (2) and invoke it only when the option price is less than the greater of Target's book value or market value. Nasdaq National Market rules contain rule (1) as well as rule (2) with the AMEX's gloss regarding the option price. Courts look carefully at the enforceability of an option which does not contain an overall cap on value or at an option exercisable by delivering consideration other than cash, such as a promissory note.

Break-up fee. Target may agree to pay Newco's reasonable expenses in the event the buyout is not consummated. In addition, Target may agree to pay a reasonable break-up fee (e.g., 2% to 3% of the consideration offered for Target). However, a court might hold a larger break-up fee or a below-market option invalid as a penalty, especially where Target's management is investing in Newco.

Financing out. Newco may seek the right to terminate the acquisition if it can not obtain financing.

Neutral or supermajority voting requirement. Target may request that (1) any Target shares owned by VC or Newco be excluded in determining whether a required shareholder vote has been achieved or (2) a supermajority of shareholders approve the transaction.

¶503.3.3.3   Negotiations with Management

Newco will negotiate (1) the terms and conditions of management's investment in Newco and management's options and other incentive compensation, (2) restrictions on transfer of Newco stock, (3) vesting or repurchase of Newco stock, and (4) other matters. See ¶202.2, ¶202.3, ¶407, ¶501.5.4 above.

¶503.3.3.4   Other Takeover Issues

States have enacted an array of takeover statutes in response to the Supreme Court's decision in *CTS Corporation v. Dynamics Corporation of America*.[6] Delaware has enacted a takeover statute requiring a supermajority shareholder vote for business combinations with an "interested" (defined as a 15%) stockholder unless the board approves such transaction before the person becomes a 15% stockholder. Some other states have enacted "control share" statutes requiring a shareholder vote before Newco is allowed to vote its "control" shares in Target. All of these statutes generally contain broad aggregation and attribution provisions and should be checked early in the process to avoid unexpected pitfalls.

In a negotiated acquisition, any poison pill will usually be redeemed by Target. This may, however, open the door to a competing offer. Courts will generally not allow Target to exempt only a favored bidder from the operation of the pill unless Target can demonstrate a reasonable relation to shareholder interest.

Finally, VC and Newco must consider any "fair price" clause or required supermajority vote in Target's charter, payments required under Target's employment contracts with "golden parachute" provisions, provisions of Target's existing loan agreements or outstanding debt securities requiring repayment on a change of control, and the identity of a trustee or other person who has the right to vote any Target voting stock held by a Target employee benefit plan.

*¶503.3.3.5   Key Issues and References on Management's Fiduciary
              Duties*

When can Newco (after acquiring control of Target through a tender offer) squeeze out Target's minority shareholders without a vote of the minority shareholders?

• Del. Gen. Corp. Law §253

What are management's fiduciary duties if they put Target in play by proposing a buyout?

Can management ask for some protection from Target against a higher third party bid?

---

[6] 481 U.S. 107 (1987).

Can Target's board favor management's bid over other similar or even higher bids?

Can Target's board take into account considerations other than the best deal for Target's public shareholders?

References:

- *Edelman v. Fruehauf Corp.*, 798 F.2d 882 (6th Cir. 1986).
- *Hanson Trust PLC v. ML SCM Acquisition Inc.*, 781 F.2d 264 (2d Cir. 1986).
- *Mills Acquisition Co. v. Macmillan, Inc.*, 559 A.2d 1261 (Del. 1989).
- *Paramount Communications Inc. v. QVC Network, Inc.*, 637 A.2d 34 (Del. 1994).
- *In re Fort Howard Corp. Shareholders Litigation*, 14 Del. J. Corp. L. 699, 1988 WL 83147 (Del. Ch. 1988).
- *Black & Decker Corp. v. American Standard Inc.*, 682 F. Supp. 772 (D. Del. 1988).

¶504 BUYOUT STRUCTURED FOR RECAP ACCOUNTING

Several years after VC has acquired Target in a buyout VC will often turn to the public equity markets to sell its Target stock. Because the price of Target's shares in a public offering is often based on a multiple of Target's book earnings, VC may want to structure its initial buyout of Target in order to obtain the benefits of recapitalization or "recap" accounting, increasing Target's post-acquisition book earnings and, hopefully, its ultimate IPO value.

Where VC simply forms Newco to acquire Target in a buyout (as described in ¶501 through ¶503 above), GAAP purchase accounting rules (as described in ¶501.8 above) generally require Target's assets to take a new aggregate book value equal to the amount Newco paid to acquire Target, *plus* Target liabilities assumed by Newco or its subsidiaries, *plus* Newco's acquisition expenses. This new aggregate book value is then allocated first to Target's current assets at FV, second to Target's fixed assets at FV, next to specific intangibles at FV, and the residual to Target's goodwill. Target's fixed assets and specific intangibles (other than goodwill) then are required to be depreciated or amortized, thus reducing Newco/Target's GAAP book earnings. Moreover, should goodwill thereafter become "impaired" (i.e., should carrying costs exceed FV), Target's goodwill must be written off to the extent of the impairment and Newco/Target's GAAP book earnings would be reduced by the amount of such impairment write off.

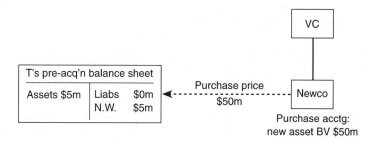

These GAAP purchase accounting rules apply regardless of whether the acquisition transaction is structured as an asset purchase, stock purchase, or merger. Hence even when the acquisition has been structured for tax purposes to achieve asset COB (e.g., a stock purchase with no Code §338 election), so that Newco has no tax savings from asset SUB, the GAAP purchase accounting rules require increased book depreciation/amortization. If Newco/Target were subsequently to go public, such GAAP purchase accounting would decrease Newco/Target's valuation.

However, where VC's buyout of Target is structured for recap accounting, there is no change in Target's asset book value, no additional goodwill is created, and hence Target's post-acquisition book earnings are not reduced as a result of increased depreciation, amortization, or impairment charges.

Where VC plans ultimately to take Target public, qualifying for recap accounting and avoiding full or partial purchase accounting may yield substantial benefits. Because Target's assets are not written up for GAAP accounting purposes in connection with a recap buyout, Target's future GAAP depreciation and amortization charges will be lower, and hence Target's future book earnings higher, than if purchase accounting had applied. Because the price of Target's shares in a public offering often is based on a multiple of Target's per share book earnings, the use of recap accounting may allow VC to realize greater proceeds in a future public offering of Target's shares.

FASB's 7/01 elimination of goodwill amortization (see ¶501.8 above) reduces (but does not eliminate) the desirability of recapitalization accounting. First, under a non-amortization/impairment approach, goodwill created by purchase accounting does not reduce earnings unless and until goodwill's FV is subsequently impaired. Thus, using recapitalization accounting to avoid goodwill creation eliminates the possibility of a future earnings reduction, should goodwill become impaired. Second, recapitalization accounting also avoids an accounting basis step-up for both tangible assets and intangible assets other than goodwill and hence avoids an earnings reduction due to increased depreciation and amortization charges for these non-goodwill assets.

As discussed in ¶501.8, FASB plans to review recap accounting in a second phase of its business combinations project, thus creating some doubt as to recap accounting's long-term viability, although (by analogy to FASB's 7/01 decision to abolish poolings prospectively) we believe any recap rule changes should apply only to acquisitions occurring after FASB finalizes new rules.

¶504.1   Recap Accounting Overview

Even where a buyout results in a change of control for Target, recap accounting—and not purchase accounting—generally applies to Target's separate financial statements so long as (1) Target survives and (2) Target's old shareholders continue to own a "significant" stake in recapitalized Target's common equity. As a practical matter, accounting firms generally take the position that where Target's old shareholders as a group own somewhere between 5.5% and 10% of recapitalized Target's common equity, depending on the circumstances such as the number and type of old Target shareholders with a continuing interest in Target's common equity, the significant continuing stake test is satisfied, as discussed further in ¶504.2.

Recap accounting may also apply in two circumstances where Target's old shareholders do not retain a significant (or indeed any) continuing interest in recapitalized Target's common equity. *First*, recap accounting generally applies where Target has publicly held debt or publicly held preferred stock outstanding prior to and independent of the recapitalization and such public debt or preferred stock remains outstanding after the recapitalization. See ¶504.3. *Second*, SEC has approved recap accounting where at least one of the new investors purchasing a significant stake in Target's recapitalized equity as part of the LBO is "independent" of the investors sponsoring the recapitalization transaction. See ¶504.4.

Where the transaction satisfies one of these routes to recap accounting (as more fully described below), recap accounting generally applies (1) whether pre-recap Target is privately owned (as in ¶502), publicly traded (as in ¶503), or a Bigco subsidiary (as in ¶501) and (2) whether Target is a corporation, an LLC, or a partnership. However, where Target is a Bigco division (not a separate entity owned by Bigco), recap accounting is more difficult to achieve (as described in ¶504.5 below).

¶504.2 Recap Accounting Where Target's Old Shareholders Have Significant Continuing Ownership In Recapitalized Target

Where Target's old shareholders as a group (1) own more than 20% of recapitalized Target's common equity, the significant continuing ownership test is satisfied, (2) own 5% or less, the test is not satisfied, and (3) own more than 5% but not more than 20%, the transaction is in the gray zone, so that the result turns on factors such as the number and type of old Target shareholders with a continuing interest in Target's common equity.

- In the event that the continuing interest in Target's stock held by old Target shareholders is "widely-held," accounting firms and SEC appear to be comfortable with continuing ownership as low as 5.5% to 7%.
- Where the continuing interest in Target's stock held by old Target shareholders is not "widely-held," but the continuing old Target shareholders are not part of Target's post-transaction management, at least some accounting firms appear to be comfortable with continuing ownership as low as 5.5% to 7%.
- However, where the only continuing old Target shareholders are part of Target's post-transaction management, 7% to 10% continuing ownership appears to be the minimum, since management is viewed as being less independent of VC due to their employment relationship (and in certain cases, accounting firms have sought a somewhat larger continuing stake).

See ¶504.2.3 below for (1) a further discussion of the continuing interest in Target which must be retained by old Target shareholders and (2) a discussion of SEC Staff's 4/01 Announcement that, effective for transactions initiated after 4/19/01, stock retained by an old Target shareholder counts toward the significant retained interest requirement only if such old Target shareholder is not part of a "collaborative group" with Target's new investors.

In the typical transaction qualifying for recap accounting because of significant continuing old T shareholders (a) VC invests new money in Target for new stock (common and/or preferred) without forming a new holding corporation for Target, (b) Target borrows additional money, (c) Target uses its new equity money and its new debt financing to redeem a portion of its outstanding stock, and (d) after the transaction Target's old shareholders continue to own a significant stake in recapitalized Target's common equity.

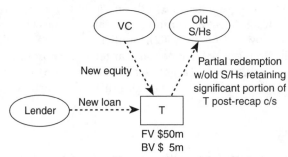

However, it is not essential that VC invests its new money in Target. The transaction can qualify for recap accounting where VC pays its new money directly to Target's old shareholders to purchase previously outstanding Target stock, so long as after the transaction Target survives and Target's old shareholders continue to own a significant stake in Target's common equity.

Where Target qualifies for recap accounting, the book value of Target's assets does not change at all (i.e., there is no purchase accounting or partial purchase accounting). Thus, Target's future depreciation/amortization charges are not increased as a result of the buyout (as they would have been if purchase accounting had applied) and Target's book earnings will be correspondingly higher.

Target's book net worth changes to reflect (a) an increase for any new equity investment and (b) a decrease for amounts paid out in the redemption. Hence Target's book net worth generally declines by the excess of (i) the amount Target paid out in the redemption of Target's old stock over (ii) the amount Target received for new Target stock. This may, in some cases, cause Target to have a negative book net worth, which should be considered in negotiating the financial covenants in Target's new debt agreements.

¶504.2.1   Use of Transitory MergerCo

In some buyouts VC forms a transitory new entity ("Transitory MergerCo" or "TMC") for purposes of merging Transitory MergerCo into Target and forcing

Target's shareholders to accept the consideration specified in the merger agreement in exchange for their Target stock.

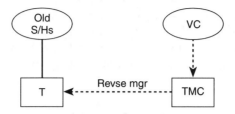

Despite the formation of Transitory MergerCo, the transaction can still qualify for recap accounting, although there is some disagreement among accountants as to the additional requirements that must be met with respect to Transitory MergerCo. Some accountants have taken the position that recap accounting will not apply if the amount of money flowing through Transitory MergerCo to Target's old shareholders is more than 50% of Target's pre-merger stock FV, i.e., where, in accounting parlance, the merger transaction results in a change of Target's control.

Thus, recap accounting is apparently precluded in the view of these accountants where a substantial portion of the money flowing to Target's old shareholders (more than 50% of Target's pre-merger stock FV) is funded into Transitory MergerCo (by VC and lenders). On the other hand, recap accounting is apparently not precluded in such accountants' view where all or a sufficient portion of the money for Target's old shareholders is funded directly into Target (by VC and lenders), i.e., not funded through Transitory MergerCo, so that the cash they receive from Transitory MergerCo constitutes 50% or less of their pre-merger Target stock FV. In the latter situation, returning once again to accounting parlance, the merger transaction (meaning the money flowing through Transitory MergerCo) did not result in a change of Target's control, rather the money funded directly into Target (without passing through Transitory MergerCo) caused the change in Target's control.

A second group of accountants takes the view that use of Transitory MergerCo does not preclude recap accounting, even where more than 50% (or even all) of the transaction consideration flows through Transitory MergerCo. These accountants adopt a position consonant with the income tax law and ignore the existence of Transitory MergerCo because it is transitory and used merely as a mechanism to effect the Target recapitalization.

A third group of accountants takes the view that use of Transitory MergerCo does not preclude recap accounting so long as Transitory MergerCo (1) is used solely as a mechanism to force, through a state law merger, all of Target's shareholders to participate in the recapitalization transaction and (2) serves no other business purpose. These accountants generally allow the new shareholders' equity money to flow through Transitory MergerCo, but believe that recap accounting is precluded if Transitory MergerCo borrows any of the debt financing employed in the recapitalization.

In 4/00, SEC staff informally enunciated a view resembling that of the third group of accountants—i.e., that use of a Transitory MergerCo in a recap transaction is permissible only if the Transitory MergerCo lacks "substance" and that "substance" is generally present—thus precluding recap accounting—if Transitory MergerCo borrows a portion of the acquisition debt. SEC's position may be evolving and hence some accountants now advise it is desirable for Transitory MergerCo to incur no debt and receive only a nominal amount of the equity financing.

¶504.2.2   Use of Newco to Acquire Target

A transaction may qualify for recap accounting at the Target level even where VC forms a Newco to hold its Target stock. As noted in ¶504.2.4 below, recap accounting would not, however, apply at the Newco level.

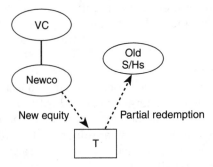

Partnership or LLC Newco. If such a Newco is formed, it will frequently be a partnership or LLC (i.e., a flow-through entity for tax purposes) so that (a) Newco can be dissolved tax free or (b) if Newco has not previously dissolved, there will be no federal income tax at the Newco level when Newco sells its Target stock (e.g.) to the public.

Newco should in most cases not be formed as a corporation because (i) Newco will be subject to corporate-level tax on its gain from selling Target stock (e.g.) to the public and (ii) VC's sale of Newco stock to the public (which would avoid Newco corporate-level tax on Newco's gain in its Target stock) would not benefit from recap accounting because Newco is required to use purchase accounting at the Newco level for its interest in Target.

Subsequent elimination of corporate Newco. Where there are reasons to form Newco as a corporation (e.g., if Target's new shareholders wish to acquire Target and make a Code §338(h)(10) election to obtain tax SUB in Target's assets—see ¶504.2.9.2), the question arises whether Newco can later be eliminated in a tax-free transaction, avoiding corporate-level tax on Newco's gain in its Target stock, with Target retaining its recap accounting.

Newco-Target merger. A simple upstream or downstream merger of Newco and Target sometime after Target's recap would eliminate Newco corporate-level tax on Newco's gain in its Target stock. However, such a merger would (in the view of the accounting profession) eliminate the benefits of recap accounting (even where the merger occurs after Target goes public), because where Newco owns more than 50% of Target's common stock when Newco and Target merge (either upstream or downstream), Newco would be viewed for accounting purposes as the surviving entity, regardless of the legal form of the merger (i.e., even if Target was the surviving entity). Accordingly, Newco's higher accounting basis in its percentage interest in Target would survive, effectively forcing push-down purchase accounting on Target.

Corporate downstream "C" or "D." In contrast, if Newco is formed as a corporation and is later eliminated in a downstream "C" or "D" reorganization (not carried out under a state law merger statute), Target should continue to qualify for recap accounting because accountants generally view a downstream "C" or "D" reorganization as a mere dissolution of Newco (since Newco corporation is dissolved for state corporate law purposes after exchanging its assets—i.e., the Target stock owned by Newco for new Target stock), even though for income tax purposes, a downstream "C" or "D" reorganization is treated as a tax-free combination of Target and Newco.

LLC downstream "C" or "D." We understand SEC has informally stated it would allow recap accounting for a transaction using a variation of the corporate downstream "C" or "D" structure described above. Under this variation, Newco is formed as an LLC but elects to be taxed as a corporation under IRS's check-the-box regulations (generally so that Newco can make a Code §338(h)(10) election with respect to its acquisition of Target). After a sufficient wait Newco exchanges its old Target shares for new Target shares, and Newco simultaneously "unchecks" the box, i.e., elects to be taxed as a partnership. Newco and its owners treat Newco's transformation for tax purposes from a corporation to a partnership (i.e., the deemed liquidation for tax purposes of Newco "corporation" into Newco partnership) and Newco's exchange of old Target shares for new Target shares as a downstream "C" or "D" reorganization of Newco "corporation" into Target. After this deemed liquidation of Newco "corporation," Newco is a partnership for tax purposes and can sell Target stock in a public offering without corporate-level tax.

Many accountants believe this LLC downstream "C" or "D" variation more desirable from an accounting standpoint than the corporate downstream "C" or "D" approach described above (where Newco is actually a corporation liquidated as part of a downstream "C" or "D" reorganization). This is because some accountants believe that where Newco is a corporation, there is risk SEC might view Newco corporation's actual liquidation during the non-merger downstream "C" or "D" reorganization as the equivalent of a Newco-Target combination (resulting in loss of Target's recap accounting) rather than as a mere Newco dissolution. In contrast, where Newco is an LLC which unchecks the box (so that it continues to exist as an LLC without change for state law purposes), there should be little or no SEC/accounting issue.

¶504.2.3   Nature of Old Target Shareholder Retained Equity Interest

As described above, recap accounting may apply even if Target's old shareholders do not own (after the buyout) more than 20% of Target's common equity, but rather in some cases may apply even if they own slightly more than 5%, with qualification for recap accounting where the old Target shareholders' ownership is in the gray zone (more than 5% but not more than 20%) presenting a factual issue.

¶504.2.3.1   Old Target Shareholders Not Part of Collaborative Group with New Target Investors

A 4/01 SEC Staff Announcement stated that "it is appropriate to aggregate the holdings of those investors who *both* 'mutually promote' the acquisition and 'collaborate' on the subsequent control of the investee company (the collaborative group)."[1] Under this standard, "a member of a collaborative group would be any investor that helps to consummate the acquisition and works or cooperates with the subsequent control of the acquired company." The Announcement also adopts "a rebuttable presumption . . . that any investor investing at the same time as or in reasonable proximity to the time others invest in the investee is part of the collaborative group with the other investor(s)."

Although the Announcement focuses primarily on the circumstances in which recap accounting is permissible after a 100% change in Target's stock ownership,[2] it also states "[p]reexisting, or rollover, investors should be evaluated for inclusion in the collaborative group on the same basis as new investors." Thus, if old Target shareholders are viewed as part of a "collaborative group" with new Target investors, their retained Target equity will apparently not be counted toward the significant retained interest test.

The 4/01 Staff Announcement contains a detailed (although non-exhaustive) list of factors SEC reviews in determining whether an investor is viewed as part of a collaborative group, divided into four categories: whether the investor is independent of the other investors, whether the investor shares the risks and rewards of ownership on the same basis as other investors, whether the investor is involved in promoting the investment to other parties, and whether the investor collaborates in Target's post-recap control.

It is not clear how SEC will apply the definition of "collaborative group" to old Target shareholders rolling over (i.e., retaining) part (or all) of their Target common stock. Because old Target shareholders made their investment in Target prior to the recapitalization, old Target shareholders are, by definition, more independent than new investors. Moreover, for the same reason, old Target continuing shareholders should escape the "rebuttable presumption" (persons investing in reasonable proximity to each other presumably are a collaborative group)

¶504   [1]SEC Staff Announcement, Topic D-97—Push Down Accounting (2001).

[2]See ¶504.4 for a discussion of the 4/01 SEC Staff Announcement where the recapitalization involves a 100% change in Target's equity ownership.

discussed above. However, even without the presumption, old Target continuing shareholders are subjected to the mutually-promote and the collaborate-on-control tests. The 4/01 Staff Announcement's concept of "collaborative group" appears to be very broad and its application to old Target shareholders may narrow significantly Target's ability to obtain recap accounting.

The 4/01 Staff Announcement "should be applied prospectively to transactions initiated after April 19, 2001."

¶504.2.3.2   *Target Voting Common Stock*

In determining whether Target's old shareholders have retained the requisite continuing common equity in Target (i.e., in applying the more-than-5%-to-20%-continuing-common-equity test), the principal measurement is the percentage of Target's post-recapitalization voting common equity owned by Target's old shareholders on account of their ownership of Target's pre-recapitalization common equity.

Although the written rules are silent, other types of voting stock with common-like features should logically count toward the requisite retained equity interest including, for example, voting participating preferred stock with common-like participation features (particularly where preferred and common stock have been amalgamated into one instrument). Voting convertible preferred stock may also count. However, there is little indication of SEC's view on these types of stock.

See ¶504.2.3.8 for a discussion of the possibility that the FV of the old Target shareholder retained equity interest must also constitute more than 5% of the aggregate FV of Target's post-recap common and preferred stock equity.

¶504.2.3.3   *Target Stock Options*

The treatment of unexercised vested options held by old Target shareholders—both pre-recapitalization and post-recapitalization—is unclear, i.e., it is not clear whether unexercised vested options held by old Target shareholders before the recapitalization or held by old Target shareholders after the recapitalization or held at both times can be counted to create the more than 5% to 20% requisite continuing common equity.

However, if old Target shareholders exercise their previously held vested options before the recapitalization transaction, the stock they receive on exercise can be counted toward the requisite continuing common equity if it is retained as Target stub common stock. Accountants believe it unlikely that newly purchased Target common stock (retained as Target stub common stock) may be counted if it is purchased pursuant to unvested options that are vested in anticipation of the transaction or pursuant to new options granted in anticipation of the transaction.

¶504.2.3.4   Newly Purchased Target Stock

Additional Target shares purchased as part of the recapitalization transaction by an old Target shareholder may constitute a favorable factor for determining qualification for recapitalization accounting where the level of continuing common ownership is in the more than 5% but not more than 20% gray zone. Most accountants, however, recommend against relying on such purchased equity in order to reach the desired threshold of retained ownership.

Where an old Target common shareholder is paid in cash for his old Target stock but as part of the recap transaction simultaneously reinvests all or a portion of the proceeds in new Target shares, logic would suggest that such new Target shares (up to the percentage of Target's post-recap common shares such old Target shareholder would have retained if his old Target common shares had not been paid off in cash in the recapitalization) should be counted as continuing common equity. However, it is not clear whether this result will be accepted by accountants and SEC, since the reinvestment by an old Target common shareholder may be viewed as a separate investment decision rather than as a continuing common equity interest, thereby precluding recap accounting treatment.

However, newly purchased Target shares would appear to fall within the rebuttable presumption discussed in ¶504.2.3.1 above.

¶504.2.3.5   Restrictions on Retained Equity Interest

If the old Target shareholders' continuing equity interest in Target is subject to significant restrictions (e.g., imposed under a shareholders' agreement, call option, etc.) which tend to eliminate the old Target shareholders' ability either to control their continuing stake or to realize the economic benefits and burdens of its ownership, it is possible that the old Target shareholders' retained equity will not count toward the continuing common ownership threshold needed for recap accounting. A 4/01 SEC Staff Announcement, effective for transactions initiated after 4/19/01, states that old Target shareholders rolling over equity in the recapitalization of Target must be tested to determine whether they are part of a "collaborative group" with Target's new investors.[3] If an old Target shareholder is part of the "collaborative group," that shareholder's retained Target stock cannot be counted toward the significant retained interest required for recap accounting.

Voting agreements. As discussed above, the old Target shareholders' continuing interest in Target must have the right to vote in order to constitute a significant retained equity interest in Target. Any agreement requiring the old Target shareholders to vote their post-recap Target stock as directed by VC would likely cause the old Target shareholders' retained stock to be treated as non-voting so that it would not count toward recap accounting.

---

[3] SEC Staff Announcement, Topic D-97—Push Down Accounting (2001). See ¶504.2.3.1 and ¶504.4 for a detailed discussion of the 4/01 Staff Announcement.

In contrast, there should be no adverse impact on recap accounting if VC merely agrees to vote for a specified number of nominees to Target's board selected by the old Target shareholders, without placing any restrictions on the old Target shareholders' right to vote their own stock. Such an agreement would strengthen the voting power of the old Target shareholders' stock, not reduce or eliminate it.

Most accountants believe that a mutual voting agreement requiring VC and the old Target shareholders to vote for a specified number of each other's board nominees should not adversely affect Target's recap accounting, so long as the old Target shareholders are entitled to select a percentage of the board nominees at least equal to their percentage ownership of Target's stock. Such an agreement merely insures that the old Target shareholders' ownership of voting stock translates into board representation. The agreement of old Target shareholders to vote for VC's board nominees constitutes a quid pro quo for VC's promise to vote for the old Target shareholders' nominees and hence should not be viewed as a limitation that reduces the old Target shareholders' voting power. Some accountants, however, have expressed concern (misplaced in our view) that any limitation on the right of old Target shareholders freely to vote their stock—even one created by a mutual voting agreement—creates risk such stock may be viewed as nonvoting for recap accounting purposes.

The 4/01 SEC Staff Announcement states that the following factors (among many others) would be favorable factors in showing that an investor is not part of a collaborative group:

- "The investor is free to exercise its voting rights in any and all shareholder votes."
- "The investor does not have disproportionate or special rights that other investors do not have, such as a guaranteed seat(s) on the investee's board, required supermajority voting rights for major or significant corporate decisions, guaranteed consent rights over corporate actions, . . . and so forth."

These two favorable factors suggest that (1) an arrangement guaranteeing old Target shareholders a board seat (or similar rights) or (2) a mutual voting agreement would be viewed as a negative factor at least suggesting the old Target shareholder was part of a collaborative group with new Target investors.

Drag-along and tag-along rights. VC often desires an agreement from old Target shareholders (as well as any other Target shareholders) to sell their Target stock when VC sells its Target stock (on the same terms and conditions as VC's sale). Most accountants believe a reasonable "drag-along" obligation should not prevent recap accounting.

Some accountants, however, are concerned that a drag-along obligation (particularly when coupled with transfer restrictions preventing old Target shareholders from selling their stock in other circumstances) may reduce the ability of old Target shareholders to control their retained stock and/or realize its economic benefits sufficiently so that the underlying stock may not count toward recap accounting. For these accountants, the form of the drag-along agreement may be important, so that an agreement obligating all shareholders to participate in a sale approved by a specified majority of all shareholders as a group (with each shareholder retaining the right to vote for or against the sale) may be less trouble-some than an agreement obligating the old Target shareholders simply to follow VC's decision on whether to sell or not.

Tag-along rights, giving old Target shareholders the right (but not the obligation) to sell their stock to the extent VC sells its Target stock, enhance the rights of old Target shareholders and should generally not create any recap accounting problems.

The 4/01 SEC Staff Announcement states "[p]ut options, call options, tag-along rights, and drag-along rights should be carefully evaluated. They may act to limit an investor's risk and rewards of ownership, effective voting rights, or ability to sell its investee shares." Drag-along rights may force old Target rollover sharehold-ers to sell, cutting off their ownership rights, and, depending on how the drag-along rights are drafted, could prevent old Target shareholders from voting against a sale of Target advocated by new investors. SEC's interest in tag-along rights is less clear, although SEC may be concerned that tag-along rights could limit an old Target continuing shareholder's ability to sell its retained Target shares, by allowing new investors to tag along on the old Target shareholder's sale. Of course, both tag-along rights and drag-along rights represent some degree of cooperation and coordination between old and new Target shareholders.

In discussing transfer restrictions in general, the 4/01 Staff Announcement states that transfer restrictions "provided by securities laws or by what is reason-able and customary in individually negotiated investment transactions for closely held companies (for example, a right of first refusal held by the investee on the investor's shares in the event of a bona fide offer from a third party)" are not to be considered a factor suggesting collaborative group membership. Thus, because drag-along and tag-along rights are customary features for investments in closely held companies, they should not cause a problem if properly drafted and of normal scope.

Transfer restrictions. Some accountants believe extensive transfer restrictions on old Target shareholders' retained stock (e.g., a blanket prohibition on sales by old Target shareholders other than in connection with a sale of Target by all shareholders) may prevent their stock from counting toward recap accounting. Accountants who take this view generally suggest that old Target shareholders must, at a minimum, have the right to sell their retained Target stock with Target's or VC's consent which will not be unreasonably withheld.

The 4/01 SEC Staff Announcement states as a factor supporting the view that an investor is not part of a collaborative group that "[t]he investor's ability to sell its investee shares is not restricted, except as provided by securities laws or by what is reasonable and customary in individually negotiated investment transactions for closely held companies (for example, a right of first refusal held by the investee on the investor's shares in the event of a bona fide offer from a third party)."

¶504.2.3.6   *Value of Retained Equity Interest*

If the value of recapitalized Target's common stock is reduced by leverage (i.e., where Target issues Target debt or Target debt-like preferred stock to fund redemptions of Target stock), old Target shareholders who retain a stub percentage of common equity in Target do not have to leave behind a similar percentage of their consideration. Thus, for example, a 1% or 2% stake in pre-recap Target could be worth 10% - 15% of post-recap Target.

As an economic matter, however, VC may insist that old Target shareholders retain a strip of Target securities, including both less desirable (i.e., lower potential return) subordinated debt or debt-like preferred stock and more desirable (i.e., higher potential return) "cheap" common stock.

See ¶504.2.3.8 for a discussion of the possibility that the FV of the old Target shareholder retained equity interest must constitute more than 5% of the aggregate FV of Target's post-recap common and preferred stock equity. If there is such a requirement, it may not be satisfied where VC purchases newly-issued Target common stock and preferred stock while old Target shareholders retain or acquire less than a pro rata portion of Target's post-recap preferred stock.

- Subordinated debt received by an old Target shareholder in exchange for old Target common stock is taxable boot.
- See ¶504.2.9.1 below for a discussion of the possibility that the receipt of Target preferred stock (constituting NQ Pfd) in exchange for Target common stock is taxable boot.

¶504.2.3.7   VC Ownership of Target Warrants or Convertibles

Whether Target's old shareholders retain a sufficiently large percentage of Target's post-recap common equity is generally determined on a fully diluted basis, so that the test is failed where VC (or certain persons considered to be closely associated with Target or VC) receives warrants or convertibles at the time of the recap transaction (or later, but prior to Target's becoming a public company—see ¶504.2.6 below), which would, if exercised, dilute Target's old shareholders below the level of a significant stake.

¶504.2.3.8   VC Ownership of Target Preferred Stock

Whether Target's old shareholders retain a sufficiently large equity stake in Target is generally determined based on their percentage ownership of Target's post-recap voting common stock. However, if VC purchases Target preferred stock with voting rights or conversion or other participation features (including a coupon rate significantly exceeding market rate), such Target preferred stock is generally taken into account in measuring the size of the old T shareholders' retained interest.

Where VC purchases newly-issued Target common stock and debt-like preferred stock (i.e., preferred stock that is non-voting, non-convertible, and non-participating), some accountants take the position that the FV of Target stub common stock retained by old Target shareholders (together with the FV of any Target preferred stock retained by old Target shareholders or acquired by them in the recapitalization in exchange for pre-recap Target common stock) must exceed 5% of recapitalized Target's aggregate common and preferred stock FV.[4] This additional requirement—if actually part of recap accounting standards—is generally satisfied if old Target shareholders retain or acquire a pro rata portion of Target's preferred stock along with their retained Target stub common stock (see ¶504.2.3.6 above), but may not be met if old Target shareholders retain or acquire less than a pro rata portion of Target's preferred stock.

Other accountants advise that where the FV of recapitalized Target's common stock in the aggregate is significant in relation to the FV of recapitalized Target's debt-like preferred stock, VC's preferred stock need not be taken into account in measuring the old Target shareholder's retained interest.

¶504.2.4   Effect of Recap Accounting on Newco's Financial Statements

Where a change in Target's stock ownership qualifies for recap accounting but one of Target's new shareholders is an entity (e.g., Newco formed by VC to acquire its interest in Target) owning sufficient Target stock so that Newco must account for its Target stock investment on the equity method of accounting (generally where Newco owns 20% or more of Target's voting power) or on the consolidated method of accounting (generally where Newco owns more than 50% of Target's voting power), Newco must use purchase accounting principles in preparing its financial statements, even though Target can use recap accounting in preparing its own separate financial statements.

Thus, even where Target qualifies for recap accounting and hence no goodwill or other accounting basis step up is reflected on Target's financial statements, Newco (which owns 20% or more of Target's voting power and hence utilizes either the equity or consolidated method of accounting for Target) must, in calculating Newco's net income, depreciate or amortize Newco's share of the accounting basis step up in tangible assets and intangible assets other than goodwill arising out of Newco's purchase of Target stock.

¶504.2.5   Uncertainty in Recap Accounting Rules

The guidelines used to determine whether Target qualifies for recap accounting are based on the rules prescribed by the SEC staff in determining whether Target must apply push down purchase accounting, i.e., where a recapitalization of Target results in such a substantial change in Target's ownership that push down purchase accounting would apply to Target, recap accounting will not apply to Target.

---

[4] Accountants taking this view may be willing to ignore debt-like preferred stock issued to a new investor who does not participate in controlling Target, e.g., an unrelated mezzanine investor purchasing preferred stock in the recapitalization.

Determining whether a transaction qualifies for recap accounting is not without its complexities. Recap accounting rules are not extensively—in truth, are only minimally—spelled out in SEC staff rules. Thus, application to varying circumstances is necessarily subject to substantial judgment and accounting firms at times disagree on the rules' application to specific circumstances. SEC staff generally dislikes recap accounting. Hence, SEC staff will generally examine Target's recap accounting when Target goes public and may challenge Target's recap accounting for its earlier buyout if SEC staff disagrees with Target's use of recap accounting.

Moreover, there is risk FASB or SEC might in the future limit or eliminate recap accounting altogether. Such a change could be effective for a Target that was not public at the time of the change, even though a previous acquisition of Target (completed before the change) was structured to obtain recap accounting.

Although not entirely clear, it is likely that Target's public offering of debt will "lock-in" Target's recap accounting so that a later change in FASB or SEC policy should not require Target to use purchase accounting for its earlier buyout, even if Target has not yet had a public stock offering.

FASB has stated that it will review recap accounting as part of a second phase of its project regarding accounting for business combinations, creating additional uncertainty regarding the future of recap accounting. By analogy to FASB's 7/01 decision abolishing pooling prospectively (see ¶501.8), we believe that any change to current recap accounting rules should apply only to transactions occurring after final FASB rules are published.

¶504.2.6   Effect of Post-Buyout Events on Recap Accounting

If, after a buyout of Target structured to achieve recap accounting but before recapitalized Target becomes public, Target or VC purchases all or part of the old Target shareholders' continuing equity stake, so that the old Target shareholders cease to have a significant continuing equity stake in Target, Target will be required to use purchase accounting, i.e., Target's earlier recap will be disqualified. This is true even if the purchase from old Target shareholders occurs a number of years after the buyout and is not part of a plan in existence at the time of the buyout.

In contrast, purchase accounting should not be required if the old Target shareholders sell all or a portion of their continuing equity stake in Target to buyers other than Target or VC (or certain persons considered to be closely associated with Target or VC).

If, after the buyout but before recapitalized Target becomes public, Target issues additional stock or options that dilute the old Target shareholders' continuing equity stake so that it is no longer significant, Target may be required to use purchase accounting if the additional stock or options are issued to VC (or to certain persons closely associated with Target or VC).

Once Target becomes public (with either publicly traded equity or publicly traded debt), subsequent events should not eliminate Target's ability to use recap accounting for the buyout.

¶504.2.7 Structuring to Obtain Recap Accounting Where Target's Shareholders Are Numerous or Recalcitrant

Where Target's shareholders are numerous or recalcitrant so that a redemption of Target shares can not be accomplished consensually, a transaction qualifying for recap accounting can nevertheless be structured as outlined below.

¶504.2.7.1 *Pro-Rata Recap with Forced Merger*

Where Target's shareholders are numerous or recalcitrant and all of Target's shareholders are to be treated identically, a recap can be accomplished through a merger of Transitory MergerCo into Target in which the merger consideration to Target's shareholders is cash and stub shares in recapitalized Target.

As an alternative, the old Target shareholders can be given the option to elect to take stub shares in recapitalized Target or to take cash. However, if an insufficient number of old Target shareholders elect to take stub shares, other Target shareholders must take stub shares in recapitalized Target in the amount necessary to qualify for recap accounting treatment. And if too many old Target shareholders elect to take Target stub shares, a proration mechanism must be in place to apportion the Target stub shares among the old Target shareholders electing continuing Target stock.

¶504.2.7.2 *Non-Pro-Rata Recap*

In many circumstances, VC desires only certain of Target's old shareholders to continue as shareholders in recapitalized Target (e.g., Target management). In the event that this cannot be accomplished by a consensual non-pro-rata redemption, there are alternative methods to accomplish this objective.

- **Alternative #1—The front-end Target recapitalization.** Target's shareholders vote to authorize a new class of equity securities (the "New Class") which are issued in a voluntary stock swap to those old Target shareholders (in exchange for a portion of their old Target common stock) who are to retain Target stub common shares. Immediately thereafter, Transitory MergerCo merges into Target, with the holders of the New Class receiving Target stub common stock and the remaining old Target shareholders receiving cash. An old Target shareholder who is to receive part cash and part Target stub common stock exchanges only a portion of his or her old Target common stock for the New Class (i.e., makes such exchange only to the extent he or she is to receive Target stub common stock).

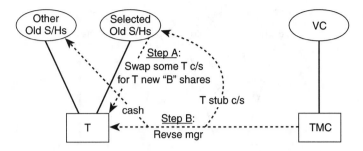

- **Alternative #2—The front-end TMC swap.** An old Target shareholder who is to retain Target stub common shares contributes Target common shares to Transitory MergerCo in exchange for stock in Transitory Merg-erCo. Transitory MergerCo then merges into Target, with Transitory Merg-erCo stock being exchanged for Target stub common stock and the remaining Target stock not held by Transitory MergerCo being redeemed for cash. An old Target shareholder who is to receive part cash and part Target stub common stock exchanges only a portion of his or her old Target common stock for Transitory MergerCo stock (i.e., makes such exchange only to the extent he or she is to receive Target stub common stock).

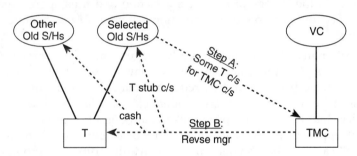

Currently, some accounting firms are more comfortable with Alternative #1 and others are more comfortable with Alternative #2.

- **Alternative #3—Merger with different consideration for different holders of T common stock.** The merger agreement between Target and Transitory MergerCo may simply state that one group of old Target shareholders is to receive cash in the merger in exchange for their Target shares (generally all Target shareholders other than those named in an exhibit to the merger agreement), while a second group of old Target shareholders (generally those Target shareholders named in an exhibit to the merger agreement), is to retain their Target stub common stock (or retain their Target stub common stock and also receive some cash).

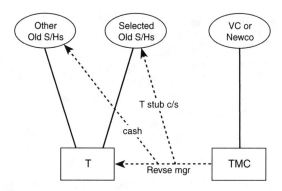

Most accounting firms are more comfortable with Alternative #3 as a method of achieving recapitalization accounting than either Alternative #1 or #2, since in Alternative #3 the old Target shareholders with a continuing interest in Target stub common stock simply retain their Target stock and do not swap their Target shares either for a new class of Target stock (as in Alternative #1) or for Transitory MergerCo stock (as in Alternative #2). The concern expressed by certain accountants appears to be that if the continuing old Target shareholders swap their old Target stock as required under Alternative #1 or #2, they may be viewed as participating in the change of control transaction and thus aggregated with the new investors for purposes of determining whether Target qualifies for recap accounting.

While Alternative #3 may have this advantage from an accounting standpoint, it may raise issues under state corporation law. Many state corporation laws traditionally have been viewed as requiring that all shareholders holding the same class of Target stock must receive identical consideration in a merger. However, under Delaware law, it appears likely, although not certain, that a merger agreement, approved by the requisite majority of Target's board and the requisite majority of Target's shareholders, may specify that different groups of Target shareholders holding the same class of Target stock prior to the merger receive different consideration in the merger, so long as *inter alia* the board has exercised in good faith its fiduciary duty to all the shareholders and the merger is fair to all shareholders (generally, the shareholders in one group are receiving consideration with roughly the same FV per share as the shareholders in the other group). See Del. Gen. Corp. Law §251.

Where only large shareholders of Target are to retain equity in recapitalized Target, two additional alternatives are available.

- **Alternative #4—Front-end reverse stock split.** Target does a reverse stock split (e.g., each 1,000 old Target shares are transformed into 1 new share), transforming smaller shareholder's stock into a fractional share which is cashed out, eliminating smaller shareholders immediately before the recapitalization.
- **Alternative #5—Fractional merger exchange ratio.** Transitory MergerCo merges into Target with consideration to old Target stockholders being

cash and a fractional share of Target stub stock (e.g., 1/1,000 of a Target stub share), so that small Target stockholders receive a fractional stub share and are cashed out, again eliminating smaller shareholders.

In any non-pro-rata transaction, Target's board of directors must ensure that the transaction is fair to all shareholders. This may require the creation of a special independent board committee to negotiate and approve the transaction on behalf of minority shareholders and may require the retention of a financial adviser to advise the board or the special committee on the economic fairness of the transaction to all shareholders.

¶504.2.8   Recap Accounting Where Target Is Partnership or an LLC

Recap accounting may be obtained, under the rules outlined above, where Target is a partnership or LLC, if T's pre-recap equity owners (i.e., its partners or members) retain a significant continuing equity stake in T (generally by owning voting common partnership or LLC interests) after the recapitalization.

¶504.2.9   Tax Issues Involved in Recap Accounting

A recap structure raises several tax issues for old Target shareholders, Target, and VC.

¶504.2.9.1   *Taxation of Continuing Old Target Shareholders*

Where an old Target shareholder retains a portion of his or her Target stock and has the balance redeemed by Target, he or she is entitled to CG treatment on the redemption only to the extent that the redemption qualifies as an exchange under Code §302. This will generally be the case where the shareholder's percentage interest (both by vote and value) in Target declines after the recapitalization. However, if an old Target shareholder's percentage interest in Target stays the same or increases (e.g., because the shareholder receives new equity in the recapitalized Target as part of its management group), such shareholder's redemption will generally not qualify under Code §302 for CG treatment and will instead be treated as a dividend to the extent of Target's tax earnings and profits.

In contrast, Code §302 does not apply to stock sold to a person other than Target (or a Target subsidiary). Thus, if the recapitalization can be structured so that the continuing shareholder sells Target stock to VC, such old Target shareholder should be entitled to CG treatment, even where his or her continuing percentage interest in Target stays the same or increases. So long as old Target shareholders retain the requisite amount of Target stock, the sale of stock from old Target shareholders to VC should not have an adverse impact on Target's ability to use recap accounting. See ¶504.1 above.

Where VC wishes to hold a strip of securities different than those purchased from old Target investors, it may in some cases be necessary for VC to swap all or a portion of the Target stock it purchases from old Target shareholders with Target for a different class or classes of Target stock. If such a swap results in Code §306 stock for VC, VC may recognize OI on redemption or sale of the Code §306 stock in some circumstances. Such a swap may also create a risk that IRS could recharacterize the old Target shareholders' sale to VC as a redemption.

Where a continuing old Target shareholder has a portion of his or her old Target stock redeemed for cash and exchanges the balance of his or her old shares for shares of one or more new classes of Target stock, there is risk IRS could treat the cash redemption and the stock-for-stock exchange as one transaction, in which case the old Target shareholder would recognize (under Code §356) all of the inherent gain in his or her stock (both the stock redeemed and the stock exchanged) up to the amount of the cash received, generally resulting in recognition of more gain than if the redemption and exchange were treated as separate transactions. This Code §356 risk is minimized where the recapitalization is structured so that the old Target shareholders merely retain a portion of their old Target stock without exchanging it for a new class of Target stock. Alternatively, if the recapitalization can be structured so that the old Target shareholder sells his or her stock to VC, as described above, the Code §356 risk should generally be eliminated.

The 1997 Tax Act treats "nonqualified preferred stock" ("NQ Pfd") (i.e., most redeemable debt-like preferred stock, discussed in more detail in ¶403(9) through (15) above) as taxable boot in an otherwise tax-free exchange. Where VC wants old Target shareholders to roll their continuing equity stake into a "strip" of Target common stock and debt-like preferred stock which constitutes NQ Pfd, the Target NQ Pfd would be taxable boot, triggering gain on the exchange. This adverse tax result can be avoided in three ways:

- The Target preferred stock may be redesigned so that it has a significant stake in corporate growth (e.g., by amalgamating the Target preferred stock and Target common stock together into a single instrument) and hence will not be NQ Pfd. As noted in ¶504.2.3.2 above, this type of stock, if voting, should count toward a significant retained equity stake for recap accounting purposes, although the GAAP rules are not wholly clear.
- The Target preferred stock may be redesigned to be evergreen (i.e., not mandatorily redeemable, puttable, or callable) and hence will not be NQ Pfd.
- The redemption, put, or call features with respect to the Target preferred stock may be limited to ones which qualify for Code §351(g)(2)(C)(i)(I)'s death-or-disability exception or Code §351(g)(2)(C)(i)(II)'s issued-in-connection-with-services exception, so that in either case the Target preferred stock will not be NQ Pfd.

IRS regulations, when ultimately promulgated, may permit old Target shareholders to defer reporting gain attributable to the receipt of Target NQ Pfd by using the installment method, even for transactions effectuated before such regulations are promulgated.

Where an old Target shareholder-executive holding vested Target shares ends up holding after the recap *unvested* Target shares, the Target shareholder-executive should generally make a Code §83(b) election within 30 days after the recap exchange in order to minimize the risk of unanticipated Code §83 OI upon subsequent vesting.

¶504.2.9.2   Tax SUB for Target's Assets

Recap accounting requires Target to survive with Target's old shareholders retaining a significant stake in recapitalized Target's common equity, thereby precluding an asset purchase as a means to achieve SUB for Target's assets. Such asset SUB for tax purposes can be achieved where a single corporate entity (here Newco formed by VC) purchases 80% or more of Target's stock by vote and by value (i.e., a QSP under Code §338) so that Newco can make a Code §338 or Code §338(h)(10) election for Target electing to treat the stock purchase as an asset purchase for income tax purposes, while still leaving Target's old shareholders with a sufficiently significant retained stake in Target to qualify for recap accounting.

In most cases, structuring for asset SUB will be tax-efficient only if Target is an S corporation or a Bigco subsidiary so that a Code §338(h)(10) election can be made with a single level of tax. However, a Code §338(h)(10) election triggers gain in all of Target's assets, so that (1) where Target is an S corporation, old Target shareholders who retain Target stock will nonetheless be taxed on their full share of the gain in Target's assets and (2) where Target is a Bigco subsidiary, Bigco will be taxed on all of the gain in Target's assets although Bigco retains some Target stock.

Use of a corporate Newco to purchase Target's stock—so that a Code §338(h)(10) election can be made to step up the tax basis of Target's assets in a transaction structured for recap accounting—is attractive only if there is a way subsequently to eliminate Newco in a tax-free manner without forcing purchase accounting on Target. As discussed in ¶504.2.2 above, if Newco corporation were to remain a Target shareholder (i) an unwanted corporate-level tax would be imposed on Newco when Newco sells its Target stock to the public (resulting in double tax) and (ii) should VC take Newco public (owning Target's stock), Newco is not entitled to utilize recap accounting.

Eliminating corporate Newco. There are several methods for eliminating Newco corporation tax-free after a sufficient wait so that Newco corporation's elimination does not jeopardize the Code §338(h)(10) election by causing Newco to be disregarded as the QSP purchaser of Target stock.

Corporate downstream "C" or "D." Eliminating Newco corporation after a sufficient wait by a non-merger downstream "C" or "D" reorganization should accomplish this goal.

While eliminating Newco corporation by an upstream or downstream merger of Newco and Target would also accomplish this tax goal (eliminating Newco corporation without corporate-level tax), such a Newco-Target merger would have the adverse result of eliminating the benefits of recap accounting (even when such merger occurs after Target goes public), because where Newco owns more than 50% of Target's common stock when Newco and Target merge (either upstream or downstream), Newco would be viewed for accounting purposes as the surviving entity so that Newco/Target would generally be required to use purchase or partial purchase accounting.

Eliminating Newco corporation by a non-merger downstream "C" or "D" reorganization, on the other hand, should be treated by accountants as a mere dissolution of Newco corporation (since Newco is dissolved for state law purposes after exchanging its assets (i.e., the old Target stock owned by Newco) for new Target stock).

LLC downstream "C" or "D." We understand SEC has informally stated it would allow recap accounting for a transaction using a variation of the corporate downstream "C" or "D" structure described above. Under this variation, Newco is formed as an LLC but elects to be taxed as a corporation under IRS's check-the-box regulations so that it can make a Code §338(h)(10) election with respect to the Newco-Target acquisition. After a sufficient wait, Newco exchanges its Target stock for new Target shares and Newco simultaneously "unchecks" the box, i.e., elects to be taxed as a partnership. Newco and its owners treat Newco's transformation for tax purposes from a corporation to a partnership (i.e., the deemed liquidation for tax purposes of Newco "corporation" into Newco partnership) and Newco's exchange of old Target stock for new Target stock as a downstream "C" or "D" reorganization of Newco "corporation" into Target. After this deemed liquidation of Newco "corporation," Newco is a partnership for tax purposes and can sell Target stock in a public offering without corporate-level tax.

Many accountants believe this LLC downstream "C" or "D" variation more desirable from an accounting standpoint than the corporate downstream "C" or "D" approach described above (where Newco is actually a corporation eliminated in a downstream "C" or "D" reorganization), because Newco continues to exist, minimizing risk SEC might argue there was a Newco-Target combination that would eliminate Target's recap accounting.

Target partnership or LLC. Where Target is a partnership or LLC, it should be possible to obtain asset SUB without double tax and without forming a corporate Newco (i) for VC's share of Target's assets, where VC purchases partnership or LLC interests from Target's equity owners (see Code §§754 and 743) and (ii) for gain recognized by old Target equity owners on redemption of their partnership or LLC interests (see Code §§754 and 734).

¶504.2.9.3   Taxation of VC

VC will generally not qualify for Code §1202's 14% long-term capital gain rate because of the substantial redemptions that take place in the recapitalization transaction.

¶504.3   *Recap Accounting Where Target Public Debt or Preferred Stock Remains Outstanding after Recap*

Recapitalization accounting also generally applies to the acquisition of Target where (1) Target continues to exist after the recapitalization *and* (2) Target has publicly held debt or publicly held preferred stock outstanding prior to and independent of the recapitalization that remains outstanding after the recapitalization, even if Target's old shareholders do not retain a significant (or indeed any) continuing interest in recapitalized Target's common equity. According to SEC, the existence of Target continuing, pre-recapitalization publicly held debt or preferred stock "might impact the parent's ability to control the form of [its] ownership [of Target]" and hence SEC allows recap accounting and "generally does not insist on . . .[purchase] push-down accounting in these circumstances."

However, recap accounting is not supported where Target's publicly held debt or preferred stock arises (1) as part of the recapitalization transaction (e.g., to finance the redemption of Target common stock) or (2) only after Target's recapitalization so that, for a period of time, Target has no outstanding publicly held debt or preferred stock.

Although SEC accounting bulletins do not explicitly impose any such requirement, an SEC staff member stated in a 12/99 speech that SEC would support recap accounting based on Target's pre-recap public debt only if the pre-recap public debt is "significant." According to the staff member, SEC applied this test to deny recap accounting in a transaction where Target's pre-recap debt was not significant in either a "quantitative" sense or a "qualitative" sense:

- Target's pre-recap public debt was not considered *quantitatively* significant because it "amounted to approximately 5 percent of [Target's] net book value and less than 1 percent of [Target's] fair value" and would have converted into approximately 1% of Target's stock.
- Target's pre-recap public debt was not considered *qualitatively* significant because "the debt holders had virtually no ability to control or influence the form of [P's] ownership of [Target], nor did the debtholders have any consent rights regarding the buying out of the existing minority interests, issuing [Target] equity, or [Target] paying dividends."

It is unclear whether SEC will require that Target pre-recap public debt be significant in *both* a quantitative *and* a qualitative sense or merely in *either* a quantitative *or* a qualitative sense. Although preferred stock was not mentioned by the SEC staff member, presumably the same significance requirement will apply to Target's pre-recap public preferred stock.

The usefulness of Target pre-recapitalization public debt or preferred stock as a route to recap accounting may be limited in some instances by restrictive covenants in the public debt or preferred stock which limit Target's ability to do a buyout recapitalization while the public debt or preferred stock remains outstanding. In such case, Target may need to negotiate a modification to the terms of the publicly held debt or preferred and/or a waiver of applicable debt or preferred covenants to permit the recapitalization and the holders may demand a fee for consenting to such modification or waiver. If the modification or waiver, including any consent fee paid to holders, results in a deemed extinguishment of the old debt or preferred and the deemed reissuance of new debt or preferred for GAAP purposes, the "new" publicly held debt or preferred would be considered issued in connection with the recapitalization and would therefore not support recap accounting. A 1996 FASB pronouncement in an analogous area (dealing with debt) suggests that there would be a deemed extinguishment and reissuance if, in general, the modification or waiver, including any consent fees, results in a 10% or greater change in the PV of the payments due under the instrument. Even where a modification or waiver does not result in a deemed extinguishment and reissuance, there may be risk (depending on the nature of the modification or waiver) SEC could take the position that the modification or waiver taints the publicly held debt or preferred (causing it to be viewed as related to the recapitalization transaction or causing the holders to be treated as acting in concert with Target or the new investors).

Target would generally cease to qualify for recap accounting and be forced to apply purchase accounting if Target's publicly held debt or preferred stock is repaid or redeemed after the recapitalization but before Target has a common stock IPO (assuming that there is no other basis to support recap accounting). However, while not entirely clear, Target's recap accounting should not be affected if Target merely refinances its pre-recapitalization public debt or preferred stock with new public debt or preferred stock so that Target continuously maintains either public debt or public preferred stock at all times after the recapitalization and before its common stock IPO. It is desirable that such refinancing not occur too soon after the recapitalization or SEC might assert that the refinancing was part of the recapitalization plan and force purchase accounting.

Of course, Target can avoid purchase accounting on a repayment/redemption of public debt or preferred stock if Target has *either* (1) sufficient pre-recap-Target-shareholder continuing voting common equity interest (as described in ¶504.2 above) *or* (2) a new independent Target shareholder (as described in ¶504.4 below), so that Target's recap accounting is not dependent on the publicly held debt or preferred stock discussed in this ¶504.3.

¶504.4   Recap Accounting Where Target Has Significant New Independent Shareholder

In 1998 SEC pre-approved recapitalization accounting for a transaction in which there was a 100% change in Target's equity ownership (so that there was no continuing equity interest on the part of old Target shareholders) and no pre-recapitalization public debt or preferred stock remained outstanding after the recapitalization. In this transaction, as we understand it, two investors (VC#1 and VC#2) acting in concert each acquired approximately 47% of Target's common stock, while a third investor who was considered independent of the first two investors acquired the remaining 6% of Target's common stock.

SEC did not require the two new investors' purchase accounting be pushed down to Target, because even though SEC aggregated the first two investors, they owned only 94% of Target, just short of the 95% threshold for mandatory pushdown purchase accounting. In SEC's view, the key fact was that the third investor was independent of the first two investors and thus not part of their "collaborative group." In effect, SEC focused more on whether one person or a group of persons properly aggregated flunked the 95% test for mandatory pushdown accounting than on the identity of the owner of Target's 6% minority stake. Had the third investor been aggregated with the first two, Target's new control group would have held 100% of Target's equity and pushdown purchase accounting would have been required for Target.[5]

The scope of SEC's approach is not entirely clear. For example, it is not clear what factors SEC will consider in determining whether an investor is not part of a collaborative group with VC or instead must be aggregated with the new investors sponsoring the recapitalization.

Because the scope of this SEC approach is unclear, it is safer to base recap accounting on old Target shareholders who retain a continuing equity stake in post-recapitalization Target (as described in ¶504.2 above). Even under SEC's 1998 approach, a continuing interest on the part of old Target shareholders may be preferable to a stake held by a new investor because it may be easier to demonstrate the required independence in the case of old Target shareholders—who acquired their Target equity stake in transactions unrelated to the recapitalization—than in the case of a new investor who purchases an interest in Target at the same time as VC#1 and VC#2.

During 1999 and 2000, SEC reconsidered its position on whether recap accounting is appropriate where old Target's shareholders do not continue to own a significant stake in Target's stock after the recapitalization. A 4/01 SEC Staff Announcement states that "it is appropriate to aggregate the holdings of those investors who both 'mutually promote' the acquisition and 'collaborate' on the subsequent control of the investee company (the collaborative group)."[6] Under this standard, "a member of a collaborative group would be any investor that helps to consummate the acquisition and works or cooperates with the subsequent control of the acquired company." The Announcement also adopts "a rebuttable presumption . . . that any investor investing at the same time as or in reasonable proximity to the time others invest in the investee is part of the collaborative group with the other investor(s)."

The 4/01 Staff Announcement contains a detailed (although non-exhaustive) list of factors SEC reviews in determining whether an investor is viewed as part of a collaborative group, divided into four categories: whether the investor is independent of the other investors, whether the investor shares the risks and rewards of ownership on the same basis as other investors, whether the investor

---

[5] It is also important that the independent shareholder invest in Target not later than simultaneously with the new investors sponsoring the recapitalization. If the independent investor invests later than the other investors, there is a moment in time during which the other investors own 100% of Target and SEC requires pushdown purchase accounting. See SEC Staff Announcement, Topic D-97—Push Down Accounting (2001).

[6] SEC Staff Announcement, Topic D-97—Push Down Accounting (2001).

is involved in promoting the investment to other parties, and whether the investor collaborates in Target's post-recap control.

The 4/01 Staff Announcement considers an example in which a financial investor C formulates a plan to acquire and consolidate companies in a fragmented industry. C approaches financial investors A and B who agree to invest in C's plan. A, B, and C are substantive entities with no employee overlap. A, B, and C have previously participated in joint investments and have other material business relationships with each other. A, B, and C acquire Target for cash and, after the recapitalization, Target's stock is held 40% each by A and B and 20% by C. A and B provide a "limited first-loss guarantee" to C with respect to C's investment. Target's bylaws are revised so that (1) A, B, and C receive equal representation on Target's board of directors (along with Target's CEO and two independent directors) and (2) any significant corporate action requires unanimous approval of all investors. A, B, and C agree not to transfer their shares for 5 years; thereafter, the shares are subject to a right of first refusal in favor of the other investors and each investor holds tag-along rights in the event of a sale by the others.

SEC concluded that A, B, and C are a collaborative group which acquired 100% of Target, so that pushdown purchase accounting is required. SEC cited the following factors as important in concluding A, B, and C are part of a single collaborative group:

- A, B, and C "acted in concert to negotiate their concurrent investments in [Target], which were made pursuant to the same contract."

- The investments in Target were "made in connection with a broader strategic initiative [A, B, and C] were pursuing."

- "There were a number of prior business relationships between [A, B, and C] that were material to" them.

- A and B provided a "limited first-loss guarantee" of C's investment.

- By virtue of bylaw provisions requiring unanimous investor approval of significant corporate actions, "A, B, and C were compelled to collaborate on the subsequent control of [Target]."

- There are restrictions on A, B, and C's ability to transfer their shares.

By taking an expansive view of the collaborative group, the 4/01 Staff Announcement appears to narrow significantly Target's ability to obtain recap accounting where there is a 100% change in Target's equity ownership.[7] The 4/01

---

[7] The SEC announcement may also narrow availability of recap accounting where Target rollover shareholders hold a significant stake in post-recap Target, since the announcement states that pre-existing Target shareholders who roll over their investment in Target as part of the recapitalization are to be tested to determine whether they are part of the collaborative group under the same standard applied to new investors (although rollover old Target shareholders should escape the rebuttable presumption (persons investing in reasonable proximity to each other presumably are a collaborative

Staff Announcement "should be applied prospectively to transactions initiated after April 19, 2001."

See ¶501.8 for a discussion of an FASB project which is reconsidering various aspects of purchase and recapitalization accounting.

¶504.5   Recap of a Bigco Division

As described above, Target must generally survive as a legal entity in order for the transaction to qualify for recap accounting. Thus, where the business to be acquired is a division of Bigco, rather than a Bigco corporate or LLC subsidiary, recap accounting does not apply if VC forms Newco (whether Newco is a corporation, partnership, or LLC) to purchase Bigco's divisional assets, even where Bigco obtains a significant continuing stake in Newco.

There are, however, three possible routes to recap accounting where the target business is a Bigco division:

Route #1. If Bigco transfers the divisional assets to a newly formed subsidiary (NewSub) before beginning the sale process, Bigco and VC could later engage in a recap transaction in which NewSub (formerly a 100% Bigco subsidiary) survives as a legal entity. Bigco's transfer of divisional assets to NewSub—whether a corporation, LLC, or partnership—causes no change to the accounting basis of the divisional assets and creates no goodwill and the subsequent recapitalization of NewSub can qualify for recap accounting so long as (1) NewSub is formed before Bigco has any substantive discussions with VC or other potential NewSub investors and (2) the transaction meets the other requirements set forth in ¶504.2 or ¶504.4 (or possibly ¶504.3).

On the other hand, if NewSub is formed only after Bigco has begun discussions with VC, most accountants take the position that recap accounting does not apply on the ground that the transaction is equivalent to a sale of assets by Bigco to Newco formed by VC.

Route #2. If Bigco has an existing subsidiary (OldSub), not formed in connection with any discussions or transaction with VC, to which the assets of the target division can be transferred prior to the recap, it may be possible to structure a recapitalization of OldSub (which owns the target Bigco division) to qualify for recap accounting, even where the drop down to OldSub takes place after Bigco and VC begin discussing a possible transaction. Most accountants take the view that a transfer of divisional assets to OldSub (rather than to NewSub), followed by OldSub's recapitalization by VC, is not the equivalent of an asset sale by Bigco to a Newco established by VC, so that recap accounting applies if the transaction meets the other requirements set forth in ¶504.2 or ¶504.4 (or possibly ¶504.3).

Two possible transactional complexities may arise where OldSub has preexisting assets and liabilities:

---

group), unless perhaps they invest new money in addition to rolling over all or a portion of their pre-existing Target stake). See ¶504.2.3.1.

First, where OldSub is a corporation with preexisting assets not wanted by VC, Bigco's extraction of such unwanted OldSub assets (generally at the same time as Bigco drops down the target division to OldSub) generally triggers any inherent gain in such unwanted assets into Bigco's taxable income (as discussed further below).

Second, VC generally seeks assurances from Bigco (in the form of representations, warranties, and indemnification) that OldSub does not have contingent liabilities from prior activities or transactions.

Route #3. If the target business is a division of an existing Bigco subsidiary (rather than a direct division of Bigco itself), an additional route to recap accounting may be available. Bigco can remove the "unwanted assets"—the assets other than the target division—from the existing subsidiary, VC can then acquire an interest in the existing subsidiary (which by then owns only the target division) in a traditional recapitalization described in ¶504.2 or ¶504.4 (or possibly ¶504.3).

Unfortunately, Bigco's extraction of the unwanted assets from the existing subsidiary generally triggers any inherent gain in such unwanted assets into Bigco's taxable income when the existing subsidiary leaves Bigco's consolidated group as part of the recapitalization. However, if the recapitalization transaction is structured for tax purposes so that a Code §338(h)(10) election is made to treat the sale of the existing subsidiary's stock as a sale of its assets followed by a tax-free deemed Code §332 liquidation of the existing subsidiary into Bigco, distribution of the unwanted assets from the existing subsidiary to Bigco would generally be part of the existing subsidiary's Code §332 liquidation so that no taxable gain is recognized with respect to the unwanted assets. See ¶504.2.9.2 for a discussion of structuring the recap of a Bigco subsidiary so that a Code §338(h)(10) election can be made.

¶504.6 *Key Recap Accounting Issues and References*

Will the buyout qualify for recap accounting or will it be subjected to purchase or part purchase accounting?

References:

- ¶501.8 of this book regarding purchase accounting
- Ginsburg and Levin M&A book ¶1703 and in particular:
  - ¶1703.2 on purchase accounting
  - ¶1703.3.1 through ¶1703.3.5 on part purchase accounting
  - ¶1703.3.6 through ¶1703.3.8 on recap accounting (containing recap accounting examples not contained in ¶504 of this book)
  - ¶1703.4 on pooling accounting

CHAPTER 6

Terms and Tax Ramifications of Debt and Equity Securities

This chapter discusses some of the terms and tax ramifications of the stock and debt investments issued in the start-up, growth-equity, and buyout transactions discussed in Chapters 2 through 5 above, as well as in the industry consolidation and turn-around transactions discussed in Chapters 7 and 8 below.

¶601   TYPES OF SECURITIES

VCs may purchase any one or a combination of the following:

- Subordinated debentures.
- Preferred stock.
- Common stock.
- Warrants.
- Convertible subordinated debentures.
- Convertible preferred stock.

¶602   SUBORDINATED DEBENTURE SAMPLE TERMS AND TAX RAMIFICATIONS

¶602.1   *Term*

Fixed maturity date (e.g., 10 years), perhaps with required principal pre-payments to the extent of Newco's excess free cash flow.

¶602.2   *Subordination*

Subordinated to all bank debt, existing and future. Infrequently subordinated to other debt, such as trade creditors.

¶602.3   *Typical Remedies*

If Newco defaults on the payment of debenture interest or principal, the debenture may give VCs the right to accelerate the debenture, an increased interest rate, a right to receive warrants to purchase additional Newco common stock at a low price (or a decrease in conversion price), the right to take control of Newco's board, and/or the right to force an IPO or sale of Newco. The terms of the senior debt will generally require VCs to agree (in a subordination agreement or in the terms of the debenture) to restrictions on their right to trigger a default (and particularly on their right to invoke the remedy of acceleration) while the senior debt is outstanding.

See also ¶402.2 above for a discussion of debenture terms.

¶602.4   *Interest Deferral*

If Newco's cash flow is expected to be negative at the outset (after taking account of required principal and interest payments on senior debt), the debenture may give Newco a front-end interest holiday for (e.g.) 18 months during which interest accretes (or is paid by PIK bunny debentures) but is not required to be paid in cash, with interest thereafter payable in cash quarterly and with the first 18 months' accreted interest payable during (e.g.) the third year (or at maturity).

¶602.5   *VC Taxed on Deferred Interest as OID*

Where there is a front-end interest holiday, VCs are nevertheless taxable on (and Newco is entitled to deduct, unless precluded by any of the prerequisites to Newco's interest deduction discussed in ¶602.8) the interest during the holiday period as it accrues (or is paid in PIK bunny debentures), calculated on the CYTM method (although the interest payment is deferred), even if VCs are cash method taxpayers. See the OID rules of Code §1273(a)(2).

¶602.6   *Imputed Interest*

Where a Newco debenture holder is also a Newco shareholder, the debenture should bear interest of at least 100% of the AFR in order to avoid the imputed interest rule of Code §7872. It is not clear whether this rule applies if the holder is not technically a shareholder but is merely the holder of a Newco warrant or convertible debenture.

¶602.7 VC Phantom OID Income

Where VCs purchase a Newco investment unit consisting of a debenture plus a security participating in Newco's upside (e.g., common stock or a warrant to purchase common stock), paying an aggregate purchase price equal to the debenture face plus a nominal amount for the upside security, IRS might take the position that VCs paid (1) less than face for the debenture and (2) more than a nominal amount for the upside security. Under IRS regulations, the aggregate price VCs pay for the investment unit is allocated among the several securities purchased by VCs based upon each security's relative FV.

Where the amount of VC's purchase price allocated to the debenture is less than the debenture's face, the excess (of face over VC's allocated purchase price) constitutes debenture OID which the holder must generally amortize into its OI (and which Newco is entitled to deduct as OID interest expense, unless precluded by any of the prerequisites to Newco's interest deduction discussed in ¶602.8), calculated on the CYTM method, even if VCs are cash method taxpayers. See the OID rules of Code §1272-§1275.

In calculating such an allocation between a Newco debenture and a Newco warrant a 2000 Ninth Circuit decision (reversing the Tax Court) concluded that warrants cannot be assigned zero or nominal value merely because (1) the warrant exercise price is at the money (i.e., the warrant exercise price is equal to the underlying stock's FV at the time of warrant issuance) and (2) the warrant's future value is highly speculative. Rather, the warrant FV at issuance must be determined (for the purpose of allocating the aggregate investment unit purchase price between the debenture and the warrant) using a reasonable method, such as the Black-Scholes warrant valuation model (see discussion at ¶407.3.3) or a calculation of the present value of the additional interest the lender would have charged had it received no warrant.

In contrast, where VCs buy only a single Newco security—a convertible debenture—and the upside potential consists of VCs' right to convert all of the debenture into Newco stock, IRS rules do not require (or permit) a separate allocation of purchase price to the conversion privilege, so that such a purchase of a traditional convertible debenture does not create OID.

¶602.8 Six Prerequisites for Newco's Interest Deduction

In order for Newco to be entitled to deduct the interest expense (including OID amortization) on the debentures for federal income tax purposes, *all* 6 of the following tests must be satisfied:

¶602.8.1 Subjective Debt/Equity Test

Interest (and OID amortization) on debt (whether such debt arises from an acquisition or not) is disallowed (and the debt is treated for tax purposes as preferred stock) if the debt instrument more closely resembles equity than debt. Under the common law of taxation, there are no objective tax rules for distinguishing between a debenture which is treated as debt for tax purposes and one which is treated as preferred stock (although there might have been if IRS had finalized regulations under Code §385). The 4 most important factors are discussed below.

If IRS treats a debenture as stock for tax purposes (and wins), there are two tax disadvantages:

(1) Newco loses the interest deduction, but VC (if a corporation) may then be entitled to a 70%, 80%, or 100% dividend received deduction ("DRD"). See ¶603.4 through ¶603.7 below.

(2) VC, on redemption of an equitized debenture, may be treated as having received a dividend rather than a return of capital. See ¶603.8 below.

Although a debt instrument which flunks the subjective debt/equity test is treated as stock (rather than as debt) for all purposes of the federal tax law,[1] this is not true for a debt instrument which flunks one of the other 5 tests set forth in ¶602.8.2 through ¶602.8.6 below. Such a debt instrument remains debt for federal tax purposes, but Newco's interest deduction is disallowed or deferred as described below.

¶602.8.1.1 DER

To pass the subjective debt/equity test, Newco shareholders should invest enough in common and preferred stock (i.e., equity) so that Newco's DER, computed on an FV (not a book value) basis, is within reasonable bounds. Although there are no clear precedents, it is generally believed that:

- DER below 3-to-1 is very good.
- DER between 3-to-1 and 5-to-1 is good.
- DER between 5-to-1 and 10-to-1 is probably acceptable (but obviously the closer to 5-to-1 the better).
- DER above 10-to-1 is questionable (and becomes more questionable as it rises).

It appears that the DER for any purported debt instrument is calculated by treating as debt the instrument being tested and all instruments senior to the instrument being tested, but by treating as equity any instruments junior to the instrument being tested.

It is unclear whether routine trade debt (as opposed to debt for borrowed money and the like) is treated as debt in measuring DER.

Start-up example. In the start-up transaction discussed in ¶202 above, Newco's DER (ignoring trade debt) was .93 to 1 ($500,000 debenture debt to $540,000

¶602 [1]However, a debt instrument satisfying the straight-debt exception of Code §1361(c)(5) is treated as debt for all purposes of the Code, so long as the issuing corporation is an S corporation, even if such debt was issued while the issuer was a C corporation.

equity), if Newco had no additional borrowing. If Newco borrowed (e.g.) an additional $500,000 from a bank, its DER (ignoring trade debt) would have been 1.85 to 1 ($1 million debt to $540,000 equity).

Growth-equity example. In testing the growth-equity investment described in Chapter 4 above, assume VC invests $1 million of its $2 million in common stock and $1 million in a subordinated debenture, that Oldco redeems $17 million of its common stock from the passive shareholders in exchange for notes as described at ¶402, and that Oldco has $7 million of old bank loans and incurs $3 million of new bank loans, so that Oldco's debts after the VC investment consist of:

New bank loan	$ 3 million
Old bank loan	7 million
New VC subordinated debentures	1 million
New notes issued to passive shareholders in redemption of common stock	17 million
Total debt for borrowed money	$28 million

Assume further that Oldco's FV equity (before the VC investment and before the redemption of Oldco stock for new notes) was $20 million, so that after the redemption and the VC investment, Oldco's FV equity is:

Old FV equity	$ 20 million
New notes issued to passive shareholders in redemption of common stock	(17 million)
New VC equity	1 million
Total equity	$4 million

In such case, Oldco's DER (ignoring trade debt) would be 7 to 1 (i.e., $28 million to $4 million).

Buyout example. In testing the $50 million buyout discussed in Chapter 5 above, Newco's DER for the $12.5 million of subordinated debt (ignoring trade debt) is 5.7-to-1:

$$\frac{\$30 \text{ million senior debt} + \$12.5 \text{ million subordinated debt}}{\$6.5 \text{ million preferred stock} + \$1 \text{ million common stock.}}$$

Taking into account an assumed $10 million of trade debt, Newco's DER would rise to 7-to-1.

¶602.8.1.2   Overlap

The higher the overlapping proportionality between the common stock and the debentures, the greater the likelihood of equity characterization for the debentures.

It is likely that warrants, conversion privileges, and other rights to acquire stock are treated as exercised/converted only if held by the creditor group whose purported debt instrument is being tested.

Growth-equity example. In the growth-equity investment discussed in Chapter 4 above, Oldco's $1 million subordinated debenture issued to VC would be held by a minority shareholder (assuming that VC receives 25% to 33% of Oldco's common stock). Such a low ratio of overlapping proportionality between Oldco's subordinated debentures and common stock is a favorable factor for debt status.

Buyout example. For the $50 million buyout discussed in Chapter 5 above, the common stock overlap with the subordinated debentures is 10%, because the subordinated debenture holders acquired 10% of Newco's common stock. Such a low ratio of overlapping proportionality is a favorable factor for debt status.

However, if VCs' $6.5 million of preferred stock in the $50 million buyout had been structured instead as junior subordinated debt (rather than as preferred stock):

- Newco's DER for this junior subordinated debt would have been 49-to-1,
- the overlap between the junior subordinated debt (held by VCs) and the common stock (held by VCs) would have been 70%, and
- the combined overlap between the subordinated debt and the junior subordinated debt, on the one hand, and the common stock, on the other, would have been 80% (10% of Newco's common stock held by the subordinated debenture holders and 70% by VCs).

Newco's DER could be reduced somewhat by structuring only a part of the $6.5 million as junior subordinated debt and the remainder as preferred stock.

¶602.8.1.3   Reasonable Terms

The more reasonable (i.e., arms length) the terms of the debenture, the more likely that debt characterization will be upheld.

¶602.8.1.4   Act Like Creditor

The more the debenture holders act like independent creditors after the transaction, the more likely that debt characterization will be upheld. For example, the more Newco complies with the debt instrument's terms, the more likely that the instrument will be debt for tax purposes.

Similarly, if Newco defaults, the more vigorously the debenture holders act, i.e., take reasonable (arms length) action to enforce their rights, the more likely that debt characterization will be upheld.

¶602.8.2   Code §279—Subordinated Debentures with Warrants or Conversion Privileges

Code §279 was enacted in 1969 in an effort to discourage acquisitions financed with complex financial instruments consisting of *either* subordinated straight debentures with warrants[2] or subordinated convertible debentures. §279 disallows Newco's interest deduction (including OID amortization) on indebtedness if the debt meets *all* 6 of the following tests:

(1) Such debt is issued to provide consideration for an acquisition of (a) stock in another corporation *or* (b) at least ⅔ of the assets of another corporation, *either by* (c) issuing such debt directly to the acquired corporation or its shareholders *or* (d) issuing such debt to lenders and using the borrowed money to consummate the acquisition.

(2) The debt instrument is issued by a C corporation. If borrower is a partnership, it is unclear whether the portion of the interest allocable to a C corporation partner is covered.

(3) The debt is *either* (a) subordinated to the claims of trade creditors generally *or* (b) expressly subordinated to any substantial amount of unsecured debt.

(4) The debt is *either* (a) convertible into stock *or* (b) issued in conjunction with an option, warrant, or other right (including convertible preferred stock) to acquire stock.

(5) Borrower has *either*:

    (a) a more than 2-to-1 DER *or*

    (b) a 3-to-1 or lower earnings-to-interest-expense ratio.

This DER compares:

- borrower's total liabilities (including trade payables and contingent liabilities that are "likely to become a reality") *to*
- the tax basis (not the FV) of its assets in excess of its total liabilities,

and is made at the end of borrower's taxable year in which borrower issues the acquisition debt. If this DER exceeds 2-to-1, borrower meets test (5) and its interest may be subject to §279.

The earnings-to-interest ratio described in (b) above compares:

- borrower's average tax EBITDA for the 36 month period ending with the close of the taxable year in which borrower issues the acquisition debt *to*

---

[2] Or a subordinated straight debenture issued in conjunction with any other instrument which gives the holder the right to acquire Newco stock, such as Newco convertible preferred stock which is convertible into Newco common stock.

- borrower's anticipated interest expense (including OID amortization) for the year following such date (calculated based on borrower's debt levels on such date).

Tax EBITDA means borrower's tax E&P before interest expense, depreciation, amortization, federal income tax, and dividend payments (but apparently after reduction for state and local income tax). If this earnings-to-interest ratio is 3-to-1 or lower, borrower meets this test (5) and its interest may be subject to §279.

(6) Borrower's total interest from all "acquisition debt" (i.e., debt described in (1) above, whether or not such debt meets any of the other 5 tests), calculated cumulatively for all acquisitions made by borrower, actually exceeds $5 million in any year.

Where borrower is a member of an affiliated group for tax purposes (under the 80-80 test of §1504), borrower and its affiliated group are treated as a single corporation for all §279 calculations, except that the acquired corporation is included only for purposes of calculating the earnings-to-interest-expense ratio described in (5)(b).

If §279 applies to Newco's debt, the amount of interest on such debt disallowed for any year is the *lesser* of:

(1) the interest on the debt which is §279 tainted (i.e., meets all 6 of the above tests) *or*

(2) the interest on all "acquisition debt" (i.e., debt described in (1) above, whether or not such debt meets any of the other 5 tests) in excess of $5 million.

§279 can be avoided by utilizing one or more of the following alternatives:

(1) Issuing no warrants or conversion privileges in conjunction with subordinated debt, i.e., if warrants or conversion privileges must be issued, issuing them only with debt which is not subordinated.

(2) If an equity kicker is necessary with subordinated debt, using contingent interest or common stock rather than warrants or conversion privileges.

(3) If warrants or conversion privileges are issued with subordinated debt, subordinating the debt only to secured debt.

(4) Using structural subordination (rather than express subordination), i.e., placing the senior debt in Target (which becomes a Newco operating subsidiary) and the junior debt in Newco (the holding company), so that the junior debt is structurally rather than expressly subordinated to the senior debt. Such structural subordination should not count as subordination for §279 purposes where the only operating subsidiary in the group is Target which was acquired in a stock acquisition.

(5) Structuring so that tainted debt (or proceeds therefrom) is used to *redeem* rather than purchase Target stock (including Target's "redemption" of part of its own stock in a taxable reverse subsidiary merger of NewSub into Target to the extent Target's shareholders are paid out of Target's cash *or* acquisition debt which becomes a Target liability).

¶602.8.3 Code §163(e)(5)—OID and PIK Debentures

Code §163(e)(5) was enacted in 1989 in an effort to discourage leveraged buyouts financed by high yield debt where all of the interest is not being paid in cash currently, and affects *OID debt* (including debt with a face greater than the amount loaned, debt where part of the basis has been allocated to warrants or common stock issued in a strip with the debt, debt where the interest accretes, and zero coupon and partial zero coupon debt) and *PIK debt* (i.e., debt which requires or permits Newco to pay interest in additional debt instruments or in stock).

For purposes of §163(e)(5), it does not matter whether the debt is (a) subordinated or (b) convertible or issued in conjunction with warrants, i.e., the Code §279 tests described above are not relevant.

Under §163(e)(5) a debt instrument is an Applicable High Yield Discount Obligation (an "AHYDO"), and hence is covered by this provision, if it meets *all* 4 of the following tests:

(1) The debt instrument has a maturity date more than 5 years after issuance.

(2) The debt instrument is issued by a C corporation. If borrower is a partnership, each partner is (under regulations) treated as borrowing its allocable portion of a loan to the partnership, so that to the extent the borrowing partnership is owned by C corporations, this test is met.

(3) The yield on the debt instrument (including interest paid currently, PIK interest, OID amortization, etc.) equals or exceeds the AFR (5.78% in 1/01 for long-term debt with semi-annual compounding) plus 5 percentage points (i.e., 10.78% in 1/01).

(4) The debt instrument has substantial OID or PIK features, i.e., the terms of the debt instrument require or permit borrower (a) to accrue without current payment or (b) to pay with bunny debentures or bunny stock a substantial portion of the interest.

- A debt instrument will not have substantial OID/PIK features if (a) no later than the 5 ½ year anniversary of its issuance all interest accrued through that date (except for an amount equal to the first year's interest/OID) is required to have been paid in cash by the terms of the instrument *and* (b) at the end of each subsequent compounding period, the total amount of interest remaining unpaid in cash will, according to the terms of the instrument, not exceed an amount equal to the first year's interest.

- The term "5 ½ year anniversary" can vary between the 5th and 6th anniversaries of the debenture's issuance and the term "each subsequent compounding period" can vary between one day and one year, depending upon the frequency of payments under the debenture and the elections made by borrower.

- This determination is made at the front end when the debt instrument is issued, based on the terms of the instrument and assuming that Newco defers any payment as long as permitted by the terms of the instrument.

If a debt instrument is an AHYDO, §163(e)(5) imposes 2 major tax disadvantages on Newco:

(1) *Deferral of interest deduction.* No OID or PIK interest will be deductible by Newco until paid in cash, although the holder will still be taxed currently under the regular OID rules.

(2) *Partial permanent disallowance of interest deduction.* If the yield on the debt instrument exceeds the AFR plus 6 percentage points, a portion of the interest deduction (including OID amortization) will be permanently disallowed, equal to the *lesser* of:

(a)   100% of the OID and PIK interest (including all non-QSI interest, i.e., interest not unconditionally payable at a fixed rate at intervals no greater than one year) or

(b)   a percentage of the total yield equal to the yield in excess of the AFR plus 6 divided by the total yield.

A 1995 revenue ruling (Rev. Rul. 95-70) interpreted narrowly the already stingy regulatory definition of QSI (which is exempt from the Code §163(e)(5) deferral/disallowance rule) by requiring that *either* (1) the debt holder must have the right to sue for the unpaid QSI *or* (2) the debt holder must receive directly a sufficiently large penalty for non-payment (e.g., an increased interest rate) to ensure that, at the time the debt is issued, it is reasonably certain (absent Newco's insolvency) that Newco will pay the interest when due. The ruling concluded that a 2 point increase in the interest rate on the defaulted portion of the interest is not large enough to meet test (2) and that a prohibition on Newco paying dividends while interest is unpaid on the debt is not adequate because it does not inure directly to the debt holder, but suggests that a 12 point increase in yield might be sufficient to meet test (2) (without stating whether such increase applies only to the unpaid interest or the entire debt instrument).

Where §163(e)(5) applies to a debt instrument and the holder of the debt is a corporation eligible for the DRD, its interest income corresponding to Newco's permanently disallowed interest deduction is treated as dividend income and hence is generally eligible for the DRD to the extent of Newco's E&P.

However, §163(e)(5) does not cause any part of the debt instrument to be treated as preferred stock.

¶602.8.4   Code §163(j) Test #1—Interest Payable to "Related" Lender Which Is TEO or FP (or Fund with TEO or FP Partners)

Code §163(j) test #1 was enacted in 1989 to combat "interest stripping," i.e., payments of deductible interest by a U.S. corporation to a "related" lender which is not taxed on the interest income. §163(j) test #1 applies if *all* 5 of the following tests are met:

(1) Borrower is a "C" corporation.

If borrower is a partnership, each partner is (under proposed regulations) treated as borrowing its allocable portion of a loan to the partnership, so that to the extent the borrowing partnership is owned by C corporations, this test is met.

(2) Borrower has a more than 1.5-to-1 DER.

For this purpose debt excludes most short-term liabilities and certain inventory financing (according to the proposed regulations) and equity is measured based on asset tax basis (not asset FV).

(3) Lender is not taxed on interest income, because lender is one of the following 3 types of persons:

- A TEO.
- An FP with a U.S. treaty tax rate below the normal 30% FP withholding rate for U.S. source interest income. In this case a portion of FP's interest income corresponding to FP's treaty rate reduction is treated as not taxed.
- A partnership (including a PE fund) with TEO-FP ownership of 10% or more (measured by either capital or profits). For an FP partner, a portion of its partnership interest is counted corresponding to its treaty rate reduction.

(4) Lender is "related" to borrower.[3] For this purpose "related" means that at least one of the following 3 is true:

(a)   Lender owns more than 50% of borrower.

- For example, assume a PE fund partnership has more than 10% TEO-FP ownership, the fund buys both debt and equity securities of a corporation (the "corporate borrower"), and the fund holds more than 50% of the corporate borrower's stock and also holds debt securities of the corporate borrower. In this case, the more-than-50% "related" test is satisfied, so that the corporate borrower's interest on the debt securities is §163(j) tainted to the extent of the fund's TEO-FP ownership (assuming the other §163(j) tests are satisfied).
- However, assume the debt securities are purchased by the PE fund's partners (even pro rata to their ownership of the fund) *or* purchased by the fund but promptly distributed to its partners. In this case, §163(j) will generally be avoided, so long as (1) no one fund partner owns (actually and by attribution from the fund and other stockholders of the corporate borrower, as described below) more than 50% of the corporate borrower's stock and (2) there are no arrangements between the fund partners that are comparable to a disguised partnership (e.g., agreements to act in regard to the corporate borrower's debt securities in accordance with a majority vote or a decision of the fund's GP and/or a carried interest in the debt securities for the fund's GP).
- Similarly, assume the PE fund is split into 2 parallel partnerships, the 2 partnerships have a common GP entity but different LPs (i.e., each LP is a partner in only one of the 2 partnerships), the 2 partnerships agree to purchase securities in tandem in a predetermined ratio, and neither of the 2 partnerships (together with the GP entity's indirect ownership through the other partnership) alone owns more than 50%

---

[3] Where lender is an FP "related" to borrower, Code §163(e)(3) imposes yet an additional limit on OID deductibility, generally deferring the borrower's OID deduction until the OID is paid, whether or not the other Code §163(j) requirements are met.

of the corporate borrower's stock. In this case, interest on the debt securities held by the 2 parallel partnerships arguably is not §163(j) tainted. However, where the split-up of the fund into 2 separate partnerships is artificial (i.e., serves no legitimate business purpose), IRS might seek to treat them both as one entity. Hence, it is desirable for the split-up into 2 partnerships to be supported by business (i.e., non-tax) reasons, e.g., different levels of carried interest or management fees in the 2 entities *or* one an offshore and the other an onshore entity.

(b) Borrower owns more than 50% of lender.

(c) The same persons own more than 50% of both borrower and lender.

- The more-than-50%-ownership test is applied in (a) through (c) above by reference to either vote or value if lender and borrower are both C corporations *and* by reference to value alone if one or both is not a C corporation.

- In addition, various attribution rules apply in making this more-than-50% ownership determination. For example: (i) each partner in a partnership and each shareholder in a corporation is treated as owning a proportionate part of stock owned by such entity, (ii) an individual is treated as owning stock owned by certain relatives, (iii) an option holder is often treated as owning outstanding stock covered by the option, and (iv) an individual is sometimes treated as owning stock owned by each of his or her partners.

- The "related" test is normally applied by reference to all of borrower's stock (common and preferred); however, where the lender is a C corporation, non-voting debt-like preferred stock, certain stock held by or for employees, and certain other stock is ignored.

- These rules are complicated and can reach unanticipated results. For example, where there are 2 partnerships—one (an "equity fund") holding more than 50% of a corporation's stock and the second (a "debt fund") holding the corporation's debentures—the corporate borrower and the debt fund are treated as "related" to each other (and hence the corporate borrower's interest paid to the debt fund is subject to §163(j) disallowance) where the debt fund is more than 50% owned by persons who also own (actually and by attribution from the equity fund and other stockholders of the corporate borrower) more than 50% of the corporate borrower's stock.

  On the other hand, where the debt fund distributes the debt securities to its partners (who hold them directly) or where the debt fund and the equity fund are each split into 2 partnerships, §163(j) may be avoided (as described in (a) above).

(5) Borrower's total interest expense for the taxable year (net of its interest income) exceeds 50% of its tax EBITDA.

Borrower's tax EBITDA is its taxable income before interest, federal income taxes, depreciation, and amortization deductions (but apparently after reduction for state and local income taxes), plus additional strange adjustments.

Where borrower is a member of an affiliated group for tax purposes (generally using an 80%-by-vote-*and*-value test), the affiliated group is treated as a single corporation for the EBITDA test, for calculating DER under (2) above, and for other purposes of §163(j).

Where borrower meets tests (1) and (2) and lender meets tests (3) and (4), borrower's interest deduction (including OID amortization) is disallowed for amounts payable to:

- such related TEO lender,
- such related FP lender (for the portion of the interest payable to such FP corresponding to its treaty rate reduction), *and*
- such related partnership lender (for the portion of the interest allocable to each TEO partner and to each FP partner corresponding to its treaty rate reduction),

but only to the extent that all of the borrower's net interest expense (whether or not disqualified) exceeds 50% of its tax EBITDA.

Borrower's disallowed interest expense is carried forward as a deduction and may be used in any subsequent year to the extent that 50% of its tax EBITDA exceeds its net interest expense. In addition, if borrower's net interest expense is less than 50% of its tax EBITDA in any year, this excess limitation can be carried forward (for up to 3 years) and added to borrower's 50%-of-EBITDA limitation (described above) for such future years.

¶602.8.5 Code §163(j) Test #2—Interest Payable on Debt "Guaranteed" by "Related" Person Who Is TEO or FP (or Possibly by Fund with TEO or FP Partners)

The 1993 Tax Act expanded §163(j) drastically so that tests (3) and (4) described in ¶602.8.4 above are treated as satisfied even where lender is a U.S. person paying U.S. taxes (i.e., lender is not a TEO or FP) but *all* 6 of the following tests are met:

(1) Borrower's debt to lender is "guaranteed" by a person "related" to borrower. "Guarantee" is defined extremely broadly as "any arrangement under which a person (directly or indirectly through an entity or otherwise) assures, on a conditional or unconditional basis, the payment of [the borrower's] obligation." According to the legislative history, this includes: "any form of credit support . . . , includ[ing] a commitment to make a capital contribution to the debtor or otherwise maintain its financial viability [and] . . . a 'comfort letter,' regardless of whether the arrangement gives rise to a legally enforceable obligation."

See ¶602.8.4(4) above for the definition of "related," which generally means more than 50% by vote or value if the guarantor is a C corporation and more than 50% by value alone if the guarantor is not a C corporation.

(2) Such "related" guarantor is a TEO or an FP, whether or not such FP is entitled to a reduced treaty withholding rate.

(a) The statutory language of §163(j) test #2 does not appear to cover the situation where a U.S. partnership (including a PE fund) with TEO-FP ownership of 10% or more (measured by either capital or profits) is "related" to borrower and such partnership guarantees the borrower's debt, even though a direct loan by the partnership would in these circumstances be covered by Code §163(j) test #1. It is not clear whether this difference in scope between tests #1 and #2 was intended.

(b) Where a partnership is organized under the laws of a foreign country, it appears that a guarantee by such a partnership is treated as a guarantee by an FP, regardless of the nationality of the partners.

(3) Borrower does not own a controlling interest in the guarantor, i.e., at least 80% by vote and value (80% of capital and profits if guarantor is not a corporation).

(4) The interest is not paid to an FP subject to a 30% U.S. withholding tax on its gross interest income.

If the interest is paid to an FP with a treaty-reduced gross withholding rate below 30%, a portion of the interest corresponding to the rate reduction is treated as meeting this test.

(5) IRS has authority (by future regulations) to exempt interest which, if paid to the guarantor, would have been subjected to a U.S. net income tax, i.e., where the guarantor is engaged in a U.S. business and the interest would be effectively connected thereto.

(6) Borrower and lender are not more than 50% "related."

Thus, under §163(j) test #2, where Newco's debt to a U.S. lender is guaranteed by a TEO or an FP and meets the other tests set forth in this ¶602.8.5, interest on such debt paid by Newco to the U.S. lender (including OID amortization) is treated as meeting tests ¶602.8.4(3) and (4) above. Such interest would then be subjected to §163(j) (as described in ¶602.8.4 above) where borrower also met tests ¶602.8.4(1) and (2) above (C corporation and DER exceeding 1.5-to-1). In such case, the interest described in this ¶602.8.5 and the interest described in ¶602.8.4 above would be combined and allowed as a deduction only to the extent permitted by the 50% EBITDA test described in ¶602.8.4 (5) above.

¶602.8.6 Code §163(*l*)—Debt Payable in, or by Reference to Value of, Issuer Equity

Code §163(*l*), enacted in 1997, permanently disallows any deduction for interest paid or accrued (including OID amortization) on a debt instrument where *all* 4 of the following tests are met:

(1) Borrower is a corporation.

If borrower is a partnership, each partner is (under legislative history) treated as borrowing its allocable portion of a loan to the partnership, so that to the extent the borrowing partnership is owned by C corporations, this test is met.

In logic, Code §163(*l*) should not apply if borrower is an S corporation, although this result is not entirely clear pending IRS guidance.

(2) The debt is payable in, or by reference to the value of, equity (*"equity-linked debt"*).

Debt is equity-linked if "a substantial amount of the principal or interest" on the debt obligation:

(a) is required to be paid in, converted into, or measured by reference to, equity of the borrower or a related party, *or*

(b) at the option of the *borrower* or a related party is payable in, convertible into, or measured by reference to, equity of the borrower or a related party (regardless of the likelihood the option will be exercised), *or*

(c) at the option of the *lender* or a related party is payable in, convertible into, or measured by reference to, equity of the borrower or a related party, but only if there is a "substantial certainty" the option will be exercised.

For this purpose, a person is a "related party" to the borrower or lender if that person and the borrower or lender, as applicable, bear a relationship described in Code §267(b) or §707(b), generally a more-than-50% equity ownership test (e.g., more-than-50% overlapping stock ownership by vote or value in the case of two corporations), as further described in ¶602.8.4.

Neither the statute nor the legislative history furnishes any guidance on what constitutes a "substantial amount" of principal or interest. More than one-third of principal or interest is likely to be treated as "a substantial amount" for this purpose, although IRS may apply a lower threshold, since the term "substantial" has been used in other areas of the Code to mean percentages as low as 20% or even 5%. The meaning of a "substantial amount" becomes even less clear where the amount of principal or interest payable in, or by reference to, borrower equity is contingent, and hence not determinable at the time the debt is issued. Presumably the determination is made at issuance, not years later when the amount of equity-based principal or interest is ultimately ascertained and paid. Some front-end determination seems necessary to permit the issuer to file its tax returns and compute estimated taxes.

If a substantial amount of principal or interest is payable in, or by reference to, equity so that Code §163(*l*) applies, *all* interest on the debt is nondeductible, not merely the portion of the interest corresponding to the amount of principal or interest payable in equity.

An option exercisable by the *lender* does not invoke Code §163(*l*) unless there is "a substantial certainty" the option will be exercised. Code §163(*l*) offers no guidance on what constitutes "a substantial certainty" of exercise in the case of a lender option. "Substantial certainty" of exercise suggests a high standard that, in other contexts, excludes at-the-money and even moderately in-the-money options. In particular, regulations concerning the treatment of options under Code §1361's one-class-of-stock requirement, which also adopt a "substantial certainty" of exercise standard, contain a safe harbor for options that are not more than 10% in the money at issuance (and at certain later testing dates).[4] Unfortunately, Code §163(*l*)'s legislative history promotes ambiguity in stating that "it is not expected that the provision will affect debt with a conversion feature where the conversion price is *significantly higher* than the market price of the stock on the issue date of

---

[4] Reg. §1.1361-1(*l*)(4)(iii)(A), (C)

the debt" (emphasis added), without similarly blessing debt with a conversion price that is only slightly out-of-the money, at-the-money, or slightly in-the-money at issuance.

Where a convertible debt is *required* to be converted upon the happening of a specified contingency (e.g., a "Qualified IPO" defined as an IPO of borrower's stock at a specified price substantially exceeding the conversion price (often 3 or 4 times the conversion price)), there is risk the debt might be viewed as (1) "*required to be . . . converted into*" borrower's equity (emphasis added) unless the possibility of the specified contingency occurring is "remote," and hence (2) as Code §163(*l*) tainted, although the statute gives no guidance. Hence a safer drafting technique would be to delete mandatory conversion upon a Qualified IPO and to substitute instead a clause terminating lender's conversion privilege upon occurrence of a Qualified IPO.

It is unclear whether (and when) debt issued with a warrant might be covered by Code §163(*l*), on the theory that either (1) quoting from Code §163(*l*)(3)(C), "the indebtedness is part of an arrangement . . . reasonably expected to result in a transaction described in [Code §163(*l*)]" or (2) under tax common law the two instruments should be treated as one, i.e., like convertible debt. Such treatment is more likely when the debt and warrant are not separately transferrable or when, although separately transferrable, the warrant requires the note to be surrendered (in whole or in part) as payment of the warrant exercise price, less likely (but possible) when, although separately transferrable, the warrant permits (but does not require) the note to be surrendered (in whole or in part) as payment of the warrant exercise price. In any event, even if the debt and warrant are viewed together, Code §163(*l*) should not apply unless the warrant holder is "substantially certain" to exercise the warrant (at least where the warrant holder is not "related" to the debt issuer).

Another difficulty is Code §163(*l*)'s silence on *when* the substantial certainty test is applied. Certainly the likelihood of exercise would be tested initially at issuance of the debt. However, the statute leaves murky whether an option would be tested only at issuance, or possibly at later dates as well. An annual or other periodic test would seem to make no sense. Code §1361's one-class-of-stock regulations and Code §1504's affiliated group regulations, which also address likelihood of option exercise, test likelihood of exercise at issuance and whenever the option is later transferred or materially modified, but at no other time.[5]

Where a conversion or similar right is exercisable by the *borrower*, the debt is treated as equity-linked even where the conversion price is significantly in-the-money so that it is unlikely the borrower will exercise this option. Moreover, where the lender is "related" to the borrower (i.e., the lender is the borrower's parent, subsidiary, or sister company), the statute can be read as taking into account any option of the related lender, regardless of the likelihood the conversion right will be exercised. For example, assume PE Fund, which owns 51% of Newco's stock (with the remaining 49% owned by unrelated persons), makes a loan to Newco that is convertible at PE Fund's option into additional Newco shares at a

---

[5] See Reg. §1.1361-1(*l*)(4)(iii)(A); Reg. §1.1504-4(g)(1), -4(c)(4).

price which is not in the money. Because the conversion right is exercisable by a person (PE Fund) related to the borrower (Newco), the debt appears to be equity-linked debt, and Code §163(*l*), literally read, apparently disallows Newco's interest deductions on the debt, even though PE Fund is not substantially certain to convert the debt.

Code §163(*l*) also appears to cover debt that is equity-linked in a technical statutory sense but whose economics do not really depend on fluctuations in equity value. For example, if a fixed dollar amount of interest or principal is payable automatically (or at the borrower's option) in the form of borrower shares having an FV at the time of payment equal to such fixed dollar amount, the debt is equity-linked, even though the debt is not participating in any meaningful sense.

Code §163(*l*) may cover debt where all of the interest and principal is payable in cash if a substantial amount of principal or interest is "determined . . . by reference to the value of [Newco's or a related person's] equity." The concept of "equity" clearly encompasses payments of principal or interest measured by the FV of Newco's stock. It is less clear whether "equity" also includes payments of principal or interest based on other measurements of Newco's performance that are related to, but not precisely the same as, Newco's stock FV (e.g., a payment based on Newco's EBITDA).

(3) The equity described in (2) is equity of the issuer or a person "related" to the issuer under Code §267(b) or §707(b).

These provisions generally apply a more-than-50% equity ownership test (e.g., more-than-50% overlapping stock ownership by vote or value in the case of two corporations), as described in ¶602.8.4.

(4) The debt is issued after 6/8/97, with limited transition relief.

Code §163(*l*) does not affect the tax treatment of the holder, who must include in income any interest paid or accrued on equity-linked debt, nor does it change the treatment of equity-linked debt as "debt" for tax purposes. Hence, for example, a corporate holder is not entitled to a dividends received deduction for yield on a debt instrument to which Code §163(*l*) applies.

¶602.8.7 References

- Code §385
- Code §279
- Code §163(e)(5) and (i)
- Code §163(j)
- Code §163(*l*)
- Code §1272–§1275
- Ginsburg and Levin M&A book ¶¶1302, 1303, 1304, 1305, 1306, and 1309

¶603   PREFERRED STOCK SAMPLE TERMS AND TAX RAMIFICATIONS

¶603.1   *Mandatory Redemption*

Mandatory redemption according to a schedule, e.g., 50% on the 7th anniversary and 50% on the 8th anniversary. A less common approach is a requirement that Newco, in addition, use any excess free cash flow for early preferred redemption. Frequently, early preferred redemption is required upon an IPO or change in control.

¶603.2   *Dividends*

Fixed cumulative dividends, e.g., dividends accrue (but are not paid currently) at a 5% rate for the first 4 years (during which they compound quarterly), dividends accrue at a 7% rate for the next 3 years and are payable currently, and dividends accrue at a 10% rate thereafter and are payable currently, with the first 4 years' accrued dividends payable only to the extent of Newco's free cash flow after year 4 (calculated after subtracting principal payments on the subordinated debenture and current dividends on the preferred stock, but before redemptions of preferred stock) or, if not previously paid, at redemption.

¶603.3   *Typical Remedies for Newco Failure to Pay Preferred Dividends or Redeem Preferred Timely*

If Newco defaults on the payment of preferred dividends or on redemptions, the preferred stock terms may give VCs compounding dividends on unpaid dividends, acceleration of Newco's preferred redemption obligation, increase in preferred dividend rate, issuance to VCs of warrants to purchase additional Newco common stock at a low price (or decrease in conversion price), right to take control of Newco's board, and/or the right to force an IPO or sale of Newco.

See also ¶403.2 above for a discussion of preferred stock terms.

¶603.4   *No Deduction for Dividends*

Newco is entitled to no federal income tax deduction for preferred dividends paid or accrued.

¶603.5 Timing of Dividend Taxation and DRDs

VC (as a holder of Newco preferred stock) has dividend income to the extent Newco has E&P at the time it pays a preferred dividend (or, in certain cases as discussed below, at the time a preferred dividend accrues).

(1) If VC is a C corporation, it is entitled to a 70% DRD for dividends out of Newco's E&P (80% if VC owns at least 20% of Newco both by vote and by value, and 100% if VC is a corporate SBIC or VC owns at least 80% of Newco both by vote and by value). Code §243. If VC is a partnership (or LLC), each partner's (or member's) entitlement to a DRD turns on such partner's (or member's) status with respect to the dividend allocated to such partner (or member).

(2) In certain cases, the 70% and 80% DRD is disallowed to the extent VC purchased the preferred stock with debt financing. There is also risk that the 70%, 80%, and 100% DRD is disallowed if preferred is puttable from the outset. Finally, in the case of certain "extraordinary dividends," the tax basis of the stock is reduced by the DRD. Code §246(c), §246A, §1059.

(3) With the exceptions discussed below, VC is generally not taxable on a preferred dividend until paid in cash or stock.

(4) Where, however, the preferred stock bears a PIK dividend (i.e., payable in bunny preferred), the PIK dividend is taxable to the holder when the bunny preferred instrument is issued (to the extent of Newco's E&P).

(5) Where the preferred stock terms state that cumulative preferred dividends will not be paid in cash or in bunny preferred (but rather will accrue and be added to liquidation value) for a specified period, it appears that such dividends are taxable to the holder as they accrue (to the extent of Newco's E&P). Code §305(b)(4) and (c).

(6) On the other hand, if the preferred terms call for payment of the cumulative preferred dividend in cash as declared by Newco's board, but Newco's board fails to declare the dividend, so that it will be paid as and when subsequently declared, or, if never declared, at redemption of the preferred stock or liquidation of Newco, the accrued dividend is apparently *not* taxable to the holder until declared and paid. Where VC is not a corporate entity entitled to a DRD, the preferred stock is frequently structured in this fashion to defer the holder's tax until the dividend is paid in cash and to convert the dividend to CG (rather than OI) by including the accrued dividends in the preferred stock redemption price (without ever declaring the dividends) when the preferred stock is redeemed.

There may be an exception to this rule (in which case (5) above would apply) if at the time the preferred was issued there was no intention to pay the cumulative preferred dividends currently, although the circumstances in which IRS would attempt to assert such an exception are uncertain in the absence of pertinent regulations.

(7) Finally, if the preferred stock has a significant participation in corporate growth (through a variable dividend rate or a redemption price based on Newco's success), VC is not taxable on preferred dividends until paid in cash (i.e., (4) through (6) above do not apply). Although illogical, a conversion privilege does not (according to the §305 regulations) constitute such a participation in growth

(unless the preferred holder participates in common dividends and redemption proceeds on an as-if-converted basis even where the preferred stock is not converted into common stock).

¶603.6   *Return of Basis*

To the extent a preferred dividend exceeds Newco's E&P, VC has a return of tax basis (i.e., no taxable income but a reduction of its tax basis in the Newco preferred stock). To the extent a dividend exceeds both Newco's E&P and the stock's tax basis, VC recognizes CG.

¶603.7   *FV Below Face*

If the preferred stock bears a below market dividend rate, IRS may assert that the Newco preferred stock has an FV less than its face, so that, in IRS's view, the Newco common stock has an FV higher than the price VC paid for its common stock and also higher than the price the executives paid for their common stock, with the tax results described immediately below.

¶603.7.1   Management Buyer Code §83 Issue

In the circumstances described in ¶603.7, an executive (i.e., a service provider) purchasing Newco common stock would have Code §83 OI equal to the bargain portion of the Newco common stock purchased (measured and taxed at the time of purchase if the executive's common stock is not subject to vesting or if the executive makes a Code §83(b) election).

For example, in the buyout described in ¶501.1 above, VC purchases $6.5 million of Newco preferred stock where VC, mezzanine lenders, and executives purchase $1 million of Newco common stock (with the executives purchasing 20% of Newco's common stock for $200,000). If the Newco preferred stock bears a below market dividend rate and hence has (e.g.) an FV of only $6 million (i.e., $500,000 below its $6.5 million face amount), IRS may take the position that Newco's common stock has an aggregate FV of $1.5 million ($500,000 more than the $1 million paid by the buyers), so that the executives' 20% of Newco's common stock has an FV of $300,000, i.e., $100,000 more than the price paid by the executives. In this case the executives would have $100,000 of Code §83 OI at the time they purchase the Newco common stock (if their common stock is not subject to vesting or if they make a Code §83(b) election).

¶603.7.2   VC Preferred OID Issue

In the circumstances described in ¶603.7, VC, an investor—as opposed to a service provider—would hold Newco preferred stock with Code §305 preferred OID equal to the preferred stock's redemption/liquidation price in excess of the preferred stock's FV at issuance. In the example discussed in ¶603.7.1 above, IRS might take the position that VC actually paid only $6 million for Newco's preferred stock (face value $6.5 million), with the additional $500,000 which VC purportedly paid for Newco's preferred stock reallocated to the Newco common stock purchased by VC. In this case VC would hold Newco preferred stock with a $6.5 million face and a $6 million issue price, i.e., VC's Newco preferred would have $500,000 of preferred OID.

VC would generally recognize phantom dividend income for tax purposes (calculated each year on a CYTM method), in an aggregate amount equal to the preferred OID. Code §305(b)(4) and (c):

(1) In any year, the preferred OID amortization constitutes dividend income to the preferred holder only to the extent of Newco's E&P. See also ¶603.6 above.

(2) No annual preferred OID amortization is required where the preferred stock is evergreen, i.e., never subject to call or mandatory redemption by Newco or to put by the holder. Although not entirely clear, IRS regulations can arguably be read as taking the position that stock which must be redeemed only upon a specified event (e.g., an IPO or change of Newco's control), rather than at a specified time, qualifies as evergreen—see Treas. Reg. §1.305-5(b)(2) mandating preferred OID amortization where "the issuer is required to redeem the stock at a *specified time* or the holder has the option (whether or not currently exercisable) to require the issuer to redeem the stock [unless there is] a contingency . . . beyond the . . . control of either the holder or the holders as a group . . . and that . . . renders remote the likelihood of redemption . . ." (emphasis added).

(3) Where the preferred stock qualifies as evergreen (as described in (2) above) except that the issuer has the right to call the preferred (whether immediately exercisable at issuance or exercisable only at a future time)—i.e., there is no mandatory redemption at "a specified time" and no holder put—the §305 regulations require preferred OID amortization only if it is "more likely than not" that the issuer will exercise the call right. Even in such circumstances, preferred OID amortization is not required when the redemption premium—in the event the preferred is called—is "solely in the nature of a penalty for premature redemption," i.e., "a premium paid as a result of changes in economic or market conditions over which neither the issuer nor the holder has control" (such as "changes in prevailing dividend rates or in the value of the common stock into which the [preferred] stock is convertible").

(4) No OID amortization is required where the excess of the preferred stock's redemption/liquidation price over the preferred stock's FV at issuance is below a specified *de minimis* amount.

(5) No annual preferred OID amortization is required if the preferred stock has a significant participation in corporate growth (through a variable dividend rate or a redemption price based on Newco's success). Although illogical, a conversion privilege does not (according to the §305 regulations) constitute such a partici-

pation in growth (unless the preferred holder participates in common dividends and redemption proceeds on an as-if-converted basis even where the preferred stock is not converted into common stock).

¶603.8 Preferred Stock Redemption Treated as Dividend

Whenever the preferred holders as a group own and are retaining a large portion of Newco's common stock, there is a risk that ultimate redemption of the preferred stock will be taxed as a dividend (rather than a return of their tax basis in the preferred stock) to the extent of Newco's E&P (on the ground that such a redemption is substantially equivalent to a dividend under Code §302):

Preferred holders (as a group) continuing percentage ownership of common stock	Extent of dividend risk
Over 80%	very high risk
60% to 80%	substantial risk
50% to 60%	moderate risk
Less than 50%	slight risk[1]

However, Rev. Rul. 85-106 can be interpreted as seeking to impose dividend treatment even where the preferred holders as a group own substantially less than 50% of Newco's common stock. The ruling suggests dividend treatment (to the extent of Newco's E&P) where the redeemed preferred holders as a group continue to own only 18% of Newco's common stock, but the preferred holders are part of Newco's control group, so that the redemption of their *non-voting* preferred stock does not alter their participation in Newco's control.

(1) If this 1985 IRS ruling is interpreted this broadly, it is highly questionable whether the ruling is a valid interpretation of Code §302.

(2) If the 1985 ruling is interpreted broadly and is valid, the risk of dividend treatment can be substantially minimized by (a) making the preferred stock *voting*, so that the post-redemption voting power of the preferred holders (here VCs) is significantly less than their pre-redemption voting power and/or (b) redeeming the preferred stock at the same time that additional common stock is being issued to third parties (e.g., in an IPO) so that the preferred holders' common stock percentage is declining.

(3) The 1985 ruling can, however, arguably be read more narrowly. The facts as set forth in the ruling demonstrate that all of the common shareholders owned the preferred stock in the same proportions as their ownership of the common stock. The taxpayer in the ruling (individual A) thus owned

---

¶603 [1] If preferred stock constitutes Code §306 stock, additional complex rules may cause a redemption—or even a sale—to be taxed as OI. See Code §306.

18% of the common stock and 18% of the preferred stock. Only A's preferred stock was redeemed. The other 82% of the preferred stock remained
outstanding. Hence, it is possible to view the ruling as turning on the fact
that when the remaining 82% of the preferred stock is ultimately redeemed,
the preferred stock proceeds will have been distributed proportionately
to the common stockholdings and hence will have been substantially
equivalent to a dividend on the common stock.

(4) While the 1985 ruling's stated facts support this narrower reading, IRS's
stated reasoning in the ruling stresses the fact that A (an 18% common
shareholder) along with two other shareholders had the ability to control
the corporation (i.e., that A was part of the corporation's control group),
and hence IRS's stated reasoning supports the broader reading.

If the redemption is taxed as a dividend, VC's tax basis in its redeemed preferred
stock hops over to the tax basis in its common stock, so that the LTCG on sale
of the common stock will be reduced.

Dividend treatment may be an advantage if VC is a corporation (or a partnership
or LLC virtually all of whose partners or members are corporations) entitled to
the DRD. However, in this case, VC's basis which hops over from the redeemed
preferred to the common stock may (under Code §1059 dealing with extraordinary
dividends) be reduced by the amount of the DRD, which would eliminate the
tax advantage of having the redemption taxed as a dividend.

However, if VC is not a corporation (or partnership or LLC owned by
corporations) entitled to a DRD, it may be desirable to give VC the right to reject
or delay a preferred stock redemption and continue to hold the preferred stock
until either Newco is sold or VC sells its common stock.

Where VC (or others) hold a debt instrument which qualifies as debt for tax
purposes under the subjective debt/equity test discussed at ¶602.8.1 above, there
is no risk that redemption of the debt may be treated as a dividend, since Code
§302 (stock redemption substantially equivalent to a dividend is taxed as a
dividend) applies only to stock, not to an instrument which is treated as debt for
tax purposes. However, where VC (or others) holds a "debt" instrument which
is treated as equity for tax purposes under the subjective debt/equity test, the
Code §302 rules apply to the redemption of such "preferred stock."

¶603.9   References

- Code §243
- Code §246A
- Code §301
- Code §302
- Code §305
- Code §318(a)
- Code §1059
- Treas. Reg. §1.305-5
- Ginsburg and Levin M&A book ¶¶1309.3, 1310

¶604   SUBORDINATED DEBT VS. PREFERRED STOCK

(1) Practical need for net worth points toward issuance of preferred stock.

- However, an SEC accounting rule (applicable only to public companies) requires that mandatorily redeemable preferred stock be carried on the balance sheet in a special section above net worth but below liabilities.
- There may be regulatory reasons for structuring a portion of a holder's investment as debt rather than stock. For example, where Newco is in the broadcasting business, FCC foreign ownership rules generally permit foreign investors (with FCC approval) to acquire debt convertible into a controlling share of Newco but do not permit an equivalent foreign equity investment.
- Similarly, where Newco is an S corporation, an entity or foreigner can generally own convertible debt or debt with warrants, but not stock, and indeed an S corporation can not issue preferred stock.

(2) A bankruptcy claim for debt ranks higher than for preferred stock, but there is risk that VC's debt claim will be equitably subordinated if VC owns substantial Newco equity and has used its equity position to cause Newco to act inequitably or unfairly to other creditors.

(3) With Newco debt which is subordinated to other creditors, an inter-creditor agreement should be carefully drafted to cover such issues as: (a) to which Newco third party debt is VC's debt claim subordinated (generally bank debt), (b) under what circumstances is there a suspension of VC's right to receive interest and principal payments on its Newco subordinated debt (generally during a default on the senior debt), and (c) under what circumstances must VC give back interest and principal payments erroneously made by Newco to VC during such a suspension period? Newco preferred stock can present all such issues, except (a).

(4) With debt, Newco is entitled to an interest deduction (if the purported debt qualifies as debt for tax purposes under the subjective debt/equity rules and satisfies the other 5 tests for interest deductibility, discussed in ¶602.8 above), but where Newco issues preferred stock, Newco cannot deduct dividend payments or preferred OID.

(5) Dividends received by a corporate holder of Newco preferred stock attract a 70%, 80%, or 100% dividends received deduction, but interest received by a corporate holder of a Newco debt instrument is fully taxable.

(6) Because different tax accounting rules apply, the timing and character of income to a holder from accrued but unpaid yield on the Newco instrument may differ depending on whether the instrument is treated as debt or equity for tax purposes. With a Newco debt instrument, both cash and accrual method holders generally are subject to constant-yield-to-maturity accrual of interest income under the Code's OID rules, whether or not the interest is paid in cash, paid in kind, or merely accrues and whether or not Newco has E&P. In contrast, with Newco preferred stock, (a) dividends (even when paid in cash) are taxable to the holder only to the extent of Newco's E&P (with excess dividends reducing the holder's

tax basis in the preferred stock) and (b) accrued but unpaid dividends generally are not includable currently in either a cash or accrual method holder's income, so long as the dividend is not payable in kind and the preferred stock terms are properly drafted.Moreover, to the extent accumulated but undeclared dividends on Newco's preferred stock have not previously been included in the holder's income, any resulting gain on a sale or redemption of the preferred stock is treated as CG. See ¶¶602.5, 603.5, and 603.7.2.

(7) Repayment of debt principal is tax free to the holder (to the extent of the holder's tax basis in the debt), but redemption of preferred stock may give rise to dividend treatment. See ¶603.8 above.

(8) If debt principal or interest is forgiven, the issuer generally has taxable income or is subject to tax attribute reduction. These consequences do not apply when stock becomes worthless or is canceled. See ¶803 below.

(9) A corporation may amortize the cost of issuing debt but mayamortize only certain "organizational expenses" of issuing stock.

CHAPTER 7

Structuring Consolidation of Fragmented Industry

VC identifies a fragmented industry, that is, an industry in which there are many small or reasonably small competitors and no or few market leaders. VC then recruits a top-flight management team with extensive experience in the industry.

VC and the management team form Newco as a "platform" to assemble a significant, ideally a leadership, presence in the fragmented industry by:

- acquiring strategically located industry players through a series of buyouts or roll-ups,
- starting up new businesses in those markets where there is no desirable target business or the existing target businesses in such market are over-priced, and
- amalgamating the buyouts and start-ups into a regionally or nationally important player in the otherwise fragmented industry.

Often the term platform is used where the consolidation begins with a reasonably large buyout of an established business, followed by numerous add-on acquisitions, and the term roll-up is generally used where there is no large initial acquisition but only a series of reasonably small acquisitions.

One important issue in properly incenting Newco's management is whether a Newco middle-management executive who is operating a particular business (as opposed to Newco's top policy makers) should receive only Newco stock *or* only stock in the Newco subsidiary such executive is operating *or* a combination.

Another crucial structuring issue for all the participants is whether to form Newco and/or its subsidiaries as C corporations or as tax flow-through entities (e.g., partnerships or LLCs none of which are subject to double tax). Where Newco is formed as a C corporation, Newco is generally subjected to federal income tax on its income at the corporate entity level, at rates ranging up to 35%. When Newco-C corporation distributes its after-tax accumulated income to its shareholders as dividends, individual shareholders are subjected to a second federal income tax—at OI rates ranging up to 38.6% for 2002 and 2003.

Thus, C corporation earnings are subjected to double tax under the U.S. federal income tax system for C corporations.[1] Indeed, even where the C corporation accumulates its after-tax income rather than distributing dividends (so that there is no shareholder-level tax on the C corporation's accumulated earnings), there is a second shareholder-level federal income tax (albeit at a 20% LTCG rate) when the shareholder sells his or her stock for a price which reflects the corporation's accumulated income, i.e., for a price which is larger than it would have been if the corporation had distributed its accumulated income, unless the shareholder retains the stock until his or her death produces SUB for the stock.[2]

This chapter discusses 7 alternative approaches to structuring the consolidation of a fragmented industry and reviews some of the principal pros and cons of each structure.

---

[1] One of the traditional methods for blunting the double tax imposed with respect to C corporations is the C corporation's payment of substantial deductible compensation to its shareholder-executives. However, compensation paid by a corporation is deductible only to the extent it constitutes "reasonable . . . compensation for personal services actually rendered." Excessive compensation (i.e., compensation in excess of this "reasonable" standard) to a shareholder is treated as a non-deductible dividend. Thus, where the economic arrangement between VC and E is that (1) Newco will pay E $100,000 per year as recompense for E's services and (2) VC and E will share Newco's profits in excess of $100,000 proportionately to their stockholdings, it is difficult to transmute Newco's taxable income in excess of $100,000 to deductible compensation when VC is not performing substantial services for Newco.

[2] A Bush administration 1/03 legislative proposal would, if enacted, (1) abolish the shareholder-level tax on dividends paid in 2003 and later by a C corporation to the extent of the corporation's after-tax profits earned in 2002 or later on which the corporation paid tax (either federal income tax or tax paid to a foreign country which qualifies for the U.S. foreign tax credit) ("taxed profits") and (2) increase shareholder-level tax basis in the corporation's stock to the extent of each shareholder's proportionate share of the corporation's taxed profits not paid out as dividends. Because future prospects for this controversial legislative proposal are highly uncertain, the text of this book is based on current law and does not further discuss this legislative proposal.

¶701 STRUCTURE #1: CORPORATE HOLDING COMPANY AND INDIVIDUAL CORPORATE SUBSIDIARIES

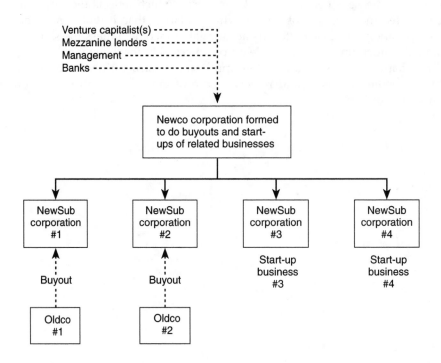

Note: One or more of the NewSubs may issue some debt and/or stock directly to subordinated lenders or management.

¶701.1 Factual Situation

(1) Newco corporation acquires a number (possibly dozens) of businesses in a previously fragmented industry, using the techniques explored in Chapter 5 dealing with buyouts. Newco corporation also starts-up one or more businesses in areas where it does not find suitable businesses available for purchase at an acceptable price, using the techniques explored in Chapter 2 dealing with start-ups.

(2) Newco corporation arranges debt and equity financing of various types (e.g., senior bank debt, subordinated debentures, preferred stock, and common stock) to fund the buyouts and start-ups described in (1) above.

(3) Some of Newco's debt and/or equity financing may go directly into one or more of Newco's subsidiaries. Hence, for example, a portion of a particular

NewSub's stock may be held by the management of that subsidiary or by the subordinated lenders to that subsidiary.

(4) Newco is a C corporation, because it can not meet the arbitrary requirements of subchapter S, including no entity shareholders (except estates and trusts and *after* 1997, charities and pension plans) and one class of stock. See ¶301 above. This is likely to be true because at least VC and subordinated lenders are likely to be entity shareholders of Newco.

If Newco were able to elect S status, the tax ramifications of structure #1 would be more like (but not identical to) structure #2 discussed at ¶702 below.

¶701.2 Analysis of Structure #1

Summary. The holding company (Newco) and each of the subsidiaries are corporate entities, thus affording Newco and each NewSub the maximum protection from the unpaid liabilities of any one business and affording Newco's shareholders the maximum protection from Newco's and the NewSubs' liabilities. So long as Newco is a C corporation and meets the 80-80 test with respect to its subsidiaries, one NewSub's income can be offset against another's losses for federal income tax purposes and funds can be freely transferred from one NewSub to another without a federal income tax liability. However, there is no tax-efficient method for selling a portion of Newco, and selling all of Newco will generally cause the buyer to take asset COB unless the sale is subjected to double tax.

¶701.2.1 Consolidated Federal Income Tax Return

As a C corporation, Newco can file a single consolidated federal income tax return including Newco and each subsidiary corporation as to which Newco's ownership meets the 80-80 test of Code §1504. By contrast, no consolidated federal income tax return is permissible under structure #2 (see ¶702 below), because no C corporation owns stock of the various NewSubs meeting the 80-80 test.

(1) Newco's ownership of a particular NewSub meets the 80-80 test so long as Newco (directly and/or indirectly through other members of its 80-80 affiliated group) owns:

- NewSub stock possessing at least 80% of the total combined voting power of NewSub's outstanding stock (the "80%-by-vote test") and
- NewSub stock with an FV of at least 80% of the FV of all NewSub's outstanding stock (the "80%-by-value test").

(2) For purposes of the 80%-by-value test:

(a) IRS's regulations treat "all shares of stock within a single class [as having] the same value" so that "control premiums and minority and blockage discounts . . . are not taken into account."

(b) A class of non-voting debt-like preferred stock will be ignored if it meets *all* of the following conditions:

- It is not entitled to vote.
- It is limited and preferred as to dividends and does not significantly participate in corporate growth.
- Its redemption and liquidation rights do not exceed its issue price plus a reasonable redemption or liquidation premium.
- It is not convertible into another class of stock.

(3) The Code defines the 80%-by-vote test as "ownership of stock [that] possesses at least 80% of the total voting power of [NewSub's] stock." For this purpose, IRS measures voting power by Newco's relative ability to elect members of New-Sub's board of directors.

Where Newco owns class A stock in NewSub which has the right to elect 4 NewSub directors while NewSub executives and subordinated lenders own class B stock in NewSub which has the right to elect 1 NewSub director (i.e., 20% of NewSub's 5 directors), Newco's ownership of NewSub stock meets the 80%-by-vote test. However, where the class B stock owned by NewSub's executives and subordinated lenders has the right to elect 2 (rather than 1) NewSub directors (i.e., 33% of NewSub's 6 directors), Newco's ownership of NewSub stock does not meet the 80%-by-vote test.

A 1999 Court of Appeals decision[1] denied Newco's right to file a consolidated return with NewSub where, although Newco owns stock possessing 80% or more of NewSub's voting power in terms of ability to elect directors, NewSub's certificate of incorporation empowers NewSub's minority shareholders (or the minority directors elected by them) to veto significant matters traditionally decided by a majority board vote. The court concluded that, although Newco's stock had the "facial power" to elect NewSub directors with 80% of NewSub directors' voting power, nevertheless the veto powers held by the minority shareholders and the minority directors elected by them allowed the minority shareholders "in essence . . . to veto . . . important matters . . . many [of which] lie at the core of the board's authority to run NewSub's business" and hence effectively reduced Newco's voting power to less than 80%. The court's decision does not, however, make clear whether granting the minority shareholders (or the minority directors elected by them) a veto power over any *one* decision traditionally determined by a majority of NewSub's board is fatal to Newco's ability to consolidate with NewSub, or whether the restrictions on decisions by a majority of NewSub's board must be significant in the aggregate (perhaps requiring the minority shareholders or the directors elected by them to have two, three, or more veto powers).

The case also does not make clear whether any contractual restriction on Newco's ability to vote its Class A NewSub stock freely (e.g., a voting trust or voting agreement), as opposed to a restriction imposed by NewSub's constitutional documents (i.e., certificate of incorporation and by-laws), would similarly be

---

¶701 [1] Alumax Inc. v. Commissioner, 165 F.3d 822, 99-1 U.S.T.C. ¶50,210 (11th Cir. 1999), affirming 109 T.C. 133 (1997).

fatal to Newco's ability to consolidate with NewSub (e.g., where Newco owns NewSub's Class A stock with the right to elect 4 NewSub directors while NewSub executives and subordinated lenders own NewSub Class B stock with the right to elect 1 NewSub director, but Newco agrees by contract to elect as one of its 4 directors a person designated by the Class B stockholders). However, in the wake of the *Alumax* decision, IRS will likely scrutinize any such arrangements more closely.

Interestingly, the court assumed without discussion that where NewSub's certificate of incorporation gives greater weight to certain directors' votes (e.g., two votes to each Class A director), such weighted voting power is taken into account in determining the relative voting power of the shareholders who elect those directors (e.g., if NewSub's Class A stock held by Newco elects 2 NewSub directors, each of whom has the right to cast 2 director votes, and NewSub's Class B stock held by minority shareholders elects 1 director, who has the right to cast 1 vote, Newco is credited with 4 director votes out of 5 and can file a consolidated return with NewSub).

(4) A complex set of IRS regulations sets forth certain circumstances when (for purposes of the 80-80 test) an option, warrant, convertible debenture, or similar instrument or right held by a third party with respect to NewSub stock will be treated as exercised where it would prevent Newco from satisfying the 80-80 test.

In general, such a third-party right to acquire NewSub stock is treated as exercised for this purpose. However, where a third-party right satisfies at least one of the following exceptions, it is not treated as exercised:

- Such a right held by an executive or other service provider in connection with the performance of services, so long as such right constitutes reasonable compensation and is not transferable except upon death.
- Such a right issued in connection with a "commercially reasonable" loan by a lender which is "actively and regularly engaged in the business of lending."
- Such a right exercisable for 24 months or less at an exercise price equal to at least 90% of the stock's FV, determined on the date of issuance (and in certain circumstances, on the date of a transfer or modification of such right).
- Such a right that is not "reasonably certain" to be exercised on the date of issue (and in certain circumstances, on the date of a transfer or modification of such right). IRS has taken the position that a right is reasonably certain to be exercised where it is 25% in the money (i.e., where the option exercise price is 75% or less of the stock's FV).

¶701.2.2   Offset of Income and Losses Within Consolidated Group

Where Newco C corporation files a consolidated federal income tax return, all the income and losses of the various members of Newco's group (i.e., the various corporate entities which meet the 80-80 test) can be freely offset against each other for federal income tax purposes, as if they were all in one entity.

Where NewSub #1 has losses and NewSub #2 has income, the income and losses can be offset, so that the consolidated group does not have to pay federal income tax on NewSub #2's income to the extent offset by NewSub #1's losses. As discussed at ¶702.2.1 and ¶702.2.2 below, this is *not* true for structure #2.

Where Newco borrows money at the parent level, so that it has substantial interest deductions, while the group's income is earned at the NewSub level, Newco's interest expense can be offset against each NewSub's income for federal income tax purposes. This is *not* true for structure #2.

State income tax law may differ from federal income tax law regarding consolidated returns. Some states prohibit a parent corporation and its subsidiaries from filing a consolidated *state* income tax return (perhaps unless they are engaged in a "unified" business). In such case, losses suffered by one NewSub or interest expense of Newco could not be offset against the income of other NewSubs.

- It may be possible to minimize this problem by merging 2 NewSubs (one expected to be profitable and one expected to suffer losses).
- It may be possible to shift the deduction for Newco's parent-level interest expense to the NewSubs by *either* (1) causing each NewSub to pay a reasonable but generous management fee to Newco *or* (2) causing Newco to supply a substantial part of the capital to each NewSub as junior subordinated debt, bearing a reasonable but generous interest rate. Through either or a combination of these approaches Newco realizes income (management fee income and/or interest income) to offset its interest expense on third-party loans at the Newco level while the NewSubs realize an equal deductible expense (management fee expense and/or interest expense) to offset their operating income.

¶701.2.3 Tax-Free Transfer of Funds Within Consolidated Group

Where Newco C corporation files a consolidated federal income tax return, each NewSub can pay dividends upstream to Newco without the imposition of any federal income tax.

Hence, Newco can freely withdraw money from a successful NewSub and contribute or loan such amount to a financially-strapped NewSub without federal income tax. This is not true for structure #2.

In a state where Newco and a particular NewSub are not allowed to file a consolidated state income tax return, there may be some state income tax on such upstream dividends.

¶701.2.4 Limitation on Amount of NewSub Stock Issued to Management and/or Subordinated Lenders

In order for a particular NewSub to be included in Newco's consolidated federal income tax return, Newco must meet the 80-80 test with regard to such NewSub. Hence, NewSub's executives, NewSub's subordinated lenders, and other persons can not (in the aggregate) own more than 20% by vote or by value of NewSub's stock (disregarding nonvoting straight preferred stock).

Persons other than Newco can own up to 20% of NewSub's stock plus, in certain circumstances, options, warrants, convertible debentures, and other such rights to acquire additional NewSub stock in the future. See ¶701.2.1(4) above regarding service provider rights to acquire future Newco stock, lender rights to acquire future Newco stock, 90%-24-month rights to acquire future Newco stock, etc.

See ¶701.2.1(3) above regarding the tax risk if Newco grants third parties the contractual right to designate one or more NewSub directors and such contractual right plus third-party-owned NewSub voting stock represents more than 20% of NewSub's voting power.

By contrast, under structures #2 and #3 there is no limitation on third-party ownership of NewSubs.

¶701.2.5 Limited Liability Protection for Newco's Owners

Because Newco is a corporation, its shareholders are generally not exposed on Newco's unpaid liabilities.

See ¶301.5 and ¶501.5.3 above for a discussion of exceptions under certain circumstances for piercing the corporate veil, CERCLA liability, unfunded pension liability, etc.

¶701.2.6 Newco's Limited Liability Protection from NewSub Obligations

Where the corporate entity owning one business (e.g., NewSub #1) falls upon hard financial times and is unable to pay its liabilities, corporate NewSub #1's unpaid liabilities are generally a claim only against assets owned by NewSub #1. Thus, the assets of Newco and the other NewSubs are generally insulated from NewSub #1's unpaid liabilities. This significant advantage follows from housing each business in a separate corporate subsidiary.

See ¶301.5 and ¶501.5.3 above for a discussion of piercing the corporate veil and several statutory doctrines that might cause Newco or the other NewSubs to be liable for NewSub #1's unpaid liabilities in certain circumstances.

With respect to structuring debt for borrowed money, where debt is incurred at the Newco parent level, such debt is a claim against all of Newco's assets, including its stock in all of the NewSub entities. On the other hand, where debt is incurred in a NewSub, the debt is a claim only against the particular NewSub which has incurred the debt (so long as neither Newco nor another NewSub has guaranteed the particular NewSub's debt). Hence with debt incurred at the NewSub level (and not guaranteed by any other entity), the failure of a particular NewSub's business does not threaten assets held by Newco or other NewSubs. For this reason, it may be desirable for Newco to provide sufficient equity to each NewSub so that it can incur its own debt without any guarantees from or cross-collateralization by other entities.

¶701.2.7 IPO or Tax-Free Merger of Newco

If Newco's shareholders decide to make a primary or secondary IPO of Newco stock or to merge Newco with another corporation tax free, there are no preliminary complications, because Newco is already a corporation. This is not true for structures #2 and #3 (where Newco partnership must be incorporated).

¶701.2.8 Sale of Newco

If Newco's shareholders decide to sell Newco C corporation in its entirety (e.g., to Bigco), it will be desirable from a federal income tax standpoint for them to sell Newco's stock.

Where a sale of Newco to Bigco is structured as a sale of Newco's stock, there is only one tax, imposed at the level of Newco's shareholders on their stock-sale gain.

By contrast, if Newco sold its assets (the stock of the various NewSubs) to Bigco and distributed the proceeds to Newco's shareholders, the sale would be subjected to double tax, i.e., Newco would pay corporate-level tax on its gain from selling NewSubs' stock and Newco's shareholders would then pay shareholder-level CG tax on receipt of the proceeds from Newco. Code §331.

Similarly, if each NewSub sold its assets to Bigco and distributed the proceeds to Newco, which in turn distributed the proceeds to its shareholders, the sale would be subjected to double tax, i.e., each NewSub would pay corporate-level tax on its gain from selling its assets (or Newco would pay such NewSub tax where a consolidated return is filed), there would be no tax at the Newco level on the liquidation of the NewSubs (Code §332), and Newco's stockholders would pay shareholder-level CG tax on receipt of the proceeds (Code §331).

Where Bigco buys Newco's stock from Newco's shareholders (including by way of a taxable reverse subsidiary merger), Bigco takes an SUB (equal to cost) for the stock of Newco but a COB for both the NewSub stock owned by Newco and the NewSub assets (absent a Code §338 election which would generally not be advantageous unless Newco and its subsidiaries had a substantial NOL—see ¶501.7 and ¶502.1.1 above). Similarly, where Bigco buys the stock of each of the NewSubs from Newco, Bigco takes an SUB (equal to cost) in the property purchased from Newco (i.e., NewSub stock) but a COB for the NewSub assets (absent a Code §338 or §338(h)(10) election). Only where Bigco buys assets from the various Newsubs (or buys stock of Newco or the NewSubs and makes a §338 or §338(h)(10) election) does Bigco obtain an SUB (equal to cost) for the NewSub assets.

In summary, the most tax-efficient way of selling Newco to Bigco is generally a sale of Newco stock, resulting in one CG tax (on Newco's shareholders) and asset COB for Newco's and each NewSub's assets. The alternative, a sale of each NewSub's assets, would result in double tax (at the NewSub level and on Newco's shareholders), but SUB for each NewSub's assets, which would generally not be economically attractive, unless Newco and its subsidiaries had a substantial NOL. See ¶501.7.4 above.

By contrast, there is a tax-efficient method for selling Newco in its entirety (i.e., asset SUB for buyer and only one level of tax on the sale) under structure #3.

¶701.2.9   Sale of Portion of Newco

If Newco C corporation decides to sell some of its businesses (e.g., to Bigco) but not all, i.e., to sell one or more NewSubs but retain and continue to operate others, there is no tax-efficient method of achieving this goal under structure #1.

This is because there is no way of eliminating Newco corporate-level federal income tax on the sale gain. Where Newco sells NewSub #1 to Bigco, Newco will bear corporate-level tax on the gain from such sale (whether Newco sells NewSub #1 stock or NewSub #1 sells its assets and liquidates tax-free into Newco under Code §332).

If Newco then retains the sales proceeds, there will be one tax on the sale (at the Newco level), and if Newco distributes the proceeds to its shareholders, there will be a second tax on the distribution (on Newco's shareholders). Newco can defer this second level of tax (on Newco's shareholders) by retaining the sales proceeds to (e.g.) pay down debt, make additional acquisitions, start-up additional businesses, etc.

Where Newco is selling only a portion of its assets, there is no procedure for avoiding Newco-level corporate federal income tax, as there was in the situation where Newco was being sold in its entirety (i.e., by a sale of Newco's stock, see ¶701.2.8 above).[2]

---

[2] If Newco is particularly patient, there are several methods of deferring the corporate-level tax on a sale of a portion of Newco's business:

- One is a sale of a Newco business to Bigco for Bigco installment notes under Code §453, to the extent Newco's assets qualify for Code §453 installment reporting.
- Another is for Newco to exchange all or a substantial part of its common stock in the NewSub being sold for NewSub preferred stock (in a tax-free recapitalization under Code §368(a)(1)(E)), with Bigco contributing to NewSub cash and/or businesses in exchange for NewSub common stock (and if Bigco is contributing appreciated businesses to NewSub, Bigco will probably want to acquire sufficient NewSub stock to invoke Code §351). However, the 1997 Tax Act adopted new rules treating an exchange of common stock or other appreciated assets for NQ Pfd stock as a taxable exchange, effective in general for exchanges after 6/8/97, making it much more difficult to effect a tax-free recapitalization or a Code §351 transaction. See ¶403.1(9)-(15) above.

By contrast, there is a modestly tax-efficient method for selling some of Newco's businesses under structure #2 (no corporate-level federal income tax and asset COB) and a very tax efficient method for selling a portion of Newco's businesses under structure #3 (no corporate-level federal income tax and also asset SUB for Bigco).

¶702   STRUCTURE #2: PARTNERSHIP OR LLC HOLDING COMPANY AND INDIVIDUAL CORPORATE SUBSIDIARIES

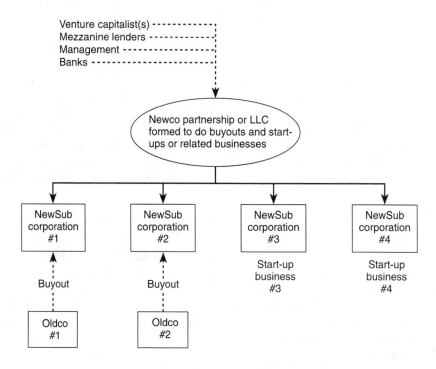

Note: One or more of the NewSubs may issue some debt and/or stock directly to subordinated lenders or management.

- A third is a drop-down of a NewSub business into a newly-formed partnership ("joint-venture partnership") in exchange for (e.g.) a large preferred partnership interest and a small common partnership interest (tax-free under Code §721), with Bigco contributing cash and/or businesses to joint-venture partnership in exchange for (e.g.) a large common partnership interest. See Ginsburg & Levin M&A book ¶1604.

¶702.1 Factual Situation

(1) Same as in ¶701.1 above, except that Newco is a partnership rather than a corporation. See ¶302 above and ¶1001 below for a discussion of partnership characteristics.

(2) Alternatively, Newco could be an LLC which qualifies for federal income tax purposes as a partnership. See ¶303 above for a discussion of LLC characteristics.

(3) Each Newsub is a C corporation, just as in ¶701 above.

¶702.2 Analysis of Structure #2

Summary. Because the holding company is a partnership or LLC, no consolidated federal income tax return is permitted, so that one incorporated NewSub's income can not be offset against another's losses for federal income tax purposes. Similarly, transfers of funds between separately incorporated NewSubs may trigger federal income tax. Each NewSub is a corporate entity, thus affording Newco's partners protection from the unpaid liabilities of a NewSub. However, when Newco is a partnership, Newco's GP is liable for Newco's unpaid liabilities. On the other hand, when Newco is an LLC, Newco's members enjoy basically the same protection from Newco's unpaid liabilities as they would have enjoyed were Newco a corporation.[1] There is a modestly tax-efficient method for selling a portion of Newco (no corporate-level federal income tax and asset COB). In a sale of all or a portion of Newco, the buyer will generally take asset COB unless the sale is subjected to double tax.

¶702.2.1 No Consolidated Federal Income Tax Return

Newco partnership/LLC can not file a consolidated federal income tax return with the various C corporation NewSubs, even where Newco owns 100% of their stock. This is because Code §1504 permits a consolidated return only where the parent entity is a C corporation.

¶702.2.2 No Offset of Income from One NewSub Against Losses of Newco or Another NewSub

Because Newco partnership/LLC and the NewSub C corporations can not file a consolidated federal income tax return, Newco's losses (e.g., from interest expense) can not be offset against the income of any NewSub corporation and

---

¶702   [1] By 1997 all 50 states and the District of Columbia had adopted LLC statutes.

any NewSub corporation's losses can not be offset against the income of any other NewSub corporation. This may make it undesirable to borrow at the Newco level.[2]

Each NewSub which has an NOL can carry it back 2 years and forward 20 years against its own income (subject to the Code §382 NOL tainting rules—see ¶809 below).

However, see ¶701.2.2 above, discussing methods for ameliorating this no-offset-of-income-and-losses problem by (1) a possible merger of a profitable and an unprofitable NewSub and (2) shifting deductions from Newco to the NewSubs, e.g., NewSub paying a management fee to Newco and/or Newco supplying a substantial part of the capital to each NewSub in the form of interest-bearing subordinated debentures.

¶702.2.3   Difficulties in Making Tax-Free Transfers of Funds Between Various NewSubs

Because Newco partnership/LLC and the NewSub C corporations can not file a consolidated federal income tax return, distributions from a NewSub to Newco will be fully subject to OI tax as dividends. Code §301.

Hence, Newco can not freely withdraw money from a successful NewSub and contribute or loan such amount to a financially-strapped NewSub without federal income tax.

A successful NewSub can loan money to Newco or to another NewSub, so long as the lender charges adequate interest and the loan qualifies as debt under the tax common-law debt/equity test. See Code §7872 regarding adequate interest and ¶602.8.1 above regarding the subjective debt/equity test.

¶702.2.4   No Limitation on Amount of NewSub Stock Issued to Management and/or Subordinated Lenders

Because Newco and its subsidiaries are not filing a consolidated federal income tax return, there is no need for Newco to comply with the 80-80 test with respect to the NewSubs, and hence there is no 20% limitation on the amount of NewSub stock third parties can own.

¶702.2.5   Limited Liability for Newco's Owners

If Newco is a partnership, its GP(s) will have unlimited liability for Newco's unpaid recourse liabilities. Newco's LPs, on the other hand, will be protected from such liabilities, subject to the ULPA and RULPA rules regarding LP participation in control or active management of Newco partnership. See ¶¶302.6 and 302.7 above

---

[2] Newco partnership and the NewSub corporation will also be unable to file a state consolidated return (even in those states which permit a parent corporation and its subsidiary corporations to file a consolidated return).

for a discussion of (1) GP and LP liability and (2) use of an S or C intermediary corporation to avoid such liability (including use of an S corporation owned by Newco's executives as Newco Partnership's GP).

If Newco is an LLC, Newco's members enjoy basically the same protection from Newco's unpaid liabilities as they would have enjoyed were Newco a corporation. See ¶303.3.

However, most of the enterprise's liabilities should be at the NewSub level. Since the various NewSubs will be corporations, Newco partnership's GP and LPs (and Newco LLC's members) have corporate limited liability protection with respect to liabilities incurred at the NewSub level. See, however, ¶¶301.5 and 501.5.3 above for a discussion of the doctrines (including piercing the corporate veil) that may cause a corporation's shareholders to be liable for its debts under certain circumstances.

It is generally desirable to avoid incurring liabilities at the Newco partnership level, except to the extent a contract creditor expressly agrees to look only to Newco's assets or a potential tort claim is adequately covered by insurance.

¶702.2.6   Newco Limited Liability Protection from NewSub Obligations

Because each business is housed in a separate corporate entity (e.g., NewSub #1), neither Newco nor the other NewSubs are exposed for the unpaid liabilities of NewSub #1, absent invocation of a doctrine that would cause a corporation's shareholders to be liable for its debts, as discussed at ¶301.5 and ¶501.5.3 above.

¶702.2.7   IPO or Tax-Free Merger of Newco

If Newco partnership's/LLC's equity owners decide to effectuate a primary or secondary IPO of Newco equity securities, it will generally be advisable first to incorporate Newco. Tax rules generally treat a publicly-traded partnership/LLC as a corporation for tax purposes (with several specific, limited exceptions). Code §7704.

If Newco partnership's/LLC's equity owners decide to merge Newco into another corporation tax-free, Newco must incorporate substantially in advance of the tax-free merger, because only a corporation (not a partnership or LLC) is permitted to use the Code §368 tax-free reorganization rules and the step-transaction doctrine precludes a tax-free incorporation of Newco immediately before the merger.

However, it is generally not necessary to incorporate Newco in order to effectuate a tax-free merger of Newco's assets into another corporation. Rather, because each of the NewSubs is already incorporated, Newco partnership or LLC can merge each of the NewSub corporations with another corporation in a series of tax-free mergers and Newco can then distribute the acquiring corporation's stock to Newco's equity owners tax free. See ¶1001.1(3) below for a tax issue which arises if the acquiring corporation's stock is publicly traded when Newco partnership/LLC distributes the stock to its equity owners.

¶702.2.8   Sale of Newco

If Newco partnership's/LLC's equity owners decide to sell Newco in its entirety (e.g., to Bigco), it will be desirable from a federal income tax standpoint for them to sell *either* the stock of each of the NewSub C corporations *or* the Newco equity interests.

Where the sale of Newco partnership/LLC to Bigco is structured as *either* a sale of the stock of each NewSub corporation *or* a sale of the equity interests in Newco, there is only one tax, imposed at the level of Newco's equity owners.

By contrast, if each NewSub corporation sells its assets to Bigco and distributes the proceeds to Newco partnership/LLC, the sale is subjected to double tax (whether or not Newco in turn distributes the proceeds to its equity owners), i.e., each NewSub pays corporate-level tax on its gain from selling its assets and Newco's equity owners pay CG tax on the proceeds distributed by a NewSub less Newco's tax basis in the NewSub's stock (Code §331).

Where Bigco buys the stock of each NewSub corporation, Bigco takes an SUB for the NewSub stock but a COB for the NewSub assets (absent a Code §338 election, which would generally not be advantageous except for a NewSub with a substantial NOL—see ¶¶501.7, 502.1.1, and 701.2.8 above). Where Bigco buys assets from the various NewSubs, Bigco takes an SUB for the NewSub assets.

In summary, the most tax-efficient way to sell Newco to Bigco is generally a sale of the stock of the various NewSubs or a sale of the equity interests in Newco, resulting in one CG tax (on Newco's equity owners) and asset COB for each NewSub's assets, similar to structure #1.

¶702.2.9   Sale of Portion of Newco

If Newco partnership/LLC decides to sell some of its businesses (e.g., to Bigco) but not all, i.e., to sell one or more C corporation NewSubs but retain and continue to operate others, this can be achieved in a way that is modestly tax-efficient (in contrast to structure #1 where Newco was a C corporation).

Newco can sell the stock of one or more NewSubs and there will be no corporate-level tax, because Newco is a flow-through entity. Thus, there will be tax only on Newco's equity owners (whether or not Newco distributes the sales proceeds). Even if Newco does distribute the sales proceeds to its equity owners, there will be no second level of tax. However, buyer will obtain asset COB, rather than asset SUB (absent a Code §338 election, which would generally not be tax advantageous unless NewSub has substantial NOLs). Hence this structure is more tax efficient than structure #1 above (single tax if Newco retains the sales proceeds and double tax if Newco distributes the sales proceeds, but asset COB for buyer in any event), but not as tax efficient as structure #3 below (single tax and buyer obtains asset SUB).

¶703   STRUCTURE #3: PARTNERSHIP OR LLC HOLDING COMPANY AND INDIVIDUAL PARTNERSHIP OR LLC SUBSIDIARIES

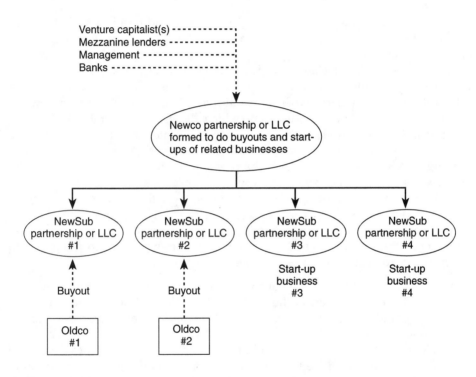

Note: One or more of the NewSubs may issue some debt and/or equity interests directly to subordinated lenders or management.

¶703.1   *Factual Situation*

(1) Same as ¶701 above, except that Newco is a partnership rather than a corporation and also each of the NewSubs is a partnership rather than a corporation. See ¶302 above or ¶1001 below for a discussion of partnership characteristics.

(2) In order for a NewSub to be a partnership, it must have at least 2 partners, i.e., at least one partner in addition to Newco.

Generally, one or more NewSub executives (or one or more S corporations owned by NewSub executives) or one or more NewSub subordinated lenders will be partners in a NewSub.

However, if Newco would be the only partner in a particular NewSub, Newco's equity owners could form a second partnership entity the ownership of which mirrors Newco ("Newco #2") and Newco #2 could own a small interest (e.g., 1%) of each NewSub which had no other second partner.

A less desirable approach to finding a second partner for such a NewSub is that another NewSub could be the second partner (holding a small interest, e.g., 1%) in the NewSub which had no other second partner. However, this approach can cause economic problems when a NewSub holding a 1% interest in one or more other NewSubs is sold separately from the NewSubs in which it holds a 1% interest.

(3) Alternatively, Newco and/or the NewSubs could be LLCs which qualify for federal income tax purposes as partnerships. See ¶303 above for a discussion of LLC characteristics.

Some states (such as Delaware) permit single-member LLCs. Effective 1/1/97, IRS generally permits a single-member LLC to be disregarded and treated as a sole proprietorship (where owned by an individual) or a division (where owned by an entity). Hence, if formed in a state which allows single-member LLCs, each NewSub LLC can be wholly owned by Newco and treated for federal tax purposes as a division of Newco (rather than as a separate entity). See ¶303.4.1. Thus, forming NewSub as an LLC avoids the problem discussed in (2) above, i.e., the need for a second partner where NewSub is formed as a partnership.

(4) Where an Oldco is being acquired in an asset purchase, this structure poses no front-end extra tax cost as compared to structure #1. However, where an Oldco is being acquired in a stock purchase with no Code §338 election (i.e., an asset COB transaction), there is a front-end tax cost to liquidating such Oldco corporation into a NewSub partnership (not present in structure #1).

- In structure #1, an Oldco corporation (acquired in a stock purchase with no §338 election) can be liquidated into a NewSub corporation without triggering corporate-level tax on such Oldco's asset appreciation under Code §332 and §337.
- However, in structure #3, liquidating an Oldco corporation into a NewSub partnership triggers federal income tax on the Oldco's asset appreciation under Code §331 and §336, in which case NewSub would take asset SUB.
- This front-end tax can, however, be avoided by keeping Oldco alive as a Newco corporate subsidiary (with asset COB), in which case, as to such Oldco corporation, the ongoing results would be more like structure #2 (corporate NewSub under partnership/LLC Newco) than like structure #3 (partnership/LLC NewSub under partnership/LLC Newco).

(5) When Newco partnership/LLC is owned in part by a TEO or an FP and there is no corporate entity between Newco and an operating business, the TEO will have taxable UBTI and the FP will have income taxable in the U.S. See ¶¶302.11 and 302.12.

¶703.2   *Analysis of Structure #3*

Summary. Because the holding company and the subsidiaries are all partnerships/LLCs, one NewSub's income can be offset against another's losses. For the same reason, there is no entity-level tax on Newco or the NewSubs and all of their net income and losses are reported on the tax returns of Newco's equity owners. Transfers of funds between various NewSubs can be effectuated without paying federal income tax. This structure permits a tax-efficient sale of all or part of Newco, i.e., asset SUB for buyer and only one tax on the sale. However, when Newco is GP of the NewSub partnerships, Newco is liable for all their unpaid liabilities, and when Newco is a partnership, its GP is liable for Newco partnership's unpaid recourse liabilities. On the other hand, when the NewSubs are LLCs, Newco enjoys basically the same protection from NewSub unpaid liabilities as Newco would have enjoyed were the NewSubs corporations, and when Newco is an LLC, its equity owners enjoy such protection.

¶703.2.1   No Entity-Level Tax

A partnership or LLC is a flow-through entity. Hence Newco's federal income tax return will reflect its share of each NewSub's income and losses. And all of Newco's income and losses (including its share of all the NewSubs' income and losses) will be reported on the tax returns of Newco's equity owners.

¶703.2.2   Offset of Income and Losses

The income and losses of all the NewSub partnerships/LLCs allocable to Newco plus the income and losses of Newco partnership/LLC are offset against each other and the net amount is reported on the federal income tax returns of Newco's equity owners.

¶703.2.3   Tax-Free Transfer of Funds Between Businesses

Because Newco and the NewSubs are all partnerships/LLCs, funds can generally flow freely between them without federal income tax.

¶703.2.4   No Limitation on Amount of NewSub Ownership
Interest Issued to Management and/or
Subordinated Lenders

Because Newco and the NewSubs are partnerships/LLCs and hence are not filing a consolidated federal income tax return, there is no 20% limitation on the amount of a NewSub's ownership interest third parties can own.

¶703.2.5   Limited Liability Protection for Newco's Owners

When Newco is a partnership, its GP will have unlimited liability for Newco's unpaid recourse liabilities. Its LPs, on the other hand, will be protected from such liabilities, subject to the ULPA and RULPA rules regarding LP participation in control or active management of Newco partnership. See ¶¶302.6 and 302.7 for a discussion of (1) GP and LP liability and (2) use of an intermediary S or C corporation to avoid such liability (including use of an S corporation owned by Newco's executives as Newco partnership's GP).

Moreover, when the NewSubs are partnerships, if Newco is GP of each NewSub, Newco will be liable for the NewSubs' unpaid recourse liabilities.

It may well be possible for the persons in control of Newco partnership to avoid GP liability with respect to both Newco partnership and the NewSub partnerships by forming a separate corporate entity ("GP Corporation") or separate LLC ("GP LLC"), owned by Newco partnership's equity owners (in the same ratio in which they own Newco), to act as (1) GP of Newco partnership and (2) GP of each of the NewSub partnerships, with GP Corporation or GP LLC holding a small (e.g., 1%) equity interest in Newco partnership and in each of the NewSub partnerships and with Newco partnership holding a 99% limited partnership interest in each NewSub partnership. See ¶¶302.6 and 302.7 above regarding use of a C or S corporate or LLC intermediary to limit GP liability. If GP corporation is a C corporation, flow-through tax treatment would be lost (and a corporate-level tax imposed) on the portion of Newco's and each NewSub's taxable income (e.g., 1%) allocated to GP Corporation.

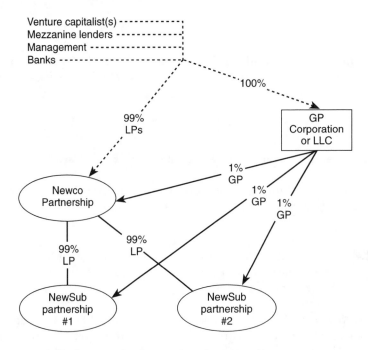

When Newco is an LLC, its equity owners enjoy basically the same protection from Newco's unpaid liabilities as they would have enjoyed were Newco a corporation, and when the NewSubs are LLCs, Newco (as an equity owner of the NewSubs) enjoys such protection. See ¶303.3 above. Moreover, so long as NewSub LLC is formed in a state which permits single-member LLCs, the problem discussed above—i.e., the need for a second partner where NewSub is formed as a partnership—is avoided.

¶703.2.6 Newco Limited Liability Protection from Obligations of NewSub

See ¶703.2.5 above.

¶703.2.7 IPO or Tax-Free Merger of Newco

If Newco partnership's/LLC's equity owners decide to effectuate a primary or secondary IPO of Newco equity securities, it will generally be advisable first to incorporate Newco. Tax rules generally treat a publicly-traded partnership/LLC as a corporation for tax purposes (with several specific, limited exceptions). Code §7704.

If Newco partnership's/LLC's equity owners decide to merge Newco with another corporation tax-free, Newco must incorporate substantially in advance of the tax-free merger, because only a corporation (not a partnership or LLC) is permitted to use the Code §368 tax-free reorganization rules and the step-transaction doctrine precludes a tax-free incorporation of Newco immediately before the merger.

¶703.2.8 Sale of Newco

If Newco partnership's/LLC's equity owners decide to sell Newco in its entirety (e.g., to Bigco), a tax-efficient result can be achieved by selling *either* the assets of each NewSub *or* the equity interests of each NewSub *or* the equity interests in Newco. Under any of these 3 approaches, Bigco obtains asset SUB while there is only one federal income tax on the sale, on Newco's equity owners (except to the extent of an intermediary C corporation's GP interest in Newco and/or the NewSubs). See ¶302 above. This is a more tax-efficient result than in structures #1 and #2 above.[1]

¶703 [1]However, to the extent the sale produces OI, the top individual 2002 and 2003 tax rate (generally 38.6%) is higher than both top corporate rate (35%) and the individual LTCG rate (generally 20%).

There may in some cases be differences in tax result (i.e., amount of gain which is OI rather than CG) depending on whether there is an asset sale or a sale of partnership/LLC interests. *See* Code §741 and §751.

¶703.2.9   Sale of Portion of Newco

If Newco partnership/LLC decides to sell some but not all of its businesses (e.g., to Bigco), i.e., to sell one or more NewSub partnerships/LLCs but retain and continue to operate others, there is a tax-efficient way to do it. Newco can sell *either* the NewSub's assets *or* the equity interests in the NewSub. Under either of these approaches, Bigco takes asset SUB while there is only one federal income tax on the sale, on Newco's equity owners (except to the extent of an intermediary C corporation's GP interest in Newco and/or the NewSub). This result (no corporate-level federal income tax and also asset SUB) is a far more tax-efficient result than obtains in structure #1 (corporate-level federal income tax and asset COB) and somewhat more tax efficient than structure #2 (no corporate-level federal income tax and asset COB).

¶704   STRUCTURE #4: SINGLE CORPORATE STRUCTURE

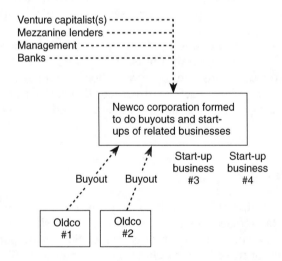

¶704.1   *Factual Situation*

(1)   Same as in ¶701 above, except that all the buyouts and start-ups are housed in a single C corporate entity, there is no holding company, and there are no subsidiaries.

(2)   All of the debt and equity financing for each business must be housed in one entity (Newco), because there are no NewSub entities to issue stock or debt to the executives who manage a particular business or the subordinated lenders to a particular business.

(3)   Newco is not likely to meet the arbitrary requirements for an S election, since (among other reasons) VC and subordinated lenders are likely to be Newco entity shareholders. If Newco were able to elect S status, the tax ramifications of structure #4 would be more like (but not identical to) structure #5 discussed in ¶705 below.

¶704.2   Analysis of Structure #4

Summary. Because a single C corporate entity holds all of the businesses, the income and losses of the various businesses are offset for federal income tax purposes, and there is no federal income tax on funds transferred among the businesses. Newco's shareholders have corporate limited liability protection from Newco's unpaid liabilities. However, Newco is liable for the unpaid liabilities of each business. Finally, there is no tax-efficient way to sell a part of Newco, and a sale of Newco as a whole will generally cause buyer to take asset COB unless the sale is subjected to double tax.

¶704.2.1   One Federal Income Tax Return

Newco C corporation will file a single federal income tax return covering the income and losses for each of the buyout and start-up businesses.

¶704.2.2   Offset of Income and Losses Within Single Income Tax Return

Because Newco C corporation files a single federal income tax return covering all the businesses, each business's income and losses are amalgamated.

State income tax laws vary on the reporting of a single corporation's profits and losses from multiple businesses conducted in more than one state. In most jurisdictions (i.e., the allocation jurisdictions), Newco reports a portion of its net income (or loss) from all of its activities based on the percentage of its property, payroll, and sales in such jurisdiction. In some jurisdictions (i.e., the separate accounting jurisdictions), however, Newco reports the income (or loss) on the particular business conducted in such jurisdiction.

¶704.2.3   Tax-Free Transfer of Funds Between Businesses

Newco, as a single C corporate entity, can freely transfer funds between businesses within the single corporate entity without the imposition of federal income tax.

¶704.2.4 No Ability to Issue Stock of Particular Business to Management and/or Subordinated Lenders

There is no limitation on the amount of Newco stock which may be issued to management and/or subordinated lenders.

However, because all the businesses are in one corporate entity, there is no ability to issue any stock to management and/or subordinated lenders with respect to a particular business. On the other hand, it would be feasible to issue an SAR or right to receive contingent interest payments based on the earnings or FV of a particular business unit within Newco. There are also circumstances where Newco can issue "tracking stock" to management of or subordinated lenders to a particular business, i.e., a separate class of Newco stock where some elements of the stock's value track the success of a specified business (e.g., dividends based on the earnings of business #1).

¶704.2.5 Limited Liability Protection for Newco's Owners

Because Newco is a corporation, its shareholders are generally entitled to protection from Newco's unpaid liabilities. See ¶701.2.5 above.

¶704.2.6 No Newco Limited Liability Protection from Obligations of Particular Business

Because all of the buyout and start-up businesses are housed in Newco (rather than in corporate subsidiaries), the unpaid liabilities of any one failed or failing business are a claim against all of Newco's assets, i.e., no business has any insulation against the liabilities of any other business.

¶704.2.7 IPO or Tax-Free Merger of Newco

There are no necessary preliminary complications to an IPO or tax-free merger of Newco C corporation. See ¶701.2.7 above.

¶704.2.8 Sale of Newco

The most tax-efficient way to sell Newco C corporation (e.g., to Bigco) is generally a sale of Newco's stock, resulting in one CG tax (on Newco's shareholders) and COB for Newco's assets. See ¶701.2.8 above.

¶704.2.9   Sale of Portion of Newco

There is no tax-efficient way to sell some but not all of Newco C corporation's businesses (e.g., to Bigco). See the discussion at ¶701.2.9 above, except that here Newco can sell to Bigco only the assets of a business unit, not the stock of a NewSub.[1]

¶705   STRUCTURE #5: SINGLE PARTNERSHIP OR LLC STRUCTURE

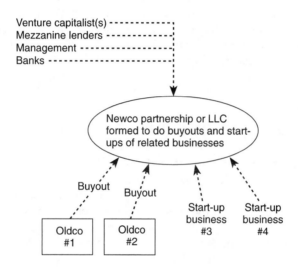

¶704   [1] If Newco is particularly patient, there are several methods for deferring the corporate-level tax on a sale of a portion of Newco's businesses to Bigco:

- One is a sale of Newco businesses for Bigco installment notes under Code §453, to the extent Newco's assets qualify for Code §453 installment reporting.
- Another is a drop-down of a Newco business into a newly-formed partnership ("joint-venture partnership") in exchange for (e.g.) a large preferred partnership interest and a small common partnership interest (tax-free under Code §721), with Bigco contributing cash and/or businesses to joint-venture partnership in exchange for (e.g.) a large common partnership interest. See Ginsburg & Levin M&A book ¶1604.
- A third is a drop-down of the business into a newly-formed corporation ("joint-venture corporation") in exchange for (e.g.) a large amount of preferred stock and a small amount of common stock (tax-free under Code §351), with Bigco contributing cash and/or businesses to joint-venture corporation in exchange for (e.g.) a large amount of common stock. However, the 1997 Tax Act adopted new rules treating a Code §351 contribution of property to a corporation in exchange for NQ Pfd stock as a taxable exchange, effective in general for exchanges after 6/8/97. See ¶403.1(9) through (15) above discussing NQ Pfd. Hence, if this third alternative is used, it is important that any preferred stock received by Newco be structured to avoid NQ Pfd characterization.

¶705.1 *Factual Situation*

(1) Same as in ¶704 above, except that all the buyouts and start-ups are housed in a single partnership (rather than a corporate) entity. See ¶302 above or ¶1001 below for a discussion of partnership characteristics.

(2) All of the debt and equity financing for each business must be housed in one entity, because there are no NewSub entities to issue stock or debt to the executives who manage a particular business or the subordinated lenders to a particular business.

(3) Alternatively, Newco could be an LLC which qualifies for federal income tax purposes as a partnership. See ¶303 above for a discussion of LLC characteristics.

(4) Where an Oldco is being acquired in a stock purchase (and no Code §338 election is permissible because the buyer is not a corporation), i.e., an asset COB transaction, there is a front-end tax cost to liquidating such Oldco corporation into Newco partnership, as described in ¶703.1(4) above.

(5) When Newco partnership/LLC is owned in part by a TEO or an FP, see ¶703.1(5) above.

¶705.2 *Analysis of Structure #5*

Summary. Because a single partnership/LLC entity holds all the businesses, the income and losses of the various businesses are offset for federal income tax purposes, and there is no federal income tax on fund transfers among the businesses. For the same reason, there is no entity-level tax on Newco and all of its income and losses are reported on the tax returns of Newco's equity owners. This structure permits a tax-efficient sale of all or part of Newco, i.e., asset SUB for buyer and only one tax on the sale. However, when Newco is a partnership, its GP is liable for Newco's unpaid recourse liabilities. On the other hand, when Newco is an LLC, Newco's equity owners enjoy basically the same protection from Newco's unpaid liabilities as they would have enjoyed were Newco a corporation.

¶705.2.1 No Entity-Level Tax

A partnership/LLC is a flow-through entity. Hence Newco's income and losses will be reported on the tax returns of Newco's equity owners.

¶705.2.2 Offset of Income and Losses

The income and losses of all the businesses are offset against each other, and the net amount is reported on the federal income tax returns of Newco's equity owners.

¶705.2.3   Tax-Free Transfer of Funds Between Businesses

Newco, as a single entity, can freely transfer funds between businesses without the imposition of federal income tax. In any event, a flow-through entity and its equity owners can generally freely transfer funds in and out of partnership/LLC solution without federal income tax.

¶705.2.4   No Ability to Issue Ownership Interests in Particular Business to Management and/or Subordinated Lenders

There is no limitation on the amount of Newco ownership interests which may be issued to management and subordinated lenders.

However, because all the businesses are in one entity, there is no ability to issue any direct ownership interests to management and/or subordinated lenders in a particular business. On the other hand, it would be feasible to issue an SAR or right to receive contingent interest payments based on the earnings or FV of a particular business unit within Newco. There are also circumstances where Newco partnership can issue "tracking partnership/LLC interests" to management of or subordinated lenders to a particular business, i.e. , a Newco partnership/LLC interest where some elements of the interest's value tracks the success of a specified business (e.g., annual distributions based on the earnings of business #1).

¶705.2.5   Limited Liability Protection for Newco's Equity Owners

When Newco is a partnership, its GP will have unlimited liability for Newco's unpaid recourse liabilities. Its LPs, on the other hand, will be protected from such liabilities, subject to ULPA and RULPA rules regarding LP participation in control or active management of Newco partnership. See ¶¶302.6 and 302.7, and ¶703.2.5 above for a discussion of GP and LP liability.

It may well be possible for the persons in control of Newco partnership to avoid GP liability by forming a separate corporate entity ("GP Corporation") or separate LLC ("GP LLC"), owned by Newco partnership's equity owners (in the same ratio in which they own Newco), to act as GP of Newco partnership, with GP Corporation or GP LLC holding a small (e.g., 1%) equity interest in Newco partnership. See ¶703.2.5 above regarding such use of an intermediary corporate entity to limit GP liability. In this case flow-through tax treatment would be lost (and a corporate-level tax imposed) on the portion of Newco's taxable income (e.g., 1%) allocated to a GP Corporation which is a C corporation.

When Newco is an LLC, its equity owners enjoy basically the same protection from Newco's unpaid liabilities as they would have enjoyed were Newco a corporation. See ¶303.3 above.

¶705.2.6   Protection from Obligations of a Particular Business

Because all of the buyouts and start-ups are housed in Newco, the unpaid liabilities of any one failed or failing business are a claim against all of Newco's assets, i.e., no business has any insulation against the liabilities of any other business.

¶705.2.7   IPO or Tax-Free Merger of Newco

There are necessary preliminary complications (incorporation of Newco partnership/LLC) to an IPO or tax-free merger of Newco with another corporation. See ¶703.2.7 above.

¶705.2.8   Sale of Newco

If Newco partnership's/LLC's equity owners decide to sell Newco in its entirety (e.g., to Bigco), a tax-efficient result can be achieved by selling *either* Newco's assets *or* the equity interests in Newco. In either of these 2 approaches, Bigco takes asset SUB while there is only one federal income tax on the sale, on Newco's equity owners (except to the extent of an intermediary C corporation's GP interest in Newco). This is a more tax-efficient result than in structures #1, #2, and #4 above.[1]

¶705.2.9   Sale of Portion of Newco

If Newco partnership/LLC decides to sell some of its businesses (e.g., to Bigco) but not all, there is a tax-efficient way to do it. Newco can sell the assets of such business, in which case Bigco will take asset SUB while there is only one tax on the sale, on Newco's equity owners. This is a more tax-efficient result than is achieved in structures #1 and #4.

¶705   [1]However, to the extent the sale produces OI, the top individual 2002 and 2003 tax rate (generally, 38.6%) is higher than both the top corporate rate (35%) and the individual LTCG rate (generally 20%).

There may in some cases be differences in tax result (i.e., amount of gain which is OI rather than CG and amount of CG which is STCG rather than LTCG) depending on whether there is an asset sale or a sale of partnership/LLC interests. *See* Code §741 and §751.

¶706 STRUCTURE #6: NO HOLDING COMPANY—DIRECT OWNERSHIP OF INDIVIDUAL CORPORATIONS BY SHAREHOLDERS

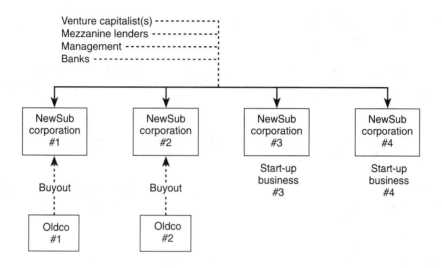

Note: The lenders to and shareholders in one NewSub may vary somewhat from the other NewSubs.

¶706.1 Factual Situation

(1) Same as in ¶701 above, except that no holding company is formed. Rather, each buyout or start-up is housed in a separate free-standing C corporation owned by the VC(s) and others.

(2) Each NewSub's debt and equity financing is housed directly in that NewSub.

(3) The shareholders of each NewSub may vary. For example, the executives who manage a particular business may hold stock only in the NewSub which owns that business or such executives may own a larger equity share in the NewSub which owns that business and a smaller equity stake in the other NewSubs. Similarly, a subordinated lender may hold stock only in the NewSub to which it has made a loan.

(4) The various NewSubs are not likely to meet the arbitrary requirements for S elections, since (among other reasons) VC and subordinated lenders are likely to be entity shareholders of the NewSubs. If the NewSubs were able to elect S status, the tax ramifications of structure #6 would be more like (but not identical to) structure #7 described in ¶707 below.

¶706.2 *Analysis of Structure #6*

¶706.2.1 No Consolidated Federal Income Tax Return

As in ¶702.2.1 above, no consolidated federal income tax return is permitted.

¶706.2.2 No Offset of Income from One NewSub Against Losses of Another NewSub

As in ¶702.2.2 above, each NewSub files its own corporate federal income tax return and can not offset the losses of one NewSub against the income of another.

¶706.2.3 Difficulties in Making Tax-Free Transfers of Funds Between Various NewSubs

As in ¶702.2.3 above, dividends from a Newsub to the shareholders will be fully subject to OI tax.

¶706.2.4 No Limitation on Amounts of NewSub Stock Issued to Management and/or Subordinated Lenders

As in ¶702.2.4 above, there is no 20% limitation on the amount of NewSub stock third parties can own. Indeed, because there is no holding partnership over the various NewSubs, the ownership of the various NewSubs' stock can be as disparate as the parties desire.

¶706.2.5 Generally No Newco Entity-Level Liabilities

Because there is no Newco holding entity over the NewSubs, there should generally be no holding-entity-level liabilities.

However, if one or more of the NewSub shareholders (singly or in concert) engage in a negligent or wrongful act toward a third party or undertake a contractual liability to a third party (e.g., borrow money to finance a NewSub or guarantee a NewSub debt), such shareholders will generally be directly liable to the third person.

Most of the enterprise's liabilities should be at the NewSub level. Since the various NewSubs will be corporations, the shareholders should enjoy corporate limited liability, subject to doctrines such as piercing the corporate veil. See ¶301.5 and ¶501.5.3 above.

¶706.2.6   NewSub Limited Liability Protection from Obligations of Another NewSub

As in ¶702.2.6 above, because each business is housed in a separate corporate entity, no NewSub should be exposed for the unpaid liabilities of another NewSub, subject to doctrines such as piercing the corporate veil.

¶706.2.7   IPO or Tax-Free Merger of the Enterprise

As in ¶702.2.7 above, there are necessary preliminary complications to an IPO of the enterprise (i.e., incorporation of a Newco to hold the stock of the NewSubs). However, there is no necessity for preliminary complications to a tax-free merger of the enterprise with another corporation, because each NewSub corporation can merge tax-free with another corporation under Code §368.

¶706.2.8   Sale of the Enterprise

As in ¶702.2.8 above, a sale of the stock of the NewSubs will result in asset COB for Bigco but only one tax on the sale, at the shareholder level.

¶706.2.9   Sale of Portion of the Enterprise

As in ¶702.2.9 above, there is a modestly tax-efficient way to sell a portion of the enterprise, i.e., the shareholders can sell the stock of one or more NewSubs, resulting in asset COB for buyer, rather than asset SUB (absent a Code §338 election, which would generally not be tax advantageous unless NewSub has substantial NOLs) with federal income tax only at the shareholder level.

¶707 STRUCTURE #7: NO HOLDING COMPANY— DIRECT OWNERSHIP OF INDIVIDUAL PARTNERSHIPS OR LLCs BY OWNERS

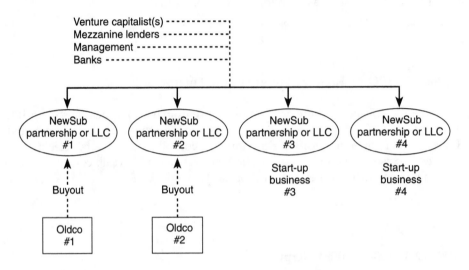

Note: The lenders to and owners of one NewSub may vary somewhat from the other NewSubs.

¶707.1 Factual Situation

(1) Same as in ¶706 above, except that each NewSub is a partnership. See ¶302 above or ¶1001 below for a discussion of partnership characteristics.

(2) Alternatively, the NewSubs could be LLCs which qualify for federal income tax purposes as partnerships. See ¶303 above for a discussion of LLC characteristics.

(3) When an Oldco is being acquired in a stock purchase with no Code §338 election (i.e., an asset COB transaction), there is a front-end tax cost to liquidating such Oldco corporation into a NewSub partnership, as described at ¶703.1(4) above.

(4) When NewSub partnership/LLC is owned in part by a TEO or an FP, see ¶703.1(5) above.

¶707.2 Analysis of Structure #7

¶707.2.1 No Entity-Level Tax

Same as in ¶703.2.1 above.

¶707.2.2   Offset of Income and Losses

Same as in ¶703.2.2 above.

¶707.2.3   Tax-Free Transfer of Funds Between Businesses

Same as in ¶703.2.3 above.

¶707.2.4   No Limitation on Amount of NewSub Ownership Interests Issued to Management and/or Subordinated Lenders

Same as in ¶703.2.4 above.

¶707.2.5   Limited Liability Protection for Enterprise's Equity Owners

Same as in ¶703.2.5 above, except that there is no holding entity.

¶707.2.6   Newco Limited Liability Protection from Obligations of NewSub

Same as ¶703.2.5 above, except that there is no Newco holding entity.

¶707.2.7   IPO or Tax-Free Merger of Newco

Same as in ¶703.2.7 above.

¶707.2.8   Sale of Enterprise

Same as in ¶703.2.8 above.

¶707.2.9   Sale of Portion of the Enterprise

Same as in ¶703.2.9 above.

¶708   OTHER KEY ISSUES

Generally the same as discussed in Chapters 2 through 5 above.

¶709   REFERENCES

- Code §1504
- Ginsburg & Levin M&A book ¶211 through ¶211.2.3.2 and ¶211.2.4
- References from ¶¶302.15 and 303.6 of this book

CHAPTER 8

Structuring Turn-Around Investment in Overleveraged or Troubled Company

Chapter 8. Structuring Troubled Company Turn-Around

VC has identified a company ("Badco") experiencing significant financial difficulties. Several years ago Badco (then called Newco) made a highly-leveraged buyout, as described in Chapter 5. However, Badco's business has not performed to expectations since the buyout, and hence Badco has not been able to service its large (and compounding) acquisition debt and does not expect to be able to do so near term.

VC is seeking to arrange an infusion of new "turn-around" capital into Badco as part of a "shared-pain" debt restructuring or workout for Badco. In this shared-pain restructuring, Badco plans to renegotiate its old debt by stretching out principal maturities, reducing interest rates, stretching out interest payments, and also canceling a portion of the debt. To induce certain of its old creditors to participate in the debt restructuring, Badco may issue shares of Badco stock to those creditors.

VC plans to invest new "turn-around" capital into Badco only if Badco's old creditors participate in the restructuring as described above. Understanding this, Badco's creditors are encouraged to participate, because their retained old debt will be more secure only if Badco receives new capital from VC.

VC intends to complete this shared-pain restructuring and simultaneously to bring new and more capable management to Badco. VC believes that Badco's business is basically sound, so that, with new management and an improved capital structure, Badco will prosper and its value will grow geometrically.

In one version of this case, VC was also the original sponsor of Badco's unfortunate highly-leveraged buyout several years ago and hence already is a large Badco shareholder. In another version, VC is new to the scene at the time Badco is seeking turn-around financing. The issues are generally the same in either event, except that in the former case there is more pressure on VC to make the new turn-around investment in order to protect both its original investment and its business reputation.

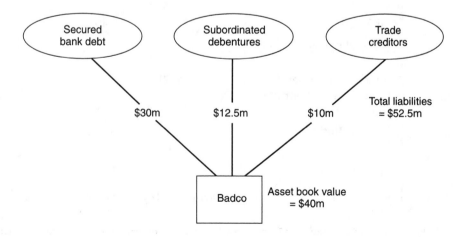

¶801 THE FAILED BUYOUT

(1) In the leveraged buyout described in Chapter 5 (as slightly altered for purposes of this Chapter 8[1]) Newco acquired Target in a highly-leveraged buyout for $50 million, borrowing $42.5 million of the purchase price (and obtaining the other $7.5 million by issuing Newco common and preferred stock) and assumed $10 million of Target's trade debt.

(2) At the time of the buyout, Newco and its VC sponsors harbored abundant optimism about the future of Target's business, believing that with Newco's superior team of executives, incented by 20% of Newco's common stock, plus the vigilant supervision of the VC sponsors, Newco's success was assured.

(3) Unfortunately, despite these well laid plans, all did not actually proceed as Newco and its VC sponsors envisioned. After the buyout, events went badly for Newco:

- Newco lost several key customers.
- One of Newco's factories was badly damaged by an errant cyclone.
- None of Newco's R&D worked out as well as expected.
- Newco suffered $20 million of accounting losses.
- Several of Newco's key executives left after repeated conflicts with Newco's VC sponsors.
- Newco ran out of cash and now is not able to meet its obligations as they mature.
- In short, Newco has turned into "Badco."

(4) **Badco's pre-restructuring balance sheet** is now as follows:

Assets	Amount (millions)	
Cash	$ 1.0	
Other assets	39.0	
Total assets		$ 40.0
Liabilities and Net Worth		
Liabilities:		
Secured bank lender	$ 30.0	
Subordinated debentures	12.5	
Trade creditors	10.0	
Total liabilities		$ 52.5

¶801 [1] For purposes of this Chapter 8, the buyout transaction described in Chapter 5 is simplified in the following respects:

- The subordinated debenture holders purchased $12.5 million of subordinated debentures (rather than buying $12.5 million of Newco subordinated debentures plus $.1 million of Newco common stock) and did not acquire any Newco stock or rights to acquire Newco stock,
- Newco issued a total of $7.5 million of common and preferred stock ($6.5 million of preferred stock to VCs and $1 million of common stock, 80% to VCs and 20% to management),

Net worth:

VC preferred stock	$ 6.5	
Common stock held by		
management and VCs (700 shares)	1.0	
Accumulated deficit	(20.0)	
Net worth		(12.5)
Total liabilities and net worth		$ 40.0

Note: Badco's balance sheet is stated in accordance with GAAP. Hence Badco's assets are carried at cost less depreciation, *not at FV*, and contingent liabilities not subject to reasonable estimation are omitted.

(5) It is now essential for Badco to:

- Raise additional cash, *either* (a) from the VCs who originally sponsored Badco (then Newco) in its now failed acquisition of Target *or* (b) if the original sponsoring VCs are unwilling or unable to invest more money in Badco (perhaps because they are out of money or have reached the limit on the amount they are permitted to invest in a single portfolio company), from one or more new VCs willing to do risky turn-around financing for a troubled company.
- Convince Badco's existing creditors to slim down their creditor claims, perhaps in exchange for a partial cash payment, new Badco debt instruments, or even some Badco stock.

(6) Unless otherwise stated, Badco is a C corporation in this chapter.

¶802   ALTERNATIVE WORKOUT TRANSACTIONS

¶802.1   *Transaction #1—Partial Payments to Creditors in Cash, New Debt, and Common Stock Where Badco Has No Market-Traded Debt Securities*

In transaction #1, Badco has no market-traded debt securities, and Badco, its creditors, its shareholders, and the VCs effectuate the shared-pain workout as follows:

¶802.1.1 $8 Million New Equity

Badco's original VCs, intending to protect their already substantial investment in Badco (or, alternatively, one or more new VCs, intending to make a new

---

- Newco took on $10 million of Target trade debt in the buyout, and
- The subordinated debentures are subordinated to debt for borrowed money (i.e., Newco's bank lender) but not to Newco's trade creditors.

high-risk, high-reward turn-around investment in Badco) contribute $8 million in new cash to Badco and receive in exchange:

- $7.9 million face of new senior preferred stock, mandatorily redeemable 10 years after issuance, *plus*
- 1,000 new common shares (at a stated price of $100 per common share, i.e., an aggregate of $0.1 million).

¶802.1.2 Stock Cancellations

Badco's original VCs surrender without payment 50% of their $6.5 million of old preferred (i.e., $3.25 million) and extend the mandatory redemption date for the remaining $3.25 million of old preferred to the 12th anniversary of the restructuring.

Badco's old common shareholders (management and the old VCs) surrender 50% of their 1,000 old common shares, retaining 500 common shares.

¶802.1.3 Creditor Compromises

Secured bank. Badco's most senior creditor, the secured bank lender, exchanges its $30 million of old secured notes for $1 million of cash *plus* $28 million of new secured notes with a lower interest rate and a stretched-out principal payment schedule.

- Haircut of $1 million plus foregone future interest.

Trade creditors. Badco's trade creditors (who are junior to the secured banks but equal in priority to the debenture holders[1]) accept $7 million in cash in complete discharge of their $10 million of claims.

- Haircut of $3 million.

Subordinated debenture holders. The subordinated debenture holders exchange their $12.5 million of old debentures for (1) $6 million of new debentures with a deferred maturity and a higher interest rate (payable in bunny debentures for the first 4 years), plus (2) 2,600 Badco common shares (FV $100 per share for a total FV of $260,000).

- Haircut of $6.24 million.

Thus, the total haircut from the 3 creditor compromises described above is $10.24 million.

¶802 [1] In most cases Badco's debentures are expressly subordinated only to its debt for borrowed money (e.g., its bank debt), although in rare cases the debentures are also expressly subordinated to trade creditors.

¶802.1.4 Badco's Post-Restructuring Stock Ownership and Balance Sheet

After the above steps, Badco's outstanding stock is:

- **Preferred stock:** $7.9 million of new senior preferred stock *plus* $3.25 million of old preferred stock = $11.15 million of preferred stock.
- **Common stock:** 4,100 total common shares outstanding, of which 2,600 shares (63.4%) are owned by the subordinated debenture holders, 1,000 shares (24.4%) are owned by the new VC investors, and 500 shares (12.2%) are owned by the old common shareholders (the original VCs and management).

After these transactions Badco's balance sheet (in accordance with GAAP) is as follows:[2]

Assets	Amount (millions)	
Cash (1 + 8 − 8)	$ 1.0	
Other assets	39.0	
Total assets		$40.0
Liabilities and Net Worth		
Liabilities:		
Secured bank lender (30 − 1 − 1)	$28.0	
Trade creditors (10 − 7 − 3)	0.0	
Sub debentures (12.5 − 6.5)	6.0	
Total liabilities		$34.0
Net worth:		
Old VC preferred (6.5 − 3.25)	$ 3.25	
New VC preferred	7.90	
Common stock held by management, VCs, and creditors (1 + .1 + .26)	1.36	

---

[2] This balance sheet (1) ignores the possibility that, under GAAP, liabilities might be stated at other than face under certain circumstances, (2) ignores the special GAAP rules for debt restructurings which vary depending on whether the restructuring occurs in or outside a bankruptcy proceeding, and (3) transfers the $3.25 million credit for the canceled old VC preferred stock to accumulated deficit, although GAAP may treat the credit differently.

Accumulated deficit (20 old deficit *less*
   10.54 aggregate debt cancellation[3]
   less 3.25 old VC preferred
   cancellation)   (6.51)

Net worth	6.0
Total liabilities and net worth	$40.0

¶802.2 Transaction #2—Badco's Subordinated Debentures Are Market Traded

Same as transaction #1, except that the old subordinated debentures (and the new debentures issued in exchange) are traded on an established securities market ("market traded"), with the following values:

- Immediately *before* the restructuring, the $12.5 million of old debentures were trading at 32% of face, for an aggregate FV of $4 million ($12.5 million face × 32%).
- Immediately *after* the restructuring, the $6 million of new debentures were trading at 66.67% of face, for an aggregate FV of $4 million ($6 million face × 66.67%).

¶802.3 Fact Pattern Variations

For each of transactions #1 and #2, there are 3 alternate fact patterns (because, as discussed below, the FV of Badco's assets and whether Badco's restructuring is conducted in bankruptcy or not are relevant to Badco's tax treatment):

Fact pattern X—High asset FV and no bankruptcy: Although Badco is cash poor and has been operating at a negative cash flow, its assets, which have a

---

[3]

Creditor Transactions	Aggreg. Debt Cancellation (millions)
Secured bank surrendered $30 million old notes for $1 million cash and $28 million new notes	$ 1.00
Trade creditors surrendered $10 million old claims for $7 million cash	3.00
Subordinated debenture holders surrendered $12.5 million old debentures for $6 million new debentures and $260,000 FV of new common shares	6.24
Aggregate debt cancelled	$10.24

GAAP book value of $40 million, have an FV of $53 million, and Badco has managed to conduct its restructuring without a bankruptcy proceeding.

- Thus, Badco is solvent by $.5 million before the restructuring and before taking account of any Badco contingent liabilities (asset FV $53 million *less* $52.5 million pre-workout liabilities).

Fact pattern Y—Low asset FV and no bankruptcy: Same as fact pattern X, except that Badco's assets have an FV of only $45 million.

- Thus, Badco is insolvent by $7.5 million before the restructuring and before taking account of any Badco contingent liabilities (asset FV $45 million *less* $52.5 million pre-workout liabilities).

Fact pattern Z—Bankruptcy: Badco conducts its restructuring in bankruptcy and (as discussed below) the FV of its assets is not relevant.

Summary of fact patterns X, Y and Z:

	X	Y	Z
FV of Badco assets	$53.0	$45.0	Not relevant
Pre-restructuring debt	52.5	52.5	Not relevant
Solvency	$ .5	$ (7.5)	Not relevant

Effect of contingent liabilities. Badco's solvency would be reduced (or its insolvency increased) in fact patterns X and Y if Badco had contingent liabilities (not on its balance sheet) for (e.g.):

- Product liability claims.
- Pollution cleanup.
- Tax disputes.
- Employment discrimination claims.

¶803   TAX RULES APPLICABLE TO DEBT RESTRUCTURING

¶803.1   *Key Badco Tax Issues*

Will the restructuring result in debt cancellation ("DC") for Badco and, if so, how much DC?

If Badco has DC, will the DC produce cancellation of debt income ("CODI"), i.e., taxable income, and, if so, how much CODI?

Will any DC that does not produce CODI result in attribute reduction ("AR"), i.e., a reduction in Badco's NOLs, asset tax basis, or other tax attributes and, if so, how much reduction and to which tax attributes?

Will the restructuring transaction result in a change in ownership of Badco that may limit future use of Badco's NOLs or other tax attributes?[1]

¶803.2   *Amount of Debt Cancellation*

In general, under the Internal Revenue Code, Badco has DC in the restructuring equal to the adjusted issue price ("AIP") of the old Badco debt canceled *less* the consideration issued by Badco in cancellation of such old debt. Code §61(a)(12).

A debt instrument's AIP is generally its face (plus any accrued unpaid interest).

However, in the case of a debt instrument initially issued with OID or original issue premium, the debt's AIP is the original issue price, *plus* any OID accrued since issuance, *plus* any accrued unpaid interest, *minus* any premium amortized since issuance, *minus* any payment of principal or OID since issuance. Code §108(e)(3).

There is no DC on cancellation of stock (common or preferred).

¶803.3   *Valuing Consideration Issued by Badco in Restructuring*

In calculating the consideration issued by Badco in a DC transaction, each item issued by Badco in cancellation of old debt is generally valued *at its FV* (including new Badco stock and other property).

However, a new Badco debt instrument issued in cancellation of an old Badco debt instrument is valued *at face* (rather than FV) where neither the old nor the new debt instrument is "traded on an established securities market" ("non market traded") and the new debt bears interest of at least the AFR. Code §108(e)(10), §1273(b)(3) and (b)(4), §1274.

Hence, Badco has no DC where the old and new debt are both non-market-traded, the new debt bears interest of at least the AFR, and the new debt's face (plus any cash, stock, or other property issued) is at least equal to the old debt's AIP.

- The relevant AFR for the new debt should be the lowest AFR for a 3 to 6 month period—the calendar month in which the parties enter into a binding written contract for the exchange of new debt for old debt that substantially sets forth the terms under which the sale is ultimately consummated and the 2 prior calendar months and the calendar month in which the exchange occurs and the 2 prior calendar months. Code §1274(d)(2); Treas. Reg. §1.1274-4(a)(1).

¶803   [1] A 1998 Tax Court opinion raises one other tax issue by suggesting that one of Badco's new VC investors would, in appropriate circumstances, recognize OI if it renders management services to Badco in connection with a restructuring and receives some Badco shares as compensation for such services, i.e., if the FV of the Badco shares received by a new VC investor who also renders services to Badco exceeds the purchase price paid by the new VC investor for such shares. See Judge Beghe's opinion (concurring in part and dissenting in part) in Venture Funding, Ltd. v. Commissioner, 110 T.C. 236 (1998) *aff'd,* 198 F.3d 248, 99-2 U.S.T.C. ¶50,972 (6th Cir. 1999).

However, where either the old or the new debt is market traded, Badco has DC equal to the old debt's AIP *over* the new debt's FV (plus any cash, stock or other property issued).

The debt of a troubled obligor (like Badco) typically trades at a substantial discount to face because of the high credit risk, so that if either the old debt or the new debt is market traded, there is likely to be sizable DC on the exchange.

¶803.4   *Meaning of Market Traded*

Debt is treated as market traded if, at any time within 29 days before or 30 days after issuance, the debt meets *any one of the following 4 tests*:

(1)   The debt is listed on (a) a national securities exchange, (b) an interdealer quotation system sponsored by a national securities association, or (c) certain specified foreign stock exchanges.

(2)   The debt is traded on a CFTC-designated contract market or on an interbank market.

(3)   The debt appears on a quotation system of general circulation that provides a reasonable basis to determine FV quotes of identified brokers and dealers (including a single dealer) or actual prices of recent sale transactions.

(4)   Price quotations for the debt are readily available from brokers and dealers.

   To reduce the potentially extreme breadth of test (4), the regulations establish a safe harbor under which test (4) does not apply if the debt instrument meets *any one of the following 4 exceptions*:

(a)   The original stated principal amount of the debt issue does not exceed $25 million.

(b)   No other outstanding debt of Badco (or a guarantor) is market traded under the tests described in (1) through (3) above.

(c)   Badco has other outstanding market-traded debt, but the conditions and covenants relating to the debt being tested are materially less restrictive than the conditions and covenants in the market-traded debt.

(d)   Badco has other outstanding market-traded debt, but the maturity date of the debt being tested is at least 3 years after the latest maturity date of the market-traded debt.

Exception (b) is not available if a debt instrument is guaranteed by a person who has outstanding market-traded debt. However, in what may have been an oversight, exceptions (c) and (d) do not, by their terms, refer to a guarantor's market-traded debt in determining whether the terms of the exception are satisfied. Treas. Reg. §1.1273-2(c).

¶803.5   *Alternative Tax Treatments of Debt Cancellation*

(1)   The amount of DC (as calculated in ¶803.1 through ¶803.4 above) constitutes cancellation of debt income ("CODI"), with the tax ramifications described in ¶803.6 below. Code §61(a)(12).

(2)   DC does not constitute CODI if one of the exceptions described in ¶803.7 through ¶803.10 below applies, including:

   - The AR-instead-of-CODI bankruptcy/insolvency exception.
   - The shareholder-contribution exception.
   - The new-debt-not-materially-different exception.

¶803.6   *Cancellation of Debt Income*

CODI constitutes taxable income for Badco's tax year in which the cancellation occurs.

Badco is entitled to offset against such CODI any tax loss suffered in its current taxable year as well as any NOLCF from a prior year. Under certain circumstances (e.g., where Code §382 or §269 applies), Badco's ability to offset its NOL against the CODI (as well as against Badco's other taxable income) may be limited or eliminated. See ¶809 below. In addition, a CL can not be offset against CODI or any type of OI.

To the extent Badco's CODI exceeds any offsetable current year loss or NOLCF, Badco owes income tax on the CODI.

The corporate alternative minimum tax ("AMT") rules allow Badco's NOLCF to offset only 90% of Badco's AMT income (remaining after the income has been offset by current year loss), so that there is a potential 2% AMT exposure for CODI which is offset by an NOLCF (20% corporate AMT rate × 10% of CODI not offset by NOLCF for AMT purposes). Code §56(d).[2]

¶803.7   *The AR-Instead-of-CODI Bankruptcy/Insolvency Exception*

The principal exception to the CODI taxation rules set forth in ¶803.6 above is that where Badco is in bankruptcy or where Badco is insolvent as defined below (but not in bankruptcy), Badco's DC does not constitute CODI but rather Badco's DC causes attribute reduction ("AR"). Code §108(a) and (b).

---

[2] The 2002 Tax Act temporarily suspended the 90% AMT NOL deduction limitation (so that 100% of AMT income could be offset by NOLs) for deductions attributable to (1) the carryback of an NOL arising in a tax year ending in 2001 or 2002 and (2) the carryforward of an NOL to a tax year ending in 2001 or 2002. The examples below all assume that the NOL does not qualify for this temporary 100% AMT offset.

¶803.7.1   Insolvency Requirement for a Non-Bankruptcy Restructuring

Where Badco is insolvent (but not in bankruptcy), this AR-instead-of-CODI rule applies only to the extent of Badco's insolvency and any DC in excess of Badco's insolvency is CODI subject to the rules of ¶803.6 above. Code §108(a)(3).

¶803.7.2   Meaning of Insolvency

Insolvency means the excess of Badco's liabilities over its aggregate asset FV, determined immediately *before* the DC (and hence before any new equity infusion which is part of the debt restructuring transaction, at least where the equity infusion does not precede the DC—see ¶803.7.6 below). Code §108(d)(3).

Assets include both tangible and intangible assets (including goodwill), whether or not shown on the balance sheet, thus creating significant asset valuation issues.

Although the law is somewhat unclear (as described below), Badco's liabilities probably include its contingent liabilities at the reasonably estimated amount Badco is likely to be obligated to pay thereon, thus creating significant liability valuation issues.

A 12/97 Tax Court case dealt with Badco's guarantee of a third party's liability when the third party had defaulted on its liability but a workout (in which Badco was not required to make any payment) was being negotiated (and was ultimately entered into). The court concluded that Badco's contingent guarantee liability could not be taken into account "unless it is more probable than not that [Badco] will be called upon to pay that obligation in the amount claimed," in which case the court indicated that Badco would take into account the full amount of the guarantee liability (rather than a discounted amount reflecting the possibility that no actual liability will arise).[3]

This court decision is not necessarily inconsistent with the rational conclusion that where Badco is the primary obligor (rather than merely the guarantor) on a lawsuit or disputed claim, Badco can (for tax insolvency purposes) take into account the reasonably estimated amount which it is more probable than not Badco will be called upon to pay when the dispute is settled or litigated—which will often be an intermediate amount, less than the claimant is seeking but more than zero.[4] On the other hand, the court's opinion could be read as adopting the less rational all-or-nothing position that where it is not more than 50% likely Badco will be liable, Badco may not take the contingent liability into account, but where it is more than 50% likely Badco will be liable, Badco can take the entire claimed amount into account.

---

[3] Merkel v. Commissioner, 109 T.C. 463 (1997), *aff'd*, 192 F.3d 844, 99-2 U.S.T.C. ¶50,848 (9th Cir. 1999).
[4] Indeed the court stated "In conclusion, a taxpayer claiming the benefit of the insolvency exclusion must prove . . . with respect to any obligation claimed to be a liability, that, as of the calculation date, it is more probable than not that he will be called upon to pay that obligation in the amount claimed . . ."

¶803.7.3   Order of AR

NOLs are reduced first, followed by credits, then CL carryovers, and then asset tax basis (but aggregate asset tax basis is not reduced below aggregate Badco liabilities immediately *after* the debt cancellation). Code §108(b); Code §1017(b)(2).

¶803.7.4   Timing of AR

Attributes are reduced immediately *after* the end of the tax year in which the debt cancellation occurs. Code §108(b)(4)(A); Code §1017(a).

Thus, NOLs can first be used to shelter any taxable income (including CODI) for the year of the discharge.

Badco can avoid tax basis reduction for a particular asset by disposing of such asset in a sale or exchange before the end of the taxable year in which the debt cancellation occurred.

Query whether Badco can avoid basis reduction for an asset by contributing the asset to a subsidiary corporation or a partnership (or LLC) prior to the end of the taxable year in which the debt cancellation occurs. If the asset transfer is respected, Badco's tax basis in the subsidiary stock or partnership (or LLC) interest would be reduced, but not the corporate subsidiary's or partnership's (or LLC's) tax basis in the asset contributed.

¶803.7.5   Insufficient Attributes to Reduce

If Badco's DC exceeds its attributes available for reduction, there is still no CODI for the excess.

¶803.7.6   Equity Capital Infusion

If Badco receives an equity capital infusion as part of the debt restructuring, the new equity infusion should be ignored in calculating the extent of Badco's insolvency (since insolvency is determined "immediately before" the debt discharge). Cf. Rev. Rul. 92-52.

In analogous contexts (e.g., Code §351), "immediately after" has been interpreted to refer to the state of affairs after all steps of a plan have been completed. Treas. Reg. §1.351-1. Similarly, "immediately before" should refer to the state of affairs before any of the steps of the restructuring plan have been implemented.

Nonetheless, it is prudent to avoid closing on a new equity infusion prior to closing on the debt exchange.

¶803.7.7   Consolidated Group

If Badco is part of a consolidated group:

- Insolvency is apparently determined on a separate company-by-company basis. Wyman-Gordon Co. v. Commissioner, 89 T.C. 207 (1987).
- It also appears that AR is calculated on a separate company-by-company basis, although IRS has taken the position that NOL reduction is done on a consolidated group basis. IRS Letter Ruling 9121017 (asset basis AR calculated on separate company basis); IRS Letter Ruling 199912007 and ILM 200149008 (NOL AR calculated on consolidated group basis).

Separate company AR may produce favorable tax results if most of the canceled debt is in a holding company and most of the consolidated group's NOLs are attributable to (and most depreciable assets are held by) operating subsidiaries. If holding company debt is canceled, separate company AR would permit the consolidated group to preserve the NOLs attributable to (and the asset tax basis of) the operating subsidiaries, while reducing only the holding company's NOLs and the holding company's tax basis in subsidiary stock.

¶803.8   *Shareholder-Contribution Exception*

If the creditor is a Badco shareholder and forgives or otherwise contributes the debt to Badco's capital, Badco is treated as satisfying the debt with an amount of money equal to the shareholder's adjusted tax basis in the old debt. Code §108(e)(6).

Hence, Badco does not have DC (or CODI) if the shareholder's adjusted tax basis for the debt is at least equal to the old debt's AIP. If the shareholder's adjusted tax basis for the old debt is less than the old debt's AIP, the excess is CODI (unless another exception applies).

The law is quite vague on when a Badco shareholder/creditor will be treated as having made a "contribution to capital." Several factors which appear to militate in favor of the exception applying:

(1) The Badco creditor/shareholder receives no consideration at all from Badco in exchange for the canceled old debt, *or* receives property (new debt, stock, cash, or other property) from Badco with an FV substantially less than the FV of the canceled old debt, so that the shareholder is contributing value to Badco.

Where the creditor/shareholder receives no consideration, the transaction looks most like a contribution to Badco's capital.

Conversely, where the creditor/shareholder receives non-stock consideration from Badco equal to the old debt's full FV, the creditor/shareholder has apparently not contributed any value to Badco and the transaction looks least like a contribution to Badco's capital.

(2) The Badco creditor/shareholder (or group thereof) transferring the old debt to Badco owns a substantial portion of Badco's stock.

The closer the transferring shareholders come to owning 100% of Badco's stock, the more the transaction looks like a contribution to Badco's capital.

(3) No holder of Badco debt who is not also a Badco shareholder is participating in the exchange/contribution on the same terms.

The following examples illustrate the 2 polar extremes of the shareholder-contribution-to-capital exception:

- The exception would surely apply if Badco had one or several shareholders (owning in the aggregate 100% of its stock) who transferred old Badco debt to Badco in the same proportions as they owned Badco's stock and received back no consideration at all.
- It is doubtful whether the exception would apply if a Badco shareholder owning 10% of Badco's stock transferred old debt to Badco and received consideration (cash, new debt, etc.) with an FV equal to the full FV of the old debt transferred, especially where other holders of the same old debt (who own no Badco stock) participate in the same transaction on the same terms.

¶803.9   New-Debt-Not-Materially-Different Exception

(1) If the terms of the new debt instrument are not "materially different" from the terms of the old debt instrument, the new debt will be treated as a continuation of the old, resulting in no DC. Reg. §§1.1001-1(a), -3.

(a) A change in the timing of interest or principal payments is treated as a material modification if it "results in the material deferral of scheduled payments." Under a safe harbor, a deferral of payments for a period not longer than the lesser of five years or 50% of the debt instrument's original term is not viewed as material. Reg. §1.1001-3(e)(3).

(b) A more than de minimis change in interest rate (i.e., more than the greater of (i) 25 basis points or (ii) 5% of the debt instrument's pre-modification yield) is generally treated as a material change. Reg. §1.1001-3(e)(2).

Where the maturity of old debt with OID is extended so that the old debt's yield is reduced, there is a change in effective interest rate (and hence, if more than de minimis, a material change), unless the stated principal amount is increased commensurate with the maturity extension.

(c) A change in the debt instrument's collateral, credit enhancement, or priority is treated as a material change if the change results in a "change in payment expectations," i.e., if (i) the obligor's payment capacity was "primarily speculative" before the change, is "substantial[ly] enhanc[ed] by the change," and is "adequate" after the change *or* (ii) the obligor's payment capacity was "adequate" before the change, is "substantial[ly] impair[ed] by the change," and is "primarily speculative" after the change. Reg. §1.1001-3(e)(4).

(d) A change in customary accounting or financial covenants is not treated as a material change. Reg. §1.1001-3(e)(6).

(e) A material payment to (or from) the lender which is not pursuant to the terms of the old debt instrument may be a material change in the old debt instrument.

- A prohibited payment to the lender includes cash, property, stock, warrants, or an increase in the principal amount of the debt. If these items were not prohibited, the rule in (b) above, prohibiting an increase in interest rate, could easily be circumvented.
- It appears that a payment to reimburse the lender for additional out-of-pocket costs incurred because of the default and/or restructuring should *not* be treated as a modification.
- However, where the AIP of the debt is being reduced, a payment to the lender which does not exceed the AIP reduction should be viewed as a partial payment on the old debt and hence should not constitute a material change (although IRS may not agree).

(2) Where the new debt is not materially different than the old debt except that the new debt's AIP is less than the old debt's AIP, the new debt should be treated as a continuation of the old debt, with DC equal to the AIP reduction. IRS may, however, attempt to treat any reduction in the old debt's AIP as a material change resulting in the deemed issuance of a new debt instrument. Rev. Rul. 89-122.

(3) Where (a) the new debt is not materially different from the old debt except for an AIP reduction, (b) Badco also issues other consideration (e.g., cash, stock or warrants) to the holder of the old debt, and (c) the other consideration does not exceed the AIP reduction, then the new consideration should be treated as a partial payment on the old debt and the new debt should be treated as a continuation of the old debt (although IRS may not agree), with DC equal to the AIP reduction less the cash and FV of property issued to the old debt holder.

The other consideration generally should be treated as first satisfying any accrued interest or OID, and then reducing principal. Treas. Reg. §1.446-2(e), §1.1275-2(a). However, if the new debt instrument represents a substantially pro rata reduction of each payment (i.e., interest and principal) remaining to be paid on the old debt, the other consideration should be treated as satisfying a proportionate part of the accrued interest/OID and principal of the old debt. Treas. Reg. §1.446-2(e)(4), §1.1275-2(f).

If the old debt's AIP exceeds the sum of the new debt's AIP plus the amount of cash or FV of other property issued by the obligor, Badco will have DC equal to such excess.

¶803.10   Related-Party Rules

If a party related to Badco acquires the Badco debt from the third-party creditor for less than its AIP (or if a party unrelated to Badco acquires Badco debt for less than its AIP in anticipation of becoming related to Badco), the result is generally the same as if Badco had acquired the old debt. Code §108(e)(4).

¶803.11   Key Issues and References on Badco's CODI and AR

What are the tax ramifications to Badco if all or a portion of Badco creditors' claims are canceled or otherwise extinguished for less than full payment?

Does it matter whether the cancellation occurs in a bankruptcy or a non-bankruptcy restructuring?

Does it matter whether Badco was insolvent before the cancellation? What does insolvent mean? How is insolvency measured? Are there significant factual issues in determining insolvency?

Does it matter whether a creditor:

- merely cancels part of its claim for no consideration,
- receives some cash and cancels the remainder of the claim,
- receives some new debt instruments of Badco, or
- receives (either alone or in a package along with other consideration) a more than "nominal or token" amount of Badco common stock (or perhaps preferred stock)?

What would induce a Badco creditor to participate in such an exchange?

How is Badco's DC measured where Badco transfers a new debt instrument to a creditor in exchange for an old debt instrument?

- Is Badco's DC measured by the new debt instrument's face or its FV, which could be radically lower because of Badco's troubled financial condition?
- When is a debt instrument market traded?
- Should the CODI rules differ for a market-traded and a non-market-traded debt instrument?

References:

- Code §61(a)(12)
- Code §108
- Code §1017
- Code §1273(b)(3) and (b)(4)
- Code §1274
- Code §163(e)(5) and (i)

How would the tax results differ if Badco were an S corporation or a partnership, rather than a C corporation?

References:

- Code §108(d)(6) and (7)

Do the tax rules applicable to the restructuring of a troubled company evidence a rational industrial policy for our nation, i.e., do they encourage the successful reorganization of a faltering business entity so that American companies will be more competitive in a global economy (or, conversely, do they discourage this salutary result)?

¶804   TAX RESULTS FROM THE ALTERNATIVE RESTRUCTURING TRANSACTIONS

¶804.1   Transaction #1—No Market-Traded Debt

Fact pattern X: Immediately before the debt cancellation, Badco's asset FV is $53 million and its liabilities are $52.5 million (assuming that all contingent liabilities have already been taken into account in such calculation). Thus Badco is solvent by $.5 million. Badco is not in bankruptcy. Hence the AR-instead-of-CODI bankruptcy/insolvency exception does not apply.

Because Badco has no market-traded debt and the new debt bears interest of at least the AFR, Badco's DC is:

	DC (millions)
Secured bank surrenders $30 million old notes for $1 million cash and $28 million new notes	$ 1.00
Trade creditors surrender $10 million old claims for $7 million cash	3.00
Subordinated debenture holders surrender $12.5 million old debentures for $6 million new debentures and $260,000 FV Badco stock	6.24
Aggregate DC	$10.24

Hence, Badco has $10.24 million of CODI.[1]

Assuming that Badco had a current-year tax loss of $1 million and an NOLCF of $7 million,[2] Badco will owe federal income tax ("FIT") of $784,000:

¶804   [1] This illustration assumes that all of the new debt is "materially different" from the old debt surrendered in exchange.

[2] Although Badco's GAAP accumulated deficit immediately before the restructuring was $20 million, tax NOLs are often smaller than GAAP losses because GAAP rules often call for loss recognition earlier than do tax rules.

	Amount
CODI	$10,240,000
Current year loss	(1,000,000)
NOLCF	(7,000,000)
Taxable income	$ 2,240,000
FIT rate	×35%[3]
FIT	$ 784,000

Fact pattern Y: The facts are the same as in fact pattern X above, except that immediately before the debt cancellation, Badco's asset FV is $45 million and its liabilities are $52.5 million (assuming that all contingent liabilities have already been taken into account in such calculation). Hence Badco is insolvent by $7.5 million. Badco is not in bankruptcy.

Badco has $10.24 million of DC, of which $7.5 million is covered by the AR-instead-of-CODI insolvency exception to CODI and the excess $2.74 million constitutes CODI.

The $2.74 million of CODI results in no regular FIT:

	Amount (millions)
CODI	$ 2.74
Current year loss	(1.00)
NOLCF	(7.00)
Taxable income	$ 0
Remaining NOLCF	$ 5.26

The $7.5 million of Badco's DC which is covered by the AR-instead-of-CODI insolvency exception causes AR immediately after year end, thus reducing Badco's remaining NOLCF from $5.26 million to zero and reducing Badco's asset tax basis by $2.24 million, but not below Badco's post-restructuring liabilities of $34 million (i.e., $28 million bank debt *plus* $0 trade creditors *plus* $6 million debentures).

In addition, in the year of the debt cancellation Badco owes AMT of $34,800:

---

[3] Although corporate tax rates are progressive up to a maximum rate of 35% for income in excess of $10 million, the examples in this chapter utilize a flat 35% rate for simplicity.

	Amount
CODI	$ 2,740,000
Current year loss	(1,000,000)
Taxable income before NOL	$ 1,740,000
90% subject to offset by NOL	(1,566,000)
AMT taxable income	$ 174,000
AMT rate	×20%
AMT	$ 34,800

- If Badco has substantial contingent liabilities in fact patterns X and Y not taken into account above, Badco's insolvency would presumably increase by the reasonably estimated amount it is more probable than not Badco will be called upon to pay.

Fact pattern Z: The facts are the same as in fact pattern X above, except that Badco is in bankruptcy. Because Badco is in bankruptcy, its entire $10.24 million of DC is covered by the AR-instead-of-CODI bankruptcy exception to CODI (and hence Badco does not utilize its $1 million current year loss or its $7 million NOLCF to offset CODI), regardless of the amount of its solvency or insolvency, if any. Hence Badco's entire $10.24 million of DC is applied to AR immediately after year end:

	Amount (millions)
Current year loss	$ 1.00
NOLCF	7.00
DC	(10.24)
Remaining NOLCF	$ 0
Asset tax basis reduction (but asset tax basis is not reduced below post-restructuring liabilities of $34 million)	$ 2.24

¶804.2   Transaction #2—Market-Traded Debt

Fact pattern X: The result differs from transaction #1 (fact pattern X) in that Badco's $12.5 million of old subordinated debentures are market traded as also are its $6 million face of new debentures issued to the old subordinated debenture holders. The old debentures had a $4 million FV immediately before the workout ($12.5 million face × 32% market-trading price), and the new debentures also have a $4 million FV immediately after the workout ($6 million face × 66.67% market-trading price).

Hence, Badco's DC in transaction #2 (fact pattern X) is substantially greater than in transaction #1 (fact pattern X):

	DC (millions)
Secured bank—same as in transaction #1 (fact pattern X)	$ 1.00
Trade creditors—same as in transaction #1 (fact pattern X)	3.00
Subordinated debentures—$12.5 million old face *less* $4 million FV of new debentures and *less* $260,000 FV Badco stock	8.24
Aggregate DC	$12.24

Thus, in transaction #2, Badco has $2 million more DC on the subordinated debentures than it had in transaction #1, because in transaction #2 the DC is measured by the FV of the market-traded debentures.[4]

Badco is solvent by $.5 million immediately before the restructuring (asset FV $53 million and liabilities $52.5 million, assuming that all contingent liabilities have already been taken into account above). There is thus no CODI exception, and Badco has $12.24 million of CODI.

Badco owes FIT of $1,484,000:

	Amount
CODI	$ 12,240,000
Current year loss	(1,000,000)
NOLCF	(7,000,000)
Taxable income	$ 4,240,000
FIT rate	×35%
FIT	$ 1,484,000

Fact pattern Y: Badco has $12.24 million of DC and is insolvent immediately before the restructuring by $7.5 million (asset FV $45 million and liabilities $52.5 million, assuming that all contingent liabilities have already been taken into account above). Hence $7.5 million of Badco's DC is covered by the AR-instead-of-CODI insolvency exception to CODI and the excess $4.74 million constitutes CODI.

The $4.74 million of CODI results in no regular FIT:

---

[4] For purposes of measuring the amount of Badco's solvency or insolvency immediately before the workout, the subordinated debentures are taken into account at their AIP, even though they are market traded and their FV is less than their AIP.

	Amount (millions)
CODI	$ 4.74
Current year loss	(1.00)
NOLCF	(7.00)
Taxable income	$ 0
Remaining NOLCF	$ 3.26

The $7.5 million of DC which is covered by the AR-instead-of-CODI insolvency exception causes AR immediately after year end, thus reducing Badco's NOLCF from $3.26 million to zero and reducing Badco's asset tax basis by $4.24 million, but not below Badco's post-restructuring liabilities of $34 million.

In addition, in the year of the debt cancellation Badco owes AMT of $74,800:

	Amount
CODI	$ 4,740,000
Current year loss	(1,000,000)
Taxable income before NOL	$ 3,740,000
90% subject to offset by NOL	(3,366,000)
AMT taxable income	$ 374,000
AMT rate	×20%
AMT	$ 74,800

- If Badco has substantial contingent liabilities in fact patterns X and Y not taken into account above, Badco's insolvency presumably would increase by the reasonably estimated amount it is more probable than not Badco will be called upon to pay.

Fact pattern Z: Because Badco is in bankruptcy, its entire $12.24 million of DC is covered by the AR-instead-of-CODI bankruptcy exception to CODI (and hence Badco does not utilize its current year loss or its NOLCF to offset CODI), regardless of the amount of its solvency or insolvency, if any. Hence Badco's entire $12.24 million of DC is applied to AR immediately after year end:

	Amount (millions)
Current year loss	$ 1.00
NOLCF	7.00
DC	(12.24)
Remaining NOLCF	$ 0
Asset tax basis reduction (but asset tax basis is not reduced below post-restructuring liabilities of $34 million)	$ 4.24

¶805   BADCO AS C CORPORATION VERSUS S CORPORATION, PARTNERSHIP, OR LLC

The tax results in all of these transactions would differ from the results described above if Badco were not a C corporation, but were instead an S corporation, a partnership, or an LLC. See Code §108(d)(6) and (7).

¶806   APPLICATION OF CODE §163(e)(5)

As described in ¶602.8.3 above, Code §163(e)(5) defers and under certain circumstances permanently disallows a corporation's deductions for amortization of OID on certain high-yield debentures (where the yield equals or exceeds AFR + 5, the instrument has substantial OID or PIK features, and certain other tests are met).

Where Badco issues market-traded debt in a restructuring, the issue price of such debt (for purposes of calculating both DC and OID) is the debt's FV. The debt's FV is frequently far below its face, because of Badco's weak credit standing. The substantial OID so created generally causes the debt to meet both of the Code §163(e)(5) requisites mentioned above—a significant OID feature and (by a combination of the stated interest and the OID amortization) a yield greater than AFR + 5.

Thus such debt is generally subject to Code §163(e)(5).

¶807   APPLICABLE SEC AND OTHER DISCLOSURE RULES

¶807.1   *Exemptions from 1933 Act Registration*

When Badco issues (or offers to issue) stock (common or preferred) or debt instruments, Badco generally must register the securities with SEC under the 1933

Act, a time-consuming and expensive endeavor. However, Badco can often avoid SEC registration by fitting the transaction into an applicable exemption.

1933 Act §3(a)(9) exempts "any security exchanged by the issuer with its existing security holders exclusively where no commission or other remuneration is paid or given directly or indirectly for soliciting such exchange," but explicitly does not apply "to a security exchanged in a case under title 11 of the United States Code" which governs bankruptcy.

1933 Act §3(a)(10) exempts "any security which is issued in exchange for one of more . . . claims . . . or partly in such exchange and partly for cash, where the terms . . . are approved after a hearing upon the fairness [thereof] . . . by any court, or by any official or agency . . . authorized by law," but explicitly does not apply "to a security exchanged in a case under title 11."

1933 Act §3(a)(7) exempts a "certificate issued by a receiver or by a trustee or debtor in possession in a case under title 11 . . . with the approval of the court."

1933 Act §3(a)(11) exempts an intra-state offering and SEC Rule 147 contains a very narrow safe-harbor definition thereof.

1933 Act §4(2) exempts "transactions by an issuer not involving any public offering" and SEC Reg. D contains a safe-harbor definition thereof. See ¶207.3 above.

Bankruptcy Code §1145(a) exempts "the offer or sale under a [bankruptcy] plan of a security . . . (A) in exchange for a claim [or] . . . an interest in . . . the debtor . . . or (B) principally such exchange and partly for cash or property," but, once Badco files for bankruptcy, Bankruptcy Code §1125(b) requires the use of a disclosure statement approved by the court containing "adequate information," which will generally require disclosure akin to an SEC registration statement. See also Bankruptcy Code §1125(e).

- See Bankruptcy Code §101(5) and §501(a) as to the meaning of "claim" and "interest."
- Query as to application of §1145 to cash sales of Badco stock to VCs, although 1933 Act §4(2) and/or Reg. D may also apply.
- SEC takes the position that §1145(a) can not be used to solicit creditor and shareholder consents to a pre-packaged bankruptcy because such consents are solicited before the actual bankruptcy filing. Bankruptcy Code §1126(b) states that a pre-bankruptcy solicitation of acceptances generally is valid if the solicitation complied with applicable non-bankruptcy law governing the adequacy of disclosure.

¶807.2   Form S-4 Registration

If none of these exemptions from SEC registration applies, Badco must register the issuance (or offer) of stock or debt under the 1933 Act, generally on form S-4 for a restructuring exchange.

¶807.3   State Securities Laws

Badco must also comply with any applicable state securities laws, except that where Badco's workout is effectuated in a bankruptcy proceeding, Bankruptcy Code §1145(a) generally exempts from state registration Badco's offers and sales of securities in exchange for a claim or interest (or principally in exchange for such) under the bankruptcy plan.

¶807.4   Other SEC Implications

Other SEC rules and securities laws that may be implicated in a restructuring include certain SEC tender offer regulations, the SEC proxy rules, the Trust Indenture Act, SEC Rule 10b-5, and related insider trading and selective disclosure laws.

¶807.5   Key Issues and References on Securities Law Impediments to Restructuring

What securities law impediments are there to issuing Badco stock and/or debt securities in a bankruptcy or non-bankruptcy restructuring?

Can a holder of securities issued in a restructuring freely resell them after the restructuring?

References:

- 1933 Act §3(a)(9), §3(a)(10), §3(a)(11), and §4(2)
- SEC Rule 144
- SEC Rule 147
- SEC Reg. D
- Bankruptcy Code §1145, §1125, §101(5), §501(a)
- ¶207, ¶903, and ¶904 of this book

¶808   BINDING DISSENTING CREDITORS TO RESTRUCTURING

¶808.1   Non-Bankruptcy Restructuring

The principal disadvantage of a non-bankruptcy restructuring is the inability to bind dissenting creditors. Hence, even if (e.g.) 95% of Badco's creditors consent to a non-bankruptcy restructuring, the 5% "free riders" can retain their full pre-restructuring claims. However, by using a pre-packaged bankruptcy plan, currently a popular technique, Badco can bind "free riders" and also induce the potentially consenting creditors to participate in the restructuring.

¶808.2   Pre-Packaged Bankruptcy Plan

Once the bulk of Badco's creditors has agreed on a restructuring plan, Badco can incorporate such agreement into a plan (a pre-packaged bankruptcy plan) and (before filing a bankruptcy petition) obtain the requisite votes from its creditors and shareholders to approve the plan.

- The requisite creditor and shareholder vote for a pre-packaged bankruptcy plan is the same as for a regular contested bankruptcy plan: *with respect to each creditor class*, at least ⅔ in dollar amount and more than ½ by number of claimants, and *with respect to each shareholder class*, ⅔ in number of shares, in both cases measured by those creditors or shareholders actually voting.

The principal advantage of a pre-packaged bankruptcy over a non-bankruptcy restructuring is that all creditors and shareholders are bound, i.e., there are no free riders.

The principal advantages of a pre-packaged bankruptcy over a regular contested Chapter 11 bankruptcy are speed, economy, and less disruption of the debtor's business.

- With a successful pre-packaged plan, Badco can exit bankruptcy in a period as short as 30 to 90 days, while a contested Chapter 11 can take many years (although a "small business" debtor with obligations below $2 million may elect a fast track bankruptcy that may well be concluded more quickly).
- The cost of a pre-packaged bankruptcy is generally less, and often much less, than the cost of a lengthy contested Chapter 11 bankruptcy.
- The inevitable negative effect of bankruptcy on Badco's business is minimized through a pre-packaged bankruptcy, because the time spent in Chapter 11 is far shorter, and hence the creditors and customers tend to react much more favorably to a pre-packaged plan.

A pre-packaged bankruptcy may not be appropriate where (1) Badco has operational problems necessitating a lengthy stay in bankruptcy or (2) Badco needs to engage in asset sales, reject contracts, and/or engage in lengthy litigation to settle the amount of its contingent liabilities.

During the pre-bankruptcy negotiation process before the pre-packaged plan is filed in court, Badco's trade credit may dry up unless it is clear that trade creditors will be paid 100% pursuant to the pre-packaged plan.

¶808.3   Procedure for Pre-Packaged Bankruptcy Plan

Badco proposes a specific restructuring plan and solicits consents from its impaired creditors and shareholders to a pre-packaged bankruptcy plan which incorporates the restructuring.

SEC takes the position that these consents must be solicited in compliance with the 1933 Act and that the 1933 Act exemption afforded by Bankruptcy Code §1145(a) is not applicable because Badco is not in bankruptcy at the time it is soliciting these consents. See ¶807.1 above. Hence, in SEC's view, if Badco's pre-bankruptcy solicitation does not fit into 1933 Act §3(a)(9) (exchange of securities without commission), Reg. D (offering to accredited investors plus limited number of non-accredited investors), or some other 1933 Act exemption (see ¶807.1 above), Badco must:

- file a 1933 Act registration statement with SEC (generally on form S-4) before soliciting creditor approval for the pre-packaged bankruptcy plan and such SEC registration statement must become effective before the creditors give final approval to the pre-packaged plan, and
- if Badco is subject to the 1934 Act proxy rules and Badco's shareholders are to vote on the plan, a proxy statement must be filed with SEC and become final before the shareholder vote.

On the facts as stated in this chapter, Badco would need consent from 5 classes of creditors and shareholders:

- Secured bank lenders.
- Trade creditors.
- Subordinated debenture holders.
- Preferred stock.
- Common stock.

It is not unusual for some classes of debt to form unofficial creditors' committees to negotiate the pre-packaged plan (or restructuring). These committees may then become the official creditors' committees once the pre-packaged bankruptcy plan is filed.

- This procedure enhances Badco's ability to confirm a pre-packaged plan quickly as the creditors' committees are ready to report to the court on the pre-bankruptcy activities and to support the pre-packaged plan.
- If trade creditors are not impaired, no creditors' committee for trade creditors would generally be formed.

¶808.4   *Restructuring Under State Compromise or Arrangement*

Applicable state law may permit Badco to effect a restructuring without resorting to bankruptcy, although such a procedure is likely possible only if all impaired creditors consent and a significant majority of impaired equity holders consent. Delaware law, for example, permits a Delaware court to approve and make binding a compromise or arrangement accepted by "a majority in number representing three fourths in value of the creditors or class of creditors, and/or the stockholders or class of stockholders" that is to be impaired by the compromise or arrangement if the debtor's certificate of incorporation so permits. Del. Gen. Corp. Law §102(b)(2).

While there is considerable doubt that non-consenting creditors may be bound by such a procedure, consenting creditors are bound. Moreover if the compromise or arrangement is accepted by the requisite majorities, it is very likely that both consenting and non-consenting equity holders are bound.

A court could approve the compromise or arrangement in as short a period as a week, without the need to resort to bankruptcy.

Such a state court proceeding would qualify for several tax advantages, including the Code §382 special elective rule discussed in ¶809.7 below and the special §382 increase in stock FV resulting from debt cancellation discussed in ¶809.3 below.

¶809   BADCO'S ABILITY TO USE ITS REMAINING NOLCF

¶809.1   NOL Reduction for DC

Badco's NOL is first reduced both (1) to the extent it is used to offset Badco's CODI and (2) by Badco's AR, as described in ¶803 above.

¶809.2   NOLCF

Badco's NOL (as so reduced) can be carried forward for the normal 20 years, subject to (1) the Code §382 tainting and elimination rules and (2) the Code §269 elimination rules.[1]

¶809.3   Code §382 Taint

Under the Code §382 tainting rule, where Badco has a more than 50 percentage point change in its stock ownership (by FV) during a 36-month period (including changes resulting from issuance of Badco stock in the workout), the amount of its pre-change NOL which Badco may thereafter use in any year is limited to a percentage (currently approximately 5%) of its stock FV *immediately before* the change in ownership (*plus*, in the case of certain *bankruptcy* or similar state court proceedings, the increase in Badco's stock FV resulting from debt cancellation and *less*, in a case where the change in ownership occurs "in connection with" a "redemption or other corporate contraction," the amount of the redemption or contraction).

¶809   [1] In addition, generally if the Code §382 rules do not apply but a corporation (including an historic Badco creditor) (P) acquires enough Badco stock in the restructuring so that Badco is included in P's consolidated federal income tax return after the restructuring, the use of Badco's NOL is limited by the "separate return limitation year" or "SRLY" rules. Under the SRLY rules, Badco's pre-acquisition NOL is usable only by Badco and possibly other pre-acquisition members of Badco's old consolidated group (and not by P or P's other subsidiaries). Badco is included in P's consolidated return if, after the restructuring, P owns at least 80% of Badco's stock both by vote and by value (determined without regard to certain nonvoting, nonparticipating, nonconvertible preferred stock).

In determining whether Badco has a more than 50 percentage point stock ownership change during a 36-month period, the current stock ownership percentage of each person who has held 5% or more of Badco's stock at any time during the past 36 months (a "5% shareholder") is identified. Next, the lowest stock ownership percentage of each such person at any time during the past 36 months is identified. Then, for each 5% shareholder whose current stock ownership percentage exceeds his or her lowest stock ownership percentage, the increase in such shareholder's stock ownership percentage is calculated. A more than 50 percentage point stock ownership change occurs if the sum of such increases in stock ownership percentages exceeds 50%.

An option is treated as exercised for purposes of causing an ownership change only if there is an abusive principal purpose, i.e., only if the Badco option was issued, rather than Badco stock, in order to avoid the §382 rules and certain other tests are met.

In identifying 5% shareholders, all of Badco's small shareholders (i.e., shareholders each of whom owns less than 5%) are generally combined and treated as a single 5% shareholder whose collective stock ownership is monitored over the 36-month tracking period. However, under so-called "segregation rules," subject to several complex regulatory relief provisions, each group of less-than-5% shareholders that acquires stock in a public offering (primary or, if from a 5% shareholder, secondary) or a private sale (primary or, if from a 5% shareholder, secondary) is generally treated as a separate 5% shareholder whose newly-acquired shares count toward the 50 percentage point ownership change. A similar rule applies to the recipient of an option (including management) where the option has an abusive principal purpose and hence is treated as exercised.

The 2 principal regulatory relief provisions ameliorating the segregation rules are as follows:

- **The small-issuance exception** applies (1) where Badco issues new stock (or options to acquire new stock), *and* (2) where the issuance does not exceed 10% of the number of shares of such class outstanding at the beginning of Badco's taxable year (or at Badco's election 10% of the FV of all Badco's stock [other than certain debt-like preferred stock] at the beginning of Badco's taxable year), adjusted for stock splits and stock dividends, *and* (3) to the extent the stock is not issued to a person who is a 5% or greater Badco shareholder immediately after the issuance. In this case, the stock issued in the small issuance (other than to a person who is a 5% or greater shareholder immediately after the issuance) is treated as acquired pro rata by all of Badco's less-than-5% shareholders immediately before the issuance, rather than by a new 5% shareholder.

  However, if Badco has made prior small issuances during such taxable year, the cumulative issuances in excess of the 10% cap do not qualify for this exception. Where a single issuance by itself exceeds the 10% cap, no part of the issuance is exempt under the small-issuance exception.

- **The cash-issuance exception** applies where (1) Badco issues new stock "solely for cash" *or* issues an option to acquire stock and the consideration for the option as well as upon exercise of the option is "solely . . . cash" (hence apparently excluding an option to a service provider) *and* (2) some or all of the stock is issued to persons who are less-than-5% Badco shareholders immediately after the issuance. Where the cash-issuance exception applies, only a portion of the issuance is exempted, equal to the lesser of (1) the amount of stock issued to persons who are less-than-5% Badco shareholders immediately after the issuance and (2) an amount determined as follows:

- calculate the percentage of Badco's stock held by less-than-5% holders immediately before the cash issuance,
- multiply such percentage by 50%, and
- multiply the resulting percentage by the stock issued for cash.

The amount so exempted is treated as acquired pro rata by all of Badco's less-than-5% shareholders immediately before the issuance, rather than by a new 5% shareholder.

If an issuance qualifies for both the small-issuance exception and the cash-issuance exception, the former is applied first and the latter is applied only to the extent the former does not apply.

In identifying Badco's 5% shareholders, if 5% or more of Badco's stock is owned by an entity (e.g., a corporation, partnership, LLC, estate, or trust), such stock is treated as owned proportionately by that entity's equity owners. Each of the entity's equity owners who is so treated as owning indirectly 5% or more of Badco's stock is a 5% shareholder of Badco. All of the entity's equity owners who are not individually so treated as owning indirectly 5% or more of Badco's stock are combined and treated as a single 5% shareholder of Badco (subject to the segregation rules and the small-issuance and cash-issuance exceptions, which, in the case of a 5% or more corporate shareholder of Badco, for example, are applied by reference to stock issuances by the corporate shareholder). Hence an ownership change of Badco can occur as a result of changes in the ownership of Badco's entity shareholders.

¶809.4   Code §382 Elimination

Under the Code §382 elimination rule, if Badco has such a 50-percentage-point change in its stock ownership (by FV) during a 36-month period and Badco fails within 2 years thereafter *either* to (1) continue at least "a significant line" of its historic business *or* (2) use "a significant portion" of its historic business assets in a business, the annual §382 limitation described in ¶809.3 above is reduced to zero, retroactive to the change in ownership.

¶809.5   Built-in Losses

If Badco suffers a Code §382 change in ownership and its aggregate asset tax basis exceeds its aggregate asset FV by more than a threshold amount (the *lesser* of 15% of Badco's asset FV or $10 million), such BIL, when recognized (during the 5-year period after the ownership change), will generally also be subject to Code §382 taint or elimination.

¶809.6   Built-in Gains

If Badco suffers a Code §382 change in ownership and its aggregate asset FV (plus built-in income items, including anticipated DC) exceeds its aggregate asset tax basis by more than a threshold amount (the *lesser* of 15% of Badco's asset FV or $10 million), then, in addition to the annual §382 limitation calculated under the formula described in ¶809.3 above, Badco can use an amount of its pre-change NOL equal to the amount of such BIG recognized during the 5-year period following the ownership change.

¶809.7   Code §382 Special Elective Bankruptcy Rule

There is a special Code §382(*l*)(5) elective rule if the more-than-50-percentage-point change in Badco's stock ownership occurs pursuant to a bankruptcy or similar state court proceeding:

Badco can elect out of the Code §382 rules described in ¶809.3 through ¶809.6 above if (1) Badco is in bankruptcy (immediately before the change in ownership) and (2) Badco's shareholders and creditors (immediately before the change in ownership) own (after the change and as a result of being Badco shareholders and creditors immediately before) at least 50% of Badco's stock by vote and by value (ignoring certain non-voting, non-participating, non-convertible preferred stock).

- A Badco creditor is counted for purposes of this 50% test only if it acquires Badco stock in exchange for Badco debt that was *either* held by the particular creditor for 18 months before bankruptcy filing *or* arose in the ordinary course of business and has been held at all times by the particular creditor.
- Badco's shareholders apparently are counted for this purpose even if they acquired their stock shortly before the ownership change, i.e., within 36 months before the ownership change.

Where Badco qualifies for, and elects to utilize, this special Code §382(*l*)(5) bankruptcy provision:

- Badco's NOL is reduced by interest paid or accrued (during an approximately 3-year to 4-year period prior to the ownership change) on the Badco debt converted into stock in the bankruptcy proceeding.
- If Badco suffers a second §382 ownership change within 2 years after the bankruptcy ownership change, (1) the special Code §382(*l*)(5) rule applies from the bankruptcy ownership change to the second ownership change, (2) the Code §382(*l*)(5) rule can not apply to the second ownership change,

and (3) after the second ownership change, Badco's §382 limitation becomes zero.

¶809.8 Code §269 Elimination

Under the Code §269 elimination rule, Badco's NOL is eliminated (notwithstanding compliance with Code §382) where a person (or persons) initially owning less than 50% of Badco's stock by vote and by value (or owning no Badco stock) thereafter becomes the owner of 50% or more of Badco's stock (by vote or by value) *and* the acquisition of such 50% control of Badco by such person (or persons) had "the principal purpose" of tax avoidance.

¶809.9 Standstill Agreement to Prevent Subsequent Changes in Badco Shareholders

In order to avoid the adverse effects of Code §382 (and in some circumstances Code §269) on Badco's NOLs, it may be advisable for Badco's shareholders to remain relatively constant for at least 36 months. Thus a stand-still agreement among Badco shareholders is highly desirable.

¶809.10 Key Issues and References on Future Usage of Badco's Pre-Workout NOLs

What are the effects on Badco's NOL if there are changes in Badco's stock ownership, including:

- issuances of new stock to creditors as part consideration for debt cancellation,
- issuances of new stock to VCs for cash,
- sales of stock (or issuances of options) to management, and
- sales of stock between existing Badco shareholders?

Is there a special rule for a bankruptcy restructuring?

References:

- Code §382
- Code §1504(a)(4)
- Code §269
- Ginsburg and Levin M&A book ¶1203.2.2 through ¶1203.2.4
- Ginsburg and Levin M&A book ¶1205.2
- Ginsburg and Levin M&A book ¶1208

See the last question in ¶803.12.

¶810   CODE §384 LIMITATION ON USE OF BADCO'S NOLCF AGAINST NEW TARGET'S BIG

If Badco (having successfully consummated its restructuring) makes an acquisition of another company (Target) in a fashion that carries over the old basis of Target's assets (e.g., a taxable purchase of Target's stock with no Code §338 or §338(h)(10) election *or* a tax-free acquisition of Target's stock or assets) *and* Target's BIG on the acquisition date exceeds a threshold amount (the *lesser* of 15% of Target's asset FV or $10 million), Badco can not use its pre-acquisition NOLCF (on its consolidated return which includes Badco and Target) to offset Target's BIG recognized during a 5-year period after the acquisition.

Key Issues and References

If Badco acquires a new target company in a manner that causes Target's old asset tax basis to carry over to Badco, is there any impediment to using Badco's NOL (on the consolidated return which includes Badco and Target) against gain recognized on a subsequent disposition of Target assets which had BIG at the time Badco acquired Target?

References:

- Code §384
- Code §1504
- Ginsburg and Levin M&A book ¶1205.1.2 (portion dealing with Code §384) and ¶1205.2.5

CHAPTER 9

Exit Strategies: Structuring IPO or Sale of VC-Financed Portfolio Company

Chapter 9.   Exit Strategies: Structuring IPO or Sale of Company

A venture capitalist does not invest in a transaction (of the types discussed in the prior chapters of this book) with the intent of holding and operating Newco, Oldco, Target, or Badco (all of which are referred to in this chapter as "Portfolio Company") into the indefinite future. Rather, VC's goal is to liquefy its investment at a substantial profit when Portfolio Company's value has been maximized through astute management and VC supervision, add-on acquisitions, and the like (i.e., when Portfolio Company has matured to the point where its value is no longer growing geometrically), generally 3 to 7 years after VC's initial investment in Portfolio Company.

Hence, when structuring VC's front-end investment—in a start-up, growth-equity, buyout, industry consolidation, or troubled company restructuring, as described in Chapters 2 through 8 above—VC will already be planning its ultimate exit strategies. Indeed, contracts signed at the time of VC's initial investment will generally give VC certain future rights to control its exit. This is especially important where VC will not (or may not) control Portfolio Company at the back end when the exit strategy is being executed. Even where VC will control Portfolio Company at the time of the endgame, the actual exit strategy employed (e.g., a sale of Portfolio Company's stock) may require cooperation from some shareholders who will not (or may not) be in agreement with the timing, price, or other terms proposed by VC.

In addition, state corporate law generally imposes fiduciary obligations on a majority shareholder (and on the board of directors) with respect to the treatment of minority shareholders, which may inhibit VC's ability to obtain certain desired advantages over other shareholders (e.g., priority in a public offering) where VC controls Portfolio Company at the back end. Such a fiduciary duty would not, however, extend to or adversely affect VC's back-end invocation of contractual rights VC obtained in connection with its initial investment in Portfolio Company.

Thus, it is important at the front end, when VC makes its investment, that VC obtain contractual rights to control the back-end exit strategies.

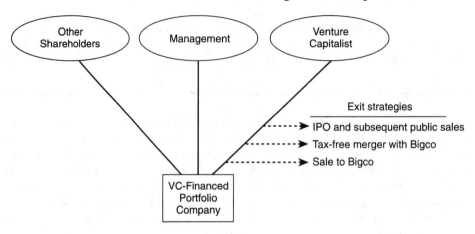

For that reason, it is typical for VC to insist at the front end that Portfolio Company and its other shareholders sign (e.g.) a registration rights agreement. Such an agreement may give VC control over the timing of a future IPO, selection of underwriters, priority over other shareholders in the public resale of its stock, the right to demand additional SEC registrations subsequent to the IPO, and the right to have VC's IPO and subsequent registration expenses paid by Portfolio Company. See ¶207.7 above regarding SEC aspects of reselling VC's Portfolio Company securities and ¶207.7.3 above regarding a front-end registration rights agreement.

Similarly, where VC is the majority or the largest single investor, it is typical for VC to insist that the Portfolio Company and its other shareholders sign "drag-along" agreements, giving VC the right to find a buyer or several buyers for part or all of Portfolio Company's stock (or a merger partner or asset buyer) and binding Portfolio Company and its shareholders to cooperate in effectuating such transactions. See ¶206 above.

Particularly where VC is a minority investor, VC will often want "tag-along" rights to sell alongside management and other principal shareholders if they sell their Portfolio Company stock (or a significant portion of their stock).

VC's exit strategy may include (1) sales of Portfolio Company stock to the public in an IPO or a post-IPO registered offering or pursuant to SEC Rule 144 *or* (2) a sale of Portfolio Company to a large company ("Bigco") in exchange for Bigco stock (in a tax-free reorganization), for cash, or partly for cash and partly for Bigco debt instruments reportable for federal income tax purposes on the installment method.

Finally, VC may (at the time of its initial investment in Portfolio Company) seek a right to put its stock back to Portfolio Company at some future time either at a formula price (e.g., 10 times earnings per share) or at appraised FV.

¶901   INITIAL PUBLIC OFFERING

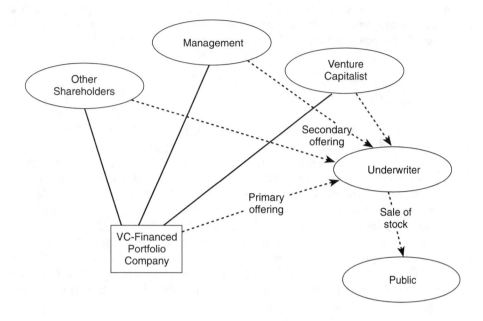

¶901.1   *Methods for Reselling Restricted Securities*

Generally VC and others originally acquired their Portfolio Company securities without SEC registration in a private placement (including a Reg. D offering) or a Rule 701 sale as described in ¶207 above. Hence their Portfolio Company securities are generally "restricted securities." A holder of "restricted securities" can generally resell such securities only:

- in a subsequent private sale (including a sale to a "qualified institutional buyer" pursuant to SEC Rule 144A), *or*
- in a public offering registered with SEC under the 1933 Act, *or*
- in a public sale under SEC Rule 144 (generally only after Portfolio Company has already become a 1934 Act reporting company), *or*
- where Portfolio Company is not already a 1934 Act reporting company, in a public sale pursuant to a Reg. A offering statement filed with SEC, usable only for up to (1) $5 million, *less* (2) sales pursuant to Reg. A during the 12 months before the start of (and during) the Reg. A offering, (3) of which $5 million only $1.5 million can be secondary sales by Portfolio Company's security holders, *or*
- in an "offshore transaction" pursuant to SEC Reg. S when there have not been any "directed selling efforts" into the U.S. market.

¶901.2 1933 Act Registration Statement on Form S-1

The most likely mode for effectuating an IPO for a privately-held Portfolio Company is a full-blown 1933 Act registration statement on form S-1. Such a registration statement on form S-1, which is generally time consuming and expensive, must be effective when the securities are actually sold to the public.

¶901.3 Underwritten Offering

The most common approach to an IPO is for VC and Portfolio Company to arrange for an underwriter (or group of underwriters) to buy the securities when the 1933 Act registration statement becomes effective and resell them to the public.

The lead underwriter will generally place a limit ("an underwriting limitation") on the number of Portfolio Company securities which can be sold in the offering.

In addition, the lead underwriter will undoubtedly require that Portfolio Company and each major holder agree not to sell additional Portfolio Company securities (including under SEC Rule 144) for a specified (and often lengthy, e.g., 90 to 180 days or occasionally longer) period after the underwritten offering (a "hold-back period"). Often the registration rights agreement will obligate holders offered the opportunity to take part in the offering not to sell (other than in the underwritten offering) during the hold-back period.

¶901.4 Primary vs. Secondary Sales

To the extent that Portfolio Company is seeking new money for expansion, redemption of VC-owned preferred stock or subordinated debentures, and other corporate purposes, the IPO will include "primary" securities to be sold by Portfolio Company. To the extent VC and the other holders want to liquify their holdings of Portfolio Company securities, the IPO will include "secondary" securities to be sold by the existing shareholders.

Frequently, in an underwritten IPO, the underwriters will insist that all or a substantial portion of the offering consist of primary securities (to demonstrate that Portfolio Company is bettering itself) and that at most a smaller portion (or possibly none) of the IPO consist of secondary securities (to demonstrate that Portfolio Company's existing holders are not bailing out).

In an underwritten offering, because there will generally be an underwriting limitation on the number of securities which can be sold, the parties should agree at the time of VC's initial investment (or where there is no front-end registration rights agreement, they should agree in advance of the underwritten offering) as to the proration of primary securities to be sold by Portfolio Company and secondary securities to be sold by the selling holders.

¶901.5   Stock Exchange Listing vs. Nasdaq National Market

Portfolio Company and VC must decide whether to seek listing of the securities on a national stock exchange (e.g., NYSE, AMEX) or on Nasdaq National Market. Each of NYSE, AMEX, and Nasdaq National Market require issuers to meet certain net tangible asset and net income thresholds to be admitted for trading. Alternatively, if an issuer is unable to meet the applicable listing standards, it is possible to be traded on the Nasdaq Small-Cap Market.

¶901.6   Special Form for Small Business Issuer

As an alternative to filing a full-blown SEC registration statement on form S-1, Portfolio Company can utilize a simplified SEC form SB-1 or SB-2 if it qualifies as a "small business issuer." A "small business issuer" is:

- a U.S. or Canadian entity,
- with revenues of less than $25 million, and
- a public float (the aggregate market FV of voting stock held by non-affiliates) of less than $25 million.

If an issuer is engaged in an IPO, the float test is calculated on the basis of the anticipated offering price.

The primary benefit to using forms SB-1 and SB-2 is a simplified disclosure format similar to that of SEC Reg. A (see ¶207.6 above) and less stringent financial statement requirements. In addition, following its IPO, a small business issuer is able to satisfy its periodic reporting requirements under the 1934 Act (see ¶207.3.1(4) above) by filing forms 10-KSB and 10-QSB which also allow simplified disclosure.

A "small business issuer" ceases to qualify for the simplified disclosure format once its revenue exceeds $25 million for two consecutive years or it exceeds the $25 million public float test for two consecutive years (tested on a date within 60 days after the end of its fiscal year).

¶901.7   Short-Form 1933 Act Registration Statement for Subsequent Offerings

Normally, Portfolio Company's IPO will be a full-blown long-form S-1 registration statement. Subsequent 1933 Act registered offerings can be on shorter form S-2 or S-3, once Portfolio Company satisfies SEC's requirements for the use of such forms. See ¶902 below.

¶901.8   Blue Sky Compliance

In addition to the SEC rules, any offering of Portfolio Company securities must comply with all applicable state blue sky laws. However, under 1996 federal legislation where Portfolio Company or a Portfolio Company shareholder sells securities to be traded on the NYSE, AMEX, or Nasdaq National Market, no state may impose merit review or require any filing.

¶901.9   No Gun Jumping

Prior to filing the preliminary registration statement with SEC, Portfolio Company and its holders must avoid statements which could be viewed as offers to sell securities ("gun jumping") and any unusual publicity about Portfolio Company designed to "condition the market" for the public offering.

¶901.10   Balanced Prospectus

It is desirable for the SEC registration statement and prospectus to give an optimistic, favorable view of Portfolio Company to assist in selling the securities to the public. However, it is essential that the prospectus also adequately describe the unfavorable aspects of Portfolio Company and set forth the risk factors, so that Portfolio Company, its directors, its control persons, and the selling holders will not be liable to public buyers of Portfolio Company securities if the securities subsequently decline in value. Hence, a well-balanced prospectus, fully describing all favorable and unfavorable aspects of Portfolio Company, its business, and its competitive and legal situation is essential.

¶901.11   Post-IPO Obligations

After the IPO, when Portfolio Company is publicly traded, it is important that Portfolio Company, its board, and its principal shareholders pay attention to a number of new legal obligations, including:

- Filing of periodic reports with SEC—annual 10-Ks, quarterly 10-Qs, periodic 8-Ks for certain events.
- Filing proxy statements with SEC, and mailing them to shareholders, in connection with each shareholder vote.
- Timely public announcements of material developments.
- 1934 Act §16(b) disgorgement of short-swing profits on a purchase and sale (or sale and purchase) of Portfolio Company stock (or certain derivatives) within a six-month period by a person who is an executive officer, director, or 10% beneficial owner of Portfolio Company.

- SEC Rule 10b-5 prohibition on a person in possession of material non-public information (an "insider" or a "temporary insider") using it to buy or sell Portfolio Company securities or "tip" others who do so. Information is "material" if a reasonable investor would consider it relevant to his or her investment decision.

  - Portfolio Company should (1) adopt a policy statement prohibiting all officers, directors, employees, and agents from buying or selling Portfolio Company securities when in possession of material non-public information or from disclosing such information to any third party not authorized by Portfolio Company to receive it and (2) consider prohibiting officers, directors, and others regularly possessing such information from ever buying or selling Portfolio Company securities except (a) during a specified window period, generally beginning two business days after the company's quarterly or annual earnings report and ending 10 business days after such report or (b) pursuant to a pre-arranged trading plan satisfying the requirements of SEC Rule 10b5-1.
  - Prohibition on Portfolio Company extending or maintaining credit in the form of a personal loan to any executive officer or director, which (as discussed in more detail in ¶501.5.4.2) likely includes an executive officer's note to Portfolio Company as the purchase price (or as part of the purchase price) for Portfolio Company stock (under Sarbanes-Oxley Act §402 which applies once Portfolio Company becomes an "issuer"— generally a company with publicly-issued or publicly-traded securities or a company which has filed with SEC a 1933 Act registration statement covering either equity or debt securities that has not yet become effective but has not yet been withdrawn).

¶902   1933 ACT REGISTERED PUBLIC OFFERINGS SUBSEQUENT TO IPO

¶902.1   *Short-Form Registrations*

Once Portfolio Company is a 1934 Act reporting company, it may qualify for short-form 1933 Act registration statements (on form S-2 or S-3) which allows Portfolio Company or holders of its restricted securities to sell securities with less delay and at less expense than a full-blown S-1 registration statement.

For the definition of a 1934 Act reporting company, see ¶207.3.1(4) above.

See ¶901.6 for a description of the simplified form available to Portfolio Company as long as it qualifies as a small business issuer.

¶902.2   Form S-3

SEC form S-3 allows Portfolio Company to incorporate most information by merely referring to Portfolio Company's periodic 1934 Act filings. To qualify for form S-3, Portfolio Company must satisfy *all* of the following Registrant Requirements:

- Portfolio Company must have been a 1934 Act reporting company for at least 12 months and filed all required material.
- Portfolio Company must have made all 1934 Act filings for the prior 12 months on a timely basis.
- Portfolio Company and its consolidated and unconsolidated subsidiaries must not have failed to make any dividend or sinking fund payments on preferred stock and not defaulted on repayment of borrowings or long-term lease rental payments for approximately a year.

In addition to meeting the Registrant Requirements, an offering on form S-3 must meet one of the following Transaction Requirements:

- For a primary or secondary offering of securities for cash, the aggregate market value of the stock held by non-affiliates (i.e., persons not in Portfolio Company's control group) of the Portfolio Company must be $75 million or more (calculated as of any date within 60 days of the SEC filing).
- Alternatively, for a secondary offering, Portfolio Company must have the same class of securities listed and registered on a national securities exchange or quoted on Nasdaq National Market, in which case it need not meet the $75 million public float test.

¶902.3   Form S-2

SEC form S-2 is not as convenient as form S-3, because form S-2 requires that certain of Portfolio Company's periodic 1934 Act filings actually be delivered to buyers. To qualify for form S-2, Portfolio Company must satisfy *all* of the following Registrant Requirements:

- Portfolio Company must have been a 1934 Act reporting company for at least 36 months and filed all required material.
- Portfolio Company must have made all 1934 Act filings for the prior 12 months on a timely basis.
- Portfolio Company and its consolidated and unconsolidated subsidiaries must not have failed to make any dividend or sinking fund payments on preferred stock and not defaulted on repayment of borrowings or long-term lease rental payments for approximately a year.

¶902.4 Demand and Piggy-Back Registrations

In a front-end registration rights agreement signed when VC made its original investment in Portfolio Company (as discussed at ¶207.7.3 above), VC will frequently have obtained the right to periodic demand registrations of its Portfolio Company restricted securities once Portfolio Company has completed its IPO and any contractual underwriter hold-back period has expired. In addition, VC will frequently also have obtained the right to piggy-back on SEC registrations filed by Portfolio Company in which Portfolio Company or any of its stockholders are selling Portfolio Company stock to the public.

¶903 SEC RULE 144 SALES AFTER IPO

Once Portfolio Company has completed its IPO, VC and other holders can begin to sell their restricted securities without filing an SEC registration statement for those securities (subject to expiration of any contractual hold-back period imposed by the underwriter in the IPO or subsequent underwritten registered offering) so long as *all* the requirements of SEC Rule 144 (as listed below) are met:

¶903.1 Information

Portfolio Company must have been a 1934 Act reporting company (see ¶207.3.1(4)) for at least 90 days prior to the sale and have filed all the reports required to be filed by the 1934 Act during the preceding 12 months (or such shorter period that Portfolio Company was required to file such reports).

¶903.2 Volume Limitation

Each holder can sell, in any 3-month period, no more than *the greater of* 1% of Portfolio Company's outstanding securities of the same class *or* 1 week's average trading volume over the past 4 weeks in securities of the same class (excluding from the reported trading volume any shares sold by the holder during that period). While nothing on this issue has been heard from SEC since 2/97, SEC had then announced that it was considering eliminating the four-week average trading volume test, so that the permitted volume would simply be 1% of the outstanding class.

All holders who are acting in concert in selling Portfolio Company securities are aggregated in applying this volume test.

¶903.3 Manner of Sale

Portfolio Company securities must be sold through a broker or to a market maker. The seller may not solicit or arrange for the solicitation of orders to buy the securities and may not make a payment in connection with the sale to any person other than the selling broker. While nothing on this issue has been heard from SEC since 2/97, SEC had then announced that it was considering eliminating these requirements.

¶903.4   1-Year Holding Period

The selling holder must have at least a 1-year SEC holding period for the securities. While nothing on this issue has been heard from SEC since 2/97, SEC had then announced that it was considering reducing this 1-year holding period to as short as 6 months. SEC was also considering how to address hedging transactions involving restricted securities and may reinstate the concept of tolling the holding period where the holder engages in puts, short sales, or other options to sell securities.

¶903.4.1   Commencement of Holding Period

If the holder purchased the securities from Portfolio Company or from a Portfolio Company affiliate (i.e., a member of Portfolio Company's control group), the SEC holding period generally does not begin until the holder has paid the full purchase price, although a full recourse note from the purchaser, secured by assets (other than the Portfolio Company securities being purchased) with an FV at least equal to the note, will also generally start the holding period, so long as the note is paid before resale of the securities.

¶903.4.2   Acquisition From a Person Other Than Portfolio Company or an Affiliate

If the holder did not acquire the securities from Portfolio Company or from a Portfolio Company affiliate, the holder tacks (i.e., adds to the holder's own SEC holding period) the transferor's SEC holding period.

¶903.4.3   Convertible Security

With a convertible debenture or convertible preferred, the SEC holding period for the debenture or preferred tacks to the common stock into which the debenture or preferred is converted.

- See ¶501.5.2.3 for a discussion of the similar IRS tacking rule for a convertible (used in determining whether a non-corporate holder has satisfied the more-than-12-month tax holding period necessary for LTCG).

¶903.4.4   Warrant

With a warrant, a new Rule 144 holding period starts at exercise, except that (1) where the warrant exercise price is paid by surrender of another Portfolio Company security (debentures, preferred stock, common stock) (i.e., a gross cashless exercise), the holder tacks the shorter of the SEC holding period for the surrendered security or the SEC holding period for the warrant to the holding period for the new common stock received upon exercise and (2) where the warrant is surrendered for common stock with an FV equal to the warrant spread (i.e., a net cashless exercise without payment of the warrant exercise price), the holder tacks the SEC holding period for the warrant to the holding period for the new common stock.

- See ¶501.5.2.2 for a discussion of the much more complex IRS tacking rules for a warrant (used in determining whether a non-corporate holder has satisfied the more-than-12-month tax period necessary for LTCG).

¶903.4.5   Possible Delay for Unvested Securities

In 1979, SEC published its position that where restricted securities are issued pursuant to "an employee benefit plan which requires the plan participants to remain as employees for a specified period of time before the securities . . . vest . . . [, the SEC] holding period . . . will commence when the securities are allocated to the account of an individual plan participant [and the] fact that the securities may not vest until some later date does not alter the result." It has long been widely believed that this salutary rule applies to all securities granted or sold to employees pursuant to a formal or informal plan.

However, the SEC staff created uncertainty in an early 1994 no-action letter where Portfolio Company granted stock to a number of executives pursuant to substantially similar individual contracts approved by the board (under which the stock would vest pro rata over 5 years, based on continued employment). The staff stated that "if the restricted securities are not issued pursuant to an employee benefit plan, the holding period does not begin to run until the date of vesting," and the staff then declined to determine whether the contracts constituted an employee benefit plan.

SEC rules define "employee benefit plan" extremely broadly, as including a "contract, authorization or arrangement, whether or not set forth in any formal documents, . . . [even if] applicable to one person." Hence, there is no rational reason for SEC to distinguish between a formal employee benefit plan and one or a set of individual contracts intended to incent one or more employees.

Discussions with the SEC staff indicate that this early 1994 no-action letter was meant merely to restate SEC's long-standing policy that it would not comment on whether a particular employment agreement constitutes an employee benefit plan. The SEC staff takes the position that such a determination must be made by the issuer and its counsel based on the facts and circumstances of each case.

Hence, it appears that SEC meant no inference in the no-action letter that the situation then presented fell short of constituting an employee benefit plan.

If Portfolio Company's original issuance of the stock to the executives qualified under SEC Rule 701, the stock can be sold free of most Rule 144 restrictions once Portfolio Company has been a 1934 Act reporting company for at least 90 days. Hence, when Rule 701 covered Portfolio Company's original issuance of the executive's stock and Portfolio Company has been a reporting company for at least 90 days, the Rule 144 issue as to when the executive's 1 year/2 year SEC holding period commences is not relevant. See ¶903.8 below.

¶903.4.6   Incorporation of Partnership or LLC

If Portfolio Company was originally formed as a partnership or LLC (e.g., in order to obtain flow-through tax treatment) and was later transformed into a corporation (e.g., in anticipation of an IPO), SEC takes the illogical position that (1) the holders' SEC holding period in the partnership or LLC interests does not tack to the corporate stock received in exchange, because the decision to incorporate is a new investment decision, but (2) the holders' SEC holding period does tack where (i) at the time of the holder's original investment in the partnership or LLC, a written agreement contemplated that the entity would be transformed into corporate form in connection with an IPO, (ii) no additional consideration is paid at the time of the transformation, (iii) the incorporation causes no shift in the holders' economic interests not contemplated by the original documents, and (iv) the holders do not retain any veto power or other voting power with respect to the transformation. However, SEC takes the position that there is no tacking for any equity owner of the partnership or LLC (e.g., the general partner) who did have a veto power or other voting power with respect to the incorporation.[1]

¶903.5   SEC Notification

If the amount of securities to be sold in reliance on Rule 144 during any three month period exceeds 500 shares or has an aggregate sale price in excess of $10,000, the selling holder must file a form 144 with SEC. The form 144 must be mailed or otherwise transmitted to SEC concurrently with placing a sell order with the broker or on sale to a market maker, and the seller must have a bona fide intention of selling the securities within a reasonable time after filing the form 144. While nothing on this issue has been heard from SEC since 2/97, SEC had then announced that it was considering raising the reporting thresholds to 1,000 shares or $40,000.

¶903 [1] If Portfolio Company partnership or LLC has an IPO (see Code §7704) or checks the box for corporate tax treatment (see ¶302.8.1), Newco will (although still a partnership or LLC for state law purposes) be treated as a corporation for federal tax purposes, but no new SEC holding period will begin. However, this technique will not transform Portfolio Company into a state law corporation (which is generally desirable for IPO purposes).

¶903.6   2-Year Holding Period for Unlimited Non-Affiliate Sales

Under Rule 144(k), where a holder who is not a Portfolio Company affiliate (i.e., not a member of Portfolio Company's control group) has at least a 2-year SEC holding period and has not been a Portfolio Company affiliate for at least 3 months, restrictions ¶903.1 through ¶903.5 lapse, so that such non-affiliate can sell an unlimited quantity of Portfolio Company securities. While nothing on this issue has been heard from SEC since 2/97, SEC had then announced that it was considering reducing the 2-year holding period to as short as 1 year.

¶903.7   Partnership Fund Distribution in Kind

If a PE fund or other partnership distributes restricted securities to its partners, the partners tack the SEC holding period of the PE fund even if the fund was an affiliate of the issuer.

Thus, once the tacked holding period reaches 1 year, the partners can begin Rule 144 sales. However, until the tacked holding period reaches 2 years, all Rule 144 sales by the partners are aggregated for purposes of the volume limitation (see ¶903.2 above).

Any partner with a tacked 2-year holding period which is not itself a Portfolio Company affiliate (i.e., a member of Portfolio Company's control group) can sell an unlimited quantity of Portfolio Company securities under Rule 144(k). Such a partner which is a Portfolio Company affiliate could begin to utilize Rule 144(k) for unlimited resales 3 months after ceasing to be an affiliate. See ¶903.6 above.

¶903.8   Rule 701 Securities

Where the holder originally acquired the restricted securities from Portfolio Company pursuant to Rule 701, the holder is generally free (once Portfolio Company has been a 1934 Act reporting company for at least 90 days) to resell the restricted securities under Rule 144 without complying with any of the Rule 144 requirements except ¶903.3 above (manner of sale).

However, if the holder is a Portfolio Company affiliate (i.e., a member of Portfolio Company's control group), such holder must also comply with Rule 144's volume limitation and SEC notification requirements.

¶904 RESALES OF PORTFOLIO COMPANY UNRESTRICTED SECURITIES BY PORTFOLIO COMPANY AFFILIATE

¶904.1 Portfolio Company Affiliate

Even where a holder's Portfolio Company securities are not restricted (e.g., the holder purchased them in the public market or under certain limited circumstances under SEC Rule 504 as described in ¶207.3.1), if the holder is a Portfolio Company affiliate (i.e., a member of Portfolio Company's control group), such holder's resale of unrestricted Portfolio Company securities must meet all of the Rule 144 requirements (as set forth in ¶903.1 through ¶903.5 above), except that ¶903.4 (the minimum 1-year holding period requirement) is not applicable. All sales of both restricted and unrestricted Portfolio Company securities by the Portfolio Company affiliate (and anyone acting in concert with such person in selling Portfolio Company securities) pursuant to Rule 144 are taken into account in determining whether such person's sales are within the 1%-of-outstanding-stock/1-week's-average-trading-volume limitation (described in ¶903.2 above).

In calculating the 1-week's-average-trading-volume limitation, sales by the affiliate (and anyone acting in concert with the affiliate) are not taken into account.

¶904.2 Portfolio Company Non-Affiliate

A person who is not a Portfolio Company affiliate can resell unrestricted Portfolio Company securities without complying with Rule 144.

¶905 SALE OF PORTFOLIO COMPANY TO, OR MERGER OF PORTFOLIO COMPANY WITH, BIGCO FOR BIGCO STOCK, NOTES, AND/OR CASH

¶905.1 Bigco Stock as Principal Consideration

Where Bigco acquires Portfolio Company principally for Bigco stock:

(1) Under the tax-free reorganization rules, (a) Portfolio Company shareholders can generally receive Bigco stock—other than NQ Pfd as described in ¶403.1(9) through (15) above—tax free and (b) any boot (including NQ Pfd) received in the reorganization will generally be taxed as LTCG. Code §354, §356, and §368.

To constitute a tax-free reorganization, a substantial portion of the consideration received by Portfolio Company's shareholders must be stock of the acquiring corporation (here Bigco) or its parent (generally at least 40%, based on a Supreme Court decision interpreting the judicial continuity-of-interest doctrine, although IRS declines to issue a ruling below 50%) and certain other technical tests must be satisfied (which are less stringent in a 2-party forward merger of Portfolio Company into Bigco than in other types of acquisition structures).

1/98 IRS regulations abolished the long-standing post-reorganization continuity-of-interest doctrine, so there is no tax law impediment if Portfolio Company's shareholders immediately sell all of the Bigco stock received in a tax-free reorganization, so long as they do not too quickly resell the stock to Bigco or a corporation related to Bigco.

(2) SEC restrictions apply to future resales of Bigco stock on the open market by Portfolio Company's shareholders.

(a) If the Bigco stock issued in its acquisition of Portfolio Company was *not* registered with SEC (e.g., because exempt under Reg. D where Portfolio Company's shareholders are a reasonably small and sophisticated group— see ¶207.3 above), former Portfolio Company shareholders will hold restricted Bigco stock, which they can resell without registration subject to Rule 144's requirements regarding (i) current public information, (ii) 1-year and 2-year holding periods for the Bigco stock (which begin anew at consummation of the merger, i.e., with no tacking of the period the shareholder held the Portfolio Company stock before the merger), (iii) volume (generally a holder of restricted stock can sell in any 3-month period the *greater of* 1% of Bigco's outstanding stock *or* 1 week's average trading volume, unless and until such holder qualifies for Rule 144(k)'s unlimited non-affiliate resales), (iv) manner of sale, and (v) notice, as described in ¶903 above.

Hence, if the Bigco stock is not registered with SEC, it is desirable for Portfolio Company's shareholders to obtain contractual registration rights from Bigco covering their resales of Bigco stock.

(b) If the Bigco stock issued in the acquisition *was* registered with SEC at the time of issuance to Portfolio Company's shareholders, the former Portfolio Company shareholders will be free to resell their Bigco stock to the public without further registration or compliance with Rule 144, except that:

- If Bigco's acquisition of Portfolio Company was structured as an asset sale or merger requiring a shareholder vote, so that it fell within SEC Rule 145, a former Portfolio Company shareholder who was an affiliate of Portfolio Company (i.e., a member of Portfolio Company's control group) immediately before the acquisition (even though not a Bigco affiliate after the acquisition) will be subject to the Rule 144 volume and other restrictions for 1 year after the acquisition but will not be subject to Rule 144's normal 1-year no sale period. Hence, it is desirable for Portfolio Company affiliates to obtain contractual registration rights from Bigco covering their resales of Bigco stock.

  While nothing on this issue has been heard from SEC since 2/97, SEC had then announced that it was considering eliminating these restrictions on a former Portfolio Company shareholder who was an affiliate of Portfolio Company immediately before the acquisition.

- A former Portfolio Company shareholder who is an affiliate of Bigco (i.e., a member of Bigco's control group) at the time of resale will be subject to Rule 144 volume and other restrictions as set forth in ¶904.1 above, but not to the 1-year no sale period.

- If the acquisition is structured to qualify for pooling (rather than purchase) accounting for GAAP purposes, in order to avoid GAAP purchase accounting—i.e., a step-up in the book value of Portfolio Company's assets and resulting goodwill amortization (see ¶501.8 above)—former Portfolio Company affiliates are prohibited from selling any Bigco stock until publication by Bigco (generally in a 10-Q) of at least 30 days' combined Bigco-Portfolio Company results (except for a de minimis rule).

¶905.2 Bigco Debt Instrument as Part of Consideration

Where Bigco issues debt instruments as part or all of the consideration for Portfolio Company:

(1) IRS installment sale rules allow Portfolio Company's shareholders to defer a pro rata portion of their gain on the sale of the Portfolio Company stock until the Bigco debt instruments are paid (so long as neither the Bigco debt instruments received nor the Portfolio Company stock sold was traded on an established securities exchange and certain other installment sale requirements are met). Code §453.

- The Rule 144 and 145 SEC limitations that apply on a resale of Bigco stock received by Portfolio Company's shareholders (see ¶905.1(2) above) also apply on a resale by Portfolio Company's shareholders of the Bigco debt instruments.

¶905.3 Bigco Asset SUB

If the transaction is structured as a taxable asset sale (or a taxable stock sale with Code §338 or §338(h)(10) election), so that Portfolio Company's assets are transferred to Bigco with an asset SUB, the transaction is generally subjected to double tax unless Portfolio Company is a S corporation or a partnership or LLC or has a sufficient NOL to shelter the corporate-level gain. Hence the transaction may be more tax efficiently structured for asset COB (as a taxable stock sale or taxable reverse subsidiary merger with no Code §338 election or as a tax-free reorganization). See ¶501.7, ¶502.1.1, and ¶503.2 above.

¶905.4 Representations, Warranties, and Indemnifications from Portfolio Company's Shareholders

Whether the sale of Portfolio Company to Bigco is structured as a tax-free reorganization, a taxable asset sale, or a taxable stock sale, there will be substantial negotiation over the extent to which Bigco has future recourse against Portfolio Company's shareholders in the event that Portfolio Company is not all that Bigco expected it to be.

Here, where VC is a seller rather than a buyer, VC will be seeking the loosest possible representation, warranty, and indemnification provisions, i.e., the opposite of VC's position at ¶501.3.1.2 above, where VC was the buyer.

¶905.4.1 Representations and Warranties

Bigco will seek extensive representations and warranties from Portfolio Company's shareholders (including VC) regarding Portfolio Company (e.g., undisclosed liabilities, inventory, receivables, condition of tangible assets, financial statements, and title to stock and/or assets).

Portfolio Company's shareholders will seek to give far fewer representations and warranties (or possibly none at all—i.e., an "as is" sale) and to qualify them with concepts of "materiality" and "knowledge."

¶905.4.2 Survival

Bigco will seek to have these representations and warranties survive the closing for a lengthy period (possibly forever) and will seek to have Portfolio Company's shareholders indemnify Bigco against any breaches Bigco discovers during the survival period.

Portfolio Company's shareholders will seek to have the representations and warranties expire at the closing (i.e., to give Bigco no right whatsoever to sue Portfolio Company's shareholders after the closing for breaches of representations and warranties) or, at least, to have the representations and warranties survive only for breaches discovered by Bigco within a brief period (e.g., 6 to 12 months after the closing).

¶905.4.3 Deductible and/or Ceiling

Bigco will desire the indemnification obligation of Portfolio Company's shareholders to begin with the first dollar of damages from breach and to be unlimited in amount.

Portfolio Company's shareholders will desire their indemnification obligation to be subject to (1) a deductible so that they pay claims only in excess of (e.g.) $1 million (or at least a minimum threshold if they can not obtain a deductible), (2) a ceiling (e.g., 50% of Bigco's purchase price for Portfolio Company), and (3) several, not joint and several, liability (so that each shareholder is liable only for his or her pro rata share).

¶905.4.4   Escrow or Other Security

Bigco will desire security for the shareholders' indemnification obligation, e.g., hold back part of the purchase price, escrow part of the purchase price, and/or set off rights against any seller paper.

Portfolio Company's shareholders ordinarily will not desire to provide any such security for their indemnification obligation.

¶905.4.5   Assumption of Liabilities

Bigco will desire to assume responsibility for only specified Portfolio Company ordinary-course-of-business liabilities and to leave the remainder (including unknown and contingent liabilities) behind for Portfolio Company's shareholders to pay (or, in a stock purchase, to have Portfolio Company's shareholders agree to hold Bigco harmless for such non-assumed liabilities).

Portfolio Company's shareholders will desire Bigco to assume responsibility for all of Portfolio Company's liabilities, known and unknown, liquidated and unliquidated, fixed and contingent.

¶906   SPECIAL LTCG TAX ADVANTAGES FOR INDIVIDUALS

The top normal federal tax rate for an individual's LTCG (i.e., gain on sale of a capital asset, including stock, held more than one year) is 20%, which is 18.6 percentage points below the top 2002 and 2003 individual OI rate (38.6%). However, three Code provisions grant further tax relief to an individual who owns stock either directly or through a partnership, LLC, or S corporation and who recognizes LTCG in special circumstances:

(1)   A 14% top rate for LTCG on sale of "qualified small business stock" held more than 5 years.

(2)   A tax-free rollover on sale of stock that would have qualified for the 14% special rate (except that the necessary holding period is more than 6 months rather than more than 5 years) where the proceeds are then reinvested in new qualified stock within 60 days.

(3)   An 18% top rate for LTCG on sale of property (not merely "qualified small business stock") acquired after 12/31/00 and held more than 5 years (with

a taxpayer election to treat pre-12/31/00 property as sold and reacquired in 1/01).

¶906.1   Code §1202 LTCG Rate Reduction to 14% on "Qualified Small Business Stock"

Code §1202 reduces the normal 20% LTCG rate to 14% for an individual's gain on disposition of a targeted stock investment. To be targeted gain, the transaction must meet every one of the onerous requirements described in ¶906.1(1)-(9) below, some relating to the corporate issuer of the stock ("Portfolio Company") and some relating to the selling shareholder.

(1) Non-corporate shareholder. The shareholder recognizing the gain must not be a corporation, i.e., the reduced rate is available only to an individual, trust, or estate. If the gain is recognized by a flow-through entity (e.g., a partnership, LLC, or S corporation), the reduced rate is available to a non-corporate partner, member, or S shareholder with respect to such non-corporate owner's proportionate share of such gain (1) if such non-corporate owner held his or her interest in the entity when the entity purchased the Portfolio Company stock and continuously thereafter and (2) to the extent that such non-corporate owner's interest in the entity is not greater than when the entity acquired the Portfolio Company stock.

(2) Stock acquired at original issuance. The shareholder recognizing the gain must have acquired the stock "at its original issue (directly or through an underwriter)." In order for this requirement to be met, the stockholder must purchase the shares in a primary offering from Portfolio Company (or Portfolio Company's underwriter), not from a third party in a secondary offering. It is not, however, necessary that the stockholder purchase the Portfolio Company shares at the time Portfolio Company first issues stock.

Where stock is received by gift, death, or partnership or LLC liquidation from a shareholder who held qualifying stock, the stock continues to qualify in the transferee's hands (so long as the transferee is a qualifying shareholder or a flow-through entity to the extent owned by a qualifying shareholder).

If the holder is a flow-through entity, the partner, member, or S shareholder (the "equity owner") must also have held his or her interest in the entity at the time the entity purchased the stock and continuously thereafter. Moreover, the equity owner cannot take advantage of the reduced rate on CG flowing through the entity to the extent that the equity owner's interest in the flow-through entity is greater than it was when the entity acquired Portfolio Company's stock, e.g., the equity owner cannot use this tax benefit to the extent he or she increased his or her interest in the entity after it acquired the Portfolio Company stock.

(3) 5-year holding period. The shareholder must have held the Portfolio Company stock for more than 5 years.

In applying requirements (2) and (3), there is tacking for a transfer by gift, upon death, on a distribution of stock by a partnership or LLC to a partner or member ((a) so long as the equity owner held his or her interest in the partnership or LLC when the partnership or LLC purchased the Portfolio Company stock and continuously thereafter and (b) to the extent that the equity owner's interest in the partnership or LLC is not greater than when the partnership or LLC acquired the Portfolio Company stock), on a conversion of convertible preferred stock (but not a convertible debenture) into common stock, or on a conversion of nonvoting into voting common stock.

Where a Portfolio Company convertible debenture is converted into stock, the §1202 holding period starts anew at the time of conversion and the measurement of whether Portfolio Company qualifies for §1202 is made at the time of conversion. Moreover, the gain which qualifies for §1202 is limited to the post-conversion appreciation in the stock. Thus, the §1202 result is sharply different for a convertible debenture than for convertible preferred, where the common stock is treated as merely a continuation of the preferred stock.

Where a Portfolio Company warrant is exercised, the transaction is treated as a new purchase of common stock with the results set forth above for conversion of a convertible debenture, except that pre-exercise appreciation in the common stock apparently does qualify for §1202.

Stock received by a service provider in connection with the performance of services is treated as issued when the resulting compensation income, if any, is included in the service provider's income in accordance with the rules of Code §83 (i.e., (a) at issuance where the stock is vested at issuance, (b) at issuance where the stock is subject to vesting but the service provider makes a timely §83(b) election, or (c) at vesting where the stock is subject to vesting and the service provider does not make a timely §83(b) election).

There are also special rules for flow-through entities, for incorporations, for reorganizations, and for certain other matters. For example, where Portfolio Company (which qualifies for §1202 treatment except that the 5-year requirement has not yet been satisfied) is acquired by Bigco in a tax-free reorganization, Bigco stock issued in exchange for Portfolio Company stock is treated as a continuation of Portfolio Company stock, except that the gain to which §1202 can apply (when the Bigco stock is later sold) is limited to the gain inherent in the Portfolio Company stock at the time of the tax-free reorganization.

(4) Post-8/10/93 issuance. The Portfolio Company stock must have been originally issued after 8/10/93, Code §1202's date of enactment.

(5) Stock acquired for cash or qualified consideration. The Portfolio Company stock must have been acquired in exchange for (a) cash, (b) stock that itself was qualified small business stock (i.e., stock meeting the requirements of ¶906.1(2) and (4) through (9)), (c) property other than stock, or (d) services.

Thus, if the Portfolio Company stock was issued to management shareholders of a target company ("Oldco") in a Code §351 rollover transaction, the Portfolio Company stock received by the management shareholders would not qualify if the Oldco stock was not "qualified small business stock" (e.g., because the Oldco stock was issued before 8/11/93).

(6) Domestic C corporation issuer. The Portfolio Company stock must have been issued by a domestic C corporation. Hence, stock of an S corporation, stock in a non-U.S. corporation, and interests in a partnership or LLC do not qualify (although stock of a C corporation indirectly owned by a qualifying shareholder through a flow-through entity does qualify).

(7) $50 million maximum assets at issuance. The "aggregate gross assets of [Portfolio Company] (or any predecessor thereof)" must not have exceeded $50 million at any time on or after 8/10/93 until "immediately after" the shareholder acquires the stock. Portfolio Company's assets are measured by their adjusted tax basis, except that a contributed asset is measured by its FV at contribution. This $50 million calculation is made *after* taking into account the amount received by Portfolio Company in the issuance.

For purposes of the $50 million test, Portfolio Company's assets generally include the assets of any 50%-or-more corporate parent and any 50%-or-more direct or indirect corporate subsidiary (measured by vote or value). Hence where a corporate VC owns or acquires 50% or more of Portfolio Company, the corporate VC's assets are apparently aggregated with Portfolio Company's assets.

Neither the statute nor the legislative history defines the term "immediately after." In the absence of specific authority, taxpayers may assert that the term should be interpreted literally to refer to the state of affairs at the instant immediately following the issuance of stock, disregarding all subsequent events. In interpreting other Code provisions, however, IRS and the courts, applying the step-transaction doctrine, have interpreted the term "immediately after" to include preplanned future events. For example, regulations under Code §351 state that:

> [t]he phrase "immediately after the exchange" does not necessarily require simultaneous exchanges by two or more persons, but comprehends a situation where the rights of the parties have been previously defined and the execution of the agreement proceeds with an expedition consistent with orderly procedure.

Hence it is unclear whether a first group of investors in Portfolio Company (who invest not more than $50 million) qualify for Code §1202 treatment where Portfolio Company has a preconceived plan to raise additional financing from a subsequent group that increases Portfolio Company's gross assets to more than $50 million shortly thereafter. Should IRS take a taxpayer-hostile (pro-step-transaction) position, the likelihood of IRS success would increase where the subsequent group's later purchase of Portfolio Company stock (a) is unconditional, (b) is intended to occur soon after the prior issuance to the first group, and (c) has been delayed only to qualify for Code §1202 treatment the prior issuance of stock to the first group. Conversely, the likelihood of IRS step-transaction victory would be reduced where the subsequent group's later purchase of Portfolio Company stock (a) is conditional (e.g., within the subsequent group's discretion or mandatory only if unpredictable future events occur), (b) is intended to occur (if at all) far in the future, and (c) was not deferred with any intent to allow the first group's prior stock purchase to qualify for Code §1202 treatment.

Where Portfolio Company is a new corporation ("Newco") formed to acquire Target's *assets*, the $50 million limitation (a) would apparently be violated where the aggregate amount received by Newco from debt and equity financing exceeded $50 million and (b) might be violated (on a step-transaction approach) even where the aggregate amount Newco received from debt and equity financing was below $50 million, if Newco's post-acquisition tax basis in the assets acquired from Target (including Target liabilities assumed by Newco) exceeded $50 million.

Where Newco is formed to acquire Target's *stock*, it is unclear whether the $50 million limitation is applied (a) by reference to the aggregate debt and equity financing raised by Newco or (b) by reference to Newco's and Target's post-acquisition assets (on a step-transaction approach) by disregarding Newco's basis in Target's *stock* and instead taking cognizance of Target's post-acquisition tax basis in its *assets*.

(8) Active business. The Portfolio Company must meet an active business requirement during "substantially all" of the stockholder's holding period for its stock. This test is met during any period while Portfolio Company uses at least 80% of its assets (by value) in conducting one or more businesses *other than*:

- Law, accounting, health, financial services, engineering, consulting, athletics, performing arts, or any other service business where the principal asset is the reputation or skill of one or more employees.
- Banking, insurance, financing, leasing, investing, and similar businesses.
- Farming.
- Production or extraction of certain minerals.
- Operating a hotel, motel, restaurant, or similar business.

Moreover, Portfolio Company is disqualified from §1202 if:

- More than 10% of its assets (by value) in excess of its liabilities consists of stock or securities in other corporations which are not 50% subsidiaries.
- More than 10% of the total value of its assets consists of real property not used in the active conduct of a business. For this purpose, owning, dealing in, or renting real property is not an active business.

For purposes of this (8), where Portfolio Company owns more than 50% by vote or value of a subsidiary's stock, there is a look-through to the Portfolio Company's pro rata share of the subsidiary's assets, liabilities, and business.

(9) No redemptions. Newly issued Portfolio Company stock is not eligible for the Code §1202 reduced tax rate if Portfolio Company has made certain types of stock redemptions. Specifically, newly issued stock will not qualify if Portfolio Company has redeemed:

(a)   any stock from the shareholder seeking the benefit of Code §1202, or from any related person (under Code §§267(b) or 707(b)), at any time during the four-year period beginning two years before and ending two years after issuance of the newly issued Portfolio Company stock, or

(b)   more than 5% of the aggregate value of all Portfolio Company stock (measured one year before issuance of the newly issued stock) from any shareholder(s) at any time during the two-year period beginning one year before and ending one year after issuance of the newly issued Portfolio Company stock.

12/97 regulations relax the above rules in several respects. First, in applying rule (a) above, redemptions of stock from the taxpayer and all related persons during the four-year period are disregarded where, aggregating all such redemptions, *either* (i) the amount paid to redeem the stock is $10,000 or less *or* (ii) the redeemed stock represents 2% or less of all Portfolio Company stock held by the taxpayer and related persons.

Second, in applying rule (b) above, redemptions of stock during the two-year period are disregarded where, aggregating all such redemptions, *either* (i) the amount paid to redeem the stock is $10,000 or less *or* (ii) the redeemed stock represents 2% or less of all Portfolio Company's outstanding stock (measured at the time of the redemption). Because the 5% threshold in rule (b) above is based on the value of Portfolio Company's stock one year before issuance of the newly issued Portfolio Company stock, the 2% regulatory threshold in (ii) above is beneficial where Portfolio Company's aggregate stock value has grown significantly between the start of the testing period and the time of the stock redemption.

Third, in applying rules (a) and (b) above, a redemption of stock is disregarded if *either* (i) the redeemed stock was acquired by the seller in connection with the performance of services as an employee or director and is redeemed incident to the seller's termination of services *or* (ii) the redeemed stock (or an option to acquire the redeemed stock) was held by a decedent or the decedent's spouse prior to the decedent's death and the redeemed stock is purchased from the decedent's estate, beneficiary, or surviving spouse within 3 years and 9 months from the date of the decedent's death *or* (iii) the redeemed stock is purchased incident to the disability or mental incompetency of the selling shareholder, *or* (iv) the redeemed stock is purchased incident to the divorce of the selling shareholder. The preamble to the 6/96 proposed regulations stated that IRS intended to extend exception (i) to independent contractors once IRS decided how to determine when a termination of an independent contractor's services has occurred, and the preamble to the 12/97 final regulations states that IRS continues to study this issue.

Finally, in applying rules (a) and (b) above, a transfer of stock from a shareholder to a corporate employee or independent contractor is not treated as a redemption of that stock, whether or not the transaction is so characterized by regulations under Code §83.

When Portfolio Company is formed to acquire Oldco's stock, it appears that redemptions of Oldco's stock would not be treated as violating this requirement. That is, Code §1202 does not contain a look-through rule for purposes of determining whether any proscribed stock redemptions have occurred.

(10) Ceiling on §1202 gain. The maximum amount of a particular non-corporate taxpayer's LTCG from stock of a single corporation eligible for the special 14% tax rate is the *greater of* (a) $10 million (taking into account his or her gain during the year of the sale and all prior years) and (b) 10 times the taxpayer's aggregate basis in targeted stock disposed of by the taxpayer during the year.

EXAMPLE

PE Fund purchases $15 million of Portfolio Company stock, holds such stock more than 5 years, and sells it for $250 million, i.e., a $235 million gain:

- 80% of which (i.e., $188 million) is allocated to PE Fund's LPs and GP in proportion to contributed capital and
- 20% of which (i.e., $47 million) is allocated to PE Fund's GP as carried interest.

Individual A, an LP who invested 10% of the PE Fund's capital, calculates the amount of his or her CG eligible for Code §1202's reduced rate as follows:

	Millions
• CG allocable to A: 10% of $188 million	$18.8
• Limitation (a): $10 million cumulative per Portfolio Company, of which none previously used	$10.0
• Limitation (b): 10 × A's stock basis (i.e., 10 × $15 million cost of PE Fund's stock × A's 10% contribution thereto)	$15.0

Hence, $15 million of A's $18.8 million CG qualifies for Code §1202's 14% rate (and the remaining $3.8 million is taxed at A's regular 20% LTCG rate). The result would be the same if PE Fund sold part of its Portfolio Company stock in one year and the remainder in another year.

Individual B, a partner of PE Fund's GP entity who, through GP, contributed 0.5% of the PE Fund's capital and holds 30% of the carried interest, calculates the amount of her CG eligible for Code §1202's reduced rate as follows:

	Millions
• CG allocable to B: 0.5% of $188 million plus 30% of $47 million	$15.040
• Limitation (a): $10 million cumulative per Portfolio Company, of which none previously used	$10.000
• Limitation (b): 10 × B's stock basis (i.e., 10 × $15 million cost of PE Fund's stock × B's 0.5% contribution thereto)	$0.075

Hence, $10 million of B's $15.04 million CG qualifies for Code §1202's 14% rate (and the remaining $5.04 million is taxed at B's regular 20% LTCG rate).

(11) AMT. For purposes of calculating the stockholder's AMT tax, 71% of the LTCG qualifying for the special 14% tax rate is included in the stockholder's AMT income.[1]

¶906.2   Code §1045 Tax-Free Rollover for "Qualified Small Business Stock"

Code §1045 allows an individual to elect to defer gain recognized on a sale of targeted stock ("old §1202 stock") held more than six months where the taxpayer uses the proceeds to purchase other targeted stock ("new §1202 stock") within the 60-day period beginning on the date of the sale.

If the Code §1045 requirements are satisfied and if the stockholder so elects (in a timely filed tax return for the year in which the old §1202 stock was sold, including extensions), gain on the sale of old §1202 stock is recognized only to the extent the sale proceeds exceed the purchase price of the new §1202 stock.

Gain realized but not recognized under Code §1045 on a sale of old §1202 stock is applied to reduce the basis of the new §1202 stock in the order such stock is acquired.

There is no need to physically trace proceeds from sale of the old §1202 stock to payment of purchase price for the new §1202 stock. Once an individual elects Code §1045 treatment with respect to a sale of the old §1202 stock, such individual is treated by Code §1045 as (a) rolling the proceeds into the first §1202 stock purchased thereafter (and within 60 days) and (b) if the purchase price for the first §1202 stock purchased is less than the proceeds from the old §1202 stock

---

¶906   [1] For purposes of the stockholder's regular income tax, 50% of the §1202 qualifying LTCG is excluded from the stockholder's regular income while 50% is included but taxed at a 28% rate, creating the special 14% regular income tax rate. In addition, 21% of the §1202 qualifying LTCG is treated as an AMT preference item. Thus, in total, 71% of the LTCG qualifying for the 14% rate is included in AMT income.

sale, as rolling the remaining proceeds into the next §1202 stock purchase, and then the next, etc., until all the proceeds from the old §1202 stock are used up (or 60 days has expired).

(1) Qualified small business stock. To satisfy Code §1045, both the old §1202 stock and the new §1202 stock must be "qualified small business stock" and, hence, must meet all eight requirements described in ¶906.1 (other than (3) and (10)).

However, the old §1202 stock need not have been held more than five years (i.e., the requirement described in ¶906.1(3) above need not be met); only a six month holding period is necessary. Moreover, the active business requirement described in ¶906.1(8) above must be satisfied with respect to the new §1202 stock only for the first six months of the stockholder's holding period for such stock. Accordingly, if the active business requirement is satisfied with respect to the new §1202 stock for at least six months after the stockholder's purchase of the new §1202 stock, but ceases to be satisfied thereafter, the stockholder's reinvestment in new §1202 stock qualifies for Code §1045 nonrecognition, but his or her gain on ultimate disposition of the new §1202 stock does *not* qualify for the 14% Code §1202 rate.

(2) Noncorporate shareholder. Code §1045 rollover treatment is not limited to old §1202 stock sold, and new §1202 stock purchased, by an individual, but also applies where the stock is sold and/or purchased by a flow-through entity (e.g., a partnership, LLC, or S corporation) to the extent the flow-through entity is owned by an individual. Where a flow-through entity *sells* old §1202 stock, an individual owner of the flow-through entity can take into account his or her proportionate share of any proceeds and gain recognized by the flow-through entity. Where a flow-through entity *buys* new §1202 stock, an individual owner of the flow-through entity can take into account his or her share of any such reinvestment in new §1202 stock.

Thus, Code §1045 rollover treatment (a) applies to a sale of old §1202 stock by a flow-through entity (to the extent of individual A's share thereof) matched with individual A's timely reinvestment in new §1202 stock and (b) appears to apply to (i) individual A's sale of old §1202 stock matched with a flow-through entity's timely reinvestment in new §1202 stock (to the extent individual A's share thereof) and (ii) individual A's share of flow-through entity #1's sale of old §1202 stock matched with individual A's share of flow-through entity #2's timely reinvestment in new §1202 stock.

Although a Code §1045 election is normally made by the individual on whose return the CG covered by the election would otherwise appear, a flow-through entity itself can make an entity-level Code §1045 rollover election on its tax return for the year in which the old §1202 stock is sold, in which case the entity is obligated to keep track of the new §1202 stock's low rollover basis and tacked holding period. When the flow-through entity holding the old §1202 stock does not make a Code §1045 election, each individual on whose return a portion of the CG from the old §1202 stock would otherwise appear can do so.

(3) Holding period of new §1202 stock. Where the acquisition of new §1202 stock results in nonrecognition of gain on old §1202 stock under Code §1045(a), the holding period for the old §1202 stock is included in the holding period for the new §1202 stock.

¶906.3   18% LTCG Tax Rate for Property Acquired After 12/31/00

Under a provision in the 1997 Tax Act which first became effective in 1/01 (Code §1(h)(2) and (9)), the top LTCG rate for an individual (noncorporate) taxpayer is reduced from 20% to 18% for property (not merely "qualified small business stock") acquired after 12/31/00 and held more than 5 years.

In determining whether property is acquired after 12/31/00, "property acquired pursuant to the exercise of an option (or other right or obligation to acquire property)" is treated as acquired when the "option (or other right or obligation)" was acquired. However, if such an option or contract right or obligation is acquired after 12/31/00 (so that the underlying property may qualify for the 18% rate if held more than 5 years), this rule does not apply in calculating whether the underlying property has been held more than 5 years. Hence this rule can work only to the taxpayer's detriment.

With respect to property acquired before 1/1/01 (pre-2001 property), a taxpayer (e.g., an individual or a flow-through entity owned in whole or in part by individuals) may elect to treat property held by such individual or flow-through entity as sold on 1/1/01, and simultaneously reacquired, at FV (in the case of "readily tradeable stock," as having been sold and reacquired on 1/2/01 at its 1/2/01 closing price). The effect of such an election is that:

- The property is treated as acquired after 12/31/00 so that upon a subsequent actual sale such property qualifies for the 18% LTCG rate if held more than 5 years after 1/1/01 (after 1/2/01 in the case of readily tradable stock). The taxpayer's pre-1/01 holding period does not count in determining whether the property has been held more than 5 years after the deemed reacquisition.
- The property is treated as sold on 1/1/01 (1/2/01 for readily tradable stock) so that the taxpayer recognizes CG on such date, LT or ST depending upon the taxpayer's holding period as of 1/1/01 (1/2/01 for readily tradable stock). However, the taxpayer does not recognize CL where the property's FV on the deemed sale date is less than its basis. Indeed any such loss is permanently disallowed, i.e., any such basis evaporates and the property takes a new basis equal to its 1/1/01 FV (its 1/2/01 closing price in the case of readily tradable stock).

The election can not be made with respect to property which the taxpayer actually sells within a year after the 1/01 deemed sale date. This rule prevents a taxpayer from starting a new holding period for a pre-2001 asset where the new holding period would cause gain or loss on the asset's actual disposition (within one year after 1/01) to be STCG or STCL.

The election to treat pre-2001 property as deemed sold and repurchased in 2001 (which is irrevocable once made) can be made by the property's owner (an individual or flow-through entity) with its timely filed tax return (including extensions) which includes the deemed sale date (i.e., its 2001 return for a calendar year taxpayer) *or,* if the taxpayer "timely filed [its] tax return without making the election *for any asset*," in an amended return within 6 months after such return's original due date (excluding extensions).[2] The election can be made on an asset by asset basis.

A deemed-sale-and-repurchase election can be disadvantageous for 4 reasons: *First,* if there is built-in-loss ("BIL") in the property as of 1/1/01 (1/2/01 for readily tradable stock), such BIL is permanently disallowed.

Second, if there is built-in gain ("BIG") in the property as of 1/1/01 (1/2/01 for readily tradable stock), such gain is recognized in 2001 although the property may not be sold for many years.

Third, if the property has been held one year or less as of the 1/01 deemed sale date, the deemed CG then recognized is ST (and hence, absent offsetting CLs, taxable as OI), although the property may thereafter be held many years.

The *fourth* potential disadvantage relates to an election made by a flow-through entity. Where pre-2001 property is owned by a flow-through entity and one or more individuals own pre-2001 equity interests in such entity, apparently (1) the individual equity owner can make the deemed-sale-and-repurchase election with respect to his or her ownership interest in the entity but (2) only the entity can make the election with respect to the property which it owns. Thus, if the flow-through entity ultimately sells the property at a gain (after holding the property more than 5 years after the 1/01 deemed repurchase), the individual equity owner is entitled to the 18% rate only where the entity made the election with respect to the property, since the character of the entity's gain flows through to the equity owner. On the other hand, if the individual ultimately sells his or her equity interest in the entity at a gain (after holding his or her equity interest more than 5 years after the 1/01 deemed repurchase), the individual is entitled to the 18% rate only where the individual made the election with respect to his equity interest in the entity.

If a flow-through entity owned partly by individuals and partly by corporations makes the deemed-sale-and-repurchase election, the statutory language is consistent with the absurd result that the entity recognizes (in 1/01) 100% of the property's BIG (not merely the portion of such BIG allocable to the entity's individual equity owners), although only the portion of the property allocable to individual equity owners can thereafter qualify (by virtue of the election) for the 18% rate (if thereafter held more than 5 years). If this is the correct reading of the statute, the corporate equity owners of a flow-through entity making the election would

---

[2] With respect to making the election on an amended return, the Form 4797 instructions are unclear on whether a taxpayer making an election for asset A on its timely filed year 2000 tax return (but making no election with respect to asset B) is precluded from subsequently making an election for asset B in an amended return within 6 months after such return's original due date (excluding extensions).

apparently recognize (on a flow- through basis) their share of the entity's 1/01 deemed-sale gain.

¶907 EXECUTIVE COMPENSATION ISSUES WHERE CORPORATION BECOMES PUBLICLY HELD—$1 MILLION DEDUCTION LIMIT

Code §162(m) (enacted by the 1993 Tax Act) limits a corporation's deduction for executive remuneration to $1 million per executive per year.

This limitation generally applies only to a publicly-held corporation. While Portfolio Company will typically be privately held after the start-up, growth-equity, buyout, industry consolidation, or turn-around investment discussed in Chapters 2, 4, 5, 7, and 8 above, Portfolio Company may subsequently become publicly held. In such case the Code §162(m) deduction limit would generally apply to executive remuneration deductions for any year in which Portfolio Company is publicly held on the last day of its taxable year.

Hence, while Portfolio Company is privately held, it should take steps to structure all executive compensation arrangements (which could give rise to tax deductions in or after the year it becomes publicly held) so as to comply with either the 2-year/4-year grandfather rule of exception #2 (discussed below)—which applies to a privately-held corporation's compensation plans and agreements in effect when it becomes publicly held—or one of the other exceptions discussed below.

¶907.1 Basic Deduction Limit

No corporation can deduct more than $1 million per executive per year for remuneration to an executive, unless the remuneration falls within one of the exceptions described in ¶907.2 through ¶907.6 below. Remuneration falling into at least one of the exceptions is deductible without regard to the §162(m) limitation and does not eat into the $1 million allowable amount for remuneration which does not meet an exception.

Remuneration for this purpose includes all amounts, whether paid in cash, stock options, the corporation's stock, or other property, and is taken into account for the corporation's taxable year in which such compensation would otherwise be deductible.

- The spread in an NQO or an SAR is generally taken into account at exercise.[1]
- Deferred compensation (i.e., compensation not payable within 2 ½ months after the end of the year in which fixed) is generally taken into account when paid.

¶907 [1] A corporation is entitled to a deduction with respect to the exercise of an ISO only if the executive makes a "disqualifying disposition" of the stock received on exercise of the ISO. In such case, the deduction would be taken into account at the time of the executive's disqualifying disposition.

- Restricted stock (i.e., stock subject to vesting[2]) is generally taken into account when transferred to the executive (if the executive chooses to be taxed on the receipt of the stock by making a §83(b) election) *or* at vesting (if the executive chooses to be taxed on the stock at vesting by making no §83(b) election).
- Phantom stock is generally taken into account when paid (in cash or unrestricted stock).

The $1 million deduction limit does not cover (1) contributions to or payments from qualified retirement plans or (2) non-taxable fringe benefits.

¶907.2   Exception #1: Privately-Held Corporation

The $1 million deduction limit does not cover remuneration paid by a corporation that is privately held on the last day of the corporation's taxable year in which the compensation is deductible.

A corporation is privately held if it has no class of "common equity securities" required to be registered under the 1934 Act.

Thus, Portfolio Company is privately held as long as it (1) has no class of common equity securities traded on a national securities exchange *and* (2) does not have both 500 or more holders of a class of common equity securities and $10 million or more of consolidated assets (based on its balance sheet prepared in accordance with GAAP).

¶907.3   Exception #2: Plan or Agreement in Place When Privately-Held Corporation Becomes Publicly Held

Compensation awarded pursuant to a plan or agreement in effect at the time a privately held corporation becomes publicly held is exempt from the $1 million deduction limit if the corporation takes certain steps (as described immediately below) with respect to the compensation during a "reliance period," which lasts approximately four years after the corporation becomes publicly held as a result of an IPO but only approximately two years after the corporation becomes publicly held without an IPO.

Stated in more detail, the reliance period ends on the earliest of: (1) the expiration of the plan or agreement, (2) a material modification to the plan or agreement, (3) the issuance of all stock or other property allocated under the plan or agreement, or (4) the first meeting of shareholders at which directors are elected occurring after the close of the third calendar year following the calendar year in which Portfolio Company becomes public as a result of an SEC registered IPO *or* the first calendar year after the year in which Portfolio Company becomes public

---

[2] In tax parlance, stock subject to a substantial risk of forfeiture.

without an SEC registered IPO. In the case of a stock option, an SAR, or property transferred subject to a substantial risk of forfeiture, exception #2 applies if the option, SAR, or property is *granted* or *transferred* during the reliance period, even if Portfolio Company's deduction is triggered after the end of the reliance period. In the case of other types of compensation, it is not sufficient to grant the compensation during the 2-year/4-year reliance period. Rather, the compensation must actually be paid during the reliance period.[3]

Because of this broad regulatory exception, Portfolio Company will generally be able to ignore Code §162(m) until it is planning the transaction which causes it to become publicly held, e.g., an SEC registered IPO, private sales of equity securities (primary or secondary) which cause Portfolio Company to exceed 500 holders, or a merger of Portfolio Company into or an acquisition of Portfolio Company by a public company or a subsidiary thereof. At such time (or in some cases earlier), Portfolio Company should structure its executive compensation arrangements either to comply with exception #2 or to fit into one of the exceptions discussed in ¶907.4 and ¶907.5 below.

¶907.4 Exception #3: Executive Not a "Covered Employee"

The $1 million deduction limit does not apply to remuneration paid to an executive unless he or she is a "covered employee."

"Covered employee" means the CEO or an individual acting in such capacity at "the close of [Portfolio Company's] taxable year" *plus* the other 4 highest compensated officers "for the taxable year" whose compensation is required to be reported to shareholders in the corporation's proxy statement and who are still employed as executive officers by Portfolio Company (or an affiliate meeting the 80-80 test) on the last day of Portfolio Company's taxable year.

Where Portfolio Company is acquired by (and becomes a subsidiary of) public Bigco, a Portfolio Company executive would be a Bigco covered employee if the executive is on the last day of Bigco's taxable year one of the 4 highest compensated officers (in addition to Bigco's CEO) whose compensation is required to be reported in Bigco's proxy statement (which, under the SEC rules, can include an executive of a Bigco subsidiary who plays a policy-making role at Bigco).

Where remuneration is *earned* by an executive while a covered employee but is not *deductible* until a year in which executive has ceased to be a covered employee, the $1 million deduction limit does *not* apply. Conversely, where remuneration is *earned* by an executive before the executive becomes a covered employee but becomes deductible in a year in which executive is a covered employee, the $1 million deduction limit *does* apply. This rule is particularly relevant for

---

[3] Because of ambiguity in the regulations, it is possible IRS might argue that the compensation must be *deductible* during the reliance period. Under some types of plans a deduction does not arise in certain circumstances until the corporation's tax year following the year the compensation was paid. See Code §83(h) and §83 regulations discussed at ¶202.3.6 above; Code §404(a)(5) discussed in Ginsburg and Levin M&A book ¶1503.1.4.

remuneration that is deductible one or more years after grant, when the executive's status may have changed, such as:

- Deferred compensation (i.e., compensation not paid within 2 ½ months after the end of the year in which fixed), which is generally deductible when paid.
- An NQO, which is generally deductible when exercised.
- Restricted stock (i.e., stock subject to vesting), which is generally deductible at vesting (where the executive makes no §83(b) election at grant).
- Phantom stock, which is generally deductible when paid (in cash or unrestricted stock).

Thus, where remuneration otherwise payable to a covered executive exceeds the $1 million deduction limit, Portfolio Company may want to grant all or a portion of such remuneration in the form of deferred compensation which is payable in a year when, through retirement or otherwise, executive is not a covered employee on the last day of Portfolio Company's taxable year.

Alternatively, Portfolio Company may want to grant NQOs, restricted stock, or phantom stock that will generate a deduction after the covered executive's retirement.

Portfolio Company may also find it desirable to structure compensation arrangements to fit the performance-based-compensation exception (exception #4 below), even where the executive is not a covered employee when the arrangement is entered into, if there is any possibility the executive may subsequently be a covered employee when the compensation becomes deductible.

¶907.5   Exception #4: Performance-Based Compensation

The $1 million deduction limit does not apply to remuneration where *all* 4 of the following tests are met:

¶907.5.1   Non-Discretionary, Pre-Established, Objective Performance Goal

In order to meet this test, the remuneration must be payable solely on account of attaining one or more non-discretionary, pre-established, objective performance goals.

A goal is pre-established if the compensation committee writes the goal before the *earlier* of (1) 90 days after commencement of the period of service *or* (2) when 25% of the service period (as measured in good faith) has elapsed and while the outcome is substantially uncertain. Such goal is objective if a third party having knowledge of the relevant facts could determine whether the goal is met. The compensation committee may retain discretion to reduce or eliminate the award but not to increase the award calculated pursuant to the objective formula goal.

A performance goal must relate to business criteria that apply to the individual, a business unit, or the corporation as a whole, e.g., stock price, market share, sales, earnings per share, return on equity, or costs. A goal would not qualify if it related to the performance (for example) of the S&P 500 or the length of the executive's future employment (e.g., a requirement of 5 years of future continuous employment for Portfolio Company).

There is risk that an objective performance goal could be disregarded on the ground that "the outcome is [not] substantially uncertain" if it is too easy to attain. The regulations clarify that a formula bonus based on a percentage of sales (with no minimum threshold) is not substantially uncertain because a company is virtually certain to have some sales. However, a formula bonus based on a percentage of profits is substantially uncertain, even if the company has consistently been profitable in the past.

A stock option or SAR that is not in the money at grant will automatically satisfy this test (although the other 3 tests described below must also be satisfied in order to invoke the performance-based-compensation exception). The legislative history explains that this rule is justified "because the amount of compensation attributable to the options or other rights . . . would be based solely on an increase in the corporation's stock price." If the stock option or SAR is in the money at all at grant, none of the compensation attributable to such grant will satisfy the performance-based-compensation exception, even with respect to post-grant appreciation.

Because a grant of restricted stock is always in the money, the legislative history makes clear that it does not qualify for the performance-based-compensation exception, "unless the grant or vesting of the restricted stock is based upon the attainment of a performance goal."

¶907.5.2   Compensation Committee Comprised Solely of 2 or More Outside Directors

The performance goal must be determined by a compensation committee of the board comprised solely of 2 or more outside directors.

In general, under the regulations, a person is not a qualified Portfolio Company outside director if such person (1) was ever an officer of Portfolio Company or any 80-80 affiliate, (2) is currently receiving payments for goods or services from Portfolio Company or an 80-80 affiliate in any capacity other than as a director or pursuant to a tax-qualified retirement plan, (3) owns more than a 50% interest in an entity that is receiving payments for goods or services from Portfolio Company, (4) owns at least a 5% but not more than a 50% interest in an entity that received from Portfolio Company during Portfolio Company's prior taxable year payments for goods or services in excess of the lesser of (i) 5% of the gross revenue of the director-owned entity or (ii) $60,000, (5) is an employee of or self-employed by an entity that received from Portfolio Company during Portfolio Company's prior taxable year payments for goods or services in excess of 5% of the entity's gross revenue, *or* (6) is an employee of or self-employed by an entity that received from Portfolio Company during Portfolio Company's prior taxable year payments as remuneration for personal services (e.g., legal, accounting, investment banking, or management consulting services) rendered to Portfolio Company (but not including services incidental to Portfolio Company's purchase of goods or services which are not personal services) in excess of the lesser of (i) 5% of the gross revenue of the entity or (ii) $60,000.

¶907.5.3   Shareholder Disclosure and Approval

The material terms under which the remuneration is to be paid must be disclosed to shareholders and approved by a majority vote. This requirement is generally met if the shareholders are informed about and approve all of the following:

- The individuals eligible to receive the compensation (who may be identified by name, by title, or by class of executive).
- A description of the business criteria on which the performance goal is based, which need not include (1) the specific targets under the goal or (2) any information determined by the compensation committee to be confidential information disclosure of which would have an adverse effect on Portfolio Company (e.g., the proposed time schedule for developing a new product), so long as the disclosure states that such information has been omitted as confidential information.
- Either (1) the maximum amount of compensation payable to an employee *or* (2) sufficient information so that shareholders can determine the maximum amount of compensation that could be paid to any employee or (3) the formula used to calculate the amount of compensation.
- Any subsequent material changes to the plan.

The executive's right to receive the compensation must be contingent on shareholder approval (i.e., the shareholders must not be voting merely on whether the corporation will receive a deduction for such compensation).

¶907.5.4   Compensation Committee Certification

Before the remuneration is paid, the compensation committee must certify that the performance goals and any other terms were satisfied. The executive's right to receive the compensation must be contingent on such certification (except for a stock option or SAR otherwise meeting the requirements of the performance-based-compensation exception).

¶907.6   *Exception #5: Compensation Not Paid for Services as an Employee*

Payments made to an individual other than for services performed as an employee are not subject to the $1 million deduction limit. Whether a payment constitutes consideration for services performed in an individual's capacity as an employee (rather than as an independent contractor) is factual in nature. Examples of payments that should not be treated as consideration for services performed in an individual's capacity as an employee include (1) a payment for consulting services made to an individual acting in the capacity of an independent contractor, regardless of whether such individual has been in the past, or becomes in the future, an employee of the public corporation and (2) a signing or hello bonus paid to an individual in connection with the commencement of such individual's employment with the public corporation, so long as the individual's retention of such bonus is not conditioned on the performance of services as an employee.

¶908   REFERENCES

- 1933 Act §4(2) and §5
- SEC Rule 144
- SEC Rule 145
- SEC Reg. D
- Code §1(h)
- Code §354, §356, §368
- Code §453
- Code §1045
- Code §1202
- Code §162(m)
- Ginsburg and Levin M&A book ¶203.4 (installment method), ¶1506 (Code §162(m)), ¶1702.2.8.5 (restrictions on resale of securities), ¶1702.3.1 (representations and warranties)

CHAPTER 10

Structuring Formation of Private Equity Fund

Several VC professionals have recently left positions as key executives at the venture capital/private equity units of a bank holding company, insurance company, and/or other large financial institution. They are planning to raise a private venture capital fund ("PE Fund") with money contributed by a limited number of sophisticated investors, including public and private employee benefit plans, university endowment funds, wealthy families, insurance companies, and bank holding companies. The VC professionals plan to form a Management Company, which they would own, to act as PE Fund's GP (or as PE Fund's managing member if PE Fund is formed as an LLC and not as a partnership).

Alternatively, these VC professionals raised a private venture capital fund several years ago. The fund has already invested most of its money, and its investments have performed very well. Hence the VC professionals are now seeking to raise a second private fund to make additional investments.

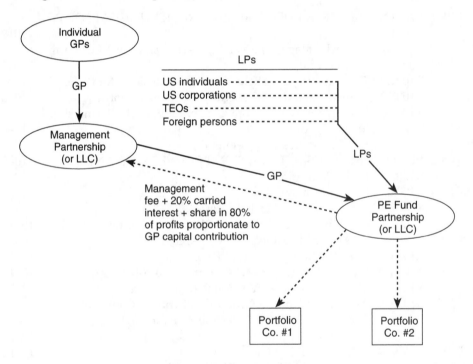

¶1001   PARTNERSHIP (OR LLC) VERSUS CORPORATE FORM FOR PE FUND

¶1001.1   *Tax Advantages of Selecting Partnership (or LLC) Form for PE Fund*

(1)   PE Fund's partners (members if PE Fund is formed as an LLC) are entitled to flow-through taxation with respect to PE Fund's CGs.

- No federal income tax at PE Fund level.
- The federal income tax rate payable at the equity owner level on the portion of PE Fund's LTCG allocable to an individual partner is 20% (14% if such gain qualifies under Code §1202—see ¶906 above) and on the portion of PE Fund's LTCG allocable to a corporate partner is 35%.
- No federal income tax at the equity owner level for a PE Fund LP which is a tax-exempt organization (a "TEO"), so long as (a) the portfolio company securities producing such CG are not debt-financed and (b) the portfolio company is not a partnership or LLC engaged in an active business (as opposed to a portfolio company formed as a C corporation or as a partnership or LLC engaged merely in investment activities). See ¶302.1 above. As to whether PE Fund's fee income allocable to a TEO may constitute an active business, see (4) below.
- No federal income tax on CG for a PE Fund LP which is a foreign person (an "FP"), so long as (a) the CG is not "effectively connected" to an active U.S. business (as opposed to a mere investment activity) conducted either by PE Fund or by a portfolio company formed as a partnership or LLC and (b) the portfolio company generating the CG does not predominantly own U.S. real estate, generally as determined under a 50%-by-FV-at-anytime-in-the-past-5-years test, but treating as a reduction in the FV of such property any mortgage liability or other debt secured by any property and either (i) "incurred to acquire" or (ii) "incurred in direct connection with" such property. See ¶302.12 above. As to whether PE Fund's fee income allocable to an FP may constitute an active business, see (4) below.

(2) PE Fund's partners (members if PE Fund is formed as an LLC) are also entitled to flow-through taxation with respect to PE Fund's OI or ordinary loss.

- PE Fund's losses flow through to its partners in the early years when PE Fund's management fee and other expenses exceed PE Fund's income.
- However, Code §67 disallows (under the 2% rule discussed below) a portion of PE Fund's expenses (including the management fee) to the extent allocable to an individual LP (as opposed to a corporate LP) where PE Fund is not, for tax purposes, deemed to be engaged in a business (but rather is engaged merely in an investment activity). This fund-expense-disallowance rule (1) does not apply to the extent a fund expense is allocable to a fund business activity, including the fund's indirect interest in a business activity conducted through a partnership, LLC, or other flow-through entity,[1] but (2) does apply where the fund owns a business activity indirectly through a corporate (i.e., non-flow-through) entity. Generally a U.S. individual may deduct his

---

¶1001   [1] However, the Code §469 passive activity loss limitations do apply to an individual partner's losses arising out of a business activity as to which such partner is passive.

or her miscellaneous investment expenses only to the extent such expenses exceed 2% of his or her adjusted gross income ("AGI"), regardless of whether PE Fund operates at a net profit or net loss for the year.

- A corporate partner in PE Fund (as distinguished from an individual partner) is entitled to a 70% or 80% DRD with respect to its allocable share of PE Fund's dividend income, so that its effective federal income tax rate is reduced to 35% times either 30% or 20% of the dividend income.

- No federal income tax on an LP which is a TEO so long as (1) the TEO's share of PE Fund's OI consists of dividends, interest, and royalties (rather than active business income) and (2) the investments which produce such OI are not debt financed.

- With respect to a PE Fund LP which is an FP, such LP's share of PE Fund's dividend and interest income which is not "effectively connected" to a U.S. active business is subject to a 0% to 30% withholding tax, depending on the applicable treaty (and, in the case of interest, depending on whether the interest qualifies for the "portfolio interest" exemption from withholding).

- Where PE Fund's dividend and interest income (as well as CG) allocable to an FP is "effectively connected" with an active U.S. business (as opposed to a mere investment activity) conducted either by PE Fund or by a portfolio company formed as a partnership or LLC, the FP is subject to regular U.S. tax on such "effectively connected" income.

(3) PE Fund's partners (members if PE Fund is formed as an LLC rather than a partnership) are entitled to receive tax-free distributions of cash or property from PE Fund.

- An entity (including an LLC) taxed as a partnership can generally distribute cash or property to its equity owners without triggering income tax to either the partnership or the recipient equity owner, as further described below.

- On a partnership's distribution of cash to an equity owner, the equity owner's basis in his or her partnership interest is reduced by the amount of cash distributed but the recipient equity owner recognizes no taxable gain.[2] Only when the cash distributed to the equity owner exceeds his or her basis in the partnership interest does the recipient equity owner recognize taxable gain, i.e., the equity owner's basis in

---

[2] ¶302.2 explains the calculation of an equity owner's basis in his or her partnership interest, i.e., generally, the equity owner's original cost for such interest, *plus* the equity owner's subsequent contributions, *plus* partnership taxable (or tax-exempt) income allocated to the equity owner, *less* distributions by the partnership to the equity owner (measured by the basis of the property distributed or the face amount of cash distributed), *less* partnership taxable loss (and non-deductible non-capitalizable expense) allocated to the equity owner, *plus* increases in the equity owner's share of partnership liabilities, *less* reductions in the equity owner's share of partnership liabilities (with the latter treated as a cash distribution for purposes of the equity owner-level gain recognition rule described in text).

the partnership is first reduced (to but not below zero) by the cash distributed and the excess of the cash distributed over the equity owner's basis in the partnership triggers gain to the equity owner, which generally constitutes CG.

- On a partnership's distribution of property (including appreciated property) to an equity owner, neither the partnership nor the equity owner generally recognizes taxable gain. Rather the equity owner's basis in his or her partnership interest is reduced by the partnership's basis in the property distributed (but not below zero) and the equity owner takes a basis in the property equal to the reduction in his or her basis in the partnership interest.

- A partnership's distribution of "marketable securities" (expansively defined) to an equity owner is treated as a distribution of cash in an amount equal to the securities' FV for purposes of applying the above rules (so that the distributee equity owner recognizes gain to the extent that the FV of marketable securities received by such equity owner exceeds his or her basis in the partnership). In this case (a) the recipient equity owner's basis in the partnership is first reduced (to but not below zero) by the FV of the marketable securities distributed to him or her, (b) the FV of marketable securities in excess of the equity owner's basis in the partnership triggers gain to the recipient equity owner (generally CG), and (c) the marketable securities take a basis in the equity owner's hands equal to FV. There are, however, several important legislative limitations and exceptions to this rule that marketable securities are treated as cash:

  - Marketable securities distributed to an equity owner are not treated as cash to the extent that gain would have been allocated to such equity owner if the partnership had sold all the marketable securities of the same class. Hence where marketable securities are distributed pro rata to the equity owners, i.e., in the same ratio as the gain on a sale of such securities would have been allocated if the partnership had sold such securities, only the cost basis of the marketable securities is treated as a cash distribution.

  - If the partnership is an "investment partnership," i.e., has never engaged in a business and substantially all its assets have always consisted of money and/or securities, the marketable securities distributed are not treated as cash. Under the regulations, PE Fund would not be disqualified from this investment-partnership exception (i.e., would not be treated as engaged in a business) because of "any activity undertaken [by PE Fund] as an investor . . . , including the receipt of commitment fees, director's fees, or similar fees . . . customary in and incidental to" PE Fund's investment activities. Morever, where an entity taxed as a partnership (e.g., Management Company which is GP of PE Fund) receives "reasonable and customary fees" for rendering "reasonable and customary management services" to an investment partnership (here PE Fund), such fee income does not disqualify Management Company from this investment-partnership exception when in turn it distributes marketable securities to its partners. However, a partnership otherwise qualifying as an investment partnership (e.g., PE Fund) would generally be disqualified from this investment-partnership exception where PE Fund owns an interest in one or more flow-through entities engaged in business (e.g., PE Fund owns an interest in one or more operating portfolio companies formed as partnerships or LLCs), because PE Fund would be treated as engaged in the business of each such flow-through entity.

- Securities which were not marketable when acquired by the partnership are not treated as cash, but only "to the extent provided in regulations." Regulations state that marketable securities will not be treated as cash if (a) when the partnership acquired the securities, the issuing entity had no outstanding marketable securities, (b) the securities acquired by the partnership remained non-marketable for at least six months after the partnership acquired them, and (c) the partnership distributes the securities within five years after they became marketable.

- Securities that were contributed to the partnership by an equity owner are not treated as cash when distributed back to the same equity owner who contributed them to the partnership.

(4) Where some PE Fund LPs are TEOs (or FPs), the TEO LPs generally prefer that PE Fund not recognize any income constituting UBTI (or effectively-connected U.S. active business income for an FP).

- If PE Fund regularly conducts an active business (e.g., rendering consulting services), PE Fund's net consulting income allocable to a TEO LP constitutes UBTI and net consulting income allocable to an FP LP constitutes effectively-connected-U.S.-active-business income (as discussed in (1) above).
  - The UBTI statutory rules make clear that "amounts received [by PE Fund] . . . as consideration for entering into agreements to make loans," such as loan commitment fees, do not constitute active income for this purpose, but the UBTI rules do not address other types of fee income received by PE Fund, such as equity commitment fees, break-up fees, buyout closing fees, and director's fees. However, regulations under an unrelated Code section (under which a partnership's distribution of marketable securities to its partners is treated as a cash distribution unless the partnership constitutes "an investment partnership," as discussed in (3) above) specifically state that a partnership is not disqualified as an investment partnership because it engaged in "activity . . . as an investor . . . , including the receipt of commitment fees, break-up fees, guarantee fees, director's fees, or similar fees . . . customary in and incidental to" the partnership's investment activities. While these

regulations promulgated under the partnership-distribution Code section by their terms apply only for purposes of that section, they suggest that the listed types of income, when received incident to an investment activity, should not constitute an active business for UBTI purposes.

- Where a PE Fund LP is an FP, there is similar risk that various types of PE Fund fee income may constitute effectively-connected-U.S.-active-business income (except that the statutory provision quoted above exempting loan commitment fees does not apply in this case).

- Income from a PE Fund portfolio company operating a manufacturing, service, or other active business in partnership or LLC form flows through as UBTI to a PE Fund LP which is a TEO (or as effectively-connected-U.S.-active-business income to a PE Fund LP which is an FP).

- Passive income (dividends, interest, royalties, CG from investments, and loan commitment fees) is not UBTI to a PE Fund LP which is a TEO where neither the TEO LP nor PE Fund borrows money to finance the acquisition of the investment which produces such passive income; to the extent the purchase price for such investment is attributable to borrowing by the TEO LP or the PE Fund partnership (i.e., to the extent the investment is debt-financed), a portion of the passive income is UBTI (except in the case of certain real estate investments).

- Where PE Fund generates UBTI, pension plan and individual retirement account LPs (but not other types of TEOs) which do not want to file tax returns reporting UBTI may invest in PE Fund through a tax-exempt "group trust" described in Rev. Rul. 81-100. The group trust (rather than the TEOs investing through the group trust) reports and pays tax on any UBTI.

- It is increasingly common for TEOs to invest in a PE Fund which is permitted to make UBTI-creating investments, although in some cases TEOs insist that the portion of PE Fund's capital commitments which can be invested in UBTI-creating transactions be limited to (e.g.) 25% to 35% of the fund's capital commitments.

(5)   Instead of forming PE Fund as a state law partnership, it is possible to form it as an LLC which is taxed as a partnership. See ¶303 above for the pros and cons of an LLC format.

¶1001.2   Tax Advantages of Selecting Corporate Form for PE Fund

Forming PE Fund in corporate form entitles it to a DRD (100% if PE Fund is an SBIC, otherwise 70% or 80%).

Forming PE Fund in corporate form provides a corporate shield for PE Fund's equity owners from liability for PE Fund's debts. See ¶301.5 above. When PE

Fund is organized in partnership form, it is possible to obtain limited liability protection through compliance with RULPA and/or formation of corporate or LLC intermediaries. See ¶¶302.6 and 302.7 and ¶705.2.5 above. When PE Fund is organized in LLC form, PE Fund's members are shielded from liability for PE Fund's debts, generally in the same manner as if PE Fund were a corporation. See ¶303.3 above.

Where PE Fund is a corporation, Code §67's 2% disallowance for PE Fund expenses allocable to individual partners does not apply.

¶1001.3 Industry Standard Generally Partnership Form

Most PE funds are formed as partnerships. However, because all 50 states have adopted LLC statutes (the last of which was effective 4/1/97), future PE funds may begin to be formed as LLCs. See ¶303 above.

¶1001.4 Midstream Switch from Corporate Form to Partnership (or LLC) Form

There is federal income tax at both the corporate level and the shareholder level on assets distributed by the dissolved corporate fund and recontributed to the new partnership/LLC fund, i.e., the corporate fund recognizes gain on its assets to the extent their FV exceeds tax basis and the shareholders recognize gain to the extent the corporate fund's net asset FV exceeds their tax basis in their stock. The result is the same if the corporate fund drops its assets into a partnership/LLC and distributes partnership/LLC interests to its shareholders. See Code §331 and §336.

In such a corporate liquidation, the new partnership/LLC fund takes asset SUB equal to the assets' FV and the assets start a new holding period for determining whether CG on ultimate sale of the assets is LTCG. A special rule applies in determining the tax basis of debt-financed property distributed in a corporate liquidation to a TEO. Code §514(d).

Any accumulated corporate-level NOL is lost to the extent such NOL is not used to shelter corporate-level gain on the corporation's distribution of its assets.

For SEC Rule 144 purposes, the corporation's holding period is tacked to the partnership's/LLC's if the assets are distributed and recontributed pro rata.

¶1001.5 Key Tax Issues and References

Should PE Fund be structured as a partnership, an LLC, a C corporation, or an S corporation?

- See precedents cited in Chapters 2 through 8 above regarding taxation of these three types of entities.

How is an equity owner that is a TEO or FP taxed?

- See precedents cited in Chapter 3 above.

¶1002 PROFIT AND LOSS ALLOCATIONS BETWEEN GP AND LPs

The remainder of this chapter assumes that PE Fund chooses the partnership form. However, if it instead selected the LLC form, the points discussed below would apply equally, except that the phrase "managing member" would generally be substituted for "GP," the phrase "members other than the managing member" would be substituted for "LPs," and the word "member" would be substituted for "partner."

¶1002.1 Profit Allocation

Industry standard—no preferential return: 20% of net profit allocated to GP as a carried interest and remaining 80% of net profit allocated according to contributed capital.

Increasingly common alternative for profit allocation—preferential return:

- *Disappearing preferential return.* 100% of net profits allocated according to contributed capital until PE Fund achieves specified IRR, and thereafter 100% (or less frequently 80% or even less frequently 50%) of net profits exceeding such IRR allocated to GP as a carried interest until GP catches up (i.e., until GP is allocated an amount equal to a full 20% carried interest in all net profits), and thereafter 20% carried interest in net profits allocated to GP and remaining 80% of net profits allocated according to contributed capital.
- *Permanent preferential return.* Less commonly, 100% of net profits allocated according to contributed capital until PE Fund achieves specified IRR, and 20% of excess net profits allocated to GP as a carried interest and remaining 80% of net profits allocated according to contributed capital.

¶1002.2 Loss Allocation

Industry standard: Losses (including fund expenses, such as management fees paid to GP) allocated same as profits were previously allocated until such loss allocations have offset all previously allocated profits, and then losses in excess of this amount allocated 100% according to contributed capital; if PE Fund has suffered losses allocated 100% according to contributed capital, subsequent profits are allocated 100% according to contributed capital until such losses have been recouped and further profits are allocated as set forth in ¶1002.1.

Special allocation of fund expenses: Occasionally fund expenses (including management fee paid to the GP) or some specific component of fund expenses (e.g., organizational expenses) are specially allocated 100% according to contributed capital.

¶1002.3   Passive Money Market Interest

Generally passive money market interest on excess cash balances is allocated 100% based on capital accounts or contributed capital, although this special allocation is less important where (as is now common) the partners pay in their commitments to PE Fund only as needed to make investments or pay expenses, so that PE Fund's cash balance is normally minimal.

¶1002.4   Old Buyout Fund Separate Partnership Structure

In the 1980s some buyout funds formed a separate partnership for each deal, so that profit on each successful partnership was allocated 20% as a carried interest to GP, with the remaining 80% allocated according to contributed capital, without offset for losses on unsuccessful deals and fund expenses (including management fees).

¶1003   TIMING OF DISTRIBUTIONS TO GP AND LPs

¶1003.1   Pro-LP Alternative—Full Payout

100% of available funds are used to make distributions to LPs and GP equal to their entire contributed capital (plus a preferential return, if the fund allocates a preferential rate of return on contributed capital), i.e., GP receives no distributions with respect to its 20% carried interest in PE Fund's net profits; once LPs and GP have received back their entire contributed capital (plus a preferential return, if any), subsequent distributions are proportionate to capital accounts which are generally equal to accumulated net profits (i.e., GP's capital account is equal to its 20% carried interest *plus* its share of the remaining 80% of net profits based on contributed capital, and LPs' capital accounts are equal to their share of the remaining 80% of net profits based on contributed capital).

¶1003.2   Pro-GP Alternative—Distribute Net Profits First

LPs and GP first receive distributions equal to net profits (i.e., realized profits *less* realized losses and expenses, including management fees) allocated to each (in the fashion described in ¶1002 above); distributions in excess of net profits (i.e., return of capital) are distributed in proportion to capital contributions. Generally, under this approach LPs would seek a back-end GP give-back which would be triggered if early profits followed by subsequent losses result in GP having received more than a 20% carried interest in profits net of losses and expenses.

¶1003.3   Middle Ground—FV Capital Account Test

All distributions are made in the proportions described in the pro-LP alternative ¶1003.1 above until the sum of LPs' FV capital accounts plus distributions received by the LPs reach a specified level (e.g., 125% of LP contributed capital), at which time GP receives all further distributions (catchup distributions) until GP has received aggregate distributions equal to the amount it would have received in the pro-GP alternative ¶1003.2 above, and further distributions are generally 20% to GP as a carried interest and 80% according to contributed capital (so long as GP's capital account never falls below zero and LPs' FV capital account plus distributions stays above the 125% specified level). Generally, under this approach LPs would seek a back-end GP give-back which would be triggered if early profits followed by subsequent losses result in GP having received more than a 20% carried interest in profits net of losses and expenses.

¶1003.4   Alternative Middle Ground—Distribute Contributed Capital on Realized Investments First

Proceeds from the sale of an investment are distributed first to return contributed capital with respect to that investment, then to return unreturned contributed capital with respect to any investment previously disposed of (or written off), then to return management fees and other expenses allocated to such realized investments, and then 20% to the GP as a carried interest and 80% according to capital commitments. Generally, under this approach LPs would seek a back-end GP give-back which would be triggered if early profits followed by subsequent losses result in GP having more than a 20% carried interest in profits net of losses and expenses.

¶1003.5   GP Tax Distributions

In any of the above distribution schemes, where GP is allocated profit but such profit is not currently distributed (e.g., ¶1003.1 full payout approach or ¶1003.3

approach while LPs have not yet achieved 125% FV capital account test), GP is generally entitled to receive tax distributions (to cover federal and state income taxes) with respect to any undistributed GP 20% carried interest which is taxable to (but not distributed to) the GP and such tax distributions are generally credited against subsequent GP distributions.

¶1004   MANAGEMENT FEE TO GP

Industry standard: Management fee ("MF") payable quarterly or semi-annually to GP in an annual amount equal to 1.5% to 2.5% of capital commitments (or more in the case of a small fund), infrequently subject to COLA adjustment.

Alternative popular in 1980s: MF payable quarterly or semi-annually to GP in an annual amount equal to 1.5% to 2.5% of PE Fund's asset FV plus uncalled capital commitments. Far less common now than in the 1980s.

- This approach creates a conflict of interest on asset valuations, because GP's MF increases if GP increases the estimated value of PE Fund's assets.
- This approach also creates a conflict of interest on timing of sales and distribution in kind, because GP's MF decreases as cash and/or securities are distributed.

Reduction after (e.g.) 5 years: Typically after PE Fund's investment period (e.g., 5 or 6 years) MF declines either (1) by 10% per year or (2) to an amount equal to 1% to 2% of PE Fund's assets on hand, valued at cost (or less frequently FV).

- Approach (2) creates a conflict of interest on timing of sales and distributions in kind, because GP's MF declines as cash and/or securities are distributed.

Offset for other fees earned by GP: MF reduced by 100% or some lesser percentage of fees earned by GP from portfolio companies (e.g., director's fees or closing fees) or from target companies (e.g., breakup fees).

Reduction for MF expense allocable to GP: The MF may be reduced by an amount equal to the portion of the unreduced MF that would be allocable to GP as an expense (generally 20%), with the entire amount of the reduced MF expense allocated to LPs, in which case GP is generally entitled to receive a distribution from PE Fund (constituting a portion of the GP's capital account) equal in amount to the MF reduction.

- Such an MF reduction is designed to avoid a situation where GP recognizes OI on receipt of the gross MF but is not able to deduct all or a portion of its share of the related MF expense because of Code §67's 2% floor on an individual's miscellaneous itemized deductions. Such MF reduction generally has no adverse impact on LPs.

Reduction in exchange for enhanced allocation of LTCG profits: Some GPs opt to reduce the MF (taxable as OI) in exchange for an enhanced allocation of PE Fund profits (generally taxable as LTCG) equal in amount to the foregone MF. In some cases the choice is made upfront on PE Fund's formation, while in other cases GP reserves the right to elect periodically to waive a portion of the MF in exchange for such an enhanced allocation of PE Fund profits.

- As long as there is economic risk GP will not receive sufficient allocations of PE Fund profits to make GP whole for the foregone MF and so long as the increased allocation of profits may not be taken from appreciation in the PE Fund's assets existing at the time of the election to reduce the MF, this technique should convert MF income which would have been taxed as OI (at a 38.6% 2002 and 2003 rate in the case of individuals) into LTCG (taxable at a 20% rate in the case of individuals).
- Calls of GP's capital commitment can be reduced dollar-for-dollar for the MF reduction or GP can receive an interest free loan from PE Fund in order to minimize the adverse impact such a strategy may have on the GP's cash flow.

¶1005 LIFE OF PE FUND AND RELATED ISSUES

Industry standard: 10-12 year life.

Issues:

- GP right to extend (e.g., for up to 3 one-year periods) if PE Fund still holds private securities or restricted public securities.
- GP right to reinvest (rather than distribute) proceeds from sales of investments or cost basis thereof.
- LPs' right to terminate PE Fund's investment period early with requisite vote (e.g., 75%) of LPs for (1) changes in individual GPs or (2) bad acts by GPs or (3) no specific reason (i.e., a no-fault divorce) or (4) less commonly, poor performance.

Time limit on call-downs: Call down of commitments for new investments limited to a period shorter than the PE Fund's life (e.g., 5 or 6 years), although commitments can generally be called down throughout PE Fund's life for add-on investments in an existing Portfolio Company, management fees, and other PE Fund expenses.

All-partner give-back: Right of GP to cause PE Fund to retrieve from the partners (both GP and LPs) all or a portion of distributions previously made to them if back-end contingent liabilities arise after PE Fund terminates or shortly before termination when PE Fund's assets are insufficient to cover the contingent liabilities.

- Otherwise GP may be liable for 100% of the back-end contingent liabilities not covered by remaining PE Fund assets, although GP's individual equity owners can gain some liability protection by forming GP as an LLC or as a limited partnership with an S corporation as its 1% general partner.

¶1006   VESTING AND TAX ASPECTS OF VC PRINCIPALS' INTERESTS IN MANAGEMENT COMPANY

The Management Company (which serves as general partner of PE Fund, receives the carried interest, and generally receives the MF) is likely to be formed as a flow-through entity, generally a partnership or an LLC. The entity most commonly used in the past was a general partnership. However, in order to afford the Management Company's individual equity owners (referred to herein for simplicity as the "VC principals") some protection against PE Fund unpaid back-end contingent liabilities, it is today more common to organize Management Company as *either* (a) a limited partnership with an LLC or S corporation (owned by the VC principals) as its 1% general partner and the VC principals as limited partners *or* (b) an LLC with the VC principals as members.

Regardless of the type of entity used, it is common for each VC principal's equity interest in Management Company to vest, usually over a period of time, contingent upon the VC principal's continued performance of services for Management Company. See ¶202.3 above for a discussion of vesting in the context of a Newco start-up. The vesting (or forfeiture) of a GP principal's equity interest in Management Company generally does not affect the economic interest of PE Fund's LPs, because under the terms of PE Fund's and Management Company's documents any equity interest in Management Company forfeited by one VC principal typically flows to the other VC principals (not to the LPs). However, the LPs may be interested in Management Company's vesting arrangements to assure that each VC principal is adequately incented to remain with PE Fund.

- Typically, each VC principal's equity interest in Management Company time vests over, e.g., 5-7 years, contingent on such VC principal's continued performance of services for Management Company, but there is generally no performance vesting.
- The VC principals must resolve the effect on a VC principal's equity interest if he or she dies, becomes disabled, or is expelled with or without cause, i.e., whether the unvested portion of his or her equity interest fully or partially vests upon such an involuntary termination of services or whether the normal vesting and forfeiture rules apply.

Whether a service partner who receives a mere profits interest (such as a carried interest) recognizes OI (either at the time such VC principal receives the equity interest or at vesting) was unclear until a 1993 Revenue Procedure (supplemented by a 2001 Revenue Procedure) clarified most of the issues.

(1) The first question is whether a mere profits interest in a partnership or LLC received by a service provider constitutes "property" for Code §83 purposes. If so, (a) a VC principal who shares in the carried interest and makes (or, as discussed below, is treated as making) a §83(b) election would have OI *at the front end* equal to the FV of his or her interest in Management Company *less* the price paid for such interest and (b) a VC principal who does *not* make (and is not treated as making) a §83(b) election would have OI *at vesting* equal to the then FV of the interest in Management Company *less* the price paid for such interest.

(2) Some pre-1993 cases held that a profits interest does constitute "property" so that §83 applies to a service provider receiving a profits interest in a partnership, but most of these cases then valued such interest on a liquidation basis, i.e., at the amount the service partner would have received if the partnership (here PE Fund and Management Company) immediately sold its assets at their then FV and distributed the proceeds. Applying such a liquidation-value ("LV") approach to newly-formed PE Fund and Management Company, a VC principal's interest would generally have a front end LV equal to the amount the VC principal is paying for the interest, so that a §83(b) election (or a deemed §83(b) election) would generally be advantageous.

(3) While virtually all of the precedents deal with a *partnership*, an LLC taxed as a partnership is subject to the same rules.

(4) Until 1993 there was some risk that a future court might adopt a speculative-value (rather than an LV) approach and hence impose OI tax on the speculative value of the VC principal's right to receive a disproportionately large share (through his or her portion of the carried interest) of future appreciation in PE Fund's portfolio, which might result in very substantial front end OI even if a §83(b) election is made (or deemed made).

(5) In 1993 IRS announced (in Rev. Proc. 93-27) that where "a person receives a profits interest in exchange for providing services to (or for the benefit of) a partnership in a partner capacity (or in anticipation of being a partner), [IRS] will not treat the receipt of such an interest as a taxable event." IRS stated, however, that this taxpayer-favorable rule would not apply in any of the following circumstances:

- Where the service provider receives "a capital interest," defined as "an interest [in Management Company] that would give the [service provider] a share of the proceeds if the partnership's assets were sold at fair market value and then the proceeds were distributed in complete liquidation of the partnership," and by implication (where the partnership owns an interest in a subpartnership) as if the assets of the subpartnership (here PE Fund) were also sold at FV and the proceeds distributed. It is possible (but illogical) to read Rev. Proc. 93-27's words and conclude that IRS intends the taxpayer-favorable LV rule not be available where either (a) the service provider's partnership interest is in the money (even by a small amount) at the time he or she receives the partnership interest (e.g., the service provider pays $100 for a partnership interest that would yield $101 if the partnership immediately sells its assets and liquidates) or (b) the service provider pays an amount for the partnership interest and, immediately after such purchase, the service provider's partnership interest is worth (on an LV basis) exactly the amount for the interest (e.g., the service provider pays $100 for a partnership interest that would yield $100 if the partnership immediately sells its assets and liquidates). However, a far more rational reading is that IRS intends the taxpayer-favorable LV rule not be available only *to the extent* the service provider's partnership interest is in the money at receipt (i.e., $1 in example (a) and zero in example (b) above), so that the taxpayer-favorable LV rule is available for a "profits interest" even if combined with a "capital interest."

- Where "the profits interest relates to a substantially certain and predictable stream of income from partnership assets, such as income from high-quality debt securities or a high-quality net lease." While a VC principal's interest in Management Company often entitles the VC principal to share in the MF which PE Fund pays to Management Company, this is not likely to meet the "certain and predictable" exception, because (a) PE Fund's documents generally call for reduction of the gross MF both as PE Fund disposes of its investments and as Management Company receives other fee income (e.g., from portfolio companies), (b) the gross MF is first used to pay Management Company's expenses (which are highly variable), with only the excess (or net MF) available for distribution to the VC principals, and (c) net MF income constitutes only a portion of Management Company's income, with the larger portion generally coming from its highly variable carried interest share of PE Fund's gains.
- Where the service provider "disposes of the profits interest" within 2 years after receipt.
- Where the profits interest is a limited partnership interest in a publicly-traded partnership.

Hence, in the typical private PE Fund where a VC principal receives a carried interest that is not in the money at the time of receipt and does not dispose of the carried interest within 2 years and where the VC principal makes (or is treated as making) a timely §83(b) election, the VC principal should recognize no front-end OI and no back-end OI.

EXAMPLE

Individuals A and B (the VC principals) organize a new Management Company in partnership (or LLC) form (owned 60% by A and 40% by B), and Management Company in turn forms a new fund (PE Fund) in partnership form. A and B invest (or commit to invest as called) $1 million in Management Company (60-40), and Management Company invests (or commits to invest as called) $1 million in PE Fund as GP, while a number of investors invest (or commit to invest as called) $99 million in PE Fund as LPs.

Each of PE Fund's partners has the right to receive back (as return of capital) its capital invested in PE Fund. Management Company has a 20%

carried interest in PE Fund's profits, and remaining PE Fund profits are shared 99-1 by the LPs and Management Company as GP.

A and B share Management Company's distributions 60-40.

Management Company's GP interest (including its 20% carried interest) in PE Fund is fully vested, although A's and B's interests in Management Company vest over 5 years. A and B make timely §83(b) elections.

The *FV* of Management Company's GP interest in PE Fund substantially exceeds Management Company's $1 million commitment to PE Fund, because (1) Management Company has the right to receive back its $1 million capital invested in PE Fund (constituting 1% of PE Fund's capital) and to receive 20.8% (a 20% carried interest plus 1% of the remaining 80%), rather than 1%, of PE Fund's future profits and appreciation from PE Fund's investments and (2) PE Fund has the right to receive $100 million of funded capital ($99 million from the LPs and $1 million from Management Company) with no interest-like compensation to the partners for the use, likely for many years, of their $100 million of committed capital.

Nonetheless, under Rev. Proc. 93-27, Management Company recognizes no OI upon receipt of the GP interest. This result follows because if (at the time Management Company receives the GP interest) PE Fund (a partnership) were to sell all its assets for FV and liquidate, the LPs and Management Company as GP would each receive back their contributed capital and there would be no further liquidating distribution to Management Company above its return of capital.

Similarly the *FV* of A's and B's interests in Management Company substantially exceeds their $1 million (60-40) commitment to Management Company, because (as discussed immediately above) Management Company's GP interest in PE Fund (including the 20% carried interest) has an FV substantially exceeding Management Company's $1 million commitment to PE Fund.

However, A and B recognize no OI upon receipt (with a timely §83(b) election) of their interests in Management Company, because if PE Fund were to make the liquidating distribution to its partners described above, Management Company would receive an amount equal to its capital contributed to PE Fund and if Management Company then liquidated, A and B would each receive (60-40) an amount equal to such person's contributed capital.

(6) Rev. Proc. 93-27 is not entirely clear on the treatment of a service provider receiving a profits interest subject to vesting who makes *no* §83(b) election. If Code §83 does apply to a profits interest in a partnership or LLC and no §83(b) election is made or deemed made (as described below), the service provider would recognize OI *at vesting*, when the carried interest's value will likely have increased greatly because of appreciation in PE Fund's investments, so that the VC principal's OI will likely be very substantial even if a Rev. Proc. 93-27 LV approach is used at such time.

(7) In 2001 IRS published Rev. Proc. 2001-43, promulgating a surprisingly pro-taxpayer answer to the question whether Rev. Proc. 93-27's taxpayer-favorable LV rule applies where the service provider's partnership interest is subject to vesting but the service provider makes no §83(b) election. In this Rev. Proc., IRS announced that a service provider "need not file [a §83(b)] election" (i.e., IRS will treat the service provider as if he or she had filed such an election — a deemed election), so that the Rev. Proc. 93-27 "determination . . . whether an interest granted to a service provider is a profits interest is . . . tested at the time the interest is granted, even if, at that time, the interest is substantially nonvested" (i.e., is subject to vesting).

However, Rev. Proc. 2001-43 conditions this deemed §83 election on surmounting several hurdles:

- The *partnership* and *all partners* must consistently report their taxes for all tax periods as if the service provider partner had made a §83 election. Thus a service provider who relies on a *deemed* §83(b) election (i.e., who does not make an *actual* election) is at risk if Management Company or any Management Company partner (perhaps a former active VC principal who left Management Company on poor terms but retains an economic interest in Management Company causing him or her to continue to be treated as a partner for tax purposes) disregards the deemed §83(b) election and claims a deduction upon the vesting of the service provider's partnership interest, as is clearly permitted by Code §83 and the regulations.
- The service provider's profits interest must meet all the requirements of Rev. Proc 93-27 (discussed in (5) above), some of which are (as discussed in (5)) a bit problematic or the satisfaction of which cannot be predicted with certainty when the service provider receives the partnership interest (e.g., no disposition within 2 years).
- Because it is often impossible for a service provider to foresee with certainty (at the time he or she receives a carried interest) whether a deemed §83(b) election may later turn out to be unavailable and because of the low cost of filing an actual §83(b) election, a service provider receiving a carried interest subject to vesting should generally make an actual §83(b) election. If such an actual election is made, it will be clear that the VC principal receives the carried interest (for tax purposes) at the front end, when it is more likely to constitute a pure interest in future profits, rather than later at vesting when it may have grown into capital interest. In addition, even if the service provider's equity interest does not qualify for Rev. Proc. 93-27's taxpayer-favorable LV rule (e.g., if the service provider disposes of the interest within 2 years *or* if the interest is in the money to some extent and Rev. Proc. 93-27 is interpreted as not applying to such an interest), it will be clear that the FV of the partnership interest is determined at the front end, rather than later at vesting when PE Fund's assets may have appreciated substantially in value.

(8) The precedents are reasonably clear that where a service provider receives an equity interest for services to be performed as a partner of Management

Company (which equity interest is fully vested or with respect to which a §83(b) election is made or deemed made) and the Management Company, through its GP interest in PE Fund, subsequently recognizes OI or CG (e.g., PE Fund receives a dividend from a portfolio company or sells the stock of a portfolio company at a gain), the character of the income in PE Fund's hands (OI or CG) passes through to the VC principal, i.e., the equity interest holder.[1]

References:

- Rev. Proc. 93-27
- Rev. Proc. 2001-43

¶1007 DEPARTMENT OF LABOR PLAN ASSET REGULATIONS

The U.S. Department of Labor (the "DOL") has issued rules under which a PE Fund which has an ERISA plan (i.e., a pension or profit sharing plan sponsored by a U.S. employer *other than* a governmental entity) as an LP becomes subject to onerous ERISA fiduciary requirements, unless it meets *one* of these exceptions:

- Less than 25% of each class of PE Fund's securities (i.e., limited partnership interests) is held by ERISA-type entities, i.e., ERISA plans *plus* retirement plans sponsored by governmental entities (public retirement plans), foreign retirement plans, individual retirement accounts ("IRAs"), and collective investment funds and insurance company accounts holding retirement plan money.
- PE Fund is a "venture capital operating company" (a "VCOC") as defined below.
- PE Fund's limited partnership interests are publicly traded.

PE Fund is a *VCOC* only if:

- At least 50% of PE Fund's investments (measured by cost) are in qualified portfolio companies, meaning those engaged in the production or sale of a product or service (i.e., entities which are not reinvestment vehicles) as to which PE Fund has direct contractual rights to substantially participate in or substantially influence the conduct of the portfolio company's management (or certain companies as to which PE Fund formerly had such management rights) and
- PE Fund actively exercises such management rights in the ordinary course of its business with respect to at least one portfolio company each year.

In general, PE Fund has the requisite management rights in a portfolio company if PE Fund has:

¶1006 [1]See Code §702; Wheeler v. Commissioner, 37 T.C.M. 883 (1978); IRS TAM 9219002 (1/27/92).

(1)   the contractual right to appoint one or more portfolio company directors or officers *or*

(2)   special contractual rights to meet periodically with portfolio company management to advise and consult regarding the conduct of portfolio company's business, and/or to appoint an observer to portfolio company's board, in either case, accompanied by rights to examine portfolio company's books and records and to receive periodic portfolio company financial statements plus additional information upon request, and, in either case, so long as PE Fund's bundle of contractual rights is more significant than those normally negotiated by institutional investors with respect to investments in established, creditworthy companies.

These management rights must be direct contractual rights between PE Fund and portfolio company; thus, management rights that may be exercised only by a group of investors acting together with PE Fund are not sufficient. However, if such investor group appoints PE Fund to exercise such rights on behalf of the group—thereby delegating the entire group's management rights solely to PE Fund—PE Fund would have VCOC management rights.

Finally, where PE Fund invests in a holding company which in turn holds an equity interest in an operating subsidiary, PE Fund must obtain management rights at the holding company level in order to satisfy the VCOC rules, although there is no prohibition on seeking similar management rights at the operating subsidiary level as well.[1]

The 50%-qualified-portfolio-company test must be met at the time of PE Fund's first long-term investment and approximately annually thereafter. Because PE Fund can not be a VCOC until its first long-term investment is made (and then only if such first long-term investment is in a qualified portfolio company), PE Fund (which is relying on the VCOC exemption) can not receive ERISA money without becoming subject to ERISA fiduciary requirements until it closes its first qualifying deal.

A solution to this problem is that, until PE Fund makes its first qualifying investment, no ERISA LP makes a capital contribution to PE Fund, and each ERISA LP pays its share of the MF and PE Fund expenses already incurred directly to the Management Company rather than running the money through PE Fund. Another option is for each ERISA LP to pay its capital contributions into an escrow fund to be released only upon PE Fund's first qualifying investment. In order to simplify PE Fund's administration, either of the foregoing alternatives may be used for all LPs (not just for ERISA LPs).

¶1007 [1] However, if PE Fund invests in a portfolio company through a wholly owned PE Fund subsidiary (e.g., a C corporation interposed to block flow-through of unrelated business taxable income), DOL has concluded that PE Fund's wholly owned subsidiary is for this purpose disregarded and PE Fund is viewed as investing directly in the portfolio company, so that PE Fund must obtain management rights directly from the portfolio company.

¶1008   INVESTMENT COMPANY ACT OF 1940

(1) PE Fund falls within the "investment company" definition as set forth in the Investment Company Act of 1940 (the "ICA") because PE Fund's "primary" activity is "investing . . . in securities" of its portfolio companies. ICA §3(a)(1)(A).[1]

- If PE Fund principally purchases positions in portfolio companies not "controlled primarily" by PE Fund, its "primary" activity clearly is "investing . . . in securities."
- On the other hand, if most of PE Fund's assets consist of (and most of its income is derived from) portfolio companies "controlled primarily" by PE Fund and such portfolio companies are engaged in active manufacturing, service, and similar businesses (as opposed to investment activities), PE Fund might take the position that it is not an investment company because it is engaging indirectly, through its controlled portfolio companies, in their active businesses. See ICA §§3(a)(1)(C) and 3(a)(2) and SEC Reg. §270.3a-1.
- SEC, however, has taken the position that a holding company (like PE Fund) which invests in "special situations" (i.e., acquires a controlling position in companies with the intent of reselling such securities at a profit after fixing or maturing the companies, rather than for the purpose of operating such companies' businesses for the long term) is an investment company. See, e.g., SEC Reg. §270.3a-1(b).[2]

(2) Thus, unless PE Fund finds an exemption, it will be an "investment company" subject to the ICA's onerous and impenetrable regulatory provisions, which can significantly restrict PE Fund's activities. Only a handful of PE Funds have registered under the ICA.

(3) However, two exemptions are potentially available to PE Fund:

- the **private investment fund exemption** afforded by long-standing ICA §3(c)(1) (discussed in (4) and (5) below), and
- the **qualified purchaser fund exemption** afforded by ICA §3(c)(7), which was newly enacted by 10/96 legislation (the "1996 Act") (discussed in (6) below).

¶1008   [1] If PE Fund invests in futures or options on futures, to hedge its portfolio investments or otherwise, PE Fund may also be subject to commodity pool regulation under the Commodity Exchange Act. In 11/02, the Commodity Futures Trading Commission ("CFTC") issued an advance notice of rulemaking and interim no-action position to provide relief from commodity pool operator regulation for a PE Fund that (1) commits a limited amount of assets to financial and commodity futures transactions or (2) limits PE Fund investors to specific types of sophisticated persons, so long as the PE Fund files a notice with CFTC.

[2] By contrast, technology incubators—i.e., companies investing in a portfolio of start up companies, frequently buying a minority stock position in each and supplying the portfolio companies with leased space, executive recruiting, software development and technology assistance, legal, accounting, financial, marketing, and purchasing assistance, in an effort to build a collaborative network of related portfolio companies—generally assert that they are primarily engaged in a business other than investing in securities and therefore do not constitute an "investment company." Several of these companies have received SEC confirmation that they are engaged in a non-investment business. See ICA §3(b)(1) and (2).

(4) Under **ICA §3(c)(1)'s private investment fund exemption,** if PE Fund (a) has no more than 100 beneficial owners of its "securities (other than short-term paper)" *and* (b) has not made (and does not plan to make) a public offering of its securities, PE Fund is exempt from the "investment company" definition and escapes virtually all the ICA's provisions. ICA §3(c)(1).

In counting to 100, each PE Fund LP and each PE Fund GP normally counts as one security holder,[3] subject to a number of complex disregard rules, look-through rules, integration rules, and two different approaches for counting participants in on-shore and off-shore funds:

- SEC Reg. §270.3c-5, discussed in (6) below, describes in some detail those PE Fund service providers (officers, directors, trustees, partners, advisory board members, or employees) and certain of their family members—called "Knowledgeable Employees"—who can be ignored (i.e., not treated as PE Fund security holders in counting to 100).

- Moreover, and apart from Knowledgeable Employees, where a human being or an entity active in PE Fund's investment activities holds a GP interest in PE Fund, such GP interest is generally not a security and hence such GP human being or entity (and such GP entity's owners) are not included in the 100 count. However, a 1997 SEC release suggests an exception to this rule where "the GP interest [although] . . . not a security [is] being used as a device to evade" ICA registration. Under this "device" exception, where a GP entity (especially a newly-formed GP entity) is in part owned by passive investors, i.e., equity owners of the GP entity who are not active in PE Fund's investment activities (especially a new equity investor injecting a substantial amount of fresh money into the GP entity which the GP entity in turn invests in PE Fund), such passive investor into the GP entity is likely to be viewed as an indirect PE Fund security holder and hence included in the 100 count.

- A husband and wife are counted as one where they jointly own a PE Fund interest (but as two where they invest separately).

- In counting PE Fund's security holders (for purposes of the 100 limitation), the ICA may apply a look-through approach where PE Fund (the "lower-tier fund") has an entity partner (the "upper-tier entity"), i.e., a partner which is a corporation, a partnership, or an LLC, as discussed in (5) below.

- Where GP forms multiple PE funds relying on ICA §3(c)(1), SEC's integration doctrine may apply, so that multiple funds are treated as one for purposes of the 100 count. SEC takes the position that such multiple funds are substantively integrated unless a reasonable investor would view the funds as materially different in terms of, e.g., investment objectives, portfolio securities to be purchased, and/or risk/return characteristics. Generally where GP forms a second fund well after completing the formation of a first fund (e.g., two years or perhaps more than one year later), the second

---

[3] Throughout this Chapter 10, unless otherwise stated, (a) LP means limited partner and GP means general partner where PE Fund is organized as a limited partnership and (b) LP means non-managing member and GP means managing member where PE Fund is organized as a manager-managed LLC.

fund is formed after the first fund has invested or committed most of its capital, and the second fund intends to invest primarily in the securities of different portfolio companies than the first fund, then the two temporally separate funds are not integrated. In addition, the ICA specifically prohibits integration of a §3(c)(1) and a §3(c)(7) fund (as discussed below). See ICA §3(c)(7)(E).

- Where PE Fund is organized under *U.S.* law (i.e., is an on-shore fund), SEC takes the position that a security holder (other than a Knowledgeable Employee and certain family members who are ignored as described above) counts (for purposes of the 100 limitation) whether a U.S. person or a foreign person. However, where PE Fund is organized under *foreign* law (an off-shore fund), SEC's position (widely referred to as the Touche Remnant doctrine) is that a PE Fund security holder who is a foreign person does not count and thus the ICA §3(c)(1) no public offering and 100 limitation applies only to PE Fund security holders who are U.S. persons.[4]

   SEC utilizes 1933 Act Reg. S in determining who is a U.S. person or a foreign person, so that any person (including a U.S. citizen) permanently residing outside the U.S. is treated as a foreign person. Since the ICA prohibits unregistered offshore PE Fund from conducting a U.S. public offering (but not a U.S. private offering), unregistered offshore PE Fund can continue to comply with ICA §3(c)(1) while simultaneously (1) publicly offering securities to foreign persons offshore and (2) privately offering securities in the U.S. In addition, unregistered offshore PE Fund may have a U.S. investment manager and/or GP and may also conduct limited administrative activities in the U.S. without adversely impacting its ICA §3(c)(1) status.

   In order for PE Fund to continue to qualify for the §3(c)(1) private investment fund exemption throughout its life, it must continue to comply with both the 100-security-holder and the no-public-offering limitations.

- Where a PE Fund security holder transfers an interest in PE Fund by gift, bequest, or pursuant to separation or divorce, the transferees stand in the transferor's shoes for purposes of determining whether PE Fund has more than 100 security holders (as do similar transferees of any such transferee), i.e., the transferor is treated as continuing to own the interest and the transferees are ignored, so long as (except in the case of a transfer to an estate upon death) the transferees are not obligated to make future contributions to PE Fund (i.e., only the transferor is obligated to make future capital contributions), although the transferees may actually make future contributions out of earmarked funds supplied by the transferor. ICA §3(c)(1)(B); SEC Reg. §270.3c-6.

(5) **Two look-through rules** apply in determining whether an ICA §3(c)(1) private investment fund has more than 100 security holders. If either rule applies, PE Fund must look through an upper-tier entity to the entity owners:

---

[4] Where PE Fund consists of two companion private investment funds, one on-shore with U.S. LPs and one off-shore with foreign LPs, which invest in tandem, there is risk they might be integrated

First, the automatic 10% statutory look-through rule applies whenever an upper-tier entity *both* (i) holds a 10% or greater voting interest in PE Fund *and* (ii) is not an operating company, but rather is itself relying on either the §3(c)(1) private investment fund exemption or the §3(c)(7) qualified purchaser fund exemption to avoid investment company status under the ICA.[5] ICA §3(c)(1)(A).

In determining whether an upper-tier entity holds a voting interest in PE Fund for purposes of the 10% look-through test, SEC generally (i) treats an LP interest as a voting interest where the LP is entitled to vote on replacing the GP under any circumstances or is entitled to vote on any other significant matter and (ii) treats even a non-voting LP interest as a voting interest where such equity interest's economic rights are large (e.g., a 25% interest, or perhaps even a 15% interest that is large compared to any other LP equity interest).

Second, even where an upper-tier entity escapes the automatic statutory look-through rule, another look-through rule nevertheless applies to such upper-tier entity (even where the upper-tier entity holds less than a 10% voting interest in PE Fund and/or is not itself an ICA §3(c)(1) or §3(c)(7) company) if the entity was "formed," "reformed," or "operated" for the purpose of investing in PE Fund. In such case, it is necessary to look through to the upper-tier entity's owners regardless of the size of such upper-tier entity's equity interest in PE Fund. See ICA §48(a), prohibiting "any person, directly or indirectly, to cause to be done any act or thing through or by means of any other person [here the upper-tier entity formed, reformed, or operated for the purpose of investing in PE Fund] which it would be unlawful for such person to do."

- Where an upper-tier entity invests a very large portion of its assets in a single PE Fund, the SEC may well take the position that the upper-tier entity was *formed* for the purpose of investing in PE Fund. While SEC has historically regarded an investment of 40% or less of an entity's assets in a single PE Fund as not giving rise to such an inference, there is no express guidance with respect to amounts greater than 40%.

- Where the upper-tier entity is operated in a manner designed to facilitate individual decision making by its equity owners (e.g., the upper-tier entity's

---

for purposes of the 100 limitation and treated as an on-shore fund, unless there is a tax or business reason (i.e., a non-ICA reason) for forming both an on-shore and an off-shore fund.

[5] Prior to the 1996 Act, the automatic statutory look-through rule applied whenever an upper-tier entity held a 10% or greater voting interest in PE Fund (regardless of whether the upper-tier entity was an operating company or a private investment fund), unless the upper-tier entity met the "10%-of-assets exception," i.e., the FV of the upper-tier entity's investment in PE Fund plus its investments in all other entities exempt from the ICA under the §3(c)(1) private investment fund exception did not, in the aggregate, exceed 10% of the FV of such entity's assets (measured at the time of the entity's subscription to PE Fund). ICA §3(c)(1)(A) before amendment by the 1996 Act. If a PE Fund formed before the 1996 Act became effective has a 10% or greater upper-tier entity which is a §3(c)(1) private investment fund (and hence is covered by the automatic statutory look-through rule described in text above), such entity continues to be eligible for the pre-1997 10%-of-assets exception (described in the immediately preceding sentence) so long as (i) the entity held a 10% or greater voting interest in PE Fund on 4/1/97 and (ii) on the date of any acquisition of PE Fund's securities, the FV of all securities owned by such upper-tier entity of issuers which are private investment funds or qualified purchaser funds does not exceed 10% of its assets. ICA Reg. §270.3c-1.

equity owners can even decide whether or how much to invest in PE Fund), SEC will likely take the position that the upper-tier entity is *reformed* or *operated* for the purpose of making the investment. For example, where an employee benefit plan allows each participant to direct investment of his or her account balance, i.e., to decide whether (and how much) to invest in (e.g.) PE Fund, each participant electing to invest employee benefit plan money in PE Fund counts as a look-through PE Fund security holder.

Where one of the two look-through rules applies to an upper-tier entity and such upper-tier entity has an owner which is itself an entity (the "super-upper-tier entity"), the look-through rules also apply to the super-upper-tier entity in order to ascertain whether there is a look through to the super-upper-tier entity's owners. There is such a look through where, for example, either of the two look-through rules applies to the upper-tier entity and the super-upper-tier entity was formed, reformed, or operated for the purpose of investing in the upper-tier entity (see Second above).

(6) **ICA §3(c)(7)'s qualified purchaser fund exemption,** the second ICA exemption available to PE Fund, newly enacted by the 1996 Act, requires that (i) PE Fund's outstanding securities be owned exclusively by persons who, at the time of acquisition, are "qualified purchasers" and (ii) PE Fund has not made (and does not plan to make) a public offering of its securities.

For purposes of this exemption, qualified purchaser ("QP") generally means (i) a human being owning at least $5 million of "investments" or (ii) an entity with at least $25 million of "investments." There are several important sub-rules in determining whether a person is a QP:

(a) Where a married person invests individually in PE Fund, the investing spouse can count all investment assets owned individually by such person plus all investment assets owned jointly with such person's spouse (including as community property or similar shared ownership interest) for the $5 million test.

(b) Where a married couple invests jointly in PE Fund, both spouses can count all of the couple's investments, whether or not jointly owned, for the $5 million test.

(c) A human being can count investment assets held in an IRA or similar retirement account the investments of which are directed by, and held for the benefit of, such human being.

(d) An entity includes investment assets owned by (i) its majority-owned subsidiaries, (ii) its majority-owning parent, and (iii) majority-owned subsidiaries of such parent.

(e) A trust qualifies as a QP where (i) it was not formed for the specific purpose of acquiring PE Fund's securities, (ii) the trustee (or other person authorized to make investment decisions) is a QP, and (iii) each person who contributed assets to the trust was a QP when the assets were contributed to the trust.

(f) For an entity (such as a partnership, LLC, corporation, or trust) owned by a single family to qualify as a QP, it must meet only the $5 million (not the $25 million) test. For this purpose, family means (i) natural persons related as siblings, spouse (including former spouse), or direct lineal descendants by birth or adoption, (ii) such persons' spouses and estates, and (iii) foundations, charitable organizations, and trusts established by or for the benefit of such persons. For this purpose, a trust's owners are generally its beneficiaries. This $5 million rule does not apply to an entity formed for the specific purpose of investing in PE Fund unless each beneficial owner of the entity is a QP. SEC Reg. §270.2a51-3(a).

(g) An entity or a human being can qualify as a QP where it (i) acts for its own account or for the accounts of other QPs and (ii) in the aggregate owns and invests on a discretionary basis at least $25 million of investments. ICA §2(a)(51)(A) and SEC Reg. §270.2a51-1. This $25 million rule does not apply to an entity formed for the specific purpose of investing in PE Fund unless each beneficial owner of the entity is a QP. SEC Reg. §270.2a51-3(a).

(h) An entity qualifies as a QP if all its beneficial owners are QPs. SEC Reg. §270.2a51-3(b).

SEC regulations define "investments" according to the following philosophy: investments are broader than securities, but not every asset is an investment. To constitute an investment, an asset must be held for investment purposes, and the nature of the asset must indicate a significant degree of investment experience and sophistication such that the investor can be expected to have the knowledge to evaluate the risks of investing in unregulated investment pools.

Thus, for example, personal residences and many family-owned businesses are not investments. More specifically, SEC by regulation has determined that a person's "investments" (i) *include* (x) securities, (y) where held for investment purposes, real estate, commodities, financial contracts, cash, and cash equivalents, and (z) for a PE Fund, unfunded binding subscriptions or capital commitments, but (ii) *exclude* securities in a company controlled by, controlling, or under common control with, the person seeking to qualify as a QP unless the security is issued by (x) a 1934 Act reporting company, (y) a company with at least $50 million stockholders' equity, *or* (z) certain registered or exempt investment companies, including a PE fund. The regulations require a person's investments to be reduced by the amount of outstanding indebtedness incurred for the purpose of acquiring investments. SEC Reg. §270.2a51-1.

In determining whether a person is a QP and whether PE Fund is a §3(c)(7) qualified purchaser fund, several special rules apply:

(a) In determining whether PE Fund's outstanding securities are owned exclusively by QPs, PE Fund securities beneficially owned by a "Knowledgeable Employee" are ignored. SEC Reg. §270.3c-5.

- "Knowledgeable Employee" generally means a human being who is:

   (1) an executive officer, director, trustee, general partner, advisory board member, or person serving in a similar capacity for PE Fund or PE Fund's GP or certain of its affiliates or

   (2) an employee of PE Fund or PE Fund's GP or certain of its affiliates (but not a high-level executive described in (1) above), who regu-

larly participates in the investment activities (other than per-forming solely clerical, secretarial, or administrative functions) of PE Fund, any other PE fund, certain insurance companies, certain employee benefit plan trusts, or any investment company man-aged by PE Fund's GP or certain of its affiliates, so long as such person has for at least 12 months so participated in investment activities on behalf of any such entities (whether or not affiliated with the GP).

For purposes of (2), SEC views the phrase "regularly participates in . . . investment activities" narrowly so that participation in such fund activities as marketing, compliance, and accounting do not qualify.

A person who is a Knowledgeable Employee at the time he or she acquires PE Fund securities is ignored (even though subsequently ceasing to be a Knowledgeable Employee).

- Interests in PE Fund owned by the following persons are also ignored:

    (i)   a Knowledgeable Employee's spouse who jointly owns an interest with the Knowledgeable Employee,

    (ii)   a person (a "donee") who acquires securities from a Knowledge-able Employee by gift, bequest, or pursuant to separation or di-vorce (as well as similar transferees of any such transferee), so long as (except in the case of a transfer to an estate upon death), such donee is not obligated to make future contributions to PE Fund (i.e., only the Knowledgeable Employee is obligated to make future capital contributions), although the donee may actually make future contributions out of earmarked funds supplied by the Knowledgeable Employee,

    (iii) a company owned exclusively by Knowledgeable Employees (e.g., PE Fund's GP entity), including joint ownership with their spouses,

    (iv)   a company established by a Knowledgeable Employee and/or his or her donees exclusively for the benefit of (or owned exclu-sively by) such Knowledgeable Employee and his or her do-nees, or

    (v)   based upon an SEC no-action letter, a trust or other estate planning vehicle for which a Knowledgeable Employee makes the invest-ment decisions and is the source of funds invested (including funds owned jointly with his or her spouse) even though not owned exclusively by the Knowledgeable Employee and spouse.

- For many years prior to the 1996 Act's enactment of the Knowledgeable Employee concept, where PE Fund's GP was an entity ("Management Company") most PE Funds assumed that such Management Company would be ignored for ICA purposes on the ground that it was an active participant in PE Fund's investment activities rather than a PE Fund security holder. After 1996, a PE Fund would probably rely on SEC's Knowledgeable Employee rules which disregard, e.g., "a company owned exclusively by Knowledgeable Employees." However, as described in (4) above, a 1997 SEC release suggests that a passive investor in an active GP Management Company who injects substantial fresh money which the GP in turn invests in PE Fund is now likely to be viewed as an indirect PE Fund security holder under the "device" test.

(b) Where an upper-tier entity is "formed," "reformed," or "operated" for the purpose of investing in PE Fund, it is necessary to look through to the upper-tier entity's security holders (as described in ¶1008(5) (Second) above) in order to ascertain whether all of PE Fund's beneficial owners (including all of the beneficial owners of the look-through upper-tier entity are QPs (or Knowledgeable Employees) as discussed above). SEC Reg. §270.2a51-3(a). For a §3(c)(7) qualified purchaser fund, there is no automatic 10% statutory look-through rule (as there is for a §3(c)(1) private investment fund — see ¶1008(5)(First)); thus, if the upper-tier entity is not formed, reformed, or operated for the purpose of investing in a §3(c)(7) fund, there is no look through even where the upper-tier entity owns more than 10% of PE Fund.

(c) Where a QP and such person's spouse jointly own an interest in PE Fund, the spouse is ignored.

(d) Where a PE Fund security holder transfers an interest in PE Fund by gift, bequest, or pursuant to separation or divorce, the transferees stand in the transferor's shoes for purposes of determining whether PE Fund has a non-QP security holder (as do similar transferees of any such transferee), i.e., the transferor is treated as continuing to own the securities and the transferees are ignored, so long as (except in the case of a transfer to an estate upon death), the transferees are not obligated to make future contributions to PE Fund (i.e., only the QP transferor is obligated to make future capital contributions), although the transferees may actually make future contributions out of earmarked funds supplied by the QP transferor. SEC Reg. §270.3c-6.

(e) Under the 1996 Act, an upper-tier §3(c)(1) private investment fund or §3(c)(7) qualified purchaser fund formed before 5/96 cannot be a QP with respect to a partnership interest in PE Fund unless all of such upper-tier fund's pre-5/96 security holders (plus in certain limited circumstances pre-5/96 security holders of any private investment fund or qualified purchaser fund which owns any securities in such upper-tier fund) consent to its treatment as a QP. ICA §2(a)(51)(C).

(f) Where VC forms two companion funds—one a §3(c)(1) private investment fund with 100 or fewer non-QPs and the other a §3(c)(7) qualified purchaser fund with an unlimited number of QPs—the two companion funds, although making their investments in operating companies in tandem, are not integrated for purposes of determining whether the first qualifies for ICA §3(c)(1)'s private investment fund exemption and the second qualifies for ICA §3(c)(7)'s qualified purchaser fund exemption. ICA §3(c)(7)(E).

- Prior to the 1996 Act, PE Fund was limited to 100 security holders plus the GP. After the 1996 Act, VC can use a dual fund approach, i.e., by forming two side-by-side funds, which have in the aggregate an unlimited number of QPs, an unlimited number of knowledgeable persons, and up to 100 persons who are neither.

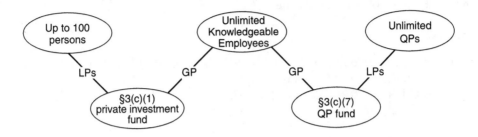

(g) Where a foreign person holds PE Fund securities, SEC takes the same position in interpreting ICA §3(c)(7)'s qualified purchaser exemption as it takes in interpreting ICA §3(c)(1)'s private investment fund exemption (see (4) above), i.e., an *on-shore* fund's qualification for the §3(c)(7) exemption is determined by taking into account each security holder (other than a Knowledgeable Employee and certain family members who are ignored as described above), whether a U.S. person or a foreign person, while an *off-shore* fund takes into account only U.S. persons. Hence an off-shore fund could qualify for the §3(c)(7) exemption although it has one or more non-QP foreign security holders, so long as all its security holders who are U.S. persons qualify as QPs (or Knowledgeable Employees).

In order for PE Fund to continue to qualify for ICA §3(c)(7)'s qualified purchaser fund exemption throughout its life, PE Fund must continue to comply with the no-public-offering limitation and must not admit as a security holder a person who is not (at the time of admission) either a QP or a Knowledgeable Employee or a disregarded person (such as a donee of a QP or Knowledgeable Employee), although PE Fund is not disqualified if a security holder ceases to be a QP or Knowledgeable Employee after admission.

(7) **Anti-pyramiding restrictions.** The ICA §3(c)(1) and §3(c)(7) exemptions discussed above are subject to certain anti-pyramiding restrictions under ICA §12. Thus, a PE Fund using either of these exemptions is restricted from acquiring more than 3% of the voting stock of any ICA registered fund, and an ICA registered fund is subject to certain restrictions on purchasing PE Fund's voting securities.

(8) **ESC.** In addition to the ICA §3(c)(1) and §3(c)(7) exemptions discussed above, an "employees security company" (or "ESC") exemption is available for an investment entity wholly-owned by the employees of a single employer (or the employees of an affiliated group of employers) and certain of their family members. In order to obtain an ESC exemption, an investment entity must file a lengthy application with SEC and any final SEC order will impose certain ICA requirements on the ESC. SEC generally permits only employees who meet speci-

fied income or net worth and educational standards to invest in an ESC. An ESC may have more than 100 investors, and investors need not meet the QP or Knowledgeable Employee tests. ICA §§6(b), 2(a)(13); SEC Reg. §270.6b-1.

(9) **Key issues and references.** Will PE Fund be subject to the ICA? Is it feasible for PE Fund to operate under the ICA?

References:

- Investment Company Act of 1940 §2(a)(2), (3), (9), (13), (24), (42), (51), §3(a), (b), (c)(1), (c)(7), §6, §48(a)
- SEC Reg. §270.2a51-1 through 51-3
- SEC Reg. §270.3a-1
- SEC Reg. §270.3a-2
- SEC Reg. §270.3a-3
- SEC Reg. §270.3c-1, -5, and -6

¶1009 PRIVATE PLACEMENT OF PE FUND's EQUITY INTERESTS

It is necessary for PE Fund's offering of its equity interests to qualify as a private placement in order to avoid (1) the registration requirements of the 1933 Act and (2) the onerous and impenetrable ICA rules (see ¶1008 above). In order to qualify the offering of equity interests as a private placement, PE Fund can comply with either the "safe harbor" contained in SEC Reg. D or the more amorphous statutory exemption of 1933 Act §4(2).

- The requirements of SEC Regulation D are reviewed at ¶207.3 above.

The offering of the LP interests must also comply with each applicable state securities (blue sky) law in order to avoid a violation of state law.

References:

- 1933 Act §4(2) and §3(a)(11)
- SEC Reg. D
- SEC Rule 147

¶1010 INVESTMENT ADVISERS ACT OF 1940

(1) PE Fund's GP (Management Company) is an "investment adviser" (an "IA") under the Investment Advisers Act of 1940 (the "IAA"), because Management Company is a "person who, for compensation, engages in the business of advising others [PE Fund] . . . as to the advisability of investing in, purchasing, or selling securities [the securities purchased by PE Fund]." IAA §202(a)(11); SEC Reg. §275.203(b)(3)-1(a)(2)(i) and (b)(3).

(2) An IA is required to register with SEC under the IAA unless an exemption is available. IAA §203(a).

- However, no IA regulated or required to be regulated as an IA in the state in which it maintains its principal office and place of business is required to (or indeed can) register with SEC under the IAA unless it *either* (a) has at least $25 million of assets under management (i.e., securities portfolios with respect to which the IA provides continuous and regular supervisory or management services) *or* (b) serves as IA to a registered investment company. Such an IA, upon attaining $25 million of assets under management, has the option to, but need not, register with SEC until it has at least $30 million of assets under management, at which point it must register with SEC. IAA §203A; SEC Reg. §275.203A-1.
- SEC Reg. §275.203A-2 allows certain IAs that meet neither (a) nor (b) above to register with SEC (rather than under state law), including (i) an affiliate of a registered IA having the same principal office and place of business as the registered IA and (ii) a new IA expecting to have at least $25 million of assets under management within 120 days after SEC IA registration.
- A state law requiring the registration, licensing, or qualification of an IA (or supervised person thereof) can not apply to an IA registered with SEC under the IAA (or a supervised person thereof), except that a state may require licensing, registration, or other qualification of IA representatives with a place of business in the state except an IA representative who advises mostly institutional clients, such as PE Funds. IAA §203A(b).
- Also, no state law requiring registration, licensing, or qualification of an IA can apply to an IA (whether or not registered with SEC) which (1) does not have a place of business located within the state and (2) during the preceding 12-month period had fewer than 6 clients resident in the state. IAA §222(d).

(3) No IA, unless exempt from SEC IA registration by the fewer-than-15-client exemption discussed in (4) below, may receive "compensation . . . on the basis of a share of capital gains [including a carried interest] upon or capital appreciation of the funds or any portion of the funds of" any investment advisory client (including here PE Fund), except as described in (6) through (9) below. IAA §205(a)(1).

- A number of states have rules applicable to IAs registered therein relative to carried interest compensation which are similar, if not identical, to the IAA rules.

(4) An IA is exempt from registering under the IAA (and hence the IAA prohibition on a carried interest would not apply) where the IA "during the course of the preceding twelve months has had fewer than fifteen clients and . . . neither holds himself out generally to the public as an investment adviser nor acts as an investment adviser to any investment company registered under" the ICA. IAA §203(b)(3). However, for a PE Fund's GP to effectively use the fewer-than-15-client exemption, the PE Fund must be located in a state with

favorable state blue sky investment adviser licensing requirements as discussed in (10) below.

(5) In determining whether PE Fund's GP has fewer than 15 advisory clients (so that it is exempt from the IAA registration requirement and the IAA carried interest prohibition), several issues arise:

(a) Where GP has formed and acts as general partner of numerous separate PE, buyout, and/or private equity funds, each such fund will generally be a separate advisory client. Hence, if GP is acting (or during the past 12 months has acted) as general partner of more than 14 such funds, GP is not exempt under the less-than-15 rule.

(b) Where GP has fewer than 15 actual fund advisees (as described in (a) above), the question arises whether each PE Fund can be counted as *one* advisory client or whether GP is treated as giving investment advice to each LP of each fund.

    (i) Under an SEC safe-harbor rule, PE Fund is counted as only one investment advisory client of GP and PE Fund's equity owners are not counted as clients of GP, so long as GP provides "investment advice to [PE Fund] based on its investment objectives rather than the individual investment objectives of its shareholders, partners, limited partners, members, or beneficiaries."[1] SEC Reg. §275.203(b)(3)-1.

    (ii) However, there is an exception to this fund-is-one safe-harbor rule: A fund LP who receives investment advice from GP "separate and apart from the investment advisory services provided to" PE Fund is counted as an additional investment advisory client of GP.

(c) Even where GP has fewer than 15 PE Fund advisees and the PE Fund's LPs do not receive investment advice from GP separate and apart from PE Fund, there is still one more hurdle to overcome in determining whether GP has fewer than 15 advisees: If GP is the "alter ego" of another investment advisory entity (an "IAE") (e.g., an entity controlling, controlled by, or under common control with the IA, such as an investment banking firm also engaged in general investment advisory activities), GP must count all of the IAE's advisees, even those who are not fund LPs. GP will be treated as the alter ego of an IAE if GP is not "separate and distinct" from the IAE. SEC has from time to time mentioned several factors in determining whether a fund's GP and a related IAE are "separate and distinct" (i.e., are not "alter egos" of each other), the most relevant of which are:

    • Whether there is an adequate buffer between the two, e.g., a board or other decision-making body at GP level a majority of whose members are independent of the IAE.

¶1010 [1] In 2002, SEC commenced an investigation of certain private funds (i.e., hedge funds) using the fewer-than-15-client exemption from IAA registration requirements. It is possible that SEC might, at the conclusion of this investigation, eliminate the fund-is-one-client safe harbor.

- GP's investment advisory personnel are not engaged in the IAE's advisory activities or vice versa.
- GP itself makes the investment decisions for its PE Fund or Funds and in making such decisions GP has and uses resources and information which are not limited to the IAE's resources and information.
- GP maintains the confidentiality of advice given to its clients (i.e., PE Fund or Funds) vis-a-vis the IAE until after the advice has been given to GP's clients.

(d) Hence, in summary, in order to meet the fewer-than-15 advisees exemption, GP must:

- count its actual advisees, including each separate fund as to which it acts as general partner (or otherwise acts as an IA),
- determine how many fund LPs must be counted as additional advisees of GP because they receive separate advice from GP,
- determine whether GP is an "alter ego" of any other IAE and hence must count such IAE's advisory clients, even though such clients are not PE Fund LPs, and
- not hold itself out generally to the public as an IA.

(6) Even if GP has more than 14 actual or deemed advisees (counting in the manner described in (5) above)—so that GP is required to register under the IAA (as described in (2) above)—GP may receive up to a 20% carried interest in PE Fund's "realized capital gains . . . net of all realized capital losses and unrealized capital depreciation," so long as PE Fund qualifies as a Business Development Company (a "BDC") and meets certain other requirements. IAA §205(b)(3). Unfortunately this statutory formulation of PE Fund's net "realized capital gains" may cause a problem when PE Fund distributes appreciated securities to its GP and LPs *in kind*, because the gain thereon may not be viewed as "realized" by such in-kind distribution.

Generally, in order for PE Fund to qualify as a BDC, at least 60% of PE Fund's assets (measured by FV) must be invested in private or troubled or certain controlled public companies. See IAA §202(a)(22) and ICA §2(a)(46), §2(a)(47), §2(a)(48), and §55.

(7) Even where GP is required to register under the IAA and PE Fund is not a BDC, an SEC exemptive rule allows GP to receive "a share of capital gains upon or capital appreciation of the funds or any portion of the funds of the client [here a carried interest in PE Fund]," so long as *either*:

(a) *an IAA statutory exemption applies* because PE Fund is "a company excepted from the definition of an investment company under" ICA §3(c)(7)'s qualified purchaser fund exemption, as described in ¶1008(6) (see IAA §205(b)(4)), *or*

(b) *SEC's "heavy hitter" regulatory exemption applies* because each PE Fund LP who is charged a carried interest is a "qualified client" (SEC Reg. §275.205-3).

For purposes of (b) above, qualified client means a person who *either:*

(i)   has at least $750,000 under the GP's management ($500,000 with respect to an LP's pre-8/20/98 commitment), *or*

(ii)   has more than $1.5 million of net worth ($1 million with respect to an LP's pre-8/20/98 commitment), counting (in the case of a human being) assets held jointly with the LP's spouse, *or*

(iii) is a "qualified purchaser" as defined in ICA §2(a)(51)(A) (as described in ¶1008(6)), i.e., in general, a natural person owning at least $5 million of investments or an entity with at least $25 million of investments, *or*

(iv)   is a human being who is a Knowledgeable Employee as described in ¶1008(6), *or*

(v)   is a donee of any of the foregoing.

In determining whether an entity LP is a qualified client for purposes of (i) through (iii) above, SEC's heavy hitter rule applies a look-through approach where both PE Fund (the "lower-tier entity") and the entity LP (the "upper-tier entity") are private investment funds exempt under ICA§3(c)(1), i.e., focuses on the upper-tier entity's equity owners (or if an upper-tier entity has an equity owner who is also a private investment fund, on the equity owners of such private investment fund), so that each equity owner must satisfy one of the qualified client tests set forth in (i) through (iv) above. Where, however, PE Fund is a qualified purchaser fund exempt under ICA §3(c)(7), so that the upper-tier entity is by definition a qualified purchaser satisfying the statutory exemption (IAA §205(b)(4)), there is no need to satisfy SEC's heavy hitter regulatory exemption and hence no need to look at or through the upper-tier entity.

(8) In addition to the exemptions from the no-carried-interest rule described above, the IAA statutory prohibition on receipt of a carried interest does not apply in the case of an IA contract with a person not a resident of the United States. IAA §205(b)(5).

(9) Certain of the IAA's provisions apply to *any* IA, whether or not required to register, including (a) general anti-fraud provisions applicable to GP's relationship with its advisees and (b) prohibitions on GP selling securities to or purchasing securities from an advisee, whether as principal or agent, without the advisee's consent. IAA §206.

(10) Even where GP is not required to register as an IA under the IAA or is precluded from registering by the $25 million/$30 million preclusion from registration described in (2) above, GP may be required to register as an IA under a state blue sky law in the state where PE Fund's principal place of business is located (since some state blue sky laws do not contain a 15-or-fewer exemption), but a few states do prohibit a state registered IA from receiving a carried interest. See however ¶1010(2) regarding federal preclusion of state IAA registration in certain circumstances.

(11) **Key issues and references.** Will GP be subject to the IAA? Will the IAA preclude GP from receiving a carried interest?

References:

- IAA §202(a)(11), §203(a), §203(b)(3), §203A(a) and (b), §205, §208(d), §215, §222(d)
- SEC Reg. §275.203(b)(3)-1
- SEC Reg. §275.203A-1 and A-2
- SEC Reg. §275.205-3 (the "heavy hitter rule")
- For the definition of a BDC for purposes of the IAA: IAA §202(a)(22) and ICA §2(a)(46) through (48) and §55

¶1011   PE FUND AS AN SBIC

(1)   Advantages to qualifying PE Fund as an SBIC.

- An SBIC has access to government financing at favorable rates, as discussed below.
- A national bank is generally not permitted to invest in PE Fund unless the fund is a licensed SBIC.
- A BHC and its non-bank subsidiaries are generally not permitted by the BHCA to invest in PE Fund unless (a) PE Fund is an SBIC (as described in ¶209.2.1.2) *or* (b) the BHC investment in PE Fund complies with Reg. Y's 5 and 25 rules (as described at ¶209.2.1.1) *or* (c) each of PE Fund's investments complies with Reg. Y's 5 and 25 rules *or* (d) the BHC is a financial holding company and the financial holding company or its non-bank subsidiary invests in PE Fund as part of its merchant banking activity (as described in ¶209.2.1.4) *or* (e) each of PE Fund's investments complies with Reg. K (as described in ¶209.2.1.3).

(2)   Disadvantages to qualifying PE Fund as an SBIC.

- An SBIC is generally permitted to make investments only in an "eligible small business" and is subject to numerous SBA regulations dealing with the terms of the SBIC's investments in eligible small businesses, conflicts of interest, reporting to SBA, and other matters, as described generally in ¶209.1 above.

    For this reason, PE Fund may wish to form two partnerships, one qualified as an SBIC which invests in only portfolio companies qualifying as "eligible small businesses" and the second a non-SBIC investing in portfolio companies not qualifying as "eligible small businesses."

- SBA regulations require a minimum contributed capital of $2.5 million in cash when the SBIC license is granted, but SBA generally requires a greater minimum committed capital (to be paid in to the SBIC over a period of time). Where the SBIC is seeking SBA financing (as described in (3) below), SBA generally requires $5 million of committed capital to obtain Debenture financing and $10 million of committed capital to obtain Participating Securities financing.
- It takes approximately 6 months or more to obtain an SBIC license, but SBA permits a PE Fund to apply for a license while raising capital

and making investments, although an investment made after SBA has accepted the license application for processing and before grant of the license qualifies as part of required capital (described immediately above) only to the extent the investment complies with SBA's regulations *and* SBA approves the investment in advance.

(3) SBA financing for an SBIC.

- An SBIC can issue "Participating Securities" to SBA. Participating Securities give SBA a preferred equity position which accrues "prioritized payments" (not interest) at a rate equal to the Treasury rate for similar maturities (generally 10-year term) plus approximately 275 basis points depending upon market conditions at the time the Participating Securities are funded, which prioritized payments are payable only out of and to the extent of the SBIC's realized earnings.

  In addition, where an SBIC issues Participating Securities, SBA is entitled to participate in profits generated by each Portfolio Company security held by the SBIC while the Participating Securities are outstanding (not merely Portfolio Company securities purchased with the proceeds of Participating Securities and not merely profits realized while the Participating Securities are outstanding).

  SBA's profit participation percentage (generally approximately 10%) varies with (a) the ratio of Participating Securities to contributed capital (the "PSCC Ratio") and (b) the rate on 10-year Treasury Notes at the time the Participating Securities are issued.

  The maximum amount of Participating Securities available to any one SBIC (or group of SBICs under common control) is generally 200% of cash contributions and commitments, but not more than an amount based on the consumer price index ($113.4 million beginning 11/02). For a 1% commitment fee, an SBIC can apply to SBA for a five-year commitment of up to the maximum amount of Participating Securities available to it. Draw-downs are permitted on short notice subject only to customary conditions. Each draw-down is generally subject to approximately 2.5% in fees, and there is a 1% per year fee on the unused portion of the commitment.

  Participating Securities are treated as equity (not debt) for tax purposes, so that where the SBIC is a flow-through entity (e.g., a partnership or LLC, although SBA has not yet blessed an LLC format for a Participating Securities SBIC) the Participating Securities do not generate debt-financed UBTI for the SBIC's TEO equity owners.

- An SBIC can seek to issue "Debentures" through SBA, bearing interest at a fixed rate (approximately 200 basis points over the Treasury rate for comparable maturities at the time the Debenture is issued) payable semi-annually, with prepayments permitted at any time.

  The maximum amount of Debentures available to any one SBIC (or group of SBICs under common control) is 300% of private capital (declining . . . toward 100% as the SBIC's private capital rises), but not more than an amount based on the consumer price index ($113.4 million beginning 11/02). It would be unusual for an SBIC to seek both Debenture and Participating Security leverage and, if it does, the formula for available leverage is more complex.

Where the SBIC is a flow-through entity and uses the proceeds from Debentures to purchase Portfolio Company securities, such Portfolio Company securities are treated as debt-financed for tax purposes, so that a TEO equity owner of the SBIC is taxed (as debt-financed UBTI) on the portion of its dividend income, interest income, and CG generated by such debt-financed securities corresponding to the percentage of the purchase price for such securities which is debt-financed.

Appendix
Statutes, Regulations, and
Other Precedents

Summary of Contents for Precedents

Many of the precedents have been abbreviated by deleting portions not relevant to this book.

¶2000

Internal Revenue Code of 1986

SEC. 1.   TAX IMPOSED.

(a) MARRIED INDIVIDUALS FILING JOINT RETURNS AND SURVIVING SPOUSES. There is hereby imposed on the taxable income of—

(1) every married individual (as defined in section 7703) who makes a single return jointly with his spouse under section 6013, and

(2) every surviving spouse (as defined in section 2(a)),

a tax [for 2002 and 2003] determined in accordance with the following table:

If Taxable Income Is:	*The Tax Is:*
Not over $36,900	[10% of the first $12,000 of taxable income and] 15% of taxable income [in excess of $12,000].
Over $36,900 but not over $89,150	. . . , plus [27%] of the excess over $36,900.
Over $89,150 but not over $140,000	. . . , plus [30%] of the excess over $89,150.
Over $140,000 but not over $250,000	. . . , plus [35%] of the excess over $140,000.
Over $250,000	. . . , plus [38.6%] of the excess over $250,000.

[Bracketed material in §1(a) above reflects enactment of Code §1(i) in 6/01.]

. . .

(h) MAXIMUM CAPITAL GAINS RATE.—

(1) IN GENERAL.—If a taxpayer has a net capital gain for any taxable year, the tax imposed by this section for such taxable year shall not exceed the sum of—

(A) a tax computed at the rates and in the same manner as if this subsection had not been enacted on the greater of—

(i) taxable income reduced by the net capital gain, or

(ii) the lesser of—

(I) the amount of taxable income taxed at a rate below 25 percent, or

(II) taxable income reduced by the adjusted net capital gain,

(B) 10 percent of so much of the adjusted net capital gain (or, if less, taxable income) as does not exceed the excess (if any) of—

(i) the amount of taxable income which would (without regard to this paragraph) be taxed at a rate below 25 percent, over

(ii) the taxable income reduced by the adjusted net capital gain,

(C) 20 percent of the adjusted net capital gain (or, if less, taxable income) in excess of the amount on which a tax is determined under subparagraph (B),

(D) 25 percent of the excess (if any) of—

(i) the unrecaptured section 1250 gain (or, if less, the net capital gain), over

(ii) the excess (if any) of—

(I) the sum of the amount on which tax is determined under subparagraph (A) plus the net capital gain, over

(II) taxable income, and

(E) 28 percent of the amount of taxable income in excess of the sum of the amounts on which tax is determined under the preceding subparagraphs of this paragraph.

(2) REDUCED CAPITAL GAIN RATES FOR QUALIFIED 5-YEAR GAIN.—

(A) REDUCTION IN 10-PERCENT RATE.—In the case of any taxable year beginning after December 31, 2000, the rate under paragraph (1)(B) shall be 8 percent with respect to so much of the amount to which the 10-percent rate would otherwise apply as does not exceed qualified 5-year gain, and 10 percent with respect to the remainder of such amount.

(B) REDUCTION IN 20-PERCENT RATE.—The rate under paragraph (1)(C) shall be 18 percent with respect to so much of the amount to which the 20-percent rate would otherwise apply as does not exceed the lesser of—

(i) the excess of qualified 5-year gain over the amount of such gain taken into account under subparagraph (A) of this paragraph; or

(ii) the amount of qualified 5-year gain (determined by taking into account only property the holding period for which begins after December 31, 2000),

and 20 percent with respect to the remainder of such amount. For purposes of determining under the preceding sentence whether the holding period of property begins after December 31, 2000, the holding period of property acquired pursuant to the exercise of an option (or other right or obligation to acquire property) shall include the period such option (or other right or obligation) was held.

An uncodified provision in the 1997 Tax Act (which enacted Code §1(h)(2)), as modified by the 12/00 legislative addition of the second sentence of (e)(3), states:

(e) ELECTION TO RECOGNIZE GAIN ON ASSETS HELD ON JANUARY 1, 2001.—For purposes of the Internal Revenue Code of 1986—

(1) IN GENERAL.—A taxpayer other than a corporation may elect to treat—

(A) any readily tradable stock (which is a capital asset) held by such taxpayer on January 1, 2001, and not sold before the next business day after such date, as having been sold on such next business day for an amount equal to its closing market price on such next business day (and as having been reacquired on such next business day for an amount equal to such closing market price), and

(B) any other capital asset or property used in the trade or business (as defined in section 1231(b) of the Internal Revenue Code of 1986) held by the taxpayer on January 1, 2001, as having been sold on such date for an amount equal to its fair market value on such date (and as having been reacquired on such date for an amount equal to such fair market value).

(2) TREATMENT OF GAIN OR LOSS.—

(A) Any gain resulting from an election under paragraph (1) shall be treated as received or accrued on the date the asset is treated as sold under paragraph (1) and shall be recognized notwithstanding any provision of the Internal Revenue Code of 1986.

(B) Any loss resulting from an election under paragraph (1) shall not be allowed for any taxable year.

(3) ELECTION.—An election under paragraph (1) shall be made in such manner as the Secretary of the Treasury or his delegate may prescribe and shall specify the assets for which such election is made. Such an election, once made with respect to any asset, shall be irrevocable. Such an election shall not apply to any asset which is disposed of (in a transaction in which gain or loss is recognized in whole or in part) before the close of the 1-year period beginning on the date that the asset would have been treated as sold under such election.

(4) READILY TRADABLE STOCK.—For purposes of this subsection, the term "readily tradable stock" means any stock which, as of January 1, 2001, is readily tradable on an established securities market or otherwise.

---

(3) NET CAPITAL GAIN TAKEN INTO ACCOUNT AS INVESTMENT INCOME.—For purposes of this subsection, the net capital gain for any taxable year shall be reduced (but not below zero) by the amount which the taxpayer takes into account as investment income under section 163(d)(4)(B)(iii).

(4) ADJUSTED NET CAPITAL GAIN.—For purposes of this subsection, the term "adjusted net capital gain" means net capital gain reduced (but not below zero) by the sum of—

(A) unrecaptured section 1250 gain, and

(B) 28 percent rate gain.

(5) 28 PERCENT RATE GAIN.—For purposes of this subsection, the term "28 percent rate gain" means the excess (if any) of—

(A) the sum of—

(i) collectibles gain; and

(ii) section 1202 gain; over

(B) the sum of—

(i) collectibles loss;

(ii) the net short-term capital loss; and

(iii) the amount of long-term capital loss carried under section 1212(b)(1)(B) to the taxable year.

(6) COLLECTIBLES GAIN AND LOSS.—For purposes of this subsection—

(A) IN GENERAL.—The terms "collectibles gain" and "collectibles loss" mean gain or loss (respectively) from the sale or exchange of a collectible (as defined in section 408(m) without regard to paragraph (3) thereof) which is a capital asset held for more than 1 year but only to the extent such gain is taken into account in computing gross income and such loss is taken into account in computing taxable income.

(B) PARTNERSHIPS, ETC. For purposes of subparagraph (A), any gain from the sale of an interest in a partnership, S corporation, or trust which is attributable to unrealized appreciation in the value of collectibles shall be treated as gain from the sale or exchange of a collectible. Rules similar to the rules of section 751 shall apply for purposes of the preceding sentence.

(7) UNRECAPTURED SECTION 1250 GAIN.—For purposes of this subsection—

(A) IN GENERAL. The term "unrecaptured section 1250 gain" means the excess (if any) of—

(i) the amount of long-term capital gain (not otherwise treated as ordinary income) which would be treated as ordinary income if section 1250(b)(1) included all depreciation and the applicable percentage under section 1250(a) were 100 percent, over

(ii) the excess (if any) of—

(I) the amount described in paragraph (5)(B), over

(II) the amount described in paragraph (5)(A).

(B) LIMITATION WITH RESPECT TO SECTION 1231 PROPERTY.—The amount described in subparagraph (A)(i) from sales, exchanges, and conversions described in section 1231(a)(3)(A) for any taxable year shall not exceed the net section 1231 gain (as defined in section 1231(c)(3)) for such year.

(8) SECTION 1202 GAIN.—For purposes of this subsection, the term "section 1202 gain" means the excess of—

(A) the gain which would be excluded from gross income under section 1202 but for the percentage limitation in section 1202(a), over

(B) the gain excluded from gross income under section 1202.

(9) QUALIFIED 5-YEAR GAIN.—For purposes of this subsection, the term "qualified 5-year gain" means the aggregate long-term capital gain from property held for more than 5 years. The determination under the preceding sentence shall be made without regard to collectibles gain, gain described in paragraph (7)(A)(i), and section 1202 gain.

(10) COORDINATION WITH RECAPTURE OF NET ORDINARY LOSSES UNDER SECTION 1231.—If any amount is treated as ordinary income under section 1231(c), such amount shall be allocated among the separate categories of net section 1231 gain (as defined in section 1231(c)(3)) in such manner as the Secretary may by forms or regulations prescribe.

(11) REGULATIONS.—The Secretary may prescribe such regulations as are appropriate (including regulations requiring reporting) to apply this subsection in the case of sales and exchanges by pass-thru entities and of interests in such entities.

(12) PASS-THRU ENTITY DEFINED.—For purposes of this subsection, the term "pass-thru entity" means—

(A) a regulated investment company;

(B) a real estate investment trust;

(C) an S corporation;

(D) a partnership;

(E) an estate or trust;

(F) a common trust fund;

(G) a foreign investment company which is described in section 1246(b)(1) and for which an election is in effect under section 1247; and

(H) a qualified electing fund (as defined in section 1295).

. . .

(i)(2) REDUCTIONS IN RATES AFTER JUNE 30, 2001.—In the case of taxable years beginning in a calendar year after 2000, the corresponding percentage specified for such calendar year in the following table shall be substituted for the otherwise applicable tax rate in the tables under subsections (a), (b), (c), (d), and (e).

In the case of taxable years beginning during calendar year:	The corresponding percentages shall be substituted for the following percentages:			
	28%	31%	36%	39.6%
2001	27.5%	30.5%	35.5%	39.1%
2002 and 2003	27.0%	30.0%	35.0%	38.6%
2004 and 2005	26.0%	29.0%	34.0%	37.6%
2006 and thereafter	25.0%	28.0%	33.0%	35.0%

SEC. 11. TAX IMPOSED.

(a) CORPORATIONS IN GENERAL.—A tax is hereby imposed for each taxable year on the taxable income of every corporation.

(b) AMOUNT OF TAX.—

(1) IN GENERAL.—The amount of the tax imposed by subsection (a) shall be the sum of—

(A) 15 percent of so much of the taxable income as does not exceed $50,000,

(B) 25 percent of so much of the taxable income as exceeds $50,000 but does not exceed $75,000,

(C) 34 percent of so much of the taxable income as exceeds $75,000 but does not exceed $10,000,000, and

(D) 35 percent of so much of the taxable income as exceeds $10,000,000.

In the case of a corporation which has taxable income in excess of $100,000 for any taxable year, the amount of tax determined under the preceding sentence for such taxable year shall be increased by the lesser of (i) 5 percent of such excess, or (ii) $11,750. In the case of a corporation which has taxable income in excess of $15,000,000, the amount of the tax determined under the foregoing provisions of this paragraph shall be increased by an additional amount equal to the lesser of (i) 3 percent of such excess, or (ii) $100,000.

(2) CERTAIN PERSONAL SERVICE CORPORATIONS NOT ELIGIBLE FOR GRADUATED RATES.—Notwithstanding paragraph (1), the amount of the tax imposed by subsection (a) on the taxable income of a qualified personal service corporation (as defined in section 448(d)(2)) shall be equal to 35 percent of the taxable income.

. . .

SEC. 61. GROSS INCOME DEFINED.

(a) GENERAL DEFINITION.—Except as otherwise provided in this subtitle, gross income means all income from whatever source derived, including (but not limited to) the following items:

(1) Compensation for services, including fees, commissions, fringe benefits, and similar items;
(2) Gross income derived from business;
(3) Gains derived from dealings in property;
(4) Interest;
(5) Rents;
(6) Royalties;
(7) Dividends;
(8) Alimony and separate maintenance payments;
(9) Annuities;
(10) Income from life insurance and endowment contracts;
(11) Pensions;
(12) Income from discharge of indebtedness;
(13) Distributive share of partnership gross income;
(14) Income in respect of a decedent; and
(15) Income from an interest in an estate or trust.

. . .

SEC. 83. PROPERTY TRANSFERRED IN CONNECTION WITH PERFORMANCE OF SERVICES.

(a) GENERAL RULE.—If, in connection with the performance of services, property is transferred to any person other than the person for whom such services are performed, the excess of—

(1) the fair market value of such property (determined without regard to any restriction other than a restriction which by its terms will never lapse) at the first time the rights of the person having the beneficial interest in such property are transferable or are not subject to a substantial risk of forfeiture, whichever occurs earlier, over

(2) the amount (if any) paid for such property,

shall be included in the gross income of the person who performed such services in the first taxable year in which the rights of the person having the beneficial interest in such property are transferable or are not subject to a substantial risk of forfeiture, whichever is applicable. The preceding sentence shall not apply if such person sells or otherwise disposes of such property in an arm's length transaction before his rights in such property become transferable or not subject to a substantial risk of forfeiture.

(b) ELECTION TO INCLUDE IN GROSS INCOME IN YEAR OF TRANSFER.—

(1) IN GENERAL.—Any person who performs services in connection with which property is transferred to any person may elect to include in his gross income, for the taxable year in which such property is transferred, the excess of—

(A) the fair market value of such property at the time of transfer (determined without regard to any restriction other than a restriction which by its terms will never lapse), over

A–10

(B) the amount (if any) paid for such property.

If such election is made, subsection (a) shall not apply with respect to the transfer of such property, and if such property is subsequently forfeited, no deduction shall be allowed in respect of such forfeiture.

(2) ELECTION.—An election under paragraph (1) with respect to any transfer of property shall be made in such manner as the Secretary prescribes and shall be made not later than 30 days after the date of such transfer. Such election may not be revoked except with the consent of the Secretary.

(c) SPECIAL RULES.—For purposes of this section—

(1) SUBSTANTIAL RISK OF FORFEITURE.—The rights of a person in property are subject to a substantial risk of forfeiture if such person's rights to full enjoyment of such property are conditioned upon the future performance of substantial services by any individual.

(2) TRANSFERABILITY OF PROPERTY.—The rights of a person in property are transferable only if the rights in such property of any transferee are not subject to a substantial risk of forfeiture.

(3) SALES WHICH MAY GIVE RISE TO SUIT UNDER SECTION 16(b) OF THE SECURITIES EXCHANGE ACT OF 1934.—So long as the sale of property at a profit could subject a person to suit under section 16(b) of the Securities Exchange Act of 1934, such person's rights in such property are—

(A) subject to a substantial risk of forfeiture, and

(B) not transferable.

(d) CERTAIN RESTRICTIONS WHICH WILL NEVER LAPSE.—

(1) VALUATION.—In the case of property subject to a restriction which by its terms will never lapse, and which allows the transferee to sell such property only at a price determined under a formula, the price so determined shall be deemed to be the fair market value of the property unless established to the contrary by the Secretary, and the burden of proof shall be on the Secretary with respect to such value.

(2) CANCELLATION.—If, in the case of property subject to a restriction which by its terms will never lapse, the restriction is cancelled, then, unless the taxpayer establishes—

(A) that such cancellation was not compensatory, and

(B) that the person, if any, who would be allowed a deduction if the cancellation were treated as compensatory, will treat the transaction as not compensatory, as evidenced in such manner as the Secretary shall prescribe by regulations, the excess of the fair market value of the property (computed without regard to the restrictions) at the time of cancellation over the sum of—

(C) the fair market value of such property (computed by taking the restriction into account) immediately before the cancellation, and

(D) the amount, if any, paid for the cancellation, shall be treated as compensation for the taxable year in which such cancellation occurs.

(e) APPLICABILITY OF SECTION.—This section shall not apply to—

(1) a transaction to which section 421 applies,

(2) a transfer to or from a trust described in section 401(a) or a transfer under an annuity plan which meets the requirements of section 404(a)(2),

(3) the transfer of an option without a readily ascertainable fair market value,

(4) the transfer of property pursuant to the exercise of an option with a readily ascertainable fair market value at the date of grant, or

(5) group-term life insurance to which section 79 applies.

(f) HOLDING PERIOD.—In determining the period for which the taxpayer has held property to which subsection (a) applies, there shall be included only the period beginning at the first time his rights in such property are transferable or are not subject to a substantial risk of forfeiture, whichever occurs earlier.

(g) CERTAIN EXCHANGES.—If property to which subsection (a) applies is exchanged for property subject to restrictions and conditions substantially similar to those to which the property given in such exchange was subject, and if section 354, 355, 356, or 1036 (or so much of section 1031 as relates to section 1036) applied to such exchange, or if such exchange was pursuant to the exercise of a conversion privilege—

(1) such exchange shall be disregarded for purposes of subsection (a), and

(2) the property received shall be treated as property to which subsection (a) applies.

(h) DEDUCTION BY EMPLOYER.—In the case of a transfer of property to which this section applies or a cancellation of a restriction described in subsection (d), there shall be allowed as a deduction under section 162, to the person for whom were performed the services in connection with which such property was transferred, an amount equal to the amount included under subsection (a), (b), or (d)(2) in the gross income of the person who performed such services. Such deduction shall be allowed for the taxable year of such person in which or with which ends the taxable year in which such amount is included in the gross income of the person who performed such services.

SEC. 108.   INCOME FROM DISCHARGE OF INDEBTEDNESS.

(a) EXCLUSION FROM GROSS INCOME.—

(1) IN GENERAL.—Gross income does not include any amount which (but for this subsection) would be includible in gross income by reason of the discharge (in whole or in part) of indebtedness of the taxpayer if—

(A) the discharge occurs in a title 11 case, or

(B) the discharge occurs when the taxpayer is insolvent,

(C) the indebtedness discharged is qualified farm indebtedness, or

(D) in the case of a taxpayer other than a C corporation, the indebtedness discharged is qualified real property business indebtedness.

(2) COORDINATION OF EXCLUSIONS.—

(A) TITLE 11 EXCLUSION TAKES PRECEDENCE.—Subparagraphs (B), (C), and (D) of paragraph (1) shall not apply to a discharge which occurs in a title 11 case.

(B) INSOLVENCY EXCLUSION TAKES PRECEDENCE OVER QUALIFIED FARM EXCLUSION AND QUALIFIED REAL PROPERTY BUSINESS

EXCLUSION.—Subparagraphs (C) and (D) of paragraph (1) shall not apply to a discharge to the extent the taxpayer is insolvent.

(3) INSOLVENCY EXCLUSION LIMITED TO AMOUNT OF INSOLVENCY.—In the case of a discharge to which paragraph (1)(B) applies, the amount excluded under paragraph (1)(B) shall not exceed the amount by which the taxpayer is insolvent.

(b) REDUCTION OF TAX ATTRIBUTES.—

(1) IN GENERAL.—The amount excluded from gross income under subparagraph (A), (B), or (C) of subsection (a)(1) shall be applied to reduce the tax attributes of the taxpayer as provided in paragraph (2).

(2) TAX ATTRIBUTES AFFECTED; ORDER OF REDUCTION.—Except as provided in paragraph (5), the reduction referred to in paragraph (1) shall be made in the following tax attributes in the following order:

(A) NOL.—Any net operating loss for the taxable year of the discharge, and any net operating loss carryover to such taxable year.

(B) GENERAL BUSINESS CREDIT.—Any carryover to or from the taxable year of a discharge of an amount for purposes for determining the amount allowable as a credit under section 38 (relating to general business credit).

(C) MINIMUM TAX CREDIT.—The amount of the minimum tax credit available under section 53(b) as of the beginning of the taxable year immediately following the taxable year of the discharge.

(D) CAPITAL LOSS CARRYOVERS.—Any net capital loss for the taxable year of the discharge, and any capital loss carryover to such taxable year under section 1212.

(E) BASIS REDUCTION.—

(i) IN GENERAL.—The basis of the property of the taxpayer.

(ii) CROSS REFERENCE.—For provisions for making the reduction described in clause (i), see section 1017.

(F) PASSIVE ACTIVITY LOSS AND CREDIT CARRYOVERS.—Any passive activity loss or credit carryover of the taxpayer under section 469(b) from the taxable year of the discharge.

(G) FOREIGN TAX CREDIT CARRYOVERS.—Any carryover to or from the taxable year of the discharge for purposes of determining the amount of the credit allowable under section 27.

(3) AMOUNT OF REDUCTION.—

(A) IN GENERAL.—Except as provided in subparagraph (B), the reductions described in paragraph (2) shall be one dollar for each dollar excluded by subsection (a).

(B) CREDIT CARRYOVER REDUCTION.—The reductions described in subparagraphs (B), (C), and (G) shall be $33\frac{1}{3}$ cents for each dollar excluded by subsection (a). The reduction described in subparagraph (F) in any passive activity credit carryover shall be $33\frac{1}{3}$ cents for each dollar excluded by subsection (a).

(4) ORDERING RULES.—

(A) REDUCTIONS MADE AFTER DETERMINATION OF TAX FOR YEAR.—The reductions described in paragraph (2) shall be made after the determination of the tax imposed by this chapter for the taxable year of the discharge.

(B) REDUCTIONS UNDER SUBPARAGRAPH (A) OR (D) OF PARA-GRAPH (2).—The reductions described in subparagraph (A) or (D) of paragraph (2) (as the case may be) shall be made first in the loss for the taxable year of the discharge and then in the carryovers to such taxable year in the order of the taxable years from which each such carryover arose.

(C) REDUCTIONS UNDER SUBPARAGRAPHS (B) AND (G) OF PARA-GRAPH (2).—The reductions described in subparagraphs (B) and (G) of paragraph (2) shall be made in the order in which carryovers are taken into account under this chapter for the taxable year of the discharge.

(5) ELECTION TO APPLY REDUCTION FIRST AGAINST DEPRECIA-BLE PROPERTY.—

(A) IN GENERAL.—The taxpayer may elect to apply any portion of the reduction referred to in paragraph (1) to the reduction under section 1017 of the basis of the depreciable property of the taxpayer.

(B) LIMITATION.—The amount to which an election under subparagraph (A) applies shall not exceed the aggregate adjusted bases of the depreciable property held by the taxpayer as of the beginning of the taxable year following the taxable year in which the discharge occurs.

(C) OTHER TAX ATTRIBUTES NOT REDUCED.—Paragraph (2) shall not apply to any amount to which an election under this paragraph applies.

(c) TREATMENT OF DISCHARGE OF QUALIFIED REAL PROPERTY BUSI-NESS INDEBTEDNESS.—

(1) BASIS REDUCTION.—

(A) IN GENERAL.—The amount excluded from gross income undersub-paragraph (D) of subsection (a)(1) shall be applied to reduce the basis of the depreciable real property of the taxpayer.

[Definitions and limitations omitted]

. . .

(d) MEANING OF TERMS; SPECIAL RULES RELATING TO CERTAIN PROVISIONS.—

(1) INDEBTEDNESS OF TAXPAYER.—For purposes of this section, the term "indebtedness of the taxpayer" means any indebtedness—

(A) for which the taxpayer is liable, or

(B) subject to which the taxpayer holds property.

(2) TITLE 11 CASE.—For purposes of this section, the term "title 11 case" means a case under title 11 of the United States Code (relating to bankruptcy), but only if the taxpayer is under the jurisdiction of the court in such case and the discharge of indebtedness is granted by the court or is pursuant to a plan approved by the court.

(3) INSOLVENT.—For purposes of this section, the term "insolvent" means the excess of liabilities over the fair market value of assets. With respect to any

discharge, whether or not the taxpayer is insolvent, and the amount by which the taxpayer is insolvent, shall be determined on the basis of the taxpayer's assets and liabilities immediately before the discharge.

(5) DEPRECIABLE PROPERTY.—The term "depreciable property" has the same meaning as when used in section 1017.

(6) CERTAIN PROVISIONS TO BE APPLIED AT PARTNER LEVEL.—In the case of a partnership, subsections (a), (b), (c), and (g) shall be applied at the partner level.

(7) SPECIAL RULES FOR S CORPORATION.—

(A) CERTAIN PROVISIONS TO BE APPLIED AT CORPORATE LEVEL.—In the case of an S corporation, subsections (a), (b), (c), and (g) shall be applied at the corporate level, including by not taking into account under section 1366(a) any amount excluded under subsection (a) of this section.

(B) REDUCTION IN CARRYOVER OF DISALLOWED LOSSES AND DEDUCTIONS.—In the case of an S corporation, for purposes of subparagraph (A) of subsection (b)(2), any loss or deduction which is disallowed for the taxable year of the discharge under section 1366(d)(1) shall be treated as a net operating loss for such taxable year. The preceding sentence shall not apply to any discharge to the extent that subsection (a)(1)(D) applies to such discharge.

(C) COORDINATION WITH BASIS ADJUSTMENTS UNDER SECTION 1367(b)(2).—For purposes of subsection (e)(6), a shareholder's adjusted basis in indebtedness of an S corporation shall be determined without regard to any adjustments made under section 1367(b)(2).

. . .

(e) GENERAL RULES FOR DISCHARGE OF INDEBTEDNESS (INCLUDING DISCHARGES NOT IN TITLE 11 CASES OR INSOLVENCY).—For purposes of this title—

(1) NO OTHER INSOLVENCY EXCEPTION.—Except as otherwise provided in this section, there shall be no insolvency exception from the general rule that gross income includes income from the discharge of indebtedness.

(2) INCOME NOT REALIZED TO EXTENT OF LOST DEDUCTIONS.—No income shall be realized from the discharge of indebtedness to the extent that payment of the liability would have given rise to a deduction.

(3) ADJUSTMENTS FOR UNAMORTIZED PREMIUM AND DISCOUNT.— The amount taken into account with respect to any discharge shall be properly adjusted for unamortized premium and unamortized discount with respect to the indebtedness discharged.

(4) ACQUISITION OF INDEBTEDNESS BY PERSON RELATED TO DEBTOR.—

(A) TREATED AS ACQUISITION BY DEBTOR.—For purposes of determining income of the debtor from discharge of indebtedness, to the extent provided in regulations prescribed by the Secretary, the acquisition of outstanding indebtedness by a person bearing a relationship to the debtor specified in section 267(b) or 707(b)(1) from a person who does not bear such a relationship to the debtor shall be treated as the acquisition of such indebtedness by the debtor. Such regulations shall provide for such adjustments in the treatment of any subsequent transactions involving the indebtedness as may be appropriate by reason of the application of the preceding sentence.

(B) MEMBERS OF FAMILY.—For purposes of this paragraph, sections 267(b) and 707(b)(1) shall be applied as if section 267(c)(4) provided that the family of an individual consists of the individual's spouse, the individual's children, grandchildren, and parents, and any spouse of the individual's children or grandchildren.

(C) ENTITIES UNDER COMMON CONTROL TREATED AS RELATED.—For purposes of this paragraph, two entities which are treated as a single employer under subsection (b) or (c) of section 414 shall be treated as bearing a relationship to each other which is described in section 267(b).

(5) PURCHASE-MONEY DEBT REDUCTION FOR SOLVENT DEBTOR TREATED AS PRICE REDUCTION.—If—

(A) the debt of a purchaser of property to the seller of such property which arose out of the purchase of such property is reduced,

(B) such reduction does not occur—

(i) in a title 11 case, or

(ii) when the purchaser is insolvent, and

(C) but for this paragraph, such reduction would be treated as income to the purchaser from the discharge of indebtedness,

then such reduction shall be treated as a purchase price adjustment.

(6) INDEBTEDNESS CONTRIBUTED TO CAPITAL.—Except as provided in regulations, for purposes of determining income of the debtor from discharge of indebtedness, if a debtor corporation acquires its indebtedness from a shareholder as a contribution to capital—

(A) section 118 shall not apply, but

(B) such corporation shall be treated as having satisfied the indebtedness with an amount of money equal to the shareholder's adjusted basis in the indebtedness.

(7) RECAPTURE OF GAIN ON SUBSEQUENT SALE OF STOCK.—

(A) IN GENERAL.—If a creditor acquires stock of a debtor corporation in satisfaction of such corporation's indebtedness, for purposes of section 1245—

(i) such stock (and any other property the basis of which is determined in whole or in part by reference to the adjusted basis of such stock) shall be treated as section 1245 property,

(ii) the aggregate amount allowed to the creditor—

(I) as deductions under subsection (a) or (b) of section 166 (by reason of the worthlessness or partial worthlessness of the indebtedness), or

(II) as an ordinary loss on the exchange,

shall be treated as an amount allowed as a deduction for depreciation, and

(iii) an exchange of such stock qualifying under section 354(a), 355(a), or 356(a) shall be treated as an exchange to which section 1245(b)(3) applies. The amount determined under clause (ii) shall be reduced by the amount (if any) included in the creditor's gross income on the exchange.

(B) SPECIAL RULE FOR CASH BASIS TAXPAYERS.—In the case of any creditor who computes his taxable income under the cash receipts and disbursements method, proper adjustment shall be made in the amount taken into account under clause (ii) of subparagraph (A) for any amount which was not included in the creditor's gross income but which would have been included in such gross income if such indebtedness had been satisfied in full.

(C) STOCK OF PARENT CORPORATION.—For purposes of this paragraph, stock of a corporation in control (within the meaning of section 368(c)) of the debtor corporation shall be treated as stock of the debtor corporation.

(D) TREATMENT OF SUCCESSOR CORPORATION.—For purposes of this paragraph, the term "debtor corporation" includes a successor corporation.

(E) PARTNERSHIP RULE.—Under regulations prescribed by the Secretary, rules similar to the rules of the foregoing subparagraphs of this paragraph shall apply with respect to the indebtedness of a partnership.

(8) INDEBTEDNESS SATISFIED BY CORPORATION'S STOCK.—For purposes of determining income of a debtor from discharge of indebtedness, if a debtor corporation transfers stock to a creditor in satisfaction of its indebtedness, such corporation shall be treated as having satisfied the indebtedness with an amount of money equal to the fair market value of the stock.

(9) DISCHARGE OF INDEBTEDNESS INCOME NOT TAKEN INTO ACCOUNT IN DETERMINING WHETHER ENTITY MEETS REIT QUALIFICATIONS.—Any amount included in gross income by reason of the discharge of indebtedness shall not be taken into account for purposes of paragraphs (2) and (3) of section 856(c).

(10) INDEBTEDNESS SATISFIED BY ISSUANCE OF DEBT INSTRUMENT.—

(A) IN GENERAL.—For purposes of determining income of a debtor from discharge of indebtedness, if a debtor issues a debt instrument in satisfaction of indebtedness, such debtor shall be treated as having satisfied the indebtedness with an amount of money equal to the issue price of such debt instrument.

(B) ISSUE PRICE.—For purposes of subparagraph (A), the issue price of any debt instrument shall be determined under sections 1273 and 1274. For purposes of the preceding sentence, section 1273(b)(4) shall be applied by reducing the stated redemption price of any instrument by the portion of such stated redemption price which is treated as interest for purposes of this chapter.

. . .

SEC. 162.   TRADE OR BUSINESS EXPENSES.

. . .

(m) CERTAIN EXCESSIVE EMPLOYEE REMUNERATION.—

(1) IN GENERAL.—In the case of any publicly held corporation, no deduction shall be allowed under this chapter for applicable employee remuneration with respect to any covered employee to the extent that the amount of such remuneration for the taxable year with respect to such employee exceeds $1,000,000.

(2) PUBLICLY HELD CORPORATION.—For purposes of this subsection, the term "publicly held corporation" means any corporation issuing any class of common equity securities required to be registered under section 12 of the Securities Exchange Act of 1934.

(3) COVERED EMPLOYEE.—For purposes of this subsection, the term "covered employee" means any employee of the taxpayer if—

(A) as of the close of the taxable year, such employee is the chief executive officer of the taxpayer or is an individual acting in such a capacity, or

(B) the total compensation of such employee for the taxable year is required to be reported to shareholders under the Securities Exchange Act of 1934 by reason of such employee being among the 4 highest compensated officers for the taxable year (other than the chief executive officer).

(4) APPLICABLE EMPLOYEE REMUNERATION.—For purposes of this subsection—

(A) IN GENERAL.—Except as otherwise provided in this paragraph, the term "applicable employee remuneration" means, with respect to any covered employee for any taxable year, the aggregate amount allowable as a deduction under this chapter for such taxable year (determined without regard to this subsection) for remuneration for services performed by such employee (whether or not during the taxable year).

(B) EXCEPTION FOR REMUNERATION PAYABLE ON COMMISSION BASIS.—The term "applicable employee remuneration" shall not include any remuneration payable on a commission basis solely on account of income generated directly by the individual performance of the individual to whom such remuneration is payable.

(C) OTHER PERFORMANCE-BASED COMPENSATION.—The term "applicable employee remuneration" shall not include any remuneration payable solely on account of the attainment of one or more performance goals, but only if—

(i) the performance goals are determined by a compensation committee of the board of directors of the taxpayer which is comprised solely of 2 or more outside directors,

(ii) the material terms under which the remuneration is to be paid, including the performance goals, are disclosed to shareholders and approved by a majority of the vote in a separate shareholder vote before the payment of such remuneration, and

(iii) before any payment of such remuneration, the compensation committee referred to in clause (i) certifies that the performance goals and any other material terms were in fact satisfied.

(D) EXCEPTION FOR EXISTING BINDING CONTRACTS.—The term "applicable employee remuneration" shall not include any remuneration payable under a written binding contract which was in effect on February 17, 1993, and which was not modified thereafter in any material respect before such remuneration is paid.

(E) REMUNERATION.—For purposes of this paragraph, the term "remuneration" includes any remuneration (including benefits) in any medium other than cash, but shall not include—

(i) any payment referred to in so much of section 3121(a)(5) as precedes subparagraph (E) thereof, and

(ii) any benefit provided to or on behalf of an employee if at the time such benefit is provided it is reasonable to believe that the employee will be able to exclude such benefit from gross income under this chapter.

For purposes of clause (i), section 3121 (a)(5) shall be applied without regard to section 3121(v)(1).

(F) COORDINATION WITH DISALLOWED GOLDEN PARACHUTE PAYMENTS.—The dollar limitation contained in paragraph (1) shall be reduced (but not below zero) by the amount (if any) which would have been included in the applicable employee remuneration of the covered employee for the taxable year but for being disallowed under section 280G.

. . .

SEC. 163.   INTEREST.

(a) GENERAL RULE.—There shall be allowed as a deduction all interest paid or accrued within the taxable year on indebtedness.

. . .

(d) LIMITATION ON INVESTMENT INTEREST.—

(1) IN GENERAL.—In the case of a taxpayer other than a corporation, the amount allowed as a deduction under this chapter for investment interest for any taxable year shall not exceed the net investment income of the taxpayer for the taxable year.

(2) CARRYFORWARD OF DISALLOWED INTEREST.—The amount not allowed as a deduction for any taxable year by reason of paragraph (1) shall be treated as investment interest paid or accrued by the taxpayer in the succeeding taxable year.

(3) INVESTMENT INTEREST.—For purposes of this subsection—

(A) IN GENERAL.—The term "investment interest" means any interest allowable as a deduction under this chapter (determined without regard to paragraph (1)) which is paid or accrued on indebtedness properly allocable to property held for investment.

(B) EXCEPTIONS.—The term "investment interest" shall not include—

(i) any qualified residence interest (as defined in subsection (h)(3)), or

(ii) any interest which is taken into account under section 469 in computing income or loss from a passive activity of the taxpayer.

(C) PERSONAL PROPERTY USED IN SHORT SALE.—For purposes of this paragraph, the term "interest" includes any amount allowable as a deduction in connection with personal property used in a short sale.

(4) NET INVESTMENT INCOME.—For purposes of this subsection—

(A) IN GENERAL.—The term "net investment income" means the excess of—

(i) investment income, over

(ii) investment expenses.

(B) INVESTMENT INCOME.—The term "investment income" means the sum of—

(i) gross income from property held for investment (other than any gain taken into account under clause (ii)(I)),

(ii) the excess (if any) of—

(I) the net gain attributable to the disposition of property held for investment, over

(II) the net capital gain determined by only taking into account gains and losses from dispositions of property held for investment, plus

(iii) so much of the net capital gain referred to in clause (ii)(II) (or, if lesser, the net gain referred to in clause (ii)(I)) as the taxpayer elects to take into account under this clause.

(C) INVESTMENT EXPENSES.—The term "investment expenses" means the deductions allowed under this chapter (other than for interest) which are directly connected with the production of investment income.

(D) INCOME AND EXPENSES FROM PASSIVE ACTIVITIES.— Investment income and investment expenses shall not include any income or expenses taken into account under section 469 in computing income or loss from a passive activity.

. . .

(5) PROPERTY HELD FOR INVESTMENT.—For purposes of this subsection—

(A) IN GENERAL.—The term "property held for investment" shall include—

(i) any property which produces income of a type described in section 469(e)(1), and

(ii) any interest held by a taxpayer in an activity involving the conduct of a trade or business—

(I) which is not a passive activity, and

(II) with respect to which the taxpayer does not materially participate.

(B) INVESTMENT EXPENSES.—In the case of property described in subparagraph (A)(i), expenses shall be allocated to such property in the same manner as under section 469.

(C) TERMS.—For purposes of this paragraph, the terms "activity," "passive activity," and "materially participate" have the meanings given such terms by section 469.

. . .

(e) ORIGINAL ISSUE DISCOUNT.—

(1) IN GENERAL.—In the case of any debt instrument issued after July 1, 1982, the portion of the original issue discount with respect to such debt instrument which is allowable as a deduction to the issuer for any taxable year shall be equal to the aggregate daily portions of the original issue discount for days during such taxable year.

(2) DEFINITIONS AND SPECIAL RULES.—For purposes of this subsection—

(A) DEBT INSTRUMENT.—The term "debt instrument" has the meaning given such term by section 1275(a)(1).

(B) DAILY PORTIONS.—The daily portion of the original issue discount for any day shall be determined under section 1272(a) (without regard to paragraph (7) thereof and without regard to section 1273(a)(3)).

. . .

(5) SPECIAL RULES FOR ORIGINAL ISSUE DISCOUNT ON CERTAIN HIGH YIELD OBLIGATIONS.—

(A) IN GENERAL.—In the case of an applicable high yield discount obligation issued by a corporation—

(i) no deduction shall be allowed under this chapter for the disqualified portion of the original issue discount on such obligation, and

(ii) the remainder of such original issue discount shall not be allowable as a deduction until paid.

For purposes of this paragraph, rules similar to the rules of subsection (i)(3)(B) shall apply in determining the amount of the original issue discount and when the original issue discount is paid.

(B) DISQUALIFIED PORTION TREATED AS STOCK DISTRIBUTION FOR PURPOSES OF DIVIDEND RECEIVED DEDUCTION.—

(i) IN GENERAL.—Solely for purposes of sections 243, 245, 246, and 246A, the dividend equivalent portion of any amount includible in gross income of a corporation under section 1272(a) in respect of an applicable high yield discount obligation shall be treated as a dividend received by such corporation from the corporation issuing such obligation.

(ii) DIVIDEND EQUIVALENT PORTION.—For purposes of clause (i), the dividend equivalent portion of any amount includible in gross income under section 1272(a) in respect of an applicable high yield discount obligation is the portion of the amount so includible—

(I) which is attributable to the disqualified portion of the original issue discount on such obligation, and

(II) which would have been treated as a dividend if it had been a distribution made by the issuing corporation with respect to stock in such corporation.

(C) DISQUALIFIED PORTION.—

(i) IN GENERAL.—For purposes of this paragraph, the disqualified portion of the original issue discount on any applicable high yield discount obligation is the lesser of—

(I) the amount of such original issue discount, or

(II) the portion of the total return on such obligation which bears the same ratio to such total return as the disqualified yield on such obligation bears to the yield to maturity on such obligation.

(ii) DEFINITIONS.—For purposes of clause (i), the term "disqualified yield" means the excess of the yield to maturity on the obligation over the sum referred to subsection (i)(1)(B) plus 1 percentage point, and the term "total return" is the amount which would have been the original issue discount on the obligation if interest described in the parenthetical in section 1273(a)(2) were included in the stated redemption price at maturity.

(D) EXCEPTION FOR S CORPORATIONS.—This paragraph shall not apply to any obligation issued by any corporation for any period for which such corporation is an S corporation.

(E) EFFECT ON EARNINGS AND PROFITS.—This paragraph shall not apply for purposes of determining earnings and profits; except that, for purposes of determining the dividend equivalent portion of any amount includible in gross income under section 1272(a) in respect of an applicable high yield discount obligation, no reduction shall be made for any amount attributable to the disqualified portion of any original issue discount on such obligation.

. . .

(h) DISALLOWANCE OF DEDUCTION FOR PERSONAL INTEREST.—

(1) IN GENERAL.—In the case of a taxpayer other than a corporation, no deduction shall be allowed under this chapter for personal interest paid or accrued during the taxable year.

(2) PERSONAL INTEREST.—For purposes of this subsection, the term "personal interest" means any interest allowable as a deduction under this chapter other than—

(A) interest paid or accrued on indebtedness properly allocable to a trade or business (other than the trade or business of performing services as an employee),

(B) any investment interest (within the meaning of subsection (d)),

(C) any interest which is taken into account under section 469 in computing income or loss from a passive activity of the taxpayer,

(D) any qualified residence interest (within the meaning of paragraph (3)),

. . .

(F) any interest allowable as a deduction under section 221 (relating to interest on educational loans).

(3) QUALIFIED RESIDENCE INTEREST.—For purposes of this subsection—

(A) IN GENERAL.—The term "qualified residence interest" means any interest which is paid or accrued during the taxable year on—

(i) acquisition indebtedness with respect to any qualified residence of the taxpayer, or

(ii) home equity indebtedness with respect to any qualified residence of the taxpayer.

For purposes of the preceding sentence, the determination of whether any property is a qualified residence of the taxpayer shall be made as of the time the interest is accrued.

(B) ACQUISITION INDEBTEDNESS.—

(i) IN GENERAL.—The term "acquisition indebtedness" means any indebtedness which—

(I) is incurred in acquiring, constructing, or substantially improving any qualified residence of the taxpayer, and

(II) is secured by such residence.

Such term also includes any indebtedness secured by such residence resulting from the refinancing of indebtedness meeting the requirements of the preceding sentence (or this sentence); but only to the extent the amount of the indebtedness resulting from such refinancing does not exceed the amount of the refinanced indebtedness.

(ii) $1,000,000 LIMITATION.—The aggregate amount treated as acquisition indebtedness for any period shall not exceed $1,000,000 ($500,000 in the case of a married individual filing a separate return).

(C) HOME EQUITY INDEBTEDNESS.—

(i) IN GENERAL.—The term "home equity indebtedness" means any indebtedness (other than acquisition indebtedness) secured by a qualified residence to the extent the aggregate amount of such indebtedness does not exceed—

(I) the fair market value of such qualified residence, reduced by

(II) the amount of acquisition indebtedness with respect to such residence.

(ii) LIMITATION.—The aggregate amount treated as home equity indebtedness for any period shall not exceed $100,000 ($50,000 in the case of a separate return by a married individual).

. . .

(5) [(4)] OTHER DEFINITIONS AND SPECIAL RULES.—For purposes of this subsection—

   (A) QUALIFIED RESIDENCE.—

      (i) IN GENERAL.—The term "qualified residence" means—

         (I) the principal residence (within the meaning of section 121) of the taxpayer, and

         (II) 1 other residence of the taxpayer which is selected by the taxpayer for purposes of this subsection for the taxable year and which is used by the taxpayer as a residence (within the meaning of section 280A(d)(1)).

. . .

      (iii) RESIDENCE NOT RENTED.—For purposes of clause (i)(II), notwithstanding section 280A(d)(1), if the taxpayer does not rent a dwelling unit at any time during a taxable year, such unit may be treated as a residence for such taxable year.

. . .

   (C) UNENFORCEABLE SECURITY INTERESTS.—Indebtedness shall not fail to be treated as secured by any property solely because, under any applicable State or local homestead or other debtor protection law in effect on August 16, 1986, the security interest is ineffective or the enforceability of the security interest is restricted.

. . .

(i) APPLICABLE HIGH YIELD DISCOUNT OBLIGATION.—

   (1) IN GENERAL.—For purposes of this section, the term "applicable high yield discount obligation" means any debt instrument if—

      (A) the maturity date of such instrument is more than 5 years from the date of issue,

      (B) the yield to maturity on such instrument equals or exceeds the sum of—

         (i) the applicable Federal rate in effect under section 1274(d) for the calendar month in which the obligation is issued, plus

         (ii) 5 percentage points, and

      (C) such instrument has significant original issue discount.

For purposes of subparagraph (B)(i), the Secretary may by regulation permit a rate to be used with respect to any debt instrument which is higher than the applicable Federal rate if the taxpayer establishes to the satisfaction of the Secretary that such higher rate is based on the same principles as the applicable Federal rate and is appropriate for the term of the instrument.

(2) SIGNIFICANT ORIGINAL ISSUE DISCOUNT.—For purposes of paragraph (1)(C), a debt instrument shall be treated as having significant original issue discount if—

(A) the aggregate amount which would be includible in gross income with respect to such instrument for periods before the close of any accrual period (as defined in section 1272(a)(5)) ending after the date 5 years after the date of issue, exceeds—

(B) the sum of—

(i) the aggregate amount of interest to be paid under the instrument before the close of such accrual period, and

(ii) the product of the issue price of such instrument (as defined in sections 1273(b) and 1274(a)) and its yield to maturity.

(3) SPECIAL RULES.—For purposes of determining whether a debt instrument is an applicable high yield discount obligation—

(A) any payment under the instrument shall be assumed to be made on the last day permitted under the instrument, and

(B) any payment to be made in the form of another obligation of the issuer (or a related person within the meaning of section 453(f)(1) shall be assumed to be made when such obligation is required to be paid in cash or in property other than such obligation).

Except for purposes of paragraph (1)(B), any reference to an obligation in subparagraph (B) of this paragraph shall be treated as including a reference to stock.

(4) DEBT INSTRUMENT.—For purposes of this subsection, the term "debt instrument" means any instrument which is a debt instrument as defined in section 1275(a).

(5) REGULATIONS.—The Secretary shall prescribe such regulations as may be appropriate to carry out the purposes of this subsection and subsection (e)(5), including—

(A) regulations providing for modifications to the provisions of this subsection and subsection (e)(5) in the case of varying rates of interest, put or call options, indefinite maturities, contingent payments, assumptions of debt instruments, conversion rights, or other circumstances where such modifications are appropriate to carry out the purposes of this subsection and subsection (e)(5), and

(B) regulations to prevent avoidance of the purposes of this subsection and subsection (e)(5) through the use of issuers other than C corporations, agreements to borrow amounts due under the debt instrument, or other arrangements.

(j) LIMITATION ON DEDUCTION FOR INTEREST ON CERTAIN INDEBTEDNESS.—

(1) LIMITATION.—

(A) IN GENERAL.—If this subsection applies to any corporation for any taxable year, no deduction shall be allowed under this chapter for disqualified interest paid or accrued by such corporation during such taxable year. The amount disallowed under the preceding sentence shall not exceed the corporation's excess interest expense for the taxable year.

(B) DISALLOWED AMOUNT CARRIED TO SUCCEEDING TAXABLE YEAR.—Any amount disallowed under subparagraph (A) for any taxable year shall be treated as disqualified interest paid or accrued in the succeeding taxable year (and clause (ii) of paragraph (2)(A) shall not apply for purposes of applying this subsection to the amout so treated).

(2) CORPORATIONS TO WHICH SUBSECTION APPLIES.—

(A) IN GENERAL.—This subsection shall apply to any corporation for any taxable year if—

(i) such corporation has excess interest expense for such taxable year, and

(ii) the ratio of debt to equity of such corporation as of the close of such taxable year (or on any other day during the taxable year as the Secretary may by regulations prescribe) exceeds 1.5 to 1.

(B) EXCESS INTEREST EXPENSE.—

(i) IN GENERAL.—For purposes of this subsection, the term "excess interest expense" means the excess (if any) of—

(I) the corporation's net interest expense, over

(II) the sum of 50 percent of the adjusted taxable income of the corporation plus any excess limitation carryforward under clause (ii).

(ii) EXCESS LIMITATION CARRYFORWARD.—If a corporation has an excess limitation for any taxable year, the amount of such excess limitation shall be an excess limitation carryforward to the 1st succeeding taxable year and to the 2nd and 3rd succeeding taxable years to the extent not previously taken into account under this clause. The amount of such a carryforward taken into account for any such succeeding taxable year shall not exceed the excess interest expense for such succeeding taxable year (determined without regard to the carryforward from the taxable year of such excess limitation).

(iii) EXCESS LIMITATION.—For purposes of clause (ii), the term "excess limitation" means the excess (if any) of—

(I) 50 percent of the adjusted taxable income of the corporation, over

(II) the corporation's net interest expense.

(C) RATIO OF DEBT TO EQUITY.—For purposes of this paragraph, the term "ratio of debt to equity" means the ratio which the total indebtedness of the corporation bears to the sum of its money and all other assets reduced (but not below zero) by such total indebtedness. For purposes of the preceding sentence—

(i) the amount taken into account with respect to any asset shall be the adjusted basis thereof for purposes of determining gain,

(ii) the amount taken into account with respect to any indebtedness with original issue discount shall be its issue price plus the portion of the original issue discount previously accrued as determined under the rules of section 1272 (determined without regard to subsection (a)(7) or (b)(4) thereof), and

(iii) there shall be such other adjustments as the Secretary may by regulations prescribe.

(3) DISQUALIFIED INTEREST.—For purposes of this subsection, the term "disqualified interest" means—

(A) any interest paid or accrued by the taxpayer (directly or indirectly) to a related person if no tax is imposed by this subtitle with respect to such interest,

(B) any interest paid or accrued by the taxpayer with respect to any indebtedness to a person who is not a related person if—

(i) there is a disqualified guarantee of such indebtedness, and

(ii) no gross basis tax is imposed by this subtitle with respect to such interest, and

. . .

(4) RELATED PERSON.—For purposes of this subsection—

(A) IN GENERAL.—Except as provided in subparagraph (B), the term "related person" means any person who is related (within the meaning of section 267(b) or 707(b)(1)) to the taxpayer.

(B) SPECIAL RULE FOR CERTAIN PARTNERSHIPS.—

(i) IN GENERAL.—Any interest paid or accrued to a partnership which (without regard to this subparagraph) is a related person shall not be treated as paid or accrued to a related person if less than 10 percent of the profits and capital interests in such partnership are held by persons with respect to whom no tax is imposed by this subtitle on such interest. The preceding sentence shall not apply to any interest allocable to any partner in such partnership who is a related person to the taxpayer.

(ii) SPECIAL RULE WHERE TREATY REDUCTION.—If any treaty between the United States and any foreign country reduces the rate of tax imposed by this subtitle on a partner's share of any interest paid or accrued to a partnership, such partner's interests in such partnership shall, for purposes of clause (i), be treated as held in part by a tax-exempt person and in part by a taxable person under rules similar to the rules of paragraph (5)(B).

(5) SPECIAL RULES FOR DETERMINING WHETHER INTEREST IS SUBJECT TO TAX.—

(A) TREATMENT OF PASS-THRU ENTITIES.—In the case of any interest paid or accrued to a partnership, the determination of whether any tax is imposed by this subtitle on such interest shall be made at the partner level. Rules similar to the rules of the preceding sentence shall apply in the case of any pass-thru entity other than a partnership and in the case of tiered partnerships and other entities.

(B) INTEREST TREATED AS TAX-EXEMPT TO EXTENT OF TREATY REDUCTION.—If any treaty between the United States and any foreign country reduces the rate of tax imposed by this subtitle on any interest paid or accrued by the taxpayer, such interest shall be treated as interest on which no tax is imposed by this subtitle to the extent of the same proportion of such interest as—

(i) the rate of tax imposed without regard to such treaty, reduced by the rate of tax imposed under the treaty, bears to

(ii) the rate of tax imposed without regard to the treaty.

(6) OTHER DEFINITIONS AND SPECIAL RULES.—For purposes of this subsection—

(A) ADJUSTED TAXABLE INCOME.—The term "adjusted taxable income" means the taxable income of the taxpayer—

(i) computed without regard to—

(I) any deduction allowable under this chapter for the net interest expense,

(II) the amount of any net operating loss deduction under section 172, and

(III) any deduction allowable for depreciation, amortization, or depletion, and

(ii) computed with such other adjustments as the Secretary may by regulations prescribe.

(B) NET INTEREST EXPENSE.—The term "net interest expense" means the excess (if any) of—

(i) the interest paid or accrued by the taxpayer during the taxable year, over

(ii) the amount of interest includible in the gross income of such taxpayer for such taxable year.

The Secretary may by regulations provide for adjustments in determining the amount of net interest expense.

(C) TREATMENT OF AFFILIATED GROUP.—All members of the same affiliated group (within the meaning of section 1504(a)) shall be treated as 1 taxpayer.

(D) DISQUALIFIED GUARANTEE.—

(i) IN GENERAL.—Except as provided in clause (ii), the term "disqualified guarantee" means any guarantee by a related person which is—

(I) an organization exempt from taxation under this subtitle, or

(II) a foreign person.

(ii) EXCEPTIONS.—The term "disqualified guarantee" shall not include a guarantee—

(I) in any circumstances identified by the Secretary by regulation, where the interest on the indebtedness would have been subject to a net basis tax if the interest had been paid to the guarantor, or

(II) if the taxpayer owns a controlling interest in the guarantor.

For purposes of subclause (II), except as provided in regulations, the term "a controlling interest" means direct or indirect ownership of at least 80 percent of the total voting power and value of all classes of stock of a corporation, or 80 percent of the profit and capital interests in any other entity. For purposes of the preceding sentence, the rules of paragraphs (1) and (5) of section 267(c) shall apply; except that such rules shall also apply to interest in entities other than corporations.

(iii) GUARANTEE.—Except as provided in regulations, the term "guarantee" includes any arrangement under which a person (directly or indirectly through an entity or otherwise) assures, on a conditional or unconditional basis, the payment of another person's obligation under any indebtedness.

(E) GROSS BASIS AND NET BASIS TAXATION.—

(i) GROSS BASIS TAX.—The term "gross basis tax" means any tax imposed by this subtitle which is determined by reference to the gross amount of any item of income without any reduction for any deduction allowed by this subtitle.

(ii) NET BASIS TAX.—The term "net basis tax" means any tax imposed by this subtitle which is not a gross basis tax.

(7) COORDINATION WITH PASSIVE LOSS RULES, ETC.—This subsection shall be applied before sections 465 and 469.

(8) REGULATIONS.—The Secretary shall prescribe such regulations as may be appropriate to carry out the purposes of this subsection, including—

(A) such regulations as may be appropriate to prevent the avoidance of the purposes of this subsection,

(B) regulations providing such adjustments in the case of corporations which are members of an affiliated group as may be appropriate to carry out the purposes of this subsection, and

(C) regulations for the coordination of this subsection with section 884.

. . .

(*l*) DISALLOWANCE OF DEDUCTION ON CERTAIN DEBT INSTRUMENTS OF CORPORATIONS.—

(1) IN GENERAL.—No deduction shall be allowed under this chapter for any interest paid or accrued on a disqualified debt instrument.

(2) DISQUALIFIED DEBT INSTRUMENT.—For purposes of this subsection, the term "disqualified debt instrument" means any indebtedness of a corporation which is payable in equity of the issuer or a related party.

(3) SPECIAL RULES FOR AMOUNTS PAYABLE IN EQUITY.—For purposes of paragraph (2), indebtedness shall be treated as payable in equity of the issuer or a related party only if—

(A) a substantial amount of the principal or interest is required to be paid or converted, or at the option of the issuer or a related party is payable in, or convertible into, such equity,

(B) a substantial amount of the principal or interest is required to be determined, or at the option of the issuer or a related party is determined, by reference to the value of such equity, or

(C) the indebtedness is part of an arrangement which is reasonably expected to result in a transaction described in subparagraph (A) or (B).

For purposes of this paragraph, principal or interest shall be treated as required to be so paid, converted, or determined if it may be required at the option of the holder or a related party and there is a substantial certainty the option will be exercised.

(4) RELATED PARTY.—For purposes of this subsection, a person is a related party with respect to another person if such person bears a relationship to such other person described in section 267(b) or 707(b).

(5) REGULATIONS.—The Secretary shall prescribe such regulations as may be necessary or appropriate to carry out the purposes of this subsection, includ-

ing regulations preventing avoidance of this subsection through the use of an issuer other than a corporation.

· · ·

SEC. 195. START-UP EXPENDITURES.

(a) CAPITALIZATION OF EXPENDITURES.—Except as otherwise provided in this section, no deduction shall be allowed for start-up expenditures.

(b) ELECTION TO AMORTIZE.—

(1) IN GENERAL.—Start-up expenditures may, at the election of the taxpayer, be treated as deferred expenses. Such deferred expenses shall be allowed as a deduction prorated equally over such period of not less than 60 months as may be selected by the taxpayer (beginning with the month in which the active trade or business begins).

(2) DISPOSITIONS BEFORE CLOSE OF AMORTIZATION PERIOD.—In any case in which a trade or business is completely disposed of by the taxpayer before the end of the period to which paragraph (1) applies, any deferred expenses attributable to such trade or business which were not allowed as a deduction by reason of this section may be deducted to the extent allowable under section 165.

(c) DEFINITIONS.—For purposes of this section—

(1) START-UP EXPENDITURES.—The term "start-up expenditure" means any amount—

(A) paid or incurred in connection with—

(i) investigating the creation or acquisition of an active trade or business, or

(ii) creating an active trade or business, or

(iii) any activity engaged in for profit and for the production of income before the day on which the active trade or business begins, in anticipation of such activity becoming an active trade or business, and

(B) which, if paid or incurred in connection with the operation of an existing active trade or business (in the same field as the trade or business referred to in subparagraph (A)), would be allowable as a deduction for the taxable year in which paid or incurred.

The term "start-up expenditure" does not include any amount with respect to which a deduction is allowable under section 163(a), 164, or 174.

(2) BEGINNING OF TRADE OR BUSINESS.—

(A) IN GENERAL.—Except as provided in subparagraph (B), the determination of when an active trade or business begins shall be made in accordance with such regulations as the Secretary may prescribe.

(B) ACQUIRED TRADE OR BUSINESS.—An acquired active trade or business shall be treated as beginning when the taxpayer acquires it.

(d) ELECTION.—

(1) TIME FOR MAKING ELECTION.—An election under subsection (b) shall be made not later than the time prescribed by law for filing the return

for the taxable year in which the trade or business begins (including extensions thereof).

(2) SCOPE OF ELECTION.—The period selected under subsection (b) shall be adhered to in computing taxable income for the taxable year for which the election is made and all subsequent taxable years.

SEC. 197. AMORTIZATION OF GOODWILL AND CERTAIN OTHER INTANGIBLES.

(a) GENERAL RULE.—A taxpayer shall be entitled to an amortization deduction with respect to any amortizable section 197 intangible. The amount of such deduction shall be determined by amortizing the adjusted basis (for purposes of determining gain) of such intangible ratably over the 15-year period beginning with the month in which such intangible was acquired.

(b) NO OTHER DEPRECIATION OR AMORTIZATION DEDUCTION ALLOWABLE.—Except as provided in subsection (a), no depreciation or amortization deduction shall be allowable with respect to any amortizable section 197 intangible.

(c) AMORTIZABLE SECTION 197 INTANGIBLE.—For purposes of this section—

(1) IN GENERAL.—Except as otherwise provided in this section, the term "amortizable section 197 intangible" means any section 197 intangible—

(A) which is acquired by the taxpayer after the date of the enactment of this section, and

(B) which is held in connection with the conduct of a trade or business or an activity described in section 212.

(2) EXCLUSION OF SELF-CREATED INTANGIBLES, ETC.—The term "amortizable section 197 intangible" shall not include any section 197 intangible—

(A) which is not described in subparagraph (D), (E), or (F) of subsection (d)(1), and

(B) which is created by the taxpayer.

This paragraph shall not apply if the intangible is created in connection with a transaction (or series of related transactions) involving the acquisition of assets constituting a trade or business or substantial portion thereof.

(3) ANTI-CHURNING RULES.—For exclusion of intangibles acquired in certain transactions, see subsection (f)(9).

(d) SECTION 197 INTANGIBLE.—For purposes of this section—

(1) IN GENERAL.—Except as otherwise provided in this section, the term "section 197 intangible" means—

(A) goodwill,

(B) going concern value,

(C) any of the following intangible items:

(i) workforce in place including its composition and terms and conditions (contractual or otherwise) of its employment,

(ii) business books and records, operating systems, or any other information base (including lists or other information with respect to current or prospective customers),

(iii) any patent, copyright, formula, process, design, pattern, knowhow, format, or other similar item,

(iv) any customer-based intangible,

(v) any supplier-based intangible, and

(vi) any other similar item,

(D) any license, permit, or other right granted by a governmental unit or an agency or instrumentality thereof,

(E) any covenant not to compete (or other arrangement to the extent such arrangement has substantially the same effect as a covenant not to compete) entered into in connection with an acquisition (directly or indirectly) of an interest in a trade or business or substantial portion thereof, and

(F) any franchise, trademark, or trade name.

(2) CUSTOMER-BASED INTANGIBLE.—

(A) IN GENERAL.—The term "customer-based intangible" means—

(i) composition of market,

(ii) market share, and

(iii) any other value resulting from future provision of goods or services pursuant to relationships (contractual or otherwise) in the ordinary course of business with customers.

(B) SPECIAL RULE FOR FINANCIAL INSTITUTIONS.—In the case of a financial institution, the term "customer-based intangible" includes deposit base and similar items.

(3) SUPPLIER-BASED INTANGIBLE.—The term "supplier-based intangible" means any value resulting from future acquisitions of goods or services pursuant to relationships (contractual or otherwise) in the ordinary course of business with suppliers of goods or services to be used or sold by the taxpayer.

(e) EXCEPTIONS.—For purposes of this section, the term "section 197 intangible" shall not include any of the following:

(1) FINANCIAL INTERESTS.—Any interest—

(A) in a corporation, partnership, trust, or estate, or

(B) under an existing futures contract, foreign currency contract, notional principal contract, or other similar financial contract.

(2) LAND.—Any interest in land.

(3) COMPUTER SOFTWARE.—

(A) IN GENERAL.—Any—

(i) computer software which is readily available for purchase by the general public, is subject to a nonexclusive license, and has not been substantially modified, and

(ii) other computer software which is not acquired in a transaction (or series of related transactions) involving the acquisition of assets constituting a trade or business or substantial portion thereof.

(B) COMPUTER SOFTWARE DEFINED.—For purposes of subparagraph (A), the term "computer software" means any program designed to cause a computer to perform a desired function. Such term shall not include any data base or similar item unless the data base or item is in the public domain and is incidental to the operation of otherwise qualifying computer software.

(4) CERTAIN INTERESTS OR RIGHTS ACQUIRED SEPARATELY.—Any of the following not acquired in a transaction (or series of related transactions) involving the acquisition of assets constituting a trade business or substantial portion thereof:

(A) Any interest in a film, sound recording, video tape, book, or similar property.

(B) Any right to receive tangible property or services under a contract or granted by a governmental unit or agency or instrumentality thereof.

(C) Any interest in a patent or copyright.

(D) To the extent provided in regulations, any right under a contract (or granted by a governmental unit or an agency or instrumentality thereof) if such right—

(i) has a fixed duration of less than 15 years, or

(ii) is fixed as to amount and, without regard to this section, would be recoverable under a method similar to the unit-of-production method.

(5) INTERESTS UNDER LEASES AND DEBT INSTRUMENTS.—Any interest under—

(A) an existing lease of tangible property, or

(B) except as provided in subsection (d)(2)(B), any existing indebtedness.

(6) TREATMENT OF SPORTS FRANCHISES.—A franchise to engage in professional football, basketball, baseball, or other professional sport, and any item acquired in connection with such a franchise.

(7) MORTGAGE SERVICING.—Any right to service indebtedness which is secured by residential real property unless such right is acquired in a transaction (or series of related transactions) involving the acquisition of assets (other than rights described in this paragraph) constituting a trade or business or substantial portion thereof.

(8) CERTAIN TRANSACTION COSTS.—Any fees for professional services, and any transaction costs, incurred by parties to a transaction with respect to which any portion of the gain or loss is not recognized under part III of subchapter C [Code §351-§368].

(f) SPECIAL RULES.—

(1) TREATMENT OF CERTAIN DISPOSITIONS, ETC.—

(A) IN GENERAL.—If there is a disposition of any amortizable section 197 intangible acquired in a transaction or series of related transactions (or any such intangible becomes worthless) and one or more other amortizable section 197 intangibles acquired in such transaction or series of related transactions are retained—

(i) no loss shall be recognized by reason of such disposition (or such worthlessness), and

(ii) appropriate adjustments to the adjusted bases of such retained intangibles shall be made for any loss not recognized under clause (i).

(B) SPECIAL RULE FOR COVENANTS NOT TO COMPETE.—In the case of any section 197 intangible which is a covenant not to compete (or other arrangement) described in subsection (d)(1)(E), in no event shall such covenant or other arrangement be treated as disposed of (or becoming worthless) before the disposition of the entire interest described in such subsection in connection with which such covenant (or other arrangement) was entered into.

(C) SPECIAL RULE.—All persons treated as a single taxpayer under section 41(f)(1) shall be so treated for purposes of this paragraph.

(2) TREATMENT OF CERTAIN TRANSFERS.—

(A) IN GENERAL.—In the case of any section 197 intangible transferred in a transaction described in subparagraph (B), the transferee shall be treated as the transferor for purposes of applying this section with respect to so much of the adjusted basis in the hands of the transferee as does not exceed the adjusted basis in the hands of the transferor.

(B) TRANSACTIONS COVERED.—The transactions described in this subparagraph are—

(i) any transaction described in section 332, 351, 361, 721, 731, 1031, or 1033, and

(ii) any transaction between members of the same affiliated group during any taxable year for which a consolidated return is made by such group.

(3) TREATMENT OF AMOUNTS PAID PURSUANT TO COVENANTS NOT TO COMPETE, ETC.—Any amount paid or incurred pursuant to a covenant or arrangement referred to in subsection (d)(1)(E) shall be treated as an amount chargeable to capital account.

(4) TREATMENT OF FRANCHISES, ETC.—

(A) FRANCHISE.—The term "franchise" has the meaning given to such term by section 1253(b)(1).

(B) TREATMENT OF RENEWALS.—Any renewal of a franchise, trademark, or trade name (or of a license, a permit, or other right referred to in subsection (d)(1)(D)) shall be treated as an acquisition. The preceding sentence shall only apply with respect to costs incurred in connection with such renewal.

(C) CERTAIN AMOUNTS NOT TAKEN INTO ACCOUNT.—Any amount to which section 1253(d)(1) applies shall not be taken into account under this section.

. . .

(6) TREATMENT OF CERTAIN SUBLEASES.—For purposes of this section, a sublease shall be treated in the same manner as a lease of the underlying property involved.

(7) TREATMENT AS DEPRECIABLE.—For purposes of this chapter, any amortizable section 197 intangible shall be treated as property which is of a character subject to the allowance for depreciation provided in section 167.

(8) TREATMENT OF CERTAIN INCREMENTS IN VALUE.—This section shall not apply to any increment in value if, without regard to this section,

such increment is properly taken into account in determining the cost of property which is not a section 197 intangible.

(9) ANTI-CHURNING RULES.—For purposes of this section—

(A) IN GENERAL.—The, term "amortizable section 197 intangible" shall not include any section 197 intangible which is described in subparagraph (A) or (B) of subsection (d)(1) (or for which depreciation or amortization would not have been allowable but for this section) and which is acquired by the taxpayer after the date of the enactment of this section, if—

(i) the intangible was held or used at any time on or after July 25, 1991, and on or before such date of enactment by the taxpayer or a related person,

(ii) the intangible was acquired from a person who held such intangible at any time on or after July 25, 1991, and on or before such date of enactment, and, as part of the transaction, the user of such intangible does not change, or

(iii) the taxpayer grants the right to use such intangible to a person (or a person related to such person) who held or used such intangible at any time on or after July 25, 1991, and on or before such date of enactment.

For purposes of this subparagraph, the determination of whether the user of property changes as part of a transaction shall be determined in accordance with regulations prescribed by the Secretary. For purposes of this subparagraph, deductions allowable under section 1253(d) shall be treated as deductions allowable for amortization.

(B) EXCEPTION WHERE GAIN RECOGNIZED.—If—

(i) subparagraph (A) would not apply to an intangible acquired by the taxpayer but for the last sentence of subparagraph (C)(i), and

(ii) the person from whom the taxpayer acquired the intangible elects, notwithstanding any other provision of this title—

(I) to recognize gain on the disposition of the intangible, and

(II) to pay a tax on such gain which, when added to any other income tax on such gain under this title, equals such gain multiplied by the highest rate of income tax applicable to such person under this title,

then subparagraph (A) shall apply to the intangible only to the extent that the taxpayer's adjusted basis in the intangible exceeds the gain recognized under clause (ii)(I).

(C) RELATED PERSON DEFINED.—For purposes of this paragraph—

(i) RELATED PERSON.—A person (hereinafter in this paragraph referred to as the "related person") is related to any person if—

(I) the related person bears a relationship to such person specified in section 267(b) or section 707(b)(1), or

(II) the related person and such person are engaged in trades or businesses under common control (within the meaning of subparagraphs (A) and (B) of section 41(f)(1)).

For purposes of subclause (I), in applying section 267(b) or 707(b)(1), "20 percent" shall be substituted for "50 percent."

(ii) TIME FOR MAKING DETERMINATION.—A person shall be treated as related to another person if such relationship exists immediately before or immediately after the acquisition of the intangible involved.

(D) ACQUISITIONS BY REASON OF DEATH.—Subparagraph (A) shall not apply to the acquisition of any property by the taxpayer if the basis of the property in the hands of the taxpayer is determined under section 1014(a).

(E) SPECIAL RULE FOR PARTNERSHIPS.—With respect to any increase in the basis of partnership property under section 732, 734, or 743, determinations under this paragraph shall be made at the partner level and each partner shall be treated as having owned and used such partner's proportionate share of the partnership assets.

(F) ANTI-ABUSE RULES.—The term "amortizable section 197 intangible" does not include any section 197 intangible acquired in a transaction, one of the principal purposes of which is to avoid the requirement of subsection (c)(1) that the intangible be acquired after the date of the enactment of this section or to avoid the provisions of subparagraph (A).

(g) REGULATIONS.—The Secretary shall prescribe such regulations as may be appropriate to carry out the purposes of this section, including such regulations as may be appropriate to prevent avoidance of the purposes of this section through related persons or otherwise.

SEC. 243.   DIVIDENDS RECEIVED BY CORPORATIONS.

(a) GENERAL RULE.—In the case of a corporation, there shall be allowed as a deduction an amount equal to the following percentages of the amount received as dividends from a domestic corporation which is subject to taxation under this chapter:

(1) 70 percent, in the case of dividends other than dividends described in paragraph (2) or (3);

(2) 100 percent, in the case of dividends received by a small business investment company operating under the Small Business Investment Act of 1958 (15 U.S.C. 661 and following); and

(3) 100 percent, in the case of qualifying dividends (as defined in subsection (b)(1)).

(b) QUALIFYING DIVIDENDS.—

(1) IN GENERAL.—For purposes of this section, the term "qualifying dividend" means any dividend received by a corporation—

(A) if at the close of the day on which such dividend is received, such corporation is a member of the same affiliated group as the corporation distributing such dividend, and

. . .

(2) AFFILIATED GROUP.—For purposes of this subsection:

(A) IN GENERAL.—The term "affiliated group" has the meaning given such term by section 1504(a), except that for such purposes sections 1504(b)(2), 1504(b)(4), and 1504(c) shall not apply.

. . .

(c) RETENTION OF 80-PERCENT DIVIDENDS RECEIVED DEDUCTION FOR DIVIDENDS FROM 20-PERCENT OWNED CORPORATIONS.—

(1) IN GENERAL.—In the case of any dividend received from a 20-percent owned corporation—

(A) subsection (a)(1) of this section, and

(B) subsections (a)(3) and (b)(2) of section 244,

shall be applied by substituting "80 percent" for "70 percent."

(2) 20-PERCENT OWNED CORPORATION.—For purposes of this section, the term "20-percent owned corporation" means any corporation if 20 percent or more of the stock of such corporation (by vote and value) is owned by the taxpayer. For purposes of the preceding sentence, stock described in section 1504(a)(4) shall not be taken into account.

. . .

SEC. 246A. DIVIDENDS RECEIVED DEDUCTION REDUCED WHERE PORTFOLIO STOCK IS DEBT FINANCED.

(a) GENERAL RULE.—In the case of any dividend on debt-financed portfolio stock, there shall be substituted for the percentage which (but for this subsection) would be used in determining the amount of the deduction allowable under section 243, 244, or 245(a) a percentage equal to the product of—

(1) 70 percent (80 percent in the case of any dividend from a 20-percent owned corporation as defined in section 243(c)(2)), and

(2) 100 percent minus the average indebtedness percentage.

(b) SECTION NOT TO APPLY TO DIVIDENDS FOR WHICH 100 PERCENT DIVIDENDS RECEIVED DEDUCTION ALLOWABLE.—Subsection (a) shall not apply to—

(1) qualifying dividends (as defined in section 243(b) without regard to section 243(c)(4)), and

(2) dividends received by a small business investment company operating under the Small Business Investment Act of 1958.

(c) DEBT FINANCED PORTFOLIO STOCK.—For purposes of this section—

(1) IN GENERAL.—The term "debt financed portfolio stock" means any portfolio stock if at some time during the base period there is portfolio indebtedness with respect to such stock.

(2) PORTFOLIO STOCK.—The term "portfolio stock" means any stock of a corporation unless—

(A) as of the beginning of the ex-dividend date, the taxpayer owns stock of such corporation—

(i) possessing at least 50 percent of the total voting power of the stock of such corporation, and

(ii) having a value equal to at least 50 percent of the total value of the stock of such corporation, or

(B) as of the beginning of the ex-dividend date—

(i) the taxpayer owns stock of such corporation which would meet the requirements of subparagraph (A) if "20 percent" were substituted for "50 percent" each place it appears in such subparagraph, and

(ii) stock meeting the requirements of subparagraph (A) is owned by 5 or fewer corporate shareholders.

. . .

(4) TREATMENT OF CERTAIN PREFERRED STOCK.—For purposes of determining whether the requirements of subparagraph (A) or (B) of paragraph (2) or of subparagraph (A) of paragraph (3) are met, stock described in section 1504(a)(4) shall not be taken into account.

(d) AVERAGE INDEBTEDNESS PERCENTAGE.—For purposes of this section—

(1) IN GENERAL.—Except as provided in paragraph (2), the term "average indebtedness percentage" means the percentage obtained by dividing—

(A) the average amount (determined under regulations prescribed by the Secretary) of the portfolio indebtedness with respect to the stock during the base period, by

(B) the average amount (determined under regulations prescribed by the Secretary) of the adjusted basis of the stock during the base period.

(2) SPECIAL RULE WHERE STOCK NOT HELD THROUGHOUT BASE PERIOD.—In the case of any stock which was not held by the taxpayer throughout the base period, paragraph (1) shall be applied as if the base period consisted only of that portion of the base period during which the stock was held by the taxpayer.

(3) PORTFOLIO INDEBTEDNESS.—

(A) IN GENERAL.—The term "portfolio indebtedness" means any indebtedness directly attributable to investment in the portfolio stock.

(B) CERTAIN AMOUNTS RECEIVED FROM SHORT SALE TREATED AS INDEBTEDNESS.—For purposes of subparagraph (A), any amount received from a short sale shall be treated as indebtedness for the period beginning on the day on which such amount is received and ending on the day the short sale is closed.

(4) BASE PERIOD.—The term "base period" means, with respect to any dividend, the shorter of—

(A) the period beginning on the ex-dividend date for the most recent previous dividend on the stock and ending on the day before the ex-dividend date for the dividend involved, or

(B) the 1-year period ending on the day before the ex-dividend date for the dividend involved.

(e) REDUCTION IN DIVIDENDS RECEIVED DEDUCTION NOT TO EXCEED ALLOCABLE INTEREST.—Under regulations prescribed by the Secretary, any reduction under this section in the amount allowable as a deduction under section 243, 244, or 245 with respect to any dividend shall not exceed the amount of any interest deduction (including any deductible short sale expense) allocable to such dividend.

(f) REGULATIONS.—The regulations prescribed for purposes of this section under section 7701(f) shall include regulations providing for the disallowance of interest deductions or other appropriate treatment (in lieu of reducing the dividend received deduction) where the obligor of the indebtedness is a person other than the person receiving the dividend.

SEC. 269.   ACQUISITIONS MADE TO EVADE OR AVOID INCOME TAX.

(a) IN GENERAL.—If—

(1) any person or persons acquire, or acquired on or after October 8, 1940, directly or indirectly, control of a corporation, or

(2) any corporation acquires, or acquired on or after October 8, 1940, directly or indirectly, property of another corporation, not controlled, directly or indirectly, immediately before such acquisition, by such acquiring corporation or its stockholders, the basis of which property, in the hands of the acquiring corporation, is determined by reference to the basis in the hands of the transferor corporation,

and the principal purpose for which such acquisition was made is evasion or avoidance of Federal income tax by securing the benefit of a deduction, credit, or other allowance which such person or corporation would not otherwise enjoy, then the Secretary may disallow such deduction, credit, or other allowance. For purposes of paragraphs (1) and (2), control means the ownership of stock possessing at least 50 percent of the total combined voting power of all classes of stock entitled to vote or at least 50 percent of the total value of shares of all classes of stock of the corporation.

(b) CERTAIN LIQUIDATIONS AFTER QUALIFIED STOCK PURCHASES.—

(1) IN GENERAL.—If—

(A) there is a qualified stock purchase by a corporation of another corporation,

(B) an election is not made under section 338 with respect to such purchase,

(C) the acquired corporation is liquidated pursuant to a plan of liquidation adopted not more than 2 years after the acquisition date, and

(D) the principal purpose for such liquidation is the evasion or avoidance of Federal income tax by securing the benefit of a deduction, credit, or other allowance which the acquiring corporation would not otherwise enjoy,
then the Secretary may disallow such deduction, credit, or other allowance.

(2) MEANING OF TERMS.—For purposes of paragraph (1), the terms "qualified stock purchase" and "acquisition date" have the same respective meanings as when used in section 338.

(c) POWER OF SECRETARY TO ALLOW DEDUCTION, ETC., IN PART.—In any case to which subsection (a) or (b) applies the Secretary is authorized—

(1) to allow as a deduction, credit, or allowance any part of any amount disallowed by such subsection, if he determines that such allowance will not result in the evasion or avoidance of Federal income tax for which the acquisition was made; or

(2) to distribute, apportion, or allocate gross income, and distribute, apportion, or allocate the deductions, credits, or allowances the benefit of which was sought to be secured, between or among the corporations, or properties, or parts thereof, involved, and to allow such deductions, credits, or allowances so distributed, apportioned, or allocated, but to give effect to such allowance only to such extent as he determines will not result in the evasion or avoidance of Federal income tax for which the acquisition was made; or

(3) to exercise his powers in part under paragraph (1) and in part under paragraph (2).

SEC. 279. INTEREST ON INDEBTEDNESS INCURRED BY CORPORATION TO ACQUIRE STOCK OR ASSETS OF ANOTHER CORPORATION.

(a) GENERAL RULE.—No deduction shall be allowed for any interest paid or incurred by a corporation during the taxable year with respect to its corporate acquisition indebtedness to the extent that such interest exceeds—

(1) $5,000,000, reduced by

(2) the amount of interest paid or incurred by such corporation during such year on obligations (A) issued after December 31, 1967, to provide consideration for an acquisition described in paragraph (1) of subsection (b), but (B) which are not corporate acquisition indebtedness.

(b) CORPORATE ACQUISITION INDEBTEDNESS.—For purposes of this section, the term "corporate acquisition indebtedness" means any obligation evidenced by a bond, debenture, note, or certificate or other evidence of indebtedness issued after October 9, 1969, by a corporation (hereinafter in this section referred to as "issuing corporation") if—

(1) such obligation is issued to provide consideration for the acquisition of—

(A) stock in another corporation (hereinafter in this section referred to as "acquired corporation"), or

(B) assets of another corporation (hereinafter in this section referred to as "acquired corporation") pursuant to a plan under which at least two-thirds (in value) of all the assets (excluding money) used in trades and businesses carried on by such corporation are acquired,

(2) such obligation is either—

(A) subordinated to the claims of trade creditors of the issuing corporation generally, or

(B) expressly subordinated in right of payment to the payment of any substantial amount of unsecured indebtedness, whether outstanding or subsequently issued, of the issuing corporation

(3) the bond or other evidence of indebtedness is either—

(A) convertible directly or indirectly into stock of the issuing corporation, or

(B) part of an investment unit or other arrangement which includes, in addition to such bond or other evidence of indebtedness, an option to acquire, directly or indirectly, stock in the issuing corporation, and

(4) as of a day determined under subsection (c)(1), either—

(A) the ratio of debt to equity (as defined in subsection (c)(2)) of the issuing corporation exceeds 2 to 1, or

(B) the projected earnings (as defined in subsection (c)(3)) do not exceed 3 times the annual interest to be paid or incurred (determined under subsection (c)(4)).

(c) RULES FOR APPLICATION OF SUBSECTION (b)(4).—For purposes of subsection (b)(4)—

(1) TIME OF DETERMINATION.—Determinations are to be made as of the last day of any taxable year of the issuing corporation in which it issues any obligation to provide consideration for an acquisition described in subsection (b)(1) of stock in, or assets of, the acquired corporation.

(2) RATIO OF DEBT TO EQUITY.—The term "ratio of debt to equity" means the ratio which the total indebtedness of the issuing corporation bears to the sum of its money and all its other assets (in an amount equal to their adjusted basis for determining gain) less such total indebtedness.

(3) PROJECTED EARNINGS.—

(A) The term "projected earnings" means the "average annual earnings" (as defined in subparagraph (B)) of—

(i) the issuing corporation only, if clause (ii) does not apply, or

(ii) both the issuing corporation and the acquired corporation, in any case where the issuing corporation has acquired control (as defined in section 368(c)), or has acquired substantially all of the properties, of the acquired corporation.

(B) The average annual earnings referred to in subparagraph (A) is, for any corporation, the amount of its earnings and profits for any 3-year period ending with the last day of a taxable year of the issuing corporation described in paragraph (1), computed without reduction for—

(i) interest paid or incurred,

(ii) depreciation or amortization allowed under this chapter,

(iii) liability for tax under this chapter, and

(iv) distributions to which section 301(c)(1) applies (other than such distributions from the acquired to the issuing corporation), and reduced to an annual average for such 3-year period pursuant to regulations prescribed by the Secretary. Such regulations shall include rules for cases where any corporation was not in existence for all of such 3-year period or such period includes only a portion of a taxable year of any corporation.

(4) ANNUAL INTEREST TO BE PAID OR INCURRED.—The term "annual interest to be paid or incurred" means—

(A) if subparagraph (B) does not apply, the annual interest to be paid or incurred by the issuing corporation only, determined by reference to its total indebtedness outstanding, or

(B) if projected earnings are determined under clause (ii) of paragraph (3)(A), the annual interest to be paid or incurred by both the issuing corporation and the acquired corporation, determined by reference to their combined total indebtedness outstanding.

. . .

(d) TAXABLE YEARS TO WHICH APPLICABLE.—In applying this section—

(1) FIRST YEAR OF DISALLOWANCE.—The deduction of interest on any obligation shall not be disallowed under subsection (a) before the first taxable year of the issuing corporation as of the last day of which the application of either subparagraph (A) or subparagraph (B) of subsection (b)(4) results in such obligation being corporate acquisition indebtedness.

(2) GENERAL RULE FOR SUCCEEDING YEARS.—Except as provided in paragraphs (3), (4), and (5), if an obligation is determined to be corporate acquisition indebtedness as of the last day of any taxable year of the issuing corporation, it shall be corporate acquisition indebtedness for such taxable year and all subsequent taxable years.

(3) REDETERMINATION WHERE CONTROL, ETC., IS ACQUIRED.—If an obligation is determined to be corporate acquisition indebtedness as of the close of a taxable year of the issuing corporation in which clause (i) of subsection (c)(3)(A) applied, but would not be corporate acquisition indebtedness if the determination were made as of the close of the first taxable year of such corporation thereafter in which clause (ii) of subsection (c)(3)(A) could apply, such obligation shall be considered not to be corporate acquisition indebtedness for such later taxable year and all taxable years thereafter.

(4) SPECIAL 3-YEAR RULE.—If an obligation which has been determined to be corporate acquisition indebtedness for any taxable year would not be such indebtedness for each of any 3 consecutive taxable years thereafter if subsection (b)(4) were applied as of the close of each of such 3 years, then such obligation shall not be corporate acquisition indebtedness for all taxable years after such 3 consecutive taxable years.

(5) 5 PERCENT STOCK RULE.—In the case of obligations issued to provide consideration for the acquisition of stock in another corporation, such obligations shall be corporate acquisition indebtedness for a taxable year only if at some time after October 9, 1969, and before the close of such year the issuing

corporation owns 5 percent or more of the total combined voting power of all classes of stock entitled to vote of such other corporation.

(e) CERTAIN NONTAXABLE TRANSACTIONS.—An acquisition of stock of a corporation of which the issuing corporation is in control (as defined in section 368 (c)) in a transaction in which gain or loss is not recognized shall be deemed an acquisition described in paragraph (1) of subsection (b) only if immediately before such transaction (1) the acquired corporation was in existence, and (2) the issuing corporation was not in control (as defined in section 368(c)) of such corporation.

(f) EXEMPTION FOR CERTAIN ACQUISITIONS OF FOREIGN CORPORATIONS.—For purposes of this section, the term "corporate acquisition indebtedness" does not include any indebtedness issued to any person to provide consideration for the acquisition of stock in, or assets of, any foreign corporation substantially all of the income of which, for the 3-year period ending with the date of such acquisition or for such part of such period as the foreign corporation was in existence, is from sources without the United States.

(g) AFFILIATED GROUPS.—In any case in which the issuing corporation is a member of an affiliated group, the application of this section shall be determined, pursuant to regulations prescribed by the Secretary, by treating all of the members of the affiliated group in the aggregate as the issuing corporation, except that the ratio of debt to equity of, projected earnings of, and annual interest to be paid or incurred by any corporation (other than the issuing corporation determined without regard to this subsection) shall be included in the determinations required under subparagraphs (A) and (B) of subsection (b)(4) as of any day only if such corporation is a member of the affiliated group on such day, and, in determining projected earnings of such corporation under subsection (c)(3), there shall be taken into account only the earnings and profits of such corporation for the period during which it was a member of the affiliated group. For purposes of the preceding sentence, the term "affiliated group" has the meaning assigned to such term by section 1504(a), except that all corporations other than the acquired corporation shall be treated as includible corporations (without any exclusion under section 1504(b)) and the acquired corporation shall not be treated as an includible corporation.

(h) CHANGES IN OBLIGATION.—For purposes of this section—

(1) Any extension, renewal, or refinancing of an obligation evidencing a preexisting indebtedness shall not be deemed to be the issuance of a new obligation.

(2) Any obligation which is corporate acquisition indebtedness of the issuing corporation is also corporate acquisition indebtedness of any corporation which becomes liable for such obligation as guarantor, endorser, or indemnitor or which assumes liability for such obligation in any transaction.

. . .

(j) EFFECT ON OTHER PROVISIONS.—No inference shall be drawn from any provision in this section that any instrument designated as a bond, debenture, note, or certificate or other evidence of indebtedness by its issuer represents an obligation or indebtedness of such issuer in applying any other provision of this title.

SEC. 280G.   GOLDEN PARACHUTE PAYMENTS.

(a) GENERAL RULE.—No deduction shall be allowed under this chapter for any excess parachute payment.

(b) EXCESS PARACHUTE PAYMENT.—For purposes of this section—

(1) IN GENERAL.—The term "excess parachute payment" means an amount equal to the excess of any parachute payment over the portion of the base amount allocated to such payment.

(2) PARACHUTE PAYMENT DEFINED.—

(A) IN GENERAL.—The term "parachute payment" means any payment in the nature of compensation to (or for the benefit of) a disqualified individual if—

(i) such payment is contingent on a change—

(I) in the ownership or effective control of the corporation, or

(II) in the ownership of a substantial portion of the assets of the corporation, and

(ii) the aggregate present value of the payments in the nature of compensation to (or for the benefit of) such individual which are contingent on such change equals or exceeds an amount equal to 3 times the base amount.

For purposes of clause (ii), payments not treated as parachute payments under paragraph (4)(A), (5), or (6) shall not be taken into account.

(B) AGREEMENTS.—The term "parachute payment" shall also include any payment in the nature of compensation to (or for the benefit of) a disqualified individual if such payment is made pursuant to an agreement which violates any generally enforced securities laws or regulations. In any proceeding involving the issue of whether any payment made to a disqualified individual is a parachute payment on account of a violation of any generally enforced securities laws or regulations, the burden of proof with respect to establishing the occurrence of a violation of such a law or regulation shall be upon the Secretary.

(C) TREATMENT OF CERTAIN AGREEMENTS ENTERED INTO WITHIN 1 YEAR BEFORE CHANGE OF OWNERSHIP.—For purposes of subparagraph (A)(i), any payment pursuant to—

(i) an agreement entered into within 1 year before the change described in subparagraph (A)(i), or

(ii) an amendment made within such 1-year period of a previous agreement,

shall be presumed to be contingent on such change unless the contrary is established by clear and convincing evidence.

(3) BASE AMOUNT.—

(A) IN GENERAL.—The term "base amount" means the individual's annualized includible compensation for the base period.

(B) ALLOCATION.—The portion of the base amount allocated to any parachute payment shall be an amount which bears the same ratio to the base amount as—

(i) the present value of such payment, bears to

(ii) the aggregate present value of all such payments.

(4) TREATMENT OF AMOUNTS WHICH TAXPAYER ESTABLISHES AS REASONABLE COMPENSATION.—In the case of any payment described in paragraph (2)(A)—

(A) the amount treated as a parachute payment shall not include the portion of such payment which the taxpayer establishes by clear and convincing evidence is reasonable compensation for personal services to be rendered on or after the date of the change described in paragraph (2)(A)(i), and

(B) the amount treated as an excess parachute payment shall be reduced by the portion of such payment which the taxpayer establishes by clear and convincing evidence is reasonable compensation for personal services actually rendered before the date of the change described in paragraph (2)(A)(i).

For purposes of subparagraph (B), reasonable compensation for services actually rendered before the date of the change described in paragraph (2)(A)(i) shall be first offset against the base amount.

(5) EXEMPTION FOR SMALL BUSINESS CORPORATIONS, ETC.—

(A) IN GENERAL.—Notwithstanding paragraph (2), the term "parachute payment" does not include—

(i) any payment to a disqualified individual with respect to a corporation which (immediately before the change described in paragraph (2)(A)(i)) was a small business corporation (as defined in section 1361(b) but without regard to paragraph (1)(C) thereof), and

(ii) any payment to a disqualified individual with respect to a corporation (other than a corporation described in clause (i)) if—

(I) immediately before the change described in paragraph (2)(A)(i), no stock in such corporation was readily tradeable on an established securities market or otherwise, and

(II) the shareholder approval requirements of subparagraph (B) are met with respect to such payment.

The Secretary may, by regulations, prescribe that the requirements of subclause (I) of clause (ii) are not met where a substantial portion of the assets of any entity consists (directly or indirectly) of stock in such corporation and interests in such other entity are readily tradeable on an established securities market, or otherwise. Stock described in section 1504(a)(4) shall not be taken into account under clause (ii)(I) if the payment does not adversely affect the shareholder's redemption and liquidation rights.

(B) SHAREHOLDER APPROVAL REQUIREMENTS.—The shareholder approval requirements of this subparagraph are met with respect to any payment if—

(i) such payment was approved by a vote of the persons who owned, immediately before the change described in paragraph (2)(A)(i), more than 75 percent of the voting power of all outstanding stock of the corporation, and

(ii) there was adequate disclosure to shareholders of all material facts concerning all payments which (but for this paragraph) would be parachute payments with respect to a disqualified individual.

The regulations prescribed under subsection (e) shall include regulations providing for the application of this subparagraph in the case of shareholders which are not individuals (including the treatment of nonvoting interests in an entity which is a shareholder) and where an entity holds a de minimis amount of stock in the corporation.

(6) EXEMPTION FOR PAYMENTS UNDER QUALIFIED PLANS.— Notwithstanding paragraph (2), the term "parachute payment" shall not include any payment to or from—

(A) a plan described in section 401(a) which includes a trust exempt from tax under section 501(a),

(B) an annuity plan described in section 403(a),

(C) a simplified employee pension (as defined in section 408(k)), or

(D) a simple retirement account described in section 408(p).

(c) DISQUALIFIED INDIVIDUALS.—For purposes of this section, the term "disqualified individual" means any individual who is—

(1) an employee, independent contractor, or other person specified in regulations by the Secretary who performs personal services for any corporation, and

(2) is an officer, shareholder, or highly-compensated individual.

For purposes of this section, a personal service corporation (or similar entity) shall be treated as an individual. For purposes of paragraph (2), the term "highly-compensated individual" only includes an individual who is (or would be if the individual were an employee) a member of the group consisting of the highest paid 1 percent of the employees of the corporation or, if less, the highest paid 250 employees of the corporation.

(d) OTHER DEFINITIONS AND SPECIAL RULES.—For purposes of this section—

(1) ANNUALIZED INCLUDIBLE COMPENSATION FOR BASE PERIOD.— The term "annualized includible compensation for the base period" means the average annual compensation which—

(A) was payable by the corporation with respect to which the change in ownership or control described in paragraph (2)(A) of subsection (b) occurs, and

(B) was includible in the gross income of the disqualified individual for taxable years in the base period.

(2) BASE PERIOD.—The term "base period" means the period consisting of the most recent 5 taxable years ending before the date on which the change in ownership or control described in paragraph (2)(A) of subsection (b) occurs (or such portion of such period during which the disqualified individual performed personal services for the corporation).

(3) PROPERTY TRANSFERS.—Any transfer of property—

(A) shall be treated as a payment, and

(B) shall be taken into account as its fair market value.

(4) PRESENT VALUE.—Present value shall be determined by using a discount rate equal to 120 percent of the applicable Federal rate (determined under section 1274(d)), compounded semiannually.

(5) TREATMENT OF AFFILIATED GROUPS.—Except as otherwise provided in regulations, all members of the same affiliated group (as defined in section 1504, determined without regard to section 1504(b)) shall be treated as 1 corporation for purposes of this section. Any person who is an officer of any member of such group shall be treated as an officer of such 1 corporation.

(e) REGULATIONS.—The Secretary shall prescribe such regulations as may be necessary or appropriate to carry out the purposes of this section (including regulations for the application of this section in the case of related corporations and in the case of personal service corporations).

SEC. 301.   DISTRIBUTIONS OF PROPERTY.

(a) IN GENERAL.—Except as otherwise provided in this chapter, a distribution of property (as defined in section 317(a)) made by a corporation to a shareholder with respect to its stock shall be treated in the manner provided in subsection (c).

(b) AMOUNT DISTRIBUTED.—

(1) GENERAL RULE.—For purposes of this section, the amount of any distribution shall be the amount of money received, plus the fair market value of the other property received.

(2) REDUCTION FOR LIABILITIES.—The amount of any distribution determined under paragraph (1) shall be reduced (but not below zero) by—

(A) the amount of any liability of the corporation assumed by the shareholder in connection with the distribution, and

(B) the amount of any liability to which the property received by the shareholder is subject immediately before, and immediately after, the distribution.

(3) DETERMINATION OF FAIR MARKET VALUE.—For purposes of this section, fair market value shall be determined as of the date of the distribution.

(c) AMOUNT TAXABLE.—In the case of a distribution to which subsection (a) applies—

(1) AMOUNT CONSTITUTING DIVIDEND.—That portion of the distribution which is a dividend (as defined in section 316) shall be included in gross income.

(2) AMOUNT APPLIED AGAINST BASIS.—That portion of the distribution which is not a dividend shall be applied against and reduce the adjusted basis of the stock.

(3) AMOUNT IN EXCESS OF BASIS.—

(A) IN GENERAL.—Except as provided in subparagraph (B), that portion of the distribution which is not a dividend, to the extent that it exceeds the adjusted basis of the stock, shall be treated as gain from the sale or exchange of property.

(B) DISTRIBUTIONS OUT OF INCREASE IN VALUE ACCRUED BEFORE MARCH 1, 1913.—That portion of the distribution which is not a dividend, to the extent that it exceeds the adjusted basis of the stock and to the extent that it is out of increase in value accrued before March 1, 1913, shall be exempt from tax.

(d) BASIS.—The basis of property received in a distribution to which subsection (a) applies shall be the fair market value of such property.

. . .

SEC. 302.   DISTRIBUTIONS IN REDEMPTION OF STOCK.

(a) GENERAL RULE.—If a corporation redeems its stock (within the meaning of section 317 (b)), and if paragraph (1), (2), (3), or (4) of subsection (b) applies, such redemption shall be treated as a distribution in part or full payment in exchange for the stock.

(b) REDEMPTIONS TREATED AS EXCHANGES.—

(1) REDEMPTIONS NOT EQUIVALENT TO DIVIDENDS.—Subsection (a) shall apply if the redemption is not essentially equivalent to a dividend.

(2) SUBSTANTIALLY DISPROPORTIONATE REDEMPTION OF STOCK.—

(A) IN GENERAL.—Subsection (a) shall apply if the distribution is substantially disproportionate with respect to the shareholder.

(B) LIMITATION.—This paragraph shall not apply unless immediately after the redemption the shareholder owns less than 50 percent of the total combined voting power of all classes of stock entitled to vote.

(C) DEFINITIONS.—For purposes of this paragraph, the distribution is substantially disproportionate if—

(i) the ratio which the voting stock of the corporation owned by the shareholder immediately after the redemption bears to all of the voting stock of the corporation at such time,

is less than 80 percent of—

(ii) the ratio which the voting stock of the corporation owned by the shareholder immediately before the redemption bears to all of the voting stock of the corporation at such time.

For purposes of this paragraph, no distribution shall be treated as substantially disproportionate unless the shareholder's ownership of the common stock of the corporation (whether voting or nonvoting) after and before redemption also meets the 80 percent requirement of the preceding sentence. For purposes of the preceding sentence, if there is more than one class of common stock, the determinations shall be made by reference to fair market value.

(D) SERIES OF REDEMPTIONS.—This paragraph shall not apply to any redemption made pursuant to a plan the purpose or effect of which is a series of redemptions resulting in a distribution which (in the aggregate) is not substantially disproportionate with respect to the shareholder.

(3) TERMINATION OF SHAREHOLDER'S INTEREST.—Subsection (a) shall apply if the redemption is in complete redemption of all of the stock of the corporation owned by the shareholder.

(4) REDEMPTION FROM NONCORPORATE SHAREHOLDER IN PARTIAL LIQUIDATION.— Subsection (a) shall apply to a distribution if such distribution is—

(A) in redemption of stock held by a shareholder who is not a corporation, and

(B) in partial liquidation of the distributing corporation.

(5) APPLICATION OF PARAGRAPHS.—In determining whether a redemption meets the requirements of paragraph (1), the fact that such redemption fails to meet the requirements of paragraph (2), (3), or (4) shall not be taken into account. If a redemption meets the requirements of paragraph (3) and also the requirements of paragraph (1), (2), or (4), then so much of subsection (c) (2) as would (but for this sentence) apply in respect of the acquisition of an interest in the corporation within the 10-year period beginning on the date of the distribution shall not apply.

(c) CONSTRUCTIVE OWNERSHIP OF STOCK.—

(1) IN GENERAL.—Except as provided in paragraph (2) of this subsection, section 318 (a) shall apply in determining the ownership of stock for purposes of this section.

(2) FOR DETERMINING TERMINATION OF INTEREST.—

(A) In the case of a distribution described in subsection (b) (3), section 318 (a) (1) shall not apply if—

(i) immediately after the distribution the distributee has no interest in the corporation (including an interest as officer, director, or employee), other than an interest as a creditor,

(ii) the distributee does not acquire any such interest (other than stock acquired by bequest or inheritance) within 10 years from the date of such distribution, and

(iii) the distributee, at such time and in such manner as the Secretary by regulations prescribes, files an agreement to notify the Secretary of any acquisition described in clause (ii) and to retain such records as may be necessary for the application of this paragraph.

If the distributee acquires such an interest in the corporation (other than by bequest or inheritance) within 10 years from the date of the distribution, then the periods of limitation provided in sections 6501 and 6502 on the making of an assessment and the collection by levy or a proceeding in court shall, with respect to any deficiency (including interest and additions to the tax) resulting from such acquisition, include one year immediately following the date on which the distributee (in accordance with regulations prescribed by the Secretary) notifies the Secretary of such acquisition; and such assessment and collection may be made notwithstanding any provision of law or rule of law which otherwise would prevent such assessment and collection.

(B) Subparagraph (A) of this paragraph shall not apply if—

(i) any portion of the stock redeemed was acquired, directly or indirectly, within the 10-year period ending on the date of the distribution by the distributee from a person the ownership of whose stock would (at the time of distribution) be attributable to the distributee under section 318 (a), or

(ii) any person owns (at the time of the distribution) stock the ownership of which is attributable to the distributee under section 318 (a) and such person acquired any stock in the corporation, directly or indirectly, from the distributee within the 10-year period ending on the date of the distribution, unless such stock so acquired from the distributee is redeemed in the same transaction.

The preceding sentence shall not apply if the acquisition (or, in the case of clause (ii), the disposition) by the distributee did not have as one of its principal purposes the avoidance of Federal income tax.

(C) SPECIAL RULE FOR WAIVERS BY ENTITIES.—

(i) IN GENERAL.—Subparagraph (A) shall not apply to a distribution to any entity unless—

(I) such entity and each related person meet the requirements of clauses (i), (ii), and (iii) of subparagraph (A), and

(II) each related person agrees to be jointly and severally liable for any deficiency (including interest and additions to tax) resulting from an acquisition described in clause (ii) of subparagraph (A).

In any case to which the preceding sentence applies, the second sentence of subparagraph (A) and subparagraph (B)(ii) shall be applied by substituting "distributee or any related person" for "distributee" each place it appears.

(ii) DEFINITIONS.—For purposes of this subparagraph—

(I) the term "entity" means a partnership, estate, trust, or corporation; and

(II) the term "related person" means any person to whom ownership of stock in the corporation is (at the time of the distribution) attributable under section 318(a)(1) if such stock is further attributable to the entity under section 318(a)(3).

(d) REDEMPTIONS TREATED AS DISTRIBUTIONS OF PROPERTY.—Except as otherwise provided in this subchapter, if a corporation redeems its stock (within the meaning of section 317 (b)), and if subsection (a) of this section does not apply, such redemption shall be treated as a distribution of property to which section 301 applies.

(e) PARTIAL LIQUIDATION DEFINED.—

(1) IN GENERAL.—For purposes of subsection (b)(4), a distribution shall be treated as in partial liquidation of a corporation if—

(A) the distribution is not essentially equivalent to a dividend (determined at the corporate level rather than at the shareholder level), and

(B) the distribution is pursuant to a plan and occurs within the taxable year in which the plan is adopted or within the succeeding taxable year.

(2) TERMINATION OF BUSINESS.—The distributions which meet the requirements of paragraph (1)(A) shall include (but shall not be limited to) a distribution which meets the requirements of subparagraphs (A) and (B) of this paragraph:

(A) The distribution is attributable to the distributing corporation's ceasing to conduct, or consists of the assets of, a qualified trade or business.

(B) Immediately after the distribution, the distributing corporation is actively engaged in the conduct of a qualified trade or business.

(3) QUALIFIED TRADE OR BUSINESS.—For purposes of paragraph (2), the term "qualified trade or business" means any trade or business which—

(A) was actively conducted throughout the 5-year period ending on the date of the redemption, and

(B) was not acquired by the corporation within such period in a transaction in which gain or loss was recognized in whole or in part.

(4) REDEMPTION MAY BE PRO RATA.—Whether or not a redemption meets the requirements of subparagraphs (A) and (B) of paragraph (2) shall be determined without regard to whether or not the redemption is pro rata with respect to all of the shareholders of the corporation.

(5) TREATMENT OF CERTAIN PASS-THRU ENTITIES.—For purposes of determining under subsection (b)(4) whether any stock is held by a shareholder who is not a corporation, any stock held by a partnership, estate, or trust shall be treated as if it were actually held proportionately by its partners or beneficiaries.

. . .

SEC. 305. DISTRIBUTIONS OF STOCK AND STOCK RIGHTS.

(a) GENERAL RULE.—Except as otherwise provided in this section, gross income does not include the amount of any distribution of the stock of a corporation made by such corporation to its shareholders with respect to its stock.

(b) EXCEPTIONS.—Subsection (a) shall not apply to a distribution by a corporation of its stock, and the distribution shall be treated as a distribution of property to which section 301 applies—

(1) DISTRIBUTIONS IN LIEU OF MONEY.—If the distribution is, at the election of any of the shareholders (whether exercised before or after the declaration thereof), payable either—

(A) in its stock, or

(B) in property.

(2) DISPROPORTIONATE DISTRIBUTIONS.—If the distribution (or a series of distributions of which such distribution is one) has the result of—

(A) the receipt of property by some shareholders, and

(B) an increase in the proportionate interests of other shareholders in the assets or earnings and profits of the corporation.

(3) DISTRIBUTIONS OF COMMON AND PREFERRED STOCK.—If the distribution (or a series of distributions of which such distribution is one) has the result of—

(A) the receipt of preferred stock by some common shareholders, and

(B) the receipt of common stock by other common shareholders.

(4) DISTRIBUTIONS ON PREFERRED STOCK.—If the distribution is with respect to preferred stock, other than an increase in the conversion ratio of

convertible preferred stock made solely to take account of a stock dividend or stock split with respect to the stock into which such convertible stock is convertible.

    (5) DISTRIBUTIONS OF CONVERTIBLE PREFERRED STOCK.—If the distribution is of convertible preferred stock, unless it is established to the satisfaction of the Secretary that such distribution will not have the result described in paragraph (2).

    (c) CERTAIN TRANSACTIONS TREATED AS DISTRIBUTIONS.—For purposes of this section and section 301, the Secretary shall prescribe regulations under which a change in conversion ratio, a change in redemption price, a difference between redemption price and issue price, a redemption which is treated as a distribution to which section 301 applies, or any transaction (including a recapitalization) having a similar effect on the interest of any shareholder shall be treated as a distribution with respect to any shareholder whose proportionate interest in the earnings and profits or assets of the corporation is increased by such change, difference, redemption, or similar transaction. Regulations prescribed under the preceding sentence shall provide that—

    (1) where the issuer of stock is required to redeem the stock at a specified time or the holder of stock has the option to require the issuer to redeem the stock, a redemption premium resulting from such requirement or option shall be treated as reasonable only if the amount of such premium does not exceed the amount determined under the principles of section 1273(a)(3),

    (2) a redemption premium shall not fail to be treated as a distribution (or series of distributions) merely because the stock is callable, and

    (3) in any case in which a redemption premium is treated as a distribution (or series of distributions), such premium shall be taken into account under principles similar to the principles of section 1272(a).

    (d) DEFINITIONS.—

    (1) RIGHTS TO ACQUIRE STOCK.—For purposes of this section, the term "stock" includes rights to acquire such stock.

    (2) SHAREHOLDERS.—For purposes of subsections (b) and (c), the term "shareholder" includes a holder of rights or of convertible securities.

. . .

SEC. 306.   DISPOSITIONS OF CERTAIN STOCK.

    (a) GENERAL RULE.—If a shareholder sells or otherwise disposes of section 306 stock (as defined in subsection (c))—

    (1) DISPOSITIONS OTHER THAN REDEMPTIONS.—If such disposition is not a redemption (within the meaning of section 317 (b))—

    (A) The amount realized shall be treated as ordinary income. This subparagraph shall not apply to the extent that—

        (i) the amount realized, exceeds

        (ii) such stock's ratable share of the amount which would have been a dividend at the time of distribution if (in lieu of section 306 stock) the corporation had distributed money in an amount equal to the fair market value of the stock at the time of distribution.

(B) Any excess of the amount realized over the sum of—

(i) the amount treated under subparagraph (A) as ordinary income, plus

(ii) the adjusted basis of the stock,

shall be treated as gain from the sale of such stock.

(C) No loss shall be recognized.

(2) REDEMPTION.—If the disposition is a redemption, the amount realized shall be treated as a distribution of property to which section 301 applies.

(b) EXCEPTIONS.—Subsection (a) shall not apply—

(1) TERMINATION OF SHAREHOLDER'S INTEREST, ETC.—

(A) NOT IN REDEMPTION.—If the disposition—

(i) is not a redemption;

(ii) is not, directly or indirectly, to a person the ownership of whose stock would (under section 318 (a)) be attributable to the shareholder; and

(iii) terminates the entire stock interest of the shareholder in the corporation (and for purposes of this clause, section 318 (a) shall apply).

(B) IN REDEMPTION.—If the disposition is a redemption and paragraph (3) or (4) of section 302(b) applies.

(2) LIQUIDATIONS.—If the section 306 stock is redeemed in a distribution in complete liquidation to which part II . . . [Code §331-§346] applies.

(3) WHERE GAIN OR LOSS IS NOT RECOGNIZED.—To the extent that, under any provision of this subtitle, gain or loss to the shareholder is not recognized with respect to the disposition of the section 306 stock.

(4) TRANSACTIONS NOT IN AVOIDANCE.—If it is established to the satisfaction of the Secretary—

(A) that the distribution, and the disposition or redemption, or

(B) in the case of a prior or simultaneous disposition (or redemption) of the stock with respect to which the section 306 stock disposed of (or redeemed) was issued, that the disposition (or redemption) of the section 306 stock,

was not in pursuance of a plan having as one of its principal purposes the avoidance of Federal income tax.

(c) SECTION 306 DEFINED.—

(1) IN GENERAL.—For purposes of this subchapter, the term "section 306 stock" means stock which meets the requirements of subparagraph (A), (B), or (C) of this paragraph.

(A) DISTRIBUTED TO SELLER.—Stock (other than common stock issued with respect to common stock) which was distributed to the shareholder selling or otherwise disposing of such stock if, by reason of section 305 (a), any part of such distribution was not includible in the gross income of the shareholder.

(B) RECEIVED IN A CORPORATE REORGANIZATION OR SEPARATION.—Stock which is not common stock and—

(i) which was received, by the shareholder selling or otherwise disposing of such stock, in pursuance of a plan of reorganization (within the meaning of section 368 (a)), or in a distribution or exchange to which section 355 (or so much of section 356 as relates to section 355) applied, and

(ii) with respect to the receipt of which gain or loss to the shareholder was to any extent not recognized by reason of part III [Code §351-§368], but only to the extent that either the effect of the transaction was substantially the same as the receipt of a stock dividend, or the stock was received in exchange for section 306 stock.

For purposes of this section, a receipt of stock to which the foregoing provisions of this subparagraph apply shall be treated as a distribution of stock.

(C) STOCK HAVING TRANSFERRED OR SUBSTITUTED BASIS.—Except as otherwise provided in subparagraph (B), stock the basis of which (in the hands of the shareholder selling or otherwise disposing of such stock) is determined by reference to the basis (in the hands of such shareholder or any other person) of section 306 stock.

(2) EXCEPTION WHERE NO EARNINGS AND PROFITS.—For purposes of this section, the term "section 306 stock" does not include any stock no part of the distribution of which would have been a dividend at the time of the distribution if money had been distributed in lieu of the stock.

(3) CERTAIN STOCK ACQUIRED IN SECTION 351 EXCHANGE.—The term "section 306 stock" also includes any stock which is not common stock acquired in an exchange to which section 351 applied if receipt of money (in lieu of the stock) would have been treated as a dividend to any extent. Rules similar to the rules of section 304(b)(2) shall apply—

(A) for purposes of the preceding sentence, and

(B) for purposes of determining the application of this section to any subsequent disposition of stock which is section 306 stock by reason of an exchange described in the preceding sentence.

(4) APPLICATION OF ATTRIBUTION RULES FOR CERTAIN PURPOSES.—For purposes of paragraphs (1)(B)(ii) and (3), section 318(a) shall apply. For purposes of applying the preceding sentence to paragraph (3), the rules of section 304(c)(3)(B) shall apply.

(d) STOCK RIGHTS.—For purposes of this section—

(1) stock rights shall be treated as stock, and

(2) stock acquired through the exercise of stock rights shall be treated as stock distributed at the time of the distribution of the stock rights, to the extent of the fair market value of such rights at the time of the distribution.

(e) CONVERTIBLE STOCK.—For purposes of subsection (c)—

(1) if section 306 stock was issued with respect to common stock and later such section 306 stock is exchanged for common stock in the same corporation (whether or not such exchange is pursuant to a conversion privilege contained in the section 306 stock), then (except as provided in paragraph (2)) the common stock so received shall not be treated as section 306 stock; and

(2) common stock with respect to which there is a privilege of converting into stock other than common stock (or into property), whether or not the

conversion privilege is contained in such stock, shall not be treated as common stock.

. . .

(g) CHANGE IN TERMS AND CONDITIONS OF STOCK.—If a substantial change is made in the terms and conditions of any stock, then, for purposes of this section—

(1) the fair market value of such stock shall be the fair market value at the time of the distribution or at the time of such change, whichever such value is higher;

(2) such stock's ratable share of the amount which would have been a dividend if money had been distributed in lieu of stock shall be determined as of the time of distribution or as of the time of such change, whichever such ratable share is higher; and

(3) subsection (c) (2) shall not apply unless the stock meets the requirements of such subsection both at the time of such distribution and at the time of such change.

SEC. 311. TAXABILITY OF CORPORATION ON DISTRIBUTION.

(a) GENERAL RULE.—Except as provided in subsection (b), no gain or loss shall be recognized to a corporation on the distribution (not in complete liquidation) with respect to its stock of—

(1) its stock (or rights to acquire its stock), or

(2) property.

(b) DISTRIBUTIONS OF APPRECIATED PROPERTY.—

(1) IN GENERAL.—If—

(A) a corporation distributes property (other than an obligation of such corporation) to a shareholder in a distribution to which subpart A applies, and

(B) the fair market value of such property exceeds its adjusted basis (in the hands of the distributing corporation), then gain shall be recognized to the distributing corporation as if such property were sold to the distributee at its fair market value.

(2) TREATMENT OF LIABILITIES.—Rules similar to the rules of section 336(b) shall apply for purposes of this subsection.

(3) SPECIAL RULE FOR CERTAIN DISTRIBUTIONS OF PARTNERSHIP OR TRUST INTERESTS.—If the property distributed consists of an interest in a partnership or trust, the Secretary may by regulations provide that the amount of the gain recognized under paragraph (1) shall be computed without regard to any loss attributable to property contributed to the partnership or trust for the principal purpose of recognizing such loss on the distribution.

SEC. 312.   EFFECT ON EARNINGS AND PROFITS.

(a) GENERAL RULE.—Except as otherwise provided in this section, on the distribution of property by a corporation with respect to its stock, the earnings and profits of the corporation (to the extent thereof) shall be decreased by the sum of—

(1) the amount of money,

(2) the principal amount of the obligations of such corporation (or, in the case of obligations having original issue discount, the aggregate issue price of such obligations), and

(3) the adjusted basis of the other property,

so distributed.

. . .

SEC. 316.   DIVIDEND DEFINED.

(a) GENERAL RULE.—For purposes of this subtitle, the term "dividend" means any distribution of property made by a corporation to its shareholders—

(1) out of its earnings and profits accumulated after February 28, 1913, or

(2) out of its earnings and profits of the taxable year (computed as of the close of the taxable year without diminution by reason of any distributions made during the taxable year), without regard to the amount of the earnings and profits at the time the distribution was made.

Except as otherwise provided in this subtitle, every distribution is made out of earnings and profits to the extent thereof, and from the most recently accumulated earnings and profits. To the extent that any distribution is, under any provision of this subchapter, treated as a distribution of property to which section 301 applies, such distribution shall be treated as a distribution of property for purposes of this subsection.

. . .

SEC. 317.   OTHER DEFINITIONS.

(a) PROPERTY.—For purposes of this part [Code §301-§318], the term "property" means money, securities, and any other property; except that such term does not include stock in the corporation making the distribution (or rights to acquire such stock).

(b) REDEMPTION OF STOCK.—For purposes of this part [Code §301-§318], stock shall be treated as redeemed by a corporation if the corporation acquires its stock from a shareholder in exchange for property, whether or not the stock so acquired is cancelled, retired, or held as treasury stock.

SEC. 318.   CONSTRUCTIVE OWNERSHIP OF STOCK.

(a) GENERAL RULE.—For purposes of those provisions of this subchapter to which the rules contained in this section are expressly made applicable—

(1) MEMBERS OF FAMILY.—

(A) IN GENERAL.—An individual shall be considered as owning the stock owned, directly or indirectly, by or for—

(i) his spouse (other than a spouse who is legally separated from the individual under a decree of divorce or separate maintenance), and

(ii) his children, grandchildren, and parents.

(B) EFFECT OF ADOPTION.—For purposes of subparagraph (A) (ii), a legally adopted child of an individual shall be treated as a child of such individual by blood.

(2) ATTRIBUTION FROM PARTNERSHIPS, ESTATES, TRUSTS, AND CORPORATIONS.—

(A) FROM PARTNERSHIPS AND ESTATES.—Stock owned, directly or indirectly, by or for a partnership or estate shall be considered as owned proportionately by its partners or beneficiaries.

(B) FROM TRUSTS.—

(i) Stock owned, directly or indirectly, by or for a trust (other than an employees' trust described in section 401(a) which is exempt from tax under section 501(a)) shall be considered as owned by its beneficiaries in proportion to the actuarial interest of such beneficiaries in such trust.

(ii) Stock owned, directly or indirectly, by or for any portion of a trust of which a person is considered the owner under subpart E of part I of subchapter J (relating to grantors and others treated as substantial owners) shall be considered as owned by such person.

(C) FROM CORPORATIONS.—If 50 percent or more in value of the stock in a corporation is owned, directly or indirectly, by or for any person, such person shall be considered as owning the stock owned, directly or indirectly, by or for such corporation, in that proportion which the value of the stock which such person so owns bears to the value of all the stock in such corporation.

(3) ATTRIBUTION TO PARTNERSHIPS, ESTATES, TRUSTS, AND CORPORATIONS.—

(A) TO PARTNERSHIPS AND ESTATES.—Stock owned, directly or indirectly, by or for a partner or a beneficiary of an estate shall be considered as owned by the partnership or estate.

(B) TO TRUSTS.—

(i) Stock owned, directly or indirectly, by or for a beneficiary of a trust (other than an employees' trust described in section 401(a) which is exempt from tax under section 501 (a)) shall be considered as owned by the trust, unless such beneficiary's interest in the trust is a remote contingent interest. For purposes of this clause, a contingent interest of a beneficiary in a trust shall be considered remote if, under the maximum exercise of discretion by the trustee in favor of such beneficiary, the value of such interest, computed actuarially, is 5 percent or less of the value of the trust property.

(ii) Stock owned, directly or indirectly, by or for a person who is considered the owner of any portion of a trust under subpart E of part I of subchapter J (relating to grantors and others treated as substantial owners) shall be considered as owned by the trust.

(C) TO CORPORATIONS.—If 50 percent or more in value of the stock in a corporation is owned, directly or indirectly, by or for any person, such corporation shall be considered as owning the stock owned, directly or indirectly, by or for such person.

(4) OPTIONS.—If any person has an option to acquire stock, such stock shall be considered as owned by such person. For purposes of this paragraph, an option to acquire such an option, and each one of a series of such options, shall be considered as an option to acquire such stock.

(5) OPERATING RULES.—

(A) IN GENERAL.—Except as provided in subparagraphs (B) and (C), stock constructively owned by a person by reason of the application of paragraph (1), (2), (3), or (4), shall, for purposes of applying paragraphs (1), (2), (3), and (4), be considered as actually owned by such person.

(B) MEMBERS OF FAMILY.—Stock constructively owned by an individual by reason of the application of paragraph (1) shall not be considered as owned by him for purposes of again applying paragraph (1) in order to make another the constructive owner of such stock.

(C) PARTNERSHIPS, ESTATES, TRUSTS, AND CORPORATIONS.— Stock constructively owned by a partnership, estate, trust, or corporation by reason of the application of paragraph (3) shall not be considered as owned by it for purposes of applying paragraph (2) in order to make another the constructive owner of such stock.

(D) OPTION RULE IN LIEU OF FAMILY RULE.—For purposes of this paragraph, if stock may be considered as owned by an individual under paragraph (1) or (4), it shall be considered as owned by him under paragraph (4).

(E) S CORPORATION TREATED AS PARTNERSHIP.—For purposes of this subsection—

(i) an S corporation shall be treated as a partnership, and

(ii) any shareholder of the S corporation shall be treated as a partner of such partnership.

The preceding sentence shall not apply for purposes of determining whether stock in the S corporation is constructively owned by any person.

. . .

SEC. 331.   GAIN OR LOSS TO SHAREHOLDERS IN CORPORATE LIQUIDATIONS.

(a) DISTRIBUTIONS IN COMPLETE LIQUIDATION TREATED AS EX- CHANGES.—Amounts received by a shareholder in a distribution in complete liquidation of a corporation shall be treated as in full payment in exchange for the stock.

(b) NONAPPLICATION OF SECTION 301.—Section 301 (relating to effects on shareholder of distributions of property) shall not apply to any distribution of property (other than a distribution referred to in paragraph (2)(B) of section 316(b)), in complete liquidation.

. . .

SEC. 332. COMPLETE LIQUIDATIONS OF SUBSIDIARIES.

(a) GENERAL RULE.—No gain or loss shall be recognized on the receipt by a corporation of property distributed in complete liquidation of another corporation.

(b) LIQUIDATIONS TO WHICH SECTION APPLIES.—For purposes of this section, a distribution shall be considered to be in complete liquidation only if—

(1) the corporation receiving such property was, on the date of the adoption of the plan of liquidation, and has continued to be at all times until the receipt of the property, the owner of stock (in such other corporation) meeting the requirements of section 1504(a)(2); and either

(2) the distribution is by such other corporation in complete cancellation or redemption of all its stock, and the transfer of all the property occurs within the taxable year; in such case the adoption by the shareholders of the resolution under which is authorized the distribution of all the assets of such corporation in complete cancellation or redemption of all its stock shall be considered an adoption of a plan of liquidation, even though no time for the completion of the transfer of the property is specified in such resolution; or

(3) such distribution is one of a series of distributions by such other corporation in complete cancellation or redemption of all its stock in accordance with a plan of liquidation under which the transfer of all the property under the liquidation is to be completed within 3 years from the close of the taxable year during which is made the first of the series of distributions under the plan, except that if such transfer is not completed within such period, or if the taxpayer does not continue qualified under paragraph (1) until the completion of such transfer, no distribution under the plan shall be considered a distribution in complete liquidation.

If such transfer of all the property does not occur within the taxable year, the Secretary may require of the taxpayer such bond, or waiver of the statute of limitations on assessment and collection, or both, as he may deem necessary to insure, if the transfer of the property is not completed within such 3-year period, or if the taxpayer does not continue qualified under paragraph (1) until the completion of such transfer, the assessment and collection of all income taxes then imposed by law for such taxable year or subsequent taxable years, to the extent attributable to property so received. A distribution otherwise constituting a distribution in complete liquidation within the meaning of this subsection shall not be considered as not constituting such a distribution merely because it does not constitute a distribution or liquidation within the meaning of the corporate law under which the distribution is made; and for purposes of this subsection a transfer of property of such other corporation to the taxpayer shall not be considered as not constituting a distribution (or one of a series of distributions) in complete cancellation or redemption of all the stock of such other corporation, merely because the carrying out of the plan involves (A) the transfer under the plan to the taxpayer by such other corporation of property, not attributable to shares owned by the taxpayer, on an exchange described in section 361, and (B) the complete cancellation or redemption under the plan, as a result of exchanges described in section 354, of the shares not owned by the taxpayer.

. . .

SEC. 334.   BASIS OF PROPERTY RECEIVED IN LIQUIDATIONS.

(a) GENERAL RULE.—If property is received in a distribution in complete liquidation, and if gain or loss is recognized on receipt of such property, then the basis of the property in the hands of the distributee shall be the fair market value of such property at the time of the distribution.

(b) LIQUIDATION OF SUBSIDIARY.—

(1) IN GENERAL.—If property is received by a corporate distributee in a distribution in a complete liquidation to which section 332 applies (or in a transfer described in section 337(b)(1)), the basis of such property in the hands of such distributee shall be the same as it would be in the hands of the transferor; except that, in any case in which gain or loss is recognized by the liquidating corporation with respect to such property, the basis of such property in the hands of such distributee shall be the fair market value of the property at the time of the distribution.

(2) CORPORATE DISTRIBUTEE.—For purposes of this subsection, the term "corporate distributee" means only the corporation which meets the stock ownership requirements specified in section 332(b).

SEC. 336.   GAIN OR LOSS RECOGNIZED ON PROPERTY DISTRIBUTED IN COMPLETE LIQUIDATION.

(a) GENERAL RULE.—Except as otherwise provided in this section or section 337, gain or loss shall be recognized to a liquidating corporation on the distribution of property in complete liquidation as if such property were sold to the distributee at its fair market value.

(b) TREATMENT OF LIABILITIES.—If any property distributed in the liquidation is subject to a liability or the shareholder assumes a liability of the liquidating corporation in connection with the distribution, for purposes of subsection (a) and section 337, the fair market value of such property shall be treated as not less than the amount of such liability.

(c) EXCEPTION FOR LIQUIDATIONS WHICH ARE PART OF A REORGANI-
ZATION.—For provision providing that this subpart does not apply to distributions in pursuance of a plan of reorganization, see section 361(c)(4).

(d) LIMITATIONS ON RECOGNITION OF LOSS.—

(1) NO LOSS RECOGNIZED IN CERTAIN DISTRIBUTIONS TO RE-
LATED PERSONS.—

(A) IN GENERAL.—No loss shall be recognized to a liquidating corporation on the distribution of any property to a related person (within the
meaning of section 267) if—

(i) such distribution is not pro rata, or

(ii) such property is disqualified property.

. . .

SEC. 337.   NONRECOGNITION FOR PROPERTY DISTRIBUTED TO PARENT IN COMPLETE LIQUIDATION OF SUBSIDIARY.

(a) IN GENERAL.—No gain or loss shall be recognized to the liquidating
corporation on the distribution to the 80-percent distributee of any property in a
complete liquidation to which section 332 applies.

(b) TREATMENT OF INDEBTEDNESS OF SUBSIDIARY, ETC.—

(1) INDEBTEDNESS OF SUBSIDIARY TO PARENT.—If—

(A) a corporation is liquidated in a liquidation to which section 332 applies, and

(B) on the date of the adoption of the plan of liquidation, such corporation
was indebted to the 80-percent distributee,

for purposes of this section and section 336, any transfer of property to the
80-percent distributee in satisfaction of such indebtedness shall be treated as
a distribution to such distributee in such liquidation.

. . .

(c) 80-PERCENT DISTRIBUTEE.—For purposes of this section, the term "80-
percent distributee" means only the corporation which meets the 80-percent stock
ownership requirements specified in section 332(b). For purposes of this section,
the determination of whether any corporation is an 80-percent distributee shall
be made without regard to any consolidated return regulation.

. . .

SEC. 338.   CERTAIN STOCK PURCHASES TREATED AS ASSET ACQUISITIONS.

(a) GENERAL RULE.—For purposes of this subtitle, if a purchasing corporation
makes an election under this section (or is treated under subsection (e) as having

made such an election), then, in the case of any qualified stock purchase, the target corporation—

(1) shall be treated as having sold all of its assets at the close of the acquisition date at fair market value in a single transaction, and

(2) shall be treated as a new corporation which purchased all of the assets referred to in paragraph (1) as of the beginning of the day after the acquisition date.

(b) BASIS OF ASSETS AFTER DEEMED PURCHASE.—

(1) IN GENERAL.—For purposes of subsection (a), the assets of the target corporation shall be treated as purchased for an amount equal to the sum of—

(A) the grossed-up basis of the purchasing corporation's recently purchased stock, and

(B) the basis of the purchasing corporation's nonrecently purchased stock.

(2) ADJUSTMENT FOR LIABILITIES AND OTHER RELEVANT ITEMS.— The amount described in paragraph (1) shall be adjusted under regulations prescribed by the Secretary for liabilities of the target corporation and other relevant items.

(3) ELECTION TO STEP-UP THE BASIS OF CERTAIN TARGET STOCK.—

(A) IN GENERAL.—Under regulations prescribed by the Secretary, the basis of the purchasing corporation's nonrecently purchased stock shall be the basis amount determined under subparagraph (B) of this paragraph if the purchasing corporation makes an election to recognize gain as if such stock were sold on the acquisition date for an amount equal to the basis amount determined under subparagraph (B).

(B) DETERMINATION OF BASIS AMOUNT.—For purposes of subparagraph (A), the basis amount determined under this subparagraph shall be an amount equal to the grossed-up basis determined under subparagraph (A) of paragraph (1) multiplied by a fraction—

(i) the numerator of which is the percentage of stock (by value) in the target corporation attributable to the purchasing corporation's nonrecently purchased stock, and

(ii) the denominator of which is 100 percent minus the percentage referred to in clause (i).

(4) GROSSED-UP BASIS.—For purposes of paragraph (1), the grossed-up basis shall be an amount equal to the basis of the corporation's recently purchased stock, multiplied by a fraction—

(A) the numerator of which is 100 percent, minus the percentage of stock (by value) in the target corporation attributable to the purchasing corporation's nonrecently purchased stock, and

(B) the denominator of which is the percentage of stock (by value) in the target corporation attributable to the purchasing corporation's recently purchased stock.

(5) ALLOCATION AMONG ASSETS.—The amount determined under paragraphs (1) and (2) shall be allocated among the assets of the target corporation under regulations prescribed by the Secretary.

(6) DEFINITIONS OF RECENTLY PURCHASED STOCK AND NONRECENTLY PURCHASED STOCK.—For purposes of this subsection—

(A) RECENTLY PURCHASED STOCK.—The term "recently purchased stock" means any stock in the target corporation which is held by the purchasing corporation on the acquisition date and which was purchased by such corporation during the 12-month acquisition period.

(B) NONRECENTLY PURCHASED STOCK.—The term "nonrecently purchased stock" means any stock in the target corporation which is held by the purchasing corporation on the acquisition date and which is not recently purchased stock.

(d) PURCHASING CORPORATION; TARGET CORPORATION; QUALIFIED STOCK PURCHASE.—For purposes of this section—

(1) PURCHASING CORPORATION.—The term "purchasing corporation" means any corporation which makes a qualified stock purchase of stock of another corporation.

(2) TARGET CORPORATION.—The term "target corporation" means any corporation the stock of which is acquired by another corporation in a qualified stock purchase.

(3) QUALIFIED STOCK PURCHASE.—The term "qualified stock purchase" means any transaction or series of transactions in which stock (meeting the requirements of section 1504(a)(2)) of 1 corporation is acquired by another corporation by purchase during the 12-month acquisition period.

. . .

(f) CONSISTENCY REQUIRED FOR ALL STOCK ACQUISITIONS FROM SAME AFFILIATED GROUP.—If a purchasing corporation makes qualified stock purchases with respect to the target corporation and 1 or more target affiliates during any consistency period, then (except as otherwise provided in subsection (e))—

(1) any election under this section with respect to the first such purchase shall apply to each other such purchase, and

(2) no election may be made under this section with respect to the second or subsequent such purchase if such an election was not made with respect to the first such purchase.

(g) ELECTION.—

(1) WHEN MADE.—Except as otherwise provided in regulations, an election under this section shall be made not later than the 15th day of the 9th month, beginning after the month in which the acquisition date occurs.

(2) MANNER.—An election by the purchasing corporation under this section shall be made in such manner as the Secretary shall by regulations prescribe.

(3) ELECTION IRREVOCABLE.—An election by a purchasing corporation under this section, once made, shall be irrevocable.

(h) DEFINITIONS AND SPECIAL RULES.—For purposes of this section—

(1) 12-MONTH ACQUISITION PERIOD.—The term "12-month acquisition period" means the 12-month period beginning with the date of the first acquisition by purchase of stock included in a qualified stock purchase (or, if any of such stock was acquired in an acquisition which is a purchase by reason of

subparagraph (C) of paragraph (3), the date on which the acquiring corporation is first considered under section 318(a) (other than paragraph (4) thereof) as owning stock owned by the corporation from which such acquisition was made).

(2) ACQUISITION DATE.—The term "acquisition date" means, with respect to any corporation, the first day on which there is a qualified stock purchase with respect to the stock of such corporation.

(3) PURCHASE.—

(A) IN GENERAL.—The term "purchase" means any acquisition of stock, but only if—

(i) the basis of the stock in the hands of the purchasing corporation is not determined (I) in whole or in part by reference to the adjusted basis of such stock in the hands of the person from whom acquired, or (II) under section 1014(a) (relating to property acquired from a decedent),

(ii) the stock is not acquired in an exchange to which section 351, 354, 355, or 356 applies and is not acquired in any other transaction described in regulations in which the transferor does not recognize the entire amount of the gain or loss realized on the transaction, and

(iii) the stock is not acquired from a person the ownership of whose stock would, under section 318(a) (other than paragraph (4) thereof), be attributed to the person acquiring such stock.

(B) DEEMED PURCHASE UNDER SUBSECTION (a).—The term "purchase" includes any deemed purchase under subsection (a)(2). The acquisition date for a corporation which is deemed purchased under subsection (a)(2) shall be determined under regulations prescribed by the Secretary.

. . .

(4) CONSISTENCY PERIOD.—

(A) IN GENERAL.—Except as provided in subparagraph (B), the term "consistency period" means the period consisting of—

(i) the 1-year period before the beginning of the 12-month acquisition period for the target corporation,

(ii) such acquisition period (up to and including the acquisition date), and

(iii) the 1-year period beginning on the day after the acquisition date.

(B) EXTENSION WHERE THERE IS PLAN.—The period referred to in subparagraph (A) shall also include any period during which the Secretary determines that there was in effect a plan to make a qualified stock purchase plus 1 or more other qualified stock purchases (or asset acquisitions described in subsection (e)) with respect to the target corporation or any target affiliate.

(5) AFFILIATED GROUP.—The term "affiliated group" has the meaning given to such term by section 1504(a) (determined without regard to the exceptions contained in section 1504(b)).

(6) TARGET AFFILIATE.—

(A) IN GENERAL.—A corporation shall be treated as a target affiliate of the target corporation if each of such corporations was, at any time during so much of the consistency period as ends on the acquisition date of the target corporation, a member of an affiliated group which had the same common parent.

. . .

(8) ACQUISITIONS BY AFFILIATED GROUP TREATED AS MADE BY 1 CORPORATION.—Except as provided in regulations prescribed by the Secretary, stock and asset acquisitions made by members of the same affiliated group shall be treated as made by 1 corporation.

(9) TARGET NOT TREATED AS MEMBER OF AFFILIATED GROUP.— Except as otherwise provided in paragraph (10) or in regulations prescribed under this paragraph, the target corporation shall not be treated as a member of an affiliated group with respect to the sale described in subsection (a)(1).

(10) ELECTIVE RECOGNITION OF GAIN OR LOSS BY TARGET CORPORATION, TOGETHER WITH NONRECOGNITION OF GAIN OR LOSS ON STOCK SOLD BY SELLING CONSOLIDATED GROUP.—

(A) IN GENERAL.—Under regulations prescribed by the Secretary, an election may be made under which if—

(i) the target corporation was, before the transaction, a member of the selling consolidated group, and

(ii) the target corporation recognizes gain or loss with respect to the transaction as if it sold all of its assets in a single transaction,

then the target corporation shall be treated as a member of the selling consolidated group with respect to such sale, and (to the extent provided in regulations) no gain or loss will be recognized on stock sold or exchanged in the transaction by members of the selling consolidated group.

(B) SELLING CONSOLIDATED GROUP.—For purposes of subparagraph (A), the term "selling consolidated group" means any group of corporations which (for the taxable period which includes the transaction)—

(i) includes the target corporation, and

(ii) files a consolidated return.

To the extent provided in regulations, such term also includes any affiliated group of corporations which includes the target corporation (whether or not such group files a consolidated return).

(C) INFORMATION REQUIRED TO BE FURNISHED TO THE SECRETARY.—Under regulations, where an election is made under subparagraph (A), the purchasing corporation and the common parent of the selling consolidated group shall, at such times and in such manner as may be provided in regulations, furnish to the Secretary the following information:

(i) The amount allocated under subsection (b)(5) to goodwill or going concern value.

(ii) Any modification of the amount described in clause (i).

(iii) Any other information as the Secretary deems necessary to carry out the provisions of this paragraph.

(11) ELECTIVE FORMULA FOR DETERMINING FAIR MARKET VALUE.— For purposes of subsection (a)(1), fair market value may be determined on the

basis of a formula provided in regulations prescribed by the Secretary which takes into account liabilities and other relevant items.

. . .

(15) COMBINED DEEMED SALE RETURN.—Under regulations prescribed by the Secretary, a combined deemed sale return may be filed by all target corporations acquired by a purchasing corporation on the same acquisition date if such target corporations were members of the same selling consolidated group (as defined in subparagraph (B) of paragraph (10)).

. . .

(i) REGULATIONS.—The Secretary shall prescribe such regulations as may be necessary or appropriate to carry out the purposes of this section, including—

(1) regulations to ensure that the purpose of this section to require consistency of treatment of stock and asset sales and purchases may not be circumvented through the use of any provision of law or regulations (including the consolidated return regulations) and

(2) regulations providing for the coordination of the provisions of this section with the provision of this title relating to foreign corporations and their shareholders.

SEC. 351.   TRANSFER TO CORPORATION CONTROLLED BY TRANSFEROR.

(a) GENERAL RULE.—No gain or loss shall be recognized if property is transferred to a corporation by one or more persons solely in exchange for stock in such corporation and immediately after the exchange such person or persons are in control (as defined in section 368(c)) of the corporation.

(b) RECEIPT OF PROPERTY.—If subsection (a) would apply to an exchange but for the fact that there is received, in addition to the stock permitted to be received under subsection (a), other property or money, then—

(1) gain (if any) to such recipient shall be recognized, but not in excess of—

(A) the amount of money received, plus

(B) the fair market value of such other property received; and

(2) no loss to such recipient shall be recognized.

. . .

(d) SERVICES, CERTAIN INDEBTEDNESS, AND ACCRUED INTEREST NOT TREATED AS PROPERTY.—For purposes of this section, stock issued for—

(1) services,

(2) indebtedness of the transferee corporation which is not evidenced by a security, or

(3) interest on indebtedness of the transferee corporation which accrued on or after the beginning of the transferor's holding period for the debt, shall not be considered as issued in return for property.

(e) EXCEPTIONS.—This section shall not apply to—

(1) TRANSFER OF PROPERTY TO AN INVESTMENT COMPANY.—A transfer of property to an investment company. For purposes of the preceding sentence, the determination of whether a company is an investment company shall be made—

(A) by taking into account all stock and securities held by the company, and

(B) by treating as stock and securities—

(i) money,

(ii) stocks and other equity interests in a corporation, evidences of indebtedness, options, forward or futures contracts, notional principal contracts and derivatives,

(iii) any foreign currency,

(iv) any interest in a real estate investment trust, a common trust fund, a regulated investment company, a publicly-traded partnership (as defined in section 7704(b)) or any other equity interest (other than in a corporation) which pursuant to its terms or any other arrangement is readily convertible into, or exchangeable for, any asset described in any preceding clause, this clause or clause (v) or (viii),

(v) except to the extent provided in regulations prescribed by the Secretary, any interest in a precious metal, unless such metal is used or held in the active conduct of a trade or business after the contribution,

(vi) except as otherwise provided in regulations prescribed by the Secretary, interests in any entity if substantially all of the assets of such entity consist (directly or indirectly) of any assets described in any preceding clause or clause (viii),

(vii) to the extent provided in regulations prescribed by the Secretary, any interest in any entity not described in clause (vi), but only to the extent of the value of such interest that is attributable to assets listed in clauses (i) through (v) or clause (viii), or

(viii) any other asset specified in regulations prescribed by the Secretary.

The Secretary may prescribe regulations that, under appropriate circumstances, treat any asset described in clauses (i) through (v) as not so listed.

. . .

(f) TREATMENT OF CONTROLLED CORPORATION.—If—(1) property is transferred to a corporation (hereinafter in this subsection referred to as the "controlled corporation") in an exchange with respect to which gain or loss is not recognized (in whole or in part) to the transferor under this section, and

(2) such exchange is not in pursuance of a plan of reorganization,
section 311 shall apply to any transfer in such exchange by the controlled corporation in the same manner as if such transfer were a distribution to which subpart
A of part I [Code §301-§307] applies.

(g) NONQUALIFIED PREFERRED STOCK NOT TREATED AS STOCK.—

(1) IN GENERAL.—In the case of a person who transfers property to a
corporation and receives nonqualified preferred stock—

(A) subsection (a) shall not apply to such transferor, and

(B) if (and only if) the transferor receives stock other than nonqualified
preferred stock—

(i) subsection (b) shall apply to such transferor; and

(ii) such nonqualified preferred stock shall be treated as other property
for purposes of applying subsection (b).

(2) NONQUALIFIED PREFERRED STOCK.—For purposes of paragraph
(1)—

(A) IN GENERAL.—The term "nonqualified preferred stock" means preferred stock if—

(i) the holder of such stock has the right to require the issuer or a
related person to redeem or purchase the stock,

(ii) the issuer or a related person is required to redeem or purchase
such stock,

(iii) the issuer or a related person has the right to redeem or purchase
the stock and, as of the issue date, it is more likely than not that such
right will be exercised, or

(iv) the dividend rate on such stock varies in whole or in part (directly
or indirectly) with reference to interest rates, commodity prices, or other
similar indices.

(B) LIMITATIONS.—Clauses (i), (ii), and (iii) of subparagraph (A) shall
apply only if the right or obligation referred to therein may be exercised
within the 20-year period beginning on the issue date of such stock and
such right or obligation is not subject to a contingency which, as of the issue
date, makes remote the likelihood of the redemption or purchase.

(C) EXCEPTIONS FOR CERTAIN RIGHTS OR OBLIGATIONS.—

(i) IN GENERAL.—A right or obligation shall not be treated as described in clause (i), (ii), or (iii) of subparagraph (A) if—

(I) it may be exercised only upon the death, disability, or mental
incompetency of the holder, or

(II) in the case of a right or obligation to redeem or purchase stock
transferred in connection with the performance of services for the issuer
or a related person (and which represents reasonable compensation),
it may be exercised only upon the holder's separation from service
from the issuer or a related person.

(ii) EXCEPTION.—Clause (i)(I) shall not apply if the stock relinquished
in the exchange, or the stock acquired in the exchange is in—

(I) a corporation if any class of stock in such corporation or a related
party is readily tradable on an established securities market or otherwise, or

(II) any other corporation if such exchange is part of a transaction or series of transactions in which such corporation is to become a corporation described in subclause (I).

(3) DEFINITIONS.—For purposes of this subsection—

(A) PREFERRED STOCK.—The term "preferred stock" means stock which is limited and preferred as to dividends and does not participate in corporate growth to any significant extent.

(B) RELATED PERSON.—A person shall be treated as related to another person if they bear a relationship to such other person described in section 267(b) or 707(b).

(4) REGULATIONS.—The Secretary may prescribe such regulations as may be necessary or appropriate to carry out the purposes of this subsection and sections 354(a)(2)(C), 355(a)(3)(D), and 356(e). The Secretary may also prescribe regulations, consistent with the treatment under this subsection and such sections, for the treatment of nonqualified preferred stock under other provisions of this title.

. . .

SEC. 354. EXCHANGES OF STOCK AND SECURITIES IN CERTAIN REORGANIZATIONS.

(a) GENERAL RULE.—

(1) IN GENERAL.—No gain or loss shall be recognized if stock or securities in a corporation a party to a reorganization are, in pursuance of the plan of reorganization, exchanged solely for stock or securities in such corporation or in another corporation a party to the reorganization.

(2) LIMITATIONS.—

(A) EXCESS PRINCIPAL AMOUNT.—Paragraph (1) shall not apply if—

(i) the principal amount of any such securities received exceeds the principal amount of any such securities surrendered, or

(ii) any such securities are received and no such securities are surrendered.

(B) PROPERTY ATTRIBUTABLE TO ACCRUED INTEREST.—Neither paragraph (1) nor so much of section 356 as relates to paragraph (1) shall apply to the extent that any stock (including nonqualified preferred stock, as defined in section 351(g)(2)), securities, or other property received is attributable to interest which has accrued on securities on or after the beginning of the holder's holding period.

(C) NONQUALIFIED PREFERRED STOCK.—

(i) IN GENERAL.—Nonqualified preferred stock (as defined in section 351(g)(2)) received in exchange for stock other than nonqualified preferred stock (as so defined) shall not be treated as stock or securities.

(ii) RECAPITALIZATIONS OF FAMILY-OWNED CORPORATIONS.—

(I) IN GENERAL.—Clause (i) shall not apply in the case of a recapitalization under section 368(a)(1)(E) of a family-owned corporation.

(II) FAMILY-OWNED CORPORATION.—For purposes of this clause, except as provided in regulations, the term "family-owned corporation" means any corporation which is described in clause (i) of section 447(d)(2)(C) throughout the 8-year period beginning on the date which is 5 years before the date of the recapitalization. For purposes of the preceding sentence, stock shall not be treated as owned by a family member during any period described in section 355(d)(6)(B).

. . .

SEC. 356.   RECEIPT OF ADDITIONAL CONSIDERATION.

(a) GAIN ON EXCHANGES.—
  (1) RECOGNITION OF GAIN.—If—
    (A) section 354 or 355 would apply to an exchange but for the fact that
    (B) the property received in the exchange consists not only of property permitted by section 354 or 355 to be received without the recognition of gain but also of other property or money, then the gain, if any, to the recipient shall be recognized, but in an amount not in excess of the sum of such money and the fair market value of such other property.
  (2) TREATMENT AS DIVIDEND.—If an exchange is described in paragraph (1) but has the effect of the distribution of a dividend (determined with the application of section 318(a)), then there shall be treated as a dividend to each distributee such an amount of the gain recognized under paragraph (1) as is not in excess of his ratable share of the undistributed earnings and profits of the corporation accumulated after February 28, 1913. The remainder, if any, of the gain recognized under paragraph (1) shall be treated as gain from the exchange of property.

. . .

(c) LOSS.—If—
  (1) section 354 would apply to an exchange, or section 355 would apply to an exchange or distribution, but for the fact that
  (2) the property received in the exchange or distribution consists not only of property permitted by section 354 or 355 to be received without the recognition of gain or loss, but also of other property or money,
then no loss from the exchange or distribution shall be recognized.
(d) SECURITIES AS OTHER PROPERTY.—For purposes of this section—
  (1) IN GENERAL.—Except as provided in paragraph (2), the term "other property" includes securities.
  (2) EXCEPTIONS.—
    (A) SECURITIES WITH RESPECT TO WHICH NONRECOGNITION OF GAIN WOULD BE PERMITTED.—The term "other property" does not include securities to the extent that, under section 354 or 355, such securities would be permitted to be received without the recognition of gain.

(B) GREATER PRINCIPAL AMOUNT IN SECTION 354 EXCHANGE.—
If—

(i) in an exchange described in section 354 (other than subsection (c) thereof), securities of a corporation a party to the reorganization are surrendered and securities of any corporation a party to the reorganization are received, and

(ii) the principal amount of such securities received exceeds the principal amount of such securities surrendered,

then, with respect to such securities received, the term "other property" means only the fair market value of such excess. For purposes of this subparagraph and subparagraph (C), if no securities are surrendered, the excess shall be the entire principal amount of the securities received.

. . .

(e) NONQUALIFIED PREFERRED STOCK TREATED AS OTHER PROPERTY.—For purposes of this section—

(1) IN GENERAL.—Except as provided in paragraph (2), the term "other property" includes nonqualified preferred stock (as defined in section 351(g)(2)).

(2) EXCEPTION.—The term "other property" does not include nonqualified preferred stock (as so defined) to the extent that, under section 354 or 355, such preferred stock would be permitted to be received without the recognition of gain.

(f) EXCHANGES FOR SECTION 306 STOCK.—Notwithstanding any other provision of this section, to the extent that any of the other property (or money) is received in exchange for section 306 stock, an amount equal to the fair market value of such other property (or the amount of such money) shall be treated as a distribution of property to which section 301 applies.

(g) TRANSACTIONS INVOLVING GIFT OR COMPENSATION.—For special rules for a transaction described in section 354, 355, or this section, but which—

(1) results in a gift, see section 2501 and following, or

(2) has the effect of the payment of compensation, see section 61(a)(1).

SEC. 358. BASIS TO DISTRIBUTEES.

(a) GENERAL RULE.—In the case of an exchange to which section 351, 354, 355, 356, or 361 applies—

(1) NONRECOGNITION PROPERTY.—The basis of the property permitted to be received under such section without the recognition of gain or loss shall be the same as that of the property exchanged—

(A) decreased by—

(i) the fair market value of any other property (except money) received by the taxpayer,

(ii) the amount of any money received by the taxpayer, and

(iii) the amount of loss to the taxpayer which was recognized on such exchange, and

(B) increased by—

(i) the amount which was treated as a dividend, and

(ii) the amount of gain to the taxpayer which was recognized on such exchange (not including any portion of such gain which was treated as a dividend).

(2) OTHER PROPERTY.—The basis of any other property (except money) received by the taxpayer shall be its fair market value.

. . .

(d) ASSUMPTION OF LIABILITY.—

(1) IN GENERAL.—Where, as part of the consideration to the taxpayer, another party to the exchange assumed a liability of the taxpayer, such assumption shall, for purposes of this section, be treated as money received by the taxpayer on the exchange.

(2) EXCEPTION.—Paragraph (1) shall not apply to the amount of any liability excluded under section 357(c)(3).

(e) EXCEPTION.—This section shall not apply to property acquired by a corporation by the exchange of its stock or securities (or the stock or securities of a corporation which is in control of the acquiring corporation) as consideration in whole or in part for the transfer of the property to it.

(f) DEFINITION OF NONRECOGNITION PROPERTY IN CASE OF SECTION 361 EXCHANGE.—For purposes of this section, the property permitted to be received under section 361 without the recognition of gain or loss shall be treated as consisting only of stock or securities in another corporation a party to the reorganization.

. . .

(h) SPECIAL RULES FOR ASSUMPTION OF LIABILITIES TO WHICH SUBSECTION (d) DOES NOT APPLY.—

(1) IN GENERAL.— If, after application of the other provisions of this section to an exchange or series of exchanges, the basis of property to which subsection (a)(1) applies exceeds the fair market value of such property, then such basis shall be reduced (but not below such fair market value) by the amount (determined as of the date of the exchange) of any liability—

(A) which is assumed by another person as part of the exchange, and

(B) with respect to which subsection (d)(1) does not apply to the assumption.

(2) EXCEPTIONS.— Except as provided by the Secretary, paragraph (1) shall not apply to any liability if—

(A) the trade or business with which the liability is associated is transferred to the person assuming the liability as part of the exchange, or

(B) substantially all of the assets with which the liability is associated are transferred to the person assuming the liability as part of the exchange.

(3) LIABILITY.— For purposes of this subsection, the term 'liability' shall include any fixed or contingent obligation to make payment, without regard to whether the obligation is otherwise taken into account for purposes of this title.

. . .

SEC. 368. DEFINITIONS RELATING TO CORPORATE REORGANIZATIONS.

(a) REORGANIZATION.—

(1) IN GENERAL.—For purposes of parts I and II and this part [Code §301-§368], the term "reorganization" means—

(A) a statutory merger or consolidation;

(B) the acquisition by one corporation, in exchange solely for all or a part of its voting stock (or in exchange solely for all or a part of the voting stock of a corporation which is in control of the acquiring corporation), of stock of another corporation if, immediately after the acquisition, the acquiring corporation has control of such other corporation (whether or not such acquiring corporation had control immediately before the acquisition);

(C) the acquisition by one corporation, in exchange solely for all or a part of its voting stock (or in exchange solely for all or a part of the voting stock of a corporation which is in control of the acquiring corporation), of substantially all of the properties of another corporation, but in determining whether the exchange is solely for stock the assumption by the acquiring corporation of a liability of the other shall be disregarded;

(D) a transfer by a corporation of all or a part of its assets to another corporation if immediately after the transfer the transferor, or one or more of its shareholders (including persons who were shareholders immediately before the transfer), or any combination thereof, is in control of the corporation to which the assets are transferred; but only if, in pursuance of the plan, stock or securities of the corporation to which the assets are transferred are distributed in a transaction which qualifies under section 354, 355, or 356;

(E) a recapitalization;

(F) a mere change in identity, form, or place of organization of one corporation, however effected; or

(G) a transfer by a corporation of all or part of its assets to another corporation in a title 11 or similar case; but only if, in pursuance of the plan, stock or securities of the corporation to which the assets are transferred are distributed in a transaction which qualifies under section 354, 355, or 356.

(2) SPECIAL RULES RELATING TO PARAGRAPH (1).—

(A) REORGANIZATIONS DESCRIBED IN BOTH PARAGRAPH (1) (C) AND PARAGRAPH (1) (D).—If a transaction is described in both paragraph (1) (C) and paragraph (1) (D), then, for purposes of this subchapter (other than for purposes of subparagraph (C)), such transaction shall be treated as described only in paragraph (1) (D).

(B) ADDITIONAL CONSIDERATION IN CERTAIN PARAGRAPH (1) (C) CASES.—If—

(i) one corporation acquires substantially all of the properties of another corporation,

(ii) the acquisition would qualify under paragraph (1) (C) but for the fact that the acquiring corporation exchanges money or other property in addition to voting stock, and

(iii) the acquiring corporation acquires, solely for voting stock described in paragraph (1) (C), property of the other corporation having a fair market value which is at least 80 percent of the fair market value of all of the property of the other corporation,

then such acquisition shall (subject to subparagraph (A) of this paragraph) be treated as qualifying under paragraph (1) (C). Solely for the purpose of determining whether clause (iii) of the preceding sentence applies, the amount of any liability assumed by the acquiring corporation, and the amount of any liability to which any property acquired by the acquiring corporation is subject, shall be treated as money paid for the property.

(C) TRANSFERS OF ASSETS OR STOCK TO SUBSIDIARIES IN CERTAIN PARAGRAPH (1)(A), (1)(B), (1)(C), AND (1)(G) CASES.—A transaction otherwise qualifying under paragraph (1)(A), (1)(B), or (1)(C) shall not be disqualified by reason of the fact that part or all of the assets or stock which were acquired in the transaction are transferred to a corporation controlled by the corporation acquiring such assets or stock. A similar rule shall apply to a transaction otherwise qualifying under paragraph (1)(G) where the requirements of subparagraphs (A) and (B) of section 354(b)(1) are met with respect to the acquisition of the assets.

(D) USE OF STOCK OF CONTROLLING CORPORATION IN PARAGRAPH (1)(A) AND (1)(G) CASES.—The acquisition by one corporation, in exchange for stock of a corporation (referred to in this subparagraph as "controlling corporation") which is in control of the acquiring corporation, of substantially all of the properties of another corporation shall not disqualify a transaction under paragraph (1)(A) or (1)(G) if—

(i) no stock of the acquiring corporation is used in the transaction, and

(ii) in the case of a transaction under paragraph (1)(A), such transaction would have qualified under paragraph (1)(A) had the merger been into the controlling corporation.

(E) STATUTORY MERGER USING VOTING STOCK OF CORPORATION CONTROLLING MERGED CORPORATION.—A transaction otherwise qualifying under paragraph (1)(A) shall not be disqualified by reason of the fact that stock of a corporation (referred to in this subparagraph as the "controlling corporation") which before the merger was in control of the merged corporation is used in the transaction, if—

(i) after the transaction, the corporation surviving the merger holds substantially all of its properties and of the properties of the merged corporation (other than stock of the controlling corporation distributed in the transaction); and

(ii) in the transaction, former shareholders of the surviving corporation exchanged, for an amount of voting stock of the controlling corporation, an amount of stock in the surviving corporation which constitutes control of such corporation.

(F) CERTAIN TRANSACTIONS INVOLVING 2 OR MORE INVESTMENT COMPANIES.—

(i) If immediately before a transaction described in paragraph (1) (other than subparagraph (E) thereof), 2 or more parties to the transaction were investment companies, then the transaction shall not be considered to be a reorganization with respect to any such investment company (and its shareholders and security holders) unless it was a regulated investment company, a real estate investment trust, or a corporation which meets the requirements of clause (ii).

(ii) A corporation meets the requirements of this clause if not more than 25 percent of the value of its total assets is invested in the stock and securities of any one issuer and not more than 50 percent of the value of its total assets is invested in the stock and securities of 5 or fewer issuers. For purposes of this clause, all members of a controlled group of corporations (within the meaning of section 1563(a)) shall be treated as one issuer. For purposes of this clause, a person holding stock in a regulated investment company, a real estate investment trust, or an investment company which meets the requirements of this clause shall, except as provided in regulations, be treated as holding its proportionate share of the assets held by such company or trust.

(iii) For purposes of this subparagraph the term "investment company" means a regulated investment company, a real estate investment trust, or a corporation 50 percent or more of the value of whose total assets are stock and securities and 80 percent or more of the value of whose total assets are assets held for investment. In making the 50-percent and 80-percent determinations under the preceding sentence, stock and securities in any subsidiary corporation shall be disregarded and the parent corporation shall be deemed to own its ratable share of the subsidiary's assets, and a corporation shall be considered a subsidiary if the parent owns 50 percent or more of the combined voting power of all classes of stock entitled to vote, or 50 percent or more of the total value of shares of all classes of stock outstanding.

(iv) For purposes of this subparagraph, in determining total assets there shall be excluded cash and cash items (including receivables), Government securities, and, under regulations prescribed by the Secretary, assets acquired (through incurring indebtedness or otherwise) for purposes of meeting the requirements of clause (ii) or ceasing to be an investment company.

(v) This subparagraph shall not apply if the stock of each investment company is owned substantially by the same persons in the same proportions.

(vi) If an investment company which does not meet the requirements of clause (ii) acquires assets of another corporation, clause (i) shall be applied to such investment company and its shareholders and security holders as though its assets had been acquired by such other corporation. If such investment company acquires stock of another corporation in a reorganization described in section 368(a)(1)(B), clause (i) shall be applied to the shareholders of such investment company as though they they had exchanged with such other corporation all of their stock in such company for stock having a fair market value equal to the fair market value of their stock of such investment company immediately after the exchange. For purposes of section 1001, the deemed acquisition or exchange referred to in the two preceding sentences shall be treated as a sale or exchange of property by the corporation and by the shareholders and security holders to which clause (i) is applied.

(vii) For purposes of clauses (ii) and (iii), the term "securities" includes obligations of State and local governments, commodity futures contracts, shares of regulated investment companies and real estate investment trusts, and other investments constituting a security within the meaning of the Investment Company Act of 1940. . . .

(G) DISTRIBUTION REQUIREMENT FOR PARAGRAPH (1)(C).—

(i) IN GENERAL.—A transaction shall fail to meet the requirements of paragraph (1)(C) unless the acquired corporation distributes the stock, securities, and other properties it receives, as well as its other properties, in pursuance of the plan of reorganization. For purposes of the preceding sentence, if the acquired corporation is liquidated pursuant to the plan of reorganization, any distribution to its creditors in connection with such liquidation shall be treated as pursuant to the plan of reorganization.

(ii) EXCEPTION.—The Secretary may waive the application of clause (i) to any transaction subject to any conditions the Secretary may prescribe.

. . .

(b) PARTY TO A REORGANIZATION.—For purposes of this part [Code §351-§368], the term "a party to a reorganization" includes—

(1) a corporation resulting from a reorganization, and

(2) both corporations, in the case of a reorganization resulting from the acquisition by one corporation of stock or properties of another.

In the case of a reorganization qualifying under paragraph (1)(B) or (1)(C) of subsection (a), if the stock exchanged for the stock or properties is stock of a corporation which is in control of the acquiring corporation, the term "a party to a reorganization" includes the corporation so controlling the acquiring corporation. In the case of a reorganization qualifying under paragraph (1)(A), (1)(B), (1)(C), or (1)(G) of subsection (a) by reason of paragraph (2)(C) of subsection (a), the term "a party to a reorganization" includes the corporation controlling the corporation to which the acquired assets or stock are transferred. In the case of a reorganization qualifying under paragraph (1)(A) or (1)(G) of subsection (a) by reason of paragraph (2)(D) of that subsection, the term "a party to a reorganization" includes the controlling corporation referred to in such paragraph (2)(D). In the case of a reorganization qualifying under subsection (a)(1)(A) by reason of subsection (a)(2)(E), the term "party to a reorganization" includes the controlling corporation referred to in subsection (a)(2)(E).

(c) CONTROL DEFINED.—For purposes of part I (other than section 304), part II, this part, and part V [Code §301–§384, except §304], the term "control" means the ownership of stock possessing at least 80 percent of the total combined voting power of all classes of stock entitled to vote and at least 80 percent of the total number of shares of all other classes of stock of the corporation.

. . .

SEC. 382. LIMITATION ON NET OPERATING LOSS CARRYFORWARDS AND CERTAIN BUILT-IN LOSSES FOLLOWING OWNERSHIP CHANGE.

(a) GENERAL RULE.—The amount of the taxable income of any new loss corporation for any post-change year which may be offset by pre-change losses shall not exceed the section 382 limitation for such year.

(b) SECTION 382 LIMITATION.—For purposes of this section—

(1) IN GENERAL.—Except as otherwise provided in this section, the section 382 limitation for any post-change year is an amount equal to—

(A) the value of the old loss corporation, multiplied by

(B) the long-term tax-exempt rate.

(2) CARRYFORWARD OF UNUSED LIMITATION.—If the section 382 limitation for any post-change year exceeds the taxable income of the new loss corporation for such year which was offset by pre-change losses, the section 382 limitation for the next post-change year shall be increased by the amount of such excess.

(3) SPECIAL RULE FOR POST-CHANGE YEAR WHICH INCLUDES CHANGE DATE.—In the case of any post-change year which includes the change date—

(A) LIMITATION DOES NOT APPLY TO TAXABLE INCOME BEFORE CHANGE.—Subsection (a) shall not apply to the portion of the taxable income for such year which is allocable to the period in such year on or before the change date. Except as provided in subsection (h)(5) and in regulations, taxable income shall be allocated ratably to each day in the year.

(B) LIMITATION FOR PERIOD AFTER CHANGE.—For purposes of applying the limitation of subsection (a) to the remainder of the taxable income for such year, the section 382 limitation shall be an amount which bears the same ratio to such limitation (determined without regard to this paragraph) as—

(i) the number of days in such year after the change date, bears to

(ii) the total number of days in such year.

(c) CARRYFORWARDS DISALLOWED IF CONTINUITY OF BUSINESS REQUIREMENTS NOT MET.—

(1) IN GENERAL.—Except as provided in paragraph (2), if the new loss corporation does not continue the business enterprise of the old loss corporation at all times during the 2-year period beginning on the change date, the section 382 limitation for any post-change year shall be zero.

(2) EXCEPTION FOR CERTAIN GAINS.—The section 382 limitation for any post-change year shall not be less than the sum of—

    (A) any increase in such limitation under—

        (i) subsection (h)(1)(A) for recognized built-in gains for such year, and

        (ii) subsection (h)(1)(C) for gain recognized by reason of an election under section 338, plus

    (B) any increase in such limitation under subsection (b)(2) for amounts described in subparagraph (A) which are carried forward to such year.

(d) PRE-CHANGE LOSS AND POST-CHANGE YEAR.—For purposes of this section—

    (1) PRE-CHANGE LOSS.—The term "pre-change loss" means—

        (A) any net operating loss carryforward of the old loss corporation to the taxable year ending with the ownership change or in which the change date occurs, and

        (B) the net operating loss of the old loss corporation for the taxable year in which the ownership change occurs to the extent such loss is allocable to the period in such year on or before the change date.

Except as provided in subsection (h)(5) and in regulations, the net operating loss shall, for purposes of subparagraph (B), be allocated ratably to each day in the year.

    (2) POST-CHANGE YEAR.—The term "post-change year" means any taxable year ending after the change date.

(e) VALUE OF OLD LOSS CORPORATION.—For purposes of this section—

    (1) IN GENERAL.—Except as otherwise provided in this subsection, the value of the old loss corporation is the value of the stock of such corporation (including any stock described in section 1504(a)(4)) immediately before the ownership change.

    (2) SPECIAL RULE IN THE CASE OF REDEMPTION OR OTHER CORPO-RATE CONTRACTION.—If a redemption or other corporate contraction occurs in connection with an ownership change, the value under paragraph (1) shall be determined after taking such redemption or other corporate contraction into account.

    (3) TREATMENT OF FOREIGN CORPORATIONS.—Except as otherwise provided in regulations, in determining the value of any old loss corporation which is a foreign corporation, there shall be taken into account only items treated as connected with the conduct of a trade or business in the United States.

(f) LONG-TERM TAX-EXEMPT RATE.—For purposes of this section—

    (1) IN GENERAL.—The long-term tax-exempt rate shall be the highest of the adjusted Federal long-term rates in effect for any month in the 3-calendar-month period ending with the calendar month in which the change date occurs.

    (2) ADJUSTED FEDERAL LONG-TERM RATE.—For purposes of paragraph (1), the term "adjusted Federal long-term rate" means the Federal long-term rate determined under section 1274(d), except that—

(A) paragraphs (2) and (3) thereof shall not apply, and

(B) such rate shall be properly adjusted for differences between rates on long-term taxable and tax-exempt obligations.

(g) OWNERSHIP CHANGE.—For purposes of this section—

(1) IN GENERAL.—There is an ownership change if, immediately after any owner shift involving a 5-percent shareholder or any equity structure shift—

(A) the percentage of the stock of the loss corporation owned by 1 or more 5-percent shareholders has increased by more than 50 percentage points, over

(B) the lowest percentage of stock of the loss corporation (or any predecessor corporation) owned by such shareholders at any time during the testing period.

(2) OWNER SHIFT INVOLVING 5-PERCENT SHAREHOLDER.—There is an owner shift involving a 5-percent shareholder if—

(A) there is any change in the respective ownership of stock of a corporation, and

(B) such change affects the percentage of stock of such corporation owned by any person who is a 5-percent shareholder before or after such change.

(3) EQUITY STRUCTURE SHIFT DEFINED.—

(A) IN GENERAL.—The term "equity structure shift" means any reorganization (within the meaning of section 368). Such term shall not include—

(i) any reorganization described in subparagraph (D) or (G) of section 368(a)(1) unless the requirements of section 354(b)(1) are met, and

(ii) any reorganization described in subparagraph (F) of section 368(a)(1).

(B) TAXABLE REORGANIZATION-TYPE TRANSACTIONS, ETC.—To the extent provided in regulations, the term "equity structure shift" includes taxable reorganization-type transactions, public offerings, and similar transactions.

(4) SPECIAL RULES FOR APPLICATION OF SUBSECTION.—

(A) TREATMENT OF LESS THAN 5-PERCENT SHAREHOLDERS.—Except as provided in subparagraphs (B)(i) and (C), in determining whether an ownership change has occurred, all stock owned by shareholders of a corporation who are not 5-percent shareholders of such corporation shall be treated as stock owned by one 5-percent shareholder of such corporation.

(B) COORDINATION WITH EQUITY STRUCTURE SHIFTS.—For purposes of determining whether an equity structure shift (or subsequent transaction) is an ownership change—

(i) LESS THAN 5-PERCENT SHAREHOLDERS.—Subparagraph (A) shall be applied separately with respect to each group of shareholders (immediately before such equity structure shift) of each corporation which was a party to the reorganization involved in such equity structure shift.

(ii) ACQUISITIONS OF STOCK.—Unless a different proportion is established, acquisitions of stock after such equity structure shift shall be treated as being made proportionately from all shareholders immediately before such acquisition.

(C) COORDINATION WITH OTHER OWNER SHIFTS.—Except as provided in regulations, rules similar to the rules of subparagraph (B) shall apply in determining whether there has been an owner shift involving a 5-percent shareholder and whether such shift (or subsequent transaction) results in an ownership change.

(D) TREATMENT OF WORTHLESS STOCK.—If any stock held by a 50-percent shareholder is treated by such shareholder as becoming worthless during any taxable year of such shareholder and such stock is held by such shareholder as of the close of such taxable year, for purposes of determining whether an ownership change occurs after the close of such taxable year, such shareholder—

(i) shall be treated as having acquired such stock on the 1st day of his 1st succeeding taxable year, and

(ii) shall not be treated as having owned such stock during any prior period.

For purposes of the preceding sentence, the term "50-percent shareholder" means any person owning 50 percent or more of the stock of the corporation at any time during the 3-year period ending on the last day of the taxable year with respect to which the stock was so treated.

(h) SPECIAL RULES FOR BUILT-IN GAINS AND LOSSES AND SECTION 338 GAINS.—For purposes of this section—

(1) IN GENERAL.—

(A) NET UNREALIZED BUILT-IN GAIN.—

(i) IN GENERAL.—If the old loss corporation has a net unrealized built-in gain, the section 382 limitation for any recognition period taxable year shall be increased by the recognized built-in gains for such taxable year.

(ii) LIMITATION.—The increase under clause (i) for any recognition period taxable year shall not exceed—

(I) the net unrealized built-in gain, reduced by

(II) recognized built-in gains for prior years ending in the recognition period.

(B) NET UNREALIZED BUILT-IN LOSS.—

(i) IN GENERAL.—If the old loss corporation has a net unrealized built-in loss, the recognized built-in loss for any recognition period taxable year shall be subject to limitation under this section in the same manner as if such loss were a pre-change loss.

(ii) LIMITATION.—Clause (i) shall apply to recognized built-in losses for any recognition period taxable year only to the extent such losses do not exceed—

(I) the net unrealized built-in loss, reduced by

(II) recognized built-in losses for prior taxable years ending in the recognition period.

(C) SPECIAL RULES FOR CERTAIN SECTION 338 GAINS.—If an election under section 338 is made in connection with an ownership change and the net unrealized built-in gain is zero by reason of paragraph (3)(B), then, with respect to such change, the section 382 limitation for the post-change year in which gain is recognized by reason of such election shall be increased by the lesser of—

(i) the recognized built-in gains by reason of such election, or

(ii) the net unrealized built-in gain (determined without regard to paragraph (3)(B)).

(2) RECOGNIZED BUILT-IN GAIN AND LOSS.—

(A) RECOGNIZED BUILT-IN GAIN.—The term "recognized built-in gain" means any gain recognized during the recognition period on the disposition of any asset to the extent the new loss corporation establishes that—

(i) such asset was held by the old loss corporation immediately before the change date, and

(ii) such gain does not exceed the excess of—

(I) the fair market value of such asset on the change date, over

(II) the adjusted basis of such asset on such date.

(B) RECOGNIZED BUILT-IN LOSS.—The term "recognized built-in loss" means any loss recognized during the recognition period on the disposition of any asset except to the extent the new loss corporation establishes that—

(i) such asset was not held by the old loss corporation immediately before the change date, or

(ii) such loss exceeds the excess of—

(I) the adjusted basis of such asset on the change date, over

(II) the fair market value of such asset on such date.

Such term includes any amount allowable as depreciation, amortization, or depletion for any period within the recognition period except to the extent the new loss corporation establishes that the amount so allowable is not attributable to the excess described in clause (ii).

(3) NET UNREALIZED BUILT-IN GAIN AND LOSS DEFINED.—

(A) NET UNREALIZED BUILT-IN GAIN AND LOSS.—

(i) IN GENERAL.—The terms "net unrealized built-in gain" and "net unrealized built-in loss" mean, with respect to any old loss corporation, the amount by which—

(I) the fair market value of the assets of such corporation immediately before an ownership change is more or less, respectively, than

(II) the aggregate adjusted basis of such assets at such time.

(ii) SPECIAL RULE FOR REDEMPTIONS OR OTHER CORPORATE CONTRACTIONS.—If a redemption or other corporate contraction occurs in connection with an ownership change, to the extent provided in regulations, determinations under clause (i) shall be made after taking such redemption or other corporate contraction into account.

(B) THRESHOLD REQUIREMENT.—

(i) IN GENERAL.—If the amount of the net unrealized built-in gain or net unrealized built-in loss (determined without regard to this subparagraph) of any old loss corporation is not greater than the lesser of—

(I) 15 percent of the amount determined for purposes of subparagraph (A)(i)(I), or

(II) $10,000,000,

the net unrealized built-in gain or net unrealized built-in loss shall be zero.

(ii) CASH AND CASH ITEMS NOT TAKEN INTO ACCOUNT.—In computing any net unrealized built-in gain or unrealized built-in loss under clause (i), except as provided in regulations, there shall not be taken into account—

(I) any cash or cash item, or

(II) any marketable security which has a value which does not substantially differ from adjusted basis.

(4) DISALLOWED LOSS ALLOWED AS A CARRYFORWARD.—If a deduction for any portion of a recognized built-in loss is disallowed for any post-change year, such portion—

(A) shall be carried forward to subsequent taxable years under rules similar to the rules for the carrying forward of net operating losses (or to the extent the amount so disallowed is attributable to capital losses, under rules similar to the rules for the carrying forward of net capital losses) but

(B) shall be subject to limitation under this section in the same manner as a pre-change loss.

(5) SPECIAL RULES FOR POST-CHANGE YEAR WHICH INCLUDES CHANGE DATE.—For purposes of subsection (b)(3)—

(A) in applying subparagraph (A) thereof, taxable income shall be computed without regard to recognized built-in gains to the extent such gains increased the section 382 limitation for the year (or recognized built-in losses to the extent such losses are treated as pre-change losses), and gain described in paragraph (1)(C), for the year, and

(B) in applying subparagraph (B) thereof, the section 382 limitation shall be computed without regard to recognized built-in gains, and gain described in paragraph (1)(C), for the year.

(6) TREATMENT OF CERTAIN BUILT-IN ITEMS.—

(A) INCOME ITEMS.—Any item of income which is properly taken into account during the recognition period but which is attributable to periods before the change date shall be treated as a recognized built-in gain for the taxable year in which it is properly taken into account.

(B) DEDUCTION ITEMS.—Any amount which is allowable as a deduction during the recognition period (determined without regard to any carryover) but which is attributable to periods before the change date shall be treated as a recognized built-in loss for the taxable year for which it is allowable as a deduction.

(C) ADJUSTMENTS.—The amount of the net unrealized built-in gain or loss shall be properly adjusted for amounts which would be treated as recognized built-in gains or losses under this paragraph if such amounts were properly taken into account (or allowable as a deduction) during the recognition period.

(7) RECOGNITION PERIOD, ETC.—

(A) RECOGNITION PERIOD.—The term "recognition period" means, with respect to any ownership change, the 5-year period beginning on the change date.

(B) RECOGNITION PERIOD TAXABLE YEAR.—The term "recognition period taxable year" means any taxable year any portion of which is in the recognition period.

(8) DETERMINATION OF FAIR MARKET VALUE IN CERTAIN CASES.—If 80 percent or more in value of the stock of a corporation is acquired in 1 transaction (or in a series of related transactions during any 12-month period), for purposes of determining the net unrealized built-in loss, the fair market value of the assets of such corporation shall not exceed the grossed up amount paid for such stock properly adjusted for indebtedness of the corporation and other relevant items.

(9) TAX-FREE EXCHANGES OR TRANSFERS.—The Secretary shall prescribe such regulations as may be necessary to carry out the purposes of this subsection where property held on the change date was acquired (or is subsequently transferred) in a transaction where gain or loss is not recognized (in whole or in part).

(i) TESTING PERIOD.—For purposes of this section—

(1) 3-YEAR PERIOD.—Except as otherwise provided in this section, the testing period is the 3-year period ending on the day of any owner shift involving a 5-percent shareholder or equity structure shift.

(2) SHORTER PERIOD WHERE THERE HAS BEEN RECENT OWNERSHIP CHANGE.—If there has been an ownership change under this section, the testing period for determining whether a 2nd ownership change has occurred shall not begin before the 1st day following the change date for such earlier ownership change.

(3) SHORTER PERIOD WHERE ALL LOSSES ARISE AFTER 3-YEAR PERIOD BEGINS.—The testing period shall not begin before the earlier of the 1st day of the 1st taxable year from which there is a carryforward of a loss or of an excess credit to the 1st post-change year or the taxable year in which the transaction being tested occurs. Except as provided in regulations, this paragraph shall not apply to any loss corporation which has a net unrealized built-in loss (determined after application of subsection (h)(3)(B)).

(j) CHANGE DATE.—For purposes of this section, the change date is—

(1) in the case where the last component of an ownership change is an owner shift involving a 5-percent shareholder, the date on which such shift occurs, and

(2) in the case where the last component of an ownership change is an equity structure shift, the date of the reorganization.

(k) DEFINITIONS AND SPECIAL RULES.—For purposes of this section—

(1) LOSS CORPORATION.—The term "loss corporation" means a corporation entitled to use a net operating loss carryover or having a net operating loss for the taxable year in which the ownership change occurs. Except to the extent provided in regulations, such term includes any corporation with a net unrealized built-in loss.

(2) OLD LOSS CORPORATION.—The term "old loss corporation" means any corporation—

(A) with respect to which there is an ownership change, and

(B) which (before the ownership change) was a loss corporation.

(3) NEW LOSS CORPORATION.—The term "new loss corporation" means a corporation which (after an ownership change) is a loss corporation. Nothing in this section shall be treated as implying that the same corporation may not be both the old loss corporation and the new loss corporation.

(4) TAXABLE INCOME.—Taxable income shall be computed with the modifications set forth in section 172(d).

(5) VALUE.—The term "value" means fair market value.

(6) RULES RELATING TO STOCK.—

(A) PREFERRED STOCK.—Except as provided in regulations and subsection (e), the term "stock" means stock other than stock described in section 1504(a)(4).

(B) TREATMENT OF CERTAIN RIGHTS, ETC.—The Secretary shall prescribe such regulations as may be necessary—

(i) to treat warrants, options, contracts to acquire stock, convertible debt interests, and other similar interests as stock, and

(ii) to treat stock as not stock,

(C) DETERMINATIONS ON BASIS OF VALUE.—Determinations of the percentage of stock of any corporation held by any person shall be made on the basis of value.

(7) 5-PERCENT SHAREHOLDER.—The term "5-percent shareholder" means any person holding 5 percent or more of the stock of the corporation at any time during the testing period.

(*l*) CERTAIN ADDITIONAL OPERATING RULES.—For purposes of this section—

(1) CERTAIN CAPITAL CONTRIBUTIONS NOT TAKEN INTO ACCOUNT.—

(A) IN GENERAL.—Any capital contribution received by an old loss corporation as part of a plan a principal purpose of which is to avoid or increase any limitation under this section shall not be taken into account for purposes of this section.

(B) CERTAIN CONTRIBUTIONS TREATED AS PART OF PLAN.—For purposes of subparagraph (A), any capital contribution made during the 2-year period ending on the change date shall, except as provided in regulations, be treated as part of a plan described in subparagraph (A).

. . .

(3) OPERATING RULES RELATING TO OWNERSHIP OF STOCK.—

(A) CONSTRUCTIVE OWNERSHIP.—Section 318 (relating to constructive ownership of stock) shall apply in determining ownership of stock, except that—

(i) paragraphs (1) and (5)(B) of section 318(a) shall not apply and an individual and all members of his family described in paragraph (1) of section 318(a) shall be treated as 1 individual for purposes of applying this section,

(ii) paragraph (2) of section 318(a) shall be applied—

(I) without regard to the 50-percent limitation contained in subparagraph (C) thereof, and

(II) except as provided in regulations, by treating stock attributed thereunder as no longer being held by the entity from which attributed,

(iii) paragraph (3) of section 318(a) shall be applied only to the extent provided in regulations,

(iv) except to the extent provided in regulations, an option to acquire stock shall be treated as exercised if such exercise results in an ownership change, and

(v) in attributing stock from an entity under paragraph (2) of section 318(a), there shall not be taken into account—

(I) in the case of attribution from a corporation, stock which is not treated as stock for purposes of this section, or

(II) in the case of attribution from another entity, an interest in such entity similar to stock described in subclause (I).

A rule similar to the rule of clause (iv) shall apply in the case of any contingent purchase, warrant, convertible debt, put, stock subject to a risk of forfeiture, contract to acquire stock, or similar interests.

(B) STOCK ACQUIRED BY REASON OF DEATH, GIFT, DIVORCE, SEPARATION, ETC.—If—

(i) the basis of any stock in the hands of any person is determined—

(I) under section 1014 (relating to property acquired from a decedent),

(II) section 1015 (relating to property acquired by a gift or transfer in trust), or

(III) section 1041(b)(2) (relating to transfers of property between spouses or incident to divorce),

(ii) stock is received by any person in satisfaction of a right to receive a pecuniary bequest, or

(iii) stock is acquired by a person pursuant to any divorce or separation instrument (within the meaning of section 71(b)(2)),

such person shall be treated as owning such stock during the period such stock was owned by the person from whom it was acquired.

(C) CERTAIN CHANGES IN PERCENTAGE OWNERSHIP WHICH ARE ATTRIBUTABLE TO FLUCTUATIONS IN VALUE NOT TAKEN INTO ACCOUNT.—Except as provided in regulations, any change in proportionate ownership which is attributable solely to fluctuations in the relative fair market values of different classes of stock shall not be taken into account.

(4) REDUCTION IN VALUE WHERE SUBSTANTIAL NONBUSINESS ASSETS.—

(A) IN GENERAL.—If, immediately after an ownership change, the new loss corporation has substantial nonbusiness assets, the value of the old loss corporation shall be reduced by the excess (if any) of

(i) the fair market value of the nonbusiness assets of the old loss corporation, over

(ii) the nonbusiness asset share of indebtedness for which such corporation is liable.

(B) CORPORATION HAVING SUBSTANTIAL NONBUSINESS ASSETS.—For purposes of subparagraph (A)—

(i) IN GENERAL.—The old loss corporation shall be treated as having substantial nonbusiness assets if at least 1/3 of the value of the total assets of such corporation consists of nonbusiness assets.

(ii) EXCEPTION FOR CERTAIN INVESTMENT ENTITIES. . . .

. . .

(C) NONBUSINESS ASSETS.—For purposes of this paragraph, the term "nonbusiness assets" means assets held for investment.

(D) NONBUSINESS ASSET SHARE.—For purposes of this paragraph, the nonbusiness asset share of the indebtedness of the corporation is an amount which bears the same ratio to such indebtedness as—

(i) the fair market value of the nonbusiness assets of the corporation, bears to

(ii) the fair market value of all assets of such corporation.

(E) TREATMENT OF SUBSIDIARIES.—For purposes of this paragraph, stock and securities in any subsidiary corporation shall be disregarded and the parent corporation shall be deemed to own its ratable share of the subsidiary's assets. For purposes of the preceding sentence, a corporation shall be treated as a subsidiary if the parent owns 50 percent or more of the combined voting power of all classes of stock entitled to vote, and 50 percent or more of the total value of shares of all classes of stock.

(5) TITLE 11 OR SIMILAR CASE.—

(A) IN GENERAL.—Subsection (a) shall not apply to any ownership change if—

(i) the old loss corporation is (immediately before such ownership change) under the jurisdiction of the court in a title 11 or similar case, and

(ii) the shareholders and creditors of the old loss corporation (determined immediately before such ownership change) own (after such ownership change and as a result of being shareholders or creditors immediately before such change) stock of the new loss corporation (or stock of a controlling corporation if also in bankruptcy) which meets the requirements of section 1504(a)(2) (determined by substituting "50 percent" for "80 percent" each place it appears).

(B) REDUCTION FOR INTEREST PAYMENTS TO CREDITORS BECOMING SHAREHOLDERS.—In any case to which subparagraph (A) applies, the pre-change losses and excess credits (within the meaning of section 383(a)(2)) which may be carried to a post-change year shall be computed as if no deduction was allowable under this chapter for the interest paid or accrued by the old loss corporation on indebtedness which was converted into stock pursuant to title 11 or similar case during—

(i) any taxable year ending during the 3-year period preceding the taxable year in which the ownership change occurs, and

(ii) the period of the taxable year in which ownership change occurs on or before the change date.

(C) COORDINATION WITH SECTION 108.—In applying section 108(e)(8) to any case to which subparagraph (A) applies, there shall not be taken into account any indebtedness for interest described in subparagraph (B).

(D) SECTION 382 LIMITATION ZERO IF ANOTHER CHANGE WITHIN 2 YEARS.—If, during the 2-year period immediately following an ownership change to which this paragraph applies, an ownership change of the new loss corporation occurs, this paragraph shall not apply and the section 382 limitation with respect to the 2nd ownership change for any post-change year ending after the change date of the 2nd ownership change shall be zero.

(E) ONLY CERTAIN STOCK TAKEN INTO ACCOUNT.—For purposes of subparagraph (A)(ii), stock transferred to a creditor shall be taken into account only to the extent such stock is transferred in satisfaction of indebtedness and only if such indebtedness—

(i) was held by the creditor at least 18 months before the date of the filing of the title 11 or similar case, or

(ii) arose in the ordinary course of the trade or business of the old loss corporation and is held by the person who at all times held the beneficial interest in such indebtedness.

. . .

(G) TITLE 11 OR SIMILAR CASE.—For purposes of this paragraph, the term "title 11 or similar case" has the meaning given such term by section 368(a)(3)(A).

(H) ELECTION NOT TO HAVE PARAGRAPH APPLY.—A new loss corporation may elect, subject to such terms and conditions as the Secretary may prescribe, not to have the provisions of this paragraph apply.

(6) SPECIAL RULE FOR INSOLVENCY TRANSACTIONS.—If paragraph (5) does not apply to any reorganization described in subparagraph (G) of section 368(a)(1) or any exchange of debt for stock in a title 11 or similar case (as defined in section 368(a)(3)(A)), the value under subsection (e) shall reflect the increase (if any) in value of the old loss corporation resulting from any surrender or cancellation of creditors' claims in the transaction.

(7) COORDINATION WITH ALTERNATIVE MINIMUM TAX.—The Secretary shall by regulation provide for the application of this section to the alternative tax net operating loss deduction under section 56(d).

(8) PREDECESSOR AND SUCCESSOR ENTITIES.—Except as provided in regulations, any entity and any predecessor or successor entities of such entity shall be treated as 1 entity.

(m) REGULATIONS.—The Secretary shall prescribe such regulations as may be necessary or appropriate to carry out the purposes of this section and section 383, including (but not limited to) regulations—

(1) providing for the application of this section and section 383 where an ownership change with respect to the old loss corporation is followed by an ownership change with respect to the new loss corporation, and

(2) providing for the application of this section and section 383 in the case of a short taxable year,

(3) providing for such adjustments to the application of this section and section 383 as is necessary to prevent the avoidance of the purposes of this section and section 383, including the avoidance of such purposes through the use of related persons, pass-thru entities, or other intermediaries,

(4) providing for the application of subsection (g)(4) where there is only 1 corporation involved, and

(5) providing, in the case of any group of corporations described in section 1563(a) (determined by substituting "50 percent" for "80 percent" each place it appears and determined without regard to paragraph (4) thereof), appropriate adjustments to value, built-in gain or loss, and other items so that items are not omitted or taken into account more than once.

SEC. 384. LIMITATION ON USE OF PREACQUISITION LOSSES TO OFFSET BUILT-IN GAINS.

(a) GENERAL RULE.—If—

(1)(A) a corporation acquires directly (or through 1 or more other corporations) control of another corporation, or

(B) the assets of a corporation are acquired by another corporation in a reorganization described in subparagraph (A), (C), or (D) of section 368(a)(1), and

(2) either of such corporations is a gain corporation,

income for any recognition period taxable year (to the extent attributable to recognized built-in gains) shall not be offset by any preacquisition loss (other than a preacquisition loss of the gain corporation).

(b) EXCEPTION WHERE CORPORATIONS UNDER COMMON CONTROL.—

(1) IN GENERAL.—Subsection (a) shall not apply to the preacquisition loss of any corporation if such corporation and the gain corporation were members of the same controlled group at all times during the 5-year period ending on the acquisition date.

(2) CONTROLLED GROUP.—For purposes of this subsection, the term "controlled group" means a controlled group of corporations (as defined in section 1563(a)); except that—

(A) "more than 50 percent" shall be substituted for "at least 80 percent" each place it appears,

(B) the ownership requirements of section 1563(a) must be met both with respect to voting power and value, and

(C) the determination shall be made without regard to subsection (a)(4) of section 1563.

(3) SHORTER PERIOD WHERE CORPORATIONS NOT IN EXISTENCE FOR 5 YEARS.—If either of the corporations referred to in paragraph (1) was

not in existence throughout the 5-year period referred to in paragraph (1), the period during which such corporation was in existence (or if both, the shorter of such periods) shall be substituted for such 5-year period.

(c) DEFINITIONS.—For purposes of this section—

(1) RECOGNIZED BUILT-IN GAIN.—

(A) IN GENERAL.—The term "recognized built-in gain" means any gain recognized during the recognition period on the disposition of any asset except to the extent the gain corporation (or, in any case described in subsection (a)(1)(B), the acquiring corporation) establishes that—

(i) such asset was not held by the gain corporation on the acquisition date, or

(ii) such gain exceeds the excess (if any) of—

(I) the fair market value of such asset on the acquisition date, over

(II) the adjusted basis of such asset on such date.

(B) TREATMENT OF CERTAIN INCOME ITEMS.—Any item of income which is properly taken into account for any recognition period taxable year but which is attributable to periods before the acquisition date shall be treated as a recognized built-in gain for the taxable year in which it is properly taken into account and shall be taken into account in determining the amount of the net unrealized built-in gain.

(C) LIMITATION.—The amount of the recognized built-in gains for any recognition period taxable year shall not exceed—

(i) the net unrealized built-in gain, reduced by

(ii) the recognized built-in gains for prior years ending in the recognition period which (but for this section) would have been offset by preacquisition losses.

(2) ACQUISITION DATE.—The term "acquisition date" means—

(A) in any case described in subsection (a)(1)(A), the date on which the acquisition of control occurs, or

(B) in any case described in subsection (a)(1)(B), the date of the transfer in the reorganization.

(3) PREACQUISITION LOSS.—

(A) IN GENERAL.—The term "preacquisition loss" means—

(i) any net operating loss carryforward to the taxable year in which the acquisition date occurs, and

(ii) any net operating loss for the taxable year in which the acquisition date occurs to the extent such loss is allocable to the period in such year on or before the acquisition date.

Except as provided in regulations, the net operating loss shall, for purposes of clause (ii), be allocated ratably to each day in the year.

(B) TREATMENT OF RECOGNIZED BUILT-IN LOSS.—In the case of a corporation with a net unrealized built-in loss, the term "preacquisition loss" includes any recognized built-in loss.

(4) GAIN CORPORATION.—The term "gain corporation" means any corporation with a net unrealized built-in gain.

(5) CONTROL.—The term "control" means ownership of stock in a corporation which meets the requirements of section 1504(a)(2).

(6) TREATMENT OF MEMBERS OF SAME GROUP.—Except as provided in regulations and except for purposes of subsection (b), all corporations which are members of the same affiliated group immediately before the acquisition date shall be treated as 1 corporation. To the extent provided in regulations, section 1504 shall be applied without regard to subsection (b) thereof for purposes of the preceding sentence.

(7) TREATMENT OF PREDECESSORS AND SUCCESSORS.—Any reference in this section to a corporation shall include a reference to any predecessor or successor thereof.

(8) OTHER DEFINITIONS.—Except as provided in regulations, the terms "net unrealized built-in gain," "net unrealized built-in loss," "recognized built-in loss," "recognition period," and "recognition period taxable year," have the same respective meanings as when used in section 382(h), except that the acquisition date shall be taken into account in lieu of the change date.

(d) LIMITATION ALSO TO APPLY TO EXCESS CREDITS OR NET CAPITAL LOSSES.—Rules similar to the rules of subsection (a) shall also apply in the case of any excess credit (as defined in section 383(a)(2)) or net capital loss.

. . .

(f) REGULATIONS.—The Secretary shall prescribe such regulations as may be necessary to carry out the purposes of this section, including regulations to ensure that the purposes of this section may not be circumvented through—

(1) the use of any provision of law or regulations (including subchapter K of this chapter), or

(2) contributions of property to a corporation.

SEC. 385. TREATMENT OF CERTAIN INTERESTS IN CORPORATIONS AS STOCK OR INDEBTEDNESS.

(a) AUTHORITY TO PRESCRIBE REGULATIONS.—The Secretary is authorized to prescribe such regulations as may be necessary or appropriate to determine whether an interest in a corporation is to be treated for purposes of this title as stock or indebtedness (or as in part stock and in part indebtedness).

(b) FACTORS.—The regulations prescribed under this section shall set forth factors which are to be taken into account in determining with respect to a particular factual situation whether a debtor-creditor relationship exists or a corporation-shareholder relationship exists. The factors so set forth in the regulations may include among other factors:

(1) whether there is a written unconditional promise to pay on demand or on a specified date a sum certain in money in return for an adequate consideration in money or money's worth, and to pay a fixed rate of interest,

(2) whether there is subordination to or preference over any indebtedness of the corporation,

(3) the ratio of debt to equity of the corporation,

(4) whether there is convertibility into the stock of the corporation, and

(5) the relationship between holdings of stock in the corporation and holdings of the interest in question.

(c) EFFECT OF CLASSIFICATION BY ISSUER.—

(1) IN GENERAL.—The characterization (as of the time of issuance) by the issuer as to whether an interest in a corporation is stock or indebtedness shall be binding on such issuer and on all holders of such interest (but shall not be binding on the Secretary).

(2) NOTIFICATION OF INCONSISTENT TREATMENT.—Except as provided in regulations, paragraph (1) shall not apply to any holder of an interest if such holder on his return discloses that he is treating such interest in a manner inconsistent with the characterization referred to in paragraph (1).

(3) REGULATIONS.—The Secretary is authorized to require such information as the Secretary determines to be necessary to carry out the provisions of this subsection.

SEC. 421.   GENERAL RULES.

(a) EFFECT OF QUALIFYING TRANSFER.—If a share of stock is transferred to an individual in a transfer in respect of which the requirements of section 422(a) or 423(a) are met—

(1) no income shall result at the time of the transfer of such share to the individual upon his exercise of the option with respect to such share;

(2) no deduction under section 162 (relating to trade or business expenses) shall be allowable at any time to the employer corporation, a parent or subsidiary corporation of such corporation, or a corporation issuing or assuming a stock option in a transaction to which section 424(a) applies, with respect to the share so transferred; and

(3) no amount other than the price paid under the option shall be considered as received by any of such corporations for the share so transferred.

(b) EFFECT OF DISQUALIFYING DISPOSITION.—If the transfer of a share of stock to an individual pursuant to his exercise of an option would otherwise meet the requirements of section 422(a) or 423(a) except that there is a failure to meet any of the holding period requirements of section 422(a)(1) or 423(a)(1), then any increase in the income of such individual or deduction from the income of his employer corporation for the taxable year in which such exercise occurred attributable to such disposition, shall be treated as an increase in income or a deduction from income in the taxable year of such individual or of such employer corporation in which such disposition occurred.

. . .

SEC. 422.   INCENTIVE STOCK OPTIONS.

(a) IN GENERAL.—Section 421(a) shall apply with respect to the transfer of a share of stock to an individual pursuant to his exercise of an incentive stock option if—

(1) no disposition of such share is made by him within 2 years from the date of the granting of the option nor within 1 year after the transfer of such share to him, and

(2) at all times during the period beginning on the date of the granting of the option and ending on the day 3 months before the date of such exercise, such individual was an employee of either the corporation granting such option, a parent or subsidiary corporation of such corporation, or a corporation or a parent or subsidiary corporation of such corporation issuing or assuming a stock option in a transaction to which section 424(a) applies.

(b) INCENTIVE STOCK OPTION.—For purposes of this part [Code §421-§424], the term "incentive stock option" means an option granted to an individual for any reason connected with his employment by a corporation, if granted by the employer corporation or its parent or subsidiary corporation, to purchase stock of any of such corporations, but only if—

(1) the option is granted pursuant to a plan which includes the aggregate number of shares which may be issued under options and the employees (or class of employees) eligible to receive options, and which is approved by the stockholders of the granting corporation within 12 months before or after the date such plan is adopted;

(2) such option is granted within 10 years from the date such plan is adopted, or the date such plan is approved by the stockholders, whichever is earlier;

(3) such option by its terms is not exercisable after the expiration of 10 years from the date such option is granted;

(4) the option price is not less than the fair market value of the stock at the time such option is granted;

(5) such option by its terms is not transferable by such individual otherwise than by will or the laws of descent and distribution, and is exercisable, during his lifetime, only by him; and

(6) such individual, at the time the option is granted, does not own stock possessing more than 10 percent of the total combined voting power of all classes of stock of the employer corporation or of its parent or subsidiary corporation.

Such term shall not include any option if (as of the time the option is granted) the terms of such option provide that it will not be treated as an incentive stock option.

(c) SPECIAL RULES.—

(1) GOOD FAITH EFFORTS TO VALUE STOCK.—If a share of stock is transferred pursuant to the exercise by an individual of an option which would fail to qualify as an incentive stock option under subsection (b) because there was a failure in an attempt, made in good faith, to meet the requirement of subsection (b)(4), the requirement of subsection (b)(4) shall be considered to have been met. To the extent provided in regulations by the Secretary, a similar rule shall apply for purposes of subsection (d).

(2) CERTAIN DISQUALIFYING DISPOSITIONS WHERE AMOUNT REAL-IZED IS LESS THAN VALUE AT EXERCISE.—If—

(A) an individual who has acquired a share of stock by the exercise of an incentive stock option makes a disposition of such share within either of the periods described in subsection (a)(1), and

(B) such disposition is a sale or exchange with respect to which a loss (if sustained) would be recognized to such individual,

then the amount which is includible in the gross income of such individual, and the amount which is deductible from the income of his employer corporation, as compensation attributable to the exercise of such option shall not exceed the excess (if any) of the amount realized on such sale or exchange over the adjusted basis of such share.

. . .

(4) PERMISSIBLE PROVISIONS.—An option which meets the requirements of subsection (b) shall be treated as an incentive stock option even if—

(A) the employee may pay for the stock with stock of the corporation granting the option,

(B) the employee has a right to receive property at the time of exercise of the option, or

(C) the option is subject to any condition not inconsistent with the provisions of subsection (b).

Subparagraph (B) shall apply to a transfer of property (other than cash) only if section 83 applies to the property so transferred.

(5) 10-PERCENT SHAREHOLDER RULE.—Subsection (b)(6) shall not apply if at the time such option is granted the option price is at least 110 percent of the fair market value of the stock subject to the option and such option by its terms is not exercisable after the expiration of 5 years from the date such option is granted.

(6) SPECIAL RULE WHEN DISABLED.—For purposes of subsection (a)(2), in the case of an employee who is disabled (within the meaning of section 22(e)(3)), the 3-month period of subsection (a)(2) shall be 1 year.

(7) FAIR MARKET VALUE.—For purposes of this section, the fair market value of stock shall be determined without regard to any restriction other than a restriction which, by its terms, will never lapse.

(d) $100,000 PER YEAR LIMITATION.—

(1) IN GENERAL.—To the extent that the aggregate fair market value of stock with respect to which incentive stock options (determined without regard to this subsection) are exercisable for the 1st time by any individual during any calendar year (under all plans of the individual's employer corporation and its parent and subsidiary corporations) exceeds $100,000, such options shall be treated as options which are not incentive stock options.

(2) ORDERING RULE.—Paragraph (1) shall be applied by taking options into account in the order in which they were granted.

(3) DETERMINATION OF FAIR MARKET VALUE.—For purposes of paragraph (1), the fair market value of any stock shall be determined as of the time the option with respect to such stock is granted.

SEC. 424.   DEFINITIONS AND SPECIAL RULES.

(a) CORPORATE REORGANIZATIONS, LIQUIDATIONS, ETC.—For purposes of this part [Code §421-§424], the term "issuing or assuming a stock option in a transaction to which section 424(a) applies" means a substitution of a new option for the old option, or an assumption of the old option, by an employer corporation, or a parent or subsidiary of such corporation, by reason of a corporate merger, consolidation, acquisition of property or stock, separation, reorganization, or liquidation, if—

(1) the excess of the aggregate fair market value of the shares subject to the option immediately after the substitution or assumption over the aggregate option price of such shares is not more than the excess of the aggregate fair market value of all shares subject to the option immediately before such substitution or assumption over the aggregate option price of such shares, and

(2) the new option or the assumption of the old option does not give the employee additional benefits which he did not have under the old option.
For purposes of this subsection, the parent-subsidiary relationship shall be determined at the time of any such transaction under this subsection.

(b) ACQUISITION OF NEW STOCK.—For purposes of this part [Code §421-§424], if stock is received by an individual in a distribution to which section 305, 354, 355, 356, or 1036 (or so much of section 1031 as relates to section 1036) applies, and such distribution was made with respect to stock transferred to him upon his exercise of the option, such stock shall be considered as having been transferred to him on his exercise of such option. A similar rule shall be applied in the case of a series of such distributions.

(c) DISPOSITION.—

(1) IN GENERAL.—Except as provided in paragraphs (2), (3), and (4), for purposes of this part [Code §421-§424], the term "disposition" includes a sale, exchange, gift, or a transfer of legal title, but does not include—

(A) a transfer from a decedent to an estate or a transfer by bequest or inheritance;

(B) an exchange to which section 354, 355, 356, or 1036 (or so much of section 1031 as relates to section 1036) applies; or

(C) a mere pledge or hypothecation.

(2) JOINT TENANCY.—The acquisition of a share of stock in the name of the employee and another jointly with the right of survivorship or a subsequent transfer of a share of stock into such joint ownership shall not be deemed a disposition, but a termination of such joint tenancy (except to the extent such employee acquires ownership of such stock) shall be treated as a disposition by him occurring at the time such joint tenancy is terminated.

(3) SPECIAL RULE WHERE INCENTIVE STOCK IS ACQUIRED THROUGH USE OF OTHER STATUTORY OPTION STOCK.—

(A) NONRECOGNITION SECTIONS NOT TO APPLY.—If—

(i) there is a transfer of statutory option stock in connection with the exercise of any incentive stock option, and

(ii) the applicable holding period requirements (under section 422(a)(1) or 423(a)(1) are not met before such transfer, then no section referred to in subparagraph (B) of paragraph (1) shall apply to such transfer.

(B) STATUTORY OPTION STOCK.—For purpose of subparagraph (A), the term "statutory option stock" means any stock acquired through the exercise of an incentive stock option or an option granted under an employee stock purchase plan.

(4) TRANSFERS BETWEEN SPOUSES OR INCIDENT TO DIVORCE.—In the case of any transfer described in subsection (a) of section 1041—

(A) such transfer shall not be treated as a disposition for purposes of this part [Code §421-§424], and

(B) the same tax treatment under this part [Code §421-§424] with respect to the transferred property shall apply to the transferee as would have applied to the transferor.

(d) ATTRIBUTION OF STOCK OWNERSHIP.—For purposes of this part [Code §421-§424], in applying the percentage limitations of sections 422(b)(6) and 423(b)(3)—

(1) the individual with respect to whom such limitation is being determined shall be considered as owning the stock owned, directly or indirectly, by or for his brothers and sisters (whether by the whole or half blood), spouse, ancestors, and lineal descendants; and

(2) stock owned, directly or indirectly, by or for a corporation, partnership, estate, or trust, shall be considered as being owned proportionately by or for its shareholders, partners, or beneficiaries.

(e) PARENT CORPORATION.—For purposes of this part [Code §421-§424], the term "parent corporation" means any corporation (other than the employer corporation) in an unbroken chain of corporations ending with the employer corporation if, at the time of the granting of the option, each of the corporations other than the employer corporation owns stock possessing 50 percent or more of the total combined voting power of all classes of stock in one of the other corporations in such chain.

(f) SUBSIDIARY CORPORATION.—For purposes of this part [Code §421-§424], the term "subsidiary corporation" means any corporation (other than the employer corporation) in an unbroken chain of corporations beginning with the employer corporation if, at the time of the granting of the option, each of the corporations other than the last corporation in the unbroken chain owns stock possessing 50 percent or more of the total combined voting power of all classes of stock in one of the other corporations in such chain.

(g) SPECIAL RULE FOR APPLYING SUBSECTIONS (e) AND (f).—In applying subsections (e) and (f) for purposes of section 422(a)(2) and 423(a)(2), there shall be substituted for the term "employer corporation" wherever it appears in subsections (e) and (f) the term "grantor corporation," or the term "corporation issuing or assuming a stock option in a transaction to which section 424(a) applies," as the case may be.

(h) MODIFICATION, EXTENSION, OR RENEWAL OF OPTION.—

(1) IN GENERAL.—For purposes of this part [Code §421-§424], if the terms of any option to purchase stock are modified, extended, or renewed, such modification, extension, or renewal shall be considered as the granting of a new option.

(2) SPECIAL RULE FOR SECTION 423 OPTIONS.—In the case of the transfer of stock pursuant to the exercise of an option to which section 423 applies and which has been so modified, extended, or renewed, the fair market value of such stock at the time of the granting of the option shall be considered as whichever of the following is the highest—

(A) the fair market value of such stock on the date of the original granting of the option,

(B) the fair market value of such stock on the date of the making of such modification, extension, or renewal, or

(C) the fair market value of such stock at the time of the making of any intervening modification, extension, or renewal.

(3) DEFINITION OF MODIFICATION.—The term "modification" means any change in the terms of the option which gives the employee additional benefits under the option, but such term shall not include a change in the terms of the option—

(A) attributable to the issuance or assumption of an option under subsection (a);

(B) to permit the option to qualify under section 423(b)(9); or

(C) in the case of an option not immediately exercisable in full, to accelerate the time at which the option may be exercised.

(i) STOCKHOLDER APPROVAL.—For purposes of this part [Code §421-§424], if the grant of an option is subject to approval by stockholders, the date of grant of the option shall be determined as if the option had not been subject to such approval.

. . .

SEC. 447.   [Definition of Family Corporation for purposes of nonqualified preferred]

. . .

(d)(2)(C) FAMILY CORPORATION.—For purposes of this section, the term "family corporation" means—

(i) any corporation if at least 50 percent of the total combined voting power of all classes of stock entitled to vote, and at least 50 percent of all other classes of stock of the corporation, are owned by members of the same family, and

. . .

(e) MEMBERS OF THE SAME FAMILY.—For purposes of subsection (d)—

(1) the members of the same family are an individual, such individual's brothers and sisters, the brothers and sisters of such individual's parents and grandparents, the ancestors and lineal descendants of any of the foregoing, a spouse of any of the foregoing, and the estate of any of the foregoing,

(2) stock owned, directly or indirectly, by or for a partnership or trust shall be treated as owned proportionately by its partners or beneficiaries, and

(3) if 50 percent or more in value of the stock in a corporation (hereinafter in this paragraph referred to as "first corporation") is owned, directly or through paragraph (2), by or for members of the same family, such members shall be considered as owning each class of stock in a second corporation (or a wholly owned subsidiary of such second corporation) owned, directly or indirectly, by or for the first corporation, in that proportion which the value of the stock in the first corporation which such members so own bears to the value of all the stock in the first corporation.

For purposes of paragraph (1), individuals related by the half blood or by legal adoption shall be treated as if they were related by the whole blood.

SEC. 453. INSTALLMENT METHOD.

(a) GENERAL RULE.—Except as otherwise provided in this section, income from an installment sale shall be taken into account for purposes of this title under the installment method.

(b) INSTALLMENT SALE DEFINED.—For purposes of this section—

(1) IN GENERAL.—The term "installment sale" means a disposition of property where at least 1 payment is to be received after the close of the taxable year in which the disposition occurs.

(2) EXCEPTIONS.—The term "installment sale" does not include—

(A) DEALER DISPOSITIONS.—Any dealer disposition (as defined in subsection (1)).

(B) INVENTORIES OF PERSONAL PROPERTY.—A disposition of personal property of a kind which is required to be included in the inventory of the taxpayer if on hand at the close of the taxable year.

(c) INSTALLMENT METHOD DEFINED.—For purposes of this section, the term "installment method" means a method under which the income recognized for any taxable year from a disposition is that proportion of the payments received in that year which the gross profit (realized or to be realized when payment is completed) bears to the total contract price.

(d) ELECTION OUT.—

(1) IN GENERAL.—Subsection (a)(1) shall not apply to any disposition if the taxpayer elects to have subsection (a)(1) not apply to such disposition.

(2) TIME AND MANNER FOR MAKING ELECTION.—Except as otherwise provided by regulations, an election under paragraph (1) with respect to a disposition may be made only on or before the due date prescribed by law (including extensions) for filing the taxpayer's return of the tax imposed by this chapter for the taxable year in which the disposition occurs. Such an election shall be made in the manner prescribed by regulations.

(3) ELECTION REVOCABLE ONLY WITH CONSENT.—An election under paragraph (1) with respect to any disposition may be revoked only with the consent of the Secretary.

. . .

(f) DEFINITIONS AND SPECIAL RULES.—For purposes of this section—

(1) RELATED PERSON.—Except for purposes of subsections (g) and (h), the term "related person" means—

(A) a person whose stock would be attributed under section 318(a) (other than paragraph (4) thereof) to the person first disposing of the property, or

(B) a person who bears a relationship described in section 267(b) to the person first disposing of the property.

(2) MARKETABLE SECURITIES.—The term "marketable securities" means any security for which, as of the date of the disposition, there was a market on an established securities market or otherwise.

(3) PAYMENT.—Except as provided in paragraph (4), the term "payment" does not include the receipt of evidences of indebtedness of the person acquiring the property (whether or not payment of such indebtedness is guaranteed by another person).

(4) PURCHASER EVIDENCES OF INDEBTEDNESS PAYABLE ON DEMAND OR READILY TRADABLE.—Receipt of a bond or other evidence of indebtedness which—

(A) is payable on demand, or

(B) is issued by a corporation or a government or political subdivision thereof and is readily tradable,

shall be treated as receipt of payment.

(5) READILY TRADABLE DEFINED.—For purposes of paragraph (4), the term "readily tradable" means a bond or other evidence of indebtedness which is issued—

(A) with interest coupons attached or in registered form (other than one in registered form which the taxpayer establishes will not be readily tradable in an established securities market), or

(B) in any other form designed to render such bond or other evidence of indebtedness readily tradable in an established securities market.

(6) LIKE-KIND EXCHANGES.—In the case of any exchange described in section 1031(b)—

(A) the total contract price shall be reduced to take into account the amount of any property permitted to be received in such exchange without recognition of gain,

(B) the gross profit from such exchange shall be reduced to take into account any amount not recognized by reason of section 1031(b), and

(C) the term "payment," when used in any provision of this section other than subsection (b)(1), shall not include any property permitted to be received in such exchange without recognition of gain.

Similar rules shall apply in the case of an exchange which is described in section 356(a) and is not treated as a dividend.

(7) DEPRECIABLE PROPERTY.—The term "depreciable property" means property of a character which (in the hands of the transferee) is subject to the allowance for depreciation provided in section 167.

(8) PAYMENTS TO BE RECEIVED DEFINED.—The term "payments to be received" includes—

(A) the aggregate amount of all payments which are not contingent as to amount, and

(B) the fair market value of any payments which are contingent as to amount.

. . .

(k) CURRENT INCLUSION IN CASE OF REVOLVING CREDIT PLANS, ETC.—In the case of—

. . .

(2) any installment obligation arising out of a sale of—

(A) stock or securities which are traded on an established securities market, or

(B) to the extent provided in regulations, property (other than stock or securities) of a kind regularly traded on an established market,

subsection (a)(1) shall not apply, and, for purposes of this title, all payments to be received shall be treated as received in the year of disposition. The Secretary may provide for the application of this subsection in whole or in part for transactions in which the rules of this subsection otherwise would be avoided through the use of related parties, pass-thru entities, or intermediaries.

. . .

SEC. 453A.   SPECIAL RULES FOR NONDEALERS.

(a) GENERAL RULE.—In the case of an installment obligation to which this section applies—

(1) interest shall be paid on the deferred tax liability with respect to such obligation in the manner provided under subsection (c), and

(2) the pledging rules under subsection (d) shall apply.

(b) INSTALLMENT OBLIGATIONS TO WHICH SECTION APPLIES.—

(1) IN GENERAL.—This section shall apply to any obligation which arises from the disposition of any property under the installment method, but only if the sales price of such property exceeds $150,000.

(2) SPECIAL RULE FOR INTEREST PAYMENTS.—For purposes of subsection (a)(1), this section shall apply to an obligation described in paragraph (1) arising during a taxable year only if—

(A) such obligation is outstanding as of the close of such taxable year, and

(B) the face amount of all such obligations held by the taxpayer which arose during, and are outstanding as of the close of, such taxable year exceeds $5,000,000.

Except as provided in regulations, all persons treated as a single employer under subsection (a) or (b) of section 52 shall be treated as one person for purposes of this paragraph and subsection (c)(4).

. . .

(5) SALES PRICE.—For purposes of paragraph (1), all sales or exchanges which are part of the same transaction (or a series of related transactions) shall be treated as 1 sale or exchange.

(c) INTEREST ON DEFERRED TAX LIABILITY.—

(1) IN GENERAL.—If an obligation to which this section applies is outstanding as of the close of any taxable year, the tax imposed by this chapter for such taxable year shall be increased by the amount of interest determined in the manner provided under paragraph (2).

(2) COMPUTATION OF INTEREST.—For purposes of paragraph (1), the interest for any taxable year shall be an amount equal to the product of—

(A) the applicable percentage of the deferred tax liability with respect to such obligation, multiplied by

(B) the underpayment rate in effect under section 6621(a)(2) for the month with or within which the taxable year ends.

(3) DEFERRED TAX LIABILITY.—For purposes of this section, the term "deferred tax liability" means, with respect to any taxable year, the product of—

(A) the amount of gain with respect to an obligation which has not been recognized as of the close of such taxable year, multiplied by

(B) the maximum rate of tax in effect under section 1 or 11, whichever is appropriate, for such taxable year.

For purposes of applying the preceding sentence with respect to so much of the gain which, when recognized, will be treated as long-term capital gain, the maximum rate on net capital gain under section 1(h) or 1201 (whichever is appropriate) shall be taken into account.

(4) APPLICABLE PERCENTAGE.—For purposes of this subsection, the term "applicable percentage" means, with respect to obligations arising in any taxable year, the percentage determined by dividing—

(A) the portion of the aggregate face amount of such obligations outstanding as of the close of such taxable year in excess of $5,000,000, by

(B) the aggregate face amount of such obligations outstanding as of the close of such taxable year.

(5) TREATMENT AS INTEREST.—Any amount payable under this subsection shall be taken into account in computing the amount of any deduction allowable to the taxpayer for interest paid or accrued during the taxable year.

(6) REGULATIONS.—The Secretary shall prescribe such regulations as may be necessary to carry out the provisions of this subsection including regulations providing for the application of this subsection in the case of contingent payments, short taxable years, and pass-thru entities.

(d) PLEDGES, ETC., OF INSTALLMENT OBLIGATIONS.—

(1) IN GENERAL.—For purposes of section 453, if any indebtedness (hereinafter in this subsection referred to as "secured indebtedness") is secured by an

installment obligation to which this section applies, the net proceeds of the secured indebtedness shall be treated as a payment received on such installment obligation as of the later of—

(A) the time the indebtedness becomes secured indebtedness, or

(B) the time the proceeds of such indebtedness are received by the taxpayer.

(2) LIMITATION BASED ON TOTAL CONTRACT PRICE.—The amount treated as received under paragraph (1) by reason of any secured indebtedness shall not exceed the excess (if any) of—

(A) the total contract price, over

(B) any portion of the total contract price received under the contract before the later of the times referred to in subparagraph (A) or (B) of paragraph (1) (including amounts previously treated as received under paragraph (1) but not including amounts not taken into account by reason of paragraph (3)).

(3) LATER PAYMENTS TREATED AS RECEIPT OF TAX PAID AMOUNTS.—If any amount is treated as received under paragraph (1) with respect to any installment obligation, subsequent payments received on such obligation shall not be taken into account for purposes of section 453 to the extent that the aggregate of such subsequent payments does not exceed the aggregate amount treated as received under paragraph (1).

(4) SECURED INDEBTEDNESS.—For purposes of this subsection indebtedness is secured by an installment obligation to the extent that payment of principal or interest on such indebtedness is directly secured (under the terms of the indebtedness or any underlying arrangements) by any interest in such installment obligation. A payment shall be treated as directly secured by an interest in an installment obligation to the extent an arrangement allows the taxpayer to satisfy all or a portion of the indebtedness with the installment obligation.

(e) REGULATIONS.—The Secretary shall prescribe such regulations as may be necessary to carry out the purposes of this section, including regulations—

(1) disallowing the use of the installment method in whole or in part for transactions in which the rules of this section otherwise would be avoided through the use of related persons, pass-thru entities, or intermediaries, and

(2) providing that the sale of an interest in a partnership or other pass-thru entity will be treated as a sale of the proportionate share of the assets of the partnership or other entity.

SEC. 453B. GAIN OR LOSS ON DISPOSITION OF INSTALLMENT OBLIGATIONS.

(a) GENERAL RULE.—If an installment obligation is satisfied at other than its face value or distributed, transmitted, sold, or otherwise disposed of, gain or loss shall result to the extent of the difference between the basis of the obligation and—

(1) the amount realized, in the case of satisfaction at other than face value or a sale or exchange, or

(2) the fair market value of the obligation at the time of distribution, transmission, or disposition, in the case of the distribution, transmission, or disposition otherwise than by sale or exchange.

Any gain or loss so resulting shall be considered as resulting from the sale or exchange of the property in respect of which the installment obligation was received.

(b) BASIS OF OBLIGATION.—The basis of an installment obligation shall be the excess of the face value of the obligation over an amount equal to the income which would be returnable were the obligation satisfied in full.

(c) SPECIAL RULE FOR TRANSMISSION AT DEATH.—Except as provided in section 691 (relating to recipients of income in respect of decedents), this section shall not apply to the transmission of installment obligations at death.

(d) EXCEPTION FOR DISTRIBUTIONS TO WHICH SECTION 337(A) APPLIES.—Subsection (a) shall not apply to any distribution to which section 337(a) applies.

. . .

(f) OBLIGATION BECOMES UNENFORCEABLE.—For purposes of this section, if any installment obligation is canceled or otherwise becomes unenforceable—

(1) the obligation shall be treated as if it were disposed of in a transaction other than a sale or exchange, and

(2) if the obligor and obligee are related persons (within the meaning of section 453(f)(1)), the fair market value of the obligation shall be treated as not less than its face amount.

(g) TRANSFERS BETWEEN SPOUSES OR INCIDENT TO DIVORCE.—In the case of any transfer described in subsection (a) of section 1041 (other than a transfer in trust)—

(1) subsection (a) of this section shall not apply, and

(2) the same tax treatment with respect to the transferred installment obligation shall apply to the transferee as would have applied to the transferor.

(h) CERTAIN LIQUIDATING DISTRIBUTIONS BY S CORPORATIONS.—If—

(1) an installment obligation is distributed by an S corporation in a complete liquidation, and

(2) receipt of the obligation is not treated as payment for the stock by reason of section 453(h)(1).

then, except for purposes of any tax imposed by subchapter S, no gain or loss with respect to the distribution of the obligation shall be recognized by the distributing corporation. Under regulations prescribed by the Secretary, the character of the gain or loss to the shareholder shall be determined in accordance with the principles of section 1366(b).

SEC. 465. DEDUCTIONS LIMITED TO AMOUNT AT RISK.

(a) LIMITATION TO AMOUNT AT RISK.—
    (1) IN GENERAL.—In the case of—
        (A) an individual, and
        (B) a C corporation with respect to which the stock ownership requirement of paragraph (2) of section 542(a) is met,
engaged in an activity to which this section applies, any loss from such activity for the taxable year shall be allowed only to the extent of the aggregate amount with respect to which the taxpayer is at risk (within the meaning of subsection (b)) for such activity at the close of the taxable year.
    (2) DEDUCTION IN SUCCEEDING YEAR.—Any loss from an activity to which this section applies not allowed under this section for the taxable year shall be treated as a deduction allocable to such activity in the first succeeding taxable year.

. . .

SEC. 469. PASSIVE ACTIVITY LOSSES AND CREDITS LIMITED.

(a) DISALLOWANCE.—
    (1) IN GENERAL.—If for any taxable year the taxpayer is described in paragraph (2), neither—
        (A) the passive activity loss, nor
        (B) the passive activity credit,
for the taxable year shall be allowed.
    (2) PERSONS DESCRIBED.—The following are described in this paragraph:
        (A) any individual, estate, or trust,
        (B) any closely held C corporation, and
        (C) any personal service corporation.
(b) DISALLOWED LOSS OR CREDIT CARRIED TO NEXT YEAR.—Except as otherwise provided in this section, any loss or credit from an activity which is disallowed under subsection (a) shall be treated as a deduction or credit allocable to such activity in the next taxable year.
(c) PASSIVE ACTIVITY DEFINED.—For purposes of this section—
    (1) IN GENERAL.—The term "passive activity" means any activity—
        (A) which involves the conduct of any trade or business, and
        (B) in which the taxpayer does not materially participate.
    (2) PASSIVE ACTIVITY INCLUDES ANY RENTAL ACTIVITY.—Except as provided in paragraph (7), the term "passive activity" includes any rental activity.

. . .

(4) MATERIAL PARTICIPATION NOT REQUIRED FOR PARAGRAPHS (2) AND (3).—Paragraphs (2) and (3) shall be applied without regard to whether or not the taxpayer materially participates in the activity.

. . .

(6) ACTIVITY IN CONNECTION WITH TRADE OR BUSINESS OR PRODUCTION OF INCOME.—To the extent provided in regulations, for purposes of paragraph (1)(A), the term "trade or business" includes—

(A) any activity in connection with a trade or business, or

(B) any activity with respect to which expenses are allowable as a deduction under section 212.

. . .

(e) SPECIAL RULES FOR DETERMINING INCOME OR LOSS FROM A PASSIVE ACTIVITY.—For purposes of this section—

(1) CERTAIN INCOME NOT TREATED AS INCOME FROM PASSIVE ACTIVITY.—In determining the income or loss from any activity—

(A) IN GENERAL.—There shall not be taken into account—

(i) any—

(I) gross income from interest, dividends, annuities, or royalties not derived in the ordinary course of a trade or business,

(II) expenses (other than interest) which are clearly and directly allocable to such gross income, and

(III) interest expense properly allocable to such gross income, and

(ii) gain or loss not derived in the ordinary course of a trade or business which is attributable to the disposition of property—

(I) producing income of a type described in clause (i), or

(II) held for investment.

For purposes of clause (ii), any interest in a passive activity shall not be treated as property held for investment.

(B) RETURN ON WORKING CAPITAL.—For purposes of subparagraph (A), any income, gain, or loss which is attributable to an investment of working capital shall be treated as not derived in the ordinary course of a trade or business.

(2) PASSIVE LOSSES OF CERTAIN CLOSELY HELD CORPORATIONS MAY OFFSET ACTIVE INCOME.—

(A) IN GENERAL.—If a closely held C corporation (other than a personal service corporation) has net active income for any taxable year, the passive activity loss of such taxpayer for such taxable year (determined without regard to this paragraph)—

(i) shall be allowable as a deduction against net active income, and

(ii) shall not be taken into account under subsection (a) to the extent so allowable as a deduction.

A similar rule shall apply in the case of any passive activity credit of the taxpayer.

(B) NET ACTIVE INCOME.—For purposes of this paragraph, the term "net active income" means the taxable income of the taxpayer for the taxable year determined without regard to—

(i) any income or loss from a passive activity, and

(ii) any item of gross income, expense, gain, or loss described in paragraph (1)(A).

(3) COMPENSATION FOR PERSONAL SERVICES.—Earned income (within the meaning of section 911(d)(2)(A)) shall not be taken into account in computing the income or loss from a passive activity for any taxable year.

(4) DIVIDENDS REDUCED BY DIVIDENDS RECEIVED DEDUCTION.—For purposes of paragraphs (1) and (2), income from dividends shall be reduced by the amount of any dividends received deduction under section 243, 244 or 245.

. . .

(g) DISPOSITIONS OF ENTIRE INTEREST IN PASSIVE ACTIVITY.—If during the taxable year a taxpayer disposes of his entire interest in any passive activity (or former passive activity), the following rules shall apply:

(1) FULLY TAXABLE TRANSACTION.—

(A) IN GENERAL.—If all gain or loss realized on such disposition is recognized, the excess of—

(i) any loss from such activity for such taxable year (determined after the application of subsection (b)), over

(ii) any net income or gain for such taxable year from all other passive activities (determined after the application of subsection (b)),

shall be treated as a loss which is not from a passive activity.

(B) SUBPARAGRAPH (A) NOT TO APPLY TO DISPOSITION INVOLVING RELATED PARTY.—If the taxpayer and the person acquiring the interest bear a relationship to each other described in section 267(b) or section 707(b)(1), then subparagraph (A) shall not apply to any loss of the taxpayer until the taxable year in which such interest is acquired (in a transaction described in subparagraph (A)) by another person who does not bear such a relationship to the taxpayer.

(C) INCOME FROM PRIOR YEARS.—To the extent provided in regulations, income or gain from the activity for preceding taxable years shall be taken into account under subparagraph (A)(ii) for the taxable year to the extent necessary to prevent the avoidance of this section.

(2) DISPOSITION BY DEATH.—If an interest in the activity is transferred by reason of the death of the taxpayer—

(A) paragraph (1)(A) shall apply to losses described in paragraph (1)(A) to the extent such losses are greater than the excess (if any) of—

(i) the basis of such property in the hands of the transferee, over

(ii) the adjusted basis of such property immediately before the death of the taxpayer, and

(B) any losses to the extent of the excess described in subparagraph (A) shall not be allowed as a deduction for any taxable year.

(3) INSTALLMENT SALE OF ENTIRE INTEREST.—In the case of an installment sale of an entire interest in an activity to which section 453 applies, paragraph (1) shall apply to the portion of such losses for each taxable year which bears the same ratio to all such losses as the gain recognized on such sale during such taxable year bears to the gross profit from such sale (realized or to be realized when payment is completed).

(h) MATERIAL PARTICIPATION DEFINED.—For purposes of this section—

(1) IN GENERAL.—A taxpayer shall be treated as materially participating in an activity only if the taxpayer is involved in the operations of the activity on a basis which is—

    (A) regular,

    (B) continuous, and

    (C) substantial.

(2) INTERESTS IN LIMITED PARTNERSHIPS.—Except as provided in regulations, no interest in a limited partnership as a limited partner shall be treated as an interest with respect to which a taxpayer materially participates.

. . .

(4) CERTAIN CLOSELY HELD C CORPORATIONS AND PERSONAL SERVICE CORPORATIONS.—A closely held C corporation or personal service corporation shall be treated as materially participating in an activity only if—

    (A) 1 or more shareholders holding stock representing more than 50 percent (by value) of the outstanding stock of such corporation materially participate in such activity, or

    (B) in the case of a closely held C corporation (other than a personal service corporation), the requirements of section 465(c)(7)(C) (without regard to clause (iv)) are met with respect to such activity.

(5) PARTICIPATION BY SPOUSE.—In determining whether a taxpayer materially participates, the participation of the spouse of the taxpayer shall be taken into account.

. . .

(*l*) REGULATIONS.—The Secretary shall prescribe such regulations as may be necessary or appropriate to carry out provisions of this section, including regulations—

    (1) which specify what constitutes an activity, material participation, or active participation for purposes of this section,

    (2) which provide that certain items of gross income will not be taken into account in determining income or loss from any activity (and the treatment of expenses allocable to such income),

    (3) requiring net income or gain from a limited partnership or other passive activity to be treated as not from a passive activity,

    (4) which provide for the determination of the allocation of interest expense for purposes of this section, and

(5) which deal with changes in marital status and changes between joint returns and separate returns.

. . .

SEC. 483. INTEREST ON CERTAIN DEFERRED PAYMENTS.

(a) AMOUNT CONSTITUTING INTEREST.—For purposes of this title, in the case of any payment—

(1) under any contract for the sale or exchange of any property, and

(2) to which this section applies,

there shall be treated as interest that portion of the total unstated interest under such contract which, as determined in a manner consistent with the method of computing interest under section 1272(a), is properly allocable to such payment.

(b) TOTAL UNSTATED INTEREST.—For purposes of this section, the term "total unstated interest" means, with respect to a contract for the sale or exchange of property, an amount equal to the excess of—

(1) the sum of the payments to which this section applies which are due under the contract, over

(2) the sum of the present values of such payments and the present values of any interest payments due under the contract.

For purposes of the preceding sentence, the present value of a payment shall be determined under the rules of section 1274(b)(2) using a discount rate equal to the applicable Federal rate determined under section 1274(d).

(c) PAYMENTS TO WHICH SUBSECTION (a) APPLIES.—

(1) IN GENERAL.—Except as provided in subsection (d), this section shall apply to any payment on account of the sale or exchange of property which constitutes part or all of the sales price and which is due more than 6 months after the date of such sale or exchange under a contract—

(A) under which some or all of the payments are due more than 1 year after the date of such sale or exchange, and

(B) under which there is total unstated interest.

(2) TREATMENT OF OTHER DEBT INSTRUMENTS.—For purposes of this section, a debt instrument of the purchaser which is given in consideration for the sale or exchange of property shall not be treated as a payment, and any payment due under such debt instrument shall be treated as due under the contract for the sale or exchange.

(3) DEBT INSTRUMENT DEFINED.—For purposes of this subsection, the term "debt instrument" has the meaning given such term by section 1275(a)(1).

(d) EXCEPTIONS AND LIMITATIONS.—

(1) COORDINATION WITH ORIGINAL ISSUE DISCOUNT RULES.—This section shall not apply to any debt instrument for which an issue price is

determined under section 1273(b) (other than paragraph (4) thereof) or section 1274.

. . .

(f) REGULATIONS.—The Secretary shall prescribe such regulations as may be necessary or appropriate to carry out the purposes of this section including regulations providing for the application of this section in the case of—

(1) any contract for the sale or exchange of property under which the liability for, or the amount or due date of, a payment cannot be determined at the time of the sale or exchange, or

(2) any change in the liability for, or the amount or due date of, any payment (including interest) under a contract for the sale or exchange of property.

. . .

SEC. 511.   IMPOSITION OF TAX ON UNRELATED BUSINESS INCOME OF CHARITABLE, ETC., ORGANIZATIONS.

(a) CHARITABLE, ETC., ORGANIZATIONS TAXABLE AT CORPORATION RATES.—

(1) IMPOSITION OF TAX.—There is hereby imposed for each taxable year on the unrelated business taxable income (as defined in section 512) of every organization described in paragraph (2) a tax computed as provided in section 11. In making such computation for purposes of this section, the term "taxable income" as used in section 11 shall be read as "unrelated business taxable income."

. . .

SEC. 512.   UNRELATED BUSINESS TAXABLE INCOME.

(a) DEFINITION.—For purposes of this title—

(1) GENERAL RULE.—Except as otherwise provided in this subsection, the term "unrelated business taxable income" means the gross income derived by any organization from any unrelated trade or business (as defined in section 513) regularly carried on by it, less the deductions allowed by this chapter which are directly connected with the carrying on of such trade or business, both computed with the modifications provided in subsection (b).

. . .

(b) MODIFICATIONS.—The modifications referred to in subsection (a) are the following:

(1) There shall be excluded all dividends, interest, payments with respect to securities loans (as defined in section 512(a)(5)), amounts received or accrued as consideration for entering into agreements to make loans, and annuities, and all deductions directly connected with such income.

. . .

(4) Notwithstanding paragraph (1), (2), (3), or (5), in the case of debt-financed property (as defined in section 514) there shall be included, as an item of gross income derived from an unrelated trade or business, the amount ascertained under section 514(a)(1), and there shall be allowed, as a deduction, the amount ascertained under section 514(a)(2).

(5) There shall be excluded all gains or losses from the sale, exchange, or other disposition of property other than—

(A) stock in trade or other property of a kind which would properly be includible in inventory if on hand at the close of the taxable year, or

(B) property held primarily for sale to customers in the ordinary course of the trade or business.

There shall also be excluded all gains or losses recognized, in connection with the organization's investment activities, from the lapse or termination of options to buy or sell securities (as defined in section 1236(c)) or real property and all gains or losses from the forfeiture of good-faith deposits (that are consistent with established business practice) for the purchase, sale, or lease of real property in connection with the organization's investment activities. This paragraph shall not apply with respect to the cutting of timber which is considered, on the application of section 631, as a sale or exchange of such timber.

. . .

(c) SPECIAL RULES FOR PARTNERSHIPS.—

(1) IN GENERAL.—If a trade or business regularly carried on by a partnership of which an organization is a member is an unrelated trade or business with respect to such organization, such organization in computing its unrelated business taxable income shall, subject to the exceptions, additions, and limitations contained in subsection (b), include its share (whether or not distributed) of the gross income of the partnership from such unrelated trade or business and its share of the partnership deductions directly connected with such gross income.

. . .

(e) SPECIAL RULES APPLICABLE TO S CORPORATIONS.—

(1) IN GENERAL.—If an organization described in section 1361(c)(6) holds stock in an S corporation—

(A) such interest shall be treated as an interest in an unrelated trade or business, and

(B) notwithstanding any other provision of this part [Code §511-§515]—

(i) all items of income, loss, or deduction taken into account under section 1366(a), and

(ii) any gain or loss on the disposition of the stock in the S corporation

shall be taken into account in computing the unrelated business taxable income of such organization.

(2) BASIS REDUCTION.—Except as provided in regulations, for purposes of paragraph (1), the basis of any stock acquired by purchase (as defined in section 1361(e)(1)(C)) shall be reduced by the amount of any dividends received by the organization with respect to the stock.

(3) EXCEPTION FOR ESOPs.—This subsection shall not apply to employer securities (within the meaning of section 409(l)) held by an employee stock ownership plan described in section 4975(e)(7).

SEC. 513.   UNRELATED TRADE OR BUSINESS.

(a) GENERAL RULE.—The term "unrelated trade or business" means, in the case of any organization subject to the tax imposed by section 511, any trade or business the conduct of which is not substantially related (aside from the need of such organization for income or funds or the use it makes of the profits derived) to the exercise or performance by such organization of its charitable, educational, or other purpose or function constituting the basis for its exemption under section 501 (or, in the case of an organization described in section 511(a)(2)(B), to the exercise or performance of any purpose or function described in section 501(c)(3)), except that such term does not include any trade or business—

(1) in which substantially all the work in carrying on such trade or business is performed for the organization without compensation; or

(2) which is carried on, in the case of an organization described in section 501(c)(3) or in the case of a college or university described in section 511(a)(2)(B), by the organization primarily for the convenience of its members, students, patients, officers, or employees, or, in the case of a local association of employees described in section 501(c)(4) organized before May 27, 1969, which is the selling by the organization of items of work-related clothes and equipment and items normally sold through vending machines, through food dispensing facilities, or by snack bars, for the convenience of its members at their usual places of employment; or

(3) which is the selling of merchandise, substantially all of which has been received by the organization as gifts or contributions.

. . .

SEC. 514.   UNRELATED DEBT-FINANCED INCOME.

(a) UNRELATED DEBT-FINANCED INCOME AND DEDUCTIONS.—In computing under section 512 the unrelated business taxable income for any taxable year—

(1) PERCENTAGE OF INCOME TAKEN INTO ACCOUNT.—There shall be included with respect to each debt-financed property as an item of gross income derived from an unrelated trade or business an amount which is the same percentage (but not in excess of 100 percent) of the total gross income derived during the taxable year from or on account of such property as (A) the average acquisition indebtedness (as defined in subsection (c)(7)) for the taxable year with respect to the property is of (B) the average amount (determined under regulations prescribed by the Secretary) of the adjusted basis of such property during the period it is held by the organization during such taxable year.

(2) PERCENTAGE OF DEDUCTIONS TAKEN INTO ACCOUNT.—There shall be allowed as a deduction with respect to each debt-financed property an amount determined by applying (except as provided in the last sentence of this paragraph) the percentage derived under paragraph (1) to the sum determined under paragraph (3). The percentage derived under this paragraph shall not be applied with respect to the deduction of any capital loss resulting from the carryback or carryover of net capital losses under section 1212.

(3) DEDUCTIONS ALLOWABLE.—The sum referred to in paragraph (2) is the sum of the deductions under this chapter which are directly connected with the debt-financed property or the income therefrom, except that if the debt-financed property is of a character which is subject to the allowance for depreciation provided in section 167, the allowance shall be computed only by use of the straight-line method.

(b) DEFINITION OF DEBT-FINANCED PROPERTY.—

(1) IN GENERAL.—For purposes of this section, the term "debt-financed property" means any property which is held to produce income and with respect to which there is an acquisition indebtedness (as defined in subsection (c)) at any time during the taxable year (or, if the property was disposed of during the taxable year, with respect to which there was an acquisition indebtedness at any time during the 12-month period ending with the date of such disposition), except that such term does not include—

(A)(i) any property substantially all the use of which is substantially related (aside from the need of the organization for income or funds) to the exercise or performance by such organization of its charitable, educational, or other purpose or function constituting the basis for its exemption under section 501 (or, in the case of an organization described in section 511(a)(2)(B), to the exercise or performance of any purpose or function designated in section 501(c)(3)), or (ii) any property to which clause (i) does not apply, to the extent that its use is so substantially related;

(B) except in the case of income excluded under section 512(b)(5), any property to the extent that the income from such property is taken into account in computing the gross income of any unrelated trade or business;

(C) any property to the extent that the income from such property is excluded by reason of the provisions of paragraph (7), (8), or (9) of section 512(b) in computing the gross income of any unrelated trade or business; or

(D) any property to the extent that it is used in any trade or business described in paragraph (1), (2), or (3) of section 513(a).

. . .

(c) ACQUISITION INDEBTEDNESS.—

(1) GENERAL RULE.—For purposes of this section, the term "acquisition indebtedness" means, with respect to any debt-financed property, the unpaid amount of—

(A) the indebtedness incurred by the organization in acquiring or improving such property;

(B) the indebtedness incurred before the acquisition or improvement of such property if such indebtedness would not have been incurred but for such acquisition or improvement; and

(C) the indebtedness incurred after the acquisition or improvement of such property if such indebtedness would not have been incurred but for such acquisition or improvement and the incurrence of such indebtedness was reasonably foreseeable at the time of such acquisition or improvement.

(2) PROPERTY ACQUIRED SUBJECT TO MORTGAGE, ETC.—For purposes of this subsection—

(A) GENERAL RULE.—Where property (no matter how acquired) is acquired subject to a mortgage or other similar lien, the amount of the indebtedness secured by such mortgage or lien shall be considered as an indebtedness of the organization incurred in acquiring such property even though the organization did not assume or agree to pay such indebtedness.

. . .

(d) BASIS OF DEBT-FINANCED PROPERTY ACQUIRED IN CORPORATE LIQUIDATION.—For purposes of this subtitle, if the property was acquired in a complete or partial liquidation of a corporation in exchange for its stock, the basis of the property shall be the same as it would be in the hands of the transferor corporation, increased by the amount of gain recognized to the transferor corporation upon such distribution and by the amount of any gain to the organization which was included, on account of such distribution, in unrelated business taxable income under subsection (a).

. . .

SEC. 691. RECIPIENTS OF INCOME IN RESPECT OF DECEDENTS.

(a) INCLUSION IN GROSS INCOME.—

(1) GENERAL RULE.—The amount of all items of gross income in respect of a decedent which are not properly includible in respect of the taxable period in which falls the date of his death or a prior period (including the amount of all items of gross income in respect of a prior decedent, if the right to receive such amount was acquired by reason of the death of the prior decedent or by bequest, devise, or inheritance from the prior decedent) shall be included in the gross income, for the taxable year when received, of:

(A) the estate of the decedent, if the right to receive the amount is acquired by the decedent's estate from the decedent;

(B) the person who, by reason of the death of the decedent, acquires the right to receive the amount, if the right to receive the amount is not acquired by the decedent's estate from the decedent; or

(C) the person who acquires from the decedent the right to receive the amount by bequest, devise, or inheritance, if the amount is received after a distribution by the decedent's estate of such right.

(2) INCOME IN CASE OF SALE, ETC.—If a right, described in paragraph (1), to receive an amount is transferred by the estate of the decedent or a person who received such right by reason of the death of the decedent or by bequest, devise, or inheritance from the decedent, there shall be included in the gross income of the estate or such person, as the case may be, for the taxable period in which the transfer occurs, the fair market value of such right at the time of such transfer plus the amount by which any consideration for the transfer exceeds such fair market value. For purposes of this paragraph, the term "transfer" includes sale, exchange, or other disposition, or the satisfaction of an installment obligation at other than face value, but does not include transmission at death to the estate of the decedent or a transfer to a person pursuant to the right of such person to receive such amount by reason of the death of the decedent or by bequest, devise, or inheritance from the decedent.

(3) CHARACTER OF INCOME DETERMINED BY REFERENCE TO DECEDENT.—The right, described in paragraph (1), to receive an amount shall be treated, in the hands of the estate of the decedent or any person who acquired such right by reason of the death of the decedent, or by bequest, devise, or inheritance from the decedent, as if it had been acquired by the estate or such person in the transaction in which the right to receive the income was originally derived and the amount includible in gross income under paragraph (1) or (2) shall be considered in the hands of the estate or such person to have the character which it would have had in the hands of the decedent if the decedent had lived and received such amount.

(4) INSTALLMENT OBLIGATIONS ACQUIRED FROM DECEDENT.—In the case of an installment obligation reportable by the decedent on the installment method under section 453, if such obligation is acquired by the decedent's estate from the decedent or by any person by reason of the death of the decedent or by bequest, devise, or inheritance from the decedent—

(A) an amount equal to the excess of the face amount of such obligation over the basis of the obligation in the hands of the decedent (determined under section 453B) shall, for the purpose of paragraph (1), be considered as an item of gross income in respect of the decedent; and

(B) such obligation shall, for purposes of paragraphs (2) and (3), be considered a right to receive an item of gross income in respect of the decedent, but the amount includible in gross income under paragraph (2) shall be reduced by an amount equal to the basis of the obligation in the hands of the decedent (determined under section 453B).

(5) OTHER RULES RELATING TO INSTALLMENT OBLIGATIONS.—

(A) IN GENERAL.—In the case of an installment obligation reportable by the decedent on the installment method under section 453, for purposes of paragraph (2)—

(i) the second sentence of paragraph (2) shall be applied by inserting "(other than the obligor)" after "or a transfer to a person,"

(ii) any cancellation of such an obligation shall be treated as a transfer, and

(iii) any cancellation of such an obligation occurring at the death of the decedent shall be treated as a transfer by the estate of the decedent (or, if held by a person other than the decedent before the death of the decedent, by such person).

(B) FACE AMOUNT TREATED AS FAIR MARKET VALUE IN CERTAIN CASES.—In any case to which the first sentence of paragraph (2) applies by reason of subparagraph (A), if the decedent and the obligor were related persons (within the meaning of section 453(f)(l)), the fair market value of the installment obligation shall be treated as not less than its face amount.

(C) CANCELLATION INCLUDES BECOMING UNENFORCEABLE.— For purposes of subparagraph (A), an installment obligation which becomes unenforceable shall be treated as if it were canceled.

(b) ALLOWANCE OF DEDUCTIONS AND CREDIT.—The amount of any deduction specified in section 162, 163, 164, 212, or 611 (relating to deductions for expenses, interest, taxes, and depletion) or credit specified in section 27 (relating to foreign tax credit), in respect of a decedent which is not properly allowable to the decedent in respect of the taxable period in which falls the date of his death, or a prior period, shall be allowed:

(1) EXPENSES, INTEREST, AND TAXES.—In the case of a deduction specified in section 162, 163, 164, or 212 and a credit specified in section 27, in the taxable year when paid—

(A) to the estate of the decedent; except that

(B) if the estate of the decedent is not liable to discharge the obligation to which the deduction or credit relates, to the person who, by reason of the death of the decedent of by bequest, devise, or inheritance acquires, subject to such obligation, from the decedent an interest in property of the decedent.

. . .

(c) DEDUCTION FOR ESTATE TAX.—
(1) ALLOWANCE OF DEDUCTION.—
(A) GENERAL RULE.—A person who includes an amount in gross income under subsection (a) shall be allowed, for the same taxable year, as a deduction an amount which bears the same ratio to the estate tax attributable to the net value for estate tax purposes of all the items described in subsection (a)(1) as the value for estate tax purposes of the items of gross income or portions thereof in respect of which such person included the amount in gross income (or the amount included in gross income, whichever is lower) bears to the value for estate tax purposes of all the items described in subsection (a)(1).
(B) ESTATES AND TRUSTS.—In the case of an estate or trust, the amount allowed as a deduction under subparagraph (A) shall be computed by excluding from the gross income of the estate or trust the portion (if any) of the items described in subsection (a) (1) which is properly paid, credited, or to be distributed to the beneficiaries during the taxable year.

. . .

(2) METHOD OF COMPUTING DEDUCTION.—For purposes of paragraph (1)—
(A) The term "estate tax" means the tax imposed on the estate of the decedent or any prior decedent under section 2001 or 2101, reduced by the credits against such tax.
(B) The net value for estate tax purposes of all the items described in subsection (a) (1) shall be the excess of the value for estate tax purposes of all the items described in subsection (a) (1) over the deductions from the gross estate in respect of claims which represent the deductions and credit described in subsection (b). Such net value shall be determined with respect to the provisions of section 421(c)(2), relating to the deduction for estate tax with respect to stock options to which part II of subchapter D [Code §421-§424] applies.
(C) The estate tax attributable to such net value shall be an amount equal to the excess of the estate tax over the estate tax computed without including in the gross estate such net value.

. . .

(4) COORDINATION WITH CAPITAL GAIN PROVISIONS.—For purposes of sections 1(h), 1201, 1202, and 1211, the amount of any gain taken into account with respect to any item described in subsection (a)(1) shall be reduced (but not below zero) by the amount of the deduction allowable under paragraph (1) of this subsection with respect to such item.

. . .

SEC. 701.   PARTNERS, NOT PARTNERSHIP, SUBJECT TO TAX.

A partnership as such shall not be subject to the income tax imposed by this chapter. Persons carrying on business as partners shall be liable for income tax only in their separate or individual capacities.

SEC. 702.   INCOME AND CREDITS OF PARTNER.

(a) GENERAL RULE.—In determining his income tax, each partner shall take into account separately his distributive share of the partnership's—

(1) gains and losses from sales or exchanges of capital assets held for not more than 1 year,

(2) gains and losses from sales or exchanges of capital assets held for more than 1 year,

(3) gains and losses from sales or exchanges of property described in section 1231 (relating to certain property used in a trade or business and involuntary conversions),

(4) charitable contributions (as defined in section 170 (c)),

(5) dividends with respect to which there is a deduction under part VIII of subchapter B [Code §241-§249],

(6) taxes, described in section 901, paid or accrued to foreign countries and to possessions of the United States,

(7) other items of income, gain, loss, deduction, or credit, to the extent provided by regulations prescribed by the Secretary, and

(8) taxable income or loss, exclusive of items requiring separate computation under other paragraphs of this subsection.

(b) CHARACTER OF ITEMS CONSTITUTING DISTRIBUTIVE SHARE.—The character of any item of income, gain, loss, deduction, or credit included in a partner's distributive share under paragraphs (1) through (7) of subsection (a) shall be determined as if such item were realized directly from the source from which realized by the partnership, or incurred in the same manner as incurred by the partnership.

(c) GROSS INCOME OF A PARTNER.—In any case where it is necessary to determine the gross income of a partner for purposes of this title, such amount shall include his distributive share of the gross income of the partnership.

. . .

SEC. 703.   PARTNERSHIP COMPUTATIONS.

(a) INCOME AND DEDUCTIONS.—The taxable income of a partnership shall be computed in the same manner as in the case of an individual except that—

(1) the items described in section 702 (a) shall be separately stated, and

(2) the following deductions shall not be allowed to the partnership:

(A) the deductions for personal exemptions provided in section 151,

(B) the deduction for taxes provided in section 164 (a) with respect to taxes, described in section 901, paid or accrued to foreign countries and to possessions of the United States,

(C) the deduction for charitable contributions provided in section 170,

(D) the net operating loss deduction provided in section 172,

(E) the additional itemized deductions for individuals provided in part VII of subchapter B . . . [Code§211-§222], and

(F) the deduction for depletion under section 611 with respect to oil and gas wells.

(b) ELECTIONS OF THE PARTNERSHIP.—Any election affecting the computation of taxable income derived from a partnership shall be made by the partnership, except that any election under—

(1) subsection (b)(5) or (c)(3) of section 108 (relating to income from discharge of indebtedness),

(2) section 617 (relating to deduction and recapture of certain mining exploration expenditures), or

(3) section 901 (relating to taxes of foreign countries and possessions of the United States),

shall be made by each partner separately.

SEC. 704.   PARTNER'S DISTRIBUTIVE SHARE.

(a) EFFECT OF PARTNERSHIP AGREEMENT.—A partner's distributive share of income, gain, loss, deduction, or credit shall, except as otherwise provided in this chapter, be determined by the partnership agreement.

(b) DETERMINATION OF DISTRIBUTIVE SHARE.—A partner's distributive share of income, gain, loss, deduction, or credit (or item thereof) shall be determined in accordance with the partner's interest in the partnership (determined by taking into account all facts and circumstances), if—

(1) the partnership agreement does not provide as to the partner's distributive share of income, gain, loss, deduction, or credit (or item thereof), or

(2) the allocation to a partner under the agreement of income, gain, loss, deduction, or credit (or item thereof) does not have substantial economic effect.

(c) CONTRIBUTED PROPERTY.—

(1) IN GENERAL.—Under regulations prescribed by the Secretary—

(A) income, gain, loss, and deduction with respect to property contributed to the partnership by a partner shall be shared among the partners so as to take account of the variation between the basis of the property to the partnership and its fair market value at the time of contribution, and

(B) if any property so contributed is distributed (directly or indirectly) by the partnership (other than to the contributing partner) within 7 years of being contributed—

(i) the contributing partner shall be treated as recognizing gain or loss (as the case may be) from the sale of such property in an amount equal to the gain or loss which would have been allocated to such partner under subparagraph (A) by reason of the variation described in subparagraph (A) if the property had been sold at its fair market value at the time of the distribution,

(ii) the character of such gain or loss shall be determined by reference to the character of the gain or loss which would have resulted if such property had been sold by the partnership to the distributee, and

(iii) appropriate adjustments shall be made to the adjusted basis of the contributing partner's interest in the partnership and to the adjusted basis of the property distributed to reflect any gain or loss recognized under this subparagraph.

(2) SPECIAL RULE FOR DISTRIBUTIONS WHERE GAIN OR LOSS WOULD NOT BE RECOGNIZED OUTSIDE PARTNERSHIPS.—Under regulations prescribed by the Secretary, if—

(A) property contributed by a partner (hereinafter referred to as the "contributing partner") is distributed by the partnership to another partner, and

(B) other property of a like kind (within the meaning of section 1031) is distributed by the partnership to the contributing partner not later than the earlier of—

(i) the 180th day after the date of the distribution described in subparagraph (A), or

(ii) the due date (determined with regard to extensions) for the contributing partner's return of the tax imposed by this chapter for the taxable year in which the distribution described in subparagraph (A) occurs,

then to the extent of the value of the property described in subparagraph (B), paragraph (1)(B) shall be applied as if the contributing partner had contributed to the partnership the property described in subparagraph (B).

(3) OTHER RULES.—Under regulations prescribed by the Secretary, rules similar to the rules of paragraph (1) shall apply to contributions by a partner (using the cash receipts and disbursements method of accounting) of accounts payable and other accrued but unpaid items. Any reference in paragraph (1) or (2) to the contributing partner shall be treated as including a reference to any successor of such partner.

(d) LIMITATION ON ALLOWANCE OF LOSSES.—A partner's distributive share of partnership loss (including capital loss) shall be allowed only to the extent of the adjusted basis of such partner's interest in the partnership at the end of the partnership year in which such loss occurred. Any excess of such loss over such basis shall be allowed as a deduction at the end of the partnership year in which such excess is repaid to the partnership.

(e) FAMILY PARTNERSHIPS.—

(1) RECOGNITION OF INTEREST CREATED BY PURCHASE OR GIFT.—A person shall be recognized as a partner for purposes of this subtitle if he owns a capital interest in a partnership in which capital is a material income-producing factor, whether or not such interest was derived by purchase or gift from any other person.

(2) DISTRIBUTIVE SHARE OF DONEE INCLUDIBLE IN GROSS INCOME.—In the case of any partnership interest created by gift, the distributive

share of the donee under the partnership agreement shall be includible in his gross income, except to the extent that such share is determined without allowance of reasonable compensation for services rendered to the partnership by the donor, and except to the extent that the portion of such share attributable to donated capital is proportionately greater than the share of the donor attributable to the donor's capital. The distributive share of a partner in the earnings of the partnership shall not be diminished because of absence due to military service.

(3) PURCHASE OF INTEREST BY MEMBER OF FAMILY.—For purposes of this section, an interest purchased by one member of a family from another shall be considered to be created by gift from the seller, and the fair market value of the purchased interest shall be considered to be donated capital. The "family" of any individual shall include only his spouse, ancestors, and lineal descendants, and any trusts for the primary benefit of such persons.

. . .

SEC. 705. DETERMINATION OF BASIS OF PARTNER'S INTEREST.

(a) GENERAL RULE.—The adjusted basis of a partner's interest in a partnership shall, except as provided in subsection (b), be the basis of such interest determined under section 722 (relating to contributions to a partnership) or section 742 (relating to transfers of partnership interests)—

(1) increased by the sum of his distributive share for the taxable year and prior taxable years of—

(A) taxable income of the partnership as determined under section 703 (a),

(B) income of the partnership exempt from tax under this title, and

(C) the excess of the deductions for depletion over the basis of the property subject to depletion;

(2) decreased (but not below zero) by distributions by the partnership as provided in section 733 and by the sum of his distributive share for the taxable year and prior taxable years of—

(A) losses of the partnership, and

(B) expenditures of the partnership not deductible in computing its taxable income and not properly chargeable to capital account; and

(3) decreased (but not below zero) by the amount of the partner's deduction for depletion for any partnership oil and gas property to the extent such deduction does not exceed the proportionate share of the adjusted basis of such property allocated to such partner under section 613A(c)(7)(D).

(b) ALTERNATIVE RULE.—The Secretary shall prescribe by regulations the circumstances under which the adjusted basis of a partner's interest in a partnership may be determined by reference to his proportionate share of the adjusted basis of partnership property upon a termination of the partnership.

SEC. 706.　TAXABLE YEARS OF PARTNER AND PARTNERSHIP.

(a) YEAR IN WHICH PARTNERSHIP INCOME IS INCLUDIBLE.—In computing the taxable income of a partner for a taxable year, the inclusions required by section 702 and section 707 (c) with respect to a partnership shall be based on the income, gain, loss, deduction, or credit of the partnership for any taxable year of the partnership ending within or with the taxable year of the partner.

(b) TAXABLE YEAR.—

(1) PARTNERSHIP'S TAXABLE YEAR.—

(A) PARTNERSHIP TREATED AS TAXPAYER.—The taxable year of a partnership shall be determined as though the partnership were a taxpayer.

(B) TAXABLE YEAR DETERMINED BY REFERENCE TO PARTNERS.— Except as provided in subparagraph (C), a partnership shall not have a taxable year other than—

(i) the majority interest taxable year (as defined in paragraph (4)),

(ii) if there is no taxable year described in clause (i), the taxable year of all the principal partners of the partnership, or

(iii) if there is no taxable year described in clause (i) or (ii), the calendar year unless the Secretary by regulations prescribes another period.

(C) BUSINESS PURPOSE.—A partnership may have a taxable year not described in subparagraph (B) if it establishes, to the satisfaction of the Secretary, a business purpose therefor. For purposes of this subparagraph, any deferral of income to partners shall not be treated as a business purpose.

(2) PARTNER'S TAXABLE YEAR.—A partner may not change to a taxable year other than that of a partnership in which he is a principal partner unless he establishes, to the satisfaction of the Secretary, a business purpose therefor.

(3) PRINCIPAL PARTNER.—For the purpose of this subsection, a principal partner is a partner having an interest of 5 percent or more in partnership profits or capital.

(4) MAJORITY INTEREST TAXABLE YEAR; LIMITATION ON REQUIRED CHANGES.—

(A) MAJORITY INTEREST TAXABLE YEAR DEFINED.—For purposes of paragraph (1)(B)(i)—

(i) IN GENERAL.—The term "majority interest taxable year" means the taxable year (if any) which, on each testing day, constituted the taxable year of 1 or more partners having (on such day) an aggregate interest in partnership profits and capital of more than 50 percent.

(ii) TESTING DATE.—The testing days shall be—

(I) the 1st day of the partnership taxable year (determined without regard to clause (i)), or

(II) the days during such representative period as the Secretary may prescribe.

. . .

(c) CLOSING OF PARTNERSHIP YEAR.—

(1) GENERAL RULE.—Except in the case of a termination of a partnership and except as provided in paragraph (2) of this subsection, the taxable year of a partnership shall not close as the result of the death of a partner, the entry of a new partner, the liquidation of a partner's interest in the partnership, or the sale or exchange of a partner's interest in the partnership.

(2) TREATMENT OF DISPOSITIONS.—

(A) DISPOSITION OF ENTIRE INTEREST.—The taxable year of a partnership shall close with respect to a partner whose entire interest in the partnership terminates (whether by reason of death, liquidation, or otherwise).

(B) DISPOSITION OF LESS THAN ENTIRE INTEREST.—The taxable year of a partnership shall not close (other than at the end of a partnership's taxable year as determined under subsection (b) (1)) with respect to a partner who sells or exchanges less than his entire interest in the partnership or with respect to a partner whose interest is reduced (whether by entry of a new partner, partial liquidation of a partner's interest, gift, or otherwise).

(d) DETERMINATION OF DISTRIBUTIVE SHARE WHEN PARTNER'S INTEREST CHANGES.—

(1) IN GENERAL.—Except as provided in paragraphs (2) and (3), if during any taxable year of the partnership there is a change in any partner's interest in the partnership, each partner's distributive share of any item of income, gain, loss, deduction, or credit of the partnership for such taxable year shall be determined by the use of any method prescribed by the Secretary by regulations which take into account the varying interests of the partners in the partnership during such taxable year.

. . .

SEC. 707. TRANSACTIONS BETWEEN PARTNER AND PARTNERSHIP.

(a) PARTNER NOT ACTING IN CAPACITY AS PARTNER.—

(1) IN GENERAL.—If a partner engages in a transaction with a partnership other than in his capacity as a member of such partnership, the transaction shall, except as otherwise provided in this section, be considered as occurring between the partnership and one who is not a partner.

(2) TREATMENT OF PAYMENTS TO PARTNERS FOR PROPERTY OR SERVICES.—Under regulations prescribed by the Secretary—

(A) TREATMENT OF CERTAIN SERVICES AND TRANSFERS OF PROPERTY.—If—

(i) a partner performs services for a partnership or transfers property to a partnership,

(ii) there is a related direct or indirect allocation and distribution to such partner, and

(iii) the performance of such services (or such transfer) and the allocation and distribution, when viewed together, are properly characterized as a transaction occurring between the partnership and a partner acting other than in his capacity as a member of the partnership,

such allocation and distribution shall be treated as a transaction described in paragraph (1).

(B) TREATMENT OF CERTAIN PROPERTY TRANSFERS.—If—

(i) there is a direct or indirect transfer of money or other property by a partner to a partnership,

(ii) there is a related direct or indirect transfer of money or other property by the partnership to such partner (or another partner), and

(iii) the transfers described in clauses (i) and (ii), when viewed together, are properly characterized as a sale or exchange of property,

such transfers shall be treated either as a transaction described in paragraph (1) or as a transaction between 2 or more partners acting other than in their capacity as members of the partnership.

(b) CERTAIN SALES OR EXCHANGES OF PROPERTY WITH RESPECT TO CONTROLLED PARTNERSHIPS.—

(1) LOSSES DISALLOWED.—No deduction shall be allowed in respect of losses from sales or exchanges of property (other than an interest in the partnership), directly or indirectly, between—

(A) a partnership and a person owning, directly or indirectly, more than 50 percent of the capital interest, or the profits interest, in such partnership, or

(B) two partnerships in which the same persons own, directly or indirectly, more than 50 percent of the capital interests or profits interests.

In the case of a subsequent sale or exchange by a transferee described in this paragraph, section 267(d) shall be applicable as if the loss were disallowed under section 267(a)(1). For purposes of section 267(a)(2), partnerships described in subparagraph (B) of this paragraph shall be treated as persons specified in section 267(b).

(2) GAINS TREATED AS ORDINARY INCOME.—In the case of a sale or exchange, directly or indirectly, of property, which, in the hands of the transferee, is property other than a capital asset as defined in section 1221—

(A) between a partnership and a person owning, directly or indirectly, more than 50 percent of the capital interest, or profits interest, in such partnership, or

(B) between two partnerships in which the same persons own, directly or indirectly, more than 50 percent of the capital interests or profits interests,

any gain recognized shall be considered as ordinary income.

(3) OWNERSHIP OF A CAPITAL OR PROFITS INTEREST.—For purposes of paragraphs (1) and (2) of this subsection, the ownership of a capital or profits interest in a partnership shall be determined in accordance with the rules for constructive ownership of stock provided in section 267 (c) other than paragraph (3) of such section.

(c) GUARANTEED PAYMENTS.—To the extent determined without regard to the income of the partnership, payments to a partner for services or the use of capital shall be considered as made to one who is not a member of the partnership, but only for the purposes of section 61 (a) (relating to gross income) and, subject to section 263, for purposes of section 162 (a) (relating to trade or business expenses).

SEC. 708. CONTINUATION OF PARTNERSHIP.

(a) GENERAL RULE.—For purposes of this subchapter, an existing partnership shall be considered as continuing if it is not terminated.

(b) TERMINATION.—

(1) GENERAL RULE.—For purposes of subsection (a), a partnership shall be considered as terminated only if—

(A) no part of any business, financial operation, or venture of the partnership continues to be carried on by any of its partners in a partnership, or

(B) within a 12-month period there is a sale or exchange of 50 percent or more of the total interest in partnership capital and profits.

(2) SPECIAL RULES.—

(A) MERGER OR CONSOLIDATION.—In the case of the merger or consolidation of two or more partnerships, the resulting partnership shall, for purposes of this section, be considered the continuation of any merging or consolidating partnership whose members own an interest of more than 50 percent in the capital and profits of the resulting partnership.

(B) DIVISION OF A PARTNERSHIP.—In the case of a division of a partnership into two or more partnerships, the resulting partnerships (other than any resulting partnership the members of which had an interest of 50 percent or less in the capital and profits of the prior partnership) shall, for purposes of this section, be considered a continuation of the prior partnership.

SEC. 709. TREATMENT OF ORGANIZATION AND SYNDICATION FEES.

(a) GENERAL RULE.—Except as provided in subsection (b), no deduction shall be allowed under this chapter to the partnership or to any partner for any amounts paid or incurred to organize a partnership or to promote the sale of (or to sell) an interest in such partnership.

(b) AMORTIZATION OF ORGANIZATION FEES.—

(1) DEDUCTION.—Amounts paid or incurred to organize a partnership may, at the election of the partnership (made in accordance with regulations prescribed by the Secretary), be treated as deferred expenses. Such deferred expenses shall be allowed as a deduction ratably over such period of not less than 60 months as may be selected by the partnership (beginning with the month in which the partnership begins business), or if the partnership is liquidated before the end of such 60-month period, such deferred expenses (to the extent not deducted under this section) may be deducted to the extent provided in section 165.

(2) ORGANIZATIONAL EXPENSES DEFINED.—The organizational expenses to which paragraph (1) applies, are expenditures which—

(A) are incident to the creation of the partnership;

(B) are chargeable to capital account; and

(C) are of a character which, if expended incident to the creation of a partnership having an ascertainable life, would be amortized over such life.

SEC. 721. NONRECOGNITION OF GAIN OR LOSS ON CONTRIBUTION.

(a) GENERAL RULE.—No gain or loss shall be recognized to a partnership or to any of its partners in the case of a contribution of property to the partnership in exchange for an interest in the partnership.

(b) SPECIAL RULE.—Subsection (a) shall not apply to gain realized on a transfer of property to a partnership which would be treated as an investment company (within the meaning of section 351) if the partnership were incorporated.

. . .

SEC. 722. BASIS OF CONTRIBUTING PARTNER'S INTEREST.

The basis of an interest in a partnership acquired by a contribution of property, including money, to the partnership shall be the amount of such money and the adjusted basis of such property to the contributing partner at the time of the contribution increased by the amount (if any) of gain recognized under section 721(b) to the contributing partner at such time.

SEC. 723. BASIS OF PROPERTY CONTRIBUTED TO PARTNERSHIP.

The basis of property contributed to a partnership by a partner shall be the adjusted basis of such property to the contributing partner at the time of the contribution increased by the amount (if any) of gain recognized under section 721(b) to the contributing partner at such time.

SEC. 731. EXTENT OF RECOGNITION OF GAIN OR LOSS ON DISTRIBUTION.

(a) PARTNERS.—In the case of a distribution by a partnership to a partner—

(1) gain shall not be recognized to such partner, except to the extent that any money distributed exceeds the adjusted basis of such partner's interest in the partnership immediately before the distribution, and

(2) loss shall not be recognized to such partner except that upon a distribution in liquidation of a partner's interest in a partnership where no property other than that described in subparagraph (A) or (B) is distributed to such partner, loss shall be recognized to the extent of the excess of the adjusted basis of such partner's interest in the partnership over the sum of—

(A) any money distributed, and

(B) the basis to the distributee, as determined under section 732, of any unrealized receivables (as defined in section 751(c)) and inventory (as defined in section 751(d)).

Any gain or loss recognized under this subsection shall be considered as gain or loss from the sale or exchange of the partnership interest of the distributee partner.

(b) PARTNERSHIPS.—No gain or loss shall be recognized to a partnership on a distribution to a partner of property, including money.

(c) TREATMENT OF MARKETABLE SECURITIES.—

(1) IN GENERAL.—For purposes of subsection (a)(1) and section 737—

(A) the term "money" includes marketable securities, and

(B) such securities shall be taken into account at their fair market value as of the date of the distribution.

(2) MARKETABLE SECURITIES.—For purposes of this subsection:

(A) IN GENERAL.—The term "marketable securities" means financial instruments and foreign currencies which are, as of the date of the distribution, actively traded (within the meaning of section 1092(d)(1)).

(B) OTHER PROPERTY.—Such term includes—

(i) any interest in—

(I) a common trust fund, or

(II) a regulated investment company which is offering for sale or has outstanding any redeemable security (as defined in section 2(a)(32) of the Investment Company Act of 1940) of which it is the issuer,

(ii) any financial instrument which, pursuant to its terms of any other arrangement, is readily convertible into, or exchangeable for, money or marketable securities,

(iii) any financial instrument the value of which is determined substantially by reference to marketable securities,

(iv) except to the extent provided in regulations prescribed by the Secretary, any interest in precious metal which, as of the date of the distribution, is actively traded (within the meaning of section 1092(d)(1)) unless such metal was produced, used, or held in the active conduct of a trade or business by the partnership,

(v) except as otherwise provided in regulations prescribed by the Secretary, interests in any entity if substantially all of the assets of such entity consist (directly or indirectly) of marketable securities, money, or both, and

(vi) to the extent provided in regulations prescribed by the Secretary, any interest in an entity not described in clause (v) but only to the extent of the value of such interest which is attributable to marketable securities, money, or both.

(C) FINANCIAL INSTRUMENT.—The term "financial instrument" includes stocks and other equity interests, evidences of indebtedness, options, forward or future contracts, notional principal contracts, and derivatives.

(3) EXCEPTIONS.—

(A) IN GENERAL.—Paragraph (1) shall not apply to the distribution from a partnership of a marketable security to a partner if—

(i) the security was contributed to the partnership by such partner, except to the extent that the value of the distributed security is attributable to marketable securities or money contributed (directly or indirectly) to the entity to which the distributed security relates,

(ii) to the extent provided in regulations prescribed by the Secretary, the property was not a marketable security when acquired by such partnership, or

(iii) such partnership is an investment partnership and such partner is an eligible partner thereof.

(B) LIMITATION ON GAIN RECOGNIZED.—In the case of a distribution of marketable securities to a partner, the amount taken into account under paragraph (1) shall be reduced (but not below zero) by the excess (if any) of—

(i) such partner's distributive share of the net gain which would be recognized if all of the marketable securities of the same class and issuer as the distributed securities held by the partnership were sold (immediately before the transaction to which the distribution relates) by the partnership for fair market value, over

(ii) such partner's distributive share of the net gain which is attributable to the marketable securities of the same class and issuer as the distributed securities held by the partnership immediately after the transaction, determined by using the same fair market value as used under clause (i).

Under regulations prescribed by the Secretary, all marketable securities held by the partnership may be treated as marketable securities of the same class and issuer as the distributed securities.

(C) DEFINITIONS RELATING TO INVESTMENT PARTNERSHIPS.—For purposes of subparagraph (A)(iii):

(i) INVESTMENT PARTNERSHIP.—The term "investment partnership" means any partnership which has never been engaged in a trade or business and substantially all of the assets (by value) of which have always consisted of—

(I) money,

(II) stock in a corporation,

(III) notes, bonds, debentures, or other evidences of indebtedness,

(IV) interest rate, currency, or equity notional principal contracts,

(V) foreign currencies,

(VI) interests in or derivative financial instruments (including options, forward or futures contracts, short positions, and similar financial instruments) in any asset described in any other subclause of this clause or in any commodity traded on or subject to the rules of a board of trade or commodity exchange,

(VII) other assets specified in regulations prescribed by the Secretary, or

(VIII) any combination of the foregoing.

(ii) EXCEPTION FOR CERTAIN ACTIVITIES.—A partnership shall not be treated as engaged in a trade or business by reason of—

(I) any activity undertaken as an investor, trader, or dealer in any asset described in clause (i), or

(II) any other activity specified in regulations prescribed by the Secretary.

(iii) ELIGIBLE PARTNER.—

(I) IN GENERAL.—The term "eligible partner" means any partner who, before the date of the distribution, did not contribute to the partnership any property other than assets described in clause (i).

(II) EXCEPTION FOR CERTAIN NONRECOGNITION TRANSACTIONS.—The term "eligible partner" shall not include the transferor or transferee in a nonrecognition transaction involving a transfer of any portion of an interest in a partnership with respect to which the transferor was not an eligible partner.

(iv) LOOK-THRU OF PARTNERSHIP TIERS.—Except as otherwise provided in regulations prescribed by the Secretary—

(I) a partnership shall be treated as engaged in any trade or business engaged in by, and as holding (instead of a partnership interest) a proportionate share of the assets of, any other partnership in which the partnership holds a partnership interest, and

(II) a partner who contributes to a partnership an interest in another partnership shall be treated as contributing a proportionate share of the assets of the other partnership.

If the preceding sentence does not apply under such regulations with respect to any interest held by a partnership in another partnership, the interest in such other partnership shall be treated as if it were specified in a subclause of clause (i).

(4) BASIS OF SECURITIES DISTRIBUTED.—

(A) IN GENERAL.—The basis of marketable securities with respect to which gain is recognized by reason of this subsection shall be—

(i) their basis determined under section 732, increased by

(ii) the amount of such gain.

(B) ALLOCATION OF BASIS INCREASE.—Any increase in basis attributable to the gain described in subparagraph (A)(ii) shall be allocated to marketable securities in proportion to their respective amounts of unrealized appreciation before such increase.

(5) SUBSECTION DISREGARDED IN DETERMINING BASIS OF PARTNER'S INTEREST IN PARTNERSHIP AND OF BASIS OF PARTNERSHIP PROPERTY.—Sections 733 and 734 shall be applied as if no gain were recognized, and no adjustment were made to the basis of property, under this subsection.

(6) CHARACTER OF GAIN RECOGNIZED.—In the case of a distribution of a marketable security which is an unrealized receivable (as defined in section 751(c)) or an inventory item (as defined in section 751(d)), any gain recognized under this subsection shall be treated as ordinary income to the extent of any increase in the basis of such security attributable to the gain described in paragraph (4)(A)(ii).

(7) REGULATIONS.—The Secretary shall prescribe such regulations as may be necessary or appropriate to carry out the purposes of this subsection, including regulations to prevent the avoidance of such purposes.

(d) EXCEPTIONS.—This section shall not apply to the extent otherwise provided by section 736 (relating to payments to a retiring partner or a deceased partner's successor in interest), section 751 (relating to unrealized receivables and inventory items), and section 737 (relating to recognition of precontribution gain in case of certain distributions).

SEC. 732.   BASIS OF DISTRIBUTED PROPERTY OTHER THAN MONEY.

(a) DISTRIBUTIONS OTHER THAN IN LIQUIDATION OF A PARTNER'S INTEREST.—

(1) GENERAL RULE.—The basis of property (other than money) distributed by a partnership to a partner other than in liquidation of the partner's interest shall, except as provided in paragraph (2), be its adjusted basis to the partnership immediately before such distribution.

(2) LIMITATION.—The basis to the distributee partner of property to which paragraph (1) is applicable shall not exceed the adjusted basis of such partner's interest in the partnership reduced by any money distributed in the same transaction.

(b) DISTRIBUTIONS IN LIQUIDATION.—The basis of property (other than money) distributed by a partnership to a partner in liquidation of the partner's interest shall be an amount equal to the adjusted basis of such partner's interest in the partnership reduced by any money distributed in the same transaction.

(c) ALLOCATION OF BASIS.—

(1) IN GENERAL.—The basis of distributed properties to which subsection (a)(2) or (b) is applicable shall be allocated—

(A)(i) first to any unrealized receivables (as defined in section 751(c)) and inventory items (as defined in section 751(d)) in an amount equal to the adjusted basis of each such property to the partnership, and

(ii) if the basis to be allocated is less than the sum of the adjusted bases of such properties to the partnership, then, to the extent any decrease is required in order to have the adjusted bases of such properties equal the basis to be allocated, in the manner provided in paragraph (3), and

(B) to the extent of any basis remaining after the allocation under subparagraph (A), to other distributed properties—

(i) first by assigning to each such other property such other property's adjusted basis to the partnership, and

(ii) then, to the extent any increase or decrease in basis is required in order to have the adjusted bases of such other distributed properties equal such remaining basis, in the manner provided in paragraph (2) or (3), whichever is appropriate.

(2) METHOD OF ALLOCATING INCREASE.—Any increase required under paragraph (1)(B) shall be allocated among the properties—

(A) first to properties with unrealized appreciation in proportion to their respective amounts of unrealized appreciation before such increase (but only to the extent of each property's unrealized appreciation), and

(B) then, to the extent such increase is not allocated under subparagraph (A), in proportion to their respective fair market values.

(3) METHOD OF ALLOCATING DECREASE.—Any decrease required under paragraph (1)(A) or (1)(B) shall be allocated—

(A) first to properties with unrealized depreciation in proportion to their respective amounts of unrealized depreciation before such decrease (but only to the extent of each property's unrealized depreciation), and

(B) then, to the extent such decrease is not allocated under subparagraph (A), in proportion to their respective adjusted bases (as adjusted under subparagraph (A)).

(d) SPECIAL PARTNERSHIP BASIS TO TRANSFEREE.—For purposes of subsections (a), (b), and (c), a partner who acquired all or part of his interest by a transfer with respect to which the election provided in section 754 is not in effect, and to whom a distribution of property (other than money) is made with respect to the transferred interest within 2 years after such transfer, may elect, under regulations prescribed by the Secretary, to treat as the adjusted partnership basis of such property the adjusted basis such property would have if the adjustment provided in section 743 (b) were in effect with respect to the partnership property. The Secretary may by regulations require the application of this subsection in the case of a distribution to a transferee partner, whether or not made within 2 years after the transfer, if at the time of the transfer the fair market value of the partnership property (other than money) exceeded 110 percent of its adjusted basis to the partnership.

(e) EXCEPTION.—This section shall not apply to the extent that a distribution is treated as a sale or exchange of property under section 751(b) (relating to unrealized receivables and inventory items).

(f) CORRESPONDING ADJUSTMENT TO BASIS OF ASSETS OF A DISTRIBUTED CORPORATION CONTROLLED BY A CORPORATE PARTNER. . . .

. . .

SEC. 733.   BASIS OF DISTRIBUTEE PARTNER'S INTEREST.

In the case of a distribution by a partnership to a partner other than in liquidation of a partner's interest, the adjusted basis to such partner of his interest in the partnership shall be reduced (but not below zero) by—

(1) the amount of any money distributed to such partner, and

(2) the amount of the basis to such partner of distributed property other than money, as determined under section 732.

SEC. 734.   OPTIONAL ADJUSTMENT TO BASIS OF UNDISTRIBUTED PARTNERSHIP PROPERTY.

(a) GENERAL RULE.—The basis of partnership property shall not be adjusted as the result of a distribution of property to a partner unless the election, provided in section 754 (relating to optional adjustment to basis of partnership property), is in effect with respect to such partnership.

(b) METHOD OF ADJUSTMENT.—In the case of a distribution of property to a partner, a partnership, with respect to which the election provided in section 754 is in effect, shall—

(1) increase the adjusted basis of partnership property by—

(A) the amount of any gain recognized to the distributee partner with respect to such distribution under section 731(a)(1), and

(B) in the case of distributed property to which section 732(a)(2) or (b) applies, the excess of the adjusted basis of the distributed property to the partnership immediately before the distribution (as adjusted by section 732(d)) over the basis of the distributed property to the distributee, as determined under section 732, or

(2) decrease the adjusted basis of partnership property by—

(A) the amount of any loss recognized to the distributee partner with respect to such distribution under section 731(a)(2), and

(B) in the case of distributed property to which section 732(b) applies, the excess of the basis of the distributed property to the distributee, as determined under section 732, over the adjusted basis of the distributed property to the partnership immediately before such distribution (as adjusted by section 732(d)).

Paragraph (1)(B) shall not apply to any distributed property which is an interest in another partnership with respect to which the election provided in section 754 is not in effect.

(c) ALLOCATION OF BASIS.—The allocation of basis among partnership properties where subsection (b) is applicable shall be made in accordance with the rules provided in section 755.

SEC. 736.   PAYMENTS TO A RETIRING PARTNER OR A DECEASED PARTNER'S SUCCESSOR IN INTEREST.

(a) PAYMENTS CONSIDERED AS DISTRIBUTIVE SHARE OR GUARANTEED PAYMENT.—Payments made in liquidation of the interest of a retiring partner or a deceased partner shall, except as provided in subsection (b), be considered—

(1) as a distributive share to the recipient of partnership income if the amount thereof is determined with regard to the income of the partnership, or

(2) as a guaranteed payment described in section 707(c) if the amount thereof is determined without regard to the income of the partnership.

(b) PAYMENTS FOR INTEREST IN PARTNERSHIP.—

(1) GENERAL RULE.—Payments made in liquidation of the interest of a retiring partner or a deceased partner shall, to the extent such payments (other than payments described in paragraph (2)) are determined, under regulations prescribed by the Secretary, to be made in exchange for the interest of such partner in partnership property, be considered as a distribution by the partnership and not as a distributive share or guaranteed payment under subsection (a).

(2) SPECIAL RULES.—For purposes of this subsection, payments in exchange for an interest in partnership property shall not include amounts paid for—

(A) unrealized receivables of the partnership (as defined in section 751(c)), or

(B) good will of the partnership, except to the extent that the partnership agreement provides for a payment with respect to good will.

(3) LIMITATION ON APPLICATION OF PARAGRAPH (2).—Paragraph (2) shall apply only if—

(A) capital is not a material income-producing factor for the partnership, and

(B) the retiring or deceased partner was a general partner in the partnership.

SEC. 737. RECOGNITION OF PRECONTRIBUTION GAIN IN CASE OF CERTAIN DISTRIBUTIONS TO CONTRIBUTING PARTNER.

(a) GENERAL RULE.—In the case of any distribution by a partnership to a partner, such partner shall be treated as recognizing gain in an amount equal to the lesser of—

(1) the excess (if any) of (A) the fair market value of property (other than money) received in the distribution over (B) the adjusted basis of such partner's interest in the partnership immediately before the distribution reduced (but not below zero) by the amount of money received in the distribution, or

(2) the net precontribution gain of the partner.

Gain recognized under the preceding sentence shall be in addition to any gain recognized under section 731. The character of such gain shall be determined by reference to the proportionate character of the net precontribution gain.

(b) NET PRECONTRIBUTION GAIN.—For purposes of this section, the term "net precontribution gain" means the net gain (if any) which would have been recognized by the distributee partner under section 704(c)(1)(B) if all property which—

(1) had been contributed to the partnership by the distributee partner within 7 years of the distribution, and

(2) is held by such partnership immediately before the distribution,

had been distributed by such partnership to another partner.

(c) BASIS RULES.—

(1) PARTNER'S INTEREST.—The adjusted basis of a partner's interest in a partnership shall be increased by the amount of any gain recognized by such partner under subsection (a). For purposes of determining the basis of the distributed property (other than money) such increase shall be treated as occurring immediately before the distribution.

(2) PARTNERSHIP'S BASIS IN CONTRIBUTED PROPERTY.—Appropriate adjustments shall be made to the adjusted basis of the partnership in the contributed property referred to in subsection (b) to reflect gain recognized under subsection (a).

(d) EXCEPTIONS.—

(1) DISTRIBUTIONS OF PREVIOUSLY CONTRIBUTED PROPERTY.—If any portion of the property distributed consists of property which had been contributed by the distributee partner to the partnership, such property shall not be taken into account under subsection (a)(1) and shall not be taken into account in determining the amount of the net precontribution gain. If the property distributed consists of an interest in an entity, the preceding sentence shall not apply to the extent that the value of such interest is attributable to property contributed to such entity after such interest had been contributed to the partnership.

(2) COORDINATION WITH SECTION 751.—This section shall not apply to the extent section 751(b) applies to such distribution.

(e) MARKETABLE SECURITIES TREATED AS MONEY.—For treatment of marketable securities as money for purposes of this section, see section 731(c).

SEC. 741.   RECOGNITION AND CHARACTER OF GAIN OR LOSS ON SALE OR EXCHANGE.

In the case of a sale or exchange of an interest in a partnership, gain or loss shall be recognized to the transferor partner. Such gain or loss shall be considered as gain or loss from the sale or exchange of a capital asset, except as otherwise provided in section 751 (relating to unrealized receivables and inventory items.

SEC. 742.   BASIS OF TRANSFEREE PARTNER'S INTEREST.

The basis of an interest in a partnership acquired other than by contribution shall be determined under part II of subchapter O . . . [Code §1011–§1023].

SEC. 743.   OPTIONAL ADJUSTMENT TO BASIS OF PARTNERSHIP PROPERTY.

(a) GENERAL RULE.—The basis of partnership property shall not be adjusted as the result of a transfer of an interest in a partnership by sale or exchange or on the death of a partner unless the election provided by section 754 (relating to optional adjustment to basis of partnership property) is in effect with respect to such partnership.

(b) ADJUSTMENT TO BASIS OF PARTNERSHIP PROPERTY.—In the case of a transfer of an interest in a partnership by sale or exchange or upon the death of a partner, a partnership with respect to which the election provided in section 754 is in effect shall—

(1) increase the adjusted basis of the partnership property by the excess of the basis to the transferee partner of his interest in the partnership over his proportionate share of the adjusted basis of the partnership property, or

(2) decrease the adjusted basis of the partnership property by the excess of the transferee partner's proportionate share of the adjusted basis of the partnership property over the basis of his interest in the partnership.

Under regulations prescribed by the Secretary, such increase or decrease shall constitute an adjustment to the basis of partnership property with respect to the transferee partner only. A partner's proportionate share of the adjusted basis of partnership property shall be determined in accordance with his interest in partnership capital and, in the case of property contributed to the partnership by a partner, section 704(c) (relating to contributed property) shall apply in determining such share. In the case of an adjustment under this subsection to the basis of partnership property subject to depletion, any depletion allowable shall be determined separately for the transferee partner with respect to his interest in such property.

(c) ALLOCATION OF BASIS.—The allocation of basis among partnership properties where subsection (b) is applicable shall be made in accordance with the rules provided in section 755.

SEC. 751.   UNREALIZED RECEIVABLES AND INVENTORY ITEMS.

(a) SALE OR EXCHANGE OF INTEREST IN PARTNERSHIP.—The amount of any money, or the fair market value of any property, received by a transferor partner in exchange for all or a part of his interest in the partnership attributable to—

(1) unrealized receivables of the partnership, or

(2) inventory items of the partnership,

shall be considered as an amount realized from the sale or exchange of property other than a capital asset.

(b) CERTAIN DISTRIBUTIONS TREATED AS SALES OR EXCHANGES.—

(1) GENERAL RULE.—To the extent a partner receives in a distribution—

(A) partnership property which is—

(i) unrealized receivables, or

(ii) inventory items which have appreciated substantially in value,

in exchange for all or a part of his interest in other partnership property (including money), or

(B) partnership property (including money) other than property described in subparagraph (A)(i) or (ii) in exchange for all or a part of his interest in partnership property described in subparagraph (A)(i) or (ii), such transactions shall, under regulations prescribed by the Secretary, be considered as a sale or exchange of such property between the distributee and the partnership (as constituted after the distribution).

(2) EXCEPTIONS.—Paragraph (1) shall not apply to—

(A) a distribution of property which the distributee contributed to the partnership, or

(B) payments, described in section 736 (a), to a retiring partner or successor in interest of a deceased partner.

(3) SUBSTANTIAL APPRECIATION—For purposes of paragraph (1)—

(A) IN GENERAL.—Inventory items of the partnership shall be considered to have appreciated substantially in value if their fair market value exceeds 120 percent of the adjusted basis to the partnership of such property.

(B) CERTAIN PROPERTY EXCLUDED.—For purposes of subparagraph (A), there shall be excluded any inventory property if a principal purpose for acquiring such property was to avoid the provisions of this subsection relating to inventory items.

(c) UNREALIZED RECEIVABLES.—For purposes of this subchapter, the term "unrealized receivables" includes, to the extent not previously includible in income under the method of accounting used by the partnership, any rights (contractual or otherwise) to payment for—

(1) goods delivered, or to be delivered, to the extent the proceeds therefrom would be treated as amounts received from the sale or exchange of property other than a capital asset, or

(2) services rendered, or to be rendered.

For purposes of this section and, sections 731, 732, and 741 (but not for purposes of section 736), such term also includes mining property (as defined in section 617(f)(2)), stock in a DISC (as described in section 992(a)), section 1245 property (as defined in section 1245(a)(3)), stock in certain foreign corporations (as described in section 1248), section 1250 property (as defined in section 1250 (c)), farm land (as defined in section 1252(a)), franchises, trademarks, or trade names (referred to in section 1253(a)), and an oil, gas, or geothermal property (described in section 1254) but only to the extent of the amount which would be treated as gain to which section 617(d)(1), 995(c), 1245(a), 1248(a), 1250(a), 1252(a), 1253(a) or 1254(a) would apply if (at the time of the transaction described in this section or section 731, 732, or 741, as the case may be) such property had been sold by the partnership at its fair market value. For purposes of this section and, sections 731, 732, and 741 (but not for purposes of section 736), such term also includes any market discount bond (as defined in section 1278) and any short-term obligation (as defined in section 1283) but only to the extent of the amount which would be treated as ordinary income if (at the time of the transaction described in this section or section 731, 732, or 741, as the case may be) such property had been sold by the partnership.

(d) INVENTORY ITEMS.—For purposes of this subchapter the term "inventory items" means—

(1) property of the partnership of the kind described in section 1221(a)(1),

(2) any other property of the partnership which, on sale or exchange by the partnership, would be considered property other than a capital asset and other than property described in section 1231,

(3) any other property of the partnership which, if sold or exchanged by the partnership, would result in a gain taxable under subsection (a) of section 1246 (relating to gain on foreign investment company stock), and

(4) any other property held by the partnership which, if held by the selling or distributee partner, would be considered property of the type described in subparagraph (1), (2), or (3).

(e) LIMITATION ON TAX ATTRIBUTABLE TO DEEMED SALES OF SECTION 1248 STOCK.—For purposes of applying this section and sections 731 and 741 to any amount resulting from the reference to section 1248(a) in the second sentence of subsection (c), in the case of an individual, the tax attributable to such amount shall be limited in the manner provided by subsection (b) of section 1248 (relating to gain from certain sales or exchanges of stock in certain foreign corporations).

(f) SPECIAL RULES IN THE CASE OF TIERED PARTNERSHIPS, ETC.—In determining whether property of a partnership is—

(1) an unrealized receivable, or

(2) an inventory item,

such partnership shall be treated as owning its proportionate share of the property of any other partnership in which it is a partner. Under regulations, rules similar to the rules of the preceding sentence shall also apply in the case of interests in trusts.

SEC. 752.   TREATMENT OF CERTAIN LIABILITIES.

(a) INCREASE IN PARTNER'S LIABILITIES.—Any increase in a partner's share of the liabilities of a partnership, or any increase in a partner's individual liabilities by reason of the assumption by such partner of partnership liabilities, shall be considered as a contribution of money by such partner to the partnership.

(b) DECREASE IN PARTNER'S LIABILITIES.—Any decrease in a partner's share of the liabilities of a partnership, or any decrease in a partner's individual liabilities by reason of the assumption by the partnership of such individual liabilities, shall be considered as a distribution of money to the partner by the partnership.

(c) LIABILITY TO WHICH PROPERTY IS SUBJECT.—For purposes of this section, a liability to which property is subject shall, to the extent of the fair market value of such property, be considered as a liability of the owner of the property.

(d) SALE OR EXCHANGE OF AN INTEREST.—In the case of a sale or exchange of an interest in a partnership, liabilities shall be treated in the same manner as liabilities in connection with the sale or exchange of property not associated with partnerships.

SEC. 753.   PARTNER RECEIVING INCOME IN RESPECT OF DECEDENT.

The amount includible in the gross income of a successor in interest of a deceased partner under section 736 (a) shall be considered income in respect of a decedent under section 691.

SEC. 754.   MANNER OF ELECTING OPTIONAL ADJUSTMENT TO BASIS OF PARTNERSHIP PROPERTY.

If a partnership files an election, in accordance with regulations prescribed by the Secretary, the basis of partnership property shall be adjusted, in the case of a distribution of property, in the manner provided in section 734 and, in the case of a transfer of a partnership interest, in the manner provided in section 743. Such an election shall apply with respect to all distributions of property by the partnership and to all transfers of interests in the partnership during the taxable year with respect to which such election was filed and all subsequent taxable years. Such election may be revoked by the partnership, subject to such limitations as may be provided by regulations prescribed by the Secretary.

SEC. 755.   RULES FOR ALLOCATION OF BASIS.

(a) GENERAL RULE.—Any increase or decrease in the adjusted basis of partnership property under section 734 (b) (relating to the optional adjustment to the basis of undistributed partnership property) or section 743 (b) (relating to the optional adjustment to the basis of partnership property in the case of a transfer of an interest in a partnership) shall, except as provided in subsection (b), be allocated—

    (1) in a manner which has the effect of reducing the difference between the fair market value and the adjusted basis of partnership properties, or

    (2) in any other manner permitted by regulations prescribed by the Secretary.

(b) SPECIAL RULE.—In applying the allocation rules provided in subsection (a), increases or decreases in the adjusted basis of partnership property arising from a distribution of, or a transfer of an interest attributable to, property consisting of—

    (1) capital assets and property described in section 1231 (b), or

    (2) any other property of the partnership,

shall be allocated to partnership property of a like character except that the basis of any such partnership property shall not be reduced below zero. If, in the case of a distribution, the adjustment to basis of property described in paragraph (1) or (2) is prevented by the absence of such property or by insufficient adjusted basis for such property, such adjustment shall be applied to subsequently acquired property of a like character in accordance with regulations prescribed by the Secretary.

SEC. 761.   TERMS DEFINED.

(a) PARTNERSHIP.—For purposes of this subtitle, the term "partnership" includes a syndicate, group, pool, joint venture or other unincorporated organization through or by means of which any business, financial operation, or venture is carried on, and which is not, within the meaning of this title [subtitle], a corporation or a trust or estate. Under regulations the Secretary may, at the election of all the members of an unincorporated organization, exclude such organization from the application of all or part of this subchapter [Code §701-§777], if it is availed of—

(1) for investment purposes only and not for the active conduct of a business,

(2) for the joint production, extraction, or use of property, but not for the purpose of selling services or property produced or extracted, or

(3) by dealers in securities for a short period for the purpose of underwriting, selling, or distributing a particular issue of securities,

if the income of the members of the organization may be adequately determined without the computation of partnership taxable income.

(b) PARTNER.—For purposes of this subtitle, the term "partner" means a member of a partnership.

(c) PARTNERSHIP AGREEMENT.—For purposes of this subchapter, a partnership agreement includes any modifications of the partnership agreement made prior to, or at, the time prescribed by law for the filing of the partnership return for the taxable year (not including extensions) which are agreed to by all the partners, or which are adopted in such other manner as may be provided by the partnership agreement.

(d) LIQUIDATION OF A PARTNER'S INTEREST.—For purposes of this subchapter, the term "liquidation of a partner's interest" means the termination of a partner's entire interest in a partnership by means of a distribution, or a series of distributions, to the partner by the partnership.

(e) DISTRIBUTIONS OF PARTNERSHIP INTERESTS TREATED AS EXCHANGES.—Except as otherwise provided in regulations, for purposes of—

(1) section 708 (relating to continuation of partnership),

(2) section 743 (relating to optional adjustment to basis of partnership property), and

(3) any other provision of this subchapter specified in regulations prescribed by the Secretary, any distribution of an interest in a partnership (not otherwise treated as an exchange) shall be treated as an exchange.

. . .

SEC. 871.   TAX ON NONRESIDENT ALIEN INDIVIDUALS.

(a) INCOME NOT CONNECTED WITH UNITED STATES BUSINESS—30 PERCENT TAX.—

(1) INCOME OTHER THAN CAPITAL GAINS.—Except as provided in subsection (h), there is hereby imposed for each taxable year a tax of 30 percent

of the amount received from sources within the United States by a nonresident alien individual as—

(A) interest (other than original issue discount as defined in section 1273), dividends, rents, salaries, wages, premiums, annuities, compensations, remunerations, emoluments, and other fixed or determinable annual or periodical gains, profits, and income,

. . .

(C) in the case of—

(i) a sale or exchange of an original issue discount obligation, the amount of the original issue discount accruing while such obligation was held by the nonresident alien individual (to the extent such discount was not theretofore taken into account under clause (ii)), and

(ii) a payment on an original issue discount obligation, an amount equal to the original issue discount accruing while such obligation was held by the nonresident alien individual (except that such original issue discount shall be taken into account under this clause only to the extent such discount was not theretofore taken into account under this clause and only to the extent that the tax thereon does not exceed the payment less the tax imposed by subparagraph (A) thereon), and

. . .

but only to the extent the amount so received is not effectively connected with the conduct of a trade or business within the United States.

(2) CAPITAL GAINS OF ALIENS PRESENT IN THE UNITED STATES 183 DAYS OR MORE.—In the case of a nonresident alien individual present in the United States for a period or periods aggregating 183 days or more during the taxable year, there is hereby imposed for such year a tax of 30 percent of the amount by which his gains, derived from sources within the United States, from the sale or exchange at any time during such year of capital assets exceed his losses, allocable to sources within the United States, from the sale or exchange at any time during such year of capital assets. For purposes of this paragraph, gains and losses shall be taken into account only if, and to the extent that, they would be recognized and taken into account if such gains and losses were effectively connected with the conduct of a trade or business within the United States, except that such gains and losses shall be determined without regard to section 1202 and such losses shall be determined without the benefits of the capital loss carryover provided in section 1212. Any gain or loss which is taken into account in determining the tax under paragraph (1) or subsection (b) shall not be taken into account in determining the tax under this paragraph. For purposes of the 183-day requirement of this paragraph, a nonresident alien

individual not engaged in trade or business within the United States who has not established a taxable year for any prior period shall be treated as having a taxable year which is the calendar year.

. . .

(b) INCOME CONNECTED WITH UNITED STATES BUSINESS—GRADUATED RATE OF TAX.—

(1) IMPOSITION OF TAX.—A nonresident alien individual engaged in trade or business within the United States during the taxable year shall be taxable as provided in section 1 or 55 on his taxable income which is effectively connected with the conduct of a trade or business within the United States.

(2) DETERMINATION OF TAXABLE INCOME.—In determining taxable income for purposes of paragraph (1), gross income includes only gross income which is effectively connected with the conduct of a trade or business within the United States.

. . .

SEC. 875. PARTNERSHIPS; BENEFICIARIES OF ESTATES AND TRUSTS.

For purposes of this subtitle—

(1) a nonresident alien individual or foreign corporation shall be considered as being engaged in a trade or business within the United States if the partnership of which such individual or corporation is a member is so engaged, and

(2) a nonresident alien individual or foreign corporation which is a beneficiary of an estate or trust which is engaged in any trade or business within the United States shall be treated as being engaged in such trade or business within the United States.

SEC. 881. TAX ON INCOME OF FOREIGN CORPORATIONS NOT CONNECTED WITH UNITED STATES BUSINESS.

(a) IMPOSITION OF TAX.—Except as provided in subsection (c), there is hereby imposed for each taxable year a tax of 30 percent of the amount received from sources within the United States by a foreign corporation as—

(1) interest (other than original issue discount as defined in section 1273), dividends, rents, salaries, wages, premiums, annuities, compensations, remu-

nerations, emoluments, and other fixed or determinable annual or periodical gains, profits, and income,

(2) gains described in section 631(b) or (c),

(3) in the case of—

(A) a sale or exchange of an original issue discount obligation, the amount of the original issue discount accruing while such obligation was held by the foreign corporation (to the extent such discount was not theretofore taken into account under subparagraph (B)), and

(B) a payment on an original issue discount obligation, an amount equal to the original issue discount accruing while such obligation was held by the foreign corporation (except that such original issue discount shall be taken into account under this subparagraph only to the extent such discount was not theretofore taken into account under this subparagraph and only to the extent that the tax thereon does not exceed the payment less the tax imposed by paragraph (1) thereon), and

. . .

but only to the extent the amount so received is not effectively connected with the conduct of a trade or business within the United States.

. . .

SEC. 882.   TAX ON INCOME OF FOREIGN CORPORATIONS CONNECTED WITH UNITED STATES BUSINESS.

(a) IMPOSITION OF TAX.—

(1) IN GENERAL.—A foreign corporation engaged in trade or business within the United States during the taxable year shall be taxable as provided in section 11, 55, 59A, or 1201(a) on its taxable income which is effectively connected with the conduct of a trade or business within the United States.

(2) DETERMINATION OF TAXABLE INCOME.—In determining taxable income for purposes of paragraph (1), gross income includes only gross income which is effectively connected with the conduct of a trade or business within the United States.

(3) For special tax treatment of gain or loss from the disposition by a foreign corporation of a United States real property interest, see section 897.

(b) GROSS INCOME.—In the case of a foreign corporation, except where the context clearly indicates otherwise, gross income includes only—

(1) gross income which is derived from sources within the United States and which is not effectively connected with the conduct of a trade or business within the United States, and

(2) gross income which is effectively connected with the conduct of a trade or business within the United States.

(c) ALLOWANCE OF DEDUCTIONS AND CREDITS.—

(1) ALLOCATION OF DEDUCTIONS.—

(A) GENERAL RULE.—In the case of a foreign corporation, the deductions shall be allowed only for purposes of subsection (a) and (except as provided by subparagraph (B)) only if and to the extent that they are connected with income which is effectively connected with the conduct of a trade or business within the United States; and the proper apportionment and allocation of the deductions for this purpose shall be determined as provided in regulations prescribed by the Secretary.

(B) CHARITABLE CONTRIBUTIONS.—The deduction for charitable contributions and gifts provided by section 170 shall be allowed whether or not connected with income which is effectively connected with the conduct of a trade or business within the United States.

(2) DEDUCTIONS AND CREDITS ALLOWED ONLY IF RETURN FILED.—A foreign corporation shall receive the benefit of the deductions and credits allowed to it in this subtitle only by filing or causing to be filed with the Secretary a true and accurate return, in the manner prescribed in subtitle F, including therein all the information which the Secretary may deem necessary for the calculation of such deductions and credits. The preceding sentence shall not apply for purposes of the tax imposed by section 541 (relating to personal holding company tax), and shall not be construed to deny the credit provided by section 33 for tax withheld at source or the credit provided by section 34 for certain uses of gasoline.

(3) FOREIGN TAX CREDIT.—Except as provided by section 906, foreign corporations shall not be allowed the credit against the tax for taxes of foreign countries and possessions of the United States allowed by section 901.

. . .

SEC. 1001. DETERMINATION OF AMOUNT OF AND RECOGNITION OF GAIN OR LOSS.

(a) COMPUTATION OF GAIN OR LOSS.—The gain from the sale or other disposition of property shall be the excess of the amount realized therefrom over the adjusted basis provided in section 1011 for determining gain, and the loss shall be the excess of the adjusted basis provided in such section for determining loss over the amount realized.

(b) AMOUNT REALIZED.—The amount realized from the sale or other disposition of property shall be the sum of any money received plus the fair market value of the property (other than money) received. . . .

. . .

(c) RECOGNITION OF GAIN OR LOSS.—Except as otherwise provided in this subtitle, the entire amount of the gain or loss, determined under this section, on the sale or exchange of property shall be recognized.

(d) INSTALLMENT SALES.—Nothing in this section shall be construed to prevent (in the case of property sold under contract providing for payment in installments) the taxation of that portion of any installment payment representing gain or profit in the year in which such payment is received.

SEC. 1014. BASIS OF PROPERTY ACQUIRED FROM A DECEDENT.

(a) IN GENERAL.—Except as otherwise provided in this section, the basis of property in the hands of a person acquiring the property from a decedent or to whom the property passed from a decedent shall, if not sold, exchanged, or otherwise disposed of before the decedent's death by such person, be—

(1) the fair market value of the property at the date of the decedent's death,

(2) in the case of an election under either section 2032 . . . its value at the applicable valuation date prescribed by those sections,

(3) in the case of an election under section 2032A, its value determined under such section. . . .

. . .

(c) PROPERTY REPRESENTING INCOME IN RESPECT OF A DECEDENT.— This section shall not apply to property which constitutes a right to receive an item of income in respect of a decedent under section 691.

. . .

SEC. 1017. DISCHARGE OF INDEBTEDNESS.

(a) GENERAL RULE.—If—

(1) an amount is excluded from gross income under subsection (a) of section 108 (relating to discharge of indebtedness), and

(2) under subsection (b)(2)(E), (b)(5), or (c)(1) of section 108, any portion of such amount is to be applied to reduce basis,

then such portion shall be applied in reduction of the basis of any property held by the taxpayer at the beginning of the taxable year following the taxable year in which the discharge occurs.

(b) AMOUNT AND PROPERTIES DETERMINED UNDER REGULATIONS.—

(1) IN GENERAL.—The amount of reduction to be applied under subsection (a) (not in excess of the portion referred to in subsection (a)), and the particular properties the bases of which are to be reduced, shall be determined under regulations prescribed by the Secretary.

(2) LIMITATION IN TITLE 11 CASE OR INSOLVENCY.—In the case of a discharge to which subparagraph (A) or (B) of section 108(a)(1) applies, the reduction in basis under subsection (a) of this section shall not exceed the excess of—

(A) the aggregate of the bases of the property held by the taxpayer immediately after the discharge, over

(B) the aggregate of the liabilities of the taxpayer immediately after the discharge.

The preceding sentence shall not apply to any reduction in basis by reason of an election under section 108(b)(5).

(3) CERTAIN REDUCTIONS MAY ONLY BE MADE IN THE BASIS OF DEPRECIABLE PROPERTY.—

(A) IN GENERAL.—Any amount which under subsection (b)(5) or (c)(1) of section 108 is to be applied to reduce basis shall be applied only to reduce the basis of depreciable property held by the taxpayer.

(B) DEPRECIABLE PROPERTY.—For purposes of this section, the term "depreciable property" means any property of a character subject to the allowance for depreciation, but only if a basis reduction under subsection (a) will reduce the amount of depreciation or amortization which otherwise would be allowable for the period immediately following such reduction.

(C) SPECIAL RULE FOR PARTNERSHIP INTERESTS.—For purposes of this section, any interest of a partner in a partnership shall be treated as depreciable property to the extent of such partner's proportionate interest in the depreciable property held by such partnership. The preceding sentence shall apply only if there is a corresponding reduction in the partnership's basis in depreciable property with respect to such partner.

(D) SPECIAL RULE IN CASE OF AFFILIATED GROUP.—For purposes of this section, if—

(i) a corporation holds stock in another corporation (hereinafter in this subparagraph referred to as the "subsidiary"), and

(ii) such corporations are members of the same affiliated group which file a consolidated return under section 1501 for the taxable year in which the discharge occurs,

then such stock shall be treated as depreciable property to the extent that such subsidiary consents to a corresponding reduction in the basis of its depreciable property.

(E) ELECTION TO TREAT CERTAIN INVENTORY AS DEPRECIABLE PROPERTY.—

(i) IN GENERAL.—At the election of the taxpayer, for purposes of this section, the term "depreciable property" includes any real property which is described in section 1221(a)(1).

(ii) ELECTION.—An election under clause (i) shall be made on the taxpayer's return for the taxable year in which the discharge occurs or at such other time as may be permitted in regulations prescribed by the Secretary. Such an election, once made, may be revoked only with the consent of the Secretary.

(F) SPECIAL RULES FOR QUALIFIED REAL PROPERTY BUSINESS INDEBTEDNESS.—In the case of any amount which under section 108(c)(1) is to be applied to reduce basis—

    (i) depreciable property shall only include depreciable real property for purposes of subparagraphs (A) and (C),

    (ii) subparagraph (E) shall not apply, and

    (iii) in the case of property taken into account under section 108(c)(2)(B), the reduction with respect to such property shall be made as of the time immediately before disposition if earlier than the time under subsection (a).

. . .

SEC. 1032.   EXCHANGE OF STOCK FOR PROPERTY.

(a) NONRECOGNITION OF GAIN OR LOSS.— No gain or loss shall be recognized to a corporation on the receipt of money or other property in exchange for stock (including treasury stock) of such corporation. No gain or loss shall be recognized by a corporation with respect to any lapse or acquisition of an option, or with respect to a securities futures contract (as defined in section 1234B), to buy or sell its stock (including treasury stock).

SEC. 1045.   ROLLOVER OF GAIN FROM QUALIFIED SMALL BUSINESS STOCK TO ANOTHER QUALIFIED SMALL BUSINESS STOCK.

(a) NONRECOGNITION OF GAIN.— In the case of any sale of qualified small business stock held by a taxpayer other than a corporation for more than 6 months and with respect to which such taxpayer elects the application of this section, gain from such sale shall be recognized only to the extent that the amount realized on such sale exceeds—

    (1) the cost of any qualified small business stock purchased by the taxpayer during the 60-day period beginning on the date of such sale, reduced by

    (2) any portion of such cost previously taken into account under this section.
This section shall not apply to any gain which is treated as ordinary income for purposes of this title.

    (b) DEFINITIONS AND SPECIAL RULES.— For purposes of this section—

    (1) QUALIFIED SMALL BUSINESS STOCK.—The term "qualified small business stock" has the meaning given such term by section 1202(c).

    (2) PURCHASE.—A taxpayer shall be treated as having purchased any property if, but for paragraph (3), the unadjusted basis of such property in the hands of the taxpayer would be its cost (within the meaning of section 1012).

    (3) BASIS ADJUSTMENTS.—If gain from any sale is not recognized by reason of subsection (a), such gain shall be applied to reduce (in the order acquired) the basis for determining gain or loss of any qualified small business stock which is purchased by the taxpayer during the 60-day period described in subsection (a).

(4) HOLDING PERIOD.—For purposes of determining whether the nonrecognition of gain under subsection (a) applies to stock which is sold—

(A) the taxpayer's holding period for such stock and the stock referred to in subsection (a)(1) shall be determined without regard to section 1223, and

(B) only the first 6 months of the taxpayer's holding period for the stock referred to in subsection (a)(1) shall be taken into account for purposes of applying section 1202(c)(2).

(5) CERTAIN RULES TO APPLY.—Rules similar to the rules of subsections (f), (g), (h), (i), (j), and (k) of section 1202 shall apply.

SEC. 1059. CORPORATE SHAREHOLDER'S BASIS IN STOCK REDUCED BY NONTAXED PORTION OF EXTRAORDINARY DIVIDENDS.

(a) GENERAL RULE.—If any corporation receives any extraordinary dividend with respect to any share of stock and such corporation has not held such stock for more than 2 years before the dividend announcement date—

(1) REDUCTION IN BASIS.—The basis of such corporation in such stock shall be reduced (but not below zero) by the nontaxed portion of such dividends.

(2) AMOUNTS IN EXCESS OF BASIS.—If the nontaxed portion of such dividends exceeds such basis, such excess shall be treated as gain from the sale or exchange of such stock for the taxable year in which the extraordinary dividend is received.

(b) NONTAXED PORTION.—For purposes of this section—

(1) IN GENERAL.—The nontaxed portion of any dividend is the excess (if any) of—

(A) the amount of such dividend, over

(B) the taxable portion of such dividend.

(2) TAXABLE PORTION.—The taxable portion of any dividend is—

(A) the portion of such dividend includible in gross income, reduced by

(B) the amount of any deduction allowable with respect to such dividend under section 243, 244, or 245.

(c) EXTRAORDINARY DIVIDEND DEFINED.—For purposes of this section—

(1) IN GENERAL.—The term "extraordinary dividend" means any dividend with respect to a share of stock if the amount of such dividend equals or exceeds the threshold percentage of the taxpayer's adjusted basis in such share of stock.

(2) THRESHOLD PERCENTAGE.—The term "threshold percentage" means—

(A) 5 percent in the case of stock which is preferred as to dividends, and

(B) 10 percent in the case of any other stock.

(3) AGGREGATION OF DIVIDENDS.—

(A) AGGREGATION WITHIN 85-DAY PERIOD.—All dividends—

(i) which are received by the taxpayer (or a person described in subparagraph (C)) with respect to any share of stock, and

(ii) which have ex-dividend dates within the same period of 85 consecutive days,

shall be treated as 1 dividend.

(B) AGGREGATION WITHIN 1 YEAR WHERE DIVIDENDS EXCEED 20 PERCENT OF ADJUSTED BASIS.—All dividends—

(i) which are received by the taxpayer . . . with respect to any share of stock, and

(ii) which have ex-dividend dates during the same period of 365 consecutive days,

shall be treated as extraordinary dividends if the aggregate of such dividends exceeds 20 percent of the taxpayer's adjusted basis in such stock (determined without regard to this section).

. . .

(4) FAIR MARKET VALUE DETERMINATION.—If the taxpayer establishes to the satisfaction of the Secretary the fair market value of any share of stock as of the day before the ex-dividend date, the taxpayer may elect to apply paragraphs (1) and (3) by substituting such value for the taxpayer's adjusted basis.

(d) SPECIAL RULES.—For purposes of this section—

(1) TIME FOR REDUCTION.—Any reduction in basis under subsection (a)(1) shall be treated as occurring at the beginning of the ex-dividend date of the extraordinary dividend to which the reduction relates.

. . .

(3) DETERMINATION OF HOLDING PERIOD.—For purposes of determining the holding period of stock under subsection (a), rules similar to the rules of paragraphs (3) and (4) of section 246(c) shall apply; except that "2 years" shall be substituted for the number of days specified in subparagraph (B) of section 246(c)(3).

(4) EX-DIVIDEND DATE.—The term "ex-dividend date" means the date on which the share of stock becomes ex-dividend.

(5) DIVIDEND ANNOUNCEMENT DATE.—The term "dividend announcement date" means, with respect to any dividend, the date on which the corporation declares, announces, or agrees to, the amount or payment of such dividend, whichever is the earliest.

(6) EXCEPTION WHERE STOCK HELD DURING ENTIRE EXISTENCE OF CORPORATION.—

(A) IN GENERAL.—Subsection (a) shall not apply to any extraordinary dividend with respect to any share of stock of a corporation if—

(i) such stock was held by the taxpayer during the entire period such corporation was in existence, and

(ii) except as provided in regulations, no earnings and profits of such corporation were attributable to transfers of property from (or earnings and profits of) a corporation which is not a qualified corporation.

(B) QUALIFIED CORPORATION.—For purposes of subparagraph (A), the term "qualified corporation" means any corporation (including a predecessor corporation)—

(i) with respect to which the taxpayer holds directly or indirectly during the entire period of such corporation's existence at least the same ownership interest as the taxpayer holds in the corporation distributing the extraordinary dividend, and

(ii) which has no earnings and profits—

(I) which were earned by, or

(II) which are attributable to gain on property which accrued during a period the corporation holding the property was,

a corporation not described in clause (i).

(C) APPLICATION OF PARAGRAPH.—This paragraph shall not apply to any extraordinary dividend to the extent such application is inconsistent with the purposes of this section.

(e) SPECIAL RULES FOR CERTAIN DISTRIBUTIONS.—

(1) TREATMENT OF PARTIAL LIQUIDATIONS AND CERTAIN REDEMPTIONS.—Except as otherwise provided in regulations—

(A) REDEMPTIONS.—In the case of any redemption of stock—

(i) which is part of a partial liquidation (within the meaning of section 302(e)) of the redeeming corporation,

(ii) which is not pro rata as to all shareholders, or

(iii) which would not have been treated (in whole or in part) as a dividend if—

(I) any options had not been taken into account under section 318(a)(4), or

(II) section 304(a) had not applied,

any amount treated as a dividend with respect to such redemption shall be treated as an extraordinary dividend to which paragraphs (1) and (2) of subsection (a) apply without regard to the period the taxpayer held such stock. In the case of a redemption described in clause (iii), only the basis in the stock redeemed shall be taken into account under subsection (a).

(B) REORGANIZATIONS, ETC.—An exchange described in section 356 which is treated as a dividend shall be treated as a redemption of stock for purposes of applying subparagraph (A).

. . .

(f) TREATMENT OF DIVIDENDS ON CERTAIN PREFERRED STOCK.—

(1) IN GENERAL.—Any dividend with respect to disqualified preferred stock shall be treated as an extraordinary dividend to which paragraphs (1) and (2) of subsection (a) apply without regard to the period the taxpayer held the stock.

(2) DISQUALIFIED PREFERRED STOCK.—For purposes of this subsection, the term "disqualified preferred stock" means any stock which is preferred as to dividends if—

(A) when issued, such stock has a dividend rate which declines (or can reasonably be expected to decline) in the future,

(B) the issue price of such stock exceeds its liquidation rights or its stated redemption price, or

(C) such stock is otherwise structured—

(i) to avoid the other provisions of this section, and

(ii) to enable corporate shareholders to reduce tax through a combination of dividend received deductions and loss on the disposition of the stock.

(g) REGULATIONS.—The Secretary shall prescribe such regulations as may be appropriate to carry out the purposes of this section, including regulations—

(1) providing for the application of this section in the case of stock dividends, stock splits, reorganizations, and other similar transactions, in the case of stock held by pass-thru entities, and in the case of consolidated groups, and

(2) providing that the rules of subsection (f) shall apply in the case of stock which is not preferred as to dividends in cases where stock is structured to avoid the purposes of this section.

SEC. 1202. PARTIAL EXCLUSION FOR GAIN FROM CERTAIN SMALL BUSINESS STOCK.

(a) EXCLUSION.—

(1) IN GENERAL.— In the case of a taxpayer other than a corporation, gross income shall not include 50 percent of any gain from the sale or exchange of qualified small business stock held for more than 5 years.

. . .

(b) PER-ISSUER LIMITATION ON TAXPAYER'S ELIGIBLE GAIN.—

(1) IN GENERAL.—If the taxpayer has eligible gain for the taxable year from 1 or more dispositions of stock issued by any corporation, the aggregate amount of such gain from dispositions of stock issued by such corporation which may be taken into account under subsection (a) for the taxable year shall not exceed the greater of—

(A) $10,000,000 reduced by the aggregate amount of eligible gain taken into account by the taxpayer under subsection (a) for prior taxable years attributable to dispositions of stock issued by such corporation, or

(B) 10 times the aggregate adjusted bases of qualified small business stock issued by such corporation and disposed of by the taxpayer during the taxable year.

For purposes of subparagraph (B), the adjusted basis of any stock shall be determined without regard to any addition to basis after the date on which such stock was originally issued.

(2) ELIGIBLE GAIN.—For purposes of this subsection, the term "eligible gain" means any gain from the sale or exchange of qualified small business stock held for more than 5 years.

(3) TREATMENT OF MARRIED INDIVIDUALS.—

(A) SEPARATE RETURNS.—In the case of a separate return by a married individual, paragraph (1)(A) shall be applied by substituting "$5,000,000" for "$10,000,000."

(B) ALLOCATION OF EXCLUSION.—In the case of any joint return, the amount of gain taken into account under subsection (a) shall be allocated equally between the spouses for purposes of applying this subsection to subsequent taxable years.

(C) MARITAL STATUS.—For purposes of this subsection, marital status shall be determined under section 7703.

(c) QUALIFIED SMALL BUSINESS STOCK.—For purposes of this section—

(1) IN GENERAL.—Except as otherwise provided in this section, the term "qualified small business stock" means any stock in a C corporation which is originally issued after the date of the enactment of the Revenue Reconciliation Act of 1993, if—

(A) as of the date of issuance, such corporation is a qualified small business, and

(B) except as provided in subsections (f) and (h), such stock is acquired by the taxpayer at its original issue (directly or through an underwriter)—

(i) in exchange for money or other property (not including stock), or

(ii) as compensation for services provided to such corporation (other than services performed as an underwriter of such stock).

(2) ACTIVE BUSINESS REQUIREMENTS; ETC.—

(A) IN GENERAL.—Stock in a corporation shall not be treated as qualified small business stock unless, during substantially all of the taxpayer's holding period for such stock, such corporation meets the active business requirements of subsection (e) and such corporation is a C corporation.

(B) SPECIAL RULE FOR CERTAIN SMALL BUSINESS INVESTMENT COMPANIES.—

(i) WAIVER OF ACTIVE BUSINESS REQUIREMENT.— Notwithstanding any provision of subsection (e), a corporation shall be treated as meeting the active business requirements of such subsection for any period during which such corporation qualifies as a specialized small business investment company.

(ii) SPECIALIZED SMALL BUSINESS INVESTMENT COMPANY.— For purposes of clause (i), the term "specialized small business investment company" means any eligible corporation (as defined in subsection (e)(4)) which is licensed to operate under section 301(d) of the Small Business Investment Act of 1958 (as in effect on May 13, 1993).

(3) CERTAIN PURCHASES BY CORPORATION OF ITS OWN STOCK.—

(A) REDEMPTIONS FROM TAXPAYER OR RELATED PERSON.—Stock acquired by the taxpayer shall not be treated as qualified small business stock if, at any time during the 4-year period beginning on the date 2 years before the issuance of such stock, the corporation issuing such stock purchased (directly or indirectly) any of its stock from the taxpayer or from a person related (within the meaning of section 267(b) or 707(b)) to the taxpayer.

(B) SIGNIFICANT REDEMPTIONS.—Stock issued by a corporation shall not be treated as qualified business stock if, during the 2-year period beginning on the date 1 year before the issuance of such stock, such corporation made 1 or more purchases of its stock with an aggregate value (as of the time of the respective purchases) exceeding 5 percent of the aggregate value of all of its stock as of the beginning of such 2-year period.

(C) TREATMENT OF CERTAIN TRANSACTIONS.—If any transaction is treated under section 304(a) as a distribution in redemption of the stock of any corporation, for purposes of subparagraphs (A) and (B), such corporation shall be treated as purchasing an amount of its stock equal to the amount treated as such a distribution under section 304(a).

(d) QUALIFIED SMALL BUSINESS.—For purposes of this section—

(1) IN GENERAL.—The term "qualified small business" means any domestic corporation which is a C corporation if—

(A) the aggregate gross assets of such corporation (or any predecessor thereof) at all times on or after the date of the enactment of the Revenue Reconciliation Act of 1993 and before the issuance did not exceed $50,000,000,

(B) the aggregate gross assets of such corporation immediately after the issuance (determined by taking into account amounts received in the issuance) do not exceed $50,000,000, and

(C) such corporation agrees to submit such reports to the Secretary and to shareholders as the Secretary may require to carry out the purposes of this section.

(2) AGGREGATE GROSS ASSETS.—

(A) IN GENERAL.—For purposes of paragraph (1), the term "aggregate gross assets" means the amount of cash and the aggregate adjusted bases of other property held by the corporation.

(B) TREATMENT OF CONTRIBUTED PROPERTY.—For purposes of subparagraph (A), the adjusted basis of any property contributed to the corporation (or other property with a basis determined in whole or in part by reference to the adjusted basis of property so contributed) shall be determined as if the basis of the property contributed to the corporation (immediately after such contribution) were equal to its fair market value as of the time of such contribution.

(3) AGGREGATION RULES.—

(A) IN GENERAL.—All corporations which are members of the same parent-subsidiary controlled group shall be treated as 1 corporation for purposes of this subsection.

(B) PARENT-SUBSIDIARY CONTROLLED GROUP.—For purposes of subparagraph (A), the term "parent-subsidiary controlled group" means any controlled group of corporations as defined in section 1563(a)(1), except that—

(i) "more than 50 percent" shall be substituted for "at least 80 percent" each place it appears in section 1563(a)(1), and

(ii) section 1563(a)(4) shall not apply.

(e) ACTIVE BUSINESS REQUIREMENT.—

(1) IN GENERAL.—For purposes of subsection (c)(2), the requirements of this subsection are met by a corporation for any period if during such period—

(A) at least 80 percent (by value) of the assets of such corporation are used by such corporation in the active conduct of 1 or more qualified trades or businesses, and

(B) such corporation is an eligible corporation.

(2) SPECIAL RULE FOR CERTAIN ACTIVITIES.—For purposes of paragraph (1), if, in connection with any future qualified trade or business, a corporation is engaged in—

(A) start-up activities described in section 195(c)(1)(A),

(B) activities resulting in the payment or incurring of expenditures which may be treated as research and experimental expenditures under section 174, or

(C) activities with respect to in-house research expenses described in section 41(b)(4),

assets used in such activities shall be treated as used in the active conduct of a qualified trade or business. Any determination under this paragraph shall be made without regard to whether a corporation has any gross income from such activities at the time of the determination.

(3) QUALIFIED TRADE OR BUSINESS.—For purposes of this subsection, the term "qualified trade or business" means any trade or business other than—

(A) any trade or business involving the performance of services in the fields of health, law, engineering, architecture, accounting, actuarial science, performing arts, consulting, athletics, financial services, brokerage services, or any trade or business where the principal asset of such trade or business is the reputation or skill of 1 or more of its employees,

(B) any banking, insurance, financing, leasing, investing, or similar business,

(C) any farming business (including the business of raising or harvesting trees),

(D) any business involving the production or extraction of products of a character with respect to which a deduction is allowable under section 613 or 613A, and

(E) any business of operating a hotel, motel, restaurant, or similar business.

(4) ELIGIBLE CORPORATION.—For purposes of this subsection, the term "eligible corporation" means any domestic corporation; except that such term shall not include—

. . .

(D) a cooperative.

(5) STOCK IN OTHER CORPORATIONS.—

(A) LOOK-THRU IN CASE OF SUBSIDIARIES.—For purposes of this subsection, stock and debt in any subsidiary corporation shall be disregarded and the parent corporation shall be deemed to own its ratable share of the subsidiary's assets, and to conduct its ratable share of the subsidiary's activities.

(B) PORTFOLIO STOCK OR SECURITIES.—A corporation shall be treated as failing to meet the requirements of paragraph (1) for any period during which more than 10 percent of the value of its assets (in excess of liabilities) consists of stock or securities in other corporations which are not subsidiaries of such corporation (other than assets described in paragraph (6)).

(C) SUBSIDIARY.—For purposes of this paragraph, a corporation shall be considered a subsidiary if the parent owns more than 50 percent of the combined voting power of all classes of stock entitled to vote, or more than 50 percent in value of all outstanding stock, of such corporation.

(6) WORKING CAPITAL.—For purposes of paragraph (1)(A), any assets which—

(A) are held as a part of the reasonably required working capital needs of a qualified trade or business of the corporation, or

(B) are held for investment and are reasonably expected to be used within 2 years to finance research and experimentation in a qualified trade or business or increases in working capital needs of a qualified trade or business,

shall be treated as used in the active conduct of a qualified trade or business. For periods after the corporation has been in existence for at least 2 years, in no event may more than 50 percent of the assets of the corporation qualify as used in the active conduct of a qualified trade or business by reason of this paragraph.

(7) MAXIMUM REAL ESTATE HOLDINGS.—A corporation shall not be treated as meeting the requirements of paragraph (1) for any period during which more than 10 percent of the total value of its assets consists of real property which is not used in the active conduct of a qualified trade or business. For purposes of the preceding sentence, the ownership of, dealing in, or renting of real property shall not be treated as the active conduct of a qualified trade or business.

(8) COMPUTER SOFTWARE ROYALTIES.—For purposes of paragraph (1), rights to computer software which produces active business computer software royalties (within the meaning of section 543(d)(1)) shall be treated as an asset used in the active conduct of a trade or business.

(f) STOCK ACQUIRED ON CONVERSION OF OTHER STOCK.—If any stock in a corporation is acquired solely through the conversion of other stock in such corporation which is qualified small business stock in the hands of the taxpayer—

(1) the stock so acquired shall be treated as qualified small business stock in the hands of the taxpayer, and

(2) the stock so acquired shall be treated as having been held during the period during which the converted stock was held.

(g) TREATMENT OF PASS-THRU ENTITIES.—

(1) IN GENERAL.—If any amount included in gross income by reason of holding an interest in a pass-thru entity meets the requirements of paragraph (2)—

(A) such amount shall be treated as gain described in subsection (a), and

(B) for purposes of applying subsection (b), such amount shall be treated as gain from a disposition of stock in the corporation issuing the stock disposed of by the pass-thru entity and the taxpayer's proportionate share of the adjusted basis of the pass-thru entity in such stock shall be taken into account.

(2) REQUIREMENTS.—An amount meets the requirements of this paragraph if—

(A) such amount is attributable to gain on the sale or exchange by the pass-thru entity of stock which is qualified small business stock in the hands of such entity (determined by treating such entity as an individual) and which was held by such entity for more than 5 years, and

(B) such amount is includible in the gross income of the taxpayer by reason of the holding of an interest in such entity which was held by the taxpayer on the date on which such pass-thru entity acquired such stock and at all times thereafter before the disposition of such stock by such pass-thru entity.

(3) LIMITATION BASED ON INTEREST ORIGINALLY HELD BY TAXPAYER.—Paragraph (1) shall not apply to any amount to the extent such amount exceeds the amount to which paragraph (1) would have applied if such amount were determined by reference to the interest the taxpayer held in the pass-thru entity on the date the qualified small business stock was acquired.

(4) PASS-THRU ENTITY.—For purposes of this subsection, the term "pass-thru entity" means—

(A) any partnership,

(B) any S corporation,

(C) any regulated investment company, and

(D) any common trust fund.

(h) CERTAIN TAX-FREE AND OTHER TRANSFERS.—For purposes of this section—

(1) IN GENERAL.—In the case of a transfer described in paragraph (2), the transferee shall be treated as—

(A) having acquired such stock in the same manner as the transferor, and

(B) having held such stock during any continuous period immediately preceding the transfer during which it was held (or treated as held under this subsection) by the transferor.

(2) DESCRIPTION OF TRANSFERS.—A transfer is described in this subsection if such transfer is—

(A) by gift,

(B) at death, or

(C) from a partnership to a partner of stock with respect to which requirements similar to the requirements of subsection (g) are met at the time of the transfer (without regard to the 5-year holding period requirement).

(3) CERTAIN RULES MADE APPLICABLE.—Rules similar to the rules of section 1244(d)(2) shall apply for purposes of this section.

(4) INCORPORATIONS AND REORGANIZATIONS INVOLVING NON-QUALIFIED STOCK.—

(A) IN GENERAL.—In the case of a transaction described in section 351 or a reorganization described in section 368, if qualified small business stock is exchanged for other stock which would not qualify as qualified small business stock but for this subparagraph, such other stock shall be treated as qualified small business stock acquired on the date on which the exchanged stock was acquired.

(B) LIMITATION.—This section shall apply to gain from the sale or exchange of stock treated as qualified small business stock by reason of subparagraph (A) only to the extent of the gain which would have been recognized at the time of the transfer described in subparagraph (A) if section 351 or 368 had not applied at such time. The preceding sentence shall not apply if the stock which is treated as qualified small business stock by reason of subparagraph (A) is issued by a corporation which (as of the time of the transfer described in subparagraph (A)) is a qualified small business.

(C) SUCCESSIVE APPLICATION.—For purposes of this paragraph, stock treated as qualified small business stock under subparagraph (A) shall be so treated for subsequent transactions or reorganizations, except that the limitation of subparagraph (B) shall be applied as of the time of the first transfer to which such limitation applied (determined after the application of the second sentence of subparagraph (B)).

(D) CONTROL TEST.—In the case of a transaction described in section 351, this paragraph shall apply only if, immediately after the transaction, the corporation issuing the stock owns directly or indirectly stock representing control (within the meaning of section 368(c)) of the corporation whose stock was exchanged.

(i) BASIS RULES.—For purposes of this section—

(1) STOCK EXCHANGED FOR PROPERTY.—In the case where the taxpayer transfers property (other than money or stock) to a corporation in exchange for stock in such corporation—

(A) such stock shall be treated as having been acquired by the taxpayer on the date of such exchange, and

(B) the basis of such stock in the hands of the taxpayer shall in no event be less than the fair market value of the property exchanged.

(2) TREATMENT OF CONTRIBUTIONS TO CAPITAL.—If the adjusted basis of any qualified small business stock is adjusted by reason of any contribution to capital after the date on which such stock was originally issued, in determining the amount of the adjustment by reason of such contribution, the basis of the contributed property shall in no event be treated as less than its fair market value on the date of the contribution.

(j) TREATMENT OF CERTAIN SHORT POSITIONS.—

(1) IN GENERAL.—If the taxpayer has an offsetting short position with respect to any qualified small business stock, subsection (a) shall not apply to any gain from the sale or exchange of such stock unless—

(A) such stock was held by the taxpayer for more than 5 years as of the first day on which there was such a short position, and

(B) the taxpayer elects to recognize gain as if such stock were sold on such first day for its fair market value.

(2) OFFSETTING SHORT POSITION.—For purposes of paragraph (1), the taxpayer shall be treated as having an offsetting short position with respect to any qualified small business stock if—

(A) the taxpayer has made a short sale of substantially identical property,

(B) the taxpayer has acquired an option to sell substantially identical property at a fixed price, or

(C) to the extent provided in regulations, the taxpayer has entered into any other transaction which substantially reduces the risk of loss from holding such qualified small business stock.

For purposes of the preceding sentence, any reference to the taxpayer shall be treated as including a reference to any person who is related (within the meaning of section 267(b) or 707(b)) to the taxpayer.

(k) REGULATIONS.—The Secretary shall prescribe such regulations as may be appropriate to carry out the purposes of this section, including regulations to prevent the avoidance of the purposes of this section through split-ups, shell corporations, partnerships, or otherwise.

SEC. 1272. CURRENT INCLUSION IN INCOME OF ORIGINAL ISSUE DISCOUNT.

(a) ORIGINAL ISSUE DISCOUNT ON DEBT INSTRUMENTS ISSUED AFTER JULY 1, 1982, INCLUDED IN INCOME ON BASIS OF CONSTANT INTEREST RATE.—

(1) GENERAL RULE.—For purposes of this title, there shall be included in the gross income of the holder of any debt instrument having original issue discount issued after July 1, 1982, an amount equal to the sum of the daily portions of the original issue discount for each day during the taxable year on which such holder held such debt instrument.

. . .

(3) DETERMINATION OF DAILY PORTIONS.—For purposes of paragraph (1), the daily portion of the original issue discount on any debt instrument shall be determined by allocating to each day in any accrual period its ratable portion of the increase during such accrual period in the adjusted issue price of the debt instrument. For purposes of the preceding sentence, the increase in the adjusted issue price for any accrual period shall be an amount equal to the excess (if any) of—

(A) the product of—

(i) the adjusted issue price of the debt instrument at the beginning of such accrual period, and

(ii) the yield to maturity (determined on the basis of compounding at the close of each accrual period and properly adjusted for the length of the accrual period), over

(B) the sum of the amounts payable as interest on such debt instrument during such accrual period.

(4) ADJUSTED ISSUE PRICE.—For purposes of this subsection, the adjusted issue price of any debt instrument at the beginning of any accrual period is the sum of—

(A) the issue price of such debt instrument, plus

(B) the adjustments under this subsection to such issue price for all periods before the first day of such accrual period.

(5) ACCRUAL PERIOD.—Except as otherwise provided in regulations prescribed by the Secretary, the term "accrual period" means a 6-month period (or shorter period from the date of original issue of the debt instrument) which ends on a day in the calendar year corresponding to the maturity date of the debt instrument or the date 6 months before such maturity date.

. . .

(7) REDUCTION WHERE SUBSEQUENT HOLDER PAYS ACQUISITION PREMIUM.—

(A) REDUCTION.—For purposes of this subsection, in the case of any purchase after its original issue of a debt instrument to which this subsection applies, the daily portion for any day shall be reduced by an amount equal to the amount which would be the daily portion for such day (without regard to this paragraph) multiplied by the fraction determined under subparagraph (B).

(B) DETERMINATION OF FRACTION.—For purposes of subparagraph (A), the fraction determined under this subparagraph is a fraction—

(i) the numerator of which is the excess (if any) of—

(I) the cost of such debt instrument incurred by the purchaser, over

(II) the issue price of such debt instrument, increased by the portion of original issue discount previously includible in the gross income of any holder (computed without regard to this paragraph), and

(ii) the denominator of which is the sum of the daily portions for such debt instrument for all days after the date of such purchase and ending on the stated maturity date (computed without regard to this paragraph).

. . .

(c) EXCEPTIONS.—This section shall not apply to any holder—

(1) who has purchased the debt instrument at a premium, or

(2) which is a life insurance company to which section 811(b) applies.

(d) DEFINITION AND SPECIAL RULE.—

(1) PURCHASE DEFINED.—For purposes of this section, the term "purchase" means—

(A) any acquisition of a debt instrument, where

(B) the basis of the debt instrument is not determined in whole or in part by reference to the adjusted basis of such debt instrument in the hands of the person from whom acquired.

(2) BASIS ADJUSTMENT.—The basis of any debt instrument in the hands of the holder thereof shall be increased by the amount included in his gross income pursuant to this section.

SEC. 1273. DETERMINATION OF AMOUNT OF ORIGINAL ISSUE DISCOUNT.

(a) GENERAL RULE.—for purposes of this subpart—

(1) IN GENERAL.—The term "original issue discount" means the excess (if any) of—

(A) the stated redemption price at maturity, over

(B) the issue price.

(2) STATED REDEMPTION PRICE AT MATURITY.—The term "stated redemption price at maturity" means the amount fixed by the last modification of the purchase agreement and includes interest and other amounts payable at that time (other than any interest based on a fixed rate, and payable unconditionally at fixed periodic intervals of 1 year or less during the entire term of the debt instrument).

(3) $\frac{1}{4}$ OF 1 PERCENT DE MINIMIS RULE.—If the original issue discount determined under paragraph (1) is less than—

(A) $\frac{1}{4}$ of 1 percent of the stated redemption price at maturity, multiplied by

(B) the number of complete years to maturity,

then the original issue discount shall be treated as zero.

(b) ISSUE PRICE.—For purposes of this subpart—

(1) PUBLICLY OFFERED DEBT INSTRUMENTS NOT ISSUED FOR PROPERTY.—In the case of any issue of debt instruments—

(A) publicly offered, and

(B) not issued for property,

the issue price is the initial offering price to the public (excluding bond houses and brokers) at which price a substantial amount of such debt instruments was sold.

(2) OTHER DEBT INSTRUMENTS NOT ISSUED FOR PROPERTY.—In the case of any issue of debt instruments not issued for property and not publicly offered, the issue price of each such instrument is the price paid by the first buyer of such debt instrument.

(3) DEBT INSTRUMENTS ISSUED FOR PROPERTY WHERE THERE IS PUBLIC TRADING.—In the case of a debt instrument which is issued for property and which—

(A) is part of an issue a portion of which is traded on an established securities market, or

(B)(i) is issued for stock or securities which are traded on an established securities market, or

(ii) to the extent provided in regulations, is issued for property (other than stock or securities) of a kind regularly traded on an established market, the issue price of such debt instrument shall be the fair market value of such property.

    (4) OTHER CASES.—Except in any case—

        (A) to which paragraph (1), (2), or (3) of this subsection applies, or

        (B) to which section 1274 applies,

the issue price of a debt instrument which is issued for property shall be the stated redemption price at maturity.

    (5) PROPERTY.—In applying this subsection, the term "property" includes services and the right to use property, but such term does not include money.

    (c) SPECIAL RULES FOR APPLYING SUBSECTION (b).—For purposes of subsection (b)—

    (1) INITIAL OFFERING PRICE; PRICE PAID BY THE FIRST BUYER.—The terms "initial offering price" and "price paid by the first buyer" include the aggregate payments made by the purchaser under the purchase agreement, including modifications thereof.

    (2) TREATMENT OF INVESTMENT UNITS.—In the case of any debt instrument and an option, security, or other property issued together as an investment unit—

        (A) the issue price for such unit shall be determined in accordance with the rules of this subsection and subsection (b) as if it were a debt instrument,

        (B) the issue price determined for such unit shall be allocated to each element of such unit on the basis of the relationship of the fair market value of such element to the fair market value of all elements in such unit, and

        (C) the issue price of any debt instrument included in such unit shall be the portion of the issue price of the unit allocated to the debt instrument under subparagraph (B).

SEC. 1274. DETERMINATION OF ISSUE PRICE IN THE CASE OF CERTAIN DEBT INSTRUMENTS ISSUED FOR PROPERTY.

    (a) IN GENERAL.—In the case of any debt instrument to which this section applies, for purposes of this subpart, the issue price shall be—

    (1) where there is adequate stated interest, the stated principal amount, or

    (2) in any other case, the imputed principal amount.

    (b) IMPUTED PRINCIPAL AMOUNT.—For purposes of this section—

    (1) IN GENERAL.—Except as provided in paragraph (3), the imputed principal amount of any debt instrument shall be equal to the sum of the present values of all payments due under such debt instrument.

    (2) DETERMINATION OF PRESENT VALUE.—For purposes of paragraph (1), the present value of a payment shall be determined in the manner provided by regulations prescribed by the Secretary—

        (A) as of the date of the sale or exchange, and

(B) by using a discount rate equal to the applicable Federal rate, compounded semiannually.

. . .

(c) DEBT INSTRUMENTS TO WHICH SECTION APPLIES.—

(1) IN GENERAL.—Except as otherwise provided in this subsection, this section shall apply to any debt instrument given in consideration for the sale or exchange of property if—

(A) the stated redemption price at maturity for such debt instrument exceeds—

(i) where there is adequate stated interest, the stated principal amount, or

(ii) in any other case, the imputed principal amount of such debt instrument determined under subsection (b), and

(B) some or all of the payments due under such debt instrument are due more than 6 months after the date of such sale or exchange.

(2) ADEQUATE STATED INTEREST.—For purposes of this section, there is adequate stated interest with respect to any debt instrument if the stated principal amount for such debt instrument is less than or equal to the imputed principal amount of such debt instrument determined under subsection (b).

(3) EXCEPTIONS.—This section shall not apply to—

. . .

(C) SALES INVOLVING TOTAL PAYMENTS OF $250,000 OR LESS.—

(i) IN GENERAL.—Any debt instrument arising from the sale or exchange of property if the sum of the following amounts does not exceed $250,000:

(I) the aggregate amount of the payments due under such debt instrument and all other debt instruments received as consideration for the sale or exchange, and

(II) the aggregate amount of any other consideration to be received for the sale or exchange.

(ii) CONSIDERATION OTHER THAN DEBT INSTRUMENT TAKEN INTO ACCOUNT AT FAIR MARKET VALUE.—For purposes of clause (i), any consideration (other than a debt instrument) shall be taken into account at its fair market value.

(iii) AGGREGATION OF TRANSACTIONS.—For purposes of this subparagraph, all sales and exchanges which are part of the same transaction (or a series of related transactions) shall be treated as 1 sale or exchange.

(D) DEBT INSTRUMENTS WHICH ARE PUBLICLY TRADED OR ISSUED FOR PUBLICLY TRADED PROPERTY.—Any debt instrument to which section 1273(b)(3) applies.

. . .

(F) SALES OR EXCHANGES TO WHICH SECTION 483(e) APPLIES.—Any debt instrument to the extent section 483(e) (relating to certain land transfers between related persons) applies to such instrument.

(4) EXCEPTION FOR ASSUMPTIONS.—If any person—

(A) in connection with the sale or exchange of property, assumes any debt instrument, or

(B) acquires any property subject to any debt instrument,

in determining whether this section or section 483 applies to such debt instrument, such assumption (or such acquisition) shall not be taken into account unless the terms and conditions of such debt instrument are modified (or the nature of the transaction is changed) in connection with the assumption (or acquisition).

(d) DETERMINATION OF APPLICABLE FEDERAL RATE.—For purposes of this section—

(1) APPLICABLE FEDERAL RATE.—

(A) IN GENERAL.—

In the Case of a Debt Instrument with a Term of:	The Applicable Federal Rate Is:
Not over 3 years	The Federal short-term rate.
Over 3 years but not over 9 years	The Federal mid-term rate.
Over 9 years	The Federal long-term rate.

(B) DETERMINATION OF RATES.—During each calendar month, the Secretary shall determine the Federal short-term rate, mid-term rate, and long-term rate which shall apply during the following calendar month.

(C) FEDERAL RATE FOR ANY CALENDAR MONTH.—For purposes of this paragraph—

(i) FEDERAL SHORT-TERM RATE.—The Federal short-term rate shall be the rate determined by the Secretary based on the average market yield (during any 1-month period selected by the Secretary and ending in the calendar month in which the determination is made) on outstanding marketable obligations of the United States with remaining periods to maturity of 3 years or less.

(ii) FEDERAL MID-TERM AND LONG-TERM RATES.—The Federal mid-term and long-term rate shall be determined in accordance with the principles of clause (i).

(D) LOWER RATE PERMITTED IN CERTAIN CASES.—The Secretary may by regulations permit a rate to be used with respect to any debt instrument which is lower than the applicable Federal rate if the taxpayer establishes to the satisfaction of the Secretary that such lower rate is based on the same principles as the applicable Federal rate and is appropriate for the term of such instrument.

(2) LOWEST 3-MONTH RATE APPLICABLE TO ANY SALE OR EXCHANGE.—

(A) IN GENERAL.—In the case of any sale or exchange, the applicable Federal rate shall be the lowest 3-month rate.

(B) LOWEST 3-MONTH RATE.—For purposes of subparagraph (A), the term "lowest 3-month rate" means the lowest of the applicable Federal rates in effect for any month in the 3-calendar-month period ending with the 1st calendar month in which there is a binding contract in writing for such sale or exchange.

(3) TERM OF DEBT INSTRUMENT.—In determining the term of a debt instrument for purposes of this subsection, under regulations prescribed by the Secretary, there shall be taken into account options to renew or extend.

. . .

SEC. 1275.   OTHER DEFINITIONS AND SPECIAL RULES.

(a) DEFINITIONS.—For purposes of this subpart—

(1) DEBT INSTRUMENT.—

(A) IN GENERAL.—Except as provided in subparagraph (B), the term "debt instrument" means a bond, debenture, note, or certificate or other evidence of indebtedness.

. . .

(2) ISSUE DATE.—

(A) PUBLICLY OFFERED DEBT INSTRUMENTS.—In the case of any debt instrument which is publicly offered, the term "date of original issue" means the date on which the issue was first issued to the public.

(B) ISSUES NOT PUBLICLY OFFERED AND NOT ISSUED FOR PROPERTY.—In the case of any debt instrument to which section 1273(b)(2) applies, the term "date of original issue" means the date on which the debt instrument was sold by the issuer.

(C) OTHER DEBT INSTRUMENTS.—In the case of any debt instrument not described in subparagraph (A) or (B), the term "date of original issue" means the date on which the debt instrument was issued in a sale or exchange.

. . .

(4) TREATMENT OF OBLIGATIONS DISTRIBUTED BY CORPORATIONS.—Any debt obligation of a corporation distributed by such corporation with respect to its stock shall be treated as if it had been issued by such corporation for property.

. . .

(c) INFORMATION REQUIREMENTS.—

(1) INFORMATION REQUIRED TO BE SET FORTH ON INSTRUMENT.—

(A) IN GENERAL.—In the case of any debt instrument having original issue discount, the Secretary may by regulations require that—

(i) the amount of the original issue discount, and

(ii) the issue date,

be set forth on such instrument.

(B) SPECIAL RULE FOR INSTRUMENTS NOT PUBLICLY OF-FERED.—In the case of any issue of debt instruments not publicly offered, the regulations prescribed under subparagraph (A) shall not require the information to be set forth on the debt instrument before any disposition of such instrument by the first buyer.

. . .

(d) REGULATION AUTHORITY.—The Secretary may prescribe regulations providing that where, by reason of varying rates of interest, put or call options, indefinite maturities, contingent payments, assumptions of debt instruments, or other circumstances, the tax treatment under this subpart (or section 163(e)) does not carry out the purposes of this subpart (or section 163(e)), such treatment shall be modified to the extent appropriate to carry out the purposes of this subpart (or section 163(e)).

SEC. 1361.   S CORPORATION DEFINED.

(a) S CORPORATION DEFINED.—

(1) IN GENERAL.—For purposes of this title, the term "S corporation" means, with respect to any taxable year, a small business corporation for which an election under section 1362(a) is in effect for such year.

(2) C CORPORATION.—For purposes of this title, the term "C corporation" means, with respect to any taxable year, a corporation which is not an S corporation for such year.

(b) SMALL BUSINESS CORPORATION.—

(1) IN GENERAL.—For purposes of this subchapter, the term "small business corporation" means a domestic corporation which is not an ineligible corporation and which does not—

(A) have more than 75 shareholders,

(B) have as a shareholder a person (other than an estate, a trust described in subsection (c)(2), or an organization described in subsection (c)(6)) who is not an individual,

(C) have a nonresident alien as a shareholder, and

(D) have more than 1 class of stock.

(2) INELIGIBLE CORPORATION DEFINED.—For purposes of paragraph (1), the term "ineligible corporation" means any corporation which is—

(A) a financial institution which uses the reserve method of accounting for bad debts described in section 585,

(B) an insurance company subject to tax under subchapter L,

(C) a corporation to which an election under section 936 applies, or

(D) a DISC or former DISC.

(3) TREATMENT OF CERTAIN WHOLLY OWNED SUBSIDIARIES.—

(A) IN GENERAL.—Except as provided in regulations prescribed by the Secretary, for purposes of this title—

(i) a corporation which is a qualified subchapter S subsidiary shall not be treated as a separate corporation, and

(ii) all assets, liabilities, and items of income, deduction, and credit of a qualified subchapter S subsidiary shall be treated as assets, liabilities, and such items (as the case may be) of the S corporation.

(B) QUALIFIED SUBCHAPTER S SUBSIDIARY.—For purposes of this paragraph, the term "qualified subchapter S subsidiary" means any domestic corporation which is not an ineligible corporation (as defined in paragraph (2)), if—

(i) 100 percent of the stock of such corporation is held by the S corporation, and

(ii) the S corporation elects to treat such corporation as a qualified subchapter S subsidiary.

(C) TREATMENT OF TERMINATIONS OF QUALIFIED SUBCHAPTER S SUBSIDIARY STATUS.—For purposes of this title, if any corporation which was a qualified subchapter S subsidiary ceases to meet the requirements of subparagraph (B), such corporation shall be treated as a new corporation acquiring all of its assets (and assuming all of its liabilities) immediately before such cessation from the S corporation in exchange for its stock.

(D) ELECTION AFTER TERMINATION.—If a corporation's status as a qualified subchapter S subsidiary terminates, such corporation (and any successor corporation) shall not be eligible to make—

(i) an election under subparagraph (B)(ii) to be treated as a qualified subchapter S subsidiary, or

(ii) an election under section 1362(a) to be treated as an S corporation, before its 5th taxable year which begins after the 1st taxable year for which such termination was effective, unless the Secretary consents to such election.

(c) SPECIAL RULES FOR APPLYING SUBSECTION (b).—

(1) HUSBAND AND WIFE TREATED AS 1 SHAREHOLDER.—For purposes of subsection (b)(1)(A), a husband and wife (and their estates) shall be treated as 1 shareholder.

(2) CERTAIN TRUSTS PERMITTED AS SHAREHOLDERS.—

(A) IN GENERAL.—For purposes of subsection (b)(1)(B), the following trusts may be shareholders:

(i) A trust all of which is treated (under subpart E of part I of subchapter J of this chapter) as owned by an individual who is a citizen or resident of the United States.

(ii) A trust which was described in clause (i) immediately before the death of the deemed owner and which continues in existence after such death, but only for the 2-year period beginning on the day of the deemed owner's death.

(iii) A trust with respect to stock transferred to it pursuant to the terms of a will, but only for the 2-year period beginning on the day on which such stock is transferred to it.

(iv) A trust created primarily to exercise the voting power of stock transferred to it.

(v) An electing small business trust.

This subparagraph shall not apply to any foreign trust.

(B) TREATMENT AS SHAREHOLDERS.—For purposes of subsection (b)(1)—

(i) In the case of a trust described in clause (i) of subparagraph (A), the deemed owner shall be treated as the shareholder.

(ii) In the case of a trust described in clause (ii) of subparagraph (A), the estate of the deemed owner shall be treated as the shareholder.

(iii) In the case of a trust described in clause (iii) of subparagraph (A), the estate of the testator shall be treated as the shareholder.

(iv) In the case of a trust described in clause (iv) of subparagraph (A), each beneficiary of the trust shall be treated as a shareholder.

(v) In the case of a trust described in clause (v) of subparagraph (A), each potential current beneficiary of such trust shall be treated as a shareholder; except that, if for any period there is no potential current beneficiary of such trust, such trust shall be treated as the shareholder during such period.

(3) ESTATE OF INDIVIDUAL IN BANKRUPTCY MAY BE SHAREHOLDER.—For purposes of subsection (b)(1)(B), the term "estate" includes the estate of an individual in a case under title 11 of the United States Code.

(4) DIFFERENCES IN COMMON STOCK VOTING RIGHTS DISREGARDED.—For purposes of subsection (b)(1)(D), a corporation shall not be treated as having more than 1 class of stock solely because there are differences in voting rights among the shares of common stock.

(5) STRAIGHT DEBT SAFE HARBOR.—

(A) IN GENERAL.—For purposes of subsection (b)(1)(D), straight debt shall not be treated as a second class of stock.

(B) STRAIGHT DEBT DEFINED.—For purposes of this paragraph, the term "straight debt" means any written unconditional promise to pay on demand or on a specified date a sum certain in money if—

(i) the interest rate (and interest payment dates) are not contingent on profits, the borrower's discretion, or similar factors,

(ii) there is no convertibility (directly or indirectly) into stock, and

(iii) the creditor is an individual (other than a nonresident alien), an estate, a trust described in paragraph (2), or a person which is actively and regularly engaged in the business of lending money.

(C) REGULATIONS.—The Secretary shall prescribe such regulations as may be necessary or appropriate to provide for the proper treatment of straight debt under this subchapter and for the coordination of such treatment with other provisions of this title.

(6) CERTAIN EXEMPT ORGANIZATIONS PERMITTED AS SHAREHOLDERS.—For purposes of subsection (b)(1)(B), an organization which is—

(A) described in section 401(a) or 501(c)(3), and

(B) exempt from taxation under section 501(a),

may be a shareholder in an S corporation.

(d) SPECIAL RULE FOR QUALIFIED SUBCHAPTER S TRUST.—

(1) IN GENERAL.—In the case of a qualified subchapter S trust with respect to which a beneficiary makes an election under paragraph (2)—

(A) such trust shall be treated as a trust described in subsection (c)(2)(A)(i), and

(B) for purposes of section 678(a), the beneficiary of such trust shall be treated as the owner of that portion of the trust which consists of stock in an S corporation with respect to which the election under paragraph (2) is made.

(2) ELECTION.—

(A) IN GENERAL.—A beneficiary of a qualified subchapter S trust (or his legal representative) may elect to have this subsection apply.

(B) MANNER AND TIME OF ELECTION.—

(i) SEPARATE ELECTION WITH RESPECT TO EACH CORPORA-TION.—An election under this paragraph shall be made separately with respect to each corporation the stock of which is held by the trust.

(ii) ELECTIONS WITH RESPECT TO SUCCESSIVE INCOME BENEFI-CIARIES.—If there is an election under this paragraph with respect to any beneficiary, an election under this paragraph shall be treated as made by each successive beneficiary unless such beneficiary affirmatively re-fuses to consent to such election.

(iii) TIME, MANNER, AND FORM OF ELECTION.—Any election, or refusal, under this paragraph shall be made in such manner and form, and at such time, as the Secretary may prescribe.

(C) ELECTION IRREVOCABLE.—An election under this paragraph, once made, may be revoked only with the consent of the Secretary.

(D) GRACE PERIOD.—An election under this paragraph shall be effective up to 15 days and 2 months before the date of the election.

(3) QUALIFIED SUBCHAPTER S TRUST.—For purposes of this subsection, the term "qualified subchapter S trust" means a trust—

(A) the terms of which require that—

(i) during the life of the current income beneficiary, there shall be only 1 income beneficiary of the trust,

(ii) any corpus distributed during the life of the current income benefi-ciary may be distributed only to such beneficiary,

(iii) the income interest of the current income beneficiary in the trust shall terminate on the earlier of such beneficiary's death or the termination of the trust, and

(iv) upon the termination of the trust during the life of the current income beneficiary, the trust shall distribute all of its assets to such benefi-ciary, and

(B) all of the income (within the meaning of section 643(b)) of which is distributed (or required to be distributed) currently to 1 individual who is a citizen or resident of the United States.

A substantially separate and independent share of a trust within the meaning of 663(c) shall be treated as a separate trust for purposes of this subsection and subsection (c).

(4) TRUST CEASING TO BE QUALIFIED.—

(A) FAILURE TO MEET REQUIREMENTS OF PARAGRAPH (3)(A).—If a qualified subchapter S trust ceases to meet any requirement of paragraph (3)(A), the provisions of this subsection shall not apply to such trust as of the date it ceases to meet such requirement.

(B) FAILURE TO MEET REQUIREMENTS OF PARAGRAPH (3)(B).—If any qualified subchapter S trust ceases to meet any requirement of paragraph (3)(B) but continues to meet the requirements of paragraph (3)(A), the provisions of this subsection shall not apply to such trust as of the first day of the first taxable year beginning after the first taxable year for which it failed to meet the requirements of paragraph (3)(B).

(e) ELECTING SMALL BUSINESS TRUST DEFINED.—

(1) ELECTING SMALL BUSINESS TRUST.—For purposes of this section—

(A) IN GENERAL.—Except as provided in subparagraph (B), the term "electing small business trust" means any trust if—

(i) such trust does not have as a beneficiary any person other than (I) an individual, (II) an estate, (III) an organization described in paragraph (2), (3), (4), or (5) of section 170(c), or (IV) an organization described in section 170(c)(1) which holds a contingent interest in such trust and is not a potential current beneficiary,

(ii) no interest in such trust was acquired by purchase, and

(iii) an election under this subsection applies to such trust.

(B) CERTAIN TRUSTS NOT ELIGIBLE.—The term "electing small business trust" shall not include—

(i) any qualified subchapter S trust (as defined in subsection (d)(3)) if an election under subsection (d)(2) applies to any corporation the stock of which is held by such trust,

(ii) any trust exempt from tax under this subtitle, and

(iii) any charitable remainder annuity trust or charitable remainder unitrust (as defined in section 664(d)).

(C) PURCHASE.—For purposes of subparagraph (A), the term "purchase" means any acquisition if the basis of the property acquired is determined under section 1012.

(2) POTENTIAL CURRENT BENEFICIARY.—For purposes of this section, the term "potential current beneficiary" means, with respect to any period, any person who at any time during such period is entitled to, or at the discretion of any person may receive, a distribution from the principal or income of the trust. If a trust disposes of all of the stock which it holds in an S corporation, then, with respect to such corporation, the term "potential current beneficiary" does not include any person who first met the requirements of the preceding sentence during the 60-day period ending on the date of such disposition.

(3) ELECTION.—An election under this subsection shall be made by the trustee. Any such election shall apply to the taxable year of the trust for which

made and all subsequent taxable years of such trust unless revoked with the consent of the Secretary.

(4) CROSS REFERENCE.—For special treatment of electing small business trusts, see section 641(c).

SEC. 1362.   ELECTION; REVOCATION; TERMINATION.

(a) ELECTION.—

(1) IN GENERAL.—Except as provided in subsection (g), a small business corporation may elect, in accordance with the provisions of this section, to be an S corporation.

(2) ALL SHAREHOLDERS MUST CONSENT TO ELECTION.—An election under this subsection shall be valid only if all persons who are shareholders in such corporation on the day on which such election is made consent to such election.

(b) WHEN MADE.—

(1) IN GENERAL.—An election under subsection (a) may be made by a small business corporation for any taxable year—

(A) at any time during the preceding taxable year, or

(B) at any time during the taxable year and on or before the 15th day of the 3d month of the taxable year.

(2) CERTAIN ELECTIONS MADE DURING 1ST $2\frac{1}{2}$ MONTHS TREATED AS MADE FOR NEXT TAXABLE YEAR.—If—

(A) an election under subsection (a) is made for any taxable year during such year and on or before the 15th day of the 3d month of such year, but

(B) either—

(i) on 1 or more days in such taxable year before the day on which the election was made the corporation did not meet the requirements of subsection (b) of section 1361, or

(ii) 1 or more of the persons who held stock in the corporation during such taxable year and before the election was made did not consent to the election,

then such election shall be treated as made for the following taxable year.

(3) ELECTION MADE AFTER 1ST $2\frac{1}{2}$ MONTHS TREATED AS MADE FOR FOLLOWING TAXABLE YEAR.—If—

(A) a small business corporation makes an election under subsection (a) for any taxable year, and

(B) such election is made after the 15th day of the 3d month of the taxable year and on or before the 15th day of the 3rd month of the following taxable year,

then such election shall be treated as made for the following taxable year.

(4) TAXABLE YEARS OF $2\frac{1}{2}$ MONTHS OR LESS.—For purposes of this subsection, an election for a taxable year made not later than 2 months and 15 days after the first day of the taxable year shall be treated as timely made during such year.

(5) AUTHORITY TO TREAT LATE ELECTIONS, ETC., AS TIMELY.—If—

(A) An election under subsection (a) is made for any taxable year (determined without regard to paragraph (3)) after the date prescribed by this subsection for making such election for such taxable year or no such election is made for any taxable year, and

(B) the Secretary determines that there was reasonable cause for the failure to timely make such election,

the Secretary may treat such an election as timely made for such taxable year (and paragraph (3) shall not apply).

(c) YEARS FOR WHICH EFFECTIVE.—An election under subsection (a) shall be effective for the taxable year of the corporation for which it is made and for all succeeding taxable years of the corporation, until such election is terminated under subsection (d).

(d) TERMINATION.—

(1) BY REVOCATION.—

(A) IN GENERAL.—An election under subsection (a) may be terminated by revocation.

(B) MORE THAN ONE-HALF OF SHARES MUST CONSENT TO REVO-CATION.—An election may be revoked only if shareholders holding more than one-half of the shares of stock of the corporation on the day on which the revocation is made consent to the revocation.

(C) WHEN EFFECTIVE.—Except as provided in subparagraph (D)—

(i) a revocation made during the taxable year and on or before the 15th day of the 3d month thereof shall be effective on the 1st day of such taxable year, and

(ii) a revocation made during the taxable year but after such 15th day shall be effective on the 1st day of the following taxable year.

(D) REVOCATION MAY SPECIFY PROSPECTIVE DATE.—If the revocation specifies a date for revocation which is on or after the day on which the revocation is made, the revocation shall be effective on and after the date so specified.

(2) BY CORPORATION CEASING TO BE SMALL BUSINESS CORPO-RATION.—

(A) IN GENERAL.—An election under subsection (a) shall be terminated whenever (at any time on or after the 1st day of the 1st taxable year for which the corporation is an S corporation) such corporation ceases to be a small business corporation.

(B) WHEN EFFECTIVE.—Any termination under this paragraph shall be effective on and after the date of cessation.

(3) WHERE PASSIVE INVESTMENT INCOME EXCEEDS 25 PERCENT OF GROSS RECEIPTS FOR 3 CONSECUTIVE TAXABLE YEARS AND CORPORA-TION HAS ACCUMULATED EARNINGS AND PROFITS.—

(A) TERMINATION.—

(i) IN GENERAL.—An election under subsection (a) shall be terminated whenever the corporation—

(I) has accumulated earnings and profits at the close of each of 3 consecutive taxable years, and

(II) has gross receipts for each of such taxable years more than 25 percent of which are passive investment income.

(ii) WHEN EFFECTIVE.—Any termination under this paragraph shall be effective on and after the first day of the first taxable year beginning after the third consecutive taxable year referred to in clause (i).

(iii) YEARS TAKEN INTO ACCOUNT.—A prior taxable year shall not be taken into account under clause (i) unless—

(I) such taxable year began after December 31, 1981, and

(II) the corporation was an S corporation for such taxable year.

(B) GROSS RECEIPTS FROM SALES OF CAPITAL ASSETS (OTHER THAN STOCK AND SECURITIES).—For purposes of this paragraph, in the case of dispositions of capital assets (other than stock and securities), gross receipts from such dispositions shall be taken into account only to the extent of the capital gain net income therefrom.

(C) PASSIVE INVESTMENT INCOME DEFINED.—For purposes of this paragraph—

(i) IN GENERAL.—Except as otherwise provided in this subparagraph, the term "passive investment income" means gross receipts derived from royalties, rents, dividends, interest, annuities, and sales or exchanges of stock or securities (gross receipts from such sales or exchanges being taken into account for purposes of this paragraph only to the extent of gains therefrom).

(ii) EXCEPTION FOR INTEREST ON NOTES FROM SALES OF INVENTORY.—The term "passive investment income" shall not include interest on any obligation acquired in the ordinary course of the corporation's trade or business from its sale of property described in section 1221(a)(1).

(iii) TREATMENT OF CERTAIN LENDING OR FINANCE COMPANIES.—If the S corporation meets the requirements of section 542(c)(6) for the taxable year, the term "passive investment income" shall not include gross receipts for the taxable year which are derived directly from the active and regular conduct of a lending or finance business (as defined in section 542(d)(1)).

(iv) TREATMENT OF CERTAIN LIQUIDATIONS.—Gross receipts derived from sales or exchanges of stock or securities shall not include amounts received by an S corporation which are treated under section 331 (relating to corporate liquidations) as payments in exchange for stock where the S corporation owned more than 50 percent of each class of stock of the liquidating corporation.

(D) SPECIAL RULE FOR OPTIONS AND COMMODITY DEALINGS.—

(i) IN GENERAL.—In the case of any options dealer or commodities dealer, passive investment income shall be determined by not taking into account any gain or loss (in the normal course of the taxpayer's activity of dealing in or trading section 1256 contracts) from any section 1256 contract or property related to such a contract.

(ii) DEFINITIONS.—For purposes of this subparagraph—

(I) OPTIONS DEALER.—The term "options dealer" has the meaning given such term by section 1256(g)(8).

(II) COMMODITIES DEALER.—The term "commodities dealer" means a person who is actively engaged in trading section 1256 contracts and is registered with a domestic board of trade which is designated as a contract market by the Commodities Futures Trading Commission.

(III) SECTION 1256 CONTRACT.—The term "section 1256 contract" has the meaning given to such term by section 1256(b).

(E) TREATMENT OF CERTAIN DIVIDENDS.—If an S corporation holds stock in a C corporation meeting the requirements of section 1504(a)(2), the term "passive investment income" shall not include dividends from such C corporation to the extent such dividends are attributable to the earnings and profits of such C corporation derived from the active conduct of a trade or business.

(e) TREATMENT OF S TERMINATION YEAR.—

(1) IN GENERAL.—In the case of an S termination year, for purposes of this title—

(A) S SHORT YEAR.—The portion of such year ending before the 1st day for which the termination is effective shall be treated as a short taxable year for which the corporation is an S corporation.

(B) C SHORT YEAR.—The portion of such year beginning on such 1st day shall be treated as a short taxable year for which the corporation is a C corporation.

(2) PRO RATA ALLOCATION.—Except as provided in paragraph (3) and subparagraphs (C) and (D) of paragraph (6), the determination of which items are to be taken into account for each of the short taxable years referred to in paragraph (1) shall be made—

(A) first by determining for the S termination year—

(i) the amount of each of the items of income, loss, deduction, or credit described in section 1366(a)(1)(A), and

(ii) the amount of the nonseparately computed income or loss, and

(B) then by assigning an equal portion of each amount determined under subparagraph (A) to each day of the S termination year.

(3) ELECTION TO HAVE ITEMS ASSIGNED TO EACH SHORT TAXABLE YEAR UNDER NORMAL TAX ACCOUNTING RULES.—

(A) IN GENERAL.—A corporation may elect to have paragraph (2) not apply.

(B) SHAREHOLDERS MUST CONSENT TO ELECTION.—An election under this subsection shall be valid only if all persons who are shareholders in the corporation at any time during the S short year and all persons who are shareholders in the corporation on the first day of the C short year consent to such election.

(4) S TERMINATION YEAR.—For purposes of this subsection, the term "S termination year" means any taxable year of a corporation (determined without

regard to this subsection) in which a termination of an election made under subsection (a) takes effect (other than on the 1st day thereof).

. . .

(f) INADVERTENT INVALID ELECTIONS OR TERMINATIONS.—If—

(1) an election under subsection (a) by any corporation—

(A) was not effective for the taxable year for which made (determined without regard to subsection (b)(2)) by reason of a failure to meet the requirements of section 1361(b) or to obtain shareholder consents, or

(B) was terminated under paragraph (2) or (3) of subsection (d),

(2) the Secretary determines that the circumstances resulting in such ineffectiveness or termination were inadvertent,

(3) no later than a reasonable period of time after discovery of the circumstances resulting in such ineffectiveness or termination, steps were taken—

(A) so that the corporation is a small business corporation, or

(B) to acquire the required shareholder consents, and

(4) the corporation, and each person who was a shareholder in the corporation at any time during the period specified pursuant to this subsection, agrees to make such adjustments (consistent with the treatment of the corporation as an S corporation) as may be required by the Secretary with respect to such period,

then, notwithstanding the circumstances resulting in such ineffectiveness or termination, such corporation shall be treated as an S corporation during the period specified by the Secretary.

(g) ELECTION AFTER TERMINATION.—If a small business corporation has made an election under subsection (a) and if such election has been terminated under subsection (d), such corporation (and any successor corporation) shall not be eligible to make an election under subsection (a) for any taxable year before its 5th taxable year which begins after the 1st taxable year for which such termination is effective, unless the Secretary consents to such election.

An uncodified 1996 statutory provision states that "For purposes of section 1362(g) of the Internal Revenue Code of 1986 (relating to election after termination), any termination under section 1362(d) of such Code in a taxable year beginning before January 1, 1997, shall not be taken into account."

SEC. 1363.   EFFECT OF ELECTION ON CORPORATION.

(a) GENERAL RULE.—Except as otherwise provided in this subchapter, an S corporation shall not be subject to the taxes imposed by this chapter.

(b) COMPUTATION OF CORPORATION'S TAXABLE INCOME.—The taxable income of an S corporation shall be computed in the same manner as in the case of an individual, except that—

(1) the items described in section 1366(a)(1)(A) shall be separately stated,

(2) the deductions referred to in section 703(a)(2) shall not be allowed to the corporation,

(3) section 248 shall apply, and

(4) section 291 shall apply if the S corporation (or any predecessor) was a C corporation for any of the 3 immediately preceding taxable years.

(c) ELECTIONS OF THE S CORPORATION.—

(1) IN GENERAL.—Except as provided in paragraph (2), any election affecting the computation of items derived from an S corporation shall be made by the corporation.

(2) EXCEPTIONS.—In the case of an S corporation, elections under the following provisions shall be made by each shareholder separately—

(A) section 617 (relating to deduction and recapture of certain mining exploration expenditures), and

(B) section 901 (relating to taxes of foreign countries and possessions of the United States).

(d) RECAPTURE OF LIFO BENEFITS.—

(1) IN GENERAL.—If—

(A) an S corporation was a C corporation for the last taxable year before the first taxable year for which the election under section 1362(a) was effective, and

(B) the corporation inventoried goods under the LIFO method for such last taxable year,

the LIFO recapture amount shall be included in the gross income of the corporation for such last taxable year (and appropriate adjustments to the basis of inventory shall be made to take into account the amount included in gross income under this paragraph).

(2) ADDITIONAL TAX PAYABLE IN INSTALLMENTS.—

(A) IN GENERAL.—Any increase in the tax imposed by this chapter by reason of this subsection shall be payable in 4 equal installments.

(B) DATE FOR PAYMENT OF INSTALLMENTS.—The first installment under subparagraph (A) shall be paid on or before the due date (determined without regard to extensions) for the return of the tax imposed by this chapter for the last taxable year for which the corporation was a C corporation and the 3 succeeding installments shall be paid on or before the due date (as so determined) for the corporation's return for the 3 succeeding taxable years.

(C) NO INTEREST FOR PERIOD OF EXTENSION.—Notwithstanding section 6601(b), for purposes of section 6601, the date prescribed for the payment of each installment under this paragraph shall be determined under this paragraph.

(3) LIFO RECAPTURE AMOUNT.—For purposes of this subsection, the term "LIFO recapture amount" means the amount (if any) by which—

(A) the inventory amount of the inventory asset under the first-in, first-out method authorized by section 471, exceeds

(B) the inventory amount of such assets under the LIFO method.

For purposes of the preceding sentence, inventory amounts shall be determined as of the close of the last taxable year referred to in paragraph (1).

(4) OTHER DEFINITIONS.—For purposes of this subsection—

(A) LIFO METHOD.—The term "LIFO method" means the method authorized by section 472.

(B) INVENTORY ASSETS.—The term "inventory assets" means stock in trade of the corporation, or other property of a kind which would properly be included in the inventory of the corporation if on hand at the close of the taxable year.

(C) METHOD OF DETERMINING INVENTORY AMOUNT.—The inventory amount of assets under a method authorized by section 471 shall be determined—

(i) if the corporation uses the retail method of valuing inventories under section 472, by using such method, or

(ii) if clause (i) does not apply, by using cost or market, whichever is lower.

(D) NOT TREATED AS MEMBER OF AFFILIATED GROUP.—Except as provided in regulations, the corporation referred to in paragraph (1) shall not be treated as a member of an affiliated group with respect to the amount included in gross income under paragraph (1).

SEC. 1366. PASS-THRU OF ITEMS TO SHAREHOLDERS.

(a) DETERMINATION OF SHAREHOLDER'S TAX LIABILITY.—

(1) IN GENERAL.—In determining the tax under this chapter of a shareholder for the shareholder's taxable year in which the taxable year of the S corporation ends (or for the final taxable year of a shareholder who dies, or of a trust or estate which terminates, before the end of the corporation's taxable year), there shall be taken into account the shareholder's pro rata share of the corporation's—

(A) items of income (including tax-exempt income), loss, deduction, or credit the separate treatment of which could affect the liability for tax of any shareholder, and

(B) nonseparately computed income or loss.

For purposes of the preceding sentence, the items referred to in subparagraph (A) shall include amounts described in paragraph (4) or (6) of section 702(a).

(2) NONSEPARATELY COMPUTED INCOME OR LOSS DEFINED.—For purposes of this subchapter, the term "nonseparately computed income or loss" means gross income minus the deductions allowed to the corporation under this chapter, determined by excluding all items described in paragraph (1)(A).

(b) CHARACTER PASSED THRU.—The character of any item included in a shareholder's pro rata share under paragraph (1) of subsection (a) shall be determined as if such item were realized directly from the source from which realized by the corporation, or incurred in the same manner as incurred by the corporation.

(c) GROSS INCOME OF A SHAREHOLDER.—In any case where it is necessary to determine the gross income of a shareholder for purposes of this title, such gross income shall include the shareholder's pro rata share of the gross income of the corporation.

(d) SPECIAL RULES FOR LOSSES AND DEDUCTIONS.—

(1) CANNOT EXCEED SHAREHOLDER'S BASIS IN STOCK AND DEBT.—The aggregate amount of losses and deductions taken into account by a shareholder under subsection (a) for any taxable year shall not exceed the sum of—

(A) the adjusted basis of the shareholder's stock in the S corporation (determined with regard to paragraphs (1) and (2)(A) of section 1367(a) for the taxable year), and

(B) the shareholder's adjusted basis of any indebtedness of the S corporation to the shareholder (determined without regard to any adjustment under paragraph (2) of section 1367(b) for the taxable year).

(2) INDEFINITE CARRYOVER OF DISALLOWED LOSSES AND DEDUCTIONS.—Any loss or deduction which is disallowed for any taxable year by reason of paragraph (1) shall be treated as incurred by the corporation in the succeeding taxable year with respect to that shareholder.

(3) CARRYOVER OF DISALLOWED LOSSES AND DEDUCTIONS TO POST-TERMINATION TRANSITION PERIOD.—

(A) IN GENERAL.—If for the last taxable year of a corporation for which it was an S corporation a loss or deduction was disallowed by reason of paragraph (1), such loss or deduction shall be treated as incurred by the shareholder on the last day of any post-termination transition period.

(B) CANNOT EXCEED SHAREHOLDER'S BASIS IN STOCK.—The aggregate amount of losses and deductions taken into account by a shareholder under subparagraph (A) shall not exceed the adjusted basis of the shareholder's stock in the corporation (determined at the close of the last day of the post-termination transition period and without regard to this paragraph).

(C) ADJUSTMENT IN BASIS OF STOCK.—The shareholder's basis in the stock of the corporation shall be reduced by the amount allowed as a deduction by reason of this paragraph.

(D) AT-RISK LIMITATIONS.—To the extent that any increase in adjusted basis described in subparagraph (B) would have increased the shareholder's amount at risk under section 465 if such increase had occurred on the day preceding the commencement of the post-termination transition period, rules similar to the rules described in subparagraphs (A) through (C) shall apply to any losses disallowed by reason of section 465(a).

(e) TREATMENT OF FAMILY GROUP.—If an individual who is a member of the family (within the meaning of section 704(e)(3)) of one or more shareholders of an S corporation renders services for the corporation or furnishes capital to the corporation without receiving reasonable compensation therefor, the Secretary shall make such adjustments in the items taken into account by such individual and such shareholders as may be necessary in order to reflect the value of such services or capital.

(f) SPECIAL RULES.—

. . .

(2) TREATMENT OF TAX IMPOSED ON BUILT-IN GAINS.—If any tax is imposed under section 1374 for any taxable year on an S corporation, for purposes of subsection (a), the amount so imposed shall be treated as a loss sustained by the S corporation during such taxable year. The character of such loss shall be determined by allocating the loss proportionately among the recognized built-in gains giving rise to such tax.

(3) REDUCTION IN PASS-THRU FOR TAX IMPOSED ON EXCESS NET PASSIVE INCOME.—If any tax is imposed under section 1375 for any taxable year on an S corporation, for purposes of subsection (a), each item of passive investment income shall be reduced by an amount which bears the same ratio to the amount of such tax as—

(A) the amount of such item, bears to

(B) the total passive investment income for the taxable year.

. . .

SEC. 1367. ADJUSTMENTS TO BASIS OF STOCK OF SHAREHOLDERS, ETC.

(a) GENERAL RULE.—

(1) INCREASES IN BASIS.—The basis of each shareholder's stock in an S corporation shall be increased for any period by the sum of the following items determined with respect to that shareholder for such period:

(A) the items of income described in subparagraph (A) of section 1366(a)(1),

(B) any nonseparately computed income determined under subparagraph (B) of section 1366(a)(1), and

(C) the excess of the deductions for depletion over the basis of the property subject to depletion.

(2) DECREASES IN BASIS.—The basis of each shareholder's stock in an S corporation shall be decreased for any period (but not below zero) by the sum of the following items determined with respect to the shareholder for such period:

(A) distributions by the corporation which were not includible in the income of the shareholder by reason of section 1368,

(B) the items of loss and deduction described in subparagraph (A) of section 1366(a)(1),

(C) any nonseparately computed loss determined under subparagraph (B) of section 1366(a)(1),

(D) any expense of the corporation not deductible in computing its taxable income and not properly chargeable to capital account, and

(E) the amount of the shareholder's deduction for depletion for any oil and gas property held by the S corporation to the extent such deduction does not exceed the proportionate share of the adjusted basis of such property allocated to such shareholder under section 613A(c)(11)(B).

(b) SPECIAL RULES.—

(1) INCOME ITEMS.—An amount which is required to be included in the gross income of a shareholder and shown on his return shall be taken into account under subparagraph (A) or (B) of subsection (a)(1) only to the extent such amount is included in the shareholder's gross income on his return, increased or decreased by any adjustment of such amount in a redetermination of the shareholder's tax liability.

(2) ADJUSTMENTS IN BASIS OF INDEBTEDNESS.—

(A) REDUCTION OF BASIS.— If for any taxable year the amounts specified in subparagraphs (B), (C), (D), and (E) of subsection (a)(2) exceed the amount which reduces the shareholder's basis to zero, such excess shall be applied to reduce (but not below zero) the shareholder's basis in any indebtedness of the S corporation to the shareholder.

(B) RESTORATION OF BASIS.— If for any taxable year beginning after December 31, 1982, there is a reduction under subparagraph (A) in the shareholder's basis in the indebtedness of an S corporation to a shareholder, any net increase (after the application of paragraphs (1) and (2) of subsection (a) for any subsequent taxable year shall be applied to restore such reduction in basis before any of it may be used to increase the shareholder's basis in the stock of the S corporation.

(3) COORDINATION WITH SECTIONS 165(g) AND 166(d).— This section and section 1366 shall be applied before the application of sections 165(g) and 166(d) to any taxable year of the shareholder or the corporation in which the security or debt becomes worthless.

(4) ADJUSTMENTS IN CASE OF INHERITED STOCK.—

(A) IN GENERAL.—If any person acquires stock in an S corporation by reason of the death of a decedent or by bequest, devise, or inheritance, section 691 shall be applied with respect to any item of income of the S corporation in the same manner as if the decedent had held directly his pro rata share of such item.

(B) ADJUSTMENTS TO BASIS.—The basis determined under section 1014 of any stock in an S corporation shall be reduced by the portion of the value of the stock which is attributable to items constituting income in respect of the decedent.

SEC. 1368. DISTRIBUTIONS.

(a) GENERAL RULE.— A distribution of property made by an S corporation with respect to its stock to which (but for this subsection) section 301(c) would apply shall be treated in the manner provided in subsection (b) or (c), whichever applies.

(b) S CORPORATION HAVING NO EARNINGS AND PROFITS.— In the case of a distribution described in subsection (a) by an S corporation which has no accumulated earnings and profits—

(1) AMOUNT APPLIED AGAINST BASIS.— The distribution shall not be included in gross income to the extent that it does not exceed the adjusted basis of the stock.

(2) AMOUNT IN EXCESS OF BASIS.— If the amount of the distribution exceeds the adjusted basis of the stock, such excess shall be treated as gain from the sale or exchange of property.

(c) S CORPORATION HAVING EARNINGS AND PROFITS.— In the case of a distribution described in subsection (a) by an S corporation which has accumulated earnings and profits—

(1) ACCUMULATED ADJUSTMENTS ACCOUNT.— That portion of the distribution which does not exceed the accumulated adjustments account shall be treated in the manner provided by subsection (b).

(2) DIVIDEND.— That portion of the distribution which remains after the application of paragraph (1) shall be treated as a dividend to the extent it does not exceed the accumulated earnings and profits of the S corporation.

(3) TREATMENT OF REMAINDER.— Any portion of the distribution remaining after the application of paragraph (2) of this subsection shall be treated in the manner provided by subsection (b).

Except to the extent provided in regulations, if the distributions during the taxable year exceed the amount in the accumulated adjustments account at the close of the taxable year, for purposes of this subsection, the balance of such account shall be allocated among such distributions in proportion to their respective sizes.

(d) CERTAIN ADJUSTMENTS TAKEN INTO ACCOUNT.— Subsections (b) and (c) shall be applied by taking into account (to the extent proper)—

(1) the adjustments to the basis of the shareholder's stock described in section 1367, and

(2) the adjustments to the accumulated adjustments account which are required by subsection (e)(1).

In the case of any distribution made during any taxable year, the adjusted basis of the stock shall be determined with regard to the adjustments provided in paragraph (1) of section 1367(a) for the taxable year.

(e) DEFINITIONS AND SPECIAL RULES.— For purposes of this section—

(1) ACCUMULATED ADJUSTMENTS ACCOUNT.—

(A) IN GENERAL.— Except as otherwise provided in this paragraph, the term "accumulated adjustments account" means an account of the S corporation which is adjusted for the S period in a manner similar to the adjustments under section 1367 (except that no adjustment shall be made for income (and related expenses) which is exempt from tax under this title and the phrase "(but not below zero)" shall be disregarded in section 1367(a)(2)) and no adjustment shall be made for Federal taxes attributable to any taxable year in which the corporation was a C corporation.

(B) AMOUNT OF ADJUSTMENT IN THE CASE OF REDEMPTIONS.— In the case of any redemption which is treated as an exchange under section

302(a) or 303(a), the adjustment in the accumulated adjustments account shall be an amount which bears the same ratio to the balance in such account as the number of shares redeemed in such redemption bears to the number of shares of stock in the corporation immediately before such redemption.

    (C) NET LOSS FOR YEAR DISREGARDED.—

        (i) IN GENERAL.—In applying this section to distributions made during any taxable year, the amount in the accumulated adjustments account as of the close of such taxable year shall be determined without regard to any net negative adjustment for such taxable year.

        (ii) NET NEGATIVE ADJUSTMENT.—For purposes of clause (i), the term "net negative adjustment" means, with respect to any taxable year, the excess (if any) of—

           (I) the reductions in the account for the taxable year (other than for distributions), over

           (II) the increases in such account for such taxable year.

  (2) S PERIOD.— The term "S period" means the most recent continuous period during which the corporation has been an S corporation. Such period shall not include any taxable year beginning before January 1, 1983.

  (3) ELECTION TO DISTRIBUTE EARNINGS FIRST.—

    (A) IN GENERAL.— An S corporation may, with the consent of all of its affected shareholders, elect to have paragraph (1) of subsection (c) not apply to all distributions made during the taxable year for which the election is made.

    (B) AFFECTED SHAREHOLDER.— For purposes of subparagraph (A), the term "affected shareholder" means any shareholder to whom a distribution is made by the S corporation during the taxable year.

SEC. 1371. COORDINATION WITH SUBCHAPTER C.

  (a) APPLICATION OF SUBCHAPTER C RULES.—Except as otherwise provided in this title, and except to the extent inconsistent with this subchapter, subchapter C shall apply to an S corporation and its shareholders.

  (b) NO CARRYOVER BETWEEN C YEAR AND S YEAR.—

  (1) FROM C YEAR TO S YEAR.— No carryforward, and no carryback, arising for a taxable year for which a corporation is a C corporation may be carried to a taxable year for which such corporation is an S corporation.

  (2) NO CARRYOVER FROM S YEAR.— No carryforward, and no carryback, shall arise at the corporate level for a taxable year for which a corporation is an S corporation.

  (3) TREATMENT OF S YEAR AS ELAPSED YEAR.—Nothing in paragraphs (1) and (2) shall prevent treating a taxable year for which a corporation is an S corporation as a taxable year for purposes of determining the number of taxable years to which an item may be carried back or carried forward.

  (c) EARNINGS AND PROFITS.—

(1) IN GENERAL.—Except as provided in paragraphs (2) and (3) and subsection (d)(3), no adjustment shall be made to the earnings and profits of an S corporation.

(2) ADJUSTMENTS FOR REDEMPTIONS, LIQUIDATIONS, REORGANIZATIONS, DIVISIVES, ETC.—In the case of any transaction involving the application of subchapter C to any S corporation, proper adjustment to any accumulated earnings and profits of the corporation shall be made.

(3) ADJUSTMENTS IN CASE OF DISTRIBUTIONS TREATED AS DIVIDENDS UNDER SECTION 1368(c)(2).—Paragraph (1) shall not apply with respect to that portion of a distribution which is treated as a dividend under section 1368(c)(2).

. . .

(e) CASH DISTRIBUTIONS DURING POST-TERMINATION TRANSITION PERIOD.—

(1) IN GENERAL.—Any distribution of money by a corporation with respect to its stock during a post-termination transition period shall be applied against and reduce the adjusted basis of the stock, to the extent that the amount of the distribution does not exceed the accumulated adjustments account (within the meaning of section 1368(e)).

(2) ELECTION TO DISTRIBUTE EARNINGS FIRST.—An S corporation may elect to have paragraph (1) not apply to all distributions made during a post-termination transition period described in section 1377(b)(1)(A). Such election shall not be effective unless all shareholders of the S corporation to whom distributions are made by the S corporation during such post-termination transition period consent to such election.

SEC. 1372. PARTNERSHIP RULES TO APPLY FOR FRINGE BENEFIT PURPOSES.

(a) GENERAL RULE.—For purposes of applying the provisions of this subtitle which relate to employee fringe benefits—

(1) the S corporation shall be treated as a partnership, and

(2) any 2-percent shareholder of the S corporation shall be treated as a partner of such partnership.

(b) 2-PERCENT SHAREHOLDER DEFINED.—For purposes of this section, the term "2-percent shareholder" means any person who owns (or is considered as owning within the meaning of section 318) on any day during the taxable year of the S corporation more than 2 percent of the outstanding stock of such corporation or stock possessing more than 2 percent of the total combined voting power of all stock of such corporation.

SEC. 1374.   TAX IMPOSED ON CERTAIN BUILT-IN
GAINS.

(a) GENERAL RULE.—If for any taxable year beginning in the recognition period an S corporation has a net recognized built-in gain, there is hereby imposed a tax (computed under subsection (b)) on the income of such corporation for such taxable year.

(b) AMOUNT OF TAX.—

(1) IN GENERAL.—The amount of the tax imposed by subsection (a) shall be computed by applying the highest rate of tax specified in section 11(b) to the net recognized built-in gain of the S corporation for the taxable year.

(2) NET OPERATING LOSS CARRYFORWARDS FROM C YEARS AL-LOWED.—Notwithstanding section 1371(b)(1), any net operating loss carryforward arising in a taxable year for which the corporation was a C corporation shall be allowed for purposes of this section as a deduction against the net recognized built-in gain of the S corporation for the taxable year. For purposes of determining the amount of any such loss which may be carried to subsequent taxable years, the amount of the net recognized built-in gain shall be treated as taxable income. Rules similar to the rules of the preceding sentences of this paragraph shall apply in the case of a capital loss carryforward arising in a taxable year for which the corporation was a C corporation.

(3) CREDITS.—

(A) IN GENERAL.—Except as provided in subparagraph (B), no credit shall be allowable under part IV if subchapter A of this chapter (other than under section 34) [Code §21-§53, other than §34] against the tax imposed by subsection (a).

(B) BUSINESS CREDIT CARRYFORWARDS FROM C YEARS AL-LOWED.—Notwithstanding section 1371(b)(1), any business credit carryforward under section 39 arising in a taxable year for which the corporation was a C corporation shall be allowed as a credit against the tax imposed by subsection (a) in the same manner as if it were imposed by section 11. A similar rule shall apply in the case of the minimum tax credit under section 53 to the extent attributable to taxable years for which the corporation was a C corporation.

(4) COORDINATION WITH SECTION 1201(a).—For purposes of section 1201(a)—

(A) the tax imposed by subsection (a) shall be treated as if it were imposed by section 11, and

(B) the amount of the net recognized built-in gain shall be treated as the taxable income.

(c) LIMITATIONS.—

(1) CORPORATIONS WHICH WERE ALWAYS S CORPORATIONS.—Subsection (a) shall not apply to any corporation if an election under section 1362(a) has been in effect with respect to such corporation for each of its taxable years. Except as provided in regulations, an S corporation and any predecessor corporation shall be treated as 1 corporation for purposes of the preceding sentence.

(2) LIMITATION ON AMOUNT OF RECOGNIZED BUILT-IN GAIN. The amount of the net recognized built-in gain taken into account under this section for any taxable year shall not exceed the excess (if any) of—

(A) the net unrealized built-in gain, over

(B) the net recognized built-in gain for prior taxable years beginning in the recognition period.

(d) DEFINITIONS AND SPECIAL RULES.—For purposes of this section—

(1) NET UNREALIZED BUILT-IN GAIN.—The term "net unrealized built-in gain" means the amount (if any) by which—

(A) the fair market value of the assets of S corporation as of the beginning of its 1st taxable year for which an election under section 1362(a) is in effect, exceeds

(B) the aggregate adjusted bases of such assets at such time.

(2) NET RECOGNIZED BUILT-IN GAIN.—

(A) IN GENERAL.—The term "net recognized built-in gain" means, with respect to any taxable year in the recognition period, the lesser of—

(i) the amount which would be taxable income of the S corporation for such taxable year if only recognized built-in gains and recognized built-in losses were taken into account, or

(ii) such corporation's taxable income for such taxable year (determined as provided in section 1375(b)(1)(B)).

(B) CARRYOVER.—If, for any taxable year, the amount referred to in clause (i) of subparagraph (A) exceeds the amount referred to in clause (ii) of subparagraph (A), such excess shall be treated as a recognized built-in gain in the succeeding taxable year. The preceding sentence shall apply only in the case of a corporation treated as an S corporation by reason of an election made on or after March 31, 1988.

(3) RECOGNIZED BUILT-IN GAIN.—The term "recognized built-in gain" means any gain recognized during the recognition period on the disposition of any asset except to the extent that the S corporation establishes that—

(A) such asset was not held by the S corporation as of the beginning of the 1st taxable year for which it was an S corporation, or

(B) such gain exceeds the excess (if any) of—

(i) the fair market value of such asset as of the beginning of such 1st taxable year, over

(ii) the adjusted basis of the asset as of such time.

(4) RECOGNIZED BUILT-IN LOSSES.—The term "recognized built-in loss" means any loss recognized during the recognition period on the disposition of any asset to the extent that the S corporation establishes that—

(A) such asset was held by the S corporation as of the beginning of the 1st taxable year referred to in paragraph (3), and

(B) such loss does not exceed the excess of—

(i) the adjusted basis of such asset as of the beginning of such 1st taxable year, over

(ii) the fair market value of such asset as of such time.

(5) TREATMENT OF CERTAIN BUILT-IN ITEMS.—

(A) INCOME ITEMS.—Any item of income which is properly taken into account during the recognition period but which is attributable to periods before the 1st taxable year for which the corporation was an S corporation shall be treated as a recognized built-in gain for the taxable year in which it is properly taken into account.

(B) DEDUCTION ITEMS.—Any amount which is allowable as a deduction during the recognition period (determined without regard to any carryover) but which is attributable to periods before the 1st taxable year referred to in subparagraph (A) shall be treated as a recognized built-in loss for the taxable year for which it is allowable as a deduction.

(C) ADJUSTMENT TO NET UNREALIZED BUILT-IN GAIN.—The amount of the net unrealized built-in gain shall be properly adjusted for amounts which would be treated as recognized built-in gains or losses under this paragraph if such amounts were properly taken into account (or allowable as a deduction) during the recognition period.

(6) TREATMENT OF CERTAIN PROPERTY.—If the adjusted basis of any asset is determined (in whole or in part) by reference to the adjusted basis of any other asset held by the S corporation as of the beginning of the 1st taxable year referred to in paragraph (3)—

(A) such asset shall be treated as held by the S corporation as of the beginning of such 1st taxable year, and

(B) any determination under paragraph (3)(B) or (4)(B) with respect to such asset shall be made by reference to the fair market value and adjusted basis of such other asset as of the beginning of such 1st taxable year.

(7) RECOGNITION PERIOD.—The term "recognition period" means the 10-year period beginning with the 1st day of the 1st taxable year for which the corporation was an S corporation.

. . .

(8) TREATMENT OF TRANSFER OF ASSETS FROM C CORPORATION TO S CORPORATION.—

(A) IN GENERAL.—Except to the extent provided in regulations, if—

(i) an S corporation acquires any asset, and

(ii) the S corporation's basis in such asset is determined (in whole or in part) by reference to the basis of such asset (or any other property) in the hands of a C corporation,

then a tax is hereby imposed on any net recognized built-in gain attributable to any such assets for any taxable year beginning in the recognition period. The amount of such tax shall be determined under the rules of this section as modified by subparagraph (B).

(B) MODIFICATIONS.—For purposes of this paragraph, the modifications of this subparagraph are as follows:

(i) IN GENERAL.—The preceding paragraphs of this subsection shall be applied by taking into account the day on which the assets were acquired by the S corporation in lieu of the beginning of the 1st taxable year for which the corporation was an S corporation.

(ii) SUBSECTION (c)(1) NOT TO APPLY.—Subsection (c)(1) shall not apply.

(9) REFERENCE TO 1ST TAXABLE YEAR.—Any reference in this section to the 1st taxable year for which the corporation was an S corporation shall be treated as a reference to the 1st taxable year for which the corporation was an S corporation pursuant to its most recent election under section 1362.

(e) REGULATIONS.—The Secretary shall prescribe such regulations as may be necessary to carry out the purposes of this section including regulations providing for the appropriate treatment of successor corporations.

SEC. 1375. TAX IMPOSED WHEN PASSIVE INVESTMENT INCOME OF CORPORATION HAVING ACCUMULATED EARNINGS AND PROFITS EXCEEDS 25 PERCENT OF GROSS RECEIPTS.

(a) GENERAL RULE.—If for the taxable year an S corporation has—

(1) accumulated earnings and profits at the close of such taxable year, and

(2) gross receipts more than 25 percent of which are passive investment income,

then there is hereby imposed a tax on the income of such corporation for such taxable year. Such tax shall be computed by multiplying the excess net passive income by the highest rate of tax specified in section 11(b).

(b) DEFINITIONS.—For purposes of this section—

(1) EXCESS NET PASSIVE INCOME.—

(A) IN GENERAL.—Except as provided in subparagraph (B), the term "excess net passive income" means an amount which bears the same ratio to the net passive income for the taxable year as—

(i) the amount by which the passive investment income for the taxable year exceeds 25 percent of the gross receipts for the taxable year, bears to

(ii) the passive investment income for the taxable year.

(B) LIMITATION.—The amount of the excess net passive income for any taxable year shall not exceed the amount of the corporation's taxable income for such taxable year as determined under section 63(a)—

(i) without regard to the deductions allowed by part VIII of subchapter B (other than the deduction allowed by section 248, relating to organization expenditures) [Code §241-§249, other than §248], and

(ii) without regard to the deduction under section 172.

(2) NET PASSIVE INCOME.—The term "net passive income" means—

(A) passive investment income, reduced by

(B) the deductions allowable under this chapter which are directly connected with the production of such income (other than deductions allowable under section 172 and part VIII of subchapter B) [Code §241-§249].

(3) PASSIVE INVESTMENT INCOME, ETC.—The terms "passive investment income" and "gross receipts" shall have the same respective meanings as when used in paragraph (3) of section 1362(d).

(4) COORDINATION WITH SECTION 1374.—Notwithstanding paragraph (3), the amount of passive investment income shall be determined by not taking into account any recognized built-in gain or loss of the S corporation for any taxable year in the recognition period. Terms used in the preceding sentence shall have the same respective meanings as when used in section 1374.

. . .

(d) WAIVER OF TAX IN CERTAIN CASES.—If the S corporation establishes to the satisfaction of the Secretary that—

(1) it determined in good faith that it had no subchapter C earnings and profits at the close of a taxable year, and

(2) during a reasonable period of time after it was determined that it did have subchapter C earnings and profits at the close of such taxable year such earnings and profits were distributed,

the Secretary may waive the tax imposed by subsection (a) for such taxable year.

SEC. 1377.   DEFINITIONS AND SPECIAL RULE.

(a) PRO RATA SHARE.—For purposes of this subchapter—

(1) IN GENERAL.—Except as provided in paragraph (2), each shareholder's pro rata share of any item for any taxable year shall be the sum of the amounts determined with respect to the shareholder—

(A) by assigning an equal portion of such item to each day of the taxable year, and

(B) then by dividing that portion pro rata among the shares outstanding on such day.

(2) ELECTION TO TERMINATE YEAR.—

(A) IN GENERAL.—Under regulations prescribed by the Secretary, if any shareholder terminates the shareholder's interest in the corporation during the taxable year and all affected shareholders and the corporation agree to the application of this paragraph, paragraph (1) shall be applied to the affected shareholders as if the taxable year consisted of 2 taxable years the first of which ends on the date of the termination.

(B) AFFECTED SHAREHOLDERS.—For purposes of subparagraph (A), the term "affected shareholders" means the shareholder whose interest is terminated and all shareholders to whom such shareholder has transferred shares during the taxable year. If such shareholder has transferred shares to the corporation, the term "affected shareholders" shall include all persons who are shareholders during the taxable year.

(b) POST-TERMINATION TRANSITION PERIOD.—

(1) IN GENERAL.—For purposes of this subchapter, the term "post-termination transition period" means—

(A) the period beginning on the day after the last day of the corporation's last taxable year as an S corporation and ending on the later of—

(i) the day which is 1 year after such last day, or

(ii) the due date for filing the return for such last year as an S corporation (including extensions),

(B) the 120-day period beginning on the date of any determination pursuant to an audit of the taxpayer which follows the termination of the corporation's election and which adjusts a subchapter S item of income, loss, or deduction of the corporation arising during the S period (as defined in section 1368(e)(2)), and

(C) the 120-day period beginning on the date of a determination that the corporation's election under section 1362(a) had terminated for a previous taxable year.

(2) DETERMINATION DEFINED.—For purposes of paragraph (1), the term "determination" means—

(A) a determination as defined in section 1313(a), or

(B) an agreement between the corporation and the Secretary that the corporation failed to qualify as an S corporation.

(c) MANNER OF MAKING ELECTIONS, ETC.—Any election under this subchapter, and any revocation under section 1362(d)(1), shall be made in such manner as the Secretary shall by regulations prescribe.

SEC. 1378. TAXABLE YEAR OF S CORPORATION.

(a) GENERAL RULE.—For purposes of this subtitle, the taxable year of an S corporation shall be a permitted year.

(b) PERMITTED YEAR DEFINED.—For purposes of this section, the term "permitted year" means a taxable year which—

(1) is a year ending December 31, or

(2) is any other accounting period for which the corporation establishes a business purpose to the satisfaction of the Secretary.

For purposes of paragraph (2), any deferral of income to shareholders shall not be treated as a business purpose.

SEC. 1501. PRIVILEGE TO FILE CONSOLIDATED RETURNS.

An affiliated group of corporations shall, subject to the provisions of this chapter, have the privilege of making a consolidated return with respect to the income tax imposed by chapter 1 for the taxable year in lieu of separate returns. The making of a consolidated return shall be upon the condition that all corporations which at any time during the taxable year have been members of the affiliated group consent to all the consolidated return regulations prescribed under section 1502 prior to the last day prescribed by law for the filing of such return. The making of a consolidated return shall be considered as such consent. In the case of a corporation which is a member of the affiliated group for a fractional part of the year, the consolidated return shall include the income of such corporation for such part of the year as it is a member of the affiliated group.

SEC. 1504.   DEFINITIONS.

(a) AFFILIATED GROUP DEFINED.—For purposes of this subtitle—

(1) IN GENERAL.—The term "affiliated group" means—

(A) 1 or more chains of includible corporations connected through stock ownership with a common parent corporation which is an includible corporation, but only if—

(B)(i) the common parent owns directly stock meeting the requirements of paragraph (2) in at least 1 of the other includible corporations, and

(ii) stock meeting the requirements of paragraph (2) in each of the includible corporations (except the common parent) is owned directly by 1 or more of the other includible corporations.

(2) 80-PERCENT VOTING AND VALUE TEST.—The ownership of stock of any corporation meets the requirements of this paragraph if it—

(A) possesses at least 80 percent of the total voting power of the stock of such corporation, and

(B) has a value equal to at least 80 percent of the total value of the stock of such corporation.

(3) 5 YEARS MUST ELAPSE BEFORE RECONSOLIDATION.—

(A) IN GENERAL.—If—

(i) a corporation is included (or required to be included) in a consolidated return filed by an affiliated group for a taxable year which includes any period after December 31, 1984, and

(ii) such corporation ceases to be a member of such group in a taxable year beginning after December 31, 1984,

with respect to periods after such cessation, such corporation (and any successor of such corporation) may not be included in any consolidated return filed by the affiliated group (or by another affiliated group with the same common parent or a successor of such common parent) before the 61st month beginning after its first taxable year in which it ceased to be a member of such affiliated group.

(B) SECRETARY MAY WAIVE APPLICATION OF SUBPARAGRAPH (A).—The Secretary may waive the application of subparagraph (A) to any corporation for any period subject to such conditions as the Secretary may prescribe.

(4) STOCK NOT TO INCLUDE CERTAIN PREFERRED STOCK.—For purposes of this subsection, the term "stock" does not include any stock which—

(A) is not entitled to vote,

(B) is limited and preferred as to dividends and does not participate in corporate growth to any significant extent,

(C) has redemption and liquidation rights which do not exceed the issue price of such stock (except for a reasonable redemption or liquidation premium), and

(D) is not convertible into another class of stock.

(5) REGULATIONS.—The Secretary shall prescribe such regulations as may be necessary or appropriate to carry out the purposes of this subsection, including (but not limited to) regulations—

(A) which treat warrants, obligations convertible into stock, and other similar interests as stock, and stock as not stock,

(B) which treat options to acquire or sell stock as having been exercised,

(C) which provide that the requirements of paragraph (2)(B) shall be treated as met if the affiliated group, in reliance on a good faith determination of value, treated such requirements as met,

(D) which disregard an inadvertent ceasing to meet the requirements of paragraph (2)(B) by reason of changes in relative values of different classes of stock,

(E) which provide that transfers of stock within the group shall not be taken into account in determining whether a corporation ceases to be a member of an affiliated group, and

(F) which disregard changes in voting power to the extent such changes are disproportionate to related changes in value.

(b) DEFINITION OF "INCLUDIBLE CORPORATION."—As used in this chapter, the term "includible corporation" means any corporation except—

(1) Corporations exempt from taxation under section 501.

(2) Insurance companies subject to taxation under section 801.

(3) Foreign corporations.

(4) Corporations with respect to which an election under section 936 (relating to possession tax credit) is in effect for the taxable year.

(5) Corporations organized under the China Trade Act, 1922 [repealed for taxable years beginning after December 31, 1977].

(6) Regulated investment companies and real estate investment trusts subject to tax under subchapter M of chapter 1.

(7) A DISC (as defined in section 992(a)(1)).

(8) An S corporation.

. . .

SEC. 4999. GOLDEN PARACHUTE PAYMENTS.

(a) IMPOSITION OF TAX.—There is hereby imposed on any person who receives an excess parachute payment a tax equal to 20 percent of the amount of such payment.

(b) EXCESS PARACHUTE PAYMENT DEFINED.—For purposes of this section, the term "excess parachute payment" has the meaning given to such term by section 280G(b).

(c) ADMINISTRATIVE PROVISIONS.—

(1) WITHHOLDING.—In the case of any excess parachute payment which is wages (within the meaning of section 3401) the amount deducted and withheld under section 3402 shall be increased by the amount of the tax imposed by this section on such payment.

(2) OTHER ADMINISTRATIVE PROVISIONS.—For purposes of subtitle F, any tax imposed by this section shall be treated as a tax imposed by subtitle A.

SEC. 7704.　CERTAIN PUBLICLY TRADED PARTNERSHIPS TREATED AS CORPORATIONS.

(a) GENERAL RULE.—For purposes of this title, except as provided in subsection (c), a publicly traded partnership shall be treated as a corporation.

(b) PUBLICLY TRADED PARTNERSHIP.—For purposes of this section, the term "publicly traded partnership" means any partnership if—

(1) interests in such partnership are traded on an established securities market, or

(2) interests in such partnership are readily tradable on a secondary market (or the substantial equivalent thereof).

(c) EXCEPTION FOR PARTNERSHIPS WITH PASSIVE-TYPE INCOME.—

(1) IN GENERAL.—Subsection (a) shall not apply to any publicly traded partnership for any taxable year if such partnership met the gross income requirements of paragraph (2) for such taxable year and each preceding taxable year beginning after December 31, 1987, during which the partnership (or any predecessor) was in existence. For purposes of the preceding sentence, a partnership shall not be treated as being in existence during any period before the 1st taxable year in which such partnership (or a predecessor) was a publicly traded partnership.

(2) GROSS INCOME REQUIREMENTS.—A partnership meets the gross income requirements of this paragraph for any taxable year if 90 percent or more of the gross income of such partnership for such taxable year consists of qualifying income.

(3) EXCEPTION NOT TO APPLY TO CERTAIN PARTNERSHIPS WHICH COULD QUALIFY AS REGULATED INVESTMENT COMPANIES.—This subsection shall not apply to any partnership which would be described in section 851(a) if such partnership were a domestic corporation. To the extent provided in regulations, the preceding sentence shall not apply to any partnership a principal activity of which is the buying and selling of commodities (not described in section 1221(1)), or options, futures, or forwards with respect to commodities.

(d) QUALIFYING INCOME.—For purposes of this section—

(1) IN GENERAL.—Except as otherwise provided in this subsection, the term "qualifying income" means—

(A) interest,

(B) dividends,

(C) real property rents,

(D) gain from the sale or other disposition of real property (including property described in section 1221(a)(1)),

(E) income and gains derived from the exploration, development, mining or production, processing, refining, transportation (including pipelines transporting gas, oil, or products thereof), or the marketing of any mineral or natural resource (including fertilizer, geothermal energy, and timber),

(F) any gain from the sale or disposition of a capital asset (or property described in section 1231(b)) held for the production of income described in any of the foregoing subparagraphs of this paragraph, and

(G) in the case of a partnership described in the second sentence of subsection (c)(3), income and gains from commodities (not described in section 1221(a)(1)) or futures, forwards, and options with respect to commodities.

For purposes of subparagraph (E), the term "mineral or natural resource" means any product of a character with respect to which a deduction for depletion is allowable under section 611; except that such term shall not include any product described in subparagraph (A) or (B) of section 613(b)(7).

(2) CERTAIN INTEREST NOT QUALIFIED.—Interest shall not be treated as qualifying income if—

(A) such interest is derived in the conduct of a financial or insurance business, or

(B) such interest would be excluded from the term "interest" under section 856(f).

(3) REAL PROPERTY RENT.—The term "real property rent" means amounts which would qualify as rent from real property under section 856(d) if—

(A) such section were applied without regard to paragraph (2)(C) thereof (relating to independent contractor requirements), and

(B) stock owned, directly or indirectly, by or for a partner would not be considered as owned under section 318(a)(3)(A) by the partnership unless 5 percent or more (by value) of the interests in such partnership are owned, directly or indirectly, by or for such partner.

(4) CERTAIN INCOME QUALIFYING UNDER REGULATED INVESTMENT COMPANY OR REAL ESTATE TRUST PROVISIONS.—The term "qualifying income" also includes any income which would qualify under section 851(b)(2) or 856(c)(2).

(5) SPECIAL RULE FOR DETERMINING GROSS INCOME FROM CERTAIN REAL PROPERTY SALES.—In the case of the sale or other disposition of real property described in section 1221(a)(1), gross income shall not be reduced by inventory costs.

(e) INADVERTENT TERMINATIONS.—If—

(1) A partnership fails to meet the gross income requirements of subsection (c)(2),

(2) the Secretary determines that such failure was inadvertent,

(3) no later than a reasonable time after the discovery of such failure, steps are taken so that such partnership once more meets such gross income requirements, and

(4) such partnership agrees to make such adjustments (including adjustments with respect to the partners) or to pay such amounts as may be required by the Secretary with respect to such period,

then, notwithstanding such failure, such entity shall be treated as continuing to meet such gross income requirements for such period.

(f) EFFECT OF BECOMING CORPORATION.—As of the 1st day that a partnership is treated as a corporation under this section, for purposes of this title, such partnership shall be treated as—

(1) transferring all of its assets (subject to its liabilities) to a newly formed corporation in exchange for the stock of the corporation, and

(2) distributing such stock to its partners in liquidation of their interests in the partnership.

(g) EXCEPTION FOR ELECTING 1987 PARTNERSHIPS.— . . .

SEC. 7872.   TREATMENT OF LOANS WITH BELOW-MARKET INTEREST RATES.

(a) TREATMENT OF GIFT LOANS AND DEMAND LOANS.—

(1) IN GENERAL.—For purposes of this title, in the case of any below-market loan to which this section applies and which is a gift loan or a demand loan, the forgone interest shall be treated as—

(A) transferred from the lender to the borrower, and

(B) retransferred by the borrower to the lender as interest.

(2) TIME WHEN TRANSFERS MADE.—Except as otherwise provided in regulations prescribed by the Secretary, any forgone interest attributable to periods during any calendar year shall be treated as transferred (and retransferred) under paragraph (1) on the last day of such calendar year.

(b) TREATMENT OF OTHER BELOW-MARKET LOANS.—

(1) IN GENERAL.—For purposes of this title, in the case of any below-market loan to which this section applies and to which subsection (a)(1) does not apply, the lender shall be treated as having transferred on the date the loan was made (or, if later, on the first day on which this section applies to such loan), and the borrower shall be treated as having received on such date, cash in an amount equal to the excess of—

(A) the amount loaned, over

(B) the present value of all payments which are required to be made under the terms of the loan.

(2) OBLIGATION TREATED AS HAVING ORIGINAL ISSUE DISCOUNT.— For purposes of this title—

(A) IN GENERAL.—Any below-market loan to which paragraph (1) applies shall be treated as having original issue discount in an amount equal to the excess described in paragraph (1).

(B) AMOUNT IN ADDITION TO OTHER ORIGINAL ISSUE DISCOUNT.—Any original issue discount which a loan is treated as having by reason of subparagraph (A) shall be in addition to any other original issue discount on such loan (determined without regard to subparagraph (A)).

(c) BELOW-MARKET LOANS TO WHICH SECTION APPLIES.—

(1) IN GENERAL.—Except as otherwise provided in this subsection and subsection (g), this section shall apply to—

(A) GIFTS.—Any below-market loan which is a gift loan.

(B) COMPENSATION-RELATED LOANS.—Any below-market loan directly or indirectly between—

(i) an employer and an employee, or

(ii) an independent contractor and a person for whom such independent contractor provides services.

(C) CORPORATION-SHAREHOLDER LOANS.—Any below-market loan directly or indirectly between a corporation and any shareholder of such corporation.

(D) TAX AVOIDANCE LOANS.—Any below-market loan 1 of the principal purposes of the interest arrangements of which is the avoidance of any Federal tax.

(E) OTHER BELOW-MARKET LOANS.—To the extent provided in regulations, any below-market loan which is not described in subparagraph (A), (B), (C) or (F) if the interest arrangements of such loan have a significant effect on any Federal tax liability of the lender or the borrower.

. . .

(2) $10,000 DE MINIMIS EXCEPTION FOR GIFT LOANS BETWEEN INDIVIDUALS.—

(A) IN GENERAL.—In the case of any gift loan directly between individuals, this section shall not apply to any day on which the aggregate outstanding amount of loans between such individuals does not exceed $10,000.

(B) DE MINIMIS EXCEPTION NOT TO APPLY TO LOANS ATTRIBUTABLE TO ACQUISITION OF INCOME-PRODUCING ASSETS.—Subparagraph (A) shall not apply to any gift loan directly attributable to the purchase or carrying of income-producing assets.

. . .

(3) $10,000 DE MINIMIS EXCEPTION FOR COMPENSATION-RELATED AND CORPORATE-SHAREHOLDER LOANS.—

(A) IN GENERAL.—In the case of any loan described in subparagraph (B) or (C) of paragraph (1), this section shall not apply to any day on which the aggregate outstanding amount of loans between the borrower and lender does not exceed $10,000.

(B) EXCEPTION NOT TO APPLY WHERE 1 OF PRINCIPAL PURPOSES IS TAX AVOIDANCE.—Subparagraph (A) shall not apply to any loan the interest arrangements of which have as 1 of their principal purposes the avoidance of any Federal tax.

(d) SPECIAL RULES FOR GIFT LOANS.—

(1) LIMITATION ON INTEREST ACCRUAL FOR PURPOSES OF INCOME TAXES WHERE LOANS DO NOT EXCEED $100,000.—

(A) IN GENERAL.—For purposes of subtitle A, in the case of a gift loan directly between individuals, the amount treated as retransferred by the borrower to the lender as of the close of any year shall not exceed the borrower's net investment income for such year.

(B) LIMITATION NOT TO APPLY WHERE 1 OF PRINCIPAL PURPOSES IS TAX AVOIDANCE.—Subparagraph (A) shall not apply to any loan the interest arrangements of which have as 1 of their principal purposes the avoidance of any Federal tax.

(C) SPECIAL RULE WHERE MORE THAN 1 GIFT LOAN OUTSTAND-ING.—For purposes of subparagraph (A), in any case in which a borrower has outstanding more than 1 gift loan, the net investment income of such borrower shall be allocated among such loans in proportion to the respective amounts which would be treated as retransferred by the borrower without regard to this paragraph.

(D) LIMITATION NOT TO APPLY WHERE AGGREGATE AMOUNT OF LOANS EXCEED $100,000.—This paragraph shall not apply to any loan made by a lender to a borrower for any day on which the aggregate outstanding amount of loans between the borrower and lender exceeds $100,000.

(E) NET INVESTMENT INCOME.—For purposes of this paragraph—

(i) IN GENERAL.—The term "net investment income" has the meaning given such term by section 163(d)(4).

(ii) DE MINIMIS RULE.—If the net investment income of any borrower for any year does not exceed $1,000, the net investment income of such borrower for such year shall be treated as zero.

(iii) ADDITIONAL AMOUNTS TREATED AS INTEREST.—In de-termining the net investment income of a person for any year, any amount which would be included in the gross income of such person for such year by reason of section 1272 if such section applied to all deferred payment obligations shall be treated as interest received by such person for such year.

(iv) DEFERRED PAYMENT OBLIGATIONS.—The term "deferred pay-ment obligation" includes any market discount bond, short-term obliga-tion, United States savings bond, annuity, or similar obligation.

(2) SPECIAL RULE FOR GIFT TAX.—In the case of any gift loan which is a term loan, subsection (b)(1) (and not subsection(a)) shall apply for purposes of chapter 12.

(e) DEFINITIONS OF BELOW-MARKET LOAN AND FORGONE INTER-EST.—For purposes of this section—

(1) BELOW-MARKET LOAN.—The term "below-market loan" means any loan if—

(A) in the case of a demand loan, interest is payable on the loan at a rate less than the applicable Federal rate, or

(B) in the case of a term loan, the amount loaned exceeds the present value of all payments due under the loan.

(2) FORGONE INTEREST.—The term "forgone interest" means, with respect to any period during which the loan is outstanding, the excess of—

(A) the amount of interest which would have been payable on the loan for the period if interest accrued on the loan at the applicable Federal rate and were payable annually on the day referred to in subsection (a)(2), over

(B) any interest payable on the loan properly allocable to such period.

(f) OTHER DEFINITIONS AND SPECIAL RULES.—For purposes of this section—

(1) PRESENT VALUE.—The present value of any payment shall be determined in the manner provided by regulations prescribed by the Secretary—

(A) as of the date of the loan, and

(B) by using a discount rate equal to the applicable Federal rate.

(2) APPLICABLE FEDERAL RATE.—

(A) TERM LOANS.—In the case of any term loan, the applicable Federal rate shall be the applicable Federal rate in effect under section 1274(d) (as of the day on which the loan was made), compounded semiannually.

(B) DEMAND LOANS.—In the case of a demand loan, the applicable Federal rate shall be the Federal short-term rate in effect under section 1274(d) for the period for which the amount of forgone interest is being determined, compounded semiannually.

(3) GIFT LOAN.—The term "gift loan" means any below-market loan where the forgoing of interest is in the nature of a gift.

(4) AMOUNT LOANED.—The term "amount loaned" means the amount received by the borrower.

(5) DEMAND LOAN.—The term "demand loan" means any loan which is payable in full at any time on the demand of the lender. Such term also includes (for purposes other than determining the applicable Federal rate under paragraph (2)) any loan if the benefits of the interest arrangements of such loan are not transferable and are conditioned on the future performance of substantial services by an individual. To the extent provided in regulations, such term also includes any loan with an indefinite maturity.

(6) TERM LOAN.—The term "term loan" means any loan which is not a demand loan.

(7) HUSBAND AND WIFE TREATED AS 1 PERSON.—A husband and wife shall be treated as 1 person.

(8) LOANS TO WHICH SECTION 483, 643(i), OR 1274 APPLIES.—This section shall not apply to any loan to which section 483, 643(i), or 1274 applies.

(9) NO WITHHOLDING.—No amount shall be withheld under chapter 24 with respect to—

(A) any amount treated as transferred or retransferred under subsection (a), and

(B) any amount treated as received under subsection (b).

(10) SPECIAL RULE FOR TERM LOANS.—If this section applies to any term loan on any day, this section shall continue to apply to such loan notwithstanding paragraphs (2) and (3) of subsection (c). In the case of a gift loan, the preceding sentence shall only apply for purposes of chapter 12.

. . .

(h) REGULATIONS.—

(1) IN GENERAL.—The Secretary shall prescribe such regulations as may be necessary or appropriate to carry out the purposes of this section, including—

(A) regulations providing that where, by reason of varying rates of interest, conditional interest payments, waivers of interest, disposition of the lender's or borrower's interest in the loan, or other circumstances, the provisions of this section do not carry out the purposes of this section, adjustments to the provisions of this section will be made to the extent necessary to carry out the purposes of this section,

(B) regulations for the purpose of assuring that the positions of the borrower and lender are consistent as to the application (or nonapplication) of this section, and

(C) regulations exempting from the application of this section any class of transactions the interest arrangements of which have no significant effect on any Federal tax liability of the lender or the borrower.

(2) ESTATE TAX COORDINATION.—Under regulations prescribed by the Secretary, any loan which is made with donative intent and which is a term loan shall be taken into account for purposes of chapter 11 in a manner consistent with the provisions of subsection (b).

¶2100

Treasury Regulations

Selected Sections

Treas. Reg. §1.83-1. Property transferred in connection with the performance of services.—(a) *Inclusion in gross income*—(1) *General rule.* Section 83 provides rules for the taxation of property transferred to an employee or independent contractor (or beneficiary thereof) in connection with the performance of services by such employee or independent contractor. In general, such property is not taxable under section 83(a) until it has been transferred (as defined in §1.83-3(a)) to such person and become substantially vested (as defined in §1.83-3(b)) in such person. In that case, the excess of—

(i) The fair market value of such property (determined without regard to any lapse restriction, as defined in §1.83-3(i)) at the time that the property becomes substantially vested, over

(ii) The amount (if any) paid for such property,

shall be included as compensation in the gross income of such employee or independent contractor for the taxable year in which the property becomes substantially vested. Until such property becomes substantially vested, the transferor shall be regarded as the owner of such property, and any income from such property received by the employee or independent contractor (or beneficiary thereof) or the right to the use of such property by the employee or independent contractor constitutes additional compensation and shall be included in the gross income of such employee or independent contractor for the taxable year in which such income is received or such use is made available. This paragraph applies to a transfer of property in connection with the performance of services even though the transferor is not the person for whom such services are performed.

(2) *Life insurance.* The cost of life insurance protection under a life insurance contract, retirement income contract, endowment contract, or other contract

providing life insurance protection is taxable generally under section 61 and the regulations thereunder during the period such contract remains substantially nonvested (as defined in §1.83-3(b)). The cost of such life insurance protection is the reasonable net premium cost, as determined by the Commissioner, of the current life insurance protection (as defined in §1.72-16(b)(3)) provided by such contract.

(3) *Cross references.* For rules concerning the treatment of employers and other transferors of property in connection with the performance of services, see section 83(h) and §1.83-6. For rules concerning the taxation of beneficiaries of an employees' trust that is not exempt under section 501(a), see section 402(b) and the regulations thereunder.

(b) *Subsequent sale, forfeiture, or other disposition of nonvested property.*—(1) If substantially nonvested property (that has been transferred in connection with the performance of services) is subsequently sold or otherwise disposed of to a third party in an arm's length transaction while still substantially nonvested, the person who performed such services shall realize compensation in an amount equal to the excess of—

      (i) The amount realized on such sale or other disposition, over

      (ii) The amount (if any) paid for such property.

Such amount of compensation is includible in his gross income in accordance with his method of accounting. Two preceding sentences also apply when the person disposing of the property has received it in a non-arm's length transaction described in paragraph (c) of this section. In addition, section 83(a) and paragraph (a) of this section shall thereafter cease to apply with respect to such property.

(2) If substantially nonvested property that has been transferred in connection with the performance of services to the person performing such services is forfeited while still substantially nonvested and held by such person, the difference between the amount paid (if any) and the amount received upon forfeiture (if any) shall be treated as an ordinary gain or loss. This paragraph (b)(2) does not apply to property to which §1.83-2(a) applies.

(3) This paragraph (b) shall not apply to, and no gain shall be recognized on, any sale, forfeiture, or other disposition described in this paragraph to the extent that any property received in exchange therefor is substantially nonvested. Instead, section 83 and this section shall apply with respect to such property received (as if it were substituted for the property disposed of).

(c) *Dispositions of nonvested property not at arm's length.* If substantially nonvested property (that has been transferred in connection with the performance of services) is disposed of in a transaction which is not at arm's length and the property remains substantially nonvested, the person who performed such services realizes compensation equal in amount to the sum of any money and the fair market value of any substantially vested property received in such disposition. Such amount of compensation is includible in his gross income in accordance with his method of accounting. However, such amount of compensation shall not exceed the fair market value of the property disposed of at the time of disposition (determined without regard to any lapse restriction), reduced by the amount paid for such property. In addition, section 83 and these regulations shall continue to apply with respect to such property, except that any amount previously includible in gross income under this paragraph (c) shall thereafter be treated as an amount paid for such property. For example, if in 1971 an employee pays $50 for a share of stock which has a fair market value of $100 and is substantially nonvested at that time and later in 1971 (at a time when the property still has a fair market value of $100 and is still substantially nonvested) the employee disposes of, in a transaction not at arm's length, the share of stock to his wife for $10, the employee realizes compensation of $10 in 1971. If in 1972, when the share of stock has a fair market value of $120, it becomes substantially vested, the employee realizes additional compensation in 1972 in the amount of $60 (the $120 fair market value of the stock less both the $50 price paid for the stock and the $10 taxed as compensation in 1971). For purposes of this paragraph, if substantially nonvested property has been transferred to a person other than the person who performed the services, and the transferee dies holding the property while the property is still substantially nonvested and while the person who performed the services is alive, the transfer which results by reason of the death of such transferee is a transfer not at arm's length.

(d) *Certain transfers upon death.* If substantially nonvested property has been transferred in connection with the performance of services and the person who performed such services dies while the property is still substantially nonvested, any income realized on or after such death with respect to such property under this section is income in respect of a decedent to which the rules of section 691 apply. In such a case the income in respect of such property shall be taxable under section 691 (except to the extent not includible under section 101(b)) to the estate or beneficiary of the person who performed the services, in accordance with section 83 and the regulations thereunder. However, if an item of income is realized upon such death before July 21, 1978, because the property became substantially vested upon death, the person responsible for filing decedent's income tax return for decedent's last taxable year may elect to treat such item as includible in gross income for decedent's last taxable year by including such item in gross income on the return or amended return filed for decedent's last taxable year.

(e) *Forfeiture after substantial vesting.* If a person is taxable under section 83(a) when the property transferred becomes substantially vested and thereafter the person's beneficial interest in such property is nevertheless forfeited pursuant to a lapse restriction, any loss incurred by such person (but not by a beneficiary of such person) upon such forfeiture shall be an ordinary loss to the extent the basis in such property has been increased as a result of the recognition of income by such person under section 83(a) with respect to such property.

(f) *Examples.* The provisions of this section may be illustrated by the following examples:

Example 1. On November 1, 1978, X corporation sells to E, an employee, 100 shares of X corporation stock at $10 per share. At the time of such sale the fair market value of the X corporation stock is $100 per share. Under the terms of the sale each share of stock is subject to a substantial risk of forfeiture which will not lapse until November 1, 1988. Evidence of this restriction is stamped on the face of E's stock certificates, which are therefore nontransferable (within the meaning of §1.83-3(d)). Since in 1978 E's stock is substantially nonvested, E does not include any of such amount in his gross income as compensation in 1978. On November 1, 1988, the fair market value of the X corporation stock is $250 per share. Since the X corporation stock becomes substantially vested in 1988, E must include $24,000 (100 shares of X corporation stock × $250 fair market value per share less $10 price paid by E for each share) as compensation for 1988. Dividends paid by X to E on E's stock after it was transferred to E on November 1, 1973, are taxable to E as additional compensation during the period E's stock is substantially nonvested and are deductible as such by X.

Example 2. Assume the facts are the same as in example 1, except that on November 1, 1985, each share of stock of X corporation in E's hands could as a matter of law be transferred to a bona fide purchaser who would not be required to forfeit the stock if the risk of forfeiture materialized. In the event, however, that the risk materializes, E would be liable in damages to X. On November 1, 1985, the fair market value of the X corporation stock is $230 per share. Since E's stock is transferable within the meaning of §1.83-3(d) in 1985, the stock is substantially vested and E must include $22,000 (100 shares of X corporation stock × $230 fair market value per share less $10 price paid by E for each share) as compensation for 1985.

Example 3. Assume the facts are the same as in example 1 except that, in 1984 E sells his 100 shares of X corporation stock in an arm's length sale to I, an investment company, for $120 per share. At the time of this sale each share of X corporation's stock has a fair market value of $200. Under paragraph (b) of this section, E must include $11,000 (100 shares of X corporation stock × $120 amount realized per share less $10 price paid by E per share) as compensation for 1984 notwithstanding that the stock remains nontransferable and is still subject to a substantial risk of forfeiture at the time of such sale. Under §1.83-4(b)(2), I's basis in the X corporation stock is $120 per share.

Treas. Reg. §1.83-2. Election to include in gross income in year of transfer.—(a) *In general.* If property is transferred (within the meaning of §1.83-3(a)) in connection with the performance of services, the person performing such services may elect to include in gross income under section 83(b) the excess (if any) of the fair market value of the property at the time of transfer (determined without regard to any lapse restriction, as defined in §1.83-3(i)) over the amount (if any) paid for such property, as compensation for services. The fact that the transferee has paid full value for the property transferred, realizing no bargain element in the transaction, does not preclude the use of the election as provided for in this section. If this election is made, the substantial vesting rules of section 83(a) and the regulations thereunder do not apply with respect to such property, and except as otherwise provided in section 83(d)(2) and the regulations thereunder (relating to the cancellation of a nonlapse restriction), any subsequent appreciation in the value of the property is not taxable as compensation to the person who performed the services. Thus, property with respect to which this election is made shall be includible in gross income as of the time of transfer, even though such property is substantially nonvested (as defined in §1.83-3(b)) at the time of transfer, and no compensation will be includible in gross income when such property becomes substantially vested (as defined in §1.83-3(b)). In computing the gain or loss from the subsequent sale or exchange of such property, its basis shall be the amount paid for the property increased by the amount included in gross income under section 83(b). If property for which a section 83(b) election is in effect is forfeited while substantially nonvested, such forfeiture shall be treated as a sale or exchange upon which there is realized a loss equal to the excess (if any) of—

(1) The amount paid (if any) for such property, over,

(2) The amount realized (if any) upon such forfeiture.

If such property is a capital asset in the hands of the taxpayer, such loss shall be a capital loss. A sale or other disposition of the property that is in substance a forfeiture, or is made in contemplation of a forfeiture, shall be treated as a forfeiture under the two immediately preceding sentences.

(b) *Time for making election.* Except as provided in the following sentence, the election referred to in paragraph (a) of this section shall be filed not later than 30 days after the date the property was transferred (or, if later, January 29, 1970) and may be filed prior to the date of transfer. Any statement filed before February 15, 1970, which was amended not later than February 16, 1970, in order to make it conform to the requirements of paragraph (e) of this section, shall be deemed a proper election under section 83(b).

(c) *Manner of making election.* The election referred to in paragraph (a) of this section is made by filing one copy of a written statement with the internal revenue officer with whom the person who performed the services files his return. In addition, one copy of such statement shall be submitted with his income tax return for the taxable year in which such property was transferred.

(d) *Additional copies.* The person who performed the services shall also submit a copy of the statement referred to in paragraph (c) of this section to the person for whom the services are performed. In addition, if the person who performs the services and the transferee of such property are not the same person, the person who performs the services shall submit a copy of such statement to the transferee of the property.

(e) *Content of statement.* The statement shall be signed by the person making the election and shall indicate that it is being made under section 83(b) of the Code, and shall contain the following information:

(1) The name, address and taxpayer identification number of the taxpayer;

(2) A description of each property with respect to which the election is being made;

(3) The date or dates on which the property is transferred and the taxable year (for example, "calendar year 1970" or "fiscal year ending May 31, 1970") for which such election was made;

(4) The nature of the restriction or restrictions to which the property is subject;

(5) The fair market value at the time of transfer (determined without regard to any lapse restriction, as defined in §1.83-3(i)) of each property with respect to which the election is being made;

(6) The amount (if any) paid for such property; and

(7) With respect to elections made after July 21, 1978, a statement to the effect that copies have been furnished to other persons as provided in paragraph (d) of this section.

(f) *Revocability of election.* An election under section 83(b) may not be revoked except with the consent of the Commissioner. Consent will be granted only in the case where the transferee is under a mistake of fact as to the underlying transaction and must be requested within 60 days of the date on which the mistake of fact first became known to the person who made the election. In any event, a mistake as to the value, or decline in the value, of the property with respect to which an election under section 83(b) has been made or a failure to perform an act contemplated at the time of transfer of such property does not constitute a mistake of fact.

Treas. Reg. §1.83-3. Meaning and use of certain terms.—(a) *Transfer*—(1) *In general.* For purposes of section 83 and the regulations thereunder, a transfer of property occurs when a person acquires a beneficial ownership interest in such property (disregarding any lapse restriction, as defined in §1.83-3(i)).

(2) *Option.* The grant of an option to purchase certain property does not constitute a transfer of such property. However, see §1.83-7 for the extent to which the grant of the option itself is subject to section 83. In addition, if the amount paid for the transfer of property is an indebtedness secured by the transferred property, on which there is no personal liability to pay all or a substantial part of such indebtedness, such transaction may be in substance the same as the grant of an option. The determination of the substance of the transaction shall be based upon all the facts and circumstances. The factors to be taken into account include the type of property involved, the extent to which the risk that the property will decline in value has been transferred, and the likelihood that the purchase price will, in fact, be paid. See also §1.83-4(c) for the treatment of forgiveness of indebtedness that has constituted an amount paid.

(3) *Requirement that property be returned.* Similarly, no transfer may have occurred where property is transferred under conditions that require its return upon the happening of an event that is certain to occur, such as the termination of employment. In such a case, whether there is, in fact, a transfer depends upon all the facts and circumstances. Factors which indicate that no transfer has occurred are described in paragraph (a)(4), (5) and (6) of this section.

(4) *Similarity to option.* An indication that no transfer has occurred is the extent to which the conditions relating to a transfer are similar to an option.

(5) *Relationship to fair market value.* An indication that no transfer has occurred is the extent to which the consideration to be paid the transferee upon surrendering the property does not approach the fair market value of the property at the time of surrender. For purposes of paragraph (a)(5) and (6) of this section, fair market value includes fair market value determined under the rules of §1.83-5(a)(1), relating to the valuation of property subject to nonlapse restrictions. Therefore, the existence of a nonlapse restriction referred to in §1.83-5(a)(1) is not a factor indicating no transfer has occurred.

(6) *Risk of loss.* An indication that no transfer has occurred is the extent to which the transferee does not incur the risk of a beneficial owner that the value of the property at the time of transfer will decline substantially. Therefore, for purposes of this (6), risk of decline in property value is not limited to the risk that any amount paid for the property may be lost.

(7) *Examples.* The provisions of this paragraph may be illustrated by the following examples:

Example 1. On January 3, 1971, X corporation sells for $500 to S, a salesman of X, 10 shares of stock in X corporation with a fair market value of $1,000. The stock is nontransferable and subject to return to the corporation (for $500) if S's sales do not reach a certain level by December 31, 1971. Disregarding the restriction concerning S's sales (since the restriction is a lapse restriction), S's interest in the stock is that of a beneficial owner and therefore a transfer occurs on January 3, 1971.

Example 2. On November 17, 1972, W sells to E 100 shares of stock in W corporation with a fair market value of $10,000 in exchange for a $10,000 note without personal liability. The note requires E to make yearly payments of $2,000 commencing in 1973. E collects the dividends, votes the stock and pays the interest on the note. However, he makes no payments towards the face amount of the note. Because E has no personal liability on the note, and since E is making no payments towards the face amount of the note, the likelihood of E paying the full purchase price is in substantial doubt. As a result, E has not incurred the risks of a beneficial owner that the value of the stock will decline. Therefore, no transfer of the stock has occurred on November 17, 1972, but an option to purchase the stock has been granted to E.

Example 3. On January 3, 1971, X corporation purports to transfer to E, an employee, 100 shares of stock in X corporation. The X stock is subject to the sole restriction that E must sell such stock to X on termination of employment for any reason for an amount which is equal to the excess (if any) of the book value of the X stock at termination of employment over book value on January 3, 1971. The stock is not transferable by E and the restrictions on transfer are stamped on the certificate. Under these facts and circumstances, there is no transfer of the X stock within the meaning of section 83.

Example 4. Assume the same facts as in example 3 except that E paid $3,000 for the stock and that the restriction required E upon termination of employment to sell the stock to M for the total amount of dividends that have been declared on the stock since September 2, 1971, or $3,000 whichever is higher. Again, under the facts and circumstances, no transfer of the X stock has occurred.

Example 5. On July 4, 1971, X corporation purports to transfer to G an employee, 100 shares of X stock. The stock is subject to the sole restriction that upon termination of employment G must sell the stock to X for the greater of its fair market value at such time or $100, the amount G paid for the stock. On July 4, 1971 the X stock has a fair market value of $100. Therefore, G does not incur the risk of a beneficial owner that the value of the stock at the time of transfer ($100) will decline substantially. Under these facts and circumstances, no transfer has occurred.

(b) *Substantially vested and substantially nonvested property.* For purposes of section 83 and the regulations thereunder, property is substantially nonvested when it is subject to a substantial risk of forfeiture, within the meaning of paragraph (c) of this section, and is nontransferable, within the meaning of paragraph (d) of this section. Property is substantially vested for such purposes when it is either transferable or not subject to a substantial risk of forfeiture.

(c) *Substantial risk of forfeiture*—(1) *In general.* For purposes of section 83 and the regulations thereunder, whether a risk of forfeiture is substantial or not depends upon the facts and circumstances. A substantial risk of forfeiture exists where rights in property that are transferred are conditioned, directly or indirectly, upon the future performance (or refraining from performance) of substantial services by any person, or the occurrence of a condition related to a purpose of the transfer, and the possibility of forfeiture is substantial if such condition is not satisfied. Property is not transferred subject to a substantial risk of forfeiture to the extent that the employer is required to pay the fair market value of a portion of such property to the employee upon the return of such property. The risk that the value of property will decline during a certain period of time does not constitute a substantial risk of forfeiture. A nonlapse restriction, standing by itself, will not result in a substantial risk of forfeiture.

(2) *Illustrations of substantial risks of forfeiture.* The regularity of the performance of services and the time spent in performing such services tend to indicate whether services required by a condition are substantial. The fact that the person performing services has the right to decline to perform such services without forfeiture may tend to establish that services are insubstantial. Where stock is transferred to an underwriter prior to a public offering and the full enjoyment of such stock is expressly or impliedly conditioned upon the successful completion of the underwriting, the stock is subject to a substantial risk of forfeiture. Where an employee receives property from an employer subject to a requirement that it be returned if the total earnings of the employer do not increase, such property is subject to a substantial risk of forfeiture. On the other hand, requirements that the property be returned to the employer if the employee is discharged for cause or for committing a crime will not be considered to result in a substantial risk of forfeiture. An enforceable requirement that the property be returned to the employer if the employee accepts a job with a competing firm will not ordinarily be considered to result in a substantial risk of forfeiture unless the particular facts and circumstances indicate to the contrary. Factors which may be taken into account in determining whether a covenant not to compete constitutes a substantial risk of forfeiture are the age of the employee, the availability of alternative employment opportunities, the likelihood of the employee's obtaining such other employment, the degree of skill possessed by the employee, the employee's health, and the practice (if any) of the employer to enforce such covenants. Similarly, rights in property transferred to a retiring employee subject to the sole requirement that it be returned unless he renders consulting services upon the request of his former employer will not be considered subject to a substantial risk of forfeiture unless he is in fact expected to perform substantial services.

(3) *Enforcement of forfeiture condition.* In determining whether the possibility of forfeiture is substantial in the case of rights in property transferred to an employee of a corporation who owns a significant amount of the total combined voting power or value of all classes of stock of the employer corporation or of its parent corporation, there will be taken into account (i) the employee's relationship to other stockholders and the extent of their control, potential control and possible loss of control of the corporation, (ii) the position of the employee in the corporation and the extent to which he is subordinate to other employees, (iii) the employee's relationship to the officers and directors of the corporation, (iv) the person or persons who must approve the employee's discharge, and (v) past actions of the employer in enforcing the provisions of the restrictions. For example, if an employee would be considered as having received rights in property subject to a substantial risk of forfeiture, but for the fact that the employee owns 20 percent of the single class of stock in the transferor corporation, and if the remaining 80 percent of the class of stock is owned by an unrelated individual (or members of such an individual's family) so that the possibility of the corporation enforcing a restriction on such rights is substantial, then such rights are subject to a substantial risk of forfeiture. On the other hand, if 4 percent of the voting power of all the stock of a corporation is owned by the president of such corporation and the remaining stock is so diversely held by the public that the president, in effect, controls the corporation, then the possibility of the corporation enforcing a restriction on rights in property transferred to the president is not substantial, and such rights are not subject to a substantial risk of forfeiture.

(4) *Examples.* The rules contained in paragraph (c)(1) of this section may be illustrated by the following examples. In each example it is assumed that, if the conditions on transfer are not satisfied, the forfeiture provision will be enforced.

Example 1. On November 1, 1971, corporation X transfers in connection with the performance of services to E, an employee, 100 shares of corporation X stock for $90 per share. Under the terms of the transfer, E will be subject to a binding commitment to resell the stock to corporation X at $90 per share if he leaves the employment of corporation X for any reason prior to the expiration of a 2-year period from the date of such transfer. Since E must perform substantial services for corporation X and will not be paid more than $90 for the stock, regardless of its value, if he fails to perform such services during such 2-year period, E's rights in the stock are subject to a substantial risk of forfeiture during such period.

Example 2. On November 10, 1971, corporation X transfers in connection with the performance of services to a trust for the benefit of employees, $100x. Under the terms of the trust any child of an employee who is an enrolled full-time student at an accredited educational institution as a candidate for a degree will receive an annual grant of cash for each academic year the student completes as a student in good standing, up to a maximum of four years. E, an employee, has a child who is enrolled as a full-time student at an accredited college as a candidate for a degree. Therefore, E has a beneficial interest in the assets of the trust equalling the value of four cash grants. Since E's child must complete one year of college in order to receive a cash grant, E's interest in the trust assets are subject to a substantial risk of forfeiture to the extent E's child has not become entitled to any grants.

Example 3. On November 25, 1971, corporation X gives to E, an employee, in connection with his performance of services to corporation X, a bonus of 100 shares of corporation X stock. Under the terms of the bonus arrangement E is obligated to return the corporation X stock to corporation X if he terminates his employment for any reason. However, for each year occurring after November 25, 1971, during which E remains employed with corporation X, E ceases to be obligated to return 10 shares of the corporation X stock. Since in each year occurring after November 25, 1971, for which E remains employed he is not required to return 10 shares of corporation X's stock, E's rights in 10 shares each year for 10 years cease to be subject to a substantial risk of forfeiture for each year he remains so employed.

Example 4. (a) Assume the same facts as in example 3 except that for each year occurring after November 25, 1971, for which E remains employed with corporation X, X agrees to pay, in redemption of the bonus shares given to E if he terminates employment for any reason, 10 percent of the fair market value of each share of stock on the date of such termination of employment. Since corporation X will pay E 10 percent of the value of his bonus stock for each of the 10 years after November 25, 1971, in which he remains employed by X, and the risk of a decline in value is not a substantial risk of forfeiture, E's interest in 10 percent of such bonus stock becomes substantially vested in each of those years.

(b) The following chart illustrates the fair market value of the bonus stock and the fair market value of the portion of bonus stock that becomes substantially vested on November 25, for the following years:

	Fair Market Value of:	
Year	*(I) All Stock*	*(II) Portion of Stock That Becomes Vested*
1972	$200	$20
1973	300	30
1974	150	15
1975	150	15
1976	100	10

If E terminates his employment on July 1, 1977, when the fair market value of the bonus stock is $100, E must return the bonus stock to X, and X must pay, in redemption of the bonus stock, $50 (50 percent of the value of the bonus stock on the date of termination of employment). E has recognized income under section 83(a) and §1.83-1(a) with respect to 50 percent of the bonus stock, and E's basis in that portion of the stock equals the amount of income recognized, $90. Under §1.83-1(e), the $40 loss E incurred upon forfeiture ($90 basis less $50 redemption payment) is an ordinary loss.

Example 5. On January 7, 1971, corporation X, a computer service company, transfers to E, 100 shares of corporation X stock for $50. E is a highly compensated salesman who sold X's products in a three-state area since 1960. At the time of transfer each share of X stock has a fair market value of $100. The stock is transferred to E in connection with his termination of employment with X. Each share of X stock is subject to the sole condition that E can keep such share only if he does not engage in competition with X for a 5-year period in the three-state area where E had previously sold X's products. E, who is 45 years old, has no intention of retiring from the work force. In order to earn a salary comparable to his current compensation, while preventing the risk of forfeiture from arising, E will have to expend a substantial amount of time and effort in another industry or market to establish the necessary business contacts. Thus, under these facts and circumstances E's rights in the stock are subject to a substantial risk of forfeiture.

(d) *Transferability of property.* For purposes of section 83 and the regulations thereunder, the rights of a person in property are transferable if such person can transfer any interest in the property to any person other than the transferor of the property, but only if the rights in such property of such transferee are not subject to a substantial risk of forfeiture. Accordingly, property is transferable if the person performing the services or receiving the property can sell, assign, or pledge (as collateral for a loan, or as security for the performance of an obligation, or for any other purpose) his interest in the property to any person other than the transferor of such property and if the transferee is not required to give up the property or its value in the event the substantial risk of forfeiture materializes. On the other hand, property is not considered to be transferable merely because the person performing the services or receiving the property may designate a beneficiary to receive the property in the event of his death.

(e) *Property.* For purposes of section 83 and the regulations thereunder, the term "property" includes real and personal property other than either money or an unfunded and unsecured promise to pay money or property in the future. The term also includes a beneficial interest in assets (including money) which are transferred or set aside from the claims of creditors of the transferor, for example, in a trust or escrow account. See, however, §1.83-8(a) with respect to employee trusts and annuity plans subject to section 402(b) and section 403(c). In the case of a transfer of a life insurance contract, retirement income contract, endowment contract, or other contract providing life insurance protection, only the cash surrender value of the contract is considered to be property. Where rights in a contract providing life insurance protection are substantially nonvested, see §1.83-1(a)(2) for rules relating to the taxation of the cost of life insurance protection.

(f) *Property transferred in connection with the performance of services.* Property transferred to an employee or an independent contractor (or beneficiary thereof) in recognition of the performance of, or the refraining from performance of, services is considered transferred in connection with the performance of services within the meaning of section 83. The existence of other persons entitled to buy stock on the same terms and conditions as an employee, whether pursuant to a public or private offering may, however, indicate that in such circumstances a transfer to the employee is not in recognition of the performance of, or the refraining from performance of, services. The transfer of property is subject to section 83 whether such transfer is in respect of past, present, or future services.

(g) *Amount paid.* For purposes of section 83 and the regulations thereunder, the term "amount paid" refers to the value of any money or property paid for the transfer of property to which section 83 applies, and does not refer to any amount paid for the right to use such property or to receive the income therefrom. Such value does not include any stated or unstated interest payments. For rules regarding the calculation of the amount of unstated interest payments, see §1.483-1(c). When section 83 applies to the transfer of property pursuant to the exercise of an option, the term "amount paid" refers to any amount paid for the grant of the option plus any amount paid as the exercise price of the option. For rules regarding the forgiveness of indebtedness treated as an amount paid, see §1.83-4(c).

(h) *Nonlapse restriction.* For purposes of section 83 and the regulations thereunder, a restriction which by its terms will never lapse (also referred to as a "nonlapse restriction") is a permanent limitation on the transferability of property—

(i) Which will require the transferee of the property to sell, or offer to sell, such property at a price determined under a formula, and

(ii) Which will continue to apply to and be enforced against the transferee or any subsequent holder (other than the transferor).

A limitation subjecting the property to a permanent right of first refusal in a particular person at a price determined under a formula is a permanent nonlapse restriction. Limitations imposed by registration requirements of State or Federal security laws or similar laws imposed with respect to sales or other dispositions of stock or securities are not nonlapse restrictions. An obligation to resell or to offer to sell property transferred in connection with the performance of services to a specific person or persons at its fair market value at the time of such sale is not a nonlapse restriction. See §1.83-5(c) for examples of nonlapse restrictions.

(i) *Lapse restriction.* For purposes of section 83 and the regulations thereunder, the term "lapse restriction" means a restriction other than a nonlapse restriction as defined in paragraph (h) of this section, and includes (but is not limited to) a restriction that carries a substantial risk of forfeiture.

(j) *Sales which may give rise to suit under section 16(b) of the Securities Exchange Act of 1934*—(1) *In general.* For purposes of section 83 and the regulations thereunder if the sale of property at a profit within six months after the purchase of the property could subject a person to suit under section 16(b) of the Securities Exchange Act of 1934, the person's rights in the property are treated as subject to a substantial risk of forfeiture and as not transferable until the earlier of (i) the expiration of such six-month period, or (ii) the first day on which the sale of such property at a profit will not subject the person to suit under section 16(b) of the Securities Exchange Act of 1934. However, whether an option is "transferable by the optionee" for purposes of §1.83-7(b)(2)(i) is determined without regard to section 83(c)(3) and this paragraph (j).

(2) *Examples.* The provisions of this paragraph may be illustrated by the following examples:

Example 1. On January 1, 1983, X corporation sells to P, a beneficial owner of 12% of X corporation stock, in connection with P's performance of services, 100 shares of X corporation stock at $10 per share. At the time of the sale the fair market value of the X corporation stock is $100 per share. P, as a beneficial owner of more than 10% of X corporation stock, is liable to suit under section 16(b) of the Securities Exchange Act of 1934 for recovery of any profit from any sale and purchase or purchase and sale of X corporation stock within a six-month period, but no other restrictions apply to the stock. Because the section 16(b) restriction is applicable to P, P's rights in the 100 shares of stock purchased on January 1, 1983, are treated as subject to a substantial risk of forfeiture and as not transferable through June 29, 1983. P chooses not to make an election under section 83(b) and therefore does not include any amount with respect to the stock purchase in gross income as compensation on the date of purchase. On June 30, 1983, the fair market value of X corporation stock is $250 per share. P must include $24,000 (100 shares of X corporation stock × $240 ($250 fair market value per share less $10 price paid by P for each share)) in gross income as compensation on June 30, 1983. If, in this example, restrictions other than section 16(b) applied to the stock, such other restrictions (but not section 16(b)) would be taken into account in determining whether the stock is subject to a substantial risk of forfeiture and is nontransferable for periods after June 29, 1983.

Example 2. Assume the same facts as in example 1 except that P is not an insider on or after May 1, 1983, and the section 16(b) restriction does not apply beginning on that date. On May 1, 1983, P must include in gross income as compensation the difference between the fair market value of the stock on that date and the amount paid for the stock.

Example 3. Assume the same facts as in example 1 except that on June 1, 1983, X corporation sells to P an additional 100 shares of X corporation stock at $20 per share. At the time of the sale the fair market value of the X corporation stock is $150 per share. On June 30, 1983, P must include $24,000 in gross income as compensation with respect to the January 1, 1983 purchase. On November 30, 1983, the fair market value of X corporation stock is $200 per share. Accordingly, on that date P must include $18,000 (100 shares of X corporation stock × $180 ($200 fair market value per share less $20 price paid for P each share)) in gross income as compensation with respect to the June 1, 1983 purchase.

(3) *Effective date.* This paragraph applies to property transferred after December 31, 1981.

(k) *Special rule for certain accounting rules.*—(1) For purposes of section 83 and the regulations thereunder, property is subject to substantial risk of forfeiture and is not transferable so long as the property is subject to a restriction on transfer to comply with the "Pooling-of-Interests Accounting" rules set forth in Accounting Series Release Numbered 130 ((10/5/72) 37 FR 20937; 17 CFR 211.130) and Accounting Series Release Numbered 135 ((1/18/73) 38 FR 1734; 17 CFR 211.135).

(2) *Effective date.* This paragraph applies to property transferred after December 31, 1981.

Treas. Reg. §1.83-4. Special rules.—(a) Holding period. Under section 83(f), the holding period of transferred property to which section 83(a) applies shall begin just after such property is substantially vested. However, if the person who has performed the services in connection with which property is transferred has made an election under section 83(b), the holding period of such property shall begin just after the date such property is transferred. If property to which section 83 and the regulations thereunder apply is transferred at arm's length, the holding period of such property in the hands of the transferee shall be determined in accordance with the rules provided in section 1223.

(b) *Basis.*—(1) Except as provided in paragraph (b) (2) of this section, if property to which section 83 and the regulations thereunder apply is acquired by any person (including a person who acquires such property in a subsequent transfer which is not at arm's length), while such property is still substantially nonvested, such person's basis for the property shall reflect any amount paid for such property and any amount includible in the gross income of the person who performed the services (including any amount so includible as a result of a disposition by the person who acquired such property). Such basis shall also reflect any adjustments to basis provided under sections 1015 and 1016.

(2) If property to which §1.83-1 applies is transferred at arm's length, the basis of the property in the hands of the transferee shall be determined under section 1012 and the regulations thereunder.

(c) *Forgiveness of indebtedness treated as an amount paid.* If an indebtedness that has been treated as an amount paid under §1.83-1 (a) (1) (ii) is subsequently cancelled, forgiven or satisfied for an amount less than the amount of such indebtedness, the amount that is not, in fact, paid shall be includible in the gross income of the service provider in the taxable year in which such cancellation, forgiveness or satisfaction occurs.

Treas. Reg. §1.83-5. Restrictions that will never lapse.—(a) Valuation. For purposes of section 83 and the regulations thereunder, in the case of property subject to a nonlapse restriction (as defined in §1.83-3(h)), the price determined under the formula price will be considered to be the fair market value of the property unless established to the contrary by the Commissioner, and the burden of proof shall be on the Commissioner with respect to such value. If stock in a corporation is subject to a nonlapse restriction which requires the transferee to sell such stock only at a formula price based on book value, a reasonable multiple of earnings or a reasonable combination thereof, the price so determined will ordinarily be regarded as determinative of the fair market value of such property for purposes of section 83. However, in certain circumstances the formula price will not be considered to be the fair market value of property subject to such a formula price restriction, even though the formula price restriction is a substantial factor in determining such value. For example, where the formula price is the current book value of stock, the book value of the stock at some time in the future may be a more accurate measure of the value of the stock than the current book value of the stock for purposes of determining the fair market value of the stock at the time the stock becomes substantially vested.

(b) *Cancellation*

(1) *In general.* Under section 83(d) (2), if a nonlapse restriction imposed on property that is subject to section 83 is cancelled, then, unless the taxpayer establishes—

(i) That such cancellation was not compensatory, and

(ii) That the person who would be allowed a deduction, if any, if the cancellation were treated as compensatory, will treat the transaction as not compensatory, as provided in paragraph (c) (2) of this section, the excess of the fair market value of such property (computed without regard to such restriction) at the time of cancellation, over the sum of—

(iii) The fair market value of such property (computed by taking the restriction into account) immediately before the cancellation, and

(iv) The amount, if any, paid for the cancellation,

shall be treated as compensation for the taxable year in which such cancellation occurs. Whether there has been a noncompensatory cancellation of a nonlapse restriction under section 83 (d) (2) depends upon the particular facts and circumstances. Ordinarily the fact that the employee or independent contractor is required to perform additional services or that the salary or payment of such a person is adjusted to take the cancellation into account indicates that such cancellation has a compensatory purpose. On the other hand, the fact that the original purpose of a restriction no longer exists may indicate that the purpose of such cancellation is noncompensatory. Thus, for example, if a so-called "buy-sell" restriction was imposed on a corporation's stock to limit ownership of such stock and is being cancelled in connection with a public offering of the stock, such cancellation will generally be regarded as noncompensatory. However, the mere fact that the employer is willing to forego a deduction under section 83(h) is insufficient evidence to establish a noncompensatory cancellation of a nonlapse restriction. The refusal by a corporation or shareholder to repurchase stock of the corporation which is subject to a permanent right of first refusal will generally be treated as a cancellation of a nonlapse restriction. The preceding sentence shall not apply where there is no nonlapse restriction, for example, where the price to be paid for the stock subject to the right of first refusal is the fair market value of the stock. Section 83 (d) (2) and this (1) do not apply where immediately after the cancellation of a nonlapse restriction the property is still substantially nonvested and no section 83 (b) election has been made with respect to such property. In such a case the rules of section 83 (a) and §1.83-1 shall apply to such property.

(2) *Evidence of noncompensatory cancellation.* In addition to the information necessary to establish the factors described in paragraph (b) (1) of this section, the taxpayer shall request the employer to furnish the taxpayer with a written statement indicating that the employer will not treat the cancellation of the nonlapse restriction as a compensatory event, and that no deduction will be taken with respect to such cancellation. The taxpayer shall file such written statement with his income tax return for the taxable year in which or with which such cancellation occurs.

(c) *Examples.* The provisions of this section may be illustrated by the following examples:

Example 1. On November 1, 1971, X corporation whose shares are closely held and not regularly traded, transfers to E, an employee, 100 shares of X corporation stock subject to the condition that, if he desires to dispose of such stock during the period of his employment, he must resell the stock to his employer at its then existing book value. In addition, E or E's estate is obligated to offer to sell the stock at his retirement or death to his employer at its then existing book value. Under these facts and circumstances, the restriction to which the shares of X corporation stock are subject is a nonlapse restriction. Consequently, the fair market value of the X stock is includible in E's gross income as compensation for taxable year 1971. However, in determining the fair market value of the X stock, the book value formula price will ordinarily be regarded as being determinative of such value.

Example 2. Assume the facts are the same as in example 1, except that the X stock is subject to the condition that if E desires to dispose of the stock during the period of his employment he must resell the stock to his employer at a multiple of earnings per share that is in this case a reasonable approximation of value at the time of transfer to E. In addition, E or E's estate is obligated to offer to sell the stock at his retirement or death to his employer at the same multiple of earnings. Under these facts and circumstances, the restriction to which the X corporation stock is subject is a nonlapse restriction. Consequently, the fair market value of the X stock is includible in E's gross income for taxable year 1971. However, in determining the fair market value of the X stock, the multiple-of-earnings formula price will ordinarily be regarded as determinative of such value.

Example 3. On January 4, 1971, X corporation transfers to E, an employee, 100 shares of stock in X corporation. Each such share of stock is subject to an agreement between X and E whereby E agrees that such shares are to be held solely for investment purposes and not for resale (a so-called investment letter restriction). E's rights in such stock are substantially vested upon transfer, causing the fair market value of each share of X corporation stock to be includible in E's gross income as compensation for taxable year 1971. Since such an investment letter restriction does not constitute a nonlapse restriction, in determining the fair market value of each share, the investment letter restriction is disregarded.

Example 4. On September 1, 1971, X corporation transfers to B, an independent contractor, 500 shares of common stock in X corporation in exchange for B's agreement to provide services in the construction of an office building on property owned by X corporation. X corporation has 100 shares of preferred stock outstanding and an additional 500 shares of common stock outstanding. The preferred stock has a liquidation value of $1,000x$, which is equal to the value of all assets owned by X. Therefore, the book value of the common stock in X corporation is $0. Under the terms of the transfer, if B wishes to dispose of the stock, B must offer to sell the stock to X for 150 percent of the then existing book value of B's common stock. The stock is also subject to a substantial risk of forfeiture until B performs the agreed-upon services. B makes a timely election under section 83(b) to include the value of the stock in gross income in 1971. Under these facts and circumstances, the restriction to which the shares of X corporation common stock are subject is a nonlapse restriction. In determining the fair market value of the

X common stock at the time of transfer, the book value formula price would ordinarily be regarded as determinative of such value. However, the fair market value of X common stock at the time of transfer, subject to the book value restriction, is greater than $0 since B was willing to agree to provide valuable personal services in exchange for the stock. In determining the fair market value of the stock, the expected book value after construction of the office building would be given great weight. The likelihood of completion of construction would be a factor in determining the expected book value after completion of construction.

Treas. Reg. §1.83-6. Deduction by employer.—(a) *Allowance of deduction*—(1) *General rule.* In the case of a transfer of property in connection with the performance of services, or a compensatory cancellation of a nonlapse restriction described in section 83(d) and section 1.83-5, a deduction is allowable under section 162 or 212 to the person for whom the services were performed. The amount of the deduction is equal to the amount included as compensation in the gross income of the service provider under section 83(a), (b), or (d)(2), but only to the extent the amount meets the requirements of section 162 or 212 and the regulations thereunder. The deduction is allowed only for the taxable year of that person in which or with which ends the taxable year of the service provider in which the amount is included as compensation. For purposes of this paragraph, any amount excluded from gross income under section 79 or section 101(b) or subchapter N is considered to have been included in gross income.

(2) *Special rule.* For purposes of paragraph (a)(1) of this section, the service provider is deemed to have included the amount as compensation in gross income if the person for whom the services were performed satisfies in a timely manner all requirements of section 6041 or section 6041A, and the regulations thereunder, with respect to that amount of compensation. For purposes of the preceding sentence, whether a person for whom services were performed satisfies all requirements of section 6041 or section 6041A, and the regulations thereunder, is determined without regard to section 1.6041-3(c) (exception for payments to corporations). In the case of a disqualifying disposition of stock described in section 421(b), an employer that otherwise satisfies all requirements of section 6041 and the regulations thereunder will be considered to have done so timely for purposes of this paragraph (a)(2) if Form W-2 or Form W-2c, as appropriate, is furnished to the employee or former employee, and is filed with the federal government, on or before the date on which the employer files the tax return claiming the deduction relating to the disqualifying disposition.

(3) *Exceptions.* Where property is substantially vested upon transfer, the deduction shall be allowed to such person in accordance with his method of accounting (in conformity with sections 446 and 461). In the case of a transfer to an employee benefit plan described in §1.162-10(a) or a transfer to an employees' trust or annuity plan described in section 404(a)(5) and the regulations thereunder, section 83(h) and this section do not apply.

(4) *Capital expenditure, etc.* No deduction is allowed under section 83(h) to the extent that the transfer of property constitutes a capital expenditure, an item of deferred expense, or an amount properly includible in the value of

inventory items. In the case of a capital expenditure, for example, the basis of the property to which such capital expenditure relates shall be increased at the same time and to the same extent as any amount includible in the employee's gross income in respect of such transfer. Thus, for example, no deduction is allowed to a corporation in respect of a transfer of its stock to a promoter upon its organization, notwithstanding that such promoter must include the value of such stock in his gross income in accordance with the rules under section 83.

. . .

(b) *Recognition of gain or loss.* Except as provided in section 1032, at the time of a transfer of property in connection with the performance of services the transferor recognizes gain to the extent that the transferor receives an amount that exceeds the transferor's basis in the property. In addition, at the time a deduction is allowed under section 83(h) and paragraph (a) of this section, gain or loss is recognized to the extent of the difference between (i) the sum of the amount paid plus the amount allowed as a deduction under section 83(h), and (ii) the sum of the taxpayer's basis in the property plus any amount recognized pursuant to the previous sentence.

(c) *Forfeitures.* If, under section 83(h) and paragraph (a) of this section, a deduction, an increase in basis, or a reduction of gross income was allowable (disregarding the reasonableness of the amount of compensation) in respect of a transfer of property and such property is subsequently forfeited, the amount of such deduction, increase in basis or reduction of gross income shall be includible in the gross income of the person to whom it was allowable for the taxable year of forfeiture. The basis of such property in the hands of the person to whom it is forfeited shall include any such amount includible in the gross income of such person, as well as any amount such person pays upon forfeiture.

(d) *Special rules for transfers by shareholders*—(1) *Transfers.* If a shareholder of a corporation transfers property to an employee of such corporation or to an independent contractor (or to a beneficiary thereof), in consideration of services performed for the corporation, the transaction shall be considered to be a contribution of such property to the capital of such corporation by the shareholder, and immediately thereafter a transfer of such property by the corporation to the employee or independent contractor under paragraphs (a) and (b) of this section. For purposes of this (1), such a transfer will be considered to be in consideration for services performed for the corporation if either the property transferred is substantially nonvested at the time of transfer or an amount is includible in the gross income of the employee or independent contractor at the time of transfer under §1.83-1(a)(1) or §1.83-2(a). In the case of such a transfer, any money or other property paid to the shareholder for such stock shall be considered to be paid to the corporation and transferred immediately thereafter by the corporation to the shareholder as a distribution to which section 302 applies.

(2) *Forfeiture.* If, following a transaction described in paragraph (d)(1) of this section, the transferred property is forfeited to the shareholder, paragraph (c) of this section shall apply both with respect to the shareholder and with respect

to the corporation. In addition, the corporation shall, in the taxable year of forfeiture be allowed a loss (or realize a gain) to offset any gain (or loss) realized under paragraph (b) of this section. For example, if a shareholder transfers property to an employee of the corporation as compensation, and as a result the shareholder's basis of $200x in such property is allocated to his stock in such corporation and such corporation recognizes a short-term capital gain of $800x, and is allowed a deduction of $1,000x on such transfer, upon a subsequent forfeiture of the property to the shareholder, the shareholder shall take $200x into gross income, and the corporation shall take $1,000x into gross income and be allowed a short-term capital loss of $800x.

(e) *Options.* [Reserved.]

(f) *Reporting requirements.* [Reserved.]

Treas. Reg. §1.83-7. Taxation of nonqualified stock options.—(a) *In general.* If there is granted to an employee or independent contractor (or beneficiary thereof) in connection with the performance of services, an option to which section 421 (relating generally to certain qualified and other options) does not apply, section 83(a) shall apply to such grant if the option has a readily ascertainable fair market value (determined in accordance with paragraph (b) of this section) at the time the option is granted. The person who performed such services realizes compensation upon such grant at the time and in the amount determined under section 83(a). If section 83(a) does not apply to the grant of such an option because the option does not have a readily ascertainable fair market value at the time of grant, sections 83(a) and 83(b) shall apply at the time the option is exercised or otherwise disposed of, even though the fair market value of such option may have become readily ascertainable before such time. If the option is exercised, sections 83(a) and 83(b) apply to the transfer of property pursuant to such exercise, and the employee or independent contractor realizes compensation upon such transfer at the time and in the amount determined under section 83(a) or 83(b). If the option is sold or otherwise disposed of in an arm's length transaction, sections 83(a) and 83(b) apply to the transfer of money or other property received in the same manner as sections 83(a) and 83(b) would have applied to the transfer of property pursuant to an exercise of the option.

(b) *Readily ascertainable defined*—(1) *Actively traded on an established market.* Options have a value at the time they are granted, but that value is ordinarily not readily ascertainable unless the option is actively traded on an established market. If an option is actively traded on an established market, the fair market value of such option is readily ascertainable for purposes of this section by applying the rules of valuation set forth in §20.2031-2.

(2) *Not actively traded on an established market.* When an option is not actively traded on an established market, it does not have a readily ascertainable fair market value unless its fair market value can otherwise be measured with reasonable accuracy. For purposes of this section, if an option is not actively traded on an established market, the option does not have a readily ascertainable fair market value when granted unless the taxpayer can show that all of the following conditions exist:

(i) The option is transferable by the optionee;

(ii) The option is exercisable immediately in full by the optionee;

(iii) The option or the property subject to the option is not subject to any restriction or condition (other than a lien or other condition to secure the payment of the purchase price) which has a significant effect upon the fair market value of the option; and

(iv) The fair market value of the option privilege is readily ascertainable in accordance with paragraph (b)(3) of this section.

(3) *Option privilege.* The option privilege in the case of an option to buy is the opportunity to benefit during the option's exercise period from any increase in the value of property subject to the option during such period, without risking any capital. Similarly, the option privilege in the case of an option to sell is the opportunity to benefit during the exercise period from a decrease in the value of property subject to the option. For example, if at some time during the exercise period of an option to buy, the fair market value of the property subject to the option is greater than the option's exercise price, a profit may be realized by exercising the option and immediately selling the property so acquired for its higher fair market value. Irrespective of whether any such gain may be realized immediately at the time an option is granted, the fair market value of an option to buy includes the value of the right to benefit from any future increase in the value of the property subject to the option (relative to the option exercise price), without risking any capital. Therefore, the fair market value of an option is not merely the difference that may exist at a particular time between the option's exercise price and the value of the property subject to the option, but also includes the value of the option privilege for the remainder of the exercise period. Accordingly, for purposes of this section, in determining whether the fair market value of an option is readily ascertainable, it is necessary to consider whether the value of the entire option privilege can be measured with reasonable accuracy. In determining whether the value of the option privilege is readily ascertainable, and in determining the amount of such value when such value is readily ascertainable, it is necessary to consider—

(i) Whether the value of the property subject to the option can be ascertained;

(ii) The probability of any ascertainable value of such property increasing or decreasing; and

(iii) The length of the period during which the option can be exercised.

(c) *Reporting requirements.* [Reserved]

Treas. Reg. §1.83-8. Applicability of section and transitional rules.—(a) *Scope of section 83.* Section 83 is not applicable to—

(1) A transaction concerning an option to which section 421 applies;

(2) A transfer to or from a trust described in section 401(a) for the benefit of employees or their beneficiaries, or a transfer under an annuity plan that meets the requirements of section 404(a)(2) for the benefit of employees or their beneficiaries;

(3) The transfer of an option without a readily ascertainable fair market value (as defined in §1.83-7(b)(1)); or

(4) The transfer of property pursuant to the exercise of an option with a readily ascertainable fair market value at the date of grant.

Section 83 applies to a transfer to or from a trust or under an annuity plan for the benefit of employees, independent contractors, or their beneficiaries (except as provided in paragraph (a)(2) of this section), but to the extent a transfer is subject to section 402(b) or 403(c), section 83 applies to such a transfer only as provided for in section 402(b) or 403(c).

. . .

Treas. Reg. §1.305-1. Stock dividends.

. . .

(b) *Amount of distribution.*—(1) In general, where a distribution of stock or rights to acquire stock of a corporation is treated as a distribution of property to which section 301 applies by reason of section 305(b), the amount of the distribution, in accordance with section 301(b) and §1.301-1, is the fair market value of such stock or rights on the date of distribution.

. . .

(c) *Adjustment in purchase price.* A transfer of stock (or rights to acquire stock) or an increase or decrease in the conversion ratio or redemption price of stock which represents an adjustment of the price to be paid by the distributing corporation in acquiring property (within the meaning of section 317(a)) is not within the purview of section 305 because it is not a distribution with respect to its stock. For example, assume that on January 1, 1970, pursuant to a reorganization, corporation X acquires all the stock of corporation Y solely in exchange for its convertible preferred class B stock. Under the terms of the class B stock, its conversion ratio is to be adjusted in 1976 under a formula based upon the earnings of corporation Y over the 6-year period ending on December 31, 1975. Such an adjustment in 1976 is not covered by section 305.

. . .

Treas. Reg. §1.305-5. Distributions on preferred stock.—(a) *In general.* Under section 305(b)(4), a distribution by a corporation of its stock (or rights to acquire its stock) made (or deemed made under section 305(c)) with respect to its preferred stock is treated as a distribution of property to which section 301 applies unless the distribution is made with respect to convertible preferred stock to take into account a stock dividend, stock split, or any similar event (such as the sale of stock at less than the fair market value pursuant to a rights offering) which would otherwise result in the dilution of the conversion right. For purposes of the preceding sentence, an adjustment in the conversion ratio of convertible preferred stock made solely to take into account the distribution by a closed-end regulated investment company of a capital gain dividend with respect to the stock into which such stock is convertible shall not be considered a "similar event." The term "preferred stock" generally refers to stock which, in relation to other classes of stock outstanding enjoys certain limited rights and privileges (generally associated with specified dividend and liquidation priorities) but does not participate in corporate growth to any significant extent. The distinguishing feature of "preferred stock" for the purposes of section 305(b)(4) is not its privileged position as such, but that such privileged position is limited and that such stock does not participate in corporate growth to any significant extent. However, a right to participate which lacks substance will not prevent a class of stock from being treated as preferred stock. Thus, stock which enjoys a priority as to dividends and on liquidation but which is entitled to participate, over and above such priority, with another less privileged class of stock in earnings and profits and upon liquidation, may nevertheless be treated as preferred stock for purposes of section 305 if, taking into account all the facts and circumstances, it is reasonable to anticipate at the time a distribution is made (or is deemed to have been made) with respect to such stock that there is little or no likelihood of such stock actually participating in current and anticipated earnings and upon liquidation beyond its preferred interest. Among the facts and circumstances to be considered are the prior and anticipated earnings per share, the cash dividends per share, the book value per share, the extent of preference and of participation of each class, both absolutely and relative to each other, and any other facts which indicate whether or not the stock has a real and meaningful probability of actually participating in the earnings and growth of the corporation. The determination of whether stock is preferred for purposes of section 305 shall be made without regard to any right to convert such stock into another class of stock of the corporation. The term "preferred stock," however, does not include convertible debentures.

(b) *Redemption premium.*—(1) *In general.* If a corporation issues preferred stock that may be redeemed under the circumstances described in this paragraph (b) at a price higher than the issue price, the difference (the redemption premium) is treated under section 305(c) as a constructive distribution (or series of constructive distributions) of additional stock on preferred stock that is taken into account under principles similar to the principles of section 1272(a). However, constructive distribution treatment does not result under this paragraph (b) if the redemption premium does not exceed a de minimis amount, as determined under the principles of section 1273(a)(3). For purposes of this paragraph (b), preferred stock that may be acquired by a person other than the issuer (the third person) is deemed to be redeemable under the circumstances described in this paragraph (b), and references to the issuer include the third person, if—

> (i) this paragraph (b) would apply to the stock if the third person were the issuer; and
>
> (ii) either—

(A) the acquisition of the stock by the third person would be treated as a redemption for federal income tax purposes (under section 304 or otherwise); or

(B) the third person and the issuer are members of the same affiliated group (having the meaning for this purpose given the term by section 1504(a), except that section 1504(b) shall not apply) and a principal purpose of the arrangement for the third person to acquire the stock is to avoid the application of section 305 and paragraph (b)(1) of this section.

(2) *Mandatory redemption or holder put.* Paragraph (b)(1) of this section applies to stock if the issuer is required to redeem the stock at a specified time or the holder has the option (whether or not currently exercisable) to require the issuer to redeem the stock. However, paragraph (b)(1) of this section will not apply if the issuer's obligation to redeem or the holder's ability to require the issuer to redeem is subject to a contingency that is beyond the legal or practical control of either the holder or the holders as a group (or through a related party within the meaning of section 267(b) or 707(b)), and that, based on all of the facts and circumstances as of the issue date, renders remote the likelihood of redemption. For purposes of this paragraph, a contingency does not include the possibility of default, insolvency, or similar circumstances, or that a redemption may be precluded by applicable law which requires that the issuer have a particular level of capital, surplus, or similar items. A contingency also does not include an issuer's option to require earlier redemption of the stock. For rules applicable if stock may be redeemed at more than one time, see paragraph (b)(4) of this section.

(3) *Issuer call.*—(i) *In general.* Paragraph (b)(1) of this section applies to stock by reason of the issuer's right to redeem the stock (even if the right is immediately exercisable), but only if, based on all of the facts and circumstances as of the issue date, redemption pursuant to that right is more likely than not to occur. However, even if redemption is more likely than not to occur, paragraph (b)(1) of this section does not apply if the redemption premium is solely in the nature of a penalty for premature redemption. A redemption premium is not a penalty for premature redemption unless it is a premium paid as a result of changes in economic or market conditions over which neither the issuer nor the holder has legal or practical control.

(ii) *Safe harbor.* For purposes of this paragraph (b)(3), redemption pursuant to an issuer's right to redeem is not treated as more likely than not to occur if—

(A) The issuer and the holder are not related within the meaning of section 267(b) or 707(b) (for purposes of applying sections 267(b) and 707(b) (including section 267(f)(1)), the phrase "20 percent" shall be substituted for the phrase "50 percent");

(B) There are no plans, arrangements, or agreements that effectively require or are intended to compel the issuer to redeem the stock (disregarding, for this purpose, a separate mandatory redemption obligation described in paragraph (b)(2) of this section); and

(C) Exercise of the right to redeem would not reduce the yield of the stock, as determined under principles similar to the principles of section 1272(a) and the regulations under sections 1271 through 1275.

(iii) *Effect of not satisfying safe harbor.* The fact that a redemption right is not described in paragraph (b)(3)(ii) of this section does not affect the determination of whether a redemption pursuant to the right to redeem is more likely than not to occur.

(4) *Coordination of multiple redemption provisions.* If stock may be redeemed at more than one time, the time and price at which redemption is most likely to occur must be determined based on all of the facts and circumstances as of the issue date. Any constructive distribution under paragraph (b)(1) of this section will result only with respect to the time and price identified in the preceding sentence. However, if redemption does not occur at that identified time, the amount of any additional premium payable on any later redemption date, to the extent not previously treated as distributed, is treated as a constructive distribution over the period from the missed call or put date to that later date, to the extent required under the principles of this paragraph (b).

(5) *Consistency.* The issuer's determination as to whether there is a constructive distribution under this paragraph (b) is binding on all holders of the stock, other than a holder that explicitly discloses that its determination as to whether there is a constructive distribution under this paragraph (b) differs from that of the issuer. Unless otherwise prescribed by the Commissioner, the disclosure must be made on a statement attached to the holder's timely filed federal income tax return for the taxable year that includes the date the holder acquired the stock. The issuer must provide the relevant information to the holder in a reasonable manner. For example, the issuer may provide the name or title and either the address or telephone number of a representative of the issuer who will make available to holders upon request the information required for holders to comply with this provision of this paragraph (b).

. . .

(d) *Examples.* The applications of sections 305(b)(4) and 305(c) may be illustrated by the following examples:

. . .

Example 4—(i) *Facts.* Corporation X is a domestic corporation with only common stock outstanding. In connection with its acquisition of Corporation T, X issues 100 shares of its 4% preferred stock to the shareholders of T, who are unrelated to X both before and after the transaction. The issue price of the preferred stock is $40 per share. Each share of preferred stock is convertible at the shareholder's election into three shares of X common stock. At the time the preferred stock is issued, the X common stock has a value of $10 per share. The preferred stock does not provide for its mandatory redemption or for redemption at the option of the holder. It is callable at the option of X at any time beginning three years from the date of issuance for $100 per share. There are no other plans, arrangements, or agreements that effectively require or are intended to compel X to redeem the stock.

(ii) *Analysis.* The preferred stock is described in the safe harbor rule of paragraph (b)(3)(ii) of this section because X and the former shareholders of T are unrelated, there are no plans, arrangements, or agreements that effectively require or are intended to compel X to redeem the stock, and calling the stock for $100 per share would not reduce the yield of the preferred stock. Therefore, the $60 per share call premium is not treated as a constructive distribution to the shareholders of the preferred stock under paragraph (b) of this section.

Example 5—(i) *Facts*—(A) Corporation Y is a domestic corporation with only common stock outstanding. On January 1, 1996, Y issues 100 shares of its 10% preferred stock to a holder. The holder is unrelated to Y both before and after the stock issuance. The issue price of the preferred stock is $100 per share. The preferred stock is—

(1) Callable at the option of Y on or before January 1, 2001, at a price of $105 per share plus any accrued but unpaid dividends; and

(2) Mandatorily redeemable on January 1, 2006, at a price of $100 per share plus any accrued but unpaid dividends.

(B) The preferred stock provides that if Y fails to exercise its option to call the preferred stock on or before January 1, 2001, the holder will be entitled to appoint a majority of Y's directors. Based on all of the facts and circumstances as of the issue date, Y is likely to have the legal and financial capacity to exercise its right to redeem. There are no other facts and circumstances as of the issue date that would affect whether Y will call the preferred stock on or before January 1, 2001.

(ii) *Analysis.* Under paragraph (b)(3)(i) of this section, paragraph (b)(1) of this section applies because, by virtue of the change of control provision and the absence of any contrary facts, it is more likely than not that Y will exercise its option to call the preferred stock on or before January 1, 2001. The safe harbor rule of paragraph (b)(3)(ii) of this section does not apply because the provision that failure to call will cause the holder to gain control of the corporation is a plan, arrangement, or agreement that effectively requires or is intended to compel Y to redeem the preferred stock. Under paragraph (b)(4) of this section, the constructive distribution occurs over the period ending on January 1, 2001. Redemption is most likely to occur on that date, because that is the date on which the corporation minimizes the rate of return to the holder while preventing the holder from gaining control. The de minimis exception of paragraph (b)(1) of this section does not apply because the $5 per share difference between the redemption price and the issue price exceeds the amount determined under the principles of section 1273(a)(3) (5 x .0025 x $105 = $1.31). Accordingly, $5 per share, the difference between the redemption price and the issue price, is treated as a constructive distribution received by the holder on an economic accrual basis over the five-year period ending on January 1, 2001, under principles similar to the principles of section 1272(a).

. . .

Example 7—(i) *Facts*—(A) Corporation Z is a domestic corporation with only common stock outstanding. On January 1, 1996, Z issues 100 shares of its 10% preferred stock to C, an individual unrelated to Z both before and after the stock issuance. The issue price of the preferred stock is $100 per share. The preferred stock is—

(1) Not callable for a period of 5 years from the issue date;

(2) Callable at the option of Z on January 1, 2001, at a price of $110 per share plus any accrued but unpaid dividends;

(3) Callable at the option of Z on July 1, 2002, at a price of $120 per share plus any accrued but unpaid dividends; and

(4) Mandatorily redeemable on January 1, 2004, at a price of $150 per share plus any accrued but unpaid dividends.

(B) There are no other plans, arrangements, or agreements between Z and C concerning redemption of the stock. Moreover, there are no other facts and circumstances as of the issue date that would affect whether Z will call the preferred stock on either January 1, 2001, or July 1, 2002.

(ii) *Analysis.* This stock is described in paragraph (b)(2) of this section because it is mandatorily redeemable. It is also potentially described in paragraph (b)(3)(i) of this section because it is callable at the option of the issuer. The safe harbor rule of paragraph (b)(3)(ii) of this section does not apply to the option to call on January 1, 2001, because the call would reduce the yield of the stock when compared to the yield produced by the January 1, 2004, mandatory redemption feature. Moreover, absent any other facts indicating a contrary result, the fact that redemption on January 1, 2001, would produce the lowest yield indicates that redemption is most likely to occur on that date. Under paragraph (b)(4) of this section, paragraph (b)(1) of this section applies with respect to the issuer's right to call on January 1, 2001, because redemption is most likely to occur on January 1, 2001, for $110 per share. The de minimis exception of paragraph (b)(1) of this section does not apply because the $10 per share difference between the redemption price payable in 2001 and the issue price exceeds the amount determined under the principles of section 1273(a)(3) (5 × .0025 × $110 = $1.38). Accordingly, $10 per share, the difference between the redemption price and the issue price, is treated as a constructive distribution received by the holder on an economic accrual basis over the five-year period ending January 1, 2001, under principles similar to the principles of section 1272(a).

(iii) *Coordination rules*—(A) If Z does not exercise its option to call the preferred stock on January 1, 2001, paragraph (b)(4) of this section provides that the principles of paragraph (b) of this section must be applied to determine if any remaining constructive distribution occurs. Under paragraphs (b)(3)(i) and (b)(4) of this section, paragraph (b)(1) of this section applies because, absent any other facts indicating a contrary result, the fact that redemption on July 1, 2002, would produce a lower yield than the yield produced by the mandatory redemption feature indicates that redemption on that date is most likely to occur. The safe harbor rule of paragraph (b)(3)(ii) of this section does not apply to the option to call on July 1, 2002, because, as of January 1, 2001, a call by Z on July 1, 2002, for $120 would reduce the yield of the stock. The de minimis exception of paragraph (b)(1) of this section does not apply because the $10 per share difference between the redemption price and the issue price (revised as of the missed call date as provided by paragraph (b)(4) of this section) exceeds the amount determined under the principles of section 1273(a)(3) (1 × .0025 × $120 = $.30). Accordingly, the $10 per share of additional redemption premium that is payable on July 1, 2002, is treated as a constructive distribution received by the holder on an economic accrual basis over the period between January 1, 2001, and July 1, 2002, under principles similar to the principles of section 1272(a).

(B) If Z does not exercise its second option to call the preferred stock on July 1, 2002, then the $30 additional redemption premium that is payable on January 1, 2004, is treated as a constructive distribution under paragraphs (b)(2) and (b)(1) of this section. The de minimis exception of paragraph (b)(1) of this section does not apply because the $30 per share difference between the redemption price and the issue price (revised as of the second missed call date) exceeds the amount determined under the principles of section 1273(a)(3) (1 × .0025 × $150 = $.38). The holder is treated as receiving the constructive distribution on an economic accrual basis over the period between July 1, 2002, and January 1, 2004, under principles similar to the principles of section 1272(a).

Example 8—(i) *Facts.* The facts are the same as in paragraph (i) of *Example 7*, except that, based on all of the facts and circumstances as of the issue date (including an expected lack of funds on the part of Z), it is unlikely that Z will exercise the right to redeem on either January 1, 2001, or July 1, 2002.

(ii) *Analysis.* The safe harbor rule of paragraph (b)(3)(ii) of this section does not apply to the option to call on either January 1, 2001, or July 1, 2002, because each call would reduce the yield of the stock. Under paragraph (b)(3)(i) of this section, neither option to call is more likely than not to occur, because, based on all of the facts and circumstances as of the issue date (including an expected lack of funds on the part of Z), it is not more likely than not that Z will exercise either option. However, the $50 per share redemption premium that is payable on January 1, 2004, is treated as a constructive distribution under paragraphs (b)(1) and (2) of this section, regardless of whether Z is anticipated to have sufficient funds to redeem on that date, because Z is required to redeem the stock on that date. The de minimis exception of paragraph (b)(1) of this section does not apply because the $50 per share difference between the redemption price and the issue price exceeds the amount determined under the principles of section 1273(a)(3) (8 × .0025 × $150 = $3).

Example 9. Corporation Q is organized with 10,000 shares of class A stock and 1,000 shares of class B stock. The terms of the class B stock require that the class B have a preference of $5 per share with respect to dividends and $100 per share with respect to liquidation. In addition, upon a distribution of $10 per share to the class A stock, class B participates equally in any additional dividends. The terms also provide that upon liquidation the class B stock participates equally after the class A stock receives $100 per share. Corporation Q has no accumulated earnings and profits. In 1971 it earned $10,000, the highest earnings in its history. The corporation is in an industry in which it is reasonable to anticipate a growth in earnings of 5 percent per year. In 1971 the book value of corporation Q's assets totalled $100,000. In that year the corporation paid a dividend of $5 per share to the class B stock and $.50 per share to the class A. In 1972 the corporation had no earnings and in lieu of a $5 dividend distributed one share of class B stock for each outstanding share of class B. No distribution was made to the class A stock. Since, in 1972, it was not reasonable to anticipate that the class B stock would participate in the current and anticipated earnings and growth of the corporation beyond its preferred interest, the class B stock is preferred stock and the distribution of class B shares to the class B shareholders is a distribution to which sections 305(b)(4) and 301 apply.

Example 10. Corporation P is organized with 10,000 shares of class A stock and 1,000 shares of class B stock. The terms of the class B stock require that the class B have a preference of $5 per share with respect to dividends and $100 per share with respect to liquidation. In addition, upon a distribution of $5 per share to the class A stock, class B participates equally in any additional dividends. The terms also provide that upon liquidation the class B stock participates equally after the class A receives $100 per share. Corporation P has accumulated earnings and profits of $100,000. In 1971 it earned $75,000. The corporation is in an industry in which it is reasonable to anticipate a growth in earnings of 10 percent per year. In 1971 the book value of corporation P's assets totalled $5 million. In that year the corporation paid a dividend of $5 per share to the class B stock, $5 per share to the class A stock, and it distributed an additional $1 per share to both class A and class B stock. In 1972 the corporation had earnings of $82,500. In that year it paid a dividend of $5 per share to the class B stock and $5 per share to the class A stock. In addition, the corporation declared stock dividends of one share of class B stock for every 10 outstanding shares of class B and one share of class A stock for every 10 outstanding shares of class A. Since, in 1972, it was reasonable to anticipate that both the class B stock and the class A stock would participate in the current and anticipated earnings and growth of the corporation beyond their preferred interests, neither class is preferred stock and the stock dividends are not distributions to which section 305(b)(4) applies.

. . .

Treas. Reg. §1.305-7. Certain transactions treated as distributions.—(a) *In general.* Under section 305(c), a change in conversion ratio, a change in redemption price, a difference between redemption price and issue price, a redemption which is treated as a distribution to which section 301 applies, or any transaction (including a recapitalization) having a similar effect on the interest of any shareholder may be treated as a distribution with respect to any shareholder whose proportionate interest in the earnings and profits or assets of the corporation is increased by such change, difference, redemption, or similar transaction. In general, such change, difference, redemption, or similar transaction will be treated as a distribution to which sections 305(b) and 301 apply where—

(1) The proportionate interest of any shareholder in the earnings and profits or assets of the corporation deemed to have made such distribution is increased by such change, difference, redemption, or similar transaction; and

(2) Such distribution has the result described in paragraph (2), (3), (4), or (5) of section 305(b).

Where such change, difference, redemption, or similar transaction is treated as a distribution under the provisions of this section, such distribution will be deemed made with respect to any shareholder whose interest in the earnings and profits or assets of the distributing corporation is increased thereby. Such distribution will be deemed to be a distribution of the stock of such corporation made by the corporation to such shareholder with respect to his stock. Depending upon the facts presented, the distribution may be deemed to be made in common or preferred stock. For example, where a redemption premium exists with respect to a class of preferred stock under the circumstances described in §1.305-5(b) and the other requirements of this section are also met, the distribution will be deemed made with respect to such preferred stock, in stock of the same class. Accordingly, the preferred shareholders are considered under sections 305(b)(4) and 305(c) to have received a distribution of preferred stock to which section 301 applies. See the examples in §§1.305-3(e) and 1.305-5(d) for further illustrations of the application of section 305(c).

(b) *Antidilution provisions.*—(1) For purposes of applying section 305(c) in conjunction with section 305(b), a change in the conversion ratio or conversion price of convertible preferred stock (or securities), or in the exercise price of rights or warrants, made pursuant to a bona fide, reasonable, adjustment formula (including, but not limited to, either the so-called "market price" or "conversion price" type of formulas) which has the effect of preventing dilution of the interest of the holders of such stock (or securities) will not be considered to result in a deemed distribution of stock. An adjustment in the conversion ratio or price to compensate for cash or property distributions to other shareholders that are taxable under section 301, 356(a)(2), 871(a)(1)(A), 881(a)(1), 852(b), or 857(b) will not be considered as made pursuant to a bona fide adjustment formula.

(2) The principles of this paragraph may be illustrated by the following example:

Example. (i) Corporation U has two classes of stock outstanding, class A and class B. Each class B share is convertible into class A stock. In accordance with a bona fide, reasonable, antidilution provision, the conversion price is adjusted if the corporation transfers class A stock to anyone for a consideration that is below the conversion price.

(ii) The corporation sells class A stock to the public at the current market price but below the conversion price. Pursuant to the antidilution provision, the conversion price is adjusted downward. Such a change in conversion price will not be deemed to be a distribution under section 305(c) for the purposes of section 305(b).

(c) *Recapitalizations.*—(1) A recapitalization (whether or not an isolated transaction) will be deemed to result in a distribution to which section 305(c) and this section apply if—

(i) It is pursuant to a plan to periodically increase a shareholder's proportionate interest in the assets or earnings and profits of the corporation, or

(ii) A shareholder owning preferred stock with dividends in arrears exchanges his stock for other stock and, as a result, increases his proportionate interest in the assets or earnings and profits of the corporation. An increase in a preferred shareholder's proportionate interest occurs in any case where the fair market value or the liquidation preference, whichever is greater, of the stock received in the exchange (determined immediately following the recapitalization), exceeds the issue price of the preferred stock surrendered.

(2) In a case to which subparagraph (1)(ii) of this paragraph applies, the amount of the distribution deemed under section 305(c) to result from the recapitalization is the lesser of (i) the amount by which the fair market value or the liquidation preference, whichever is greater, of the stock received in the exchange (determined immediately following the recapitalization) exceeds the issue price of the preferred stock surrendered, or (ii) the amount of the dividends in arrears.

. . .

Treas. Reg. §1.338(h)(10)-1. Deemed asset sale and liquidation.— (a) *Scope.* This section prescribes rules for qualification for a section 338(h)(10) election and for making a section 338(h)(10) election. This section also prescribes the consequences of such election. The rules of this section are in addition to the rules of §§1.338-1 through 1.338-10 and, in appropriate cases, apply instead of the rules of §§1.338-1 through 1.338-10.

(b) *Definitions*—(1) *Consolidated target.* A consolidated target is a target that is a member of a consolidated group within the meaning of section 1.1502-1(h) on the acquisition date and is not the common parent of the group on that date.

(2) *Selling consolidated group.* A selling consolidated group is the consolidated group of which the consolidated target is a member on the acquisition date.

(3) *Selling affiliate; affiliated target.* A selling affiliate is a domestic corporation that owns on the acquisition date an amount of stock in a domestic target, which amount of stock is described in section 1504(a)(2), and does not join in filing a consolidated return with the target. In such case, the target is an affiliated target.

(4) *S corporation target.* An S corporation target is a target that is an S corporation immediately before the acquisition date.

(5) *S corporation shareholders.* S corporation shareholders are the S corporation target's shareholders. Unless otherwise indicated, a reference to S corporation shareholders refers both to S corporation shareholders who do and those who do not sell their target stock.

(6) *Liquidation.* Any reference in this section to a liquidation is treated as a reference to the transfer described in paragraph (d)(4) of this section notwithstanding its ultimate characterization for Federal income tax purposes.

(c) *Section 338(h)(10) election—(1) In general.* A section 338(h)(10) election may be made for T if P acquires stock meeting the requirements of section 1504(a)(2) from a selling consolidated group, a selling affiliate, or the S corporation shareholders in a qualified stock purchase.

(2) *Simultaneous joint election requirement.* A section 338(h)(10) election is made jointly by P and the selling consolidated group (or the selling affiliate or the S corporation shareholders) on Form 8023 in accordance with the instructions to the form. S corporation shareholders who do not sell their stock must also consent to the election. The section 338(h)(10) election must be made not later than the 15th day of the 9th month beginning after the month in which the acquisition date occurs.

(3) *Irrevocability.* A section 338(h)(10) election is irrevocable. If a section 338(h)(10) election is made for T, a section 338 election is deemed made for T.

(4) *Effect of invalid election.* If a section 338(h)(10) election for T is not valid, the section 338 election for T is also not valid.

(d) *Certain consequences of section 338(h)(10) election.* For purposes of subtitle A of the Internal Revenue Code (except as provided in §1.338-1(b)(2)), the consequences to the parties of making a section 338(h)(10) election for T are as follows:

(1) *P.* P is automatically deemed to have made a gain recognition election for its nonrecently purchased T stock, if any. The effect of a gain recognition election includes a taxable deemed sale by P on the acquisition date of any nonrecently purchased target stock. See §1.338-5(d).

(2) *New T.* The AGUB for new T's assets is determined under §1.338-5 and is allocated among the acquisition date assets under sections 1.338-6 and 1.338-7. Notwithstanding paragraph (d)(4) of this section (deemed liquidation of old T), new T remains liable for the tax liabilities of old T (including the tax liability for the deemed sale tax consequences). For example, new T remains liable for the tax liabilities of the members of any consolidated group that are attributable to taxable years in which those corporations and old T joined in the same consolidated return. See §1.1502-6(a).

(3) *Old T—deemed sale—*

(i) *In general.* Old T is treated as transferring all of its assets to an unrelated person in exchange for consideration that includes the discharge of its liabilities in a single transaction at the close of the acquisition date (but before the deemed liquidation). See §1.338-1(a) regarding the tax characterization of the deemed asset sale. Except as provided in §1.338(h)(10)-1(d)(8) (regarding the installment method), old T recognizes all of the gain realized on the deemed transfer of its assets in consideration for the ADSP. ADSP for old T is determined under §1.338-4 and allocated among the acquisition date assets under §§1.338-6 and 1.338-7. Old T realizes the deemed sale tax consequences from the deemed asset sale before the close of the acquisition date while old T is a member of the selling consolidated group (or owned by the selling affiliate or owned by the S corporation shareholders). If T is an affiliated target, or an S corporation target, the principles of §§1.338-2(c)(10) and 1.338-10(a)(1), (5), and (6)(i) apply to the return on which the deemed sale tax consequences are reported. When T is an S corporation target, T's S election continues in effect through the close of the acquisition date (including the time of the deemed asset sale and the deemed liquidation) notwithstanding section 1362(d)(2)(B). Also, when T is an S corporation target (but not a qualified subchapter S subsidiary), any direct and indirect subsidiaries of T which T has elected to treat as qualified subchapter S subsidiaries under section 1361(b)(3) remain qualified subchapter S subsidiaries through the close of the acquisition date.

(ii) *Tiered targets.* In the case of parent-subsidiary chains of corporations making elections under section 338(h)(10), the deemed asset sale of a parent corporation is considered to precede that of its subsidiary. See §1.338- 3(b)(4)(i).

(4) *Old T and selling consolidated group, selling affiliate, or S corporation shareholders—deemed liquidation; tax characterization—*

(i) *In general.* Old T is treated as if, before the close of the acquisition date, after the deemed asset sale in paragraph (d)(3) of this section, and while old T is a member of the selling consolidated group (or owned by the selling affiliate or owned by the S corporation shareholders), it transferred all of its assets to members of the selling consolidated group, the selling affiliate, or S corporation shareholders and ceased to exist. The transfer from old T is characterized for Federal income tax purposes in the same manner as if the parties had actually engaged in the transactions deemed to occur because of this section and taking into account other transactions that actually occurred or are deemed to occur. For example, the transfer may be treated as a distribution in pursuance of a plan of reorganization, a distribution in complete cancellation or redemption of all its stock, one of a series of distributions in complete cancellation or redemption of all its stock in accordance with a plan of liquidation, or part of a circular flow of cash. In most cases, the transfer will be treated as a distribution in complete liquidation to which section 336 or 337 applies.

(ii) *Tiered targets.* In the case of parent-subsidiary chains of corporations making elections under section 338(h)(10), the deemed liquidation of a subsidiary corporation is considered to precede the deemed liquidation of its parent.

(5) *Selling consolidated group, selling affiliate, or S corporation shareholders—*

(i) *In general.* If T is an S corporation target, S corporation shareholders (whether or not they sell their stock) take their pro rata share of the deemed sale tax consequences into account under section 1366 and increase or decrease their basis in T stock under section 1367. Members of the selling consolidated group, the selling affiliate, or S corporation shareholders are treated as if, after the deemed asset sale in paragraph (d)(3) of this section and before the close of the acquisition date, they received the assets transferred by old T in the transaction described in paragraph (d)(4)(i) of this section. In most cases, the transfer will be treated as a distribution in complete liquidation to which section 331 or 332 applies.

(ii) *Basis and holding period of T stock not acquired.* A member of the selling consolidated group (or the selling affiliate or an S corporation shareholder) retaining T stock is treated as acquiring the stock so retained on the day after the acquisition date for its fair market value. The holding period for the retained stock starts on the day after the acquisition date. For purposes of this paragraph, the fair market value of all of the T stock equals the grossed-up amount realized on the sale to P of P's recently purchased target stock. See §1.338-4(c).

(iii) *T stock sale.* Members of the selling consolidated group (or the selling affiliate or S corporation shareholders) recognize no gain or loss on the sale or exchange of T stock included in the qualified stock purchase (although they may recognize gain or loss on the T stock in the deemed liquidation).

(6) *Nonselling minority shareholders other than nonselling S corporation shareholders—*

(i) *In general.* This paragraph (d)(6) describes the treatment of shareholders of old T other than the following: Members of the selling consolidated group, the selling affiliate, S corporation shareholders (whether or not they sell their stock), and P. For a description of the treatment of S corporation shareholders, see paragraph (d)(5) of this section. A shareholder to which this paragraph (d)(6) applies is called a minority shareholder.

(ii) *T stock sale.* A minority shareholder recognizes gain or loss on the shareholder's sale or exchange of T stock included in the qualified stock purchase.

(iii) *T stock not acquired.* A minority shareholder does not recognize gain or loss under this section with respect to shares of T stock retained by the shareholder. The shareholder's basis and holding period for that T stock is not affected by the section 338(h)(10) election.

(7) *Consolidated return of selling consolidated group.* If P acquires T in a qualified stock purchase from a selling consolidated group—

(i) The selling consolidated group must file a consolidated return for the taxable period that includes the acquisition date;

(ii) A consolidated return for the selling consolidated group for that period may not be withdrawn on or after the day that a section 338(h)(10) election is made for T; and

(iii) Permission to discontinue filing consolidated returns cannot be granted for, and cannot apply to, that period or any of the immediately preceding taxable periods during which consolidated returns continuously have been filed.

(8) *Availability of the section 453 installment method.* Solely for purposes of applying sections 453, 453A, and 453B, and the regulations thereunder (the installment method) to determine the consequences to old T in the deemed asset sale and to old T (and its shareholders, if relevant) in the deemed liquidation, the rules in paragraphs (d)(1) through (7) of this section are modified as follows:

(i) *In deemed asset sale.* Old T is treated as receiving in the deemed asset sale new T installment obligations, the terms of which are identical (except as to the obligor) to P installment obligations issued in exchange for recently purchased stock of T. Old T is treated as receiving in cash all other consideration in the deemed asset sale other than the assumption of, or taking subject to, old T liabilities. For example, old T is treated as receiving in cash any amounts attributable to the grossing-up of amount realized under §1.338-4(c). The amount realized for recently purchased stock taken into account in determining ADSP is adjusted (and, thus, ADSP is redetermined) to reflect the amounts paid under an installment obligation for the stock when the total payments under the installment obligation are greater or less than the amount realized.

(ii) *In deemed liquidation*. Old T is treated as distributing in the deemed liquidation the new T installment obligations that it is treated as receiving in the deemed asset sale. The members of the selling consolidated group, the selling affiliate, or the S corporation shareholders are treated as receiving in the deemed liquidation the new T installment obligations that correspond to the P installment obligations they actually received individually in exchange for their recently purchased stock. The new T installment obligations may be recharacterized under other rules. See for example §1.453-11(a)(2) which, in certain circumstances, treats the new T installment obligations deemed distributed by old T as if they were issued by new T in exchange for the stock in old T owned by members of the selling consolidated group, the selling affiliate, or the S corporation shareholders. The members of the selling consolidated group, the selling affiliate, or the S corporation shareholders are treated as receiving all other consideration in the deemed liquidation in cash.

(9) *Treatment consistent with an actual asset sale.* No provision in section 338(h)(10) or this section shall produce a Federal income tax result under subtitle A of the Internal Revenue Code that would not occur if the parties had actually engaged in the transactions deemed to occur because of this section and taking into account other transactions that actually occurred or are deemed to occur. See, however, §1.338-1(b)(2) for certain exceptions to this rule.

(e) *Examples.* The following examples illustrate this section:

Example 1. (i) S1 owns all of the T stock and T owns all of the stock of T1 and T2. S1 is the common parent of a consolidated group that includes T, T1, and T2. P makes a qualified stock purchase of all of the T stock from S1. S1 joins with P in making a section 338(h)(10) election for T and for the deemed purchase of T1. A section 338 election is not made for T2.

(ii) S1 does not recognize gain or loss on the sale of the T stock and T does not recognize gain or loss on the sale of the T1 stock because section 338(h)(10) elections are made for T and T1. Thus, for example, gain or loss realized on the sale of the T or T1 stock is not taken into account in earnings and profits. However, because a section 338 election is not made for T2, T must recognize any gain or loss realized on the deemed sale of the T2 stock. See §1.338-4(h).

(iii) The results would be the same if S1, T, T1, and T2 are not members of any consolidated group, because S1 and T are selling affiliates.

Example 2. (i) S and T are solvent corporations. S owns all of the outstanding stock of T. S and P agree to undertake the following transaction: T will distribute half its assets to S, and S will assume half of T's liabilities. Then, P will purchase the stock of T from S. S and P will jointly make a section 338(h)(10) election with respect to the sale of T. The corporations then complete the transaction as agreed.

(ii) Under section 338(a), the assets present in T at the close of the acquisition date are deemed sold by old T to new T. Under paragraph (d)(4) of this section, the transactions described in paragraph (d) of this section are treated in the same manner as if they had actually occurred. Because S and P had agreed that, after T's actual distribution to S of part of its assets, S would sell T to P pursuant to an election under section 338(h)(10), and because paragraph (d)(4) of this section deems T subsequently to have transferred all its assets to its shareholder, T is deemed to have adopted a plan of complete liquidation under section 332. T's actual transfer of assets to S is treated as a distribution pursuant to that plan of complete liquidation.

Example 3. (i) S1 owns all of the outstanding stock of both T and S2. All three are corporations. S1 and P agree to undertake the following transaction. T will transfer substantially all of its assets and liabilities to S2, with S2 issuing no stock in exchange therefor, and retaining its other assets and liabilities. Then, P will purchase the stock of T from S1. S1 and P will jointly make a section 338(h)(10) election with respect to the sale of T. The corporations then complete the transaction as agreed.

(ii) Under section 338(a), the remaining assets present in T at the close of the acquisition date are deemed sold by old T to new T. Under paragraph (d)(4) of this section, the transactions described in this section are treated in the same manner as if they had actually occurred. Because old T transferred substantially all of its assets to S2, and is deemed to have distributed all its remaining assets and gone out of existence, the transfer of assets to S2, taking into account the related transfers, deemed and actual, qualifies as a reorganization under section 368(a)(1)(D). Section 361(c)(1) and not section 332 applies to T's deemed liquidation.

Example 4. (i) T owns two assets: an actively traded security (Class II) with a fair market value of $100 and an adjusted basis of $100, and inventory (Class IV) with a fair market value of $100 and an adjusted basis of $100. T has no liabilities. S is negotiating to sell all the stock in T to P for $100 cash and contingent consideration. Assume that under generally applicable tax accounting rules, P's adjusted basis in the T stock immediately after the purchase would be $100, because the contingent consideration is not taken into account. Thus, under the rules of §1.338-5, AGUB would be $100. Under the allocation rules of §1.338-6, the entire $100 would be allocated to the Class II asset, the actively traded security, and no amount would be allocated to the inventory. P, however, plans immediately to cause T to sell the inventory, but not the actively traded security, so it requests that, prior to the stock sale, S cause T to create a new subsidiary, Newco, and contribute the actively traded security to the capital of Newco. Because the stock in Newco, which would not be actively traded, is a Class V asset, under the rules of §1.338-6 $100 of AGUB would be allocated to the inventory and no amount of AGUB would be allocated to the Newco stock. Newco's own AGUB, $0 under the rules of §1.338-5, would be allocated to the actively traded security. When P subsequently causes T to sell the inventory, T would realize no gain or loss instead of realizing gain of $100.

(ii) Assume that, if the T stock had not itself been sold but T had instead sold both its inventory and the Newco stock to P, T would for tax purposes be deemed instead to have sold both its inventory and actively traded security directly to P, with P deemed then to have created Newco and contributed the actively traded security to the capital of Newco. Section 338, if elected, generally recharacterizes a stock sale as a deemed sale of assets. However, paragraph (d)(9) of this section states, in general, that no provision of section 338(h)(10) or the regulations thereunder shall produce a Federal income tax result under subtitle A of the Internal Revenue Code that would not occur if the parties had actually engaged in the transactions deemed to occur by virtue of the section 338(h)(10) election, taking into account other transactions that actually occurred or are deemed to occur. Hence, the deemed sale of assets under section 338(h)(10) should be treated as one of the inventory and actively traded security themselves, not of the inventory and Newco stock. The anti-abuse rule of §1.338-1(c) does not apply, because the substance of the deemed sale of assets is a sale of the inventory and the actively traded security themselves, not of the inventory and the Newco stock. Otherwise, the anti-abuse rule might apply.

Example 5. (i) T, a member of a selling consolidated group, has only one class of stock, all of which is owned by S1. On March 1 of Year 2, S1 sells its T stock to P for $80,000, and joins with P in making a section 338(h)(10) election for T. There are no selling costs or acquisition costs. On March 1 of Year 2, T owns land with a $50,000 basis and $75,000 fair market value and equipment with a $30,000 adjusted basis, $70,000 recomputed basis, and $60,000 fair market value. T also has a $40,000 liability. S1 pays old T's allocable share of the selling group's consolidated tax liability for Year 2 including the tax liability for the deemed sale tax consequences (a total of $13,600).

(ii) ADSP of $120,000 ($80,000 + $40,000 + 0) is allocated to each asset as follows:

Assets	Basis	FMV	Fraction	Allocable ADSP
Land	$50,000	$ 75,000	$5/9$	$ 66,637
Equipment	30,000	60,000	$4/9$	53,333
Total	$80,000	$135,000	1	$120,000

(iii) Under paragraph (d)(3) of this section, old T has gain on the deemed sale of $40,000 (consisting of $16,667 of capital gain and $23,333 of ordinary income).

(iv) Under paragraph (d)(5)(iii) of this section, S1 recognizes no gain or loss upon its sale of the old T stock to P. S1 also recognizes no gain or loss upon the deemed liquidation of T. See paragraph (d)(4) of this section and section 332.

(v) P's basis in new T stock is P's cost for the stock, $80,000. See section 1012.

(vi) Under §1.338-5, the AGUB for new T is $120,000, i.e., P's cost for the old T stock ($80,000) plus T's liability ($40,000). This AGUB is allocated as basis among the new T assets under §§1.338-6 and 1.338-7.

Example 6. (i) The facts are the same as in Example 5, except that S1 sells 80 percent of the old T stock to P for $64,000, rather than 100 percent of the old T stock for $80,000.

(ii) The consequences to P, T, and S1 are the same as in Example 5, except that:

(A) P's basis for its 80-percent interest in the new T stock is P's $64,000 cost for the stock. See section 1012.

(B) Under §1.338-5, the AGUB for new T is $120,000 (i.e., $64,000/.8 + $40,000 + $0).

(C) Under paragraph (d)(4) of this section, S1 recognizes no gain or loss with respect to the retained stock in T. See section 332.

(D) Under paragraph (d)(5)(ii) of this section, the basis of the T stock retained by S1 is $16,000 (i.e., $120,000 - $40,000 (the ADSP amount for the old T assets over the sum of new T's liabilities immediately after the acquisition date) x .20 (the proportion of T stock retained by S1)).

Example 7. (i) The facts are the same as in Example 6, except that K, a shareholder unrelated to T or P, owns the 20 percent of the T stock that is not acquired by P in the qualified stock purchase. K's basis in its T stock is $5,000.

(ii) The consequences to P, T, and S1 are the same as in Example 6.

(iii) Under paragraph (d)(6)(iii) of this section, K recognizes no gain or loss, and K's basis in its T stock remains at $5,000.

Example 8. (i) The facts are the same as in Example 5, except that the equipment is held by T1, a wholly-owned subsidiary of T, and a section 338(h)(10) election is also made for T1. The T1 stock has a fair market value of $60,000. T1 has no assets other than the equipment and no liabilities. S1 pays old T's and old T1's allocable shares of the selling group's consolidated tax liability for Year 2 including the tax liability for T and T1's deemed sale tax consequences.

(ii) ADSP for T is $120,000, allocated $66,667 to the land and $53,333 to the stock. Old T's deemed sale results in $16,667 of capital gain on its deemed sale of the land. Under paragraph (d)(5)(iii) of this section, old T does not recognize gain or loss on its deemed sale of the T1 stock. See section 332.

(iii) ADSP for T1 is $53,333 (i.e., $53,333 + $0 + $0). On the deemed sale of the equipment, T1 recognizes ordinary income of $23,333.

(iv) Under paragraph (d)(5)(iii) of this section, S1 does not recognize gain or loss upon its sale of the old T stock to P.

Example 9. (i) The facts are the same as in Example 8, except that P already owns 20 percent of the T stock, which is nonrecently purchased stock with a basis of $6,000, and that P purchases the remaining 80 percent of the T stock from S1 for $64,000.

(ii) The results are the same as in Example 8, except that under paragraph (d)(1) of this section and §1.338-5(d), P is deemed to have made a gain recognition election for its nonrecently purchased T stock. As a result, P recognizes gain of $10,000 and its basis in the nonrecently purchased T stock is increased from $6,000 to $16,000. P's basis in all the T stock is $80,000 (i.e., $64,000 + $16,000). The computations are as follows:

(A) P's grossed-up basis for the recently purchased T stock is $64,000 (i.e., $64,000 (the basis of the recently purchased T stock) x (1 − .2)/(.8) (the fraction in section 338(b)(4))).

(B) P's basis amount for the nonrecently purchased T stock is $16,000 (i.e., $64,000 (the grossed-up basis in the recently purchased T stock) x (.2)/(1.0 − .2) (the fraction in section 338(b)(3)(B))).

(C) The gain recognized on the nonrecently purchased stock is $10,000 (i.e., $16,000 − $6,000).

Example 10. (i) T is an S corporation whose sole class of stock is owned 40 percent each by A and B and 20 percent by C. T, A, B, and C all use the cash method of accounting. A and B each has an adjusted basis of $10,000 in the stock. C has an adjusted basis of $5,000 in the stock. A, B, and C hold no installment obligations to which section 453A applies. On March 1 of Year 1, A sells its stock to P for $40,000 in cash and B sells its stock to P for a $25,000 note issued by P and real estate having a fair market value of $15,000. The $25,000 note, due in full in Year 7, is not publicly traded and bears adequate stated interest. A and B have no selling expenses. T's sole asset is real estate, which has a value of $110,000 and an adjusted basis of $35,000. Also, T's real estate is encumbered by long-outstanding purchase-money indebtedness of $10,000. The real estate does not have built-in gain subject to section 1374. A, B, and C join with P in making a section 338(h)(10) election for T.

(ii) Solely for purposes of application of sections 453, 453A, and 453B, old T is considered in its deemed asset sale to receive back from new T the $25,000 note (considered issued by new T) and $75,000 of cash (total consideration of $80,000 paid for all the stock sold, which is then divided by .80 in the grossing-up, with the resulting figure of $100,000 then reduced by the amount of the installment note). Absent an election under section 453(d), gain is reported by old T under the installment method.

(iii) In applying the installment method to old T's deemed asset sale, the contract price for old T's assets deemed sold is $100,000, the $110,000 selling price reduced by the indebtedness of $10,000 to which the assets are subject. (The $110,000 selling price is itself the sum of the $80,000 grossed-up in paragraph (ii) above to $100,000 and the $10,000 liability.) Gross profit is $75,000 ($110,000 selling price − old T's basis of $35,000). Old T's gross profit ratio is 0.75 (gross profit of $75,000 ÷ $100,000 contract price). Thus, $56,250

(0.75 x the $75,000 cash old T is deemed to receive in Year 1) is Year 1 gain attributable to the sale, and $18,750 ($75,000 - $56,250) is recovery of basis.

(iv) In its liquidation, old T is deemed to distribute the $25,000 note to B, since B actually sold the stock partly for that consideration. To the extent of the remaining liquidating distribution to B, it is deemed to receive, along with A and C, the balance of old T's liquidating assets in the form of cash. Under section 453(h), B, unless it makes an election under section 453(d), is not required to treat the receipt of the note as a payment for the T stock; P's payment of the $25,000 note in Year 7 to B is a payment for the T stock. Because section 453(h) applies to B, old T's deemed liquidating distribution of the note is, under section 453B(h), not treated as a taxable disposition by old T.

(v) Under section 1366, A reports 40 percent, or $22,500, of old T's $56,250 gain recognized in Year 1. Under section 1367, this increases A's $10,000 adjusted basis in the T stock to $32,500. Next, in old T's deemed liquidation, A is considered to receive $40,000 for its old T shares, causing it to recognize an additional $7,500 gain in Year 1.

(vi) Under section 1366, B reports 40 percent, or $22,500, of old T's $56,250 gain recognized in Year 1. Under section 1367, this increases B's $10,000 adjusted basis in its T stock to $32,500. Next, in old T's deemed liquidation, B is considered to receive the $25,000 note and $15,000 of other consideration. Applying section 453, including section 453(h), to the deemed liquidation, B's selling price and contract price are both $40,000. Gross profit is $7,500 ($40,000 selling price - B's basis of $32,500). B's gross profit ratio is 0.1875 (gross profit of $7,500 + $40,000 contract price). Thus, $2,812.50 (0.1875 x $15,000) is Year 1 gain attributable to the deemed liquidation. In Year 7, when the $25,000 note is paid, B has $4,687.50 (0.1875 x $25,000) of additional gain.

(vii) Under section 1366, C reports 20 percent, or $11,250, of old T's $56,250 gain recognized in Year 1. Under section 1367, this increases C's $5,000 adjusted basis in its T stock to $16,250. Next, in old T's deemed liquidation, C is considered to receive $20,000 for its old T shares, causing it to recognize an additional $3,750 gain in Year 1. Finally, under paragraph (d)(5)(ii) of this section, C is considered to acquire its stock in T on the day after the acquisition date for $20,000 (fair market value = grossed-up amount realized of $100,000 x 20%). C's holding period in the stock deemed received in new T begins at that time.

(f) *Inapplicability of provisions.* The provisions of section 6043, §1.331-1(d), and §1.332-6 (relating to information returns and recordkeeping requirements for corporate liquidations) do not apply to the deemed liquidation of old T under paragraph (d)(4) of this section.

(g) *Required information.* The Commissioner may exercise the authority granted in section 338(h)(10)(C)(iii) to require provision of any information deemed necessary to carry out the provisions of section 338(h)(10) by requiring submission of information on any tax reporting form.

. . .

[*Code §351 was amended in 1989 to delete "or securities" from the phrase "stock or securities" but the Regulations have not yet been conformed.*]

Treas. Reg. §1.351-1. Transfer to corporation controlled by transferor.—(a) (1) Section 351(a) provides, in general, for the nonrecognition of gain or loss upon the transfer by one or more persons of property to a corporation solely in exchange for stock or securities in such corporation if, immediately after the exchange, such person or persons are in control of the corporation to which the property was transferred. As used in section 351, the phrase "one or more persons" includes individuals, trusts, estates, partnerships, associations, companies, or corporations (see section 7701(a)(1)). To be in control of the transferee corporation, such person or persons must own immediately after the transfer stock possessing at least 80 percent of the total combined voting power of all classes of stock entitled to vote and at least 80 percent of the total number of shares of all other classes of stock of such corporation (see section 368(c)). In determining control under this section, the fact that any corporate transferor distributes part or all of the stock which it receives in the exchange to its shareholders shall not be taken into account. The phrase "immediately after the exchange" does not necessarily require simultaneous exchanges by two or more persons, but comprehends a situation where the rights of the parties have been previously defined and the execution of the agreement proceeds with an expedition consistent with orderly procedure. For purposes of this section—

> (i) stock or securities issued for services rendered or to be rendered to or for the benefit of the issuing corporation will not be treated as having been issued in return for property, and

> (ii) stock or securities issued for property which is of relatively small value in comparison to the value of the stock and securities already owned (or to be received for services) by the person who transferred such property, shall not be treated as having been issued in return for property if the primary purpose of the transfer is to qualify under this section the exchanges of property by other persons transferring property.

For the purpose of section 351, stock rights or stock warrants are not included in the term "stock or securities."

(2) The application of section 351(a) is illustrated by the following examples:

Example 1. C owns a patent right worth $25,000 and D owns a manufacturing plant worth $75,000. C and D organize the R Corporation with an authorized capital stock of $100,000. C transfers his patent right to the R Corporation for $25,000 of its stock and D transfers his plant to the new corporation for $75,000 of its stock. No gain or loss to C or D is recognized.

Example 2. B owns certain real estate which cost him $50,000 in 1930, but which has a fair market value of $200,000 in 1955. He transfers the property to the N Corporation in 1955 for 78 percent of each class of stock of the corporation having a fair market value of $200,000, the remaining 22 percent of the stock of the corporation having been issued by the corporation in 1940 to other persons for cash. B realized a taxable gain of $150,000 on this transaction.

Example 3. E, an individual, owns property with a basis of $10,000 but which has a fair market value of $18,000. E also had rendered services valued at $2,000 to Corporation F. Corporation F has outstanding 100 shares of common stock all of which are held by G. Corporation F issues 400 shares of its common stock (having a fair market value of $20,000) to E in exchange for his property worth $18,000 and in compensation for the services he has rendered worth $2,000. Since immediately after the transaction, E owns 80 percent of the outstanding stock of Corporation F, no gain is recognized upon the exchange of the property for the stock. However, E realized $2,000 of ordinary income as compensation for services rendered to Corporation F.

(3) *Underwritings of stock*—(i) *In general.* For the purpose of section 351, if a person acquires stock of a corporation from an underwriter in exchange for cash in a qualified underwriting transaction, the person who acquires stock from the underwriter is treated as transferring cash directly to the corporation in exchange for stock of the corporation and the underwriter is disregarded. A qualified underwriting transaction is a transaction in which a corporation issues stock for cash in an underwriting in which either the underwriter is an agent of the corporation or the underwriter's ownership of the stock is transitory.

. . .

(b) (1) Where property is transferred to a corporation by two or more persons in exchange for stock or securities, as described in paragraph (a) of this section, it is not required that the stock and securities received by each be substantially in proportion to his interest in the property immediately prior to the transfer. However, where the stock and securities received are received in disproportion to such interest, the entire transaction will be given tax effect in accordance with its true nature, and in appropriate cases the transaction may be treated as if the stock and securities had first been received in proportion and then some of such stock and securities had been used to make gifts (section 2501 and following), to pay compensation (section 61(a)(1)), or to satisfy obligations of the transferor of any kind.

(2) The application of paragraph (b)(1) of this section may be illustrated as follows:

Example 1. Individuals A and B, father and son, organize a corporation with 100 shares of common stock to which A transfers property worth $8,000 in exchange for 20 shares of stock, and B transfers property worth $2,000 in exchange for 80 shares of stock. No gain or loss will be recognized under section 351. However, if it is determined that A in fact made a gift to B, such gift will be subject to tax under section 2501 and following. Similarly, if B had rendered services to A (such services having no relation to the assets transferred or to the business of the corporation) and the disproportion in the amount of stock received constituted the payment of compensation by A to B, B will be taxable upon the fair market value of the 60 shares of stock received as compensation for services rendered, and A will realize gain or loss upon the difference between the basis to him of the 60 shares and their fair market value at the time of the exchange.

Example 2. Individuals C and D each transferred, to a newly organized corporation, property having a fair market value of $4,500 in exchange for the issuance by the corporation of 45 shares of its capital stock to each transferor. At the same time, the corporation issued to E, an individual, 10 shares of its capital stock in payment for organizational and promotional services rendered by E for the benefit of the corporation. E transferred no property to the corporation. C and D were under no obligation to pay for E's services. No gain or loss is recognized to C or D. E received compensation taxable as ordinary income to the extent of the fair market value of the 10 shares of stock received by him.

(c) (1) The general rule of section 351 does not apply, and consequently gain or loss will be recognized, where property is transferred to an investment company after June 30, 1967. A transfer of property after June 30, 1967, will be considered to be a transfer to an investment company if—

(i) The transfer results, directly or indirectly, in diversification of the transferors' interests, and

(ii) The transferee is *(a)* a regulated investment company, *(b)* a real estate investment trust, or *(c)* a corporation more than 80 percent of the value of whose assets (excluding cash and nonconvertible debt obligations from consideration) are held for investment and are readily marketable stocks or securities, or interests in regulated investment companies or real estate investment trusts.

(2) The determination of whether a corporation is an investment company shall ordinarily be made by reference to the circumstances in existence immediately after the transfer in question. However, where circumstances change thereafter pursuant to a plan in existence at the time of the transfer, this determination shall be made by reference to the later circumstances.

(3) Stocks and securities will be considered readily marketable if (and only if) they are part of a class of stock or securities which is traded on a securities exchange or traded or quoted regularly in the over-the-counter market. For purposes of subparagraph (1)(ii)*(c)* of this paragraph, the term "readily marketable stocks or securities" includes convertible debentures, convertible preferred stock, warrants, and other stock rights if the stock for which they may be converted or exchanged is readily marketable. Stocks and securities will be considered to be held for investment unless they are (i) held primarily for sale to customers in the ordinary course of business, or (ii) used in the trade or business of banking, insurance, brokerage, or a similar trade or business.

(4) In making the determination required under subparagraph (1)(ii)*(c)* of this paragraph, stock and securities in subsidiary corporations shall be disregarded and the parent corporation shall be deemed to own its ratable share of its subsidiaries' assets. A corporation shall be considered a subsidiary if the parent owns 50 percent or more of (i) the combined voting power of all classes of stock entitled to vote, or (ii) the total value of shares of all classes of stock outstanding.

(5) A transfer ordinarily results in the diversification of the transferors' interests if two or more persons transfer nonidentical assets to a corporation in the exchange. For this purpose, if any transaction involves one or more transfers of nonidentical assets which, taken in the aggregate, constitute an insignificant portion of the total value of assets transferred, such transfers shall be disregarded in determining whether diversification has occurred. If there is only one transferor (or two or more transferors of identical assets) to a newly organized corporation, the transfer will generally be treated as not resulting in diversification. If a transfer is part of a plan to achieve diversification without recognition of gain, such as a plan which contemplates a subsequent transfer, however delayed, of the corporate assets (or of the stock or securities received in the earlier exchange) to an investment company in a transaction purporting to qualify for nonrecognition treatment, the original transfer will be treated as resulting in diversification.

(6) (i) For purposes of paragraph (c)(5) of this section, a transfer of stocks and securities will not be treated as resulting in a diversification of the transferors' interests if each transferor transfers a diversified portfolio of stocks and securities. For purposes of this paragraph (c)(6), a portfolio of stocks and securities is diversified if it satisfies the 25 and 50-percent tests of section 368(a)(2)(F)(ii), applying the relevant provisions of section 368(a)(2)(F). However, Government securities are included in total assets for purposes of the denominator of the 25 and 50-percent tests (unless the Government securities are acquired to meet the 25 and 50-percent tests), but are not treated as securities of an issuer for purposes of the numerator of the 25 and 50-percent tests.

. . .

(7) The application of subparagraph (5) of this paragraph may be illustrated as follows:

Example 1. Individuals A, B, and C organize a corporation with 101 shares of common stock. A and B each transfers to it $10,000 worth of the only class of stock of corporation X, listed on the New York Stock Exchange, in exchange for 50 shares of stock. C transfers $200 worth of readily marketable securities in corporation Y for one share of stock. In determining whether or not diversification has occurred, C's participation in the transaction will be disregarded. There is, therefore, no diversification, and gain or loss will not be recognized.

Example 2. A, together with 50 other transferors, organizes a corporation with 100 shares of stock. A transfers $10,000 worth of stock in corporation X, listed on the New York Stock Exchange, in exchange for 50 shares of stock. Each of the other 50 transferors transfers $200 worth of readily marketable securities in corporations other than X in exchange for one share of stock. In determining whether or not diversification has occurred, all transfers will be taken into account. Therefore, diversification is present, and gain or loss will be recognized.

Treas. Reg. §1.351-2. Receipt of property.—(a) If an exchange would be within the provisions of section 351(a) if it were not for the fact that the property received in exchange consists not only of property permitted by such subsection to be received without the recognition of gain, but also of other property or money, then the gain, if any, to the recipient shall be recognized, but in an amount not in excess of the sum of such money and the fair market value of such other property. No loss to the recipient shall be recognized.

(b) See section 357 and the regulations pertaining to that section for applicable rules as to the treatment of liabilities as "other property" in cases subject to section 351, where another party to the exchange assumes a liability, or acquires property subject to a liability.

(c) See sections 358 and 362 and the regulations pertaining to those sections for applicable rules with respect to the determination of the basis of stock, securities, or other property received in exchanges subject to section 351.

(d) See part 1 (section 301 and following), subchapter C, chapter 1 of the Code, and the regulations thereunder for applicable rules with respect to the taxation of dividends where a distribution by a corporation of its stock or securities in connection with an exchange subject to section 351(a) has the effect of the distribution of a taxable dividend.

. . .

Treas. Reg. §1.1361-1. S corporation defined.—(a) *In general.* For purposes of this title, with respect to any taxable year—

(1) The term *S corporation* means a small business corporation (as defined in paragraph (b) of this section) for which an election under section 1362(a) is in effect for that taxable year.

(2) The term *C corporation* means a corporation that is not an S corporation for that taxable year.

(b) *Small business corporation defined*—

(1) *In general.* For purposes of subchapter S, chapter 1 of the Code and the regulations thereunder, the term *small business corporation* means a domestic corporation that is not an ineligible corporation (as defined in section 1361(b)(2)) and that does not have—

(i) More than 35 shareholders;

(ii) As a shareholder, a person (other than an estate and other than certain trusts described in section 1361(c)(2)) who is not an individual;

(iii) A nonresident alien as a shareholder; or

(iv) More than one class of stock.

(2) *Estate in bankruptcy.* The term *estate*, for purposes of this paragraph, includes the estate of an individual in a case under title 11 of the United States Code.

(3) Treatment of restricted stock. For purposes of subchapter S, stock that is issued in connection with the performance of services (within the meaning of §1.83-3(f)) and that is substantially nonvested (within the meaning of §1.83-3(b)) is not treated as outstanding stock of the corporation, and the holder

of that stock is not treated as a shareholder solely by reason of holding the stock, unless the holder makes an election with respect to the stock under section 83(b). In the event of such an election, the stock is treated as outstanding stock of the corporation, and the holder of the stock is treated as a shareholder for purposes of subchapter S. See paragraphs (l)(1) and (3) of this section for rules for determining whether substantially nonvested stock with respect to which an election under section 83(b) has been made is treated as a second class of stock.

(4) *Treatment of deferred compensation plans.* For purposes of subchapter S, an instrument, obligation, or arrangement is not outstanding stock if it—

(i) Does not convey the right to vote;

(ii) Is an unfunded and unsecured promise to pay money or property in the future;

(iii) Is issued to an individual who is an employee in connection with the performance of services for the corporation or to an individual who is an independent contractor in connection with the performance of services for the corporation (and is not excessive by reference to the services performed); and

(iv) Is issued pursuant to a plan with respect to which the employee or independent contractor is not taxed currently on income.

A deferred compensation plan that has a current payment feature (*e.g.*, payment of dividend equivalent amounts that are taxed currently as compensation) is not for that reason excluded from this paragraph (b)(4).

(5) *Treatment of straight debt.* For purposes of subchapter S, an instrument or obligation that satisfies the definition of straight debt in paragraph (l)(5) of this section is not treated as outstanding stock.

. . .

(e) *Number of shareholders*—(1) *General rule.* A corporation does not qualify as a small business corporation if it has more than 35 shareholders. Ordinarily, the person who would have to include in gross income dividends distributed with respect to the stock of the corporation (if the corporation were a C corporation) is considered to be the shareholder of the corporation. For example, if stock (owned other than by a husband and wife) is owned by tenants in common or joint tenants, each tenant in common or joint tenant is generally considered to be a shareholder of the corporation. (For special rules relating to stock owned by husband and wife, see paragraph (e)(2) of this section; for special rules relating to restricted stock, see paragraphs (b)(3) and (6) of this section.) The person for whom stock of a corporation is held by a nominee, guardian, custodian, or an agent is considered to be the shareholder of the corporation for purposes of this paragraph (e) and paragraphs (f) and (g) of this section. For example, a partnership may be a nominee of S corporation stock for a person who qualifies as a shareholder of an S corporation. However, if the partnership is the beneficial owner of the stock, then the partnership is the shareholder, and the corporation does not qualify as a small business corporation. In addition, in the case of stock held for a minor under a uniform gifts to minors or similar statute, the minor and not the custodian is the shareholder. For purposes of this paragraph (e) and paragraphs (f) and (g) of this section, if stock is held by a decedent's estate, the estate (and not the beneficiaries of the estate) is considered to be the shareholder; however, if stock is held by a subpart E trust (which includes voting trusts), the deemed owner is considered to be the shareholder.

(2) *Special rules relating to stock owned by husband and wife.* For purposes of paragraph (e)(1) of this section, stock owned by a husband and wife (or by either or both of their estates) is treated as if owned by one shareholder, regardless of the form in which they own the stock. For example, if husband and wife are owners of a subpart E trust, they will be treated as one individual. Both husband and wife must be U.S. citizens or residents, and a decedent spouse's estate must not be a foreign estate as defined in section 7701(a)(31). The treatment described in this paragraph (e)(2) will cease upon dissolution of the marriage for any reason other than death.

. . .

(g) *Nonresident alien shareholder*—(1) *General rule.* (i) A corporation having a shareholder who is a nonresident alien as defined in section 7701(b)(1)(B) does not qualify as a small business corporation. If a U.S. shareholder's spouse is a nonresident alien who has a current ownership interest (as opposed, for example, to a survivorship interest) in the stock of the corporation by reason of any applicable law, such as a state community property law or a foreign country's law, the corporation does not qualify as a small business corporation from the time the nonresident alien spouse acquires the interest in the stock. If a corporation's Selection is inadvertently terminated as a result of a nonresident alien spouse being considered a shareholder, the corporation may request relief under section 1362(f).

. . .

(*l*) *Classes of stock*—(1) *General rule.* A corporation that has more than one class of stock does not qualify as a small business corporation. Except as provided in paragraph (l)(4) of this section (relating to instruments, obligations, or arrangements treated as a second class of stock), a corporation is treated as having only one class of stock if all outstanding shares of stock of the corporation confer identical rights to distribution and liquidation proceeds. Differences in voting rights among shares of stock of a corporation are disregarded in determining whether a corporation has more than one class of stock. Thus, if all shares of stock of an S corporation have identical rights to distribution and liquidation proceeds, the corporation may have voting and nonvoting common stock, a class of stock that may vote only on certain issues, irrevocable proxy agreements, or groups of shares that differ with respect to rights to elect members of the board of directors.

(2) *Determination of whether stock confers identical rights to distribution and liquidation proceeds*—(i) *In general.* The determination of whether all outstanding

shares of stock confer identical rights to distribution and liquidation proceeds is made based on the corporate charter, articles of incorporation, bylaws, applicable state law, and binding agreements relating to distribution and liquidation proceeds (collectively, the governing provisions). A commercial contractual agreement, such as a lease, employment agreement, or loan agreement, is not a binding agreement relating to distribution and liquidation proceeds and thus is not a governing provision unless a principal purpose of the agreement is to circumvent the one class of stock requirement of section 1361(b)(1)(D) and this paragraph (l). Although a corporation is not treated as having more than one class of stock so long as the governing provisions provide for identical distribution and liquidation rights, any distributions (including actual, constructive, or deemed distributions) that differ in timing or amount are to be given appropriate tax effect in accordance with the facts and circumstances.

(ii) *State law requirements for payment and withholding of income tax.* State laws may require a corporation to pay or withhold state income taxes on behalf of some or all of the corporation's shareholders. Such laws are disregarded in determining whether all outstanding shares of stock of the corporation confer identical rights to distribution and liquidation proceeds, within the meaning of paragraph (l)(1) of this section, provided that, when the constructive distributions resulting from the payment or withholding of taxes by the corporation are taken into account, the outstanding shares confer identical rights to distribution and liquidation proceeds. A difference in timing between the constructive distributions and the actual distributions to the other shareholders does not cause the corporation to be treated as having more than one class of stock.

(iii) *Buy-sell and redemption agreements—(A) In general.* Buy-sell agreements among shareholders, agreements restricting the transferability of stock, and redemption agreements are disregarded in determining whether a corporation's outstanding shares of stock confer identical distribution and liquidation rights unless—

(1) A principal purpose of the agreement is to circumvent the one class of stock requirement of section 1361(b)(l)(D) and this paragraph (1), and

(2) The agreement establishes a purchase price that, at the time the agreement is entered into, is significantly in excess of or below the fair market value of the stock.

Agreements that provide for the purchase or redemption of stock at book value or at a price between fair market value and book value are not considered to establish a price that is significantly in excess of or below the fair market value of the stock and, thus, are disregarded in determining whether the outstanding shares of stock confer identical rights. For purposes of this paragraph (l)(2)(iii)(A), a good faith determination of fair market value will be respected unless it can be shown that the value was substantially in error and the determination of the value was not performed with reasonable diligence. Although an agreement may be disregarded in determining whether shares of stock confer identical distribution and liquidation rights, payments pursuant to the agreement may have income or transfer tax consequences.

(B) *Exception for certain agreements.* Bona fide agreements to redeem or purchase stock at the time of death, divorce, disability, or termination of employment are disregarded in determining whether a corporation's shares of stock confer identical rights. In addition, if stock that is substantially nonvested (within the meaning of §1.83-3(b)) is treated as outstanding under these regulations, the forfeiture provisions that cause the stock to be substantially nonvested are disregarded. Furthermore, the Commissioner may provide by revenue ruling or other published guidance that other types of bona fide agreements to redeem or purchase stock are disregarded.

(C) *Safe harbors for determinations of book value.* A determination of book value will be respected if—

(1) The book value is determined in accordance with Generally Accepted Accounting Principles (including permitted optional adjustments); or

(2) The book value is used for any substantial nontax purpose.

(iv) *Distributions that take into account varying interests in stock during a taxable year.* A governing provision does not, within the meaning of paragraph (l)(2)(i) of this section, alter the rights to liquidation and distribution proceeds conferred by an S corporation's stock merely because the governing provision provides that, as a result of a change in stock ownership, distributions in a taxable year are to be made on the basis of the shareholders' varying interests in the S corporation's income in the current or immediately preceding taxable year. If distributions pursuant to the provision are not made within a reasonable time after the close of the taxable year in which the varying interests occur, the distributions may be recharacterized depending on the facts and circumstances, but will not result in a second class of stock.

(v) *Special rule for section 338(h)(10) elections.* If the shareholders of an S corporation sell their stock in a transaction for which an election is made under section 338(h)(10) and §1.338(h)(10)-1, the receipt of varying amounts per share by the shareholder will not cause the S corporation to have more than one class of stock, provided that the varying amounts are determined in arm's length negotiations with the purchaser.

(vi) *Examples.* The application of paragraph (l)(2) of this section may be illustrated by the following examples. In each of the examples, the S corporation requirements of section 1361 are satisfied except as otherwise stated, the corporation has in effect an S election under section 1362, and the corporation has only the shareholders described.

Example 1. Determination of whether stock confers identical rights to distribution and liquidation proceeds. (i) The law of State A requires that permission be obtained from the State Commissioner of Corporations before stock may be issued by a corporation. The Commissioner grants permission to S, a corporation, to issue its stock subject to the restriction that any person who is issued stock in exchange for property, and not cash, must waive all rights to receive distributions until the shareholders who contributed cash for stock have received distributions in the amount of their cash contributions.

(ii) The condition imposed by the Commissioner pursuant to state law alters the rights to distribution and liquidation proceeds conferred by the outstanding stock of S so that those rights are not identical. Accordingly, under paragraph (l)(2)(i) of this section, S is treated as having more than one class of stock and does not qualify as a small business corporation.

Example 2. Distributions that differ in timing. (i) S, a corporation, has two equal shareholders, A and B. Under S's bylaws, A and B are entitled to equal distributions. S distributes $50,000 to A in the current year, but does not distribute $50,000 to B until one year later. The circumstances indicate that the difference in timing did not occur by reason of a binding agreement relating to distribution or liquidation proceeds.

(ii) Under paragraph (l)(2)(i) of this section, the difference in timing of the distributions to A and B does not cause S to be treated as having more than one class of stock. However, section 7872 or other recharacterization principles may apply to determine the appropriate tax consequences.

Example 3. Treatment of excessive compensation. (i) S, a corporation, has two equal shareholders, C and D, who are each employed by S and have binding employment agreements with S. The compensation paid by S to C under C's employment agreement is reasonable. The compensation paid by S to D under D's employment agreement, however, is found to be excessive. The facts and circumstances do not reflect that a principal purpose of D's employment agreement is to circumvent the one class of stock requirement of section 1361(b)(1)(D) and this paragraph (l).

(ii) Under paragraph (l)(2)(i) of this section, the employment agreements are not governing provisions. Accordingly, S is not treated as having more than one class of stock by reason of the employment agreements, even though S is not allowed a deduction for the excessive compensation paid to D.

Example 4. Agreement to pay fringe benefits. (i) S, a corporation, is required under binding agreements to pay accident and health insurance premiums on behalf of certain of its employees who are also shareholders. Different premium amounts are paid by S for each employee-shareholder. The facts and circumstances do not reflect that a principal purpose of the agreements is to circumvent the one class of stock requirement of section 1361(b)(1)(D) and this paragraph (l).

(ii) Under paragraph (l)(2)(i) of this section, the agreements are not governing provisions. Accordingly, S is not treated as having more than one class of stock by reason of the agreements. In addition, S is not treated as having more than one class of stock by reason of the payment of fringe benefits.

Example 5. Below-market corporation-shareholder loan. (i) E is a shareholder of S, a corporation. S makes a below-market loan to E that is a corporation-shareholder loan to which section 7872 applies. Under section 7872, E is deemed to receive a distribution with respect to S stock by reason of the loan. The facts and circumstances do not reflect that a principal purpose of the loan is to circumvent the one class of stock requirement of section 1361(b)(1)(D) and this paragraph (l).

(ii) Under paragraph (l)(2)(i) of this section, the loan agreement is not a governing provision. Accordingly, S is not treated as having more than one class of stock by reason of the below-market loan to E.

Example 6. Agreement to adjust distributions for state tax burdens. (i) S, a corporation, executes a binding agreement with its shareholders to modify its normal distribution policy by making upward adjustments of its distributions to those shareholders who bear heavier state tax burdens. The adjustments are based on a formula that will give the shareholders equal after-tax distributions.

(ii) The binding agreement relates to distribution or liquidation proceeds. The agreement is thus a governing provision that alters the rights conferred by the outstanding stock of S to distribution proceeds so that those rights are not identical. Therefore, under paragraph (l)(2)(i) of this section, S is treated as having more than one class of stock.

Example 7. State law requirements for payment and withholding of income tax. (i) The law of State X requires corporations to pay state income taxes on behalf of nonresident shareholders. The law of State X does not require corporations to pay state income taxes on behalf of resident shareholders. S is incorporated in State X. S's resident shareholders have the right (for example, under the law of State X or pursuant to S's bylaws or a binding agreement) to distributions that take into account the payments S makes on behalf of its nonresident shareholders.

(ii) The payment by S of state income taxes on behalf of its nonresident shareholders are generally treated as constructive distributions to those shareholders. Because S's resident shareholders have the right to equal distributions, taking into account the constructive distributions to the nonresident shareholders, S's shares confer identical rights to distribution proceeds. Accordingly, under paragraph (l)(2)(ii) of this section, the state law requiring S to pay state income taxes on behalf of its nonresident shareholders is disregarded in determining whether S has more than one class of stock.

(iii) The same result would follow if the payments of state income taxes on behalf of nonresident shareholders are instead treated as advances to those shareholders and the governing provisions require the advances to be repaid or offset by reductions in distributions to those shareholders.

Example 8. Redemption agreements. (i) F, G, and H are shareholders of S, a corporation. F is also an employee of S. By agreement, S is to redeem F's shares on the termination of F's employment.

(ii) On these facts, under paragraph (l)(2)(iii)(B) of this section, the agreement is disregarded in determining whether all outstanding shares of S's stock confer identical rights to distribution and liquidation proceeds.

Example 9. Analysis of redemption agreements. (i) J, K, and L are shareholders of S, a corporation. L is also an employee of S. L's shares were not issued to L in connection with the performance of services. By agreement, S is to redeem L's shares for an amount significantly below their fair market value on the termination of L's employment or if S's sales fall below certain levels.

(ii) Under paragraph (l)(2)(iii)(B) of this section, the portion of the agreement providing for redemption of L's stock on termination of employment is disregarded. Under paragraph (l)(2)(iii)(A), the portion of the agreement providing for redemption of L's stock if S's sales fall below certain levels is disregarded unless a principal purpose of that portion of the agreement is to circumvent the one class of stock requirement of section 1361(b)(1)(D) and this paragraph (l).

(3) *Stock taken into account.* Except as provided in paragraphs (b)(3), (4), and (5) of this section (relating to restricted stock, deferred compensation plans, and straight debt), in determining whether all outstanding shares of stock confer identical rights to distribution and liquidation proceeds, all outstanding shares of stock of a corporation are taken into account. For example, substantially nonvested stock with respect to which an election under section 83(b) has been made is taken into account in determining whether a corporation has a second class of stock, and such stock is not treated as a second class of stock if the stock confers rights to distribution and liquidation proceeds that are identical, within the meaning of paragraph (l)(1) of this section, to the rights conferred by the other outstanding shares of stock.

(4) *Other instruments, obligations, or arrangements treated as a second class of stock*—(i) *In general.* Instruments, obligations, or arrangements are not treated as a second class of stock for purposes of this paragraph (l) unless they are described in paragraphs (l)(4)(ii) or (iii) of this section. However, in no event are instruments, obligations, or arrangements described in paragraph (b)(4) of this section (relating to deferred compensation plans), paragraphs (l)(4)(iii)(B) and (C) of this section (relating to the exceptions and safe harbor for options), paragraph (l)(4)(ii)(B) of this section (relating to the safe harbors for certain short-term unwritten advances and proportionally-held debt), or paragraph (l)(5) of this section (relating to the safe harbor for straight debt), treated as a second class of stock for purposes of this paragraph (l).

(ii) *Instruments, obligations, or arrangements treated as equity under general principles*—(A) *In general.* Except as provided in paragraph (l)(4)(i) of this section, any instrument, obligation, or arrangement issued by a corporation (other than outstanding shares of stock described in paragraph (l)(3) of this section), regardless of whether designated as debt, is treated as a second class of stock of the corporation—

(1) If the instrument, obligation, or arrangement constitutes equity or otherwise results in the holder being treated as the owner of stock under general principles of Federal tax law; and

(2) A principal purpose of issuing or entering into the instrument, obligation, or arrangement is to circumvent the rights to distribution or liquidation proceeds conferred by the outstanding shares of stock or to circumvent the limitation on eligible shareholders contained in paragraph (b)(1) of this section.

(B) *Safe harbor for certain short-term unwritten advances and proportionately held obligations—(1) Short-term unwritten advances.* Unwritten advances from a shareholder that do not exceed $10,000 in the aggregate at any time during the taxable year of the corporation, are treated as debt by the parties, and are expected to be repaid within a reasonable time are not treated as a second class of stock for that taxable year, even if the advances are considered equity under general principles of Federal tax law. The failure of an unwritten advance to meet this safe harbor will not result in a second class of stock unless the advance is considered equity under paragraph (l)(4)(ii)(A)*(1)* of this section and a principal purpose of the advance is to circumvent the rights of the outstanding shares of stock or the limitation on eligible shareholders under paragraph (l)(4)(ii)(A)*(2)* of this section.

(2) *Proportionately-held obligations.* Obligations of the same class that are considered equity under general principles of Federal tax law, but are owned solely by the owners of, and in the same proportion as, the outstanding stock of the corporation, are not treated as a second class of stock. Furthermore, an obligation or obligations owned by the sole shareholder of a corporation are always held proportionately to the corporation's outstanding stock. The obligations that are considered equity that do not meet this safe harbor will not result in a second class of stock unless a principal purpose of the obligations is to circumvent the rights of the outstanding shares of stock or the limitation on eligible shareholders under paragraph (l)(4)(ii)(A)(2) of this section.

(iii) *Certain call options, warrants or similar instruments—(A) In general.* Except as otherwise provided in this paragraph (l)(4)(iii), a call option, warrant, or similar instrument (collectively, call option) issued by a corporation is treated as a second class of stock of the corporation if, taking into account all the facts and circumstances, the call option is substantially certain to be exercised (by the holder or a potential transferee) and has a strike price substantially below the fair market value of the underlying stock on the date that the call option is issued, transferred by a person who is an eligible shareholder under paragraph (b)(1) of this section to a person who is not an eligible shareholder under paragraph (b)(1) of this section, or materially modified. For purposes of this paragraph (l)(4)(iii), if an option is issued in connection with a loan and the time period in which the option can be exercised is extended in connection with (and consistent with) a modification of the terms of the loan, the extension of the time period in which the option may be exercised is not considered a material modification. In addition, a call option does not have a strike price substantially below fair market value if the price at the time of exercise cannot, pursuant to the terms of the instrument, be substantially below the fair market value of the underlying stock at the time of exercise.

(B) *Certain exceptions.—(1)* A call option is not treated as a second class of stock for purposes of this paragraph (l) if it is issued to a person that is actively and regularly engaged in the business of lending and issued in connection with a commercially reasonable loan to the corporation. This paragraph (l)(4)(iii)(B)*(1)* continues to apply if the call option is transferred with the loan (or if a portion of the call option is transferred with a corresponding portion of the loan). However, if the call option is transferred without a corresponding portion of the loan, this paragraph (l)(4)(iii)(B)*(1)* ceases to apply. Upon that transfer, the call option is tested under paragraph (l)(4)(iii)(A) (notwithstanding anything in that paragraph to the contrary) if, but for this paragraph, the call option would have been treated as a second class of stock on the date it was issued.

(2) A call option that is issued to an individual who is either an employee or an independent contractor in connection with the performance of services for the corporation or a related corporation (and that is not excessive by reference to the services performed) is not treated as a second class of stock for purposes of this paragraph (l) if—

(i) The call option is nontransferable within the meaning of §1.83-3(d); and

(ii) The call option does not have a readily ascertainable fair market value as defined in §1.83-7(b) at the time the option is issued.

If the call option becomes transferable, this paragraph (l)(4)(iii)(B)(2) ceases to apply. Solely for purposes of this paragraph (l)(4)(iii)(B)*(2)*, a corporation is related to the issuing corporation if more than 50 percent of the total voting power and total value of its stock is owned by the issuing corporation.

(3) The Commissioner may provide other exceptions by Revenue Ruling or other published guidance.

(C) *Safe harbor for certain options.* A call option is not treated as a second class of stock if, on the date the call option is issued, transferred by a person who is an eligible shareholder under paragraph (b)(1) of this section to a person who is not an eligible shareholder under paragraph (b)(1) of this section, or materially modified, the strike price of the call option is at least 90 percent of the fair market value of the underlying stock on that date. For purposes of this paragraph (l)(4)(iii)(C), a good faith determination of fair market value by the corporation will be respected unless it can be shown that the value was substantially in error and the determination of the value was not performed with reasonable diligence to obtain a fair value. Failure of an option to meet this safe harbor will not necessarily result in the option being treated as a second class of stock.

(iv) *Convertible debt.* A convertible debt instrument is considered a second class of stock if—

(A) It would be treated as a second class of stock under paragraph (l)(4)(ii) of this section (relating to instruments, obligations, or arrangements treated as equity under general principles); or

(B) It embodies rights equivalent to those of a call option that would be treated as a second class of stock under paragraph (l)(4)(iii) of this section (relating to certain call options, warrants, and similar instruments).

(v) *Examples.* The application of this paragraph (1)(4) may be illustrated by the following examples. In each of the examples, the S corporation requirements of section 1361 are satisfied except as otherwise stated, the corporation has in effect an S election under section 1362, and the corporation has only the shareholders described.

Example 1. Transfer of call option by eligible shareholder to ineligible shareholder. (i) S, a corporation, has 10 shareholders. S issues call options to A, B, and C, individuals who are U.S. residents. A, B, and C are not shareholders, employees, or independent contractors of S. The options have a strike price of $40 and are issued on a date when the fair market value of S stock is also $40. A year later, P, a partnership, purchases A's option. On the date of transfer, the fair market value of S stock is $80.

(ii) On the date the call option is issued, its strike price is not substantially below the fair market value of the S stock. Under paragraph (l)(4)(iii)(A) of this section, whether a call option is a second class of stock must be redetermined if the call option is transferred by a person who is an eligible shareholder under paragraph (b)(1) of this section to a person who is not an eligible shareholder under paragraph (b)(1) of this section. In this case, A is an eligible shareholder of S under paragraph (b)(1) of this section, but P is not. Accordingly, the option is retested on the date it is transferred to D.

(iii) Because on the date the call option is transferred to P its strike price is 50% of the fair market value, the strike price is substantially below the fair market value of the S stock. Accordingly, the call option is treated as a second class of stock as of the date it is transferred to P if, at that time, it is determined that the option is substantially certain to be exercised. The determination of whether the option is substantially certain to be exercised is made on the basis of all the facts and circumstances.

Example 2. Call option issued in connection with the performance of services. (i) E is a bona fide employee of S, a corporation. S issues to E a call option in connection with E's performance of services. At the time the call option is issued, it is not transferable and does not have a readily ascertainable fair market value. However, the call option becomes transferable before it is exercised by E.

(ii) While the option is not transferable, under paragraph (l)(4)(iii)(B)(2) of this section, it is not treated as a second class of stock, regardless of its strike price. When the option becomes transferable, that paragraph ceases to apply, and the general rule of paragraph (l)(4)(iii)(A) of this section applies. Accordingly, if the option is materially modified or is transferred to a person who is not an eligible shareholder under paragraph (b)(1) of this section, and on the date of such modification or transfer, the option is substantially certain to be exercised and has a strike price substantially below the fair market value of the underlying stock, the option is treated as a second class of stock.

(iii) If E left S's employment before the option became transferable, the exception provided by paragraph (l)(4)(iii)(B)*(2)* would continue to apply until the option became transferable.

(5) *Straight debt safe harbor*—(i) *In general.* Notwithstanding paragraph (l)(4) of this section, straight debt is not treated as a second class of stock. For purposes of section 1361(c)(5) and this section, the term straight debt means a written unconditional obligation, regardless of whether embodied in a formal note, to pay a sum certain on demand, or on a specified due date, which—

(A) Does not provide for an interest rate or payment dates that are contingent on profits, the borrower's discretion, the payment of dividends with respect to common stock, or similar factors;

(B) Is not convertible (directly or indirectly) into stock or any other equity interest of the S corporation; and

(C) Is held by an individual (other than a nonresident alien), an estate, or a trust described in section 1361(c)(2).

(ii) *Subordination.* The fact that an obligation is subordinated to other debt of the corporation does not prevent the obligation from qualifying as straight debt.

(iii) *Modification or transfer.* An obligation that originally qualifies as straight debt ceases to so qualify if the obligation—

(A) Is materially modified so that it no longer satisfies the definition of straight debt; or

(B) Is transferred to a third party who is not an eligible shareholder under paragraph (b)(1) of this section.

(iv) *Treatment of straight debt for other purposes.* An obligation of an S corporation that satisfies the definition of straight debt in paragraph (l)(5)(i) of this section is not treated as a second class of stock even if it is considered equity under general principles of Federal tax law. Such an obligation is generally treated as debt and when so treated is subject to the applicable rules governing indebtedness for other purposes of the Code. Accordingly, interest paid or accrued with respect to a straight debt obligation is generally treated as interest by the corporation and the recipient and does not constitute a distribution to which section 1368 applies. However, if a straight debt obligation bears a rate of interest that is unreasonably high, an appropriate portion of the interest may be recharacterized and treated as a payment that is not interest. Such a recharacterization does not result in a second class of stock.

(v) *Treatment of C corporation debt upon conversion to S status.* If a C corporation has outstanding an obligation that satisfies the definition of straight debt in paragraph (l)(5)(i) of this section, but that is considered equity under general principles of Federal tax law, the obligation is not treated as a second class of stock for purposes of this section if the C corporation converts to S status. In addition, the conversion from C corporation status to S corporation status is not treated as an exchange of debt for stock with respect to such an instrument.

(6) *Inadvertent terminations.* See section 1362(f) and the regulations thereunder for rules relating to inadvertent terminations in cases where the one class of stock requirement has been inadvertently breached.

. . .

Treas. Reg. §1.1502-6. Liability for tax.—(a) *Several liability of members of group.* Except as provided in paragraph (b) of this section, the common parent corporation and each subsidiary which was a member of the group during any part of the consolidated return year shall be severally liable for the tax for such year computed in accordance with the regulations under section 1502 prescribed on or before the due date (not including extensions of time) for the filing of the consolidated return for such year.

(b) *Liability of subsidiary after withdrawal.* If a subsidiary has ceased to be a member of the group and if such cessation resulted from a bona fide sale or exchange of its stock for fair value and occurred prior to the date upon which any deficiency is assessed, the Commissioner may, if he believes that the assessment or collection of the balance of the deficiency will not be jeopardized, make assessment and collection of such deficiency from such former subsidiary in an amount not exceeding the portion of such deficiency which the Commissioner may determine to be allocable to it. If the Commissioner makes assessment and collection of any part of a deficiency from such former subsidiary, then for purposes of any credit or refund of the amount collected from such former subsidiary the agency of the common parent under the provisions of §1.1502-77 shall not apply.

(c) *Effect of intercompany agreements.* No agreement entered into by one or more members of the group with any other member of such group or with any other person shall in any case have the effect of reducing the liability prescribed under this section.

. . .

Treas. Reg. §301.7701-2. Business entities; definitions. ["Check-the-box" regulations]—(a) *Business entities.* For purposes of this section and §301.7701-3, a *business entity* is any entity recognized for federal tax purposes (including an entity with a single owner that may be disregarded as an entity separate from its owner under §301.7701-3) that is not properly classified as a trust under §301.7701-4 or otherwise subject to special treatment under the Internal Revenue Code. A business entity with two or more members is classified for federal tax purposes as either a corporation or a partnership. A business entity with only one owner is classified as a corporation or is disregarded; if the entity is disregarded, its activities are treated in the same manner as a sole proprietorship, branch, or division of the owner.

(b) *Corporations.* For federal tax purposes, the term *corporation* means—

(1) A business entity organized under a Federal or State statute, or under a statute of a federally recognized Indian tribe, if the statute describes or refers to the entity as incorporated or as a corporation, body corporate, or body politic;

(2) An association (as determined under §301.7701-3);

(3) A business entity organized under a State statute, if the statute describes or refers to the entity as a joint-stock company or joint-stock association;

(4) An insurance company;

(5) A State-chartered business entity conducting banking activities, if any of its deposits are insured under the Federal Deposit Insurance Act, as amended, 12 U.S.C. 1811 et seq., or a similar federal statute;

(6) A business entity wholly owned by a State or any political subdivision thereof, or a business entity wholly owned by a foreign government or any other entity described in §1.892-2T;

(7) A business entity that is taxable as a corporation under a provision of the Internal Revenue Code other than section 7701(a)(3); and

(8) *Certain foreign entities*—(i) *In general.* Except as provided in paragraphs (b)(8)(ii) and (d) of this section, the following business entities formed in the following jurisdictions:

[lengthy list by country omitted]

. . .

(c) *Other business entities.* For federal tax purposes—

(1) The term *partnership* means a business entity that is not a corporation under paragraph (b) of this section and that has at least two members.

(2) *Wholly owned entities —*

(i) *In general.* A business entity that has a single owner and is not a corporation under paragraph (b) of this section is disregarded as an entity separate from its owner.

(ii) *Special rule for certain business entities.* If the single owner of a business entity is a bank (as defined in section 581, or, in the case of a foreign bank, as defined in section 585(a)(2)(B) without regard to the second sentence thereof), then the special rules applicable to banks under the Internal Revenue Code will continue to apply to the single owner as if the wholly owned entity were a separate entity. For this purpose, the special rules applicable to banks under the Internal Revenue Code do not include the rules under sections 864(c), 882(c), and 884.

. . .

(d) Special rule for certain foreign business entities—[omitted]

. . .

(e) Effective date. The rules of this section are effective as of January 1, 1997.

Treas. Reg. §301.7701-3. Classification of certain business entities.—(a) *In general.* A business entity that is not classified as a corporation under §301.7701-2(b)(1), (3), (4), (5), (6), (7), or (8) (an eligible entity) can elect its classification for federal tax purposes as provided in this section. An eligible entity with at least two members can elect to be classified as either an association (and thus a corporation under §301.7701- 2(b)(2)) or a partnership, and an eligible entity with a single owner can elect to be classified as an association or to be disregarded as an entity separate from its owner. Paragraph (b) of this section provides a default classification for an eligible entity that does not make an election. Thus, elections are necessary only when an eligible entity chooses to be classified initially as other than the default classification or when an eligible entity chooses to change its classification. An entity whose classification is determined under the default classification retains that classification (regardless of any changes in the members' liability that occurs at any time during the time that the entity's classification is relevant as defined in paragraph (d) of this section) until the entity makes an election to change that classification under paragraph (c)(1) of this section. Paragraph (c) of this section provides rules for making express elections. Paragraph (d) of this section provides special rules for foreign eligible entities. . . .

(b) *Classification of eligible entities that do not file an election—*

(1) *Domestic eligible entities.* Except as provided in paragraph (b)(3) of this section, unless the entity elects otherwise, a domestic eligible entity is—

(i) A partnership if it has two or more members; or

(ii) Disregarded as an entity separate from its owner if it has a single owner.

(2) *Foreign eligible entities—*

(i) In general. Except as provided in paragraph (b)(3) of this section, unless the entity elects otherwise, a foreign eligible entity is—

(A) A partnership if it has two or more members and at least one member does not have limited liability;

(B) An association if all members have limited liability; or

(C) Disregarded as an entity separate from its owner if it has a single owner that does not have limited liability.

(ii) Definition of limited liability. For purposes of paragraph (b)(2)(i) of this section, a member of a foreign eligible entity has limited liability if the member has no personal liability for the debts of or claims against the entity by reason of being a member. This determination is based solely on the statute or law pursuant to which the entity is organized, except that if the underlying statute or law allows the entity to specify in its organizational documents whether the members will have limited liability, the organizational documents may also be relevant. For purposes of this section, a member has personal liability if the creditors of the entity may seek satisfaction of all or any portion of the debts or claims against the entity from the member as such. A member has personal liability for purposes of this paragraph even if the member makes an agreement under which another person (whether or not a member of the entity) assumes such liability or agrees to indemnify that member for any such liability.

(3) *Existing eligible entities—*

(i) In general. Unless the entity elects otherwise, an eligible entity in existence prior to the effective date of this section will have the same classification that the entity claimed under §§301.7701-1 through 301.7701-3 as in effect on the date prior to the effective date of this section; except that if an eligible entity with a single owner claimed to be a partnership under those regulations, the entity will be disregarded as an entity separate from its owner under this paragraph (b)(3)(i). For special rules regarding the classification of such entities for periods prior to the effective date of this section, see paragraph (f)(2) of this section.

(ii) Special rules. For purposes of paragraph (b)(3)(i) of this section, a foreign eligible entity is treated as being in existence prior to the effective date of this section only if the entity's classification was relevant (as defined in paragraph (d) of this section) at any time during the sixty months prior to the effective date of this section. If an entity claimed different classifications prior to the effective date of this section, the entity's classification for purposes of paragraph (b)(3)(i) of this section is the last classification claimed by the entity. If a foreign eligible entity's classification is relevant prior to the effective date of this section, but no federal tax or information return is filed or the federal tax or information return does not indicate the classification of the entity, the entity's classification for the period prior to the effective date of this section is determined under the regulations in effect on the date prior to the effective date of this section.

(c) *Elections—*

(1) *Time and place for filing—*

(i) In general. Except as provided in paragraphs (c)(1)(iv) and (v) of this section, an eligible entity may elect to be classified other than as provided under paragraph (b) of this section, or to change its classification, by filing Form 8832, Entity Classification Election, with the service center designated on Form 8832. An election will not be accepted unless all of the information required by the form and instructions, including the taxpayer identifying number of the entity, is provided on Form 8832. See §301.6109-1 for rules on applying for and displaying Employer Identification Numbers.

(ii) Further notification of elections. An eligible entity required to file a federal tax or information return for the taxable year for which an election is made under paragraph (c)(1)(i) of this section must attach a copy of its Form 8832 to its federal tax or information return for that year. If the entity is not required to file a return for that year, a copy of its Form 8832 must be attached to the federal income tax or information return of any direct or indirect owner of the entity for the taxable year of the owner that includes the date on which the election was effective. An indirect owner of the entity does not have to attach a copy of the Form 8832 to its return if an entity in which it has an interest is already filing a copy of the Form 8832 with its return. If an entity, or one of its direct or indirect owners, fails to attach a copy of a Form 8832 to its return as directed in this section, an otherwise valid election under paragraph (c)(1)(i) of this section will not be invalidated, but the non-filing party may be subject to penalties, including any applicable penalties if the federal tax or information returns are inconsistent with the entity's election under paragraph (c)(1)(i) of this section.

(iii) Effective date of election. An election made under paragraph (c)(1)(i) of this section will be effective on the date specified by the entity on Form 8832 or on the date filed if no such date is specified on the election form. The effective date specified on Form 8832 can not be more than 75 days prior to the date on which the election is filed and can not be more than 12 months after the date on which the election is filed. If an election specifies an effective date more than 75 days prior to the date on which the election is filed, it will be effective 75 days prior to the date it was filed. If an election specifies an effective date more than 12 months from the date on which the election is filed, it will be effective 12 months after the date it was filed. If an election specifies an effective date before January 1, 1997, it will be effective as of January 1, 1997. If a purchasing corporation makes an election under section 338 regarding an acquired subsidiary, an election under paragraph (c)(1)(i) of this section for the acquired subsidiary can be effective no earlier than the day after the acquisition date (within the meaning of section 338(h)(2)).

(iv) Limitation. If an eligible entity makes an election under paragraph (c)(1)(i) of this section to change its classification (other than an election made by an existing entity to change its classification as of the effective date of this section), the entity cannot change its classification by election again during the sixty months succeeding the effective date of the election. However, the Commissioner may permit the entity to change its classification by election within the sixty months if more than fifty percent of the ownership interests in the entity as of the effective date of the subsequent election are owned by persons that did not own any interests in the entity on the filing date or on the effective date of the entity's prior election. An election by a newly formed eligible entity that is effective on the date of formation is not considered a change for purposes of this paragraph (c)(1)(iv).

. . .

(2) Authorized signatures—

(i) *In general.* An election made under paragraph (c)(1)(i) of this section must be signed by—

(A) Each member of the electing entity who is an owner at the time the election is filed; or

(B) Any officer, manager, or member of the electing entity who is authorized (under local law or the entity's organizational documents) to make the election and who represents to having such authorization under penalties of perjury.

(ii) *Retroactive elections.* For purposes of paragraph (c)(2)(i) of this section, if an election under paragraph (c)(1)(i) of this section is to be effective for any period prior to the time that it is filed, each person who was an owner between the date the election is to be effective and the date the election is filed, and who is not an owner at the time the election is filed, must also sign the election.

(iii) *Changes in classification.* For paragraph (c)(2)(i) of this section, if an election under paragraph (c)(1)(i) of this section is made to change the classification of an entity, each person who was an owner on the date that any transactions under paragraph (g) of this section are deemed to occur, and who is not an owner at the time the election is filed, must also sign the election. This paragraph (c)(2)(iii) applies to elections filed on or after November 29, 1999.

(d) *Special rules for foreign eligible entities* —

(1) *Definition of relevance.* For purposes of this section, a foreign eligible entity's classification is relevant when its classification affects the liability of any person for federal tax or information purposes. For example, a foreign entity's classification would be relevant if U.S. income was paid to the entity and the determination by the withholding agent of the amount to be withheld under chapter 3 of the Internal Revenue Code (if any) would vary depending upon whether the entity is classified as a partnership or as an association. Thus, the classification might affect the documentation that the withholding agent must receive from the entity, the type of tax or information return to file, or how the return must be prepared. The date that the classification of a foreign eligible entity is relevant is the date an event occurs that creates an obligation to file a federal tax return, information return, or statement for which the classification of the entity must be determined. Thus, the classification of a foreign entity is relevant, for example, on the date that an interest in the entity is acquired which will require a U.S. person to file an information return on Form 5471.

(2) *Special rule when classification is no longer relevant.* If the classification of a foreign eligible entity which was previously relevant for federal tax purposes ceases to be relevant for sixty consecutive months, the entity's classification will initially be determined under the default classification when the classification of the foreign eligible entity again becomes relevant. The date that the classification of a foreign entity ceases to be relevant is the date an event occurs that causes the classification to no longer be relevant, or, if no event occurs in a taxable year that causes the classification to be relevant, then the date is the first day of that taxable year.

. . .

(h) *Effective date* —

(1) *In general.* Except as otherwise provided in this section, the rules of this section are effective as of January 1, 1997.

(2) *Prior treatment of existing entities.* In the case of a business entity that is not described in §301.7701-2(b)(1), (3), (4), (5), (6), or (7), and that was in existence prior to January 1, 1997, the entity's claimed classification(s) will be respected for all periods prior to January 1, 1997, if—

(i) The entity had a reasonable basis (within the meaning of section 6662) for its claimed classification;

(ii) The entity and all members of the entity recognized the federal tax consequences of any change in the entity's classification within the sixty months prior to January 1, 1997; and

(iii) Neither the entity nor any member was notified in writing on or before May 8, 1996, that the classification of the entity was under examination (in which case the entity's classification will be determined in the examination).

¶2200

Revenue Procedures and Revenue Rulings

REV. PROC. 93-27 (1993-2 C.B. 343)

SEC. 1.   PURPOSE

This revenue procedure provides guidance on the treatment of the receipt of a partnership profits interest for services provided to or for the benefit of the partnership.

SEC. 2.   DEFINITIONS

The following definitions apply for purposes of this revenue procedure.

.01 A capital interest is an interest that would give the holder a share of the proceeds if the partnership's assets were sold at fair market value and then the proceeds were distributed in a complete liquidation of the partnership. This determination generally is made at the time of receipt of the partnership interest.

.02 A profits interest is a partnership interest other than a capital interest.

SEC. 3.   BACKGROUND

Under section 1.721-1(b)(1) of the Income Tax Regulations, the receipt of a partnership capital interest for services provided to or for the benefit of the partnership is taxable as compensation. On the other hand, the issue of whether the receipt of a partnership profits interest for services is taxable has been the subject of litigation. Most recently, in Campbell v. Commissioner, 943 F.2d 815 (8th Cir. 1991), the Eighth Circuit in dictum suggested that the taxpayer's receipt of a partnership profits interest received for services was not taxable, but decided the case on valuation. Other courts have determined that in certain circumstances the receipt of a partnership profits interest for services is a taxable event under section 83 of the Internal Revenue Code. *See, e.g.,* Campbell v. Commissioner, T.C.M. 1990-236, rev'd, 943 F.2d 815 (8th Cir. 1991); St. John v. United States, No. 82-1134 (C.D. Ill. Nov. 16, 1983). The courts have also found that typically the profits interest received has speculative or no determinable value at the time of receipt. *See Campbell*, 943 F.2d at 823; *St. John.* In Diamond v. Commissioner, 56 T.C. 530 (1971), *aff'd*, 492 F.2d 286 (7th Cir. 1974), however, the court assumed that the interest received by the taxpayer was a partnership profits interest and found the value of the interest was readily determinable. In that case, the interest was sold soon after receipt.

SEC. 4. APPLICATION

.01 Other than as provided below, if a person receives a profits interest for the provision of services to or for the benefit of a partnership in a partner capacity or in anticipation of being a partner, the Internal Revenue Service will not treat the receipt of such an interest as a taxable event for the partner or the partnership.
.02 This revenue procedure does not apply:
(1) If the profits interest relates to a substantially certain and predictable stream of income from partnership assets, such as income from high-quality debt securities or a high-quality net lease;
(2) If within two years of receipt, the partner disposes of the profits interest; or
(3) If the profits interest is a limited partnership interest in a "publicly traded partnership" within the meaning of section 7704(b) of the Internal Revenue Code.

REV. PROC. 2001-43 (2001-34 I.R.B. 191)

SEC. 1. PURPOSE

This revenue procedure clarifies Rev. Proc. 93-27 (1993-2 C.B. 343) by providing guidance on the treatment of the grant of a partnership profits interest that is substantially nonvested for the provision of services to or for the benefit of the partnership.

SEC. 2. BACKGROUND

Rev. Proc. 93-27 provides that (except as otherwise provided in section 4.02 of the revenue procedure), if a person receives a profits interest for the provision of services to or for the benefit of a partnership in a partner capacity or in anticipation of being a partner, the Internal Revenue Service will not treat the receipt of the interest as a taxable event for the partner or the partnership. For this purpose, section 2.02 of Rev. Proc. 93-27 defines a profits interest as a partnership interest other than a capital interest. Section 2.01 of Rev. Proc. 93-27 defines a capital interest as an interest that would give the holder a share of the proceeds if the partnership's assets were sold at fair market value and then the proceeds were distributed in a complete liquidation of the partnership. Section 2.01 of Rev. Proc. 93-27 provides that the determination as to whether an interest is a capital interest generally is made at the time of receipt of the partnership interest.

SEC. 3. SCOPE

This revenue procedure clarifies Rev. Proc. 93-27 by providing that the determination under Rev. Proc. 93-27 of whether an interest granted to a service provider is a profits interest is, under the circumstances described below, tested at the time the interest is granted, even if, at that time, the interest is substantially nonvested (within the meaning of §1.83-3(b) of the Income Tax Regulations). Accordingly, where a partnership grants a profits interest to a service provider in a transaction meeting the requirements of this revenue procedure and Rev. Proc. 93-27, the Internal Revenue Service will not treat the grant of the interest or the event that causes the interest to become substantially vested (within the meaning of §1.83-3(b) of the Income Tax Regulations) as a taxable event for the partner or the partnership. Taxpayers to which this revenue procedure applies need not file an election under section 83(b) of the Code.

SEC. 4. APPLICATION

This revenue procedure clarifies that, for purposes of Rev. Proc. 93-27, where a partnership grants an interest in the partnership that is substantially nonvested to a service provider, the service provider will be treated as receiving the interest on the date of its grant, provided that:

.01 The partnership and the service provider treat the service provider as the owner of the partnership interest from the date of its grant and the service provider takes into account the distributive share of partnership income, gain, loss, deduction, and credit associated with that interest in computing the service provider's income tax liability for the entire period during which the service provider has the interest;

.02 Upon the grant of the interest or at the time that the interest becomes substantially vested, neither the partnership nor any of the partners deducts any amount (as wages, compensation, or otherwise) for the fair market value of the interest; and

.03 All other conditions of Rev. Proc. 93-27 are satisfied.

REV. RUL. 69-6 (1969-1 C.B. 104)

Advice has been requested whether, under the facts outlined below, the acquisition of all of the assets and liabilities of a state chartered savings and loan association having outstanding capital stock, by a federally chartered nonstock savings and loan association constitutes a reorganization under either section 368(a)(1)(A) or section 368(a)(1)(C) of the Internal Revenue Code of 1954.

X is a state chartered savings and loan association having permanent shares of stock outstanding. The stock of X has a fair market value of $25x$ dollars per share. It proposes to merge, under the laws of its state of incorporation and of the United States, into Y, a federally chartered nonstock membership savings and loan association owned entirely by its share account holders. The share accounts are evidenced by passbooks in the association. Each X shareholder who consents to the merger will exchange his stock for a voting membership in the form of a voting share account of Y evidenced by a passbook in an amount equal to the number of his shares in X multiplied by $25x$ dollars. Following the merger, X will be dissolved. Both X and Y are domestic building and loan associations within the meaning of section 7701(a)(19) of the Code.

Section 368(a)(1)(A) of the Code provides that the term "reorganization" includes a statutory merger or consolidation. Section 368(a)(1)(C) of the Code describes a reorganization as the acquisition by one corporation, "in exchange solely for all or a part of its voting stock (or in exchange solely for all or a part of the voting stock of a corporation which is in control of the acquiring corporation)," of substantially all the properties of another corporation.

The courts in interpreting the above sections of the Code have held that an otherwise qualified transaction does not constitute a reorganization within the meaning of the Code or prior revenue acts unless those persons who were shareholders prior to the transaction have a substantial continuing proprietary interest in the enterprise after the transaction. Pinellas Ice & Cold Storage Co. v. Commissioner, 287 U.S. 462 (1933), Ct. D. 630, C.B. XII-1, 161 (1933); Minnesota Tea Co. v. Helvering, 302 U.S. 609 (1938), Ct. D. 1305, C.B. 1938-1, 288; section 1.368-1(b) of the Income Tax Regulations. The continuity of interest requirement, under which the owners of an acquired corporation must receive a substantial proprietary or equity interest in the acquiring corporation, is necessary in order to distinguish sales transactions from reorganizations. LeTulle v. Scofield, 308 U.S. 415 (1940), Ct. D. 1432, C.B. 1940-1, 151.

The continuing proprietary interest of the owners of the transferor in the assets of the transferee must represent a substantial part of the value of the property transferred. See Southwest Natural Gas Co. v. Commissioner, 189 F.2d 332 (5th Cir. 1951), certiorari denied, 342 U.S. 860, where the fact that less than one percent of the total consideration received by the transferor consisted of stock of the transferee disqualified the transaction as a merger under section 112(g)(1)(A) of the Internal Revenue Code of 1939.

In the instant case it is necessary to ascertain the nature of the consideration to be received by the shareholders of X in exchange for their stock. Y's entire equity interest, including the right to vote on matters affecting Y, the right to share in current earnings and the right to share in its assets upon liquidation, is vested in the share account holders who, as members of Y, own passbooks evidencing their interests. The rights of a share account holder in a federally chartered mutual association include a proprietary interest. See sections 7701(a)(7) and (8) of the 1954 Code; Rev. Rul. 54-624, C.B. 1954-2, 16.

However, Revenue Ruling 66-290, C.B. 1966-2, 112, holds that for purposes of section 1.334-1(c)(4)(v) of the regulations dealing with the allocation of basis to assets received in certain liquidations the phrase "cash and its equivalent" includes share accounts in savings and loan associations. Thus, share accounts in a Federal association also include cash equivalents in the face amounts of the account balances. See section 1.451-2 of the regulations dealing with amounts credited to the accounts of shareholders of savings and loan associations.

Consequently, the members of a Federal nonstock mutual association have a dual relationship to the association: (1) as members of a mutual association they possess proprietary interests therein, and (2) as share account holders they possess withdrawable deposits which are the equivalent of cash.

In the instant case Y's obligation to deliver cash deposits to X's shareholders is not severable from its obligation to deliver them a proprietary interest. Both the cash equivalents and the proprietary interests are evidenced by passbooks.

The X shareholders will receive passbooks having withdrawable amounts equal to the fair market value of the stock surrendered. Only minimal value can be assigned the proprietary interests in Y received by the X shareholders inasmuch as the principal property received by them consists of withdrawable cash deposits as reflected by their passbook balances. Since their rights as members are insignificant in value as compared to the cash equivalent received by the X shareholders, the passbooks distributed to them do not constitute solely "stock" within the meaning of section 368(a)(1)(C) of the Code, nor is there a sufficient continuity of interest on the part of the X shareholders to qualify the transaction as a reorganization within the meaning of section 368(a)(1)(A) of the Code.

The transfer by X of all of its assets to Y will be considered a sale by X of all of its assets to Y. See section 1.368-1(b) of the regulations which provides in part that a sale is nevertheless to be treated as a sale even though the mechanics of a reorganization have been set up.

Since X will be dissolved, the withdrawable share accounts as represented by the passbooks will be distributed to the X shareholders in complete liquidation of X. Corporation X may avail itself of the provisions of section 337 of the Code if the liquidation meets the requirements of that section.[1]

2200 [1] [The version of Code §337 referenced in text exempted a corporation from paying tax on gains realized from sales of corporate assets shortly before the corporation's liquidation, but was repealed in 1986, as part of the repeal of the General Utilities doctrine.]

Section 331(a)(1) of the Code states that amounts distributed in complete liquidation of a corporation will be treated as in full payment in exchange for the stock.

Accordingly, the transfer by X of all of its assets to Y constitutes a sale on which gain or loss will be recognized to X measured by the difference between the basis of the property transferred and the amount received from Y. (See section 337 of the Code for circumstances under which gain may not be recognized.) The withdrawable share accounts distributed to the shareholders of X as represented by the passbooks of Y will be treated as in full payment in exchange for their stock of X as provided in section 331(a)(1) of the Code. Gain or loss will be realized by each shareholder measured by the difference between the balance shown in his passbook account and the cost or other basis of the stock of X surrendered. Such gain or loss will represent capital gain or loss and will be taxable as provided in Subchapter P of Chapter 1 of the Code provided the stock of X constitutes a capital asset in the hands of such shareholder. . . .

REV. RUL. 73-427 (1973-2 C.B. 301)

Advice has been requested concerning the Federal income tax treatment of the transaction described below.

Corporation P wanted to acquire all of the outstanding stock of corporation Y for cash and thereby become the sole shareholder of Y. Pursuant to the plan of acquisition, P was only able to purchase 97.9 percent of the outstanding stock of Y for cash. In order to complete the acquisition, P, as part of the same plan, acquired the remaining 2.1 percent of the outstanding stock of Y in the following manner.

P transferred to S, a wholly owned subsidiary formed solely to effectuate the acquisition, 5x dollars (solely to satisfy capital requirements of state law) and 10x shares of P stock in exchange for 10x shares of S stock. Pursuant to the applicable state laws, S was merged with and into Y, with Y acquiring all the assets of S (the 5x dollars and the 10x shares of P stock). Y distributed the 10x shares of P stock received in the merger to the minority shareholders of Y in exchange for their stock, and by operation of state law the S stock held by P was automatically converted into Y stock. Y, as part of the plan, returned the 5x dollars to P.

The result of the entire plan described above was that P acquired all of the stock of Y partly in exchange for cash and partly in exchange for P voting stock, with Y becoming a wholly owned subsidiary of P. This result is not negated because part of the acquisition was cast in the form of a redemption by Y of its stock from the minority shareholders of Y in exchange for the P stock received by Y in the merger of S into Y. Therefore, the transaction will be treated for Federal income tax purposes as though P transferred its stock directly to the minority shareholders of Y in exchange for their Y stock. Furthermore, the transitory existence of S, and therefore the transactions described above involving S, will be disregarded.

Accordingly, it is held as follows:

1. No gain or loss will be recognized to P upon the receipt of the Y stock from the minority shareholders of Y in exchange for P stock under section 1032(a) of the Internal Revenue Code of 1954.

2. No gain or loss is realized by S or Y as a result of the transactions described above.

3. Gain or loss is realized and recognized to the minority shareholders of Y upon the receipt by them from P of P stock in exchange for their Y stock under sections 1001 and 1002 of the Code. Gain or loss is also realized and recognized by those former shareholders of Y who received cash from P in exchange for their Y stock under sections 1001 and 1002.

4. The 5x dollars transferred by P to S to satisfy capital requirements and which was returned to P by Y is disregarded and results in no tax consequences.

The same results would obtain if:

1. P actually received Y stock in exchange for the S stock rather than, as in the instant case, the S stock held by P being converted into Y stock by operation of law;

2. no stock of P was transferred to S and the Y stock held by the minority shareholders of Y was converted into P stock by operation of law; or

3. the 5x dollars transferred to S to satisfy capital requirements was not returned to P by Y. In such case the 5x dollars is a contribution by P to the capital of Y.

In Rev. Rul. 67-448, 1967-2 C.B. 144, pursuant to a plan of reorganization, a parent corporation, P, issued some of its voting stock to its new subsidiary S which, pursuant to the plan, merged into unrelated corporation Y, with some of the Y shareholders exchanging their Y stock, in an amount constituting control of Y, for the P stock received by Y in the merger of S into Y. Rev. Rul. 67-448 states that the net effect of this series of steps for Federal income tax purposes is a direct acquisition by P of the stock of Y from the Y shareholders in exchange solely for P voting stock, with the transitory existence of S being disregarded, and holds that the transaction is a reorganization within the meaning of section 368(a)(1)(B) of the Code. In the instant case, the net effect of the transaction (that is, a direct acquisition by P of all of the Y stock from the Y shareholders partly in exchange for cash and partly in exchange for P stock) does not qualify as a reorganization described in section 368(a)(1)(B) since such acquisition was not made by P solely for P voting stock as required by section 368(a)(1)(B). Furthermore, the merger of S into Y does not qualify as a reorganization under section 368(a)(1)(A) by reason of section 368(a)(2)(E) since 97.9 percent of the total consideration received by the shareholders of Y consisted of cash, and only 2.1 percent of the total consideration received by the Y shareholders consisted of stock of the acquiring corporation. Consequently, the continuity-of-interest requirement was not satisfied. See section 1.368-1(b) of the Income Tax Regulations.

Rev. Rul. 67-448 distinguished.

REV. RUL. 78-250 (1978-1 C.B. 83)

Advice has been requested concerning the Federal income tax treatment of the transaction set forth below.

Corporation X had outstanding only common stock, which was owned 65 percent by individual A, president and a director of X. The balance of the X stock was widely held.

For various business reasons, X desired to operate without any ownership of its stock by the public. Under a plan to eliminate the minority stock interests, a new corporation, Y, was formed by A who received all of the Y stock in exchange for A's X stock on a share-for-share basis. Upon approval of a plan of merger by the shareholders of both corporations, Y was then merged with and into X under applicable state law. In the merger each share of A's Y stock was converted into a share of X stock and the minority shareholders of X received cash in exchange for their X stock, in an amount equal in value to the stock exchanged.

In Rev. Rul. 67-448, 1967-2 C.B. 144, a series of inter-related steps involving the transitory existence of a newly created corporation is disregarded and the transaction is treated for Federal income tax purposes as the mere exchange by a corporation of shares of its voting stock for the outside minority stock interest in its subsidiary, which transaction qualified as a reorganization under section 368(a)(1)(B) of the Internal Revenue Code of 1954. See also Rev. Rul. 73-427, 1973-2 C.B. 301, which disregards the creation and elimination of a corporation in an integrated transaction.

In the instant case, the net result of the overall plan is that the minority shareholders of X received cash from X for their shares, after which they were no longer shareholders.

Accordingly, the creation of Y followed by the merger of Y into X with A exchanging X stock for Y stock, with the minority shareholders receiving cash and the conversion of the Y stock into X stock is disregarded for Federal income tax purposes. Rev. Rul. 73-427. The transaction is treated as if A never transferred any X stock, with the net effect that the minority shareholders of X received cash in exchange for their stock. Such cash is treated as received by the minority shareholders as distributions in redemption of their X stock subject to the provisions and limitations of section 302 of the Code.

REV. RUL. 79-273 (1979-2 C.B. 125)

ISSUE

Does a statutory merger in which shareholders of a corporation (P) receive cash from the acquiring corporation (X) and also receive stock in a subsidiary corporation of P represent a sale by the shareholders of part of their P stock to the acquiring corporation, and a redemption of the remainder of the P stock under section 302(b)(3) of the Internal Revenue Code?

FACTS

X and P are domestic manufacturing corporations that have unrelated shareholders. X and P have only common stock outstanding and their stock is widely held. For many years, P had been engaged directly in one business, and indirectly in a different business through its wholly owned subsidiary, S; P has transferred no property to S within the past 5 years and will transfer none prior to the transaction described below. The fair market value of the outstanding P stock was 100x dollars. The fair market value of the S stock held by P was 15x dollars. P has both current and accumulated earnings and profits. X desired to purchase for cash the stock in P, but X did not desire to acquire the S business.

Under a plan designed to make P a wholly owned subsidiary of X, the following steps were taken:

(1) X formed corporation Z as a wholly owned subsidiary and contributed 85x dollars cash to Z.

(2) Z was then merged into P under applicable state law and P was the surviving corporation. The 85x dollars cash transferred by X to Z was, upon merger, transferred by P pro rata to the P shareholders in exchange for P stock of equal value. Also, in the merger, the Z stock held by X was automatically converted into P stock of equal fair market value by operation of state law.

In addition, pursuant to the merger agreement, all the stock in S was transferred by P pro rata to the P shareholders in exchange for the remainder of their P stock. X thus became the sole shareholder of P, and the former P shareholders held all of the stock of S. P and S continued their respective businesses.

LAW AND ANALYSIS

The applicable sections of the Code and Income Tax Regulations thereunder are 368 and 1.368-2(a) relating to corporate reorganizations, 302 relating to redemptions treated as distributions in part or full payment for the stock; 355 and 1.355-2(c) relating to the nonapplicability of the nonrecognition provisions of section 355 to certain transactions where shareholders sell stock in either the distributing or the controlled corporation, and 1001 relating to the recognition of gain or loss on the sale or exchange of property.

Section 1.368-2(a) of the regulations provides that a transaction will not qualify as a reorganization defined in section 368(a)(1) of the Code if there is no continuity of interest on the part of the transferor or its shareholders in the properties transferred.

Section 302(b)(3) of the Code provides that section 302(a) of the Code will apply to redemptions that are a complete termination of a shareholder's stock interest in the redeeming company. Section 302(a) of the Code provides that a distribution of property shall be treated as in part or full payment in exchange for the stock.

Section 1001 of the Code provides for the recognition of gain from the sale or other disposition of property to the extent of the excess of the amount realized therefrom over the property's adjusted basis, and for the recognition of loss to the extent of the excess of the property's adjusted basis over the amount realized.

Section 1.355-2(c) of the regulations states that section 355 contemplates a continuity of interest in all or part of the business enterprise on the part of those persons who were the owners of the enterprise prior to the distribution or exchange. Where such continuity does not exist, section 355 of the Code will not apply to the transaction.

Rev. Rul. 73-427, 1973-2 C.B. 301, holds that the transitory existence of a new subsidiary corporation, and the transfer to it of parent stock, will be disregarded where such subsidiary is organized by the parent corporation to participate in a statutory merger merely as a conduit to enable parent to acquire stock of another corporation (target). In the merger, the subsidiary goes out of existence and the parent's stock received by the target corporation in the merger is issued to its shareholders in exchange for their stock in the target corporation. In addition, the parent's stock in the transitory subsidiary is automatically converted into target corporation stock by operation of state law. Rev. Rul. 73-427, states that the net effect of the steps for federal income tax purposes is a direct acquisition by the parent of target corporation's stock from the target shareholders in exchange for stock of the parent.

As in Rev. Rul. 73-427, the net effect here of steps (1) and (2) is a direct acquisition by X of 85 percent of P's stock from the P shareholders. Since X acquired P stock solely for cash this acquisition is not a reorganization as defined in section 368(a)(1) of the Code because the P shareholders did not continue their interest in P.

Under the rationale of Zenz v. Quinlivan, 213 F.2d 914 (6th Cir. 1954) termination of a shareholder's interest under section 302(b)(3) of the Code will result where a shareholder disposes of his or her entire stock interest in a company partly through redemption and partly through sale, or gift, pursuant to an integrated plan. Rev. Rul. 55-745, 1955-2 C.B. 223, and Rev. Rul. 77-226, 1977-2 C.B. 90.

The transfer of the S stock by P to its shareholders in exchange for 15 percent of their P stock and the P shareholders' sale to X of the other 85 percent of their P stock were pursuant to an integrated plan that terminated their entire stock interest in P, in accord with the *Zenz* rationale.

The distribution by P of the S stock does not meet the requirements of section 355 of the Code because the P shareholders did not have a continuing stock interest in P after the transaction.

HOLDING

The cash acquisition by X of 85 percent of the P stock, by means of a statutory merger, represents a sale of such stock by the P shareholders to X. The distribution by P to its shareholders of its S stock in exchange for 15 percent of their P stock, together with their sale of the other 85 percent of their P stock to X, completely terminate the interest of the P shareholders in P within the meaning of section 302(b)(3) of the Code. Gain or loss is recognized to the P shareholders on the sale and redemption of their P stock in accordance with the provisions of section 1001. . . .

REV. RUL. 85-106 (1985-2 C.B. 116)

ISSUE

Is a redemption of nonvoting preferred stock not essentially equivalent to a dividend within the meaning of section 302(b)(1) of the Internal Revenue Code when there is no reduction in the percentage of voting and nonvoting common stock owned by the redeemed shareholder, and when the redeemed shareholder continues to have an undiminished opportunity to act in concert with other shareholders as a control group, under the circumstances described below?

FACTS

Corporation X had outstanding three classes of stock consisting of 100 shares of voting common stock, 100 shares of nonvoting common stock, and 50 shares of nonvoting 9 percent cumulative preferred stock. The fair market value of each share of common stock was approximately half the fair market value of each share of preferred stock. The voting common stock was held as follows:

Shareholders	Shares
A	19
B	19
C	18
Minority shareholders	44
Total	100

None of the minority shareholders owned more than five shares. None of the holders of the voting common stock were related within the meaning of section 318(a) of the Code. The combined voting power of A, B, and C was sufficient to elect a majority of the board of directors of X.

The nonvoting common stock and the preferred stock were held (directly and indirectly) in approximately the same proportions as the common stock. C held no nonvoting common stock or preferred stock directly, but was the sole remaining beneficiary of a trust, T, which owned 18 percent of both the nonvoting common stock and the preferred stock.

The trustees of T decided that it would be in the best interests of that trust if most of the X preferred stock held by T could be converted into cash. After negotiation, X redeemed six shares of preferred stock for its fair market value of 6x dollars. Following this redemption, T continued to hold three shares of preferred stock, and 18 percent of the nonvoting common stock. Under section 318(a)(3)(B) of the Code, T is also considered to own the voting common stock owned by its sole beneficiary, C.

LAW AND ANALYSIS

Section 302(a) of the Code provides, in part, that if a corporation redeems its stock, and if section 302(b)(1), (2), (3), or (4) applies, such redemption will be treated as a distribution in part or full payment in exchange for the stock.

Section 302(b)(1) of the Code provides that section 302(a) will apply if the redemption is not essentially equivalent to a dividend. Section 302(b)(2) provides that section 302(a) will apply if (in addition to other requirements) the redemption substantially reduces the voting power of the shareholder. Section 302(b)(3) provides that section 302(a) will apply if the redemption completely terminates the shareholder's interest in the corporation. Section 302(b)(4) does not deal with the type of redemption under consideration. Section 302(c)(1) provides, with an exception not here relevant, that the constructive ownership rules of section 318(a) apply in determining the ownership of stock for purposes of section 302.

The lack of any reduction in T's 18 percent vote prevented this redemption from qualifying under section 302(b)(2) of the Code, and the lack of complete termination of interest prevented it from qualifying under section 302(b)(3). The question remains whether the redemption should be considered not essentially equivalent to a dividend so as to qualify under section 302(b)(1). Under section 1.302-2(b) of the Income Tax Regulations, this determination depends upon the facts and circumstances of each case.

In United States v. Davis, 397 U.S. 301 (1970), 1970-1 C.B. 62, the Supreme Court of the United States held that in order to qualify under section 302(b)(1) of the Code, a redemption must result in a meaningful reduction of the shareholder's proportionate interest in the corporation, and that, for this purpose, the attribution rules of section 318 apply.

In determining whether a reduction in interest is "meaningful", the rights inherent in a shareholder's interest must be examined. The three elements of a shareholder's interest that are generally considered most significant are: (1) the right to vote and thereby exercise control; (2) the right to participate in current earnings and accumulated surplus; and (3) the right to share in net assets on liquidation. Rev. Rul. 81-289, 1981-2 C.B. 82.

In applying the above principles, it is significant that (as a result of section 318(a)(3)(B) of the Code) the redemption did not reduce T's percentage of the vote in X. It is true that T reduced its percentage interest in current earnings, accumulated surplus, and net assets upon liquidation, and reduced the fair market value of its ownership in X. However, when the redeemed shareholder has a voting interest (either directly or by attribution), a reduction in voting power is a key factor in determining the applicability of section 302(b)(1) of the Code. Johnson Trust v. Commissioner, 71 T.C. 941, 947, 948 (1979). Rev. Rul. 78-401, 1978-2 C.B. 127; Rev. Rul. 77-218, 1977-1 C.B. 81; Rev. Rul. 75-502, 1975-2 C.B. 111; Rev. Rul. 75-512, 1975-2 C.B. 112.

It is also true that T was not the largest shareholder. A and B each held slightly larger voting interests, and larger interests measured by fair market value. T, however, was not in the position of a minority shareholder isolated from corporate management and control. Compare Rev. Rul. 75-512, where the majority of the redeeming corporation's voting stock was held by a shareholder unrelated (within the meaning of section 318(a)) to the redeemed trust. Also compare Rev. Rul. 76-385, 1976-2 C.B. 92, when the redeemed shareholder's total interest was *de minimis*.

In the present situation, a significant aspect of *T*'s failure to reduce voting power is the fact that the redemption leaves unchanged *T*'s potential (by attribution from C) for participating in a control group by acting in concert with *A* and *B*. Compare Rev. Rul. 76-364, 1976-2 C.B. 91, where a reduction in voting interest was found meaningful in itself when it caused the redeemed shareholder to give up a potential for control by acting in concert with one other shareholder. In addition, the Tax Court has indicated significance for this factor of potential group control (Johnson Trust, at 947). See also Bloch v. United States, 261 F.Supp. 597, 611-612 (S.D.Tex. 1966), aff'd per curiam, 386 F.2d 839 (5th Cir. 1967), where, in finding that "the distributions in question were essentially equivalent to a dividend," the court noted that there was no change in the redeemed shareholder's potential for exercising control "by aligning himself with one or more of the other stockholders."

Although there was a reduction of *T*'s economic interest in *X*, such reduction was not sufficiently large to result in a meaningful reduction of *T*'s interest. The absence of any reduction of *T*'s voting interest in *X* (through C) and *T*'s potential (through C) for control group participation are compelling factors in this situation.

In Himmel v. Commissioner, 338 F.2d 815 (2d Cir. 1964), dealing with a similar question, a decision was reached permitting the applicability of section 302(b)(1) of the Code. That case, however, was decided prior to the decision of the Supreme Court in *Davis*. Thus, *Himmel* fails to reflect the development in the law represented by the *Davis* limitation on section 302(b)(1) applicability where there is no meaningful reduction of the shareholder's proportionate interest in the corporation. Thus, pursuant to *Davis*, it is proper to view *Himmel* as incorrect to the extent it conflicts with the position contained in this revenue ruling.

HOLDING

The redemption of nonvoting preferred stock held by *T* does not qualify as a redemption under section 302(b)(1) of the Code, under the facts of this ruling when there is no reduction in the percentage of voting and nonvoting common stock owned by T, and when *T* continuous [sic] to have an undiminished opportunity to act in concert with other shareholders as a control group. Since the redemption does not otherwise qualify under section 302(b), it is not a distribution in part or full payment for the stock under section 302(a). Consequently, under section 302(d), the redemption will be treated as a distribution of property to which section 301 applies.

REV. RUL. 90-95 (1990-2 C.B. 67)

ISSUES

(1) If a corporation organizes a subsidiary solely for the purpose of acquiring the stock of a target corporation in a reverse subsidiary cash merger, is the corporation treated on the occurrence of a merger as having acquired the stock of the target in a qualified stock purchase under section 338 of the Internal Revenue Code?

(2) If the corporation makes a qualified stock purchase of the target stock and immediately liquidates the target as part of a plan to acquire the assets of the target, is the corporation treated as having made an asset acquisition pursuant to the *Kimbell-Diamond* doctrine or a section 338 qualified stock purchase followed by a liquidation of the target?

FACTS

Situation 1. P, a domestic corporation, formed a wholly owned domestic subsidiary corporation, *S*, for the sole purpose of acquiring all of the stock of an unrelated domestic target corporation, *T*, by means of a reverse subsidiary cash merger. Prior to the merger, *S* conducted no activities other than those required for the merger.

Pursuant to the plan of merger, *S* merged into *T* with *T* surviving. The shareholders of *T* exchanged all of their *T* stock for cash from *S*. Part of the cash used to carry out the acquisition was received by *S* from *P*; the remaining cash was borrowed by *S*. Following the merger, *P* owned all of the outstanding *T* stock.

Situation 2. The facts are the same as in *Situation 1*, except that *P* planned to acquire *T*'s assets through a prompt liquidation of *T*. State law prohibited *P* from owning the stock of *T*. Pursuant to the plan, *T* merged into *P* immediately following the merger of *S* into *T*. The merger of *T* into *P* satisfied the requirements for a tax-free liquidation under section 332 of the Code. The liquidation was not motivated by the evasion or avoidance of federal income tax.

LAW AND ANALYSIS

In Kimbell-Diamond Milling Co. v. Commissioner, 14 T.C. 74 (1950), aff'd per curiam, 187 F.2d 718 (5th Cir. 1951), cert. denied, 342 U.S. 827 (1951), the court held that the purchase of the stock of a target corporation for the purpose of obtaining its assets through a prompt liquidation should be treated by the purchaser as one transaction, namely, a purchase of the target's assets with the purchaser receiving a cost basis in the assets. Old section 334(b)(2) of the Code was added in 1954 to codify the principles of *Kimbell-Diamond*. See S. Rep. No. 1622, 83d Cong. 2d Sess. 257 (1954).

In 1982, Congress repealed old section 334(b)(2) of the Code and enacted section 338. Section 338 was "intended to replace any nonstatutory treatment of a stock purchase as an asset purchase under the Kimbell-Diamond doctrine." H.R. Conf. Rep. No. 760, 97th Cong., 2d Sess. 536 (1982), 1982-2 C.B. 600, 632. Under section 338, in the case of any qualified stock purchase, rules are provided governing whether the transaction gives rise to purchase of target stock treatment or purchase of target asset treatment. Under these rules, stock purchase or asset purchase treatment generally results whether or not the target is liquidated, merged into another corporation, or otherwise disposed of by the purchasing corporation. See section 1.338-4T(d) Question and Answer 1, temporary Income Tax Regulations.

A qualified stock purchase is generally the purchase by a corporation of at least 80 percent of a target's stock, by vote and value, within a 12-month period. Section 338(d)(3). The requirements for a qualified stock purchase may be satisfied through a combination of purchases of target stock by the purchasing corporation and redemptions by the target. Section 1.338-4T(c)(4) of the temporary regulations.

Stock purchase or asset purchase treatment generally turns on whether the purchasing corporation makes or is deemed to make a section 338 election. If the election is made or deemed made, asset purchase treatment results and section 338 of the Code generally treats all of the assets of the target as having been sold by the target at fair market value on the date of the qualified stock purchase and then repurchased by the target on the following day. The basis of the target's assets is adjusted to reflect the stock purchase price and other relevant items. If an election is not made or deemed made, stock purchase treatment generally results. In such a case, the basis of the target's assets is not adjusted to reflect the stock purchase price and other relevant items.

Question and Answer 3 of section 1.338-4T(d) of the temporary regulations provides that the parent of the subsidiary corporation in a reverse subsidiary cash merger is considered to have made a qualified stock purchase of the target if the subsidiary's existence is properly disregarded under the step-transaction doctrine and the requirements of a qualified stock purchase are satisfied. A subsidiary used to acquire target stock in a reverse subsidiary cash merger is ordinarily disregarded for federal income tax purposes if it was formed solely for the purpose of acquiring the stock and did not conduct any activities other than those required for the merger. See Rev. Rul. 79-273, 1979-2 C.B. 125; Rev. Rul. 73-427, 1973-2 C.B. 301.

Section 269 of the Code generally provides that the Secretary may disallow certain tax benefits when evasion or avoidance of federal income tax is the principal purpose for the acquisition of a corporation or its assets. The section 269 disallowance may apply to a qualified stock purchase followed by a liquidation of the target pursuant to a plan of liquidation adopted not more than two years after the purchase if the principal purpose of the liquidation was the evasion or avoidance of federal income tax by securing tax benefits that the purchasing corporation would not otherwise enjoy. Section 269(b).

In *Situations 1 and 2*, the step-transaction doctrine is properly applied to disregard the existence of S for federal income tax purposes. S had no significance apart from P's acquisition of the T stock. S was formed for the sole purpose of enabling P to acquire the T stock, and S did not conduct any activities that were not rated to that acquisition. Accordingly, the transaction is treated as a qualified stock purchase of T stock by P.

In *Situation 2*, the step-transaction doctrine does not apply to treat the stock acquisition and liquidation as an asset purchase. Section 338 of the Code replaced the *Kimbell-Diamond* doctrine and governs whether a corporation's acquisition of stock is treated as an asset purchase. Under section 338, asset purchase treatment turns on whether a section 338 election is made (or is deemed made) following a qualified stock purchase of target stock and not on whether the target's stock is acquired to obtain the assets through a prompt liquidation of the target. The acquiring corporation may receive stock purchase treatment or asset purchase treatment whether or not the target is subsequently liquidated. A qualified stock purchase of target stock is accorded independent significance from a subsequent liquidation of the target regardless of whether a section 338 election is made or deemed made. This treatment results even if the liquidation occurs to comply with state law. Accordingly, in *Situation 2*, the acquisition is treated as a qualified stock purchase by *P* of *T* stock followed by a tax-free liquidation of *T* into *P*.

HOLDINGS

(1) In *Situations 1 and 2*, *P* is treated as having acquired stock of *T* in a qualified stock purchase under section 338 of the Code.

(2) In *Situation 2*, *P* is treated as having acquired stock of *T* in a qualified stock purchase under section 338 followed by a liquidation of *T* into *P*, rather than having made an acquisition of assets pursuant to the *Kimbell-Diamond* doctrine.

REV. RUL. 95-70 (1995-2 C.B. 124)

ISSUE

For purposes of the definition of "qualified stated interest" in §1.1273-1(c) of the Income Tax Regulations, are scheduled interest payments on a debt instrument "unconditionally payable" if, under the terms of the debt instrument, the failure to make interest payments when due requires (1) that the issuer forgo paying dividends or (2) that interest accrue on the past-due payments at a rate that is 2 percentage points greater than the stated yield?

FACTS

Situation 1. On January 1, 1995, *Y* corporation issued a 15-year debt instrument to *A* for $100x. The debt instrument provides for a principal payment of $100x at maturity and for quarterly interest payments of $2x, beginning on March 31, 1995, and ending on the maturity date. Thus, the yield on the debt instrument is 8 percent, compounded quarterly. Under the terms of the debt instrument, if *Y* corporation fails to make one or more interest payments when due, interest will accrue on the past-due interest at the 8 percent yield. The failure of *Y* corporation to make interest payments when due for 12 consecutive quarters will entitle *A* to sue for payment.

If past-due interest is outstanding, the terms of the debt instrument provide that *Y* corporation may not declare or pay any dividend on, redeem, purchase, acquire, or make a liquidation payment with respect to, its stock. *Y* corporation has a policy and a long-established history of regularly paying dividends on its stock. Any failure of *Y* corporation to pay regular dividends on its stock is reasonably expected to result in a significant decline in the value of its stock.

Situation 2. The facts are the same as in *Situation 1*, except that, under the terms of the debt instrument, if *Y* corporation fails to make one or more interest payments when due, interest will accrue on the past-due interest at the rate of 10 percent, compounded quarterly, rather than 8 percent. This higher interest rate, which the documents describe as a "penalty" rate, is in addition to the restriction on dividend payments.

LAW AND ANALYSIS

Sections 163(e) and 1271 through 1275 of the Internal Revenue Code provide rules for the treatment of debt instruments that have original issue discount. If a debt instrument is issued with original issue discount, the discount is includible in income by the holder of the instrument, and deductible by the issuer of the instrument, as it accrues. See §§163(e) and 1272.

Section 1273(a)(1) defines original issue discount as the excess (if any) of a debt instrument's stated redemption price at maturity over the debt instrument's issue price. Under 1273(a)(2), a debt instrument's stated redemption price at maturity includes all amounts payable on the instrument (other than any interest based on a fixed rate, and payable unconditionally at fixed periodic intervals of 1 year or less during the entire term of the debt instrument).

The regulations under §1273-(a)(2) refer to interest that is excluded from the definition of stated redemption price at maturity as "qualified stated interest." See §1.1273-1(b). In general, §1.1273-1(c)(1)(i) defines qualified stated interest as stated interest that is unconditionally payable at least annually at a single fixed rate. Under §1.1273-1(c)(1)(ii), interest is unconditionally payable only if late payment or nonpayment is expected to be penalized or reasonable remedies exist to compel payment. Interest is not unconditionally payable, however, if the lending transaction does not reflect arm's length dealing and the holder does not intend to enforce such remedies. For purposes of determining whether interest is unconditionally payable, the possibility of nonpayment due to default, insolvency, or similar circumstances is ignored.

The definition of unconditionally payable in §1.1273-1(c)(1)(ii) is designed to limit qualified stated interest to interest that must be paid on a current basis. Stated interest is unconditionally payable only if the holder has the right to compel payment or to extract a penalty from the issuer for nonpayment. *See* S. Rep. No. 169 (Vol. 1), 98th Cong., 2d Sess. 255 (1984) ("[I]n general, interest will be considered payable unconditionally only if the failure to timely pay interest results in an acceleration of all amounts under the debt obligation or similar consequences.") If the terms of the debt instrument do not provide the holder with the right to compel payment, they must provide for a penalty that inures directly to the benefit of the holder and that is large enough to ensure that, at the time the debt instrument is issued, it is reasonably certain that, absent insolvency, the issuer will make interest payments when due.

In *Situation 1*, the failure of Y corporation to make interest payments when due limits Y corporation's ability to pay dividends on its stock. This dividend restriction is not a penalty within the meaning of §1.1273-1(c)(1)(ii) because it does not inure directly to the benefit of the holder, A.

In *Situation 2*, if Y corporation fails to make interest payments when due, interest will accrue on the past-due interest at the "penalty" rate of 10 percent, compounded quarterly. This 10 percent rate increases the yield on the entire debt instrument above its stated 8 percent rate, and, therefore, inures directly to the benefit of the holder. Nevertheless, the increase in yield is not large enough to ensure that it is reasonably certain that, absent insolvency, Y corporation will make interest payments when due. It is possible that there may be circumstances in which the benefit of deferring is worth the additional cost. This increase in yield is thus not a penalty within the meaning of §1.1273-1(c)(1)(ii). Depending on the facts and circumstances, however, an increase in yield that is 12 percentage points greater than the stated yield might be sufficient to ensure that, absent insolvency, interest payments are reasonably certain to be paid when due.

HOLDING

For purposes of the definition of "qualified stated interest" in §1.1273- 1(c), scheduled interest payments on a debt instrument are not "unconditionally payable" merely because, under the terms of the debt instrument, the failure to make interest payments when due requires (1) that the issuer forgo paying dividends, or (2) that interest accrue on the past-due payments at a rate that is 2 percentage points greater than the stated yield.

REV. RUL. 98-21 (1998-1 C.B. 975)

ISSUE

When is the transfer of a nonstatutory stock option (i.e., a compensatory stock option that is not subject to the provisions of §421 of the Internal Revenue Code) by the optionee to a family member, for no consideration, a completed gift under §2511?

FACTS

A is employed by Company. Company has one class of stock. Company has a stock option under which employees can be awarded nonstatutory stock options to purchase shares of Company's stock. These stock options are not traded on an established market. The shares acquired on the exercise of an option are freely transferable, subject only to generally applicable securities laws, and subject to no other restrictions or limitations.

Company grants to A, in consideration for services to be performed by A, a nonstatutory stock option to purchase shares of Company common stock. Company's stock option plan provides that the stock option is exercisable by A only after A performs additional services.

All options granted under Company's stock option plan expire 10 years from the grant date. The exercise price per share of A's option is the fair market value of one share of Company's common stock on the grant date. Company's stock option plan permits the transfer of nonstatutory stock options to a member of an optionee's immediate family or to a trust for the benefit of those individuals. The effect of such a transfer is that the transferee (after the required service is completed and before the option's expiration date) will determine whether and when to exercise the stock option and will also be obligated to pay the exercise price.

Before A performs the additional services necessary to allow A's option to be exercised, A transfers A's option to B, one of A's children, for no consideration.

LAW AND ANALYSIS

Section 2501 imposes a tax on the transfer of property by gift by any individual. The gift tax is not imposed upon the receipt of the property by the donee, is not necessarily determined by the measure of enrichment resulting to the donee from the transfer, and is not conditioned upon the ability to identify the donee at the time of the transfer. The tax is a primary and personal liability of the donor, is an excise upon the donor's act of making the transfer, is measured by the value of the property passing from the donor, and attaches regardless of the fact that the identity of the donee may not then be known or ascertainable. Section 25.2511–2(a) of the Gift Tax Regulations.

The gift tax applies to a transfer of property by way of gift, whether the transfer is in trust or otherwise, whether the gift is direct or indirect, and whether the property is real or personal, tangible or intangible. Section 25.2511-1(a). For this purpose, the term property is used in its broadest and most comprehensive sense and reaches "every species of right or interest protected by law and having an exchangeable value." H.R. Rep. No. 708, 72d Cong., 1st Sess. 27 (1932); S. Rep. No. 665, 72d Cong., 1st Sess. 39 (1932); both reprinted in 1939-1 (Part 2) C.B. 476, 524. Some rights, however, are not property. See e.g., Estate of Howell v. Commissioner, 15 T.C. 224 (1950) (nonvested pension rights were not property rights includible in gross estate under §811(c) of the 1939 Code); Estate of Barr v. Commissioner, 40 T.C. 227 (1963) acq., 1964-1 C.B. 4 (death benefits payable at discretion of board of directors who usually but not always, agreed to payment, were in the nature of hope or expectancy and not property rights includible in gross estate for estate tax purposes).

Generally, a gift is complete when the donor has so parted with dominion and control over the property as to leave the donor no power to change its disposition, whether for the donor's own benefit or for the benefit of another. Section 25.2511-2(b).

In Estate of Copley v. Commissioner, 15 T.C. 17 (1950), aff'd, 194 F.2d 364 (7th Cir. 1952), acq., 1965-2 C.B. 4, the petitioner entered into an antenuptial agreement in which the petitioner promised to give the future spouse a sum of money in consideration of the marriage and in lieu of all the spouse's marital rights in the petitioner's property. The agreement became legally enforceable under state law on the date of the marriage in 1931. The petitioner transferred part of the sum of money in 1936 and the rest in 1944. The court concluded that a gift tax would have been due in 1931 if there had been a gift tax law in effect at that time.

In Rev. Rul. 79-384, 1979-2 C.B. 344, a parent promised to pay a child $10,000 if the child graduated from college. Rev. Rul. 79-384 holds that the parent made a gift on the day the child graduated from college, the date when the parent's promise became enforceable and determinable in value.

In Rev. Rul. 80-186, 1980-2 C.B. 280, a parent transferred to a child, for nominal consideration, an option to purchase real property for a specified period of time at a price below fair value. Rev. Rul. 80-186 holds that the transfer is a completed gift at the time the option is transferred provided the option is binding and enforceable under state law on the date of the transfer.

In the present case, Company grants to A a nonstatutory stock option conditioned on the performance of additional services by A. If A fails to perform the services, the option cannot be exercised. Therefore, before A performs the services, the rights that A possesses in the stock option have not acquired the character of enforceable property rights susceptible of transfer for federal gift tax purposes. A can make a gift of the stock option to B for federal gift tax purposes only after A has completed the additional required services because only upon completion of the services does the right to exercise the option become binding and enforceable. In the event the option were to become exercisable in stages, each portion of the option that becomes exercisable at a different time is treated as a separate option for the purpose of applying this analysis. In the event that B is a skip person (within the meaning of §2613(a)), the generation-skipping transfer tax would apply at the same time as the gift tax. See Rev. Proc. 98-34, 1998-18 I.R.B. 15, which sets forth a methodology to value certain compensatory stock options for gift, estate, and generation-skipping transfer tax purposes.

HOLDING

On the facts stated above, the transfer to a family member, for no consideration, of a nonstatutory stock option, is a completed gift under §2511 on the later of (i) the transfer of (ii) the time when the donee's right to exercise the option is no longer conditioned on the performance of services by the transferor.

¶2300

Federal Securities Laws

SECURITIES ACT OF 1933
Act of May 27, 1933; 48 Stat. 74; 15 U.S. Code, Secs. 77a-77aa, as amended.

Selected Sections

DEFINITIONS

Sec. 2. (a) When used in this Act, unless the context otherwise requires—

(1) The term "security" means any note, stock, . . . , evidence of indebtedness, certificate of interest or participation in any profit-sharing agreement, . . . , preorganization certificate or subscription, transferable share, investment contract, . . . , certificate of deposit for a security, fractional undivided interest in oil, gas, or other mineral rights, any put, call, straddle, option, or privilege on any security, . . . , or, in general, any interest or instrument commonly known as a "security," or any . . . participation in . . . or warrant or right to subscribe to or purchase . . . any of the foregoing.

(4) The term "issuer" means every person who issues or proposes to issue any security . . .

. . .

(11) The term "underwriter" means any person who has purchased from an issuer with a view to, or offers or sells for an issuer in connection with, the distribution of any security, or participates or has a direct or indirect participation in any such undertaking, or participates or has a participation in the direct or indirect underwriting of any such undertaking; but such term shall not include a person whose interest is limited to a commission from an underwriter or dealer not in excess of the usual and customary distributors' or sellers' commission. As used in this paragraph the term "issuer" shall include, in addition to an issuer, any person directly or indirectly controlling or controlled by the issuer, or any person under direct or indirect common control with the issuer.

(12) The term "dealer" means any person who engages either for all or part of his time, directly or indirectly, as agent, broker, or principal, in the business of offering, buying, selling, or otherwise dealing or trading in securities issued by another person.

EXEMPTED SECURITIES

Sec. 3. (a) Except as hereinafter expressly provided the provisions of this title shall not apply to any of the following classes of securities:

. . .

(9) Except with respect to a security exchanged in a case under title 11 of the United States Code, any security exchanged by the issuer with its existing security holders exclusively where no commission or other remuneration is paid or given directly or indirectly for soliciting such exchange;

(10) Except with respect to a security exchanged in a case under title 11 of the United States Code, any security which is issued in exchange for one or more bona fide outstanding securities, claims or property interests, or partly in such exchange and partly for cash, where the terms and conditions of such issuance and exchange are approved, after a hearing upon the fairness of such terms and conditions at which all persons to whom it is proposed to issue securities in such exchange shall have the right to appear, by any court, or by any official or agency of the United States, or by any State or Territorial banking or insurance commission or other governmental authority expressly authorized by law to grant such approval;

(11) Any security which is a part of an issue offered and sold only to persons resident within a single State or Territory, where the issuer of such security is a person resident and doing business within, or, if a corporation, incorporated by and doing business within, such State or Territory.

. . .

(b) The Commission may from time to time by its rules and regulations, and subject to such terms and conditions as may be prescribed therein, add any class of securities to the securities exempted as provided in this section, if it finds that the enforcement of this Act with respect to such securities is not necessary in the public interest and for the protection of investors by reason of the small amount involved or the limited character of the public offering; but no issue of securities shall be exempted under this subsection where the aggregate amount at which such issue is offered to the public exceeds $5,000,000.

. . .

EXEMPTED TRANSACTIONS

Sec. 4. The provisions of section 5 shall not apply to—

(1) transactions by any person other than an issuer, underwriter, or dealer.

(2) transactions by an issuer not involving any public offering.

(3) transactions by a dealer . . . .

(4) brokers' transactions executed upon customers' orders on any exchange or in the over-the-counter market but not the solicitation of such orders.

. . .

(6) transactions involving offers or sales by an issuer solely to one or more accredited investors, if the aggregate offering price of an issue of securities offered in reliance on this paragraph does not exceed the amount allowed under section 3(b) of the Act, if there is no advertising or public solicitation in connection with the transaction by the issuer or anyone acting on the issuer's behalf, and if the issuer files such notice with the Commission as the Commission shall prescribe.

. . .

PROHIBITIONS RELATING TO INTERSTATE COMMERCE AND THE MAILS

Sec. 5. (a) Unless a registration statement is in effect as to a security, it shall be unlawful for any person, directly or indirectly—

(1) to make use of any means or instruments of transportation or communication in interstate commerce or of the mails to sell such security through the use or medium of any prospectus or otherwise; or

(2) to carry or cause to be carried through the mails or in interstate commerce, by any means or instruments of transportation, any such security for the purpose of sale or for delivery after sale.

(b) It shall be unlawful for any person, directly or indirectly—

(1) to make use of any means or instruments of transportation or communication in interstate commerce or of the mails to carry or transmit any prospectus relating to any security with respect to which a registration statement has been filed under this title, unless such prospectus meets the requirements of section 10, or

(2) to carry or to cause to be carried through the mails or in interstate commerce any such security for the purpose of sale or for delivery after sale, unless accompanied or preceded by a prospectus that meets the requirements of subsection (a) of section 10.

(c) It shall be unlawful for any person, directly or indirectly, to make use of any means or instruments of transportation or communication in interstate commerce or of the mails to offer to sell or offer to buy through the use or medium of any prospectus or otherwise any security, unless a registration statement has been filed as to such security, or while the registration statement is the subject of the refusal order or stop order or (prior to the effective date of the registration statement) any public proceeding or examination under section 8.

. . .

1933 ACT RULES AND REGULATIONS

Selected Sections

SEC RULE 144

Reg. §230.144 (Rule 144) Persons Deemed Not to Be Engaged in a Distribution and Therefore Not Underwriters

Preliminary Note to Rule 144

Rule 144 is designed to implement the fundamental purposes of the Act, as expressed in its preamble, "To provide full and fair disclosure of the character of the securities sold in interstate commerce and through the mails, and to prevent fraud in the sale thereof . . ." The rule is designed to prohibit the creation of public markets in securities of issuers concerning which adequate current information is not available to the public. At the same time, where adequate current information concerning the issuer is available to the public, the rule permits the public sale in ordinary trading transactions of limited amounts of securities owned by persons controlling, controlled by or under common control with the issuer and by persons who have acquired restricted securities of the issuer.

Certain basic principles are essential to an understanding of the requirement of registration in the Act:

(1) If any person utilizes the jurisdictional means to sell any non-exempt security to any other person, the security must be registered unless a statutory exemption can be found for the transaction.

(2) In addition to the exemptions found in Section 3, four exemptions applicable to transactions in securities are contained in Section 4. Three of these Section 4 exemptions are clearly not available to anyone acting as an "underwriter" of securities. (The fourth, found in Section 4(4), is available only to those who act as brokers under certain limited circumstances.) An understanding of the term "underwriter" is therefore important to anyone who wishes to determine whether or not an exemption from registration is available for his sale of securities.

The term underwriter is broadly defined in Section 2(11) of the Act to mean any person who has purchased from an issuer with a view to, or offers or sells for an issuer in connection with, the distribution of any security, or participates or has a direct or indirect participation in any such undertaking, or participates or has a participation in the direct or indirect underwriting of any such undertaking. The interpretation of this definition has traditionally focused on the words "with the view to" in the phrase "purchased from an issuer with a view to . . . distribution." Thus, an investment banking firm which arranges with an issuer for the public sale of its securities is clearly an "underwriter" under that section. Individual investors who are not professionals in the securities business may also be "underwriters" within the meaning of that term as used in the Act if they act as links in a chain of transactions through which securities move from an issuer to the public. Since it is difficult to ascertain the mental state of the purchaser at the time of his acquisition, subsequent acts and circumstances have been considered to determine whether such person took with a view to distribution at the time of his acquisition. Emphasis has been placed on factors such as the length of time the person has held the securities and whether there has been an unforeseeable change in circumstances of the holder. Experience has shown, however, that reliance upon such factors as the above has not assured adequate protection of investors through the maintenance of informed trading markets and has led to uncertainty in the application of the registration provisions of the Act.

It should be noted that the statutory language of Section 2(11) is in the disjunctive. Thus, it is insufficient to conclude that a person is not an underwriter solely because he did not purchase securities from an issuer with a view to their distribution. It must also be established that the person is not offering or selling for an issuer in connection with the distribution of the securities, does not participate or have a direct or indirect participation in any such undertaking, and does not participate or have a participation in the direct or indirect underwriting of such an undertaking.

In determining when a person is deemed not to be engaged in a distribution several factors must be considered.

First, the purpose and underlying policy of the Act to protect investors requires that there be adequate current information concerning the issuer, whether the resales of securities by persons result in a distribution or are effected in trading transactions. Accordingly, the availability of the rule is conditioned on the existence of adequate current public information.

Secondly, a holding period prior to resale is essential, among other reasons, to assure that those persons who buy under a claim of a Section 4(2) exemption have assumed the economic risks of investment, and therefore are not acting as conduits for sale to the public of unregistered securities, directly or indirectly, on behalf of an issuer. It should be noted that there is nothing in Section 2(11) which places a time limit on a person's status as an underwriter. The public has the same need for protection afforded by registration whether the securities are distributed shortly after their purchase or after a considerable length of time.

A third factor, which must be considered in determining what is deemed not to constitute a "distribution," is the impact of the particular transaction or transactions on the trading markets. Section 4(1) was intended to exempt only routine trading transactions between individual investors with respect to securities already issued and not to exempt distributions by issuers or acts of other individuals who engage in steps necessary to such distributions. Therefore, a person reselling securities under Section 4(1) of the Act must sell the securities in such limited quantities and in such a manner as not to disrupt the trading markets. The larger the amount of securities involved, the more likely it is that such resales may involve methods of offering and amounts of compensation usually associated with a distribution rather than routine trading transactions. Thus, solicitation of buy orders or the payment of extra compensation are not permitted by the rule.

In summary, if the sale in question is made in accordance with *all* of the provisions of the rule, as set forth below, any person who sells restricted securities shall be deemed not to be engaged in a distribution of such securities and therefore not an underwriter thereof. The rule also provides that any person who sells restricted or other securities on behalf of a person in a control relationship with the issuer shall be deemed not to be engaged in a distribution of such securities and therefore not to be an underwriter thereof, if the sale is made in accordance with *all* the conditions of the rule.

Reg. §230.144.

(a) *Definitions.* The following definitions shall apply for the purposes of this rule.

(1) An "affiliate" of an issuer is a person that directly, or indirectly through one or more intermediaries, controls, or is controlled by, or is under common control with, such issuer.

(2) The term "person" when used with reference to a person for whose account securities are to be sold in reliance upon this rule includes, in addition to such person, all of the following persons:

(i) Any relative or spouse of such person, or any relative of such spouse, any one of whom has the same home as such person;

(ii) Any trust or estate in which such person or any of the persons specified in paragraph (a)(2)(i) of this section collectively own ten percent or more of the total beneficial interest or of which any of such persons serve as trustee, executor or in any similar capacity; and

(iii) Any corporation or other organization (other than the issuer) in which such person or any of the persons specified in paragraph (a)(2)(i) of this section are the beneficial owners collectively of ten percent or more of any class of equity securities or ten percent or more of the equity interest.

(3) The term "restricted securities" means:

(i) Securities that are acquired directly or indirectly from the issuer, or from an affiliate of the issuer, in a transaction or chain of transactions not involving any public offering;

(ii) Securities acquired from the issuer that are subject to the resale limitations of §230.502(d) under Regulation D or §230.701(c);

(iii) Securities acquired in a transaction or chain of transactions meeting the requirements of §230.144A;

(iv) Securities acquired from the issuer in a transaction subject to the conditions of Regulation CE (§230.1001);

(v) Equity securities of domestic issuers acquired in a transaction or chain of transactions subject to the conditions of §230.901 or §230.903 under Regulation S (§203.901 through §203.905, and Preliminary Notes);

(vi) Securities acquired in a transaction made under §230.801 to the same extent and proportion that the securities held by the security holder of the class with respect to which the rights offering was made were as of the record date for the rights offering "restricted securities" within the meaning of this paragraph (a) (3); and

(vii) Securities acquired in a transaction made under §230.802 to the same extent and proportion that the securities that were tendered or exchanged in the exchange offer or business combination were "restricted securities" within the meaning of this paragraph (a) (3).

(b) *Conditions to be Met.* Any affiliate or other person who sells restricted securities of an issuer for his own account, or any person who sells restricted or any other securities for the account of an affiliate of the issuer of such securities, shall be deemed not to be engaged in a distribution of such securities and therefore not to be an underwriter thereof within the meaning of Section 2(11) of the Act if all of the conditions of this rule are met.

(c) *Current Public Information.* There shall be available adequate current public information with respect to the issuer of the securities. Such information shall be deemed to be available only if either of the following conditions is met:

(1) *Filing of Reports.* The issuer has securities registered pursuant to Section 12 of the Securities Exchange Act of 1934, has been subject to the reporting requirements of Section 13 of that Act for a period of at least 90 days immediately preceding the sale of the securities and has filed all the reports required to be filed thereunder during the 12 months preceding such sale (or for such shorter period that the issuer was required to file such reports); or has securities registered pursuant to the Securities Act of 1933, has been subject to the re-porting requirements of Section 15(d) of the Securities Exchange Act of 1934 for a period of at least 90 days immediately preceding the sale of the securities and has filed all the reports required to be filed thereunder during the 12 months preceding such sale (or for such shorter period that the issuer was required to file such reports). The person for whose account the securities are to be sold shall be entitled to rely upon a statement in whichever is the most recent report, quarterly or annual, required to be filed and filed by the issuer that such issuer has filed all reports required to be filed by Section 13 or 15(d) of the Securities Exchange Act of 1934 during the preceding 12 months (or for such shorter period that the issuer was required to file such reports) and has been subject to such filing requirements for the past 90 days, unless he knows or has reason to believe that the issuer has not complied with such requirements. Such person shall also be entitled to rely upon a written statement from the issuer that it has complied with such reporting requirements unless he knows or has reason to believe that the issuer has not complied with such requirements.

(2) *Other Public Information.* If the issuer is not subject to Section 13 or 15(d) of the Securities Exchange Act of 1934, there is publicly available the information concerning the issuer specified in paragraphs (a)(5)(i) to (xiv), inclusive, and paragraph (a)(5)(xvi) of Rule 15c2-11 (§240.15c2-11 of this chapter) under that Act or, if the issuer is an insurance company, the information specified in Section 12(g)(2)(G)(i) of that Act.

(d) *Holding Period for Restricted Securities.* If the securities sold are restricted securities, the following provisions apply:

(1) *General Rule.* A minimum of one year must elapse between the later of the date of the acquisition of the securities from the issuer or from an affiliate of the issuer, and any resale of such securities in reliance on this section for the account of either the acquiror or any subsequent holder of those securities. If the acquiror takes the securities by purchase, the one-year period shall not begin until the full purchase price or other consideration is paid or given by the person acquiring the securities from the issuer or from an affiliate of the issuer.

(2) *Promissory Notes, Other Obligations or Installment Contracts.* Giving the issuer or affiliate of the issuer from whom the securities were purchased a promissory note or other obligation to pay the purchase price, or entering into an installment purchase contract with such seller, shall not be deemed full payment of the purchase price unless the promissory note, obligation or contract:

(i) provides for full recourse against the purchaser of the securities;

(ii) is secured by collateral, other than the securities purchased, having a fair market value at least equal to the purchase price of the securities purchased; and

(iii) shall have been discharged by payment in full prior to the sale of the securities.

(3) *Determination of Holding Period.* The following provisions shall apply for the purpose of determining the period securities have been held:

(i) *Stock Dividends, Splits and Recapitalizations.* Securities acquired from the issuer as a dividend or pursuant to a stock split, reverse split or recapitalization shall be deemed to have been acquired at the same time as the securities on which the dividend or, if more than one, the initial dividend was paid, the securities involved in the split or reverse split, or the securities surrendered in connection with the recapitalization;

(ii) *Conversions.* If the securities sold were acquired from the issuer for a consideration consisting solely of other securities of the same issuer surrendered for conversion, the securities so acquired shall be deemed to have been acquired at the same time as the securities surrendered for conversion;

(iii) *Contingent Issuance of Securities.* Securities acquired as a contingent payment of the purchase price of an equity interest in a business, or the assets of a business, sold to the issuer or an affiliate of the issuer shall be deemed to have been acquired at the time of such sale if the issuer or affiliate was then committed to issue the securities subject only to conditions other than the payment of further consideration for such securities. An agreement entered into in connection with any such purchase to remain in the employment of, or not to compete with, the issuer or affiliate or the rendering of services pursuant to such agreement shall not be deemed to be the payment of further consideration for such securities.

(iv) *Pledged Securities.* Securities which are bona-fide pledged by an affiliate of the issuer when sold by the pledgee, or by a purchaser, after a default in the obligation secured by the pledge, shall be deemed to have been acquired when they were acquired by the pledgor, except that if the securities were pledged without recourse they shall be deemed to have been acquired by the pledgee at the time of the pledge or by the purchaser at the time of purchase.

(v) *Gifts of Securities.* Securities acquired from an affiliate of the issuer by gift shall be deemed to have been acquired by the donee when they were acquired by the donor.

(vi) *Trusts.* Where a trust settlor is an affiliate of the issuer, securities acquired from the settlor by the trust, or acquired from the trust by the beneficiaries thereof, shall be deemed to have been acquired when such securities were acquired by the settlor.

(vii) *Estates.* Where a deceased person was an affiliate of the issuer, securities held by the estate of such person or acquired from such estate by the beneficiaries thereof shall be deemed to have been acquired when they were acquired by the deceased person, except that no holding period is required if the estate is not an affiliate of the issuer or if the securities are sold by a beneficiary of the estate who is not such an affiliate.

> Note. While there is no holding period or amount limitation for estates and beneficiaries thereof which are not affiliates of the issuer, paragraphs (c), (h) and (i) of the rule apply to securities sold by such persons in reliance upon the rule.

(viii) *Rule 145(a) transactions.* The holding period for securities acquired in a transaction specified in Rule 145(a) shall be deemed to commence on the date the securities were acquired by the purchaser in such transaction. This provision shall not apply, however, to a transaction effected solely for the purpose of forming a holding company.

(e) *Limitation on Amount of Securities Sold.* Except as hereinafter provided, the amount of securities which may be sold in reliance upon this rule shall be determined as follows:

(1) *Sales by affiliates.* If restricted or other securities are sold for the account of an affiliate of the issuer, the amount of securities sold, together with all sales of restricted and other securities of the same class for the account of such person within the preceding three months, shall not exceed the greater of (i) one percent of the shares or other units of the class outstanding as shown by the most recent report or statement published by the issuer, or (ii) the average weekly reported volume of trading in such securities on all national securities exchanges and/or reported through the automated quotation system of a registered securities association during the four calendar weeks preceding the filing of notice required by paragraph (h), or if no such notice is required the date of receipt of the order to execute the transaction by the broker or the date of execution of the transaction directly with a market maker, or (iii) the average weekly volume of trading in such securities reported through the consolidated transaction reporting system, contemplated by Rule 11Aa3-1 under the Securities Exchange Act of 1934 (§240.11Aa3-1) during the four-week period specified in subdivision (ii) of this paragraph.

(2) *Sales by persons other than affiliates.* The amount of restricted securities sold for the account of any person other than an affiliate of the issuer, together with all other sales of restricted securities of the same class for the account of such person within the preceding three months, shall not exceed the amount specified in paragraphs (e)(1)(i), (1)(ii) or (1)(iii) of this section, whichever is applicable, unless the conditions in paragraph (k) of this rule are satisfied.

(3) *Determination of Amount.* For the purpose of determining the amount of securities specified in paragraphs (e)(1) and (2) of this rule, the following provisions shall apply:

(i) Where both convertible securities and securities of the class into which they are convertible are sold, the amount of convertible securities sold shall be deemed to be the amount of securities of the class into which they are convertible for the purpose of determining the aggregate amount of securities of both classes sold;

(ii) The amount of securities sold for the account of a pledgee thereof, or for the account of a purchaser of the pledged securities, during any period of three months within one year after a default in the obligation secured by the pledge, and the amount of securities sold during the same three-month period for the account of the pledgor shall not exceed, in the aggregate, the amount specified in paragraph (e)(1) or (2) of this section, whichever is applicable;

(iii) The amount of securities sold for the account of a donee thereof during any period of three months within one year after the donation, and the amount of securities sold during the same three-month period for the account of the donor, shall not exceed, in the aggregate, the amount specified in paragraph (e)(1) or (2) of this section, whichever is applicable;

(iv) Where securities were acquired by a trust from the settlor of the trust, the amount of such securities sold for the account of the trust during any period of three months within one year after the acquisition of the securities by the trust, and the amount of securities sold during the same three-month period for the account of the settlor, shall not exceed, in the aggregate, the amount specified in paragraph (e)(1) or (2) of this section, whichever is applicable;

(v) The amount of securities sold for the account of the estate of a deceased person, or for the account of a beneficiary of such estate, during any period of three months and the amount of securities sold during the same period for the account of the deceased person prior to his death shall not exceed, in the aggregate, the amount specified in subparagraph (1) or (2) of this paragraph, whichever is applicable; *Provided*, That no limitation on amount shall apply if the estate or beneficiary thereof is not an affiliate of the issuer;

(vi) When two or more affiliates or other persons agree to act in concert for the purpose of selling securities of an issuer, all securities of the same class sold for the account of all such persons during any period of three months shall be aggregated for the purpose of determining the limitation on the amount of securities sold;

(vii) The following sales of securities need not be included in determining the amount of securities sold in reliance upon this section: securities sold pursuant to an effective registration statement under the Act; securities sold pursuant to an exemption provided by Regulation A (§230.251 through §230.263) under the Act; securities sold in a transaction exempt pursuant to Section 4 of the Act and not involving any public offering; and securities sold offshore pursuant to Regulation S (§230.901 through §230.905, and Preliminary Notes) under the Act.

(f) *Manner of sale.* The securities shall be sold in "brokers' transactions" within the meaning of section 4(4) of the Act or in transactions directly with a "market maker," as that term is defined in section 3(a)(38) of the Securities Exchange Act of 1934, and the person selling the securities shall not (1) solicit or arrange for the solicitation of orders to buy the securities in anticipation of or in connection with such transaction, or (2) make any payment in connection with the offer or sale of the securities to any person other than the broker who executes the order to sell the securities. The requirements of this paragraph, however, shall not apply to securities sold for the account of the estate of a deceased person or for the account of a beneficiary of such estate provided the estate or beneficiary thereof is not an affiliate of the issuer; nor shall they apply to securities sold for the account of any person other than an affiliate of the issuer, provided the conditions of paragraph (k) of this rule are satisfied.

(g) *Brokers' Transactions.* The term "brokers' transactions" in Section 4(4) of the Act shall for the purposes of this rule be deemed to include transactions by a broker in which such broker—

(1) does no more than execute the order or orders to sell the securities as agent for the person for whose account the securities are sold; and receives no more than the usual and customary broker's commission;

(2) neither solicits nor arranges for the solicitation of customers' orders to buy the securities in anticipation of or in connection with the transaction; provided, that the foregoing shall not preclude (i) inquiries by the broker of other brokers or dealers who have indicated an interest in the securities within the preceding 60 days, (ii) inquiries by the broker of his customers who have indicated an unsolicited bona fide interest in the securities within the preceding 10 business days; or (iii) the publication by the broker of bid and ask quotations for the security in an inter-dealer quotation system provided that such quotations are incident to the maintenance of a bona fide inter-dealer market for the security for the broker's own account and that the broker has published bona fide bid and ask quotations for the security in an inter-dealer quotation system on each of at least twelve days within the preceding thirty calendar days with no more than four business days in succession without such two-way quotations;

> *Note to Subparagraph g(2)(ii)*: The broker should obtain and retain in his files written evidence of indications of bona fide unsolicited interest by his customers in the securities at the time such indications are received.

(3) after reasonable inquiry is not aware of circumstances indicating that the person for whose account the securities are sold is an underwriter with respect to the securities or that the transaction is a part of a distribution of securities of the issuer. Without limiting the foregoing, the broker shall be deemed to be aware of any facts or statements contained in the notice required by paragraph (h) below.

> *Notes.* (i) The broker, for his own protection, should obtain and retain in his files a copy of the notice required by paragraph (h).
>
> (ii) The reasonable inquiry required by paragraph (g)(3) of this section should include, but not necessarily be limited to, inquiry as to the following matters:
>
> > (a) The length of time the securities have been held by the person for whose account they are to be sold. If practicable, the inquiry should include physical inspection of the securities;

(b) The nature of the transaction in which the securities were acquired by such person;

(c) The amount of securities of the same class sold during the past three months by all persons whose sales are required to be taken into consideration pursuant to paragraph (e) of this section;

(d) Whether such person intends to sell additional securities of the same class through any other means;

(e) Whether such person has solicited or made any arrangement for the solicitation of buy orders in connection with the proposed sale of securities;

(f) Whether such person has made any payment to any other person in connection with the proposed sale of the securities; and

(g) The number of shares or other units of the class outstanding, or the relevant trading volume.

(h) *Notice of proposed sale.* If the amount of securities to be sold in reliance upon the rule during any period of three months exceeds 500 shares or other units or has an aggregate sale price in excess of $10,000, three copies of a notice on Form 144 shall be filed with the Commission at its principal office in Washington, D.C.; and if such securities are admitted to trading on any national securities exchange, one copy of such notice shall also be transmitted to the principal exchange on which such securities are so admitted. The Form 144 shall be signed by the person for whose account the securities are to be sold and shall be transmitted for filing concurrently with either the placing with a broker of an order to execute a sale of securities in reliance upon this rule or the execution directly with a market maker of such a sale. Neither the filing of such notice nor the failure of the Commission to comment thereon shall be deemed to preclude the Commission from taking any action it deems necessary or appropriate with respect to the sale of the securities referred to in such notice. The requirements of this paragraph, however, shall not apply to securities sold for the account of any person other than an affiliate of the issuer, provided the conditions of paragraph (k) of this rule are satisfied.

(i) *Bona Fide Intention to Sell.* The person filing the notice required by paragraph (h) shall have a bona fide intention to sell the securities referred to therein within a reasonable time after the filing of such notice.

(j) *Non-exclusive rule.* Although this rule provides a means for reselling restricted securities and securities held by affiliates without registration, it is not the exclusive means for reselling such securities in that manner. Therefore, it does not eliminate or otherwise affect the availability of any exemption for resales under the Securities Act that a person or entity may be able to rely upon.

(k) *Termination of certain restrictions on sales of restricted securities by persons other than affiliates.* The requirements of paragraphs (c), (e), (f) and (h) of this section shall not apply to restricted securities sold for the account of a person who is not an affiliate of the issuer at the time of the sale and has not been an affiliate during the preceding three months, provided a period of at least two years has elapsed since the later of the date the securities were acquired from the issuer or from an affiliate of the issuer. The two-year period shall be calculated as described in paragraph (d) of this section.

SEC RULE 145

Reg. §230.145 (Rule 145) Reclassification of Securities, Mergers, Consolidations and Acquisitions of Assets

Preliminary Note to Rule 145

Rule 145 (§230.145 of this chapter) is designed to make available the protection provided by registration under the Securities Act of 1933, as amended (Act), to persons who are offered securities in a business combination of the type described in paragraphs (a)(1), (2) and (3) of the rule. The thrust of the rule is that an "offer," "offer to sell," "offer for sale," or "sale" occurs when there is submitted to security holders a plan or agreement pursuant to which such holders are required to elect, on the basis of what is in substance a new investment decision, whether to accept a new or different security in exchange for their existing security. Rule 145 embodies the Commission's determination that such transactions are subject to the registration requirements of the Act, and that the previously existing "no-sale" theory of Rule 133 is no longer consistent with the statutory purposes of the Act. See Release No. 33-5316 (October 6, 1972). Securities issued in transactions described in paragraph (a) of Rule 145 may be registered on Form S-4 or F-4 (§239.25 or §239.34 of this chapter) or Form N-14 (§239.23 of this chapter) under the Act.

Transactions for which statutory exemptions under the Act, including those contained in sections 3(a)(9), (10), (11) and 4(2), are otherwise available and are not affected by Rule 145.

Note 1.—Reference is made to Rule 153a (§230.153a of this chapter) describing the prospectus delivery required in a transaction of the type referred to in Rule 145.

Note 2.—A reclassification of securities covered by Rule 145 would be exempt from registration pursuant to section 3(a)(9) or (11) of the Act if the conditions of either of these sections are satisfied.

Reg. §230.145

(a) *Transactions Within the Rule.* An "offer," "offer to sell," "offer for sale," or "sale" shall be deemed to be involved, within the meaning of section 2(3) of the Act, so far as the security holders of a corporation or other person are concerned where, pursuant to statutory provisions of the jurisdiction under which such corporation or other person is organized, or pursuant to provisions contained in its certificate of incorporation or similar controlling instruments, or otherwise, there is submitted for the vote or consent of such security holders a plan or agreement for—

(1) Reclassifications. A reclassification of securities of such corporation or other person, other than a stock split, reverse stock split, or change in par value, which involves the substitution of a security for another security;

(2) Mergers or Consolidations. A statutory merger or consolidation or similar plan or acquisition in which securities of such corporation or other person held by such security holders will become or be exchanged for securities of any person, unless the sole purpose of the transaction is to change an issuer's domicile solely within the United States; or

(3) *Transfers of Assets.* A transfer of assets of such corporation or other person, to another person in consideration of the issuance of securities of such other person or any of its affiliates, if:

(i) Such plan or agreement provides for dissolution of the corporation or other person whose security holders are voting or consenting; or

(ii) Such plan or agreement provides for a pro rata or similar distribution of such securities to the security holders voting or consenting; or

(iii) The board of directors or similar representatives of such corporation or other person, adopts resolutions relative to paragraph (a)(3)(i) or (ii) of this section within 1 year after the taking of such vote or consent; or

(iv) The transfer of assets is a part of a preexisting plan for distribution of such securities, notwithstanding paragraph (a)(3)(i), (ii), or (iii) of this section.

(b) *Communications Before a Registration Statement is Filed.* Communications made in connection with or relating to a transaction described in paragraph (a) of this section that will be registered under the Act may be made under §230.135, §230.165 or §230.166.

(c) *Persons and Parties Deemed to be Underwriters.* For purposes of this rule, any party to any transaction specified in paragraph (a) of this section, other than the issuer, or any person who is an affiliate of such party at the time any such transaction is submitted for vote or consent, who publicly offers or sells securities of the issuer acquired in connection with any such transaction, shall be deemed to be engaged in a distribution and therefore to be an underwriter thereof within the meaning of section 2(11) of the Act. The term "party" as used in this paragraph (c) shall mean the corporations, business entities, or other persons, other than the issuer, whose assets or capital structure are affected by the transactions specified in paragraph (a) of this section.

(d) *Resale Provisions for Persons and Parties Deemed Underwriters.* Notwithstanding the provisions of paragraph (c), a person or party specified therein shall not be deemed to be engaged in a distribution and therefore not to be an underwriter of registered securities acquired in a transaction specified in paragraph (a) of this section if:

(1) Such securities are sold by such person or party in accordance with the provisions of paragraphs (c), (e), (f) and (g) of §230.144;

(2) Such person or party is not an affiliate of the issuer, and a period of at least one year, as determined in accordance with paragraph (d) of §230.144, has elapsed since the date the securities were acquired from the issuer in such transaction, and the issuer meets the requirements of paragraph (c) of §230.144; or

(3) Such person or party is not, and has not been for at least three months, an affiliate of the issuer, and a period of at least two years, as determined in accordance with paragraph (d) of §230.144, has elapsed since the date the securities were acquired from the issuer in such transaction.

(e) *Definition of "Person."* The term "person" as used in paragraphs (c) and (d) of this rule, when used with reference to a person for whose account securities are to be sold, shall have the same meaning as the definition of that term in paragraph (a)(2) of Rule 144 under the Act.

SEC RULE 147

Reg. §230.147 (Rule 147) "Part of an Issue," "Person Resident," and "Doing Business Within" for Purposes of Section 3(a)(11)

Preliminary Notes

1. This rule shall not raise any presumption that the exemption provided by Section 3(a)(11) of the Act is not available for transactions by an issuer which do not satisfy all of the provisions of the rule.

2. Nothing in this rule obviates the need for compliance with any state law relating to the offer and sale of the securities.

3. Section 5 of the Act requires that all securities offered by the use of the mails or by any means or instruments of transportation or communication in interstate commerce be registered with the Commission. Congress, however, provided certain exemptions in the Act from such registration provisions where there was no practical need for registration or where the benefits of registration were too remote. Among those exemptions is that provided by Section 3(a)(11) of the Act for transactions in "any security which is a part of an issue offered and sold only to persons resident within a single State or Territory, where the issuer of such security is a person resident and doing business within . . . such State or Territory." The legislative history of that Section suggests that the exemption was intended to apply only to issues genuinely local in character, which in reality represent local financing by local industries, carried out through local investment. Rule 147 is intended to provide more objective standards upon which responsible local businessmen intending to raise capital from local sources may rely in claiming the Section 3(a)(11) exemption.

All of the terms and conditions of the rule must be satisfied in order for the rule to be available. These are: (i) that the issuer be a resident of and doing business within the state or territory in which all offers and sales are made; and (ii) that no part of the issue be offered or sold to nonresidents within the period of time specified in the rule. For purposes of the rule the definition of "issuer" in Section 2(4) of the Act shall apply.

All offers, offers to sell, offers for sale, and sales which are part of the same issue must meet all of the conditions of Rule 147 for the rule to be available. The determination whether offers, offers to sell, offers for sale and sales of securities are part of the same issue (i.e., are deemed to be "integrated") will continue to be a question of fact and will depend on the particular circumstances. See Securities Act of 1933 Release No. 4434 (December 6, 1961). Release 33-4434 indicates that in determining whether offers and sales should be regarded as part of the same issue and thus should be integrated any one or more of the following factors may be determinative:

   (i)   Are the offerings part of a single plan of financing;
   (ii)   Do the offerings involve issuance of the same class of securities;
   (iii)   Are the offerings made at or about the same time;
   (iv)   Is the same type of consideration to be received; and
   (v)   Are the offerings made for the same general purpose.

Subparagraph (b)(2) of the rule, however, is designed to provide certainty to the extent feasible by identifying certain types of offers and sales of securities which will be deemed not part of an issue, for purposes of the rule *only*.

Persons claiming the availability of the rule have the burden of proving that they have satisfied all of its provisions. However, the rule does not establish exclusive standards for complying with the Section 3(a)(11) exemption. The exemption would also be available if the issuer satisfied the standards set forth in relevant administrative and judicial interpretations at the time of the offering but the issuer would have the burden of proving the availability of the exemption. Rule 147 relates to transactions exempted from the registration requirements of Section 5 of the Act by Section 3(a)(11). Neither the rule nor Section 3(a)(11) provides an exemption from the registration requirements of Section 12(g) of the Securities Exchange Act of 1934, the anti-fraud provisions of the federal securities laws, the civil liability provisions of Section 12(2) of the Act or other provisions of the federal securities laws.

Finally, in view of the objectives of the rule and the purposes and policies underlying the Act, the rule shall not be available to any person with respect to any offering which, although in technical compliance with the rule, is part of a plan or scheme by such person to make interstate offers or sales of securities. In such cases registration pursuant to the Act is required.

4. The rule provides an exemption for offers and sales by the issuer *only*. It is not available for offers or sales of securities by other persons. Section 3(a)(11) of the Act has been interpreted to permit offers and sales by persons controlling the issuer, if the exemption provided by that Section would have been available to the issuer at the time of the offering. See Securities Act Release No. 4434 (December 6, 1961). Controlling persons who want to offer or sell securities pursuant to Section 3(a)(11) may continue to do so in accordance with applicable judicial and administrative interpretations.

Reg. §230.147.

(a) *Transactions Covered.* Offers, offers to sell, offers for sale and sales by an issuer of its securities made in accordance with all of the terms and conditions of this rule shall be deemed to be part of an issue offered and sold only to persons resident and doing business within such state or territory, within the meaning of Section 3(a)(11) of the Act.

(b) *Part of an Issue.*

(1) For purposes of this rule, all securities of the issuer which are part of an issue shall be offered, offered for sale or sold in accordance with all of the terms and conditions of this rule.

(2) For purposes of this rule only, an issue shall be deemed not to include offers, offers to sell, offers for sale or sales of securities of the issuer pursuant to the exemptions provided by Section 3 or Section 4(2) of the Act or pursuant to a registration statement filed under the Act, that take place prior to the six month period immediately preceding or after the six month period immediately following any offers, offers for sale or sales pursuant to this rule, *provided that,* there are during either of said six month periods no offers, offers for sale or

sales of securities by or for the issuer of the same or similar class as those offered, offered for sale or sold pursuant to the rule.

NOTE: In the event that securities of the same or similar class as those offered pursuant to the rule are offered, offered for sale or sold less than six months prior to or subsequent to any offer, offer for sale or sale pursuant to this rule, see Preliminary Note 3 hereof, as to which offers, offers to sell, offers for sale, or sales are part of an issue.

(c) *Nature of the Issuer.*

The issuer of the securities shall at the time of any offers and the sales be a person resident and doing business within the state or territory in which all of the offers, offers to sell, offers for sale and sales are made.

(1) The issuer shall be deemed to be a resident of the state or territory in which:

(i) it is incorporated or organized, if a corporation, limited partnership, trust or other form of business organization that is organized under state or territorial law;

(ii) its principal office is located, if a general partnership or other form of business organization that is not organized under any state or territorial law;

(iii) his principal residence is located, if an individual.

(2) The issuer shall be deemed to be doing business within a state or territory if:

(i) the issuer derived at least 80% of its gross revenues and those of its subsidiaries on a consolidated basis;

(A) for its most recent fiscal year, if the first offer of any part of the issue is made during the first six months of the issuer's current fiscal year; or

(B) for the first six months of its current fiscal year or during the twelve month fiscal period ending with such six month period, if the first offer of any part of the issue is made during the last six months of the issuer's current fiscal year from the operation of a business or of real property located in or from the rendering of services within such state or territory; provided, however, that this provision does not apply to any issuer which has not had gross revenues in excess of $5,000 from the sale of products or services or other conduct of its business for its most recent twelve month fiscal period;

(ii) the issuer had at the end of its most recent semi-annual fiscal period prior to the first offer of any part of the issue, at least 80 percent of its assets and those of its subsidiaries on a consolidated basis located within such state or territory;

(iii) the issuer intends to use and uses at least 80% of the net proceeds to the issuer from sales made pursuant to this rule in connection with the operation of a business or of real property, the purchase of real property located in, or the rendering of services within such state or territory; and

(iv) the principal office of the issuer is located within such state or territory.

(d) *Offerees and Purchasers: Person Resident.* Offers, offers to sell, offers for sale and sales of securities that are part of an issue shall be made only to persons resident within the state or territory of which the issuer is a resident. For purposes of determining the residence of offerees and purchasers:

(1) A corporation, partnership, trust or other form of business organization shall be deemed to be a resident of a state or territory if, at the time of the offer and sale to it, it has its principal office within such state or territory.

(2) An individual shall be deemed to be a resident of a state or territory if such individual has, at the time of the offer and sale to him, his principal residence in the state or territory.

(3) A corporation, partnership, trust or other form of business organization which is organized for the specific purpose of acquiring part of an issue offered pursuant to this rule shall be deemed not to be a resident of a state or territory unless all of the beneficial owners of such organization are residents of such state or territory.

(e) *Limitation of Resales.* During the period in which securities that are part of an issue are being offered and sold by the issuer, and for a period of nine months from the date of the last sale by the issuer of such securities, all resales of any part of the issue, by any person, shall be made only to persons resident within such state or territory.

NOTES: (1) In the case of convertible securities resales of either the convertible security, or if it is converted, the underlying security, could be made during the period described in paragraph (e) only to persons resident within such state or territory. For purposes of this rule a conversion in reliance on Section 3(a)(9) of the Act does not begin a new period.

(2) Dealers must satisfy the requirements of Rule 15c2-11 under the Securities Exchange Act of 1934 prior to publishing any quotation for a security, or submitting any quotation for publication, in any quotation medium.

(f) *Precautions Against Interstate Offers and Sales.*

(1) The issuer shall, in connection with any securities sold by it pursuant to this rule:

(i) Place a legend on the certificate or other document evidencing the security stating that the securities have not been registered under the Act and setting forth the limitations on resale contained in paragraph (e);

(ii) Issue stop transfer instructions to the issuer's transfer agent, if any, with respect to the securities, or, if the issuer transfers its own securities, make a notation in the appropriate records of the issuer; and

(iii) Obtain a written representation from each purchaser as to his residence.

(2) The issuer shall, in connection with the issuance of new certificates for any of the securities that are part of the same issue that are presented for transfer during the time period specified in paragraph (e), take the steps required by subsections (f)(1)(i) and (ii).

(3) The issuer shall, in connection with any offers, offers to sell, offers for sale or sales by it pursuant to this rule, disclose, in writing, the limitations on resale contained in paragraph (e) and the provisions of subsections (f)(1)(i) and (ii) and subparagraph (f)(2).

SEC REGULATION D (Rules 501 through 508)

Rules Governing the Limited Offer and Sale of Securities Without Registration Under the Securities Act of 1933

Preliminary Notes

(1) The following rules relate to transactions exempted from the registration requirements of section 5 of the Securities Act of 1933 (the "Act"). Such transactions are not exempt from the antifraud, civil liability, or other provisions of the federal securities laws. Issuers are reminded of their obligation to provide such further material information, if any, as may be necessary to make the information required under this regulation, in light of the circumstances under which it is furnished, not misleading.

(2) Nothing in these rules obviates the need to comply with any applicable state law relating to the offer and sale of securities. Regulation D is intended to be a basic element in a uniform system of federal-state limited offering exemptions consistent with the provisions of sections 18 and 19(c) of the Act. In those states that have adopted Regulation D, or any version of Regulation D, special attention should be directed to the applicable state laws and regulations, including those relating to registration of persons who receive remuneration in connection with the offer and sale of securities, to disqualification of issuers and other persons associated with offerings based on state administrative orders or judgments, and to requirements for filings of notices of sales.

(3) Attempted compliance with any rule in Regulation D does not act as an exclusive election; the issuer can also claim the availability of any other applicable exemption. For instance, an issuer's failure to satisfy all the terms and conditions of Rule 506 shall not raise any presumption that the exemption provided by section 4(2) of the Act is not available.

(4) These rules are available only to the issuer of the securities and not to any affiliate of that issuer or to any other person for resales of the issuer's securities. The rules provide an exemption only for the transactions in which the securities are offered or sold by the issuer, not for the securities themselves.

(5) These rules may be used for business combinations that involve sales by virtue of Rule 145(a) or otherwise.

(6) In view of the objectives of these rules and the policies underlying the Act, Regulation D is not available to any issuer for any transaction or chain of transactions that, although in technical compliance with these rules, is part of a plan or scheme to evade the registration provisions of the Act. In such cases, registration under the Act is required.

(7) Securities offered and sold outside the United States in accordance with Regulation S need not be registered under the Act. See Release No. 33-6863. Regulation S may be relied upon for such offers and sales even if coincident offers and sales are made in accordance with Regulation D inside the United States. Thus, for example, persons who are offered and sold securities in accordance with Regulation S would not be counted in the calculation of the number of purchasers under Regulation D. Similarly, proceeds from such sales would not

be included in the aggregate offering price. The provisions of this note, however, do not apply if the issuer elects to rely solely on Regulation D for offers or sales to persons made outside the United States.

Definitions and Terms Used in Regulation D

Reg. §230.501.

As used in Regulation D (§§230.501-230.508), the following terms shall have the meaning indicated:

(a) *Accredited investor.* "Accredited investor" shall mean any person who comes within any of the following categories, or who the issuer reasonably believes comes within any of the following categories, at the time of the sale of the securities to that person:

(1) Any bank as defined in section 3(a)(2) of the Act, or any savings and loan association or other institution as defined in section 3(a)(5)(A) of the Act whether acting in its individual or fiduciary capacity; any broker or dealer registered pursuant to section 15 of the Securities Exchange Act of 1934; any insurance company as defined in section 2(13) of the Act; any investment company registered under the Investment Company Act of 1940 or a business development company as defined in section 2(a)(48) of that Act; any Small Business Investment Company licensed by the U.S. Small Business Administration under section 301(c) or (d) of the Small Business Investment Act of 1958; any plan established and maintained by a state, its political subdivisions, or any agency or instrumentality of a state or its political subdivisions for the benefit of its employees, if such plan has total assets in excess of $5,000,000; any employee benefit plan within the meaning of the Employee Retirement Income Security Act of 1974 if the investment decision is made by a plan fiduciary, as defined in section 3(21) of such Act, which is either a bank, savings and loan association, insurance company, or registered investment adviser, or if the employee benefit plan has total assets in excess of $5,000,000 or, if a self-directed plan, with investment decisions made solely by persons that are accredited investors;

(2) Any private business development company as defined in section 202(a)(22) of the Investment Advisers Act of 1940;

(3) Any organization described in section 501(c)(3) of the Internal Revenue Code, corporation, Massachusetts or similar business trust, or partnership, not formed for the specific purpose of acquiring the securities offered, with total assets in excess of $5,000,000;

(4) Any director, executive officer, or general partner of the issuer of the securities being offered or sold, or any director, executive officer, or general partner of a general partner of that issuer;

(5) Any natural person whose individual net worth, or joint net worth with that person's spouse, at the time of his purchase exceeds $1,000,000;

(6) Any natural person who had an individual income in excess of $200,000 in each of the two most recent years or joint income with that person's spouse

in excess of $300,000 in each of those years and has a reasonable expectation of reaching the same income level in the current year;

(7) Any trust, with total assets in excess of $5,000,000, not formed for the specific purpose of acquiring the securities offered, whose purchase is directed by a sophisticated person as described in §230.506(b)(2)(ii); and

(8) Any entity in which all of the equity owners are accredited investors.

(b) *Affiliate.* An "affiliate" of, or person "affiliated" with, a specified person shall mean a person that directly, or indirectly through one or more intermediaries, controls or is controlled by, or is under common control with, the person specified.

(c) *Aggregate offering price.* "Aggregate offering price" shall mean the sum of all cash, services, property, notes, cancellation of debt, or other consideration to be received by an issuer for issuance of its securities. Where securities are being offered for both cash and non-cash consideration, the aggregate offering price shall be based on the price at which the securities are offered for cash. Any portion of the aggregate offering price attributable to cash received in a foreign currency shall be translated into United States currency at the currency exchange rate in effect at a reasonable time prior to or on the date of the sale of the securities. If securities are not offered for cash, the aggregate offering price shall be based on the value of the consideration as established by bona fide sales of that consideration made within a reasonable time, or, in the absence of sales, on the fair value as determined by an accepted standard. Such valuations of non-cash consideration must be reasonable at the time made.

(d) *Business combination.* "Business combination" shall mean any transaction of the type specified in paragraph (a) of Rule 145 under the Act and any transaction involving the acquisition by one issuer, in exchange for all or a part of its own or its parent's stock, of stock of another issuer if, immediately after the acquisition, the acquiring issuer has control of the other issuer (whether or not it had control before the acquisition).

(e) *Calculation of number of purchasers.* For purposes of calculating the number of purchasers under §§230.505(b) and 230.506(b) only, the following shall apply:

(1) The following purchasers shall be excluded:

(i) Any relative, spouse or relative of the spouse of a purchaser who has the same principal residence as the purchaser;

(ii) Any trust or estate in which a purchaser and any of the persons related to him as specified in paragraph (e)(1)(i) or (e)(1)(iii) of this §230.501 collectively have more than 50 percent of the beneficial interest (excluding contingent interests);

(iii) Any corporation or other organization of which a purchaser and any of the persons related to him as specified in paragraph (e)(1)(i) or (e)(1)(ii) of this §230.501 collectively are beneficial owners of more than 50 percent of the equity securities (excluding directors' qualifying shares) or equity interests; and

(iv) Any accredited investor.

(2) A corporation, partnership or other entity shall be counted as one purchaser. If, however, that entity is organized for the specific purpose of acquiring

the securities offered and is not an accredited investor under paragraph (a)(8) of this section, then each beneficial owner of equity securities or equity interests in the entity shall count as a separate purchaser for all provisions of Regulation D (§§230.501-230.508), except to the extent provided in subdivision (1) of this paragraph (e).

(3) A non-contributory employee benefit plan within the meaning of Title I of the Employee Retirement Income Security Act of 1974 shall be counted as one purchaser where the trustee makes all investment decisions for the plan.

Note: The issuer must satisfy all the other provisions of Regulation D for all purchasers whether or not they are included in calculating the number of purchasers. Clients of an investment adviser or customers of a broker or dealer shall be considered the "purchasers" under Regulation D regardless of the amount of discretion given to the investment adviser or broker or dealer to act on behalf of the client or customer.

(f) *Executive officer.* "Executive officer" shall mean the president, any vice president in charge of a principal business unit, division or function (such as sales, administration or finance), any other officer who performs a policy making function, or any other person who performs similar policy making functions for the issuer. Executive officers of subsidiaries may be deemed executive officers of the issuer if they perform such policy making functions for the issuer.

(g) *Issuer.* The definition of the term "issuer" in section 2(4) of the Act shall apply, except that in the case of a proceeding under the Federal Bankruptcy Code, the trustee or debtor in possession shall be considered the issuer in an offering under a plan or reorganization, if the securities are to be issued under the plan.

(h) *Purchaser representative.* "Purchaser representative" shall mean any person who satisfies all of the following conditions or who the issuer reasonably believes satisfies all of the following conditions:

(1) Is not an affiliate, director, officer or other employee of the issuer, or beneficial owner of 10 percent or more of any class of the equity securities or 10 percent or more of the equity interest in the issuer, except where the purchaser is:

(i) A relative of the purchaser representative by blood, marriage or adoption and not more remote than a first cousin;

(ii) A trust or estate in which the purchaser representative and any persons related to him as specified in paragraph (h)(1)(i) or (h)(1)(iii) of this §230.501 collectively have more than 50 percent of the beneficial interest (excluding contingent interest) or of which the purchaser representative serves as trustee, executor, or in any similar capacity; or

(iii) A corporation or other organization of which the purchaser representative and any persons related to him as specified in paragraph (h)(1)(i) or (h)(1)(ii) of this §230.501 collectively are the beneficial owners of more than 50 percent of the equity securities (excluding directors' qualifying shares) or equity interests;

(2) Has such knowledge and experience in financial and business matters that he is capable of evaluating, alone, or together with other purchaser repre-

sentatives of the purchaser, or together with the purchaser, the merits and risks of the prospective investment;

(3) Is acknowledged by the purchaser in writing, during the course of the transaction, to be his purchaser representative in connection with evaluating the merits and risks of the prospective investment; and

(4) Discloses to the purchaser in writing a reasonable time prior to the sale of securities to that purchaser any material relationship between himself or his affiliates and the issuer or its affiliates that then exists, that is mutually understood to be contemplated, or that has existed at any time during the previous two years, and any compensation received or to be received as a result of such relationship.

Note 1: A person acting as a purchaser representative should consider the applicability of the registration and antifraud provisions relating to brokers and dealers under the Securities Exchange Act of 1934 ("Exchange Act") and relating to investment advisers under the Investment Advisers Act of 1940.

Note 2: The acknowledgment required by paragraph (h)(3) and the disclosure required by paragraph (h)(4) of this §230.501 must be made with specific reference to each prospective investment. Advance blanket acknowledgment, such as for "all securities transactions" or "all private placements," is not sufficient.

Note 3: Disclosure of any material relationships between the purchaser representative or his affiliates and the issuer or its affiliates does not relieve the purchaser representative of his obligation to act in the interest of the purchaser.

General Conditions to Be Met

Reg. §230.502.

The following conditions shall be applicable to offers and sales made under Regulation D (§§230.501-230.508):

(a) *Integration.* All sales that are part of the same Regulation D offering must meet all of the terms and conditions of Regulation D. Offers and sales that are made more than six months before the start of a Regulation D offering or are made more than six months after completion of a Regulation D offering will not be considered part of that Regulation D offering, so long as during those six month periods there are no offers or sales of securities by or for the issuer that are of the same or a similar class as those offered or sold under Regulation D, other than those offers or sales of securities under an employee benefit plan as defined in Rule 405 under the Act.

Note: The term "offering" is not defined in the Act or in Regulation D. If the issuer offers or sells securities for which the safe harbor rule in paragraph (a) of this §230.502 is unavailable, the determination as to whether separate sales of securities are part of the same offering (i.e., are considered "integrated") depends on the particular facts and circumstances. Generally, transactions otherwise meeting the requirements of an exemption will not be integrated with simultaneous offerings being made outside the United States in compliance with Regulation S. See Release No. 33-6863.

The following factors should be considered in determining whether offers and sales should be integrated for purposes of the exemptions under Regulation D:

(a) whether the sales are part of a single plan of financing;

(b) whether the sales involve issuance of the same class of securities;

(c) whether the sales have been made at or about the same time;

(d) whether the same type of consideration is received; and

(e) whether the sales are made for the same general purpose.

See Release No. 33-4552 (November 6, 1962).

(b) *Information requirements.*

(1) *When information must be furnished.*

If the issuer sells securities under §230.505 or §230.506 to any purchaser that is not an accredited investor, the issuer shall furnish the information specified in paragraph (b)(2) of this section to such purchaser a reasonable time prior to sale. The issuer is not required to furnish the specified information to purchasers when it sells securities under §230.504, or to any accredited investor.

Note: When an issuer provides information to investors pursuant to paragraph (b)(1), it should consider providing such information to accredited investors as well, in view of the anti-fraud provisions of the federal securities laws.

(2) *Type of information to be furnished.*

(i) If the issuer is not subject to the reporting requirements of section 13 or 15(d) of the Exchange Act, at a reasonable time prior to the sale of securities the issuer shall furnish to the purchaser, to the extent material to an understanding of the issuer, its business and the securities being offered:

(A) *Non-financial statement information.* If the issuer is eligible to use Regulation A (§230.251-263), the same kind of information as would be required in Part II of Form 1-A (§239.90 of this chapter). If the issuer is not eligible to use Regulation A, the same kind of information as required in Part I of a registration statement filed under the Securities Act on the form that the issuer would be entitled to use.

(B) *Financial statement information.* (1) Offering up to $2,000,000. The information required in Item 310 of Regulation S-B (§228.310 of this chapter), except that only the issuer's balance sheet, which shall be dated within 120 days of the start of the offering, must be audited.

(2) *Offerings up to $7,500,000.* The financial statement information required in Form SB-2 (§239.10 of this chapter). If an issuer, other than a limited partnership, cannot obtain audited financial statements without unreasonable effort or expense, then only the issuer's balance sheet, which shall be dated within 120 days of the start of the offering, must be audited. If the issuer is a limited partnership and cannot obtain the required financial statements without unreasonable effort or expense, it may furnish financial statements that have been prepared on the basis of Federal income tax requirements and examined and reported on in accordance with generally accepted auditing standards by an independent public or certified accountant.

(3) *Offerings over $7,500,000.* The financial statement as would be required in a registration statement filed under the Act on the form that the issuer would be entitled to use. If an issuer, other than a limited partnership, cannot obtain audited financial statements without unreasonable effort or expense, then only the issuer's balance sheet, which shall be dated within 120 days of the start of the offering, must be audited. If the issuer is a limited partnership and cannot obtain the required financial statements without unreasonable effort or expense, it may furnish financial statements that have been prepared on the basis of Federal income tax requirements and examined and reported on in accordance with generally accepted auditing standards by an independent public or certified accountant.

(C) If the issuer is a foreign private issuer eligible to use Form 20-F (§249.220f of this chapter), the issuer shall disclose the same kind of information required to be included in a registration statement filed under the Act on the form that the issuer would be entitled to use. The financial statements need be certified only to the extent required by paragraph (b)(2)(i)(B)(*1*), (2) or (3) of this section, as appropriate.

(ii) If the issuer is subject to the reporting requirements of section 13 or 15(d) of the Exchange Act, at a reasonable time prior to the sale of securities the issuer shall furnish to the purchaser the information specified in paragraph (b)(2)(ii)(A) or (B) of this section, and in either event the information specified in paragraph (b)(2)(ii)(C) of this section:

(A) The issuer's annual report to shareholders for the most recent fiscal year, if such annual report meets the requirements of §240.14a-3 or 240.14c-3 under the Exchange Act, the definitive proxy statement filed in connection with that annual report, and, if requested by the purchaser in writing, a copy of the issuer's most recent Form 10-K and Form 10-KSB under the Exchange Act.

(B) The information contained in an annual report on Form 10-K (§249.310 of this chapter) or 10-KSB (§249.310b of this chapter) under the Exchange Act or in a registration statement on Form S-1 (§239.11 of this chapter), SB-1 (§239.9 of this chapter), SB-2 (§239.10 of this chapter) or S-11 (§239.18 of this chapter) under the Act or on Form 10 (§249.210 of this chapter) or Form 10-SB (§249.210b of this chapter) under the Exchange Act, whichever filing is the most recent required to be filed.

(C) The information contained in any reports or documents required to be filed by the issuer under sections 13(a), 14(a), 14(c), and 15(d) of the Exchange Act since the distribution or filing of the report or registration statement specified in paragraph (A) or (B), and a brief description of the securities being offered, the use of the proceeds from the offering, and any material changes in the issuer's affairs that are not disclosed in the documents furnished.

(D) If the issuer is a foreign private issuer, the issuer may provide in lieu of the information specified in paragraph (b)(2)(ii)(A) or (B) of this section, the information contained in its most recent filing on Form 20-F or Form F-1 (§239.31 of the chapter).

(iii) Exhibits required to be filed with the Commission as part of a registration statement or report, other than an annual report to shareholders or parts of that report incorporated by reference in a Form 10-K and Form 10-KSB report, need not be furnished to each purchaser that is not an accredited investor if the contents of material exhibits are identified and such exhibits are made available to a purchaser, upon his written request, a reasonable time prior to his purchase.

(iv) At a reasonable time prior to the sale of securities to any purchaser that is not an accredited investor in a transaction under §230.505 or §230.506, the issuer shall furnish to the purchaser a brief description in writing of any material written information concerning the offering that has been provided by the issuer to any accredited investor but not previously delivered to such unaccredited purchaser. The issuer shall furnish any portion or all of this information to the purchaser, upon his written request a reasonable time prior to his purchase.

(v) The issuer shall also make available to each purchaser at a reasonable time prior to his purchase of securities in a transaction under §230.505 or 230.506 the opportunity to ask questions and receive answers concerning the terms and conditions of the offering and to obtain any additional information which the issuer possesses or can acquire without unreasonable effort or expense that is necessary to verify the accuracy of information furnished under paragraph (b)(2)(i) or (ii) of this §230.502.

(vi) For business combinations or exchange offers, in addition to information required by Form S-4, the issuer shall provide to each purchaser at the time the plan is submitted to security holders, or, with an exchange, during the course of the transaction and prior to sale, written information about any terms or arrangements of the proposed transactions that are materially different from those for all other security holders. For purposes of this subsection, an issuer which is not subject to the reporting requirements of section 13 or 15(d) of the Exchange Act may satisfy the requirements of Part I.B. or C. of Form S-4 by compliance with paragraph (b)(2)(i) of this §230.502.

(vii) At a reasonable time prior to the sale of securities to any purchaser that is not an accredited investor in a transaction under §230.505 or §230.506, the issuer shall advise the purchaser of the limitations on resale in the manner contained in paragraph (d)(2) of this section. Such disclosure may be contained in other materials required to be provided by this paragraph.

(c) *Limitation on manner of offering.* Except as provided in §230.504(b)(1), neither the issuer nor any person acting on its behalf shall offer or sell the securities by any form of general solicitation or general advertising, including, but not limited to, the following:

(1) Any advertisement, article, notice or other communication published in any newspaper, magazine, or similar media or broadcast over television or radio; and

(2) Any seminar or meeting whose attendees have been invited by any general solicitation or general advertising.

Provided, however, that publication by an issuer of a notice in accordance with §230.135c shall not be deemed to constitute general solicitation or general advertising for purposes of this section; *provided further,* that, if the requirements of §230.135e are satisfied, proving any journalist with access to press conferences held outside of the United States, to meeting with issuer or selling security holder representatives conducted outside the United States, or to written press-related materials released outside the United States, at or in which a present or proposed offering of securities is discussed, will not be deemed to constitute general solicitation or general advertising for purposes of this section.

(d) *Limitations on resale.* Except as provided in §230.504(b)(1), securities acquired in a transaction under Regulation D shall have the status of securities acquired in a transaction under section 4(2) of the Act and cannot be resold without registration under the Act or an exemption therefrom. The issuer shall exercise reasonable care to assure that the purchasers of the securities are not underwriters within the meaning of section 2(11) of the Act, which reasonable care may be demonstrated by the following:

(1) Reasonable inquiry to determine if the purchaser is acquiring the securities for himself or for other persons;

(2) Written disclosure to each purchaser prior to sale that the securities have not been registered under the Act and, therefore, cannot be resold unless they are registered under the Act or unless an exemption from registration is available; and

(3) Placement of a legend on the certificate or other document that evidences the securities stating that the securities have not been registered under the Act and setting forth or referring to the restrictions on transferability and sale of the securities.

While taking these actions will establish the requisite reasonable care, it is not the exclusive method to demonstrate such care. Other actions by the issuer may satisfy this provision. In addition, §230.502(b)(2)(vii) requires the delivery of written disclosure of the limitations on resale to investors in certain instances.

Filing of Notice of Sales

Reg. §230.503.

(a) An issuer offering or selling securities in reliance on §230.504, §230.505 or §230.506 shall file with the Commission five copies of a notice on Form D no later than 15 days after the first sale of securities.

(b) One copy of every notice on Form D shall be manually signed by a person duly authorized by the issuer.

(c) If sales are made under §230.505, the notice shall contain an undertaking by the issuer to furnish to the Commission, upon the written request of its staff, the information furnished by the issuer under §230.502(b)(2) to any purchaser that is not an accredited investor.

(d) Amendments to notices filed under paragraph (a) of this §230.503 need only report the issuer's name and the information required by Part C and any material change in the facts from those set forth in Parts A and B.

(e) A notice on Form D shall be considered filed with the Commission under paragraph (a) of this §230.503:

(1) As of the date on which it is received at the Commission's principal office in Washington, D.C.; or

(2) As of the date on which the notice is mailed by means of United States registered or certified mail to the Commission's principal office in Washington, D.C., if the notice is delivered to such office after the date on which it is required to be filed.

Exemption for Limited Offerings and Sales of Securities Not Exceeding $1,000,000

Reg. §230.504.

(a) *Exemption.* Offers and sales of securities that satisfy the conditions in paragraph (b) of this §230.504 by an issuer that is not:

(1) subject to the reporting requirements of section 13 or 15(d) of the Exchange Act;

(2) an investment company; or

(3) a development stage company that either has no specific business plan or purpose or has indicated that its business plan is to engage in a merger or acquisition with an unidentified company or companies, or other entity or person, shall be exempt from the provision of section 5 of the Act under section 3(b) of the Act.

(b) *Conditions to be met.*

(1) *General conditions.* To qualify for exemption under this §230.504, offers and sales must satisfy the terms and conditions of §§230.501 and 230.502(a), (c) and (d), except that the provisions of §230.502(c) and (d) will not apply to offers and sales of securities under this §230.504 that are made:

(i) Exclusively in one or more states that provide for the registration of the securities, and require the public filing and delivery to investors of a substantive disclosure document before sale, and are made in accordance with those state provisions;

(ii) In one or more states that have no provision for the registration of the securities or the public filing or delivery of a disclosure document before sale, if the securities have been registered in at least one state that provides for such registration, public filing and delivery before sale, offers and sales are made in that state in accordance with such provisions, and the disclosure document is delivered before sale to all purchasers (including those in the states that have no such procedure); or

(iii) Exclusively according to state law exemptions from registration that permit general solicitation and general advertising so long as sales are made only to "accredited investors" as defined in §230.501(a).

(2) The aggregate offering price for an offering of securities under this §230.504, as defined in §230.501(c), shall not exceed $1,000,000, less the aggregate offering price for all securities sold within the twelve months before the start of and during the offering of securities under this §230.504, in reliance on any exemption under Section 3(b), or in violation of section 5(a) of the Securities Act.

Note 1: The calculation of the aggregate offering price is illustrated as follows:

If an issuer sold $900,000 on June 1, 1987 under this §230.504 and an additional $4,100,000 on December 1, 1987 under §230.505, the issuer could not sell any of its securities under this §230.504 until December 1, 1988. Until then the issuer must count the December 1, 1987 sale towards the $1,000,000 limit within the preceding twelve months.

Note 2: If a transaction under §230.504 fails to meet the limitation on the aggregate offering price, it does not affect the availability of this §230.504 for the other transactions considered in applying such limitation. For example, if an issuer sold $1,000,000 worth of its securities on January 1, 1988 under this §230.504 and an additional $500,000 worth on July 1, 1988, this §230.504 would not be available for the later sale, but would still be applicable to the January 1, 1988 sale.

Exemption for Limited Offers and Sales of Securities Not Exceeding $5,000,000

Reg. §230.505.

(a) *Exemption.* Offers and sales of securities that satisfy the conditions in paragraph (b) of this §230.505 by an issuer that is not an investment company shall be exempt from the provisions of section 5 of the Act under section 3(b) of the Act.

(b) *Conditions to be met.*

(1) *General conditions.* To qualify for exemption under this section, offers and sales must satisfy the terms and conditions of §§230.501 and 230.502.

(2) *Specific conditions.*

(i) Limitation on aggregate offering price. The aggregate offering price for an offering of securities under this §230.505, as defined in §230.501(c), shall not exceed $5,000,000, less the aggregate offering price for all securities sold within the twelve months before the start of and during the offering of securities under this §230.505 in reliance on any exemption under section 3(b) of the Act or in violation of section 5(a) of the Act.

Note: The calculation of the aggregate offering price is illustrated as follows:

Example 1. If an issuer sold $2,000,000 of its securities on June 1, 1982 under this §230.505 and an additional $1,000,000 on September 1, 1982, the issuer would be permitted to sell only $2,000,000 more under this §230.505 until June 1, 1983. Until that date the issuer must count both prior sales towards the $5,000,000 limit. However, if the issuer made its third sale on June 1, 1983, the issuer could then sell $4,000,000 of its securities because the June 1, 1982 sale would not be within the preceding twelve months.

Example 2. If an issuer sold $500,000 of its securities on June 1, 1982 under §230.504 and an additional $4,500,000 on December 1, 1982 under this §230.505, then the issuer could not sell any of its securities under this §230.505 until June 1, 1983. At that time it could sell an additional $500,000 of its securities.

(ii) *Limitation on number of purchasers.* There are no more than or the issuer reasonably believes that there are no more than 35 purchasers of securities from the issuer in any offering under this section.

Note: See §230.501(e) for the calculation of the number of purchasers and §230.502(a) for what may or may not constitute an offering under this section.

(iii) *Disqualifications.* No exemption under this section shall be available for the securities of any issuer described in §230.262 of Regulation A, except that for purposes of this section only:

(A) The term "filing of the offering statement required by §230.252" as used in §230.262(a), (b) and (c) shall mean the first sale of securities under this section;

(B) The term "underwriter" as used in §230.262(b) and (c) shall mean a person that has been or will be paid directly or indirectly remuneration for solicitation of purchasers in connection with sales of securities under this section; and

(C) Paragraph (b)(2)(iii) of this §230.505 shall not apply to any issuer if the Commission determines, upon a showing of good cause, that it is not necessary under the circumstances that the exemption be denied. Any such determination shall be without prejudice to any other action by the Commission in any other proceeding or matter with respect to the issuer or any other person.

Exemption for Limited Offers and Sales Without Regard to Dollar Amount of Offering

Reg. §230.506.

(a) *Exemption.* Offers and sales of securities by an issuer that satisfy the conditions in paragraph (b) of this §230.506 shall be deemed to be transactions not involving any public offering within the meaning of section 4(2) of the Act.

(b) *Conditions to be met.*—(1) *General conditions.* To qualify for exemption under this section, offers and sales must satisfy all the terms and conditions of §230.501 and §230.502.

(2) *Specific conditions.*—

(i) *Limitation on number of purchasers.* There are no more than or the issuer reasonably believes that there are no more than 35 purchasers of securities from the issuer in any offering under this section.

Note: See §230.501(e) for the calculation of the number of purchasers and §230.502(a) for what may or may not constitute an offering under this section 230.506.

(ii) *Nature of purchasers.* Each purchaser who is not an accredited investor either alone or with his purchaser representative(s) has such knowledge and experience in financial and business matters that he is capable of evaluating the merits and risks of the prospective investment, or the issuer reasonably believes immediately prior to making any sale that such purchaser comes within this description.

Disqualifying Provision Relating to Exemptions Under §§230.504, 230.505 and 230.506

Reg. §230.507.

(a) No exemption under §§230.504, 230.505 or 230.506 shall be available for an issuer if such issuer, any of its predecessors or affiliates have been subject to any order, judgment, or decree of any court of competent jurisdiction temporarily, preliminarily or permanently enjoining such person for failure to comply with §230.503.

(b) Paragraph (a) of this section shall not apply if the Commission determines, upon a showing of good cause, that it is not necessary under the circumstances that exemption be denied.

Insignificant Deviations from a Term, Condition or Requirement of Regulation D

Reg. §230.508.

(a) A failure to comply with a term, condition or requirement of §§230.504, 230.505 or 230.506 will not result in the loss of the exemption from the requirements of section 5 of the Act for any offer or sale to a particular individual or entity, if the person relying on the exemption shows:

(1) the failure to comply did not pertain to a term, condition or requirement directly intended to protect that particular individual or entity; and

(2) the failure to comply was insignificant with respect to the offering as a whole, provided that any failure to comply with paragraph (c) of §230.502, paragraph (b)(2) of §230.504, paragraphs (b)(2)(i) and (ii) of §230.505 and paragraph (b)(2)(i) of §230.506 shall be deemed to be significant to the offering as a whole; and

(3) a good faith and reasonable attempt was made to comply with all applicable terms, conditions and requirements of §§230.504, 230.505 or 230.506.

(b) A transaction made in reliance on §§230.504, 230.505 or 230.506 shall comply with all applicable terms, conditions and requirements of Regulation D. Where an exemption is established only through reliance upon paragraph (a) of this section, the failure to comply shall nonetheless be actionable by the Commission under section 20 of the Act.

SEC Rule 701

Exemption for Offers and Sales of Securities Pursuant to Certain Compensatory Benefit Plans and Contracts Relating to Compensation

Preliminary Notes

(1) This section relates to transactions exempted from the registration requirements of section 5 of the Act. These transactions are not exempt from the antifraud, civil liability, or other provisions of the federal securities laws. Issuers and persons acting on their behalf have an obligation to provide investors with disclosure adequate to satisfy the antifraud provisions of the federal securities laws.

(2) In addition to complying with this section, the issuer also must comply with any applicable state law relating to the offer and sale of securities.

(3) An issuer that attempts to comply with this section, but fails to do so, may claim any other exemption that is available.

(4) This section is available only to the issuer of the securities. Affiliates of the issuer may not use this section to offer or sell securities. This section also does not cover resales of securities by any person. This section provides an exemption only for the transactions in which the securities are offered or sold by the issuer, not for the securities themselves.

(5) The purpose of this section is to provide an exemption from the registration requirements of the Act for securities issued in compensatory circumstances. This section is not available for plans or schemes to circumvent this purpose, such as to raise capital. This section also is not available to exempt any transaction that is in technical compliance with this section but is part of a plan or scheme to evade the registration provisions of the Act. In any of these cases, registration under the Act is required unless another exemption is available.

Reg. §230.701.

(a) *Exemption.* Offers and sales made in compliance with all of the conditions of this section are exempt from section 5 of the Act.

(b) *Issuers eligible to use this section.*

(1) *General.* This section is available to any issuer that is not subject to the reporting requirements of section 13 or 15(d) of the Securities Exchange Act of 1934 (the "Exchange Act") and is not an investment company registered or required to be registered under the Investment Company Act of 1940.

(2) *Issuers that become subject to reporting.* If an issuer becomes subject to the reporting requirements of section 13 or 15(d) of the Exchange Act after it has made offers complying with this section, the issuer may nevertheless rely on this section to sell the securities previously offered to the persons to whom those offers were made.

(3) *Guarantees by reporting companies.* An issuer subject to the reporting requirements of section 13 or 15(d) of the Exchange Act may rely on this section if it is merely guaranteeing the payment of a subsidiary's securities that are sold under this section.

(c) *Transactions exempted by this section.* This section exempts offers and sales of securities (including plan interests and guarantees pursuant to paragraph (d)(2)(ii) of this section) under a written compensatory benefit plan (or written compensation contract) established by the issuer, its parents, its majority-owned subsidiaries or majority-owned subsidiaries of the issuer's parent, for the participation of their employees, directors, general partners, trustees (where the issuer is a business trust), officers, or consultants and advisors, and their family members who acquire such securities from such persons through gifts or domestic relations orders. This section exempts offers and sales to former employees, directors, general partners, trustees, officers, consultants and advisors only if such persons were employed by or providing services to the issuer at the time the securities were offered. In addition, the term "employee" includes insurance agents who are exclusive agents of the issuer, its subsidiaries or parents, or derive more than 50% of their annual income from those entities.

(1) *Special requirements for consultants and advisors.* This section is available to consultants and advisors only if:

(i) They are natural persons;

(ii) They provide bona fide services to the issuer, its parents, its majority-owned subsidiaries or majority-owned subsidiaries of the issuer's parent; and

(iii) The services are not in connection with the offer or sale of securities in a capital-raising transaction, and do not directly or indirectly promote or maintain a market for the issuer's securities.

(2) *Definition of "Compensatory Benefit Plan."* For purposes of this section, a compensatory benefit plan is any purchase, savings, option, bonus, stock appreciation, profit sharing, thrift, incentive, deferred compensation, pension or similar plan.

(3) *Definition of "Family Member."* For purposes of this section, family member includes any child, stepchild, grandchild, parent, stepparent, grandparent, spouse, former spouse, sibling, niece, nephew, mother-in-law, father-in-law, son-in-law, daughter-in-law, brother-in-law, or sister-in-law, including adoptive relationships, any person sharing the employee's household (other than a tenant or employee), a trust in which these persons have more than fifty percent of the beneficial interest, a foundation in which these persons (or the employee) control the management of assets, and any other entity in which these persons (or the employee) own more than fifty percent of the voting interests.

(d) *Amounts that may be sold.*

(1) *Offers.* Any amount of securities may be offered in reliance on this section. However, for purposes of this section, sales of securities underlying options must be counted as sales on the date of the option grant.

(2) *Sales.* The aggregate sales price or amount of securities sold in reliance on this section during any consecutive 12-month period must not exceed the greatest of the following:

(i) $1,000,000;

(ii) 15% of the total assets of the issuer (or of the issuer's parent if the issuer is a wholly-owned subsidiary and the securities represent obligations that the parent fully and unconditionally guarantees), measured at the issuer's most recent balance sheet date (if no older than its last fiscal year end); or

(iii) 15% of the outstanding amount of the class of securities being offered and sold in reliance on this section, measured at the issuer's most recent balance sheet date (if no older than its last fiscal year end).

(3) *Rules for calculating prices and amounts.*

(i) *Aggregate sales price.* The term aggregate sales price means the sum of all cash, property, notes, cancellation of debt or other consideration received or to be received by the issuer for the sale of the securities. Non-cash consideration must be valued by reference to bona fide sales of that consideration made within a reasonable time or, in the absence of such sales, on the fair value as determined by an accepted standard. The value of services exchanged for securities issued must be measured by reference to the value of the securities issued. Options must be valued based on the exercise price of the option.

(ii) *Time of the calculation.* With respect to options to purchase securities, the aggregate sales price is determined when an option grant is made (without regard to when the option becomes exercisable). With respect to other securities, the calculation is made on the date of sale. With respect to deferred compensation or similar plans, the calculation is made when the irrevocable election to defer is made.

(iii) *Derivative securities.* In calculating outstanding securities for purposes of paragraph (d)(2)(iii) of this section, treat the securities underlying all currently exercisable or convertible options, warrants, rights or other securities, other than those issued under this exemption, as outstanding. In calculating the amount of securities sold for other purposes of paragraph (d)(2) of this section, count the amount of securities that would be acquired upon exercise or conversion in connection with sales of options, warrants, rights or other exercisable or convertible securities, including those to be issued under this exemption.

(iv) *Other exemptions.* Amounts of securities sold in reliance on this section do not affect "aggregate offering prices" in other exemptions, and amounts of securities sold in reliance on other exemptions do not affect the amount that may be sold in reliance on this section.

(e) *Disclosure that must be provided.* The issuer must deliver to investors a copy of the compensatory benefit plan or the contract, as applicable. In addition, if the aggregate sales price or amount of securities sold during any consecutive 12-month period exceeds $5 million, the issuer must deliver the following disclosure to investors a reasonable period of time before the date of sale:

(1) If the plan is subject to the Employee Retirement Income Security Act of 1974 ("ERISA"), a copy of the summary plan description required by ERISA;

(2) If the plan is not subject to ERISA, a summary of the material terms of the plan;

(3) Information about the risks associated with investment in the securities sold pursuant to the compensatory benefit plan or compensation contract; and

(4) Financial statements required to be furnished by Part F/S of Form 1-A (Regulation A Offering Statement) under Regulation A. Foreign private issuers as defined in §230.405 must provide a reconciliation to generally accepted accounting principles in the United States (U.S. GAAP) if their financial statements are not prepared in accordance with U.S. GAAP (Item 17 of Form 20-F). The financial statements required by this section must be as of a date no more than 180 days before the sale of securities in reliance on this exemption.

(5) If the issuer is relying on paragraph (d)(2)(ii) of this section to use its parent's total assets to determine the amount of securities that may be sold, the parent's financial statements must be delivered. If the parent is subject to the reporting requirements of section 13 or 15(d) of the Exchange Act, the financial statements of the parent required by Rule 10-01 of Regulation S-X and Item 310 of Regulation S-B, as applicable, must be delivered.

(6) If the sale involves a stock option or other derivative security, the issuer must deliver disclosure a reasonable period of time before the date of exercise or conversion. For deferred compensation or similar plans, the issuer must deliver disclosure to investors a reasonable period of time before the date the irrevocable election to defer is made.

(f) *No integration with other offerings.* Offers and sales exempt under this section are deemed to be a part of a single, discrete offering and are not subject to integration with any other offers or sales, whether registered under the Act or otherwise exempt from the registration requirements of the Act.

(g) *Resale limitations.*

(1) Securities issued under this section are deemed to be "restricted securities" as defined in §230.144.

(2) Resales of securities issued pursuant to this section must be in compliance with the registration requirements of the Act or an exemption from those requirements.

(3) Ninety days after the issuer becomes subject to the reporting requirements of section 13 or 15(d) of the Exchange Act, securities issued under this section may be resold by persons who are not affiliates (as defined in §230.144) in reliance on §230.144, without compliance with paragraphs (c), (d), (e) and (h) of §230.144, and by affiliates without compliance with paragraph (d) of §230.144.

SECURITIES EXCHANGE ACT OF 1934

Act of June 6, 1934; 48 Stat. 881; 15 U.S. Code Secs. 78a—78jj; as amended.

Selected Sections

REGULATION OF THE USE OF MANIPULATIVE AND DECEPTIVE DEVICES

Sec. 10. It shall be unlawful for any person, directly or indirectly, by the use of any means or instrumentality of interstate commerce or of the mails, or of any facility of any national securities exchange—

. . .

(b) To use or employ, in connection with the purchase or sale of any security registered on a national securities exchange or any security not so registered, any manipulative or deceptive device or contrivance in contravention of such rules and regulations as the commission may prescribe as necessary or appropriate in the public interest or for the protection of investors.

PROHIBITION ON PERSONAL LOANS TO EXECUTIVES [ENACTED BY SARBANES-OXLEY ACT OF 2002 §402]

Sec. 13 (k)(1). It shall be unlawful for any issuer (as defined in section 2 of the Sarbanes-Oxley Act of 2002[1]), directly or indirectly, including through any subsidiary, to extend or maintain credit, to arrange for the extension of credit, or to renew an extension of credit, in the form of a personal loan to or for any director or executive officer (or equivalent thereof) of that issuer. An extension of credit maintained by the issuer on the date of enactment of this subsection shall not be subject to the provisions of this subsection, provided that there is no material modification to any term of any such extension of credit or any renewal of any such extension of credit on or after that date of enactment.

---

[1] Sarbanes-Oxley Act of 2002 §2 defines issuer as follows: an issuer (as defined in section 3 of the Securities Exchange Act of 1934), the securities of which are registered under section 12 of that Act, or that is required to file reports under section 15(d), or that files or has filed a registration statement that has not yet become effective under the Securities Act of 1933, and that it has not withdrawn.

1934 ACT RULES AND REGULATIONS

Selected Sections

SEC Reg. §240.10b-5

Employment of Manipulative and Deceptive Devices.

Reg. §240.10b-5.

It shall be unlawful for any person, directly or indirectly, by the use of any means or instrumentality of interstate commerce, or of the mails, or of any facility of any national securities exchange,

(a) to employ any device, scheme, or artifice to defraud,

(b) to make any untrue statement of a material fact or to omit to state a material fact necessary in order to make the statements made, in the light of the circumstances under which they were made, not misleading, or

(c) to engage in any act, practice, or course of business which operates or would operate as a fraud or deceit upon any person, in connection with the purchase or sale of any security.

INVESTMENT COMPANY ACT OF 1940

Act of August 22, 1940, 54 Stat. 789, 15 U.S. Code Secs. 80a-1—80a-52, as amended.

Selected Sections

GENERAL DEFINITIONS

Sec. 2. (a) When used in this title, unless the context otherwise requires—

. . .

(2) "Affiliated company" means a company which is an affiliated person.

(3) "Affiliated person" of another person means (A) any person directly or indirectly owning, controlling, or holding with power to vote, 5 per centum or more of the outstanding voting securities of such other person; (B) any person 5 per centum or more of whose outstanding voting securities are directly or indirectly owned, controlled, or held with power to vote, by such other person; (C) any person directly or indirectly controlling, controlled by, or under common control with, such other person; (D) any officer, director, partners,

co-partner, or employee of such other person; (E) if such other person is an investment company, any investment adviser thereof or any member of an advisory board thereof; and (F) if such other person is an unincorporated investment company not having a board of directors, the depositor thereof.

. . .

(9) "Control" means the power to exercise a controlling influence over the management or policies of a company, unless such power is solely the result of an official position with such company.

Any person who owns beneficially, either directly or through one or more controlled companies, more than 25 per centum of the voting securities of a company shall be presumed to control such company. Any person who does not so own more then 25 per centum of the voting securities of any company shall be presumed not to control such company . . .

. . .

(13) "Employees' securities company" means any investment company or similar issuer all of the outstanding securities of which (other than short-term paper) are beneficially owned

(A) by the employees or persons on retainer of a single employer or of two or more employers each of which is an affiliated company of the other,

(B) by former employees of such employer or employers,

(C) by members of the immediate family of such employees, persons on retainer, or former employees,

(D) by any two or more of the foregoing classes of persons, or

(E) by such employer or employers together with any one or more of the foregoing classes of persons.

. . .

(24) "Majority-owned subsidiary" of a person means a company 50 per centum or more of the outstanding voting securities of which are owned by such person, or by a company which, within the meaning of this paragraph, is a majority-owned subsidiary of such person.

. . .

(42) "Voting security" means any security presently entitling the owner or holder thereof to vote for the election of directors of a company. A specified percentage of the outstanding voting securities of a company means such amount of its outstanding voting securities as entitles the holder or holders thereof to cast said specified percentage of the aggregate votes which the holders of all the outstanding voting securities of such company are entitled

to cast. The vote of a majority of the outstanding voting securities of a company means the vote, at the annual or a special meeting of the security holders of such company duly called,

(A) of 67 per centum or more of the voting securities present at such meeting, if the holders of more than 50 per centum of the outstanding voting securities of such company are present or represented by proxy; or

(B) of more than 50 per centum of the outstanding voting securities of such company, whichever is the less.

(43) "Wholly-owned subsidiary" of a person means a company 95 per centum or more of the outstanding voting securities of which are owned by such person, or by a company which, within the meaning of this paragraph, is a wholly-owned subsidiary of such person.

. . .

(46) "Eligible portfolio company" means any issuer which—

(A) is organized under the laws of, and has its principal place of business in, any State or States;

(B) is neither an investment company as defined in section 3 (other than a small business investment company which is licensed by the Small Business Administration to operate under the Small Business Investment Act of 1958 and which is a wholly-owned subsidiary of the business development company) nor a company which would be an investment company except for the exclusion from the definition of investment company in section 3(c); and

(C) satisfies one of the following:

(i) it does not have any class of securities with respect to which a member of a national securities exchange, broker, or dealer may extend or maintain credit to or for a customer pursuant to rules or regulations adopted by the Board of Governors of the Federal Reserve System under section 7 of the Securities Exchange Act of 1934;

(ii) it is controlled by a business development company, either alone or as part of a group acting together, and such business development company in fact exercises a controlling influence over the management or policies of such eligible portfolio company and, as a result of such control, has an affiliated person who is a director of such eligible portfolio company;

(iii) it has total assets of not more than $4,000,000, and capital and surplus (shareholders' equity less retained earnings) of not less than $2,000,000, except that the Commission may adjust such amounts by rule, regulation, or order to reflect changes in 1 or more generally accepted indices or other indicators for small businesses; or

(iv) it meets such other criteria as the Commission may, by rule, establish as consistent with the public interest, the protection of investors, and the purposes fairly intended by the policy and provisions of this title.

(47) "Making available significant managerial assistance" by a business development company means—

(A) any arrangement whereby a business development company, through its directors, officers, employees, or general partners, offers to provide, and, if accepted, does so provide, significant guidance and counsel concerning the management, operations, or business objectives and policies of a portfolio company;

(B) the exercise by a business development company of a controlling influence over the management or policies of a portfolio company by the business development company acting individually or as part of a group acting together which controls such portfolio company; or

(C) with respect to a small business investment company licensed by the Small Business Administration to operate under the Small Business Investment Act of 1958, the making of loans to a portfolio company.

For purposes of subparagraph (A), the requirement that a business development company make available significant managerial assistance shall be deemed to be satisfied with respect to any particular portfolio company where the business development company purchases securities of such portfolio company in conjunction with one or more other persons acting together, and at least one of the persons in the group makes available significant managerial assistance to such portfolio company, except that such requirement will not be deemed to be satisfied if the business development company, in all cases, makes available significant managerial assistance solely in the manner described in this sentence.

(48) "Business development company" means any closed-end company which—

(A) is organized under the laws of, and has its principal place of business in, any State or States:

(B) is operated for the purpose of making investments in securities described in paragraphs (1) through (3) of section 55(a), and makes available significant managerial assistance with respect to the issuers of such securities, provided that a business development company must make available significant managerial assistance only with respect to the companies which are treated by such business development company as satisfying the 70 per centum of the value of its total assets condition of section 55; and provided further that a business development company need not make available significant managerial assistance with respect to any company described in paragraph (46)(C)(iii), or with respect to any other company that meets such criteria as the Commission may by rule, regulation, or order permit, as consistent with the public interest, the protection of investors, and the purposes of this title; and

(C) has elected pursuant to section 54(a) to be subject to the provisions of sections 55 through 65.

. . .

(51) (A) "Qualified purchaser" means—

(i) any natural person (including any person who holds a joint, community property, or other similar shared ownership interest in an issuer that is excepted under section 3(c)(7) with that person's qualified purchaser spouse) who owns not less than $5,000,000 in investments, as defined by the Commission;

(ii) any company that owns not less than $5,000,000 in investments and that is owned directly or indirectly by or for 2 or more natural persons who are related as siblings or spouse (including former spouses), or direct lineal descendants by birth or adoption, spouses of such persons, the estates of such persons, or foundations, charitable organizations, or trusts established by or for the benefit of such persons;

(iii) any trust that is not covered by clause (ii) and that was not formed for the specific purpose of acquiring the securities offered, as to which the trustee or other person authorized to make decisions with respect to the trust, and each settlor or other person who has contributed assets to the trust, is a person described in clause (i), (ii), or (iv); or

(iv) any person, acting for its own account or the accounts of other qualified purchasers, who in the aggregate owns and invests on a discretionary basis, not less than $25,000,000 in investments.

(B) The Commission may adopt such rules and regulations applicable to the persons and trusts specified in clauses (i) through (iv) of subparagraph (A) as it determines are necessary or appropriate in the public interest or for the protection of investors.

(C) The term "qualified purchaser" does not include a company that, but for the exceptions provided for in paragraph (1) or (7) of section 3(c), would be an investment company (hereafter in this paragraph referred to as an "excepted investment company"), unless all beneficial owners of its outstanding securities (other than short-term paper), determined in accordance with section 3(c)(1)(A), that acquired such securities on or before April 30, 1996 (hereafter in this paragraph referred to as "pre-amendment beneficial owners"), and all pre-amendment beneficial owners of the outstanding securities (other than short-term paper) of any excepted investment company that, directly or indirectly, owns any outstanding securities of such excepted investment company, have consented to its treatment as a qualified purchaser. Unanimous consent of all trustees, directors, or general partners of a company or trust referred to in clause (ii) or (iii) of subparagraph (A) shall constitute consent for purposes of this subparagraph.

DEFINITION OF INVESTMENT COMPANY

Sec. 3. (a) (1) When used in this title, "investment company" means any issuer which—

(A) is or holds itself out as being engaged primarily, or proposes to engage primarily, in the business of investing, reinvesting, or trading in securities . . . or

(C) is engaged or proposes to engage in the business of investing, reinvesting, owning, holding, or trading in securities, and owns or proposes to acquire investment securities having a value exceeding 40 per centum of the value of such issuer's total assets (exclusive of Government securities and cash items) on an unconsolidated basis.

(2) As used in this section, "investment securities" includes all securities except (A) Government securities, (B) securities issued by employees' securities companies, and (C) securities issued by majority-owned subsidiaries of the owner which (i) are not investment companies, and (ii) are not relying on the exception from the definition of investment company in paragraph (1) or (7) of subsection (c).

(b) Notwithstanding paragraph (1)(C) of subsection (a), none of the following persons is an investment company within the meaning of this title:

(1) Any issuer primarily engaged, directly or through a wholly-owned subsidiary or subsidiaries, in a business or businesses other than that of investing, reinvesting, owning, holding, or trading in securities.

(2) Any issuer which the Commission, upon application by such issuer, finds and by order declares to be primarily engaged in a business or businesses other than that of investing, reinvesting, owning, holding, or trading in securities either directly or (A) through majority-owned subsidiaries or (B) through controlled companies conducting similar types of businesses. The filing of an application under this paragraph in good faith by an issuer other than a registered investment company shall exempt the applicant for a period of sixty days from all provisions of this title applicable to investment companies as such. For cause shown, the Commission by order may extend such period of exemption for an additional period or periods. Whenever the Commission, upon its own motion or upon application, finds that the circumstances which gave rise to the issuance of an order granting an application under this paragraph no longer exist, the Commission shall by order revoke such order.

(3) Any issuer all the outstanding securities of which (other than short-term paper and directors' qualifying shares) are directly or indirectly owned by a company excepted from the definition of investment company by paragraph (1) or (2) of this subsection.

(c) Notwithstanding subsection (a), none of the following persons is an investment company within the meaning of this title.

(1) Any issuer whose outstanding securities (other than short-term paper) are beneficially owned by not more than one hundred persons and which is not making and does not presently propose to make a public offering of its securities . . . . For the purposes of this paragraph:

(A) Beneficial ownership by a company shall be deemed to be beneficial ownership by one person, except that, if the company owns 10 per centum or more of the outstanding voting securities of the issuer and is or, but for the exception provided for in this paragraph or paragraph (7), would be an investment company, the beneficial ownership shall be deemed to be that of the holders of such company's outstanding securities (other than short-term paper).

(B) Beneficial ownership by any person who acquires securities or interests in securities of an issuer described in the first sentence of this paragraph shall be deemed to be beneficial ownership by the person from whom such transfer was made, pursuant to such rules and regulations as the Commission shall prescribe as necessary or appropriate in the public interest and consistent with the protection of investors and the purposes fairly intended by the policy and provisions of this title, where the transfer was caused by legal separation, divorce, death, or other involuntary event.

. . .

(3) Any bank or insurance company; any savings and loan association, building and loan association, cooperative bank, homestead association, or similar institution, or any receiver, conservator, liquidator, liquidating agent, or similar official or person thereof or therefor; or any common trust fund or similar fund maintained by a bank exclusively for the collective investment and reinvestment of moneys contributed thereto by the bank in its capacity as a trustee, executor, administrator, or guardian, if—

(A) such fund is employed by the bank solely as an aid to the administration of trusts, estates, or other accounts created and maintained for a fiduciary purpose;

(B) except in connection with the ordinary advertising of the bank's fiduciary services, interests in such fund are not—

(i) advertised; or

(ii) offered for sale to the general public; and

(C) fees and expenses charged by such fund are not in contravention of fiduciary principles established under applicable Federal or State law.

. . .

(7) (A) Any issuer, the outstanding securities of which are owned exclusively by persons who, at the time of acquisition of such securities, are qualified purchasers, and which is not making and does not at that time propose to make a public offering of such securities. Securities that are owned by persons who received the securities from a qualified purchaser as a gift or bequest, or in a case in which the transfer was caused by legal separation, divorce, death, or other involuntary event, shall be deemed to

be owned by a qualified purchaser, subject to such rules, regulations, and orders as the Commission may prescribe as necessary or appropriate in the public interest or for the protection of investors.

. . .

(E) For purposes of determining compliance with this paragraph and paragraph (1), an issuer that is otherwise excepted under this paragraph and an issuer that is otherwise excepted under paragraph (1) shall not be treated by the Commission as being a single issuer for purposes of determining whether the outstanding securities of the issuer excepted under paragraph (1) are beneficially owned by not more than 100 persons or whether the outstanding securities of the issuer excepted under this paragraph are owned by persons that are not qualified purchasers. Nothing in this subparagraph shall be construed to establish that a person is a bona fide qualified purchaser for purposes of this paragraph or a bona fide beneficial owner for purposes of paragraph (1).

EXEMPTIONS

Sec. 6 . . .

. . .

(b) Upon application by any employees' security company, the Commission shall by order exempt such company from the provisions of this Act and of the rules and regulations hereunder, if and to the extent that such exemption is consistent with the protection of investors. In determining the provisions to which such an order of exemption shall apply, the Commission shall give due weight, among other things, to the form of organization and the capital structure of such company, the persons by whom its voting securities, evidences of indebtedness, and other securities are owned and controlled, the prices at which securities issued by such company are sold and the sales load thereon, the disposition of the proceeds of such sales, the character of the securities in which such proceeds are invested, and any relationship between such company and the issuer of any such security.

LIABILITY OF CONTROLLING PERSONS; PREVENTING COMPLIANCE WITH TITLE

Sec. 48. (a) It shall be unlawful for any person, directly or indirectly, to cause to be done any act or thing through or by means of any other person which it would be unlawful for such person to do under the provisions of this title or any rule, regulation, or order thereunder.

. . .

FUNCTIONS AND ACTIVITIES OF BUSINESS DEVELOPMENT COMPANIES

Sec. 55. (a) It shall be unlawful for a business development company to acquire any assets (other than those described in paragraphs (1) through (7) of this subsection) unless, at the time the acquisition is made, assets described in paragraphs (1) through (6) below represent at least 70 per centum of the value of its total assets (other than assets described in paragraph (7) below):

(1) securities purchased, in transactions not involving any public offering or in such other transactions as the Commission may, by rule, prescribe if it finds that enforcement of this title and of the Securities Act of 1933 with respect to such transactions is not necessary in the public interest or for the protection of investors by reason of the small amount, or the limited nature of the public offering, involved in such transactions—

(A) from the issuer of such securities, which issuer is an eligible portfolio company, from any person who is, or who within the preceding thirteen months has been, an affiliated person of such eligible portfolio company, or from any other person, subject to such rules and regulations as the Commission may prescribe as necessary or appropriate in the public interest or for the protection of investors; or

(B) from the issuer of such securities, which issuer is described in section 2(a)(46)(A) and (B) but is not an eligible portfolio company because it has issued a class of securities with respect to which a member of a national securities exchange, broker, or dealer may extend or maintain credit to or for a customer pursuant to rules or regulations adopted by the Board of Governors of the Federal Reserve System under section 7 of the Securities Exchange Act of 1934, or from any person who is an officer or employee of such issuer, if—

(i) at the time of the purchase, the business development company owns at least 50 per centum of—

(I) the greatest number of equity securities of such issuer and securities convertible into or exchangeable for such securities; and

(II) the greatest amount of debt securities of such issuer, held by such business development company at any point in time during the period when such issuer was an eligible portfolio company, except that options, warrants, and similar securities which have by their terms expired and debt securities which have been converted, or repaid or prepaid in the ordinary course of business or incident to a public offering of securities of such issuer, shall not be considered to have been held by such business development company for purposes of this requirement; and

(ii) the business development company is one of the 20 largest holders of record of such issuer's outstanding voting securities;

(2) securities of any eligible portfolio company with respect to which the business development company satisfies the requirements of section 2(a)(46)(C)(ii);

(3) securities purchased in transactions not involving any public offering from an issuer described in sections 2(a)(46)(A) and (B) or from a person who is, or who within the preceding thirteen months has been, an affiliated person of such issuer, or from any person in transactions incident thereto, if such securities were—

(A) issued by an issuer that is, or was immediately prior to the purchase of its securities by the business development company, in bankruptcy proceedings, subject to reorganization under the supervision of a court of competent jurisdiction, or subject to a plan or arrangement resulting from such bankruptcy proceedings or reorganization;

(B) issued by an issuer pursuant to or in consummation of such a plan or arrangement; or

(C) issued by an issuer that, immediately prior to the purchase of such issuer's securities by the business development company, was not in bankruptcy proceedings but was unable to meet its obligations as they came due without material assistance other than conventional lending or financing arrangements;

(4) securities of eligible portfolio companies purchased from any person in transactions not involving any public offering, if there is no ready market for such securities and if immediately prior to such purchase the business development company owns at least 60 percentum of the outstanding equity securities of such issuer (giving effect to all securities presently convertible into or exchangeable for equity securities of such issuer as if such securities were so converted or exchanged);

(5) securities received in exchange for or distributed on or with respect to securities described in paragraphs (1) through (4) of this subsection, or pursuant to the exercise of options, warrants, or rights relating to securities described in such paragraphs;

(6) cash, cash items, Government securities, or high quality debt securities maturing in one year or less from the time of investment in such high quality debt securities; and

(7) office furniture and equipment, interests in real estate and lease-hold improvements and facilities maintained to conduct the business operations of the business development company, deferred organization and operating expenses, and other noninvestment assets necessary and appropriate to its operations as a business development company, including notes of indebtedness of directors, officers, employees, and general partners held by a business development company as payment for securities of such company issued in connection with an executive compensation plan described in section 57(j).

(b) For purposes of this section, the value of a business development company's assets shall be determined as of the date of the most recent financial statements filed by such company with the Commission pursuant to section 13 of the Securities Exchange Act of 1934, and shall be determined no less frequently than annually.

INVESTMENT COMPANY ACT RULES AND REGULATIONS

Selected Sections

Definition of investments for purposes of §2(a)(51) (definition of "qualified purchaser"); certain calculations.

SEC Reg. §270.2a51-1.

(a) *Definitions.* As used in this section:

. . .

(3) The term *Investment Vehicle* means an investment company, a company that would be an investment company but for the exclusions provided by sections 3(c)(1) through 3(c)(9) of the Act or the exemptions provided by §§270.3a-6 or 270.3a-7, or a commodity pool.

. . .

(6) The term *Prospective Qualified Purchaser* means a person seeking to purchase a security of a Section 3(c)(7) Company.

(7) The term *Public Company* means a company that:

(i) Files reports pursuant to section 13 or 15(d) of the Securities Exchange Act of 1934; or

(ii) Has a class of securities that are listed on a "designated offshore securities market" as such term is defined by Regulation S under the Securities Act of 1933.

(8) The term *Related Person* means a person who is related to a Prospective Qualified Purchaser as a sibling, spouse or former spouse, or is a direct lineal descendant or ancestor by birth or adoption of the Prospective Qualified Purchaser, or is a spouse of such descendant or ancestor, *provided that*, in the case of a Family Company, a Related Person includes any owner of the Family Company and any person who is a Related Person of such owner.

(9) The term *Relying Person* means a Section 3(c)(7) Company or a person acting on its behalf.

(10) The term *Section 3(c)(7) Company* means a company that would be an investment company but for the exclusion provided by section 3(c)(7) of the Act.

(b) *Types of Investments.* For purposes of section 2(a)(51) of the Act, the term *Investments* means:

(1) Securities (as defined by section 2(a)(1) of the Securities Act of 1933), other than securities of an issuer that controls, is controlled by, or is under common control with, the Prospective Qualified Purchaser that owns such securities, unless the issuer of such securities is:

(i) An Investment Vehicle;

(ii) A Public Company; or

(iii) A company with shareholders' equity of not less than $50 million (determined in accordance with generally accepted accounting principles) as reflected on the company's most recent financial statements, *provided that* such financial statements present the information as of a date within 16 months preceding the date on which the Prospective Qualified Purchaser acquires the securities of a Section 3(c)(7) Company;

(2) Real estate held for investment purposes;

(3) Commodity Interests held for investment purposes;

(4) Physical Commodities held for investment purposes;

(5) To the extent not securities, financial contracts (as such term is defined in section 3(c)(2)(B)(ii) of the Act) entered into for investment purposes;

(6) In the case of a Prospective Qualified Purchaser that is a Section 3(c)(7) Company, a company that would be an investment company but for the exclusion provided by section 3(c)(1) of the Act, or a commodity pool, any amounts payable to such Prospective Qualified Purchaser pursuant to a firm agreement or similar binding commitment pursuant to which a person has agreed to acquire an interest in, or make capital contributions to, the Prospective Qualified Purchaser upon the demand of the Prospective Qualified Purchaser; and

(7) Cash and cash equivalents (including foreign currencies) held for investment purposes. For purposes of this section, cash and cash equivalents include:

(i) Bank deposits, certificates of deposit, bankers acceptances and similar bank instruments held for investment purposes; and

(ii) The net cash surrender value of an insurance policy.

(c) *Investment Purposes.* For purposes of this section:

(1) Real estate shall not be considered to be held for investment purposes by a Prospective Qualified Purchaser if it is used by the Prospective Qualified Purchaser or a Related Person for personal purposes or as a place of business, or in connection with the conduct of the trade or business of the Prospective Qualified Purchaser or a Related Person, *provided that* real estate owned by a Prospective Qualified Purchaser who is engaged primarily in the business of investing, trading or developing real estate in connection with such business may be deemed to be held for investment purposes. Residential real estate shall not be deemed to be used for personal purposes if deductions with respect to such real estate are not disallowed by section 280A of the Internal Revenue Code.

(2) A Commodity Interest or Physical Commodity owned, or a financial contract entered into, by the Prospective Qualified Purchaser who is engaged primarily in the business of investing, reinvesting, or trading in Commodity

Interests, Physical Commodities or financial contracts in connection with such business may be deemed to be held for investment purposes.

(d) *Valuation.* For purposes of determining whether a Prospective Qualified Purchaser is a qualified purchaser, the aggregate amount of Investments owned and invested on a discretionary basis by the Prospective Qualified Purchaser shall be the Investments' fair market value on the most recent practicable date or their cost, *provided that:*

(1) In the case of Commodity Interests, the amount of Investments shall be the value of the initial margin or option premium deposited in connection with such Commodity Interests; and

(2) In each case, there shall be deducted from the amount of Investments owned by the Prospective Qualified Purchaser the amounts specified in paragraphs (e) and (f) of this section, as applicable.

(e) *Deductions.* In determining whether any person is a qualified purchaser there shall be deducted from the amount of such person's Investments the amount of any outstanding indebtedness incurred to acquire or for the purpose of acquiring the Investments owned by such person.

(f) *Deductions: Family Companies.* In determining whether a Family Company is a qualified purchaser, in addition to the amounts specified in paragraph (e) of this section, there shall be deducted from the value of such Family Company's Investments any outstanding indebtedness incurred by an owner of the Family Company to acquire such Investments.

(g) *Special Rules for Certain Prospective Qualified Purchasers.*

(1) *Qualified Institutional Buyers.* Any Prospective Qualified Purchaser who is, or who a Relying Person reasonably believes is, a qualified institutional buyer as defined in paragraph (a) of §230.144A(a) of this chapter, acting for its own account, the account of another qualified institutional buyer, or the account of a qualified purchaser, shall be deemed to be a qualified purchaser *provided:*

(i) That a dealer described in paragraph (a)(1)(ii) of §230.144A of this chapter shall own and invest on a discretionary basis at least $25 million in securities of issuers that are not affiliated persons of the dealer; and

(ii) That a plan referred to in paragraph (a)(1)(i)(D) or (a)(1)(i)(E) of §230.144A of this chapter, or a trust fund referred to in paragraph (a)(1)(i)(F) of §230.144A of this chapter that holds the assets of such a plan, will not be deemed to be acting for its own account if investment decisions with respect to the plan are made by the beneficiaries of the plan, except with respect to investment decisions made solely by the fiduciary, trustee or sponsor of such plan.

(2) *Joint Investments.* In determining whether a natural person is a qualified purchaser, there may be included in the amount of such person's Investments any Investments held jointly with such person's spouse, or Investments in which such person shares with such person's spouse a community property or similar shared ownership interest. In determining whether spouses who are making a joint investment in a Section 3(c)(7) Company are qualified purchasers, there may be included in the amount of each spouse's Investments any Invest-

ments owned by the other spouse (whether or not such Investments are held jointly). In each case, there shall be deducted from the amount of any such Investments the amounts specified in paragraph (e) of this section incurred by each spouse.

(3) *Investments by Subsidiaries.* For purposes of determining the amount of Investments owned by a company under section 2(a)(51)(A)(iv) of the Act, there may be included Investments owned by majority-owned subsidiaries of the company and Investments owned by a company ("Parent Company") of which the company is a majority-owned subsidiary, or by a majority-owned subsidiary of the company and other majority-owned subsidiaries of the Parent Company.

(4) *Certain Retirement Plans and Trusts.* In determining whether a natural person is a qualified purchaser, there may be included in the amount of such person's Investments any Investments held in an individual retirement account or similar account the Investments of which are directed by and held for the benefit of such person.

(h) *Reasonable Belief.* The term "qualified purchaser" as used in section 3(c)(7) of the Act means any person that meets the definition of qualified purchaser in section 2(a)(51)(A) of the Act and the rules thereunder, or that a Relying Person reasonably believes meets such definition.

Definitions of beneficial owner for certain purposes under §§2(a)(51) and 3(c)(7) and determining indirect ownership interests.

SEC Reg. 270.2a51-2.

(a) *Beneficial Ownership: General.* Except as set forth in this section, for purposes of sections 2(a)(51)(C) and 3(c)(7)(B)(ii) of the Act, the beneficial owners of securities of an excepted investment company (as defined in section 2(a)(51)(C) of the Act) shall be determined in accordance with section 3(c)(1) of the Act.

(b) *Beneficial Ownership: Grandfather Provision.* For purposes of section 3(c)(7)(B)(ii) of the Act, securities of an issuer beneficially owned by a company (without giving effect to section 3(c)(1)(A) of the Act) ("owning company") shall be deemed to be beneficially owned by one person unless:

(1) The owning company is an investment company or an excepted investment company:

(2) The owning company, directly or indirectly, controls, is controlled by, or is under common control with, the issuer; and

(3) On October 11, 1996, under section 3(c)(1)(A) of the Act as then in effect, the voting securities of the issuer were deemed to be beneficially owned by the holders of the owning company's outstanding securities (other than short-term paper), in which case, such holders shall be deemed to be beneficial owners of the issuer's outstanding voting securities.

(c) *Beneficial Ownership: Consent Provision.* For purposes of section 2(a)(51)(C) of the Act, securities of an excepted investment company beneficially owned by a company (without giving effect to section 3(c)(1)(A) of the Act)("owning company") shall be deemed to be beneficially owned by one person unless:

(1) The owning company is an excepted investment company;

(2) The owning company directly or indirectly controls, is controlled by, or is under common control with, the excepted investment company or the company with respect to which the excepted investment company is, or will be, a qualified purchaser; and

(3) On April 30, 1996, under section 3(c)(1)(A) of the Act as then in effect, the voting securities of the excepted investment company were deemed to be beneficially owned by the holders of the owning company's outstanding securities (other than short-term paper), in which case the holders of such excepted company's securities shall be deemed to be beneficial owners of the excepted investment company's outstanding voting securities.

(d) *Indirect Ownership: Consent Provision.* For purposes of section 2(a)(51)(C) of the Act, an excepted investment company shall not be deemed to indirectly own the securities of an excepted investment company seeking a consent to be treated as a qualified purchaser ("qualified purchaser company") unless such excepted investment company, directly or indirectly, controls, is controlled by, or is under common control with, the qualified purchaser company or a company with respect to which the qualified purchaser company is or will be a qualified purchaser.

(e) *Required Consent: Consent Provision.* For purposes of section 2(a)(51)(C) of the Act, the consent of the beneficial owners of an excepted investment company ("owning company") that beneficially owns securities of an excepted investment company that is seeking the consents required by section 2(a)(51)(C) ("consent company") shall not be required unless the owning company directly or indirectly controls, is controlled by, or is under common control with, the consent company or the company with respect to which the consent company is, or will be, a qualified purchaser.

NOTES to §270.2a51-2:

1. On both April 30, 1996 and October 11, 1996, section 3(c)(1)(A) of the Act as then in effect provided that: (A) Beneficial ownership by a company shall be deemed to be beneficial ownership by one person, except that, if the company owns 10 per centum or more of the outstanding voting securities of the issuer, the beneficial ownership shall be deemed to be that of the holders of such company's outstanding securities (other than short-term paper) unless, as of the date of the most recent acquisition by such company of securities of that issuer, the value of all securities owned by such company of all issuers which are or would, but for the exception set forth in this subparagraph, be excluded from the definition of investment company solely by this paragraph, does not exceed 10 per centum of the value of the company's total assets. Such issuer nonetheless is deemed to be an investment company for purposes of section 12(d)(1).

2. Issuers seeking the consent required by section 2(a)(51)(C) of the Act should note that section 2(a)(51)(C) requires an issuer to obtain the consent of the beneficial owners of its securities and the beneficial owners of securities of any "excepted investment company" that directly or indirectly owns the securities of the issuer. Except as set forth in paragraphs (d) (with respect to indirect owners) and (e)

(with respect to direct owners) of this section, nothing in this section is designed to limit this consent requirement.

Certain companies as qualified purchasers.

SEC Reg. §270.2a51-3.

(a) For purposes of section 2(a)(51)(A)(ii) and (iv) of the Act, a company shall not be deemed to be a qualified purchaser if it was formed for the specific purpose of acquiring the securities offered by a company excluded from the definition of investment company by section 3(c)(7) of the Act unless each beneficial owner of the company's securities or other interest in the company is a qualified purchaser.

(b) For purposes of section 2(a)(51) of the Act, a company may be deemed to be a qualified purchaser if each beneficial owner of the company's securities is a qualified purchaser.

Certain Prima Facie Investment Companies

SEC Reg. §270.3a-1.

Notwithstanding section 3(a)(1)(C) of the Act . . . , an issuer will be deemed not to be an investment company under the act; Provided, That:

(a) No more than 45 percent of the value (as defined in section 2(a)(41) of the Act) of such issuer's total assets (exclusive of Government securities and cash items) consists of, and no more than 45 percent of such issuer's net income after taxes (for the last four fiscal quarters combined) is derived from, securities other than:

(1) Government securities;

(2) Securities issued by employees' securities companies;

(3) Securities issued by majority-owned subsidiaries of the issuer (other than subsidiaries relying on the exclusion from the definition of investment companies in section 3(b)(3) or section 3(c)(1) of the Act) which are not investment companies; and

(4) Securities issued by companies:

(i) Which are controlled primarily by such issuer;

(ii) Through which such issuer engages in a business other than that of investing, reinvesting, owning, holding or trading in securities; and

(iii) Which are not investment companies;

(b) The issuer is not an investment company as defined in section 3(a)(1)(A) or 3(a)(1)(B) of the Act . . . and is not a special situation investment company; and

(c) The percentages described in paragraph (a) of this section are determined on an unconsolidated basis, except that the issuer shall consolidate its financial statements with the financial statements of any wholly-owned subsidiaries.

Transient investment companies

SEC Reg. §270.3a-2.

(a) For purposes of sections 3(a)(1)(A) and 3(a)(1)(C) of the Act . . . , an issuer is deemed not to be engaged in the business of investing, reinvesting, owning, holding or trading in securities during a period of time not to exceed one year; Provided, That the issuer has a bona fide intent to be engaged primarily, as soon as is reasonably possible (in any event by the termination of such period of time), in a business other than that of investing, reinvesting, owning, holding or trading in securities, such intent to be evidenced by:

(1) The issuer's business activities; and

(2) An appropriate resolution of the issuer's board of directors, or by an appropriate action of the person or persons performing similar functions for any issuer not having a board of directors, which resolution or action has been recorded contemporaneously in its minute books or comparable documents.

(b) For purposes of this rule, the period of time described in paragraph (a) shall commence on the earlier of:

(1) The date on which an issuer owns securities and/or cash having a value exceeding 50 percent of the value of such issuer's total assets on either a consolidated or unconsolidated basis; or

(2) The date on which an issuer owns or proposes to acquire investment securities (as defined in section 3(a) of the Act) having a value exceeding 40 per centum of the value of such issuer's total assets (exclusive of Government securities and cash items) on an unconsolidated basis.

(c) No issuer may rely on this section more frequently than once during any three-year period.

Certain Investment Companies Owned by Companies Which Are Not Investment Companies

SEC Reg. §270.3a-3.

Notwithstanding section 3(a)(1)(A) or section 3(a)(1)(C) of the Act . . . , an issuer will be deemed not to be an investment company for purposes of the Act; Provided, That all of the outstanding securities of the issuer (other than short-term paper, directors' qualifying shares, and debt securities owned by the Small Business Administration) are directly or indirectly owned by a company which satisfies the conditions of Sec. 270.3a-1(a) and which is:

(a) A company that is not an investment company as defined in section 3(a) of the Act;

(b) A company that is an investment company as defined in section 3(a)(1)(C) of the Act . . . , but which is excluded from the definition of the term "investment company" by section 3(b)(1) or 3(b)(2) of the Act . . . ; or

(c) A company that is deemed not to be an investment company for purposes of the Act by rule 3a-1.

Definition of beneficial ownership for certain §3(c)(1) funds.

SEC Reg. §270.3c-1.

(a) As used in this section:

(1) The term *Covered Company* shall mean a company that is an investment company, a Section 3(c)(1) Company or a Section 3(c)(7) Company.

(2) The term *Section 3(c)(1) Company* shall mean a company that would be an investment company but for the exclusion provided by section 3(c)(1) of the Act.

(3) The term *Section 3(c)(7) Company* shall mean a company that would be an investment company but for the exclusion provided by section 3(c)(7) of the Act.

(b) For purposes of section 3(c)(1)(A) of the Act, beneficial ownership by a Covered Company owning 10 percent or more of the outstanding voting securities of a Section 3(c)(1) Company shall be deemed to be beneficial ownership by one person, *provided that*:

(1) On April 1, 1997, the Covered Company owned 10 percent or more of the outstanding voting securities of the Section 3(c)(1) Company or non-voting securities that, on such date and in accordance with the terms of such securities, were convertible into or exchangeable for voting securities that, if converted or exchanged on or after such date, would have constituted 10 percent or more of the outstanding voting securities of the Section 3(c)(1) Company; and

(2) On the date of any acquisition of securities of the Section 3(c)(1) Company by the Covered Company, the value of all securities owned by the Covered Company of all issuers that are Section 3(c)(1) or Section 3(c)(7) Companies does not exceed 10 percent of the value of the Covered Company's total assets.

Beneficial ownership by knowledgeable employees and certain other persons.

SEC Reg. §270.3c-5.

(a) As used in this section:

(1) The term *Affiliated Management Person* means an affiliated person, as such term is defined in section 2(a)(3) of the Act, that manages the investment activities of a Covered Company. For purposes of this definition, the term "investment company" as used in section 2(a)(3) of the Act includes a Covered Company.

(2) The term *Covered Company* means a Section 3(c)(1) Company or a Section 3(c)(7) Company.

(3) The term *Executive Officer* means the president, any vice president in charge of a principal business unit, division or function (such as sales, administration or finance), any other officer who performs a policy-making function, or any other person who performs similar policy-making functions, for a Covered Company or for an Affiliated Management Person of the Covered Company.

(4) The term *Knowledgeable Employee* with respect to any Covered Company means any natural person who is:

(i) An Executive Officer, director, trustee, general partner, advisory board member, or person serving in a similar capacity, of the Covered Company or an Affiliated Management Person of the Covered Company; or

(ii) An employee of the Covered Company or an Affiliated Management Person of the Covered Company (other than an employee performing solely clerical, secretarial or administrative functions with regard to such company or its investments) who, in connection with his or her regular functions or duties, participates in the investment activities of such Covered Company, other Covered Companies, or investment companies the investment activities of which are managed by such Affiliated Management Person of the Covered Company, *provided that* such employee has been performing such functions and duties for or on behalf of the Covered Company or the Affiliated Management Person of the Covered Company, or substantially similar functions or duties for or on behalf of another company for at least 12 months.

(5) The term *Section 3(c)(1) Company* means a company that would be an investment company but for the exclusion provided by section 3(c)(1) of the Act.

(6) The term *Section 3(c)(7) Company* means a company that would be an investment company but for the exclusion provided by section 3(c)(7) of the Act.

(b) For purposes of determining the number of beneficial owners of a Section 3(c)(1) Company, and whether the outstanding securities of a Section 3(c)(7) Company are owned exclusively by qualified purchasers, there shall be excluded securities beneficially owned by:

(1) A person who at the time such securities were acquired was a Knowledgeable Employee of such Company;

(2) A company owned exclusively by Knowledgeable Employees;

(3) Any person who acquires securities originally acquired by a Knowledgeable Employee in accordance with this section, provided that such securities were acquired by such person in accordance with §270.3c-6.

Certain transfers of interests in §3(c)(1) and §3(c)(7) funds.

SEC Reg. §270.3c-6.

(a) As used in this section:

(1) The term *Donee* means a person who acquires a security of a Covered Company (or a security or other interest in a company referred to in paragraph (b)(3) of this section) as a gift or bequest or pursuant to an agreement relating to a legal separation or divorce.

(2) The term *Section 3(c)(1) Company* means a company that would be an investment company but for the exclusion provided by section 3(c)(1) of the Act.

(3) The term *Section 3(c)(7) Company* means a company that would be an investment company but for the exclusion provided by section 3(c)(7) of the Act.

(4) The term *Transferee* means a Section 3(c)(1) Transferee or a Qualified Purchaser Transferee, in each case as defined in paragraph (b) of this section.

(5) The term *Transferor* means a Section 3(c)(1) Transferor or a Qualified Purchaser Transferor, in each case as defined in paragraph (b) of this section.

(b) Beneficial ownership by any person ("Section 3(c)(1) Transferee") who acquires securities or interests in securities of a Section 3(c)(1) Company from a person other than the Section 3(c)(1) Company shall be deemed to be beneficial ownership by the person from whom such transfer was made ("Section 3(c)(1) Transferor"), and securities of a Section 3(c)(7) Company that are owned by persons who received the securities from a qualified purchaser other than the Section 3(c)(7) Company ("Qualified Purchaser Transferor") or a person deemed to be a qualified purchaser by this section shall be deemed to be acquired by a qualified purchaser ("Qualified Purchaser Transferee"), provided that the Transferee is:

(1) The estate of the Transferor;

(2) A Donee; or

(3) A company established by the Transferor exclusively for the benefit of (or owned exclusively by) the Transferor and the persons specified in paragraphs (b)(1) and (b)(2) of this section.

INVESTMENT ADVISERS ACT OF 1940

Act of August 22, 1940, 54 Stat. 847, 15 U.S. Code, Secs. 80b-1—80b-21, as amended.

Selected Sections

DEFINITIONS

Sec. 202. (a) When used in this title, unless the context otherwise requires—

. . .

(11) "Investment adviser" means any person who, for compensation, engages in the business of advising others, either directly or through publications or writings, as to the value of securities or as to the advisability of investing in, purchasing, or selling securities, or who, for compensation and as part of a regular business, issues or promulgates analyses or reports concerning securities; but does not include (A) a bank, or any bank holding company as defined in the Bank Holding Company Act of 1956, which is not an investment company, except that the term "investment adviser" includes any bank or bank holding company to the extent that such bank or bank holding company serves or acts

as an investment adviser to a registered investment company, but if, in the case of a bank, such services or actions are performed through a separately identifiable department or division, the department or division, and not the bank itself, shall be deemed to be the investment adviser; (B) any lawyer, accountant, engineer, or teacher whose performance of such services is solely incidental to the practice of his profession; (C) any broker or dealer whose performance of such services is solely incidental to the conduct of his business as a broker or dealer and who receives no special compensation therefor; (D) the publisher of any bona fide newspaper, news magazine or business or financial publication of general and regular circulation; (E) any person whose advice, analyses, or reports relate to no securities other than securities which are direct obligations of or obligations guaranteed as to principal or interest by the United States, or securities issued or guaranteed by corporations in which the United States has a direct or indirect interest which shall have been designated by the Secretary of the Treasury, pursuant to section 3(a)(12) of the Securities Exchange Act of 1934, as exempted securities for the purposes of that Act; or (F) such other persons not within the intent of this paragraph, as the Commission may designate by rules and regulations or order.

. . .

(22) "Business development company" means any company which is a business development company as defined in section 2(a)(48) of title I of this Act and which complies with section 55 of title I of this Act, except that—

(A) the 70 per centum of the value of the total assets condition referred to in sections 2(a)(48) and 55 of title I of this Act shall be 60 per centum for purposes of determining compliance therewith;

(B) such company need not be a closed-end company and need not elect to be subject to the provisions of sections 55 through 65 of title I of this Act; and

(C) the securities which may be purchased pursuant to section 55(a) of title I of this Act may be purchased from any person.

For purposes of this paragraph, all terms in sections 2(a)(48) and 55 of title I of this Act shall have the same meaning set forth in such title as if such company were a registered closed-end investment company, except that the value of the assets of a business development company which is not subject to the provisions of sections 55 through 65 of title I of this Act shall be determined as of the date of the most recent financial statements which it furnished to all holders of its securities and shall be determined no less frequently than annually.

. . .

REGISTRATION OF INVESTMENT ADVISERS

Sec. 203. (a) Except as provided in subsection (b) and section 203A, it shall be unlawful for any investment adviser, unless registered under this section, to make use of the mails or any means or instrumentality of interstate commerce in connection with his or its business as an investment adviser.

. . .

(b) The provisions of subsection (a) shall not apply to—

. . .

(3) any investment adviser who during the course of the preceding twelve months has had fewer than fifteen clients and who neither holds himself out generally to the public as an investment adviser nor acts as an investment adviser to any investment company registered under title I of this Act, or a company which has elected to be a business development company pursuant to section 54 of title I of this Act and has not withdrawn its election. For purposes of determining the number of clients of an investment adviser under this paragraph, no share-holder, partner, or beneficial owner of a business development company, as defined in this title, shall be deemed to be a client of such investment adviser unless such person is a client of such investment adviser separate and apart from his status as a shareholder, partner, or beneficial owner;

. . .

STATE AND FEDERAL RESPONSIBILITIES

Sec 203A. (a) Advisers Subject To State Authorities.—
(1) In General.—No investment adviser that is regulated or required to be regulated as an investment adviser in the State in which it maintains its principal office and place of business shall register under section 203, unless the invest-ment adviser—

(A) has assets under management of not less than $25,000,000, or such higher amount as the Commission may; by rule, deem appropriate in accordance with the purposes of this title; or

(B) is an adviser to an investment company registered under title I of this Act.

(2) Definition.—For purposes of this subsection, the term "assets under manage-ment" means the securities portfolios with respect to which an investment adviser provides continuous and regular supervisory or management services.

(b) Advisers Subject To Commission Authority.—
(1) In General.—No law of any State or political subdivision thereof requiring the registration, licensing, or qualification as an investment adviser or supervised person of an investment adviser shall apply to any person—

(A) that is registered under section 203 as an investment adviser, or that is a supervised person of such person, except that a State may license, register, or otherwise qualify any investment adviser representative who has a place of business located within that State; or

(B) that is not registered under section 203 because that person is excepted from the definition of an investment adviser under section 202(a)(11).

(2) Limitation.—Nothing in this subsection shall prohibit the securities commission (or any agency or office performing like functions) of any State from investigating and bringing enforcement actions with respect to fraud or deceit against an investment adviser or person associated with an investment adviser.

. . .

INVESTMENT ADVISORY CONTRACTS

Sec. 205. (a) No investment adviser, unless exempt from registration pursuant to section 203(b), shall make use of the mails or any means or instrumentality of interstate commerce, directly or indirectly, to enter into, extend, or renew any investment advisory contract, or in any way to perform any investment advisory contract entered into, extended, or renewed on or after the effective date of this title, if such contract—

(1) provides for compensation to the investment adviser on the basis of a share of capital gains upon or capital appreciation of the funds or any portion of the funds of the client;

(2) fails to provide, in substance, that no assignment of such contract shall be made by the investment adviser without the consent of the other party to the contract; or

(3) fails to provide, in substance, that the investment adviser, if a partnership, will notify the other party to the contract of any change in the membership of such partnership within a reasonable time after such change.

(b) Paragraph (1) of subsection (a) shall not—

(1) be construed to prohibit an investment advisory contract which provides for compensation based upon the total value of a fund averaged over a definite period, or as of definite dates, or taken as of a definite date;

(2) apply to an investment advisory contract with—

(A) an investment company registered under title I of this Act, or

(B) any other person (except a trust, governmental plan, collective trust fund, or separate account referred to in section 3(c)(11) of title I of this Act), provided that the contract relates to the investment of assets in excess of $1 million,

if the contract provides for compensation based on the asset value of the company or fund under management averaged over a specified period and increasing and decreasing proportionately with the investment performance of the company or fund over a specified period in relation to the investment record of an appropriate index of securities prices or such other measure of investment performance as the Commission by rule, regulation, or order may specify;

(3) apply with respect to any investment advisory contract between an investment adviser and a business development company, as defined in this title, if (A) the compensation provided for in such contract does not exceed 20 per centum of the realized capital gains upon the funds of the business development company over a specified period or as of definite dates, computed net of all realized capital losses and unrealized capital depreciation, and the condition of section 61(a)(3)(B)(iii) of title I of this Act is satisfied, and (B) the business

development company does not have outstanding any option, warrant, or right issued pursuant to section 61(a)(3)(B) of title I of this Act and does not have a profit-sharing plan described in section 57(n) of title I of this Act; or

(4) apply to an investment advisory contract with a company excepted from the definition of an investment company under section 3(c)(7) of title I of this Act; or

(5) apply to an investment advisory contract with a person who is not a resident of the United States.

(c) For purposes of paragraph (2) of subsection (b), the point from which increases and decreases in compensation are measured shall be the fee which is paid or earned when the investment performance of such company or fund is equivalent to that of the index or other measure of performance, and an index of securities prices shall be deemed appropriate unless the Commission by order shall determine otherwise.

(d) As used in paragraphs (2) and (3) of this subsection (a), "investment advisory contract" means any contract or agreement whereby a person agrees to act as investment adviser to or to manage any investment or trading account of another person other than an investment company registered under title I of this Act.

(e) The Commission, by rule or regulation, upon its own motion, or by order upon application, may conditionally or unconditionally exempt any person or transaction, or any class or classes of persons or transactions, from subsection (a)(1), if and to the extent that the exemption relates to an investment advisory contract with any person that the Commission determines does not need the protections of subsection (a)(1), on the basis of such factors as financial sophistication, net worth, knowledge of and experience in financial matters, amount of assets under management, relationship with a registered investment adviser, and such other factors as the Commission determines are consistent with this section.

GENERAL PROHIBITIONS

Sec. 208.

. . .

(d) It shall be unlawful for any person indirectly, or through or by any other person, to do any act or thing which it would be unlawful for such person to do directly under the provisions of this title or any rule or regulation thereunder.

VALIDITY OF CONTRACTS

Sec. 215. (a) Any condition, stipulation, or provision binding any person to waive compliance with any provision of this title or with any rule, regulation, or order thereunder shall be void.

(b) Every contract made in violation of any provision of this title and every contract heretofore or hereafter made, the performance of which involves the violation of, or the continuance of any relationship or practice in violation of any provision of this title, or any rule, regulation, or order thereunder, shall be void (1) as regards the rights of any person who, in violation of any such provision, rule, regulation, or order, shall have made or engaged in the performance of any such contract, and (2) as regards the rights of any person who, not being a party to such contract, shall have acquired any right thereunder with actual knowledge of the facts by reason of which the making or performance of such contract was in violation of any such provision.

STATE REGULATION OF INVESTMENT ADVISERS

Sec. 222.

. . .

(d) National De Minimis Standard.—No law of any State or political subdivision thereof requiring the registration, licensing, or qualification as an investment adviser shall require an investment adviser to register with the securities commissioner of the State (or any agency or officer performing like functions) or to comply with such law (other than any provision thereof prohibiting fraudulent conduct) if the investment adviser—

(1) does not have a place of business located within the State; and

(2) during the preceding 12-month period, has had fewer than 6 clients who are residents of that State.

INVESTMENT ADVISERS ACT RULES AND REGULATIONS

Selected Sections

SEC Reg. §275.203(b)(3)-1

Definition of "client" of an investment adviser.

Preliminary Note to §203(b)(3)-1

This rule is a safe harbor and is not intended to specify the exclusive method for determining who may be deemed a single client for purposes of section 203(b)(3) of the Act.

SEC Reg. §275.203(b)(3)-1.

(a) *General.* For purposes of section 203(b)(3) of the Act, the following are deemed a single client:

(1) A natural person, and:

(i) Any minor child of the natural person;

(ii) Any relative, spouse, or relative of the spouse of the natural person who has the same principal residence;

(iii) All accounts of which the natural person and/or the persons referred to in this paragraph (a)(1) are the only primary beneficiaries; and

(iv) All trusts of which the natural person and/or the persons referred to in this paragraph (a)(1) are the only primary beneficiaries;

(2) (i) A corporation, general partnership, limited partnership, limited liability company, trust (other than a trust referred to in paragraph (a)(1)(iv) of this section), or other legal organization (any of which are referred to hereinafter as a "legal organization") that receives investment advice based on its investment objectives rather than the individual investment objectives of its shareholders, partners, limited partners, members, or beneficiaries (any of which are referred to hereinafter as an "owner"); and

(ii) Two or more legal organizations referred to in paragraph (a)(2)(i) of this section that have identical owners.

(b) *Special Rules.* For purposes of this section:

(1) An owner must be counted as a client if the investment adviser provides investment advisory services to the owner separate and apart from the investment advisory services provided to the legal organization, Provided, however, that the determination that an owner is a client will not affect the applicability of this section with regard to any other owner;

(2) An owner need not be counted as a client of an investment adviser solely because the investment adviser, on behalf of the legal organization, offers, promotes, or sells interests in the legal organization to the owner, or reports periodically to the owners as a group solely with respect to the performance of or plans for the legal organization's assets or similar matters;

(3) A limited partnership is a client of any general partner or other person acting as investment adviser to the partnership;

(4) Any person for whom an investment adviser provides investment advisory services without compensation need not be counted as a client; and

(5) An investment adviser that has its principal office and place of business outside of the United States must count only clients that are United States residents; an investment adviser that has its principal office and place of business in the United States must count all clients.

(c) *Holding Out.* Any investment adviser relying on this section shall not be deemed to be holding itself out generally to the public as an investment adviser, within the meaning of section 203(b)(3) of the Act, solely because such investment adviser participates in a non-public offering of interests in a limited partnership under the Securities Act of 1933.

SEC Reg. §275.203A-1

Eligibility for SEC registration; switching to or from SEC registration.

Reg. §275.203A-1.

(a) *Eligibility for SEC registration.*

(1) *Threshold for SEC registration—$30 million of assets under management.* If the State where you maintain your principal office and place of business has enacted an investment adviser statute, you are not required to register with the Commission, unless:

(i) You have assets under management of at least $30,000,000, as reported on your Form ADV; or

(ii) You are an investment adviser to an investment company registered under the Investment Company Act of 1940.

(2) *Exemption for investment advisers having between $25 and $30 million of assets under management.* If the State where you maintain your principal office and place of business has enacted an investment adviser statute, you may register with the Commission if you have assets under management of at least $25,000,000 but less than $30,000,000, as reported on your Form ADV. This paragraph (a)(2) shall not apply if:

(i) You are an investment adviser to an investment company registered under the Investment Company Act of 1940; or

(ii) You are eligible for an exemption described in §275.203A-2 of this chapter.

Note to Paragraphs (a)(1) and (a)(2):

Paragraphs (a)(1) and (a)(2) of this section together make SEC registration optional for certain investment advisers that have between $25 and $30 million of assets under management.

(b) *Switching to or from SEC registration.*

(1) *State-registered advisers—switching to SEC registration.* If you are registered with a State securities authority, you must apply for registration with the Commission within 90 days of filing an annual updating amendment to your Form ADV reporting that you have at least $30 million of assets under management.

(2) *SEC-registered advisers—switching to State registration.* If you are registered with the Commission and file an annual updating amendment to your Form ADV reporting that you no longer have $25 million of assets under management (or are not otherwise eligible for SEC registration), you must file Form ADV-W to withdraw your SEC registration within 180 days of your fiscal year end (unless you then have at least $25 million of assets under management or are otherwise eligible for SEC registration). During this period while you are registered with both the Commission and one or more State securities authori-

ties, the Investment Advisers Act of 1940 and applicable State law will apply to your advisory activities.

. . .

SEC Reg. §275.203A-2

Exemptions from Prohibition on SEC Registration.

Reg. §275.203A-2.

The prohibition of section 203A(a) of the Act does not apply to:

. . .

(c) *Investment Advisers Controlling, Controlled By, or Under Common Control with an Investment Adviser Registered with the Commission.* An investment adviser that controls, is controlled by, or is under common control with, an investment adviser eligible to register, and registered with, the Commission ("registered adviser"), provided that the principal office and place of business of the investment adviser is the same as that of the registered adviser. For purposes of this paragraph, control means the power to direct or cause the direction of the management or policies of an investment adviser, whether through ownership of securities, by contract, or otherwise. Any person that directly or indirectly has the right to vote 25 percent or more of the voting securities, or is entitled to 25 percent or more of the profits, of an investment adviser is presumed to control that investment adviser.

. . .

SEC Reg. §275.205-3 (the "heavy hitter rule")

Exemption from the Compensation Prohibition of Section 205(a)(1) for Investment Advisers

Reg. §275.205-3.

(a) *General.* The provisions of section 205(a)(1) of the Act will not be deemed to prohibit an investment adviser from entering into, performing, renewing or extending an investment advisory contract that provides for compensation to the investment adviser on the basis of a share of the capital gains upon, or the capital appreciation of, the funds, or any portion of the funds, of a client, *Provided,* That the client entering into the contract subject to this section is a qualified client, as defined in paragraph (d)(1) of this section.

(b) *Identification of the client.* In the case of a private investment company, as defined in paragraph (d)(3) of this section, an investment company registered under the Investment Company Act of 1940, or a business development company, as defined in section 202(a)(22) of the Act, each equity owner of any such company (except for the investment adviser entering into the contract and any other equity owners not charged a fee on the basis of a share of capital gains or capital appreciation) will be considered a client for purposes of paragraph (a) of this section.

(c) *Transition rule.* An investment adviser that entered into a contract before August 20, 1998 and satisfied the conditions of this section as in effect on the date that the contract was entered into will be considered to satisfy the conditions of this section; *Provided, however,* that this section will apply with respect to any natural person or company who is not a party to the contract prior to and becomes a party to the contract after August 20, 1998.

(d) *Definitions.* For the purposes of this section:

(1) The term qualified client means:

(i) A natural person who or a company that immediately after entering into the contract has at least $750,000 under the management of the investment adviser;

(ii) A natural person who or a company that the investment adviser entering into the contract (and any person acting on his behalf) reasonably believes, immediately prior to entering into the contract, either:

(A) Has a net worth (together, in the case of a natural person, with assets held jointly with a spouse) of more than $1,500,000 at the time the contract is entered into; or

(B) Is a qualified purchaser as defined in section 2(a)(51)(A) of the Investment Company Act of 1940 at the time the contract is entered into; or

(iii) A natural person who immediately prior to entering into the contract is:

(A) An executive officer, director, trustee, general partner, or person serving in a similar capacity, of the investment adviser; or

(B) An employee of the investment adviser (other than an employee performing solely clerical, secretarial or administrative functions with regard to the investment adviser) who, in connection with his or her regular functions or duties, participates in the investment activities of such investment adviser, provided that such employee has been performing such functions and duties for or on behalf of the investment adviser, or substantially similar functions or duties for or on behalf of another company for at least 12 months.

(2) The term company has the same meaning as in section 202(a)(5) of the Act, but does not include a company that is required to be registered under the Investment Company Act of 1940 but is not registered.

(3) The term "private investment company" means a company that would be defined as an investment company under section 3(a) of the Investment

Company Act of 1940 but for the exception provided from that definition by section 3(c)(1) of such Act.

(4) The term "executive officer" means the president, any vice president in charge of a principal business unit, division or function (such as sales, administration or finance), any other officer who performs a policy-making function, or any other person who performs similar policy-making functions, for the investment adviser.

¶2400

Bankruptcy Code

Selected Sections

§101.   Definitions

In this title—

. . .

(5) "claim" means—
   (A) right to payment, whether or not such right is reduced to judgment, liquidated, unliquidated, fixed, contingent, matured, unmatured, disputed, undisputed, legal, equitable, secured, or unsecured; or
   (B) right to an equitable remedy for breach of performance if such breach gives rise to a right to payment, whether or not such right to an equitable remedy is reduced to judgment, fixed, contingent, matured, unmatured, disputed, undisputed, secured, or unsecured;

. . .

(32) "insolvent" means—
   (A) with reference to an entity other than a partnership and a municipality, financial condition such that the sum of such entity's debts is greater than all of such entity's property, at a fair valuation, exclusive of—
      (i) property transferred, concealed, or removed with intent to hinder, delay, or defraud such entity's creditors; and
      (ii) property that may be exempted from property of the estate under section 522 of this title;

(B) with reference to a partnership, financial condition such that the sum of such partnership's debts is greater than the aggregate of, at a fair valuation—

(i) all of such partnership's property, exclusive of property of the kind specified in subparagraph (A)(i) of this paragraph; and

(ii) the sum of the excess of the value of each general partner's nonpartnership property, exclusive of property of the kind specified in subparagraph (A) of this paragraph, over such partner's nonpartnership debts; and

(C) with reference to a municipality, financial condition such that the municipality is—

(i) generally not paying its debts as they become due unless such debts are the subject of a bona fide dispute; or

(ii) unable to pay its debts as they become due;

. . .

§501.   *Filing of proofs of claims or interests*

(a) A creditor or an indenture trustee may file a proof of claim. An equity security holder may file a proof of interest.

. . .

§544.   *Trustee as lien creditor and as successor to certain creditors and purchasers*

. . .

(b)(1) Except as provided in paragraph (2), the trustee may avoid any transfer of an interest of the debtor in property or any obligation incurred by the debtor that is voidable under applicable law by a creditor holding an unsecured claim that is allowable under section 502 of this title or that is not allowable only under section 502(e) of this title.

. . .

§548.   *Fraudulent transfers and obligations*

(a)(1) The trustee may avoid any transfer of an interest of the debtor in property, or any obligation incurred by the debtor, that was made or incurred on or within one year before the date of the filing of the petition, if the debtor voluntarily or involuntarily—

(A) made such transfer or incurred such obligation with actual intent to hinder, delay, or defraud any entity to which the debtor was or became, on or after the date that such transfer was made or such obligation was incurred, indebted; or

(B)(i) received less than a reasonably equivalent value in exchange for such transfer or obligation; and

(ii)(I) was insolvent on the date that such transfer was made or such obligation was incurred, or became insolvent as a result of such transfer or obligation;

(II) was engaged in business or a transaction, or was about to engage in business or a transaction, for which any property remaining with the debtor was an unreasonably small capital; or

(III) intended to incur, or believed that the debtor would incur, debts that would be beyond the debtor's ability to pay as such debts matured.

. . .

(b) The trustee of a partnership debtor may avoid any transfer of an interest of the debtor in property, or any obligation incurred by the debtor, that was made or incurred on or within one year before the date of the filing of the petition, to a general partner in the debtor, if the debtor was insolvent on the date such transfer was made or such obligation was incurred, or became insolvent as a result of such transfer or obligation.

(c) Except to the extent that a transfer or obligation voidable under this section is voidable under section 544, 545, or 547 of this title, a transferee or obligee of such a transfer or obligation that takes for value and in good faith has a lien on or may retain any interest transferred or may enforce any obligation incurred, as the case may be, to the extent that such transferee or obligee gave value to the debtor in exchange for such transfer or obligation.

(d)(1) For the purposes of this section, a transfer is made when such transfer is so perfected that a bona fide purchaser from the debtor against whom applicable law permits such transfer to be perfected cannot acquire an interest in the property transferred that is superior to the interest in such property of the transferee, but if such transfer is not so perfected before the commencement of that case, such transfer is made immediately before the date of the filing of the petition.

(2) In this section—

(A) "value" means property, or satisfaction or securing of a present or an antecedent debt of the debtor, but does not include an unperformed promise to furnish support to the debtor or to a relative of the debtor;

. . .

§550. *Liability of transferee of avoided transfer*

(a) Except as otherwise provided in this section, to the extent that a transfer is avoided under section 544, 545, 547, 548, 549, 553(b), or 724(a) of this title, the trustee may recover, for the benefit of the estate, the property transferred, or, if the court so orders, the value of such property, from—

(1) the initial transferee of such transfer or the entity for whose benefit such transfer was made; or

(2) any immediate or mediate transferee of such initial transferee.

(b) The trustee may not recover under section (a)(2) of this section from—

(1) a transferee that takes for value, including satisfaction or securing of a present or antecedent debt, in good faith, and without knowledge of the voidability of the transfer avoided; or

(2) any immediate or mediate good faith transferee of such transferee.

(c) If a transfer made between 90 days and one year before the filing of the petition—

(1) is avoided under section 547(b) of this title; and

(2) was made for the benefit of a creditor that at the time of such transfer was an insider;

the trustee may not recover under subsection (a) from a transferee that is not an insider.

(d) The trustee is entitled to only a single satisfaction under subsection (a) of this section.

(e)(1) A good faith transferee from whom the trustee may recover under subsection (a) of this section has a lien on the property recovered to secure the lessor of—

(A) the cost, to such transferee, of any improvement made after the transfer, less the amount of any profit realized by or accruing to such transferee from such property; and

(B) any increase in the value of such property as a result of such improvement, of the property transferred.

(2) In this subsection, "improvement" includes—

(A) physical additions or changes to the property transferred;

(B) repairs to such property;

(C) payment of any tax on such property;

(D) payment of any debt secured by a lien on such property that is superior or equal to the rights of the trustee; and

(E) preservation of such property.

(f) An action or proceeding under this section may not be commenced after the earlier of—

(1) one year after the avoidance of the transfer on account of which recovery under this section is sought; or

(2) the time the case is closed or dismissed.

§1125. *Postpetition disclosure and solicitation*

(a) In this section—

(1) "adequate information" means information of a kind, and in sufficient detail, as far as is reasonably practicable in light of the nature and history of the debtor and the condition of the debtor's books and records, that would enable a hypothetical reasonable investor typical of holders of claims or interests of the relevant class to make an informed judgment about the plan, but adequate information need not include such information about any other possible or proposed plan; and

(2) "investor typical of holders of claims or interests of the relevant class" means investor having—

(A) a claim or interest of the relevant class;

(B) such a relationship with the debtor as the holders of other claims or interest of such class generally have; and

(C) such ability to obtain such information from sources other than the disclosure required by this section as holders of claims or interest in such class generally have.

(b) An acceptance or rejection of a plan may not be solicited after the commencement of the case under this title from a holder of a claim or interest with respect to such claim or interest, unless, at the time of or before such solicitation, there is transmitted to such holder the plan or a summary of the plan, and a written disclosure statement approved, after notice and a hearing, by the court as containing adequate information. The court may approve a disclosure statement without a valuation of the debtor or an appraisal of the debtor's assets.

(c) The same disclosure statement shall be transmitted to each holder of a claim or interest of a particular class, but there may be transmitted different disclosure statements, differing in amount, detail, or kind of information, as between classes.

(d) Whether a disclosure statement required under subsection (b) of this section contains adequate information is not governed by any otherwise applicable non-bankruptcy law, rule, or regulation, but an agency or official whose duty is to administer or enforce such a law, rule, or regulation may be heard on the issue of whether a disclosure statement contains adequate information. Such an agency or official may not appeal from, or otherwise seek review of, an order approving a disclosure statement.

(e) A person that solicits acceptance or rejection of a plan, in good faith and in compliance with the applicable provisions of this title, or that participates, in good faith and in compliance with the applicable provisions of this title, in the offer, issuance, sale, or purchase of a security, offered or sold under the plan, of the debtor, of an affiliate participating in a joint plan with the debtor, or of a newly organized successor to the debtor under the plan, is not liable, on account of such solicitation or participation, for violation of any applicable law, rule, or regulation governing solicitation of acceptance or rejection of a plan or the offer, issuance, sale, or purchase of securities.

(f) Notwithstanding subsection (b), in a case in which the debtor has elected under section 1121(e) to be considered a small business—

(1) the court may conditionally approve a disclosure statement subject to final approval after notice and a hearing;

(2) acceptances and rejections of a plan may be solicited based on a conditionally approved disclosure statement as long as the debtor provides adequate information to each holder of a claim or interest that is solicited, but a conditionally approved disclosure statement shall be mailed at least 10 days prior to the date of the hearing on confirmation of the plan; and

(3) a hearing on the disclosure statement may be combined with a hearing on confirmation of a plan.

§1145.   *Exemption from securities laws*

(a) Except with respect to an entity that is an underwriter as defined in subsection (b) of this section, section 5 of the Securities Act of 1933 and any State or local law requiring registration for offer or sale of a security or registration or licensing of an issuer of, underwriter of, or broker or dealer in, a security do not apply to—

(1) the offer or sale under a plan of a security of the debtor, of an affiliate participating in a joint plan with the debtor, or of a successor to the debtor under the plan—

(A) in exchange for a claim against, an interest in, or a claim for an administrative expense in the case concerning, the debtor or such affiliate; or

(B) principally in such exchange and partly for cash or property;

(2) the offer of a security through any warrant, option, right to subscribe, or conversion privilege that was sold in the manner specified in paragraph (1) of this subsection, or the sale of a security upon the exercise of such a warrant, option, right, or privilege;

. . .

(b)(1) Except as provided in paragraph (2) of this subsection and except with respect to ordinary trading transactions of an entity that is not an issuer, an entity is an underwriter under section 2(11) of the Securities Act of 1933, if such entity—

(A) purchases a claim against, interest in, or claim for an administrative expense in the case concerning, the debtor, if such purchase is with a view to distribution of any security received or to be received in exchange for such a claim or interest;

(B) offers to sell securities offered or sold under the plan for the holders of such securities;

(C) offers to buy securities offered or sold under the plan from the holders of such securities, if such offer to buy is—

(i) with a view to distribution of such securities; and

(ii) under an agreement made in connection with the plan, with the consummation of the plan, or with the offer or sale of securities under the plan; or

(D) is an issuer, as used in such section 2(11), with respect to such securities.

(2) An entity is not an underwriter under section 2(11) of the Securities Act of 1933 or under paragraph (1) of this subsection with respect to an agreement that provides only for—

(A)(i) the matching or combining of fractional interests in securities offered or sold under the plan into whole interests; or

(ii) the purchase or sale of such fractional interests from or to entities receiving such fractional interests under the plan; or

(B) the purchase or sale for such entities of such fractional or whole interests as are necessary to adjust for any remaining fractional interests after such matching.

(3) An entity other than an entity of the kind specified in paragraph (1) of this subsection is not an underwriter under section 2(11) of the Securities Act of 1933 with respect to any securities offered or sold to such entity in the manner specified in subsection (a)(1) of this section.

(c) An offer or sale of securities of the kind and in the manner specified under subsection (a)(1) of this section is deemed to be a public offering.

. . .

¶2500

State Fraudulent Conveyance Statutes

EXAMPLES OF STATUTE OF ELIZABETH STATES

Virginia

§55-81. Voluntary gifts, etc., void as to prior creditors

Every gift, conveyance, assignment, transfer or charge which is not upon consideration deemed valuable in law . . . by an insolvent transferor, or by a transferor who is thereby rendered insolvent, shall be void as to creditors whose debts shall have been contracted at the time it was made, but shall not, on that account merely, be void as to creditors whose debts shall have been contracted or as to purchasers who shall have purchased after it was made. Even though it is decreed to be void as to a prior creditor, because voluntary . . . , it shall not, for that cause, be decreed to be void as to subsequent creditors or purchasers.

South Carolina

§27-23-10. Conveyances to defraud creditors . . .

(A) Every gift, . . . transfer, and conveyance of . . . for any intent or purpose to delay, hinder, or defraud creditors and others of their just and lawful actions, suits, debts, accounts, damages, penalties, and forfeitures must be deemed and taken (only as against that person or persons, his . . . successors, . . . whose actions, suits, debts, accounts, damages, penalties, and forfeitures by guileful, covinous, or fraudulent devices and practices . . . might be in any ways disturbed, hindered, delayed, or defrauded) to be clearly and utterly void, frustrate and of no effect. . . .

UNIFORM FRAUDULENT CONVEYANCE ACT

§1. Definition of Terms

In this act "Assets" of a debtor means property not exempt from liability for his debts. To the extent that any property is liable for any debts of the debtor, such property shall be included in his assets.

"Conveyance" includes every payment of money, assignment, release, transfer, lease, mortgage or pledge of tangible or intangible property, and also the creation of any lien or incumbrance.

"Creditor" is a person having any claim, whether matured or unmatured, liquidated or unliquidated, absolute, fixed or contingent.

"Debt" includes any legal liability, whether matured or unmatured, liquidated or unliquidated, absolute, fixed or contingent.

§2. Insolvency

(1) A person is insolvent when the present fair salable value of his assets is less than the amount that will be required to pay his probable liability on his existing debts as they become absolute and matured.

(2) In determining whether a partnership is insolvent there shall be added to the partnership property the present fair salable value of the separate assets of each general partner in excess of the amount probably sufficient to meet the claims of his separate creditors, and also the amount of any unpaid subscription to the partnership of each limited partner, provided the present fair salable value of the assets of such limited partner is probably sufficient to pay his debts, including such unpaid subscription.

§3. Fair Consideration

Fair consideration is given for property, or obligation,
(a) When in exchange for such property, or obligation, as a fair equivalent therefor, and in good faith, property is conveyed or an antecedent debt is satisfied, or
(b) When such property, or obligation is received in good faith to secure a present advance or antecedent debt in amount not disproportionately small as compared with the value of the property, or obligation obtained.

§4. Conveyances by Insolvent

Every conveyance made and every obligation incurred by a person who is or will be thereby rendered insolvent is fraudulent as to creditors without regard to his actual intent if the conveyance is made or the obligation is incurred without a fair consideration.

§5. Conveyances by Persons in Business

Every conveyance made without fair consideration when the person making it is engaged or is about to engage in a business or transaction for which the property remaining in his hands after the conveyance is an unreasonably small capital, is fraudulent as to creditors and as to other persons who become creditors during the continuance of such business or transaction without regard to his actual intent.

§6. Conveyances by a Person About to Incur Debts

Every conveyance made and every obligation incurred without fair consideration when the person making the conveyance or entering into the obligation intends or believes that he will incur debts beyond his ability to pay as they mature, is fraudulent as to both present and future creditors.

§7. Conveyance Made With Intent to Defraud

Every conveyance made and every obligation incurred with actual intent, as distinguished from intent presumed in law, to hinder, delay, or defraud either present or future creditors, is fraudulent as to both present and future creditors.

§8. Conveyance of Partnership Property

Every conveyance of partnership property and every partnership obligation incurred when the partnership is or will be thereby rendered insolvent, is fraudulent as to partnership creditors, if the conveyance is made or obligation is incurred,

    (a) To a partner, whether with or without a promise by him to pay partnership debts, or

    (b) To a person not a partner without fair consideration to the partnership as distinguished from consideration to the individual partners.

§9. Rights of Creditors Whose Claims Have Matured

(1) Where a conveyance or obligation is fraudulent as to a creditor, such creditor, when his claim has matured, may, as against any person except a purchaser for fair consideration without knowledge of the fraud at the time of the purchase, or one who has derived title immediately or mediately from such a purchaser,

    (a) Have the conveyance set aside or obligation annulled to the extent necessary to satisfy his claim, or

    (b) Disregard the conveyance and attach or levy execution upon the property conveyed.

(2) A purchaser who without actual fraudulent intent has given less than a fair consideration for the conveyance or obligation, may retain the property or obligation as security for repayment.

§10. Rights of Creditors Whose Claims Have Not Matured

Where a conveyance made or obligation incurred is fraudulent as to a creditor whose claim has not matured he may proceed in a court of competent jurisdiction against any person against whom he could have proceeded had his claim matured, and the court may,

(a) Restrain the defendant from disposing of his property,
(b) Appoint a receiver to take charge of the property,
(c) Set aside the conveyance or annul the obligation, or
(d) Make any order which the circumstances of the case may require.

§11. Cases Not Provided For in Act

In any case not provided for in this Act the rules of law and equity including the law merchant, and in particular the rules relating to the law of principal and agent, and the effect of fraud, misrepresentation duress or coercion, mistake, bankruptcy or other invalidating cause shall govern.

§12. Construction of Act

This act shall be so interpreted and construed as to effectuate its general purpose to make uniform the law of those states which enact it.

. . .

UNIFORM FRAUDULENT TRANSFER ACT

§1. Definitions

As used in this [Act]:
(1) "Affiliate" means:
(i) a person who directly or indirectly owns, controls, or holds with power to vote, 20 percent or more of the outstanding voting securities of the debtor, other than a person who holds the securities,

(A) as a fiduciary or agent without sole discretionary power to vote the securities; or

(B) solely to secure a debt, if the person has not exercised the power to vote;

(ii) a corporation 20 percent or more of whose outstanding voting securities are directly or indirectly owned, controlled, or held with power to vote, by the debtor or a person who directly or indirectly owns, controls, or holds, with power to vote, 20 percent or more of the outstanding voting securities of the debtor, other than a person who holds the securities,

(A) as a fiduciary or agent without sole power to vote the securities; or

(B) solely to secure a debt, if the person has not in fact exercised the power to vote;

(iii) a person whose business is operated by the debtor under a lease or other agreement, or a person substantially all of whose assets are controlled by the debtor; or

(iv) a person who operates the debtor's business under a lease or other agreement or controls substantially all of the debtor's assets.

(2) "Asset" means property of a debtor, but the term does not include:

(i) property to the extent it is encumbered by a valid lien;

(ii) property to the extent it is generally exempt under nonbankruptcy law; or

(iii) an interest in property held in tenancy by the entireties to the extent it is not subject to process by a creditor holding a claim against only one tenant.

(3) "Claim" means a right to payment, whether or not the right is reduced to judgment, liquidated, unliquidated, fixed, contingent, matured, unmatured, disputed, undisputed, legal, equitable, secured, or unsecured.

(4) "Creditor" means a person who has a claim.

(5) "Debt" means liability on a claim.

(6) "Debtor" means a person who is liable on a claim.

(7) "Insider" includes:

(i) if the debtor is an individual,

(A) a relative of the debtor or of a general partner of the debtor;

(B) a partnership in which the debtor is a general partner;

(C) a general partner in a partnership described in clause (B); or

(D) a corporation of which the debtor is a director, officer, or person in control;

(ii) if the debtor is a corporation,

(A) a director of the debtor;

(B) an officer of the debtor;

(C) a person in control of the debtor;

(D) a partnership in which the debtor is a general partner;

(E) a general partner in a partnership described in clause (D); or

(F) a relative of a general partner, director, officer, or person in control of the debtor;

(iii) if the debtor is a partnership,

(A) a general partner in the debtor;

(B) a relative of a general partner in, a general partner of, or a person in control of the debtor;

(C) another partnership in which the debtor is a general partner;

(D) a general partner in a partnership described in clause (C); or

(E) a person in control of the debtor;

(iv) an affiliate, or an insider of an affiliate as if the affiliate were the debtor; and

(v) a managing agent of the debtor.

(8) "Lien" means a charge against or an interest in property to secure payment of a debt or performance of an obligation, and includes a security interest created by agreement, a judicial lien obtained by legal or equitable process or proceedings, a common-law lien, or a statutory lien.

(9) "Person" means an individual, partnership, corporation, association, organization, government or governmental subdivision or agency, business trust, estate, trust, or any other legal or commercial entity.

(10) "Property" means anything that may be the subject of ownership.

(11) "Relative" means an individual related by consanguinity within the third degree as determined by the common law, a spouse, or an individual related to a spouse within the third degree as so determined, and includes an individual in an adoptive relationship within the third degree.

(12) "Transfer" means every mode, direct or indirect, absolute or conditional, voluntary or involuntary, of disposing of or parting with an asset or an interest in an asset, and includes payment of money, release, lease, and creation of a lien or other encumbrance.

(13) "Valid lien" means a lien that is effective against the holder of a judicial lien subsequently obtained by legal or equitable process or proceedings.

§2. Insolvency

(a) A debtor is insolvent if the sum of the debtor's debts is greater than all of the debtor's assets at a fair valuation.

(b) A debtor who is generally not paying his [or her] debts as they become due is presumed to be insolvent.

(c) A partnership is insolvent under subsection (a) if the sum of the partnership's debts is greater than the aggregate, at a fair valuation, of all of the partnership's assets and the sum of the excess of the value of each general partner's nonpartnership assets over the partner's nonpartnership debts.

(d) Assets under this section do not include property that has been transferred, concealed, or removed with intent to hinder, delay, or defraud creditors or that has been transferred in a manner making the transfer voidable under this [Act].

(e) Debts under this section do not include an obligation to the extent it is secured by a valid lien on property of the debtor not included as an asset.

§3. Value

(a) Value is given for a transfer or an obligation if, in exchange for the transfer or obligation, property is transferred or an antecedent debt is secured or satisfied, but value does not include an unperformed promise made otherwise than in the ordinary course of the promisor's business to furnish support to the debtor or another person.

(b) For the purposes of Sections 4(a)(2) and 5, a person gives a reasonably equivalent value if the person acquires an interest of the debtor in an asset pursuant to a regularly conducted, noncollusive foreclosure sale or execution of a power of sale for the acquisition or disposition of the interest of the debtor upon default under a mortgage, deed of trust, or security agreement.

(c) A transfer is made for present value if the exchange between the debtor and the transferee is intended by them to be contemporaneous and is in fact substantially contemporaneous.

§4. Transfers Fraudulent as to Present and Future Creditors

(a) A transfer made or obligation incurred by a debtor is fraudulent as to a creditor, whether the creditor's claim arose before or after the transfer was made or the obligation was incurred, if the debtor made the transfer or incurred the obligation:

(1) with actual intent to hinder, delay, or defraud any creditor of the debtor; or

(2) without receiving a reasonably equivalent value in exchange for the transfer or obligation, and the debtor:

(i) was engaged or was about to engage in a business or a transaction for which the remaining assets of the debtor were unreasonably small in relation to the business or transaction; or

(ii) intended to incur, or believed or reasonably should have believed that he [or she] would incur, debts beyond his [or her] ability to pay as they became due.

(b) In determining actual intent under subsection (a)(1), consideration may be given, among other factors, to whether:

(1) the transfer or obligation was to an insider;

(2) the debtor retained possession or control of the property transferred after the transfer;

(3) the transfer or obligation was disclosed or concealed;

(4) before the transfer was made or obligation was incurred, the debtor had been sued or threatened with suit;

(5) the transfer was of substantially all the debtor's assets;

(6) the debtor absconded;

(7) the debtor removed or concealed assets;

(8) the value of the consideration received by the debtor was reasonably equivalent to the value of the asset transferred or the amount of the obligation incurred;

(9) the debtor was insolvent or became insolvent shortly after the transfer was made or the obligation was incurred;

(10) the transfer occurred shortly before or shortly after a substantial debt was incurred; and

(11) the debtor transferred the essential assets of the business to a lienor who transferred the assets to an insider of the debtor.

§5. Transfers Fraudulent as to Present Creditors

(a) A transfer made or obligation incurred by a debtor is fraudulent as to a creditor whose claim arose before the transfer was made or the obligation was incurred if the debtor made the transfer or incurred the obligation without receiving a reasonably equivalent value in exchange for the transfer or obligation and the debtor was insolvent at that time or the debtor became insolvent as a result of the transfer or obligation.

(b) A transfer made by a debtor is fraudulent as to a creditor whose claim arose before the transfer was made if the transfer was made to an insider for an antecedent debt, the debtor was insolvent at that time, and the insider had reasonable cause to believe that the debtor was insolvent.

§6. When Transfer is Made or Obligation is Incurred

For the purposes of this [Act]:

(1) a transfer is made:

(i) with respect to an asset that is real property other than a fixture, but including the interest of a seller or purchaser under a contract for the sale of the asset, when the transfer is so far perfected that a good-faith purchaser of the asset from the debtor against whom applicable law permits the transfer to be perfected cannot acquire an interest in the asset that is superior to the interest of the transferee; and

(ii) with respect to an asset that is not real property or that is a fixture, when the transfer is so far perfected that a creditor on a simple contract cannot acquire a judicial lien otherwise than under this [Act] that is superior to the interest of the transferee;

(2) if applicable law permits the transfer to be perfected as provided in paragraph (1) and the transfer is not so perfected before the commencement of an action for relief under this [Act], the transfer is deemed made immediately before the commencement of the action;

(3) if applicable law does not permit the transfer to be perfected as provided in paragraph (1), the transfer is made when it becomes effective between the debtor and the transferee;

(4) a transfer is not made until the debtor has acquired rights in the asset transferred;

(5) an obligation is incurred:

(i) if oral, when it becomes effective between the parties; or

(ii) if evidenced by a writing, when the writing executed by the obligor is delivered to or for the benefit of the obligee.

§7. Remedies of Creditors

(a) In an action for relief against a transfer or obligation under this [Act], a creditor, subject to the limitations in Section 8, may obtain:

(1) avoidance of the transfer or obligation to the extent necessary to satisfy the creditor's claim;

[(2) an attachment or other provisional remedy against the asset transferred or other property of the transferee in accordance with the procedure prescribed by [ ];]

(3) subject to applicable principles of equity and in accordance with applicable rules of civil procedure,

(i) an injunction against further disposition by the debtor or a transferee, or both, of the asset transferred or of other property;

(ii) appointment of a receiver to take charge of the asset transferred or of other property of the transferee; or

(iii) any other relief the circumstances may require.

(b) If a creditor has obtained a judgment on a claim against the debtor, the creditor, if the court so orders, may levy execution on the asset transferred or its proceeds.

§8. Defenses, Liability, and Protection of Transferee

(a) A transfer or obligation is not voidable under Section 4(a)(1) against a person who took in good faith and for a reasonably equivalent value or against any subsequent transferee or obligee.

(b) Except as otherwise provided in this section, to the extent a transfer is voidable in an action by a creditor under Section 7(a)(1), the creditor may recover judgment for the value of the asset transferred, as adjusted under subsection (c), or the amount necessary to satisfy the creditor's claim, whichever is less. The judgment may be entered against:

(1) the first transferee of the asset or the person for whose benefit the transfer was made; or

(2) any subsequent transferee other than a good faith transferee who took for value or from any subsequent transferee.

(c) If the judgment under subsection (b) is based upon the value of the asset transferred, the judgment must be for an amount equal to the value of the asset at the time of the transfer, subject to adjustment as the equities may require.

(d) Notwithstanding voidability of a transfer or an obligation under this [Act], a good-faith transferee or obligee is entitled, to the extent of the value given the debtor for the transfer or obligation, to

(1) a lien on or a right to retain any interest in the asset transferred;

(2) enforcement of any obligation incurred; or

(3) a reduction in the amount of the liability on the judgment.

(e) A transfer is not voidable under Section 4(a)(2) or Section 5 if the transfer results from:

(1) termination of a lease upon default by the debtor when the termination is pursuant to the lease and applicable law; or

(2) enforcement of a security interest in compliance with Article 9 of the Uniform Commercial Code.

(f) A transfer is not voidable under Section 5(b):

(1) to the extent the insider gave new value to or for the benefit of the debtor after the transfer was made unless the new value was secured by a valid lien;

(2) if made in the ordinary course of business or financial affairs of the debtor and the insider; or

(3) if made pursuant to a good-faith effort to rehabilitate the debtor and the transfer secured present value given for that purpose as well as an antecedent debt of the debtor.

§9. Extinguishment of [Claim for Relief] [Cause of Action]

A [claim for relief] [cause of action] with respect to a fraudulent transfer or obligation under this [Act] is extinguished unless action is brought:

(a) under Section 4(a)(1), within 4 years after the transfer was made or the obligation was incurred or, if later, within one year after the transfer or obligation was or could reasonably have been discovered by the claimant;

(b) under Section 4(a)(2) or 5(a), within 4 years after the transfer was made or the obligation was incurred; or

(c) under Section 5(b), within one year after the transfer was made or the obligation was incurred.

§10. Supplementary Provisions

Unless displaced by the provisions of this [Act], the principles of law and equity, including the law merchant and the law relating to principal and agent, estoppel, laches, fraud, misrepresentation, duress, coercion, mistake, insolvency, or other validating or invalidating cause, supplement its provisions.

¶2600

Delaware Corporate, Partnership, and LLC Statutes

DELAWARE GENERAL CORPORATION LAW

Selected Sections

§102.   Contents of certificate of incorporation.

(a) The certificate of incorporation shall set forth:

. . .

(4) If the corporation is to be authorized to issue only 1 class of stock, the total number of shares of stock which the corporation shall have authority to issue and the par value of each of such shares, or a statement that all such shares are to be without par value. If the corporation is to be authorized to issue more than 1 class of stock, the certificate of incorporation shall set forth the total number of shares of all classes of stock which the corporation shall have authority to issue and the number of shares of each class and shall specify each class the shares of which are to be without par value and each class the shares of which are to have par value and the par value of the shares of each such class. The certificate of incorporation shall also set forth a statement of the designations and the powers, preferences and rights, and the qualifications, limitations or restrictions thereof, which are permitted by §151 of this title in respect of any class or classes of stock or any series of any class of stock of the corporation and the fixing of which by the certificate of incorporation is desired, and an express grant of such authority as it may then be desired to grant to the board of directors to fix by resolution or resolutions any thereof that may be desired but which shall not be fixed by the certificate of incorporation.

. . .

(b) In addition to the matters required to be set forth in the certificate of incorporation by subsection (a) of this section, the certificate of incorporation may also contain any or all of the following matters:

. . .

(4) Provisions requiring for any corporate action, the vote of a larger portion of the stock or of any class or series thereof, or of any other securities having voting power, or a larger number of the directors, than is required by this chapter;

. . .

(6) A provision imposing personal liability for the debts of the corporation on its stockholders or members to a specified extent and upon specified conditions; otherwise, the stockholders or members of a corporation shall not be personally liable for the payment of the corporation's debts except as they may be liable by reason of their own conduct or acts;

(7) A provision eliminating or limiting the personal liability of a director to the corporation or its stockholders for monetary damages for breach of fiduciary duty as a director, provided that such provision shall not eliminate or limit the liability of a director: (i) for any breach of the director's duty of loyalty to the corporation or its stockholders; (ii) for acts or omissions not in good faith or which involve intentional misconduct or a knowing violation of law; (iii) under §174 of this title; or (iv) for any transaction from which the director derived an improper personal benefit. No such provision shall eliminate or limit the liability of a director for any act or omission occurring prior to the date when such provision becomes effective. All references in this paragraph to a director shall also be deemed to refer . . . to such other person or persons, if any, who, pursuant to a provision of the certificate of incorporation in accordance with §141(a) of this title, exercise or perform any of the powers or duties otherwise conferred or imposed upon the board of directors by this title.

. . .

§145.   Indemnification of officers, directors, employees and agents; insurance.

(a) A corporation shall have power to indemnify any person who was or is a party or is threatened to be made a party to any threatened, pending or completed action, suit or proceeding, whether civil, criminal, administrative or investigative (other than an action by or in the right of the corporation) by reason of the fact that the person is or was a director, officer, employee or agent of the corporation, or is or was serving at the request of the corporation as a director, officer, employee or agent of another corporation, partnership, joint venture, trust or other enterprise, against expenses (including attorneys' fees), judgments, fines and amounts paid in settlement actually and reasonably incurred by the person in connection with such action, suit or proceeding if the person acted in good faith and in a manner the person reasonably believed to be in or not opposed to the best interests of the corporation, and, with respect to any criminal action or proceeding, had no reasonable cause to believe the person's conduct was unlawful. The termination of any action, suit or proceeding by judgment, order, settlement, conviction, or upon a plea of nolo contendere or its equivalent, shall not, of itself, create a presumption that the person did not act in good faith and in a manner which the person reasonably believed to be in or not opposed to the best interests of the corporation, and, with respect to any criminal action or proceeding, had reasonable cause to believe that the person's conduct was unlawful.

(b) A corporation shall have power to indemnify any person who was or is a party or is threatened to be made a party to any threatened, pending or completed action or suit by or in the right of the corporation to procure a judgment in its favor by reason of the fact that the person is or was a director, officer, employee or agent of the corporation, or is or was serving at the request of the corporation as a director, officer, employee or agent of another corporation, partnership, joint venture, trust or other enterprise against expenses (including attorneys' fees) actually and reasonably incurred by the person in connection with the defense or settlement of such action or suit if the person acted in good faith and in a manner the person reasonably believed to be in or not opposed to the best interests of the corporation and except that no indemnification shall be made in respect of any claim, issue or matter as to which such person shall have been adjudged to be liable to the corporation unless and only to the extent that the Court of Chancery or the court in which such action or suit was brought shall determine upon application that, despite the adjudication of liability but in view of all the circumstances of the case, such person is fairly and reasonably entitled to indemnity for such expenses which the Court of Chancery or such other court shall deem proper.

(c) To the extent that a present or former director or officer of a corporation has been successful on the merits or otherwise in defense of any action, suit or proceeding referred to in subsections (a) and (b) of this section, or in defense of any claim, issue or matter therein, such person shall be indemnified against expenses (including attorneys' fees) actually and reasonably incurred by such person in connection therewith.

. . .

(f) The indemnification and advancement of expenses provided by, or granted pursuant to, the other subsections of this section shall not be deemed exclusive of any other rights to which those seeking indemnification or advancement of expenses may be entitled under any bylaw, agreement, vote of stockholders or disinterested directors or otherwise, both as to action in such person's official capacity and as to action in another capacity while holding such office.

(g) A corporation shall have power to purchase and maintain insurance on behalf of any person who is or was a director, officer, employee or agent of the corporation, or is or was serving at the request of the corporation as a director, officer, employee or agent of another corporation, partnership, joint venture, trust or other enterprise against any liability asserted against such person and incurred by such person in any such capacity, or arising out of such person's status as such, whether or not the corporation would have the power to indemnify such person against such liability under this section.

. . .

(j) The indemnification and advancement of expenses provided by, or granted pursuant to, this section shall, unless otherwise provided when authorized or ratified, continue as to a person who has ceased to be a director, officer, employee or agent and shall inure to the benefit of the heirs, executors and administrators of such a person.

§154.   Determination of amount of capital; capital, surplus and net assets defined.

Any corporation may, by resolution of its board of directors, determine that only a part of the consideration which shall be received by the corporation for any of the shares of its capital stock which it shall issue from time to time shall be capital; but, in case any of the shares issued shall be shares having a par value, the amount of the part of such consideration so determined to be capital shall be in excess of the aggregate par value of the shares issued for such consideration having a par value, unless all the shares issued shall be shares having a par value, in which case the amount of the part of such consideration so determined to be capital need be only equal to the aggregate par value of such shares. In each such case the board of directors shall specify in dollars the part of such consideration which shall be capital. If the board of directors shall not have determined (1) at the time of issue of any shares of the capital stock of the corporation issued for cash or (2) within 60 days after the issue of any shares of the capital stock of the corporation issued for property other than cash what part of the consideration for such shares shall be capital, the capital of the corporation in respect of such shares shall be an amount equal to the aggregate par value of such shares having a par value, plus the amount of the consideration for such shares without par value. The amount of the consideration so determined to be capital in respect of any shares without par value shall be the stated capital of such shares. The capital of the corporation may be increased from time to time by resolution of the board of directors directing that a portion of the net assets of the corporation in excess of the amount so determined to be capital be transferred to the capital account. The board of directors may direct that the portion of such net assets so transferred shall be treated as capital in respect of any shares of the corporation of any designated class or classes. The excess, if any, at any given time, of the net assets of the corporation over the amount so determined to be capital shall be surplus. Net assets means the amount by which total assets exceed total liabilities. Capital and surplus are not liabilities for this purpose.

§160. **Corporation's powers respecting ownership, voting, etc., of its own stock; rights of stock called for redemption.**

(a) Every corporation may purchase, redeem, receive, take or otherwise acquire, own and hold, sell, lend, exchange, transfer or otherwise dispose of, pledge, use and otherwise deal in and with its own shares; provided, however, that no corporation shall:

(1) Purchase or redeem its own shares of capital stock for cash or other property when the capital of the corporation is impaired or when such purchase or redemption would cause any impairment of the capital of the corporation, except that a corporation may purchase or redeem out of capital any of its own shares which are entitled upon any distribution of its assets, whether by dividend or in liquidation, to a preference over another class or series of its stock or, if no shares entitled to such a preference are outstanding, any of its own shares, if such shares will be retired upon their acquisition and the capital of the corporation reduced in accordance with §§243 and 244 of this title. Nothing in this subsection shall invalidate or otherwise affect a note, debenture or other obligation of a corporation given by it as consideration for its acquisition by purchase, redemption or exchange of its shares of stock if at the time such note, debenture or obligation was delivered by the corporation its capital was not then impaired or did not thereby become impaired;

(2) Purchase, for more than the price at which they may then be redeemed, any of its shares which are redeemable at the option of the corporation; or

(3) Redeem any of its shares unless their redemption is authorized by subsection (b) of §151 of this title and then only in accordance with such section and the certificate of incorporation.

(b) Nothing in this section limits or affects a corporation's right to resell any of its shares theretofore purchased or redeemed out of surplus and which have not been retired, for such consideration as shall be fixed by the board of directors.

(c) Shares of its own capital stock belonging to the corporation or to another corporation, if a majority of the shares entitled to vote in the election of directors of such other corporation is held, directly or indirectly, by the corporation, shall neither be entitled to vote nor be counted for quorum purposes. Nothing in this section shall be construed as limiting the right of any corporation to vote stock, including but not limited to its own stock, held by it in a fiduciary capacity.

(d) Shares which have been called for redemption shall not be deemed to be outstanding shares for the purpose of voting or determining the total number of shares entitled to vote on any matter on and after the date on which written notice of redemption has been sent to holders thereof and a sum sufficient to redeem such shares has been irrevocably deposited or set aside to pay the redemption price to the holders of the shares upon surrender of certificates therefor.

§170. **Dividends; payment; ...**

(a) The directors of every corporation, subject to any restrictions contained in its certificate of incorporation, may declare and pay dividends upon the shares of its capital stock ... either (1) out of its surplus, as defined in and computed in accordance with §§154 and 244 of this title, or (2) in case there shall be no such surplus, out of its net profits for the fiscal year in which the dividend is declared and/or the preceding fiscal year. If the capital of the corporation, computed in accordance with §§154 and 244 of this title, shall have been diminished by depreciation in the value of its property, or by losses, or otherwise, to an amount less than the aggregate amount of the capital represented by the issued and outstanding stock of all classes having a preference upon the distribution of assets, the directors of such corporation shall not declare and pay out of such net profits any dividends upon any shares of any classes of its capital stock until the deficiency in the amount of capital represented by the issued and outstanding stock of all classes having a preference upon the distribution of assets shall have been repaired. Nothing in this subsection shall invalidate or otherwise affect a note, debenture or other obligation of the corporation paid by it as a dividend on shares of its stock, or any payment made thereon, if at the time such note, debenture or obligation was delivered by the corporation, the corporation had either surplus or net profits as provided in clauses (1) or (2) of this subsection from which the dividend could lawfully have been paid.

. . .

§172. Liability of directors and committee members as to dividends or stock redemption.

A member of the board of directors, or a member of any committee designated by the board of directors, shall be fully protected in relying in good faith upon the records of the corporation and upon such information, opinions, reports or statements presented to the corporation by any of its officers or employees, or committees of the board of directors, or by any other person as to matters the director reasonably believes are within such other person's professional or expert competence and who has been selected with reasonable care by or on behalf of the corporation, as to the value and amount of the assets, liabilities and/or net profits of the corporation, or any other facts pertinent to the existence and amount of surplus or other funds from which dividends might properly be declared and paid, or with which the corporation's stock might properly be purchased or redeemed.

§173. Declaration and payment of dividends.

No corporation shall pay dividends except in accordance with this chapter. Dividends may be paid in cash, in property, or in shares of the corporation's capital stock. If the dividend is to be paid in shares of the corporation's theretofore unissued capital stock the board of directors shall, by resolution, direct that there be designated as capital in respect of such shares an amount which is not less than the aggregate par value of par value shares being declared as a dividend and, in the case of shares without par value being declared as a dividend, such amount as shall be determined by the board of directors. No such designation as capital shall be necessary if shares are being distributed by a corporation pursuant to a split-up or division of its stock rather than as payment of a dividend declared payable in stock of the corporation.

§202.   Restrictions on transfer and ownership of securities.

(a) A written restriction or restrictions on the transfer or registration of transfer of a security of a corporation, or on the amount of the corporation's securities that may be owned by any person or group of persons, if permitted by this section and noted conspicuously on the certificate or certificates representing the security or securities so restricted . . . , may be enforced against the holder of the restricted security or securities or any successor or transferee of the holder including an executor, administrator, trustee, guardian or other fiduciary entrusted with like responsibility for the person or estate of the holder. Unless noted conspicuously on the certificate or certificates representing the security or securities so restricted . . . , a restriction, even though permitted by this section, is ineffective except against a person with actual knowledge of the restriction.

(b) A restriction on the transfer or registration of transfer of securities of a corporation, or on the amount of a corporation's securities that may be owned by any person or group of persons, may be imposed by the certificate of incorporation or by the bylaws or by an agreement among any number of security holders or among such holders and the corporation. No restrictions so imposed shall be binding with respect to securities issued prior to the adoption of the restriction unless the holders of the securities are parties to an agreement or voted in favor of the restriction.

(c) A restriction on the transfer or registration of transfer of securities of a corporation or on the amount of such securities that may be owned by any person or group of persons is permitted by this section if it:

(1) Obligates the holder of the restricted securities to offer to the corporation or to any other holders of securities of the corporation or to any other person or to any combination of the foregoing, a prior opportunity, to be exercised within a reasonable time, to acquire the restricted securities; or

(2) Obligates the corporation or any holder of securities of the corporation or any other person or any combination of the foregoing, to purchase the securities which are the subject of an agreement respecting the purchase and sale of the restricted securities; or

(3) Requires the corporation or the holders of any class or series of securities of the corporation to consent to any proposed transfer of the restricted securities or to approve the proposed transferee of the restricted securities, or to approve the amount of securities of the corporation that may be owned by a person or group of persons; or

(4) Obligates the holder of the restricted securities to sell or transfer an amount of restricted securities to the corporation or to any other holders of securities of the corporation or to any other person or to any combination of the foregoing, or causes or results in the automatic sale or transfer of an amount

of restricted securities to the corporation or to any other holders of securities of the corporation or to any other person or to any combination of the foregoing; or

(5) Prohibits or restricts the transfer of the restricted securities to, or the ownership of restricted securities by, designated persons or classes of persons or groups of persons, and such designation is not manifestly unreasonable.

(d) Any restriction on the transfer or the registration of transfer of the securities of a corporation, or on the amount of securities of a corporation that may be owned by a person or group of persons, for any of the following purposes shall be conclusively presumed to be for a reasonable purpose:

(1) maintaining any local, state, federal, or foreign tax advantage to the corporation or its stockholders, including without limitation (i) maintaining the corporation's status as an electing small business corporation under subchapter S of the United States Internal Revenue Code, or (ii) maintaining or preserving any tax attribute (including without limitation net operating losses), or (iii) qualifying or maintaining the qualification of the corporation as a real estate investment trust pursuant to the United States Internal Revenue Code or regulations adopted pursuant to the United States Internal Revenue Code, or

(2) maintaining any statutory or regulatory advantage or complying with any statutory or regulatory requirements under applicable local, state, federal, or foreign law.

(e) Any other lawful restriction on transfer or registration of transfer of securities, or on the amount of securities that may be owned by any person or group of persons, is permitted by this section.

§244.   Reduction of capital.

(a) A corporation, by resolution of its board of directors, may reduce its capital in any of the following ways:

(1) By reducing or eliminating the capital represented by shares of capital stock which have been retired;

(2) By applying to an otherwise authorized purchase or redemption of outstanding shares of its capital stock some or all of the capital represented by the shares being purchased or redeemed, or any capital that has not been allocated to any particular class of its capital stock;

(3) By applying to an otherwise authorized conversion or exchange of outstanding shares of its capital stock some or all of the capital represented by the shares being converted or exchanged, or some or all of any capital that has not been allocated to any particular class of its capital stock, or both, to the extent that such capital in the aggregate exceeds the total aggregate par value or the stated capital of any previously unissued shares issuable upon such conversion or exchange; or

(4) By transferring to surplus (i) some or all of the capital not represented by any particular class of its capital stock; (ii) some or all of the capital represented by issued shares of its par value capital stock, which capital is in excess of the aggregate par value of such shares; or (iii) some of the capital represented by issued shares of its capital stock without par value.

(b) Notwithstanding the other provisions of this section, no reduction of capital shall be made or effected unless the assets of the corporation remaining after such reduction shall be sufficient to pay any debts of the corporation for which payment has not been otherwise provided. No reduction of capital shall release any liability of any stockholder whose shares have not been fully paid.

§251.   Merger or consolidation of domestic corporations.

(a) Any 2 or more corporations existing under the laws of this State may merge into a single corporation, which may be any 1 of the constituent corporations or may consolidate into a new corporation formed by the consolidation, pursuant to an agreement of merger or consolidation, as the case may be, complying and approved in accordance with this section.

(b) The board of directors of each corporation which desires to merge or consolidate shall adopt a resolution approving an agreement of merger or consolidation and declaring its advisability. The agreement shall state:

(1) The terms and conditions of the merger or consolidation;

(2) the mode of carrying the same into effect;

(3) in the case of a merger, such amendments or changes in the certificate of incorporation of the surviving corporation as are desired to be effected by the merger, or, if no such amendments or changes are desired, a statement that the certificate of incorporation of the surviving corporation shall be its certificate of incorporation;

(4) in the case of a consolidation, that the certificate of incorporation of the resulting corporation shall be as is set forth in an attachment to the agreement;

(5) the manner of converting the shares of each of the constituent corporations into shares or other securities of the corporation surviving or resulting from the merger or consolidation and, if any shares of any of the constituent corporations are not to be converted solely into shares or other securities of the surviving or resulting corporation, the cash, property, rights or securities of any other corporation or entity which the holders of such shares are to receive in exchange for, or upon conversion of such shares and the surrender of any certificates evidencing them, which cash, property, rights or securities of any other corporation or entity may be in addition to or in lieu of shares or other securities of the surviving or resulting corporation; and

(6) such other details or provisions as are deemed desirable, including, without limiting the generality of the foregoing, a provision for the payment of cash in lieu of the issuance or recognition of fractional shares, interests or rights, or for any other arrangement with respect thereto, consistent with §155 of this title. . . . Any of the terms of the agreement of merger or consolidation may be made dependent upon facts ascertainable outside of such agreement, provided that the manner in which such facts shall operate upon the terms of the agreement is clearly and expressly set forth in the agreement of merger or consolidation. The term "facts," as used in the preceding sentence, includes, but is not limited to, the occurrence of any event, including a determination or action by any person or body, including the corporation.

(c) The agreement required by subsection (b) of this section shall be submitted to the stockholders of each constituent corporation at an annual or special meeting for the purpose of acting on the agreement. The terms of the agreement may require that the agreement be submitted to the stockholders whether or not the board of directors determines at any time subsequent to declaring its advisability that the agreement is no longer advisable and recommends that the stockholders reject it. Due notice of the time, place and purpose of the meeting shall be mailed to each holder of stock, whether voting or nonvoting, of the corporation at the holder's address as it appears on the records of the corporation, at least 20 days prior to the date of the meeting. The notice shall contain a copy of the agreement or a brief summary thereof, as the directors shall deem advisable. At the meeting, the agreement shall be considered and a vote taken for its adoption or rejection. If a majority of the outstanding stock of the corporation entitled to vote thereon shall be voted for the adoption of the agreement, that fact shall be certified on the agreement by the secretary or assistant secretary of the corporation. If the agreement shall be so adopted and certified by each constituent corporation, it shall then be filed and shall become effective, in accordance with §103 of this title. In lieu of filing the agreement of merger or consolidation required by this section, the surviving or resulting corporation may file a certificate of merger or consolidation, executed in accordance with §103 of this title, which states:

(1) The name and state of incorporation of each of the constituent corporations;

(2) That an agreement of merger or consolidation has been approved, adopted, certified, executed and acknowledged by each of the constituent corporations in accordance with this section;

(3) The name of the surviving or resulting corporation;

(4) In the case of a merger, such amendments or changes in the certificate of incorporation of the surviving corporation as are desired to be effected by the merger, or, if no such amendments or changes are desired, a statement that the certificate of incorporation of the surviving corporation shall be its certificate of incorporation;

(5) In the case of a consolidation, that the certificate of incorporation of the resulting corporation shall be as set forth in an attachment to the certificate;

(6) That the executed agreement of consolidation or merger is on file at an office of the surviving corporation, stating the address thereof; and

(7) That a copy of the agreement of consolidation or merger will be furnished by the surviving corporation, on request and without cost, to any stockholder of any constituent corporation.

(d) Any agreement of merger or consolidation may contain a provision that at any time prior to the time that the agreement (or a certificate in lieu thereof) filed with the Secretary of State becomes effective in accordance with §103 of this title, the agreement may be terminated by the board of directors of any constituent corporation notwithstanding approval of the agreement by the stockholders of all or any of the constituent corporations; in the event the agreement of merger or consolidation is terminated after the filing of the agreement (or a certificate in lieu thereof) with the Secretary of State but before the agreement (or a certificate in lieu thereof) has become effective, a certificate of termination or merger or consolidation shall be filed in accordance with §103 of this title. Any agreement of merger or consolidation may contain a provision that the boards of directors of the constituent corporations may amend the agreement at any time prior to the time that the agreement (or a certificate in lieu thereof) filed with the Secretary of State becomes effective in accordance with §103 of this title, provided that an amendment made subsequent to the adoption of the agreement by the stockholders of any constituent corporation shall not (1) alter or change the amount or kind of shares, securities, cash, property and/or rights to be received in exchange for or on conversion of all or any of the shares of any class or series thereof of such constituent corporation, (2) alter or change any term of the certificate of incorporation of the surviving corporation to be effected by the merger or consolidation, or (3) alter or change any of the terms and conditions of the agreement if such alteration or change would adversely affect the holders of any class or series thereof of such constituent corporation; in the event the agreement of merger or consolidation is amended after the filing thereof with the Secretary of State but before the agreement has become effective, a certificate of amendment of merger or consolidation shall be filed in accordance with §103 of this title.

(e) In the case of a merger, the certificate of incorporation of the surviving corporation shall automatically be amended to the extent, if any, that changes in the certificate of incorporation are set forth in the agreement of merger.

(f) Notwithstanding the requirements of subsection (c) of this section, unless required by its certificate of incorporation, no vote of stockholders of a constituent corporation surviving a merger shall be necessary to authorize a merger if (1) the agreement of merger does not amend in any respect the certificate of incorporation of such constituent corporation, (2) each share of stock of such constituent corporation outstanding immediately prior to the effective date of the merger is to be an identical outstanding or treasury share of the surviving corporation after the effective date of the merger, and (3) either no shares of common stock of the surviving corporation and no shares, securities or obligations convertible into such stock are to be issued or delivered under the plan of merger, or the authorized unissued shares or the treasury shares of common stock of the surviving corporation to be issued or delivered under the plan of merger plus those initially issuable upon conversion of any other shares, securities or obligations to be issued or delivered under such plan do not exceed 20% of the shares of common stock of such constituent corporation outstanding immediately prior to the effective date of the merger. No vote of stockholders of a constituent corporation shall be necessary to authorize a merger or consolidation if no shares of the stock of such corporation shall have been issued prior to the adoption by the board of directors of the resolution approving the agreement of merger or consolidation. If an agreement of merger is adopted by the constituent corporation surviving the merger, by action of its board of directors and without any vote of its stockholders pursuant to this subsection, the secretary or assistant secretary of that corporation shall certify on the agreement that the agreement has been adopted pursuant to this subsection and, (i) if it has been adopted pursuant to the first sentence of this subsection, that the conditions specified in that sentence have been satisfied, or (ii) if it has been adopted pursuant to the second sentence of this subsection, that no shares of stock of such corporation were issued prior to the adoption by the board of directors of the resolution approving the agreement of merger or consolidation. The agreement so adopted and certified shall then be filed and shall become effective, in accordance with §103 of this title. Such filing shall constitute a representation by the person who executes the agreement that the facts stated in the certificate remain true immediately prior to such filing.

(g) Notwithstanding the requirements of subsection (c) of this section, unless expressly required by its certificate of incorporation, no vote of stockholders of a constituent corporation shall be necessary to authorize a merger with or into a single direct or indirect wholly-owned subsidiary of such constituent corporation if: (1) such constituent corporation and the direct or indirect wholly-owned subsidiary of such constituent corporation are the only constituent entities to the merger; (2) each share or fraction of a share of the capital stock of the constituent corporation outstanding immediately prior to the effective time of the merger is converted in the merger into a share or equal fraction of share of capital stock of a holding company having the same designations, rights, powers and preferences, and the qualifications, limitations and restrictions thereof, as the share of stock of the constituent corporation being converted in the merger; (3) the holding company and the constituent corporation are corporations of this State and the direct or indirect wholly-owned subsidiary that is the other constituent entity to the merger is a corporation or limited liability company of this State; (4) the certificate of incorporation and by-laws of the holding company immediately following the effective time of the merger contain provisions identical to the certificate of incorporation and by-laws of the constituent corporation immediately prior to the effective time of the merger . . . ; (5) as a result of the merger the constituent corporation or its successor becomes or remains a direct or indirect wholly-owned subsidiary of the holding company; (6) the directors of the constituent corporation become or remain the directors of the holding company upon the effective time of the merger; (7) the organizational documents of the surviving entity immediately following the effective time of the merger contain provisions [as discussed in omitted language] . . . (8) the stockholders of the constituent corporation do not recognize gain or loss for United States federal income tax purposes as determined by the board of directors of the constituent corporation. . . .

As used in this subsection only, the term "holding company" means a corporation which, from its incorporation until consummation of a merger governed by this subsection, was at all times a direct or indirect wholly-owned subsidiary of the constituent corporation and whose capital stock is issued in such merger. . . .

§252. Merger or consolidation of domestic and foreign corporations; service of process upon surviving or resulting corporation.

(a) Any 1 or more corporations of this State may merge or consolidate with 1 or more other corporations of any other state or states of the United States, or of the District of Columbia if the laws of the other state or states, or of the District permit a corporation of such jurisdiction to merge or consolidate with a corporation of another jurisdiction. The constituent corporations may merge into a single corporation, which may be any 1 of the constituent corporations, or they may consolidate into a new corporation formed by the consolidation, which may be a corporation of the state of incorporation of any 1 of the constituent corporations, pursuant to an agreement of merger or consolidation, as the case may be, complying and approved in accordance with this section. In addition, any 1 or more corporations existing under the laws of this State may merge or consolidate with 1 or more corporations organized under the laws of any jurisdiction other than 1 of the United States if the laws under which the other corporation or corporations are organized permit a corporation of such jurisdiction to merge or consolidate with a corporation of another jurisdiction.

(b) All the constituent corporations shall enter into an agreement of merger or consolidation. The agreement shall state:

(1) The terms and conditions of the merger or consolidation;

(2) the mode of carrying the same into effect;

(3) the manner of converting the shares of each of the constituent corporations into shares or other securities of the corporation surviving or resulting from the merger or consolidation and, if any shares of any of the constituent corporations are not to be converted solely into shares or other securities of the surviving or resulting corporation, the cash, property, rights or securities of any other corporation or entity which the holders of such shares are to receive in exchange for, or upon conversion of, such shares and the surrender of any certificates evidencing them, which cash, property, rights or securities of any other corporation or entity may be in addition to or in lieu of the shares or other securities of the surviving or resulting corporation;

(4) such other details or provisions as are deemed desirable, including, without limiting the generality of the foregoing, a provision for the payment of cash in lieu of the issuance or recognition of fractional shares of the surviving or resulting corporation or of any other corporation the securities of which are to be received in the merger or consolidation, or for some other arrangement with respect thereto consistent with §155 of this title; and

(5) such other provisions or facts as shall be required to be set forth in certificates of incorporation by the laws of the state which are stated in the agreement to be the laws that shall govern the surviving or resulting corporation and that can be stated in the case of a merger or consolidation. Any of the terms of the agreement of merger or consolidation may be made dependent upon facts ascertainable outside of such agreement, provided that the manner in which such facts shall operate upon the terms of the agreement is clearly and expressly set forth in the agreement of merger or consolidation. The term "facts," as used in the preceding sentence, includes, but is not limited to, the occurrence of any event, including a determination or action by any person or body, including the corporation.

(c) The agreement shall be adopted, approved, certified, executed and acknowledged by each of the constituent corporations in accordance with the laws under which it is formed, and, in the case of a Delaware corporation, in the same manner as is provided in §251 of this title. The agreement shall be filed and shall become effective for all purposes of the laws of this State when and as provided in §251 of this title with respect to the merger or consolidation of corporations of this State. In lieu of filing the agreement of merger or consolidation, the surviving or resulting corporation may file a certificate of merger or consolidation, executed in accordance with §103 of this title, which states:

(1) The name and state or jurisdiction of incorporation of each of the constituent corporations;

(2) That an agreement of merger or consolidation has been approved, adopted, certified, executed and acknowledged by each of the constituent corporations in accordance with this subsection;

(3) The name of the surviving or resulting corporation;

(4) In the case of a merger, such amendments or changes in the certificate of incorporation of the surviving corporation as are desired to be effected by the merger, or, if no such amendments or changes are desired, a statement that the certificate of incorporation of the surviving corporation shall be its certificate of incorporation;

(5) In the case of a consolidation, that the certificate of incorporation of the resulting corporation shall be as is set forth in an attachment to the certificate;

(6) That the executed agreement of consolidation or merger is on file at an office of the surviving corporation and the address thereof;

(7) That a copy of the agreement of consolidation or merger will be furnished by the surviving corporation, on request and without cost, to any stockholder of any constituent corporation;

(8) If the corporation surviving or resulting from the merger or consolidation is to be a corporation of this State, the authorized capital stock of each constituent corporation which is not a corporation of this State; and

(9) The agreement, if any, required by subsection (d) of this section.

(d) If the corporation surviving or resulting from the merger or consolidation is to be governed by the laws of the District of Columbia or any state other than this State, it shall agree that it may be served with process in this State in any proceeding for enforcement of any obligation of any constituent corporation of this State, as well as for enforcement of any obligation of the surviving or resulting corporation arising from the merger or consolidation, including any suit or other proceeding to enforce the right of any stockholders as determined in appraisal proceedings pursuant to §262 of this title, and shall irrevocably appoint the Secretary of State as its agent to accept service of process in any such suit or other proceedings and shall specify the address to which a copy of such process shall be mailed by the Secretary of State. In the event of such service upon the Secretary of State in accordance with this subsection, the Secretary of State shall forthwith notify such surviving or resulting corporation thereof . . .

(e) Subsection (d) and the second sentence of subsection (c) of §251 of this title shall apply to any merger or consolidation under this section; subsection (e) of §251 shall apply to a merger under this section in which the surviving corporation is a corporation of this State; subsection (f) of §251 shall apply to any merger under this section.

§253. Merger of parent corporation and subsidiary or subsidiaries.

(a) In any case in which at least 90% of the outstanding shares of each class of the stock of a corporation or corporations (other than a corporation which has in its certificate of incorporation the provision required by §251(g)(7)(i) of this title), of which class there are outstanding shares that, absent this subsection, would be entitled to vote on such merger, is owned by another corporation and 1 of the corporations is a corporation of this State and the other or others are corporations of this State, or any other state or states, or the District of Columbia and the laws of other state or states, or the District permit a corporation of such jurisdiction to merge with a corporation of another jurisdiction, the corporation having such stock ownership may either merge the other corporation or corporations into itself and assume all of its or their obligations, or merge itself, or itself and 1 or more of such other corporations, into 1 of the other corporations by executing, acknowledging and filing, in accordance with §103 of this title, a certificate of such ownership and merger setting forth a copy of the resolution of its board of directors to so merge and the date of the adoption; provided, however, that in case the parent corporation shall not own all the outstanding stock of all the subsidiary corporations, parties to a merger as aforesaid, the resolution of the board of directors of the parent corporation shall state the terms and conditions of the merger, including the securities, cash, property, or rights to be issued, paid, delivered or granted by the surviving corporation upon surrender of each share of the subsidiary corporation or corporations not owned by the parent corporation. Any of the terms of the resolution of the board of directors to so merge may be made dependent upon facts ascertainable outside of such resolution, provided that the manner in which such facts shall operate upon the terms of the resolution is clearly and expressly set forth in the resolution. The term "facts," as used in the preceding sentence, includes, but is not limited to, the occurrence of any event, including a determination or action by any person or body, including the corporation. If the parent corporation be not the surviving corporation, the resolution shall include provision for the pro rata issuance of stock of the surviving corporation of the holders of the stock of the parent corporation on surrender of any certificates therefor, and the certificate of ownership and merger shall state that the proposed merger has been approved by a majority of the outstanding stock of the parent corporation entitled to vote thereon at a meeting duly called and held after 20 days' notice of the purpose of the meeting mailed to each such stockholder at the stockholder's address as it appears on the records of the corporation if the parent corporation is a corporation of this State or state that the proposed merger has been adopted, approved, certified, executed and acknowledged by the parent corporation in accordance with the laws under which it is organized if the parent corporation is not a corporation of this State. If the surviving corporation exists under the laws of the District of Columbia or any state or jurisdiction other than this State, subsection (d) of §252 of this title shall also apply to a merger under this section.

(b) If the surviving corporation is a Delaware corporation, it may change its corporate name by the inclusion of a provision to that effect in the resolution of merger adopted by the directors of the parent corporation and set forth in the certificate of ownership and merger, and upon the effective date of the merger, the name of the corporation shall be so changed.

(c) Subsection (d) of §251 of this title shall apply to a merger under this section, and subsection (e) of §251 of this title shall apply to a merger under this section in which the surviving corporation is the subsidiary corporation and is a corporation of this State. References to "agreement of merger" in subsections (d) and (e) of §251 of this title shall mean for purposes of this subsection the resolution of merger adopted by the board of directors of the parent corporation. Any merger which effects any changes other than those authorized by this section or made applicable by this subsection shall be accomplished under §251 or §252 of this title. Section 262 of this title shall not apply to any merger effected under this section, except as provided in subsection (d) of this section.

(d) In the event all of the stock of a subsidiary Delaware corporation party to a merger effected under this section is not owned by the parent corporation immediately prior to the merger, the stockholders of the subsidiary Delaware corporation party to the merger shall have appraisal rights as set forth in §262 of this title.

(e) A merger may be effected under this section although 1 or more of the corporations parties to the merger is a corporation organized under the laws of a jurisdiction other than 1 of the United States; provided that the laws of such jurisdiction permit a corporation of such jurisdiction to merge with a corporation of another jurisdiction.

§259. Status, rights, liabilities, etc. of constituent and surviving or resulting corporations following merger or consolidation.

(a) When any merger or consolidation shall have become effective under this chapter, for all purposes of the laws of this State the separate existence of all the constituent corporations, or of all such constituent corporations except the one into which the other or others of such constituent corporations have been merged, as the case may be, shall cease and the constituent corporations shall become a new corporation, or be merged into 1 of such corporations, as the case may be, possessing all the rights, privileges, powers and franchises as well of a public as of a private nature, and being subject to all the restrictions, disabilities and duties of each of such corporations so merged or consolidated; and all and singular, the rights, privileges, powers and franchises of each of said corporations, and all property, real, personal and mixed, and all debts due to any of said constituent corporations on whatever account, as well for stock subscriptions as all other things in action or belonging to each of such corporations shall be vested in the corporation surviving or resulting from such merger or consolidation; and all property, rights, privileges, powers and franchises, and all and every other interest shall be thereafter as effectually the property of the surviving or resulting corporation as they were of the several and respective constituent corporations, and the title to any real estate vested by deed or otherwise, under the laws of this State, in any of such constituent corporations, shall not revert or be in any way impaired by reason of this chapter; but all rights of creditors and all liens upon any property of any of said constituent corporations shall be preserved unimpaired, and all debts, liabilities and duties of the respective constituent corporations shall thenceforth attach to said surviving or resulting corporation, and may be enforced against it to the same extent as if said debts, liabilities and duties had been incurred or contracted by it.

. . .

§261. Effect of merger upon pending actions.

Any action or proceeding, whether civil, criminal or administrative, pending by or against any corporation which is a party to a merger or consolidation shall be prosecuted as if such merger or consolidation had not taken place, or the corporation surviving or resulting from such merger or consolidation may be substituted in such action or proceeding.

§262. Appraisal rights.

(a) Any stockholder of a corporation of this State who holds shares of stock on the date of the making of a demand pursuant to subsection (d) of this section with respect to such shares, who continuously holds such shares through the effective date of the merger or consolidation, who has otherwise complied with subsection (d) of this section and who has neither voted in favor of the merger or consolidation nor consented thereto in writing pursuant to §228 of this title shall be entitled to an appraisal by the Court of Chancery of the fair value of the stockholder's shares of stock under the circumstances described in subsections (b) and (c) of this section. . . .

(b) Appraisal rights shall be available for the shares of any class or series of stock of a constituent corporation in a merger or consolidation to be effected pursuant to §251 (other than a merger effected pursuant to §251(g) of this title), §252, §254, §257, §258, §263 or §264 of this title:

(1) Provided, however, that no appraisal rights under this section shall be available for the shares of any class or series of stock, which stock, or depository receipts in respect thereof, at the record date fixed to determine the stockholders entitled to receive notice of and to vote at the meeting of stockholders to act upon the agreement of merger or consolidation, were either (i) listed on a national securities exchange or designated as a national market system security on an interdealer quotation system by the National Association of Securities Dealers, Inc. or (ii) held of record by more than 2,000 holders; and further provided that no appraisal rights shall be available for any shares of stock of the constituent corporation surviving a merger if the merger did not require for its approval the vote of the holders of the surviving corporation as provided in subsection (f) of §251 of this title.

(2) Notwithstanding paragraph (1) of this subsection, appraisal rights under this section shall be available for the shares of any class or series of stock of a constituent corporation if the holders thereof required by the terms of an

agreement of merger or consolidation pursuant to §§251, 252, 254, 257, 258, 263 and 264 of this title to accept for such stock anything except:

a. Shares of stock of the corporation surviving or resulting from such merger or consolidation;

b. Shares of stock of any other corporation, or depository receipts in respect thereof, which shares of stock (or depository receipts in respect thereof) or depository receipts at the effective date of the merger or consolidation will be either listed on a national securities exchange or designated as a national market system security on an interdealer quotation system by the National Association of Securities Dealers, Inc. or held of record by more than 2,000 holders;

c. Cash in lieu of fractional shares or fractional depository receipts described in the foregoing subparagraphs a. and b. of this paragraph; or

d. Any combination of the shares of stock, depository receipts and cash in lieu of fractional shares or fractional depository receipts described in the foregoing subparagraphs a., b. and c. of this paragraph.

(3) In the event all of the stock of a subsidiary Delaware corporation party to a merger effected under §253 of this title is not owned by the parent corporation immediately prior to the merger, appraisal rights shall be available for the shares of the subsidiary Delaware corporation.

(c) Any corporation may provide in its certificate of incorporation that appraisal rights under this section shall be available for the shares of any class or series of its stock as a result of an amendment to its certificate of incorporation, any merger or consolidation in which the corporation is a constituent corporation or the sale of all or substantially all of the assets of the corporation. If the certificate of incorporation contains such a provision, the procedures of this section, including those set forth in subsections (d) and (e) of this section, shall apply as nearly as is practicable.

(d) Appraisal rights shall be perfected as follows:

(1) If a proposed merger or consolidation for which appraisal rights are provided under this section is to be submitted for approval at a meeting of stockholders, the corporation, not less than 20 days prior to the meeting, shall notify each of its stockholders who was such on the record date for such meeting with respect to shares for which appraisal rights are available pursuant to subsection (b) or (c) hereof that appraisal rights are available for any or all of the shares of the constituent corporations, and shall include in such notice a copy of this section. Each stockholder electing to demand the appraisal of such stockholder's shares shall deliver to the corporation, before the taking of the vote on the merger or consolidation, a written demand for appraisal of such stockholder's shares. Such demand will be sufficient if it reasonably informs the corporation of the identity of the stockholder and that the stockholder intends thereby to demand the appraisal of such stockholder's shares. A proxy or vote against the merger or consolidation shall not constitute such a demand. A stockholder electing to take such action must do so by a separate written demand as herein provided. Within 10 days after the effective date of such merger or consolidation, the surviving or resulting corporation shall notify

each stockholder of each constituent corporation who has complied with this subsection and has not voted in favor of or consented to the merger or consolidation of the date that the merger or consolidation has become effective; or

(2) If the merger or consolidation was approved pursuant to §228 or §253 of this title, then, either a constituent corporation before the effective date of the merger or consolidation, or the surviving or resulting corporation within ten days thereafter, shall notify each of the holders of any class or series of stock of such constituent corporation who are entitled to appraisal rights of the approval of the merger or consolidation and that appraisal rights are available for any or all shares of such class or series of stock of such constituent corporation, and shall include in such notice a copy of this section. Such notice may, and, if given on or after the effective date of the merger or consolidation, shall, also notify such stockholders of the effective date of the merger or consolidation. Any stockholder entitled to appraisal rights may, within 20 days after the date of mailing of such notice, demand in writing from the surviving or resulting corporation the appraisal of such holder's shares. Such demand will be sufficient if it reasonably informs the corporation of the identity of the stockholder and that the stockholder intends thereby to demand the appraisal of such holder's shares. If such notice did not notify stockholders of the effective date of the merger or consolidation, either (i) each such constituent corporation shall send a second notice before the effective date of the merger or consolidation notifying each of the holders of any class or series of stock of such constituent corporation that are entitled to appraisal rights of the effective date of the merger or consolidation or (ii) the surviving or resulting corporation shall send such a second notice to all such holders on or within 10 days after such effective date; provided, however, that if such second notice is sent more than 20 days following the sending of the first notice, such second notice need only be sent to each stockholder who is entitled to appraisal rights and who has demanded appraisal of such holder's shares in accordance with this subsection. . . . For purposes of determining the stockholders entitled to receive either notice, each constituent corporation may fix, in advance, a record date that shall be not more than 10 days prior to the date the notice is given, provided, that if the notice is given on or after the effective date of the merger or consolidation, the record date shall be such effective date. If no record date is fixed and the notice is given prior to the effective date, the record date shall be the close of business on the day next preceding the day on which the notice is given.

(e) Within 120 days after the effective date of the merger or consolidation, the surviving or resulting corporation or any stockholder who has complied with subsections (a) and (d) hereof and who is otherwise entitled to appraisal rights, may file a petition in the Court of Chancery demanding a determination of the value of the stock of all such stockholders. Notwithstanding the foregoing, at any time within 60 days after the effective date of the merger or consolidation, any stockholder shall have the right to withdraw such stockholder's demand for appraisal and to accept the terms offered upon the merger or consolidation. . . .

. . .

(g) At the hearing on such petition, the Court shall determine the stockholders who have complied with this section and who have become entitled to appraisal rights. The Court may require the stockholders who have demanded an appraisal for their shares and who hold stock represented by certificates to submit their certificates of stock to the Register in Chancery for notation thereon of the pendency of the appraisal proceedings; and if any stockholder fails to comply with such direction, the Court may dismiss the proceedings as to such stockholder.

(h) After determining the stockholders entitled to an appraisal, the Court shall appraise the shares, determining their fair value exclusive of any element of value arising from the accomplishment or expectation of the merger or consolidation, together with a fair rate of interest, if any, to be paid upon the amount determined to be the fair value. In determining such fair value, the Court shall take into account all relevant factors. In determining the fair rate of interest, the Court may consider all relevant factors, including the rate of interest which the surviving or resulting corporation would have had to pay to borrow money during the pendency of the proceeding. Upon application by the surviving or resulting corporation or by any stockholder entitled to participate in the appraisal proceeding, the Court may, in its discretion, permit discovery or other pretrial proceedings and may proceed to trial upon the appraisal prior to the final determination of the stockholder entitled to an appraisal. . . .

. . .

(j) The costs of the proceeding may be determined by the Court and taxed upon the parties as the Court deems equitable in the circumstances. Upon application of a stockholder, the Court may order all or a portion of the expenses incurred by any stockholder in connection with the appraisal proceeding, including, without limitation, reasonable attorney's fees and the fees and expenses of experts, to be charged pro rata against the value of all the shares entitled to an appraisal.

(k) From and after the effective date of the merger or consolidation, no stockholder who has demanded appraisal rights as provided in subsection (d) of this section shall be entitled to vote such stock for any purpose or to receive payment of dividends or other distributions on the stock (except dividends or other distributions payable to stockholders of record at a date which is prior to the effective date of the merger or consolidation); provided, however, that if no petition for an appraisal shall be filed within the time provided in subsection (e) of this section, or if such stockholder shall deliver to the surviving or resulting corporation a written withdrawal of such stockholder's demand for an appraisal and an acceptance of the merger or consolidation, either within 60 days after the effective date of the merger or consolidation as provided in subsection (e) of this section or thereafter with the written approval of the corporation, then the right of such stockholder to an appraisal shall cease. Notwithstanding the foregoing, no appraisal proceeding in the Court of Chancery shall be dismissed as to any stockholder without the approval of the Court, and such approval may be conditioned upon such terms as the Court deems just.

. . .

§263. Merger or consolidation of domestic corporation and partnership.

(a) Any 1 or more corporations of this State may merge or consolidate with 1 or more partnerships (whether general (including a limited liability partnership) or limited (including a limited liability limited partnership)), of this State or of any other state or states of the United States, or of the District of Columbia, unless the laws of such other state or states or the District of Columbia forbid such merger or consolidation. Such corporation or corporations and such 1 or more partnerships may merge with or into a corporation, which may be any 1 of such corporations, or they may merge with or into a partnership, which may be any 1 of such partnerships, or they may consolidate into a new corporation or partnership formed by the consolidation, which shall be a corporation or partnership of this State or any other state of the United States, or the District of Columbia, which permits such merger or consolidation, pursuant to an agreement of merger or consolidation, as the case may be, complying and approved in accordance with this section.

. . .

§264. Merger or consolidation of domestic corporation and limited liability company.

(a) Any 1 or more corporations of this State may merge or consolidate with 1 or more limited liability companies, of this State or of any other state or states of the United States, or of the District of Columbia, unless the laws of such other state or states or the District of Columbia forbid such merger or consolidation. Such corporation or corporations and such 1 or more limited liability companies may merge with or into a corporation, which may be any 1 of such corporations, or they may merge with or into a limited liability company, which may be any 1 of such limited liability companies, or they may consolidate into a new corporation or limited liability company formed by the consolidation, which shall be a corporation or limited liability company of this State or any other state of the United States, or the District of Columbia, which permits such merger or consolidation, pursuant to an agreement of merger or consolidation, as the case may be, complying and approved in accordance with this section.

§265. Conversion of other entities to a domestic corporation.

(a) As used in this section, the term 'other entity' means a limited liability company, partnership (whether general (including a limited liability partnership) or limited (including a limited liability limited partnership)), or statutory trust of this State.

(b) Any other entity may convert to a corporation incorporated under the laws of this State by complying with subsection (g) of this section and filing in the office of the Secretary of State:

(1) A certificate of conversion that has been executed in accordance with subsection (h) of this section and filed in accordance with §103 of this title; and

(2) A certificate of incorporation that has been executed, acknowledged and filed in accordance with §103 of this title.

. . .

§266.   Conversion of a domestic corporation to other entities.

(a) A corporation of this State may, upon the authorization of such conversion in accordance with this section, convert to a limited liability company, partnership (whether general (including a limited liability partnership) or limited (including a limited liability limited partnership)), or statutory trust of this State.

(b) The board of directors of the corporation which desires to convert under this section shall adopt a resolution approving such conversion, specifying the type of entity into which the corporation shall be converted and recommending the approval of such conversion by the stockholders of the corporation. Such resolution shall be submitted to the stockholders of the corporation at an annual or special meeting. Due notice of the time, and purpose of the meeting shall be mailed to each holder of stock, whether voting or nonvoting, of the corporation at the address of the stockholder as it appears on the records of the corporation, at least 20 days prior to the date of the meeting. At the meeting, the resolution shall be considered and a vote taken for its adoption or rejection. If all outstanding shares of stock of the corporation, whether voting or nonvoting, shall be voted for the adoption of the resolution, the corporation shall file with the Secretary of State a certificate of conversion executed in accordance with §103 of this title . . .

. . .

§271.   Sale, Lease or Exchange of Assets; Consideration; Procedure.

(a) Every corporation may at any meeting of its board of directors or governing body sell, lease or exchange all or substantially all of its property and assets, including its goodwill and its corporate franchises, upon such terms and conditions and for such consideration, which may consist in whole or in part of money or other property, including shares of stock in, and/or other securities of, and other corporation or corporations, as its board of directors or governing body deems expedient and for the best interests of the corporation, when and as authorized by a resolution adopted by the holders of a majority of the outstanding stock of the corporation entitled to vote thereon, . . . at a meeting duly called upon at least 20 days notice. The notice of the meeting shall state that such a resolution will be considered.

(b) Notwithstanding authorization or consent to a proposed sale, lease or exchange of a corporation's property and assets by the stockholders or members, the board of directors or governing body may abandon such proposed sale, lease or exchange without further action by the stockholders or members, subject to the rights, if any, of third parties under any contract relating thereto.

§388. Domestication of non-United States corporations.

(a) As used in this section, the term:

(1) "Corporation" includes any incorporated organization, private law corporation (whether or not organized for business purposes), public law corporation, partnership, proprietorship, joint venture, foundation, trust, association or similar entity; and

(2) "Non-United States corporation" means any corporation the internal affairs of which are governed by the laws of any jurisdiction other than the United States, any state, the District of Columbia, Puerto Rico, Guam or any possession or territory of the United States.

(b) Any non-United States corporation may become domesticated in this State by filing with the Secretary of State . . .

. . .

DELAWARE REVISED UNIFORM LIMITED PARTNERSHIP ACT

Selected Sections

§17-208. Notice.

The fact that a certificate of limited partnership is on file in the Office of the Secretary of State is notice that the partnership is a limited partnership and is notice of all other facts set forth therein which are required to be set forth in a certificate of limited partnership. . .

§17-211. Merger and consolidation.

(a) As used in this section, "other business entity" means a corporation, a statutory trust or association, a real estate investment trust, a common-law trust, a limited liability company, or an unincorporated business, including a partnership (whether general (including a limited liability partnership) or limited (including a foreign limited liability limited partnership), but excluding a domestic limited partnership).

(b) Pursuant to an agreement of merger or consolidation, 1 or more domestic limited partnerships may merge or consolidate with or into 1 or more domestic limited partnerships or 1 or more other business entities formed or organized under the laws of the State of Delaware or any other state or the United States or any foreign country or other foreign jurisdiction, or any combination thereof, with such domestic limited partnership or other business entity as the agreement shall provide being the surviving or resulting domestic limited partnership or other business entity. Unless otherwise provided in the partnership agreement, a merger or consolidation shall be approved by each domestic limited partnership which is to merge or consolidate (1) by all general partners, and (2) by the limited partners or, if there is more than 1 class or group of limited partners, then by each class or group of limited partners, in either case, by limited partners who own more than 50 percent of the then current percentage or other interest in the profits of the domestic limited partnership owned by all of the limited partners or by the limited partners in each class or group, as appropriate. In connection with a merger or consolidation hereunder, rights or securities of, or interests in, a limited partnership or other business entity which is a constituent party to the merger or consolidation may be exchanged for or converted into cash, property, rights or securities of, or interests in, the surviving or resulting limited partnership or other business entity or, in addition to or in lieu thereof, may be exchanged for or converted into cash, property, rights or securities of, or interests in, a limited partnership or other business entity which is not the surviving or resulting limited partnership or other business entity in the merger or consolidation.

. . .

(h) When any merger or consolidation shall have become effective under this section, for all purposes of the laws of the State of Delaware, all of the rights, privileges and powers of each of the domestic limited partnerships and other business entities that have merged or consolidated, and all property, real, personal and mixed, and all debts due to any of said domestic limited partnerships and other business entities, as well as all other things and causes of action belonging to each of such domestic limited partnerships and other business entities, shall be vested in the surviving or resulting domestic limited partnership or other business entity, and shall thereafter be the property of the surviving or resulting domestic limited partnership or other business entity as they were of each of the domestic limited partnerships and other business entities that have merged or consolidated, and the title to any real property vested by deed or otherwise, under the laws of the State of Delaware, in any of such domestic limited partnerships and other business entities, shall not revert or be in any way impaired by reason of this chapter; but all rights of creditors and all liens upon any property of any of said domestic limited partnerships and other business entities shall be preserved unimpaired, and all debts, liabilities and duties of each of the said domestic limited partnerships and other business entities that have merged or consolidated shall thenceforth attach to the surviving or resulting domestic limited partnership or other business entity, and may be enforced against it to the same extent as if said debts, liabilities and duties had been incurred or contracted by it.

. . .

§17-212. Contractual appraisal rights.

A partnership agreement or an agreement of merger or consolidation may provide that contractual appraisal rights with respect to a partnership interest or another interest in a limited partnership shall be available for any class or group of partners or partnership interests in connection with any amendment of a partnership agreement, any merger or consolidation in which the limited partnership is a constituent party to the merger or consolidation, any conversion of the limited partnership to another business form, any transfer to or domestication in any jurisdiction by the limited partnership, or the sale of all or substantially all of the limited partnership's assets. The Court of Chancery shall have jurisdiction to hear and determine any matter relating to any such appraisal rights.

§17-215. Domestication of non-United States entities.

(a) As used in this section, "non-United States entity" means a foreign limited partnership (other than one formed under the laws of a state) (including a foreign limited liability limited partnership (other than one formed under the laws of a state)), or a corporation, a business trust or association, a real estate investment trust, a common-law trust, or any other unincorporated business, including a general partnership (including a limited liability partnership) or a limited liability company, formed, incorporated, created or that otherwise came into being under the laws of any foreign country or other foreign jurisdiction (other than any state).

(b) Any non-United States entity may become domesticated as a limited partnership in the State of Delaware by complying with subsection (g) of this section and filing in the office of the Secretary of State . . .

. . .

(g) Prior to filing a certificate of limited partnership domestication with the office of the Secretary of State, the domestication shall be approved in the manner provided for by the document, instrument, agreement or other writing, as the case may be, governing the internal affairs of the non-United States entity and the conduct of its business or by applicable non-Delaware law, as appropriate, and a partnership agreement shall be approved by the same authorization required to approve the domestication; provided that, in any event, such approval shall include the approval of any person who, at the effective date or time of the domestication, shall be a general partner of the limited partnership.

§17-217. Conversion of certain entities to a limited partnership.

(a) As used in this section, the term "other entity" means a corporation, statutory trust or association, a real estate investment trust, a common-law trust, or any other unincorporated business, including a general partnership (including a limited liability partnership) or a foreign limited partnership (including a foreign limited liability limited partnership) or a limited liability company.

(b) Any other entity may convert to a domestic limited partnership by complying with subsection (h) of this section and filing in the office of the Secretary of State . . .

. . .

(i) In connection with a conversion hereunder, rights or securities of, or interests in, the other entity which is to be converted to a domestic limited partnership may be exchanged for or converted into cash, property, rights or securities of, or interests in, such domestic limited partnership or, in addition to or in lieu thereof, may be exchanged for or converted into cash, property, rights or securities of, or interests in, another domestic limited partnership or other entity.

§17-218.   Series of limited partners, general partners or partnership interests.

(a) A partnership agreement may establish or provide for the establishment of designated series of limited partners, general partners or partnership interests having separate rights, powers or duties with respect to specified property or obligations of the limited partnership or profits and losses associated with specified property or obligations, and, to the extent provided in the partnership agreement, any such series may have a separate business purpose or investment objective.

(b) Notwithstanding anything to the contrary set forth in this chapter or under other applicable law, in the event that a partnership agreement creates 1 or more series or states that the liabilities of a general partner are limited to the liabilities of a designated series, and if separate and distinct records are maintained for any such series and the assets associated with any such series are held (directly or indirectly, including through a nominee or otherwise) and accounted for separately from the other assets of the limited partnership, or any other series thereof, and if the partnership agreement so provides, and notice of the limitation on liabilities of a series or a general partner as referenced in this subsection is set forth in the certificate of limited partnership, then the debts, liabilities and obligations incurred, contracted for or otherwise existing with respect to a particular series or general partner shall be enforceable only against the assets of such series or a general partner associated with such series and not against the assets of the limited partnership generally, any other series thereof, or any general partner not associated with such series, and, unless otherwise provided in the partnership agreement, none of the debts, liabilities, obligations and expenses incurred, contracted for or otherwise existing with respect to the limited partnership generally or any other series thereof shall be enforceable against the assets of such series or a general partner associated with such series.

(c) The fact that a certificate of limited partnership that contains the notice of the limitation on liabilities of a series or a general partner as referenced in subsection (b) of this section is on file in the office of the Secretary of State shall constitute notice of such limitation on liabilities.

(d) A limited partner may possess or exercise any of the rights and powers or act or attempt to act in 1 or more of the capacities as permitted under §17-303 of this title, with respect to any series, without participating in the control of the business of the limited partnership or with respect to any series thereof within the meaning of §17-303(a) of this title. A partnership agreement may provide for classes or groups of general partners or limited partners associated with a series having such relative rights, powers and duties as the partnership agreement may provide, and may make provision for the future creation in the manner provided in the partnership agreement of additional classes or groups of general partners or limited partners associated with the series having such relative rights, powers and duties as may from time to time be established, including rights, powers and duties senior to existing classes and groups of general partners or limited partners associated with the series. A partnership agreement may provide for the taking of an action, including the amendment of the partnership agreement, without the vote or approval of any general partner or limited partner or class or group of general partners or limited partners, including an action to create under the provisions of the partnership agreement a class or group of the series of partnership interests that was not previously outstanding.

(e) A partnership agreement may grant to all or certain identified general partners or limited partners or a specified class or group of the general partners or limited partners associated with a series the right to vote separately or with all or any class or group of the general partners or limited partners associated with the series, on any matter. Voting by general partners or limited partners associated with a series may be on a per capita, number, financial interest, class, group or any other basis.

. . .

(i) Notwithstanding §17-607(a) of this title, a limited partnership may make a distribution with respect to a series that has been established in accordance with subsection (b) of this section. A limited partnership shall not make a distribution with respect to a series that has been established in accordance with subsection (b) of this section to a partner to the extent that at the time of the distribution, after giving effect to the distribution, all liabilities of such series, other than liabilities to partners on account of their partnership interests with respect to such series and liabilities for which the recourse of creditors is limited to specified property of such series, exceed the fair value of the assets associated with such series, except that the fair value of property of the series that is subject to a liability for which the recourse of creditors is limited shall be included in the assets associated with such series only to the extent that the fair value of that property exceeds that liability. For purposes of the immediately preceding sentence, the term "distribution" shall not include amounts constituting reasonable compensation for present or past services or reasonable payments made in the ordinary course of business pursuant to a bona fide retirement plan or other benefits program. A limited partner who receives a distribution in violation of this subsection, and who knew at the time of the distribution that the distribution violated this subsection, shall be liable to a series for the amount of the distribution. A limited partner who receives a distribution in violation of this subsection, and who did not know at the time of the distribution that the distribution violated this subsection, shall not be liable for the amount of the distribution. Subject to §17-607(c) of this title, which shall apply to any distribution made with respect to a series under this subsection, this subsection shall not affect any obligation or liability of a limited partner under an agreement or other applicable law for the amount of a distribution.

. . .

§17-219. Approval of conversion of a limited partnership.

A domestic limited partnership may convert to a corporation, statutory trust or association, a real estate investment trust, a common-law trust, a general partnership (including a limited liability partnership) or a limited liability company, organized, formed or created under the laws of the State of Delaware, upon the authorization of such conversion in accordance with this section. If the partnership agreement specifies the manner of authorizing a conversion of the limited partnership, the conversion shall be authorized as specified in the partnership agreement. If the partnership agreement does not specify the manner of authorizing a conversion of the limited partnership and does not prohibit a conversion of the limited partnership, the conversion shall be authorized in the same manner as is specified in the partnership agreement for authorizing a merger or consolidation that involves the limited partnership as a constituent party to the merger or consolidation. If the partnership agreement does not specify the manner of authorizing a conversion of the limited partnership or a merger or consolidation that involves the limited partnership as a constituent party and does not prohibit a conversion of the limited partnership, the conversion shall be authorized by the approval (1) by all general partners, and (2) by the limited partners or, if there is more than one class or group of limited partners, then by each class or group of limited partners, in either case, by limited partners who own more than 50 percent of the then current percentage or other interest in the profits of the domestic limited partnership owned by all of the limited partners or by the limited partners in each class or group, as appropriate. Unless otherwise agreed, the conversion of a domestic limited partnership to another business form pursuant to this section shall not require such limited partnership to wind up its affairs under §17-803 of this title or pay its liabilities and distribute its assets under §17-804 of this title. In connection with a conversion of a domestic limited partnership to another business form pursuant to this section, rights or securities of, or interests in, the domestic limited partnership which is to be converted may be exchanged for or converted into cash, property, rights or securities of, or interests in, the business form into which the domestic limited partnership is being converted or, in addition to or in lieu thereof, may be exchanged for or converted into cash, property, rights or securities of, or interests in, another business form.

§17-301. Admission of limited partners.

. . .

(d) A person may be admitted to a limited partnership as a limited partner of the limited partnership and may receive a partnership interest in the limited partnership without making a contribution or being obligated to make a contribution to the limited partnership. Unless otherwise provided in a partnership agreement, a person may be admitted to a limited partnership as a limited partner of the limited partnership without acquiring a partnership interest in the limited partnership. Unless otherwise provided in a partnership agreement, a person may be admitted as the sole limited partner of a limited partnership without making a contribution or being obligated to make a contribution to the limited partnership or without acquiring a partnership interest in the limited partnership.

§17-302. Classes and voting.

(a) A partnership agreement may provide for classes or groups of limited partners having such relative rights, powers and duties as the partnership agreement may provide, and may make provision for the future creation in the manner provided in the partnership agreement of additional classes or groups of limited partners having such relative rights, powers and duties as may from time to time be established, including rights, powers and duties senior to existing classes and groups of limited partners. A partnership agreement may provide for the taking of an action, including the amendment of the partnership agreement, without the vote or approval of any limited partner or class or group of limited partners, including an action to create under the provisions of the partnership agreement a class or group of partnership interests that was not previously outstanding.

(b) Subject to §17-303 of this title, the partnership agreement may grant to all or certain identified limited partners or a specified class or group of the limited partners the right to vote separately or with all or any class or group of the limited partners or the general partners, on any matter. Voting by limited partners may be on a per capita, number, financial interest, class, group or any other basis.

. . .

(d) Any right or power, including voting rights, granted to limited partners as permitted under §17-303 of this title shall be deemed to be permitted by this section.

(e) Unless otherwise provided in a partnership agreement, on any matter that is to be voted on, consented to or approved by limited partners, the limited partners may take such action without a meeting, without prior notice and without a vote, if a consent or consents in writing, setting forth the action so taken, shall be signed by the limited partners having not less than the minimum number of votes that would be necessary to authorize or take such action at a meeting at which all limited partners entitled to vote thereon were present and voted. Unless otherwise provided in a partnership agreement, on any matter that is to be voted on by limited partners, the limited partners may vote in person or by proxy. . . .

(f) If a partnership agreement provides for the manner in which it may be amended, it may be amended in that manner or with the approval of all the partners or as otherwise permitted by law. If a partnership agreement does not provide for the manner in which it may be amended, the partnership agreement may be amended with the approval of all the partners or as otherwise permitted by law. A limited partner and any class or group of limited partners have the right to vote only on matters as specifically set forth in this chapter, on matters specifically provided by agreement, including a partnership agreement, and on any matter with respect to which a general partner may determine in its discretion to seek a vote of a limited partner or a class or group of limited partners if a vote on such matter is not contrary to a partnership agreement or another agreement to which a general partner or the limited partnership is a party. A limited partner and any class or group of limited partners have no other voting rights. A partnership agreement may provide that any limited partner or class or group of limited partners shall have no voting rights.

§17-303.   Liability to third parties.

(a) A limited partner is not liable for the obligations of a limited partnership unless he is also a general partner or, in addition to the exercise of his rights and powers as a limited partner, he participates in the control of the business. However, if the limited partner does participate in the control of the business, he is liable only to persons who transact business with the limited partnership reasonably believing, based upon the limited partner's conduct, that the limited partner is a general partner.

(b) A limited partner does not participate in the control of the business within the meaning of subsection (a) of this section by virtue of his possessing or, regardless of whether or not the limited partner has the rights or powers, exercising or attempting to exercise 1 or more of the following rights or powers or having or, regardless of whether or not the limited partner has the rights or powers, acting or attempting to act in 1 or more of the following capacities:

(1) To be an independent contractor for or to transact business with, including being a contractor for, or to be an agent or employee of, the limited partnership or a general partner, or to be an officer, director or stockholder of a corporate general partner, or to be a limited partner of a partnership that is a general partner of the limited partnership, or to be a trustee, administrator, executor, custodian or other fiduciary or beneficiary of an estate or trust which is a general partner, or to be a trustee, officer, advisor, stockholder or beneficiary of a business trust or a statutory trust which is a general partner or to be a

member, manager, agent or employee of a limited liability company which is a general partner;

(2) To consult with or advise a general partner or any other person with respect to any matter, including the business of the limited partnership, or to act or to cause a general partner or any other person to take or refrain from taking any action, including by proposing, approving, consenting or disapproving, by voting or otherwise, with respect to any matter, including the business of the limited partnership;

(3) To act as surety, guarantor or endorser for the limited partnership or a general partner, to guaranty or assume one or more obligations of the limited partnership or a general partner, to borrow money from the limited partnership or a general partner, to lend money to the limited partnership or a general partner, or to provide collateral for the limited partnership or a general partner;

(4) To call, request, or attend or participate at a meeting of the partners or the limited partners;

(5) To wind up a limited partnership pursuant to §17-803 of this title;

(6) To take any action required or permitted by law to bring, pursue or settle or otherwise terminate a derivative action in the right of the limited partnership;

(7) To serve on a committee of the limited partnership or the limited partners or partners or to appoint, elect or otherwise participate in the choice of a representative or another person to serve on any such committee, and to act as a member of any such committee directly or by or through any such representative or other person;

(8) To act or cause the taking or refraining from the taking of any action, including by proposing, approving, consenting or disapproving, by voting or otherwise, with respect to 1 or more of the following matters:

a. The dissolution and winding up of the limited partnership or an election to continue the limited partnership or an election to continue the business of the limited partnership;

b. The sale, exchange, lease, mortgage, assignment, pledge or other transfer of, or granting of a security interest in, any asset or assets of the limited partnership;

c. The incurrence, renewal, refinancing or payment or other discharge of indebtedness by the limited partnership;

d. A change in the nature of the business;

e. The admission, removal or retention of a general partner;

f. The admission, removal or retention of a limited partner;

g. A transaction or other matter involving an actual or potential conflict of interest;

h. An amendment to the partnership agreement or certificate of limited partnership;

i. The merger or consolidation of a limited partnership;

j. In respect of a limited partnership which is registered as an investment company under the Investment Company Act of 1940, as amended, any matter required by the Investment Company Act of 1940, as amended, or the rules and regulations of the Securities and Exchange Commission there-under, to be approved by the holders of beneficial interests in an investment company, including the electing of directors or trustees of the investment company, the approving or terminating of investment advisory or underwriting contracts and the approving of auditors;

k. The indemnification of any partner or other person; or

l. The making of, or calling for, or the making of other determinations in connection with contributions;

m. The making of, or the making of other determinations in connection with or concerning, investments, including investments in property, whether real, personal or mixed, either directly or indirectly, by the limited partnership; or

n. Such other matters as are stated in the partnership agreement or in any other agreement or in writing;

(9) To serve on the board of directors or a committee of, to consult with or advise, to be an officer, director, stockholder, partner (other than a general partner of a general partner of the limited partnership), member, manager, trustee, agent or employee of, or to be a fiduciary or contractor for, any person in which the limited partnership has an interest or any person providing management, consulting, advisory, custody or other services or products for, to or on behalf of, or otherwise having a business or other relationship with, the limited partnership or a general partner of the limited partnership; or

(10) Any right or power granted or permitted to limited partners under this chapter and not specifically enumerated in this subsection.

(c) The enumeration in subsection (b) of this section does not mean that the possession or exercise of any other powers or having or acting in other capacities by a limited partner constitutes participation by him in the control of the business of the limited partnership.

(d) A limited partner does not participate in the control of the business within the meaning of subsection (a) of this section by virtue of the fact that all or any part of the name of such limited partner is included in the name of the limited partnership.

(e) This section does not create rights or powers of limited partners. Such rights and powers may be created only by a certificate of limited partnership, a partnership agreement or any other agreement or in writing, or other sections of this chapter.

(f) A limited partner does not participate in the control of the business within the meaning of subsection (a) of this section regardless of the nature, extent, scope, number or frequency of the limited partner's possessing or, regardless of whether or not the limited partner has the rights or powers, exercising or attempting to exercise 1 or more of the rights or powers or having or, regardless of whether or not the limited partner has the rights or powers, acting or attempting to act in 1 or more of the capacities which are permitted under this section.

§17-401. Admission of general partners.

(a) A person may be admitted to a limited partnership as a general partner of the limited partnership and may receive a partnership interest in the limited partnership without making a contribution or being obligated to make a contribution to the limited partnership. Unless otherwise provided in a partnership agreement, a person may be admitted to a limited partnership as a general partner of the limited partnership without acquiring a partnership interest in the limited partnership. Unless otherwise provided in a partnership agreement, a person may be admitted as the sole general partner of a limited partnership without making a contribution or being obligated to make a contribution to the limited partnership or without acquiring a partnership interest in the limited partnership. . . .

. . .

(b) After the filing of the limited partnership's initial certificate of limited partnership, unless otherwise provided in the partnership agreement, additional general partners may be admitted only with the written consent of each partner.

(c) Unless otherwise provided in a partnership agreement or another agreement, a general partner shall have no preemptive right to subscribe to any additional issue of partnership interests or another interest in a limited partnership.

§17-402. Events of withdrawal.

(a) A person ceases to be a general partner of a limited partnership upon the happening of any of the following events:

(1) The general partner withdraws from the limited partnership as provided in §17-602 of this title;

(2) The general partner ceases to be a general partner of the limited partnership as provided in §17-702 of this title;

(3) The general partner is removed as a general partner in accordance with the partnership agreement;

(4) Unless otherwise provided in the partnership agreement, or with the written consent of all partners, the general partner [voluntarily or involuntarily becomes bankrupt or makes an assignment for the benefit of creditors];

. . .

(5) Unless otherwise provided in the partnership agreement, or with the written consent of all partners, 120 days after the commencement of a proceeding against the general partner seeking reorganization, arrangement, composition, readjustment, liquidation, dissolution or similar relief under any statute, law or regulation, the proceeding has not been dismissed . . .

(6) In the case of a general partner who is a natural person:

a. His death; or

b. The entry by a court of competent jurisdiction adjudicating him incompetent to manage his person or his property;

. . .

(8) In the case of a general partner that is a separate partnership, the dissolution and commencement of winding up of the separate partnership;

(9) In the case of a general partner that is a corporation, the filing of a certificate of dissolution, or its equivalent . . .

. . .

(11) In the case of a general partner that is a limited liability company, the dissolution and commencement of winding up of the limited liability company; or

(12) In the case of a general partner who is not an individual, partnership, corporation, trust or estate, the termination of the general partner.

. . .

§17-403. General powers and liabilities.

. . .

(b) Except as provided in this chapter, a general partner of a limited partnership has the liabilities of a partner in a partnership that is governed by the Delaware Uniform Limited Partnership Law to persons other than the partnership and the other partners. Except as provided in this chapter or in the partnership agreement, a general partner of a limited partnership has the liabilities of a partner in a partnership that is governed by the Delaware Uniform Limited Partnership Law to the partnership and to the other partners.

§17-404. Contributions by a general partner.

A general partner of a limited partnership may make contributions to the limited partnership and share in the profits and losses of, and in distributions from, the limited partnership as a general partner. A general partner also may make contributions to and share in profits, losses and distributions as a limited partner. A person who is both a general partner and a limited partner has the rights and powers, and is subject to the restrictions and liabilities, of a general partner and, except as provided in the partnership agreement, also has the rights and powers, and is subject to the restrictions, of a limited partner to the extent of his participation in the partnership as a limited partner.

§17-405. Classes and voting.

(a) A partnership agreement may provide for classes or groups of general partners having such relative rights, powers and duties as the partnership agreement may provide, and may make provision for the future creation in the manner provided in the partnership agreement of additional classes or groups of general partners having such relative rights, powers and duties as may from time to time be established, including rights, powers and duties senior to existing classes and groups of general partners.

A partnership agreement may provide for the taking of an action, including the amendment of the partnership agreement, without the vote or approval of any general partner or class or group of general partners, including an action to create under the provisions of the partnership agreement a class or group of partnership interests that was not previously outstanding.

(b) The partnership agreement may grant to all or certain identified general partners or a specified class or group of the general partners the right to vote, separately or with all or any class or group of the limited partners or the general partners, on any matter. Voting by general partners may be on a per capita, number, financial interest, class, group or any other basis.

. . .

(d) Unless otherwise provided in a partnership agreement, on any matter that is to be voted on, consented to or approved by general partners, the general partners may take such action without a meeting, without prior notice and without a vote, if a consent or consents in writing, setting forth the action so taken, shall be signed by the general partners having not less than the minimum number of votes that would be necessary to authorize or take such action at a meeting at which all general partners entitled to vote thereon were present and voted. Unless otherwise provided in a partnership agreement, on any matter that is to be voted on by general partners, the general partners may vote in person or by proxy. . . .

§17-501. Form of contribution.

The contribution of a partner may be in cash, property or services rendered, or a promissory note or other obligation to contribute cash or property or to perform services.

§17-502. Liability for contribution.

(a)(1) Except as provided in the partnership agreement, a partner is obligated to the limited partnership to perform any promise to contribute cash or property or to perform services, even if he is unable to perform because of death, disability or any other reason. . . .

. . .

§17-503. Allocation of profits and losses.

The profits and losses of a limited partnership shall be allocated among the partners, and among classes or groups of partners, in the manner provided in the partnership agreement. If the partnership agreement does not so provide, profits and losses shall be allocated on the basis of the agreed value (as stated in the records of the limited partnership) of the contributions made by each partner to the extent they have been received by the limited partnership and have not been returned.

§17-504.   Allocation of distributions.

Distributions of cash or other assets of a limited partnership shall be allocated among the partners, and among classes or groups of partners, in the manner provided in the partnership agreement. If the partnership agreement does not so provide, distributions shall be made on the basis of the agreed value (as stated in the records of the limited partnership) of the contributions made by each partner to the extent they have been received by the limited partnership and have not been returned.

§17-602.   Withdrawal of general partner and assignment of general partner's partnership interest

(a) A general partner may withdraw from a limited partnership at the time or upon the happening of events specified in the partnership agreement and in accordance with the partnership agreement. A partnership agreement may provide that a general partner shall not have the right to withdraw as a general partner of a limited partnership. Notwithstanding that a partnership agreement provides that a general partner does not have the right to withdraw as a general partner of a limited partnership, a general partner may withdraw from a limited partnership at any time by giving written notice to the other partners. If the withdrawal of a general partner violates a partnership agreement, in addition to any remedies otherwise available under applicable law, the limited partnership may recover from the withdrawing general partner damages for breach of the partnership agreement and offset the damages against the amount otherwise distributable to the withdrawing general partner.

. . .

§17-603.   Withdrawal of limited partner.

A limited partner may withdraw from a limited partnership only at the time or upon the happening of events specified in the partnership agreement and in accordance with the partnership agreement. Notwithstanding anything to the contrary under applicable law, unless a partnership agreement provides otherwise, a limited partner may not withdraw from a limited partnership prior to the dissolution and winding up of the limited partnership. Notwithstanding anything to the contrary under applicable law, a partnership agreement may provide that a partnership interest may not be assigned prior to the dissolution and winding up of the limited partnership.

Unless otherwise provided in a partnership agreement, a limited partnership whose original certificate of limited partnership was filed with the Secretary of State and effective on or prior to July 31, 1996, shall continue to be governed by 6 Del. C. §17-603 as in effect on July 31, 1996, and shall not be governed by this section.

§17-604.   Distribution upon withdrawal.

Except as provided in this subchapter, upon withdrawal any withdrawing partner is entitled to receive any distribution to which such partner is entitled under a partnership agreement and, if not otherwise provided in a partnership agreement, such partner is entitled to receive, within a reasonable time after withdrawal, the fair value of such partner's partnership interest in the limited partnership as of the date of withdrawal based upon such partner's right to share in distributions from the limited partnership.

§17-605.   Distribution in kind.

Except as provided in the partnership agreement, a partner, regardless of the nature of his contribution, has no right to demand and receive any distribution from a limited partnership in any form other than cash. Except as provided in the partnership agreement, a partner may not be compelled to accept a distribution of any asset in kind from a limited partnership to the extent that the percentage of the asset distributed to him exceeds a percentage of that asset which is equal to the percentage in which he shares in distributions from the limited partnership. Except as provided in the partnership agreement, a partner may be compelled to accept a distribution of any asset in kind from a limited partnership to the extent that the percentage of the asset distributed to him is equal to a percentage of that asset which is equal to the percentage in which he shares in distributions from the limited partnership.

§17-607.   Limitations on distribution.

(a) A limited partnership shall not make a distribution to a partner to the extent that at the time of the distribution, after giving effect to the distribution, all liabilities of the limited partnership, other than liabilities to partners on account of their partnership interests and liabilities for which the recourse of creditors is limited to specified property of the limited partnership, exceed the fair value of the assets of the limited partnership, except that the fair value of property that is subject to a liability for which the recourse of creditors is limited shall be included in the assets of the limited partnership only to the extent that the fair value of that property exceeds that liability. For purposes of this subsection (a), the term "distribution" shall not include amounts constituting reasonable compensation for present or past services or reasonable payments made in the ordinary course of business pursuant to a bona fide retirement plan or other benefits program.

(b) A limited partner who receives a distribution in violation of subsection (a) of this section, and who knew at the time of the distribution that the distribution violated subsection (a) of this section, shall be liable to the limited partnership for the amount of the distribution. A limited partner who receives a distribution in violation of subsection (a) of this section, and who did not know at the time of the distribution that the distribution violated subsection (a) of this section, shall not be liable for the amount of the distribution. Subject to subsection (c) of this section, this subsection shall not affect any obligation or liability of a limited partner under an agreement or other applicable law for the amount of a distribution.

(c) Unless otherwise agreed, a limited partner who receives a distribution from a limited partnership shall have no liability under this chapter or other applicable law for the amount of the distribution after the expiration of 3 years from the date of the distribution.

§17-702.   Assignment of partnership interest.

(a) Unless otherwise provided in the partnership agreement:

(1) A partnership interest is assignable in whole or in part;

(2) An assignment of a partnership interest does not dissolve a limited partnership or entitle the assignee to become or to exercise any rights or powers of a partner;

(3) An assignment of a partnership interest entitles the assignee to share in such profits and losses, to receive such distribution or distributions, and to receive such allocation of income, gain, loss, deduction, or credit or similar item to which the assignor was entitled, to the extent assigned; and

(4) A partner ceases to be a partner and to have the power to exercise any rights or powers of a partner upon assignment of all of his partnership interest. . . .

. . .

(d) Unless otherwise provided in the partnership agreement, a limited partnership may acquire, by purchase, redemption or otherwise, any partnership interest or other interest of a partner in the limited partnership. Unless otherwise provided in the partnership agreement, any such interest so acquired by the limited partnership shall be deemed canceled.

. . .

§17-704.   Right of assignee to become limited partner.

(a) An assignee of a partnership interest, including an assignee of a general partner, may become a limited partner if and to the extent that:

(1) The partnership agreement so provides; or

(2) All partners consent.

. . .

§17-801.   Nonjudicial dissolution.

A limited partnership is dissolved and its affairs shall be wound up upon the first to occur of the following:

(1) At the time specified in the partnership agreement, but if no such time is set forth in the partnership agreement, then the limited partnership shall have a perpetual existence.

(2) Unless otherwise provided in a partnership agreement, upon the affirmative vote or written consent of (a) all general partners and (b) the limited partners of a limited partnership or, if there is more than one class or group of limited partners, then by each class or group of limited partners, in either case, by limited partners who own more than two-thirds of the then current percentage or other interest in the profits of the limited partnership owned by all of the limited partners or by the limited partners in each class or group, as appropriate.

(3) An event of withdrawal of a general partner unless at the time there is at least 1 other general partner and the partnership agreement permits the business of the limited partnership to be carried on by the remaining general partner and that partner does so, but the limited partnership is not dissolved and is not required to be wound up by reason of any event of withdrawal if (i) within 90 days or such other period as is provided for in a partnership agreement after the withdrawal either (A) if provided for in the partnership agreement, the then-current percentage or other interest in the profits of the limited partnership specified in the partnership agreement owned by the remaining partners agree in writing or vote to continue the business of the limited partnership and to appoint, effective as of the date of withdrawal, one or more additional general partners if necessary or desired, or (B) if no such right to agree or vote to continue the business of the limited partnership and to appoint one or more additional general partners is provided for in the partnership agreement, then more than 50% of the then current percentage or other interest in the profits of the limited partnership owned by the remaining partners or, if there is more than one class or group of remaining partners, then more than 50% of the then current percentage or other interest in the profits of the limited partnership owned by each class or classes or group or groups of remaining partners agree in writing or vote to continue the business of the limited partnership and to appoint, effective as of the date of withdrawal, one or more additional general partners if necessary or desired, or (ii) the business of the limited partnership is continued pursuant to a right to continue stated in the partnership agreement and; the appointment, effective as of the date of withdrawal, of 1 or more additional general partners if necessary or desired.

(4) At the time there are no limited partners; provided that the limited partnership is not dissolved and is not required to be wound up if, (i) unless

otherwise provided in a partnership agreement, within 90 days or such other period as is provided for in the partnership agreement after the occurrence of the event that caused the last remaining limited partner to cease to be a limited partner, the personal representative of the last remaining limited partner and all of the general partners agree, in writing or by vote, to continue the business of the limited partnership and to the admission of the personal representative of such limited partner or its nominee or designee to the limited partnership as a limited partner, effective as of the occurrence of the event that caused the last remaining limited partner to cease to be a limited partner; provided that a partnership agreement may provide that the general partners or the personal representative of the last remaining limited partner shall be obligated to agree in writing to continue the business of the limited partnership and to the admission of the personal representative of such limited partner or its nominee or designee to the limited partnership as a limited partner, effective as of the occurrence of the event that caused the last limited partner to cease to be a limited partner or (ii) a limited partner is admitted to the limited partnership in the manner provided for in the partnership agreement, effective as of the occurrence of the event that caused the last remaining limited partner to cease to be a limited partner, within 90 days or such other period as is provided for in the partnership agreement after the occurrence of the event that caused the last remaining limited partner to cease to be a limited partner, pursuant to a provision of the partnership agreement that specifically provides for the admission of a limited partner to the limited partnership after there is no longer a remaining limited partner of the limited partnership.

(5) Upon the happening of events specified in a partnership agreement; or

(6) Entry of a decree of judicial dissolution under §17-802 of this title.

§17-804.   Distribution of assets.

(a) Upon the winding up of a limited partnership, the assets shall be distributed as follows:

(1) To creditors, including partners who are creditors, to the extent otherwise permitted by law, in satisfaction of liabilities of the limited partnership (whether by payment or the making of reasonable provision for payment thereof) other than liabilities for which reasonable provision for payment has been made and liabilities for distributions to partners and former partners under §17-601 or §17-604 of this title;

(2) Unless otherwise provided in the partnership agreement, to partners and former partners in satisfaction of liabilities for distributions under §17-601 or §17-604 of this title; and

(3) Unless otherwise provided in the partnership agreement, to partners first for the return of their contributions and second respecting their partnership interests, in the proportions in which the partners share in distributions.

(b) A limited partnership which has dissolved (i) shall pay or make reasonable provision to pay all claims and obligations, including all contingent, conditional or unmatured contractual claims, known to the limited partnership, (ii) shall make such provision as will be reasonably likely to be sufficient to provide compensation for any claim against the limited partnership which is the subject of a pending action, suit or proceeding to which the limited partnership is a party and (iii) shall make such provision as will be reasonably likely to be sufficient to provide compensation for claims that have not been made known to the limited partnership or that have not arisen but that, based on facts known to the limited partnership, are likely to arise or to become known to the limited partnership within 10 years after the date of dissolution. If there are sufficient assets, such claims and obligations shall be paid in full and any such provision for payment made shall be made in full. If there are insufficient assets, such claims and obligations shall be paid or provided for according to their priority and, among claims of equal priority, ratably to the extent of assets available therefor. Unless otherwise provided in the partnership agreement, any remaining assets shall be distributed as provided in this chapter. Any liquidating trustee winding up a limited partner ship's affairs who has complied with this section shall not be personally liable to the claimants of the dissolved limited partnership by reason of such person's actions in winding up the limited partnership.

(c) A limited partner who receives a distribution in violation of subsection (a) of this section, and who knew at the time of the distribution that the distribution violated subsection (a) of this section, shall be liable to the limited partnership for the amount of the distribution. For purposes of the immediately preceding sentence, the term "distribution" shall not include amounts constituting reasonable compensation for present or past services or reasonable payments made in the ordinary course of business pursuant to a bona fide retirement plan or other benefits program. A limited partner who receives a distribution in violation of subsection (a) of this section, and who did not know at the time of the distribution that the distribution violated subsection (a) of this section, shall not be liable for the amount of the distribution. Subject to subsection (d) of this section, this subsection shall not affect any obligation or liability of a limited partner under an agreement or other applicable law for the amount of a distribution.

(d) Unless otherwise agreed, a limited partner who receives a distribution from a limited partnership to which this section applies shall have no liability under this chapter or other applicable law for the amount of the distribution after the expiration of 3 years from the date of the distribution.

(e) Section 17-607 of this title shall not apply to a distribution to which this section applies.

§17-901. Law governing.

(a) Subject to the Constitution of the State of Delaware:

(1) The laws of the State, territory, possession, or other jurisdiction or country under which a foreign limited partnership is organized govern its organization and internal affairs and the liability of its limited partners; and

(2) A foreign limited partnership may not be denied registration by reason of any difference between those laws and the laws of the State of Delaware.

. . .

§17-902.   Registration required; application.

(a) Before doing business in the State of Delaware, a foreign limited partnership shall register with the Secretary of State. . . .

§17-907.   Doing business without registration.

(a) A foreign limited partnership doing business in the State of Delaware may not maintain any action, suit or proceeding in the State of Delaware until it has registered in the State of Delaware . . .

(b) The failure of a foreign limited partnership to register in the State of Delaware does not impair:

(1) The validity of any contract or act of the foreign limited partnership;

(2) The right of any other party to the contract to maintain any action, suit or proceeding on the contract; or

(3) Prevent the foreign limited partnership from defending any action, suit or proceeding in any court of the State of Delaware.

(c) A limited partner of a foreign limited partnership is not liable as a general partner of the foreign limited partnership solely by reason of the foreign limited partnership's having done business in the State of Delaware without registration.

. . .

DELAWARE LIMITED LIABILITY COMPANY ACT

Selected Sections

§18-101.   Definitions.—As used in this chapter unless the context otherwise requires:

. . .

(4) "Foreign limited liability company" means a limited liability company formed under the laws of any state or under the laws of any foreign country or other foreign jurisdiction and denominated as such under the laws of such state or foreign country or other foreign jurisdiction.

. . .

(6) "Limited liability company" and "domestic limited liability company" means a limited liability company formed under the laws of the State of Delaware and having 1 or more members.

(7) "Limited liability company agreement" means any agreement, (whether referred to as a limited liability company agreement, operating agreement or otherwise) written or oral, of the member or members as to the affairs of a limited liability company and the conduct of its business. A limited liability company is not required to execute its limited liability company agreement. A limited liability company is bound by its limited liability company agreement whether or not the limited liability company executes the limited liability company agreement. A limited liability company agreement of a limited liability company having only one member shall not be unenforceable by reason of there being only one person who is a party to the limited liability company agreement. . . .

. . .

(10) "Manager" means a person who is named as a manager of a limited liability company in, or designated as a manager of a limited liability company pursuant to, a limited liability company agreement or similar instrument under which the limited liability company is formed.

(11) "Member" means a person who has been admitted to a limited liability company as a member as provided in §18-301 of this chapter or, in the case of a foreign limited liability company, in accordance with the laws of the state or foreign country or other foreign jurisdiction under which the foreign limited liability company is organized.

. . .

§18-107. Business transactions of member or manager with the limited liability company.

Except as provided in a limited liability company agreement, a member or manager may lend money to, borrow money from, act as a surety, guarantor or endorser for, guarantee or assume 1 or more obligations of, provide collateral for, and transact other business with, a limited liability company and, subject to other applicable law, has the same rights and obligations with respect to any such matter as a person who is not a member or manager.

§18-108. Indemnification.

Subject to such standards and restrictions, if any, as are set forth in its limited liability company agreement, a limited liability company may, and shall have the power to, indemnify and hold harmless any member or manager or other person from and against any and all claims and demands whatsoever.

§18-207.   Notice.

The fact that a certificate of formation is on file in the office of the Secretary of State is notice that the entity formed in connection with the filing of the certificate of formation is a limited liability company formed under the laws of the State of Delaware and is notice of all other facts set forth therein which are required to be set forth in a certificate of formation . . .

§18-209.   Merger and consolidation.

(a) As used in this section, "other business entity" means a corporation, a statutory trust, or a business trust or association, a real estate investment trust, a common-law trust, or any other unincorporated business, including a partnership (whether general (including a limited liability partnership) or limited (including a limited liability limited partnership)), and a foreign limited liability company, but excluding a domestic limited liability company.

(b) Pursuant to an agreement of merger or consolidation, 1 or more domestic limited liability companies may merge or consolidate with or into 1 or more domestic limited liability companies or 1 or more other business entities formed or organized under the laws of the State of Delaware or any other state or the United States or any foreign country or other foreign jurisdiction, or any combination thereof, with such domestic limited liability companies or other business entity as the agreement shall provide being the surviving or resulting domestic limited liability companies or other business entity. Unless otherwise provided in the limited liability company agreement, a merger or consolidation shall be approved by each domestic limited liability company which is to merge or consolidate by the members or, if there is more than one class or group of members, then by each class or group of members, in either case, by members who own more than 50 percent of the then current percentage or other interest in the profits of the domestic limited liability company owned by all of the members or by the members in each class or group, as appropriate. In connection with a merger or consolidation hereunder, rights or securities of, or interests in, a domestic limited liability company or other business entity which is a constituent party to the merger or consolidation may be exchanged for or converted into cash, property, rights or securities of, or interests in, the surviving or resulting domestic limited liability company or other business entity or, in addition to or in lieu thereof, may be exchanged for or converted into cash, property, rights or securities of, or interests in, a domestic limited liability company or other business entity which is not the surviving or resulting limited liability company or other business entity in the merger or consolidation. . . .

. . .

(g) When any merger or consolidation shall have become effective under this section, for all purposes of the laws of the State of Delaware, all of the rights, privileges and powers of each of the domestic limited liability companies and other business entities that have merged or consolidated, and all property, real, personal and mixed, and all debts due to any of said domestic limited liability companies and other business entities, as well as all other things and causes of action belonging to each of such domestic limited liability companies and other business entities, shall be vested in the surviving or resulting domestic limited liability company or other business entity, and shall thereafter be the property of the surviving or resulting domestic limited liability company or other business entity as they were of each of the domestic limited liability companies and other business entities that have merged or consolidated, and the title to any real property vested by deed or otherwise, under the laws of the State of Delaware, in any of such domestic limited liability companies and other business entities, shall not revert or be in any way impaired by reason of this chapter; but all rights of creditors and all liens upon any property of any of said domestic limited liability companies and other business entities shall be preserved unimpaired, and all debts, liabilities and duties of each of the said domestic limited liability companies and other business entities that have merged or consolidated shall thenceforth attach to the surviving or resulting domestic limited liability company or other business entity, and may be enforced against it to the same extent as if said debts, liabilities and duties had been incurred or contracted by it. . . .

. . .

§18-210.   Contractual appraisal rights.

A limited liability company agreement or an agreement of merger or consolidation may provide that contractual appraisal rights with respect to a limited liability company interest or another interest in a limited liability company shall be available for any class or group of members or limited liability company interests in connection with any amendment of a limited liability company agreement, any merger or consolidation in which the limited liability company is a constituent party to the merger or consolidation, any conversion of the limited liability company to another business form, any transfer to or domestication in any jurisdiction by the limited liability company, or the sale of all or substantially all of the limited liability company's assets. The Court of Chancery shall have jurisdiction to hear and determine any matter relating to any such appraisal rights.

§18-212.   Domestication of non-United States entities.

(a) As used in this section, "non-United States entity" means a foreign limited liability company (other than one formed under the laws of a state) or a corporation, a business trust or association, a real estate investment trust, a common-law trust or any other unincorporated business, including a partnership (whether general (including a limited liability partnership) or limited (including a limited liability limited partnership)) formed, incorporated, created or that otherwise came into being under the laws of any foreign country or other foreign jurisdiction (other than any state).

(b) Any non-United States entity may become domesticated as a limited liability company in the State of Delaware by complying with subsection (g) of this section and filing in the office of the Secretary of State . . .

. . .

(g) Prior to filing a certificate of limited liability company domestication with the Office of the Secretary of State, the domestication shall be approved in the manner provided for by the document, instrument, agreement or other writing, as the case may be, governing the internal affairs of the non-United States entity and the conduct of its business or by applicable non-Delaware law, as appropriate, and a limited liability company agreement shall be approved by the same authorization required to approve the domestication.

§18-214. Conversion of certain entities to a limited liability company.

(a) As used in this section, the term "other entity" means a corporation, statutory trust, business trust or association, a real estate investment trust, a common-law trust or any other unincorporated business, including a partnership (whether general (including a limited liability partnership) or limited (including a limited liability limited partnership)) or a foreign limited liability company.

(b) Any other entity may convert to a domestic limited liability company by complying with subsection (h) of this section and filing in the office of the Secretary of State . . .

. . .

(h) Prior to filing a certificate of conversion to limited liability company with the office of the Secretary of State, the conversion shall be approved in the manner provided for by the document, instrument, agreement or other writing, as the case may be, governing the internal affairs of the other entity and the conduct of its business or by applicable law, as appropriate and a limited liability company agreement shall be approved by the same authorization required to approve the conversion.

(i) In connection with a conversion hereunder, rights or securities of, or interests in, the other entity which is to be converted to a domestic limited liability company may be exchanged for or converted into cash, property, rights or securities of, or interests in, such domestic limited liability company or, in addition to or in lieu thereof, may be exchanged for or converted into cash, property, rights or securities of, or interests in, another domestic limited liability company or other entity.

§18-215. Series of members, managers or limited liability company interests.

(a) A limited liability company agreement may establish or provide for the establishment of designated series of members, managers or limited liability company interests having separate rights, powers or duties with respect to specified property or obligations of the limited liability company or profits and losses associated with specified property or obligations, and, to the extent provided in the limited liability company agreement, any such series may have a separate business purpose or investment objective.

(b) Notwithstanding anything to the contrary set forth in this chapter or under other applicable law, in the event that a limited liability company agreement creates 1 or more series, and if separate and distinct records are maintained for any such series and the assets associated with any such series are held (directly or indirectly, including through a nominee or otherwise) and accounted for separately from the other assets of the limited liability company, or any other series thereof, and if the limited liability company agreement so provides, and notice of the limitation on liabilities of a series as referenced in this subsection is set forth in the certificate of formation of the limited liability company, then the debts, liabilities and obligations incurred, contracted for or otherwise existing with respect to a particular series shall be enforceable against the assets of such series only, and not against the assets of the limited liability company generally or any other series thereof, and, unless otherwise provided in the limited liability company agreement, none of the debts, liabilities, obligations and expenses incurred, contracted for or otherwise existing with respect to the limited liability company generally or any other series thereof shall be enforceable against the assets of such series. The fact that a certificate of formation that contains the foregoing notice of the limitation on liabilities of a series is on file in the office of the Secretary of State shall constitute notice of such limitation on liabilities of a series.

. . .

(d) A limited liability company agreement may provide for classes or groups of members or managers associated with a series having such relative rights, powers and duties as the limited liability company agreement may provide, and may make provision for the future creation in the manner provided in the limited liability company agreement of additional classes or groups of members or managers associated with the series having such relative rights, powers and duties as may from time to time be established, including rights, powers and duties senior to existing classes and groups of members or managers associated with the series. A limited liability company agreement may provide for the taking of an action, including the amendment of the limited liability company agreement, without the vote or approval of any member or manager or class or group of members or managers, including an action to create under the provisions of the limited liability company agreement a class or group of the series of limited liability company interests that was not previously outstanding. A limited liability company agreement may provide that any member or class or group of members associated with a series shall have no voting rights.

(e) A limited liability company agreement may grant to all or certain identified members or managers or a specified class or group of the members or managers associated with a series the right to vote separately or with all or any class or group of the members or managers associated with the series, on any matter. Voting by members or managers associated with a series may be on a per capita, number, financial interest, class, group or any other basis.

(f) Unless otherwise provided in a limited liability company agreement, the management of a series shall be vested in the members associated with such series in proportion to the then current percentage or other interest of members in the profits of the series owned by all of the members associated with such series, the decision of members owning more than 50 percent of the said percentage or other interest in the profits controlling; provided, however, that if a limited liability company agreement provides for the management of the series, in whole or in part, by a manager, the management of the series, to the extent so provided, shall be vested in the manager who shall be chosen in the manner provided in the limited liability company agreement. The manager of the series shall also hold the offices and have the responsibilities accorded to the manager as set forth in a limited liability company agreement. A series may have more than 1 manager. Subject to §18-602 of this title, a manager shall cease to be a manager with respect to a series as provided in a limited liability company agreement. Except as otherwise provided in a limited liability company agreement, any event under this chapter or in a limited liability company agreement that causes a manager to cease to be a manager with respect to a series shall not, in itself, cause such manager to cease to be a manager of the limited liability company or with respect to any other series thereof.

. . .

(h) Notwithstanding §18-607(a) of this title, a limited liability company may make a distribution with respect to a series that has been established in accordance with subsection (b) of this section. A limited liability company shall not make a distribution with respect to a series that has been established in accordance with subsection (b) of this section to a member to the extent that at the time of the distribution, after giving effect to the distribution, all liabilities of such series, other than liabilities to members on account of their limited liability company interests with respect to such series and liabilities for which the recourse of creditors is limited to specified property of such series, exceed the fair value of the assets associated with such series, except that the fair value of property of the series that is subject to a liability for which the recourse of creditors is limited shall be included in the assets associated with such series only to the extent that the fair value of that property exceeds that liability. For purposes of the immediately preceding sentence, the term "distribution" shall not include amounts constituting reasonable compensation for present or past services or reasonable payments made in the ordinary course of business pursuant to a bona fide retirement plan or other benefits program. A member who receives a distribution in violation of this subsection, and who knew at the time of the distribution that the distribution violated this subsection, shall be liable to a series for the amount of the distribution. A member who receives a distribution in violation of this subsection, and who did not know at the time of the distribution that the distribution violated this subsection, shall not be liable for the amount of the distribution. Subject to §18-607(c) of this title, which shall apply to any distribution made with respect to a series under this subsection, this subsection shall not affect any obligation or liability of a member under an agreement or other applicable law for the amount of a distribution.

. . .

§18-216. Approval of conversion of a limited liability company.

A domestic limited liability company may convert to a corporation, statutory trust or association, a real estate investment trust, a common-law trust, a general partnership (including a limited liability partnership) or a limited partnership (including a limited liability limited partnership), organized, formed or created under the laws of the State of Delaware, upon the authorization of such conversion in accordance with this section. If the limited liability company agreement specifies the manner of authorizing a conversion of the limited liability company, the conversion shall be authorized as specified in the limited liability company agreement. If the limited liability company agreement does not specify the manner of authorizing a conversion of the limited liability company and does not prohibit a conversion of the limited liability company, the conversion shall be authorized in the same manner as is specified in the limited liability company agreement for authorizing a merger or consolidation that involves the limited liability company as a constituent party to the merger or consolidation. If the limited liability company agreement does not specify the manner of authorizing a conversion of the limited liability company or a merger or consolidation that involves the limited liability company as a constituent party and does not prohibit a conversion of the limited liability company, the conversion shall be authorized by the approval by the members or, if there is more than 1 class or group of members, then by each class or group of members, in either case, by members who own more than 50 percent of the then current percentage or other interest in the profits of the domestic limited liability company owned by all of the members or by the members in each class or group, as appropriate. Unless otherwise agreed, the conversion of a domestic limited liability company to another business form pursuant to this section shall not require such limited liability company to wind up its affairs under §18-803 of this title or pay its liabilities and distribute its assets under §18-804 of this title. In connection with a conversion of a domestic limited liability company to another business form pursuant to this section, rights or securities of, or interests in, the domestic limited liability company which is to be converted may be exchanged for or converted into cash, property, rights or securities of, or interests in, the business form into which the domestic limited liability company is being converted or, in addition to or in lieu thereof, may be exchanged for or converted into cash, property, rights or securities of, or interests in, another business form.

§18-301.   Admission of members.

. . .

(b) After the formation of a limited liability company, a person is admitted as a member of the limited liability company:

(1) In the case of a person who is not an assignee of a limited liability company interest, including a person acquiring a limited liability company interest directly from the limited liability company and a person to be admitted as a member of the limited liability company without acquiring a limited liability company interest in the limited liability company, at the time provided in and upon compliance with the limited liability company agreement or, if the limited liability company agreement does not so provide, upon the consent of all members and when the person's admission is reflected in the records of the limited liability company;

. . .

(d) A person may be admitted to a limited liability company as a member of the limited liability company and may receive a limited liability company interest in the limited liability company without making a contribution or being obligated to make a contribution to the limited liability company. Unless otherwise provided in a limited liability company agreement, a person may be admitted to a limited liability company as a member of the limited liability company without acquiring a limited liability company interest in the limited liability company. Unless otherwise provided in a limited liability company agreement, a person may be admitted as the sole member of a limited liability company without making a contribution or being obligated to make a contribution to the limited liability company or without acquiring a limited liability company interest in the limited liability company.

(e) Unless otherwise provided in a limited liability company agreement or another agreement, a member shall have no preemptive right to subscribe to any additional issue of limited liability company interests or another interest in a limited liability company.

§18-302.   Classes and voting.

(a) A limited liability company agreement may provide for classes or groups of members having such relative rights, powers and duties as the limited liability company agreement may provide, and may make provision for the future creation in the manner provided in the limited liability company agreement of additional classes or groups of members having such relative rights, powers and duties as may from time to time be established, including rights, powers and duties senior to existing classes and groups of members. A limited liability company agreement may provide for the taking of an action, including the amendment of the limited liability company agreement, without the vote or approval of any member or class or group of members, including an action to create under the provisions of the limited liability company agreement a class or group of limited liability company interests that was not previously outstanding. A limited liability company agreement may provide that any member or class or group of members shall have no voting rights.

(b) A limited liability company agreement may grant to all or certain identified members or a specified class or group of the members the right to vote separately or with all or any class or group of the members or managers, on any matter. Voting by members may be on a per capita, number, financial interest, class, group or any other basis.

. . .

(d) Unless otherwise provided in a limited liability company agreement, on any matter that is to be voted on, consented to or approved by members, the members may take such action without a meeting, without prior notice and without a vote if a consent or consents in writing, setting forth the action so taken, shall be signed by the members having not less than the minimum of votes that would be necessary to authorize or take such action at a meeting at which all members entitled to vote thereon were present and voted. Unless otherwise provided in a limited liability company agreement, on any matter that is to be voted on by members, the members may vote in person or by proxy. . . .

. . .

§18-303. Liability to third parties.

(a) Except as otherwise provided by this chapter, the debts, obligations and liabilities of a limited liability company, whether arising in contract, tort or otherwise, shall be solely the debts, obligations and liabilities of the limited liability company, and no member or manager of a limited liability company shall be obligated personally for any such debt, obligation or liability of the limited liability company solely by reason of being a member or acting as a manager of the limited liability company.

(b) Notwithstanding the provisions of §18-303(a) of this chapter, under a limited liability company agreement or under another agreement, a member or manager may agree to be obligated personally for any or all of the debts, obligations and liabilities of the limited liability company.

§18-305. Access to and confidentiality of information; records.

. . .

(g) The rights of a member or manager to obtain information as provided in this section may be restricted in an original limited liability company agreement or in any subsequent amendment approved or adopted by all of the members and in compliance with any applicable requirements of the limited liability company agreement. The provisions of this subsection shall not be construed to limit the ability to impose restrictions on the rights of a member or manager to obtain information by any other means permitted under this section.

§18-306. Remedies for breach of limited liability company agreement by member.

A limited liability company agreement may provide that (1) a member who fails to perform in accordance with, or to comply with the terms and conditions of, the limited liability company agreement shall be subject to specified penalties or specified consequences, and (2) at the time or upon the happening of events specified in the limited liability company agreement, a member shall be subject to specified penalties or specified consequences. Such specified penalties or specified consequences may include and take the form of any penalty or consequence set forth in §18-502(c) of this chapter.

§18-402.   Management of limited liability company.

Unless otherwise provided in a limited liability company agreement, the management of a limited liability company shall be vested in its members in proportion to the then current percentage or other interest of members in the profits of the limited liability company owned by all of the members, the decision of members owning more than 50 percent of the said percentage or other interest in the profits controlling; provided however, that if a limited liability company agreement provides for the management, in whole or in part, of a limited liability company by a manager, the management of the limited liability company, to the extent so provided, shall be vested in the manager who shall be chosen in the manner provided in the limited liability company agreement. The manager shall also hold the offices and have the responsibilities accorded to the manager by or in the manner provided in a limited liability company agreement. Subject to §18-602 of this chapter, a manager shall cease to be a manager as provided in a limited liability company agreement. A limited liability company may have more than 1 manager. Unless otherwise provided in a limited liability company agreement, each member and manager has the authority to bind the limited liability company.

§18-403.   Contributions by a manager.

A manager of a limited liability company may make contributions to the limited liability company and share in the profits and losses of, and in distributions from, the limited liability company as a member. A person who is both a manager and a member has the rights and powers, and is subject to the restrictions and liabilities, of a manager and, except as provided in a limited liability company agreement, also has the rights and powers, and is subject to the restrictions and liabilities, of a member to the extent of his participation in the limited liability company as a member.

§18-404. Classes and voting.

(a) A limited liability company agreement may provide for classes or groups of managers having such relative rights, powers and duties as the limited liability company agreement may provide, and may make provision for the future creation in the manner provided in the limited liability company agreement of additional classes or groups of managers having such relative rights, powers and duties as may from time to time be established, including rights, powers and duties senior to existing classes and groups of managers. A limited liability company agreement may provide for the taking of an action, including the amendment of the limited liability company agreement, without the vote or approval of any manager or class or group of managers, including an action to create under the provisions of the limited liability company agreement a class or group of limited liability company interests that was not previously outstanding.

(b) A limited liability company agreement may grant to all or certain identified managers or a specified class or group of the managers the right to vote, separately or with all or any class or group of managers or members, on any matter. Voting by managers may be on a per capita, number, financial interest, class, group or any other basis.

. . .

(d) Unless otherwise provided in a limited liability company agreement, on any matter that is to be voted on, consented to or approved by managers, the managers may take such action without a meeting, without prior notice and without a vote if a consent or consents in writing, setting forth the action so taken, shall be signed by the managers having not less than the minimum number of votes that would be necessary to authorize or take such action at a meeting at which all managers entitled to vote thereon were present and voted. Unless otherwise provided in a limited liability company agreement, on any matter that is to be voted on by managers, the managers may vote in person or by proxy. . . .

§18-405. Remedies for breach of limited liability company agreement by manager.

A limited liability company agreement may provide that (1) a manager who fails to perform in accordance with, or to comply with the terms and conditions of, the limited liability company agreement shall be subject to specified penalties or specified consequences, and (2) at the time or upon the happening of events specified in the limited liability company agreement, a manager shall be subject to specified penalties or specified consequences.

§18-407. Delegation of rights and powers to manage.

Unless otherwise provided in the limited liability company agreement, a member or manager of a limited liability company has the power and authority to delegate to 1 or more other persons the member's or manager's, as the case may be, rights and powers to manage and control the business and affairs of the limited liability company, . . . Unless otherwise provided in the limited liability company agreement, such delegation by a member or manager of a limited liability company shall not cause the member or manager to cease to be a member or manager, as the case may be, of the limited liability company or cause the person to whom any such rights and powers have been delegated to be a member or manager, as the case may be, of the limited liability company.

§18-501.   Form of contribution.

The contribution of a member to a limited liability company may be in cash, property or services rendered, or a promissory note or other obligation to contribute cash or property or to perform services.

§18-502.   Liability for contribution.

(a) Except as provided in a limited liability company agreement, a member is obligated to a limited liability company to perform any promise to contribute cash or property or to perform services, even if he is unable to perform because of death, disability or any other reason. . . .

. . .

§18-503.   Allocation of profits and losses.

The profits and losses of a limited liability company shall be allocated among the members, and among classes or groups of members, in the manner provided in a limited liability company agreement. If the limited liability company agreement does not so provide, profits and losses shall be allocated on the basis of the agreed value (as stated in the records of the limited liability company) of the contributions made by each member to the extent they have been received by the limited liability company and have not been returned.

§18-504.   Allocation of distributions.

Distributions of cash or other assets of a limited liability company shall be allocated among the members, and among classes or groups of members, in the manner provided in a limited liability company agreement. If the limited liability company agreement does not so provide, distributions shall be made on the basis of the agreed value (as stated in the records of the limited liability company) of the contributions made by each member to the extent they have been received by the limited liability company and have not been returned.

§18-602.   Resignation of Manager.

A manager may resign as a manager of a limited liability company at the time or upon the happening of events specified in a limited liability company agreement and in accordance with the limited liability company agreement. A limited liability company agreement may provide that a manager shall not have the right to resign as a manager of a limited liability company. Notwithstanding that a limited liability company agreement provides that a manager does not have the right to resign as a manager of a limited liability company, a manager may resign as a manager of a limited liability company at any time by giving written notice to the members and other managers. If the resignation of a manager violates a limited liability company agreement, in addition to any remedies otherwise available under applicable law, a limited liability company may recover from the resigning manager damages for breach of the limited liability company agreement and offset the damages against the amount otherwise distributable to the resigning manager.

§18-603.   Resignation of member.

A member may resign from a limited liability company only at the time or upon the happening of events specified in a limited liability company agreement and in accordance with the limited liability company agreement. Notwithstanding anything to the contrary under applicable law, unless a limited liability company agreement provides otherwise, a member may not resign from a limited liability company prior to the dissolution and winding up of the limited liability company. Notwithstanding anything to the contrary under applicable law, a limited liability company agreement may provide that a limited liability company interest may not be assigned prior to the dissolution and winding up of the limited liability company.

Unless otherwise provided in a limited liability company agreement, a limited liability company whose original certificate of formation was filed with the Secretary of State and effective on or prior to July 31, 1996, shall continue to be governed by this section as in effect on July 31, 1996, and shall not be governed by this section.

§18-604.   Distribution upon resignation.

Except as provided in this subchapter, upon resignation any resigning member is entitled to receive any distribution to which such member is entitled under a limited liability company agreement and, if not otherwise provided in a limited liability company agreement, such member is entitled to receive, within a reasonable time after resignation, the fair value of such member's limited liability company interest as of the date of resignation based upon such member's right to share in distributions from the limited liability company.

§18-605.   Distribution in kind.

Except as provided in a limited liability company agreement, a member, regardless of the nature of the member's contribution, has no right to demand and receive any distribution from a limited liability company in any form other than cash. Except as provided in a limited liability company agreement, a member may not be compelled to accept a distribution of any asset in kind from a limited liability company to the extent that the percentage of the asset distributed exceeds a percentage of that asset which is equal to the percentage in which the member shares in distributions from the limited liability company. Except as provided in the limited liability company agreement, a member may be compelled to accept a distribution of any asset in kind from a limited liability company to the extent that the percentage of the asset distributed is equal to a percentage of that asset which is equal to the percentage in which the member shares in distributions from the limited liability company.

§18-607.   Limitations on distribution.

(a) A limited liability company shall not make a distribution to a member to the extent that at the time of the distribution, after giving effect to the distribution, all liabilities of the limited liability company, other than liabilities to members on account of their limited liability company interests and liabilities for which the recourse of creditors is limited to specified property of the limited liability company, exceed the fair value of the assets of the limited liability company, except that the fair value of property that is subject to a liability for which the recourse of creditors is limited shall be included in the assets of the limited liability company only to the extent that the fair value of that property exceeds that liability. For purposes of this subsection (a), the term "distribution" shall not include amounts constituting reasonable compensation for present or past services or reasonable payments made in the ordinary course of business pursuant to a bona fide retirement plan or other benefits program.

(b) A member who receives a distribution in violation of subsection (a) of this section, and who knew at the time of the distribution that the distribution violated subsection (a) of this section, shall be liable to a limited liability company for the amount of the distribution. A member who receives a distribution in violation of subsection (a) of this section, and who did not know at the time of the distribution that the distribution violated subsection (a) of this section, shall not be liable for the amount of the distribution. Subject to subsection (c) of this section, this subsection shall not affect any obligation or liability of a member under an agreement or other applicable law for the amount of a distribution.

(c) Unless otherwise agreed, a member who receives a distribution from a limited liability company shall have no liability under this chapter or other applicable law for the amount of the distribution after the expiration of three years from the date of the distribution unless an action to recover the distribution from such member is commenced prior to the expiration of the said three-year period and an adjudication of liability against such member is made in the said action.

§18-702. Assignment of limited liability company interest.

(a) A limited liability company interest is assignable in whole or in part except as provided in a limited liability company agreement. The assignee of a member's limited liability company interest shall have no right to participate in the management of the business and affairs of a limited liability company except as provided in a limited liability company agreement and upon:

(1) The approval of all of the members of the limited liability company other than the member assigning his limited liability company interest; or

(2) Compliance with any procedure provided for in the limited liability company agreement.

(b) Unless otherwise provided in a limited liability company agreement:

(1) An assignment of a limited liability company interest does not entitle the assignee to become or to exercise any rights or powers of a member;

(2) An assignment of a limited liability company interest entitles the assignee to share in such profits and losses, to receive such distribution or distributions, and to receive such allocation of income, gain, loss, deduction, or credit or similar item to which the assignor was entitled, to the extent assigned; and

(3) A member ceases to be a member and to have the power to exercise any rights or powers of a member upon assignment of all of the member's limited liability company interest. . . .

. . .

(e) Unless otherwise provided in the limited liability company agreement, a limited liability company may acquire, by purchase, redemption or otherwise, any limited liability company interest or other interest of a member or manager in the limited liability company. Unless otherwise provided in the limited liability company agreement, any such interest so acquired by the limited liability company shall be deemed canceled.

§18-704. Right of assignee to become member.

(a) An assignee of a limited liability company interest may become a member as provided in a limited liability company agreement and upon:

(1) The approval of all of the members of the limited liability company other than the member assigning his limited liability company interest; or

(2) Compliance with any procedure provided for in the limited liability company agreement.

(b) An assignee who has become a member has, to the extent assigned, the rights and powers, and is subject to the restrictions and liabilities, of a member under a limited liability company agreement and this chapter. Notwithstanding the foregoing, unless otherwise provided in a limited liability company agreement, an assignee who becomes a member is liable for the obligations of his assignor to make contributions as provided in §18-502 of this chapter, but shall not be liable for the obligations of his assignor under subchapter VI [§18-601 through §18-607] of this chapter. However, the assignee is not obligated for liabilities, including the obligations of his assignor to make contributions as provided in §18-502 of this chapter, unknown to the assignee at the time he became a member and which could not be ascertained from a limited liability company agreement.

(c) Whether or not an assignee of a limited liability company interest becomes a member, the assignor is not released from his liability to a limited liability company under subchapters V and VI [§18-501 through §18-607] of this chapter.

§18-705.   Powers of estate of deceased or incompetent member.

If a member who is an individual dies or a court of competent jurisdiction adjudges him to be incompetent to manage the member's person or property, the member's personal representative may exercise all of the member's rights for the purpose of settling the member's estate or administering the member's property, including any power under a limited liability company agreement of an assignee to become a member. If a member is a corporation, trust or other entity and is dissolved or terminated, the powers of that member may be exercised by its personal representative.

§18-801.   Dissolution.

(a) A limited liability company is dissolved and its affairs shall be wound up upon the first to occur of the following:

(1) At the time specified in a limited liability company agreement, but if no such time is set forth in the limited liability company agreement, then the limited liability company shall have a perpetual existence;

(2) Upon the happening of events specified in a limited liability company agreement;

(3) Unless otherwise provided in a limited liability company agreement, upon the affirmative vote or written consent of the members of the limited liability company or, if there is more than 1 class or group of members, then by each class or group of members, in either case, by members who own more than two-thirds of the then-current percentage or other interest in the profits of the limited liability company owned by all of the members or by the members in each class or group, as appropriate;

(4) At any time there are no members; provided that the limited liability company is not dissolved and is not required to be wound up if, (i) unless otherwise provided in a limited liability company agreement, within 90 days or such other period as is provided for in the limited liability company agreement after the occurrence of the event that terminated the continued membership of the last remaining member, the personal representative of the last remaining member agrees in writing to continue the limited liability company and to the admission of the personal representative of such member or its nominee or designee to the limited liability company as a member, effective

as of the occurrence of the event that terminated the continued membership of the last remaining member; provided that a limited liability company agreement may provide that the personal representative of the last remaining member shall be obligated to agree in writing to continue the limited liability company and to the admission of the personal representative of such member or its nominee or designee to the limited liability company as a member, effective as of the occurrence of the event that terminated the continued membership of the last remaining member, or, (ii) a member is admitted to the limited liability company in the manner provided for in the limited liability company agreement, effective as of the occurrence of the event that terminated the continued membership of the last remaining member, within 90 days or such other period as is provided for in the limited liability company agreement after the occurrence of the event that terminated the continued membership of the last remaining member, pursuant to a provision of the limited liability company agreement that specifically provides for the admission of a member to the limited liability company after there is no longer a remaining member of the limited liability company.

(5) The entry of a decree of judicial dissolution under §18-802 of this title.

(b) Unless otherwise provided in a limited liability company agreement, the death, retirement, resignation, expulsion, bankruptcy or dissolution of any member or the occurrence of any other event that terminates the continued membership of any member shall not cause the limited liability company to be dissolved or its affairs to be wound up, and upon the occurrence of any such event, the limited liability company shall be continued without dissolution.

§18-803.   Winding up.

(a) Unless otherwise provided in a limited liability company agreement, a manager who has not wrongfully dissolved a limited liability company or, if none, the members or a person approved by the members or, if there is more than 1 class or group of members, then by each class or group of members, in either case, by members who own more than 50 percent of the then current percentage or other interest in the profits of the limited liability company owned by all of the members or by the members in each class or group, as appropriate, may wind up the limited liability company's affairs; but the Court of Chancery, upon cause shown, may wind up the limited liability company's affairs upon application of any member or manager, the member's or manager's personal representative or assignee, and in connection therewith, may appoint a liquidating trustee.

. . .

§18-804.   Distribution of assets.

(a) Upon the winding up of a limited liability company, the assets shall be distributed as follows:

(1) To creditors, including members and managers who are creditors, to the extent otherwise permitted by law, in satisfaction of liabilities of the limited liability company (whether by payment or the making of reasonable provision for payment thereof) other than liabilities for which reasonable provision for payment has been made and liabilities for distributions to members and former members under section 18-601 or section 18-604 of this title;

(2) Unless otherwise provided in a limited liability company agreement, to members and former members in satisfaction of liabilities for distributions under section 18-601 or section 18-604 of this title; and

(3) Unless otherwise provided in a limited liability company agreement, to members first for the return of their contributions and second respecting their limited liability company interests, in the proportions in which the members share in distributions.

(b) A limited liability company which has dissolved (i) shall pay or make reasonable provision to pay all claims and obligations, including all contingent, conditional or unmatured contractual claims, known to the limited liability company, (ii) shall make such provision as will be reasonably likely to be sufficient to provide compensation for any claim against the limited liability company which is the subject of a pending action, suit or proceeding to which the limited liability company is a party and (iii) shall make such provision as will be reasonably likely to be sufficient to provide compensation for claims that have not been made known to the limited liability company or that have not arisen but that, based on facts known to the limited liability company, are likely to arise or to become known to the limited liability company within 10 years after the date of dissolution. If there are sufficient assets, such claims and obligations shall be paid in full and any such provision for payment made shall be made in full. If there are insufficient assets, such claims and obligations shall be paid or provided for according to their priority and, among claims of equal priority, ratably to the extent of assets available therefor. Unless otherwise provided in the limited liability company agreement, any remaining assets shall be distributed as provided in this chapter. Any liquidating trustee winding up a limited liability company's affairs who has complied with this section shall not be personally liable to the claimants of the dissolved limited liability company by reason of such person's actions in winding up the limited liability company.

(c) A member who receives a distribution in violation of subsection (a) of this section, and who knew at the time of the distribution that the distribution violated subsection (a) of this section, shall be liable to the limited liability company for the amount of the distribution. For purposes of the immediately preceding sentence, the term "distribution" shall not include amounts constituting reasonable compensation for present or past services or reasonable payments made in the ordinary course of business pursuant to a bona fide retirement plan or other benefits program. A member who receives a distribution in violation of subsection (a) of this section, and who did not know at the time of the distribution that the distribution violated subsection (a) of this section, shall not be liable for the amount of the distribution. Subject to subsection (d) of this section, this subsection shall not affect any obligation or liability of a member under an agreement or other applicable law for the amount of a distribution.

(d) Unless otherwise agreed, a member who receives a distribution from a limited liability company to which this section applies shall have no liability under this chapter or other applicable law for the amount of the distribution after the expiration of 3 years from the date of the distribution unless an action to recover the distribution from such member is commenced prior to the expiration of the said 3-year period and an adjudication of liability against such member is made in the said action.

(e) section 18-607 of this title shall not apply to a distribution to which this section applies.

§18-901.   Law governing.

(a) Subject to the Constitution of the State of Delaware:

(1) The laws of the state, territory, possession, or other jurisdiction or country under which a foreign limited liability company is organized govern its organization and internal affairs and the liability of its members and managers; and

(2) A foreign limited liability company may not be denied registration by reason of any difference between those laws and the laws of the State of Delaware.

. . .

§18-902.   Registration required; application.

(a) Before doing business in the State of Delaware, a foreign limited liability company shall register with the Secretary of State. . . .

. . .

§18-907.   Doing business without registration.

(a) A foreign limited liability company doing business in the State of Delaware may not maintain any action, suit or proceeding in the State of Delaware until it has registered . . .

(b) The failure of a foreign limited liability company to register in the State of Delaware does not impair:

(1) The validity of any contract or act of the foreign limited liability company;

(2) The right of any other party to the contract to maintain any action, suit or proceeding on the contract; or

(3) Prevent the foreign limited liability company from defending any action, suit or proceeding in any court of the State of Delaware.

(c) A member or a manager of a foreign limited liability company is not liable for the obligations of the foreign limited liability company solely by reason of the limited liability company's having done business in the State of Delaware without registration.

. . .

§18-1107.   Taxation of limited liability companies.

(a) For purposes of any tax imposed by the State of Delaware or any instrumentality, agency or political subdivision of the State of Delaware, a limited liability company formed under this chapter or qualified to do business in the State of Delaware as a foreign limited liability company shall be classified as a partnership unless classified otherwise for federal income tax purposes, in which case the limited liability company shall be classified in the same manner as it is classified for federal income tax purposes. For purposes of any tax imposed by the State of Delaware or any instrumentality, agency or political subdivision of the State of Delaware, a member or assignee of a member of a limited liability company formed under this chapter or qualified to do business in the State of Delaware as a foreign limited liability company shall be treated as either a resident or nonresident partner unless classified otherwise for federal income tax purposes, in which case the member or assignee of a member shall have the same status as such member or assignee of a member has for federal income tax purposes.

. . .

¶2700

Cases

In re INTERNATIONAL RADIATOR CO.

Court of Chancery of Delaware

92 A. 255 (1914)

. . .

THE CHANCELLOR.

This claim is for $7,500 for damages based on the failure of the company to comply with an agreement with Harris, whereby Harris in April, 1913, gave to the company his notes aggregating $5,000 in payment for 1,000 shares of stock of the company, of par value of $10, which shares the company agreed to sell for him to net him $7.50 per share, to be paid to him on or before August 1, 1913. The notes were given to, and the proceeds thereof by a discount thereof were received by the company. The stock was not sold, and the notes were paid by Harris. In substance, for $5,000, the company agreed to pay $7,500 from the proceeds of the sale by it of shares of its capital stock subscribed for by Harris. The legal effect of the agreement is, of course, that in case it was unable to sell the shares of stock it would buy them back, and the claim filed by Harris is necessarily based on this principle.

It may be considered doubtful whether the corporation had a right to make such a contract, even if solvent, and if the rights of creditors were not affected. Subscriptions to capital stock should not be made subterfuges to borrow money under unusual terms, nor should countenance by [be] given to sales made by a corporation of shares of its capital stock in such irregular ways, especially where the advantage is disproportionately in favor of the purchaser. But when at the time the bargain is made the rights, of creditors of the company are, or would be, affected by it, then clearly such an agreement is unenforcible [sic] against the assets of the company in the hands of a receiver subsequently appointed by reason of insolvency.

The undoubted weight of authority is that a corporation, without express authority, and when not prohibited by their charter, or by statute, may buy its own shares, provided they do so in good faith, without intending to injure its creditors and without in fact injuring them. . . . A corporation cannot purchase its own shares of stock when the purchase diminishes the ability of the company to pay its debts, or lessens the security of its creditors. . . .

The claim is further affected by the statute in Delaware. By the General Corporation Act, under which the company was incorporated, the company could not use its funds or property to purchase shares of its own capital 'when such use would cause an impairment of the capital of the corporation.' At the time when the agreement was made with Harris, and at the time the receiver was appointed, the capital stock of the company was about $400,000, presumably issued for value, while its assets were appraised at $13,000 by the appraisers in the receivership cause. It is said that about $75,000 of stock was issued for patents, etc. But even adding this sum to the appraised value of the assets of the company, still the payment of the claim of Harris from the assets to come into the hands of the receiver will, of course, deplete the capital.

Therefore, the question is whether an agreement of a corporation to sell shares of its own capital stock for a stockholder, is not as to a claim by the stockholder for the sum of money at which the company agreed to sell it, a purchase by the company of such shares?

A claim for the price at which the company agreed to sell the shares is certainly equivalent to an agreement to purchase at that price, and equally within the spirit of the act and equally unlawful, if the enforcement of such an agreement impaired the capital of the company. Any one dealing with the corporation is bound to know the limitations put on it by the statute under which it was created. In the statute the impairment of the 'capital' of the company is mentioned. As here used, this means the reduction of the amount of the assets of the company below the amount represented by the aggregate outstanding shares of the capital stock of the company. In other words, a corporation may use only its surplus for the purchase of shares of its own capital stock. 'Capital' does not in this connection mean the assets of the company, for, of course, the assets are reduced when any of it is used by a corporation to purchase shares of its own capital stock. It must have some other meaning then. The statute must mean, therefore, that the funds and property of the company shall not be used for the purchase of shares of its own capital stock when the value of its assets is less than the aggregate amount of all the shares of its capital stock. A use by a corporation of its assets to purchase shares of its own capital stock under such conditions impairs the capital of the company.

¶2700 In re International Radiator Co.

As these conditions existed when the contract was made between Harris and the International Radiator Company, the contract is not now enforceable against the assets in the hands of the receiver, and the claim is disallowed. . . .

Stuart TURNER et al., Plaintiffs, v.
Joel E. BERNSTEIN, et al., Defendants.

Court of Chancery of Delaware

1999 WL 66532 (1999)

Before it was acquired by Medicis in the merger, GenDerm . . . was a non-public Delaware corporation . . .

[GenDerm mailed to certain (but not all) of its shareholders some (but not extensive) information and the merger was then approved by written consent of shareholders owning sufficient stock to approve the merger. The plaintiff shareholders (who did not consent to the merger) accepted the merger consideration and did not seek statutory appraisal rights.]

. . .

The Complaint . . . alleges that the former directors of GenDerm . . . failed to provide material information about GenDerm that would enable its stockholders to decide whether or not to execute a written consent approving the merger or demand appraisal. Specifically, the plaintiffs claim that they were not furnished basic financial information concerning GenDerm's business; information about business plans or recent or planned transactions or agreements; or any description of GenDerm's material products, pharmacological categories, or markets in which such products compete. That failure to disclose is said to constitute a breach of the former GenDerm directors' fiduciary duties of loyalty and disclosure, and to entitle the shareholder class to damages and an accounting in a "quasi-appraisal action" to determine GenDerm's fair value.

. . .

For purposes of this motion, the Court assumes . . . that GenDerm's former shareholders did not receive all material information necessary to an informed decision on whether or not to elect their appraisal remedy.

. . .

The fiduciary duty of disclosure flows from the broader fiduciary duties of care and loyalty. . . . That disclosure duty is triggered (inter alia) where directors (as GenDerm's former directors did here) present to stockholders for their consideration a transaction that requires them to cast a vote and/or make an investment decision, such as whether or not to accept a merger or demand appraisal. . . . Stockholders confronted with that choice are entitled to disclosure of the available material facts needed to make such an informed decision. . . . Specifically in the merger context, the directors of a constituent corporation whose shareholders are to vote on a proposed merger, have a fiduciary duty to disclose to the shareholders the available material facts that would enable them to make an informed decision, . . . , whether to accept the merger consideration or demand appraisal. . . .

Our case law recognizes that a stockholder who surrenders his shares in a merger and accepts the merger consideration and the other benefits of the merger, will be deemed to have waived his right to seek appraisal or otherwise to challenge the transaction, provided that the decision to accept the merger was fully informed. . . . The question presented here is whether the undisputed facts are sufficient to establish as a matter of law that the plaintiffs were not fully informed when they elected to accept the merger consideration.

. . .

The former directors argue that . . . the plaintiffs received GenDerm's most recent financial statements shortly before the merger. . . . The defendants underscore that both plaintiffs signed consent forms that expressly and pointedly told them that signing the consents would operate as a waiver of appraisal rights, and that the plaintiffs then accepted the merger consideration. Lastly, the defendants point out that although the Letter of Transmittal invited the recipients to call a telephone number if they needed more information, the plaintiffs did not do so. These facts, the defendants argue, create sufficient reason to doubt the plaintiffs' professions of ignorance of GenDerm's pre-merger financial condition, and preclude the entry of judgment as a matter of law.

I agree that a grant of summary judgment would be imprudent. Further discovery is needed to flesh out what specific facts the plaintiffs knew or had available to them when they decided to accept the merger consideration. . . .

Doran MALONE et al., Plaintiffs-Appellants, v. John. N. BRINCAT et al., - Appellees.

Supreme Court of Delaware

722 A.2d 5 (1998)

. . .

It is well-established that the duty of disclosure "represents nothing more than the well-recognized proposition that directors of Delaware corporations are under a fiduciary duty to disclose fully and fairly all material information within the board's control when it seeks shareholder action.". . .

. . . The director's fiduciary duty to both the corporation and its shareholders has been characterized by this Court as a triad: due care, good faith, and loyalty. . . .

. . . The duty of disclosure is, and always has been, a specific application of the general fiduciary duty owed by directors. The duty of disclosure obligates directors to provide the stockholders with accurate and complete information material to a transaction or other corporate event that is being presented to them for action.

. . .

Shareholders are entitled to rely upon the truthfulness of all information disseminated to them by the directors . . . Delaware directors disseminate information in at least three contexts: public statements made to the market, including shareholders; statements informing shareholders about the affairs of the corporation without a request for shareholder action; and, statements to shareholders in conjunction with a request for shareholder action. Inaccurate information in these contexts may be the result of a violation of the fiduciary duties of care, loyalty or good faith.

. . .

. . . When the directors disseminate information to stockholders when no stockholder action is sought, the fiduciary duties of care, loyalty and good faith apply. . . .

. . .

The directors' duty to disclose all available material information in connection with a request for shareholder action must be balanced against its concomitant duty to protect the corporate enterprise, in particular, by keeping certain financial information confidential. . . . Directors are required to provide shareholders with all information that is material to the action being requested and to provide a balanced, truthful account of all matters disclosed in the communications with shareholders. . . . Accordingly, directors have definitive guidance in discharging their fiduciary duty by an analysis of the factual circumstances relating to the specific shareholder action being requested and an inquiry into the potential for deception or misinformation. . . .

Asher B. EDELMAN et al., Plaintiffs-Appellees v. FRUEHAUF CORPORATION, a Michigan corporation, et al., Defendants-Appellants.

United States Court of Appeals, Sixth Circuit

798 F.2d 882 (1986)

Affirmed.
Ralph B. Guy, Jr., Circuit Judge, dissented and filed opinion.
Before MERRITT, MARTIN and GUY, Circuit Judges.
MERRITT, Circuit Judge.

In this corporate takeover case arising under the Securities Exchange Act and the Williams Act and under Michigan law governing corporate self-dealing, the District Court issued a preliminary injunction restraining the defendant directors of Fruehauf Corporation, the target corporation, from using corporate funds and from preempting the bidding in order to assist Fruehauf management in effectuating a leveraged buyout made in response to a hostile tender offer by plaintiffs, the Edelman group. The District Court also required the disclosure of certain information to shareholders in connection with management's buyout offer and ordered that the Fruehauf directors establish a fair auction process and reopen the bidding for the company instead of closing it off prematurely by accepting management's bid. It ordered the defendants to give the Edelman group an opportunity to continue the bidding on an equal basis with management. The basic issues before us concern the steps that management and the directors of a target corporation may take in attempting to beat a hostile takeover by formulating a management buyout of the company. The basic question is: once the company has been put up for sale, to what extent should Michigan corporation law be interpreted to require open bidding on an equal basis by all parties including management and to what extent should the law allow the directors of the target corporation to tilt the contest in management's favor. . . .

Fruehauf Corporation was incorporated under the laws of Michigan. The company is a leading producer of truck trailers and cargo containers. It owns a finance company and has subsidiaries in a number of industries: auto parts production, conversion of cargo ships to container operations, construction and repair of ships, and manufacture of container handling equipment. In 1985, Fruehauf and its subsidiaries had sales of $2.5 billion and net profit of $70 million. It has over 21 million shares of common stock outstanding, and in 1985, Fruehauf stock traded publicly at between $20.3 and $28.8 per share.

In February 1986, the Edelman group began acquiring Fruehauf stock on the open market. At that time, the stock was trading in the mid $20 range. The Edelman group attempted, unsuccessfully, to negotiate a "friendly" acquisition of Fruehauf and then proposed a cash merger in which Fruehauf shareholders would receive $41 per share for their stock. Later, this price was increased to $42 per share. Fruehauf's Board rejected this proposal. On June 11, 1986, the Edelman group announced its intention to make an all-cash tender offer for all Fruehauf shares at $44 per share. Fruehauf's financial advisors told the Board that if the Edelman group made the offer, the shares would probably be tendered. At that time, the Board realized that a change of ownership of Fruehauf was imminent and that the company would end up being sold. The market responded to the Edelman group's overtures, and the market price of Fruehauf stock climbed to the mid $40 range.

In response to the Edelman group's offer, members of Fruehauf's management negotiated with Merrill Lynch to arrange a two-tier leveraged buyout by management and Merrill Lynch. Under this deal, a corporation formed for purposes of the buyout would purchase approximately 77% of Fruehauf's stock in a cash tender offer for $48.50 per share. This tender offer would be funded using $375 million borrowed from Merrill Lynch, $375 million borrowed from Manufacturers Hanover, and $100 million contributed by Fruehauf Corporation. Next, Fruehauf would be merged with the acquiring corporation, and the remaining Fruehauf shareholders would receive securities in the new corporation valued at $48.50. Total equity contribution to the new company would be only $25 million—$10 to $15 million from management and the rest from Merrill Lynch. In return for their equity contribution, management would receive between 40 and 60 percent control of the new company (depending on the amount of their equity contribution). Under this arrangement, Fruehauf would also pay approximately $30 million to Merrill Lynch for loan commitment fees, advisory fees, and a "breakup fee" that Merrill Lynch would keep even if the deal did not go through. Additionally, the deal would contain a "no-shop" clause restricting Fruehauf's ability to attempt to negotiate a better deal with another bidder. A special committee composed of Fruehauf's outside directors approved the proposed management leveraged buyout, and Fruehauf's board authorized the buyout. We must determine whether these outside directors and the board as a whole fulfilled their fiduciary duty to Fruehauf's shareholders when they approved management's buyout proposal.

Like the District Court, we conclude on the basis of strong evidence that Fruehauf's Board of Directors unreasonably preferred incumbent management in the bidding process—acting without objectivity and requisite loyalty to the corporation. Their actions were not taken in a good faith effort to negotiate the best deal for the shareholders. They acted as interested parties and did not treat the Fruehauf managers and the Edelman group in an even handed way but rather gave their colleagues on the Board, the inside managers, the inside track and accepted their proposal without fostering a real bidding process.

The evidence for this conclusion is clear. Several directors admitted their bias in their depositions. In disclosing the management transaction to the stockholders, the Board made it appear that the management proposal was the best bid obtainable after giving Edelman a reasonable opportunity to top the bid. In fact the Board accepted the leverage[d] buyout proposal of the management and Merrill Lynch without giving Edelman an opportunity to bid further and then rejected out of hand Edelman's offer a couple of days later to acquire the company on the same terms as management but at a higher price. While refusing to talk to Edelman or promote an open bidding process, the Board agreed to pay well over $30 million in corporate funds to Merrill Lynch as financing and advisory fees so that the management buyout could be consummated. (Over half of this amount would be paid even if another bidder prevailed.) The Board also made available $100 million of corporate funds for management's use in the purchase of shares and entered into an agreement severely limiting the Board's ability to negotiate another offer.

There are other indicia of the Board's intention to preempt the bidding in favor of management. For example, the committee of outside directors employed as its advisor the investment banker that was in the process of negotiating management's buyout proposal and clearly favored that course. Then no effort was made to get a counter offer. Additionally, the Board amended Fruehauf's stock option plan, incentive compensation plan, and pension plan to provide that if anyone obtained a 40% interest in Fruehauf without the Board's approval, all company-issued options in Fruehauf stock would be immediately exercisable, all incentive compensation payments normally due Fruehauf's salaried employees in due course would become immediately due, and the $70 to $100 million of overfunding in the pension plan, which had been available for corporate use, would be irrevocably committed to the pension fund. These measures had the effect of making Fruehauf a less attractive takeover target, and thereby, of dampening the bidding process. Later, in response to the threat of litigation, the Board again amended these plans to provide for acceleration of stock options and incentive compensation payments in the event anyone became a 40% shareholder, even with Board approval. Counsel admits that it is from these plans that members of management would obtain the money for their equity contributions to the management buyout. The Board also further amended the pension plan to give advance board approval to any 40% acquiror who pays at least $48.50 per share. In short, it appears that the Board simply decided to make a deal with management no matter what other bidders might offer. The entire factual pattern is consistent with that purpose.

Under Michigan law, a "transaction between a corporation and 1 or more of its directors or officers" is invalid unless the transaction is "fair and reasonable" or is properly authorized or ratified by disinterested directors or shareholders after complete disclosure. Mich.Comp.Laws §450.1545. "When the validity of [such] a contract . . . is questioned, the burden of establishing its validity" is on the Board. Id. at §450.1546. Michigan law is similar to the general law on this subject. See Radol v. Thomas, 772 F.2d 244, 257 (6th Cir. 1985).

In this case, the Board has failed to carry its burden of establishing that the management buyout was fair and reasonable in light of the circumstances. The Board argues that the transaction was valid under section 450.1545 because it was authorized by Fruehauf's disinterested directors after complete disclosure. This argument assumes that any authorization by disinterested directors will suffice. However, the Board must also show that the disinterested directors did not act in dereliction of their fiduciary duty to the corporation and its shareholders when they authorized the management buyout. The evidence compels the conclusion that the directors simply "rubber stamped" the management buyout proposal. In so doing, they breached their fiduciary duty. See Hanson Trust PLC v. ML SCM Acquisition, Inc., 781 F.2d 264 (2d Cir.1986), in which the Second Circuit was faced with another leveraged buyout of a takeover target by an investment group composed of Merrill Lynch and members of the target's management. In Hanson, as in this case, the disinterested directors had approved the buyout and later argued that the business judgment rule proscribed judicial inquiry into their decision. Construing New York law, the court rejected the directors' argument, holding:

> [T]he exercise of fiduciary duties by a corporate board member includes more than avoiding fraud, bad faith and self-dealing. Directors must exercise their "honest judgment in the lawful and legitimate furtherance of corporate purposes." It is not enough that directors merely be disinterested and thus not disposed to self-dealing or other indicia of a breach of the duty of loyalty. Directors are also held to a standard of due care. They must meet this standard with "conscientious fairness." For example, where their "methodologies and procedures" are "so restricted in scope, so shallow in execution, or otherwise so *pro forma* or halfhearted as to constitute a pretext or sham," then inquiry into their acts is not shielded by the business judgment rule. ... [W]hile directors are protected to the extent that their actions evidence their business judgment, such protection assumes that courts must not reflexively decline to consider the content of their "judgment" and the extent of the information on which it is based.

781 F.2d at 274-75 (citations omitted, emphasis in original). The court found that the directors had breached their fiduciary duty. It enjoined a "lock-up option" that was part of the buyout arrangement.

Given the Board's unreasonable conduct in violation of Michigan law, as found by the District Court, we agree with the District Court that the remedy should be injunctive relief. All sides agree that Fruehauf is on the auction block. Once it becomes apparent that a takeover target will be acquired by new owners, whether by an alleged "raider" or by a team consisting of management and a "white knight," it becomes the duty of the target's directors to see that the shareholders obtain the best price possible for their stock. "The directors' role change[s] from defenders of the corporate bastion to auctioneers charged with getting the best price for the stockholders at a sale of the company." Revlon, Inc. v. MacAndrews & Forbes Holdings, Inc., 506 A.2d 173, 182 (Del. Sup. 1986). When, in violation of this duty, directors take measures that are intended to put an end to the bidding, those measures may be enjoined. See Revlon, 506 A.2d at 184 (enjoining directors from agreeing to a "no-shop" clause, which prevented them from negotiating with other bidders). In light of the clear failure of the Board to provide for a fair auction, the District Court was correct to devise injunctive relief setting a framework for an open bidding process. ...

As Judge Guy pointed out in dissent at the hearing, the most controversial provisions of the District Court's injunction are its provisions restraining the defendants from using corporate funds to effectuate the buyout, including financing, commitment, legal and other similar fees. Our treatment of those provisions should not suggest that under the business judgment rule we would never allow corporate funds to be used to encourage bidders or even to encourage management buyouts. Obviously some marginal costs to finance the flow of information are necessary, and advisory fees for lawyers and investment bankers to structure and conduct the bidding process will have to be paid. It may be that in some instances—where the neutrality and objectivity of the Board is clearly present— commitment fees of various bankers should be paid.

But in this case, as the District Court found, the degree of the Board's largesse in favor of the managers, their bankers, and Merrill Lynch, is out of proportion. The Board was willing to make over $130 million available to its managers to insure their success. The evidence clearly suggests that the Board's purpose was not to create a fair bidding process but to make sure that the managers and Merrill Lynch bought the company and that other bidders would be turned away. In light of this conduct, the District Court was correct in restraining the Board from making Fruehauf money available to fund the management buyout. Where evidence of bias is clearly present, an injunction ensuring neutrality is necessary and each bidder must stand on its own bottom in respect to funding.

We believe this position is consistent with the development of the law. The original common law rule prohibiting transactions with interested directors was found to be too inflexible and was gradually modified. See Model Business Corp. Act §41 and accompanying notes (2nd ed. 1971) (stating that such transactions should not be void *per se* and tracing history of development); W. Cary & M. Eisenberg, Cases and Materials on Corporations 563-74, 613-37 (5th ed. 1980). Vague principles granting deference to managers and directors whose interests clearly conflict with the corporation have not worked well in buyout situations and firm rules ensuring open bidding are considered necessary by most scholars who have investigated the problem. See generally, Lowenstein, Management Buyouts, 85 Colum.L.Rev. 730 (1985).

Accordingly, the judgment of the District Court, as modified herein, is affirmed.

RALPH B. GUY, Jr., Circuit Judge, dissenting. . . .

We are presented here with a relatively typical takeover case. Fruehauf, upon becoming aware that a takeover attempt was underway, decided to resist. It is not really clear from the record whether the resistance was for the purpose of forcing a higher tender offer, keeping control of the company, or some combination of both. In any event, Fruehauf went to the now relatively common arsenal of defenses and came forward with the usual assortment of lockups, poison pills, and other devices designed to make things more difficult for the raider and easier to find a white knight. The trial court enjoined *all* of the defensive actions taken by Fruehauf and ordered them rescinded. It also ordered that to the degree corporate funds were going to be used, they must be available to all on an equal basis. On appeal, the majority extends the "available to all" principle even further. For example, unlike the trial court, they have allowed the poison pills to remain so long as everyone has to swallow them.

Philosophically, there is a wide divergence of opinion as to the proper role of management in the face of a legitimate takeover attempt. Some urge almost complete passivity on the part of management, while others would allow active resistance and consideration of not only stockholder interests, but such things as employee interests as well.[1] Although the varying philosophies make an interesting backdrop for the decision of this case, we are not free to roam the landscape in the same manner as the commentators. Essentially, courts must look to applicable state and federal statutes, the business judgment rule, and the judicial decisions which offer at least some guidance in this area.

It is my feeling that undue weight in the decision making process has been given to the fact that members of Fruehauf management will be part of the white knight group. Although such action may well require close scrutiny, it is certainly not *per se* illegal or improper. Regardless of how one would characterize management actions here, the fact remains that the net result of that action was to increase the firm offer to shareholders from $44.00 a share to $48.50 a share. I would also note that to the degree shareholders have become a party to this litigation, they have supported, not attacked, what management has done. Unless you adopt the view, which no court has yet done, that management must be totally passive in the face of a takeover, I cannot see where the shareholders have been harmed to date by the action taken by the defendants. My view is not changed on this issue by the fact that plaintiff has offered to "negotiate" a higher offer. However, I am not prepared to hold that management's "cold shoulder" to the offer to negotiate was appropriate either. I just don't think there is a record here on which that decision can be made. It involves an evaluation of the upside benefit of getting perhaps a dollar more per share versus the downside benefit of possibly losing the white knight in the process. The business judgment rule does not require a decision by a court that the actions taken were correct in some absolute or hindsight sense, but only that they be reasonable at the time. At least part of the rationale of the business judgment rule is that managers know more about running their businesses than courts do.

Admittedly, these are difficult cases; the surroundings are unfamiliar, the argot is strange, the financial transactions are complex, and the time limit for decision making is extremely short. Nonetheless, in this case we are presented with a clear record as to exactly what steps management took to resist the takeover and find a white knight. The district court reviewed these actions and found them improper, but no reasons are given as to why they are improper or what judicial precedent is being specifically violated. Although all of the actions taken may be pigeonholed by category, e.g., lock up, no-shop provision, the mere affixing of the label does not resolve the question of the propriety or impropriety of the action taken. Revlon, Inc. v. MacAndrews & Forbes Holdings, 506 A.2d 173, 176 (Del. 1986). Nothing could illustrate this point better than the majority's allowance of that which the district court ordered rescinded, conditioned only upon an even-handedness of application. I cannot subscribe to this reasoning. If what management did was illegal, as the majority opinion concludes, it should be enjoined. If it wasn't illegal, it should be allowed even if philosophically unpalatable and, if a court cannot tell, it seems to me that this is what the business judgment rule is

---

Edelman v. Fruehauf Corporation [1] See, e.g., Esterbrook & Fischel, *The Proper Role of a Target Management in Responding to a Tender Offer.* 94 Harv.L.Rev. 1161 (1981).

all about and the nod should be given to those who are vested with the business decision making responsibility.

I think that what is required here is a careful analysis of each of the alleged wrongful actions taken and a decision as to whether the defendants violated their responsibilities as to each such action. We have spent too much time looking at the chaff and ignored the seed. The plaintiffs have skillfully merchandised such things as the fact that the outside directors did not engage personally in any negotiations with Merrill Lynch or any other party. We are given no authority for the proposition that they must. I do not understand that to be the role of outside directors in a takeover situation. Rather, they are to exercise independent judgment as to the general fairness and reasonableness of the actions contemplated. Here, they knew that the $48.50 offer was $4.50 higher than the existing tender offer; that it was in excess of $20.00 higher than what the stock was trading for prior to the takeover attempt; and that it was in the ballpark as far as being a fair price for shareholders was concerned. The constraints of time alone, coupled with the lack of familiarity of the outside directors with the day-to-day operations of Fruehauf, place practical limits on their function and responsibility.

Notwithstanding that time is of the essence, I would remand to the district court for an evidentiary hearing on the actual effect, if any, of the alleged wrongful actions taken by the defendants, and whether such actions violate their duty to the shareholders. I would note in this regard that in the face of all the defensive actions taken by the defendants, the plaintiffs have still aggressively pursued this acquisition. The question has never been answered or even addressed as to whether measures short of those taken by Fruehauf would have resulted in anyone stepping forward to top the original tender offer of $44.00. This is not to suggest that the ends justify the means, however, as the court's responsibility is to call a halt when that line has been crossed that separates improper self dealing from advancing the interest of the shareholders. The majority may be correct in ruling that that line has been crossed here, however, on the state of the record before me, I cannot comfortably join in that conclusion. . . .

HANSON TRUST PLC et al., Plaintiffs-Appellants v. ML SCM ACQUISITION INC. et al., Defendants-Appellees.

United States Court of Appeals, Second Circuit

781 F.2d 264 (1986)

Reversed and remanded.
Oakes, Circuit Judge, filed a concurring opinion.
Kearse, Circuit Judge, filed a dissenting opinion.
Before OAKES, KEARSE, and PIERCE, Circuit Judges.
PIERCE, Circuit Judge:

¶2700 Hanson Trust PLC v. ML SCM Acquisition Inc.

Hanson Trust PLC, HSCM Industries Inc., Hanson Holdings Netherlands B.V., and HMAC Investments Inc. (hereinafter sometimes referred to collectively as "Hanson") appeal from an order, dated November 26, 1985, in the United States District Court for the Southern District of New York, Shirley Wohl Kram, Judge, denying their motion for a preliminary injunction restraining Merrill Lynch, Pierce, Fenner & Smith Incorporated and related entities, including ML SCM Acquisition Inc. (hereinafter "Merrill"), and SCM Corporation (hereinafter "SCM"), and their respective officers, agents and employees, and all persons acting in concert with them, from exercising or seeking to exercise an asset purchase option (hereinafter sometimes referred to as a "lock-up option") pursuant to an Asset Option Agreement and a Merger Agreement between those corporate entities. Under those Agreements, in the event that by March 1, 1986, any third party acquires one third or more of SCM's outstanding common stock or rights to acquire such stock, Merrill would have the right to purchase SCM's Pigments and Consumer Foods Divisions for $350 million and $80 million, respectively. After an eight-day evidentiary hearing, the district court denied Hanson's motion for a preliminary injunction, principally because it found that under New York law approval of the lock-up option by the SCM directors (hereinafter sometimes referred to as the "Board"), and the lock-up option itself, were, in the exercise of business judgment, "part of a viable business strategy, as the law currently defines those terms," and because "Hanson failed to adduce sufficient credible proof to the contrary." Hanson Trust PLC v. SCM Corp., 623 F.Supp. 848, 859-60 (S.D.N.Y. 1985). . . . We reverse and remand.

Background

This is the second suit arising out of an intense struggle for control of a large public corporation, SCM. In the first case, Hanson Trust PLC v. SCM Corp., 774 F.2d 47 (2d Cir.1985) (hereinafter referred to as *Hanson I*), we held that Hanson's termination of a $72 offer and nearly immediate purchases of several large blocks of stock amounting to approximately twenty-five per cent of the outstanding shares of SCM privately from five sophisticated institutional investors and in one open market transaction did not violate §§14(d)(1) and (6) of the Williams Act, 15 U.S.C. §78n(d)(1) and (6) and rules promulgated by the Securities and Exchange Commission thereunder. In the present case, the issue presented is whether it was proper under New York law for SCM and Merrill to execute a lock-up option agreement as part of a $74 offer by Merrill for SCM common stock. In *Hanson I*, Judge Mansfield summarized the "fast-moving bidding contest" as follows: first, a $60 per share cash tender offer by Hanson, for any and all shares of SCM; next, a counter tender offer of $70, part cash and part debenture, by the SCM Board and their "white knight," Merrill Lynch Capital Markets (with underwriting participation by Prudential Insurance Co.), for a "leveraged buyout" (hereinafter sometimes referred to as an "LBO"); then an increase by Hanson to $72 cash, conditioned on SCM not locking up corporate assets; then a revised $74 cash and debenture offer by SCM-Merrill, with "a 'crown jewel' irrevocable lock-up option to Merrill designed to discourage Hanson from seeking control by providing that if any other party (in this case Hanson) should acquire more than one-third of SCM's outstanding shares (66 $\frac{2}{3}$ being needed under N.Y.Bus. Corp.L. §903(a)(2) to effectuate a merger) Merrill would have the right to buy SCM's two most profitable businesses" (Pigments and Consumer Foods) at $350 million and $80 million, respectively. *Hanson I* at 50-51. Hanson, evidently deterred by the option and faced with the $74 LBO offer, terminated its $72 offer, but made the September 11 purchases upheld in *Hanson I*, and later announced a $75 cash tender offer conditioned on the withdrawal or judicial invalidation of the subject lock-up options. A more detailed account of the relevant background follows.

SCM is a New York corporation with its principal place of business in New York City. It consists of several divisions, including Chemicals, Coatings and Resins, Paper Products, Foods, and Typewriters. Pigments, a subdivision of Chemicals, and Consumer Foods, a subdivision of Foods, referred to by Hanson as the "crown jewels" of the SCM Corporation, have generated approximately 50% of SCM's net operating income in recent years. SCM's Board of Directors consists of twelve members. Three directors, Messrs. Elicker, Hall, and Harris, are also members of SCM's management: Elicker is Chairman of the Board and Chief Executive Officer; Harris is SCM's President and Chief Operating Officer; Hall is a Senior Vice President of SCM. The remaining nine members of the board are "outside" or "independent" directors. None of the nine holds a management position in SCM, owns significant amounts of SCM common stock, or receives any remuneration from SCM other than the standard directors' fee. The district court also found that none is affiliated with any entity that does business with SCM and that all of the directors have considerable business experience and working knowledge of SCM and its operations. . . .

Hanson Trust PLC is a corporation organized under the laws of the United Kingdom. HSCM Industries Inc. is a Delaware corporation and an indirectly wholly owned subsidiary of Hanson Trust PLC. Hanson Holdings Netherlands B.V. is a limited liability company incorporated under the laws of the Kingdom of the Netherlands, and is an indirectly wholly owned subsidiary of Hanson Trust PLC. HMAC Investments Inc. is also a Delaware corporation and is a wholly owned subsidiary of Hanson Trust PLC.

On August 21, 1985, Hanson announced its intention to make a $60 cash tender offer for any and all shares of SCM common stock. The evidence showed that SCM common stock traded below $50 per share in July 1985, and that between August 1 and August 19, Hanson had purchased over 87,000 shares for between approximately $54 and $56. . . . On August 22, 1985, the day after the Hanson offer was announced, the price of SCM stock closed on the New York Stock Exchange at 64$\frac{1}{8}$.

It is not disputed that also on August 22—three days prior to the SCM Board's first meeting regarding Hanson's offer—SCM management met with representatives of the investment banking firm of Goldman Sachs & Co. and the law firm of Wachtell, Lipton, Rosen & Katz to discuss a response to Hanson's bid. . . . Among the alternatives considered in response to Hansons offer was the possibility of a leveraged buyout that would include SCM management participation. . . . By August 23 or 24, SCM management and Goldman Sachs had initiated discussions with the leveraged buyout firms of Kohlberg, Kravis, Roberts & Co. and Merrill Lynch. . . . SCM's Board met on August 25, and approved the retention of Goldman Sachs and Wachtell Lipton on behalf of SCM and the SCM Board. . . .

The parties agree that the August 25 Board meeting was called to discuss alternatives to the Hanson offer; that discussions focused principally on finding either another public company to act as a "white knight" or one or more financial institutions to underwrite a leveraged buyout. Willard J. Overlock, Jr., SCM's principal adviser at Goldman Sachs, advised that because SCM was a highly diversified conglomerate, finding another company to act as a "white knight" in time to defeat Hanson was unlikely. Martin Lipton of Wachtell Lipton advised that a leveraged buyout might be the best approach, assuming SCM could find institutional or private investors. The minutes show that the Board delegated to management the responsibility of investigating both options with Goldman Sachs and Wachtell Lipton. During the next five days, Goldman Sachs and SCM management, pursuing the Board's mandate, found that none of over forty companies contacted were willing to act as a "white knight," and that of three LBO firms contacted, by August 30 only Merrill was interested in participating in a leveraged buyout. Meanwhile, Hanson's $60 tender offer had become effective as of August 26, notwithstanding that the market price for SCM shares on that day was in the mid 60's. SCM did not respond to Hanson's overtures for discussions.

Following five days of negotiations, SCM management and Goldman Sachs reached an LBO agreement with Merrill, pending approval of the SCM Board. Under the proposal, Merrill, through a corporate shell called ML SCM Acquisition Inc., would make a $70 cash tender offer for up to 10,500,000 SCM shares (approximately 85% of the outstanding shares), to be followed by a second step in which the remaining shareholders would either have to exchange their shares for "high risk, high yield" subordinated debentures (commonly called "junk bonds") priced so as to be valued at $70 per share or resort to their appraisal rights under New York law. N.Y.Bus.Corp.L. §623. Proportionately, the proposed buyout would be $59.50 per share in cash and $10.50 per share in to-be-newly-issued debentures. SCM management would have the right to purchase up to 15% of the resulting ML SCM Acquisition Inc.

Merrill, concerned that it be compensated for its work and that it not become a mere "stalking horse" in the looming battle between Hanson and SCM, insisted on some protective assurances that it would profit for its efforts whether or not they proved fruitful. Although SCM's management would not accede to Merrill's demand for stock options, it granted a $1.5 million engagement fee (the so-called "hello" fee), and a $9 million "break-up" fee (the so-called "goodbye" fee), the latter to be paid to Merrill in the event that any third party should acquire one third or more of the outstanding shares of SCM common stock for $62 or more per share prior to March 1, 1986. The obvious significance of a third party acquiring one third of the shares was that such acquisition would enable that party to "block" the planned merger of tendered shares into the new ML SCM Acquisition entity, since under New York law a merger requires the approval of "two thirds of the outstanding shares entitled to vote." N.Y.Bus.Corp.L. §903(a)(2).

On August 30, the SCM Management-Merrill LBO proposal was presented to the SCM Board via a telephonic conference call meeting. The terms of the proposal were reduced to a two-page Letter Agreement, which was described to the nine independent directors in detail, but which was not available for them to read until after they had unanimously voted to approve it and to authorize SCM management and Merrill to negotiate a definitive merger agreement. The three management directors did not vote. The meeting was conducted from SCM's offices where SCM management, Goldman Sachs and Wachtell Lipton representatives, but not outside directors, were present.

The Merger Agreement was negotiated and drafted over Labor Day weekend, and presented to a special meeting of the Board of Directors on September 3. Overlock from Goldman Sachs explained to the Board that the proposal remained the only firm offer to counter Hanson's still-outstanding $60 bid, and delivered Goldman Sach's opinion that Merrill's $70 bid was "fair" to SCM shareholders. Overlock further informed the Board that the $70 debentures would be priced by Goldman Sachs and Merrill (or, if they disagreed, by a third nationally recognized investment banker) to ensure that the debentures would have a market value of $70 per share at the time of their issuance. The SCM Board understood that some SCM officers, as yet unidentified, would participate in the LBO, and would obtain an equity position in the new entity of up to 15 percent. The three management directors, though present at the meeting, did not vote. Again, the nine outside directors unanimously approved the Agreement, which was subsequently publicly announced.

In response to this Agreement, on that same day, September 3, Hanson announced that it would raise the price of its tender offer to $72 all cash, for any and all shares of SCM's common stock. Hanson conditioned this new offer on SCM's refraining from "grant[ing] to a person or group proposing to acquire the Company . . . any type of option, warrant or right which, in the sole judgment of [Hanson], constitutes a 'lock-up' device . . . and . . . makes it inadvisable to proceed with the Offer or with such acceptance for payment or payments." . . . Upon making this offer, Hanson again made unsuccessful overtures to SCM to discuss a "friendly" takeover. . . .

On September 6, Merrill and SCM management announced termination of the $70 offer under the broad authority that the Board had given to management to take all "necessary and advisable" actions regarding the offer. Negotiations between Merrill and SCM management for a second LBO-Merger Agreement resumed, and on September 10, the parties prepared a new proposal for the SCM Board. Merrill proposed to make a $74 cash tender offer for a minimum of two-thirds on a fully diluted basis and up to 80 percent (as opposed to the earlier 85%) of SCM's common stock. This would be followed by a second-step merger in which each of the remaining 20% of the shares of SCM common stock would be exchanged for a high risk, high yield debenture, subordinated to other corporate debt and not accruing interest for five years, valued at $74. Given the greater proportion of debenture financing in this offer as compared to Merrill's earlier $70 offer, the effective cash component of the new offer on a proportionate basis was $59.20 per share, or thirty cents less per share than under the $70 offer, and the effective debenture component overall was $14.80 per share, or $4.30 more per share than under the $70 offer. The net result was that under the $74 offer Merrill was not putting up any more cash than it was under the $70 offer.

As consideration for this new offer, SCM agreed to place the $9 million break-up fee into an escrow account, payable should a third party acquire one third of SCM stock, paid Merrill an additional $6 million "hello again" fee, and, most importantly, proposed to grant Merrill an option to purchase SCM's Pigments and Consumer Foods businesses. . . . Merrill also sought stock options for 18½% of SCM's stock, but SCM refused that request.

Under the proposed asset option provision, Merrill would have the irrevocable right to purchase SCM's Pigments business for $350,000,000, and SCM's Durkee Famous Foods (sometimes referred to herein as "Consumer Foods") for $80,000,000, in the event that a third party acquired more than one third of SCM's common stock. . . . The district court found that Merrill had made clear that it would not proceed without the asset options, and that the lock-up option prices were the product of "arm's length negotiations" between Goldman Sachs and Merrill. . . . There is evidence that Merrill initially proposed $260 million for Pigments and $65 to 70 million for Consumer Foods; that Goldman Sachs, negotiating on behalf of SCM, counteroffered $400 million for Pigments and $90-95 million for Consumer Foods; and that the parties ultimately settled at $350 million for Pigments and $80 million for Consumer Foods. . . .

On September 10, 1985, at the special meeting of the Board, the nine independent directors for the first time were informed of and considered the new LBO merger agreement and the proposed lock-up options. The meeting began at nine o'clock in the evening, and lasted approximately three hours. Goldman Sachs advised the Board that the $74 offer was the best available, and was fair to SCM shareholders. . . . This opinion was later confirmed in a formal letter to the SCM Board. . . . As to the Asset Option Agreement, Overlock advised the Board that the option prices were "within the range of fair value," though he did not inform the Board as to what that range was.[5] Overlock stated that he believed that SCM could obtain a higher price for each business if an orderly sale were conducted. . . . He also stated that "the current trading value" of Merrill's $74 offer would be above $72 per share. . . . He testified that, giving effect just to the time value of money, the Merrill $74 LBO was in fact worth $1.25 to $1.50 more per share than the Hanson $72 cash offer, but it would trade at about $72.50 per share. . . .

The testimony at the evidentiary hearing shows that Goldman Sachs never advised the Board, and the Board never asked, what the fair value of the two businesses was, or what the range of such value was. . . . Further, Goldman Sachs had not calculated such values—and had not informed the Board that it had not made such calculations. . . . Nor was there any discussion of the significance for

---

Hanson Trust [5] The minutes of the September 10 Board meeting indicate that Overlock informed the Board that the book value of Consumer Foods was $56 million, that the 1985 and projected 1986 earnings were $6 million and $5.2 million respectively, that the price-earnings ratios for those years were 13.3 times and 15.4 times respectively, and that the option price of $80 million represented 43.6% over book value. . . .

As to Pigments, the minutes indicate that Overlock informed the Board that the book value was $280 million, that 1985 and projected 1986 earnings were $34.4 million and $44 million respectively, that the price-earnings ratios for those years were 10.2 times and 8 times respectively, and that the option price of $350 million represented 25% over book value. . . .

SCM of selling these two businesses, which represent approximately one half of SCM's present and projected operating income. No documents or pro forma financial statements were given out at the meeting, and none were requested. . . . None of the directors suggested postponing a decision on the lock-up option. . . . Nor did the Board suggest contacting Hanson to see if it might top the proposed $74 offer, including the lock-up option. . . .

Martin Lipton advised the Board that in Wachtell Lipton's opinion, the decision whether to approve the Asset Option Agreement was within the discretion of the Board's business judgment. . . . There was evidence that one director asked Merrill's chief negotiator whether Merrill would proceed with its $74 proposal without the lock-up option. The negotiator responded that neither Merrill nor its partner, Prudential, would go forward without the asset option. After the three management directors left the room, SCM's independent directors unanimously approved the Asset Option Agreement. The district court found that the directors "approved the lock-up options after concluding that they could not secure the $74 LBO offer without the options." . . .

In response to Merrill's new proposed tender offer, on September 11 Hanson announced the termination of its $72 all cash tender offer, which had been expressly conditioned upon SCM's not granting a lock-up option. Within hours following this announcement, Hanson purchased approximately twenty-five percent of SCM's common stock in transactions that this court upheld in *Hanson I* as not constituting a *de facto* tender offer in violation of the Williams Act. In the present action, the district court found that Hanson's September 11 purchases triggered Merrill's rights to exercise the lock-up option. . . . Following this court's decision in *Hanson I* on September 30, Hanson purchased an additional 545,000 shares of SCM stock between October 2 and October 4, bringing its aggregate holdings to some 37.4% on a primary basis and approximately 32.1% on a fully diluted basis. . . .

On October 8, after commencing the present suit in district court, Hanson announced its intention to make a $75 cash tender offer for any and all shares of SCM common stock, conditioned on the withdrawal or judicial invalidation of the lock-up option,[7] to commence on October 11. . . . On October 8, Merrill announced that it was exercising the lock-up option and on October 9 it announced that it had withdrawn the $9 million break-up fee from escrow for its own use. On October 10, the SCM Board approved an Exchange Offer whereby if both the Hanson and Merrill offers fail, all SCM shareholders could exchange each SCM share for $10 cash and $64 in a new series of SCM preferred stock. The offer was made for up to 8,254,000 shares, or two thirds of the outstanding shares on a fully diluted basis.

In the evidentiary hearings before the district court, the parties presented extensive evidence regarding not only the decision-making process of the SCM directors in approving the lock-up option but also the substantive fairness to SCM shareholders of the option and the option prices. This evidence included testimony by Overlock that, based on acceptable price-earnings ratios applied to Goldman

---

[7] Specifically, Hanson stated that the offer was conditioned on the return of the optioned businesses and the $9 million break-up fee to SCM from the escrow account. On October 9, Hanson announced that its offer would no longer be conditioned on the return of the $9 million fee to SCM. . . .

Sachs' own data, the value of Pigments could be substantially higher than the option price agreed to by SCM for Pigments. There was also evidence that the Consumer Foods business was seriously undervalued in the Option Agreement. Notwithstanding the extensive evidence adduced from both sides as to the value of the optioned businesses, the district court declined to make findings regarding such evidence. Hanson appeals from the district court's denial of the motion for a preliminary injunction.

Discussion

In this second phase of litigation in this takeover dispute, we are asked to determine whether SCM's Board of Directors' approval of a lock-up option of substantial corporate assets is protected by the business judgment rule. More specifically, we are to consider whether the district court was correct in holding, as it did, that the appellants did not "make a strong showing that the directors somehow breached their fiduciary duties,". . . such as to shift to the SCM directors the burden of justifying the fairness of the lock-up option. We believe that the district court erred in holding that Hanson has failed to make a prima facie showing of a breach of a fiduciary duty; we also believe that, once the burden shifted, the extensive evidence presented during the eight-day evidentiary hearing clearly shows that, for preliminary injunction purposes, the appellees did not sustain their burden of justifying the fairness of the lock-up option.

I.

To obtain a preliminary injunction, Hanson faces the formidable task of showing: (a) irreparable harm and (b) either (1) likelihood of success on the merits or (2) sufficiently serious questions going to the merits to make them a fair ground for litigation and a balance of hardships tipping decidedly toward the party requesting the preliminary relief. . . .

Our standard of review is whether the district court abused its discretion in denying the preliminary injunction, . . . i.e., whether it "relie[d] on clearly erroneous findings of fact or on an error of law in [not] issuing the injunction," *Hanson I*, 774 F.2d at 54.

SCM is a New York corporation, and no party disputes that the acts of its directors are to be considered in light of New York law. Under New York corporation law, a director's obligation to a corporation and its shareholders includes a duty of care in the execution of directorial responsibilities. Under the duty of care, a director, as a corporate fiduciary, in the discharge of his responsibilities must use at least that degree of diligence that an "ordinarily prudent" person under similar circumstances would use. See N.Y.Bus. Corp.L. §717. In evaluating this duty, New York courts adhere to the business judgment rule, which "bars judicial inquiry into actions of corporate directors taken in good faith and in the exercise of honest judgment in the lawful and legitimate furtherance of corporate purposes." . . .

Thus, in duty of care analysis, a presumption of propriety inures to the benefit of directors; absent a prima facie showing to the contrary, directors enjoy "wide latitude in devising strategies to resist unfriendly [takeover] advances" under the business judgment rule. See Norlin, 744 F.2d at 264-65 (citing Treadway v. Care Corp., 638 F.2d 357, 380-84 (2d Cir.1980); Crouse-Hinds Co. v. Internorth, Inc., 634 F.2d 690, 701-04 (2d Cir.1980)). However, even if a board concludes that a takeover attempt is not in the best interests of the company, it does not hold a blank check to use all possible strategies to forestall the acquisition moves. Norlin, 744 F.2d at 265-66.

Although in other jurisdictions, directors may not enjoy the same presumptions per the business judgment rule, at least in a takeover context, see, e.g., Unocal Corp. v. Mesa Petroleum Co., 493 A.2d 946, 954-55 (Del. Sup. 1985) (initial burden on directors in takeover context to show reasonable grounds for believing that takeover would endanger corporate policy; satisfied by directors' showing good faith and reasonable investigation), under New York law, the initial burden of proving directors' breach of fiduciary duty rests with the plaintiff. See Crouse-Hinds, 634 F.2d at 702; see also Auerbach, 419 N.Y.S.2d at 926-27, 393 N.E.2d at 1000-01.

In the present case, the challenged acts of the directors concern the grant of the lock-up option. This takeover defensive tactic is not per se illegal. See, e.g., Buffalo Forge Co. v. Ogden Corp., 717 F.2d 757 (2d.Cir.), *cert. denied*, 464 U.S. 1018, 104 S.Ct. 550, 78 L.Ed.2d 724 (1983) (validating a stock lock-up under the business judgment rule), but it may nonetheless be illegal in particular cases, see e.g., Data Probe, Inc. v. C.R.C. Information Systems, No. 92138-1983 (Sup.Ct.N.Y. Co. Dec. 11, 1984), reprinted in N.Y.L.J. Dec. 28, 1984 at 7, Col. 2. See also MacAndrews & Forbes Holdings, Inc. v. Revlon, Inc., 501 A.2d 1239, 1250 (Del. Ch. 1985) *aff'd*, Nos. 353 & 354 (Del. Sup. Nov. 1, 1985) (noting that lock-up options are not per se illegal, but preliminarily enjoining asset option agreement as likely misapplication of directorial authority). Further, in evaluating the acts of SCM's directors in the present case, we remain mindful of our overriding concern in *Hanson I* that the role of the court in an action to enjoin takeover measures is to allow the forces of the free market to determine the outcome to the greatest extent possible within the bounds of the law. See Hanson I, 774 F.2d at 60. In this regard, we are especially mindful that some lock-up options may be beneficial to the shareholders, such as those that induce a bidder to compete for control of a corporation, while others may be harmful, such as those that effectively preclude bidders from competing with the optionee bidder. See Thompson v. Enstar Corp., Nos. 7641, 7643 at 7-13 (Del. Ch. June 20, 1984), at 7-13 *revised*, Aug. 16, 1984 (distinguishing options that attract or foreclose competing bids); see also Note, Lock-Up Options: Towards a State Law Standard, 96 Harv.L.Rev. 1068, 1076-82 (1983).

II.

Under the circumstances presented in this case, the business judgment doctrine is misapplied when it is extended to provide protection to corporate board members where there is an abundance of evidence strongly suggesting breach of fiduciary duty, as we develop below. See generally, Arsht, The Business Judgment Rule Revisited, 8 Hofstra L.Rev. 93 (1979) (noting limits of business judgment rule).

The district court herein found no fraud, no bad faith and no self-dealing by SCM's directors; we do not disagree with these findings. However, the exercise of fiduciary duties by a corporate board member includes more than avoiding fraud, bad faith and self-dealing. Directors must exercise their "honest judgment in the lawful and legitimate furtherance of corporate purposes," Auerbach, 419 N.Y.S.2d at 926, 393 N.E.2d at 1000. It is not enough that directors merely be disinterested and thus not disposed to self-dealing or other indicia of a breach of the duty of loyalty. Directors are also held to a standard of due care. They must meet this standard with "conscientious fairness," Alpert v. 28 Williams St. Corp., 63 N.Y.2d 554, 569, 483 N.Y.S.2d 667, 674, 473 N.E.2d 19, 26 (1984) (citing cases). For example, where their "methodologies and procedures" are "so restricted in scope, so shallow in execution, or otherwise so *pro forma* or halfhearted as to constitute a pretext or sham," then inquiry into their acts is not shielded by the business judgment rule. Auerbach, 419 N.Y.S.2d at 929, 393 N.E.2d at 1002-03.

The law is settled that, particularly where directors make decisions likely to affect shareholder welfare, the duty of due care requires that a director's decision be made on the basis of "reasonable diligence" in gathering and considering material information. In short, a director's decision must be an informed one. See American Law Institute, Principles of Corporate Governance: Analysis and Recommendations §4.01(c)(2) (Tent.Draft No. 4, April 12, 1985) ("informed with respect to the subject of his business judgment to the extent he reasonably believes to be appropriate under the circumstances"); H. Ballantine, Law of Corporations §63a at 161 (rev. ed. 1946) ("presupposed that reasonable diligence and care have been exercised"); Arsht, *supra*, at 111 (business judgment rule should not be available to directors who do "not exercise due care to ascertain the relevant and available facts before voting"). Directors may be liable to shareholders for failing reasonably to obtain material information or to make a reasonable inquiry into material matters. See e.g., Manheim Dairy Co. v. Little Falls Nat. Bank, 54 N.Y.S.2d 345, 365-66 (Sup.Ct.1945), cited in Platt Corp. v. Platt, et al., 42 Misc.2d 640, 249 N.Y.S.2d 1, 6 (Sup.Ct.l964), *affd*, 23 A.D.2d 823, 258 N.Y.S.2d 629 (1st Dep't.1965), *rev'd on other grounds*, 17 N.Y.2d 234, 270 N.Y.S.2d 408, 217 N.E.2d 134 (1966). Cf. Beveridge v. New York El. R. Co., 112 N.Y. 1, 22, 19 N.E. 489, 494 (1889) (directors owe to shareholders duties "of the most responsible kind"). Thus, while directors are protected to the extent that their actions evidence their business *judgment*, such protection assumes that courts must not reflexively decline to consider the content of their "judgment" and the extent of the information on which it is based.

The actions of the SCM Board do not rise to that level of gross negligence found in Smith v. Van Gorkom, 488 A.2d 858, 874-78 & n. 19 (Del. Sup. 1985). There, in making its decision after only two hours of consideration, the board relied primarily on a twenty-minute presentation by the chief executive officer who had arranged the proposed merger without informing other Board members or management and despite the advice of senior management that the merger price was inadequate. On the other hand, the SCM directors failed to take many of the affirmative directorial steps that underlie the finding of due care in *Treadway, supra*, on which the district court herein relied. In *Treadway*, the directors "armed" their bankers with financial questions to evaluate; they requested balance sheets; they adjourned deliberations for one week to consider the requisitioned advice; and they conditioned approval of the deal on the securing of a fairness opinion from their bankers. See Treadway, 638 F.2d at 384. By contrast, the SCM directors, in a three-hour late-night meeting, apparently contented themselves with their financial advisor's conclusory opinion that the option prices were "within the range of fair value," although had the directors inquired, they would have learned that Goldman Sachs had not calculated a range of fairness. There was not even a written opinion from Goldman Sachs as to the value of the two optioned businesses. . . . Moreover, the Board never asked what the top value was or why two businesses that generated half of SCM's income were being sold for one third of the total purchase price of the company under the second LBO merger agreement, or what the company would look like if the options were exercised. . . . There was little or no discussion of how likely it was that the option "trigger" would be pulled, or who would make that decision—Merrill, the Board, or management. Also, as was noted in *Van Gorkom*, the directors can hardly substantiate their claim that Hanson' efforts created an emergency need for a hasty decision, given that Hanson would not acquire shares under the tender offer until September 17. . . . The directors manifestly declined to use "time available for obtaining information" that might be critical, given "the importance of the business judgment to be made." See ALI *supra* §4.01 at 66. In short, the SCM directors' paucity of information and their swiftness of decision-making strongly suggest a breach of the duty of due care.

Nor is SCM's argument that it was entitled to rely on advice of Wachtell Lipton and Goldman Sachs dispositive of Hanson's claim that the SCM directors failed adequately to inform themselves under the duty of care. In general, directors have some oversight obligations to become reasonably familiar with an opinion, report, or other source of advice before becoming entitled to rely on it. In our view, the test of reasonableness should suffice with respect to the area of expertise relied upon, whether that area be legal or financial. See ALI, *supra* §4.02 at 76-79. Cf. Harris v. Pearsall, 116 Misc. 366, 384, 190 N.Y.S. 61, 71 (Sup.Ct.1921) (reliance unwarranted); Hawes & Sherrard, Reliance on Advice of Counsel as a Defense in Corporate and Securities Cases, 62 Va.L.Rev. 1, 48-49 (1976); Longstreth, Reliance on Advice of Counsel as a Defense to Securities Law Violations, 37 Bus.Law. 1185, 1190-93 (1982); Small, The Evolving Role of the Director in Corporate Governance, 30 Hastings L.J. 1353, 1359-62, 1382-83 (1979).

The district court in the present case notes that the Board failed to read or review carefully the various offers and agreements and instead relied on the advisers' descriptions. In particular, the district court found that at the September 10 Board meeting, the directors accepted Goldman Sachs' conclusion that the prices of the optioned assets were fair, without ever inquiring about the range of fair value. Had the directors so inquired, and had Goldman Sachs revealed that they had not investigated the range of fair value as such, the directors might have then discovered that the prices represented lower valuations than their own experienced business judgment would allow them to approve. The directors did not seek any documents in support of Goldman Sachs' conclusory opinion. Nor would the costs of obtaining documentation have outweighed any conceivable legitimate needs of the directors to conserve time and rely on Goldman Sachs' "conclusion." Cf. ALI *supra* §4.01 at 66 (considering "the costs related to obtaining information"). After all, only one week earlier, Goldman Sachs had compiled an extensive set of financial data, which, while not stating a value or range of values for the Pigments and Consumer Foods businesses, at least offered some quantitative bases for assessing whether the option prices indeed were "within the range of fair value." Given that Hanson would not acquire stock through its $72 tender offer until one week after the September 10 meeting, there was certainly time to consider these data. Moreover, the fact that Overlock opined at the September 10 board meeting that an "orderly sale" could achieve higher prices for Pigments and Consumer Foods should have led the directors to investigate, rather than rely baldly upon, the oral opinion as to fairness. Finally, Goldman Sachs offered no opinion as to what kind of company SCM would be without its "core" businesses. On this issue, of which there is no evidence of any inquiry by the directors, there is thus not even a conclusory opinion from its advisors on which the directors plausibly might have relied.

We find unpersuasive SCM's defense that this "working board" was already familiar with SCM, and hence was capable of making the swift decisions that it made. Given this "working board's" considerable familiarity with SCM, we must question why it did not find the option prices troublesome in light of the considerable evidence—from Overlock, its own investment banker, and others, and from valuations made by SCM's management and Merrill—that the optioned assets were worth considerably more than their option prices. Indeed, given that the very purpose of an asset option in a takeover context is to give the optionee a bargain as an incentive to bid and an assured benefit should its bid fail, see Fraidin & Franco, Lock-Up Arrangements, 14 Rev.Sec.Reg. 821, 823, 827 (1981), one again might have expected under such circumstances a *heightened* duty of care. The price may be low enough to entice a reluctant potential bidder, but no lower than "reasonable pessimism will allow." Cf. Brudney & Chirelstein, Fair Shares in Corporate Mergers and Takeovers, 88 Harv.L.Rev. 297, 298 (1974). To ascertain that management's proposal has not crossed this critical line, the Board certainly should have subjected the proposal to some substantial analysis. Instead, we view the board as only minimally fulfilling, if not abdicating, its role.

The proper exercise of due care by a director in informing himself of material information and in overseeing the outside advice on which he might appropriately rely is, of necessity, a pre-condition to performing his ultimate duty of acting in good faith to protect the best interests of the corporation. See Auerbach, 419 N.Y.S.2d at 927, 393 N.E.2d at 1001. Although the SCM independent directors have not been shown to have acted out of self-interest or to have been fraudulent or self-dealing in breach of their duty of loyalty, they do not appear to have pursued adequately their obligation to ensure the shareholders' fundamental right to make the "decisions affecting [the] corporation's ultimate destiny," Norlin, 744 F.2d at 258, as required by their duty of care.

In the context of a self-interested management proposing a defensive LBO, the independent directors have an important duty to protect shareholder interests, as it would be unreasonable to expect management, with financial expectancies in an LBO, fully to represent the shareholders. Cf. Longstreth, Fairness of Management Buyouts Needs Evaluation, Legal Times, Oct. 10, 1983, at 15 (noting that independent directors, even without evidencing "wrongdoing, venality or antisocial behavior," may improperly defer to management at the expense of shareholders). See also Cox & Munsinger, Bias in the Boardroom: Psychological Foundations and Legal Implications of Corporate Cohesion, 48 Law & Contemp. Probs. 83 (1985). We do not say that the independent directors of SCM were required to appoint an independent negotiating committee of outside directors to negotiate with Merrill, as the court suggested in Weinberger v. UOP, Inc., 457 A.2d 701, 709 n. 7 (Del. Sup. 1983), though that certainly would have constituted one appropriate procedure under the circumstances. But in approving *post hoc* the LBO negotiated and proposed by management directors with a not insubstantial potential 15% equity interest in the arrangement, the independent directors should have taken at least some of the prophylactic steps that were identified as constituting due care in Treadway, 638 F.2d at 384.

SCM's board delegated to management broad authority to work directly with Merrill to structure an LBO proposal, . . . and then appears to have swiftly approved management's proposals. Such broad delegations of authority are not uncommon and generally are quite proper as conforming to the way that a Board acts in generating proposals for its own consideration. However, when management has a self-interest in consummating an LBO, standard *post hoc* review procedures may be insufficient. See Longstreth, *supra*. Even before the Board first met on August 25, 1985, in reaction to Hanson's offer, Goldman Sachs and Wachtell Lipton, who were later to become the *Board's* advisers, were already discussing an LBO with management. When Hanson raised its bid to $72, it was SCM's *management* and these advisers who caucused to develop a response. Even after Wachtell Lipton was formally retained by the Board, there was sufficient confusion for one of Prudential's participants in the negotiations to note in a confidential notebook: "Lipton rep[resentin]g m[ana]g[emen]t." . . . It was SCM's management that put the $9 million break-up fee and the optioned assets into escrow accounts over which Merrill apparently exercised unilateral control. SCM's management and the Board's advisers presented the various agreements to the SCM directors more or less as *faits accompli*, which the Board quite hastily approved. As the district court found, the Board "knew or should have known" that its approval of the Asset Option Agreement would effectively foreclose further bidding for SCM. . . . The effect was to preclude shareholders from achieving any value higher than that agreed upon by SCM management and Merrill. In short, the Board appears to have failed to ensure that alternative bids were negotiated or scrutinized by those whose only loyalty was to the shareholders.

III.

Having determined that the synergies of evidence showing a prima facie case of breach of the duty of care effectively shifted the burden of justification to SCM, we now consider SCM's claims of justification. First, SCM argues that it presented evidence to rebut Hanson's extensive evidence that the option prices were undervalued. A director's obligation to protect the financial interests of the corporation, and thereby the shareholders, see, e.g., Data Probe, No. 92138-1983 at 8, may not be compromised by a competing interest in other legitimate corporate purposes, such as fending off a hostile takeover bid. When engaging in defensive maneuvers, such as a lock-up option, a director's primary obligation is to ensure the overall fairness, including a fair option price, to the shareholders. See Revlon, 501 A.2d at 1249 (noting differential of $75,000,000.00 between option price and lowest estimate of value in target's investment banker's opinion); cf. Norlin, 744 F.2d at 266 n. 11 (noting lack of cash consideration for defensive stock issuance). Of course, a court need not, and here the district court clearly did not, ascertain "the 'precise value' " of the optioned assets to determine the validity of the lock-up option, at least for preliminary injunction purposes. Cf. Alpert v. 28 Williams St. Corp., 483 N.Y.S.2d at 675, 473 N.E.2d at 27 (analyzing fairness of cash-out merger transaction). The inquiry is not whether the asset option prices represented fair value as a factual matter, but whether SCM met its burden of justifying the fairness of the lock-up option by adducing legally sufficient evidence to render inappropriate the remedy of a preliminary injunction. SCM contends that the sale of Pigments for $350 million would represent the highest price per ton (over $1000 per ton) of industrial capacity for which a Pigments business has ever been sold. Assuming this to be true, the assertion is nonetheless unpersuasive. On cross examination, Overlock of Goldman Sachs was asked whether he had told the board that "tonnage" represented "a lousy way to value [Pigments], but you talked about tonnage, correct?" Overlock answered "Yes, we did." . . . Indeed, the minutes of the September 10 board meeting reflect that Overlock told the Board that capacity is "not necessarily the best" benchmark of the value of Pigments. . . . The Board does not appear to have posed follow-up questions. Further, Overlock testified, as is surely the case, that "a very significant" measure of the real value of Pigments, as with Consumer Foods, is in the expected *earnings* of the business, . . . and it was clear to one and all that Pigments was most likely to continue to bring the most promising and important share of earnings to the corporation. And it is undisputed that in valuing Pigments SCM's litigation analysis looks to only 1985 and 1986 earnings, the two *lowest* actual and projected earnings years in a ten-year sequence.

SCM also points to a document prepared on August 7, 1985 by Rothschild Inc., Hanson's investment bank, which estimated the value of Pigments at $345 million. . . . However, these notes were based on admittedly incomplete data—Rothschild did not then have available the fiscal year-end Form 10-K filed September 27—and were not intended to provide comprehensive or final valuation determinations. In composing the document, Rothschild estimated the value of the Chemicals Division at $490 to $565 million, . . . but its estimation of the value of Pigments quite clearly did not reflect—because Rothschild was not aware of—the fact that Pigments accounted for some 88% of the operating income of the Chemicals Division in 1985, according to testimony by Overlock. . . . Given that the *Discussion Notes* provide only brief descriptive vignettes of SCM businesses without the year-end 10-K, this oversight is hardly surprising. Rothschild reevaluated its estimate of the value of the Pigments business on the basis of documents, including those of Goldman Sachs, and depositions that became available in the course of this litigation. Noting SCM's high quality Dupont technology, Rothschild valued the titanium dioxide business, which generates 85% or 90% of Pigments' operating income, in excess of $400 million. Adding in the rest of SCM's Pigments business and taking into account the price-earnings multiples, Rothschild valued the total Pigments business at $450 to 500 million.

Hanson produced substantial evidence at the eight-day hearing that the optioning of the "crown jewels" demonstrates that the directors failed to meet their duty of inquiry and had an inadequate basis for concluding one way or the other that the prices were "within the range of fair value." First, as to Pigments, optioned at $350 million, Overlock, SCM's own investment banker at Goldman Sachs, testified that, using Goldman Sachs' own valuation charts, . . . and applying thereto price-earnings ratios that Overlock accepted as appropriate, the value of that division is between $420 and $544 million. . . . Applying an average ratio of market price to book value for companies that Goldman Sachs compared to SCM's Pigments, a value of $465 million was obtained. . . . Indeed, in addition to Rothschild, two other financial institutions valued Pigments at substantially higher than the options price. Bear Stearns, one of Hanson's deponents, valued Pigments at $420 to 500 million based on Goldman Sachs data. . . . Kohlberg, Kravis, Roberts & Co., one of the first potential "white knight" leveraged buyout firms that SCM management contacted in August, valued Pigments at about $550 million as part of its consideration as to whether it would make a tender offer for SCM stock. R-43. The *lowest* of all of these estimates of value, $420 million, suggests a $70 million undervaluation in the optioned price as to Pigments, a differential that would suggest serious undervaluation. See Revlon, 501 A.2d at 1248-1249 (questioning shareholder benefit where, to secure additional $1 per share, Board optioned certain divisions at price $75 million below Revlon's own investment banker's lowest estimate of fair value).[9]

---

[9] We note that a prima facie showing of lack of due care is distinct from a prima facie showing of corporate waste, which may constitute a cause of action against directors separate and distinct from breach of the duty of loyalty or due care. See Ludlum v. Riverhead Bond & Mortgage Corp., 244 A.D. 113, 278 N.Y.S. 487 (2d Dep't 1935). It might well be that Hanson's evidence was sufficient to establish a prima facie case of waste, even given the considerable burden of proof required under that cause of action. See Cohen v. Ayers, 596 F.2d 733, 739 (7th Cir.1979) (applying New York law) (plaintiff must show that "no reasonable businessman could find that adequate consideration had been supplied"); accord, Aronoff v. Albanese, 85 A.D.2d 3, 5, 446 N.Y.S.2d 368, 371 (2d Dep't 1982) ("The objecting stockholder must demonstrate that no person of ordinary sound business judgment would say that the corporation received fair benefit."). However, we need not reach the issue of waste given the sufficient grounds presented herein in support of a preliminary injunction. See Revlon, 501 A.2d (enjoining lock-up option without specifically noting waste); Data Probe, No. 92138-1983 (same).

We find unpersuasive the district court's efforts to distinguish *Revlon*. . . . First, although Revlon's fourteen-member board included six directors who held prominent management positions, and while most of the remaining directors had associations with entities that did business with Revlon, *Revlon*, 501 A.2d at 1243 n. 2, the absence in the present case of such indicia of disloyalty does not limit the likelihood of a breach of the duty of due care. Second, although the hostile bidder in *Revlon* expressly intended to outbid every offer by the "white knight," *id.* at 1245, here the district court expressly found that the SCM directors "knew or should have known" that the lock-up would foreclose additional bidding—by Hanson or any other bidder. Op. at 855. Third, while the *Revlon* court noted that the option price was $75,000,000.00 below the lowest fair value placed upon it by Revlon's own investment banker (Goldman Sachs), *Revlon*, 501 A.2d at 1249, here the option price of Pigments *alone* was $70,000,000.00 below the lowest fair value placed upon it in any of the testimony specifying a purported fair value—and this differential represents a *greater proportion* of the option price than that represented

Regarding Consumer Foods, Hanson again adduced considerable evidence that the business was optioned at a considerably undervalued price. Simonson from Prudential testified that Borden was interested in buying Consumer Foods for $105 million and that Merrill hoped to get $125 million. . . . "Base Case #10," a document prepared by Merrill and SCM management, placed a July 1, 1986 sale value on Consumer Foods of $100 million. . . . On the basis of this document and deposition testimony of representatives of SCM, Merrill, Prudential and Goldman Sachs, a partner at Bear Stearns valued Consumer Foods at approximately $100 million or a range between $90 and 110 million. . . . Cooper-Mullin from Rothschild noted that "no document was produced in discovery which reflects a valuation or divestiture of the Consumer Foods business at less than $100 million prior to the grant of the Lock-Up Option." . . . Indeed, Overlock, the principal negotiator for SCM at the negotiations with Merrill regarding the asset options admitted that he had never seen the above-mentioned Base Case #10 document. . . . It is also undisputed that the Goldman Sachs negotiator's first counteroffer to Merrill regarding Consumer Foods was $90 to 95 million.[10]

The above evidence notwithstanding, the district court made no findings as to Hanson's claim that the Pigments and Consumer Foods businesses were optioned at prices far below their fair value. Rather, the district court held:

> Questions involving valuation of particular segments of large companies are precisely the type of questions into which the business judgment rule is designed to preclude courts from inquiring. Courts cannot become mired in valuation issues and should not second-guess directors' decisions on such issues absent a strong showing that the directors somehow breached their fiduciary duties.
>
> No such showing has been made in the instant case.

. . . Although the district court conceded that "[t]here are several aspects of the independent directors' actions which trouble the Court," . . . and made clear that its decision "is by no means intended to convey the impression that this Court condones or approves of the actions taken by SCM's board in granting the lock-up options," . . . the court denied Hanson's motion for a preliminary injunction to restrain SCM and Merrill from exercising the lock-up option.

---

by the differential in *Revlon*. Finally, while the Revlon board acted to protect note or debtholders instead of shareholders. *Revlon*, 501 A.2d at 1249-1250, here the SCM board appears to have failed to protect steadfastly shareholders interests in the face of a management-interested LBO, and, through junk bond financing, to have subordinated in significant part the equity of existing SCM shareholders to the future debt of the acquired company.

[10] $420 million, which the evidence suggests may represent the low end of the range of fair value for Pigments, is 20% higher than the $350 million option price. This differential is greater than the percent differential between $600 million, the apparently lowest material valuation of Revlon's health aids divisions, and $525 million, the option price therefor. See Revlon, 501 A.2d at 1245, 1249. $90 million, the lowest value for Consumer Foods adduced in Hanson's evidence, is 12 1/2% above the option price. Significantly, the Bear Stearns partner stated that although he could understand how one could conceivably value Consumer Foods at $80 million, he could not "conceive of the basis at which someone arrives at 350" million dollars for Pigments. . . .

We conclude that the district court erred in declining to consider evidence, which the court admittedly found troublesome, which was importantly related to the critical issue of the value of the optioned assets. The court erred in failing to recognize that Hanson had presented a prima facie case of breach of fiduciary duty, and thus should have considered the extensive evidence on whether the option prices were indeed "within the range of fair value." On the crucial issue of valuation, then, the district court presents no findings of fact for us either to uphold or to find clearly erroneous. Appellate courts, of course, are not precluded from inquiring into the evidence in the record when necessary to resolve legal issues. Even where the district court has made specific findings, a reviewing court can overturn those findings when it "is left with the definite and firm conviction that a mistake has been committed." Anderson v. City of Bessemer, 470 U.S. 564, 105 S.Ct. 1504, 1511, 84 L.Ed.2d 518 (1985) (quoting United States v. Gypsum Co., 333 U.S. 364, 395, 68 S.Ct. 525, 542, 92 L.Ed. 746 (1948)). Because we need not make a specific determination as to value of the optioned assets at this preliminary injunction stage of the proceedings, we do not remand to the District Court to make a finding of valuation. However, we believe that the appellants present evidence sufficient to raise a very serious question that the assets, in terms of what may be the outer parameters of valuation, were significantly undervalued, and that the SCM directors failed in the evidentiary hearings before the district court to present legally sufficient evidence to the contrary, or to otherwise justify their actions. Thus, the district court's legal error in declining to reach the important evidence of valuation does not preclude this court from reversing with directions to grant a preliminary injunction, pursuant to Congress' mandate to us under 28 U.S.C. §1292(a)(1). . . .

SCM's second attempt at justification is to argue that the purpose of the lock-up option is to achieve a better bid for the shareholders. Primary purpose analysis is undoubtedly a sound theory of lock-up option justification, and is tested in pertinent part according to whether the lock-up option objectively benefits share-holders. Cf. N.Y.Bus.Corp.L. §717 ("ordinarily prudent person" standard); see also Revlon, 501 A.2d at 1250 ("objective needs of shareholders"); Bennett v. Propp, 41 Del. Ch. 14, 22, 187 A.2d 405, 409 (Del. Sup. 1962) (directors may justify stock purchase as "in the corporate interest"); Norlin, 744 F.2d at 265-66. Whatever good intentions the directors might have had, they have pointed to little or no evidence to rebut the evidence discussed above that suggested that they failed to ensure that their acts would redound to the benefit of SCM and its shareholders. Indeed, the district court found that the directors "knew or should have known" that the lock-up option would end the bidding. . . . The directors thus face the difficult task of justifying a lock-up option that is suspect for foreclosing bidding, see Thompson v. Enstar, Nos. 7641, 7643 and for thereby impinging upon share-holder decisional rights regarding corporate governance, see Norlin, 744 F.2d at 258.

Viewing the LBO proposal in its entirety, we cannot see how the deal redounds to the benefit of SCM and its shareholders. For the benefit of an offer superior to Hanson's $72 cash bid by at best one dollar and change, and which arbitrageurs would value at no more than $.75 to $1.00 higher than Hanson's $72 bid, according to Overlock,[11] the board approved immediate release of a $6 million "hello again" fee, and approved management's transfer into escrow of the $9 million "break-up" fee payable upon a third party's acquisition of one-third of SCM's common stock. The Board additionally optioned 50 percent of SCM's operating income from two prime businesses at conceivably well below fair value, according to the abundant evidence before the district court. Cf. Revlon, 501 A.2d at 1249 (noting costs of securing additional $1 per share). Of course, the tendering shareholders would appear to get the benefits but not pay the costs of this arrangement if the LBO were to be consummated and the new entity were a financial success. However, serious questions are presented as to whether the shareholders would be economically harmed by effectively being forced to tender if the lock-up option is not enjoined. Those who do not tender will either become remaining twenty percent holders with appraisal rights which may be valued less because of the lock-up options, and who will be forced out in the second-step of the merger, or, if the requisite two thirds do not tender to Merrill, will be left facing the prospect of the transfer of effectively half the company for inadequate consideration, in addition to the already effected diminution of the corporate treasury resulting from the considerable fees paid by SCM in the course of its defensive tactics.[12] Thus, the SCM-Merrill LBO appears to benefit shareholders, if at all, only so long as it succeeds all the way through the merger stage and the new entity is a financial success. But if the buyout falls short of its ultimate goal, non-tendering shareholders may bear all of the potential risks of an aborted effort, including the risk of significant undervaluation. Indeed, it is the prospect of inadequate consideration that coerces shareholders to tender, and thereby serves as the means by which SCM's managers and directors could wrest from the shareholders the power to make the *independent* ownership choices that Judge Kaufman saw as the prerogative of shareholders alone, "in accordance with democratic procedures." See Norlin, 744 F.2d at 258.

SCM argues that the above concerns notwithstanding, its offer must be upheld as *facilitating* competition in the market for control of SCM. The argument is flawed because it assumes that a competing bidder is not handicapped by the existence of the option. This is not a case where only in hindsight could the directors have known that the terms of their offer could ultimately harm shareholders. Cf. Thompson v. Enstar, Nos. 7641, 7643 at 9-10. Here, as the district court found, the directors knew or should have known that the lock-up option would foreclose any better offers. . . . Since the option threatens inadequate consideration, a competing bidder is deterred from making a tender offer, unless conditioned

---

[11] According to Overlock, arbitrageurs, who are among the most sophisticated investors, would value the $74 LBO offer at about $72.50 in view of not just the cost of money but the "risk" involved in connection with the use of the "junk bonds." . . . Precisely what risk or risks he was referring to was not developed in the record, although such risk or risks might involve the collapse of the "junk bond" market or the failure of the new corporate entity due to an unserviceable debt resulting from the LBO. According to Overlock, arbitrageurs would also value Hanson's $72 cash offer between $71.50 and $71.75.

[12] The $16.5 million in fees to Merrill represents a dimunition [sic] in value equal to approximately $1.25 per share if the $74 LBO does not succeed.

on the withdrawal or invalidation of the subject lock-up, for substantially the same reasons that shareholders are deterred from resisting the SCM-Merrill offer. Both Hanson and other SCM shareholders must be concerned that if the SCM-Merrill deal is consummated through the merger stage, then to be left holding shares is to bear the risk of undervaluation.

Indeed, the deterrence to Hanson is even greater than to a small shareholder who does not have or expect to have a blocking position. For, assuming SCM and Merrill achieve a two-thirds majority, the small shareholder most likely risks only being forced to tender under the 20% debenture provision in the SCM-Merrill $74 offer or resorting to appraisal rights. By contrast, hypothetically, Hanson, as the likely largest minority shareholder, holds enough shares to thwart not only the merger but also the 20% freeze-out, and consequently risks holding over one third of a denuded company, a risk that it concededly took in acquiring the additional shares involved in *Hanson I*. Thus, if the lock-up option is not invalidated, and if it indeed threatens to dissipate the company for inadequate consideration, then Hanson's only rational move is to tender into the SCM-Merrill offer, thereby ending the bidding. In sum, we think the offer forecloses rather than facilitates, competitive bidding. Cf. Thompson v. Enstar, Nos. 7641, 7643.

The foregoing compels us to ask the question that the district court failed to consider, but that the court in *Revlon* wisely raised: "What motivated the directors to end the auction with so little objective improvement?" Revlon, 501 A.2d at 1249. In *Revlon*, the inescapable conclusion was that the Board seemed to want the LBO partner "in the picture at all costs." . . . In the present case, the SCM Board, by its lack of due care, appears to have achieved the same questionable result.

IV.

For all the above reasons, we think that Hanson has raised serious questions going to the merits sufficient to make them a fair ground for litigation. We further believe that irreparable injury to the stockholders, including Hanson, is at stake, and that the balance of hardships in this case tips decidedly in Hanson's favor. For if the lock-up option is exercised without completion of the merger, SCM will likely be broken up for inadequate consideration, thus effectively precluding Hanson or any other bidder from seeking to gain control. Once shareholders tender into the SCM-Merrill $74 offer, the company will essentially become privately held, and Hanson would be virtually precluded from seeking to acquire it, short of the virtually inconceivable possibility of judicial valuation and forced sale. It certainly seems "doubtful that any damage claim against the directors can reasonably be a meaningful alternative." Gimbel v. The Signal Companies, 316 A.2d 599, 603 (Del. Ch.), *aff'd*, 316 A.2d 619 (Del. Sup. 1974). This harm is not protected by the business judgment rule, given Hanson's prima facie showing of breach of the duty of due care as discussed above. Further, the mere threat of the exercise of the option, as discussed above, operates to coerce Hanson and other SCM shareholders into tendering for potentially less than optimal consideration, now tangible in the form of Hanson's higher cash offer of $75. Cf. Asarco, Inc. v. M.R.H. Holmes A Court et al., 611 F.Supp. 468, 480 (D.N.J.1985); Applied Digital Data Systems, Inc. v. Milgo Electronic Corp., 425 F.Supp. 1145, 1162 (S.D.N.Y.1977).

Further, the consequences portend irreparable harm to Hanson, a substantial shareholder, given the possibility of major structural changes to the corporation, even though SCM will have the $430 million in cash that it receives for the exercise of the option. Another possibility is that Merrill might later sell corporate assets to finance its LBO debt. Cf. Mobil Corp. v. Marathon Oil Co., 66 F.2d 366 (6th Cir.1981), *cert. denied*, 455 U.S. 982, 102 S.Ct. 1490, 71 L.Ed.2d 691 (1982) (injunctive relief necessary to ensure that "Crown Jewel Option" (oil field) will not be depleted by white knight option grantee). We believe that the market forces can best be permitted to determine the outcome of this contest if the lock-up option is preliminarily enjoined. See Seagram & Son, Inc. v. Abrams, 510 F.Supp. 860, 862 (S.D.N.Y.1981). This remedy, of course, does not preclude SCM from renewing its defensive efforts on other legitimate terms, or on a basis that is beyond challenge, cf. Revlon, 501 A.2d at 1251, a possibility that we view as highly significant in weighing the balance of hardships.

The order of the district court is reversed, and the case is remanded for prompt issuance of a preliminary injunction enjoining SCM, Merrill, and any other parties acting in concert with or on behalf of SCM or Merrill from exercising or purporting to or seeking to exercise the lock-up option considered herein. Judgment to be entered in accordance with this opinion.

It is so ordered.

OAKES, Circuit Judge (concurring):

Concurring fully in Judge Pierce's opinion and its reference to the shift in the burden of proof, I write solely in partial reply to points made in Judge Kearse's dissent.

I do not think that the New York "business judgment" rule . . . goes so far as to immunize directors merely because they act in good faith, without self-dealing. Rather, even though "independent directors" make a decision, they have a duty to exercise due care, a duty which I think the dissent recognizes. Due care requires full inquiry. To obtain the benefit of the business judgment rule, then, directors must make certain that they are fully informed, and, to the extent that they are relying on advisers, that the advisers are fully informed and in turn fully inform the directors. This is particularly true, it seems to me, when the decision is whether to agree to an asset lock-up, which by definition implies making some asset available to the potential buyer at a price less than those assets would bring in an orderly sale, thereby tending to foreclose further bidding for the target company. And this duty of care is, if anything, heightened—it certainly is not weakened—when the favored buyer obtaining the lock-up is a consortium including within it the management/non-independent directors who will have a substantial participation in the future equity of the potential buyer and whose interests by virtue of that participation, at that stage, are to favor the buyout at the lowest price. This directorial duty of care is heightened because management interests are then in direct conflict with those of the shareholders of the target corporation to obtain the highest price either for their shares or for the company's assets. In other words, a management-participation leveraged buyout, when coupled with a lock-up option, calls for close scrutiny of the exercise of care on the part of independent directors to make certain that their collective judgment is informed sufficiently to enable them objectively to weigh the delicate balance of potential gain, if any, to the stockholders from the lock-up, as against possible loss from closing out the bidding or, in the event of a tender-offer standoff, having some of the corporate assets sold at an unconscionably low price. That there was some concern about the possibility of a standoff is evident from SCM's own "exchange offer" made October 10, 1985, in which it proposed to offer $10 in cash and $64 in preferred stock for two-thirds of its outstanding stock, in the event neither the management-Merrill Lynch tender offer nor the Hanson tender offer is completed. . . .

This is an extremely close case, I have no doubt. It is also an important one since the federal courts seem to attract tender offer cases and the substantive New York law will govern many of them, at least in this circuit. I note parenthetically that this would be, I think, a much easier case for the plaintiffs were Delaware's the governing law, under MacAndrew & Forbes Holdings, Inc. v. Revlon, Inc., 501 A.2d 1239 (Del. Ch. 1985), *aff'd*, Nos. 353 & 354 (Del. Sup. Nov. 1, 1985). In any event, I thought it worth noting these few points in the light of the persuasiveness of the dissent, though I by no means want to detract from the force of Judge Pierce's majority opinion, in which, as I say, I fully concur.

KEARSE, Circuit Judge, dissenting . . .

Conclusion

In sum, according to the district court's amply supported findings, the Directors had no self-interest, engaged in no fraud or bad faith, and were not improperly influenced by management. The agreement for Merrill Lynch's $74 offer in exchange for the assets option was negotiated at arm's-length by the Directors' legal and financial advisors, who also had no conflict of interest. The Directors at all times acted from a desire to secure offers for SCM and its shareholders that would be superior to the offers of Hanson. Without the $74 offer from Merrill Lynch, the bidding would have died at $72, Hanson's then-current offer. The Directors had extensive business experience and a thorough working knowledge of SCM, its operations, and its financial condition. They relied on their legal and financial advisors. They also relied on their own business experience and their own knowledge of SCM's operations and financial condition. They were informed of, *inter alia*, at least three bases for the Goldman Sachs conclusion that the option prices were fair—price-earnings ratios, book values, and, with respect to pigments, capacity—and had other data offering quantitative bases for assessing whether the option prices were within the range of fair value. The Directors were informed that a more leisurely sale of these businesses might, but might not, bring higher prices. They asked many questions before approving the transaction. They were informed that Merrill Lynch would not make its $74 offer without receiving the assets option. They "exercised independent judgment." . . .

MILLS ACQUISITION CO., a Delaware Corporation, et al., Plaintiffs Below, Appellants, v. MACMILLAN, INC., a Delaware Corporation, et al., Defendants Below, Appellees.

Supreme Court of Delaware

559 A.2d 1261 (1989)

Reversed.
Upon appeal from the Court of Chancery. REVERSED AND REMANDED.
Before CHRISTIE, C.J., MOORE and HOLLAND, JJ.
MOORE, Justice.

In this interlocutory appeal from the Court of Chancery, we review the denial of injunctive relief to Mills Acquisition Co., a Delaware corporation, and its affiliates Tendclass Limited and Maxwell Communications Corp., PLC, both United Kingdom corporations substantially controlled by Robert Maxwell. . . . Plaintiffs sought control of Macmillan, Inc. ("Macmillan" or the "company"), and moved to enjoin an asset option agreement—commonly known as a "lockup"—between Macmillan and Kohlberg Kravis Roberts & Co. ("KKR"), an investment firm specializing in leveraged buyouts. The lockup was granted by Macmillan's board of directors to KKR, as the purported high bidder, in an "auction" for control of Macmillan.

Although the trial court found that the conduct of the board during the auction was not "evenhanded or neutral," it declined to enjoin the lockup agreement between KKR and Macmillan. That action had the effect of prematurely ending the auction before the board had achieved the highest price reasonably available for the company. Even though the trial court found that KKR had received improper favor in the auction, including a wrongful "tip" of Maxwell's bid by Macmillan's chairman of the board and chief executive officer, and that Macmillan's board was uninformed as to such clandestine advantages, the Vice Chancellor nevertheless concluded that such misconduct neither misled Maxwell nor deterred it from submitting a prevailing bid.

Given our scope and standard of review under Levitt v. Bouvier, Del.Supr., 287 A.2d 671, 673 (1972), we find that the legal conclusions of the trial court, refusing to enjoin the KKR lockup agreement, are inconsistent with its factual findings respecting the unfairness of the bidding process. Our decision in Revlon, Inc. v. MacAndrews & Forbes Holdings, Inc., Del.Supr., 506 A.2d 173 (1986), requires the most scrupulous adherence to ordinary standards of fairness in the interest of promoting the highest values reasonably attainable for the stockholders' benefit. When conducting an auction for the sale of corporate control, this concept of fairness must be viewed solely from the standpoint of advancing general, rather than individual, shareholder interests. Here, the record reflects breaches of the duties of loyalty and care by various corporate fiduciaries which tainted the evaluative and deliberative processes of the Macmillan board, thus adversely affecting general stockholder interests. With the divided loyalties that existed on the part of certain directors, and the absence of any serious oversight by the allegedly independent directors, the governing standard was one of intrinsic fairness. Weinberger v. UOP, Inc., Del.Supr., 457 A.2d 701, 710-11 (1983). The record here does not meet that rigorous test, and the Court of Chancery failed to apply it. We take it as a cardinal principle of Delaware law that such conduct of an auction for corporate control is insupportable. Accordingly, we reverse. . . .

I.

The lengthy factual background and evolution of the present battle for control of Macmillan are found in earlier opinions of the trial court. See Robert M. Bass Group, Inc. v. Evans, Del. Ch., 552 A.2d 1227 (1988) (*Macmillan I*); Mills Acquisition Co. v. Macmillan, Inc., C.A. No. 10168, 1988 WL 108332 (October 17, 1988) (*Macmillan II*). However, a detailed review of certain major and other salient facts is essential to a proper understanding and analysis of the issues, and the context in which we address them.

Macmillan is a large publishing, educational and informational services company. It had approximately 27,870,000 common shares listed and traded on the New York Stock Exchange. In May, 1987, Macmillan's chairman and chief executive officer, Edward P. Evans, and its president and chief operating officer, William F. Reilly, recognized that the company was a likely target of an unsolicited takeover bid. They began exploring various defensive measures, including a corporate restructuring of the company. The genesis of this idea was a plan undertaken by another publishing company, Harcourt Brace Jovanovich, Inc., to defeat an earlier hostile bid by Robert Maxwell in May, 1987. . . . See Macmillan I, 552 A.2d at 1229. Indeed, Macmillan's management began exploring such a recapitalization or restructuring just one day after the public announcement of Harcourt's plan. . . . See 552 A.2d at 1229.

As the Vice Chancellor noted in *Macmillan I*, for one year following the initial study of management's proposed restructuring plans:

> two central concepts remained constant. First Evans, Reilly and certain other members of management would end up owning absolute majority control of the restructured company. Second, management would acquire that majority control, not by investing new capital at prevailing market prices, but by being granted several hundred thousand restricted Macmillan shares and stock options. . . .

Management's plan was to "exchange" these options and shares granted by the company into "several million shares of the recapitalized company." . . . In addition, a Macmillan Employee Stock Option Plan ("ESOP") would purchase, with borrowed funds provided by the company, a large block of Macmillan shares. The then-existing independent ESOP trustee would be replaced by Evans, Reilly, Beverly C. Chell, Vice President, General Counsel, and Secretary, and John D. Limpitlaw, Vice President—Personnel and Administration. . . . This arrangement would have given these persons voting control over all of the unallocated ESOP shares.

¶2700 Mills Acquisition Co. v. Macmillan, Inc.

At a meeting held on June 11, 1987, the Macmillan board authorized the above transactions. During the pendency of *Macmillan I*, the directors maintained that no relationship existed between the management-proposed restructuring and the June 11 approval of the ESOP transactions along with the grant of options and restricted shares to management. In rejecting this claim the Vice Chancellor observed that "[i]f the directors were unaware of the implications of their actions for the restructuring, it can only be because management failed appropriately to disclose those implications."... This apparent domination of the allegedly "independent" board by the financially interested members of management, coupled with the directors' evident passivity in the face of their fiduciary duties, which so marked *Macmillan I*, continued unchanged throughout *Macmillan II*.

After the June 11 board meeting, management initiated various anti-takeover measures, including new lucrative severance contracts, known as "golden parachute" agreements, for several top executives in the event of a hostile takeover. Earlier, at the June 11 meeting, the board had approved generous five year "golden parachute" agreements for Evans and Reilly. The board also approved the adoption of a rights plan, commonly known as a "poison pill," from which the management-controlled ESOP was exempted. ...

Until August, 1987, the restructuring plan contemplated a "one company" surviving entity. This concept was changed, however, to provide for the company to be split into two distinct and separately traded parts: the Information business ("Information") and the Publishing business ("Publishing"). ... Many "business related" reasons were advanced by management for the two company concept. It appears, however, that the real reason for this move was to greatly enhance management's control over the entities, thus making a hostile acquisition even more difficult. ...

As initially planned, Information would trade two classes of common stock. One class, wholly owned by management, would be entitled to ten votes per share (constituting absolute voting control). ... The second class would have one vote per share and would be held by the public stockholders. The management owned shares were all to be deposited in a voting trust designating Evans as the sole voting trustee. Further, Information would hold a "blocking preferred" stock in Publishing (constituting 20% of Publishing's voting power). ...

At the September 22, 1987 board meeting the directors were informed of the new two company restructuring concept, including its anti-takeover features and management's substantial voting and equity participation in Information. The board approved the plan without objection.[5] ...

On October 21, 1987, the Robert M. Bass Group, Inc., a Texas corporation controlled by Robert M. Bass, together with certain affiliates (hereafter collectively, "the Bass Group" or "Bass"), emerged as a potential bidder. By then, Bass had acquired approximately 7.5% of Macmillan's common stock. Management immediately called a special board meeting on October 29, where a rather grim and uncomplimentary picture of Bass and its supposed "*modus operandi*" in prior

Mills Acquisition Co. [5] In addition, the board granted options to management to purchase 202,500 shares of Macmillan at an exercise price of $74.24 per share. ...

investments was painted by management. Bass was portrayed, among other things, as a "greenmailer." . . . At the meeting, the previously adopted poison pill was modified to reduce the "flip-in" trigger from 30% to 15%.[6] . . .

In its decisions the Macmillan board completely relied on management's portrayal of Bass. As it turned out, and the Vice Chancellor so found in *Macmillan I*, management's characterization of the Bass Group, including most if not all of the underlying "factual" data in support thereof, was "less than accurate." . . . Indeed, it was false. As the Vice Chancellor found: "[t]here is . . . no evidence that Macmillan management made any effort to accurately inform the board of [the true] facts. On the present record, I must conclude (preliminarily) that management's pejorative characterization of the Bass Group, even if honestly believed, served more to propagandize the board than to enlighten it."[7] . . .

As the Bass Group increased its holdings in the company, the Macmillan board's executive committee, at the behest of management, examined two charts (initially) outlining the proposed restructuring. The first chart contemplated management's ownership in Information at 50.6%. The second chart, prepared two days later, increased Evans, Reilly and Chell's share to 60%. The committee studied other such charts at a later date, but according to the Vice Chancellor: "[a]ll restructuring proposals clearly contemplated that management would own an absolute majority of Information's stock." . . .

At a regularly scheduled board meeting on March 22, 1988, the Macmillan directors voted to: (1) grant 130,000 more shares of restricted stock to Evans, Reilly, Chell and Charles G. McCurdy, Vice President—Corporate Finance; (2) seek shareholder approval of a "1988 stock option and incentive plan" and the issuance of "blank check" preferred stock "having disparate voting rights;" (3) increase the directors' compensation by some 25% per year; and (4) adopt a "non-Employee Director Retirement Plan."[8] . . .

Due to the significant financial interests of Evans, Reilly, Chell, McCurdy and other managers in the proposed restructuring, management decided in February or March to establish a "Special Committee" of the Board to serve as an "independent" evaluator of the plan. The Special Committee was hand picked by Evans, but not actually formed until the May 18, 1988 board meeting. . . . This fact is

---

[6] A "flip-in" poison pill is one which grants shareholders additional financial rights in the target corporation when the pill is triggered by a cash offer or a large acquisition of target shares—here a threshold level of 15%. . . .

[7] Further, the Vice Chancellor found that "[n]either management nor the board engaged in a reasonable investigation of the Bass Group, as required by Unocal [Corp. v. Mesa Petroleum Co., 493 A.2d 946 (Del.Supr., 1985)]." 552 A.2d at 1240. Management's characterization of Bass is belied by testimony to the contrary of some of the Macmillan managers themselves. Ironically, after Bass' interest in Macmillan became known, Evans himself had contacted Robert Bass and expressed an interest in joining Bass in his investment in Bell & Howell and other transactions. . . .

[8] Under this plan, all directors aged sixty years or older who had served on the Macmillan Board for at least five years (constituting seven of the eleven non-management directors) would be paid lifetime benefits equal to the directors' fees being paid at the time of "termination." In addition to the seven directors who would immediately qualify, three of the five members of the Special Committee who were considering the restructuring would also instantly qualify. Under this plan, as later amended, benefits also were to be paid to surviving spouses of board members. . . .

significant because the events that transpired between the time that the Special Committee was conceived and the time it was formed illuminate the actual working relationship between management and the allegedly "independent" directors. It calls into serious question the actual independence of the board in *Macmillan I* and *II*.

As the Vice Chancellor observed, starting in April, 1988, Evans and others in management interviewed, and for four weeks thereafter maintained intensive contact with, the investment banking firm of Lazard Freres & Co. ("Lazard"), which was to eventually become the Special Committee's financial advisor. . . . On April 14 representatives of Lazard met alone with Evans, and later with Evans, Chell and McCurdy. A few days later, Evans, Reilly, Chell, McCurdy and Samuel Bell, a Macmillan executive, again met with Lazard. All of these meetings involved extensive discussions concerning the proposed recapitalization. . . .

Thus, the Vice Chancellor found that "[i]n total, Lazard professionals worked with management on the proposed restructuring for over 500 hours before their 'client,' the Special Committee, formally came into existence and retained them." . . . Further, the restructuring plan that was presented to Lazard was chosen by Evans alone—with management owning 55% of the planned Information company. . . .

On May 17, the day before the Macmillan annual stockholders' meeting, Evans received a letter from the Bass Group offering to purchase, consensually, all of Macmillan's common stock for $64 per share. The offer was left open for further negotiation. On May 18, the annual meeting was held at which the board recommended, and the shareholders approved, the previously mentioned 1988 Stock Option Plan and the "blank check" preferred stock. The Bass offer was not disclosed to the shareholders, although Bass had made the offer public in a filing with the Securities and Exchange Commission, which occurred simultaneously with the delivery of Bass' offer to Evans. . . .

The Macmillan board convened immediately after the shareholders' meeting. Evans disclosed the Bass offer to the board. He then described the proposed restructuring, including the management group's planned equity position in Information. Thereafter, the Special Committee was selected.[9] However, the Committee was not given any negotiating authority regarding the terms of the restructuring. Evans apparently designated himself to "negotiate" that matter with the board.

At this May 18 meeting, the directors also amended the earlier "golden parachute" agreements; authorized a $125 million mortgage on Macmillan's building in New York City in order to finance the contemplated restructuring; and further amended the "Retirement Plan" to include severance benefits for *spouses* of directors. . . . However, the board deferred discussion of the Bass proposal.

The Special Committee remained dormant for one week following its formation, and met for the first time on May 24, 1988. Before its first meeting, Evans and Reilly again met with Lazard, allegedly the Special Committee's advisor, and

---

[9] The Special Committee consisted of Lewis A. Lapham, an old college classmate of Evans' father, (Chairman), James H. Knowles, Jr., Dorsey A. Gardner, Abraham L. Gitlow and Eric M. Hart. Hart failed to attend a single meeting of the Committee. . . .

Wasserstein, Perella, apparently to discuss the recapitalization plan. Evans, Reilly, Chell and McCurdy attended the May 24 Special Committee meeting, at which Lazard, as financial advisor, and the law firm of Wachtell, Lipton, Rosen & Katz were formally retained, having been invited to the meeting by Evans.[10] Significantly, Evans and his management colleagues did not inform the Committee of their substantial prior discussions with Lazard over the preceding month. . . . One of the outside directors, Thomas J. Neff, testified that if he had known of the extent of the activities between Lazard and management, it would have raised "serious doubts" concerning Lazard's independence. . . . The restructuring plan, including management's proposed 55% ownership of Information, was presented to the Committee, which then directed Lazard to "evaluate" it further, along with the Bass offer.

Concurrent with the Special Committee meeting of May 24, Evans directed McCurdy to meet with John Scully, a Bass representative, that same day in Chicago. As the Vice Chancellor found, however, "Evans [had so] limited McCurdy's authority as to make it a foregone conclusion that the meeting would yield no meaningful result." . . . In fact, the Vice Chancellor termed the meeting "little more than a charade," . . . since McCurdy's only mission was to tell Scully that "Evans wanted the Bass Group to go away." . . . The Vice Chancellor also observed that "[m]anagement . . . had no desire to negotiate. They chose to close their eyes and to treat the Bass offer as firm and unalterable. *The Board and the Special Committee followed in lockstep. Neither took reasonable efforts to uncover the facts.*". . .

Notwithstanding this fruitless approach, Scully, Bass' representative, explained the background of the prior Bass investments about which the Macmillan board had been misinformed. Scully even offered to make other Bass representatives available to resolve these concerns. However, Scully's offer was never accepted, and the May 24 meeting was the only time that a Macmillan representative would meet with a Bass delegate until after the final board approval of the restructuring on May 30. . . .

At the May 27 Macmillan board meeting, McCurdy reported on his meeting with Scully. The Vice Chancellor found that "[a]t least one director developed the misimpression from McCurdy's report that McCurdy had tried unsuccessfully to get Scully to amplify or clarify the terms of the Bass offer." . . .

The Special Committee met on May 28 to hear Lazard's presentation. Evans, Reilly, Chell and McCurdy attended. . . . Lazard reported that management would ultimately own 39% of Information, instead of the previous 55%. This reduction occurred, ostensibly, to prevent the restructuring from being "regarded as a transfer of corporate control from the public shareholders to management." . . . The Vice Chancellor found, however, that: "[d]ocuments internally generated by Macmillan reported that the management group would have effective control over Information even with less than 50% of its stock." . . . In addition: "the conclusion that

---

[10] It appears that none of the committee members had even met with the advisors before the May 24 meeting. The method by which the advisors to the Special Committee was chosen is quite revealing. While the chairman, Mr. Lapham, remembered little about the matter, it is clear that Evans, Chell, and a Pittsburgh lawyer, Charles J. Queenan, Jr., directed the choices. . . .

effective control will pass to management is consistent with the intent and histori-cal evolution of the restructuring which, in every proposed permutation, had management owning over 50% of Information." . . .

Macmillan's financial advisors valued the recapitalization at $64.15 per share. Lazard valued Macmillan at $72.57 per share, on a pre-tax basis, but advised the "independent" directors that it found the restructuring, valued at $64.15 per share, to be "fair." Lazard also recommended rejection of the $64 Bass offer because it was "inadequate." Wasserstein, Perella valued Macmillan at between $63 and $68 per share and made the same recommendations as Lazard concerning the restructuring and the Bass offer. All of these valuations will gain added signifi-cance in *Macmillan II*.

On the Special Committee's recommendation, the Macmillan board adopted the restructuring and rejected the Bass offer. The committee, however, had not negotiated any aspect of the transaction with management. . . .

On May 31, Macmillan publicly announced the May 30 approval of the restruc-turing. This was the first disclosure to the shareholders of Evans' plans to signifi-cantly benefit himself and others in management at the stockholders' expense.

The restructuring that was approved, and later preliminarily enjoined, treated the public shareholders and the management group differently. In exchange for their Macmillan shares, the public stockholders were to receive a dividend of $52.35 cash, a $4.50 debenture, a "stub share" of Publishing ($5.10) and a one-half share of Information ($2.20). The management group, and the ESOP, would not receive the cash and debenture components. Instead, they would "exchange" their restricted stock and options for restricted shares of Information, representing a 39.2% stake in that company. . . .

The Information stock received by management could not be sold, pledged, or transferred for two years, and would not fully vest for five years. The management holders could, however, vote the shares and receive dividends. Management would also own 3.2% of Publishing. The ESOP would own 26% of Publishing.[13] . . .

The effect of all this would increase management's then-combined holdings of 4.5% in Macmillan to 39% in Information. Additionally, management would re-ceive substantial cash and other benefits from the transaction. . . .

Following the board's public announcement on May 31, the Bass Group made a second offer for all Macmillan stock at $73 per share. In the alternative, Bass proposed a restructuring, much like the one the board had approved, differing only in the respect that it would offer $5.65 per share more, and management would be treated the same as the public stockholders.[14]

---

[13] Although the *Macmillan I* opinion did not further discuss this point, it appears that the combination of the ESOP and management holdings, along with the 20% "blocking preferred" that Information holds in Publishing, would give management effective control over Publishing as well.

[14] The Vice Chancellor determined that "[t]here is no evidence that any member of the Board or the Special Committee questioned how a sale of 39% of Information would constitute a sale of the company if sold to the Bass Group, yet would not be if that same 39% interest is sold to the management group. The defendants have failed to explain that reasoning, and its logic continues to elude the Court." . . .

Two days after the revised offer was announced, Lazard concluded that it could furnish an 'adequacy' opinion that would enable the Special Committee to reject the $73 per share cash portion of Bass' offer. They gave an oral opinion the following day, June 7, at a joint meeting of the Special Committee and the board that the Bass $73 cash offer, as distinguished from Bass' alternative restructuring proposal, was inadequate, given Lazard's earlier opinion that the "pre-tax break up" value of Macmillan was between $72 and $80 per share. Wasserstein, Perella expressed a similar opinion, having previously valued the company at between $66 and $80 per share. . . . These valuation ranges, obviously intended to accord with management's restructuring in *Macmillan I*, will assume an interesting significance in *Macmillan II*, when less than three months later, on August 25, these same advisors, at Evans' behest, found Maxwell's $80 all cash offer inadequate.

Upon the Special Committee's recommendation, the board again rejected the revised Bass offer and reaffirmed its approval of the management restructuring. It is noteworthy that Bass' alternative restructuring proposal was never determined to be financially inadequate or unfair by Lazard or Wasserstein, Perella. . . .

However, after suit was filed in *Macmillan I*, and in an apparent effort to lessen the appearance of impropriety surrounding the restructuring, Evans, Reilly, Chell and McCurdy agreed in writing that "they would vote Information shares for a slate of nominees, a majority of which are independent directors." . . . However, the Vice Chancellor noted that "the record indisputably shows that these individuals have always acted in unison, and that Reilly, Chell, and McCurdy will have strong incentives to remain on good terms with Evans, who would be their immediate supervisor and Information's largest single stockholder." . . . Further, "the undertaking to elect independent directors has been carefully drafted, so that its terms would permit the management group to select directors that might not act independently of management, but would prevent the selection of directors who would be likely to act independently."[15] . . .

On July 14, 1988, the Vice Chancellor preliminarily enjoined the Evans designed restructuring, and held that both of the revised Bass offers were "clearly superior to the restructuring." The Court further inferred that the only real "threat" posed by the Bass offers was to the incumbency of the board "or to the management group's expectation of garnering a 39% ownership interest in Information on extremely favorable terms."[16] . . .

Thus, *Macmillan I* essentially ended on July 14, 1988. However, it only set the stage for the saga of *Macmillan II* to begin that same day. It opened with Macmillan's senior management holding extensive discussions with KKR in an attempt to develop defensive measures to thwart the Bass Group offer. This included a management-sponsored buyout of the company by KKR. There is nothing in the

---

[15] The definition, given in the written undertaking, of the term "independent director" would, in the Vice Chancellor's opinion, "enable the management group to nominate officers or other employees of Publishing or close personal friends of the management group. . . ." . . .

[16] Consistent with the trial court's strong implication that any "threat" posed by the Bass offer was being used merely as a pretext, the court found that "management was . . . able to use the 'threat' posed by the Bass offers to '[avail] themselves of the takeover threat to increase their, and their employees' ownership interest in the company.'" . . .

record to suggest that this was done pursuant to board action. If anything, it was Evans acting alone in his own personal interest.

Within a few hours after the Court of Chancery issued its preliminary injunction, Evans and Reilly formally authorized Macmillan's investment advisors to explore a possible sale of the entire company. This procedure eventually identified six potential bidders.[17] That search process appears to have been motivated by two primary objectives: (1) to repel any third party suitors unacceptable to Evans and Reilly, and (2) to transfer an enhanced equity position in a restructured Macmillan to Evans and his management group. While these goals may not have constituted *prima facie* breaches of the duty of loyalty owed by senior management to the company and its shareholders, it is evident that such objectives undoubtedly led to the tainted process which we now confront.

On July 20, a most significant development occurred when Maxwell intervened in the Bass-Macmillan bidding contest by proposing to Evans a consensual merger between Macmillan and Maxwell at an all-cash price of $80 per share. This was $5.00 higher than any other outstanding offer for the company.[18] Maxwell further stated his intention to retain the company's management, and additionally, to negotiate appropriate programs of executive incentives and compensation.

Macmillan did not respond to Maxwell's overture for five weeks. Instead, during this period, Macmillan's management intensified their discussions with KKR concerning a buyout in which senior management, particularly Evans and Reilly, would have a substantial ownership interest in the new company. Upon execution of a confidentiality agreement, KKR was given detailed internal, non-public, financial information of Macmillan, culminating in a series of formal "due diligence" presentations to KKR representatives by Macmillan senior management on August 4 and 5, 1988.

On August 12, 1988, after more than three weeks of silence from the company, Maxwell made an $80 per share, all-cash tender offer for Macmillan, conditioned solely upon receiving the same nonpublic information which Macmillan had given to KKR three weeks earlier. Additionally, Maxwell filed this action in the Court of Chancery seeking a declaration that the Delaware Takeover statute, 8 *Del.C.* §203, was inapplicable to the tender offer.[19]

Later that day, Evans received a letter from Maxwell confirming that he had initiated a tender offer, but also reiterating his desire to reach a friendly accord with Macmillan's management. Alternatively, Maxwell offered to purchase Information from the company for $1.1 billion. Significantly, no Macmillan representative ever attempted to negotiate with Maxwell on any of these matters. Notwithstanding the fact that on May 30 both Wasserstein, Perella and Lazard

---

[17] These entities were the Bass Group, Maxwell, KKR, Gulf & Western, McGraw-Hill and News-America Corp.

[18] Two days before the initial Maxwell bid, the Bass Group had raised its offer for the company to $75 per share. Although this final Bass offer remained open into September, the entry of Maxwell into the fray, for all practical purposes, rendered the Bass bid academic.

[19] Macmillan eventually conceded that 8 *Del.C.* §203 was inapplicable to Maxwell's offer. Later, the complaint in the Court of Chancery was amended on September 15 seeking to enjoin use of Macmillan's "poison pill" against Maxwell.

had given opinions that the management restructuring, with a value of $64.15, was fair, and on June 7 had advised the board that the company had a maximum breakup value of $80 per share, Wasserstein, Perella and Lazard issued new opinions on August 25 that $80 was unfair and inadequate. Accordingly, the Maxwell offer was rejected by the Macmillan board.

On August 30 a meeting was arranged with Maxwell at Evans' request at which Maxwell executed a confidentiality agreement, and was furnished with some, but not all, of the confidential financial information that KKR had received. At this meeting, Evans told Robert Maxwell that he was an unwelcome bidder for the whole company, but that a sale to Maxwell of up to $1 billion of Macmillan's assets would be considered. Undeterred, Maxwell indicated his intent and ability to prevail in an auction for the company, as "nobody could afford" to top a Maxwell bid due to the operational economies and synergies available through a merger of Maxwell's companies with Macmillan.

Nonetheless, on September 6, 1988, representatives of Macmillan and KKR met to negotiate and finalize KKR's buyout of the company. In this transaction Macmillan senior management would receive up to 20% ownership in the newly formed company. During this meeting, Evans and his senior managers suggested that they would endorse the concept and structure of the buyout to the board of directors, *even though KKR had not yet disclosed to Evans and his group the amount of its bid*. With this extraordinary commitment, KKR indicated that it would submit a firm offer by the end of the week—September 9. Following this meeting with KKR, Macmillan's financial advisors were instructed by Evans to notify the six remaining potential bidders, during September 7 and 8, that "the process seems to be coming to a close" and that any bids for Macmillan were due by Friday afternoon, September 9. It is particularly noteworthy that Maxwell was given less than 24 hours to prepare its bid, not having received this notification until the night of September 8.

In a September 8 meeting with Robert Maxwell and his representatives, Evans announced that the company's management planned to recommend a management-KKR leveraged buyout to the directors of Macmillan, and that he would not consider Maxwell's outstanding offer despite Maxwell's stated claim that he would pay "top dollar" for the entire company. Evans then declared that now he would only discuss the possible sale of up to $750 million worth of assets to Maxwell in order to facilitate this buyout. Furthermore, Evans flatly told Maxwell that senior management would leave the company if any other bidder prevailed over the management sponsored buyout offer. Following this meeting, Robert Maxwell expressed his concern to Evans that no lockup or other "break up" arrangements should be made until Macmillan had properly considered his proposal. Additionally, he volunteered to either negotiate his offering price or to purchase Information for $1.4 billion, subject to a minimal due diligence investigation.

On the morning of September 9, Maxwell representatives were granted a limited due diligence review with respect to certain divisions of the company. However, during these sessions Macmillan provided little additional material information to Maxwell. Indeed, throughout the bidding process, and despite its repeated requests Maxwell was not given complete information until September 25—almost two months after such data had been furnished to KKR.

In the late afternoon of September 9, Evans received another letter from Robert Maxwell, offering to increase his all-cash bid for the company to $84 per share. This revised offer was conditioned solely upon Maxwell receiving a clear understanding of which managers would be leaving Macmillan upon his acquisition of the company. However, Maxwell ended this correspondence with the statement:

> If you have a financed binding alternative proposal which will generate a greater present value for shareholders, I will withdraw my bid.

In their deliberations that weekend, Macmillan's advisors inferred from this remark that Maxwell was unwilling to bid over $84 per share for the company.

By 5:30 p.m. on September 9, two bidders remained in the auction: Maxwell, by virtue of his written $84 all-cash offer, and KKR, which had submitted only an oral bid to Macmillan's advisors. However, Macmillan representatives continued to negotiate overnight with KKR until an offer was reduced to writing on the next day, September 10, despite the bid deadline previously mandated by the company. In their written bid, KKR offered to acquire 94% of Macmillan's shares through a management participation, highly-leveraged, two-tier, transaction, with a "face value" of $85 per share and payable in a mix of cash and subordinated debt securities. Additionally, this offer was strictly conditioned upon the payment of KKR's expenses and an additional $29.3 million "break up" fee if a merger agreement between KKR and Macmillan was terminated by virtue of a higher bid for the company.

On September 10 and 11, Macmillan's directors met to consider Maxwell's all-cash $84 bid and KKR's blended bid of $85. Although Macmillan's financial advisors discounted KKR's offer at $84.76 per share, they nevertheless formally opined that the KKR offer was both higher than Maxwell's bid and was fair to Macmillan shareholders from a financial point of view. The Macmillan board, inferring from Maxwell's September 9 letter that he would not top a bid higher than $84 per share, approved the KKR offer and agreed to recommend KKR's offer to the shareholders. The Macmillan-KKR merger agreement was publicly announced the following day, accompanied by Macmillan's affirmation that it would take all action necessary to insure the inapplicability of its shareholder rights plan, i.e., "poison pill," to the KKR offer.

Subsequently, on September 15—and in seeming contradiction to his September 9 statement that he would not top his previous offer—Maxwell announced that he was increasing his all-cash offer to $86.60 per share. Additionally, Maxwell asked the Court of Chancery to enjoin the operation of Macmillan's "poison pill" rights plan against the revised Maxwell offer.

After considering the increased Maxwell bid, on September 22 the Macmillan board withdrew its recommendation of the KKR offer to shareholders, and declared its willingness to consider higher bids for the company. The board therefore instructed its investment advisors to attempt to solicit higher bids from Maxwell, KKR or any other potential bidders, in an effort to maximize the company's value for shareholders. Additionally, the board directed that the shareholder rights plan be applied to all bidders in order to enhance the auction process.

On September 23, 1988, Wasserstein, Perella began establishing the procedures for submission of the Maxwell and KKR final bids. In partial deference to Maxwell's vocal belief that the auction would be "rigged" in KKR's favor, and in order to promote an appearance of fairness in the bidding process, a "script" was developed which would be read over the telephone to both KKR and Maxwell. According to this script, both bidders were called and advised on September 24 that "the process appears to be drawing to a close" and that any final amended bids were due by 5:30 p.m., September 26.

After receiving this information on September 24, Robert Pirie, Maxwell's financial advisor, once again expressed concern to Macmillan that KKR would be favored in the auction process, and would receive "break up" fees or a lockup agreement without Maxwell first being allowed to increase its bid. Perhaps as a result of this concern, Robert Maxwell stated unequivocally in a September 25 letter to Macmillan that he was prepared, if necessary, to exceed a higher competing offer from KKR.[20]

KKR had further discussions with Macmillan's advisors during the afternoon of September 25. One of the primary topics was an agreement that KKR's amended offer would include a "no-shop" clause. KKR's stated interpretation of this "blanket prohibition" was that disclosure by Macmillan of any element of KKR's bid, including price, would automatically revoke the offer. . . . Macmillan's advisors thus knew that KKR would insist upon conditions that could hinder maximization of the auction process to the detriment of Macmillan's shareholders.

On September 26, the Court of Chancery heard Maxwell's application for a temporary restraining order, seeking to prevent Macmillan from acting unfairly in the auction to be held later that evening. Although the Vice Chancellor observed that the auction process should be fair, he denied Maxwell's motion, based in part upon Macmillan's representation that there would be "no irrevocable scrambling of transactions" in the auction.

By the auction deadline on that evening, both Maxwell and KKR had submitted bids. Maxwell made an all-cash offer, consistent with its previous bids, of $89 per share. Like its past bids, KKR submitted another "blended," front-loaded offer of $89.50 per share, consisting of $82 in cash and the balance in subordinated securities. However, this nominally higher KKR bid was subject to three conditions effectively designed to end the auction: (1) imposition of the "no-shop" rule, (2) the grant to KKR of a lockup option to purchase eight Macmillan subsidiaries for $950 million, and (3) the execution of a definitive merger agreement by 12:00 noon, the following day, September 27.

While Macmillan's financial analysts considered the value of KKR's bid to be slightly higher, they decided that the bids were too close to permit the recommendation of either offer, and that the auction should therefore continue. However, shortly after the bids were received, Evans and Reilly, who were present in the

---

[20] Later that day, Maxwell was finally given the additional financial information which KKR received in early August.

Macmillan offices at the time, asked unidentified financial advisors about the status of the auction process. Inexplicably, these advisors told Evans and Reilly that both bids had been received, informed them of the respective price and forms of the bids, and stated that the financial advisors were unable to recommend either bid to the board.[22]

Thereafter, in the presence of Reilly and Charles J. Queenan, a Pittsburgh lawyer previously mentioned in note 10, *supra*, but who did not appear before us in this action, Evans telephoned a KKR representative and "tipped" Maxwell's bid to him. In this call, Evans informed KKR that Maxwell had offered "$89, all cash" for the company and that the respective bids were considered "a little close." After a few minutes of conversation, the KKR representative realized the impropriety of the call and abruptly terminated it.[23]

Meanwhile, Macmillan's financial advisors, apparently ignorant of Evans' "tip" to KKR, began developing procedures for a supplemental round of bidding. Bruce Wasserstein, the leading financial advisor to Macmillan management, who primarily orchestrated the auction process, developed a second "script" which was to be read over the telephone to both bidders. It stated:

> We are not in a position at this time to recommend any bid. If you would like to increase your bid price, let us know by 10:00 p.m.

At approximately 8:15 p.m., Wasserstein first read this prepared text to a Maxwell representative, and then relayed the same message to KKR. However, the actual document in evidence, which purports to be the "script," significantly varies in what was said to KKR. Allegedly in response to questions from KKR, Wasserstein and other financial advisors impressed upon KKR "the need to go as high as [KKR] could go" in terms of price. Additionally, the Wasserstein "script" discloses the further statement:

> To KKR: Focus on price but be advised that we do not want to give a lockup. If we granted a lockup, we would need: (1) a significant gap in your bid over the competing bid; (2) a smaller group of assets to be bought; and (3) a higher price for the assets to be bought.

At approximately 10:00 p.m., near the auction deadline of midnight, Pirie on behalf of Maxwell telephoned Wasserstein to inquire whether Macmillan had received a bid higher than the Maxwell offer. During the call, Pirie flatly stated that upon being informed that a higher bid had been received by Macmillan, Maxwell would promptly notify the company whether it would increase its stand-

---

[22] This epitomizes the problem of conducting an auction without board oversight, and under uncontrolled circumstances that gave Evans and Reilly, themselves interested bidders with KKR, complete and improper access to the process.

[23] In fairness to KKR even Maxwell concedes that but for the integrity of KKR's counsel, it is unlikely that Evans' tip would have been publicly disclosed. . . . It also appears that counsel, who appeared in this action for the defendants, were unaware of the "tip" until it was disclosed by KKR.

ing offer. Pirie also said that if Maxwell had already submitted the highest bid for the company, he would not "bid against himself" by increasing his offer.

While Wasserstein could reasonably infer from this message that Maxwell intended to top any KKR offer, it is clear that Pirie wanted to know whether KKR had in fact submitted a higher bid. Wasserstein claims to have believed that such a revelation might violate KKR's "no-shop" condition, and would have terminated the KKR offer.[24] Therefore, he replied that if Maxwell had "anything further to say, tell us by midnight." Additionally, Wasserstein told Pirie to assume that Macmillan would not call Maxwell to inform it of a higher offer. After this conversation, and upon the advice of legal counsel, Wasserstein called Pirie back and reemphasized that he was not in a position to recommend a bid to the Macmillan board, and that Maxwell should submit its highest bid to the company by 12:00 midnight.

From the bulk of these conversations, Maxwell and Pirie reasonably, but erroneously, concluded that Wasserstein was attempting to force Maxwell to bid against itself, and that its offer was indeed higher than the competing KKR bid. Furthermore, the record is clear that Wasserstein, who later acknowledged this fact to the Macmillan board, knew that Pirie mistakenly believed that Maxwell was already the high bidder for the company. Yet, despite his responsibilities as "auctioneer" for the company, Wasserstein never sought to correct Maxwell's mistaken belief that it had prevailed in the auction. The cumulative effect of all this was that Maxwell did not increase its bid before the Macmillan board met on the next day, September 27.

At 11:50 p.m., September 26, ten minutes before the bid deadline, KKR submitted a final revised offer with a face value of $90 per share. Furthermore, the bid was predicated upon the same three previous conditions—except that the revised lockup option, apparently reflecting the additional information relayed by Wasserstein in his special KKR "script," was reduced to include only four subsidiaries at a purchase price of $775 million.

In the early morning hours of September 27, after the midnight auction deadline, Macmillan negotiated with both parties over wholly different matters. Macmillan's advisors negotiated with Maxwell's representatives for several hours over the specific and unresolved terms of Maxwell's otherwise unconditional merger proposal. However, during these sessions Macmillan never suggested that Maxwell increase its bid. On the other hand, for almost eight hours Macmillan and KKR negotiated to increase KKR's offer. By the next morning, while only increasing its total bid by approximately $1.6 million, to $90.05 ($.05 per share), KKR extracted concessions from Macmillan which increased KKR's exercise price under the lockup by $90 million after adding three more Macmillan divisions to the group of optioned assets.

Significantly, the sale of the assets under the KKR lockup agreement was structured on a "cash" basis, which would immediately result in a $250 million current tax liability for Macmillan. Moreover, both KKR and Macmillan knew

---

[24] At oral argument the parties, including KKR, could not seriously claim that disclosing the mere existence of a higher bid would violate the "no-shop" clause. . . .

that this tax liability could have been avoided through an "installment" basis sale of the assets. Above all, they knew that it would produce a *de facto* financial "poison pill" which would effectively end the auction process.

On the morning of September 27, the Macmillan board met with its investment advisors to consider these competing bids. During the course of the meeting, chaired by Evans and with Reilly present, the company's financial advisors with Wasserstein as the lead spokesman (some directors said he presided), made presentations describing their communications with both Maxwell and KKR during the auction process. Wasserstein falsely claimed that the advisors had conducted "a level-playing field auction where both parties had equal opportunity to participate." Additionally, in answer to questioning, Wasserstein mistakenly assured the board that he had been the "only conduit of information" during the process and, falsely, that both parties had received *identical* information during the auction. Despite the obvious untruth of these assertions, Evans and Reilly remained silent, knowing also that Evans had clandestinely, and wrongfully, tipped Maxwell's bid to KKR.

Wasserstein then announced the results of the second round of the auction along with the specific aspects of KKR's $90.05 "face amount" offer and Maxwell's $89 cash bid. Wasserstein, whose firm was originally retained as *management's* financial advisor, not the board's, then opined that the KKR offer was the higher of the two bids. The Lazard representative, who was retained as the financial advisor to the independent directors of the board, but throughout acquiesced in Wasserstein's predominant role, thereafter concurred in Wasserstein's assessment. Wasserstein additionally explained the ramifications of the conditions of KKR's offer, including the "deterrent" effect of the $250 million tax liability produced by the KKR lockup agreement.

However, through its deliberations on September 27, Macmillan's board, whether justified or not, was under the impression that the two bids were the product of a fair and unbiased auction process, designed to encourage KKR and Maxwell to submit their best bids.[25] The directors were not informed of Evans' and Reilly's "tip" to KKR on the previous day. Nor were they told of Wasserstein's extended "script" giving to KKR, but denying to Maxwell, additional information about the bidding process. Throughout the board meeting Evans and Reilly remained silent, deliberately concealing from their fellow directors their misconduct of tipping Maxwell's bid to KKR. . . .

After these presentations, the Macmillan directors held extensive and closed discussions concerning the choices available to the board, including the possibility that Maxwell might increase its bid if the board "shopped" the KKR offer. Yet, as they believed that the risk of terminating the KKR offer outweighed the potential advantage of an increased Maxwell bid, the directors decided to accept the higher face value KKR proposal, and granted the KKR merger and lockup option agreements.

---

[25] Even though neither the Board as a whole, nor the allegedly "independent" directors, had taken any action to ensure such a process.

On the next day, Maxwell promptly amended its original complaint in the Court of Chancery, added KKR as a co-defendant, and among other things, sought to enjoin the lockup agreement, the break-up fees and expenses granted to KKR.

On September 29, 1988, KKR filed documents required by the Securities and Exchange Commission, amending its outstanding tender offer to reflect the increased $90.05 face amount bid accepted by the Macmillan board. In this filing, and for the first time, KKR disclosed Evans' September 26 "tip" to KKR that Maxwell's cash bid was $.50 lower than KKR's.

On that same day, Robert Maxwell delivered a letter to Evans announcing that he had amended his cash tender offer to $90.25 per share, conditioned upon invalidation of the KKR lockup agreement. In his letter, Maxwell emphasized that he had previously stated his willingness to top any offer higher than his earlier $89 offer, and that he was nevertheless willing to purchase for $900 million the same four divisions which KKR originally proposed to purchase for $775 million.

On October 4, the Macmillan board met to consider both the revised Maxwell bid and Evans' September 26 "tip" to KKR. After some discussion and deliberation, the board rejected Maxwell's increased offer because it was conditioned on invalidating the KKR lockup. Furthermore, the board considered that Evans' "tip" to KKR was immaterial in light of the second round of bidding that occurred. Additionally, after consultation with counsel, the board concluded that their ignorance of this "tip," at the time they approved the merger with KKR, was insufficient grounds for repudiating the lockup agreement.

After a hearing on Maxwell's motion for a preliminary injunction, on October 17, the Court of Chancery denied Maxwell's request to enjoin the lockup agreement, the break-up fees and expenses granted by the Macmillan board to KKR. In ruling for Macmillan, the trial court found that although KKR was consistently and deliberately favored throughout the auction process, Maxwell was not prevented from, or otherwise misled to refrain from, submitting a higher bid for the company. However, the court found that Macmillan's shareholders should have the opportunity to consider an alternative offer for the company, and therefore enjoined the operation of Macmillan's "poison pill" shareholder rights plan as a defensive measure to Maxwell's still open tender offer. In this appeal neither party has challenged that limited injunction. Thus, the sole issue before us is the validity, under all of the foregoing circumstances, of the asset lockup option granted pursuant to the KKR-Macmillan merger agreement with its attendant breakup fees and expenses.

II.

. . .

When seeking a preliminary injunction, a plaintiff must demonstrate a reasonable probability of success on the merits and that some irreparable harm will occur in the absence of the injunction. . . . Furthermore, in evaluating the need for a preliminary injunction, the Court must balance the plaintiff's need for protection against any harm that can reasonably be expected to befall the defendants if the injunction is granted. When the former outweighs the latter, then the injunction should issue. . . .

A.

. . .

While it is apparent that the Court of Chancery seemingly attempted to evaluate this case under the relatively broad parameters of the business judgment rule, it nevertheless held that the relevant inquiry must focus upon the "fairness" of the auction process in light of promoting the maximum shareholder value as mandated by this Court in *Revlon*. In denying Maxwell's motion for an injunction, the Vice-Chancellor concluded that the auction-related deficiencies could be deemed "material" only upon a showing that they actually deterred a higher bid from Maxwell.

We have held that when a court reviews a board action, challenged as a breach of duty, it should decline to evaluate the wisdom and merits of a business decision unless sufficient facts are alleged with particularity, or the record otherwise demonstrates, that the decision was not the product of an informed, disinterested, and independent board. See Aronson v. Lewis, Del.Supr., 473 A.2d 805, 812 (1984); Pogostin v. Rice, Del.Supr., 480 A.2d 619, 624 (1984); Smith v. Van Gorkom, Del.Supr., 488 A.2d 858, 872 (1985). Yet, this judicial reluctance to assess the merits of a business decision ends in the face of illicit manipulation of a board's deliberative processes by self-interested corporate fiduciaries. Here, not only was there such deception, but the board's own lack of oversight in structuring and directing the auction afforded management the opportunity to indulge in the misconduct which occurred. In such a context, the challenged transaction must withstand rigorous judicial scrutiny under the exacting standards of entire fairness. Weinberger v. UOP, Inc., Del.Supr., 457 A.2d 701, 710 (1983); Gottlieb v. Heyden Chemical Corp., Del. Supr., 33 Del. Ch. 177, 91 A.2d 57, 58 (1952). Compare Rosenblatt v. Getty Oil Co., Del. Supr., 493 A.2d 929, 937-40 (1985). What occurred here cannot survive that analysis.[27]

The Vice Chancellor correctly found that Evans and Reilly, as participants in the leveraged buyout, had significant self-interest in ensuring the success of a KKR bid. Given this finding, Evans' and Reilly's deliberate concealment of material information from the Macmillan board must necessarily have been motivated by an interest adverse to Macmillan's shareholders. Evans' and Reilly's conduct throughout was resolutely intended to deliver the company to themselves in *Macmillan I*, and to their favored bidder, KKR, and thus themselves, in *Macmillan II*. The board was torpid, if not supine, in its efforts to establish a truly independent

---

[27] See AC Acquisitions v. Anderson, Clayton & Co., Del. Ch., 519 A. 2d 103, 111(1986) wherein the court correctly noted that "where a self-interested corporate fiduciary has set the terms of a transaction and caused its effectuation, it will be required to establish the entire fairness of the transaction to a reviewing court's satisfaction." Id. [citing Weinberger v. UOP Inc., Del.Supr., 457 A.2d 701 (1983); Sterling v. Mayflower Hotel Corp., Del.Supr., 33 Del. Ch. 293, 93 A.2d 107 (1952); Guth v. Loft, Del.Supr., 23 Del. Ch. 255, 5 A.2d 503 (1939)]. We could conceive no clearer instance of the proper application of this most basic rule of law than the present case.

auction, free of Evans' interference and access to confidential data. By placing the entire process in the hands of Evans, through his own chosen financial advisors, with little or no board oversight, the board materially contributed to the unprincipled conduct of those upon whom it looked with a blind eye.

B.

It is basic to our law that the board of directors has the ultimate responsibility for managing the business and affairs of a corporation. 8 *Del. C.* §141(a). In discharging this function, the directors owe fiduciary duties of care and loyalty to the corporation and its shareholders, Revlon, 506 A.2d at 179; Aronson, 473 A.2d at 811; Guth v. Loft, Inc., Del.Supr., 23 Del. Ch. 255, 5 A.2d 503, 510 (1939). This unremitting obligation extends equally to board conduct in a sale of corporate control. Smith v. Van Gorkom, Del.Supr., 488 A.2d 858, 872-73 (1985).

The fiduciary nature of a corporate office is immutable. As this Court stated long ago:

> Corporate officers and directors are not permitted to use their position of trust and confidence to further their private interests. While technically not trustees, they stand in a fiduciary relation to the corporation and its shareholders. . . . This rule, inveterate and uncompromising in its rigidity, does not rest upon the narrow ground of injury or damage to the corporation resulting from a betrayal of confidence, but upon a broader foundation of a wise public policy that, for the purpose of removing all temptation, extinguishes all possibility of profit flowing from a breach of the confidence imposed by fiduciary relation.

Guth v. Loft, 5 A.2d at 510. Not only do these principles demand that corporate fiduciaries absolutely refrain from any act which breaches the trust reposed in them, but also to affirmatively protect and defend those interests entrusted to them. Officers and directors must exert all reasonable and lawful efforts to ensure that the corporation is not deprived of any advantage to which it is entitled. Weinberger, 457 A.2d at 710 (citing Guth v. Loft, 5 A.2d at 510).

Thus, directors are required to demonstrate both their utmost good faith and the most scrupulous inherent fairness of transactions in which they possess a financial, business or other personal interest which does not devolve upon the corporation or all stockholders generally. Aronson, 473 A.2d at 812; Pogostin, 480 A.2d at 624; Weinberger, 457 A.2d at 710. When faced with such divided loyalties, directors have the burden of establishing the entire fairness of the transaction to survive careful scrutiny by the courts.

Under Delaware law this concept of fairness has two aspects: fair dealing and fair price. Weinberger, 457 A.2d at 711. "Fair dealing" focuses upon the actual conduct of corporate fiduciaries in effecting a transaction, such as its initiation, structure, and negotiation. This element also embraces the duty of candor owed by corporate fiduciaries to disclose all material information relevant to corporate decisions from which they may derive a personal benefit. See 8 *Del.C.* §144. "Fair price," in the context of an auction for corporate control, mandates that directors commit themselves, inexorably, to obtaining the highest value reasonably available to the shareholders under all the circumstances. Weinberger, 457 A.2d at 711.

III.

The voluminous record in this case discloses conduct that fails all basic standards of fairness. While any one of the identifiable breaches of fiduciary duty, standing alone, should easily foretell the outcome, what occurred here, including the lack of oversight by the directors, irremediably taints the design and execution of the transaction.

It is clear that on July 14, 1988, the day that the Court of Chancery enjoined the management-induced reorganization, and with Bass' $73 offer outstanding, Macmillan's management met with KKR to discuss a management sponsored buyout. This was done without prior board approval. By early September, Macmillan's financial and legal advisors, originally chosen by Evans, independently constructed and managed the process by which bids for the company were solicited. Although the Macmillan board was fully aware of its ultimate responsibility for ensuring the integrity of the auction, the directors wholly delegated the creation and administration of the auction to an array of Evans' hand-picked investment advisors. It is undisputed that Wasserstein, who was originally retained as an investment advisor to Macmillan's senior management, was a principal, if not the primary, "auctioneer" of the company. While it is unnecessary to hold that Wasserstein lacked independence, or was necessarily "beholden" to management, it appears that Lazard Freres, allegedly the investment advisor to the independent directors, was a far more appropriate candidate to conduct this process on behalf of the board. Yet, both the board and Lazard acceded to Wasserstein's, and through him Evans', primacy.

While a board of directors may rely in good faith upon "information, opinions, reports or statements presented" by corporate officers, employees and experts "selected with reasonable care," 8 *Del. C.* §141(e), it may not avoid its active and direct duty of oversight in a matter as significant as the sale of corporate control. That would seem particularly obvious where insiders are among the bidders. This failure of the Macmillan board significantly contributed to the resulting mismanagement of the bidding process. When presumably well-intentioned outside directors remove themselves from the design and execution of an auction, then what occurred here, given the human temptations left unchecked, was virtually inevitable.

Clearly, this auction was clandestinely and impermissibly skewed in favor of KKR. The record amply demonstrates that KKR repeatedly received significant material advantages to the exclusion and detriment of Maxwell to stymie, rather than enhance, the bidding process.

As for any "negotiations" between Macmillan and Maxwell, they are noteworthy only for the peremptory and curt attitude of Macmillan, through its self-interested chief executive officer Evans, to reject every overture from Maxwell. In Robert Maxwell's initial letter to Evans of July 21, he proposed an $80 all-cash offer for the company. This represented a substantial increase over any other outstanding offer. Indeed, it equalled the highest per share price, which both Wasserstein, Perella and Lazard had previously ascribed to the value of the company on June 7, when the Evans' sponsored restructuring was before the board. Now, not only was Maxwell ignored, but Evans convinced Wasserstein,

Perella and Lazard, contrary to their June 7 opinions, ascribing a maximum value to the company of $80 per share, to declare Maxwell's August 12 bid of $80 inadequate.[28] Not only did Macmillan's financial advisors dismiss all Maxwell offers for negotiations, but they also deliberately misled Maxwell in the final stage of the auction by perpetuating the mistaken belief that Maxwell had the high bid. Additionally, Maxwell was subjected to a series of short bid deadlines in a seeming effort to prevent the submission of a meaningful bid. The defendants have totally failed to justify this calculated campaign of resistance and misinformation, despite the strict duties of care and loyalty demanded of them. See Revlon, 506 A.2d at 181.

The tone and substance of the communications between Macmillan and Maxwell dispel any further doubt that Maxwell was seen as an unwelcome, unfriendly and unwanted bidder. Evans, a self-interested fiduciary, repeatedly stated that *he* had no intention of considering a merger with Maxwell, and that *he* would do everything to prevent Maxwell from acquiring Macmillan. Nonetheless, Robert Maxwell's response was a diplomatic, yet persistent, pursuit of Macmillan, emphasizing his desire to work with existing management and his intent to operate the company as a going concern. With the sole exception of his September 9th letter, declining to exceed a "fully financed" offer above $84, Maxwell never retreated from his stated intent to continue bidding for Macmillan, or his willingness to negotiate any other aspect of his offer.

This continuing hostility toward Maxwell cannot be justified after the Macmillan board actually decided on September 10-11 to abandon any further restructuring attempts, and to sell the entire company. Although Evans had begun negotiations with KKR on July 14, the board's action in September formally initiated the auction process. Further discriminatory treatment of a bidder, without any rational benefit to the shareholders, was unwarranted. The proper objective of Macmillan's fiduciaries was to obtain the highest price reasonably available for the company, provided it was offered by a reputable and responsible bidder.[29] Revlon, 506 A.2d at 182, 184. At this point, there was no justification for denying Maxwell the same courtesies and access to information as had been extended to KKR. Id. at 184. Without board planning and oversight to insulate the self-interested management from improper access to the bidding process, and to ensure the proper conduct of the auction by truly independent advisors selected by, and answerable only to, the independent directors, the legal complications which a challenged transaction faces under *Revlon* are unnecessarily intensified. See Weinberger, 457 A.2d at 709 n. 7. Compare Rosenblatt, 493 A.2d at 937-40, where an authentic independent negotiating structure had been established.

---

[28] Yet, on May 30 these same advisors had found management's $64.15 restructuring to be fair.

[29] In assessing the bid and the bidder's responsibility, a board may consider, among various proper factors, the adequacy and terms of the offer; its fairness and feasibility; the proposed or actual financing for the offer, and the consequences of that financing; questions of illegality; the impact of both the bid and the potential acquisition on other constituencies, provided that it bears some reasonable relationship to general shareholder interests; the risk of nonconsumation; the basic stockholder interests at stake; the bidder's identity, prior background and other business venture experiences; and the bidder's business plans for the corporation and their effects on stockholder interests. Cf. Ivanhoe, 535 A.2d at 1341-42; Unocal, 493 A.2d at 955-56; Revlon, 506 A.2d at 182-83.

IV.

In examining the actual conduct of this auction, there can be no justification for the telephonic "tip" to KKR of Maxwell's $89 all-cash offer following the first round of bidding held on September 26th. Although the defendants contend that this tip was made "innocently" and under the impression that the auction process had already ended, this assertion is refuted by the record. The recipient of the "tip," KKR, immediately recognized its impropriety.[30] Evans' and Reilly's knowing concealment of the tip at the critical board meeting of September 27th utterly destroys their credibility. Given their duty of disclosure under the circumstances, this silence is an explicit acknowledgment of their culpability. . . .

As the duty of candor is one of the elementary principles of fair dealing, Delaware law imposes this unremitting obligation not only on officers and directors, but also upon those who are privy to material information obtained in the course of representing corporate interests. See Weinberger, 457 A.2d at 710; Marciano v. Nakash, Del. Supr., 535 A.2d 400, 406-407 (1987); Brophy v. Cities Service Co, Del. Supr., 31 Del. Ch. 241, 70 A.2d 5, 7 (1949). At a minimum, this rule dictates that fiduciaries, corporate or otherwise, may not use superior information or knowledge to mislead others in the performance of their own fiduciary obligations. The actions of those who join in such misconduct are equally tainted. See e.g. Penn Mart Realty v. Becker, Del. Ch., 298 A.2d 349, 351 (1972).

Defendants maintain that the Evans-Reilly tip was immaterial, because it did not prevent Maxwell from submitting a higher bid in the second and final round of the auction on September 26th. However, this "immaterial" tip revealed both the price and form of Maxwell's first round bid, which constituted the two principal strategic components of their otherwise unconditional offer. With this information, KKR knew every crucial element of Maxwell's initial bid. The unfair tactical advantage this gave KKR, since no aspect of its own bid could be shopped, becomes manifest in light of the situation created by Maxwell's belief that it had submitted the higher offer. . . . Absent an unprompted and unexpected improvement in Maxwell's bid, the tip provided vital information to enable KKR to prevail in the auction.

Similarly, the defendants argue that the subsequent Wasserstein "long script"—in reality another form of tip—was an immaterial and "appropriate response" to questions by KKR, providing no tactical information useful to KKR. As to this claim, the eventual auction results demonstrate that Wasserstein's tip relayed crucial information to KKR: the methods by which KKR should tailor its bid in order to satisfy Macmillan's financial advisors. It is highly significant that both aspects of the advice conveyed by the tip—to "focus on price" and to amend the terms of its lockup agreement—were adopted by KKR. They were the very improvements upon which the board subsequently accepted the KKR bid on Wasserstein's recommendation. Nothing could have been more material under

[30] Although the KKR representative initially was unaware of the unauthorized nature of the tip, it is revealing that he abruptly terminated the call when he realized that Evans and Reilly were acting improperly. At the least, it stands in stark contrast to the later efforts of KKR, Evans and other defendants to trivialize this extraordinary act of misconduct.

the circumstances. It violated every principle of fair dealing, and of the exacting role demanded of those entrusted with the conduct of an auction for the sale of corporate control. Weinberger, 457 A.2d at 710-711; Revlon, 506 A.2d at 182, 184.

V.

Given the materiality of these tips, and the silence of Evans, Reilly and Wasserstein in the face of their rigorous affirmative duty of disclosure at the September 27 board meeting, there can be no dispute but that such silence was misleading and deceptive. In short, it was a fraud upon the board. . . .

VI.

In *Revlon*, we addressed for the first time the parameters of a board of directors' fiduciary duties in a sale of corporate control. There, we affirmed the Court of Chancery's decision to enjoin the lockup and no-shop provisions accepted by the Revlon directors, holding that the board had breached its fiduciary duties of care and loyalty.[34]

Although we have held that such agreements are not *per se* illegal, we recognized that like measures often foreclose further bidding to the detriment of shareholders, and end active auctions prematurely. Revlon, 506 A.2d at 183-84; see also Thompson v. Enstar Corp., Del. Ch., 509 A.2d 578 (1984). If the grant of an auction-ending provision is appropriate, it must confer a substantial benefit upon the stockholders in order to withstand exacting scrutiny by the courts. Cf. Revlon, 506 A.2d at 183-85; see also Hanson Trust PLC v. ML SCM Acquisition Inc., 781 F.2d 264, 274 (2nd Cir.1986). Moreover, where the decision of the directors, granting the lockup option, was not informed or was induced by breaches of fiduciary duties, such as those here, they cannot survive. See Revlon, 506 A.2d at 184; Hanson Trust, 781 F.2d at 278-81; Guth, 5 A.2d at 503.

A.

Perhaps the most significant aspect of *Revlon* was our holding that when the Revlon board authorized its management to negotiate a sale of the company:

> [t]he duty of the board had thus changed from the preservation of Revlon as a corporate entity to the maximization of the company's value at a sale for the stockholders' benefit. . . . [The board] no longer faced threats to corporate policy and effectiveness, or to the stockholders' interests, from a grossly inadequate bid. The whole question of defensive measures became moot. The directors' role changed from defenders of the corporate bastion to auctioneers charged with getting the best price for the stockholders at a sale of the company.

Revlon, 506 A.2d at 182.

---

[34] Following *Revlon*, there appeared to be a degree of "scholarly" debate about the particular fiduciary duty that had been breached in that case, i.e. the duty of care or the duty of loyalty. In Ivanhoe, 535 A.2d at 1345, we made it abundantly clear that *both* duties were involved in *Revlon*, and that both had been breached.

This case does not require a judicial determination of *when* Macmillan was "for sale." . . . By any standards this company was for sale both in *Macmillan I and II*. In any event, the board of directors formally concluded on September 11 that it would be in the best interests of the stockholders to sell the company. . . . Evidently, they reached this decision with the prospect of a KKR-management sponsored buyout in mind. Although Evans apparently made the decision to pursue a KKR buyout on July 14, the day the Court of Chancery enjoined his "restructuring," there is no evidence in the record that Evans had acted with board authority on that date.

What we are required to determine here is the scope of the board's responsibility in an active bidding contest once their role as auctioneer has been invoked under *Revlon*. Particularly, we are concerned with the use of lockup and no-shop clauses.

At a minimum, Revlon requires that there be the most scrupulous adherence to ordinary principles of fairness in the sense that stockholder interests are enhanced, rather than diminished, in the conduct of an auction for the sale of corporate control. This is so whether the "sale" takes the form of an active auction, a management buyout, or a "restructuring" such as that which the Court of Chancery enjoined in *Macmillan I. Revlon*, 506 A.2d at 181-82. Under these special circumstances the duties of the board are "significantly altered." Id. at 182. The defensive aspects of *Unocal* no longer apply. Id. The sole responsibility of the directors in such a sale is for the shareholders' benefit. The board may not allow any impermissible influence, inconsistent with the best interests of the shareholders, to alter the strict fulfillment of these duties. Id. Clearly, this requires the intense scrutiny and participation of the independent directors, whose conduct comports with the standards of independence enunciated by us in Aronson v. Lewis, 473 A.2d at 816.

The Macmillan directors argue that a "blind auction" is a desirable means to fulfill their primary duty to the shareholders. That may be so, but it did not happen here. Only Maxwell was blind.

B.

Turning to the lockup option, in *Revlon* we held that such an agreement is not *per se* unlawful under Delaware law. Revlon, 506 A.2d at 183. We recognized its proper function in a contest for corporate control. Apparently, it has escaped some that in *Revlon* we distinguished the potentially valid uses of a lockup from those that are impermissible:

> "[W]hile those lock-ups which draw bidders into a battle benefit shareholders, similar measures which end an active auction and foreclose further bidding operate to the shareholders' detriment."

Id. at 183. See also Hanson Trust, 781 F.2d at 272.

In this case, a lockup agreement was not necessary to draw any of the bidders into the contest. Macmillan cannot seriously contend that they received a final bid from KKR that materially enhanced general stockholder interests. By all rational indications it was intended to have a directly opposite effect. As the record clearly shows, on numerous occasions Maxwell requested opportunities to further negotiate the price and structure of his proposal. When he learned of KKR's higher offer, he increased his bid to $90.25 per share. Compare Revlon, 506 A.2d at 179, 184; Hanson Trust, 781 F.2d at 272. Further, KKR's "enhanced" bid, being nominal at best, was a *de minimis* justification for the lockup. When one compares what KKR received for the lockup, in contrast to its inconsiderable offer, the invalidity of the agreement becomes patent. Cf. Revlon, 506 A.2d at 184.

Here, the assets covered by the lockup agreement were some of Macmillan's most valued properties, its "crown jewels." [37] Even if the lockup is permissible, when it involves "crown jewel" assets careful board scrutiny attends the decision. When the intended effect is to end an active auction, at the very least the independent members of the board must attempt to negotiate alternative bids before granting such a significant concession. See Revlon, 506 A.2d at 183; Hanson Trust, 781 F.2d at 277. Maxwell invited negotiations for a purchase of the same four divisions, which KKR originally sought to buy for $775 million. Maxwell was prepared to pay $900 million. Instead of serious negotiations with Maxwell, there were only concessions to KKR by giving it a lockup of seven divisions for $865 million.

Thus, when directors in a *Revlon* bidding contest grant a crown jewel lockup, serious questions are raised, particularly where, as here, there is little or no improvement in the final bid. Revlon, 506 A.2d at 184, 187. The care and attention which independent directors bring to this decision are crucial to its success. Cf. Weinberger, 457 A.2d at 709 n. 7; Rosenblatt, 493 A.2d at 937-38.

C.

As for the no-shop clause, *Revlon* teaches that the use of such a device is even more limited than a lockup agreement. Absent a material advantage to the stockholders from the terms or structure of a bid that is contingent on a no-shop clause, a successful bidder imposing such a condition must be prepared to survive the careful scrutiny which that concession demands. Revlon, 506 A.2d at 184.

VII.

A.

Directors are not required by Delaware law to conduct an auction according to some standard formula, only that they observe the significant requirement of fairness for the purpose of enhancing general shareholder interests. That does not preclude differing treatment of bidders when necessary to advance those interests. Variables may occur which necessitate such treatment.[38] However, the

---

[37] In the current takeover parlance, these are valuable assets or lines of business owned by a target company. The attempt is to sell them to third parties or place them under option at bargain prices as a device to defeat an unwanted takeover attempt. . . .

[38] For example, this Court has upheld actions of directors when a board is confronted with a coercive "two-tiered" bust-up tender offer. See Unocal, 493 A.2d at 956; Ivanhoe, 535 A.2d at 1342. Compare Revlon, 506 A.2d at 184.

board's primary objective, and essential purpose, must remain the enhancement of the bidding process for the benefit of the stockholders.

We recognize that the conduct of a corporate auction is a complex undertaking both in its design and execution. . . . We do not intend to limit the broad negotiating authority of the directors to achieve the best price available to the stockholders. To properly secure that end may require the board to invoke a panoply of devices, and the giving or receiving of concessions that may benefit one bidder over another. See e.g., In re J.P. Stevens & Co., Inc. Shareholders Litigation, Del. Ch., 542 A.2d 770, 781-784 (1988); *appeal* refused, 540 A.2d 1088 (1988). But when that happens, there must be a rational basis for the action such that the interests of the stockholders are manifestly the board's paramount objective.

B.

In the absence of self-interest, and upon meeting the enhanced duty mandated by *Unocal*, the actions of an independent board of directors in designing and conducting a corporate auction are protected by the business judgment rule. Ivanhoe, 535 A.2d at 1341; Unocal, 493 A.2d at 954; Pogostin, 480 A.2d at 627. Thus, like any other business decision, the board has a duty in the design and conduct of an auction to act in "the best interests of the corporation and its shareholders." Unocal, 493 A.2d at 954-56; Ivanhoe, 535 A.2d at 1341-42.

However, as we recognized in *Unocal*, where issues of corporate control are at stake, there exists "the omnipresent specter that a board may be acting primarily in its own interests, rather than those of the corporation and its shareholders." Unocal, 493 A.2d at 954. For that reason, an "enhanced duty" must be met at the threshold before the board receives the normal protections of the business judgment rule. Id. Directors may not act out of a sole or primary desire to "perpetuate themselves in office." Id. at 955; Cf. Cheff v. Mathes, Del.Supr., 41 Del. Ch. 494, 199 A.2d 548, 556 (1964); Kors v. Carey, 39 Del. Ch. 47, 158 A.2d 136, 140 (1960).

As we held in *Revlon*, when management of a target company determines that the company is for sale, the board's *responsibilities* under the enhanced *Unocal* standards are significantly altered. Revlon, 506 A.2d at 182. Although the board's *responsibilities* under *Unocal* are far different, the enhanced *duties* of the directors in responding to a potential shift in control, recognized in *Unocal*, remain unchanged. This principle pervades *Revlon*,[39] and when directors conclude that an auction is appropriate, the standard by which their ensuing actions will be judged continues to be the enhanced duty imposed by this Court in *Unocal*. . . .

When *Revlon* duties devolve upon directors, this Court will continue to exact an enhanced judicial scrutiny at the threshold, as in *Unocal*, before the normal presumptions of the business judgment rule will apply. However, as we recog-

---

[39] See e.g. Revlon, 506 A.2d at 184 ("Thus, when a board ends an intense bidding contest on an insubstantial basis, and where a significant byproduct of that action is to protect the directors against a perceived threat of personal liability. . .the action cannot withstand the enhanced scrutiny which *Unocal* requires of director conduct."). Further, "when bidders make relatively similar offers, or dissolution of the company becomes inevitable, the directors cannot fulfill their enhanced *Unocal* duties by playing favorites with the contending factions." Id.

nized in *Revlon*, the two part threshold test, of necessity, is slightly different. Revlon, 506 A.2d at 182.

At the outset, the plaintiff must show, and the trial court must find, that the directors of the target company treated one or more of the respective bidders on unequal terms. It is only then that the two-part threshold requirement of *Unocal* is truly invoked, for in *Revlon* we held that "[f]avoritism for a white knight to the total exclusion of a hostile bidder might be justifiable when the latter's offer adversely affects shareholder interests, but . . . the directors cannot fulfill their enhanced *Unocal* duties by playing favorites with the contending factions." Id. 506 A.2d at 184.

In the face of disparate treatment, the trial court must first examine whether the directors properly perceived that shareholder interests were enhanced. In any event the board's action must be reasonable in relation to the advantage sought to be achieved, or conversely, to the threat which a particular bid allegedly poses to stockholder interests. Unocal, 493 A.2d at 955.

If on the basis of this enhanced *Unocal* scrutiny the trial court is satisfied that the test has been met, then the directors' actions necessarily are entitled to the protections of the business judgment rule. The latitude a board will have in responding to differing bids will vary according to the degree of benefit or detriment to the shareholders' general interests that the amount or terms of the bids pose. We stated in *Revlon*, and again here, that in a sale of corporate control the responsibility of the directors is to get the highest value reasonably attainable for the shareholders. Revlon, 506 A.2d at 182. Beyond that, there are no special and distinct "Revlon duties." Once a finding has been made by a court that the directors have fulfilled their fundamental duties of care and loyalty under the foregoing standards, there is no further judicial inquiry into the matter. See In re R.J.R. Nabisco, supra at 53-56. See also In re J. P. Stevens & Co., supra; In re Fort Howard, supra; compare In re Holly Farms, supra.

For the foregoing reasons, the judgment of the Court of Chancery, denying Maxwell's motion for a preliminary injunction, is REVERSED.

PARAMOUNT COMMUNICATIONS INC., et al., Defendants Below, Appellants, v. QVC NETWORK INC., Plaintiff Below, Appellee.

Supreme Court of Delaware

637 A.2d 34 (1994)

Affirmed.
Upon appeal from the Court of Chancery
Before VEASEY, C.J., MOORE and HOLLAND, JJ.
VEASEY, Chief Justice.

In this appeal we review an order of the Court of Chancery dated November 24, 1993 (the "November 24 Order"), preliminarily enjoining certain defensive measures designed to facilitate a so-called strategic alliance between Viacom Inc. ("Viacom") and Paramount Communications Inc. ("Paramount") approved by the board of directors of Paramount (the "Paramount Board" or the "Paramount directors") and to thwart an unsolicited, more valuable, tender offer by QVC Network Inc. ("QVC"). In affirming, we hold that the sale of control in this case, which is at the heart of the proposed strategic alliance, implicates enhanced judicial scrutiny of the conduct of the Paramount Board under Unocal Corp. v. Mesa Petroleum Co., Del. Supr., 493 A.2d 946 (1985), and Revlon, Inc. v. MacAndrews & Forbes Holdings, Inc., Del. Supr., 506 A.2d 173 (1986). We further hold that the conduct of the Paramount Board was not reasonable as to process or result.

QVC and certain stockholders of Paramount commenced separate actions (later consolidated) in the Court of Chancery seeking preliminary and permanent injunctive relief against Paramount, certain members of the Paramount Board, and Viacom. This action arises out of a proposed acquisition of Paramount by Viacom through a tender offer followed by a second-step merger (the "Paramount-Viacom transaction"), and a competing unsolicited tender offer by QVC. The Court of Chancery granted a preliminary injunction. . . .

The Court of Chancery found that the Paramount directors violated their fiduciary duties by favoring the Paramount-Viacom transaction over the more valuable unsolicited offer of QVC. The Court of Chancery preliminarily enjoined Paramount and the individual defendants (the "Paramount defendants") from amending or modifying Paramount's stockholder rights agreement (the "Rights Agreement"), including the redemption of the Rights, or taking other action to facilitate the consummation of the pending tender offer by Viacom or any proposed second-step merger, including the Merger Agreement between Paramount and Viacom dated September 12, 1993 (the "Original Merger Agreement"), as amended on October 24, 1993 (the "Amended Merger Agreement"). Viacom and the Paramount defendants were enjoined from taking any action to exercise any provision of the Stock Option Agreement between Paramount and Viacom dated September 12, 1993 (the "Stock Option Agreement"), as amended on October 24, 1993. The Court of Chancery did not grant preliminary injunctive relief as to the termination fee provided for the benefit of Viacom in Section 8.05 of the Original Merger Agreement and the Amended Merger Agreement (the "Termination Fee").

Under the circumstances of this case, the pending sale of control implicated in the Paramount-Viacom transaction required the Paramount Board to act on an informed basis to secure the best value reasonably available to the stockholders. . . . we agree with the Court of Chancery that the Paramount directors violated their fiduciary duties . . .

I. Facts

. . .

Paramount is a Delaware corporation with its principal offices in New York City. Approximately 118 million shares of Paramount's common stock are outstanding and traded on the New York Stock Exchange. The majority of Paramount's stock is publicly held by numerous unaffiliated investors. Paramount owns and operates a diverse group of entertainment businesses, including motion picture and television studios, book publishers, professional sports teams, and amusement parks.

There are 15 persons serving on the Paramount Board. Four directors are officer-employees of Paramount: Martin S. Davis ("Davis"), Paramount's Chairman and Chief Executive Officer since 1983; Donald Oresman ("Oresman"), Executive Vice-President, Chief Administrative Officer, and General Counsel; Stanley R. Jaffe, President and Chief Operating Officer; and Ronald L. Nelson, Executive Vice President and Chief Financial Officer. Paramount's 11 outside directors are distinguished and experienced business persons who are present or former senior executives of public corporations or financial institutions. . . .

Viacom is a Delaware corporation with its headquarters in Massachusetts. Viacom is controlled by Sumner M. Redstone ("Redstone"), its Chairman and Chief Executive Officer, who owns indirectly approximately 85.2 percent of Viacom's voting Class A stock and approximately 69.2 percent of Viacom's nonvoting Class B stock through National Amusements, Inc. ("NAI"), an entity 91.7 percent owned by Redstone. Viacom has a wide range of entertainment operations, including a number of well-known cable television channels such as MTV, Nickelodeon, Showtime, and The Movie Channel. Viacom's equity co-investors in the Paramount-Viacom transaction include NYNEX Corporation and Blockbuster Entertainment Corporation.

QVC is a Delaware corporation with its headquarters in West Chester, Pennsylvania. QVC has several large stockholders, including Liberty Media Corporation, Comcast Corporation, Advance Publications, Inc., and Cox Enterprises Inc. Barry Diller ("Diller"), the Chairman and Chief Executive Officer of QVC, is also a substantial stockholder. QVC sells a variety of merchandise through a televised shopping channel. QVC has several equity co- investors in its proposed combination with Paramount including BellSouth Corporation and Comcast Corporation.

Beginning in the late 1980s, Paramount investigated the possibility of acquiring or merging with other companies in the entertainment, media, or communications industry. Paramount considered such transactions to be desirable, and perhaps necessary, in order to keep pace with competitors in the rapidly evolving field of entertainment and communications. Consistent with its goal of strategic expansion, Paramount made a tender offer for Time Inc. in 1989, but was ultimately unsuccessful. See Paramount Communications, Inc. v. Time Inc., Del. Supr., 571 A.2d 1140 (1990) ("Time-Warner").

Although Paramount had considered a possible combination of Paramount and Viacom as early as 1990, recent efforts to explore such a transaction began at a dinner meeting between Redstone and Davis on April 20, 1993. . . .

On September 12, 1993, the Paramount Board met again and unanimously approved the Original Merger Agreement whereby Paramount would merge with and into Viacom. The terms of the merger provided that each share of Paramount common stock would be converted into 0.10 shares of Viacom Class A voting stock, 0.90 shares of Viacom Class B nonvoting stock, and $9.10 in cash. In addition, the Paramount Board agreed to amend its "poison pill" Rights Agreement to exempt the proposed merger with Viacom. The Original Merger Agreement also contained several provisions designed to make it more difficult for a potential competing bid to succeed. We focus, as did the Court of Chancery, on three of these defensive provisions: a "no-shop" provision (the "No-Shop Provision"), the Termination Fee, and the Stock Option Agreement.

First, under the No-Shop Provision, the Paramount Board agreed that Paramount would not solicit, encourage, discuss, negotiate, or endorse any competing transaction unless: (a) a third party "makes an unsolicited written, bona fide proposal, which is not subject to any material contingencies relating to financing"; and (b) the Paramount Board determines that discussions or negotiations with the third party are necessary for the Paramount Board to comply with its fiduciary duties.

Second, under the Termination Fee provision, Viacom would receive a $100 million termination fee if: (a) Paramount terminated the Original Merger Agreement because of a competing transaction; (b) Paramount's stockholders did not approve the merger; or (c) the Paramount Board recommended a competing transaction.

The third and most significant deterrent device was the Stock Option Agreement, which granted to Viacom an option to purchase approximately 19.9 percent (23,699,000 shares) of Paramount's outstanding common stock at $69.14 per share if any of the triggering events for the Termination Fee occurred. In addition to the customary terms that are normally associated with a stock option, the Stock Option Agreement contained two provisions that were both unusual and highly beneficial to Viacom: (a) Viacom was permitted to pay for the shares with a senior subordinated note of questionable marketability instead of cash, thereby avoiding the need to raise the $1.6 billion purchase price (the "Note Feature"); and (b) Viacom could elect to require Paramount to pay Viacom in cash a sum equal to the difference between the purchase price and the market price of Paramount's stock (the "Put Feature"). Because the Stock Option Agreement was not "capped" to limit its maximum dollar value, it had the potential to reach (and in this case did reach) unreasonable levels.

After the execution of the Original Merger Agreement and the Stock Option Agreement on September 12, 1993, Paramount and Viacom announced their proposed merger. In a number of public statements, the parties indicated that the pending transaction was a virtual certainty. Redstone described it as a "marriage" that would "never be torn asunder" and stated that only a "nuclear attack" could break the deal. Redstone also called Diller and John Malone of Tele-Communications Inc., a major stockholder of QVC, to dissuade them from making a competing bid.

Despite these attempts to discourage a competing bid, Diller sent a letter to Davis on September 20, 1993, proposing a merger in which QVC would acquire Paramount for approximately $80 per share, consisting of 0.893 shares of QVC common stock and $30 in cash. QVC also expressed its eagerness to meet with Paramount to negotiate the details of a transaction. When the Paramount Board met on September 27, it was advised by Davis that the Original Merger Agreement prohibited Paramount from having discussions with QVC (or anyone else) unless certain conditions were satisfied. In particular, QVC had to supply evidence that its proposal was not subject to financing contingencies. . . .

On October 21, 1993, QVC filed this action and publicly announced an $80 cash tender offer for 51 percent of Paramount's outstanding shares (the "QVC tender offer"). Each remaining share of Paramount common stock would be converted into 1.42857 shares of QVC common stock in a second-step merger. The tender offer was conditioned on, among other things, the invalidation of the Stock Option Agreement, which was worth over $200 million by that point.[5] . . .

Confronted by QVC's hostile bid, which on its face offered over $10 per share more than the consideration provided by the Original Merger Agreement, Viacom realized that it would need to raise its bid in order to remain competitive. Within hours after QVC's tender offer was announced, Viacom entered into discussions with Paramount concerning a revised transaction. These discussions led to serious negotiations concerning a comprehensive amendment to the original Paramount-Viacom transaction. In effect, the opportunity for a "new deal" with Viacom was at hand for the Paramount Board. With the QVC hostile bid offering greater value to the Paramount stockholders, the Paramount Board had considerable leverage with Viacom.

At a special meeting on October 24, 1993, the Paramount Board approved the Amended Merger Agreement and an amendment to the Stock Option Agreement. The Amended Merger Agreement was, however, essentially the same as the Original Merger Agreement, except that it included a few new provisions. One provision related to an $80 per share cash tender offer by Viacom for 51 percent of Paramount's stock, and another changed the merger consideration so that each share of Paramount would be converted into 0.20408 shares of Viacom Class A voting stock, 1.08317 shares of Viacom Class B nonvoting stock, and 0.20408 shares of a new series of Viacom convertible preferred stock. The Amended Merger Agreement also added a provision giving Paramount the right not to amend its Rights Agreement to exempt Viacom if the Paramount Board determined that such an amendment would be inconsistent with its fiduciary duties because another offer constituted a "better alternative." . . . Finally, the Paramount Board was given the power to terminate the Amended Merger Agreement if it withdrew its recommendation of the Viacom transaction or recommended a competing transaction.

Although the Amended Merger Agreement offered more consideration to the Paramount stockholders and somewhat more flexibility to the Paramount Board than did the Original Merger Agreement, the defensive measures designed to make a competing bid more difficult were not removed or modified. In particular, there is no evidence in the record that Paramount sought to use its newly-acquired leverage to eliminate or modify the No-Shop Provision, the Termination Fee, or the Stock Option Agreement when the subject of amending the Original Merger Agreement was on the table.

Paramount Communications Inc. [5] By November 15, 1993, the value of the Stock Option Agreement had increased to nearly $500 million based on the $90 QVC bid. . . .

Viacom's tender offer commenced on October 25, 1993, and QVC's tender offer was formally launched on October 27, 1993. . . .

On November 6, 1993, Viacom unilaterally raised its tender offer price to $85 per share in cash and offered a comparable increase in the value of the securities being proposed in the second-step merger. . . .

QVC responded to Viacom's higher bid on November 12 by increasing its tender offer to $90 per share and by increasing the securities for its second-step merger by a similar amount. . . .

At its meeting on November 15, 1993, the Paramount Board determined that the new QVC offer was not in the best interests of the stockholders. The purported basis for this conclusion was that QVC's bid was excessively conditional. The Paramount Board did not communicate with QVC regarding the status of the conditions because it believed that the No-Shop Provision prevented such communication in the absence of firm financing. Several Paramount directors also testified that they believed the Viacom transaction would be more advantageous to Paramount's future business prospects than a QVC transaction. . . . Although a number of materials were distributed to the Paramount Board describing the Viacom and QVC transactions, the only quantitative analysis of the consideration to be received by the stockholders under each proposal was based on then-current market prices of the securities involved, not on the anticipated value of such securities at the time when the stockholders would receive them.[8]

The preliminary injunction hearing in this case took place on November 16, 1993. On November 19, Diller wrote to the Paramount Board to inform it that QVC had obtained financing commitments for its tender offer and that there was no antitrust obstacle to the offer. On November 24, 1993, the Court of Chancery issued its decision granting a preliminary injunction in favor of QVC and the plaintiff stockholders. This appeal followed.

II. Applicable Principles of Established Delaware Law

The General Corporation Law of the State of Delaware (the "General Corporation Law") and the decisions of this Court have repeatedly recognized the fundamental principle that the management of the business and affairs of a Delaware corporation is entrusted to its directors, who are the duly elected and authorized representatives of the stockholders. 8 Del.C. §141(a); Aronson v. Lewis, Del. Supr., 473 A.2d 805, 811-12 (1984); Pogostin v. Rice, Del. Supr., 480 A.2d 619, 624 (1984). Under normal circumstances, neither the courts nor the stockholders should interfere with the managerial decisions of the directors. The business judgment rule embodies the deference to which such decisions are entitled. Aronson, 473 A.2d at 812.

Nevertheless, there are rare situations which mandate that a court take a more direct and active role in overseeing the decisions made and actions taken by directors. In these situations, a court subjects the directors' conduct to enhanced

---

[8] The market prices of Viacom's and QVC's stock were poor measures of their actual values because such prices constantly fluctuated depending upon which company was perceived to be the more likely to acquire Paramount.

scrutiny to ensure that it is reasonable.[9] The decisions of this Court have clearly established the circumstances where such enhanced scrutiny will be applied. E.g., Unocal, 493 A.2d 946; Moran v. Household Int'l, Inc., Del. Supr., 500 A.2d 1346 (1985); Revlon, 506 A.2d 173; Mills Acquisition Co. v. Macmillan, Inc., Del. Supr., 559 A.2d 1261 (1989); Gilbert v. El Paso Co., Del. Supr., 575 A.2d 1131 (1990). The case at bar implicates two such circumstances: (1) the approval of a transaction resulting in a sale of control, and (2) the adoption of defensive measures in response to a threat to corporate control.

A. The Significance of a Sale or Change[10] of Control

When a majority of a corporation's voting shares are acquired by a single person or entity, or by a cohesive group acting together, there is a significant diminution in the voting power of those who thereby become minority stockholders. Under the statutory framework of the General Corporation Law, many of the most fundamental corporate changes can be implemented only if they are approved by a majority vote of the stockholders. Such actions include elections of directors, amendments to the certificate of incorporation, mergers, consolidations, sales of all or substantially all of the assets of the corporation, and dissolution. 8 Del.C. §§211, 242, 251-258, 263, 271, 275. Because of the overriding importance of voting rights, this Court and the Court of Chancery have consistently acted to protect stockholders from unwarranted interference with such rights. . . .

In the absence of devices protecting the minority stockholders, . . . stockholder votes are likely to become mere formalities where there is a majority stockholder. For example, minority stockholders can be deprived of a continuing equity interest in their corporation by means of a cash-out merger. Weinberger, 457 A.2d at 703. Absent effective protective provisions, minority stockholders must rely for protection solely on the fiduciary duties owed to them by the directors and the majority stockholder, since the minority stockholders have lost the power to influence corporate direction through the ballot. The acquisition of majority status and the consequent privilege of exerting the powers of majority ownership come at a price. That price is usually a control premium which recognizes not only the value of a control block of shares, but also compensates the minority stockholders for their resulting loss of voting power.

In the case before us, the public stockholders (in the aggregate) currently own a majority of Paramount's voting stock. Control of the corporation is not vested in a single person, entity, or group, but vested in the fluid aggregation of unaffiliated stockholders. In the event the Paramount-Viacom transaction is consummated, the public stockholders will receive cash and a minority equity voting position in the surviving corporation. Following such consummation, there will be a controlling stockholder who will have the voting power to: (a) elect directors; (b)

---

[9] Where actual self-interest is present and affects a majority of the directors approving a transaction, a court will apply even more exacting scrutiny to determine whether the transaction is entirely fair to the stockholders. E.g., Weinberger v. UOP, Inc., Del. Supr., 457 A.2d 701, 710-11 (1983); Nixon v. Blackwell, Del. Supr., 626 A.2d 1366, 1376 (1993).

[10] . . . we have used the terms "sale of control" and "change of control" interchangeably without intending any doctrinal distinction.

cause a break-up of the corporation; (c) merge it with another company; (d) cash-out the public stockholders; (e) amend the certificate of incorporation; (f) sell all or substantially all of the corporate assets; or (g) otherwise alter materially the nature of the corporation and the public stockholders' interests. Irrespective of the present Paramount Board's vision of a long-term strategic alliance with Viacom, the proposed sale of control would provide the new controlling stockholder with the power to alter that vision.

Because of the intended sale of control, the Paramount-Viacom transaction has economic consequences of considerable significance to the Paramount stockholders. Once control has shifted, the current Paramount stockholders will have no leverage in the future to demand another control premium. As a result, the Paramount stockholders are entitled to receive, and should receive, a control premium and/or protective devices of significant value. There being no such protective provisions in the Viacom-Paramount transaction, the Paramount directors had an obligation to take the maximum advantage of the current opportunity to realize for the stockholders the best value reasonably available.

B. The Obligations of Directors in a Sale or Change of Control Transaction

The consequences of a sale of control impose special obligations on the directors of a corporation.[13] In particular, they have the obligation of acting reasonably to seek the transaction offering the best value reasonably available to the stockholders. The courts will apply enhanced scrutiny to ensure that the directors have acted reasonably. The obligations of the directors and the enhanced scrutiny of the courts are well-established by the decisions of this Court. The directors' fiduciary duties in a sale of control context are those which generally attach. In short, "the directors must act in accordance with their fundamental duties of care and loyalty." Barkan v. Amsted Indus., Inc., Del. Supr., 567 A.2d 1279, 1286 (1989). . . .

In the sale of control context, the directors must focus on one primary objective—to secure the transaction offering the best value reasonably available for the stockholders—and they must exercise their fiduciary duties to further that end. The decisions of this Court have consistently emphasized this goal. Revlon, 506 A.2d at 182 ("The duty of the board . . . [is] the maximization of the company's value at a sale for the stockholders' benefit."); Macmillan, 559 A.2d at 1288 ("[I]n a sale of corporate control the responsibility of the directors is to get the highest value reasonably attainable for the shareholders."); Barkan, 567 A.2d at 1286 ("[T]he board must act in a neutral manner to encourage the highest possible

---

[13] We express no opinion on any scenario except the actual facts before the Court, and our precise holding herein. Unsolicited tender offers in other contexts may be governed by different precedent. For example, where a potential sale of control by a corporation is not the consequence of a board's action, this Court has recognized the prerogative of a board of directors to resist a third party's unsolicited acquisition proposal or offer. See Pogostin, 480 A.2d at 627; Time-Warner, 571 A.2d at 1152; Bershad v. Curtiss-Wright Corp., Del. Supr., 535 A.2d 840, 845 (1987); Macmillan, 559 A.2d at 1285 n. 35. The decision of a board to resist such an acquisition, like all decisions of a properly-functioning board, must be informed, Unocal, 493 A.2d at 954-55, and the circumstances of each particular case will determine the steps that a board must take to inform itself, and what other action, if any, is required as a matter of fiduciary duty.

price for shareholders."). See also Wilmington Trust Co. v. Coulter, Del. Supr., 200 A.2d 441, 448 (1964) (in the context of the duty of a trustee, "[w]hen all is equal . . . it is plain that the Trustee is bound to obtain the best price obtainable").

In pursuing this objective, the directors must be especially diligent. See Citron v. Fairchild Camera and Instrument Corp., Del. Supr., 569 A.2d 53, 66 (1989) (discussing "a board's active and direct role in the sale process"). In particular, this Court has stressed the importance of the board being adequately informed in negotiating a sale of control: "The need for adequate information is central to the enlightened evaluation of a transaction that a board must make." Barkan, 567 A.2d at 1287. This requirement is consistent with the general principle that "directors have a duty to inform themselves, prior to making a business decision, of all material information reasonably available to them." Aronson, 473 A.2d at 812. See also Cede & Co. v. Technicolor, Inc., Del. Supr., 634 A.2d 345, 367 (1993); Smith v. Van Gorkom, Del. Supr., 488 A.2d 858, 872 (1985). Moreover, the role of outside, independent directors becomes particularly important because of the magnitude of a sale of control transaction and the possibility, in certain cases, that management may not necessarily be impartial. See Macmillan, 559 A.2d at 1285 (requiring "the intense scrutiny and participation of the independent directors").

Barkan teaches some of the methods by which a board can fulfill its obligation to seek the best value reasonably available to the stockholders. 567 A.2d at 1286-87. These methods are designed to determine the existence and viability of possible alternatives. They include conducting an auction, canvassing the market, etc. Delaware law recognizes that there is "no single blueprint" that directors must follow. Id. at 1286-87; Citron 569 A.2d at 68; Macmillan, 559 A.2d at 1287.

In determining which alternative provides the best value for the stockholders, a board of directors is not limited to considering only the amount of cash involved, and is not required to ignore totally its view of the future value of a strategic alliance. See Macmillan, 559 A.2d at 1282 n. 29. Instead, the directors should analyze the entire situation and evaluate in a disciplined manner the consideration being offered. Where stock or other non-cash consideration is involved, the board should try to quantify its value, if feasible, to achieve an objective comparison of the alternatives.[14] In addition, the board may assess a variety of practical considerations relating to each alternative, including:

> [an offer's] fairness and feasibility; the proposed or actual financing for the offer, and the consequences of that financing; questions of illegality; . . . the risk of non-consum[m]ation; . . . the bidder's identity, prior background and other business venture experiences; and the bidder's business plans for the corporation and their effects on stockholder interests.

Macmillan, 559 A.2d at 1282 n. 29. These considerations are important because the selection of one alternative may permanently foreclose other opportunities.

---

[14] When assessing the value of non-cash consideration, a board should focus on its value as of the date it will be received by the stockholders. . . .

While the assessment of these factors may be complex, the board's goal is straight-forward: Having informed themselves of all material information reasonably available, the directors must decide which alternative is most likely to offer the best value reasonably available to the stockholders.

C. Enhanced Judicial Scrutiny of a Sale or Change of Control Transaction

Board action in the circumstances presented here is subject to enhanced scrutiny. Such scrutiny is mandated by: (a) the threatened diminution of the current stockholders' voting power; (b) the fact that an asset belonging to public stockholders (a control premium) is being sold and may never be available again; and (c) the traditional concern of Delaware courts for actions which impair or impede stockholder voting rights (see supra note 11). In Macmillan, this Court held:

> When *Revlon* duties devolve upon directors, this Court will continue to exact an enhanced judicial scrutiny at the threshold, as in *Unocal*, before the normal presumptions of the business judgment rule will apply.[15]

559 A.2d at 1288. The *Macmillan* decision articulates a specific two-part test for analyzing board action where competing bidders are not treated equally:[16]

> In the face of disparate treatment, the trial court must first examine whether the directors properly perceived that shareholder interests were enhanced. In any event the board's action must be reasonable in relation to the advantage sought to be achieved, or conversely, to the threat which a particular bid allegedly poses to stockholder interests.

Id. See also Roberts v. General Instrument Corp., Del. Ch., C.A. No. 11639, 1990 WL 118356, Allen, C. (Aug. 13, 1990), reprinted at 16 Del. J. Corp. L. 1540, 1554 ("This enhanced test requires a judicial judgment of reasonableness in the circumstances.").

The key features of an enhanced scrutiny test are: (a) a judicial determination regarding the adequacy of the decisionmaking process employed by the directors, including the information on which the directors based their decision; and (b) a judicial examination of the reasonableness of the directors' action in light of the circumstances then existing. The directors have the burden of proving that they were adequately informed and acted reasonably.

Although an enhanced scrutiny test involves a review of the reasonableness of the substantive merits of a board's actions,[17] a court should not ignore the

---

[15] Because the Paramount Board acted unreasonably as to process and result in this sale of control situation, the business judgment rule did not become operative.

[16] Before this test is invoked, "the plaintiff must show, and the trial court must find, that the directors of the target company treated one or more of the respective bidders on unequal terms." Macmillan, 559 A.2d at 1288.

[17] It is to be remembered that, in cases where the traditional business judgment rule is applicable and the board acted with due care, in good faith, and in the honest belief that they are acting in the best interests of the stockholders (which is not this case), the Court gives great deference to the substance of the directors' decision and will not invalidate the decision, will not examine its reasonableness, and

complexity of the directors' task in a sale of control. There are many business and financial considerations implicated in investigating and selecting the best value reasonably available. The board of directors is the corporate decisionmaking body best equipped to make these judgments. Accordingly, a court applying enhanced judicial scrutiny should be deciding whether the directors made a reasonable decision, not a perfect decision. If a board selected one of several reasonable alternatives, a court should not second-guess that choice even though it might have decided otherwise or subsequent events may have cast doubt on the board's determination. Thus, courts will not substitute their business judgment for that of the directors, but will determine if the directors' decision was, on balance, within a range of reasonableness. See Unocal, 493 A.2d at 955-56; Macmillan, 559 A.2d at 1288; Nixon, 626 A.2d at 1378.

D. Revlon and Time-Warner Distinguished

The Paramount defendants and Viacom assert that the fiduciary obligations and the enhanced judicial scrutiny discussed above are not implicated in this case in the absence of a "break-up" of the corporation, and that the order granting the preliminary injunction should be reversed. This argument is based on their erroneous interpretation of our decisions in *Revlon* and *Time-Warner*.

. . . . [I]n *Revlon*, we held that "[t]he directors' role changed from defenders of the corporate bastion to auctioneers charged with getting the best price for the stockholders at a sale of the company." 506 A.2d at 182. We further held that "when a board ends an intense bidding contest on an insubstantial basis, . . . [that] action cannot withstand the enhanced scrutiny which Unocal requires of director conduct." Id. at 184. . . .

Although . . . a change of control imposes on directors the obligation to obtain the best value reasonably available to the stockholders, the Paramount defendants have interpreted our decision in *Time-Warner* as requiring a corporate break-up in order for that obligation to apply. The facts in *Time-Warner*, however, were quite different from the facts of this case, and refute Paramount's position here. In *Time-Warner*, the Chancellor held that there was no change of control in the original stock-for-stock merger between Time and Warner because Time would be owned by a fluid aggregation of unaffiliated stockholders both before and after the merger:

> If the appropriate inquiry is whether a change in control is contemplated, the answer must be sought in the specific circumstances surrounding the transaction. Surely under some circumstances a stock for stock merger could reflect a transfer of corporate control. That would, for example, plainly be the case here if Warner were a private company. But where, as here, the shares of both constituent corporations are widely held, corporate control can be expected to remain unaffected by a stock for stock merger. This in my judgment was the situation with respect to the original merger agreement. When the specifics of that situation are reviewed, it is seen that, aside from legal technicalities and aside from arrangements thought to enhance the prospect for

---

"will not substitute our views for those of the board if the latter's decision can be 'attributed to any rational business purpose.'" Unocal, 493 A.2d at 949 (quoting Sinclair Oil Corp. v. Levien, Del. Supr., 280 A.2d 717, 720 (1971)). See Aronson, 473 A.2d at 812.

the ultimate succession of [Nicholas J. Nicholas, Jr., president of Time], neither corporation could be said to be acquiring the other. Control of both remained in a large, fluid, changeable and changing market.

The existence of a control block of stock in the hands of a single shareholder or a group with loyalty to each other does have real consequences to the financial value of "minority" stock. The law offers some protection to such shares through the imposition of a fiduciary duty upon controlling shareholders. But here, effectuation of the merger would not have subjected Time shareholders to the risks and consequences of holders of minority shares. This is a reflection of the fact that no control passed to anyone in the transaction contemplated. The shareholders of Time would have "suffered" dilution, of course, but they would suffer the same type of dilution upon the public distribution of new stock.

Paramount Communications Inc. v. Time Inc., Del. Ch., No. 10866, 1990 WL 118356, Allen, C. (July 17, 1989), reprinted at 15 Del. J. Corp. L. 700, 739 (emphasis added). Moreover, the transaction actually consummated in *Time-Warner* was not a merger, as originally planned, but a sale of Warner's stock to Time.

In our affirmance of the Court of Chancery's well-reasoned decision, this Court held that "The Chancellor's findings of fact are supported by the record and his conclusion is correct as a matter of law." 571 A.2d at 1150 (emphasis added). . . .

Accordingly, when a corporation undertakes a transaction which will cause: (a) a change in corporate control; or (b) a break-up of the corporate entity, the directors' obligation is to seek the best value reasonably available to the stockholders. This obligation arises because the effect of the Viacom-Paramount transaction, if consummated, is to shift control of Paramount from the public stockholders to a controlling stockholder, Viacom. Neither *Time-Warner* nor any other decision of this Court holds that a "break-up" of the company is essential to give rise to this obligation where there is a sale of control.

III. Breach of Fiduciary Duties by Paramount Board

. . .

A. The Specific Obligations of the Paramount Board

Under the facts of this case, the Paramount directors had the obligation: (a) to be diligent and vigilant in examining critically the Paramount-Viacom transaction and the QVC tender offers; (b) to act in good faith; (c) to obtain, and act with due care on, all material information reasonably available, including information necessary to compare the two offers to determine which of these transactions, or an alternative course of action, would provide the best value reasonably available to the stockholders; and (d) to negotiate actively and in good faith with both Viacom and QVC to that end.

Having decided to sell control of the corporation, the Paramount directors were required to evaluate critically whether or not all material aspects of the Paramount-Viacom transaction (separately and in the aggregate) were reasonable and in the best interests of the Paramount stockholders in light of current circumstances, including: the change of control premium, the Stock Option Agreement, the Termination Fee, the coercive nature of both the Viacom and QVC tender offers,[18] the No-Shop Provision, and the proposed disparate use of the Rights Agreement as to the Viacom and QVC tender offers, respectively.

These obligations necessarily implicated various issues, including the questions of whether or not those provisions and other aspects of the Paramount-Viacom transaction (separately and in the aggregate): (a) adversely affected the value provided to the Paramount stockholders; (b) inhibited or encouraged alternative bids; (c) were enforceable contractual obligations in light of the directors' fiduciary duties; and (d) in the end would advance or retard the Paramount directors' obligation to secure for the Paramount stockholders the best value reasonably available under the circumstances.

The Paramount defendants contend that they were precluded by certain contractual provisions, including the No-Shop Provision, from negotiating with QVC or seeking alternatives. Such provisions, whether or not they are presumptively valid in the abstract, may not validly define or limit the directors' fiduciary duties under Delaware law or prevent the Paramount directors from carrying out their fiduciary duties under Delaware law. To the extent such provisions are inconsistent with those duties, they are invalid and unenforceable. See Revlon, 506 A.2d at 184-85. . . .

B. The Breaches of Fiduciary Duty by the Paramount Board

The Paramount directors made the decision on September 12, 1993, that, in their judgment, a strategic merger with Viacom on the economic terms of the Original Merger Agreement was in the best interests of Paramount and its stockholders. Those terms provided a modest change of control premium to the stockholders. The directors also decided at that time that it was appropriate to agree to certain defensive measures (the Stock Option Agreement, the Termination Fee, and the No-Shop Provision) insisted upon by Viacom as part of that economic transaction. Those defensive measures, coupled with the sale of control and subsequent disparate treatment of competing bidders, implicated the judicial scrutiny of Unocal, Revlon, Macmillan, and their progeny. We conclude that the Paramount directors' process was not reasonable, and the result achieved for the stockholders was not reasonable under the circumstances.

When entering into the Original Merger Agreement, and thereafter, the Paramount Board clearly gave insufficient attention to the potential consequences of the defensive measures demanded by Viacom. The Stock Option Agreement had a number of unusual and potentially "draconian"[19] provisions, including the Note

---

[18] Both the Viacom and the QVC tender offers were for 51 percent cash and a "back-end" of various securities, the value of each of which depended on the fluctuating value of Viacom and QVC stock at any given time. Thus, both tender offers were two-tiered, front-end loaded, and coercive. Such coercive offers are inherently problematic and should be expected to receive particularly careful analysis by a target board. See Unocal, 493 A.2d at 956.

[19] The Vice Chancellor so characterized the Stock Option Agreement. . . . We express no opinion whether a stock option agreement of essentially this magnitude, but with a reasonable "cap" and without the Note and Put Features, would be valid or invalid under other circumstances. See Hecco Ventures v. Sea-Land Corp., Del. Ch., C.A. No. 8486, 1986 WL 5840, Jacobs, V.C. (May 19, 1986) (21.7 percent stock option); In re Vitalink Communications Corp. Shareholders Litig., Del. Ch., C.A. No. 12085, Chandler, V.C. (May 16, 1990) (19.9 percent stock option).

Feature and the Put Feature. Furthermore, the Termination Fee, whether or not unreasonable by itself, clearly made Paramount less attractive to other bidders, when coupled with the Stock Option Agreement. Finally, the No-Shop Provision inhibited the Paramount Board's ability to negotiate with other potential bidders, particularly QVC which had already expressed an interest in Paramount.[20] ...

The Paramount directors had the opportunity in the October 23-24 time frame, when the Original Merger Agreement was renegotiated, to take appropriate action to modify the improper defensive measures as well as to improve the economic terms of the Paramount-Viacom transaction. Under the circumstances existing at that time, it should have been clear to the Paramount Board that the Stock Option Agreement, coupled with the Termination Fee and the No-Shop Clause, were impeding the realization of the best value reasonably available to the Paramount stockholders. Nevertheless, the Paramount Board made no effort to eliminate or modify these counterproductive devices, and instead continued to cling to its vision of a strategic alliance with Viacom. Moreover, based on advice from the Paramount management, the Paramount directors considered the QVC offer to be "conditional" and asserted that they were precluded by the No-Shop Provision from seeking more information from, or negotiating with, QVC.

By November 12, 1993, the value of the revised QVC offer on its face exceeded that of the Viacom offer by over $1 billion at then current values. This significant disparity of value cannot be justified on the basis of the directors' vision of future strategy, primarily because the change of control would supplant the authority of the current Paramount Board to continue to hold and implement their strategic vision in any meaningful way. Moreover, their uninformed process had deprived their strategic vision of much of its credibility. See Van Gorkom, 488 A.2d at 872; Cede v. Technicolor, 634 A.2d at 367; Hanson Trust PLC v. ML SCM Acquisition Inc., 2d Cir., 781 F.2d 264, 274 (1986).

When the Paramount directors met on November 15 to consider QVC's increased tender offer, they remained prisoners of their own misconceptions and missed opportunities to eliminate the restrictions they had imposed on themselves. Yet, it was not "too late" to reconsider negotiating with QVC. The circumstances existing on November 15 made it clear that the defensive measures, taken as a whole, were problematic: (a) the No-Shop Provision could not define or limit their fiduciary duties; (b) the Stock Option Agreement had become "draconian"; and (c) the Termination Fee, in context with all the circumstances, was similarly deterring the realization of possibly higher bids. Nevertheless, the Paramount directors remained paralyzed by

---

[20] We express no opinion whether certain aspects of the No-Shop Provision here could be valid in another context. Whether or not it could validly have operated here at an early stage solely to prevent Paramount from actively "shopping" the company, it could not prevent the Paramount directors from carrying out their fiduciary duties in considering unsolicited bids or in negotiating for the best value reasonably available to the stockholders. Macmillan, 559 A.2d at 1287. As we said in Barkan: " Where a board has no reasonable basis upon which to judge the adequacy of a contemplated transaction, a no-shop restriction gives rise to the inference that the board seeks to forestall competing bids." 567 A.2d at 1288. See also Revlon, 506 A.2d at 184 (holding that "[t]he no-shop provision, like the lock-up option, while not per se illegal, is impermissible under the Unocal standards when a board's primary duty becomes that of an auctioneer responsible for selling the company to the highest bidder").

their uninformed belief that the QVC offer was "illusory." This final opportunity to negotiate on the stockholders' behalf and to fulfill their obligation to seek the best value reasonably available was thereby squandered. . . .

IV. Viacom's Claim of Vested Contract Rights

Viacom argues that it had certain "vested" contract rights with respect to the No-Shop Provision and the Stock Option Agreement.[22] In effect, Viacom's argument is that the Paramount directors could enter into an agreement in violation of their fiduciary duties and then render Paramount, and ultimately its stockholders, liable for failing to carry out an agreement in violation of those duties. Viacom's protestations about vested rights are without merit. This Court has found that those defensive measures were improperly designed to deter potential bidders, and that such measures do not meet the reasonableness test to which they must be subjected. They are consequently invalid and unenforceable under the facts of this case. . . .

V. Conclusion

The realization of the best value reasonably available to the stockholders became the Paramount directors' primary obligation under these facts in light of the change of control. That obligation was not satisfied, and the Paramount Board's process was deficient. The directors' initial hope and expectation for a strategic alliance with Viacom was allowed to dominate their decisionmaking process to the point where the arsenal of defensive measures established at the outset was perpetuated (not modified or eliminated) when the situation was dramatically altered. QVC's unsolicited bid presented the opportunity for significantly greater value for the stockholders and enhanced negotiating leverage for the directors. Rather than seizing those opportunities, the Paramount directors chose to wall themselves off from material information which was reasonably available and to hide behind the defensive measures as a rationalization for refusing to negotiate with QVC or seeking other alternatives. Their view of the strategic alliance likewise became an empty rationalization as the opportunities for higher value for the stockholders continued to develop.

It is the nature of the judicial process that we decide only the case before us—a case which, on its facts, is clearly controlled by established Delaware law. Here, the proposed change of control and the implications thereof were crystal clear. In other cases they may be less clear. The holding of this case on its facts, coupled with the holdings of the principal cases discussed herein where the issue of sale of control is implicated, should provide a workable precedent against which to measure future cases. . . .

---

[22] Presumably this argument would have included the Termination Fee had the Vice Chancellor invalidated that provision or if appellees had cross-appealed from the Vice Chancellor's refusal to invalidate that provision.

In re FORT HOWARD CORP. SHAREHOLDERS LITIGATION

Court of Chancery of the State of Delaware, New Castle

14 Del. J. Corp. L. 699, 1988 WL 83147 (1988)

ALLEN, *Chancellor*

Pending is a motion to preliminarily enjoin the closing of a public tender offer for up to all of the currently outstanding shares of Fort Howard Corporation at $53 cash per share. The offer has been made by FH Acquistion Corp., an entity organized by Morgan Stanley Group, Inc., a Delaware Corporation, through the Morgan Stanley Leveraged Equity Fund II, L.P., a Delaware limited partnership (together, "Morgan Stanley"). The offer was extended on July 1, 1988. Pursuant to its original terms, which are still in effect, it may close no sooner than midnight August 8, 1988.

The tender offer represents the planned first stage in a two step leveraged buyout transaction. The CEO and other senior management of Fort Howard have affiliated themselves with Morgan Stanley in extending the offer. The transaction is a large one. Morgan Stanley and those affiliated with it will contribute $400 million and the balance of the required $3.7 billion purchase price will be borrowed, largely from banks.

Plaintiffs claim that the process followed by the directors of Fort Howard in negotiating the agreement pursuant to which the offer was made, and their conduct since, constitutes a violation of a duty arising when a sale of the company is being considered. That duty is said to require the directors to search, in good faith and advisedly, for the best available alternative and to remain perfectly neutral as between competing potential buyers. Plaintiffs claim that a realistic assessment of what occurred here shows the board, acting through a special committee, favored the management-affiliated prospective buyer from the beginning of the process; did all it could to push the transaction in its direction and to discourage the development of an active and effective auction for the Company.

Plaintiffs also claim that the Morgan Stanley Offer to Purchase omits material information and thus violates a duty of candor owed by the management directors and, in this case, shared by their co-venturer, Morgan Stanley.

The relief plaintiffs seek is delay in the closing of the tender offer in order to permit (that is, to require) a supplemental disclosure. They also seek an order requiring First Boston Corporation, the financial advisor to the Special Committee, to render a new opinion on the fairness of the $53 price after it has had access to certain financial information that it has heretofore neither seen nor sought to see.

Plaintiffs have not seriously attacked the $53 cash price as unfairly low. They have, for example, put in no expert affidavit to that effect. They do claim that it is an undependable price because the market has not been effectively explored and, putting disclosure points to one side, the correctness of that factual assertion is at the core of the matter presented by this motion.

It is essential for valid director action that it be taken on an informed basis. Indeed, it is essential of any rational human choice that alternatives to the proposed action be considered. The more significant the subject matter of the decision, obviously, the greater will be the need to probe and consider alternatives. When the decision is to sell the company, or to engage in a recapitalization that will change control of the firm, the gravity of the transaction places a special burden upon the directors to make sure that they have a basis for an informed view. Here the Special Committee did not conduct an auction of any kind before signing an agreement of merger with Morgan Stanley. It did, however, negotiate provisions purportedly intended to permit an effective check of the market before the Morgan Stanley offer could close. For purposes of this motion, I have concluded that this approach was adopted in good faith and was effective to give the board an informed, dependable basis for the view that the Morgan Stanley offer is the best available transaction from the point of view of the Fort Howard shareholders. (See Part IV, *infra*.) So concluding, I may not issue a preliminary injunction predicated upon plaintiffs' *Revlon* theory. See Revlon, Inc. v. MacAndrews & Forbes Holdings, Inc., Del. Supr., 506 A.2d 173 (1986).

As to the disclosure claims, I have considered them in the light cast by Rosenblatt v. Getty Oil Co., Del. Supr. 493 A.2d 929, 944 (1985). I cannot conclude now that the matters raised by plaintiffs would likely be of actual significance to shareholders. The reasons for this view are set forth below. (See Parts V and VI, *infra*.)

Thus, finding at this time that plaintiffs have not established a reasonable probability of ultimate success, I will for the reasons more fully set forth below decline to issue the remedy sought.

I.

Fort Howard is a Delaware corporation with its principal executive offices in Green Bay, Wisconsin. It is a manufacturer and marketer of diversified lines of paper products, including tissues. In fiscal year 1987 Fort Howard had net sales of $1.75 billion, net income of $158 million and balance sheet assets of $2.19 billion. Its stock price has not recovered from the market break of October 19, 1987 to the extent that the market generally has recovered, nor to the extent others in the paper products industry have. In late May, 1988, just prior to the emergence of the Morgan Stanley interest, its stock traded in the mid 30's. It had traded in the high 50's within the prior year.

Fearing that a temporarily depressed stock price might render the Company particularly vulnerable to an unfairly low and perhaps coercive takeover attempt, the Company's management on March 30, 1988, met with representatives of Morgan Stanley at Morgan Stanley's New York office and sought its advice concerning possible steps to protect Fort Howard shareholders from the perceived threat. Morgan Stanley had been engaged on a number of occasions in recent years to give investment banking advice or services to the Company. Defendant Paul Schierl, the CEO of Fort Howard and defendant Kathleen J. Hempel, its first Vice President and CFO, met with Donald Brennan, and others from Morgan Stanley. Mr. Schierl asked about a wide range of possible types of transactions that the Company might consider engaging in [, in] order to evaluate its stock price. He mentioned recapitalizations, spin-offs, acquisitions and other structural transactions. Mr. Brennan apparently gave a description of the structure and mechanics of types of recapitalizations, commented on other possibilities and indicated that a possible alternative to recapitalization would be a leveraged buyout of the Company's shareholders with Morgan Stanley acting as a principal and management participating in such a transaction. No decisions were made at the March 30 meeting.

On May 3 management did ask Morgan Stanley to evaluate the various alternatives open to the Company. Morgan Stanley responded with a written report at a May 24 meeting with Messrs. Schierl and Donald DeMeuse, President of the Company and Ms. Hempel. According to Mr. Brennan, "all the possibilities were gone through, with the objective of what alternative would produce the highest value." . . . The session was "an analytical presentation"; the financial feasibility of each alternative was not discussed. Mr. Brennan reported that in Morgan Stanley's view, a leveraged buyout would generate greater value for shareholders than would a recapitalization transaction, a share repurchase or a spin-off. He stated that, in Morgan Stanley's view, a leverage[d] buyout in the $48-50 range was feasible and the preferred alternative. It was again stated that Morgan Stanley would be interested in participating with senior management in such a transaction. Management did not commit to participate in such a transaction at that time, but rather took the matter under advisement.

On May 31 Mr. Schierl informed Mr. Brennan that he and others of the senior management of the Company were interested in pursuing such a transaction, but only if the Fort Howard board gave prior approval to their effort to structure a transaction and agreed to receive such a proposal.

That same day, Mr. Schierl met with director Thomas L. Shaffer at the Roanoke, Virginia Airport to advise him that senior management had decided to pursue a possible leveraged buyout of the Company in partnership with Morgan Stanley. Schierl informed Shaffer that a Special Committee of the board would have to be formed to consider the buyout proposal and that Schierl wanted Shaffer to serve as its chairman. They discussed other possible members of a Special Committee and agreed that directors Ziemer and Cuene were best suited for the job.

Mr. Shaffer, who was a law school classmate of Mr. Schierl's, has been on the Fort Howard board longer than any other outside director. He is a professor of law specializing in ethics. Mr. Cuene has been on the board for ten years; he owns a new car dealership in Green Bay. Mr. Ziemer has been on the board about one year; he is the retired chairman of a Wisconsin gas and electric utility company.

Over the next several days, Mr. Schierl flew to Florida to talk with Dr. Cofrin, a director and large shareholder, and spoke as well with Mr. Ziemer, Mr. Cuene and director Diane Rees, who had recently been named to the Fort Howard board. Mr. Schierl invited Dr. Cofrin to participate in the transaction. Cofrin asked that his children be given the opportunity to participate. Mr. Schierl declined that request.

The June 7 Board Meeting

Fort Howard's ten member board was scheduled to meet on June 7, 1988 to consider the adoption of a Shareholders Rights Plan as a defensive measure against hostile takeovers. Such a plan, however, was never considered by the board. Instead Mr. Schierl and Mr. Brennan presented the board with a "proposal to make a proposal." . . . Mr. Schierl discussed the results of the Morgan Stanley analysis and informed the board that Morgan Stanley and the three management directors, and possibly Dr. Cofrin were interested in exploring a leverage[d] buyout of Fort Howard. In addition, the board was told that director Koerber's law firm might serve as counsel to the management directors in any such transaction. Mr. Schierl stated that if the board were willing to entertain a proposal, he would "seek to make one" but there was "no commitment that it could be done because we [are] collectively ignorant of the ability to get appropriate bank financing." . . .

The three management directors then left the meeting and (judging from the draft minutes of the meeting) outside legal counsel then guided the remaining directors through adopting the necessary resolutions to appoint a Special Committee and to select outside legal counsel, began the process of selecting a financial adviser and acted affirmatively on the request to indicate an interest in receiving a proposal.

The Special Committee was comprised [of] the three outside directors discussed by Mr. Schierl and Mr. Shaffer. Shaffer was designated Chairman. The Special Committee made a determination at the June 7 meeting to keep these developments confidential. Outside legal counsel advised that disclosure was not legally required at that time. In the absence of advice that there was a legal obligation to do so, the Special Committee elected secrecy. As its chairman testified:

> It was very important to keep this matter confidential, until they [the buyout group] were in a position to present their proposal and we could listen to it.
> The reason for that was that it might be a good deal and if we introduce prematurely some sort of bidding war, we would lose it and we might lose in the bidding war as well; that all we would have done then is to invite a hostile takeover, and it had been our concern for two years to avoid a hostile takeover.
> So for that reason we determined among ourselves, talked about it a good deal, confidentiality until we had a proposal. . . .

The Special Committee acknowledged that the management group was served by this decision:

> They didn't want to be in the middle of a bidding war . . . their concern from the beginning was that there not be any third party offers. . . .

The Special Committee retains First Boston and prepares to receive a proposal.

On June 9, 1988, the Special Committee met and retained First Boston Corporation as its independent financial advisor. On June 10, Morgan Stanley entered into a confidentiality and standstill agreement with Fort Howard pursuant to which Morgan Stanley agreed not to purchase (without the board's consent) any shares in furtherance of any acquisition of the Company for a period of one year. Over the next few weeks, Morgan Stanley received confidential information concerning the Company, including management's financial projection not earlier disclosed to shareholders or the market. First Boston was provided with the same information. Promptly following the June 7 meeting, Morgan Stanley started contacting sources of financing to arrange the more than $3 billion that, in addition to its own $400 million equity investment, would be needed to close a transaction.

The Special Committee met again on June 17. At that time, First Boston distributed a preliminary written analysis of the Company and of possible transactions. While apparently no specific range of fair values was mentioned at that meeting, defendant Shaffer drew the inference from it that First Boston and Morgan Stanley might be very far apart with respect to opinions on that subject. The Special Committee then requested First Boston and Morgan Stanley to meet "to insure that everybody was dealing with the same factual information." . . . Plaintiffs in this action contend that views about fair value were expressed at this meeting and, as a result, First Boston brought its estimates down to the neighborhood that Morgan Stanley was thinking about. The record developed to date, however, does not support that assertion. Rather, it now appears that the matters discussed were general valuation issues and the types of information being used by the two firms in their work. After the meeting, First Boston informed the Special Committee that both firms were using generally the same financial information and factual data.

On June 21, 1988 the Special Committee held a 7-hour meeting at which First Boston delivered and reviewed a second written report to the committee. Draft stock option and merger agreements, prepared by counsel for Morgan Stanley, were distributed. First Boston was not yet prepared to opine on a range of fair values for Fort Howard. Under questioning, however, it did opine that there were a number of factors that suggested that this might be a good time to sell the Company. The Special Committee also discussed at this meeting the need to test any acquisition proposal in the market. It was suggested that the need for such a test would, in part, be a function of the adequacy of the price proposed.

Towards the end of this meeting, a report came in that there had been remarkable high trading volume that day in the Company's stock. There was, of course, concern that there had been a leak of information concerning the prospect of a buyout. The Special Committee chairman reports that this gave rise to concern:

> If there was going to be some profit-taking on it, we felt that it was more important to give the old time shareholders an opportunity to take their profits and not to leave it all to the speculators. That led us to the conclusion that perhaps we ought to issue a press release. Mr. Atkins drafted one.
>
> In the process of these discussions, we also got in touch with Mr. Schierl, who was in New York at Morgan with people there, and there were a few phone calls back and forth about that and the two groups negotiated a bit over it with speaker phones. They were very reluctant to have any press release at all. . . .
>
> We did not concede that we would not issue the press release in any case . . . [but concluded to reconsider the matter the following day].

The next day, there was a telephone inquiry to the Company reporting on a rumor that there was a management LBO in the works. Promptly thereafter, Fort Howard did issue a press release stating, in part, that "members of [Fort Howard's] management intend to seek a proposal with third parties to acquire the Company in a leveraged buyout."

The June 23 Special Committee Meeting

The Special Committee next met on June 23, augmented by independent directors Rees and Schoshinski. At that meeting, the directors received a presentation from First Boston reflecting its analysis of Fort Howard and several potential alternative transactions. A First Boston representative stated its opinion that it was not an inappropriate time to consider selling the Company. The Special Committee was told that, in First Boston's view, a recapitalization would not result in greater value to stockholders than a leveraged buyout, in part because the value of the resulting stub share would be highly speculative. First Boston recommended that if the board accepted a leveraged buyout proposal, that it provide for a test of any such proposal in the market to determine whether another acquiror would make a better offer.

The Special Committee then reviewed the terms of the draft merger agreement and a proposed stock option agreement calling for the creation of rights to acquire 18½% of the Company's shares. These had been prepared by Morgan Stanley. The committee found the option and several other provisions unacceptable. Among the provisions rejected were provisions calling for unspecified "breakup fees"; unlimited expense reimbursement; a broad prohibition against shopping the Company; and a provision acknowledging Morgan Stanley's right to commence and complete any tender offer within twenty days from the announcement of its agreement.

After about six hours, the Special Committee recessed to reconvene at 8 p.m. at which time the management directors and Morgan Stanley were invited to address the committee. Morgan Stanley then presented a proposal to purchase all outstanding Fort Howard stock at $50.00 per share in cash pursuant to the merger agreement. First Boston, in private, shared its view with the Special Committee that that price was below the low end of the range of fair values and stated that it could not opine that the price proposed was fair.

At about 9:35 p.m. the Special Committee announced that its members had "unanimously determined that they were disappointed with the price offered . . . and the group's financing arrangement." The Special Committee also told the buyout group that the limitation upon its ability to shop the transaction were "unacceptable, that we were not going to go forward at any price without a market test and depending on what the price was, that market test was going to have to be pretty broad. . . ." . . . The Special Committee named no price that it would consider fair. The Special Committee stated that it would enter into negotiations only if there was a substantial improvement in the price offered and that, if any price improvement was at the low end of the range of fairness, the committee would require more time to test the market and fewer restrictions on its ability to do so. . . . The committee also said that it would not accept a provision precluding it from furnishing third parties with the same information provided to Morgan Stanley.

¶2700 In re Fort Howard Corp.

The June 24 Special Committee Meeting and the $53.00 Offer

The Special Committee reconvened at 7:30 a.m. on June 24. A further revised draft merger agreement was distributed and discussed. At 9:20 a.m., Mr. Brennan and the management directors joined the Special Committee. Mr. Brennan put forward a revised "final" proposal. The price was $53.00 per share cash for all shares. The tender offer will begin five business days after the public announcement of the transaction and remain open for twenty-five business days. Thus, the tender offer transaction was designed to be publicly known for a period of thirty business days after announcement (forty-three calendar days). During that period, the Special Committee would be free to negotiate with, and provide information to, any potential acquiror who contacted the Company or First Boston. This would be expressly disclosed in any press release announcing the transaction. If a competing party outbid the buyout group, the "final" proposal provided that the buyout group would be entitled to be paid up to $1.00 per share, including actual expenses (i.e., up to $67.8 million).

After receipt of the revised buyout proposal and after consulting with its counsel, the Special Committee informed Morgan Stanley, before making any decision with respect to that proposal, that, in the committee's view, it would be necessary for the Company to issue a press release which the Special Committee and its counsel had prepared. The Company then issued the following press release:

> Fort Howard Corporation (NYSE:NHP) announced today that it is engaged in negotiations with a group comprised of members of its senior management and an affiliate of Morgan Stanley Group, Inc. for the acquisition of the Company in a leveraged buyout. There can be no assurance that any transaction will be agreed upon or consummated.

After this press release was issued, the Special Committee and its advisers considered the further proposal. First Boston advised the Special Committee that the $53.00 per share was clearly within the range of acceptable prices for the Company and that the revised ability to check the existence of other opportunities—that is, the contemplation of a public announcement that the Company was willing to entertain third party interests and the extension of the tender offer to include a thirty business day period from the date of the announcement—would, even considering the size of the transaction, provide a reasonable opportunity for third party interests to present themselves. First Boston also advised the Special Committee that the buyout group would be able to finance the transaction, but $53.00 per share was the most it could finance. After a three-hour discussion, Mr. Shaffer announced that at $53.00 per share cash, the Special Committee was prepared to go forward with negotiating other aspects of the transaction.

The June 25th Meeting

The Special Committee reconvened at 8:30, on Saturday, June 25. Counsel reviewed with the directors the most recent draft of the merger agreement page by page. First Boston delivered a written opinion that $53.00 per share was fair from a financial point of view. At approximately 2:30 that afternoon, the Special Committee determined to approve the merger agreement (the proposed topping fee and expense reimbursement provision having been reduced to $67 million in the interim) and recommend that the entire board adopt the agreement. Immediately thereafter, the full board met (with Dr. Cofrin absent) and unanimously approved the execution of the merger agreement, with Mr. Koerber abstaining.

The Market Test

The Company and Morgan Stanley prepared a joint press release for release first thing Monday morning, June 27. In delaying public announcement while the markets in the U.S. were closed, the parties, in effect, extended slightly the time during which an alternative transaction might present itself. While the merger agreement permitted the Company to receive and consider alternative transactions, it did not permit the Company to shop the Company actively by soliciting offers. The Special Committee had, however, negotiated a provision to make clear in the initial press releases that the Company has the right and would entertain alternative proposals and would cooperate with any such person in the development of a competing bid. The press release that was issued provided, in part, as follows:

> The transaction was unanimously recommended by a Special Committee of Fort Howard's outside directors, which was advised by the First Boston Corporation. Notwithstanding its recommendation, and consistent with the terms of the merger agreement, the Special Committee directed the Company's management and the First Boston Corporation to be available to receive inquires [inquiries] from any other parties interested in the possible acquisition of the Company and, as appropriate, to provide information and, in First Boston's case in conjunction with the Special Committee, enter into discussions and negotiations with such parties in connection with any such indicated interest. . . .

This press release and the news accounts that it stimulated received widespread attention. The record shows that the story was reported prominently in the business section of *The New York Times*, *The Wall Street Journal*, *The Los Angeles Times* and in other publications. Within days, eight inquiries were received.

The Special Committee instructed First Boston to screen these inquiries initially to filter out any that could not be considered serious possibilities in a transaction of this size. The next day, it reported back that all eight inquiries came from persons or entities that seemed worthy of further attention. The Committee then authorized First Boston to deliver to each all of the materials that had been given to Morgan Stanley and to First Boston including management's financial projections. These materials were those that were later filed pursuant to Section 13E-3 of the Securities Exchange Act by Morgan Stanley. The Special Committee instructed First Boston that further particular information, facility inspections or discussions with management would only be available if an inquirer was willing to sign a confidentiality and standstill agreement.

Only two of the eight entities that received the 13E-3 materials sought further access to information, to facilities and to management. The first of these did so promptly. It was a financial entity. It signed a confidentiality and standstill agreement similar to that signed by Morgan Stanley. It has not proposed a transaction.

After some delay the other of these two entities sought further information. This firm was a competitor of Fort Howard. On July 22, approximately three weeks after receiving the information Morgan Stanley had, an investment banker, representing such entity, asked First Boston whether, if his client signed a confidentiality/standstill agreement, it could see specific types of information. This party was interested in certain financial data on a plant by plant basis; financial data broken down by broad product group and business segments; cost data for fiber by grade and site; capability of mills; total labor cost and headcount per site and other data of a kind that would be of interest to a competitor. . . .

At a meeting on July 22, the Special Committee discussed this second request from the competitor that had only been identified as "Company A" in this litigation. Company A is said to be a substantial competitor of Fort Howard in the tissue business. At the July 22 meeting, it was noted that much of the information sought could be provided, but that Company A would have significant antitrust problems in acquiring Fort Howard and, perhaps, would have some financing problems, as well. The Special Committee wanted to find out how Company A proposed to deal with the antitrust problems that its acquisition of Fort Howard would occasion. The Committee's outside legal counsel was instructed to propose to Company A discussion between its antitrust lawyers and the Committee's advisors and between the investment bankers for the two firms.

The Special Committee met by telephone on July 25 and its lawyer reported no agreement on the suggestion for direct discussion among advisors. Company A took the position that it was willing to "bear the antitrust risk" and that a merger agreement could so provide. Therefore, conversations as to how it might address the antitrust problem were said to be unnecessary. Such an approach would mean, however, that the provisions that would have such an effect would have to be agreed upon before the confidential materials were furnished.

The Special Committee reports that it was concerned to explore this potential opportunity but concerned as well to protect against risks to the Morgan Stanley deal that announcement of this interest might pose, especially if the antitrust or financing problems were not solvable. The concern for confidentiality of competitive information, while noted, is somewhat underplayed.

The Committee thus says that, acting through its counsel, it attempted to negotiate an agreement that balanced these concerns. Its counsel prepared a draft form of confidentiality/standstill agreement that had several unusual features designed, it is claimed, to deal with these special problems. Those special features, not included in the confidentiality agreement that Morgan Stanley had signed or that the earlier post-agreement potential bidder had signed, included the astonishing proposal that in order to see further information about the Company, Company A would have to agree to be liable to Fort Howard in the amount of $67.8 million if Company A (1) was provided with access to the information sought, (2) made no bid, (3) the Management Group's tender offer did not close, and (4) a substitute for it did not eventuate. Not surprisingly, Company A refused to put $67 million subject to risks it could not control simply to get a look at more detailed information.

Plaintiffs point to this most recent development as the most dramatic confirmation of their contention that the "market check" period purportedly negotiated for the purpose of providing to the Special Committee a technique to assure itself that the Management Group's offer was the most beneficial one available—was a sham. No one could believe that a potiential bidder would take on the risk the Special Committee proposed. The proposal in fact was designed, it is said, to deter active interests from a logical source that First Boston has admitted could likely do the deal.

The Special Committee answers this charge by referring to further negotiations that did occur which removed the $67.8 risk and offered in substitution another approach that would have required Company A to make an offer, if any, by August 5th. Under that approach, the market would know with certainty on August 8th, the date of the scheduled closing of the Morgan Stanley offer, whether Company A intended to make an offer. Other special provisions treating the antitrust problems that Company A raised were also further negotiated. Before these matters reached conclusion, the CEO of Company A spoke to Mr. Shaffer, the Chairman of the Special Committee, informing him that Company A was suspending its activities with Mr. Howard.

II.

The pending motion is for a preliminary injunction. Such a remedy is discretionary in the sense that, in determining to issue such an order, a number of competing factors, whose weight is not scientifically ascertainable, must be evaluated. The factors themselves are not controversial. They include first, a preliminary determination of the likelihood that plaintiff will be able to prove his claims at trial. To issue the provisional remedy, the court must be satisfied that a reasonable probability of such success has been shown. Secondly, plaintiff must show that he is threatened with irreparable injury before final relief may be afforded to him. Should the court determine that both of these elements appear, it is necessary to consider what sort of injury, if any, may be visited upon defendant by the improvident granting of the remedy, how great might that injury be in relation to the injury with which plaintiff is faced, and whether a bond may offer adequate protection against that risk or whether it might be avoided by the shaping of relief. Lastly, the court must be alert to the legitimate interests of the public or innocent third parties whose property rights or other legitimate interests might be affected by the issuance of the remedy. All of this, of course, is perfectly well settled.

III.

To simplify, plaintiffs assert that the facts set forth above constitute at least four distinct legal or equitable wrongs accomplished by the management directors and the other directors working in sympathetic coordination with them. Morgan Stanley is, of course, seen as a co-venturer and an active participant in these wrongs which is jointly liable for resulting injury to the class of Fort Howard shareholders.

The first theory of liability is predicated upon plaintiffs' reading of Revlon, Inc. v. MacAndrews & Forbes Holdings, Inc., Del. Supr., 506 A.2d 173 (1986). It asserts that the independent committee engaged in a course of conduct that has had the effect of never shopping the Company; that the board never took steps that any prudent person seeking to locate the best available transaction would have taken and that, indeed, its actions throughout—from the secrecy designed to permit the management group to make its offer in a nonbidding context, to its direction to First Boston to meet with Morgan before a price was put forward and to the chilly reception it gave Company A—are consistent only with an inappropriate motive. That motive, of course, is the accommodation of management and its financial partners' desire to buy the enterprise in a highly leveraged transaction. This course of conduct is said to offend the central teaching of *Revlon*, that once a corporation is for sale, it is the board's duty to show no preference, but to seek the best transaction available.

The next proposed theory of liability relates to the disclosures contained in the July 1, 1988 Offering Circular. These are called grossly inadequate because they are said to fail to disclose the centrally important fact concerning Fort Howard—that, because it possesses a proprietary process, a deinking process, that permits it to use cheaper paper in the manufacture of tissues than do any of its competitors, it is the "superstar" of its industry. Plaintiffs contrast the lack of any description of the special nature of the Company with the descriptive material supplied by Bankers Trust to a prospective investor. Those materials, plaintiffs say, emphasized the special character of the Company's advantage. The details of this argument are treated below.

The third theory of liability involves a claim that First Boston's opinion as to the fairness of the $53 price is based upon inadequate information and the Special Committee's role in restricting First Boston's access to relevant information constitutes a breach of a duty of fair dealing. The specifics can be summarized: First Boston did not have access to Company data relating to the deinking process—either the technical information or the cost accounting information relating to the process. First Boston did not seek such information, however, stating now that it is irrelevant to the financial analysis of stock price that it was engaged to perform. Plaintiffs then join issue with First Boston on the question of what information is necessary to render a fairness opinion for a company such as Fort Howard and join issue with the Special Committee on the question whether one could, in good faith and competently, rely upon an opinion by First Boston, knowing that First Boston did not have and did not want access to such information in rendering its opinion.

The fourth theory of liability has two aspects. It relates to the attempt by defendants to keep confidential or secret such contacts, action and prospects relating to a possible management affiliated leveraged buyout as occurred prior to the announcement of the signed merger agreement. From June 7, 1988 forward, it is contended that the defendants had an obligation to disclose to the market an evolving transaction of enormous importance to existing stockholders. Silence violated that duty, it is contended. The two press releases that were issued were misleadingly vague and compounded the wrong. During the period, many stockholders sold their stock for very much less than the defendants knew or should have realized would be available in a premium commanding LBO transaction. Indeed, it is asserted that many sold on the market to Morgan Stanley during this period.

This is said both to constitute a violation of a state law imposed fiduciary duty (compare Bershad v. Curtiss-Wright Corp., Del. Supr., 535 A.2d 840 (1987)) and, equally importantly, to be reflective of the lack of good faith that is necessarily intertwined with plaintiff's *Revlon* argument. The pending motion for preliminary injunction with respect to the Morgan Stanley tender offer, however, presents no occasion to express any preliminary view with respect to the questions raised by this theory insofar as it attempts to supply an independent basis for recovery. If class members were disadvantaged in a way that is legally compensable and if defendants or some of them are accountable in damages for some or all of the injury suffered, a money judgment can be made available. But the closing of the current offer has, as I see it, no current impact upon persons who have sold their stock prior to this time. Thus, I see no reason to further address this theory directly on this application.

IV.

I turn first to plaintiffs' argument built on their understanding of the *Revlon* case. On June 7, the Fort Howard Special Committee faced two important questions. The first of course was whether the board of directors would receive and consider a proposal by the management affiliated leveraged buyout group to acquire all of the stock of the Company. The other question was whether, in evaluating any such offer from management as it did receive, it would be necessary or prudent to shop the Company, that is, to explore whether others might be interested in such a transaction and on what terms. The board, or rather its Special Committee, decided that it was unnecessary to announce an interest in selling the Company and that prudence in the circumstances dictated that it not do so. Two related critical issues that this motion presents are thus raised: first, whether that decision was legally permissible in light of the holding of *Revlon*, and second, whether, if legally permissible, it was made in a good faith effort to promote or protect the interests of the corporation and its shareholders.

The former issue is a legal one and is susceptible of resolution now. For the reasons that follow, I am of the view that—even assuming that the board action of June 7 was the equivalent of a board decision that the Company was for sale—*Revlon* does not so constrain the functioning of a board acting without a conflicting interest as to preclude the approach that was here followed when undertaken competently and in good faith. The second issue is essentially factual and may not be finally resolved now. Nevertheless, it is at the heart of the matter and decision of the pending motion does require a preliminary judgment concerning the *bona fides* of the board's action on June 7th and throughout the following period. I will discuss it first.

A.

Having read much of the testimony taken in the matter, reviewed all of the briefs and affidavits and inspected relevant documents, I am unable to conclude provisionally that the Special Committee was not motivated throughout to achieve a transaction, if there was to be one, that offered the assurance of being the best available transaction from the point of view of the shareholders. . . .

It cannot . . . be the best practice to have the interested CEO in effect handpick the members of the Special Committee as was, I am satisfied, done here. Nor can it be the best procedure for him to, in effect, choose special counsel for the committee as it appears was done here. It is obvious that no role is more critical with respect to protection of shareholder interests in these matters than that of the expert lawyers who guide sometimes inexperienced directors through the process. A suspicious mind is made uneasy contemplating the possibilities when the interested CEO is so active in choosing his adversary. The June 7 decision to keep the management interest secret, in a sense, represents a decision to sell the Company to management if it would pay a fair price, but not to inquire whether another would pay a fair price if management would not do so. It implies a bias that, while as explained below, I accept as valid for purposes of this motion, nevertheless is a source of concern to a suspicious mind. Similarly, the requested meeting between First Boston and Morgan Stanley. For present purposes, I cannot conclude that plaintiffs' reading of that affair will be shown to be correct. But it is still odd for the Special Committee to risk infecting the independence of the valuation upon which it would necessarily place such weight, by requiring its expert to talk directly with Morgan Stanley. And that risk is run for what can only be seen as a minor benefit to the convenience of the individuals involved. So there is ground for suspicion with respect to the good faith of the Special Committee, but, on balance, not such that seem at this stage persuasive.

Here, I draw no inference of bad faith on the part of the Special Committee from its course of conduct in part because I am persuaded that the alternative course pursued[1] was reasonably calculated to (and did) effectively probe the market for alternative possible transactions. The alternative "market check" that was achieved was not so hobbled by lock-ups, termination fees or topping fees; so constrained in time or so administered (with respect to access to pertinent information or manner of announcing "window shopping" rights) as to permit the inference that this alternative was a sham designed from the outset to be ineffective or minimally effective. I am particularly impressed with the announcement in the financial press and with the rapid and full-hearted response to the eight inquiries received. Very full information was provided very promptly. The later developments with Company A have been explained to my satisfaction for purposes of this motion.

Moreover, the rationale for adopting this approach—for permitting the negotiations with the management affiliated buyout group to be completed before turning to the market in any respect—makes sense (and thus, cannot alone justify an inference of bad faith). Management had proposed to make an all cash bid for all shares if and only if the board endorsed it. The rest of the world was not bound by any of these three important qualifications. To start a bidding contest before it was known that an all cash bid for all shares could and would be made, would increase the risk of a possible takeover attempt at less than a "fair" price or for less than all shares. Accordingly, even if the approach adopted could be said to favor the management affiliated group—in the sense that it negotiated its deal without the imposition of time constraints and in a setting in which no other bidders were present—it does not do so in a way that would support the inference that the decision to do so was not made in the good faith pursuit of the interests of the stockholders.

---

[1] **In re Fort Howard Corp.** That is alternative to announcing an auction on June 7.

B.

While plaintiffs contend that the Special Committee acted in bad faith, they also argue that without regard to that fact, the members of the Special Committee violated duties recognized by *Revlon*. The argument is as follows. The Company was for sale as of June 7 when the board indicated it would receive Morgan Stanley's offer, appointed a Special Committee, hired special counsel, etc. This, it is said, "established *Revlon* duties. From that point on, the Special Committee was required to maintain a neutral stance towards management and any competitor bidder in order to obtain the best possible transaction for the shareholders." . . . Three specific examples are cited of favoritism, two of which (the claim that the Special Committee "implored First Boston to adjust its valuation in order to achieve a management buyout" and that the treatment of Company A was designed to discourage its interest) do not appear to be factual at this stage. But the basic decision on June 7 to keep the process secret was, or so its seems to me, not a wholly neutral step as between potential bidders.

For the reasons set forth above, that decision may plainly be thought to serve stockholder interests, and, as stated above, I have concluded, for present purposes, that it was a decision made in good faith. Thus, the question does arise whether *Revlon* establishes rules that came into play whenever the Company is for sale, such as once the Company is for sale, the board must, in all events, be neutral as between offerors or, what is the same thing, the board must maintain a "level playing field" or the board must not interfere with the free workings of an auction market. If so, and if plaintiffs have identified such a rule with its claim to neutrality, then I would think such a duty was breached here. As the recent case of In Re J.P. Stevens & Co., Inc. Stockholder Litigation, Del. Ch., C.A. No. 9634, Allen, C. (April 8, 1988) makes clear however, that is not my understanding of the thrust of *Revlon*. I understand that case as essentially a breach of loyalty case in which the board was not seen as acting in the good faith pursuit of the shareholders' interests. *Revlon* explicitly recognized that a disinterested board acting in good faith and in an informed manner may enter into lock-up agreements if the effect was to promote, not impede, shareholder interests. (That can only mean if the *intended* effect is such, for the validity of the agreement itself cannot be made to turn upon how accurately the board did foresee the future.)

More generally, a board need not be passive even in an auction setting. It may never appropriately favor one buyer over another for a selfish or inappropriate reason, such as occurred in *Revlon*, but it may favor one over another if in good faith and advisedly it believes shareholder interests would be thereby advanced. Even in the auction context, if one deal is all cash and more likely to close and sooner, a disinterested board might prefer it to a deal that may be thought to represent a somewhat higher price, but is not all cash and not capable of closing as quickly. See Citron v. Fairchild Industries, Inc., Del. Ch., C.A. No. 6085, Allen, C. (May 19, 1988). The need to exercise judgment is *inescapably* put on the board at points in an auction process and the validity of the exercise of that judgment is appropriately subjected to a business judgment form of judicial review. In *J.P. Stevens, supra*, the board did favor one bidder by granting it a substantial topping fee. While some aspects of the case made the question of good faith or not a quite close one, once one found good faith, it was clear that granting that fee could (and as things worked out, did) benefit shareholders.

Accordingly, I cannot share plaintiffs' views that *Revlon* duties were violated by the procedure adopted here, which I am persuaded, for present purposes, was followed in good faith and was sufficient to inform the exercise of judgment that the board made in entering the merger agreement, and, in a sense, continues to make while it awaits the close of the offer or the announcement of another bidder.

V.

With respect to plaintiffs' claim concerning First Boston's role in this process, I conclude that they have not established a probability of success on the merits of their claim that the withholding of information relating to Fort Howard's proprietary manufacturing process from First Boston constitutes a breach of fiduciary duty to the shareholders or renders the First Boston opinion unreliable. . . .

VI.

With respect to the claim concerning the allegedly flawed disclosure contained in the Offer to Purchase, I also conclude that plaintiffs have failed to establish a probability of success on their claim. . . .

For the foregoing reasons, the application for a preliminary injunction will be denied. IT IS SO ORDERED.

The **BLACK & DECKER CORPORATION, a Maryland corporation, et al., Plaintiffs, v. AMERICAN STANDARD, INC., a Delaware corporation, et al., Defendants.**
Albert OMINSKY, Trustee, et al., Plaintiffs, v. AMERICAN STANDARD, INC., et. al., Defendants.

United States District Court, D. Delaware

682 F. Supp 772 (1988)

Motion for preliminary injunction granted.

Opinion

LONGOBARDI, District Judge.

. . .

Background

In late November, 1987, Black & Decker approached William A. Marquard, director and former Chairman of American Standard to discuss Black & Decker's acquisition of American Standard. From November until the present date, Black & Decker has repeatedly written and called American Standard's Chairman, William B. Boyd, in order to arrange a meeting to discuss a business combination between Black & Decker and American Standard. In early January, Boyd called Nolan Archibald, Chairman of Black & Decker, and stated that "he was not interested in pursuing a business combination of Black & Decker and [American Standard]." Docket Item ("D.I.") 47C at 1254.

On January 27, 1988, Black & Decker commenced an all cash tender offer for all the shares of American Standard at $56.00 per share. On the very day of the offer, Boyd retained Goldman, Sachs & Co. ("Goldman Sachs") to serve as American Standard's investment advisor and to work in conjunction with Sullivan & Cromwell, outside legal counsel, on the newly announced offer. The formal retainer letter was signed by Boyd on February 4, 1988. . . . Without knowing the details, without Board approval, it is obvious from the contents that Goldman Sachs and Boyd had definite ideas about how to resolve the hostile takeover attempt by Black & Decker. As it was presented to the Board on February 4, 1988, the keystone of the proposed defensive tactics to be adopted was a recapitalization plan which, if implemented, would earn Goldman Sachs $17,500,000.00. Interestingly, anticipating its success, Goldman Sachs also provided additional compensation for itself in the event assets were sold after the recapitalization. . . .

February 4, 1988 Meeting

At the February 4 meeting, the Board began considering the issues surrounding the Black & Decker offer. The directors received copies of a summary of the Interim Rights Plan and a copy of the Goldman Sachs' presentation entitled Project Lion at the meeting. . . .

The Goldman Sachs presentation, which took about an hour, covered (i) an analysis of Black & Decker's offer, including Black & Decker's capability of completing the offer and the tender offer timetable; (ii) the valuation of American Standard in terms of the price of its common stock and trading history and in terms of a summary analysis by division; (iii) a discussion of the various responses available to American Standard; and (iv) a discussion of selected alternatives, including a recapitalization and White Knights. . . .

The Goldman Sachs' report concluded with a range of values for American Standard on a per share basis. This valuation, however, is "before pensions adjustments, other assets and liabilities, transaction costs or taxes." . . .

The Sullivan & Cromwell presentation on the Poison Pill followed the Goldman Sachs presentation and lasted a little less than an hour. . . . Sullivan & Cromwell based its presentation upon a three page summary of terms which was distributed to the directors. . . . The Poison Pill called for a dividend of one contingent Right in respect to each share of common stock held of record as of February 19, 1988, and also authorized the issuance of one Right in respect of each share of common stock that was outstanding after February 19, 1988. Each Right entitled the holder thereof to purchase 5 shares of American Standard common stock for $28.00 a share when one party acquired 30% or more of the outstanding common stock. . . . Any Rights owned by the person who crossed the 30% threshold would be void for all purposes. . . . Unless the trigger date had occurred, the expiration time was set for March 16, 1988. . . . The Board of Directors could extend the expiration date until June 30, 1988, if the Board deemed it necessary in order to pursue a course of action which would result in enhanced value for the shareholders. . . . The Poison Pill could also be amended without the consent of the shareholders in order to cure any ambiguities or to make any change that did not materially affect the holders' interest adversely, or in any way at the time the expiration date is extended. . . . The Rights Plan was not redeemable.

During its presentation, Sullivan & Cromwell explained that the Poison Pill had a twofold purpose: (i) to give the directors of American Standard more time to consider other reasonable alternatives that would enhance shareholder values, . . . and (ii) to prevent a possible street sweep by Black & Decker. . . . Boyd explained that the nonredeemability of the Rights Plan was in the shareholders' best interest because "the board and management can spend its time looking at reasonable alternatives and not have to think about redeeming the rights as a result of subsequent action." . . . The purpose of the plan was that "to have a level playing field it was necessary to give a moderate amount of time to offer bidders, including possibly the company itself, and that a rights plan of this type which ran, I think, until mid-March, would permit a short but adequate amount of time for alternative propositions to be developed." . . . It is clear from the testimony that the "company" referred to was American Standard.

Although the Poison Pill was adopted to facilitate the pursuit of reasonable alternatives, the testimony of one of the directors suggests that no alternatives were being pursued and that the Board was only considering the Recapitalization Plan. Indeed, as of February 18, the Board had not considered alternatives to the Black & Decker offer other than the Recapitalization Plan. In response to the question as to whether Goldman Sachs should be permitted to provide confidential non-public information to industrial firms or leveraged buy out companies, the Chairman of American Standard stated: "I expressed the belief that we should not foreclose the future possibilities and alternatives that might have to be examined by the board and that under certain circumstances and with proper safeguard, we may wish to release information." . . . As of February 18, the Chairman testified that the Board was under no "obligation to consider reasonable alternatives to Black & Decker's offer." . . .

In addition, Goldman Sachs believed that there was the possibility of Black & Decker sweeping the street. Since sweeping the street is a widely publicized takeover tactic, Goldman Sachs saw this as a possible threat to American Standard. Furthermore, Black & Decker, in particular, was capable of sweeping the street once it achieved its financing and passed the timely requirements of Hart-Scott-Rodino.

At the conclusion of the February 4, 1988, Board meeting, the directors retained copies of the Goldman Sachs presentation book to review over the weekend. . . .

On February 5, 1988, Black & Decker increased its offer to $65.00 per share.

February 8, 1988 Meeting

The one hour Goldman Sachs presentation followed management's one hour presentation of its five year business plan. . . .

In order to determine the adequacy of Black & Decker's increased offer, Goldman Sachs presented its valuation of American Standard. This valuation, however, was exactly the same one as that presented at the February 4, 1988, Board meeting. Compare Goldman Sachs presentation of February 4, 1988. . . .

Goldman Sachs, furthermore, based its determination that the Black & Decker offer was inadequate on two other factors. First, great interest was shown in the company by Black & Decker and other possible candidates. Secondly, restructuring the company could yield immediate values exceeding the $65.00 per share offer. . . . The values for the Recapitalization Plan were increased from the February 4, 1988, Board meeting. Somehow, Goldman Sachs was able to find an additional $5.00. During the presentation of the Recapitalization proposal, the Board expressed concern as to whether the company could be successfully operated at the degree of leverage required. . . . Based upon its discussions with Goldman Sachs, "the Board unanimously concluded that the $65.00 offer was inadequate and recommended that stockholders reject." . . .

The presentation of the Poison Pill lasted approximately one half hour. Once again, the twofold rationale for adopting the Pill was set forth and discussed. . . . At the meeting, Sullivan & Cromwell presented changes in the proposed plan which included raising the exercise price to $32.50 per share and lowering the threshold for triggering the rights to 15%.

February 10 and 11, 1988

On February 10, 1988, Black & Decker announced that it would begin a consent solicitation to gain control of the American Standard Board. After gaining control, Black & Decker would take action to amend the Poison Pill and make the Rights Plan redeemable.

Following Black & Decker's announcement, American Standard amended the Poison Pill. The amendment provides:

> Pursuant to section 4.4(ii) of the Agreement,
> Section 4.4(i) of the Agreement is hereby amended to read in its entirety as follows: in any respect at any time the board of directors acts to extend the 'Expiration Time' [March 16] as provided in the proviso to section 1.1(i) hereof, but no such supplement or amendment so made shall be effective before the time which would have been the Expiration Time in the absence of such extension.

Boyd explained that the amendment was adopted without consultation of the Board because he was advised that the change was not material and that the Poison Pill authorized certain technical changes without consultation. . . . Notwithstanding American Standard's characterization of the amendment as merely a "technical change," its adoption has the effect of preventing Black & Decker, were it to gain control of the Board, from making the Rights redeemable until after March 16. (This date was later extended by another amendment.)

February 18, 1988

At the February 18 Board meeting, the Board considered and discussed three separate proposals: Amendment to its retirement and savings plan and the creation of a severance plan, an amendment to the Poison Pill and the Recapitalization proposal. This meeting lasted between two to three hours. . . . The Board amended the company's retirement and savings plan and established a severance plan for salaried employees assigned to corporate staff functions in order to provide that, "in the event of a potential change of control" payments will be accelerated under the retirement and savings plan and specified salaried employees will be entitled to severance benefits. . . . This proposal was brought to the Board by the Management Development Committee which was assisted in the formulation and presentation of the proposal by Handy Associates, a professional compensation consultant. . . . Certain financial aspects of the proposed change were discussed by the Board. . . . Black & Decker has presented an uncontroverted affidavit which states that these amendments will cost approximately 130 million dollars. . . . American Standard, however, has specifically exempted from the definition of "changes in control" the Recapitalization Plan. . . .

Also at this meeting, the Board adopted the second amendment to the Poison Pill. This amendment extended the expiration date of the Poison Pill to the earlier of June 30, 1988, or the date on which the shareholders vote on the Recapitalization Plan. . . . The amendment further provides that only directors elected at a regularly scheduled annual meeting of the shareholders may terminate the Poison Pill if they determine that it is in the best interest of the shareholders. . . . Thus, the amendment effectively removes the possibility of Black & Decker terminating the Poison Pill before the termination date by gaining control of American Standard pursuant to a consent solicitation.

Testimony revealed that there were three reasons for adopting this second amendment on February 18. The first reason was that the amendment was thought to be helpful in preventing a drop and sweep. . . . Secondly, the effect of the amendment would be to provide time for the Board to consider reasonable alternatives. Thirdly, the Chairman of American Standard testified that "it also would provide the time for us to get out to our stockholders after approval by the SEC of all the facts relative to our recapitalization program so that the stockholders could make an informed judgment." . . .

At this meeting, the Board also discussed and unanimously passed the proposed Recapitalization Plan. Prior to the adoption of the Recapitalization Plan, Goldman Sachs explained and discussed various features of the proposal. The Board discussed the value of the Recapitalization Plan and its effect on any offer from Black & Decker or any other party. . . . Several directors also questioned Goldman Sachs about the proposal and the assumptions underlying it. . . . Finally, "some directors observed that the proposal was the most conservative and prudent course the Board could follow because it would provide a significant increase in value over Black & Decker's $65 offer while preserving flexibility." . . .

Although some discussion was held, it appears that important questions were not asked nor issues raised concerning the Recapitalization Plan and the Employee Stock Ownership Plan ("ESOP"). The Board did not consider the selection of a trustee who will ensure that the ESOP is managed in the best interests of the beneficiaries. . . . Furthermore, the Board did not consider the terms of the ESOP setting forth the beneficiaries' rights or the authority of the trustee. . . . In point of fact, a draft plan of the ESOP was not presented to the Board at this meeting and testimony by one of the directors revealed that the drafting of the ESOP had not proceeded far enough to deal with some of these issues. . . . In addition, the Board failed to consider whether there was adequate surplus to pay the dividend under the proposed Recapitalization Plan. . . . Black & Decker points out that the Goldman Sachs' material shows that a $59.00 dividend requires $1,761,000,000.00 in cash. . . . American Standard does not have enough surplus to pay this dividend. . . .

Subsequent Developments

On Tuesday, February 23, 1988, Black & Decker increased its offer to $68.00 and extended its offer to March 7, 1988. In addition, Black & Decker set a new record date for its Consent Solicitation seeking to attain a majority on American Standard's Board.

On March 3, 1988, the Board for American Standard met once again to reconsider the Recapitalization Plan. The Board approved the sale of debentures to Emerson Electric. . . . This revision to the Recapitalization Plan will result in the cash component of the dividend increasing to $64.00. . . . The Board believes that "the enhanced recapitalization could produce total value to shareholders of at least $74 per share, although [Goldman Sachs] did not expect the market to reflect the full value of the plan until full information had been disclosed in the proxy statement and the stockholders have approved it." . . . Furthermore, the Board was informed that Goldman Sachs will render a fairness opinion as to the enhanced Recapitalization Plan and "would have expected to do so as to the original plan as well." . . . Counsel also advised the Board that "there appeared to exist sufficient surplus for the company to make the distribution to the stockholders provided for in the recapitalization." . . . Lastly, the company had retained a valuation firm to provide the Board an appropriate basis for revaluation of the company and to render an opinion as to whether adequate surplus exists. . . .

On March 3, Black & Decker also increased its bid to $73.00 a share and extended the offer until March 17, 1988.

On March 14, 1988, this Court's opinion was literally interrupted by additional developments that have resulted in a modification of the relief sought by Plaintiff. The Court received a hand delivered letter from the Defendant to advise the Court of the factual developments. . . . The letter stated, *inter alia*, that American Standard expects to receive at least one additional bid over $75.00 per share which is both higher than Black & Decker's offer and the Board's proposed Recapitalization Plan. The Board intends to meet on Wednesday, March 16, to consider competitive bids. In addition, on Sunday, March 13, the Board voted to terminate the Rights Plan if a majority of American Standard's shares are purchased pursuant to a formal tender offer. As a result of these developments, the Court conducted a telephone conference on the afternoon of March 14 in order to ascertain Plaintiff's response. The Court was informed by counsel for Black &

Decker that in light of the Board's actions to terminate the Rights Plan if a majority of shares are tendered, Plaintiff was withdrawing its motion for a preliminary injunction with respect to the Rights Plan. Plaintiff's application for injunctive relief as to the severance plan and amendments to the retirement plans, however, remains alive.

On the other hand, Class Plaintiffs informed the Court during the telephone conference that they no longer seek injunctive relief based on the current facts. As a result, the only remaining issue before the Court is whether or not a preliminary injunction as to both the severance plan and amendments to the retirements plan is proper under the circumstances.

Arguments of the Parties

Black & Decker argues that the Recapitalization Plan and the ESOP ensures management's control over 55% of American Standard's common stock. Thus, the Board has agreed to a transaction involving the sale of control of the company. . . . (Black & Decker suggests that American Standard's Board recognized that a sale of control of the corporation is equivalent to a sale of the corporation. As a matter of fact, American Standard has not contested that pure legal issue. . . .) This contention is supported by the facts that (i) American Standard has amended its "change in control" agreements so that the Recapitalization Plan is exempted; (ii) American Standard's news release of February 18, 1988, explained that management and the ESOP together would control 55% of the company, . . . and (iii) Goldman Sachs presented the Recapitalization Plan as one in which management, together with the ESOP, would own a controlling interest in American Standard. . . . Black & Decker further contends that American Standard has granted itself a lock-up by amending the retirement plans so that, in the event of a change in control, the excess surplus will be dedicated to the retiree group life insurance and medical plans with no reversion of the surplus. Thus, because the Recapitalization Plan is exempted from the definition of change in control, management can utilize the 80 million dollars surplus which Black & Decker cannot. . . . In addition, American Standard established an executive severance plan. Black & Decker argues, furthermore, that under Revlon, Inc. v. MacAndrews & Forbes Holdings, 506 A.2d 173 (Del.1986), any lock-up must be instituted not to stop or impede bidding, as done here, but to maximize the amount to be received by the shareholders. Finally, Black & Decker contends that as in *Revlon, Inc.*, there has been active bidding for a change in control in American Standard. Black & Decker has raised its bid three times and American Standard has increased the value of its Recapitalization Plan twice.

American Standard, needless to say, counters that the *Revlon* doctrine does not apply to the facts of this case. First, management will not gain control as a result of the Recapitalization Plan. Even on a fully diluted basis, management will control only 24% of the new common shares and the ESOP will control 30% with 46% remaining with the general public. . . . The Savings Plan and ESOP will be administered by a trustee and each will have "full confidential, pass-through voting of their American Standard shares (with unallocated shares voted in the same proportion as allocated shares)." . . . Second, American Standard argues that the *Revlon* doctrine does not apply because the Board has acted consistently to preserve the independence of the company and does not, in fact, intend to sell. ... Third, the Recapitalization Plan does not involve a lock-up condemned by *Revlon* for two reasons: (i) the recapitalization will occur only upon a shareholder vote and shareholders will vote for the recapitalization only if there is not a better outstanding bid; and (ii) management will not obtain a majority of stock under the recapitalization since the ESOP provides for confidential pass-through voting. ... Finally, American Standard's Board, contrary to what Black & Decker would like, does not have a duty to negotiate with an offeror. ...

American Standard's Duty to Auction

Black & Decker's allegations that American Standard has instituted an impermissible lock-up under *Revlon, Inc.*, and that American Standard should be negotiating with Black & Decker, including the disclosure of confidential information, are predicated on this Court concluding that the facts here implicate the *Revlon* principle. In *Revlon*, the court was confronted with a fact situation involving an auction-ending lock-up agreement in the midst of a bidding war between a hostile and a friendly bidder. Revlon, Inc., 506 A.2d at 182. The court pointed out that it was "apparent to all that the break-up of the company was inevitable. The Revlon board's authorization permitting management to negotiate a merger or buy out with a third party was a *recognition* that the company was for sale." ... (emphasis added). Once this happened, "the whole question of defensive measures became moot." ... Consequently, the directors were to take on the role of "auctioneers charged with getting the best price for the stockholders at a sale of the company." ...

The Delaware Supreme Court has recently addressed the *Revlon* principle in Ivanhoe Partners v. Newmont Mining Corp., Del.Supr., 535 A.2d 1334, [current] Fed. Sec. L.Rep. (CCH) ¶93,552 at 97,485 (Nov. 18, 1987). In that case, Ivanhoe Partners and Ivanhoe Acquisition Corporation ("Ivanhoe") engaged in a hostile tender offer for 42% of Newmont Mining Corporation ("Newmont") at $105.00 per share. In response to that threat, Newmont adopted a restructuring proposal in order to declare a $33.00 dividend and negotiated a standstill agreement with Consolidated Gold Fields PLC ("Gold Fields"), a major shareholder in Newmont. Id. at 97,486. The dividend enabled Gold Fields to sweep the street and acquire 15.8 million Newmont shares, and the standstill agreement ensured both that Gold Fields' interest in Newmont would not exceed 49.9% and that its representation on Newmont's board would be limited to 40%. Id. As a result, Ivanhoe's hostile bid was thwarted. The next predictable step was Ivanhoe's seeking a preliminary injunction enjoining the dividend and the street sweep. Id. On appeal, the Delaware Supreme Court addressed, *inter alia*, the issue of whether Newmont's directors breached their duties imposed upon them by *Revlon, Inc.* Id. at 97,489.

After explaining the duties of care and loyalty involved when a director acts as an auctioneer, Id. at 97,489-97,490, the court stated that "*Revlon* applies here only if it was apparent that the sale of Newmont was 'inevitable.'" Id. at 97,490. The court found that *Revlon, Inc.* was inapplicable for two reasons. First, the court pointed out that Newmont was never for sale. "[T]he Newmont board held fast to its decision to keep the company independent." Id. at 97,490; see also Buckhorn,

Inc. v. Ropak Corp., 656 F.Supp. 209, 228 (S.D.Ohio 1987) (Unlike the circumstances in *Revlon, Inc.*, the directors of Buckhorn [the target] did not commit themselves to the sale of the company or its assets). Secondly, the court found that there was neither a bidding contest nor a sale. *Ivanhoe* at 97,490. "The only bidder for Newmont was Ivanhoe. Gold Fields was not a bidder, but wished only to protect its already substantial interest in the company. It did this through the street sweep." Id. Since Gold Fields' purchases were in the open market (i.e., from private sellers), the court declined to hold that Newmont "sold" the company.[1] Id.

The fact the court considered persuasive in finding that the board of directors for Newmont did not "sell" the company was that Gold Fields, because of the standstill agreement, acquired neither a majority of the outstanding voting common stock nor a majority representation on Newmont's board of directors. Id. Thus, even after the restructuring proposal was implemented, the public shareholders still controlled the corporation.[2]

In order for the *Revlon* principle to apply to American Standard's proposed Recapitalization Plan, this Court must determine whether the Board intends for American Standard to be for sale or whether there is a bidding contest or a potential sale. The duty of an auctioneer cannot be imposed upon the Board, until this Court determines that the "sale" of American Standard is inevitable. *Ivanhoe Partners* at 97,490; Revlon, Inc., 506 A.2d at 182 (it was apparent to all that the "break-up of the company was inevitable," and the board's conduct "was a recognition that the company was for sale."); Freedman v. Restaurant Associates Industries, Inc., Del. Ch., C.A. No. 9212, slip op. at 16, Allen, C. (Oct. 16, 1987), [Available on WESTLAW, 1987 WL 14323]. (The board takes on the duty of an auctioneer "once it is clear to the board that the corporation is to be subject to a change in control.") In light of the stage of these proceedings, the question becomes, as in *Ivanhoe Partners*, whether Black & Decker would be successful in showing that American Standard is for sale. That court satisfied itself, in part, on this point by inferring from the decision of the directors to keep the company independent that Newmont was not for sale. Id. The court informed this conclusion, however, by finding that the negotiations and final transaction between Newmont and Gold Fields did not result in the sale of the company. Id.

In the instant case, it is true that the Chairman of American Standard has testified that the Board intended to keep the company independent. . . . Unlike the facts in *Ivanhoe Partners*, however, the record before this Court reveals the probability that the actions taken by the Board, while at the same time mouthing

---

Black and Decker Corporation [1] The court addressed the fact that Gold Fields used the $33.00 dividend to carry out the street sweep. "Even though Newmont's declaration of the dividend facilitated the street sweep, it did not constitute a 'sale' of the company by Newmont." Id. This is because Gold Fields purchases, though using the money from the dividend, were made on the open market from private sellers. The dividend itself was not considered improper since it served its purpose in defending against the coercive tender offer by distributing the undervalued non-gold assets to *all* of Newmont's shareholders. Id. at 97-488 (emphasis added).

[2] The general public's voice in the governances of Newmont, in light of Gold Fields' large holdings, was further assured of being heard through Gold Fields and Newmont's agreement to use their best efforts to establish cumulative voting. *Ivanhoe Partners* at 97,486.

cliches about a desire to remain independent, paint a picture of deliberate actions calculated to culminate in a sale of the corporation.

To reach that conclusion, the first issue that must be resolved is whether a transaction which results in a change in control of a corporation amounts to a "sale" under *Revlon, Inc.*[3] It seems unreasonable to conclude that the Delaware Supreme Court would limit the applicability of the duties under *Revlon, Inc.* to only those situations involving the complete sale of all shares of the company. Indeed, the Court of Chancery has recognized that the directors of a company have an obligation to maximize the amount received by shareholders once it is clear to them that the "corporation is to be subject to a change in control."[4] Freedman v. Restaurant Associates, Del. Ch., C.A. No. 9212 at 16 (emphasis added). To conclude otherwise would immunize directors from the duty of an auctioneer when forced with a bid involving a two-tiered tender offer because that kind of bid is, in fact, a bid for control of the company followed by a squeeze out merger effectuated through acquired control.[5]

Furthermore, the conclusion that a sale of control amounts to a "sale" under *Revlon, Inc.* is further supported by the facts in *Edelman v. Fruehauf Corp.* Here, the Sixth Circuit, relying upon *Revlon, Inc.*, recognized that the board of directors knew that Fruehauf was on the auction block. Edelman v. Fruehauf Corp., 798 F.2d 882, 884, 886 (6th Cir. 1986). In response to the hostile bidder's offer, the board approved a management led leveraged buy out with Merrill Lynch. Id. at 884. This was a two-tiered transaction with the first tier being a tender offer for 77% of the company's stock. Id. The second tier was a merger of Fruehauf into management's newly created corporation, and the remaining shareholders received securities in the new company. Id. at 885.[6] There was no dispute that, if

---

[3] None of the parties has cited authority to support the view that a Recapitalization Plan does or does not trigger the duties required under *Revlon, Inc.* Consequently, based upon the development of the case law under *Revlon, Inc.* and its progeny, this court must determine the course the Delaware Supreme Court would undertake were it confronted with the facts of this case.

[4] To require that the *Revlon* principle apply only to an offer to purchase 100% of a company's stock would ignore the inevitability of a break-up which could follow a partial tender offer. The effect of a partial tender offer is that "it allows a raider to gain control of a target and hold a minority interest captive, with little protection for the stockholder against self-dealing or a squeeze-out merger." Martin Lipton, "Corporate Governance in the Age of Finance Corporatism," 136 U. Penn.L.Rev. 1, 17-18.

[5] In a two-tiered tender offer, the raider makes a cash tender offer for a controlling interest in the target and, upon obtaining gaining control, merges the target into itself at a lower second-tier price. Martin Lipton, "Corporate Governance in the Age of Finance Corporatism," 136 U.Penn.L.Rev. 18.

[6] The management led leveraged buy out in *Fruehauf Corp.* achieves a similar result from the public shareholder's perspective as the Recapitalization Proposal would here. In *Fruehauf Corp.*, as here, the funding for the transaction was derived from loans. *Fruehauf Corp.*, 798 F.2d at 884-85. The leveraged buy out called for a tender offer for only 77% of the company's stock. Section 14(d)(6) of the Securities and Exchange Act of 1934 [sic] requires the management led group to take up the shares tendered on a pro rata basis. Section 14(d)(6). Consequently, if more than 77% of the company's shares are tendered, which could be the likely result in a coercive two-tiered tender offer, the shareholders would effectively be exchanging a fraction of their ownership interest in the corporation in exchange for cash. This must be the result since not all the shares tendered will be purchased. In addition, because the second step of the transaction called for a merger of Fruehauf into the management's corporation, the shareholders were merely exchanging their ownership interest in Fruehauf for that in the resulting corporation. There is no doubt that this was considered a sale. Here, the shareholders are exchanging

the management led leveraged buy out were permitted to go forward, this would result in the sale of the company. This is true even though management was only acquiring control, i.e., less than 100% of the shares, of Fruehauf.

Finally, the conclusion that a sale of control of a corporation could amount to a sale under *Revlon, Inc.* is not precluded by *Ivanhoe Partners*. In finding that the Newmont board did not "sell" the company, the court focused on two factors. The Court noted that Gold Fields purchased its stock not from Newmont but from private sellers. Ivanhoe Partners at 97,490. Secondly, the court also found it important that by agreement of the parties, Gold Fields would not gain control of the company as a result of the street sweep. (Thus, Ivanhoe Partners leaves unresolved the intriguing question of whether the directors would have breached their duty under *Revlon, Inc.* if the adoption of the restructuring proposal and the standstill agreement would have resulted in Golds [sic] Fields obtaining a controlling interest in Newmont directly from the company.)

Having concluded that a sale of control of a corporation could amount to a "sale" under *Revlon, Inc.*, this Court must consider the Recapitalization Plan. The Recapitalization Plan provides for the distribution to shareholders of $59.00 in cash and $10.80 in face value junior subordinated discount debentures intended to have a $5.00 market value. The shareholders would retain their common shares with the stub equity valued by Goldman Sachs to be between $6.00—$8.00. The total value of the Recapitalization Plan was estimated to be $70.00—$72.00 per share. . . . This proposal was to be financed by bank debt, senior subordinated debt, junior subordinated discount debt, proceeds from the sale of the corporate headquarters, common equity and excess cash. . . . A necessary element of the Recapitalization Plan is the creation of an ESOP which would purchase 80 million dollars worth of stub equity . . . . The plan also provides that each share of common stock owned by management and the directors would be exchanged for 11.7 shares of the new common stock. . . . But other shareholders of the corporation would not be entitled to this exchange right. As American Standard now exists, public shareholders own 92.6% of the outstanding common stock, management owns 4.8% and the Savings Plan controls 2.6%[7] . . . If the Recapitalization Plan were implemented, the public shareholders would own 45.5% of the outstanding common stock, management would own 23.9% and the Savings Plan and ESOP would control 30.6% of the outstanding common stock. . . .

Needless to say, both parties differ on whether management is gaining control of American Standard through the Recapitalization Plan. Black & Decker would have the Court find that the Recapitalization Plan results in a change in control because management and the combined ESOP and Savings Plan will control 55.5% of the outstanding stock. American Standard, however, contends not only that the options may not be exercised but also that the ESOP and Savings Plan should

---

a fraction of their ownership interest in American Standard for cash. This, in turn, results in the general public not having control of the company, as in *Fruehauf Corp.*, yet still retaining some ownership interest. The only difference between the facts before this Court and those in *Fruehauf Corp.* is that the Recapitalization Plan achieves the same result without the second step merger.

[7] These percentages are based on a fully diluted basis, assuming that all of the outstanding options are exercised on a primary basis, the general public owns 95.9%.

not be considered in conjunction with the holdings of management since the ESOP and Savings Plan provide for confidential pass through voting.

While both arguments have some merit, this Court must follow its own understanding of the Recapitalization Plan and its effect on the corporation. American Standard is correct to point out that immediately after the Recapitalization Plan has been enacted, the public shareholders will control 55% of the outstanding common stock. Merely stopping at this point, however, does not do justice to the situation faced by American Standard's shareholders. To ignore the presence of the stock options would result in overlooking the complete offer to the public shareholders.

The entire Recapitalization Plan is an offer to gain control of American Standard. American Standard's public shareholders are being offered $59.00 in cash and $5.00 in a bond. In return, they are immediately giving up on a primary basis 40.9% of their collective ownership interest in American Standard; plus management will receive the exclusive right to remove control from the public shareholders. Thus, while the Recapitalization Plan calls for a reduction in public ownership in American Standard to 55%, it inherently affects the acquisition of control of the corporation. For disclosure purposes and otherwise, American Standard could not describe the transaction in any other way. This right of control in the form of stock options may be exercised at any time without a vote of the public shareholders.

Unlike *Ivanhoe Partners*, this is a sale of control in American Standard. In *Ivanhoe Partners*, the Delaware Supreme Court found that the dividend did not constitute a "sale" of the company by Newmont because all the shareholders received a dividend not just Gold Fields. *Ivanhoe Partners* at 97,488, 97,490. Also, Gold Fields could not purchase control in Newmont and what stock it did buy was not from Newmont but from the market place. Id. at 97,490.

The differences from *Ivanhoe Partners* are informative in this case. Unlike the Newmont board of directors, the Board here is not merely declaring a dividend in order to distribute equity built up in the company. Rather, the Board is proposing that each shareholder "sell" a percentage of his or her ownership interest in the company for $59.00 in cash plus $5.00 in a bond. Thus, this situation is more analogous to that in *Fruehauf Corp.*, which was acknowledged to be a sale, than in *Ivanhoe Partners*. Secondly, the shareholders are transferring control in American Standard. The Delaware Supreme Court found it important that the standstill agreement between Gold Fields and Newmont limited Gold Fields' purchase to 49.9% of the outstanding common stock and to 40% representation on the board of Newmont. The Recapitalization Plan, however, provides for no mechanism to stop a change in control. Quite the contrary, here the sale of the public shareholders control in American Standard takes the form of options exercisable at the sole discretion of management. Thus, the transfer of control occurs now, while the relegation to minority status occurs sometime in the future under the exclusive control of management. Thirdly, unlike the acquisitions by Gold Fields from private sellers, the Board is "selling" American Standard. The Recapitalization Plan calls for management and directors alone to receive 11.7 shares of common stock in exchange for every one share presently owned. In addition, the ESOP will purchase stock from the company for its needs. Thus, while the public shareholders are receiving money in exchange for a percentage of their ownership interest in American Standard, the company is selling stock and options to management (in exchange for the value of the presently held common stock) and stock to the ESOP and Savings Plan (in exchange for 80 million dollars). Whereas all Newmont shareholders were treated equally with the distribution of the dividend, and whereas Gold Fields purchased its stock on the open market, American Standard's Recapitalization Plan provides for the transfer of stock and options to management and the ESOP without providing for the same opportunity to the public shareholder. Thus, the facts before this Court are sufficiently distinguishable from those in *Ivanhoe Partners* for this Court to conclude that on an expanded record the Recapitalization Plan would be found to amount to a sale of American Standard.

The Court, therefore, is presented with a situation in which management has said it wants to remain independent, yet its actions reveal that the company is for sale. The Court is struck by the different meanings that "independence" has. In *Ivanhoe Partners*, "independence" meant that the public shareholders retained a majority of the outstanding stock and majority representation in the board; that Gold Fields was absolutely limited in the amount of stock it could own and its representation on the board; and the directors of Newmont did not take advantage of the takeover threat as an opportunity to increase their, or employee, ownership interest in the company. "Independence" for the Newmont board meant finding a solution which had the least effect on the status quo. On the facts of this case, however, "independence" has a different meaning. Here, the shareholders are acceding control in the corporation through the medium of stock options. The shareholders are not protected from the discretionary exercise of these options and the possible effect on the corporation. And management is availing themselves of the takeover threat to increase their, and the employee's, ownership interest in the company. Thus, while American Standard's board mimics Newmont's board's statement that they decided to keep the company independent, their understanding does not mean maintaining the status quo; rather, independence is achieved only through a change in control in American Standard.[9]

Furthermore, American Standard's conduct reveals the probability that it is in a bidding contest for the company. In response to Black & Decker's $65.00 per share offer, "American Standard, Inc. countered . . . with a cash-and-debt recapitalization plan analysts and traders valued at between $68.00 and $70.00 a share, or $2.13 billion to $2.19 billion." . . . In response to American Standard's announced

---

[9] American Standard's own recent conduct belatedly implies that it understands it has reached the auction stage and the company is up for sale. On March 8, 1988, the Wall Street Journal reported that "sources close to American Standard have suggested that the company could auction itself, writing Black & Decker and others to review its books." Wall Street Journal, Mar. 8, 1985 at 26. The very next day it was reported that American Standard planned to "provide confidential information to hostile suitor Black & Decker Corp. and to hold talks with the Towson, Maryland based concern and 'other potential purchasers of the company.'" Wall Street Journal, Mar. 9, 1988, at 3. Strangely, the belated public concession comes 33 days after one of the company's own directors, as early as February 4, privately understood that American Standard was taking actions in order to create a level playing field so that alternative bids, including the company's, could be developed . . . .

plan, Black & Decker announced a sweetened bid for $68.00 a share. . . . The latest escalation in this bidding war occurred on Friday, March 4, 1988, when American Standard announced that morning an increase in the cash portion of the Recapitalization Plan to $64.00 a share. . . . In response, Black & Decker announced that afternoon that it would increase its offer to $73.00 a share. . . . Although American Standard's attorneys may contend in the courthouse that there is no bidding contest, the objective reports of the conduct of the two parties reveal something quite different. The public must perceive, and the Court concludes, that Black & Decker has established the probability that this is a bidding contest and American Standard is for sale.

Having determined that the approval of the Recapitalization Plan "was a recognition that the company was for sale,"Revlon, Inc., 506 A.2d at 182, this Court must now determine whether the adoption of the severance plan and the amendments to the retirement and savings plans were actions consonant with the Board's duty of an auctioneer. The Delaware Supreme Court has made clear that once the Board is faced with the inevitable break up of the company, the use of defensive measures is no longer an option. Id. at 182. Rather, the Board's role "changes from defenders of the corporate bastion to auctioneers charged with getting the best price for the stockholders at a sale of the company." Id. Consequently, any action taken by the Board must be directed at obtaining the highest price for the benefit of the stockholders. Id.

The validity of the Board's conduct must be evaluated in light of its duty as an auctioneer. See id. at 183 (lock-up option is not *per se* illegal but is impermissible if it puts an end to the bidding process). Furthermore, any action taken must be evaluated in terms of the timing of the auction process. A lock-up option, for example, which draws a bidder into the bidding process, may not be invalid under *Revlon, Inc.* Id. That same lock-up option, entered into in the middle of an active auction, however, would be impermissible if it forecloses further bidding to the shareholders' detriment. Id. Thus, the Delaware Supreme Court concluded that one of the reasons for holding Revlon's lock-up with Forstmann invalid was because Forstmann had already been induced to enter the bidding contest. Id. The lock-up option, therefore, resulted in destroying the bidding process, not fostering it. Id.

Any action taken which favors one bidder over another is also examined by comparing the outstanding bids. In *Revlon, Inc.,* one of the reasons given for adopting the lock-up was that Forstmann had better financing. Id. at 183. The court, however, disagreed with the board's view of the financing and stated that "any distinctions between the rival bidders' methods of financing the proposal were nominal at best, and such a consideration has little or no significance in a cash offer for any and all shares." Id. at 184. The court also considered the value of the two competing offers and pointed out that the lock-up was given in return for a minimal improvement in the bids. Id. As a result, the court concluded the board had granted the lock-up on an insubstantial basis. Id.

Finally, the Delaware Supreme Court considered who derived the benefit from the board's action.[10] In *Revlon, Inc.*, it was apparent to the court that the shareholders and the directors of Revlon were going to derive the greatest benefit from the lock-up and subsequent sale to Forstmann. Id. at 182, 184. When a board of directors takes some action either to stimulate or initiate the bidding process, the board's main concern must be to benefit the shareholders.

> A board may have regard for various constituencies in discharging its responsibilities, provided there are rationally related benefits accruing to the stockholders. However, such concern for non-stockholder interests is inappropriate when an auction among active bidders is in progress, and the object no longer is to protect or maintain the corporate enterprise but to sell it to the highest bidder.

Revlon, Inc., 506 A.2d at 183 (citations omitted). The court rejected the board's action that favored corporate noteholders pointing out that the directors sought merely to protect themselves from possible lawsuits. Id. at 184. When this impermissible purpose was coupled with the insubstantial increase in the offer, the directors' action could not "withstand the enhanced scrutiny which *Unocal* requires of director conduct." Id., citing Unocal Corp. v. Mesa Petroleum Company, Del. Supr., 493 A.2d 946, 954-55 (1985). The court concluded its discussion of a director's duty of an auctioneer and the action that can be taken in compliance with this duty by explaining that,

> [W]hen bidders make relatively similar offers, or dissolution of the company becomes inevitable, the directors cannot fulfill their enhanced *Unocal* duties by playing favorites with the contending factions. Market forces must be allowed to operate freely to bring the target's shareholders the best price available for their equity. Thus, as the trial court ruled, the shareholders' interests necessitated that the board remain free to negotiate in the fulfillment of that duty.

Revlon, Inc, 506 A.2d at 184.

With these principles established, this Court must now consider the actions taken by the Board in amending the Executive Supplement Retirement Benefit Program, the Excess Retirement Plan, the Retirement Plans, the Savings and Stock Ownership Plans (the "Retirement Plans") and the creation of the severance plan triggered by a change in control. This plan was designed to cover salaried employees assigned to corporate staff functions who were not currently a party to a "change in control agreement" with American Standard (the "Severance Plan" sometimes referred to collectively as the "Plans"). All of the Retirement Plans were amended to provide that "(i) all accrued benefits will vest, subject to collective

---

[10] One treatise points out that, "[T]he key ingredient should be an examination of the effect of the lock-up on the primary (or intended) beneficiaries of the agreement . . . Where, however, the directors allow considerations other than price to affect their analysis in a context where sale of the company appears inevitable, the courts will scrutinize closely the actions of directors, especially where the lock-up has essentially terminated an active competitive bidding contest."

Balotti and Finkelstein, 5 The Delaware Law of Corporations and Business Organizations, Ch. 6.34 (1986 Supplement).

bargaining requirements, upon a change in control and (ii) if they are terminated in whole or in part after a change in control, any surplus will be dedicated to provide retiree group life insurance and medical programs ... with no reversion of any portion of the surplus to American Standard." ... The savings and stock ownership Plans were amended, furthermore, so that all matching accounts would vest upon a change in control. ... In addition, a severance plan was adopted to provide for payments to salaried employees assigned to corporate staff functions in the event of a change in control. ... The Board also amended the definition of a "change in control" to provide for the exemption of the Recapitalization Plan. ... Consequently, if there were a change in control pursuant to the Recapitalization Plan, the actions taken on February 18 would not take effect.

The effect of the Plan is to treat the competing bidders unfairly.[11] In the event of a change in control, such as a successful Black & Decker takeover, the Retirement Plans call for an acceleration of payments. This would result in an immediate loss of 80 million dollars to American Standard shareholders. ... Furthermore, in the event of that same change in control, it has been estimated that the cost of the Severance Plan to a successful bidder would be 50 million dollars. ... The Board, on the other hand, as discussed *supra*, has exempted the Recapitalization Plan from the definition of a change in control. So a successful vote on the Recapitalization Plan provides management and employees a 130 million dollar advantage. Thus, it is clear that the Board's actions places [sic] Black & Decker on an unequal footing in its bid for control.

Moreover, it does not appear that there is any justification for such continuing unequal treatment. Indeed the value of the competing offers are substantially similar. At the time the Retirement Plans were amended and the Severance Plan was created, the Recapitalization Plan's estimated value was between $70.00—$72.00 a share and Black & Decker's offer was at $65.00 a share. Black & Decker then increased its offer to $68.00 a share. At the present, the Recapitalization Plan's value is now estimated at $74.00—$75.00 and Black & Decker's offer is at $73.00. Although it initially appears that the competing bids were far apart, the Recapitalization Plan, at the time it was approved, may not have been a viable offer. The Recapitalization Plan contemplated a $59.00 dividend which would have required $1,761,000.00 in cash in order to provide the necessary surplus. ... Consequently, one need not conclude that the favored Recapitalization Plan was a clearly superior offer. Furthermore, since Black & Decker's offer is an offer for any and all shares, any alleged differences in the methods of financing in an attempt to justify the unequal treatment has "little or no significance." Revlon, Inc., 506 A.2d at 184.

---

[11] During a telephone conference call with all of the parties on March 14, 1988, counsel for American Standard stated that there was a possible higher bid from an undisclosed third party. At this time, however, this unknown potential bidder remains a mere possibility. In fact, the Court is presented with only two actual bidders. Thus, American Standard's argument that the effect of the Plans may be the subject of negotiations is not relevant since the Recapitalization Plan is exempt from the effect of these Plans. The possibility of negotiations, therefore, is illusory since it is only Black & Decker who must give up something in order to be placed in the same position as management and the employees.

Finally, it is difficult to see how the amendment to the Retirement Plans and the enactment of the Severance Plan benefit the shareholders. *Revlon, Inc.* makes clear that "concern for non-stockholder interests is inappropriate when an auction among active bidders is in progress, and the object is no longer to protect or maintain the corporate enterprise but to sell it to the highest bidder." Revlon, Inc., 506 A.2d at 182. Thus, it is probable that the Board abrogated its duty when it adopted the amendments to the Retirement Plans and enacted the Severance Plan in order to provide for its employees when its concern should have been to sell the company to the highest bidder. No doubt one could conclude in a different situation with different timing that severance and retirement plans are legitimate corporate functions designed to reward corporate officers fidelity and performance. Indeed, in other situations, courts have found the plans due to the deference accorded the business judgment rule. Cf. Buckhorn, Inc., 656 F.Supp. at 232. But these Plans were designed to deter bidding and, in the *Revlon* context, provide a substantial basis for concluding that Black & Decker will succeed on the merits.

In conclusion, Black & Decker has carried its burden of showing a probability of success on the question of whether the Board breached its duty under *Revlon, Inc.* by amending the Retirement Plans and enacting the Severance Plan. At this time, it appears that the Plans do not foster the bidding process. Rather, Black & Decker has preliminarily shown that they, in fact, unfairly favor the Recapitalization Plan. . . .

¶2800

Other Materials

1916 UNIFORM LIMITED PARTNERSHIP ACT

Selected Sections

§7. Limited partner not liable to creditors

A limited partner shall not become liable as a general partner unless, in addition to the exercise of his rights and powers as a limited partner, he takes part in the control of the business.

1985 REVISED UNIFORM LIMITED PARTNERSHIP ACT

Selected Sections

§303. Liability to third parties.

(a) Except as provided in subsection (d), a limited partner is not liable for the obligations of a limited partnership unless he [or she] is also a general partner or, in addition to the exercise of his [or her] rights and powers as a limited partner, he [or she] participates in the control of the business. However, if the limited partner participates in the control of the business, he [or she] is liable only to persons who transact business with the limited partnership reasonably believing, based upon the limited partner's conduct, that the limited partner is a general partner.

(b) A limited partner does not participate in the control of the business within the meaning of subsection (a) solely by doing one or more of the following:

(1) being a contractor for or an agent or employee of the limited partnership or of a general partner or being an officer, director, or shareholder of a general partner that is a corporation;

(2) consulting with and advising a general partner with respect to the business of the limited partnership;

(3) acting as surety for the limited partnership or guaranteeing or assuming one or more specific obligations of the limited partnership;

(4) taking any action required or permitted by law to bring or pursue a derivative action in the right of the limited partnership;

(5) requesting or attending a meeting of partners;

(6) proposing, approving, or disapproving, by voting or otherwise, one or more of the following matters:

(i) the dissolution and winding up of the limited partnership;

(ii) the sale, exchange, lease, mortgage, pledge, or other transfer of all or substantially all of the assets of the limited partnership;

(iii) the incurrence of indebtedness by the limited partnership other than in the ordinary course of its business;

(iv) a change in the nature of the business;

(v) the admission or removal of a general partner;

(vi) the admission or removal of a limited partner;

(vii) a transaction involving an actual or potential conflict of interest between a general partner and the limited partnership or the limited partners;

(viii) an amendment to the partnership agreement or certificate of limited partnership; or

(ix) matters related to the business of the limited partnership not otherwise enumerated in this subsection (b), which the partnership agreement states in writing may be subject to the approval or disapproval of limited partners;

(7) winding up the limited partnership pursuant to Section 803; or

(8) exercising any right or power permitted to limited partners under this [Act] and not specifically enumerated in this subsection (b).

(c) The enumeration in subsection (b) does not mean that the possession or exercise of any other powers by a limited partner constitutes participation by him [or her] in the business of the limited partnership.

(d) A limited partner who knowingly permits his [or her] name to be used in the name of the limited partnership, except under circumstances permitted by Section 102(2), is liable to creditors who extend credit to the limited partnership without actual knowledge that the limited partner is not a general partner.

Comment

Section 303 makes several important changes in Section 7 of the 1916 Act. The first sentence of Section 303(a) differs from the text of Section 7 of the 1916 Act in that it speaks of participating (rather than taking part) in the control of the business; this was done for the sake of consistency with the second sentence of Section 303(a), not to change the meaning of the text. It is intended that judicial decisions interpreting the phrase "takes part in the control of the business" under the prior uniform law will remain applicable to the extent that a different result is not called for by other provisions of Section 303 and other provisions of the Act. The second sentence of Section 303(a) reflects a wholly new concept in the 1976 Act that has been further modified in the 1985 Act. It was adopted partly because of the difficulty of determining when the "control" line has been overstepped, but also (and more importantly) because of a determination that it is not sound public policy to hold a limited partner who is not also a general partner liable for the obligations of the partnership except to persons who have done business with the limited partnership reasonably believing, based on the limited partner's conduct, that he is a general partner. Paragraph (b) is intended to provide a "safe harbor" by enumerating certain activities which a limited partner may carry on for the partnership without being deemed to have taken part in control of the business. This "safe harbor" list has been expanded beyond that set out in the 1976 Act to reflect case law and statutory developments and more clearly to assure that limited partners are not subjected to general liability where such liability is inappropriate. Paragraph (d) is derived from Section 5 of the 1916 Act, but adds as a condition to the limited partner's liability the requirement that a limited partner must have knowingly permitted his name to be used in the name of the limited partnership.

. . .

§607. Limitations on distribution.

A partner may not receive a distribution from a limited partnership to the extent that, after giving effect to the distribution, all liabilities of the limited partnership, other than liabilities to partners on account of their partnership interests, exceed the fair value of the partnership assets.

. . .

§608. Liability upon return of contribution.

(a) If a partner has received the return of any part of his [or her] contribution without violation of the partnership agreement or this [Act], he [or she] is liable to the limited partnership for a period of one year thereafter for the amount of the returned contribution, but only to the extent necessary to discharge the limited partnership's liabilities to creditors who extended credit to the limited partnership during the period the contribution was held by the partnership.

(b) If a partner has received the return of any part of his [or her] contribution in violation of the partnership agreement or this [Act], he [or she] is liable to the limited partnership for a period of six years thereafter for the amount of the contribution wrongfully returned.

(c) A partner receives a return of his [or her] contribution to the extent that a distribution to him [or her] reduces his [or her] share of the fair value of the net assets of the limited partnership below the value, as set forth in the partnership records required to be kept pursuant to Section 105, of his [or her] contribution which has not been distributed to him [or her].

. . .

§901. Law governing [foreign limited partnerships].

Subject to the Constitution of this State, (i) the laws of the state under which a foreign limited partnership is organized govern its organization and internal affairs and the liability of its limited partners, and (ii) a foreign limited partnership may not be denied registration by reason of any difference between those laws and the laws of this State.

Comment

Section 901 first appeared in the 1976 Act.

2001 UNIFORM LIMITED PARTNERSHIP ACT

Selected Sections

§201. Formation of limited partnership; certificate of limited partnership.

(a) In order for a limited partnership to be formed, a certificate of limited partnership must be delivered to the [Secretary of State] for filing. The certificate must state:

. . .

(4) whether the limited partnership is a limited liability limited partnership. . . .

§303. No liability as limited partner for limited partnership obligations. An obligation of a limited partnership, whether arising in contract, tort, or otherwise, is not the obligation of a limited partner. A limited partner is not personally liable, directly or indirectly, by way of contribution or otherwise, for an obligation of the limited partnership solely by reason of being a limited partner, even if the limited partner participates in the management and control of the limited partnership.

Comment

This section provides a full, status-based liability shield for each limited partner, "even if the limited partner participates in the management and control of the limited partnership." The section thus eliminates the so-called "control rule" with respect to personal liability for entity obligations and brings limited partners into parity with LLC members, LLP partners and corporate shareholders.

The "control rule" first appeared in an uniform act in 1916, although the concept is much older. Section 7 of the original Uniform Limited Partnership Act provided that "A limited partner shall not become liable as a general partner [i.e., for the obligations of the limited partnership] unless . . . he takes part in the control of the business." The 1976 Uniform Limited Partnership Act (ULPA-1976) "carrie[d] over the basic test from former Section 7," but recognized "the difficulty of determining when the 'control' line has been overstepped." Comment to ULPA-1976, Section 303. Accordingly, ULPA-1976 tried to buttress the limited partner's shield by (i) providing a safe harbor for a lengthy list of activities deemed not to constitute participating in control, ULPA-1976, Section 303(b), and (ii) limiting a limited partner's "control rule" liability "only to persons who transact business with the limited partnership with actual knowledge of [the limited partner's] participation in control." ULPA-1976, Section 303(a). However, these protections were complicated by a countervailing rule which made a limited partner generally liable for the limited partnership's obligations "if the limited partner's participation in the control of the business is . . . substantially the same as the exercise of the powers of a general partner." ULPA-1976, Section 303(a).

The 1985 amendments to ULPA-1976 (i.e., RULPA) further buttressed the limited partner's shield, removing the "substantially the same" rule, expanding the list of safe harbor activities and limiting "control rule" liability "only to persons who transact business with the limited partnership reasonably believing, based upon the limited partner's conduct, that the limited partner is a general partner."

In a world with LLPs, LLCs and, most importantly, LLLPs, the control rule has become an anachronism. This Act therefore takes the next logical step in the evolution of the limited partner's liability shield and renders the control rule extinct.

The shield established by this section protects only against liability for the limited partnership's obligations and only to the extent that the limited partner is claimed to be liable on account of being a limited partner. Thus, a person that is both a general and limited partner will be liable as a general partner for the limited partnership's obligations. Moreover, this section does not prevent a limited partner from being liable as a result of the limited partner's own conduct and is therefore inapplicable when a third party asserts that a limited partner's own wrongful conduct has injured the third party. This section is likewise inapplicable to claims by the limited partnership or another partner that a limited partner has breached a duty under this Act or the partnership agreement.

This section does not eliminate a limited partner's liability for promised contributions, Section 502 or improper distributions. Section 509. That liability pertains to a person's status as a limited partner but is not liability for an obligation of the limited partnership.

The shield provided by this section applies whether or not a limited partnership is a limited liability limited partnership.

. . .

§404. General partner's liability.

(a) Except as otherwise provided in subsections (b) and (c), all general partners are liable jointly and severally for all obligations of the limited partnership unless otherwise agreed by the claimant or provided by law.

(b) A person that becomes a general partner of an existing limited partnership is not personally liable for an obligation of a limited partnership incurred before the person became a general partner.

(c) An obligation of a limited partnership incurred while the limited partnership is a limited liability limited partnership, whether arising in contract, tort, or otherwise, is solely the obligation of the limited partnership. A general partner is not personally liable, directly or indirectly, by way of contribution or otherwise, for such an obligation solely by reason of being or acting as a general partner. This subsection applies despite anything inconsistent in the partnership agreement that existed immediately before the consent required to become a limited liability limited partnership under Section 406(b)(2).

. . .

§508. Limitations on distribution.

(a) A limited partnership may not make a distribution in violation of the partnership agreement.

(b) A limited partnership may not make a distribution if after the distribution:

(1) the limited partnership would not be able to pay its debts as they become due in the ordinary course of the limited partnership's activities; or

(2) the limited partnership's total assets would be less than the sum of its total liabilities plus the amount that would be needed, if the limited partnership were to be dissolved, wound up, and terminated at the time of the distribution, to satisfy the preferential rights upon dissolution, winding up, and termination of partners whose preferential rights are superior to those of persons receiving the distribution.

(c) A limited partnership may base a determination that a distribution is not prohibited under subsection (b) on financial statements prepared on the basis of accounting practices and principles that are reasonable in the circumstances or on a fair valuation or other method that is reasonable in the circumstances.

(d) Except as otherwise provided in subsection (g), the effect of a distribution under subsection (b) is measured:

(1) in the case of distribution by purchase, redemption, or other acquisition of a transferable interest in the limited partnership, as of the date money or other property is transferred or debt incurred by the limited partnership; and

(2) in all other cases, as of the date: (A) the distribution is authorized, if the payment occurs within 120 days after that date; or (B) the payment is made, if payment occurs more than 120 days after the distribution is authorized.

(e) A limited partnership's indebtedness to a partner incurred by reason of a distribution made in accordance with this section is at parity with the limited partnership's indebtedness to its general, unsecured creditors.

(f) A limited partnership's indebtedness, including indebtedness issued in connection with or as part of a distribution, is not considered a liability for purposes of subsection (b) if the terms of the indebtedness provide that payment of principal and interest are made only to the extent that a distribution could then be made to partners under this section.

(g) If indebtedness is issued as a distribution, each payment of principal or interest on the indebtedness is treated as a distribution, the effect of which is measured on the date the payment is made.

. . .

§509. Liability for improper distributions.

(a) A general partner that consents to a distribution made in violation of Section 508 is personally liable to the limited partnership for the amount of the distribution which exceeds the amount that could have been distributed without the violation if it is established that in consenting to the distribution the general partner failed to comply with Section 408.

(b) A partner or transferee that received a distribution knowing that the distribution to that partner or transferee was made in violation of Section 508 is personally liable to the limited partnership but only to the extent that the distribution received by the partner or transferee exceeded the amount that could have been properly paid under Section 508.

(c) A general partner against which an action is commenced under subsection (a) may:

(1) implead in the action any other person that is liable under subsection (a) and compel contribution from the person; and

(2) implead in the action any person that received a distribution in violation of subsection (b) and compel contribution from the person in the amount the person received in violation of subsection (b).

(d) An action under this section is barred if it is not commenced within two years after the distribution.

. . .

§901. Governing law.

(a) The laws of the State or other jurisdiction under which a foreign limited partnership is organized govern relations among the partners of the foreign limited partnership and between the partners and the foreign limited partnership and the liability of partners as partners for an obligation of the foreign limited partnership.

AMERICAN BAR ASSOCIATION MODEL RULES[1]

Selected Rules

RULE 1.7   CONFLICT OF INTEREST: CURRENT CLIENTS

(a) Except as provided in paragraph (b), a lawyer shall not represent a client if the representation involves a concurrent conflict of interest. A concurrent conflict of interest exists if:

(1) the representation of one client will be directly adverse to another client; or

(2) there is a significant risk that the representation of one or more clients will be materially limited by the lawyer's responsibilities to another client, a former client or a third person or by a personal interest of the lawyer.

(b) Notwithstanding the existence of a concurrent conflict of interest under paragraph (a), a lawyer may represent a client if:

(1) the lawyer reasonably believes that the lawyer will be able to provide competent and diligent representation to each affected client;

(2) the representation is not prohibited by law;

(3) the representation does not involve the assertion of a claim by one client against another client represented by the lawyer in the same litigation or other proceeding before a tribunal; and

(4) each affected client gives informed consent, confirmed in writing.

. . .

Identifying Conflicts of Interest: Directly Adverse

[7] Directly adverse conflicts can also arise in transactional matters. For example, if a lawyer is asked to represent the seller of a business in negotiations with a buyer represented by the lawyer, not in the same transaction but in another, unrelated matter, the lawyer could not undertake the representation without the informed consent of each client.

Identifying Conflicts of Interest: Material Limitation

[8] Even where there is no direct adverseness, a conflict of interest exists if there is a significant risk that a lawyer's ability to consider, recommend or carry

out an appropriate course of action for the client will be materially limited as a result of the lawyer's other responsibilities or interests. For example, a lawyer asked to represent several individuals seeking to form a joint venture is likely to be materially limited in the lawyer's ability to recommend or advocate all possible positions that each might take because of the lawyer's duty of loyalty to the others. The conflict in effect forecloses alternatives that would otherwise be available to the client. The mere possibility of subsequent harm does not itself require disclosure and consent. The critical questions are the likelihood that a difference in interests will eventuate and, if it does, whether it will materially interfere with the lawyer's independent professional judgment in considering alternatives or foreclose courses of action that reasonably should be pursued on behalf of the client.

. . .

Prohibited Representations

[14] Ordinarily, clients may consent to representation notwithstanding a conflict. However, as indicated in paragraph (b), some conflicts are nonconsentable, meaning that the lawyer involved cannot properly ask for such agreement or provide representation on the basis of the client's consent. When the lawyer is representing more than one client, the question of consentability must be resolved as to each client.

[15] Consentability is typically determined by considering whether the interests of the clients will be adequately protected if the clients are permitted to give their informed consent to representation burdened by a conflict of interest. Thus, under paragraph (b)(1), representation is prohibited if in the circumstances the lawyer cannot reasonably conclude that the lawyer will be able to provide competent and diligent representation. . . .

. . .

Consent to Future Conflict

[22] Whether a lawyer may properly request a client to waive conflicts that might arise in the future is subject to the test of paragraph (b). The effectiveness of such waivers is generally determined by the extent to which the client reasonably understands the material risks that the waiver entails. The more comprehensive the explanation of the types of future representations that might arise and the actual and reasonably foreseeable adverse consequences of those representations, the greater the likelihood that the client will have the requisite understanding. Thus, if the client agrees to consent to a particular type of conflict with which the client is already familiar, then the consent ordinarily will be effective with regard to that type of conflict. If the consent is general and open-ended, then the consent ordinarily will be ineffective, because it is not reasonably likely that the client will have understood the material risks involved. On the other hand, if the client is an experienced user of the legal services involved and is reasonably

informed regarding the risk that a conflict may arise, such consent is more likely to be effective, particularly if, e.g., the client is independently represented by other counsel in giving consent and the consent is limited to future conflicts unrelated to the subject of the representation. In any case, advance consent cannot be effective if the circumstances that materialize in the future are such as would make the conflict nonconsentable under paragraph (b).

· · ·

Nonlitigation Conflicts

[26] Conflicts of interest under paragraphs (a)(1) and (a)(2) arise in contexts other than litigation. For a discussion of directly adverse conflicts in transactional matters, see Comment [7]. Relevant factors in determining whether there is significant potential for material limitation include the duration and intimacy of the lawyer's relationship with the client or clients involved, the functions being performed by the lawyer, the likelihood that disagreements will arise and the likely prejudice to the client from the conflict. The question is often one of proximity and degree. See Comment [8].

· · ·

[28] Whether a conflict is consentable depends on the circumstances. For example, a lawyer may not represent multiple parties to a negotiation whose interests are fundamentally antagonistic to each other, but common representation is permissible where the clients are generally aligned in interest even though there is some difference in interest among them. Thus, a lawyer may seek to establish or adjust a relationship between clients on an amicable and mutually advantageous basis; for example, in helping to organize a business in which two or more clients are entrepreneurs, working out the financial reorganization of an enterprise in which two or more clients have an interest or arranging a property distribution in settlement of an estate. The lawyer seeks to resolve potentially adverse interests by developing the parties' mutual interests. Otherwise, each party might have to obtain separate representation, with the possibility of incurring additional cost, complication or even litigation. Given these and other relevant factors, the clients may prefer that the lawyer act for all of them.

Special Considerations in Common Representation

[29] In considering whether to represent multiple clients in the same matter, a lawyer should be mindful that if the common representation fails because the potentially adverse interests cannot be reconciled, the result can be additional cost, embarrassment and recrimination. Ordinarily, the lawyer will be forced to withdraw from representing all of the clients if the common representation fails. In some situations, the risk of failure is so great that multiple representation is plainly impossible. For example, a lawyer cannot undertake common representa-

tion of clients where contentious litigation or negotiations between them are imminent or contemplated. Moreover, because the lawyer is required to be impartial between commonly represented clients, representation of multiple clients is improper when it is unlikely that impartiality can be maintained. Generally, if the relationship between the parties has already assumed antagonism, the possibility that the clients' interests can be adequately served by common representation is not very good. Other relevant factors are whether the lawyer subsequently will represent both parties on a continuing basis and whether the situation involves creating or terminating a relationship between the parties.

. . .

[31] As to the duty of confidentiality, continued common representation will almost certainly be inadequate if one client asks the lawyer not to disclose to the other client information relevant to the common representation. This is so because the lawyer has an equal duty of loyalty to each client, and each client has the right to be informed of anything bearing on the representation that might affect that client's interests and the right to expect that the lawyer will use that information to that client's benefit. See Rule 1.4. The lawyer should, at the outset of the common representation and as part of the process of obtaining each client's informed consent, advise each client that information will be shared and that the lawyer will have to withdraw if one client decides that some matter material to the representation should be kept from the other. In limited circumstances, it may be appropriate for the lawyer to proceed with the representation when the clients have agreed, after being properly informed, that the lawyer will keep certain information confidential. For example, the lawyer may reasonably conclude that failure to disclose one client's trade secrets to another client will not adversely affect representation involving a joint venture between the clients and agree to keep that information confidential with the informed consent of both clients.

[32] When seeking to establish or adjust a relationship between clients, the lawyer should make clear that the lawyer's role is not that of partisanship normally expected in other circumstances and, thus, that the clients may be required to assume greater responsibility for decisions than when each client is separately represented. Any limitations on the scope of the representation made necessary as a result of the common representation should be fully explained to the clients at the outset of the representation. See Rule 1.2(c).

[33] Subject to the above limitations, each client in the common representation has the right to loyal and diligent representation and the protection of Rule 1.9 concerning the obligations to a former client. The client also has the right to discharge the lawyer as stated in Rule 1.16.

THE AMERICAN LAW INSTITUTE FEDERAL INCOME TAX PROJECT*

Reporter's Study Draft

(June 1, 1989)

SUBCHAPTER C (SUPPLEMENTAL STUDY)

Selected Portions

B. Corporate Financial Practice in the 1980s

During the 1980s there has been a proliferation of corporate financial transactions that have the effect of distributing corporate funds or other assets out of corporate solution, without the offsetting tax burden that would accompany ordinary dividend distributions.

These transactions include an unusually persistent wave of corporate acquisitions, some negotiated (friendly) and others by tender offer over the objection of incumbent management and directors (hostile). They have mostly been for cash or debt, rather than stock of acquiring corporations.

There has also been a proliferation of other, nonacquisition transactions that involve a net exchange of corporate funds for previously outstanding stock of the distributing corporation itself. Such transactions include some leveraged buyouts and also simple redemptions of stock for cash or debt. These transactions have often been entered into for defense against threatened or potential hostile takeover attempts. Most recently there have even been simple extraordinary dividends, representing the proceeds from borrowing a substantial portion (sometimes exceeding 100 percent) of the prior value of a corporation's stock.

Transactions like these (except the last) have long been standard fare among close corporations and their shareholders. Stock redemptions in particular are at the heart of close corporation tax planning. Debt-for-stock recapitalizations have been tried, and shoestring purchases are a common, continuing tactic. What is new in the 1980s is the diffusion of these transactions, on a widespread basis, into the public corporate sector.

Cash acquisitions commonly go forward at prices substantially above the market price prior to announcement of the acquisition plan, and this has been something of a puzzle to explain. In practice, as soon as a serious acquisition plan becomes known, the market price rises; stock in such a situation is said to be "in play." A large fraction of the total market gains from acquisition transactions have therefore gone to target shareholders. The Williams Act requires disclosure

---

within 10 days after acquiring 5 percent of a target corporation's stock; an acquiror will often attempt to keep his intentions unknown until then, by which time he may have acquired a total of around 10 percent, since stock purchased at the pre-play price may be his main source of profit.[13]

But what accounts for premia of this magnitude at all?

. . .

c) *Elimination of prospective corporate income taxes.* Almost all current acquisition transactions, and a good many of the rest of the financial transactions characteristic of the 1980s, have this in common: that they remove funds from corporate solution, and thus bring about a reduction in the amount of net capital producing taxable corporate income in the future. For debt-financed acquisitions and distributions, the reduction in taxable income will be achieved through increased interest deductions. For internally financed acquisitions and distributions, it will generally take the immediate form of a reduction in investment income.

The volume of scholarly writing that simply ignores tax effects suggests that reduction in tax liabilities may not have been focused on as an end in itself, as in the case of net operating losses, or GU basis step-ups, or common tax-shelter investments. But the concomitant of reduced taxes is an increase in aggregate income streams for corporate investors, and the reduction therefore gets taken into account automatically if cash-flow predictions are done in any sensible manner.

The *effect* of the present tax laws therefore is to create a reward for investors, in the aggregate, from carrying out these various sorts of transactions, provided only that taxes on the transactions themselves are not too high and that pre-tax earnings hold steady or do not decline too much.

This effect may not be any better than carryover of tax benefits or tax-free basis step-up in explaining which acquisitions occur, because the advantage does not depend on any special characteristic of the target corporation; all that is required is the prospect of paying corporate income taxes if the transaction does not occur. Furthermore this effect does not explain the increase in LBO and acquisition activity in the present decade, since the provisions of law that make it possible predate 1980 by a lot. The *change* is apparently due to innovations in the securities markets; a willingness to tolerate high debt/equity ratios, and the presence in the market of persons who threaten to take over companies that do not themselves take steps to capture for their investors income streams previously flowing to the government as corporate income taxes.

The matter is easiest to see, perhaps, when an acquisition or stock retirement is debt-financed. In that case the effect is simply to increase total investor returns by an amount equal to the loss of tax receipts imposed on the government by turning nondeductible dividends into deductible interest payments.

---

[13] 15 U.S.C. §78n(d)(1) (1982). See Kraakman, Taking Discounts Seriously: The Implications of "Discounted" Share Prices as an Acquisition Motive, 88 Colum. L. Rev. 891, 923-24 (1988).

Example (1). Swiftco has annual earnings of $1,000,000, and 100,000 outstanding shares, or earnings per share of $10. The stock sells at about $70 per share or 7 times earnings. There is virtually no debt.

New Director, who teaches finance at a highly respected business school, has complained about the absence of debt, on the ground that debt provides a needed discipline for corporate managers. And so the company plans an issue of $6,000,000 of 12 percent bonds, with the proceeds to be used to retire shares, at $91 a share. This represents a premium of 30 percent over the present market value of $70, but with the discipline of debt, New Director asserts, the stock value will readily rise to something like that in value. At $91 per share, $6,000,000 will buy in 65.9 percent of the outstanding stock.

The plan is announced. The stock value rises indeed to about $91 per share, but enough shareholders come forward to permit the transaction to happen. Thereafter the stock value remains in the 85-90 range for some time, making it appear that something more than the pending tender offer produced the increase. Looking behind market prices, we find that earnings per share have risen dramatically from $10 to $15.30, in quick response to the transaction. The price per share has risen somewhat less, proportionately, reflecting the increase in the stock's leverage.

New Director is widely acclaimed for the astuteness of his prediction and wisdom of his advice, and it is thought by many that the transaction must have produced a genuine social benefit of some sort, since everyone involved has come out ahead as a result of it.

Well almost everyone: if the People of the United States of America, as beneficiaries of corporate income tax collections are taken into account, the picture is not so rosy (nor so remarkable either). The corporate income tax share of Swiftco operating income has declined by almost half; by the same *dollar amount*, indeed, as the Swiftco investors' shares have risen.

Indeed if one digs below earnings per share to see whether this transaction has had any effect on corporate operations, as reflected in operating income,[23] the answer is nothing has happened at all. The only effect of the transaction has been to *shift* about one sixth of operating income, from this point forward, from the IRS to the Swiftco investors.[24]

Under the old capital structure, earnings of $1,000,000 required operating income of about $1,500,000, of which about a third went in corporate income taxes. Under the new structure nearly half, $720,000, goes out in interest. But then one-third of what is left, which is what the government gets, is only $260,000 instead of $500,000. That reduces corporate earnings from $1,000,000 to $520,000, but those earnings are now to be divided among 34,100 shares instead of 100,000, with the result that earnings per share have *risen* from $10 to $15.30.

---

[23] Operating income means corporate revenues minus all deductions except returns to investors and income taxes.

[24] Self-help privatization, perhaps. But privatization usually involves a distribution to citizens at large, or the payment into the public fisc of some price for what goes into private hands. This version of privatization involves an uncompensated bonus to the investors whose New Director thought it up.

In sum, the effect of the transaction is simply to redistribute operating income as follows:

Income Flows	Before	After
Redeeming shareholders	$ 659,000	—
New Bondholders	—	$ 720,000
Continuing shareholders	341,000	520,000
Corporate Income Taxes	500,000	260,000
Total Operating Income	$1,500,000	$1,500,000

The added value detected by the market in this transaction, is essentially the present value of $240,000 per year shifted from the government to the investors, capitalized at 12 percent; i.e., $2,000,000, which at the redemption price of $91 was effectively split almost pro rata among the continuing and redeeming shareholders.

Indeed the effect on values can be conveniently summarized as follows:

Capitalized Values	Before	After
Redeeming shareholders	$ 4,613,000	—
New Bondholders	—	$ 6,000,000
Continuing shareholders	2,387,000	3,000,000
Corporate Income Taxes	3,500,000	1,500,000
Total Value	$10,500,000	$10,500,000

Figures in the first column, being essentially equity shares, are all simply seven times the earnings shares shown in the prior table. In the second column, the bondholders' share is capitalized at the bond interest rate of 12 percent, and then the remaining value is divided 2:1 between continuing shareholders and corporate income taxes. In effect the price/earnings ratio for the equity, including taxes, has gone down from 7 to 5.77, to reflect the risk associated with increased leverage.[25]

Example (2). Slowco had figures like Swiftco's, but unfortunately no New Director. Its need for discipline was discovered instead by Rapco, a corporate acquisition specialist.

Rapco first borrowed $350,000 from a bank with which it surreptitiously bought nearly 5 percent of Slowco's stock at $70 a share. It then announced its plan to acquire the rest of Slowco's stock for $100 a share, a premium of 43 percent over its prior market value of $70, and thus the stock was put in play at about that price. Next, Rapco issued 13.5 percent bonds in the amount of $9,850,000, with the proceeds of which it paid off the bank loan (350,000) and bought the rest of Slowco's stock (95,000 × 100 = 9,500,000).

Some might wonder how Rapco can profit by spending $9,850,000 for the stock of a company valued by the market at only $7,000,000. Indeed, how can it avoid serious losses? But Rapco has done it before, without serious losses, which seems

---

[25] The underlying assumption here is that the sum of the values of all the claims against operating income is the same, whatever the number and shape of the claims. . . .

to suggest that Rapco is able to supply some combination of better management, stricter financial controls, and good connections that improves the productivity of companies it acquires. The present acquisition proves, in fact, to add over $100,000 to Rapco's annual earnings right away, and the market value of Rapco's stock is not depressed by the acquisition.

One puzzle is why the gains from carrying out this transaction are divided the way they are, with Slowco shareholders receiving a 43 percent premium for their shares while Rapco shares go up only marginally. But if Rapco had not offered a very substantial premium experience indicates that other bidders would likely have entered the fray, driven up the price, and perhaps made off with the quarry. Whatever the answer to this puzzle about distribution, the market's message is clear about total value which has gone up by nearly half the prior value of the Slowco stock.

Again, the matter wears a very different aspect if operating income is examined as a gauge of performance, and the corporate income tax share of it is taken into account, along with investors' shares. Operating income, it turns out, has again held steady at $1,500,000. And again all that has happened is a redistribution of this income stream. Slowco shareholders used to get $1,000,000; now they are out. In their place now stand the bondholders, who receive interest of 13.5 percent on $9,850,000, or $1,330,000; 33 percent more than the whole amount of earnings before. And in addition Rapco makes a profit of $113,000. But since the return to investors has all been converted from dividends into interest, taxable income is reduced from $1,500,000 to $170,000, and taxes from $500,000 to $57,000. That reduction exactly pays for the immediate increase in aggregate investors' returns achieved by the acquisition.

In sum, the Slowco operating income is shared as follows:

Income Flows	Before	After
Slowco shareholders	$1,000,000	—
New Bondholders	—	$1,330,000
Rapco	—	113,000
Corporate Income Taxes	500,000	57,000
Total Operating Income	$1,500,000	$1,500,000

As with Swiftco, everyone comes up a winner without the slightest improvement in economic performance as reflected in operating income. Indeed the transaction has a considerable cushion in it for ineptitude on Rapco's part: operating income could drop by 11 percent and still cover the interest on the bonds. Of course Rapco might do something good, or lucky, or efficient, so that operating income goes up; in that case it will be handsomely rewarded indeed.

Example (3). Suppose Slowco (in *Example (2)*) brought in a new CEO before Rapco or anyone else made his bid. New CEO looked around at other companies and saw that shareholders were enjoying substantial enhancements in value through LBO's (as in *Example (1)*), and even more through acquisitions (as in *Example (2)*), and decided he had better show something similar, quick. Rather than take the time for an LBO, New CEO simply consulted underwriters to determine how much the company could borrow, and then had the borrowing proceeds paid out as a dividend. The company name was changed from Slowco to Rushco, to indicate its new age attitude toward corporate finance.

In a conservative version of this ploy, Rushco might borrow $7,000,000, just about the market value of its stock, and pay that out as a dividend. The stock value and earnings would apparently be largely depleted by such a manoeuvre, and the stock has been dubbed "stub stock." But a significant part of the distributed value is restored to the stock itself by diversion from the collector of Corporate Income Taxes, and so the stub stock might be expected to have a value of as much as a third of its prior value ($23.33), as indicated in the following tables:

Income Flows	Before	After
New Bondholders	—	$ 980,000
Shareholders	$ 1,000,000	346,667
Corporate Income Taxes	500,000	173,333
Total Operating Income	$ 1,500,000	$ 1,500,000

Capitalized Values	Before	After
New Bondholders	—	$ 7,000,000
Continuing shareholders	$ 7,000,000	2,333,333
Corporate Income Taxes	3,500,000	1,166,667
Total Value	$10,500,000	$10,500,000

The shareholders are quite happy to eat their cake and still have about a third of it left. Total security values have risen from $7 million to $9.3, so the shareholders feel good about New CEO. Moreover, the value to be released through a cash acquisition, as in Example (2), is substantially diminished. Moreover, the lower share price, together with the distribution of funds, may make it feasible for management to increase its proportionate ownership without any additional investment.

Of course there still is some value in the stock and some corporate income taxes still to pay, and so one might have been a little more aggressive. Instead of $7 million, why not $8? The interest rate would be higher, but still the effect on values will be enhanced. Suppose it is $8 million at 16 percent. Then earnings per share will be cut down to $1.47, and shareholders equity down below $17 per share, but total values of stock and bonds will be even higher than before and the lure of values still to be released in an acquisition even less.

Income Flows	Before	After
New Bondholders	—	$ 1,280,000
Shareholders	$ 1,000,000	146,667
Corporate Income Taxes	500,000	73,333
Total Operating Income	$ 1,500,000	$ 1,500,000

Capitalized Values	Before	After
New Bondholders	—	$ 8,000,000
Continuing shareholders	$ 7,000,000	1,666,667
Corporate Income Taxes	3,500,000	833,333
Total Operating Income	$10,500,000	$10,500,000

Debt financing puts the matter in bold relief, but the effect of these transactions would be essentially the same if they were paid for with corporate funds on hand in the form of money or financial assets. Indeed borrowing by itself has no spectacular effect since the deduction for interest on the resulting liability only offsets the income to be received from investment of the borrowed funds. The essential source of the gains in these transactions is the elimination of corporate income tax on financial assets, by distributing them to shareholders, whether or not they represent borrowing proceeds.

Example (4). Assume the same facts as in *Example (2),* except that another bidder, Fatco, made the acquisition, utilizing cash on hand in the amount of $11,000,000, to pay $110 per share for the Slowco stock. In this case no interest expense arises from the transaction and so Slowco earnings remain fully subject to corporate income tax without diminution by interest deductions. Fatco also remains fully taxable on its other businesses, whatever they may be. Fatco is nevertheless willing to pay this premium because its investment will return 13.6 percent ($1,500,000/$11,000,000) right off the bat, which is considerably better than the 10 percent it has been making on CD's. It believes, indeed, that Slowco reported earnings understate true growth in value, but even if that is wrong the investment will bring about some improvement in Fatco's earnings as long as Slowco earnings do not diminish by more than a third. The fact that Fatco can make this acquisition at a 57 percent premium over market and still show a modest increase in its own earnings will be taken by some to demonstrate yet again the social and economic utility of a free market in corporate control.

But again the feat is less magical if one takes account of corporate income taxes. Before the transaction the corporate income tax base included the earnings of Slowco and of Fatco's other businesses *and of $11,000,000 of CD's in Fatco's treasury.* The effect of the transaction is to take the last item out from under the corporate income tax, at a saving to investors of $366,667 (1/3 of 10 percent of $11,000,000) per year. This saving is essentially just what is needed to finance the premium to Slowco's shareholders.

The saving is an after-tax item. Its present value is therefore to be measured by discounting at an after-tax rate of return, which for 10 percent CD's would be 6.67 percent. $366,667 represents a 6.67 percent return on $5,500,000. In effect, the distribution of the CD's out of corporate solution increases their value to investors by 50 percent, the share of their return previously going to the government in corporate income taxes. $4,000,000 of that $5,500,000 was used to pay the premium for Slowco stock; the rest is captured by Fatco, in the form of a $266,667 increase in earnings, as a reward for its contribution to imaginative finance.

In sum, the transaction is essentially a redistribution of the operating income of Slowco ($1,500,000) plus the interest on the CD's ($1,100,000), as follows:

Income Flows	Before	After
Investors (aside from Fatco)		
Old Slowco shareholders	$1,000,000	—
New holders of CD's	—	$1,100,000
Fatco		
from CD's	733,333	—
from Slowco business	—	1,000,000
Corporate Income Taxes		
from Slowco business	500,000	500,000
from CD's	366,667	
Total Operating Income	$2,600,000	$2,600,000
from Slowco business	1,500,000	1,500,000
from interest on CD's	1,100,000	1,100,000

This example shows that an important source of the savings in a simple cash acquisition is the elimination of corporate income taxes previously being imposed on the income from investment of the funds used in the acquisition, in this example CD's. Elimination of income from financial assets is indeed the exact equivalent of incurring interest on borrowing for a debt-financed acquisition as in *Example (2)*.[26]

This suggests that the saving could be realized without acquiring a whole company in place of the CD's, and this is true. One possibility is just to replace the CD's with a portfolio investment in a small portion of the stock of another corporation; to the extent the return on that investment is protected from tax by the dividend-received deduction, the same result will be achieved. *Example (5)*. And if no other stock is appealing, a purchase of some of the issuer's own shares will do the trick nicely, without reliance on the dividend-received deduction. *Example (6)*.

Example (5). Portco has CD's worth $10,000,000, paying interest at 10 percent.

Privatco has outstanding issues of preferred stock, distributed as dividends to common shareholders at various points in the company's history in order to bring the price of common down to a level at which key employees could afford to make significant investments. A large portion of that preferred (100,000 shares) was owned by Privatco's founder, until his recent death. The Privatco preferred

---

[26] What if the corporate funds used in an acquisition had already been invested in tax preferred financial assets? If the preference is like that for municipal bond interest, available to all taxable investors alike, then the resulting bias is much the same, though reached by a different route. While the municipal bonds are in corporate solution, there is indeed no corporate income tax on the interest but there is a shareholder tax on dividends or other distributions paid with that interest; transferring the bonds into individual hands will eliminate that shareholder tax. Another way of thinking about it is to consider the bond interest rate to contain an implicit tax, so that there is double taxation (implicit at the corporate level, explicit to shareholders) before the distribution and only a single level (implicit to investors) afterward. One need not be concerned about the actual level of implicit tax since it continues after the distribution; the one level of explicit tax is what gets eliminated.

If the preference is peculiar to a corporate holder, like the dividends-received deduction, then indeed the tax gains from using such assets to finance an acquisition will be diminished. That simply indicates that tax preferences of this sort are part of the problem to be dealt with. See *Example (5)*.

has a liquidation preference of $100 a share, and annual dividends of $8.00 a year, fully cumulative, with standard provisions for control to pass to the preferred shareholders if dividends fall into arrears. It has no fixed redemption date and no provisions giving the holder any kind of right to redeem.

An alert Investment Banker named Irvana (IB) is urging Portco to sell its CD's and buy preferred stock instead. She is simultaneously urging Privatco's Founder's Executor (PFE) to sell the preferred stock and invest the proceeds in CD's.

Who profits how much depends, of course, on price; but anywhere within a suitable range of prices everyone stands to gain substantially.

Pointing to the fact that the preferred yields only $8, while CD's yield 10 percent, Irvana has offered to buy the preferred for $85 a share or $8,500,000, and that offer has been accepted. She next seeks to sell the Privatco preferred to Portco, pointing to the fact that the preferred dividends would be 70 percent taxfree, thus yielding $7.20 per share after tax, as compared to $6.67 on $100 of CD's. She calculates that Portco could pay up to $108 per share and maintain the same after-tax return as on the CD's, and offers the Privatco shares to Portco at the bargain price of $100, on which $7.20 will still represent a 7.2 percent after-tax return. That offer too was accepted.

Before either branch of the transaction was carried out, one of the Portco directors encountered PFE on the golf course, and they got into a heated discussion of the relative merits of CD's and preferred stock as portfolio investments, each ultimately echoing what they had been taught by Irvana and citing her by name as authority. This story has alternative endings. According to one, Irvana was able to calm everyone down with a lecture on pareto optimality, and a reminder that Portco's and PFE's improvements in income might never have occurred but for her acuity, for which she richly deserved to be duly rewarded.

The redistribution of income streams ($1,000,000 on the CD's plus $800,000 on the Privatco preferred) resulting from these transactions can be summarized as follows:

Income Flows	Before	After
Portco	$ 666,667	$ 720,000
Privatco's Founder's Executor	800,000	850,000
Irvana	—	150,000[27]
Corporate Income Taxes	333,333	80,000
Total Return on CD's and Privatco preferred	$1,800,000	$1,800,000

Example (6). Selfco, like Portco, had $10,000,000 of surplus funds invested in CD's paying 10 percent. IB convinced Selfco that this was not a good long-term

---

[27] This is Irvana's return, at 10 percent, on the $1,500,000 profit she made by buying the Privatco preferred at 85 and reselling it at 100. Her individual income taxes might well take a substantial part of that profit, and a substantial part of the return from investment of what is left. But the present series of examples all show the effects of corporate income taxes only. See the next section for an appraisal of the effect of individual investor taxes.

investment, and that it ought to sell those and buy stock. But the Selfco directors were unable to find any stock to invest in, since they could not find any other company in the world in which they had as much confidence as they had in Selfco itself. Finally someone suggested that in such a case they ought to buy shares in Selfco itself, a suggestion that seemed to make preeminent good sense because the Selfco stock, in the directors' opinions, was consistently underpriced.

In point of fact, Selfco has total earnings of $10,000,000 and 1,000,000 shares outstanding, selling at $70 a share, or 7 times earnings. Over a period of time Selfco sold off its CD's for $10,000,000 and used the proceeds to purchase its own shares. This action pushed the market up a little, so Selfco ended up acquiring only 133,333 shares, at an average price of $75. Even at that price the purchase has turned out well.

Selfco earnings dropped by $666,667 as a result of this transaction, from $10,000,000 to $9,333,333 ($1,000,000 lost interest minus $333,333 saved taxes). This is a drop of 6.67 percent. But the number of shares outstanding dropped 13.3 percent, from 1,000,000 to 866,667, and so earnings per share actually rose, 7.7 percent, from $10 to $10.77. In sum:

Income Flows	Before	After
Redeeming shareholders	$ 1,333,333	—
New holders of CDs	—	$ 1,000,000
Continuing shareholders	8,666,667	9,333,333
Corporate Income Tax	5,000,000	4,666,667
Total Operating Income plus interest on CD's	$15,000,000	$15,000,000

The market value of Selfco shares went up less than 7.7 percent, because distribution of the CD's made the shares somewhat more volatile. Or put differently, the new holders of the CD's have taken a larger portion of value than of income, since the CD's are worth 10 times earnings instead of 7. But still the price of the continuing shares settled at about $73 a share, representing a 4.3 percent gain over $70 and a price/earnings ratio of 6.8. And this represents nothing but a rearrangement of values based on the foregoing rearrangement of income flows, as follows:

Capitalized Values	Before	After
Redeeming shareholders	$ 9,333,333	—
New holders of CD's	—	$ 10,000,000
Continuing shareholders	60,666,667	63,333,333
Corporate Income Taxes	35,000,000	31,666,667
Total	$105,000,000	$105,000,000

The BEFORE column shows shareholder and CIT values at 7 times the earnings shown on the last table. The AFTER column shows $10,000,000 of value removed and the remaining equity value then divided 2/1 between shareholders and CIT. Note that the CIT share of value goes down about 9.5 percent, which is more than its share of operating income declines (6.7 percent), because the CIT share, like the shareholders' share, is now more volatile. . . .

These last examples illustrate tax advantages without leverage, if a corporation has financial assets available for a nondividend or extraordinary distribution. One can also have leverage without tax advantage, if there is no retirement of outstanding shares.

Example (7). Horatio was general manager of the battery division of Universal Foodstuffs. He felt that the needs of a battery business were poorly understood by managers preoccupied with foods; those managers themselves also were mystified by the special needs of battery makers and marketers.

Accordingly Universal agreed to sell the battery business to Horatio, and Horatio arranged to borrow substantially the whole purchase price through a firm specializing in leveraged buyouts. Universal will use the proceeds to construct a new grain storage facility.

Although Horatio's new company will be highly leveraged, Universal will have no reduction in net worth as a result of this transaction, since the battery assets will be replaced in its hands by the storage facility. Universal's earnings will increase from this transaction only if it makes more from the storage facility than it previously made on batteries. Similarly, Horatio will make money if and only if the battery business, out from under Universal's care, makes more than the interest payable on the notes issued to make the purchase. So for both parties this is a transaction in which economic incentives will work correctly, undistorted by income tax effects.

This is indeed the sort of LBO in which the firm that arranged it should take special pride. Horatio would be an excellent witness to testify before congressional committees about the social utility of LBO's and the undesirability of tax changes that might hamper them. . . . A careful evaluation of Horatio's case would confirm that it is indeed an LBO with likely social value and no tax subsidy. It is also an LBO in which no noncorporate shareholders have been bought out, no equity retired or acquired, and therefore one that would not be affected in any way by the proposals in this Reporter's Study Draft.

Examples (1) to (6) should be carefully taken for just what they are. They are all constructed on the *assumption* that operating income remains unchanged by the restructuring transaction. What they show is that even on that assumption investors' returns and security values should be expected to rise by amounts running up to 50 percent as a simple result of revenue streams being diverted from the government into private investors' hands. That prediction is generally consistent with observed premia over prior market values in many acquisition and restructuring transactions.

Operating income may in fact go up (or down) as a result of particular acquisition or restructuring transactions, and then investors' gains should be even more (or less); nothing in the examples refutes that. But the examples do show that an increase in operating income or underlying economic value cannot be inferred solely from an increase in market value of securities or after-tax returns to investors.

2) *Investor income taxes: the broken counterbalance.* The immediately preceding discussion shows increases in security values to be had by substituting corporate debt for equity or by transferring ownership of income-producing financial assets from corporate into individual hands. The gains result from a reduction in prospective corporate income taxes and a transfer of the income streams represented by those prospective taxes into the hands of private investors. The game is basically quite simple. The harder question is why it has not been played more extensively throughout the history of the corporate income tax.

A large part of the answer lies in the effects of shareholder income taxes. Transactions involving substitution of corporate debt for equity or distribution of financial assets other than corporate stock are taxable to the recipient shareholders, on either an exchange or a dividend basis. The question arises under what circumstances individual investor income taxes due on the consummation of a restructuring transaction will be adequate to compensate for the loss of prospective corporate income taxes described in the last section.[30]

It is sometimes assumed that corporate income taxes can be considered in isolation, since all income, corporate and noncorporate alike, is ultimately subject to individual income tax. But the timing of shareholder taxes operates strongly to favor accumulation of corporate profits. Shareholder taxes are generally deferred until corporate income is distributed. And deferral, we all now know, is tantamount to a permanent exemption for the return on the amount whose taxation is deferred—i.e., the amount accumulated. For a prosperous going corporation with fully taxable shareholders, therefore, the corporate income tax operates, at the margin, more as a substitute than a supplement for individual investor taxes.

In many circumstances this investor-tax bias against distribution has apparently outweighed the corporate-tax savings that would result from distribution as illustrated in the last section, but recent developments have impaired this counterbalancing effect.

(a) *The paradigm case.* It is instructive, at least as a benchmark, to consider conditions under which the counterbalancing effect of investor taxes would just equal and offset the corporate income tax savings to be achieved by substituting debt for equity or distributing funds out of corporate solution. These are—

1. that corporate and investor rates of tax on interest income are the same, and that corporate interest paid is fully deductible;
2. that investors are not taxed on gains from investment in a corporation unless and until there is a distribution; and
3. that distributions from corporations are subject to a uniform tax, at the same rate, applied to the whole distribution, whatever form (dividend,

---

[30] Taxes on sellers do not offset or diminish the power of prospective corporate income tax reductions to explain the premia over market at which LBO and similar transactions often occur, since that explanatory power has to do with why a buyer would pay more. Indeed taxes on sellers will themselves tend to push transaction prices up on the supply side.

redemption, etc.) they may take, and whenever they may occur. (The uniform rate on distributions in this condition need not be the same, however, as the rates of tax on interest income referred to in the first condition.)

Under these conditions there would be a perfect balance between corporate and investor tax effects on distributions. Taxes would be differently timed in the two cases, but the outcome would be the same for (1) current distribution and investment by shareholders, as for (2) current accumulation and later distribution.

Consider a sum of 300x inside a corporation. If the rate of tax on distributions were a flat 33⅓ percent, uniformly and permanently, then this 300x would represent 200x of value to shareholders and whatever it may grow to would represent a value of two-thirds of that amount to shareholders. If investment opportunities are the same inside and outside the corporation, and corporate and investor taxes on the returns from such investment are the same, and there are no differences in investment opportunity between having 200x to invest and 300x, then it will be a matter of indifference when distribution occurs. Investments in and outside the corporation will grow at the same rate, and $3 inside the corporation will consistently represent net value of $2 to shareholders, whenever distribution may occur.

Example (8). X corporation has 300x invested in interest bearing deposits, which it could distribute as a dividend or retain for future distribution. Its investors are all in a 33 percent marginal income tax bracket, while X is in the 34 percent corporate tax bracket. All distributions are taxable in full to investors, at 33 percent, when they occur.

In this case it will make hardly any difference whether distribution occurs now or sometime in the future. If it occurs now, the government would take l00x and the investors would have 200x to invest on their own. If they invest, for example, at 9 percent, taxes would leave about 6 percent to accumulate, and their money would double to 400x in about 12 years.

If distribution is deferred, on the other hand, there would be no immediate tax, and the whole 300x would be available for investment. Invested at 9 percent, that would yield *almost* 6 percent after tax (5.94 to be exact), and it would double to 600x in about 12 years. But if the whole fund were then distributed, the tax would take 1/3, leaving about 400x as in the first case.

A uniform distribution tax of 33 percent has the effect that $1.00 in the corporation always corresponds to 67 cents in the shareholders' hands, since 33 cents will go to the government on any distribution. That proportion remaining constant, the shareholders can afford to be quite indifferent about whether distribution occurs sooner or later, except to the extent of any difference between after-tax rates of return inside and outside the corporation.

The equivalence in this case is actually only approximate, since the rate of tax in the corporation is 34 percent while the rate outside is 33. For that reason it would take a little longer for funds to double within the corporation than in the hands of investors. If the investors were in a 28 percent marginal rate bracket, and the deferral went on for long, the difference would be more significant.[31]

Example (9). The facts are the same as in the last example except that distributions are uniformly taxed at 15 percent instead of 33. Even though this rate is less than half the corporate income tax rate, or the savings in corporate income tax burden described in the previous section, it will still be a matter of relative indifference whether a distribution occurs sooner or later.

If there is an immediate distribution, the government will take 45x leaving 255x, and that will still take the same amount of time to double to 510x. If distribution is deferred, there will again be 600x to distribute, but this time the distribution tax would only take 15 percent of that, so the ultimate fund would be the same, 510x. The tax that substitutes for the corporate income tax is not the tax on distributions but rather the investors' tax on the income realized directly at the investor level after the property is distributed.

b) *Real life.* These several conditions have obviously never been met in any form our income tax has actually taken. The first condition, that corporate and individual rates be the same on interest income, cannot be met so long as investors are taxed at different rates (including zero). Even for particular investors, in the same rate bracket year after year, nondividend distributions have never been uniformly taxed in relation to the amount distributed. . . . [N]ondividend distributions [are] taxed at the favorable rate applicable to capital gains. They are still only taxed to the extent of gain, which may be a small portion of the amount distributed.

Until recently, however, failures to meet these conditions ran in both directions, and in many circumstances (perhaps most) investor tax biases against distribution have tended to outweigh corporate tax biases against accumulation. In particular, from almost the beginning of the modern income tax until the beginning of the present decade [in 1980 and then again after 1993], the corporate income tax rate was significantly below the top rate of tax on investment income for individuals.[32] The corporate income tax rate was thus a recognized shelter for active business profits of a growing corporation, as compared with the rates its shareholders would have borne if the income accrued directly to them. Moreover, exchange treatment of some distributions, together with basis step-up at death, has often provided a strong incentive to accumulate corporate funds until after the death of an investor from whose estate the shares could then be redeemed without tax.

---

[31] An investment of $100 at 9 percent before tax, compounded annually after tax, would grow as follows:

Tax Rate	After 12 Years	After 24 Years
34	$199.86	$399.43
33 ⅓	201.22	404.89
33	201.90	407.65
28	212.43	451.27
15	242.20	586.59
0	281.27	791.11

[32] Pechman, Federal Tax Policy, 302-303, 308-309 (4th ed. 1983). Excess profits taxes, if considered part of the corporate income tax, might require some qualifications.

(In general, however, the differential treatment of distributions has provided an incentive to do nondividend distributions whenever the opportunity arises, even if that would entail borrowing against future earnings to finance the redemption).

Recent developments in the tax law and in corporate practice, however, have upset whatever balance there was between corporate tax savings arising from distribution and investor tax savings resulting from accumulation.

For one thing there has been a marked increase in nondividend distributions by public corporations. Purchases of a corporation's own shares have grown in volume, so that they have regularly exceeded new stock issues, in dollar terms, during the present decade. (Net stock issues are reported as negative.) Leveraged buy-outs have become common, and we have witnessed an unusually persistent boom in corporate acquisitions for debt or cash. Some of these transactions, redemptions in particular, have long been familiar for close corporations, but their widespread use in the public sector is something new.

There is a puzzle about why this has not happened earlier. Indeed it has long been a paradox why public corporations pay dividends at all, given the more favorable tax treatment for shareholders if all distributions were made by share repurchase. One reason for recent changes may just be increased sophistication and decreased conservatism in financial circles. And one can easily imagine that the change has also to do with the pressure of the acquisitions market. Whether or not they have thought of it that way, persons conducting acquisitions for cash or debt have had the benefit of corporate income tax reductions helping to make a success of their transactions. Leveraged buyouts and recapitalizations have been used as defenses, and have worked as such, in part because they preempt the acquisition in seizing the benefit of corporate income tax reductions. One can picture a world in which opportunities to avoid future corporate income taxes were not widely exploited in the case of public corporations, for whatever reason, until the presence of acquirors ready to do the exploitation made it a matter of survival for those who did not wish to be taken over, to do the exploitation first.

Even extraordinary dividend transactions now largely escape the tax burdens associated with ordinary dividends. At least extraordinary dividends have been resorted to as defensive measures against threatened acquisitions, and they have produced increases in market value which have led others to do them even if no acquisition is immediately threatened. It seems likely that such transactions do not produce anything like the burden of taxes on ordinary dividends, since shareholders who care can sell their shares, and there will presumably be plenty of purchasers for whom the dividend will not be substantially burdensome. (Dealers in the stock for whom the offsetting loss on resale is an ordinary loss; persons with substantial excess capital gains to absorb the loss; persons with ordinary losses to absorb the dividend; pension funds, foreigners and others in a zero tax bracket.)

Another factor accounting for recent changes in financial practice may have been the increase in stock ownership by tax exempt institutions, especially pension funds, for whom there is no tax burden on dividends. Such shareholders should rationally prefer a policy of high payout, whether or not by dividend, with growth to be financed by debt rather than accumulated equity. It would not be surprising to find that corporate financial policies become more responsive to the interests of tax-exempt investors as the latter become more significant shareholders, even if there were not a lot of direct intervention by tax exempts in the determination of corporate financial policy.

. . .

Organizing the Corporate Venture
(Practising Law Institute, "Tax Strategies for Corporate Acquisitions, Dispositions, Spin-Offs, Joint Ventures, Reorganizations and Restructurings," vol. 8, 2000)

by Jeffrey T. Sheffield and Christian E. Kimball

Selected Portions

. . .

"Property" and the Transfer and Exchange Requirements

§301 TRANSFERS IN EXCHANGE FOR STOCK

On the formation of Newco, the founders receive Newco stock. The receipt of stock will be tax-free in the following circumstances:

(a) The stock is received in exchange for property and the value of the stock is no greater than the contributor's tax basis in the property (i.e., where there is no gain "realized").[1]

(b) The stock is received in exchange for property and the persons transferring property, as a group, are in "control" of Newco immediately after the exchange

This chapter discusses the meaning of "property" as that term is used in Code §351 and discusses the requirement that such property be "transferred" in "exchange" for Newco stock.

§302 EXPANSIVE DEFINITION OF "PROPERTY"

Code §351 prevents recognition of gain or loss when the owner of property parts with ownership through the transfer of such property to a corporation that he and other transferors control.[2]

---

[1] Where the tax basis is higher than the value of the stock received, a loss may or may not be recognized. See Code §§267 and 351.

[2] See, e.g., American Compress & Warehouse Co. v. Bender, 70 F.2d 655, 657-658 (5th Cir. 1934), *cert. denied*, 293 U.S. 607 (1934); Portland Oil Co. v. Commissioner, 109 F.2d 479, 488 (1st Cir. 1940), *cert. denied*, 310 U.S. 650 (1940).

The Code and regulations define property only indirectly, stating that property does *not* include (1) services, (2) Newco indebtedness not evidenced by a security, or (3) interest on Newco debt accruing while the transferor held the debt.[3] The inference is that stock issued for other rights, property, or interests will be considered as issued in return for property.[4] The courts have given an expansive construction to the term "property" stating, for example, that it "encompasses whatever may be transferred."[5] Consequently, a wide variety of rights and interests have been held to constitute property.

§303 MONEY AS PROPERTY

Cash contributed to Newco in exchange for stock will be treated as a transfer of property to Newco.[6] This is clearly a necessary and reasonable interpretation of Code §351, since in nearly all cases Newco will require cash to begin operation of its business. In addition, foreign currency should qualify as property both because it is money and because it is treated as property for other Code purposes.[7]

Including money in the definition of property is essentially irrelevant to the transferor of money because he is transferring full-basis assets. However, it is important that money be treated as property so that the person receiving Newco stock in exchange for cash will be included in the transferor group in determining whether the transferor group controls Newco.

Example: A transfers $100,000 to Newco, and B transfers land with a fair market value of $100,000 and a basis of zero to Newco, each in exchange for 50% of Newco's outstanding stock. If A's cash transfer were not treated as a transfer of property to Newco (and thus A was not treated as a transferor), the transaction would not qualify under Code §351 because B, the only transferor of property in that case, does not control Newco immediately after the transfer. As a result, B would be taxed on the $100,000 of gain inherent in the land transferred to Newco. However, since cash is treated as property, A is included in the transferor group, the transferor group owns 100% of Newco's stock, and Code §351 will apply to the transaction.[8]

§304 INTANGIBLE PROPERTY

Intangible property includes proprietary rights such as patents, trademarks, trade names, know-how, and secret processes and can also include such diverse

---

[3] Code §351(d).

[4] See H.B. Zachry Co. v. Commissioner, 49 T.C. 73, 80 n.6 (1967).

[5] United States v. Stafford, 727 F. Supp. 1043 (11th Cir. 1984), quoting Hempt Bros., Inc. v. United States, 354 F.2d 1172, 1175 (1973), aff'd, 490 F.2d 1172 (3d Cir. 1974), cert. denied, 419 U.S. 826 (1974).

[6] Rev. Rul. 69-357, 1969-1 C.B. 101; Dillard v. Commissioner, 20 T.C.M. 137 (1961).

[7] See, e.g., Rev. Rul. 74-7, 1974-1 C.B. 198.

[8] See generally, B. Bittker & J. Eustice, Federal Income Taxation of Corporations and Shareholders, ¶3.02 (6th ed. 1998).

property interests as going concern value and goodwill. This section discusses when such rights and interests will be considered property under Code §351.

§304.1   Patents and Other Proprietary Rights

The regulations provide that patents are considered property.[9] In addition, the IRS has indicated that a wide variety of intangible property, including trademarks, trade names, trade secrets, know-how, secret formulas, goodwill, and other types of intangible assets will be considered in certain defined instances to be property for Code §351 purposes.[10] Thus, Code §351 applies to the transfer of many types of intangible rights to Newco in exchange for Newco stock.

In general, no distinction is drawn between intangible property that is developed by the individual efforts of the transferor and intangible property that was purchased by the transferor and then later contributed for Newco stock.[11] Thus, the creation of intangible property rights may be considered a way of transmuting services into property, which can then be transferred to Newco without triggering gain under Code §351. . . .

In part because of the blurred distinction between intangible property rights and services, and in part because of the ephemeral nature of interests that can be considered property rights, it is not always clear when intangible property rights will be considered property under Code §351. The most comprehensive IRS pronouncement in this area is Revenue Ruling 64-56.[13] While this revenue ruling specifically deals only with know-how, secret processes, and secret formulas, the IRS also applies these rules to patents and generally can be expected to apply them to all intangible property rights.[14]

Much of the precedent regarding the treatment of intangible rights under Code §351 was developed in connection with Code §367. This Code provision is designed to prevent the avoidance of U.S. tax through the tax-free transfer of assets to a foreign corporation followed by a tax-free disposition of the assets by the same corporation. Accordingly, Code §367 states in part that the transfer of property by a U.S. person to a foreign corporation will not qualify for Code §351 treatment unless the U.S. person complies with certain IRS guidelines designed to prevent any potential tax avoidance.[15] Thus, a case or ruling holding that Code §367 applies to a cross-border transfer implies that, except for Code §367, the transfer would be tax-free under Code §351. In other words, transfers of "property"

---

[9] Reg. § 1.351-1(a)(2) example 1.

[10] See Rev. Rul. 64-56, 1964-1 (Part 1) C.B. 133; Rev. Rul. 71-564, 1971-2 C.B. 179 (trade secret); Rev. Proc. 74-36, 1974-2 C.B. 491 (software); Rev. Rul. 79-288, 1979-2 C.B. 139 (corporate name and goodwill).

[11] See, e.g., Reg. § 1.351-1(a)(2) example 1.

[13] 1964-1 (Part 1) C.B. 133.

[14] See, e.g., Rev. Proc. 83-59, 1983-2 C.B. 575; Rev. Proc. 74-36, 1974-2 C.B. 491; Rev. Proc. 69-19, 1969-2 C.B. 301.

[15] See Code §367(a)(1).

subject to Code §367 must necessarily be transfers of "property" for purposes of Code §351.[16]

§304.2 Other Intangible Rights

Outside the context of Code §351, intangibles such as going concern value,[17] customer lists,[18] subscription lists,[19] and insurance in force[20] have long been considered property. These precedents appear to be strong support for treating intangible assets as property for purposes of Code §351. For example, the IRS has often contended in a taxable acquisition of a business that part of the purchase price for the business should be allocated to going concern value or goodwill. It would appear difficult for the IRS to also argue that such an asset does not constitute property that can be transferred to Newco tax-free in exchange for stock.

§304.3 Legal Protection for Intangibles

The IRS requires that a property right be afforded legal protection under local law before it will be considered property for tax purposes. Thus, where relevant federal or state law affords the owner of intangible property substantial legal protection against its unauthorized disclosure or use (e.g., the right to prevent an ex-employee from using the employer's secret processes), such intangible right should be considered "property" that can be transferred under Code §351.[21]

When no such legal protection exists, it is less clear whether such intangible rights can constitute property. The IRS has contended that such intangible rights cannot constitute property, presumably because the intangible does not give the owner any right vis-a-vis other persons.[22] However, the IRS has recognized property rights in going concern value, customer lists and related assets without specific reference to legal protection under local law.

In contrast, the courts have not insisted on substantial legal protection in order to find that property exists. Specifically, in connection with Code §351, at least one court has held that a contract to purchase real estate constituted property even though the contract was not legally enforceable.[23] Arguably, property may be considered to exist for Code §351 purposes so long as it can be said to possess value to a third party. . . .

---

[16] See, e.g., Rev. Rul. 79-288, 1979-2 C.B. 139; Abegg v. Commissioner, 50 T.C. 145 (1968), aff'd on other grounds, 429 F.2d 1209 (2d Cir. 1970).

[17] Black Industries, Inc., 38 T.C.M. 242 (1979); Rev. Proc. 75-39, 1975-2 C.B. 569.

[18] Rev. Rul. 74-456, 1974-2 C.B. 65.

[19] Id. and Houston Chronicle Publishing Co. v. United States, 481 F.2d 1240 (5th Cir. 1973), cert. denied, 414 U.S. 1129 (1974).

[20] See Hill v. Commissioner, 3 B.T.A. 761 (1926) (acq.).

[21] See Rev. Rul. 64-56, 1964-1 (Part 1) C.B. 133.

[22] See id. and Rev. Rul. 79-288, 1979-2 C.B. 139.

[23] United States v. Stafford, 727 F.2d 1043 (11th Cir. 1984).

§304.4   Distinguishing Intangibles from Services

Determining whether Newco is issuing stock in exchange for property or for services is discussed at §203.

In general, if A develops intangible property specifically for Newco, stock received in exchange for such intangibles will be considered received in exchange for services. Thus, A will not be treated as a transferor of property to Newco for Code §351 purposes.

Example: A and VC enter into an agreement that states that A will use his best efforts to develop a certain software program for Newco. Upon A's successful completion of the program, A will transfer the software rights to Newco in exchange for 50% of Newco's stock, and VC will contribute $500,000 (for marketing of the software) to Newco in exchange for 50% of Newco's stock. In this situation, since A is under an obligation to transfer the property to Newco if and when the program is completed, the software is not likely to qualify as property.

A transfer of property may require certain services to make the property useful. In Rev. Rul. 64-56, the IRS ruled that services performed for Newco by a transferor will be disregarded if the services are "merely ancillary and subsidiary to the property transfer." Examples of ancillary and subsidiary services include "promoting the transaction by demonstrating and explaining the use of the property, . . . assisting in the effective 'starting-up' of the property transferred, or . . . performing under a guarantee relating to effective starting-up." In general, training Newco's personnel is considered services (so that payment is for services, not for property). However, if Newco's employees are already sufficiently skilled, instruction on how to use certain machines or other property should be considered "ancillary and subsidiary services."

The revenue ruling also states that continuing technical assistance will be considered services, whether or not styled as part of a guarantee agreement between A and Newco. Any assistance in helping design housing for machinery or layout for a plant will normally be considered services and not ancillary to the property transferred.

To the extent that both property and services are furnished as consideration to Newco in exchange for Newco stock, and the services are not merely ancillary and subsidiary to the property transferred, an allocation must be made between the amount of stock delivered for services and the amount of stock delivered for the intangible property. The stock received for services should be taxable under Code §83. However, where there is a transfer of some property and the transferor is not treated as an accommodation transferor, the transferor should normally be considered part of the transferor group, and Code §351 should apply with respect to the transfer.[25]

---

[25] See Reg. § 1.351-1(a)(2) example 3.

Example: A has developed a secret process for manufacturing widgets. He transfers all rights to the process to Newco in exchange for all 100 shares of Newco stock. In addition to transferring the secret process to Newco, A agrees to train unskilled labor to apply the secret process and to design the building in which the process will be carried out. Such services are considered more than ancillary and subsidiary to the transfer of the secret process. Thus, the 100 shares of Newco stock received by A must be apportioned between those received for property and those received for services. If 30 shares are considered received for services and 70 shares are considered received for property, then A will be taxed on the fair market value of the 30 shares. However, A in fact transferred property to Newco (the secret process), and the property so transferred was not an accommodation for the rendering of services. Therefore, A should be treated as a transferor of property, and Code §351 should apply with respect to the 70 shares of Newco received by A, so that no gain or loss will be recognized with respect to the secret process transferred to Newco.

TESTIMONY BEFORE THE HOUSE WAYS AND MEANS COMMITTEE

by Jack S. Levin, Lecturer, University of Chicago Law School

Regarding The Tax Policy Aspects of Mergers & Acquisitions

February 2, 1989[1]

Introduction

. . .

I believe that most mergers, acquisitions, and buyouts in recent years have, on the whole, been beneficial for our country. While I am not an economist, I have observed at short range hundreds of transactions in recent years. Many of these transactions have moved inefficient companies into the hands of more efficient managers, reduced unnecessary corporate overhead, caused acquired business to be operated in a more entrepreneurial fashion, created jobs, allowed selling shareholders to realize enhanced values, and allowed buying shareholders to build values.

These transactions have given public shareholders, pension plans, mutual funds, and the like the opportunity to share in a control premium rather than requiring them merely to sell their shares in small lots at the discounted minority price.

This does not mean that every merger, acquisition, and buyout has been good for our economy and has been soundly structured. Inevitably there are excesses; when a pendulum swings in a good direction, it often swings a bit too far. If we knew the magic formula, this Committee could adopt legislation imposing a stiff tax on bad buyouts which are unsoundly structured, but draft the legislation so that it would not impede soundly structured buyouts which are beneficial for our economy. However, experience tells us that we can not effectively legislate such a fine distinction.

I therefore urge legislative moderation at this time. Do not enact drastic legislation which will break or severely bend the pendulum. Our economy would feel the adverse effects of such legislation for a decade to come. The market is self-correcting. It will deal effectively with excesses. Investors will quickly learn not to invest in unsound buyouts.

Three misconceptions

Before dealing specifically with the moderate steps this Committee might take at this time, I would like to deal with three oft-repeated misconceptions.

---

[1] This testimony occurred shortly prior to enactment of Code §163(e)(5) and §163(j).

First misconception: LBOs are creatures of the tax law

The first misconception is that leveraged buyouts are creatures of the tax law, i.e., they are largely motivated by the desire to obtain interest deductions. That is, in my experience, simply not true. Buyouts occur because a business is undervalued by the market and the buyer believes it can improve the business so that it will be more valuable than the purchase price. Many factors play a much larger role in this process: interest rates, the business climate, foreign and domestic competition, the management team's skills, and expectations as to the ability to expand the company's sales. Taxes play a very minor role in this process.

Second misconception: LBOs reduce tax collections

The second misconception is that leveraged buyouts reduce tax collections. Although LBOs substitute debt for equity, I do not believe that they reduce the government's tax collections. When an LBO takes place, the old shareholders receive a very large premium over the prior market price of their stock. Their gain on the sale of their shares is immediately taxable. There are four reasons this front-end capital gain tax is particularly sweet for the Treasury:

1. The LBO accelerates the timing of a sale. All of the company's shareholders must sell now rather than selling their stock in dribs and drabs over the next twenty years. Hence the present value of the tax is vastly enhanced.
2. Capital gains are now taxed at the same rates as ordinary income. There is no longer a low preferential rate for capital gains.
3. All those shareholders who expected to hold their stock until death eradicated the capital gain tax must pay tax at the time of the LBO.
4. The premium price over market swells the amount of capital gain.

Thus the present value of the front-end capital gain tax very likely more than offsets any corporate tax lost over the life of the debt, taking account of the obvious fact that the company repays the debt as quickly as possible.

Moreover, it is simply not accurate to say that the interest expense paid by the company avoids corporate-level tax. Much of the LBO interest is paid to banks, insurance companies, and other corporate lenders so it is subject to corporate taxation and ultimately shareholder-level taxation—the income simply hops over from the LBO company to the corporate lender.

As described in the Joint Committee Staff's excellent pamphlet of 1/18/89, a portion (less than half) of the lenders are foreign or tax-exempt entities. As I will discuss in a moment, perhaps one of the fine-tuning provisions you should adopt is to tax foreign and tax-exempt entities on all or part of the interest income arising out of transactions of this type.

Third misconception: Debt and equity should now be treated the same

The third misconception is that the problem can be cured by treating debt and equity the same and allowing a deduction (or credit) for corporate dividends. While such a change in the tax law would be excellent, we clearly can not now afford the billions of dollars of revenue loss that integration would inevitably entail. Moreover, to adopt only prospective integration (in order to reduce the revenue loss) would bring more complexity: If you enacted a deduction (or credit) for dividends only on *new* equity, we would need complex anti-churning rules to prevent every corporation in America from issuing new equity securities and using the proceeds to redeem its old equity securities. This would entail tracing rules and rules regarding extraordinary dividends and other complex financial transactions. Hence I do not believe that a practical solution lies in granting a deduction (or credit) for dividends paid.

First sound course of action: Begin a comprehensive study

There are in my opinion two sound courses for this Committee: First, listen to all the pros and cons regarding this extremely complicated set of economic issues, instruct Treasury to make a comprehensive study, but do not enact any piecemeal tax legislation at this time. The issues we are dealing with are too complex for a quick fix; more harm than good can result from bending the complex economic pendulum in mid-swing.

October 1987 experience. One example of bending the pendulum is the proposed 1987 House Bill, introduced in early October 1987, which would have disallowed acquisition interest in excess of $5 million per year. Within a few days after this proposal, on October 19, 1987, the patient nearly expired. While there is no clear evidence that the House proposal caused or contributed to the crash, the dramatic juxtaposition of the events counsels for even more caution in the future.

Competitive disadvantages for U.S. buyers. We must also be vigilant that the solution to one illness does not exacerbate another even more serious illness. Disallowing a deduction under U.S. tax law for acquisition interest would put American buyers at a severe disadvantage to many foreign buyers. It would prevent an American buyer from deducting acquisition interest. But a foreign buyer's home jurisdiction may well allow it to deduct on its foreign tax return all of its acquisition interest. Such a solution may therefore reduce buyouts of *American* companies by American buyers but exacerbate buyouts of American companies by *foreign* buyers.

Second sound course of action: Fine-tuning changes in the tax law

A second sound course for this Committee, if it believes that a change in the tax law is necessary now, would be to avoid a drastic legislative change which may impede legitimate transactions for years to come, and instead adopt one or several fine-tuning changes which may redress the pendulum a bit but not bend it beyond repair. I will suggest several such fine-tuning changes which would not disrupt our economy but would deal specifically with several possibly tax-abusive situations.

First fine-tuning proposal: Zero coupon and PIK debentures

First, there are two categories of debt instruments that do not pay interest in cash, but under current tax law the corporate obligor is nevertheless entitled to a tax deduction each year for the interest not paid. One type is called "zeros" or zero-coupon debentures. This means that the corporate obligor pays no interest; rather, the interest accrues and is paid when the bond matures, perhaps after ten years. A second type is called "PIK" or payment-in-kind debentures. This means that each year the corporate obligor pays the interest by issuing another PIK debenture, so that at maturity, perhaps after ten years, the obligor pays both the original debenture plus all the little PIK progeny. In a theoretical world it does not matter that the corporate obligor deducts the interest not paid each year on a zero or a PIK debenture, because the tax law requires the holder to pay tax on the interest income he does not receive. However, in a real world virtually all zeros and PIKs are held by tax-exempt or foreign entities (e.g., pension plans, IRAs, university endowment funds).

So if I were to single out a type of debt that is fueling buyouts in a possibly tax-abusive manner, it would probably be those that deliver a tax deduction to the corporate obligor without requiring it to pay any interest in cash. Therefore, I believe it may be appropriate to impose an additional tax burden on this type of instrument. The proper tax burden could be either (a) to disallow the company's interest deduction until it actually pays the interest in cash or (b) to tax even a tax-exempt or foreign holder on interest accrued on such an instrument.

Second fine-tuning proposal: Interest in excess of a maximum rate

A second fine-tuning legislative proposal would focus on the fact that some buyouts use debentures carrying yields markedly above normal debt rates. It may be appropriate to impose an additional tax burden on the interest in excess of a maximum rate, for example, eight points over the rate payable by the Treasury on debt with a comparable maturity. The additional tax burden might be imposed on the corporate obligor in the form of a deduction disallowance or on the holder, perhaps by taxing holders otherwise tax-exempt. Because of the difficult definitional issues, it would not in my view be proper to taint an entire debt instrument merely because the yield may be slightly higher than the established rate—it would be fairer to taint only the interest in excess of the established rate.

Third fine-tuning proposal: Reduce the ESOP incentives

A third fine-tuning proposal would be to withdraw some of the tax incentives for ESOPs. ESOPs have frequently sponsored leveraged buyouts of their employer companies and in light of recent judicial decisions, ESOPs may now become a defensive takeover device. Current tax law grants a crazy-quilt of tax benefits to ESOPs:

1. Rollover exemption from capital gain recognition to a shareholder selling stock to certain types of ESOPs.

2. Estate tax reduction to an estate selling stock to certain types of ESOPs.
3. Reduced tax rate on the interest income received by a lender to an ESOP.
4. Tax deduction for the sponsoring company when it repays both the principal and interest on an ESOP's borrowing.
5. Tax deduction for a company paying dividends on its stock held by an ESOP.

If you reexamine the tax benefits of leverage, it would be worthwhile also to reexamine these ESOP tax incentives which encourage greater leverage.

Fourth fine-tuning proposal: Tax foreign and tax-exempt entities on income from leveraged investments

A fourth, and somewhat more drastic, fine-tuning proposal would focus on the fact that some investors in highly leveraged securities, namely tax-exempt entities and foreigners, are exempt from U.S. tax on certain types of passive income (or under certain circumstances pay tax at a drastically reduced rate). It may be appropriate to tax such an investor on its interest income, dividend income, and capital gain income from highly leveraged investments at full U.S. rates regardless of its special status. (Any change in the tax treatment of a foreign person suggested in this testimony would, of course, have to be consistent with our treaty obligations. In addition, if special rules are applied to "highly leveraged investments" or a similar category, the definitional issues would be formidable.)

Alternatively, a somewhat less drastic approach would be to focus on the difference between short-term and long-term holders of highly leveraged investments and to tax persons currently exempt from tax, i.e., foreign and tax-exempt entities, on gains from such stock and debt instruments not held for at least a prescribed period—with the tax rate declining as the holding period increases.

These four legislative proposals have, in my view, one thing in common: They are fine-tuning adjustments to cure possible tax abuses and would redress the pendulum a bit, but not bend it beyond repair, i.e., they are not so drastic as to threaten the free market system.

Cumulative effect of tax and non-tax legislation and regulations

Finally, I believe it crucially important that any action by this Committee must be viewed in conjunction with action by the eight other Congressional Committees and the many federal agencies reviewing LBOs, so that the *cumulative* effect does not overwhelm the free market and drastically affect our economy. Among the non-tax points which may now be addressed, and would in my view, fit within the fine-tuning framework, are:

1. Make clear that trustees (of a pension plan, a university endowment fund, etc.) are not required by fiduciary duty to sell whenever a buyout proposal is made at a premium over market, but rather that trustees are entitled to take into account their good faith expectations as to future share performance of the company if the buyout is rejected.

2. Require institutional investors (such as banks, pension plans, university endowment funds) to disclose separately in their financial statements all risky investments, whether oil and gas, real estate in depressed areas, or LBO investments, so that appropriate regulators and the people to whom the institution's management are responsible can judge management's performance.
3. Where an institution is regulated (e.g., a bank), make sure the appropriate regulators are empowered and encouraged to require additional reserves on new capital whenever the institution's overall financial condition (including the risky investments) warrant.

[Shortly after this testimony and other hearings, Congress enacted Code §163(e)(5) and §163(j).]

Table of Internal Revenue Code Sections

Most of these Code sections are reprinted in Appendix ¶2000

References are to sections.

Table of Internal Revenue Code Sections

Table of Treasury Regulations

Many of these Regulations are reprinted in Appendix ¶2100

References are to sections.

Table of Treasury/IRS Rulings

Most of these precedents are reprinted in Appendix ¶2200

References are to sections.

Revenue Procedures

93-27 . . . . .302.14, 302.15, 1006
98-34 . . . . 407.1.2
2001-43. . . . . .302.14, 302.15, 1006

Revenue Rulings

69-6 . . . . .501.7.6, 502.8
73-427 . . . . .501.7.6, 502.8
78-250 . . . . .501.7.6, 502.8
79-273 . . . . .501.7.6, 502.8
81-100 . . . . .1001.1
85-106 . . . . 409, 603.8
89-122 . . . . .803.9
90-95 . . . . .501.7.6, 502.8
92-52 . . . . 803.7.6

95-70 . . . . 602.8.3
98-21 . . . . .407.1.2, 407.6

Letter Rulings

9121017 . . . . 803.7.7
199912007. . . . . 803.7.7
200204005. . . . . 202.3.8
200212005. . . . . 202.3.8

Technical Advice Memoranda

9219002 1006

IRS Legal Memoranda

200149008. . . . . 803.7.7

Table of Federal Securities Laws, Rules, and Regulations

Most of these SEC precedents are reprinted in Appendix ¶2300

References are to sections.

Investment Company Act Regulations

Investment Advisers Act of 1940

Investment Advisers Act Regulations

Table of Bankruptcy Code Sections

Many of these Bankruptcy Code sections are reprinted in Appendix ¶2400

References are to sections.

Table of State Fraudulent Conveyance Statutes

These fraudulent conveyance statutes are reprinted in Appendix ¶2500

References are to sections.

Table of Delaware Corporate, Partnership, and LLC Statutes

Most of these Delaware statutory provisions are reprinted in Appendix ¶2600

References are to sections.

Table of Cases

Excerpts from some of these cases are reprinted in Appendix ¶2700

References are to sections.

Table of Other Laws

Some of these precedents are reprinted in Appendix ¶2800

References are to sections.

Table of Other Materials

Some of these precedents are reprinted in Appendix ¶2800

References are to sections.

Organizing the Corporate Venture

**Testimony Before the House Ways &
Means Committee of Jack S. Levin**

Index

Index

Index